CASES AND MATERIALS ON
EU PRIVATE INTERNATIONAL LAW

Since the Amsterdam Treaty of 1997 empowered the EC to adopt rules in the field of conflicts of laws, legal instruments have been adopted that provide common rules on issues that touch upon the day-to-day life of European citizens. There are now instruments covering jurisdiction and the recognition and enforcement of judgments in civil and commercial matters, family matters and maintenance obligations, and the law applicable to contractual and non-contractual obligations, legal separations and divorces. There are also acts establishing swift procedures for recovering claims abroad, ie the European Enforcement Order, the European Order for Payment Procedure and the European Small Claims Procedure, and acts regulating cross-border insolvency proceedings and judicial assistance in the field of service of documents, taking of evidence and access to justice. This long list of EU legislation is not exhaustive of EU conflicts of laws rules: numerous further provisions are scattered among other EU legislation, eg directives on consumer, labour and insurance contracts; company law; IP rights; securities; privacy; and so on. Besides this the European Court of Justice has issued many judgments addressing relevant aspects of the conflict of laws found in the *acquis communautaire* in this field. This book, which assembles all the relevant EU legislation and ECJ decisions in one place, provides a guide to the maze of legal instruments now in place, supplemented by brief commentaries identifying the leading principles and anticipating future developments.

Volume 4 in the series Studies in Private International Law

Studies in Private International Law

Cases and Materials on EU Private International Law

Stefania Bariatti

·HART·
PUBLISHING

OXFORD AND PORTLAND, OREGON
2011

Published in the United Kingdom by Hart Publishing Ltd
16C Worcester Place, Oxford, OX1 2JW
Telephone: +44 (0)1865 517530
Fax: +44 (0)1865 510710
E-mail: mail@hartpub.co.uk
Website: http://www.hartpub.co.uk

Published in North America (US and Canada) by
Hart Publishing
c/o International Specialized Book Services
920 NE 58th Avenue, Suite 300
Portland, OR 97213-3786
USA
Tel: +1 503 287 3093 or toll-free: (1) 800 944 6190
Fax: +1 503 280 8832
E-mail: orders@isbs.com
Website: http://www.isbs.com

British Library Cataloguing in Publication Data

Data Available

ISBN: 978-1-84946-027-9

Typeset by Columns Design XML Ltd, Reading
Printed and bound in Great Britain by
TJ International Ltd, Padstow, Cornwall

Studies in Private International Law
Series Editors' Preface

For even the most dedicated private international law scholar or practitioner, it has become increasingly difficult to keep up in recent years with the tidal wave of EU legislation and judgments of the ECJ that impact upon the discipline. Ever more fields are the subject of harmonised rules of private international law in the European Union, or proposals for harmonisation. As the ambit and influence of those harmonised rules develops, so the role of national rules of private international law is diminished.

In compiling this volume, Professor Stefania Bariatti, a leading figure in the field of private international law, has performed an outstanding service for those engaged in the study and practice of private international law. Professor Bariatti has assembled and catalogued a remarkable range of cases and materials covering the panoply of private international law matters which have been subject to harmonisation at a European level. Beginning with a most interesting chapter in which Professor Bariatti charts the development of EU private international law and reflects upon its future directions, the author goes on skilfully to organise, present and analyse a vast array of materials in a format that is extremely accessible to the reader.

Professor Bariatti includes extremely helpful summaries and extracts of ECJ judgments, including the numerous rulings on the interpretation of the Brussels I Regulation, which are organised by reference to the Article or Articles to which they relate. There are also chapters covering such matters as: the law applicable to contractual obligations; the law applicable to non-contractual obligations; insolvency; companies; rights in rem, securities and intellectual property; social security; personality rights, status and family relations; succession; and judicial assistance in civil matters.

The book addresses other initiatives that may influence the application of European rules of private international law. It includes Regulations and Directives in relation to particular matters that affect the operation of European rules of private international law. It also incorporates international conventions to which Member States are parties and which affect the application of European rules of private international law. The author also considers in some detail the impact of general principles of European law, such as the concept of citizenship, the protection of fundamental rights and the role of public policy and overriding mandatory provisions.

The author has incorporated recent developments in European private international law, including, most notably, the Commission Proposal of 14 December 2010 to reform the Brussels I Regulation. The author reflects that the proposed extension of the Brussels I Regulation generally to defendants domiciled in non-Member States, coupled with the universal scope of other recent harmonisation initiatives, suggests that, in the future, all, or almost all, aspects of private international law will be the subject of European rules.

Professor Bariatti has produced an indispensible resource and we are delighted to welcome *Cases and Materials on EU Private International Law* to the Studies in Private International Law series.

Paul Beaumont (University of Aberdeen)

Jonathan Harris (University of Birmingham)

21 March 2011

Preface

This book aims primarily to provide a support for university courses on private international and EU law, as well as an instrument for practitioners who face conflicts of laws issues in their day-to-day legal practice. The development of EU legislation in this field has affected the competence of national legislatures and has substantially reduced the scope of domestic law. A considerable number of provisions have been adopted and are scattered throughout many legislative instruments based upon Article 81 TFEU or on other provisions of the Treaty (directives on consumer, labour and insurance contracts, company law, IP rights, securities, privacy, and so on). Moreover, the European Court of Justice has issued many interpretative judgments that concur with the *acquis communautaire* in this field.

The cases and materials are presented in chapters, devoted to specific issues or relationships. An introduction provides an overview of the development of the competence of the European Union, from Article 220 of the EEC Treaty to Article 81 of the Treaty on the Functioning of the European Union, and of its external dimension, as well as a preliminary tentative assessment of the principles and solutions adopted in respect of the general issues of private international law for further discussion.

I wish to express my gratitude to the team of young scholars who – after two Italian editions in 2002 and 2009 – have helped me in preparing this English edition, Professor Carola Ricci, PhD Serena Crespi, PhD Giuseppe Serranò and Dr Eva De Goetzen. Comments and suggestions by readers will be most welcome and will help in limiting errors and gaps in a new edition.

Stefania Bariatti
Milan, 20 December 2010

Table of contents

CASES AND MATERIALS

Table of EU Cases
(Chronological)

General Court (previously Court of First Instance - CFI)

Table of EU Cases
(Alphabetical)

General Court (previously Court of First Instance - CFI)

Table of Legislation

Protocols to the Treaty on the European Union and to the Treaty on the Functioning of the European Union

Declarations annexed to the Final Act of the Intergovernmental Conference which adopted the Treaty of Lisbon

B) Previous versions

Treaty of Maastricht (1991)

Resolutions and declarations

Guidelines, Notices and Recommendations

The Development of EU Private International Law: Instruments, Principles, Rules

1. Cooperation in the Field of Justice and Home Affairs under the Treaty of Maastricht

Cooperation among the Member States of the European Union on matters of justice and home affairs was formally established by the Treaty of Maastricht on the European Union in 1991, which entered into force in November 1993. Under Title VI, at Articles K–K9 numerous 'matters of common interest' deemed relevant for purposes of realising the free movement of persons — such as asylum policy, the crossing of the external borders and related controls, immigration policy and, more generally, policy vis-à-vis citizens of third countries, the ongoing fight against unauthorised immigration, residence and work by nationals of third countries, the fight against drug addiction, the fight against fraud on an international scale, judicial cooperation in civil matters, judicial cooperation in criminal matters, customs cooperation, police cooperation to prevent and fight terrorism, unlawful drug trafficking and other serious forms of international crimes — were governed at the inter-governmental level (Article K.2 Treaty on the European Union (TEU)).

At the institutional level, this sector fell under the responsibility of the Council, which was supported by a Coordinating Committee. The Commission was involved in these works, while the European Parliament was merely informed or consulted on the main issues. The Council could take joint positions or actions, whose effectiveness was not mentioned. In addition, it could draw up conventions to be submitted to the Member States for ratification. The Court of Justice had no duties or responsibilities with the exception of those conferred under such conventions. It was possible to establish an enhanced cooperation among a restricted group of States and the Council could decide to submit the adoption of measures in any of the above-mentioned fields to the procedure set out under the former Article 100c EC, subject to a decision by the Member States in accordance with their respective constitutional requirements.

In reality, the Member States had already commenced intensive cooperation on these matters at the inter-governmental level, which had developed over time. In fact, some of these activities date back many years, even prior to the conclusion of the Single European Act, with the aim of completing the freedoms envisaged under the EC Treaty. From the very outset, Article 220 of the EEC Treaty (which later became Article 293 EC) assigned to the Member States the power to commence negotiations to the extent necessary in order to guarantee their citizens, inter alia, the protection of persons, the enjoyment and protection of the rights under the same conditions granted by each State to its own citizens, the mutual recognition of companies, the retention of legal personality in the event of

1

transfer of their seat within the EC, the possibility of mergers of companies subject to different national legislations, the simplification of formalities governing the reciprocal recognition and enforcement of court judgments and arbitration awards. In these matters and in that initial phase of the European Economic Community, the selected method was the inter-governmental method, through the establishment of treaties among the Member States on certain specific matters.

It is well-known that various texts based upon this provision were negotiated, but only one of them, the Brussels Convention on jurisdiction, recognition and the enforcement of judgments in civil and commercial matters was adopted in 1968, was ratified by the Member States and entered into force in 1973. Its objective was to guarantee legal certainty for citizens and economic operators and equality of rights in raising their claims and in obtaining satisfaction for their rights, allowing for the exercise of what has come to be known as the 'fifth freedom', ie, the free circulation of judgments. The Brussels Convention marked the beginning of the European judicial area and established over the years a complex system that was extended to some third countries through the Lugano Convention of 1988.

This area was based from the outset upon certain fundamental principles, which were later explicitly expressed at the Tampere summit in December 1999. In particular, access to justice in any Member State was guaranteed to all persons domiciled in the Community, at the same conditions applicable to the citizens of such State, both as plaintiffs (Articles 2(2) and 4(2) of the Brussels Convention), and as defendants (Article 4(1) of the Convention). The enjoyment of these rights was ensured regardless of citizenship, and therefore also for citizens of third countries, well beyond what would be imposed under the principle of non-discrimination set out under Article 12 EC. The automatic recognition of judgments and a facilitated uniform enforcement procedure throughout all of the Member States have facilitated the circulation of decisions and reduced discriminations among individuals in this phase as well. Moreover, Article 44 permitted legal aid in order to ensure that the same treatment in place in the State of origin would be available in the State of enforcement of the judgment, as it is generally available nowadays for all cross-border disputes under a specific directive.

Subsequently — but outside the provisions of former Article 220 EEC — on 19 June 1980 the Rome Convention on the law applicable to contractual obligations was concluded, which was supposed to be followed shortly thereafter by a parallel agreement on the law applicable to non-contractual obligations. While this latter project was later abandoned, the Rome Convention was ratified by the Member States and entered into force a few years after its signing, on 1 April 1991, contributing to legal certainty before the courts of the Member States and reducing the effects of forum shopping. It is important to recall that the Rome Convention contained conflicts rules that were universal in scope, and therefore rendered applicable also the law of third countries, thus replacing national conflict rules within its scope of application.

On the basis of the new provisions set out under Title VI of the Treaty of Maastricht, over just a few years a broad range of acts were formulated — resolutions, common positions, common actions, decisions, recommendations, agreements and conventions among the Member States, which created a quite vast body of provisions that produced varying effects, depending upon the type of act used. As regards judicial cooperation in civil matters, two conventions based upon Article K.3 were adopted and negotiations were initiated regarding other matters. In particular, a Convention on service of documents, as well as a Protocol on its interpretation by the Court of Justice (1997) and a Convention on jurisdiction and the enforcement of judgments in matrimonial matters (known as Brussels II) (1998) were signed. A short time prior, in 1995, the Convention on insolvency procedures had been adopted, based upon Article 293 EC, that concluded a process which had continued over the span of many years in a sector falling under civil and commercial matters, that had been excluded from the outset from the scope of the 1968 Brussels Convention.

2. The Area of Freedom, Security and Justice in the Treaty of Amsterdam

With the Treaty of Amsterdam, which entered into force on 1 May 1999, very important changes were made to the third pillar of the European Union and the prospects of achieving cooperation in the justice and home affairs area changed dramatically with regard to both the scope of cooperation among the Member States and the instruments and institutional structure used in order to take into account the requirements related to the future development of the European Union. The cooperation in this area changed its name and objectives as the result of, on the one hand, the expansion of the matters that remained under the scope of Title VI TEU, and on the other, the communitarisation of a portion of activities which fell under its scope and which became an integral part of the EC Treaty, with important consequences from an institutional and regulatory standpoint.

The notion of 'area of freedom, security and justice' had already been used in Article B (later Article 2) TEU, which indicated among the objectives of the European Union that of preserving and developing the European Union as an area of freedom, security and justice in which the free movement of persons was guaranteed, together with measures for the control of external borders, asylum, immigration, the prevention of crime and the battle against crime. It was only with the Treaty of Amsterdam, however, and with certain acts which immediately followed it that the notion's contents became precise. We are talking about, first of all, the Action Plan of the Council and the Commission on how best to implement the provisions of the Treaty of Amsterdam on an area of freedom, security and justice, prepared prior to the entry into force of the said Treaty and adopted by the European Council of Vienna in December 1998 (known as the Vienna Action Plan), and later developed in the conclusions of the extraordinary European Council held in Tampere on 15 and 16 October 1999.

The Vienna Action Plan states that the notion of freedom, which is based upon the Schengen system, does not only lead to free circulation within the European Union, but also to the freedom to live in an environment that is respectful of the law and is subject to control by public authorities in order to prevent the abuse of such freedom and to punish those who commit such abuse. It leads to the enjoyment of human rights, including the protection from any form of discrimination, as well as protection of personal data and privacy, which are particularly important from a criminal law standpoint. In the field of immigration and asylum, the primary objectives are the battle against clandestine immigration and the integration of legal residents, and the protection of those who require international protection even if they do not officially meet the parameters and conditions of the Geneva Convention. Their transfer to Title IV EC, which we will return to later, allows for the adoption of binding acts and the establishment of control procedures.

The need to guarantee security in the European Union does not lead to a need to call upon the duties and responsibilities of the individual Member States for the maintenance of internal safety, nor is it meant to lead to the creation of a common investigation area. On the contrary, it has to do with improving and reinforcing cooperation on criminal law matters, including in favour of the Union. The objective is the battle against crime (whether organised or not), such as terrorism, human trafficking, crimes against minors, unlawful trafficking of drugs and arms, corruption and fraud.

The pursuit of the objective of justice, finally, should facilitate the day-to-day life of citizens, in affirming a common sense of justice and legal certainty throughout Europe, which ensures that those who pose a threat to the area of freedom and security are called before courts of law. This area encompasses both access to justice and legal cooperation among Member States on civil law matters (aimed at facilitating the identification of the competent court, the applicable law, the conduct of fast and fair proceedings, and effective enforcement procedures) and on criminal law matters (especially through the coordination of courts, equality in procedural guarantees through the establishment of standards and codes of conduct, in addition to the guarantees provided under the European Convention on human rights). The facilitation of cross-border proceedings through the development of more streamlined instruments for the exchange of documents and information, the use of multi-lingual forms, the creation of mechanisms for consultancy and legal assistance such as legal aid are also mentioned.

The European Council at Tampere also specified the need for conditions ensuring that security and justice are accessible to all. In the European area of justice 'people can approach courts and authorities in any Member State as easily as in their own. Criminals must find no ways of exploiting differences in the judicial systems of Member States. Judgements and decisions should be respected and enforced throughout the Union, while safeguarding the basic legal certainty of people and economic operators. Better compatibility and more convergence between the legal systems of Member States must be achieved'.

Under the Treaty of Amsterdam, cooperation on justice and home affairs has made great progress. The cooperation on police and judicial cooperation in criminal matters remained in the third pillar of the European Union, while the other areas of cooperation on matters of justice and home affairs were transferred under the first pillar, the Community pillar, where a new dedicated heading was created concerning 'visas, asylum, immigration and other policies related to free movement of persons' (Title IV, Articles 61–69) after Title III concerning the four freedoms of circulation of goods, persons, services and capital.

In particular, responsibilities on the following matters were transferred under the EC Treaty:

a.   measures concerning the implementation of free movement of persons and directly related flanking measures with respect to controls on external borders, asylum and immigration, indicated in Article 62 and intended to be introduced within five years from the entry into force of the Treaty of Amsterdam, aimed at governing the movement of citizens of Member States and third countries at internal borders, and controls at external borders and various matters concerning visas for stay and the freedom of stay for non-EC citizens;

b.   measures on the matter of asylum, in accordance with the Geneva Convention of 1951 and any other treaty on the matter, and related to the temporary acceptance and protection of refugees and displaced people, and on the matter of immigration policy in order to govern in a uniform manner visas and stays of lawful immigrants and the entry and stay of clandestine immigrants (Article 63);

c.   measures in the area of judicial cooperation in civil matters having cross-border implications, which include measures aimed at improving and simplifying the system for the cross-border service of judicial and extrajudicial documents, cooperation in the taking of evidence, recognition and enforcement of judgments on civil and commercial matters, including decisions in extrajudicial cases, to promote compatibility of the national rules on conflicts of laws and jurisdiction, to eliminate impediments to the proper conduct of civil proceedings, possibly promoting compatibility of national procedural rules (Article 65);

d.   measures aimed at encouraging and reinforcing administrative cooperation on the above-mentioned matters (Article 66).

3.   Judicial Cooperation on Civil Matters in the Treaty of Lisbon

The Treaty of Lisbon, which entered into force on 1 December 2009, has introduced various important changes, both at the institutional level, and specifically with regard to the area of freedom, security and justice. From the first standpoint, two treaties were adopted: the Treaty on the European Union (TEU), containing provisions of a general institutional nature, and the Treaty on the functioning of the European Union (TFEU), to which the provisions on the policies of the Union were moved. From the second standpoint, the area of freedom, security and justice is now governed under Title V TFEU, into which the activities related to cooperation on criminal law matters are integrated as well.

As regards private international law, a separate chapter is now dedicated to judicial cooperation in civil matters (Chapter 3, comprised only of Article 81), which finally overcomes the limited and limiting reference to the policy on visas, asylum and immigration. It has to be noted, however, that the new Title still expresses itself in reductive terms with respect to the forms and contents of the activities falling in this field and which have been and will be carried out by the Union and by the Member States. The European legislature, unfortunately, did not take advantage of this opportunity — after the attempt made at the European Constitution, which never entered into force — to adopt a text which best reflects the actual situation of cooperation on this matter. Indeed, on one hand it is simplistic to talk about 'judicial' cooperation since these provisions do not involve merely cooperation among judicial authorities; but, on the other hand it is simplistic to speak of merely 'cooperation' if, as has occurred so far, regulations will continue to be adopted which lead to the uniformity of national legislations. In addition, it is also highly simplistic to condense these matters at Article 67(4) TFEU, at the beginning of Title V, mentioning as the sole express objective that of access to justice, which should be achieved 'in particular through the principle of mutual recognition of judicial and extrajudicial decisions in civil matters', when in reality the scope of the action is much broader.

From a standpoint of substance, Article 81 TFEU is broader than Article 65 EC since not only does it cover mutual recognition and enforcement between Member States of judgments and of decisions in extrajudicial cases; cross-border service of judicial and extrajudicial documents; compatibility of the rules applicable in the Member States concerning conflict of laws and of jurisdiction; cooperation in the taking of evidence; elimination of obstacles to the proper functioning of civil proceedings, if necessary by promoting the compatibility of the rules on civil procedure applicable in the Member States; but it also covers effective access to justice, the development of alternative methods of dispute settlement, and support for the training of the judiciary and judicial staff.

4.   The Type of Acts to be Adopted on the Basis of Article 81 TFEU

The Treaty of Lisbon, unlike the Constitution, does not affect the traditional and consolidated type of legislative acts of the Union, which instead, as regards the matter of judicial cooperation on civil matters, had been revolutionised by the Treaty of Amsterdam. Indeed, the communitarisation decided in 1997 had led to important changes to the prior structure as regards the instruments used, the adoption procedures and the related controls, as well as the relationships with other EU and international acts.

First of all, as regards legislative acts, the inclusion of these matters within Title IV EC had led to the possibility of making use of all binding and non-binding acts, whether typical or atypical, provided under the same or which had affirmed in practice. From a concrete standpoint the communitarisation has therefore resolved two problems related to the nature and adoption of international conventions, which had served so far as instrument of the cooperation in this field. On the one hand, through the adoption of a Community act the timeframe for the entry into force of the agreed rules is greatly reduced as compared with a convention, which requires long negotiations and long ratification procedures by Member States. Consider for instance the outcome of the protocols to the 1980 Rome Convention which, after being adopted eight years later, entered into force in 2004. On the other hand, the law of the European Union is meant to produce the same effects throughout all Member States simultaneously.

The text of Article 81 TFEU now retains the flexibility that had already made its appearance in Article 65 EC with reference to the type of measures that may be adopted.

In practice, besides certain general acts which indicate future plans for the implementation of the area of freedom, security and justice and besides Directive 2003/8/EC on access to justice, until now the legislature has adopted regulations on virtually an exclusive basis and would appear to be leaning toward continuing along this route, which better ensures the uniformity of the rights of the parties within the Member States through uniformity of applicable rules. On the other hand, differences deriving from the domestic implementation of directives already adopted in other fields and setting out rules of private international law — eg on consumer protection, employment and insurance — did not lend supporting evidence in favour this instrument in an area that is so close to the ambit of personal, and not only economic rights of individuals.

As for the lawfulness of this practice, the Protocol on the application of principles of subsidiarity and proportionality attached to the EC Treaty established under point 6 that '[o]ther things being equal, directives should be preferred to regulations and framework directives to detailed measures'. However, when the Commission proposed a draft directive on service of documents in May 1999, the European Parliament submitted an amendment (No 1) in order to have a regulation adopted due to the advantage of guaranteeing a fast, clear and consistent implementation of the text in line with its objectives,[1] which was approved without any roadblocks.

The following use of regulations should not be criticised. It is true that in the context of an international organisation the institutions have to comply with the instituting treaty and with all related acts, as the Protocol on subsidiarity certainly is; and it is also well-known that, according to the ECJ, 'a mere practice on the part of the Council cannot… create a precedent binding on Community institutions with regard to the correct legal basis'.[2] The provisions of Title IV EC, however, vest the institutions with a certain level of discretionality in the selection of the measures to be adopted. Moreover, the role of subsequent practice in the application of treaties and the will of the Contracting Parties in interpreting and applying them, including treaties instituting international organisations, cannot be forgotten.[3] In addition, the regulation constitutes the EU act whose effects most resemble those of an international treaty, such as the conventions entered into among the Member States that have been transformed into Community instruments.

Article 81 TFEU does not introduce any substantive innovations in this regard, except the indication that 'measures for the approximation of the laws and regulations of the Member States' may be adopted (paragraph 1). Moreover, the principle of mutual recognition of judgments and of decisions in extrajudicial cases is expressly identified as the basis for actions in this area. Article 81(2), however, is more precise than Article 65 EC in defining the objectives, which no longer consist in merely improving and simplifying the matters subject to cooperation, but in guaranteeing their effective implementation.

5.   The Procedure for the Adoption of Acts Based upon Article 81 TFEU

The procedure for the adoption of acts based upon Article 65 EC, as in all cases of application of Title IV EC, was governed by Article 67, which provided for a range of different procedures and majorities, depending upon the moment in which the act was adopted and the type of measure. The power in such regard was initially granted exclusively to the Council, which for the first five years from the entry into force of the Treaty of

---

[1]   Amended proposal for a Council Regulation for the service in the Member States of judicial and extrajudicial documents in civil or commercial matters, COM (2000) 75 of 29 March 2000, paragraph 2.1.

[2]   Judgment 23 February 1988, case 68/86, *United Kingdom v Council*.

[3]   The importance of the practice followed by Member State is also highlighted by A Borrás, 'Derecho internacional privado y Tratado de Amsterdam', (1999) 1 *Revista Espanola de Derecho Internacional* (1999) 395, 400 *et seq*.

Amsterdam, and therefore until 30 April 2004, would have decided unanimously,[4] upon the Commission's proposal or the initiative of a Member State, and after consulting the European Parliament. After such date, the power of initiative of the Member States ceased to apply and the acts have been adopted only upon proposal by the Commission, which has gathered the Member States' requests.

The Treaty of Amsterdam had also granted to the Council the power to directly amend certain of such provisions, without waiting for future amendments to the Treaties. Article 67(2), second hyphen, provided that the Council, acting unanimously after consulting the European Parliament, could take a decision with a view to providing for all or parts of the areas covered Title IV to be governed by the co-decision procedure. This would entail a closer involvement of the Parliament in the decision-making process and the abandonment of unanimity within the Council.

The Treaty of Nice, entered into force on 1 February 2003, had added in Article 67 EC a fifth paragraph, pursuant to which the Council, as an exception to paragraph 1, could adopt measures based upon Article 65 EC through the co-decision procedure set out under Article 251 EC, with the exception of family law matters. Ever since, such measures have been enacted in accordance with the co-decision procedure.

The Treaty of Lisbon maintains this procedure — now defined ordinary legislative procedure — for all of the acts based upon Article 81 TFEU, except for family law measures having cross-border implications, with respect to which the Council decides by unanimous vote, in accordance with the special procedure, and following consultation of the European Parliament. Through a special decision, also adopted unanimously and following consultation of the European Parliament, the Council may establish that certain acts on family law matters may follow the ordinary procedure. National parliaments may oppose the adoption of such decision within six months from the date on which the proposal is notified to them. In such case, the decision may not be adopted.

6.   The Judicial Control over Acts Based upon Article 81 TFEU

Acts adopted under the framework of Title IV EC were already subject, in principle, to the control procedures set out under the Treaty, with certain exceptions that had been widely criticised precisely with regard to the acts in the field of judicial cooperation in civil matters. The Court of Justice had jurisdiction to issue a preliminary ruling on the interpretation of the provisions set out in Title IV and on the interpretation and validity of acts adopted on its basis pursuant to Article 234 EC, which was explicitly cited at Article 68(1) EC. The obligation to refer a question to the ECJ, however, was imposed only to courts of last resort and did not cover any 'measure or decision taken pursuant to Article 62(1) relating to the maintenance of law and order and the safeguarding of internal security' (Article 68(2)).

---

[4]   Reference was made to the unanimity of the Member States which participate in Title IV EC, from which Denmark was always excluded and from which the United Kingdom and Ireland could opt in (see below, at para 7).

The first limit, in particular, was difficult to justify considering the positive experience within the system created by and around the 1968 Brussels Convention, where the 1971 Luxembourg Protocol permitted courts of second instance to turn to the Court, thus guaranteeing uniformity of interpretation and unified control by the ECJ starting from the decision on the merits.

Upon invitation by the European Council, the Commission had presented a proposal for a decision aimed at rendering Article 234 EC fully applicable to issues related to the interpretation of Title IV EC or the validity and interpretation of acts adopted on the basis of its provisions.[5] The proposal was then abandoned in view of the entry into force of the European Constitution, first, and the Treaty of Lisbon, later, which achieved this aim. Indeed, the TFEU does not provide for any exception in the field of judicial cooperation in civil matters to the general rules on the control over the lawfulness of acts and preliminary interpretation, now governed by Articles 263 and 267 TFEU.[6]

The full application of the general provisions of the Treaty in this field is proved by the infringement procedure under Article 227 EC (now Article 259 TFEU) that was commenced by Latvia against Italy in 2008 alleging the violation of Regulation (EC) No 2201/2003 on matrimonial matters. In particular, the case concerned a decision of the Rome Tribunal that had ordered the return of a child to Italy after his removal to Latvia. The Commission, however, found that the Italian court had not infringed either the provisions of the Regulation or Article 24 of the Charter of fundamental rights, the UN Convention on the rights of children, and the principle of due process.[7]

It should be noted that in 2006 an urgent procedure for deciding upon references for preliminary rulings in the area of freedom, security and justice was introduced, which allows for the timeframe for proceedings before the Court of Justice in this area to be significantly shortened (Article 104(b) of the Rules of procedure).[8] The urgent nature of the situation is not clearly defined, but the Information note provides the example of 'proceedings concerning parental authority or custody of children, where the identity of the court having jurisdiction under European Union law depends on the answer to the question referred for a preliminary ruling'. The national court must set out the matters of fact and law which establish the urgency and, in particular, the risks involved in following the normal preliminary ruling procedure. The case is decided by a special chamber and significant simplifications in the procedure are envisaged, from the limited number of persons entitled to submit written observations (generally, only the parties involved in the national proceedings, the Member State to which the requesting court belongs and the

---

[5]   COM (2006) 346 of 28 June 2006. The request was set out in the Hague Programme of 2004 (OJ, C 53 of 3 March 2005).

[6]   With the entry into force of the Lisbon Treaty also the power of the Council, the Commission and Member States to request the ECJ to interpret Title IV EC and the acts based upon it pursuant to Article 68(3) EC was abandoned. The ECJ rejected a request for preliminary interpretation of Regulation (EC) No 44/2001 presented by a French court of first instance and based upon the Treaty of Lisbon prior to its entry into force (judgment 20 November 2009, case C-278/09, *Martinez*).

[7]   R Baratta, 'Un recente procedimento di infrazione 'interstatale' dinanzi alla Commissione europea' (2010) 115 *Rivista di Diritto Internazionale*, 115. It is worth mentioning that proceedings were initiated by Belgium against Switzerland before the International Court of Justice concerning the application of the 1988 Lugano Convention: see ICJ, Press Release No 2009/36 of 22 December 2009.

[8]   Council Decision 2008/79/EC, Euratom dated 20 December 2007 (OJ, L 24 of 29 January 2008), and the ECJ's 'Information note on references by national courts for preliminary rulings', as amended after the entry into force of the Treaty of Lisbon (OJ, C 297 of 5 December 2009), at para 34 *et seq*.

Commission), to the reduction of the written phase, to the use of electronic communication means. This procedure has proved very effective since some judgments have been adopted in less than three months from the application.

7.   The Position of Certain Member States and Enhanced Cooperations

Not all of the Member States of the European Union participate in the judicial cooperation in civil matters. Since the Amsterdam Treaty, a special form of enhanced cooperation has been established which in principle excludes the United Kingdom, Ireland and Denmark, with the following clarifications.

Under Articles 3 and 4 of the Protocol on the position of the United Kingdom and Ireland entered into in Amsterdam and updated in Lisbon, these States may participate in the adoption of a measure already proposed by notifying their intention to the President of the Council within three months from the presentation of the proposal itself, and may notify at any time their intention of participating in a measure that has already been adopted. The two States had, however, already issued a general declaration in which they expressed their willingness to be included in the judicial cooperation on civil law matters at the meeting of the Council JHA held on 12 March 1999. Ireland has renewed such declaration in Lisbon, undertaking to review once again the functioning of the Protocol within three years from the entry into force of the Treaty of Lisbon.[9] Both countries have participated in all of the acts adopted so far, but the United Kingdom has decided to participate in the Rome I Regulation and in Regulation (EC) No 4/2009 on maintenance obligations only after their adoption.[10]

The Protocol on the position of the United Kingdom and Ireland adopted in Lisbon further provides, under Article 4a, that the above-mentioned provisions also apply in the event of amendments to acts already adopted and binding upon these two States. However, if their non-participation in the amended version of an act in force were to render its application inoperable for the other Member States or for the European Union — in case it consists of a 'unitary' act that could not be applied in different versions on a bilateral basis — the Council may invite Ireland and the UK to notify their participation in accordance with Article 3. The two States have two months to submit the notification. Should they fail to do so, the act in force would cease to apply to such States.

This situation is addressed also by Declaration No 26 on non-participation by a Member State in a measure based on Title V of Part Three TFEU, according to which, if a Member State opts not to participate in such a measure, the Council will discuss the implications and effects of that Member State's non-participation in the measure. Moreover, any Member State may ask the Commission to examine the situation on the basis of Article 116 TFEU.

---

[9] See Declaration (No 56) by Ireland on Article 3 of the Protocol on the position of the United Kingdom and Ireland in respect of the area of freedom, security and justice.

[10] See the Commission Decisions 2009/26/EC of 22 December 2008 (OJ, L 10 of 15 January 2009) and 2009/451/EC of 8 June 2009 (OJ, L 149 of 12 June 2009).

Denmark's position is different, since it may not render any declaration of participation in individual legislative acts, but — in accordance with the Protocol entered into in Amsterdam and renewed in Lisbon — it may accept one or more parts of Title V TFEU, thus becoming bound to all of the acts adopted until such declaration. From a standpoint of external relationships, Denmark is not bound by any conventions concluded by the Union in this field.

This situation, which has generated difficulties and complications that emerged with clarity at the time of the transformation of the 1968 Brussels Convention into a regulation, has resulted in the need for the execution of two agreements between the Community and Denmark, based upon Article 61(c) EC, in order to render applicable to Denmark the Brussels I Regulation and Regulation (EC) No 1348/2000 on the service of documents, later amended through Regulation (EC) No 1393/2007. The exclusive competence of the Community to enter into these agreements has never been called into question and, in any case, they were entered into on 27 April 2006, following the ECJ opinion 1/03 concerning the Lugano Convention. The agreements with Denmark entered into force on 1 July 2007. It is interesting to note that they also provide for a procedure that allows Denmark to adapt to any amendments to Regulations (EC) No 44/2001 and No 1348/2000 (see Article 3 of the agreements). A similar provision concerns the measures adopted in accordance with Article 17 and the opinions of the committee referred to under Article 18 of the Regulation on service.

Article 8 of the Protocol attached to the Treaty of Lisbon, however, allows Denmark to revisit its constitutional position and to put itself in a situation substantially analogous to that of Ireland and the United Kingdom. The Protocol, indeed, includes a schedule which Denmark may render applicable by way of notification to the other Member States at any time, which amends Articles 1–4 of the Protocol through provisions that are virtually identical to those set out in the protocol concerning the other two States.

The judicial cooperation in civil matters has thus been since the beginning a sort of enhanced cooperation as not all of the Member States did participate in it.

Very recently in this same field the first enhanced cooperation formally founded upon Article 20 TEU and Article 326 *et seq*. TFEU has been proposed in the area of the law applicable to divorce and legal separation. In fact, following lack of unanimity within the Council on the proposal for a regulation amending Regulation (EC) No 2201/2003 as regards jurisdiction and introducing rules concerning applicable law in matrimonial matters ('Rome III'),[11] 10 Member States[12] requested the Commission to submit a proposal in the area of applicable law in matrimonial matters. The Commission proposed two draft instruments, aimed respectively at authorising the establishment of the enhanced cooperation and at implementing it. The former was adopted by the Council on 12 July 2010, while the Council adopted the latter on 20 December 2010. The enhanced cooperation will initially bind 14 Member States (Belgium, Bulgaria, Germany, Spain, France, Italy, Latvia, Luxembourg, Hungary, Malta, Austria, Portugal, Romania and Slovenia).[13]

---

[11] COM (2006) 399 of 17 July 2006.

[12] Bulgaria, Greece, Spain, France, Italy, Luxembourg, Hungary, Austria, Romania and Slovenia. Greece later withdrew the request.

[13] See Council Decision No 2010/405 authorising enhanced cooperation in the area of the law applicable to divorce and legal separation and Council Regulation No 1259/2010 of 20 December 2010.

8.   The Scope of Judicial Cooperation on Civil Matters: Actions Already Performed and Plans for the Future

As anticipated above, prior to the Amsterdam Treaty the Member States had already established a solid intergovernmental cooperation in the field of judicial cooperation in civil matters, both among themselves and with third countries.

First of all, over the years the Members States have signed numerous conventions in this field, both among the Member States and with third countries. Certain of them have undergone considerable developments, so much as to be considered a self-standing system, such as the above-mentioned Brussels Convention of 27 September 1968 on jurisdiction and the enforcement of judgments on civil and commercial matters, which was based upon Article 220 EC and has been in force since 1 February 1973 and updated repeatedly on the occasion of accession by new States to the EU. It was accompanied by a Protocol on interpretation entered into force in 1971 and by the parallel Lugano Convention of 1988, which was also binding upon Switzerland, Norway and Iceland, and has now been replaced by the new Convention signed in 2007 between the Community and these States.[14] The Brussels Convention was followed by the Rome Convention of 19 June 1980 on the law applicable to contractual obligations, in force since 1 April 1991, which, while lacking any legal basis under the Treaty, was aimed at continuing 'in the field of private international law the work of unification of law which has already been done within the Community, in particular in the field of jurisdiction and enforcement of judgments'. The Convention of 23 November 1995 on insolvency proceedings was also based upon the same provision of the EC Treaty. The Convention was concluded following lengthy and difficult negotiations, but it never entered into force and was eventually superseded by Regulation (EC) No 1346/2000 to which we will return shortly.

In the area of intergovernmental cooperation without any basis in specific provisions of the Treaties, two conventions were signed aimed at facilitating relations between the Member States, but they never entered into force at the international level. These were the Convention dated 25 May 1987 abolishing the legalisation of documents in the Member States, which is applied on a temporary basis on the basis of reciprocal declarations among Italy, Belgium, Denmark, Ireland and France, and the Convention dated 6 November 1990 on the simplification of procedures for the recovery of maintenance claims.

Finally, Article 31 (formerly K.3) TEU had provided a legal basis for the Convention of 26 May 1997 on the service of judicial and extrajudicial documents in civil and commercial matters and the Convention of 28 May 1998 concerning jurisdiction, recognition and enforcement of matrimonial judgments (known as Brussels II). These agreements also never entered into force, but their provisions have been introduced to the new regulations adopted under Title IV EC.

---

[14] The Lugano Convention of 2007 entered into force in the relationships with Norway and Iceland on 1 January 2010 and will enter into force in relationships with Switzerland on 1 January 2011.

8.1.   The Vienna Action Plan of 1998

Between the signature and the entry into force of the Amsterdam Treaty, in December 1998 the Council and the Commission adopted an Action Plan on the implementation of the provisions of the Treaty of Amsterdam in the area of freedom, security and justice, which acknowledged the acts already adopted under Article 293 CE and Article 31 TEU and indicated certain priorities following a rather precise timetable.

The Vienna Action Plan defined the priorities and the programme of future works on judicial cooperation on civil matters, with the aim 'to make life simpler for European citizens by improving and simplifying the rules and procedures on cooperation and communication between authorities and on enforcing decisions, by promoting the compatibility of conflict of law rules and on jurisdiction and by eliminating obstacles to the good functioning of civil proceedings in a European judicial area'. This is clearly a paraphrase of the text of Article 65 EC, which is supplemented with the improvement of coordination of European judicial bodies and knowledge of the laws and regulations of the Member States, which did not appear in the text of the Treaty.

The Action Plan further indicated certain measures to be adopted over the short term (two years) and certain others over a longer term (five years). The first included, first of all, the revision of the Brussels and Lugano Conventions, which had already been commenced prior to the entry into force of the Treaty of Amsterdam following a Communication of the Commission 'Towards greater efficiency in obtaining and enforcing judgments in the European Union' and a draft text of a new Brussels Convention, limited at such time to the Member States of the Union.[15] Secondly, the Action Plan envisaged the drafting of a legal instrument, which was not better specified, on non-contractual obligations (known as Rome II); thirdly, it envisaged the revision of certain provisions of the Rome Convention on contractual obligations (Rome I) in order to implement a coordination between it and the choice-of-law rules provided in numerous directives, which in many cases had led to divergences and confusion. Finally, the possibility of creating a judicial European network in civil matters based on the model already in place in the criminal law area was proposed in order to facilitate the knowledge of the law of the Member States and the coordination of the proceedings.

For the medium term, the Vienna Action Plan included a study on the possibility of adopting two legal instruments, respectively on the law applicable to divorce (Rome III) and on jurisdiction, applicable law and the enforcement of judgments on matrimonial property and successions. The first instrument, given the existence of the Convention on jurisdiction and the enforcement of judgments in matrimonial matters (Brussels II), was supposed to be aimed at identifying the applicable law in order to avoid *forum shopping* in this field. The second was supposed to take into consideration the connection between the two matters and the work conducted at the Hague Conference on Private International Law. Further, the Action Plan proposed the preparation of models for non-judicial solutions to disputes, mainly in family law matters; the identification of procedural rules to be harmonised in order to facilitate access to justice and the measures necessary in order to improve the compatibility of the rules on civil procedure, such as the rules on the deposition of security for litigation costs and expenses or those related to legal aid;

---

[15]   OJ, C 33 of 31 January 1998.

cooperation among judicial authorities in the taking of evidence; the assessment of the possibility of approximating certain areas of civil law through, for example, uniform private international law rules applicable to the acquisition in good faith of corporal movables.[16]

In this initial phase, therefore, certain studies were announced aimed at allowing for the analysis of prospects for development in certain areas or matters, but most importantly, the regulatory model of the convention was maintained, which had been successful for many years.

8.2.   The Conclusions of the European Council at Tampere (1999)

Following the entry into force of the Treaty of Amsterdam, the Vienna Action Plan was confirmed at the Tampere European Council of December 1999 and by a subsequent Draft Programme of measures for implementation of the principle of mutual recognition of decisions in civil and commercial matters, which was quite ambitious, presented at the end of 2000 upon the European Council's request.

The Tampere conclusions, in particular, indicated three priorities for the development of a European judicial area. First of all, improved access to justice in Europe, to be guaranteed through a series of actions, the preparation of which had been assigned to the Commission, also in cooperation with other competent bodies such as the Council of Europe. The plan involved starting with the launch of an information campaign on judicial cooperation in the European Union and on legal systems of the Member States, with the publication of user guides and the establishment of an easy access information system, delegated to a network of competent national authorities. It also envisaged the drafting of minimum rules in order to ensure an adequate level of judicial assistance in cross-border disputes and common procedural rules to simplify and accelerate the resolution of small cross-border claims on commercial matters regarding consumers, disputes on maintenance obligations and on non-contested claims, including through the establishment of alternative national out-of-court procedures; the preparation of multilingual forms and documents for cross-border disputes, which would be accepted in all proceedings within the EU; the preparation of minimum rules for the protection of victims of crimes, particularly on the matter of access by victims to justice and the right to receive compensation for damages.

Secondly, the Council of Tampere, as already mentioned, had approved the principle of mutual recognition of court decisions, which was meant to apply to both judgments and other decisions issued by judicial authorities, on civil and criminal matters, in order to facilitate cooperation between authorities and judicial protection of the rights of individuals. In the field of civil matters, the Commission was requested to present a proposal to reduce intermediate procedures for the recognition of judgments, first for

---

[16] It should be noted that there is a discrepancy among the various language versions of para 41(f), on the acquisition in good faith of movables: while the Spanish, Italian, English, Danish and Dutch texts refer to the adoption of rules of uniform private international law, the French and German versions make reference to uniform provisions of private law. Perhaps it is the second version that is correct, given that the approximation of certain areas of civil law is at stake.

small claims in commercial matters or consumers disputes or for certain family disputes, clearly accompanied by minimal rules on certain procedural matters.

Finally, the European Council had indicated the need to achieve greater convergence in the area of civil law, at both the procedural and the substantive level. The Council and the Commission had been asked to prepare legal provisions on certain procedural aspects pertaining to cross-border disputes, such as preliminary measures, taking of evidence, payment orders, and the commencement of a study on the approximation of national legislations on civil matters.

It is clear that over the course of one year, from the Vienna Council to the Tampere Council, the prospects of this sector had changed considerably and the scope of Article 65 EC had expanded significantly. It is also worth noting that the structure of the programme was independent of the list of measures set out under Article 65 EC — which was non-exhaustive and thus did not pose any limit upon Community action in the field of civil justice — and made no reference to it, even when the planned measures would have fallen under its scope.

Many acts have been adopted since 2000 implementing the provisions of the Treaty of Amsterdam and the indications of the European Council of Tampere. Certain are the result of activities already under way, which have been adapted to the changing legal framework, while others represented a development of the same, which has not always been natural.

As regards the first priority of Tampere, access to justice, Directive 2003/8/EC was adopted, with a view to improving access to justice in cross-border disputes through the definition of minimum common rules related to legal aid. It addresses various aspects of assistance in legal proceedings and legal advice, including exemption from legal expenses, free legal representation and contribution for legal expenses. In addition, on 28 May 2001, the Council adopted a Decision on the establishment of a European judicial network in civil and commercial matters, modelled after the one already in place in the criminal area, having the objective of improving judicial cooperation and providing information to the public in order to facilitate access to justice.[17]

More recently, a Directive on compensation to victims of crimes has been adopted (2004/80/EC of 29 April 2004), which establishes cooperation between the authorities of the Member States in order to ensure compensation for harm suffered as the result of an intentional crime committed in a Member State against life, health and personal integrity. It is based upon Article 308 EC (now Article 352 TFEU) since, as stated in the attached report, the State compensation is strictly related to civil law, but it is not a civil matter pursuant to Article 61(c) since it does not pertain to rights and duties between individuals.

As for the third priority, ie, the convergence in the civil law sector, the Commission responded to the Tampere Council's exhortation with a Communication on European contract law of September 2001,[18] that opened a debate on the legal options in order to

---

[17] The legal basis for the funding of all activities necessary for the development of the European judicial area in civil matters is set out in Regulation (EC) No 743/2002 of 25 April 2002 establishing a general Community framework of activities to facilitate the implementation of judicial cooperation in civil matters (OJ, L 115 of 1 May 2002).

[18] OJ, C 255 of 13 September 2001. The reactions to the Communication are available on the website europa.eu.int/comm/consumers/policy/developments/contract_law/comments/summaries/sum_it.pdf.   The Commission also submitted to the Council a draft report of the Council on the need to approximate the law of the Member States in civil matters (11621/01 REV 1-JUSTCIV 110, of 2 October 2001).

harmonise private law. This Communication has been subject to significant discussion since it traces a direct link between this action and judicial cooperation in civil matters under Title IV. It was followed by an Action Plan in 2003 and more recently by a Common Frame of Reference for European contract law.[19]

Many acts have been adopted for purposes of implementing the second priority and the principle of mutual recognition, which is now the explicit basis for judicial cooperation in civil matters under Article 81 TFEU. At the time of the revision of the Brussels and Lugano Conventions, a few days prior to the entry into force of the Treaty of Amsterdam, it was already clear that an international treaty could no longer be maintained as a viable legislative instrument and that the cooperation would have to be implemented by means of the standard EU acts provided under Article 249 EC (now 288 TFEU). We have already mentioned that the regulation was chosen since, according to the Commission, it best guarantees legal certainty for citizens and economic operators and meets the needs for clarity and homogeneity of Member States. In addition, the European Court of Justice's interpretation was thus made possible without any additional instruments.[20]

Within slightly over a year, the Council adopted Regulation (EC) No 1346/2000 on insolvency proceedings, Regulation (EC) No 1347/2000 on jurisdiction and the recognition and enforcement of judgments in matrimonial matters and in matters of parental responsibility for children of both spouses (known as Brussels II), Regulation (EC) No 1348/2000 on the service in the Member States of judicial and extrajudicial documents in civil or commercial matters, Regulation (EC) No 44/2001 on jurisdiction, recognition and enforcement of judgments in civil and commercial matters (known as Brussels I) and Regulation (EC) No 1206/2001 on cooperation between the courts of the Member States in the taking of evidence in civil or commercial matters.

8.3.   The Draft Programme of 2000

These acts were part of the Draft Programme of measures for implementation of the principle of mutual recognition of decisions in civil and commercial matters mentioned above, adopted by the Council on 30 November 2000. This plan addressed both the methodological aspects and the substantive aspects of the sector, also indicating the subsequent deadlines, which provided a precise idea of the future of private international law in the European Union in the following years.

The document laid down various levels of recognition, corresponding to the status of the areas in question and their future development. The minimum level is that of sectors that are not yet governed at EU level, which are subject to the national rules of the requested State and international conventions in force. Just above that, there is the first level, comprised of the procedure of the Brussels Convention and the Brussels II Regulation: the recognition is automatic and the enforcement is granted under a facilitated procedure, generally simpler than that envisaged at the lower level. The rules are common

---

[19]   See ec.europa.eu/consumers/cons_int/safe_shop/fair_bus_pract/cont_law/common_frame_ref_en.htm.
[20]   Proposal for a Council Regulation on jurisdiction and the recognition and enforcement of judgments in civil and commercial matters, COM (1999) 348 of 14 July 1999 (OJ, C 376/1999 E).

to all of the Member States and the recognition and enforcement may be refused only on the basis of reasons provided under the relevant act. At the higher level, the second level, we find the proceedings of the Brussels I Regulation and the Regulation on insolvency: the recognition is automatic, the enforcement must be granted after few formalities and it is possible to challenge it only subsequently, in any case after the grant of the *exequatur* by the judge receiving the request. At the even higher ('new level') of recognition, there is no longer any control over the foreign decision by the requested court: in certain areas, judgments may circulate freely and the European enforcement order is instituted.

With regard to the matters for which the Community proposed to intervene, the intensity of the action was graduated depending upon whether they involved areas for which acts had already been issued by the European Union or areas newly subject to communitarisation. As for the first, it was deemed necessary to improve the functioning of the existing mechanisms, reducing or eliminating the obstacles to free circulation of court decisions, passing in other words to higher levels of recognition. In the area of family law, for example, an instrument was envisaged for the facilitation of the procedure for the recovery of maintenance claims, possibly through the elimination of enforcement proceedings. It should be recalled that the Member States had already entered into a convention on this matter in 1990, which never entered into force.

In the context of commercial law, on the other hand, passage to the higher level of recognition was envisaged, involving the suppression of intermediate procedures, for non-contested claims and for small claims. The reduction of intermediate procedures involved the reduction of grounds for the refusal to recognise or enforce a foreign judgment, and the introduction of the possibility to obtain temporary enforcement thereof, to enforce precautionary injunctions throughout the European Union on the basis of a decision issued in a Member State, and to carry out precautionary seizures over bank accounts at the European level. The elimination of intermediate procedures led to the complete free movement of the foreign judgments, no longer subject to any jurisdictional control.

Where no prior Community acts existed, a lower level of recognition was envisaged, with the exception of particular cases, including certain aspects of disputes related to divorce or personal separation falling outside the scope of the Brussels II Regulation, such as parental custody and family situations falling outside the matrimonial sphere, matrimonial property regimes, wills and successions.

Finally, certain supporting measures were indicated, such as the adoption of minimal common rules of procedure or, on occasion, harmonisation of procedures to ensure access to fair proceedings and, in any case, compliance with the European Convention on human rights, and to improve and accelerate the service of judicial documents, the preparation of measures aimed at improving efficiency in enforcement, such as the exchange of information on the debtor's assets, in compliance, moreover, with the rules on the protection of personal data and on the confidential nature of certain information; the improvement of cooperation between judicial authorities of the Member States through the judicial network on civil and commercial law matters and the Regulation on the taking of evidence, mentioned above, the guarantee of access to justice for all, and the harmonisation of conflicts of laws rules. It is well-known that this latter measure has beneficial effects at the procedural level, since it reduces both forum shopping and the need for control over the law applied by the foreign court, particularly used in sensitive areas such as family law.

Actually, the subsequent developments were achieved particularly in the area of family law through an amendment to the Brussels II Regulation, replaced by Regulation (EC) No 2201/2003 (Brussels IIa). An initiative by France for the adoption of a regulation the mutual enforcement of judgments on rights of access to children[21] and a proposal by the Commission for a regulation related to jurisdiction, recognition and the enforcement of judgments in matters of parental responsibility[22] had been presented to the Council, but the debate had expanded to reconsider the private international law framework applicable to the entire area following the publication of a complex working paper prepared by the Commission on the 'Mutual recognition of decisions on parental responsibility'.[23] A discussion was opened also on the signing and ratification by the Member States of the Hague Convention on jurisdiction, applicable law, recognition, enforcement and cooperation in respect of parental responsibility and measures for the protection of children of 1996. Parallel to the adoption of the decision which authorised the Member States to sign this Convention, a draft regulation of the Council had been presented, which was adopted in 2003.[24]

More recently, the Council adopted a decision which finally authorised the Member States to ratify the above-mentioned Hague Convention, thus posing an end to a deadlock situation which persisted for many years and which, after the latest expansion of the Union, had led to an asymmetry in international obligations of the Member States on this matter. In fact, for certain of the new Member States, the 1996 Hague Convention was already in force.

In the area of jurisdiction, recognition and enforcement of decisions on civil and commercial matters, a draft amendment to Article 20 of the Brussels I Regulation had been presented by the Netherlands, in order to allow the employer to lodge a claim against the employee upon the termination of the employment contract also in the State where the employee habitually carries out his work or, if he carries out his works in more than one country, before the court of the place where the business which engaged him is situated. The Commission, on its part, had presented a 'two phase strategy': on the one hand, a draft regulation aimed at instituting a European enforcement order for non-contested claims, ie, a sort of 'certificate' for a judicial decision related to such claims in order to guarantee the free circulation of the same and the enforceability in all Member States without the need for any *exequatur*, to complement the procedure for recognition and enforcement of the Brussels I Regulation; on the other hand, a Green Paper on a European order for payment procedure and on measures to simplify and speed up small claims litigation, with the view to adopting an act aimed at completing Directive 2000/35/EC of 29 June 2000 on combating late payment in commercial transactions through the establishment of a special harmonised procedure for the recovery of non-contested claims. These were two complementary initiatives which were neither mutually exclusive nor overlapping.

---

[21] OJ, C 234 of 15 August 2000.

[22] COM (2001) 505 of 6 September 2001.

[23] COM (2001) 166 of 27 March 2001.

[24] The Commission's proposal included a provision aimed at amending Regulation (EC) No 44/2001 with reference to maintenance obligations, but this provision was abandoned. The Regulation was eventually amended in this respect by Regulation (EC) No 4/2009. It is worth mentioning that a European Parliament Mediator for international parental child abduction was created in 1987, with the task of helping children from binational marriages who have been abducted by one of their parents (http://www.europarl.europa.eu/parliament/public/staticDisplay.do?id=154).

On the contrary, according to the Commission, 'the existence of a European order for payment procedure would not only create a level playing field for creditors and debtors throughout the Member States in terms of affording them equal access to justice. It could also bring about further progress in the field of recognition and enforcement by rendering superfluous even the requirement of certification envisaged under the proposal for a European Enforcement Order'.[25]

8.4. The Hague Programme of 2004

Subsequently, the objectives of the judicial cooperation in civil matters were confirmed in the Hague Programme on the reinforcement of freedom, security and justice, adopted by the European Council on 4 November 2004, which proposed to reinforce mutual trust and to develop gradually a European judicial culture based upon the diversity of the legal systems of the Member States and the unity of European law. As regards the measures to be adopted,[26] it stated that the programme of measures on mutual recognition was supposed to have been completed in 2011 with the adoption of instruments on the law applicable to contractual and extra-contractual obligations, on the European order for payment procedure and on the European small claims procedure. The standardisation of procedures and documents and the elaboration of minimum rules concerning aspects of procedural law were also envisaged, such as service, the commencement of proceedings, the enforcement of judgments and the transparency of costs.

In the field of family law and successions, the Commission was asked to present a proposal for an instrument on the recognition and enforcement of decisions concerning maintenance obligations and some green papers on conflicts of laws and jurisdiction in the area of successions, matrimonial property regimes and divorce. It is worth pointing out that in the field of family law it was not required that the acts be based upon harmonised concepts of 'family' or 'marriage': uniform provisions of substantive law could constitute merely supporting rules and were not deemed necessary.[27]

Finally, the Hague Programme of 2004 purported to guarantee consistency and improve the quality of the Community legal framework, particularly through the adoption of provisions which allowed the Council to proceed with a more systematic review of the quality and consistency of the legal instruments concerning cooperation on civil matters.

The Hague Programme was implemented over a very short period of time. Within four years, regulations were adopted which established a European Enforcement Order (No 805/2004), a European order for payment procedure (No 1896/2006) and a European Small Claims Procedure (No 861/2007), in addition to Regulation (EC) No 1393/2007 amending Regulation (EC) No 1348/00 on service, Regulation (EC) No 4/2009 on

---

[25] COM (2002) 746 def of 20 December 2002, para 2.9.
[26] On developments of the external action in this area, as envisaged under the Plan of 2004, see para 10 below.
[27] This should not be surprising: private international law has developed for purposes of providing a solution for cross-border cases which present points of contact with more than one State, having different substantive laws. The harmonisation of national substantive laws was neither deemed necessary nor required for the adoption of national rules of private international law, and it has developed in certain areas through international conventions and model laws.

maintenance obligations and the above-mentioned Directive 2004/80/EC on compensation to victims of crime. In the area of conflicts of laws, Regulation (EC) No 864/2007 on the law applicable to non-contractual obligations (Rome II) and Regulation (EC) No 593/2008 on the law applicable to contractual obligations (Rome I) were adopted.[28] Instead, as mentioned above, the draft regulation which was supposed to amend the Brussels IIa Regulation only with respect to jurisdiction and which aimed at introducing rules on the law applicable in the matrimonial area (Rome III) was abandoned in June 2008 since unanimity could not be reached. The Council concluded that the conditions set forth by Article 20 TEU for the establishment of an enhanced cooperation in the area of the law applicable to divorce and legal separation were satisfied and, upon the request of nine Member States, the Commission submitted two proposals to this end, which were adopted by the Council in 2010.[29] In addition, the Commission answered the European Council's invitation, presenting a draft regulation on successions and a green paper on matrimonial property.[30]

8.5.   The Stockholm Programme of 2009

Finally, in October 2009 the European Council adopted the Stockholm Programme, providing guidance for the activities in the area of freedom, security and justice for the period 2010–2014.[31] The future actions will be centred on the citizen and other persons for whom the EU has a responsibility and will aim at promoting European citizenship and fundamental rights of individuals, and developing the external dimension. The European Council has noted that the development of legislation has been impressive, but it has shortcomings in terms of overlapping and a certain lack of coherence, and the quality of the legislation could be improved.

As concerns the protection of fundamental rights, the European Council has invited the Commission to submit a proposal on the accession of the EU to the European Convention on Human Rights. The protection of personal data at international level should be enhanced through the adoption of a recommendation for the negotiation of a data protection and, where necessary, data sharing agreements for law enforcement purposes with third countries.

The European Council has underlined the improvements achieved in respect to the application of the principle of mutual recognition, and has considered that the process of abolishing all intermediate measures should be continued, to be accompanied by a series of safeguards, especially regarding judgments taken by default. Mutual recognition should be extended to succession and wills, matrimonial property rights and the property consequences of the separation of couples. The harmonisation of conflict-of-law rules

---

[28] It should be noted that in the meantime, on 1 August 2004, the two Protocols on the interpretation by the Court of Justice of the 1980 Rome Convention had entered into force. The Rome Convention remains in force for contracts entered into prior to the date of application of the Rome I Regulation, ie 17 December 2010.

[29] See above at fn 13.

[30] COM (2009) 154 of 14 October 2009 and COM (2006) 400 of 17 July 2006.

[31] On 10 June 2009 the Commission had adopted the communication 'An area of freedom, security and justice serving the citizen' (COM (2009) 262).

should also continue in the areas of separation and divorces, company law, insurance contracts and security interests. The European Council also requested the Commission to follow up on the recent study on the possible problems encountered with regard to civil status documents and access to registers of such documents and to submit appropriate proposals with the aim of setting up a system whereby citizens would be able to obtain their own civil status documents and eventually the effects of civil status documents would be mutually recognised. Moreover, the possibility of abolishing all formalities for the legalisation of documents between Member States should be studied with the aim of creating, in the long term, authentic European documents.

In order to support economic activity in the single market the Commission was invited to assess the need for, and the feasibility of, providing for certain provisional, including protective, measures to prevent the disappearance of assets before the enforcement of a claim, and to submit a proposal for improving the efficiency of enforcement of judgments regarding bank accounts and debtors' assets.

As concerns the external dimension, the European Council noted that the Lugano Convention is open to the accession of other States and it should be assessed, in cooperation with the other Contracting Parties, which third countries could be encouraged to accede to it. The participation in the Hague Conference should help in promoting the widest possible accession to the most relevant Conventions and to offer as much assistance as possible to other States with a view to the proper implementation of the instruments.

More generally, the European Council noticed that the Lisbon Treaty offers new possibilities for the European Union to act more efficiently in external relations and that the new legal basis for concluding international agreements will ensure that the Union can negotiate more effectively with key partners, ie candidate countries and countries with a European Union membership perspective, European neighbourhood countries, EEA/ Schengen States having a close relationship with the EU, the United States of America, the Russian Federation and other strategic partners, other countries or regions of priority, in terms of their contribution to EU strategic or geographical priorities, international organisations such as the UN and the Council of Europe with whom the Union need to continue to work and within which the Union should coordinate its position.

On 20 April 2010 the Commission adopted the Action Plan implementing the Stockholm Programme,[32] and announced the presentation of proposals for regulations amending the Brussels I Regulation (which was actually presented on 15 December 2010), the Brussels II Regulation (2011) and the insolvency Regulation (2012), as well as proposals for instruments on matrimonial property regimes, on a European attachment of bank accounts and on contract law by the end of 2010. Finally, the Commission announced that it will carry out studies concerning the recognition of civil status documents with the aim of presenting a green paper in 2010 and a legislative proposal by the end of 2013, when also a proposal for a regulation on the transparency of debtor's assets with the aim of improving the efficiency of the enforcement of judgments and a legislative proposal on the abolition of legalisation would be ready. A green paper on private international law aspects relating to companies, associations and other legal entities is scheduled for 2014.

---

[32] COM (2010) 171.

9.   The Relationship of Article 65 EC and Article 81 TFEU with other Provisions of the Treaty

One problem that was debated at length by the first commentators on the communitarisation of the judicial cooperation in civil law matters related to the position of art 65 CE within the system established by the Treaty. This problem concerns primarily the existence of possible limits upon the Community's activities, ie, whether Articles 61 and 65 EC granted to it a general competence in this field or if the Community's powers were limited to only what is necessary in order to develop the other matters falling under the scope of Title IV. An additional issue was connected and interwoven with this one, concerning possible connections with Article 293 (formerly 220) EC and with Article 95 (formerly 100a) CE. While the issue of the relationships between Article 81 TFEU and Article 293 EC is no longer relevant, since the Treaty of Lisbon definitively abrogated the latter, the other problems still remain open.

9.1.   The Relationship with Article 293 EC

As concerns the relationship of between Article 65 EC and Article 293 EC, it had been argued that the former should be positioned within Title VI TEU since the provisions and the position of the new Title IV EC had been designed for the free circulation of persons and for the Schengen *acquis* and not for cooperation in the field of private international law. The inclusion of this cooperation within Title IV EC would have led to an overlapping with Article 293 EC, which had remained unaltered from 1957, and which ordered the commencement of negotiations among the Member States in order to mutually ensure to their citizens, through international conventions, the protection of persons and the enjoyment of rights, the elimination of double taxation, mutual recognition of companies, maintenance of legal personality in the event of transfer of a registered office and the merger of companies subject to different laws, the simplification of formalities for the recognition and enforcement of judgments and arbitration awards.[33]

This view could not be shared and, in any case, it has been superseded by practice over the past 10 years. Indeed, Article 293 EC did not apply to all of the matters falling under the scope of Article 65 EC, but concerned only certain aspects of procedural law in cross-border matters. In fact, the Rome Convention on the law applicable to contractual obligations had been entered into outside the EC Treaty as a continuation and completion

---

[33] According to the scholarly position under discussion here, since under the Commission's proposal to the inter-governmental conference which led to the Treaty of Amsterdam, Article 220 EC was supposed to disappear, the fact that it remained (see Article 293) confirms the nature and scope of Article 65: this would be limited to what is necessary in the area of visas and free movement of persons, while choice-of-law rules would remain included under Article 293 and subject to the inter-governmental method: Ch Kohler, 'Interrogations sur les Sources du Droit International Privé Européen après le Traité d'Amsterdam' (1999) *Revue critique* 8 *et seq*, 11, 15, 22. On the theory that Article 65 is limited to the measures necessary for purposes of the policies indicated under the heading of Title IV and would have merely the function of supplementing Article 95 EC, see also J Basedow, 'The Communitarization of the Conflict of Laws under the Treaty of Amsterdam'(2000) *Common Market Law Review* 697.

of the 1968 Brussels Convention. In addition, the scope of Article 293 EC was limited to measures in favour of citizens of the Member States, while the provisions contained in Title IV EC also concerned the citizens of third countries.

In any case, Article 293 EC already appeared to have been superseded following the Treaty of Maastricht: Article K.3 TEU, indeed, has provided the basis for certain of the above-mentioned conventions, with the sole exception of the Convention on insolvency proceedings concluded in 1995. It was therefore difficult to avoid concluding that Article 61(c) EC was broad in scope and capable of vesting the Community with the powers to adopt acts related to any aspect of judicial cooperation in civil matters, of which the rules on conflicts of laws and jurisdiction are only one of the sectors, indicated by way of example ('shall include', stated the text of Article 65 EC). The same wording appears now in Article 81 TFEU, with reference to the Union, which also restates the two conditions already provided under Article 65 EC, ie, that there are cross-border implications and that the action is taken 'particularly when necessary for the proper functioning of the internal market'.

9.2. The Relationship with Article 114 TFEU (Formerly Article 95 EC)

The notion of 'proper functioning of the internal market' has a rather wide scope, not limited to persons, but also encompassing entire sectors of economic life. Consequently, Article 81 TFEU, like Article 65 EC beforehand, does not supplement Article 114 TFEU (formerly Article 95 EC), which provides for measures aiming at the approximation of rules of law having as their object the establishment and functioning of the internal market. It has been properly noted, inter alia, that if until the Treaty of Amsterdam the main provisions on conflicts of laws and jurisdiction were those founded upon Article 293 EC or Article K.3 TEU or agreed in an inter-governmental context, there is no reason why the communitarisation should bring them under the scope of Article 114 TFEU (formerly Article 95 EC). Indeed, in sectors that are not related to the free movement of persons in which this provision could well have fully applied in the past, it was never used: the unification of the rules on the law applicable to contractual obligations, which was deemed necessary given the existence of 'legal fields in which the differences between national legal systems and the lack of unified rules of conflict definitely impede the free movement of persons, goods, services and capital among the Member States',[34] was reached through the Rome Convention of 1980 on the law applicable to contractual obligations, concluded outside the scope of Article 220 EC. The reference to the internal market contained in the two provisions — Article 65 CE/81 TFEU and Article 95 CE/114 TFEU — must therefore not lead to confusion as to their respective scopes and objectives.

In addition, as it has been highlighted, the practice of EC institutions in these years from the entry into force of the Treaty of Amsterdam has gone in the direction of a

---

[34] M Giuliano and P Lagarde, *Report on the Convention on the law applicable to contractual obligations*, OJ, C 282 of 31 October 1980, at para 2, citing the speech by the general director Vogelaar at the inaugural meeting of the government experts in charge of drafting the Convention.

utilization of Article 65 EC and, in any case, of the reference to the 'area of freedom, security and justice' or the 'European judicial area' as a basis for the measures adopted or planned. No mention has ever been made of Article 95 EC, although in various cases the measures for harmonisation of substantive law adopted on the basis of the latter may contain, and in fact do contain, provisions on conflicts of laws and jurisdictions. Moreover, the last acts adopted on the basis of Article 65 EC show that the presence of a rule granting general competence to the institutions ensures greater attention to the matter and tends to ensure better coordination among provisions contained in different acts than has occurred in the past.

As a final note on this point, the conclusions in the *Fundación Gaia-Salvador Dalí* case are worth recalling. In that case, in order to rule out the possibility that Directive 2001/84/EC on the resale right contains choice-of-law rules for the identification of the beneficiaries after the author's death, Attorney general Sharpston stated that 'had there been any intention to harmonise choice of law rules in the field of succession, the Directive could not have been based, as it is, simply on Article 95 EC, but would have had to refer… to Article 61 EC and 67 EC'.[35]

The limit posed upon the adoption of measures within the context of Article 81 TFEU — 'particularly when necessary for the proper functioning of the internal market' — merits further discussion. While it is certainly different from the general limit under Article 115 TFEU (formerly Article 94 CE) concerning measures that 'directly affect the establishment or functioning of the internal market', it is not so clear precisely what the former consists of. On the contrary, the limit established at Article 81 TFEU appears close or similar to the limit posed on measures referred to under Article 114 TFEU, having 'as their object the establishment and functioning of the internal market', so much so as to lead to refer to the criteria laid down by the Court of Justice in its judgment concerning the Directive 98/43/EC on advertising and sponsorship of tobacco products. According to the ECJ, the objective of Article 95 EC does not allow for it to be interpreted as granting to the Community (now to the Union) the general power to regulate the internal market. This would not only be contrary to the tenor of such provisions, 'but would also be incompatible with the principle embodied in Article 3b of the EC Treaty [now Article 5 TEU] that the powers of the Community are limited to those specifically conferred on it. Moreover, a measure adopted on the basis of Article 100a of the Treaty must genuinely have as its object the improvement of the conditions for the establishment and functioning of the internal market. If a mere finding of disparities between national rules and of the abstract risk of obstacles to the exercise of fundamental freedoms or of distortions of competition liable to result therefrom were sufficient to justify the choice of Article 100a as a legal basis, judicial review of compliance with the proper legal basis might be rendered nugatory. The Court would then be prevented from discharging the function entrusted to it by Article 164 of the EC Treaty (now Article 220 EC) of ensuring that the law is observed in the interpretation and application of the Treaty'.[36]

These considerations still apply with reference to Article 81 TFEU, but with one clarification: the institutions have not been granted general carte blanche power to render uniform or to promote the compatibility of national rules on conflicts of laws and

---

[35] Case C-518/08. The judgment was given on 15 April 2010.

[36] Judgment 5 October 2000, case C-376/98, *Germany v European Parliament and Council*, points 83 and 84.

jurisdiction, but only to the extent necessary for the proper functioning of the internal market. This notion appears to have a more complex meaning than the mere 'functioning', so as to be capable of forming the basis of Union power in a broader number of cases as compared with Article 114 TFEU, which always had a broad scope of application. If the existence of divergences between the legal systems of the Member States and the resulting risk of impediments to the fundamental freedoms or distortions in competition are perhaps insufficient, the qualification of the functioning as 'proper' might suggest a more incisive evaluation and control. Furthermore, Article 81 TFEU would appear to diminish the role of the need for the measure adopted with reference to the functioning of the internal market where it grants to the institutions regulatory power in this field '*in particular* if necessary to the proper functioning of the internal market'.

10.   The Conflict-of-Law Rules Set Out in Acts Based upon Other Provisions of the TFEU

The significant production of laws, which in just a few years reduced the scope of national systems of private international law, does not constitute the entire legal framework of reference of the Union in this field, which includes numerous acts and instruments adopted in the context of other policies, containing rules on conflicts of laws and jurisdiction. Take, for example, the directives on employment, insurance and consumer contracts, the regulations on EU intellectual property rights, and so on. As we may see from the vastness of the material presented in this volume, the provisions that are relevant for purposes of our analysis are very numerous and may be found in an extensive range of acts pertaining to a very broad range of areas.

In addition, the presence of the general rule on the matter, Article 65 EC and today Article 81 TFEU, has granted greater attention to the problems of private international law, thus facilitating and improving coordination between provisions contained in various acts. This is a concern which has been the focus of attention on the part of the Member States since the adoption of the Rome Convention, which included as an attachment a common declaration that, in order to avoid the possible 'dispersion of choice of law rules among several instruments and differences between these rules', trusted that the institutions would 'endeavour' to adopt provisions that were consistent with those set out in the Convention, to the extent possible. Recital No 35 of the Rome II Regulation leans in this direction, where it states that '[a] situation where conflict-of-law rules are dispersed among several instruments and where there are differences between those rules should be avoided. This Regulation, however, does not exclude the possibility of inclusion of conflict-of-law rules relating to non-contractual obligations in provisions of Community law with regard to particular matters.' Substantially the same wording appears at Recital No 40 of the Rome I Regulation.[37]

The fact that the general provisions on conflicts of laws and jurisdiction in certain areas are gathered together under general acts, leaving the possibility of providing only

---

[37] Recital No 40 of the Rome I Regulation states that 'this regulation *should not exclude*' (italics added).

for exceptions that may be necessary or opportune in particular areas precisely to the acts dealing with those particular areas, better ensures the consistency of the system and the uniformity of the connecting factors used and the objectives to be achieved.[38] Indeed, it should be noted that actually these widely dispersed provisions adopted so far in specific areas not only reflect the complexity of the decision-making mechanisms which govern the division of powers within the EU institutions, but document the presence of incongruities and the lack of uniformity even within the same area.

By way of example, in order to illustrate the difficulties deriving from the fragmentation of the legal framework, we may mention the directives related to consumer contracts[39] in which the objective of guaranteeing a minimum common level of protection of the weaker contractual party was achieved using modalities which changed over time. The first directives provided only substantive rules, with a provision of the scope of application and on minimum treatment, as well as provisions that could not be derogated by the parties.[40] Some later directives, however, such as that on distance contracts, that on unfair terms and that on the sale of consumer goods and associated warranties, operate also at the level of private international law where they provide that the consumer may not be deprived of the protection granted by the directive through the choice of the law of a third country where the contract is connected to the territory of one or more Member States. This provision, which apparently reiterates Article 5 of the Rome Convention, in reality adds certain elements: on the one hand, the protection is granted for all contracts entered into by the consumer using the modalities envisaged under the directive in question; on the other hand, the protection is granted only if the law of the non-EU country, in theory less protective, was chosen by the parties (Article 5(2) of the Convention and Article 6(2) of the Rome I Regulation), but no protection is granted if such law applies pursuant to Article 5(3) of the same Convention (or Article 6(1) of the said Regulation, ie, as the law of the consumer's State of residence lacking any choice by the parties). Therefore, the rule protects only the consumer domiciled in the EU, who enters into a contract where the parties contractually agree that the law of a third country will apply.

The Directive on timeshare provides an exception, in so far as, for obvious reasons, it links the protection to the presence of the real estate asset within the Union, regardless of the location of the consumer and the law governing the contract.[41]

---

[38] See the *Position Paper* presented by P Beaumont, at the hearing on the proposed directive on services held at the European Parliament on 11 November 2004, and the *Position of the European Group of Private International Law on the draft directive of the European Parliament and the Council on services in the internal market* of 24 November 2004, www.drt.ucl.ac.be/gedip/DirservicesE.html.

[39] In this area, directives contain rules of general application, such as those on misleading and comparative advertising, on unfair terms, on the sale of consumer goods and associated guarantees, and directives which specifically concern sales sectors and methods, such as food products, cosmetics, denominations in the textile sector, pharmaceutical for human use, 'all-inclusive' travel packages, consumer credit, timeshare, distance contracts (see for the related data the EC Commission's communication 'Green paper on the protection of consumers in the European Union', COM (2001) 531 of 2 October 2001). Recently, the Commission presented a proposed directive on consumer rights which aims at reformulating certain of the above-mentioned directives (COM (2008) 614 of 8 October 2008).

[40] See Articles 5(3) and 8 of Directive 90/314/CEE on package travel, package holidays and package tours (OJ, L 158 of 23 June 1990).

[41] The relevant provisions of these directives are set out below under Chapter VI, as well as the decision issued by the Court of Justice in case C-70/03, *Commission v Spain*, concerning the implementation of the protection clauses contained in Directive 93/13/EEC on unfair terms.

The limitation of protection in favour of solely the EU consumer is explained by the objective of the above-mentioned directives, ie, the approximation of the provisions laid down by law, regulation or administrative action in Member States which have as their object the establishment and functioning of the internal market pursuant to Article 114 TFEU, cited by Article 169 TFEU on consumers' protection. Any extension of this protection to consumers resident outside the European Union is merely a secondary effect of the conflict rules considered here, but not the expression of a specific intention that the directives apply as super-mandatory rules for the protection of all consumers, regardless of their location. Consequently, in connection with the above-mentioned directives, the consumer resident outside the European Union who decides to bring action against its counterparty before the court of a Member State of its registered office in order to benefit from the protection of the Directive on distance contracts, for example, will be granted such protection only if the contract contains a choice of law clause selecting the law of the State of the consumer which is less favourable to his interests, but will not succeed if the law of such State applies as the result of Article 5(3) of the Rome Convention or Article 6(1) of the Rome I Regulation.

The Commission recently presented a draft directive on consumer rights,[42] which will introduce considerable changes to the substantive law of the Member States and the functioning of the system in the context of the application of Directives 85/577/ CEE, 93/13/CEE, 97/7/CE and 1999/44/CE, for the main purpose of eliminating the fragmentation of the *acquis* concerning consumers, which hinders cross-border sales within the Union. Based upon the assumption that under the Rome I Regulation, consumers which enter into an agreement with a foreign commercial operator may not be deprived of the protection arising under mandatory provision of law of their country of residence, the proposal distances itself from the minimum harmonisation approach followed in the four mentioned directives in favour of complete harmonisation, on the basis of which Member States will not be empowered to maintain or adopt provisions diverging from those set out under the future directive. Therefore, the above-mentioned protection clause on the choice of applicable law made by the parties is abandoned, while in reality the consumer who resides in the Union may not be deprived of the rights granted by the future directive. Indeed, if the parties choose the law of a non-EU country, Article 6 of the Rome I Regulation will determine, on the basis of the consumer's habitual residence, whether he will be entitled to the protection granted under EU law.

If we look at the conflict rules applicable to non-contractual obligations, it should be noted that no provision of the TFEU indicates the law applicable to extra-contractual liability of the Union, unlike the situation for the law applicable to contractual liability. Article 340(2) TFEU makes reference to the general common principles of the Member States for the determination of compensation for damages caused by the institutions and agents of the Community. Thus, the Court of Justice has been assigned the task of identifying such principles as well as the conditions and scope of liability of the Community, of 'creating' the applicable substantive law, autonomous from the law of the Members States.

Certain acts contain specific provisions, designating the law of the State where the action is carried out or the law of the State where the event took place, or even both, including through a reference to national conflicts rules. An example of the third type is

---

[42]   COM (2008) 614 of 8 October 2008.

found in Article 2(2) of Directive 2009/22 on injunctions for the protection of consumers' interests, pursuant to which '[t]his Directive shall be without prejudice to the rules of private international law with respect to the applicable law, that is, normally, either the law of the Member State where the infringement originated or the law of the Member State where the infringement has its effects.' In the area of infringement of a Union trade mark, on the other hand, Article 14 of Regulation (EC) No 207/2009 provides that national rules apply, while Article 102(2) imposes the application of the 'the law of the Member State in which the acts of infringement or threatened infringement were committed, including the private international law'.[43] On the matter of intellectual property rights, Article 10 of Regulation (EC) No 1383/2003 concerning customs action against goods suspected of infringing certain intellectual property rights subjects the assessment of the existence of a breach of such right to the law of the State of location of the goods, which also regulates the liability of the customs authorities and the owner of the right (Article 19).

Numerous ECJ decisions have affirmed that the law which governs extra-contractual liability is, generally speaking, the law of the Member State where the damages occur: 'the rights that the victim or those entitled under him have against the person who caused the injury and the requirements to be satisfied to enable an action in damages to be brought before the courts of the Member State where the injury was sustained must be determined in accordance with the law of that State, including any applicable rules of private international law'.[44] This context also includes now the Rome II Regulation, which designates as the governing law of the tort the law of the country where the damage occurs, regardless of the place of the event and of the indirect consequences thereof.

An additional problem concerns the evaluation of the respective scope of application and of the relationships between the various types of acts that have been used. Aside from the institutional aspects, it is well-known that in general, there is no hierarchical relationship between regulations and directives, given the difference in their objectives and effects, also because the rules set out under the directives apply generally by way of the national implementing provisions. The solution is provided by the principle of speciality: already a number of the regulations adopted so far on the basis of Article 65 EC (now 81 TFEU), indeed leave intact the directives and, in general, the Union acts which, in particular areas, govern the matters governed by the regulations. An example of a general provision to this end is provided by Article 67 of Regulation (EC) No 44/2001. Recital No 27 of Regulation (EC) No 1346/2000 expressly cites the specificity of the Directive on settlement finality in order to justify the fact that it prevails over general rules set out in the Regulation itself. Likewise, always in this context, the Directive on the reorganisation and winding up of credit institutions and the analogous provisions concerning insurance companies now set out in Directive 2009/138/EC establish special rules vis-à-vis Regulation (EC) No 1346/2000. The rules set out in the above-mentioned Directives on contracts entered into by consumers also apply in this manner, as they prevail over the general rules established under the Rome Convention, as per its Article 20, and under the Rome I Regulation (Article 23). Article 27 of the Rome II Regulation provides similarly with reference to non-contractual obligations.

---

[43]   See also Article 89 of Regulation (EC) No 6/2002 on Union designs and models.
[44]   Judgments 21 September 1999, case C-397/96, *Kordel*; 9 December 1965, case 44/65, *Singer*; 16 May 1973, case 78/72, *De Waal*; 2 June 1994, case C-428/92, *DAK*; 9 September 2004, case C-397/02, *Clinique la Ramée*.

11.   The 'Cross-Border Implications' of Judicial Cooperation in Civil Matters

In addition to the condition related to the 'correct functioning of the internal market' discussed above, Article 81 TFEU, like Article 65 EC before it, imposes a second general requirement for the EU competence in so far as it refers to the 'cross-border implications' of judicial cooperation in civil matters. Two different approaches have been proposed so far with reference to this provision. According to the first, the Union would be empowered to adopt only measures aimed at regulating cases connected exclusively to the Member States, relationships located within the borders of the Union, as the reference to the functioning of the internal market would appear to suggest. In this case, we are merely dealing with a different formulation of a general condition for the application of EU law, which may not come into play for situations which pertain entirely to one Member State. According to other authors, however, cases linked to third countries could be regulated as well, and therefore the Union competence would be general and exclusive in nature and would completely replace national jurisdiction.

In practice and in the scholarly doctrine this condition and the scope of cross-border implications which would justify the exercise of EU competence have been discussed at length.

The issue has been explicitly addressed and resolved at the institutional level on the occasion of the adoption of the Rome II Regulation. The initial proposal by the Commission contained under Article 2 a provision corresponding to Article 2 of the 1980 Rome Convention and indicated the intention of determining the law applicable to non-contractual obligations even when the law of a third country was made applicable. The majority of the States within the Council had supported the *erga omnes* application of the future regulation considering that the proper functioning on the internal market would require the application of uniform conflicts rules also vis-à-vis third countries in order to eliminate forum shopping and the obstacles to the recognition and enforcement of judgments.

This position may be shared since it would appear quite difficult to establish the border between the respective competence of the EU and of the Member States, especially if the parties to the dispute retain the possibility of choosing the applicable law, naturally on the assumption that they may continue to choose the competent forum pursuant to the Brussels I Regulation or in accordance with national procedural rules. It is clear that the achievement of the objectives of the future Rome II Regulation would be hindered if its application were subject to the fact that the parties had chosen the law of a Member State.

Certain Member States, however, were of the view that it was necessary to condition the application of the future Rome II Regulation to the existence of an effective link between the actual case and the Union. The objective of facilitating the proper functioning of the internal market, upon which Article 81 TFEU still conditions the competence of the EU, would operate as a limit upon the application of the Regulation which should not come into consideration if all or the majority of the factual elements are located outside the European Union.

In order to establish an objective connection between the dispute and the territory of the European Union, under the text prepared by the Committee on Civil Law Matters of the Council, Article 2 remained intact, but three different options for Article 1 had been proposed. Under the first, the Regulation would not have applied if the only connecting factor with the Union was the selection of the competent forum within the Union (and none of the parties was domiciled therein); under the second option, the Regulation would not have applied if the judge of a Member State had based his jurisdiction on a jurisdictional criterion provided under domestic law; under the third, finally, the Regulation would have applied only if the judge of a Member State had jurisdiction. In cases where the effective connecting factor existed, it would have been justified to apply the law of a non-EU country. In this manner, reconciliation was sought between the desire to apply the Regulation not only in cases of conflicts between the laws of Member States, but also to conflicts between the law of a Member State and that of a third country, with the need to exclude cases that were connected too tenuously with the Community.

The second option was the least convincing since the Brussels I Regulation not only envisages the recognition of judgments issued on the basis of exorbitant national rules against a defendant domiciled in a third country, but in certain cases it applies directly in order to determine the jurisdiction of a Member State regardless of the defendant's domicile within the European Union (Articles 22 and 23). For this reason as well, the third option was preferable since it was broader and was more consistent with the current structure of the Union's conflict-of-laws system, broadly speaking.[45] It should not be forgotten that already the Rome Convention applies not only *erga omnes*, but without any condition with regard to the link of the particular case with the EU legal system. It is clear that, generally speaking, it may not apply directly except where the judge of a Member State has jurisdiction,[46] but this is independent of the jurisdiction criterion that comes into play. It is also clear that from this perspective, it is preferable that the conflict rule may designate either the law of a Member State or that of a third country since two parallel systems of rules would give rise to confusion for operators as well as room for manipulation by the parties involved.

The solution adopted in the Rome II Regulation, later followed also for the Rome I Regulation, was that of avoiding any specific objective or subjective connection of the dispute with the territory of the Union. The cross-border implications are therefore general and not limited to the relationships among Member States. As stated in the press release of the meeting of the JHA Council on 19–20 April 2007, during which the future regulation on maintenance obligations was discussed, '[t]he Presidency therefore takes the view, in the light of other civil law instruments adopted as well, that an explicit definition of the cross-border nature of the instrument is not essential. The Presidency accordingly suggests making it clear in a recital that the Regulation applies only in situations having cross-border implications and hence an international aspect'.[47]

---

[45]   S Bariatti 'The Future Community Rules in the Framework of the Communitarization of Private International Law' in A Malatesta (ed), *The Unification of Choice of Law Rules on Torts and Other Non-Contractual Obligations in Europe. The Rome II Proposal* (Padua, 2006).

[46]   It may be applied indirectly by a non-EU judge whose conflicts-of-laws system designates the law of a State party to the Convention.

[47]   Doc 8364/07.

12.   The External Dimension of EU Activities in the Field of Private International Law: The Relationships with Third Countries

The solution adopted with reference to the treatment of cross-border cases that are connected to non-EU countries have significant consequences upon the structure of external relationships and, in particular, on the respective competence of the Member States and the Union in the conclusion of treaties with third countries on the matters falling under Title V TFEU. In this regard, reference may be made on a preliminary basis to the indications provided by the ECJ in certain judgments concerning other areas.

12.1.   The ECJ Case-Law on External Powers

First of all, following *AETR*, where the Court had affirmed that external competence is an expression of internal jurisdiction and may be exercised after the Community has adopted an internal act,[48] in opinion 1/76 it clearly limited the exclusive external competence of the Union to the assumption of international undertakings necessary for the achievement of a specific objective imposed under the Treaty.[49] Certainly, the realisation of an area of freedom, security and justice and, within it, judicial cooperation in civil matters are objectives expressed under the Treaty in its current version, but it should not be forgotten that in this area the Union may adopt only those actions which are necessary for the proper functioning of the internal market. In the following opinion 1/94, the Court stated that '[w]henever the Community has included in its internal legislative acts provisions relating to the treatment of nationals of non-member countries or expressly conferred on its institutions powers to negotiate with non-member countries, it acquires exclusive external competence in the spheres covered by those acts. The same applies in any event, even in the absence of any express provision authorizing its institutions to negotiate with non-member countries, where the Community has achieved complete harmonization of the rules governing access to a self-employed activity, because the common rules thus adopted could be affected within the meaning of the *AETR* judgment if the Member States retained freedom to negotiate with non-member countries'.[50]

It is therefore well accepted that the establishment of exclusive Union competence deprives Member States of external competence, except for a transitional period until the exercise by the Union of internal jurisdiction. Member States, in this case, are nonetheless bound, pursuant to Article Article 4(3) TEU (formerly Article 10 CE), to adopt all of the general and specific measures aimed at ensuring fulfilment of the obligations arising under the Treaty and the acts issued by the institutions, and at facilitating the Union in the performance of their duties. Where, on the contrary, it is believed that there exists a

---

[48]   31 March 1971, case 22/70, *Commission v Council.*
[49]   Opinion 1/76 of 26 April 1977 on the Draft Agreement establishing a European laying-up fund for inland waterway vessels.
[50]   Opinion 1/94 of 15 November 1994 on the WTO, GATS and TRIPS agreements, points 95 and 96.

possibility of shared or concurrent jurisdiction, the power to enter into agreements with third countries would be shared among the Union and the Member States, which would be under a duty to cooperate with one another both during the negotiation and conclusion of such agreements and during the subsequent phase involving the performance of the duties deriving therefrom.

12.2.   The Vienna Action Plan of 1998

Although the genesis of Title IV EC, based upon Article K TEU, would appear to indicate that the attention was directed at the intra-Union relationships and not at those with third countries, the practice of the EU institutions within the framework of Article 65 EC has shown from the outset a tendency toward establishing exclusive jurisdiction and universalisation. As discussed above, such tendency was already present both in the conflict rules contained in the directives adopted on the basis of Article 95 EC, and in the universal nature of the rules set out in the 1980 Rome Convention, although this is not a 'Community convention'.

Indeed, the Vienna Action Plan of 1998, with regard to the relationships with third countries and international organisations stated that 'the "communitarisation" of the matters relating to asylum, immigration and judicial cooperation in civil matters permit the Community, to the extent permitted by the established case-law of the European Court of Justice related to the external competence of the Community, to exercise its influence internationally in these matters' (point 22). With specific reference to Article 65 EC, an opinion by the legal service of the Council issued on 5 February 1999 stated some time later that the exercise of internal competence by the Commission would have deprived the Member States of power to enter into treaties with third countries which could have prejudiced European Union law.[51]

This approach was set very clearly in connection with the negotiations held at the Hague Conference on Private International Law for the conclusion of a universal convention on jurisdiction, recognition and enforcement of judgments on civil and commercial matters. It is important to point out that while the Brussels Convention did not affect conventions on special matters to which the Contracting States were or would have been party (Article 57), Regulation (EC) No 44/2001 states that it does not prejudice only those agreements to which the Member States were already party at the time of its entry into force (Article 71).[52] On the occasion of its adoption, the Council and the Commission issued a common statement 'on Articles 71 and 72 and on the negotiations within the Hague Conference on Private International Law', on the basis of which the two institutions would have assessed the possibility to commence negotiations with third countries for the conclusion of agreements aimed at limiting, for parties domiciled in such countries, the consequences of Article 4 of the Regulation and its provisions on the recognition and enforcement of judgments, as well as the conclusions of conventions with third countries

---

[51]   The opinion is cited by A Borrás, *Derecho internacional privado* (n 3), at 406.
[52]   On the scope of Article 71 and the relationship of the Brussels I Regulation with the CMR Convention see the *TNT Express Nederland* judgment of the ECJ, 4 May 2010, case C-533/08.

in certain of the areas covered by the Regulation, as provided Article 57 of the Brussels Convention. Indeed, the conclusion of international agreements was considered favourably as an instrument that 'might allow the creation of a global or regional legal environment conducive to the circulation of judgments in civil and commercial matters.' Precisely for purposes of the negotiations at the Hague Conference, the statement emphasised the importance of works carried out so far and indicated a particular method of works which, without prejudicing the scope of the external powers of the Union, intended 'to ensure the continuity of the current negotiations, while making sure that Community positions are consistent and that Member States take an effective part in the negotiations.'[53] The statement attached to Regulation (EC) No 44/2001 ended with a declaration by the two institutions that 'the Regulation does not prevent a Member State from concluding agreements with third States on matters covered by the Regulation, where the latter is unaffected by those agreements'.[54]

Even at the time of adoption of certain of the prior regulations, in May 2000, the Council, the Member States and the Commission had adopted declarations on the possibility of entering into agreements with third countries. Some declarations are published in the *Official Journal*, while others appear only in the minutes of the meetings of the Council and are available on the site of the Council. In particular, a declaration by the Council was published which, with reference to Regulation (EC) No 1346/2000 on insolvency proceedings, states that the Regulation 'shall not prevent a Member State from concluding agreements with non-Member States, which cover the same matter as this Regulation, where the agreement in question does not affect this Regulation'.[55] Regulation (EC) No 1346/2000 contains under Article 44(3) a provision that is entirely similar to Article 71 of the Brussels I Regulation, which leaves intact only those agreements already in force between Member States and third countries. Also Article 22 of the Regulation on the European Enforcement Order states that it does not affect bilateral conventions with third countries adopted on the basis of Article 59 of the Brussels Convention prior to the entry into force of the Brussels I Regulation.

The situation with regard to Regulation (EC) No 1347/2000 on matrimonial matters (Brussels II) is more complex: on the one hand it stated that it prevailed over certain conventions specifically listed under Article 37, while on the other it did not affect agreements entered into by certain Member States with the Holy See (Article 40).

---

[53] The method indicated in the declaration provided for the adoption of negotiating directives by the Council which, on the basis of consultations among the institutions and the Member States during special coordination meetings, could be adapted to the development of the negotiations. The Community's proposals within the negotiations were presented by the Council and by the Commission, and the Member States could express their opinion only if it is not incompatible with such proposals. They could also make proposals and answer proposals presented by other States, provided that they submitted notice of the same to the President-in-Office of the Council and to the Commission. In the event of serious difficulties, in particular in the event of disagreement among Member States or need to define new approaches, the matter was referred to the Council. This procedure was later followed also with respect to subsequent negotiations for the adoption of the more recent Hague conventions, ie the Convention of 5 July 2006 on certain rights over securities held with an intermediary, the Convention of 30 June 2005 on choice of court agreement and the Convention of 23 November 2007 on maintenance obligations.

[54] Such declaration was first attached to the proposal for the Brussels I Regulation (doc 13 742/00, JUST-CIV 131 of 24 November 2000).

[55] According to E Jayme and Ch Kohler, this declaration refers to Regulation (EC) No 1347/2000 on matrimonial matters (*Europäisches Kollisionsrecht 2000: Interlokales Privatrecht oder universelles Gemeinschaftsrecht?*, *IPRax*, 2000, 454, fn 6). This Regulation, however, is accompanied by other declarations of a different tenor that are mentioned in the text above.

Furthermore, Article 16 provided that the courts of a Member State could refuse — on the basis of a treaty with a non-EU State on the recognition and enforcement of judgments — to recognise a decision adopted in another Member State based upon criteria other than those set out under Articles 2–7 of the Regulation.

The silence on other agreements with third countries was accompanied by several statements which appear to lean in the direction of supporting the existence of the power on the part of Member States to enter into such agreements. The Council had declared that 'the Member States undertake to inform the Commission of any agreements which they envisage concluding with third States in accordance with Article 16 and of any changes to or repeal of such agreements, such as amendments or complaints'. This position was reinforced by two statements by the United Kingdom: the first clarified that Member States should be able to conclude agreements with third States that allowed them not to recognise decisions adopted by other Member States based upon criteria other than those established under the Regulation or agreements which did not interfere with the application of the Regulation itself; the second stated that Article 16 of the Regulation and the above-mentioned statement by the Council ensured that the Member States were able to enter into treaties with third countries and that such ability should be formulated in an explicit manner. On its part, the Commission had adopted a statement on Article 16 which cited the *AETR* case-law as a parameter of compliance of the future application of Regulation (EC) No 1347/2000.

The situation is essentially the same on this issue following the entry into force of the Brussels IIa Regulation, which abrogated Regulation (EC) No 1347/2000 and contains at Articles 60 and 63 provisions similar to Articles 37 and 40 of the latter. Following the decision to participate in the 1996 Hague Convention on the protection of minors, a specific provision — Article 61 — is dedicated to this, which specifies when the Regulation prevails over the Convention in relationships between Member States. No rule has been provided on the power of the Member States to enter into new agreements with third countries in general, and Article 16 has been discharged.

Some scholars have tried to limit the scope of the general principles developed by the ECJ on the issue of the Union's external competence in order to resist the expansion of EU powers in the field of judicial cooperation in civil matters with the aim of affirming at least the concurring powers of the Member States. In particular, reference has been made to a second element pointed out by the ECJ, where in its opinion 1/94 it distinguished between the EU and Member States' powers on the basis of a detailed analysis of the scope of application of the WTO, GATS and TRIPS agreements in order to identify on a concrete basis which activities fall under the exclusive competence of the European Union and which are shared or concurrent. It was therefore suggested that the acts adopted pursuant to Article 65 CE be analysed and that the respective powers of the States and the Union be determined on a sector-by-sector basis according to the contents of such acts.[56]

---

[56] S Bariatti 'Le Competenze comunitarie in materia di diritto internazionale privato e processuale'. in S Bariatti (ed), *Casi e materiali di diritto internazionale privato e processuale comunitario* (Milan, 2003), 45 *et seq.*

12.3.   The Hague Programme and the ECJ Opinion Concerning the Lugano Convention

In May 2004, the Hague Programme indicated the future steps of the external action concerning the area of freedom, security and justice, which was given absolute priority. The Commission and the Secretary-General of the Council were called to prepare by 2005 a general strategy of the external aspects of the Union's policy in this area, based upon the measures contained in the same Programme. This strategy was supposed to concentrate on the specific requirements of the cooperation with third countries, groups of States and regions of the world in order to solidly affirm the area of freedom, security and justice in an integrated and consistent way. To this end, the European Council indicated a number of guidelines, ie, 'the existence of internal policies as the major parameter justifying external action; need for value added in relation to projects carried out by the Member States; contribution to the general political objectives of the foreign policies of the Union; possibility of achieving the goals during a period of reasonable time; the possibility of long-term action'. Moreover, the Hague Programme stressed the need to ensure consistency between the law of the Union and international law and the importance of cooperating with international organisations such as the Council of Europe and the Hague Conference on Private International Law. Finally, the European Council recommended that the Community acceded to the latter as soon as possible.

On these issues the ECJ intervened in a decisive but not entirely unexpected manner, in its opinion 1/03, which affirmed the Community's exclusive powers to enter into the new Lugano Convention in very broad terms, going well beyond the question submitted to the Court and the agreement in question. The Court adopted a very generous approach, which was also (if not mainly) based upon Article 4 of the Brussels I Regulation: this provision was interpreted in such a way that it would have 'communitarised' national rules on jurisdiction within the scope of a unified system that defines the borders of the Union's jurisdiction with respect to defendants domiciled abroad.[57]

This interpretation has an immediate and direct effect upon the generally accepted notion that the domicile of the defendant serves both as a criterion for the application of the Convention — and now of the Brussels I Regulation — and as a jurisdiction criterion since the Regulation, according to the Court's position in opinion 1/03, would also apply when the defendant is domiciled in a non-EU country, even if for the sole purpose of applying the national jurisdiction criterion through Article 4. In this manner, all of the national jurisdiction criteria considered jointly contribute to defining the perimeter of the

---

[57] On opinion 1/03, see F Pocar (ed.), *The External Competence of the European Union and Private International Law. The EC Court's Opinion on the Lugano Convention* (Padua, 2007). The Court of Justice had already mentioned this approach in the *Nürnberger Allgemeine Versicherungs AG* case (case C-148/03) with reference to the jurisdiction criteria set out in conventions on special matters referred to under Article 57 of the Brussels Convention. According to the Court, if the judges of a State party to the Convention affirm their jurisdiction on the basis of a convention on special matters, such jurisdiction must be deemed to derive from the Brussels Convention. For a reconstruction of the role of Article 4 of the Brussels Convention very similar to that adopted by the ECJ in opinion 1/03 to the end of assessing the duty to revert to the Court of Justice in the event of issues concerning the interpretation of the provisions of the Convention when applied following a reference by national law, such as Article 3(2), first sentence of the Italian PIL Act (Law No 218/95), see S Bariatti, *Article 2*, in S Bariatti (ed), *Legge 31 Maggio 1995, n 218, Riforma del sistema italiano di diritto internazionale privato*, in *Nuove leggi civili commentate*, 1996, 896 *et seq.*

Union's jurisdiction, including in other areas. Such jurisdiction would not be uncertain or indeterminate since the national criteria are well-known and easily determinable, but certainly the overall result is close to that of a federal state, whose jurisdiction is determined through reference to the jurisdiction of its single territorial units.

The Court's position, however, has certain weak points and negative consequences which should not be underestimated. The weakest point lies in the fact that lacking any specific provisions in the Brussels I Regulation, Member States are entirely free to change national rules on jurisdiction, as confirmed under Article 74 of the same Regulation.[58] Consequently, the scope of the jurisdiction of the Union depends upon national rules, or in other words, upon the will of the Member States, which is not and has not been subject to coordination at all. Another consequence is that the scope of the Union's jurisdiction against defendants domiciled in third countries varies in each Member State, depending upon the court seised. In certain Member States the two may coincide, where for example the jurisdiction criteria of Regulation (EC) No 44/2001 are extended unilaterally to defendants domiciled outside the European Union, as it happens in Italy. In addition, the Court of Justice's position would seem to conflict with Recital No 9 of the Brussels I Regulation, according to which '[a] defendant not domiciled in a Member State is in general subject to national rules of jurisdiction applicable in the territory of the Member State of the court seised'.

The Court then apparently overlooked (maybe intentionally) that several years ago, in the *Kleinwort Benson* case, it had refused to interpret the provisions of the *Civil Jurisdiction and Judgments Act* of the UK concerning the respective scope of the jurisdiction of its territorial units, that were based upon the criteria set forth in the 1968 Brussels Convention. At that time the ECJ stated that in this respect the Act consisted of national provisions, independent of the Convention.[59] Yet, in opinion 1/03 the Court has stated that such national provisions are not so independent of the Regulation which replaced the Convention and that, on the contrary, they constitute an essential part of the Union's jurisdiction system. We may ask ourselves whether this change in perspective derives from the different nature of the Regulation as compared with the Convention, notwithstanding the fact that the wording of Article 4 is substantially the same in the two acts.

At the more general level of external relations, after the '*AETR* doctrine' and the 'doctrine of potential competence', opinion 1/03 appears to have introduced a new 'doctrine of effects', which grant exclusive powers to the institutions where the international agreement may produce effects on EU acts.[60] This is clearly a position which greatly expands the exclusive powers of the Union since potentially any convention with third countries which contains provisions aimed at allocating jurisdiction among Contracting Parties is capable of affecting EU rules as interpreted by the Court.

Notwithstanding the apparent generalisation made by the Court, the scope of opinion 1/03 would appear nonetheless limited to bilateral and multilateral conventions, having the same or a more limited scope of application as compared with the Brussels I Regulation, like the Lugano Convention. The institutions' practice in recent years would appear to lean in this direction, especially when one considers the numerous international agreements concerning issues falling under Article 81 TFEU entered into after the entry into force of

---

[58]   See also the view of the European Parliament reported at point 72 of opinion 1/03.
[59]   Judgment 28 March 1995, case C-346/93.
[60]   LS Rossi, in F Pocar (ed), *The External Competence* (fn 57), 54.

the Treaty of Amsterdam, in which the accession of an international organisation is not envisaged and thus the Union may not participate directly. The Council authorised the Member States to sign, ratify or accede to such treaties in the name of the European Union, stating that the latter has exclusive competence on matters covered by certain provisions of the conventions in question, which could affect the Brussels I Regulation.[61] These conventions provide for jurisdiction criteria applicable both to intra-Union cases and cases with third countries and the Union's competence does not appear to derive from the fact that the rules on jurisdiction vis-à-vis third countries could affect an EU act only where such rules apply to intra-Union cases. Consequently, the Council's decisions establish a clear border between the respective powers of the Union and of the Member States on the basis of the contents of each convention: while the latter are competent in connection with substantive rules, the rules on jurisdiction fall under the exclusive competence of the former. Consequently, opinion 1/03 would have a limited impact on conventions on jurisdiction and enforcement of the judgments that are broader in scope than the Brussels I Regulation.

12.4.   The New Procedure for the Negotiation and Conclusion of Agreements between the Member States and Third Countries

Immediately after such opinion, the Council adopted a document setting out the general framework of the future strategy for the external dimension in the area of judicial cooperation in civil matters consisting in the conclusion of multilateral or bilateral agreements or in the establishment of good practices, with an indication of the geographical priorities. As possible areas of cooperation such document listed jurisdiction, recognition and enforcement of decisions, applicable law, cross-border transmission of judicial and extra-judicial documents, taking of evidence and administrative cooperation between authorities involved in international legal aid. To this end, the main steps of the procedure for the definition of priorities and negotiations with third countries were indicated.[62] This document also touched upon the conclusion of the procedure for the accession of the Community to the Hague Conference on Private International Law, to which we shall return shortly.

In the subsequent document No 8364/07 of 19–20 April 2007, with regard to the (then) future regulation on maintenance obligations, the Council acknowledged the desire on the part of the various Member States to be able to maintain in force or enter into bilateral agreements with certain non-EU countries in these matters. As regards pre-existing agreements, the Council proposed that Article 307 EC (now 351 TFEU) applied and that they should not affect the system to be established by the future regulation. As regards future bilateral agreements and amendments to existing bilateral agreements with certain third countries, the Presidency-in-Office suggested the elaboration of a procedure for the negotiation and conclusion of such agreements, to be based upon existing precedents. This

---

[61]   See, eg, Recitals 2, 3 and 6 of Decision 2002/762 on the International Convention on Civil Liability for Bunker Oil Pollution Damage, which also cites decisions concerning other relevant international conventions.

[62]   Doc Consilium No 8140/06 of 11 April 2006.

procedure should set the criteria and conditions that will allow to assess whether the Union will have an interest in entering into the agreement. If not, the procedure should establish the criteria and the conditions for the negotiation and conclusion of such agreements by the Member States, in particular where the contents of the provisions of the envisaged agreement diverges from the contents of European Union acts, in order to ensure that the agreements do not affect the system established under the proposed regulation. The Council approved the principle of allowing the Member States to maintain or enter into bilateral agreements on maintenance obligations with third countries, without prejudice to the Union's exclusive external powers.

The possibility for the Member States to negotiate and conclude agreements with third countries or international organisations in this area was confirmed by the Conference which adopted the Lisbon Treaty through Declaration No 36, in so far as such agreements comply with Union law. Prior of the entry into force of the Treaty, two regulations were adopted establishing a procedure for the negotiation and conclusion of agreements between Member States and third countries on particular matters concerning the law applicable to contractual and non-contractual obligations (No 662/2009) and in matrimonial matters, matters of parental responsibility and matters relating to maintenance obligations, and the law applicable to matters relating to maintenance obligations (No 664/2009). This procedure will allow the Member States to enter into bilateral agreements or regional agreements with third countries where the European Union has no interest in entering into such agreements. In particular, the Commission may propose negotiating directives, may request the inclusion of specific provisions and may participate in the negotiations as an observer. If the Commission is of the view that it must not authorise the negotiations or the signing of the agreement, following a discussion with the Member State involved, it issues a reasoned decision.

12.5.   The Extent of EU External Powers in case of Treaties on Conflicts-of-Laws and on Judicial Assistance

On the basis of this recent practice, we may infer that with regard to the general issue of the existence of the Union's powers, the institutions of the Union do not differentiate between the various categories of rules set out in an agreement with non-EU countries (jurisdiction, applicable law, recognition of judgments, judicial cooperation) or the area under consideration (obligations, separation and divorce, etc.). The extension of external powers of the Union does not change for this reason. With reference to conventions concerning the applicable law, for example, Article 24 of the Rome Convention already limited the right of the Contracting States to participate in other conventions in the same area, imposing the same consultation procedure used for the amendment of national laws on this matter, pursuant to Article 23. A common declaration attached to the Rome Convention, moreover, included a similar consultation in the period prior to its entry into force. The Rome I and Rome II Regulations confirm the Union's jurisdiction with respect to international agreements containing provisions on the law applicable to contractual and non-contractual obligations: Article 25(1) of the former and Article 27(1) of the latter, indeed, exempt only the conventions to which the Member States are already a party, which had to be communicated to the Commission[63]. However, the Regulations shall apply in lieu of the bilateral or multilateral conventions in force only between Member States in so far as they concern the matters covered by the same.

Therefore, in this area as well, the model adopted under the Brussels I Regulation is reproduced. As indicated by the proposal for a decision of the Council on the signing of the Hague Convention on securities held by intermediaries (abandoned in 2009) and the related legal assessment submitted by the Commission in July 2007, in case of agreements having a substantive scope of application broader than EU rules, the Community enjoys exclusive powers only over convention rules governing matters subject to such EU rules, while the rest of the convention falls under the jurisdiction of the Member States. This Convention in fact applies also when the law designated is the law of a non-Contracting Party and in this area there are certain EU directives based upon Article 95 EC which contain conflicts of law rules.

The same applies to agreements with third countries aimed at improving and simplifying procedures for service of documents and taking of evidence and, more generally, cooperation between judicial and administrative authorities. Actually, in this area it would be more appropriate to vest the Union with the power to regulate only the transmission of documents and the means and modalities of collaboration among the Member States, that would maintain full jurisdiction for cooperation with non-EU countries at the bilateral or multilateral level.[64] Instead, as already mentioned, the document issued by the Council in April 2007, in indicating a general strategy for relationships with third countries, makes no distinction between the various matters pertaining to cooperation on civil matters and, in fact, also includes agreements concerning civil judicial assistance among those agreements to which the new negotiation procedures will apply.

The allocation of powers has been definitively established under the Treaty of Lisbon. The new Article 4(2)(j) TFEU indeed establishes explicitly that in the area of freedom, security and justice, the Union and the Member States have concurrent competence.[65] Article 3(2) also reproduces the principles established by the Court of Justice in the judgments and opinions mentioned above, granting the Union exclusive powers for the conclusion of an international agreement 'when its conclusion is provided for in a legislative act of the Union or is necessary to enable the Union to exercise its internal competence, or in so far as its conclusion may affect common rules or alter their scope.'

---

[63] The list of the conventions notified by the Member States was published in the OJ C 343 of 17 December 2010.

[64] According to Article 20 of Regulation (EC) No 1348/2000 and, in a more precise and correct way, to Article 21 of Regulation (EC) No 1206/2001, their provisions prevail over other agreements concerning the same subject matters (such as the Hague Conventions of 1954, 1965 and 1970, as well as Article 4 of the protocol annexed to the 1968 Brussels Convention) within their scope of application, ie in the relationships among Member States. They also allow Member States to maintain in force or enter into agreements aimed at facilitating the service of documents and the taking of evidence, provided that they are compatible with the Regulations. Thus, they apparently intended to operate as special supplementary instruments among the Contracting States of the Hague Conventions aimed at simplifying the convention regimes (Article 11 of the 1965 Convention on service and Articles 31 and 32 of the 1970 Convention on evidence).

[65] The text of the Treaty seems to supersede the statement made by the ECJ in opinion 1/03 that the exclusive Union powers would also arise when future developments of EU legislation are foreseen, ie even as early as at the adoption of a green paper. This statement was in contrast to opinion 1/76, that in the event that the Community had not exercise its internal competence yet, established that the competence was shared between the Community and the Member States. See also Articles 2(1) and (2) TFEU, Protocol (No 25) on the exercise of shared competence and Declaration in relation to the delimitation of competences (No 18).

12.6.   The Accession to the Hague Conference on Private International Law and Declarations of Competence

At the international level, non-EU States had already acknowledged this situation and the more recent conventions contain specific provisions which allow for the participation of the Union together with the Member States. They envisage the filing of special declarations which indicate to third countries the precise scope of the respective spheres of competence and the acts adopted by the Union on the matter in question. This would satisfy the need of such countries of knowing, with an adequate degree of certainty, the entity that is internationally responsible for complying with the international obligations arising from each convention.

The most relevant example in this area, is the accession of the Community (now the Union) to the Hague Conference on Private International Law, that was envisaged under the Hague Programme of 2004 and was realised through an amendment to the Statute of the Conference. Under the amended Statute a regional organisation to which the Member States have transferred certain powers on the matters covered by the Conference may accede to the Conference. The accession of the EC, with regard to which discussions had begun within the Council in 2001,[66] took effect on 3 April 2007. On the matters transferred to it, the Union exercises voting rights of all of the Member States which have transferred such competence, that shall abstain from the vote. Pursuant to Article 3(4) of the Statute, the Community filed a declaration in which it indicated the allocation of external powers with Member States and listed the instruments adopted so far.

Indeed, the final Act of the XX Session of the Hague Conference provided that the Community would have examined the conventions which it would have had an interest in ratifying even in the absence of a specific accession clause. The review was immediately commenced on the basis of a document prepared by the Secretary-General of the Conference, at the same time as the accession,[67] and led to classifying such conventions under four categories.[68] The first included the conventions to which the Union should accede, or in any case which should enter into force for the Union, to which different modalities apply on a case to case basis. In particular, (i) the Conventions of 1965 on service of documents and of 1970 on taking of evidence, to which almost all of the Member States are already party will be ratified by the remaining Member States on the basis of a decision by the Council; (ii) the 1996 Convention on the protection of minors will be ratified by the Member States in the interest of the Union following a procedure that has already been commenced; (iii) the 2005 Convention on choice of court will be signed on the basis of a proposal prepared by the Commission, (iv) as well as the 2007 Convention on child support and its Protocol.[69]

---

[66] Just prior to the commencement of the works on the first part of Session XIX of the Conference, in June 2001, the Council acknowledged a declaration approved by the Committee of Permanent Representatives on the relationships with the Hague Conference on Private International Law concerning the new powers of the Community in the area of judicial cooperation on civil and commercial matters, which lead the Community to consider its status in the context of the Conference and the possibility of participating as a full member: 2350th meeting of the Council (JHA) 28–29 May 2001, Doc Consilium No 9118/01, Press Release No 203 of 28 May 2001.

[67] Doc Consilium No 7783/07.

[68] Doc Consilium No 9522/08.

[69] The European Union signed and ratified the Protocol on the law applicable to maintenance obligations on 8 April 2010.

Additional reflection will be given to the 1970 Convention on the recognition of divorces, the 1980 Convention on access to justice and the 2005 Convention on the law applicable to securities held through an intermediary. Numerous Member States already participate in the first one and it could turn out to be a useful instrument in relationships with third countries. In order to carry out a more in-depth analysis, the Member States that are already party to it have been asked to share their experience with the other States in the Committee on Civil Law Matters (General Questions). The second convention may also be useful in the relationships with third countries and the Commission was asked to present a proposal to invite the Member States which did not yet participate, to ratify and sign it. The third one was subject to further reflection, and the proposal for a decision for its signing was abandoned in 2009.

No action will be taken in connection with the 1971 Convention on the law applicable to traffic accidents and the 1973 Convention on the law applicable to product liability, matters on which EU conflicts rules have been adopted in the Rome II Regulation. The same applies in respect to the 1978 Convention on the law applicable to agency, which is also covered in part by EU rules. Finally, the Member States should be free to participate in a series of other conventions, in particular the 1961 Convention on the form of testamentary dispositions, the 1978 Conventions on the celebration and recognition of validity of marriages and on the law applicable to matrimonial property regimes, the 1985 Convention on the law applicable to trusts, the 1989 Convention on the law applicable to succession to the estates of deceased persons, the 1993 Convention on international adoption, and the 2000 Convention on the international protection of adults.

At the international level the examples of declarations concerning the respective competence of the Union and the Member States are numerous. In particular, declarations on the allocation of powers are envisaged for the conclusion of the Montreal Convention for the Unification of Certain Rules for International Carriage by Air, the Cape Town Convention on international interests in mobile equipment and its Protocols on aircraft equipment and railway rolling stock, for the COTIF Convention and the related Conventions on carriage by rail.

13.   General Considerations on the Relationships Between Private International Law and EU Law

Apart from the brief indication of the contents of the acts adopted on the basis of Article 65 EC (now 81 TFEU) and the analysis of the related institutional issues, after more than 10 years from the communitarisation of private international law, it is possible to start evaluating the results achieved by the Union legislator also from a methodological standpoint. Indeed, the quantity of acts adopted clearly shows the serious intention of achieving as soon as possible the realisation of an area of freedom, security and justice in order to ensure that the persons subject to the jurisdiction (broadly speaking) of the Member States will enjoy the protection clearly delineated since the European Council at Tampere. The creation of a consistent system of uniform rules of private international law, however, calls also for a strategy and a general vision which must be carefully verified, as indicated by the European Parliament in its Resolution on the Action Plan implementing the Stockholm Programme,[70] possibly with the final aim of a comprehensive codification of private international law.[71] This analysis should be conducted on the basis of the actual development of the legal framework, which has occurred over the years, without pursuing a priori dogmatic positions that, while consistent with the plan of relationships among national legal systems, may not necessarily be capable of being transposed at the level of the European Union. The drawing of fixed borders and the pre-establishment of rigid and mandatory models does not appear to provide particular advantages compared with the use of empirical methods, in search of classifications, if possible, starting from the basic acts and then moving onward to address general categories, by identifying and eventually accepting innovative aspects of the system.

In this analysis, the practice of the institutions and of the Member States within the institutions should not be underestimated, since they prove their assessment of the scope of the rules and, in some circumstances and under certain conditions, they are capable of changing the legislature's perspective in order to achieve results that are considered 'better' or necessary or in any case preferable to the text of the acts. One must not forget that public international law is at the basis of both the European Union — even if such origin is often overlooked or ignored — and of many developments of private international law, that is comprised also of uniform rules established through treaties and international conventions. Moreover, the purposes of the Union and the specific objectives of the area of freedom, security and justice must not be forgotten, since they are the ultimate objective of the activities in the area of judicial cooperation in civil matters.

Certain preliminary observations are necessary, even if they appear quite clear.

EU private international law is today comprised of a vast number of binding acts and various instruments relevant only for interpretative purposes, which use various methods to resolve conflicts of laws and jurisdiction issues.[72] These methods are, in part, derived from the private international law tradition and are faithful to it, and differ in part in order to take into consideration the characteristics of the legal system of the European Union, in which the rules are elaborated and to which they belong, even though they apply and are implemented through national legal systems. We must not forget that the rules of the Union prevail over the domestic laws of the Member States, but they are not self-sufficient either within the European legal system, or vis-à-vis other legal systems. The legal system of the Union, in fact, is far from being considered 'complete' and therefore the rules of private international law set out in the its acts are 'assisted' by substantive rules that are elaborated at the same level only sporadically. Indeed, in many areas of the law, no regulatory power has been granted to the Community or the Union, and therefore many EU choice-of-law rules lack any corresponding substantive rules. Consequently, while in certain areas there exist harmonised national rules based upon EU models, which are part of the national legal systems, in other areas there are no harmonised rules and it is likely that this will continue to be the case for some time.

---

[70] European Parliament Resolution of 23 November 2010 on civil law, commercial law, family law and private international law aspects of the Action Plan Implementing the Stockholm Programme (2010/2080/INI), P7_TA-PROV(2010)0426, Recital D.

[71] European Parliament Resolution of 7 September 2010 on the implementation and review of Council Regulation (EC) No 44/2001 on jurisdiction and the recognition and enforcement of judgments in civil and commercial matters (2009/2140/INI), P7_TA-PROV(2010)0304.

[72] P Picone, 'Diritto internazionale privato comunitario e pluralità dei metodi di coordinamento tra ordinamenti' in P Picone (ed), *Diritto internazionale privato e diritto comunitario*, (Padova, 2004) 485 *et seq.*

Furthermore, the perspective of the Union appears different from that of national legal systems since the rules are not adopted by one State, which effects a comparison internally with its own legal framework and externally with other legal systems, of equally sovereign States. The Union is neither super-State nor a federal State, but an international organisation which exercises certain legal powers, granted to it by the Member States, at times together with such States, and which legislates in particular in cases within its boundaries, but which is presenting itself as a unitary system vis-à-vis third countries in this area.

14. Mutual Recognition, Conflict-of-Law Method and the Country-of-Origin Principle

First of all, it is worth noting that so far, the role of the principle of mutual recognition of judgments has been emphasised as the basis for judicial cooperation in civil matters in general, and has been explicitly mentioned in Article 81 TFEU. This may be explained by the fact that for many years civil judicial cooperation has developed through acts concerning procedural issues, aimed at facilitating the recognition of judgments through uniform rules on jurisdiction. In this regard, the role of public policy has been very limited, also because in the civil and commercial matters that have been subject to the Brussels Convention for many years, it could very rarely be invoked for substantive issues.[73] Reliance has been placed upon the respect of the rules on jurisdiction and on the simplified procedure for the recognition and enforcement of judgments.

The implications of the principle of mutual recognition with reference to choice-of-law rules are entirely new and not yet studied in full since they have come to the foreground with the adoption of the Rome I and Rome II Regulations. Even though certain such rules were already present in several EU acts, the adoption of these general instruments opens a new sphere of investigation.

In reality, when the first general acts setting out the conflicts rules for general categories of obligations were adopted, the EU legislature would not appear to have followed particularly innovative route from a methodological standpoint. Rather, it decided to follow the traditional conflicts method rather than a different method, which according to some commentators would have better fostered consistency within the EU legal system. We are referring to the State of origin principle, upon which the freedom of movement and the freedom to provide services are modelled and which has already served as a guiding principle for many EU acts in various areas. The basic principle in the area of freedom, security and justice is the mutual recognition of decisions, as set out in the Tampere Conclusions, the European Constitution and now the Treaty of Lisbon and the Hague Programme, under which the main objective to be achieved in this area is ensuring that the borders of the Member States do not pose an obstacle to the resolution of civil disputes, the commencement of civil proceedings and the enforcement of judgments concerning civil matters. Mutual recognition and the enactment of common rules on

---

[73] This was more relevant for issues of due process.

applicable law are the means for achieving this general objective.[74] Indeed, according to the Committee on Civil Law Matters of the Council, 'the country-of-origin principle, in the context of building an internal market in the field of justice, is best expressed by the free movement of decisions within the Community'.[75]

This general objective is achieved, or at least we come closer to achieving it, when the conflicts rule is uniform within the Member States, ie when the same dispute is subject to the same law regardless of the court that is seised within the Union, with the sole exception of public policy, which is rarely used in intra-Union relationships. In other words, mutual recognition in the area of freedom, security and justice does not exclude conflicts-of-laws rules, that are a fundamental instrument for its realisation. As stated under Recital 6 of the Rome I and Rome II Regulations, '[t]he proper functioning of the internal market creates a need, in order to improve the predictability of the outcome of litigation, certainty as to the law applicable and the free movement of judgments, for the conflict-of-law rules in the Member States to designate the same national law irrespective of the country of the court in which an action is brought'.[76]

The country-of-origin principle or 'internal market method', on the other hand, means that the service provider is subject to the legislation and control of the State in which it is established as regards access to the activity and conditions for their performance, in so far as they fall under the harmonised area, even where it provides services in another Member State: thus recognition of entitlement to exercise activities based upon the law of a Member State is granted and restrictions imposed by the laws of a different Member State are avoided. The latter State, indeed, cannot impose additional conditions to the supply of the services unless justified by particular and entirely exceptional reasons. This principle is well established in order to protect the freedoms granted under the Treaty, but it does not constitute a general EU legal principle since it is not established under Articles 2 and 3 EC. Indeed, it was identified by the institutions and confirmed by the ECJ as the simplest route for achieving the objective of free movement. Its functioning is conditional upon harmonisation or, at the very least, equivalence of national laws, since otherwise it could lead to distortions and a race to the bottom on the level of guarantees and conditions applicable to the provision of the service.

The country-of-origin principle therefore excludes a priori the application of the 'traditional' conflicts rule, since it prevents any other law, and in particular the law of the country of destination, to apply and to govern the provision of the service or the exercise of free movement. Yet, it leaves intact the possibility for the law of another State to apply to agreements entered into in the context of the activities and to the liability of the service provider. In other words, the country-of-origin principle has so far served solely in favour

---

[74] Communication by the Commission 'Assessment of the Tampere programme and future orientations', COM (2004) 401 of 2 June 2004, 19.

[75] The opinion of the Committee is cited in Doc Consilium No 13858/04 of 22 October 2004, paragraph 7. In the sense that the so-called fifth freedom, the free movement of judgments, has not yet involved the harmonisation of conflicts rules see also Doc Consilium No 12 655/04 of 24 September 2004.

[76] The use of conflicts rules functions well and should be maintained exclusively when there is a conflict between interests of private parties, such as in the area of contractual obligations and extra-contractual obligations: P Lagarde, 'Développements futurs du droit international privé dans une Europe en voie d'unification : quelques conjectures' (2004) *RabelsZ* 225 *et seq*, at 230. In its Resolution of 23 November 2010 on civil law, commercial law, family law and private international law aspects of the Action Plan Implementing the Stockholm Programme (fn 70 above), the European Parliament stated that 'private international law is the means *par excellence* of achieving mutual recognition of, and respect for, each others' legal systems' (Recital E).

of the service provider, allowing him to avoid satisfying the conditions imposed under the laws and regulations of all of the Member States in which it intends to carry out its business. The recipients of the services, however, have been subjected to the uncertainty of having the services received governed by different laws, depending upon the State of origin of the providers.

If we look more closely at the development of the country-of-origin principle, we find that it has never been applied in an absolute and generalised manner. All of the sector-specific acts implementing such principle contemplate the possibility of exemptions from the application of the law of the State of origin and allow Member States to maintain restrictions on free movement, provided they are justified by imperative reasons of general interest, are applied in a non-discriminatory manner, and comply with the principle of proportionality, ie they are capable of achieving the purpose and do not go beyond what is necessary in order to do so. An additional condition for the legitimacy of restrictions on free movement consists in the absence of harmonisation rules in the sector in question, since no restrictions are allowed in circumstances where, and to the extent that, the internal implementation of EU directives has introduced equivalent national provisions.

The country-of-origin principle is not applied in a general manner, but rather is subject to exemptions and exceptions aimed at honouring different requirements and interests worthy of specific protection, which show the intrinsic inadequacy of such principle which prevents it from becoming a general method for the resolution of conflicts of laws. In addition, given the current state of EU law, it would not appear that it offers advantages, in terms of certainty and predictability, of such a nature as to justify the elimination of the conflicts method. It is certainly true that economic reasons justify its expansion since it better addresses the needs of businesses, but there is no doubt that its use as a conflicts rule could lead to a reduction in protection of other needs, which are equally important. As the Committee on Civil Law Matters of the Council has noted, the country-of-origin principle in the conflicts of law sector on matters of services leads to the risk that businesses are favoured to the detriment of a more general interest in justice, which would call for a solution that is more fair and reasonable to all of the parties involved.[77]

Despite the fact that the principle is based upon the harmonisation of the substantive rules, the limits on harmonisation deriving from the exemptions and exceptions applied to it mean that it leaves the determination of the level of protection in the country of destination entirely in the hands of the service provider: by allowing him to establish himself in a less protective country, there remains a risk of a race to the bottom, which the State of destination is empowered to fight only in exceptional circumstances. Moreover, the issue as to whether and to what extent the country-of-origin principle addresses the principle of proportionality with respect to the objectives to be achieved has never been raised, even if the latter is a fundamental principle of EU law.

In any case, the country-of-origin principle has been eliminated from the proposal for the Rome II Regulation, in favour of traditional connecting factors, just like — more or less over the same period — its scope in the Bolkenstein Directive on services was also reduced. As already mentioned, the Rome I Regulation later confirmed the EU legislature's full support for the conflicts method.

---

[77] Doc Consilium No 13858/04, para 10.

Finally, the mutual recognition principle may play a more important role in the area of conflicts of laws with regard to the recognition of status and civil status certificates which are among the objectives for the coming years under the Stockholm Programme of 2009. This is a function which has been elaborated in the national legal systems through the application of conflicts rules, but which could be enhanced by the ECJ, emphasising its positive effect for purposes of free movement, as it has done in the *Centros* and *Grunkin and Paul* cases.

15.   Preliminary Considerations on the Function of EU Conflicts-of-Laws Rules, the Connecting Factors and the Relationship with Principles of EU Law

With reference to the approach followed by the EU legislature, we may observe that in both the Rome I and Rome II Regulations, the various connecting factors have been put on the same level and may designate either the law of the Member States or that of third country, on an equivalent basis. The same occurred already for the conflicts rules already included in prior EU acts. Using the terminology of the traditional doctrine of private international law, we may therefore affirm that these rules are perfectly bilateral, provided that we keep in mind that we are dealing with conflicts rules that have been created in the context of an international organisation: they do not designate the substantive law of the legal system that has established them — ie EU law, which provides substantive rules meant to operate only within the Member States through their own legal systems, either directly or following implementation –, but the domestic law of the Member States or of third countries, on an equivalent basis. The only direct and partial exception to the bilateral nature of the EU conflicts rules appears to arise in situations where the competent court and the law applicable to the dispute coincide, as it happens for example in matters of insolvency, where Regulation (EC) No 1346/2000 grants jurisdiction for the opening of insolvency proceedings to the court of the State where the debtor's centre of main interests is located (see Article 3), that will apply the *lex fori* to the proceedings and to the issues which could arise over the course of the same (Article 4).[78]

Thus, as for the nature and the function of the conflicts rules set out in directives or regulations, there would not appear to exist any differences in the functioning, for example, of Article 9 of Directive 2002/47/EC on collaterals and the conflicts rules set out in the Rome I and Rome II Regulations, despite the different modalities of application / implementation in the Member States. Indeed, the direct applicability of the second set of rules would not appear to change the application of the same with regard to the designation of the law applicable to a specific case.

An additional problem of a general nature consists in the identification of the limits imposed by substantive EU law upon the rules of private international law set out in EU

---

[78] M Benedettelli, 'Connecting factors, principles of coordination between conflict systems, criteria of applicability: three different notions for a "European Community private international law"'(2005) *Diritto dell'Unione Europea*, 433. This conclusion would not appear to be hindered by the fact that the following Articles 5–15 introduce certain exceptions to the application of the *lex concursus* since they are indeed mere exceptions.

acts. This issue has been the focus of attention relatively recently and is separate and distinct from that related to the limitations which substantive EU rules, with particular regard to the four freedoms, impose upon the substantive rules of private international law of the Member States, which has been closely studied in the past. It is well-settled in this regard that national rules, of whatever nature, may not restrict the exercise of the freedoms unless certain conditions specified by the Court of Justice in numerous decisions have been met: in particular, such national rules (i) must be justified by mandatory reasons of general interest, (ii) must be applied in a non-discriminatory manner and (iii) must comply with the principle of proportionality, or in other words (a) they must be suitable to achieve the purpose pursued and (b) they must not go beyond what is necessary in order to achieve such purpose. An additional condition consists in the absence of harmonisation rules in the sector in question, since restrictions are not allowed in cases in which and to the extent that the internal implementation of EU directives has introduced equivalent provisions under the national legal systems.

In this context, it is often asserted — and we believe correctly, at least in the area of commercial transactions — that such limitations derive from the application of the substantive domestic rule designated by the conflicts rules rather than from the conflicts rules considered per se, their functioning mechanism and the connecting factor adopted. This opinion is reiterated in certain EU acts that are not immediately binding[79] and is confirmed by the ECJ case-law, which has focused its attention mainly upon the restrictions imposed under national substantive rules and their possible justification within the framework of EU rules on free movement, without assessing the mechanism for the designation of the applicable law. In part, the fact that in the cases at stake the restrictions were always imposed by the *lex fori*, being the law of the State of destination of the good or service, or more rarely, being the law of the State of origin, may have had a relatively important influence in such regard. Secondly, these were cases in which the effect of national rules on free movement of the good or service were the object of the complaint, and not the interpersonal contractual relationships of private parties. Thus, for purposes of the decision no analysis on the private international law mechanism per se was required.

Yet, more recently the ECJ resolved by following the same structure — ie avoiding an assessment of compatibility with EU law of the connecting factors used by the national legislatures — some disputes where personal relationships or status were discussed. Already in the *Johannes* case, in 1999, the ECJ did not specifically address the alleged breach of the principle of non-discrimination triggered by the application of the husband's national law to the dissolution of the marriage for divorce, asserting that the national rules on divorce, both the substantive rules and the rules of private international law, do not fall within the scope of application of the EC Treaty, and are therefore subtracted from its control from a standpoint of their compatibility with the prohibition on discriminations based upon nationality.[80] The same approach was followed in the well-known cases concerning companies, in which the Court did not directly give precedence to the connecting factor of incorporation as opposed to the real seat, but criticised the negative consequences that the application of the law of the latter country would have on the

---

[79]   See the Communications of the Commission 'Freedom to provide services and the interest of the general good in the Second Banking Directive' and 'Freedom to provide services and the general good in the insurance sector' and Recital 23 of Directive 2000/31/EC on e-commerce.

[80]   Judgment 10 June 1999, case C-430/97.

freedom of establishment of shareholders, who choose to establish a company on the basis of the law which they deem to be most favourable for purposes of conducting their business activity.[81]

Also in the following *Garcia Avello* case,[82] the Court resolved the issue posed to it — focused upon the conflict between Belgian law and Spanish law with regard to the name of two minors with both nationalities resident in Belgium — by avoiding favouring one or the other law and not making any reference to the use of nationality as a connecting factor. From the first standpoint, the negative assessment of national rules which discriminate by giving preference to one citizenship or the other of a person with dual citizenship, in breach of the non-discrimination principle against citizens of other Member States, was therefore reaffirmed.[83] As compared with prior decisions, in which the citizenship of a Member State other than the forum concurred with the citizenship of a non-EU country, *Garcia Avello* concerned precedence of the local nationality as opposed to the nationality of another Member State for purposes of the application of internal rules concerning the right to name, but the solution did not change.

From the second standpoint, the Court did not touch upon the Belgian private international law provision on the right to name per se. Instead, the ECJ stated, on the one hand, that such matter falls under the jurisdiction of the Member States and, on the other hand, that the national rules must nonetheless comply with EU law. Yet, it is not clear from the ECJ decision, whether this statement concerns only national substantive rules or also national conflicts rules. The Court concluded that the Belgian provisions preventing the children of a Spanish citizen who resides in Belgium, who are in turn both Belgian and Spanish citizens, from having the last name of their mother recognised in accordance with the laws of Spain, were in breach of Articles 12 and 17 EC (now Arts 18 and 20 TFEU).[84]

More recently, in the *Grunkin and Paul* case, the ECJ dealt with the right to name of a minor with German citizenship who resided in Denmark, where he was registered under the last name of both parents by a civil status officer on the basis of Danish law, which was applicable as the law of residence according to Danish conflicts rules. The German civil status officers, on the contrary, had refused to register the double last name of the child, invoking the application of German law on the basis of German private international law rules, that designate the law of the country of nationality. In this case as well, the Court carefully avoided taking a position on the issue of compatibility of the connecting factors used in national legal systems with EU law, and once again it proposed a solution focused upon the freedom of movement of the individual, for whom the situation of uncertainty as to his personal identity deriving from differing data in the identity documents issued by

---

[81]   These are the very well-known judgments in *Centros* (9 March 1999, case C-212/97), *Überseering* (5 November 2002, case C-208/00) and *Inspire Art* (30 September 2003, case C-167/01).

[82]   Judgment 2 October 2003, case C-148/02.

[83]   Judgments 7 July 1992, case C-369/90, *Micheletti*, and 2 October 1997, case C-122/96, *Saldanha*. On this point, see also judgment 16 July 2009, case C-168/08, *Hadadi*.

[84]   It would not appear of secondary importance in this case that the parents had first registered their children in the registers of the Spanish consulate in Brussels with the surname of both in accordance with Spanish law. One could ask what would have happened had this case occurred in Spain, had the parents requested the registration of the children according to Belgian law with the Spanish registrar (S Bariatti, *Prime considerazioni sugli effetti dei principi generali e delle norme materiali del Trattato CE sul diritto internazionale privato comunitario*, *Rivista di diritto internazionale privato e processuale*, 2003, 32).

the different competent national authorities would give rise to difficulties.[85] It should be underlined that in this case the Court was not dealing with the application of two domestic laws which both came into consideration as national laws, but rather with a comparison between the law of the State of residence and that of the State of nationality.

The Court therefore posed on the same level the situation of the individual who is subject to the application of two different substantive laws on the basis of his dual citizenship, such as the Garcia-Weber minors, and that in which the person finds himself in such situation due to the designation of two different substantive laws by the conflicts-of-laws provisions of two States which apply different connecting factors, such as the Grunkin-Paul minor. Indeed, while from a dogmatic standpoint the two situations are entirely different, they are fully comparable in practice and must necessarily be treated the same: irrespective of the reason why two different laws may apply, according to the Court the result must be the same, ie any solution that ends up hindering free circulation, imposing upon a person an identity in which he does not recognise himself, whatever the connecting factor used, is incompatible with EU law.

In this manner, the Court, once again, lacking uniform conflicts rules at the EU level, used the general principles of EU law to pursue the coordination of national legal systems[86] and avoided any assessment on connecting factors in general, in order to avoid prejudicing in advance any future decisions by the EU legislature. The ECJ also confirmed that, as already mentioned, it is not the conflicts rules which cause restrictions on free movement, but rather the applicable substantive rules.

Moreover, it is entirely clear that for now the approach followed by the Court favours the will of the individual, who through his own conduct chooses the legal system — that we may qualify as the legal system of origin — in which to establish his own personal identity. This identity must then be recognised in all Member States, regardless of the connecting factor used, and therefore also in the Member State of which the individual is a national.[87] Such a choice had been made by Mr Garcia Avello and his wife when they registered their children as Garcia Weber in the registers of the Spanish consulate, later invoking such name before the Belgian authorities. The same was made also by the parents of the Grunkin-Paul minor. If the solution may be acceptable in cases dealing with personal identity and name, which characterise a person in his/her relationships with a multitude of parties, it may not work in cases dealing with personal statuses which are affirmed as the result of relationships with other persons, such as marriage and matters related to marriage. Clearly, the adoption of uniform connecting factors, whatever they may be, through an act by the EU on the matter such as the Rome III Regulation, will allow for the conflict between national connecting factors to be overcome, as already happens in the area of obligations thanks to the Rome I and Rome II Regulations. It is in any case important to highlight that the Court abstained from any assessment, leaving it entirely to the EU legislature.

In this general framework, there are only few elements which allow for an assessment of the main issue of the relationship between the substantive rules and the general

---

[85] Judgment 14 October 2008, case C-353/06; but see also judgment 30 March 1993, case C-168/91, *Konstantinidis*, and the pending case C-391/09, *Runevič-Vardyn*.

[86] See M Benedettelli, (above n 75) 431 *et seq.*

[87] Similar to what takes place with reference to the freedom of choice of legal system under which to establish a company in order to exercise the right of establishment.

principles of EU law, on the one side, and the rules of EU private international law on the other, which involves an assessment of the 'space' which private international law may occupy in the legal system of the Union and the role that the principles that inspire it may play with respect to the general principles of the same legal system. As already mentioned, we are not dealing with problems related to the relationship between the rules of different legal systems, one of which is deemed to prevail over the other, but rather with problems related to interests that are protected by different rules belonging to the same legal system, that have the same rank, that compete with one another.[88]

Firstly, we may conclude that the EU conflicts rules must comply with the general principles of EU law, and in particular the principles concerning the allocation of powers, proportionality, subsidiarity, the prohibition on discrimination, and respect for basic human rights.[89] Secondly, they are also subject to the provisions and principles related to free movement, which, since they are linked to the implementation of the internal market, are necessary to achieve the purposes of the EU, with the well-known exception of the 'general interest'[90]. In assessing the general interest, it is necessary in this case to compare the interests in play with their balancing through the use of instruments of substantive law or private international law, as the case may be, which must be posed by the legislature on the same level, at least at the outset. Indeed it is possible that the notions of 'general interest', 'non-discrimination' and 'proportionality' have a different scope and, perhaps, a narrower one, where they pose limits upon EU rules of private international law as compared with cases in which they refer to national substantive and conflicts rules. The reasons which lead to limiting the application of the latter, indeed, do not apply to the former since they involve the assessment of relationships between rules that belong to the same legal system, the EU legal system, that are imposed by the same legislature. The consideration of needs and interests that are different from those guaranteed by the rules on free movement introduces a significant element of novelty. It should also be noted that while a national provision that conflicts with free movement must be discarded since the EU rule would prevail over it, the same conclusion would not appear so obvious in the case of an EU conflicts rule which, even if it may produce restrictive effects on free movement, is nonetheless aimed at protecting a different interest that is just as worthy.[91]

---

[88] For a preliminary evaluation, see our *Prime considerazioni* cited above and *Restrictions Resulting from the EC Treaty Provisions for Brussels I and Rome I*, in J Meeusen, M Pertegás and G Straetmans (eds), *Enforcement of International Contracts in the European Union, Convergence and Divergence between Brussels I and Rome I* (Antwerp–Oxford–New York, 2004), 77 *et seq*. Along the same lines, see H Duintjer Tebbens, 'Les règles de conflit contenues dans les instruments de droit dérivé', in A Fuchs, H Muir Watt and E Pataut, *Les conflits de lois et le système juridique communautaire* (Paris, 2004); LS Rossi, 'L'incidenza dei principi del diritto comunitario cit. sul diritto internazionale privato: dalla "comunitarizzazione" alla "costituzionalizzazione"'(2003) *Rivista didiritto internazionale privato e processuale* 63 *et seq*.

[89] It must be noted, in this regard, that in connection with the determination of applicable law, the prohibition on discriminations imposes an additional condition other than those usually considered, in the sense that no prevalence may be granted to the *lex fori* over the laws of other Member States which are posed on the same level. As already mentioned above, the bilateral nature of EU conflicts rules, which also allows for the application of the law of third countries, means that the *lex fori* may not prevail even over the law of third States since it is impossible to predict a priori whether the pre-established connected factor will indicate one Member State or a non-EU country. Limits may be imposed on the application of the law of non-EU countries in certain cases, see Articles 3(4) of the Rome I Regulation and Article 14(3) of the Rome II Regulation.

[90] Judgment 13 April 2000, case C-292/97, *Karlsson*.

[91] See along these lines M Wilderspin and X Lewis, 'Les relations entre le droit communautaire et les règles de conflits de lois des Etats membres' (2002) *Revue critique*, 23.

16.   Preliminary Remarks on the Solutions Adopted by the EU Conflicts Rules on Certain General Issues of Private International Law

Only recently scholars have begun to reflect on solutions concerning the general issues of private international law, which could be found within the EU legal system. In particular, it should be assessed whether they are posed just as they would be under the national legal systems, or whether the structure of the EU legal system calls for different dogmatic solutions. The answer would appear to be affirmative, in the sense that general issues are presented and must be generally resolved as they would be within national legal systems, if for no other reason than the fact that EU rules are meant to apply within national legal systems. However, certain specifications are necessary deriving from the interplay between the needs of the EU legal system and its mechanisms.

16.1.   Characterisation

On the issue of characterisation, in particular, it has been noted that, unlike what occurs in the national systems where the qualification of the case at stake generally takes place on the basis of the *lex fori* or the *lex causae*, the notions used in the acts and instruments of EU private international law should be interpreted on the basis of substantive EU law, where it exists, ie the rules belonging to the same legal system which imposes the conflicts rule to be applied, as if we were dealing with a *lex fori*. Consequently, notions such as 'services', 'transport', 'consumer', and the like, should have the same meaning that they have under the Treaty and secondary law. It is possible, however, that specific notions are affirmed in the field of judicial cooperation in civil matters. For example, in the *Falco* case, the ECJ declared that the notion of 'provision of services' under Article 5(1) of Regulation (EC) No 44/2001 must be interpreted in light of the genesis, objectives and systematic structure of the Regulation, and this does not necessarily mean that the interpretation followed for a Treaty provision would need to be followed in this field. In this case the Court stated that the notion of 'provision of services' means at least that the party who provides the service carries out a particular activity in return for remuneration, which does not occur in the case of the owner of an intellectual property right granting a licence, who only undertakes not to challenge the use of the right by its counterparty. Moreover, the Court excluded that possibility that the case-law related to Article 50 EC (now Article 57 TFEU) or to VAT Directives might come into consideration, since their rationale is different from that underlying the Brussels I Regulation and in particular its Article 5(1).[92]

Where a given term has different meanings in different sectors of EU law, such as, for example, 'residence', 'permanent establishment', 'domicile', the solution which would appear to best ensure uniformity in application of the rule and the consequent equality of

---

[92] Judgment 23 April 2009, case C-533/2007, *Falco Privatstiftung*, §20, 29 *et seq.*

rights and obligations for the persons affected in all of the Member States consists in the adoption of specific material definitions directly in the act, depending upon the subject matter in question, rather than delegating this task, and this responsibility, entirely to the Court of Justice or to national courts. The EU legislature took this approach, for example, in the definition of the domicile of companies under Article 60 of Regulation (EC) No 44/2001 and of the residence of companies under Article 29 of the Rome I Regulation and Article 23 of the Rome II Regulation. On the contrary, lacking a common definition, for the interpretation of the notion of 'habitual residence' of minors, pursuant to Article 8.1 of the Brussels IIa Regulation, the ECJ in case *A* indicated that its case-law on the notion of habitual residence concerning other areas of EU law may not be taken into consideration, but rather that such notion will have to be established on the basis of the facts and circumstances of each particular case.[93]

Where common substantive rules, and therefore an 'EU *lex fori*', are lacking, other instruments must be used for the interpretation of the notions used in the conflicts provisions of EU acts. Eventually national rules and principles may be taken into consideration, under the conditions and in the circumstances to be discussed below. Given the nature and the origin of EU rules, which are the result of a complex elaboration through international negotiations even if they are meant to be applied — and implemented, in case of directives — within the Member States, it is difficult to support the view that characterisation should be made in accordance with the *lex causae*, especially when the conflicts rule of the EU is universal in character, and is therefore suitable to designate both the law of a Member State and that of a third country: characterisation under the *lex causae* can lead to the use of notions and concepts of a non-Member State in the interpretation of categories and notions established under EU rules, which to a certain extent are often inspired by the legal rules and principles of the Member States or by pre-existing acts of the EU and are justified by the achievement of common objectives. This limitation would appear particularly necessary where dealing with the interpretation of notions that are necessary to determine the scope of application of the legal instrument and therefore play a particularly important role.

It should be noticed, finally, that under the EU legal system a jurisdictional body that has been vested with the exclusive power to interpret the Treaties and the acts of secondary law with binding effects in all Member States, which uses specific interpretative instruments, aimed both at ensuring uniformity of the rights and obligations of the Member States and of all parties subject to the EU legal system and at achieving the purposes of the EU.

Therefore, in consideration of the factors indicated above, although within the EU legal system the problem of the interpretation of notions and legal terms used in conflicts rules is posed in the same ways and on occasions that are similar to those that arise within the national legal systems, it would appear justifiable to conclude that the solution to the problem of the characterisation under EU private international law may be different from

---

[93] Judgment 2 April 2009, case C-523/07, point 36 *et seq*, where in addition to the physical presence of the minor, it is necessary that such presence not be temporary or occasional, but rather that such presence reflects 'some degree of integration by the child in a social and family environment', for whose assessment the ECJ provided some factors. Article 11 of Regulation (EC) No 284/2009 on the matter of social security contains a list of elements to be taken into consideration in order to determine the residence of the beneficiary of the service.

that reached in the national legal systems. This may indeed give way to the more general problem of the interpretation of notions set out under EU rules, which dates back to the establishment of the EC, thus losing the characteristic features which define it with respect to any other general issue under the national conflicts systems.

It would appear that the solutions provided by the Court over the course of the years – and mainly autonomous interpretation - may also apply for purposes of the interpretation of legal notions used by the conflicts rules of the EU, regardless of their role under such rule (eg indication of the subject matter, or the connecting factor). In general, from the standpoint of the interpreter, but also of the legal system, there would not appear to be much difference between the qualification of 'divorce' or 'marriage' for purposes of identifying the applicable law and the interpretation of the same notions in order to assess the applicability of the Brussels IIa Regulation. The same occurs for the connecting factors, or for the terms and notions used in other acts on jurisdiction and recognition of judgments, as well as in the case of provisions which use the same notions for purposes of the application of substantive rules.

As already mentioned, the interpreter must address the additional and specific problem, deriving from the need for EU law to produce the same effects in all Member States, for purposes of ensuring that there are no discriminations between similar situations and that the same rights and obligations are granted to the parties regardless of the Member State in question. In light of this objective, there can be no doubt that the search for autonomous meaning of the terms used constitutes the ideal solution for the interpretation of the legal categories used, thus avoiding the use of notions that are specific to national legal systems. This is particularly true for those categories that define the scope of application of a given act, which may not depend upon the *lex fori*, or any other national law. The Court of Justice has always followed this fundamental rule in the interpretation of the Brussels Convention, thus contributing greatly to its uniform application.

In this regard, we must also recall that at times a provision refers to a general category, but later it restricts its scope through clauses which exclude or exempt certain matters. These are in any case part of the general notion, but are excluded from the scope of the EU act for a broad range of reasons. For example, a dispute concerning matrimonial property regimes falls under 'civil and commercial matters', but not under the scope of application of Regulation (EC) No 44/2001, while it is subject to the Regulations on service and the taking of evidence. Sometimes, on the other hand, the opposite solution is followed and a provision broadens the scope of an act through a clause pursuant to which a legal situation or category is deemed similar to those falling under the scope of such act. Out of many possible examples, it suffices for our purposes to mention the new paragraph recently added to Article 1 of Regulation (EEC) No 422/67 on the emoluments of certain members of the Commission and the EU Courts, which equates non-marital partnerships and marriages.

Case-law does not provide clear and systematic guidance on this point, or on the specific conditions for referring to national law. On the contrary, one is under the impression that so far the solution must be found on a case-by-case basis, depending upon the term in question. We could conclude that reference to national conflicts rules is preferable, especially where we are dealing with rules that are common to all of the Member States or are established under the same act. The main issue concerns the identification of the law to apply for the interpretation of legal notions, especially when the notion at stake concerns a status that has been acquired or must be acquired on the basis of a national law. The need for coherence and consistency among EU instruments adopted in this area, however, should lead to giving the same meaning to certain concepts that are used throughout, such as *lis pendens*, civil and commercial matters, and so on.[94]

16.2.   Public Policy

Finally, a few remarks on public policy and overriding mandatory rules under the acts adopted on the basis of Article 81 TFEU, also in light of the case-law of the ECJ. In this regard, it must be noted that the Rome I and Rome II Regulations on the law applicable to contractual and non-contractual obligations adopted the same solutions with a view to ensuring consistency among EU rules regulating conflicts of laws and jurisdiction.

As for the public policy of the Member States, Article 26 of the Rome II Regulation and Article 21 of the Rome I Regulation would not appear to introduce noteworthy novelties with respect to the national conflicts rules since they allow for its application as a limit to the application of foreign law, where the latter is manifestly incompatible with the public policy order of the forum. Moreover, it is well-known that within the European judicial area the EU freedoms greatly limit the possibility by a State to invoke general interests and the grounds listed in Article 36 TFEU, which are subject to control by the ECJ.

Indeed, in the *Krombach* case, the Court has asserted its power to control the limits within which the courts of a Member State may use public policy as a ground for refusing recognition of a judgment issued in another Member State, and has limited the effects of national public policy to entirely exceptional cases, where the guarantees established by the law of the State of origin and under the Brussels Convention are not adequate to protect the defendant from a manifest breach of his right to raise a defence in the State of origin of the judgment.[95] Two months later, in the *Renault* decision, the Court of Justice stated that a Member State may not invoke public policy as a justification for refusing to recognise a decision issued by another Member State, even if it believes that the court of origin has breached or erroneously applied provisions of EU law, such as those on free movement of goods and on competition. According to the Court, a limitation on the free movement of judgments would violate the principle of proportionality since there are other possible remedies under EU and national law for the protection of individuals against this type of errors, such as the exhaustion of remedies in the State of origin and the mechanism of preliminary interpretation pursuant to Article 267 TFEU.[96] In such case, therefore, the free movement of judgments ended up prevailing over the correct application of the provisions on the other EU freedoms.

---

[94]   In its Resolution on the review of Council Regulation (EC) No 44/2001 (above, fn 71), the European Parliament considered that 'the terminology in all subject-matters and all the concepts and requirements for similar rules in all subject-matters should be unified and harmonised (*e.g. lis pendens*, jurisdiction clauses, *etc.*) (at Point 1).

[95]   Judgment 28 March 2000, case C-7/98. The need for a restrictive interpretation of the notion of the public policy and control by the ECJ had already been affirmed in connection with free movement in the *Van Duyn* case (4 December 1974, case 41/74), where the Court concluded that public policy may vary over space and time. See also the judgments 28 October 1975, case 36–75, *Rutili*, 27 October 1977, case 30–77, *Bouchereau*, and 23 November 1999, joined case C-369/96 and C-376/96, *Arblade*.

[96]   Judgment 11 May 2000, case C-38/98.

If we consider the issue from another perspective, this decision would appear to mean that the court of the State where recognition is sought may not invoke public policy in order to avoid recognising a judgment rendered in another Member State which applied a national provision of law that was contrary to the EU freedoms. This result would appear compatible with that reached in the context of a unified legal system, even if the difficulties in challenging a judgment before the foreign court should not be underestimated.

On the other hand, public policy could be invoked where EU harmonising provisions have been adopted and recognition is sought of a decision in which national rules have been applied that are in conflict with harmonised rules, that have not yet been transposed in the State of origin of the provider, even after the envisaged deadline. In light of Article 16 of Directive 2002/65 on distance contracts for financial services, it would appear that the State that regularly adopted the harmonised rules may limit the free provision of financial services by providers established in States that infringed the duty to timely implement such harmonised rules.

Regulation (EC) No 1436/2000 on insolvency proceedings envisages limited recourse to public policy under Article 26, pursuant to which recognition or enforcement may be refused if they produce effects that are 'would be manifestly contrary to that State's public policy, in particular its fundamental principles or the constitutional rights and liberties of the individual'. In interpreting this provision, the ECJ cited the *Krombach* case, reiterating the exceptional nature of the use of the public policy exception in the European judicial area and its power to assess the grounds invoked by the State, and it confirmed the full importance of the principle of fair trial.[97]

It is likely that this structure and this control will be maintained by the Court of Justice even in connection with the assessment of compatibility with public policy of the forum of the rules of other Member States. One would expect, however, that the above-mentioned provisions of the Rome I and Rome II Regulations will be interpreted as making a distinction between the case in which the rules that are incompatible with the public policy of the forum belong to third countries and that in which they belong to other Member States, since the notion of public policy in the latter case might be more restricted than that in the former one. It is likely that a distinction will develop through the case-law, where necessary, in order to avoid the production in the Member States of effects that conflict with fundamental principles and are not justified by the fulfilment of international obligations.

Finally, it should be noted on this point that Recital 32 of the Rome II Regulation authorises the Member States to invoke public policy in order to reject the application of a foreign provision which 'would have the effect of causing non-compensatory exemplary or punitive damages of an excessive nature to be awarded', taking into account the circumstances of the particular case in question. This is a reference that is much more moderate than Article 24 of the proposal, which established that such provisions were contrary to EU public policy.

---

[97] Judgment 2 May 2006, case C-341/04, *Eurofood*.

16.3.   Provisions Which Cannot Be Derogated from by Agreement and Overriding Mandatory Provisions

Also with regard to provisions which cannot be derogated from by agreement, or mandatory rules, it would not appear that the Rome I and Rome II Regulations have introduced noteworthy novelties. In the former Regulation, as already was the case under the 1980 Rome Convention, the choice of the applicable law by the parties may not prejudice the application of provisions of the law which cannot be derogated from by agreement of the country where all other elements relevant to the situation at the time of the choice are located (Article 3(3)) or, for consumers and employment contracts, the law which would be applicable in the absence of choice (Articles 6(2) and 8(1)). In the latter Regulation, the choice of applicable law may not prejudice the application of the provisions which may not be contractually opted out of, of the law of the country in which the event causing the damages occurred (Article 14(2)). It may be expected that the Court of Justice will tend to assert its control over these national rules, in order to assess the compatibility with EU law of the restrictions that they pose upon the application of the law of another Member State.

Yet, important novelties may be found with regard to overriding mandatory provisions, that are defined at Article 9 of the Rome I Regulation as 'provisions the respect for which is regarded as crucial by a country for safeguarding its public interests, such as its political, social or economic organization, to such an extent that they are applicable to any situation falling within their scope, irrespective of the law otherwise applicable to the contract' under the Regulation. While the application of overriding mandatory provisions of the forum is identical in the two acts (Article 9(2) of the Rome I Regulation and Article 16 of the Rome II Regulation) and mirrors Article 7(2) of the Rome Convention, the treatment of such provisions when they belong to a law other than the *lex fori* and the *lex causae* is different.

Indeed, room has been given only to overriding mandatory provisions of certain pre-established countries: in the Rome II Regulation '[i]n assessing the conduct of the person claimed to be liable, account shall be taken, as a matter of fact and in so far as is appropriate, of the rules of safety and conduct which were in force at the place and time of the event giving rise to the liability' (Article 17). In the Rome I Regulation, the possibility of considering the overriding mandatory provisions of a country strictly related to the case at stake — as the court was empowered to do under Article 7(1) of the Rome Convention — has been eliminated. Such possibility exists only in respect 'the law of the country where the obligations arising out of the contract have to be or have been performed, in so far as those overriding mandatory provisions render the performance of the contract unlawful' (Article 9(3)).

It is also interesting to note the developments related to EU public policy and mandatory provisions of EU law, which came on the scene, respectively, in the *Eco Swiss* and *Ingmar* cases, and which have been formalised in certain provisions of the Rome I and Rome II Regulations. In the first case, the Court of Justice affirmed that Article 81 EC (now Article 101 TFEU) may be considered a provision of public policy pursuant to the New York Convention of 1958 on the recognition of arbitral awards, since it establishes a provision of fundamental importance for the functioning of the internal market: in fact, any agreement or contract infringing such provision is null and void.[98] In the second case, the Court, with certain uncertainties in the qualification of the rules and principles the application of which it intended to ensure, and the mechanisms on the basis of which they should apply, transformed provisions that were mandatory for the parties to a contract (internal public policy) into overriding mandatory provisions, which also apply when the law chosen by the parties is the law of a non-EU country.[99]

This decision has been criticised from a particular standpoint which is relevant for our purposes. Indeed, the Court of Justice intended to extend to the sales agent the protection which the directives on consumer protection, which were more recent than those on agents, guarantee to the weaker party within a contractual relationship. The generalisation of this approach, however, would mean that all of the rules of these directives which the parties may not opt out of contractually would have to be considered mandatory provisions, giving rise to perhaps an excessive expansion in protection. The Rome I and Rome II Regulations, moreover, followed the Court's approach under Articles 3(4) and 14(3), respectively, which establish that provisions of EU law, 'where appropriate as implemented in the Member State of the forum, which cannot be derogated from by agreement' prevail over provisions of the law of a third country chosen by the parties 'where all other elements relevant to the situation at the time of the choice are located in one or more Member States'.

This is the first time that an EU provision contains an express and clear indication of the effect of the existence of overriding mandatory EU rules, with respect to the application of the law of a third country, with consequences that are much broader than the general provisions contained in the directives on consumer protection, which have varying conditions of application and make reference to the protection guaranteed by the substantive harmonisation rules contained therein. With respect to the *Ingmar* decision, the provisions of the Rome I and Rome II Regulations limit the effect of the application of the law chosen by the parties since the overriding mandatory EU rules are safeguarded only where the only element of contact of the case with the non-EU legal system consists in the choice of its law by the parties. In this manner, the court aims at ensuring that the law of a third country does not lead to a result that is not acceptable from a standpoint of the EU legal system. It should be pointed out, however, that these provisions do not appear to cover the *Ingmar* situation, thus leaving the ECJ's judgment fully applicable.

17.   Towards a EU System of Private International Law?

May the general framework that is described above be defined as an 'autonomous system' of private international law? Or is the EU prevented from creating such a system for general dogmatic reasons?

---

[98]   Judgment 1 June 1999, case C-126/97.
[99]   Judgment 9 November 2000, case C-381/98. On the public policy nature of certain provisions in directives concerning consumer contracts see *Mostaza Claro* (judgment 26 October 2006, case C-168/05) and *Asturcom* (judgment 6 October 2009, case C-40/08).

Certainly, as the European Parliament indicated in the Resolution of 7 September 2010 concerning the review of the Brussels I Regulation, the EU institutions would appear to be leaning towards achieving this objective over the medium/long-term, on the basis of action plans and programmes that have been adopted and gradually implemented, as well as on the basis of the broad provision of Article 81 TFEU. It would appear that a general vision of the purposes pursued by the EU in this area is slowly being affirmed, despite the different area-specific responsibilities within the single institutions and the different principles which sometimes influence such areas, with a view toward reaching solutions that ensure certainty of law for the parties within the EU legal system.

The set of acts which have so far been adopted would suggest that solutions are being sought out that are consistent with one another and with the rules and general principles of the Treaty, as interpreted by the ECJ over the course of the years. A positive signal in this regard may be gleaned from the recent proposal for a directive on consumer rights,[100] which reorganises the matter within the framework of the Rome I Regulation and in harmony with its provisions.

Despite opinions to the contrary, we are of the view that the set of rules adopted by the EU which are directly or indirectly linked — by function or objective — to Article 81 TFEU is being developed in a system of EU private international law to the extent in which the coordination or replacement of national provisions on conflicts of law and jurisdictions is proposed, as the case may be, making them consistent with one another. Such set of rules is even more than a system now that all hesitations on the extension of external EU powers in this area has been overcome, even if reluctantly. Indeed, if and to the extent that the EU rule is assigned the function of regulating relationships with third countries, through *erga omnes* conflict rules, which may designate also the law of third States, it would appear difficult to argue that it does not allocate the legislative powers among Member States and third countries, should this be one of the functions of EU conflicts rules. Likewise, when common jurisdiction criteria vis-à-vis non-EU States will be established through a revision of Article 4 of the Brussels I Regulation — that has always contained certain provisions which apply regardless of the domicile of the defendant — and adopting common provisions on the recognition and enforcement of decisions issued in third countries, it will be difficult to deny that the rules in question allocate jurisdiction not only among Member States, but also vis-à-vis third States. The Member States' approach on the occasion of the adoption of the Rome II Regulation and the debate on the Regulation on maintenance obligations with regard to the need to identify elements linking the cases with the territory of the Union for the application of EU instruments would appear to be a clear demonstration of the intention to overcome objections of principle and to use mechanisms that are well-known and tested at the national level also for common purposes.

It is possible that the use of the entire set of armaments comprising private international law, in the broad sense, that has developed over time leads to changes in certain dogmatic approaches, to the elaboration of new methods, to the application of old methods with a view to achieving new objectives or to the attribution of new functions to such instruments. In this regard, let us just mention the interpretation of EU public policy as a set provision that may not be derogated from by the choice of the law of a third

---

[100] COM (2008) 614 of 8 October 2008.

country where all of the elements of the case are located within the EU (Article 3(4) of the Rome I Regulation). In the almost 30 years since the signing of the Rome Convention, principles and rules have clearly evolved, the application of which the EU is not willing to relinquish when a dispute is raised before the courts of the Member States. In light of the considerations made by the ECJ in the *Eco Swiss* case, however, it would not be surprising if the same principles are not relinquished even with regard to the recognition of a decision issued in a non-EU State, thus ensuring internal consistency of the legal system in this case as well.

Shall we therefore deny that this phenomenon is 'systemic' in nature since it bends traditional instruments and methods to its needs? Or since Article 81 TFEU provides that the Union powers are limited to the 'compatibility' of the national conflicts rules? It would seem difficult to accept these rigidities, especially in light of the fact that the legislature has clearly overcome this limit through the adoption of regulations, with the agreement of all of the institutions and without any dissenting voices from the Member States. The fact that their application is later realised through national legal systems would not appear to be of predominant importance, especially since in any case the compliance with the general principles and interpretation criteria of the EU legal system must be guaranteed. Consider, furthermore, that such rules and instruments are used by the institutions in order to resolve cases that pertain exclusively to the EU level. It would be rather odd, to say the least, if such rules were deemed to serve a different and 'classic' function in these cases. Take, for example, issues concerning family relationships in disputes between the EU and its agents and officers, or disputes concerning the applicable law to contracts between the EU and its suppliers, or the recognition of a decision for purposes of affirming a status before the institutions.

By this, we do not mean to underestimate the fact that EU private international law rules are established by means of a range of acts and instruments that vary widely as to their nature and scope, which at present are not always coordinated, and at times present conspicuous gaps. Yet this volume shows that the system is growing even outside the framework of the acts founded upon Article 81 TFEU, also through the case-law of the ECJ, which has the difficult task of fostering the internal consistency of the system, as well as of ensuring uniformity in its application within the Member States.

Essential Bibliography

M Audit, H Muir Watt and E Pataut, *Conflits de lois et régulation économique, l'expérience du marché intérieur* (Paris, 2008).

G Badiali, 'Le droit international privé des Communautés européennes' (1985) 191 *Recueil des Cours de l'Académie de Droit International de La Haye* 9 et seq.

P Bertoli, *Corte di giustizia, integrazione comunitaria e diritto internazionale privato e processuale* (Milan, 2005).

M Bogdan, *Concise Introduction to EU Private International Law* (Groningen, 2006).

A Borrás, 'Le droit international privé communautaire: réalités, problèmes et perspectives d'avenir' (2005) 317 *Recueil des Cours de l'Académie de Droit International de La Haye* 313 et seq.

N Boschiero 'Cooperazione giudiziaria in materia civile e commerciale (diritto comunitario)', *Enciclopedia del diritto, Annali I*, 344 *et seq.*

SM Carbone, M Frigo and L Fumagalli, *Diritto processuale civile e commerciale comunitario* (Milan, 2004).

G Carella (a cura di), *Cooperazione giudiziaria ed efficacia delle sentenze: problematiche di diritto internazionale ed europeo* (Bari, 2007).

P De Cesari, *Diritto internazionale privato e processuale comunitario*, 2nd edn (Turin, 2005).

M Fallon, 'Les conflits de lois et de juridictions dans un espace économique intégré. L'expérience de la Communauté européenne' (1995) 253 *Recueil des Cours de l'Académie de Droit International de La Haye* 9 *et seq.*

M Fallon, P Lagarde and S Poillot-Peruzzetto (dir), *La matière civile et commerciale, socle d'un code européen de droit international privé* (Paris, 2009).

R Fentiman, A Nuyts, H Tagaras and N Watté, *L'espace judiciaire européen en matières civile et commerciale* (Brussels, 1999).

IF Fletcher, *Conflict of Laws and European Community Law* (Amsterdam, 1982).

S Francq, *L'applicabilité du droit communautaire dérivé au regard des méthodes de droit international privé* (Brussels, 2005).

A Fuchs, H Muir Watt and E Pataut (dir), *Les conflits de lois et le système juridique communautaire* (Paris, 2004).

P Hommelhoff, E Jayme and W Mangold (Hrsg), *Europäisches Binnenmarkt, IPR und Rechstangleichung* (Heidelberg, 1995).

U Höpping, *Auswirkungen der Warenverkehrsfreiheit auf das IPR* (Frankfurt a.M., 1997).

E Jayme, *Ein Internationales Privatrecht für Europa* (Heidelberg, 1991).

B Jud, WH Rechberger and G Reichelt, *Kollisionsrecht in der Europäischen Union* (Wien, 2008).

P Lagarde and B von Hoffmann (dir), *L'européisation du droit international privé* (Köln, 1996).

O Lando, U Magnus and M Novak-Stief (Hrsg), *Angleichung des Materielles und des Internationalen Privatrechts in der EU* (Bern, 2003).

D Lasok and PA Stone, *Conflict of Laws in the European Community* (Abingdon, 1987).

A Malatesta, S Bariatti and F Pocar (eds), *The External Dimension of EC Private International Law in Family and Succession Matters* (Padua, 2008).

S Marinai, *I valori comuni nel diritto internazionale privato e processuale comunitario* (Turin, 2007).

J Meeusen, M Pertegás and G Straetmans (eds), *Enforcement of International Contracts in the European Union* (Antwerpen-Oxford-New York, 2004).

J Meeusen, M Pertegás, G Straetmans and F Swennen (eds), *International Family Law for the European Union* (Antwerpen-Oxford, 2007).

P-Ch Müller-Graff (Hrsg), *Gemeinsames Privatrecht in der Europäischen Gemeinschaft*, 2. Aufl (Baden-Baden, 1998).

A Nuyts and N Watté (eds), *International Civil Litigation in Europe and Relations with Third States* (Brussels, 2005).

P-E Partsch, *Le droit international privé européen. De Rome à Nice* (Brussels, 2003).

P Picone (a cura di), *Diritto internazionale privato e diritto comunitario* (Padua, 2004).

F Pocar (ed), *The External Competence of the European Union and Private International Law* (Padua, 2007).

JA Pontier and E Burg, *EU Principles on Jurisdiction and Recognition and Enforcement of Judgments in Civil and Commercial Matters According to the Case Law of the European Court of Justice* (The Hague, 2004).

G Rossolillo, *Mutuo riconoscimento e tecniche conflittuali* (Padua, 2002).

P Stone, *EU Private International Law — Harmonization of Laws* (Cheltenham-Northampton, 2006).

AVM Struycken, 'Les conséquences de l'intégration européenne sur le développement du droit international privé' (1992i) 232 *Recueil des Cours de l'Academie de Droit International de La Haye* 257 et seq.

Ch von Bar (Hrsg), *Europäisches Gemeinschaftsrecht und Internationales Privatrecht* (Köln, 1991).

B von Hoffmann (ed), *European Private International Law* (Nijmegen, 1998).

Numerous articles on the developments in the field of judicial cooperation in civil matters are also included in Essays in honour, including the following: *Private International Law in the International Arena — From National Conflict Rules Towards Harmonization and Unification, Liber Amicorum Kurt Siehr* (The Hague, 2000); *International Conflicts of Laws for the Third Millennium, Essays in Honor of Friedrich K Juenger* (New York, 2001); *Law and Justice in a Multi-State World, Essays in Honor of Arthur T Von Mehren* (New York, 2002); *Intercontinental Cooperation Through Private International Law, Essays in Memory of Peter E. Nygh* (The Hague, 2004); *Le droit international privé: esprit et méthodes, Mélanges en l'honneur de Paul Lagarde* (Paris, 2005); *Vers des nouveaux équilibres entre ordres juridiques, Liber amicorum Helène Gaudemet-Tallon* (Paris, 2008); *New Instruments of Private International Law, Liber Fausto Pocar* (Milan, 2009); *Convergence and Divergence in Private International Law: Liber Amicorum Kurt Siehr* (Zurich, 2010).

I

General Provisions on Judicial Cooperation in Civil Matters

General provisions

A.1. Treaty on the European Union

Article 2. The Union is founded on the values of respect for human dignity, freedom, democracy, equality, the rule of law and respect for human rights, including the rights of persons belonging to minorities. These values are common to the Member States in a society in which pluralism, non-discrimination, tolerance, justice, solidarity and equality between women and men prevail.

Article 3 (ex Article 2 TEU).   1.   The Union's aim is to promote peace, its values and the well-being of its peoples.

2.   The Union shall offer its citizens an area of freedom, security and justice without internal frontiers, in which the free movement of persons is ensured in conjunction with appropriate measures with respect to external border controls, asylum, immigration and the prevention and combating of crime.

3.   The Union shall establish an internal market. It shall work for the sustainable development of Europe based on balanced economic growth and price stability, a highly competitive social market economy, aiming at full employment and social progress, and a high level of protection and improvement of the quality of the environment. It shall promote scientific and technological advance. It shall combat social exclusion and discrimination, and shall promote social justice and protection, equality between women and men, solidarity between generations and protection of the rights of the child. It shall promote economic, social and territorial cohesion, and solidarity among Member States. It shall respect its rich cultural and linguistic diversity, and shall ensure that Europe's cultural heritage is safeguarded and enhanced...

5.   In its relations with the wider world, the Union shall uphold and promote its values and interests and contribute to the protection of its citizens. It shall contribute to peace, security, the sustainable development of the Earth, solidarity and mutual respect among peoples, free and fair trade, eradication of poverty and the protection of human rights, in particular the rights of the child, as well as to the strict observance and the development of international law, including respect for the principles of the United Nations Charter...

Article 4.   3.   Pursuant to the principle of sincere cooperation, the Union and the Member States shall, in full mutual respect, assist each other in carrying out tasks which flow from the Treaties. The Member States shall take any appropriate measure, general or particular, to ensure fulfilment of the obligations arising out of the Treaties or resulting from the acts of the institutions of the Union. The Member States shall facilitate the achievement of the Union's tasks and refrain from any measure which could jeopardise the attainment of the Union's objectives.

Article 5 (ex Article 5 TEC).   1.   The limits of Union competences are governed by the principle of conferral. The use of Union competences is governed by the principles of subsidiarity and proportionality.
2.   Under the principle of conferral, the Union shall act only within the limits of the competences conferred upon it by the Member States in the Treaties to attain the objectives set out therein. Competences not conferred upon the Union in the Treaties remain with the Member States.
3.   Under the principle of subsidiarity, in areas which do not fall within its exclusive competence, the Union shall act only if and in so far as the objectives of the proposed action cannot be sufficiently achieved by the Member States, either at central level or at regional and local level, but can rather, by reason of the scale or effects of the proposed action, be better achieved at Union level. The institutions of the Union shall apply the principle of subsidiarity as laid down in the Protocol on the application of the principles of subsidiarity and proportionality. National Parliaments ensure compliance with the principle of subsidiarity in accordance with the procedure set out in that Protocol.
4.   Under the principle of proportionality, the content and form of Union action shall not exceed what is necessary to achieve the objectives of the Treaties. The institutions of the Union shall apply the principle of proportionality as laid down in the Protocol on the application of the principles of subsidiarity and proportionality.

Article 20 (ex Articles 27a to 27e, 40 to 40b and 43 to 45 TEU and ex Articles 11 and 11a TEC).   1.   Member States which wish to establish enhanced cooperation between themselves within the framework of the Union's non-exclusive competences may make use of its institutions and exercise those competences by applying the relevant provisions of the Treaties, subject to the limits and in accordance with the detailed arrangements laid down in this Article and in Articles 326 to 334 of the Treaty on the Functioning of the European Union.
Enhanced cooperation shall aim to further the objectives of the Union, protect its interests and reinforce its integration process. Such cooperation shall be open at any time to all Member States, in accordance with Article 328 of the Treaty on the Functioning of the European Union.
2.   The decision authorising enhanced cooperation shall be adopted by the Council as a last resort, when it has established that the objectives of such cooperation cannot be attained within a reasonable period by the Union as a whole, and provided that at least nine Member States participate in it. The Council shall act in accordance with the procedure laid down in Article 329 of the Treaty on the Functioning of the European Union.
3.   All members of the Council may participate in its deliberations, but only members of the Council representing the Member States participating in enhanced cooperation shall take part in the vote. The voting rules are set out in Article 330 of the Treaty on the Functioning of the European Union.

4.   Acts adopted in the framework of enhanced cooperation shall bind only participating Member States. They shall not be regarded as part of the *acquis* which has to be accepted by candidate States for accession to the Union.

A.2.   Treaty on the Functioning of the European Union

Part Three — Union Policies and Internal Actions

Title V — Area of Freedom, Security and Justice

Chapter 1 — General provisions

Article 67 (ex Article 61 TEC and ex Article 29 TEU).   1.   The Union shall constitute an area of freedom, security and justice with respect for fundamental rights and the different legal systems and traditions of the Member States.

2.   It shall ensure the absence of internal border controls for persons and shall frame a common policy on asylum, immigration and external border control, based on solidarity between Member States, which is fair towards third-country nationals. For the purpose of this Title, stateless persons shall be treated as third-country nationals.

3.   The Union shall endeavour to ensure a high level of security through measures to prevent and combat crime, racism and xenophobia, and through measures for coordination and cooperation between police and judicial authorities and other competent authorities, as well as through the mutual recognition of judgments in criminal matters and, if necessary, through the approximation of criminal laws.

4.   The Union shall facilitate access to justice, in particular through the principle of mutual recognition of judicial and extrajudicial decisions in civil matters.

Article 68.   The European Council shall define the strategic guidelines for legislative and operational planning within the area of freedom, security and justice.

Chapter 3 — Judicial cooperation in civil matters

Article 81 (ex Article 65 TEC).   1.   The Union shall develop judicial cooperation in civil matters having cross-border implications, based on the principle of mutual recognition of judgments and of decisions in extrajudicial cases. Such cooperation may include the adoption of measures for the approximation of the laws and regulations of the Member States.

2.   For the purposes of paragraph 1, the European Parliament and the Council, acting in accordance with the ordinary legislative procedure, shall adopt measures, particularly when necessary for the proper functioning of the internal market, aimed at ensuring:

(a)   the mutual recognition and enforcement between Member States of judgments and of decisions in extrajudicial cases;

(b)   the cross-border service of judicial and extrajudicial documents;

(c)   the compatibility of the rules applicable in the Member States concerning conflict of laws and of jurisdiction;

(d)   cooperation in the taking of evidence;

(e)   effective access to justice;

(f)   the elimination of obstacles to the proper functioning of civil proceedings, if necessary by promoting the compatibility of the rules on civil procedure applicable in the Member States;

(g)   the development of alternative methods of dispute settlement;

(h)   support for the training of the judiciary and judicial staff.

3.   Notwithstanding paragraph 2, measures concerning family law with cross-border implications shall be established by the Council, acting in accordance with a special legislative procedure. The Council shall act unanimously after consulting the European Parliament.

The Council, on a proposal from the Commission, may adopt a decision determining those aspects of family law with cross-border implications which may be the subject of acts adopted by the ordinary legislative procedure. The Council shall act unanimously after consulting the European Parliament.

The proposal referred to in the second subparagraph shall be notified to the national Parliaments. If a national Parliament makes known its opposition within six months of the date of such notification, the decision shall not be adopted. In the absence of opposition, the Council may adopt the decision.

Title VII — Common rules on competition, taxation and approximation of laws

Chapter 3 — Approximation of laws

Article 114 (ex Article 95 TEC).   1.   Save where otherwise provided in the Treaties, the following provisions shall apply for the achievement of the objectives set out in Article 26. The European Parliament and the Council shall, acting in accordance with the ordinary legislative procedure and after consulting the Economic and Social Committee, adopt the measures for the approximation of the provisions laid down by law, regulation or administrative action in Member States which have as their object the establishment and functioning of the internal market.

2.   Paragraph 1 shall not apply to fiscal provisions, to those relating to the free movement of persons nor to those relating to the rights and interests of employed persons.

3.   The Commission, in its proposals envisaged in paragraph 1 concerning health, safety, environmental protection and consumer protection, will take as a base a high level of protection, taking account in particular of any new development based on scientific facts. Within their respective powers, the European Parliament and the Council will also seek to achieve this objective.

4.   If, after the adoption of a harmonisation measure by the European Parliament and the Council, by the Council or by the Commission, a Member State deems it necessary to maintain national provisions on grounds of major needs referred to in Article 36, or relating to the protection of the environment or the working environment, it shall notify the Commission of these provisions as well as the grounds for maintaining them.

5.   Moreover, without prejudice to paragraph 4, if, after the adoption of a harmonisation measure by the European Parliament and the Council, by the Council or by the Commission, a Member State deems it necessary to introduce national provisions based on new scientific evidence relating to the protection of the environment or the working environment on grounds of a problem specific to that Member State arising after the adoption of the harmonisation measure, it shall notify the Commission of the envisaged provisions as well as the grounds for introducing them.

6.   The Commission shall, within six months of the notifications as referred to in paragraphs 4 and 5, approve or reject the national provisions involved after having verified whether or not they are a means of arbitrary discrimination or a disguised restriction on trade between Member States and whether or not they shall constitute an obstacle to the functioning of the internal market. In the absence of a decision by the Commission within this period the national provisions referred to in paragraphs 4 and 5 shall be deemed to have been approved. When justified by the complexity of the matter and in the absence of danger for human health, the Commission may notify the Member State concerned that the period referred to in this paragraph may be extended for a further period of up to six months.

7.   When, pursuant to paragraph 6, a Member State is authorised to maintain or introduce national provisions derogating from a harmonisation measure, the Commission shall immediately examine whether to propose an adaptation to that measure.

8.   When a Member State raises a specific problem on public health in a field which has been the subject of prior harmonisation measures, it shall bring it to the attention of the Commission which shall immediately examine whether to propose appropriate measures to the Council.

9.   By way of derogation from the procedure laid down in Articles 258 and 259, the Commission and any Member State may bring the matter directly before the Court of Justice of the European Union if it considers that another Member State is making improper use of the powers provided for in this Article.

10.   The harmonisation measures referred to above shall, in appropriate cases, include a safeguard clause authorising the Member States to take, for one or more of the non-economic reasons referred to in Article 36, provisional measures subject to a Union control procedure.

Part Six — Institutional and Financial Provisions

Title III — Enhanced Cooperation

Article 326 (ex Articles 27a to 27e, 40 to 40b and 43 to 45 TEU and ex Articles 11 and 11a TEC).   Any enhanced cooperation shall comply with the Treaties and Union law.

Such cooperation shall not undermine the internal market or economic, social and territorial cohesion. It shall not constitute a barrier to or discrimination in trade between Member States, nor shall it distort competition between them.

Article 327 (ex Articles 27a to 27e, 40 to 40b and 43 to 45 TEU and ex Articles 11 and 11a TEC).   Any enhanced cooperation shall respect the competences, rights and obligations of those Member States which do not participate in it. Those Member States shall not impede its implementation by the participating Member States.

Article 328 (ex Articles 27a to 27e, 40 to 40b and 43 to 45 TEU and ex Articles 11 and 11a TEC).   1.   When enhanced cooperation is being established, it shall be open to all Member States, subject to compliance with any conditions of participation laid down by the authorising decision. It shall also be open to them at any other time, subject to compliance with the acts already adopted within that framework, in addition to those conditions.

The Commission and the Member States participating in enhanced cooperation shall ensure that they promote participation by as many Member States as possible.

2.   The Commission and, where appropriate, the High Representative of the Union for Foreign Affairs and Security Policy shall keep the European Parliament and the Council regularly informed regarding developments in enhanced cooperation.

Article 329 (ex Articles 27a to 27e, 40 to 40b and 43 to 45 TEU and ex Articles 11 and 11a TEC).   1.   Member States which wish to establish enhanced cooperation between themselves in one of the areas covered by the Treaties, with the exception of fields of exclusive competence and the common foreign and security policy, shall address a request to the Commission, specifying the scope and objectives of the enhanced cooperation proposed. The Commission may submit a proposal to the Council to that effect. In the event of the Commission not submitting a proposal, it shall inform the Member States concerned of the reasons for not doing so.

Authorisation to proceed with the enhanced cooperation referred to in the first subparagraph shall be granted by the Council, on a proposal from the Commission and after obtaining the consent of the European Parliament.

2.   The request of the Member States which wish to establish enhanced cooperation between themselves within the framework of the common foreign and security policy shall be addressed to the Council. It shall be forwarded to the High Representative of the Union for Foreign Affairs and Security Policy, who shall give an opinion on whether the enhanced cooperation proposed is consistent with the Union's common foreign and security policy and to the Commission, which shall give its opinion in particular on whether the enhanced cooperation proposed is consistent with other Union policies. It shall also be forwarded to the European Parliament for information.

Authorisation to proceed with enhanced cooperation shall be granted by a decision of the Council acting unanimously.

Article 330 (ex Articles 27a to 27e, 40 to 40b and 43 to 45 TEU and ex Articles 11 and 11a TEC).   All members of the Council may participate in its deliberations, but only members of the Council representing the Member States participating in enhanced cooperation shall take part in the vote.

Unanimity shall be constituted by the votes of the representatives of the participating Member States only.

A qualified majority shall be defined in accordance with Article 238(3).

Article 331 (ex Articles 27a to 27e, 40 to 40b and 43 to 45 TEU and ex Articles 11 and 11a TEC).   1.   Any Member State which wishes to participate in enhanced cooperation in progress in one of the areas referred to in Article 329(1) shall notify its intention to the Council and the Commission.

The Commission shall, within four months of the date of receipt of the notification, confirm the participation of the Member State concerned. It shall note where necessary that the conditions of participation have been fulfilled and shall adopt any transitional measures necessary with regard to the application of the acts already adopted within the framework of enhanced cooperation.

However, if the Commission considers that the conditions of participation have not been fulfilled, it shall indicate the arrangements to be adopted to fulfil those conditions and shall set a deadline for re-examining the request. On the expiry of that deadline, it shall re-examine the request, in accordance with the procedure set out in the second subparagraph. If the Commission considers that the conditions of participation have still not been met, the Member State concerned may refer the matter to the Council, which shall decide on the request. The Council shall act in accordance with Article 330. It may also adopt the transitional measures referred to in the second subparagraph on a proposal from the Commission.

2.   Any Member State which wishes to participate in enhanced cooperation in progress in the framework of the common foreign and security policy shall notify its intention to the Council, the High Representative of the Union for Foreign Affairs and Security Policy and the Commission.

The Council shall confirm the participation of the Member State concerned, after consulting the High Representative of the Union for Foreign Affairs and Security Policy and after noting, where necessary, that the conditions of participation have been fulfilled. The Council, on a proposal from the High Representative, may also adopt any transitional measures necessary with regard to the application of the acts already adopted within the framework of enhanced cooperation. However, if the Council considers that the conditions of participation have not been fulfilled, it shall indicate the arrangements to be adopted to fulfil those conditions and shall set a deadline for re-examining the request for participation.

For the purposes of this paragraph, the Council shall act unanimously and in accordance with Article 330.

Article 332 (ex Articles 27a to 27e, 40 to 40b and 43 to 45 TEU and ex Articles 11 and 11a TEC).   Expenditure resulting from implementation of enhanced cooperation, other than administrative costs entailed for the institutions, shall be borne by the participating Member States, unless all members of the Council, acting unanimously after consulting the European Parliament, decide otherwise.

Article 333 (ex Articles 27a to 27e, 40 to 40b and 43 to 45 TEU and ex Articles 11 and 11a TEC).   1.   Where a provision of the Treaties which may be applied in the context of enhanced cooperation stipulates that the Council shall act unanimously, the Council, acting unanimously in accordance with the arrangements laid down in Article 330, may adopt a decision stipulating that it will act by a qualified majority.

2.   Where a provision of the Treaties which may be applied in the context of enhanced cooperation stipulates that the Council shall adopt acts under a special legislative procedure, the Council, acting unanimously in accordance with the arrangements laid down in Article 330, may adopt a decision stipulating that it will act under the ordinary legislative procedure. The Council shall act after consulting the European Parliament.

3.   Paragraphs 1 and 2 shall not apply to decisions having military or defence implications.

Article 334 (ex Articles 27a to 27e, 40 to 40b and 43 to 45 TEU and ex Articles 11 and 11a TEC).   The Council and the Commission shall ensure the consistency of activities undertaken in the context of enhanced cooperation and the consistency of such activities with the policies of the Union, and shall cooperate to that end.

A.3.   Protocols to the Treaty on the European Union and to the Treaty on the Functioning of the European Union

Protocol (No 21) on the position of the United Kingdom and Ireland in respect of the area of freedom, security and justice

The High Contracting Parties,

Desiring to settle certain questions relating to the United Kingdom and Ireland,

Having regard to the Protocol on the application of certain aspects of Article 26 of the Treaty on the Functioning of the European Union to the United Kingdom and to Ireland,

Have agreed upon the following provisions, which shall be annexed to the Treaty on European Union and the Treaty on the Functioning of the European Union:

Article 1.   Subject to Article 3, the United Kingdom and Ireland shall not take part in the adoption by the Council of proposed measures pursuant to Title V of Part Three of the Treaty on the Functioning of the European Union. The unanimity of the members of the Council, with the exception of the representatives of the governments of the United Kingdom and Ireland, shall be necessary for decisions of the Council which must be adopted unanimously.

For the purposes of this Article, a qualified majority shall be defined in accordance with Article 238(3) of the Treaty on the Functioning of the European Union.

Article 2.   In consequence of Article 1 and subject to Articles 3, 4 and 6, none of the provisions of Title V of Part Three of the Treaty on the Functioning of the European Union, no measure adopted pursuant to that Title, no provision of any international agreement concluded by the Union pursuant to that Title, and no decision of the Court of Justice interpreting any such provision or measure shall be binding upon or applicable in the United Kingdom or Ireland; and no such provision, measure or decision shall in any way affect the competences, rights and obligations of those States; and no such provision, measure or decision shall in any way affect the Community or Union acquis nor form part of Union law as they apply to the United Kingdom or Ireland.

Article 3.   1.   The United Kingdom or Ireland may notify the President of the Council in writing, within three months after a proposal or initiative has been presented to the Council pursuant to Title V of Part Three of the Treaty on the Functioning of the European Union, that it wishes to take part in the adoption and application of any such proposed measure, whereupon that State shall be entitled to do so.

The unanimity of the members of the Council, with the exception of a member which has not made such a notification, shall be necessary for decisions of the Council which must be adopted unanimously. A measure adopted under this paragraph shall be binding upon all Member States which took part in its adoption.

Measures adopted pursuant to Article 70 of the Treaty on the Functioning of the European Union shall lay down the conditions for the participation of the United Kingdom and Ireland in the evaluations concerning the areas covered by Title V of Part Three of that Treaty.

For the purposes of this Article, a qualified majority shall be defined in accordance with Article 238(3) of the Treaty on the Functioning of the European Union.

2. If after a reasonable period of time a measure referred to in paragraph 1 cannot be adopted with the United Kingdom or Ireland taking part, the Council may adopt such measure in accordance with Article 1 without the participation of the United Kingdom or Ireland. In that case Article 2 applies.

Article 4. The United Kingdom or Ireland may at any time after the adoption of a measure by the Council pursuant to Title V of Part Three of the Treaty on the Functioning of the European Union notify its intention to the Council and to the Commission that it wishes to accept that measure. In that case, the procedure provided for in Article 331(1) of the Treaty on the Functioning of the European Union shall apply mutatis mutandis.

Article 4a. 1. The provisions of this Protocol apply for the United Kingdom and Ireland also to measures proposed or adopted pursuant to Title V of Part Three of the Treaty on the Functioning of the European Union amending an existing measure by which they are bound.

2. However, in cases where the Council, acting on a proposal from the Commission, determines that the non-participation of the United Kingdom or Ireland in the amended version of an existing measure makes the application of that measure inoperable for other Member States or the Union, it may urge them to make a notification under Article 3 or 4. For the purposes of Article 3, a further period of two months starts to run as from the date of such determination by the Council.

If at the expiry of that period of two months from the Council's determination the United Kingdom or Ireland has not made a notification under Article 3 or Article 4, the existing measure shall no longer be binding upon or applicable to it, unless the Member State concerned has made a notification under Article 4 before the entry into force of the amending measure. This shall take effect from the date of entry into force of the amending measure or of expiry of the period of two months, whichever is the later.

For the purpose of this paragraph, the Council shall, after a full discussion of the matter, act by a qualified majority of its members representing the Member States participating or having participated in the adoption of the amending measure. A qualified majority of the Council shall be defined in accordance with Article 238(3)(a) of the Treaty on the Functioning of the European Union.

3. The Council, acting by a qualified majority on a proposal from the Commission, may determine that the United Kingdom or Ireland shall bear the direct financial consequences, if any, necessarily and unavoidably incurred as a result of the cessation of its participation in the existing measure.

4. This Article shall be without prejudice to Article 4.

Article 5.   A Member State which is not bound by a measure adopted pursuant to Title V of Part Three of the Treaty on the Functioning of the European Union shall bear no financial consequences of that measure other than administrative costs entailed for the institutions, unless all members of the Council, acting unanimously after consulting the European Parliament, decide otherwise.

Article 6.   Where, in cases referred to in this Protocol, the United Kingdom or Ireland is bound by a measure adopted by the Council pursuant to Title V of Part Three of the Treaty on the Functioning of the European Union, the relevant provisions of the Treaties shall apply to that State in relation to that measure.

Article 8.   Ireland may notify the Council in writing that it no longer wishes to be covered by the terms of this Protocol. In that case, the normal treaty provisions will apply to Ireland.

Protocol (No 22) on the position of Denmark

The High Contracting Parties,

Recalling the Decision of the Heads of State or Government, meeting within the European Council at Edinburgh on 12 December 1992, concerning certain problems raised by Denmark on the Treaty on European Union,

Having noted the position of Denmark with regard to Citizenship, Economic and Monetary Union, Defence Policy and Justice and Home Affairs as laid down in the Edinburgh Decision,

Conscious of the fact that a continuation under the Treaties of the legal regime originating in the Edinburgh decision will significantly limit Denmark's participation in important areas of cooperation of the Union, and that it would be in the best interest of the Union to ensure the integrity of the *acquis* in the area of freedom, security and justice,

Wishing therefore to establish a legal framework that will provide an option for Denmark to participate in the adoption of measures proposed on the basis of Title V of Part Three of the Treaty on the Functioning of the European Union and welcoming the intention of Denmark to avail itself of this option when possible in accordance with its constitutional requirements,

Noting that Denmark will not prevent the other Member States from further developing their cooperation with respect to measures not binding on Denmark,

Bearing in mind Article 3 of the Protocol on the Schengen *acquis* integrated into the framework of the European Union,

Have agreed upon the following provisions, which shall be annexed to the Treaty on European Union and the Treaty on the Functioning of the European Union:

Part I

Article 1.   Denmark shall not take part in the adoption by the Council of proposed measures pursuant to Title V of Part Three of the Treaty on the Functioning of the European Union. The unanimity of the members of the Council, with the exception of the representative of the government of Denmark, shall be necessary for the decisions of the Council which must be adopted unanimously.

For the purposes of this Article, a qualified majority shall be defined in accordance with Article 238(3) of the Treaty on the Functioning of the European Union.

Article 2.   None of the provisions of Title V of Part Three of the Treaty on the Functioning of the European Union, no measure adopted pursuant to that Title, no provision of any international agreement concluded by the Union pursuant to that Title, and no decision of the Court of Justice of the European Union interpreting any such provision or measure or any measure amended or amendable pursuant to that Title shall be binding upon or applicable in Denmark; and no such provision, measure or decision shall in any way affect the competences, rights and obligations of Denmark; and no such provision, measure or decision shall in any way affect the Community or Union *acquis* nor form part of Union law as they apply to Denmark. In particular, acts of the Union in the field of police cooperation and judicial cooperation in criminal matters adopted before the entry into force of the Treaty of Lisbon which are amended shall continue to be binding upon and applicable to Denmark unchanged.

Article 2a.   Article 2 of this Protocol shall also apply in respect of those rules laid down on the basis of Article 16 of the Treaty on the Functioning of the European Union which relate to the processing of personal data by the Member States when carrying out activities which fall within the scope of Chapter 4 or Chapter 5 of Title V of Part Three of that Treaty.

Article 3.   Denmark shall bear no financial consequences of measures referred to in Article 1, other than administrative costs entailed for the institutions.

Part IV

Article 7.   At any time Denmark may, in accordance with its constitutional requirements, inform the other Member States that it no longer wishes to avail itself of all or part of this Protocol. In that event, Denmark will apply in full all relevant measures then in force taken within the framework of the European Union.

Article 8.   1.   At any time and without prejudice to Article 7, Denmark may, in accordance with its constitutional requirements, notify the other Member States that, with effect from the first day of the month following the notification, Part I shall consist of the provisions in the Annex. In that case Articles 5 to 8 shall be renumbered in consequence.

Annex

Article 1.   Subject to Article 3, Denmark shall not take part in the adoption by the Council of measures proposed pursuant to Title V of Part Three of the Treaty on the Functioning of the European Union. The unanimity of the members of the Council, with the exception of the representative of the government of Denmark, shall be necessary for the acts of the Council which must be adopted unanimously.

For the purposes of this Article, a qualified majority shall be defined in accordance with Article 238(3) of the Treaty on the Functioning of the European Union.

Article 2.   Pursuant to Article 1 and subject to Articles 3, 4 and 8, none of the provisions in Title V of Part Three of the Treaty on the Functioning of the European Union, no measure adopted pursuant to that Title, no provision of any international agreements concluded by the Union pursuant to that Title, no decision of the Court of Justice of the European Union interpreting any such provision or measure shall be binding upon or applicable in Denmark; and no such provision, measure or decision shall in any way affect the competences, rights and obligations of Denmark; and no such provision, measure or decision shall in any way affect the Community or Union *acquis* nor form part of Union law as they apply to Denmark.

Article 3.   1.   Denmark may notify the President of the Council in writing, within three months after a proposal or initiative has been presented to the Council pursuant to Title V of Part Three of the Treaty on the Functioning of the European Union, that it wishes to take part in the adoption and application of any such proposed measure, whereupon Denmark shall be entitled to do so.
    2.   If after a reasonable period of time a measure referred to in paragraph 1 cannot be adopted with Denmark taking part, the Council may adopt that measure referred to in paragraph 1 in accordance with Article 1 without the participation of Denmark. In that case Article 2 applies.

Article 4.   Denmark may at any time after the adoption of a measure pursuant to Title V of Part Three of the Treaty on the Functioning of the European Union notify its intention to the Council and the Commission that it wishes to accept that measure. In that case, the procedure provided for in Article 331(1) of that Treaty shall apply mutatis mutandis.

Article 5.   1.   The provisions of this Protocol apply for Denmark also to measures proposed or adopted pursuant to Title V of Part Three of the Treaty on the Functioning of the European Union amending an existing measure by which it is bound.
    2.   However, in cases where the Council, acting on a proposal from the Commission, determines that the non-participation of Denmark in the amended version of an existing measure makes the application of that measure inoperable for other Member States or the Union, it may urge it to make a notification under Article 3 or 4. For the purposes of Article 3 a further period of two months starts to run as from the date of such determination by the Council.
    If, at the expiry of that period of two months from the Council's determination, Denmark has not made a notification under Article 3 or Article 4, the existing measure shall no longer be binding upon or applicable to it, unless it has made a notification under Article 4 before the entry into force of the amending measure. This shall take effect from the date of entry into force of the amending measure or of expiry of the period of two months, whichever is the later.
    For the purpose of this paragraph, the Council shall, after a full discussion of the matter, act by a qualified majority of its members representing the Member States participating or having participated in the adoption of the amending measure. A qualified

majority of the Council shall be defined in accordance with Article 238(3)(a) of the Treaty on the Functioning of the European Union.

3.   The Council, acting by a qualified majority on a proposal from the Commission, may determine that Denmark shall bear the direct financial consequences, if any, necessarily and unavoidably incurred as a result of the cessation of its participation in the existing measure.

4.   This Article shall be without prejudice to Article 4.

Article 6.   1.   Notification pursuant to Article 4 shall be submitted no later than six months after the final adoption of a measure if this measure builds upon the Schengen *acquis*.

If Denmark does not submit a notification in accordance with Articles 3 or 4 regarding a measure building upon the Schengen *acquis*, the Member States bound by that measure and Denmark will consider appropriate measures to be taken.

2.   A notification pursuant to Article 3 with respect to a measure building upon the Schengen *acquis* shall be deemed irrevocably to be a notification pursuant to Article 3 with respect to any further proposal or initiative aiming to build upon that measure to the extent that such proposal or initiative builds upon the Schengen *acquis*.

Article 7.   Denmark shall not be bound by the rules laid down on the basis of Article 16 of the Treaty on the Functioning of the European Union which relate to the processing of personal data by the Mem ber States when carrying out activities which fall within the scope of Chapter 4 or Chapter 5 of Title V of Part Three of that Treaty where Denmark is not bound by the rules governing the forms of judicial cooperation in criminal matters or police cooperation which require compliance with the provisions laid down on the basis of Article 16.

Article 8.   Where, in cases referred to in this Part, Denmark is bound by a measure adopted by the Council pursuant to Title V of Part Three of the Treaty on the Functioning of the European Union, the relevant provisions of the Treaties shall apply to Denmark in relation to that measure.

Article 9.   Where Denmark is not bound by a measure adopted pursuant to Title V of Part Three of the Treaty on the Functioning of the European Union, it shall bear no financial consequences of that measure other than administrative costs entailed for the institutions unless the Council, with all its Members acting unanimously after consulting the European Parliament, decides otherwise.

A.4. Declarations annexed to the Final Act of the Intergovernmental Conference which adopted the Treaty of Lisbon, signed on 13 December 2007

Declaration on non-participation by a Member State in a measure based on Title V of Part Three of the Treaty on the Functioning of the European Union (No 26).

The Conference declares that, where a Member State opts not to participate in a measure based on Title V of Part Three of the Treaty on the Functioning of the European Union, the Council will hold a full discussion on the possible implications and effects of that Member State's non-participation in the measure.

In addition, any Member State may ask the Commission to examine the situation on the basis of Article 116 of the Treaty on the Functioning of the European Union.

The above paragraphs are without prejudice to the entitlement of a Member State to refer the matter to the European Council.

Declaration concerning the Protocol on the position of Denmark (No 48)

The Conference notes that with respect to legal acts to be adopted by the Council acting alone or jointly with the European Parliament and containing provisions applicable to Denmark as well as provisions not applicable to Denmark because they have a legal basis to which Part I of the Protocol on the position of Denmark applies, Denmark declares that it will not use its voting right to prevent the adoption of the provisions which are not applicable to Denmark....

Declaration by Ireland on Article 3 of the Protocol on the position of the United Kingdom and Ireland in respect of the area of freedom, security and justice (No 56)

Ireland affirms its commitment to the Union as an area of freedom, security and justice respecting fundamental rights and the different legal systems and traditions of the Member States within which citizens are provided with a high level of safety.

Accordingly, Ireland declares its firm intention to exercise its right under Article 3 of the Protocol on the position of the United Kingdom and Ireland in respect of the area of freedom, security and justice to take part in the adoption of measures pursuant to Title V of Part Three of the Treaty on the Functioning of the European Union to the maximum extent it deems possible.

Ireland will, in particular, participate to the maximum possible extent in measures in the field of police cooperation.

Furthermore, Ireland recalls that in accordance with Article 8 of the Protocol it may notify the Council in writing that it no longer wishes to be covered by the terms of the Protocol. Ireland intends to review the operation of these arrangements within three years of the entry into force of the Treaty of Lisbon.

B.   Action Plan of the Council and the Commission on how best to implement the provisions of the Treaty of Amsterdam on an area of freedom, security and justice — Vienna Action Plan (OJ, C 19 of 23 January 1999)

1.   The European Council, meeting at Cardiff called on the Council and the Commission to submit at its meeting in Vienna an action plan on 'how best to implement the provisions of the Treaty of Amsterdam on an area of freedom, security and justice'.

Heads of State or Government at Pörtschach further confirmed the importance they attach to this subject by agreeing to hold a special European Council in Tampere in October 1999.

Under the Amsterdam Treaty, the areas of visa, asylum, immigration and other policies related to free movement of persons, like judicial cooperation in civil matters, are transferred from the EU's third pillar to its first pillar (albeit not all of the first pillar procedures will be applicable), whereas provisions on police and judicial cooperation in criminal matters contained in the new Title VI of the Treaty on European Union remain within the EU's third pillar. In addition to these changes in responsibilities, the Amsterdam Treaty also lays down the broad lines of action in the areas currently assigned to the third pillar.

2.   When the Cardiff European Council called on the Council and the Commission to present the action plan, it clearly indicated its view that those provisions offer new opportunities to tackle an area of major public concern and thus to bring the European Union closer to the people.

3.   Without underestimating what has already been achieved in this area under the EC Treaty, under the Title VI provisions of the Maastricht Treaty and within Schengen, it is worth recalling the reasons why the new provisions adopted in Amsterdam open up improved possibilities. First, the objective of maintaining and developing the Union as an area of freedom, security and justice is asserted and the various aspects involved are reviewed. Secondly, the Union has been given the necessary framework in which to accommodate it and the instruments required have been strengthened and at the same time, thanks to the enhanced role foreseen for the European Court of Justice and the European Parliament, made subject to tighter judicial and democratic review. The Community method is extended: several of the areas of the current third pillar are brought under Community arrangements and restrictions which used to apply to the Community institutions in the areas of police and criminal justice cooperation have been lifted. Access to the Community budget has been made less cumbersome. Finally, the integration of Schengen recognises the efforts of the Member States which embarked on this cooperation and gives the Union a base on which to build further.

4.   In drawing up this action plan, the Council and the Commission take as their starting point that one of the keys to its success lies in ensuring that the spirit of interinstitutional cooperation inherent in the Amsterdam Treaty is translated into reality. This applies in particular to the new responsibilities, including an extended right of initiative, which Amsterdam bestows on the Commission. What is important is not so much where the right of initiative lies, be it shared or exclusive, as the way in which this right is exercised. In any case the Treaty provides that for the five years earmarked for the full attainment of the free movement of persons, the right of initiative will be

shared between the Commission and the Member States for matters transferred to the Community framework.

5.   Although any action plan drawn up must, in concrete terms, necessarily reflect the priorities and timetable set out in the Amsterdam Treaty itself, it needs to reflect also the general approach and philosophy inherent in the concept of an 'area of freedom, security and justice'. These three notions are closely interlinked. Freedom loses much of its meaning if it cannot be enjoyed in a secure environment and with the full backing of a system of justice in which all Union citizens and residents can have confidence. These three inseparable concepts have one common denominator 'people' and one cannot be achieved in full without the other two. Maintaining the right balance between them must be the guiding thread for Union action. It should be noted in this context that the Treaty establishing the European Communities (Article 61 (ex) Article 73(i)(a), makes a direct link between the measures establishing freedom of movement of persons and the specific measures seeking to combat and prevent crime (Article 31(e) of the Treaty on European Union), thus creating a conditional link between the two areas.

A.   An Area of Freedom

(a)   A Wider Concept of Freedom

6.   Freedom in the sense of free movement of people within the European Union remains a fundamental objective of the Treaty, and one to which the flanking measures associated with the concepts of security and justice must make their essential contribution. The Schengen achievement has shown the way and provides the foundation on which to build. However, the Treaty of Amsterdam also opens the way to giving 'freedom' a meaning beyond free movement of people across internal borders. It is also freedom to live in a law-abiding environment in the knowledge that public authorities are using everything in their individual and collective power (nationally, at the level of the Union and beyond) to combat and contain those who seek to deny or abuse that freedom. Freedom must also be complemented by the full range of fundamental human rights, including protection from any form of discrimination as foreseen by Articles 12 and 13 of TEC and 6 of the TEU.

7.   Another fundamental freedom deserving special attention in today's fast-developing information society is that of respect for privacy and in particular the protection of personal data. When, in support of the development of police and judicial cooperation in criminal matters, personal data files are set up and information exchanged, it is indeed essential to strike the right balance between public security and the protection of individuals' privacy.

B.   An Area of Security

9.   The full benefits of any area of freedom will never be enjoyed unless they are exercised in an area where people can feel safe and secure.

10.   The agreed aim of the Treaty is not to create a European security area in the sense of a common territory where uniform detection and investigation procedures would be applicable to all law enforcement agencies in Europe in the handling of security matters. Nor do the new provisions affect the exercise of the responsibilities incumbent on Member States to maintain law and order and safeguard internal security.

11. Amsterdam rather provides an institutional framework to develop common action among the Member States in the indissociable fields of police cooperation and judicial cooperation in criminal matters and thus not only to offer enhanced security to their citizens but also to defend the Union's interests, including its financial interests. The declared objective is to prevent and combat crime at the appropriate level, 'organised or otherwise, in particular terrorism, trafficking in persons and offences against children, illicit drug trafficking and illicit arms trafficking, corruption and fraud'.

C.   An Area of Justice

15.   The new impetus and instruments introduced by Amsterdam provide the opportunity to examine what the area of 'justice' should seek to achieve, while respecting the reality that, for reasons deeply imbedded in history and tradition, judicial systems differ substantially between Member States. The ambition is to give citizens a common sense of justice throughout the Union. Justice must be seen as facilitating the day-to-day life of people and bringing to justice those who threaten the freedom and security of individuals and society. This includes both access to justice and full judicial cooperation among Member States. What Amsterdam provides is both in civil and criminal matters speedy ratification and effective implementation of adopted conventions are crucial for achieving an area of Justice.

(a)   Judicial cooperation in civil matters

16.   Reinforcement of judicial cooperation in civil matters, which many believe has developed too slowly, represents a fundamental stage in the creation of a European judicial area which will bring tangible benefits for every Union citizen. Law-abiding citizens have a right to look to the Union to simplify and facilitate the judicial environment in which they live in the European Union context. Here principles such as legal certainty and equal access to justice should be a main objective, implying identification of the competent jurisdiction, clear designation of the applicable law, availability of speedy and fair proceedings and effective enforcement procedures.

(c)   Procedures

19.   Procedural rules should respond to broadly the same guarantees, ensuring that people will not be treated unevenly according to the jurisdiction dealing with their case. In principle, this function of adequate and comparable procedural guarantees is already achieved by the safeguards of the European Convention on Human Rights and Fundamental Freedoms and their dynamic interpretation by the European Court of Human Rights, in particular regarding the rights of the defence in criminal proceedings. It appears useful, however, to complement those basic principles by standards and codes of good practice in areas of Transnational relevance and common concern (eg interpretation) which may also extend to certain parts of the enforcement of criminal decisions, including, for instance, confiscation of assets and to aspects of offender reintegration and victim support.

(d)   Cross-border litigation

20. Difficulties with which citizens are intrinsically confronted in cross-border litigation, be it in civil or in criminal matters, should be neutralised as much as possible. This means, for example, streamlined communication of documents and information, use of multilingual forms, creation of mechanisms or networks to assist and advise in transnational cases and possible legal aid schemes in such cases.

E.   *Relations with third countries and international organisations*

22. The advances introduced by the Amsterdam Treaty will also enhance the Union's role as a player and partner on the international stage, both bilaterally and in multilateral forums. As a result, and building on the dialogue that it has already started in Justice and Home Affairs cooperation with an increasing number of third countries and international organisations and bodies (eg Interpol, UNHCR, Council of Europe, G8 and the OECD), this external aspect of the Union's action can be expected to take on a new and more demanding dimension. Full use will need to be made of the new instruments available under the Treaty. In particular, the 'communitarisation' of the matters relating to asylum, immigration and judicial cooperation in civil matters permit the Community, to the extent permitted by the established case-law of the European Court of Justice related to the external competence of the Community, to exercise its influence internationally in these matters. In those subjects which remain in Title VI of the TEU, the Union can also make use of the possibility for the Council to conclude international agreements in matters relating to Title VI of the Treaty, as well as for the Presidency, assisted by the General Secretariat of the Council and in full association with the Commission, to represent the Union in these areas.

F.   *Structure of Work in the Field of Justice and Home Affairs*

23. The new provisions of the Amsterdam Treaty as well as its Protocol integrating the Schengen *acquis* into the framework of the European Union, with their emphatically cross-pillar characteristic, will need to be reflected also in the working structures of the Council. It was clearly not the intention of the Treaty to compartmentalise the way in which the different components of this area of freedom, security and justice are handled as between the structures of the European Community on the one hand and the European Union on the other, particularly since in both cases the responsibility for taking the objective forward will fall irrespective whether they are first or third pillar competence, to the Council in its composition of Ministers for Justice and Home Affairs. It will therefore be essential to establish before the entry into force of the Treaty of Amsterdam for this purpose appropriate arrangements which both respect the provisions of the Treaty and facilitate the coordinating role of the Committee of Permanent Representatives.

It will also be important to establish the appropriate arrangement to cover the particular case of the Schengen information system in order to ensure smooth transition, with no reduction in the system's efficiency. A discussion could, also, be started in the medium term on the prospects for developing SIS II after it has been expanded.

Work on the necessary structural arrangements, including reflexions on the need for further coordination in the fields of migration and asylum as well as in the area of civil law by committees composed of high officials is already under way within the K4 Committee acting on the basis of Article K4(1) of the TEU.

This reform of the working structures should be based on the following principles: rationalisation and simplification (an appropriate number of working parties to meet the objectives laid down in the Treaty, no duplication), specialisation and responsibility (working parties to consist of experts having an adequate degree of responsibility in their Member States, appropriate allowance for operational structures — Europol, European judicial network), continuity (permanence of working parties to reflect the permanent objectives of the Treaty, mechanism for following-up all the instruments adopted), transparency (clarity of terms of reference and of relations between working parties) and flexibility (possibility of extremely short-term adjustment of structures to deal with new problems requiring urgent specific handling).

The entry into force of the Treaty of Amsterdam also raises a number of legal questions resulting from the transition of certain policies from the third pillar to the first pillar as well as from the transition to new forms of acts and procedures in the third pillar. This concerns, for example, the question of how to handle conventions in the field to be transferred to Community competence which will be signed but not yet ratified at the time of entry into force of the Treaty of Amsterdam.

II.   *Judicial Cooperation in Civil Matters*

39.   The aim is to make life simpler for European citizens by improving and simplifying the rules and procedures on cooperation and communication between authorities and on enforcing decisions, by promoting the compatibility of conflict of law rules and on jurisdiction and by eliminating obstacles to the good functioning of civil proceedings in a European judicial area. It will be necessary to improve the coordination of Europe's courts and the awareness of Member States' laws, particularly in cases with important human dimensions, having an impact on the everyday life of the citizens.

Measures to be taken within two years

40.   The following measures should be taken within two years after the entry into force of the Treaty:

(a)   finalisation, if it has not been completed, of work on the revision of the Brussels and Lugano Conventions,

(b)   drawing up a legal instrument on the law applicable to non-contractual obligations (Rome I),

(c)   begin revision, where necessary, of certain provisions of the Convention on the Law applicable to contractual obligations, taking into account special provisions on conflict of law rules in other Community instruments (Rome I),

(d)   examine the possibility of extending the concept of the European judicial network in criminal matters to embrace civil proceedings.

Highly individualised contact points in each Member State could permit greater awareness of Member States' laws and ensure better coordination of proceedings in cases with important human dimensions (cross-border parental disputes, for example).

Measures to be taken within five years

41.   The following measures should be taken within five years after the entry into force of the Treaty:

(a) examine the possibilities to draw up a legal instrument on the law applicable to divorce (Rome III):

After the first step on divorce matters taken with Brussels II in the field of jurisdiction and the recognition and enforcement of judgments, the possibilities to agree on rules determining the law applicable in order to prevent forum shopping needs to be explored on the basis of an in-depth study,

(b) examine the possibility of drawing up models for non-judicial solutions to disputes with particular reference to transnational family conflicts. In this context, the possibility of mediation as a means of solving family conflicts should be examined,

(c) examine the possibility of drawing up a legal instruments on international jurisdiction, applicable law, recognition and enforcement of judgments relating to matrimonial property regimes and those relating to succession.

In elaborating such instruments, the connection between matrimonial property and rules relating to succession should be taken into account.

Work already undertaken within the framework of the Hague Conference of Private International Law should be taken into account,

(d) identifying the rules on civil procedure having cross-border implications which are urgent to approximate for the purpose of facilitating access to justice for the citizens of Europe and examine the elaboration of additional measures accordingly to improve compatibility of civil procedures.

This could include the examination of the rules on deposition of security for litigation costs and expenses of the defendant in a civil procedure, the granting of legal aid as well as other possible obstacles of an economic nature,

(e) improving and simplifying cooperation between courts in the taking of evidence,

(f) examine the possibility of approximating certain areas of civil law, such as creating uniform private international law applicable to the acquisition in good faith of corporal movables.

C.   Presidency Conclusions, Tampere European Council, 15–16 October 1999

The European Council is determined to develop the Union as an area of freedom, security and justice by making full use of the possibilities offered by the Treaty of Amsterdam. The European Council sends a strong political message to reaffirm the importance of this objective and has agreed on a number of policy orientations and priorities which will speedily make this area a reality.

The European Council will place and maintain this objective at the very top of the political agenda. It will keep under constant review progress made towards implementing the necessary measures and meeting the deadlines set by the Treaty of Amsterdam, the Vienna Action Plan and the present conclusions. The Commission is invited to make a proposal for an appropriate scoreboard to that end. The European Council underlines the importance of ensuring the necessary transparency and of keeping the European Parliament regularly informed. It will hold a full debate assessing progress at its December meeting in 2001.

Towards a Union of Freedom, Security and Justice: The Tampere Milestones

1.   From its very beginning European integration has been firmly rooted in a shared commitment to freedom based on human rights, democratic institutions and the rule of law. These common values have proved necessary for securing peace and developing prosperity in the European Union. They will also serve as a cornerstone for the enlarging Union.

2.   The European Union has already put in place for its citizens the major ingredients of a shared area of prosperity and peace: a single market, economic and monetary union, and the capacity to take on global political and economic challenges. The challenge of the Amsterdam Treaty is now to ensure that freedom, which includes the right to move freely throughout the Union, can be enjoyed in conditions of security and justice accessible to all. It is a project which responds to the frequently expressed concerns of citizens and has a direct bearing on their daily lives.

3.   This freedom should not, however, be regarded as the exclusive preserve of the Union's own citizens. Its very existence acts as a draw to many others world-wide who cannot enjoy the freedom Union citizens take for granted. It would be in contradiction with Europe's traditions to deny such freedom to those whose circumstances lead them justifiably to seek access to our territory. This in turn requires the Union to develop common policies on asylum and immigration, while taking into account the need for a consistent control of external borders to stop illegal immigration and to combat those who organise it and commit related international crimes. These common policies must be based on principles which are both clear to our own citizens and also offer guarantees to those who seek protection in or access to the European Union.

4.   The aim is an open and secure European Union, fully committed to the obligations of the Geneva Refugee Convention and other relevant human rights instruments, and able to respond to humanitarian needs on the basis of solidarity. A common approach must also be developed to ensure the integration into our societies of those third country nationals who are lawfully resident in the Union.

5.   The enjoyment of freedom requires a genuine area of justice, where people can approach courts and authorities in any Member State as easily as in their own. Criminals must find no ways of exploiting differences in the judicial systems of Member States. Judgments and decisions should be respected and enforced throughout the Union, while safeguarding the basic legal certainty of people and economic operators. Better compatibility and more convergence between the legal systems of Member States must be achieved.

6.   People have the right to expect the Union to address the threat to their freedom and legal rights posed by serious crime. To counter these threats a common effort is needed to prevent and fight crime and criminal organisations throughout the Union. The joint mobilisation of police and judicial resources is needed to guarantee that there is no hiding place for criminals or the proceeds of crime within the Union.

7.   The area of freedom, security and justice should be based on the principles of transparency and democratic control. We must develop an open dialogue with civil society on the aims and principles of this area in order to strengthen citizens' acceptance and support. In order to maintain confidence in authorities, common standards on the integrity of authorities should be developed.

8.   The European Council considers it essential that in these areas the Union should also develop a capacity to act and be regarded as a significant partner on

the international scene. This requires close cooperation with partner countries and international organisations, in particular the Council of Europe, OSCE, OECD and the United Nations.

9.   The European Council invites the Council and the Commission, in close cooperation with the European Parliament, to promote the full and immediate implementation of the Treaty of Amsterdam on the basis of the Vienna Action Plan and of the following political guidelines and concrete objectives agreed here in Tampere.

B.   *A genuine European area of justice*

28.   In a genuine European Area of Justice individuals and businesses should not be prevented or discouraged from exercising their rights by the incompatibility or complexity of legal and administrative systems in the Member States.

V.   Better access to justice in Europe

29.   In order to facilitate access to justice the European Council invites the Commission, in cooperation with other relevant fora, such as the Council of Europe, to launch an information campaign and to publish appropriate 'user guides' on judicial cooperation within the Union and on the legal systems of the Member States. It also calls for the establishment of an easily accessible information system to be maintained and up-dated by a network of competent national authorities.

30.   The European Council invites the Council, on the basis of proposals by the Commission, to establish minimum standards ensuring an adequate level of legal aid in cross-border cases throughout the Union as well as special common procedural rules for simplified and accelerated cross-border litigation on small consumer and commercial claims, as well as maintenance claims, and on uncontested claims. Alternative, extra-judicial procedures should also be created by Member States.

31.   Common minimum standards should be set for multilingual forms or documents to be used in cross-border court cases throughout the Union. Such documents or forms should then be accepted mutually as valid documents in all legal proceedings in the Union.

32.   Having regard to the Commission's communication, minimum standards should be drawn up on the protection of the victims of crime, in particular on crime victims' access to justice and on their rights to compensation for damages, including legal costs. In addition, national programmes should be set up to finance measures, public and non-governmental, for assistance to and protection of victims.

VI.   Mutual recognition of judicial decisions

33.   Enhanced mutual recognition of judicial decisions and judgments and the necessary approximation of legislation would facilitate cooperation between authorities and the judicial protection of individual rights. The European Council therefore endorses the principle of mutual recognition which, in its view, should become the cornerstone of judicial cooperation in both civil and criminal matters within the Union. The principle should apply both to judgments and to other decisions of judicial authorities.

34.   In civil matters the European Council calls upon the Commission to make a proposal for further reduction of the intermediate measures which are still required to

enable the recognition and enforcement of a decision or judgment in the requested State. As a first step these intermediate procedures should be abolished for titles in respect of small consumer or commercial claims and for certain judgments in the field of family litigation (eg on maintenance claims and visiting rights). Such decisions would be automatically recognised throughout the Union without any intermediate proceedings or grounds for refusal of enforcement. This could be accompanied by the setting of minimum standards on specific aspects of civil procedural law.

36. The principle of mutual recognition should also apply to pre-trial orders, in particular to those which would enable competent authorities quickly to secure evidence and to seize assets which are easily movable; evidence lawfully gathered by one Member State's authorities should be admissible before the courts of other Member States, taking into account the standards that apply there.

37. The European Council asks the Council and the Commission to adopt, by December 2000, a programme of measures to implement the principle of mutual recognition. In this programme, work should also be launched on a European Enforcement Order and on those aspects of procedural law on which common minimum standards are considered necessary in order to facilitate the application of the principle of mutual recognition, respecting the fundamental legal principles of Member States.

VII. Greater convergence in civil law

38. The European Council invites the Council and the Commission to prepare new procedural legislation in cross-border cases, in particular on those elements which are instrumental to smooth judicial cooperation and to enhanced access to law, eg provisional measures, taking of evidence, orders for money payment and time limits.

39. As regards substantive law, an overall study is requested on the need to approximate Member States' legislation in civil matters in order to eliminate obstacles to the good functioning of civil proceedings. The Council should report back by 2001.

D. Stronger external action

59. The European Council underlines that all competences and instruments at the disposal of the Union and in particular, in external relations must be used in an integrated and consistent way to build the area of freedom, security and justice. Justice and Home Affairs concerns must be integrated in the definition and implementation of other Union policies and activities.

60. Full use must be made of the new possibilities offered by the Treaty of Amsterdam for external action and in particular of Common Strategies as well as Community agreements and agreements based on Article 38 TEU.

61. Clear priorities, policy objectives and measures for the Union's external action in Justice and Home Affairs should be defined. Specific recommendations should be drawn up by the Council in close cooperation with the Commission on policy objectives and measures for the Union's external action in Justice and Home Affairs, including questions of working structure, prior to the European Council in June 2000.

62. The European Council expresses its support for regional cooperation against organised crime involving the Member States and third countries bordering on the Union. In this context it notes with satisfaction the concrete and practical results obtained by the surrounding countries in the Baltic Sea region. The European Council attaches particular

importance to regional cooperation and development in the Balkan region. The European Union welcomes and intends to participate in a European Conference on Development and Security in the Adriatic and Ionian area, to be organised by the Italian Government in Italy in the first half of the year 2000. This initiative will provide valuable support in the context of the South Eastern Europe Stability Pact.

D. Draft Programme of measures for implementation of the principle of mutual recognition of decisions in civil and commercial matters (OJ, C 12 of 15 January 2001)

Introduction

The Treaty of Amsterdam inserted into the Treaty establishing the European Community a new Title IV containing specific provisions on judicial cooperation in civil matters.

In order to lend impetus to this cooperation and to set precise guidelines therefore, the European Council meeting in Tampere on 15 and 16 October 1999 held that 'enhanced mutual recognition of judicial decisions and judgments and the necessary approximation of legislation would facilitate cooperation between authorities and the judicial protection of individual rights'. It approved the principle of mutual recognition, which should become 'the cornerstone of judicial cooperation in both civil and criminal matters within the Union'.

In civil matters, the Tampere European Council advocated 'further reduction of the intermediate measures which are still required to enable the recognition and enforcement of a decision or judgment in the requested State'. 'As a first step these intermediate procedures should be abolished for titles in respect of small consumer or commercial claims and for certain judgments in the field of family litigation (eg on maintenance claims and visiting rights). Such decisions would be automatically recognised throughout the Union without any intermediate proceedings or grounds for refusal of enforcement. This could be accompanied by the setting of minimum standards on specific aspects of civil procedural law'.

It asked the Council and the Commission to adopt, by the end of 2000, a programme of measures to implement the principle of mutual recognition, and added that 'in this programme, work should also be launched on a European Enforcement Order and on those aspects of procedural law on which common minimum standards are considered necessary in order to facilitate the application of the principle of mutual recognition, respecting the fundamental legal principles of Member States'.

The Brussels Convention of 27 September 1968 lays down rules on jurisdiction and the recognition and enforcement of judgments in civil and commercial matters. This Convention has undergone several amendments with the accession of new States to the Community and is now in the process of being converted into a regulation.

The Community has other major achievements to its credit: the 'Brussels II' Regulation on jurisdiction and the recognition and enforcement of judgments in matrimonial matters and in matters of parental responsibility for children of both spouses, and the Regulation on insolvency proceedings.

The principle of mutual recognition of civil and commercial judgments between Member States is therefore not new. However, its implementation has had limited effect to date, for two main reasons. The first relates to the fact that many areas of private law do not come within the ambit of the existing instruments. This applies, for example, to family situations arising through relationships other than marriage, rights in property arising out of a matrimonial relationship, and succession.

The second reason lies with the fact that the existing texts retain certain barriers to the free movement of judicial decisions. The intermediate procedures enabling a ruling handed down in one Member State to be enforced in another are still too restrictive. Thus, despite the changes and simplifications it makes with regard to recognition and enforcement of judgments, the future Brussels I Regulation does not remove all the obstacles to the unhindered movement of judgments within the European Union.

Discussions on the subject were held at the informal meeting of Justice and Home Affairs Ministers in Marseilles on 28 and 29 July 2000.

The current programme of measures establishes objectives and stages for the work to be undertaken within the Union in the coming years to implement the principle of mutual recognition. It advocates the adoption of measures that can facilitate both the activity of economic agents and the everyday lives of citizens.

This programme contains measures that concern the recognition and enforcement in one Member State of a decision taken in another Member State, which implies that harmonised jurisdiction rules should be adopted, as was the case in the Brussels Convention and the Brussels II Regulation. It in no way prejudges work that will be undertaken in other areas under judicial cooperation in civil matters, particularly with regard to conflicts of law. The measures relating to harmonisation of conflict-of-law rules, which may sometimes be incorporated in the same instruments as those relating to jurisdiction, recognition and enforcement of judgments, actually do help facilitate the mutual recognition of judgments.

In the implementation of the measures advocated, account will be taken of the instruments adopted and ongoing work in other international forums.

The approach adopted to establish the programme is threefold:
— identifying the areas in which progress should be made;
— determining the nature, detailed procedures and scope of potential progress;
— fixing the stages for the progress to be made.

I.   Areas of mutual recognition

State of play

The 1968 Brussels Convention is the basic instrument. It covers all areas of civil and commercial law except for those which are expressly excluded from its scope, which are listed exhaustively in the text: the status or legal capacity of natural persons, rights in property arising out of a matrimonial relationship, wills and succession; bankruptcy; social security; and arbitration. The scope will not be changed by the future Brussels I Regulation, which is to replace the Brussels Convention.

Supplementary instruments: the areas excluded from the scope of the Brussels Convention are not yet all covered by instruments supplementing the 1968 provisions.

The Brussels II Regulation of 29 May 2000 applies to civil proceedings relating to divorce, legal separation or marriage annulment and to civil proceedings relating to parental responsibility for the children of both spouses on the occasion of such matrimonial proceedings.

The following are therefore not covered, and remain outside the ambit of any instrument applicable between the Member States:

— certain aspects of divorce litigation or legal separation that are not covered by the Brussels II Regulation (particularly decisions concerning parental responsibility amending decisions taken at the time of the divorce or legal separation),

— family situations arising through relationships other than marriage,

— rights in property arising out of a matrimonial relationship,

— wills and succession.

The Regulation of 29 May 2000 on insolvency proceedings applies to collective proceedings which entail the partial or total divestment of the debtor and the appointment of a liquidator.

Proposals

A.   In areas not yet covered by existing instruments

It is mainly in the area of family law that progress is needed. Legal instruments will be drawn up in both the following areas.

1.   INTERNATIONAL JURISDICTION, RECOGNITION AND ENFORCEMENT OF JUDGMENTS RELATING TO THE DISSOLUTION OF RIGHTS IN PROPERTY ARISING OUT OF A MATRIMONIAL RELATIONSHIP, TO PROPERTY CONSEQUENCES OF THE SEPARATION OF UNMARRIED COUPLES AND TO SUCCESSION

Rights in property arising out of a matrimonial relationship and succession were already featured among the priorities of the Vienna action plan (December 1998). The economic consequences of judgments delivered when matrimonial ties are loosened or dissolved, during the lifetime of the spouses, or on the death of a spouse, are clearly of major interest in the creation of a European Judicial Area. In this context it is possible that, when drawing up instruments, a distinction needs to be drawn between rights in property arising out of a matrimonial relationship and succession. In this respect the relationship existing in Member States' law between rights in property arising out of a matrimonial relationship and succession will be examined.

The question of property consequences of the separation of unmarried couples will also be dealt with, so that all property aspects of family law can be examined.

2.   INTERNATIONAL JURISDICTION, RECOGNITION AND ENFORCEMENT OF JUDGMENTS RELATING TO PARENTAL RESPONSIBILITY AND OTHER NON-PROPERTY ASPECTS OF THE SEPARATION OF COUPLES

(a)   Family situations arising through relationships other than marriage

Here it is a matter of supplementing the area covered by the Brussels II Regulation to take account of sociological reality: increasingly, couples are choosing to dispense with any matrimonial formalities, and there is a marked rise in the number of children born out of wedlock.

In order to take this new social reality into consideration, the scope of the Brussels II Regulation should be extended, by means of a separate instrument if necessary, notably to judgments concerning the exercise of parental responsibility with regard to the children of unmarried couples.

(b) Judgments on parental responsibility other than those taken at the time of the divorce or separation

The provisions of the Brussels II Regulation relate only to judgments in matrimonial proceedings. In view of the frequency and importance of judgments that are made subsequently and may modify the conditions under which parental responsibility is exercised, as fixed in judgments made at the time of the divorce or separation, it is necessary to apply to them the rules governing jurisdiction, recognition and enforcement contained in the Brussels II Regulation. This development must relate both to judgments concerning married couples and to those made in the context of the separation of unmarried couples.

In these new areas, which are not at present covered by any instrument, it will be useful to examine the legal situation in Member States' national law, as well as existing international instruments, in order to gauge the scope that should be given to any instruments that might be drawn up.

B. In areas already covered by existing instruments

Here, the aim is to make the existing machinery work better by reducing or abolishing obstacles to the free movement of judicial decisions. The Tampere conclusions refer generally to all 'civil matters', but also stress that as a first step these intermediate procedures should be abolished for titles in respect of small consumer or commercial claims and for certain judgments in the field of family litigation (eg on maintenance claims and rights of access).

Thus, two areas are involved: family law on the one hand, more especially rights of access and maintenance claims, and commercial and consumer law on the other. These areas are thus identified as being priorities.

1. RIGHTS OF ACCESS

France has already tabled an initiative. It is designed to abolish the exequatur procedure for the cross-border exercise of rights of access arising from a judgment falling within the scope of the Brussels II Regulation.

2. MAINTENANCE CLAIMS

This matter, expressly mentioned in the conclusions of the Tampere European Council, directly concerns the everyday lives of citizens in the same way as the previous matter. Although the guarantee of effective and rapid recovery of maintenance claims is indeed essential to the welfare of very large numbers of people in Europe, this does not necessarily imply that a separate legal instrument has to be drawn up. Maintenance creditors are already covered by provisions of the Brussels Convention and of the future Brussels I Regulation, but it would also be advisable in the long term to abolish the exequatur procedure for maintenance creditors, thus boosting the effectiveness of the means by which they safeguard their rights.

3.   UNCONTESTED CLAIMS

The abolition of exequatur for uncontested claims should feature among the Community's priorities.

The substance of the concept of 'uncontested claims' will be specified when the limits of the instruments drawn up in application of the programme are defined. At present, that concept generally covers situations in which a creditor, given the verifiable absence of any dispute by the debtor over the nature or extent of the debt, has obtained an enforcement order against that debtor.

The fact that an exequatur procedure can delay the enforcement of judgments concerning uncontested claims is a contradiction in terms. It fully justifies this area being the first in which exequatur is abolished. Rapid recovery of outstanding payments is an absolute necessity for business and is a constant concern for the economic sectors whose interest lies in the proper operation of the internal market.

4.   LITIGATION ON SMALL CLAIMS

The concept of litigation on small claims referred to by the Tampere European Council covers various situations of varying degrees of importance that give rise to different procedures according to the Member State concerned. Discussions on simplifying and speeding up the settlement of cross-border litigation on small claims, in line with the Tampere conclusions, will also, through the establishment of specific common rules of procedure or minimum standards, facilitate the recognition and enforcement of judgments.

II.   *Degrees of mutual recognition*

State of play

Current degrees of mutual recognition

In areas not covered by existing instruments, recognition and enforcement of foreign judgments is governed by the law of the requested State and by existing international, bilateral or multilateral agreements on the subject.

In areas already covered, there are two degrees of mutual recognition.

The first degree still features today in the 1968 Brussels Convention and the Brussels II Regulation: recognition is automatic unless contested; a declaration of enforceability (exequatur) may be obtained upon application and can be refused on one of the grounds on the exhaustive list in the relevant instrument. This exequatur procedure is therefore less complex than would generally result from the application of national law.

The second degree resulted from the review of the Brussels and Lugano Conventions and will be implemented following adoption of the Brussels I Regulation, which is due to replace the 1968 Brussels Convention: the procedure for obtaining a declaration of enforceability is considerably streamlined; it is obtained on completion of certain formalities and can only be contested by the other party at the second stage (system of 'reversing the responsibility for action'). This streamlined exequatur will apply to all areas covered by the current 1968 Brussels Convention and to insolvency procedures covered by the Regulation of 29 May 2000.

Proposals

Achieving further degrees of mutual recognition

A.   MEASURES DIRECTLY AFFECTING MUTUAL RECOGNITION

1.   *Areas not covered by the existing instruments*

The approach must be to follow a gradual method to reach the degree of mutual recognition currently achieved by the Brussels II Regulation, before attaining the degree achieved by the future Brussels I Regulation, and then to progress beyond it. However, it will be possible in certain cases to reach new degrees of mutual recognition directly, without any intermediate step.

2.   *Areas already covered by the existing instruments*

In these areas, further progress should be made, with two series of measures.
    (a)   First series of measures: further streamlining of intermediate measures and strengthening the effects in the requested State of judgments made in the State of origin
    (i)   Limiting the reasons which can be given for challenging recognition or enforcement of a foreign judgment (for example, removal of the test of public policy, taking account of cases in which this reason is currently used by the Member States' courts).
    (ii)   Establishing provisional enforcement: the decision stating enforceability in the requested country would thus be enforceable on a provisional basis, despite the possibility of appeal.
    Such a development requires an amendment of Article 47(3) of the draft Brussels I Regulation (Article 39(1) of the Brussels Convention).
    (iii)   Establishing protective measures at European level will enable a decision given in one Member State to embrace the authorisation to take protective measures against the debtor's assets in the whole territory of the Union.
    This possibility, which is currently not afforded by the draft Brussels I Regulation, would, for example, enable a person who has obtained judgment against a debtor in one Member State, in the event of the latter challenging recovery of his debt, to have the debtor's property forthwith frozen in another Member State as a protective measure, without recourse to a further procedure. These measures would be without prejudice to the fact that certain types of property may not be seized under domestic law.
    (iv)   Improving attachment measures concerning banks, eg by establishing a European system for the attachment of bank accounts: with a judgment certified as enforceable in

the Member State of origin, measures could be taken in any other Member State, without exequatur and ipso jure, for attachment of the debtor's bank accounts. The judgment would become enforceable in the country of attachment, at least for the purposes of the latter, unless contested by the debtor.

(b) Second series of measures: abolition of intermediate measures

Abolition, pure and simple, of any checks on the foreign judgment by courts in the requested country allows national judgments to move freely throughout the Community. Each requested State treats these national judgments as if they had been delivered by one of its own courts.

In some areas, abolition of the exequatur might take the form of establishing a true European enforcement order, obtained following a specific, uniform and harmonised procedure laid down within the Community.

B.   MEASURES ANCILLARY TO MUTUAL RECOGNITION

1.   Minimum standards for certain aspects of civil procedure

It will sometimes be necessary, or even essential, to lay down a number of procedural rules at European level, which will constitute common minimum guarantees intended to strengthen mutual trust between the Member States' legal systems. These guarantees will make it possible, inter alia, to ensure that the requirements for a fair trial are strictly observed, in keeping with the European Convention for the Protection of Human Rights and Fundamental Freedoms.

For each measure under consideration, the question of drawing up some of these minimum guarantees will be examined, in order to determine their usefulness and their role. In certain areas, and particularly where abolition of the exequatur is planned, drawing up such minimum guarantees may be a precondition for the desired progress.

If the establishment of minimum guarantees appears to be insufficient, discussions should be directed towards a certain degree of harmonisation of the procedures.

In order to take into account the fundamental principles of law recognised by Member States, measures aiming at the establishment of minimum guarantees or at a certain degree of harmonisation of procedures will be sought most particularly in the case of the mutual recognition of decisions relating to parental responsibility (including those concerning rights of access). Questions relating to the child's best interests and the child's place in the procedure will, inter alia, be discussed in this context.

In order to increase the certainty, efficiency and rapidity of service of legal documents, which is clearly one of the foundations of mutual trust between national legal systems, consideration will be given to harmonising the applicable rules or setting minimum standards.

If the parties to proceedings are able to adduce their arguments in a manner recognised as valid by all the Member States, this clearly increases confidence in the proper administration of justice at an early stage in the proceedings, making it easier to dispense with checks later on.

Such a development will take duly into account progress already made on account of the entry into force of Council Regulation (EC) No 1348/2000 of 29 May 2000 on the service in the Member States of judicial and extrajudicial documents in civil or commercial matters.

2.   Efficiency of measures providing for improved enforcement of decisions

Another series of ancillary measures would consist in seeking to make more efficient the enforcement, in the requested State, of judgments delivered in another Member State.

Some of these measures could concern more specifically debtors' assets. It would in fact be much easier to enforce judgments within the European Union if it were possible to obtain accurate information on the debtor's financial position. Measures could therefore be taken to enable precise identification of a debtor's assets in the territory of the Member States.

When devising measures of this kind, account should be taken of the impact they could have on data protection and the confidential nature of certain information as provided for in Member States' domestic law or in international law.

3.   Improving judicial cooperation on civil matters in general

These would include measures conducive to implementation of the principle of mutual recognition, ie which would make for a climate of improved cooperation between national judicial authorities.

The establishment of the European Judicial Network on civil and commercial matters should accordingly feature in the programme of measures, as an ancillary measure.

Mention should also be made of an instrument for enhancing cooperation between Member States' courts on the taking of evidence in civil and commercial matters.

Similarly, the programme includes the development of measures giving easier access to justice. Here, account will be taken of the follow-up to the Green Paper on legal aid submitted by the Commission in February 2000, with a view to taking initiatives with regard to legal aid in cross-border cases.

Likewise, it would seem particularly useful to make the public better informed on the rules on mutual recognition.

Lastly, implementation of the mutual recognition principle may be facilitated through harmonisation of conflict-of-law rules.

III.   Stages

Method

It is always difficult to set deadlines for work to be achieved in the Community: deadlines which are too short are unrealistic, while those set too far ahead do not provide sufficient incentive for States. Progress should be made in stages, without any precise deadlines, but simply some broad guidelines.

1.   The programme will be put in hand as from adoption of the Brussels I Regulation, which is the basic instrument for mutual recognition.

2.   The programme distinguishes between the following four areas of action:

— areas of civil and commercial law covered by the Brussels I Regulation,

— areas of family law covered by the Brussels II Regulation, and family situations arising through relationships other than marriage,

— rights in property arising out of a matrimonial relationship and the property consequences of the separation of unmarried couples,

— wills and succession.

3.   In each area stages are established with a view to making gradual progress. A stage is begun when the previous one has ended, at least as regards essentials (for example, Council agreement on an instrument, even if it has not yet been formally adopted for technical reasons); however, this requirement must not prohibit more rapid progress from being made in certain subjects.

4.   Several initiatives may be taken at the same time in several areas.

5.   Ancillary measures mentioned in the programme are taken whenever they seem necessary, in all areas and at all stages of the programme.

Launching, monitoring and completion of the programme

The programme starts with the launching of work on the first stage in one or more areas. It continues by following the order of stages in each area, on the understanding that progress may be achieved more rapidly in one area than in another.

Five years after adoption of the programme, the Commission will submit to the Council and the Parliament a report on its implementation. The Commission will make any recommendations to the Council that it deems useful for the proper execution of the programme, indicating in particular those areas in which it considers that special efforts should be made.

The monitoring report drawn up by the Commission may also contain recommendations concerning measures which were not initially planned in the programme but which it seemed necessary to adopt subsequently.

The programme of measures is completed by the general abolition of exequatur.

E.   The Hague Programme: strengthening freedom, security and justice in the European Union (OJ, C 53 of 3 March 2005)

I.   Introduction

The European Council reaffirms the priority it attaches to the development of an area of freedom, security and justice, responding to a central concern of the peoples of the States brought together in the Union.

Over the past years the European Union has increased its role in securing police, customs and judicial cooperation and in developing a coordinated policy with regard to asylum, immigration and external border controls. This development will continue with the firmer establishment of a common area of freedom, security and justice by the Treaty establishing a Constitution for Europe, signed in Rome on 29 October 2004. This Treaty and the preceding Treaties of Maastricht, Amsterdam and Nice have progressively brought about a common legal framework in the field of justice and home affairs, and the integration of this policy area with other policy areas of the Union.

Since the Tampere European Council in 1999, the Union's policy in the area of justice and home affairs has been developed in the framework of a general programme. Even if not all the original aims were achieved, comprehensive and coordinated progress has been made. The European Council welcomes the results that have been achieved in the first five-year period: the foundations for a common asylum and immigration policy have been laid, the harmonisation of border controls has been prepared, police cooperation has been improved, and the groundwork for judicial cooperation on the basis of the principle of mutual recognition of judicial decisions and judgments has been well advanced.

The security of the European Union and its Member States has acquired a new urgency, especially in the light of the terrorist attacks in the United States on 11 September 2001 and in Madrid on 11 March 2004. The citizens of Europe rightly expect the European Union, while guaranteeing respect for fundamental freedoms and rights, to take a more effective, joint approach to cross-border problems such as illegal migration, trafficking in and smuggling of human beings, terrorism and organised crime, as well as the prevention thereof. Notably in the field of security, the coordination and coherence between the internal and the external dimension has been growing in importance and needs to continue to be vigorously pursued.

Five years after the European Council's meeting in Tampere, it is time for a new agenda to enable the Union to build on the achievements and to meet effectively the new challenges it will face. To this end, the European Council has adopted this new multi-annual programme to be known as the Hague Programme. It reflects the ambitions as expressed in the Treaty establishing a Constitution for Europe and contributes to preparing the Union for its entry into force. It takes account of the evaluation by the Commission as welcomed by the European Council in June 2004 as well as the Recommendation adopted by the European Parliament on 14 October 2004, in particular in respect of the passage to qualified majority voting and co-decision as foreseen by Article 67(2) TEC.

In the light of this Programme, the European Council invites the Commission to present to the Council an Action Plan in 2005 in which the aims and priorities of this programme will be translated into concrete actions. The plan shall contain a timetable for the adoption and implementation of all the actions. The European Council calls on the Council to ensure that the timetable for each of the various measures is observed. The Commission is invited to present to the Council a yearly report on the implementation of the Hague programme ('scoreboard').

II.   General orientations

1.   General principles

The programme set out below seeks to respond to the challenge and the expectations of our citizens. It is based on a pragmatic approach and builds on ongoing work arising from the Tampere programme, current action plans and an evaluation of first generation measures. It is also grounded in the general principles of subsidiarity, proportionality, solidarity and respect for the different legal systems and traditions of the Member States.

The Treaty establishing a Constitution of Europe (hereinafter 'the Constitutional Treaty') served as a guideline for the level of ambition, but the existing Treaties provide the legal basis for Council action until such time as the Constitutional Treaty takes effect. Accordingly, the various policy areas have been examined to determine whether preparatory work or studies could already commence, so that measures provided for in the Constitutional Treaty can be taken as soon as it enters into force.

Fundamental rights, as guaranteed by the European Convention on Human Rights and the Charter of Fundamental Rights in Part II of the Constitutional Treaty, including the explanatory notes, as well as the Geneva Convention on Refugees, must be fully respected. At the same time, the programme aims at real and substantial progress towards enhancing mutual confidence and promoting common policies to the benefit of all our citizens.

3.   Implementation and evaluation

The evaluation by the Commission of the Tampere programme showed a clear need for adequate and timely implementation and evaluation of all types of measures in the area of freedom, security and justice.

It is vital for the Council to develop in 2005 practical methods to facilitate timely implementation in all policy areas: measures requiring national authorities' resources should be accompanied by proper plans to ensure more effective implementation, and the length of the implementation period should be more closely related to the complexity of the measure concerned. Regular progress reports by the Commission to the Council during the implementation period should provide an incentive for action in Member States.

Evaluation of the implementation as well as of the effects of all measures is, in the European Council's opinion, essential to the effectiveness of Union action. The evaluations undertaken as from 1 July 2005 must be systematic, objective, impartial and efficient, while avoiding too heavy an administrative burden on national authorities and the Commission. Their goal should be to address the functioning of the measure and to suggest solutions for problems encountered in its implementation and/or application. The Commission should prepare a yearly evaluation report of measures to be submitted to the Council and to inform the European Parliament and the national parliaments.

The European Commission is invited to prepare proposals, to be tabled as soon as the Constitutional Treaty has entered into force, relating to the role of the European Parliament and national parliaments in the evaluation of Eurojust's activities and the scrutiny of Europol's activities.

III.   *Specific orientations*

1.   Strengthening freedom

1.1.   *Citizenship of the Union*

The right of all EU citizens to move and reside freely in the territory of the Member States is the central right of citizenship of the Union. Practical significance of citizenship of the Union will be enhanced by full implementation of Directive 2004/38, which codifies Community law in this field and brings clarity and simplicity. The Commission is asked to submit in 2008 a report to the Council and the European Parliament, accompanied by proposals, if appropriate, for allowing EU citizens to move within the European Union on similar terms to nationals of a Member State moving around or changing their place of residence in their own country, in conformity with established principles of Community law.

The European Council encourages the Union's institutions, within the framework of their competences, to maintain an open, transparent and regular dialogue with representative associations and civil society and to promote and facilitate citizens' participation in public life. In particular, the European Council invites the Council and the Commission to give special attention to the fight against anti-semitism, racism and xenophobia.

3. Strengthening justice

The European Council underlines the need further to enhance work on the creation of a Europe for citizens and the essential role that the setting up of a European Area for Justice will play in this respect. A number of measures have already been carried out. Further efforts should be made to facilitate access to justice and judicial cooperation as well as the full employment of mutual recognition. It is of particular importance that borders between countries in Europe no longer constitute an obstacle to the settlement of civil law matters or to the bringing of court proceedings and the enforcement of decisions in civil matters.

3.1. *European Court of Justice*

The European Council underlines the importance of the European Court of Justice in the relatively new area of freedom, security and justice and is satisfied that the Constitutional Treaty greatly increases the powers of the European Court of Justice in that area.

To ensure, both for European citizens and for the functioning of the area of freedom, security and justice, that questions on points of law brought before the Court are answered quickly, it is necessary to enable the Court to respond quickly as required by Article III-369 of the Constitutional Treaty.

In this context and with the Constitutional Treaty in prospect, thought should be given to creating a solution for the speedy and appropriate handling of requests for preliminary rulings concerning the area of freedom, security and justice, where appropriate, by amending the Statutes of the Court. The Commission is invited to bring forward — after consultation of the Court of Justice — a proposal to that effect.

3.2. *Confidence-building and mutual trust*

Judicial cooperation both in criminal and civil matters could be further enhanced by strengthening mutual trust and by progressive development of a European judicial culture based on diversity of the legal systems of the Member States and unity through European law. In an enlarged European Union, mutual confidence shall be based on the certainty that all European citizens have access to a judicial system meeting high standards of quality. In order to facilitate full implementation of the principle of mutual recognition, a system providing for objective and impartial evaluation of the implementation of EU policies in the field of justice, while fully respecting the independence of the judiciary and consistent with all the existing European mechanisms, must be established.

Strengthening mutual confidence requires an explicit effort to improve mutual understanding among judicial authorities and different legal systems. In this regard, networks of judicial organisations and institutions, such as the network of the Councils for the Judiciary, the European Network of Supreme Courts and the European Judicial Training Network, should be supported by the Union.

Exchange programmes for judicial authorities will facilitate cooperation and help develop mutual trust. An EU component should be systematically included in the training of judicial authorities. The Commission is invited to prepare as soon as possible a proposal aimed at creating, from the existing structures, an effective European training network for judicial authorities for both civil and criminal matters, as envisaged by Articles III-269 and III-270 of the Constitutional Treaty.

3.4.   *Judicial cooperation in civil matters*

3.4.1.   FACILITATING CIVIL LAW PROCEDURE ACROSS BORDERS

Civil law, including family law, concerns citizens in their everyday lives. The European Council therefore attaches great importance to the continued development of judicial cooperation in civil matters and full completion of the programme of mutual recognition adopted in 2000. The main policy objective in this area is that borders between countries in Europe should no longer constitute an obstacle to the settlement of civil law matters or to the bringing of court proceedings and the enforcement of decisions in civil matters.

3.4.2.   MUTUAL RECOGNITION OF DECISIONS

Mutual recognition of decisions is an effective means of protecting citizens' rights and securing the enforcement of such rights across European borders.

Continued implementation of the programme of measures on mutual recognition must therefore be a main priority in the coming years to ensure its completion by 2011. Work concerning the following projects should be actively pursued: the conflict of laws regarding non-contractual obligations ('Rome II') and contractual obligations ('Rome I'), a European Payment Order and instruments concerning alternative dispute resolution and concerning small claims. In timing the completion of these projects, due regard should be given to current work in related areas.

The effectiveness of existing instruments on mutual recognition should be increased by standardising procedures and documents and developing minimum standards for aspects of procedural law, such as the service of judicial and extra-judicial documents, the commencement of proceedings, enforcement of judgments and transparency of costs.

Regarding family and succession law, the Commission is invited to submit the following proposals:

— a draft instrument on the recognition and enforcement of decisions on maintenance, including precautionary measures and provisional enforcement in 2005,

— a green paper on the conflict of laws in matters of succession, including the question of jurisdiction, mutual recognition and enforcement of decisions in this area, a European certificate of inheritance and a mechanism allowing precise knowledge of the existence of last wills and testaments of residents of European Union in 2005, and

— a green paper on the conflict of laws in matters concerning matrimonial property regimes, including the question of jurisdiction and mutual recognition in 2006,

— a green paper on the conflict of laws in matters relating to divorce (Rome III) in 2005.

Instruments in these areas should be completed by 2011. Such instruments should cover matters of private international law and should not be based on harmonised concepts of 'family', 'marriage', or other. Rules of uniform substantive law should only be introduced as an accompanying measure, whenever necessary to effect mutual recognition of decisions or to improve judicial cooperation in civil matters.

Implementation of the programme of mutual recognition should be accompanied by a careful review of the operation of instruments that have recently been adopted. The outcome of such reviews should provide the necessary input for the preparation of new measures.

3.4.3.   ENHANCING COOPERATION

With a view to achieving smooth operation of instruments involving cooperation of judicial or other bodies, Member States should be required to designate liaison judges or other competent authorities based in their own country. Where appropriate they could use their national contact point within the European Judicial Network in civil matters. The Commission is invited to organise EU workshops on the application of EU law and promote cooperation between members of the legal professions (such as bailiffs and notaries public) with a view to establishing best practice.

3.4.4.   ENSURING COHERENCE AND UPGRADING THE QUALITY OF EU LEGISLATION

In matters of contract law, the quality of existing and future Community law should be improved by measures of consolidation, codification and rationalisation of legal instruments in force and by developing a common frame of reference. A framework should be set up to explore the possibilities to develop EU-wide standard terms and conditions of contract law which could be used by companies and trade associations in the Union.

Measures should be taken to enable the Council to effect a more systematic scrutiny of the quality and coherence of all Community law instruments relating to cooperation on civil law matters.

3.4.5.   INTERNATIONAL LEGAL ORDER

The Commission and the Council are urged to ensure coherence between the EU and the international legal order and continue to engage in closer relations and cooperation with international organisations such as The Hague Conference on Private International Law and the Council of Europe, particularly in order to coordinate initiatives and to maximise synergies between these organisations' activities and instruments and the EU instruments. Accession of the Community to the Hague Conference should be concluded as soon as possible.

4.   EXTERNAL RELATIONS

The European Council considers the development of a coherent external dimension of the Union policy of freedom, security and justice as a growing priority.

In addition to the aspects already addressed in the previous chapters, the European Council calls on the Commission and the Secretary-General/High Representative to present, by the end of 2005, a strategy covering all external aspects of the Union policy on freedom, security and justice, based on the measures developed in this programme to the Council. The strategy should reflect the Union's special relations with third countries, groups of countries and regions, and focus on the specific needs for JHA cooperation with them.

All powers available to the Union, including external relations, should be used in an integrated and consistent way to establish the area of freedom, security and justice. The following guidelines should be taken into account: the existence of internal policies as the major parameter justifying external action; need for value added in relation to projects carried out by the Member States; contribution to the general political objectives of the foreign policies of the Union; possibility of achieving the goals during a period of reasonable time; the possibility of long-term action.

F.   The Stockholm Programme — An open and secure Europe serving and protecting the citizens, adopted by the European Council on 10–11 December 2009 (Doc. Consilium No 17024/09)[1]

1.   *Towards a Citizens' Europe in the area of freedom, security and justice*

The European Council reaffirms the priority it attaches to the development of an area of freedom, security and justice (JLS), responding to a central concern of the peoples of the States brought together in the Union.

Building on the achievements of the Tampere and Hague Programmes, significant progress has been achieved to date in this field.... Cooperation in civil law is facilitating the everyday life of citizens and law enforcement cooperation provides for enhanced security.

In spite of these and other important achievements in the area of freedom, security and justice Europe still faces challenges. These challenges must be addressed in a comprehensive manner. Further efforts are thus needed in order to improve coherence between policy areas. In addition cooperation with partner countries should be intensified.

It is therefore time for a new agenda to enable the Union and its Member States to build on the achievements and to meet future challenges. To this end the European Council has adopted this new multi-annual programme to be known as the Stockholm Programme, for the period 2010–2014.

The European Council welcomes the increased role that the European Parliament and National Parliaments will play following the entry into force of the Lisbon Treaty. Citizens and representative associations will have an increased opportunity to make known and publicly exchange their views in all areas of Union action in accordance with article 11

---

[1]   The Programme was published in the OJ, C 115 of 4 May 2010, with minor linguistic changes. See also the Communication from the Commission to the European Parliament and the Council — An area of freedom, security and justice serving the citizen (COM (2009) 262) and the Communication from the Commission to the Council, the European Parliament, the European Economic and Social Committee and the Committee of the Regions — Justice, freedom and security in Europe since 2005: an evaluation of The Hague programme and action plan, COM (2009) 263 of of 19 June 2009. The Action Plan implementing the Stockholm Programme was adopted by the Commission on 20 April 2010 (COM (2010) 171).

TEU. This will reinforce the open and democratic character of the European Union for the benefit of its people.

The Treaty facilitates the process of reaching the goals outlined in this programme, both for the institutions and for the Member States. The role of the Commission in preparing initiatives is confirmed, as well as the right for a group of at least seven Member States to submit legislative proposals. The legislative process is improved by the use, in most sectors, of co-decision procedure, thereby granting full involvement of the European Parliament. National Parliaments will play an increasing role in the legislative process. By enhancing also the role of the Court of Justice, it will improve the European capacity to fully implement policy in this area and ensure the consistency of interpretation.

All opportunities offered by the Lisbon Treaty to strengthen the European area of freedom, security and justice for the benefit of EU citizens should be used by the European institutions.

The present programme defines strategic guidelines for legislative and operational planning within the area of freedom, security and justice in accordance with Article 68 TFEU.

1.1.   Political priorities

The European Council considers that a priority for the coming years will be to focus on the interests and needs of citizens. The challenge will be to ensure respect for fundamental freedoms and integrity while guaranteeing security in Europe. It is of paramount importance that law enforcement measures and measures to safeguard individual rights, the rule of law, international protection rules go hand in hand in the same direction and are mutually reinforced.

As it is commonly known, the Treaty is actually two treaties: the Treaty on European Union (TEU) and the Treaty of the Functioning of the European Union (TFEU). For ease of reading, the 'Lisbon Treaty' or 'the Treaty' will sometimes be used in the Programme.

All actions taken in the future should be centred on the citizen and other persons for whom the EU has a responsibility. The EU should in the years to come work towards the following main priorities:

Promoting citizenship and fundamental rights: European citizenship must become a tangible reality. The area of freedom, security and justice must above all be a single area in which fundamental rights are protected. The enlargement of the Schengen area must continue. Respect for the human person and human dignity and for the other rights set out in the Charter of Fundamental Rights and the European Convention on Human Rights are core values. For example, the exercise of these freedoms and citizens' privacy must be preserved beyond national borders, especially by protecting personal data. Allowance must be made for the special needs of vulnerable people and European citizens and others must be able to exercise their specific rights to the full within the European Union, even, where relevant, outside the Union.

A Europe of law and justice: The achievement of a European area of justice must be consolidated so as to move beyond the current fragmentation. Priority should be given to mechanisms that facilitate access to justice, so that people can enforce their rights throughout the Union. Cooperation between public professionals and their training should also be improved, and resources should be mobilised to eliminate barriers to the recognition of legal acts in other Member States.

The role of Europe in a globalised world — the external dimension: The importance of the external dimension of the EU's policy in the area of freedom, security and justice underlines the need for increased integration of these policies into the general policies of the European Union. The external dimension is essential to address the key challenges we face and providing greater opportunities for EU citizens to work and do business with countries across the world. The external dimension of JLS is crucial to the successful implementation of the objectives of this programme and should in particular be taken into account in, and be fully coherent with, all other aspects of EU foreign policy.

1.2.   The tools

If the next multi-annual programme is to be implemented successfully, the following tools are important.

1.2.1.   *Mutual trust*

Mutual trust between authorities and services in the different Member States as well as decision-makers is the basis for efficient cooperation in this area. Ensuring trust and finding new ways to increase reliance on, and mutual understanding between, the different systems in the Member States will thus be one of the main challenges for the future.

For ease of reading, the Programme only attributes the Commission the right of initiative. This does not hinder that Member States may take initiatives in accordance with Article 76 TFEU.

1.2.2.   *Implementation*

Increased attention needs to be paid in the coming years to the full and effective implementation, enforcement and evaluation of existing instruments. Legal transposition should be ensured using, to its fullest extent, wherever necessary, existing institutional tools.

The time taken to respond to the needs of citizens and businesses must also be shorter in the future. The Union should focus on identifying the needs of citizens and practitioners and the appropriate responses. The development of action at Union level should involve Member States' expertise and consider a range of measures, including non-legislative solutions such as agreed handbooks, sharing of best practice (among other things, making best use of the European Judicial Networks) and regional projects that address those needs, in particular where they can produce a fast response.

1.2.3.   *Legislation*

In general, new legislative initiatives, by the Commission or by Member States where the Treaty so provides, should be tabled only after verification of the respect for the principles of proportionality and subsidiarity, a thorough preparation, including prior impact assessments, also involving identifying needs and financial consequences and using Member States' expertise. It is crucial to evaluate the implications of new legislative initiatives on the four freedoms under the Treaty and to ensure that such initiatives are fully compatible with internal market principles.

The European Council considers that the development of legislation in the area of freedom, security and justice is impressive, but it has shortcomings in terms of overlapping and a certain lack of coherence. At the same time, the quality of the legislation including the language used in some of the legal acts could be improved.

A horizontal review of the instruments adopted should be considered, where appropriate, in order to improve consistency and consolidation of legislation. Legal coherence and ease of accessibility is particularly important. Better regulation and lawmaking principles should be strengthened throughout the decision-making procedure. The inter-institutional agreement on simplification reached between the EU institutions should be applied in full. All EU institutions at all stages of the inter-institutional procedure should make an effort to draft EU legislation in clear and comprehensible language.

1.2.4. Increased coherence

The European Council invites the Council and the Commission to enhance the internal coordination in order to achieve greater coherence between external and internal elements of JLS work. The same need for coherence and improved coordination applies to the EU agencies (Europol, Eurojust, Frontex, CEPOL, the Lisbon Drugs Observatory, the future European Asylum Support Office and the Fundamental Rights Agency). The Council should exercise more political oversight over the agencies, by, for instance, drawing conclusions on annual reports. Special rules in relation to some agencies apply as regards oversight by the European Parliament.

1.2.10. Action Plan

In light of the Stockholm Programme, the European Council invites the Commission to present promptly an Action Plan in the first 6 months of 2010 to be adopted by the Council. This Action Plan will translate the aims and priorities of the Stockholm Programme into concrete actions with a clear timetable for adoption and implementation. It should include a proposal for a timetable for the transformation of instruments with a new legal basis.

1.2.11. Review of the Stockholm Programme

The European Council invites the Commission to submit a mid-term review before June 2012 of the implementation of the Stockholm Programme. Trio Presidency programmes and Commission legislative programmes should be published as soon as possible so as to enable national Parliaments to have early sight of proposals.

2. Promoting citizens' rights: a Europe of rights

2.1. A Europe built on fundamental rights

The European Union is based on common values and respect for fundamental rights. After the entry into force of the Lisbon Treaty, the rapid accession of the EU to the European Convention on Human Rights is of key importance. This will reinforce the obligation of the Union, including its institutions, to ensure that in all its areas of activity, fundamental rights are actively promoted. The case law of the Court of Justice of the European Union and the European Court of Human Rights will be able to continue to develop in step, reinforcing the creation of a uniform European fundamental and human rights system based on the European Convention and those set out in the Charter of Fundamental Rights.

The European Council invites

— the Commission to submit a proposal on the accession of the EU to the European Convention on Human Rights as a matter of urgency,

— the EU Institutions and the Member States to ensure that legal initiatives are and remain consistent with fundamental rights throughout the legislative process by way of strengthening the application of the methodology for a systematic and rigorous monitoring of compliance with the Convention and the rights set out in the Charter of Fundamental Rights.

The European Council invites the EU institutions to

— make full use of the expertise of the European Union, Agency for Fundamental Rights and to consult, where appropriate, with the Agency, in line with its mandate, on the development of policies and legislation with implications for fundamental rights, and to use it for the communication to citizens of human rights issues affecting them in their everyday life.

2.3.   Living together in an area that respects diversity and protects the most vulnerable

Since diversity enriches the Union, the EU and its Member States must provide a safe environment where differences are respected and the most vulnerable protected. Measures to tackle discrimination, racism, anti-semitism, xenophobia and homophobia must be vigorously pursued.

2.3.1.   *Racism and xenophobia*

The European Council invites the Commission to

— report during the period of the Stockholm Programme on the transposition of the 2008 Framework Decision on racism and xenophobia by 28 November 2013, and, if appropriate, to make proposals for amending it,

— make full use of the existing instruments, in particular the financing programmes to combat racism and xenophobia.

The Member States should implement the Framework Decision as soon as possible and at the latest by 28 November 2010.

2.3.2.   *Rights of the child*

The rights of the child — ie the principle of the best interest of the child being the child's right to life, survival and development, non-discrimination and respect for the children's right to express their opinion and be genuinely heard in all matters concerning them according to their age and level of development as proclaimed in the Charter and the

United Nations Convention on the Rights of the Child, concern all EU policies. They must be systematically and strategically taken into account with a view to ensuring an integrated approach. The Commission Communication 'Towards an EU Strategy on the rights of the child' (2006) reflect important considerations in this regard. An ambitious EU strategy on the rights of the child should be developed.

The European Council calls upon the Commission to

— identify measures, to which the Union can bring added value, in order to protect and promote the rights of the child. Children in particularly vulnerable situations should receive special attention, notably children that are victims of sexual exploitation and abuse as well as children that are victims of trafficking and unaccompanied minors in the context of immigration policy.

As regards parental child abduction, apart from effectively implementing existing legal instruments in this area, the possibility to use family mediation at international level should be explored, while taking account of good practices in the Member States. The Union should continue to develop criminal child abduction alert mechanisms, by promoting cooperation between national authorities and interoperability of systems.

2.3.3. *Vulnerable groups*

All forms of discrimination remain unacceptable. The EU and the Member States must make a concerted effort to fully integrate vulnerable groups, in particular the Roma community, into society by promoting their inclusion in the education system and labour market and by taking action to prevent violence against them. For this purpose, Member States should ensure that the existing legislation is properly applied to tackle potential discrimination. The EU will offer practical support and promote best practice to help Member States achieve this. Civil society will have a special role to play.

Vulnerable groups in particularly exposed situations, such as women victim of violence or of genital mutilation or persons who are harmed in a Member State of which they are not nationals or residents, are in need of greater protection, including legal protection. Appropriate financial support will be provided, through the available financing programmes.

The need for additional proposals as regards vulnerable adults should be assessed in the light of the experience acquired from the application of the 2000 Hague Convention on the International Protection of Adults by the Member States which are parties or which will become parties in the future. The Member States are encouraged to join the Convention as soon as possible.

2.3.4. *Victims of crime, including terrorism*

Those who are most vulnerable or who find themselves in particularly exposed situations, such as persons subjected to repeated violence in close relationships, victims of gender based violence, or persons who fall victim to other types of crimes in a Member State of which they are not nationals or residents, are in need of special support and legal protection. Victims of terrorism also need special attention, support and social recognition. An integrated and coordinated approach to victims is needed, in line with the Council conclusions on a strategy to ensure fulfilment of the rights of, and improve support for, persons who fall victims of crime.

The European Council calls on the Commission and the Member States to

— examine how to improve legislation and practical support measures for protection of victims and to improve implementation of existing instruments,

— offer better support to victims otherwise, possibly through existing European networks that provide practical help and put forward proposals to that end,

— examine the opportunity of making one comprehensive legal instrument on the protection of victims, by joining together the Directive on compensation to victims and the Framework Decision on victims, on the basis of an evaluation of the two instruments.

Increased use of the financing programmes should be made in accordance with their respective legal frameworks.

2.5.   Protecting citizen's rights in the information society

When it comes to assessing the individual's privacy in the area of freedom, security and justice, the right to freedom is overarching. The right to privacy and the right to the protection of personal data are set out in the Charter of Fundamental Rights. The Union must therefore respond to the challenge posed by the increasing exchange of personal data and the need to ensure the protection of privacy. The Union must secure a comprehensive strategy to protect data within the EU and in its relations with other countries. In that context, it should promote the application of the principles set out in relevant EU instruments on data protection and the 1981 Council of Europe Convention on data protection as well as promoting accession to that convention. It must also foresee and regulate the circumstances in which interference by public authorities with the exercise of these rights is justified and also apply data protection principles in the private sphere.

The Union must address the necessity for increased exchange of personal data while ensuring the utmost respect for the protection of privacy. The European Council is convinced that the technological developments not only present new challenges to the protection of personal data, but also offer new possibilities to better protect personal data.

Basic principles such as purpose limitation, proportionality, legitimacy of processing, limits on storage time, security and confidentiality as well as respect for the rights of the individual, control by national independent supervisory authorities, and access to effective judicial redress need to be ensured and a comprehensive protection scheme must be established. These issues are also dealt with in the context of the EU Information Management Strategy set out in Chapter 4.

The European Council invites the Commission to:

— evaluate the functioning of the various instruments on data protection and present, where necessary, further legislative and non-legislative initiatives to maintain the effective application of the above principles,

— propose a Recommendation for the negotiation of a data protection and, where necessary, data sharing agreements for law enforcement purposes with the United States of America, building on the work carried out by the EU-US High Level Contact Group on data protection,

— consider core elements for data protection agreements with third states for law enforcement purposes, which may include, where necessary, privately held data, based on a high level of data protection,

— improve compliance with the principles of data protection through the development of appropriate new technologies, improving cooperation between the public and private sector, particularly in the field of research,

— examine the introduction of a European certification scheme for 'privacy-aware' technologies, products and services,

— conduct information campaigns, in particular to raise awareness among the public.

On a broader front, the Union must be a driving force behind the development and promotion of international standards for personal data protection, based on relevant EU instruments on data protection and the 1981 Council of Europe Convention, and in the conclusion of appropriate bilateral or multilateral instruments.

3. *Making people's lives easier: a Europe of law and justice*

The European Council declared at its meeting in Tampere in 1999 that enhanced mutual recognition of judicial decisions and judgments and the necessary approximation of legislation would facilitate cooperation between authorities and the judicial protection of individual rights and that the principle of mutual recognition should be the cornerstone of judicial cooperation in both civil and criminal matters. This principle is now expressed in the Treaty.

In the Hague Programme, adopted in 2004, the European Council noted that in order for the principle of mutual recognition to become effective, mutual trust needed to be strengthened by progressively developing a European judicial culture based on the diversity of legal systems and unity through European law. The judicial systems of the Member States should be able to work together coherently and effectively in accordance with their national legal traditions.

The EU should continue to enhance mutual trust in the legal systems of the Member States by establishing minimum rights as necessary for the development of the principle of mutual recognition and by establishing minimum rules concerning the definition of criminal offences and sanctions as defined by the Treaty. The European judicial area must also allow citizens to assert their rights anywhere in the Union by significantly raising overall awareness of rights and by facilitating their access to justice.

In this respect, the European Council emphasises the horizontal importance of e-Justice, which is not confined to specific areas of law. It should be integrated into all areas of civil, criminal and administrative law in order to ensure better access to justice and strengthened cooperation between administrative and judicial authorities.

3.1. Furthering the implementation of mutual recognition

The European Council notes with satisfaction that considerable progress has been achieved in implementing the two programmes on mutual recognition adopted by the Council in 2000 and emphasises that the Member States should take all necessary measures to transpose at national level the rules agreed at European level. In this context the European Council emphasises the need to evaluate the implementation of these measures and to continue the work on mutual recognition.

3.1.2. Civil law

As regards civil matters, the European Council considers that the process of abolishing all intermediate measures (the exequatur), should be continued during the period covered by the Stockholm Programme. At the same time the abolition of the exequatur will also be accompanied by a series of safeguards, which may be measures in respect of procedural law as well as of conflict-of-law rules.

Mutual recognition should, moreover, be extended to fields that are not yet covered but essential to everyday life, eg succession and wills, matrimonial property rights and the property consequences of the separation of couples, while taking into consideration Member States' legal systems, including public policy, and national traditions in this area.

The European Council considers that the process of harmonising conflict-of-law rules at Union level should also continue in areas where it is necessary, like separation and divorces. It could also include the area of company law, insurance contracts and security interests.

The European Council also highlights the importance of starting work on consolidation of the instruments adopted so far in the area of judicial cooperation in civil matters. First and foremost the consistency of Union legislation should be enhanced by streamlining the existing instruments. The aim should be to ensure the coherence and user-friendliness of the instruments, thus ensuring a more efficient and uniform application thereof.

The European Council invites the Commission to

— assess which safeguards are needed to accompany the abolition of exequatur and how these could be streamlined,

— assess whether there are grounds for consolidation and simplification in order to improve the consistency of existing Union legislation,

— follow up on the recent study on the possible problems encountered with regard to civil status documents and access to registers of such documents.

In light of the findings, the Commission could submit appropriate proposals taking into account the different legal systems and traditions in the Member States. In the short term a system allowing citizens to obtain their own civil status documents easily could be envisaged. In the long term, it might be considered whether mutual recognition of the effects of civil status documents could be appropriate, at least in certain areas. Work developed by the International Commission on Civil Status should be taken into account in this particular field.

3.2. Strengthening mutual trust

One of the consequences of mutual recognition is that rulings made at national level have an impact in other Member States, in particular in their judicial systems. Measures aimed at strengthening mutual trust are therefore necessary in order to take full advantage of these developments.

The Union should support Member States' efforts to improve the efficiency of their judicial systems by encouraging exchanges of best practice and the development of innovative projects relating to the modernisation of justice.

3.2.5.   *Implementation*

A priority of the Union should be the implementation of decisions which have already been taken. This should be done in several ways: by accompanying the implementation of Union legislation more closely, through the better use of the financing instruments, by increasing the training of judges and other professionals and by enhancing evaluation mechanisms and practical measures.

Without prejudice to the role of the Commission and the Court of Justice, implementation is primarily a matter for the Member States, but as mutual recognition instruments are common tools, the Union should better accompany implementation of them by enabling the sharing of experiences and best practices.

The European Council invites the Commission to

— ensure the sharing of information by way of developing handbooks or national facts sheets together with experts in civil and criminal law and Member States, on the use of mutual recognition instruments, in the same manner as what has been done for the European Arrest Warrant. The aim should be to have a handbook or national fact sheet for each of the instruments that have been adopted so far at the end of the five-year period.

The European Council also considers that all modern means of electronic communication should be used to the full, and that the judicial authorities as soon as possible should be given means for secure electronic communications to enable safe correspondence. The Union should also put an emphasis on videoconferencing and on assisting the development of translation tools in order to make them as accurate as possible. These developments should be accompanied by and form part of the implementation of the e-justice action plan. In addition, measures should be taken to enhance cooperation, while taking full account of data protection rules, between competent authorities so as to detect addresses where persons live as their habitual residence, in connection with service of documents.

3.3.   Developing a core of common minimum rules

To the extent necessary to facilitate mutual recognition of judgments and judicial decisions and police and judicial cooperation in criminal matters, the Union may adopt common minimum rules. The European Council considers that a certain level of approximation of laws is necessary to foster a common understanding of issues among judges and prosecutors, and hence to enable the principle of mutual recognition to be applied properly, taking into account the differences between legal traditions and systems of Member States.

3.3.2.   *Civil law*

The abolition of exequatur will be accompanied by a series of safeguards, especially regarding judgments taken by default, which may be measures in respect of procedural law as well as of conflict of law rules (eg the right to be heard, the servicing of documents, time required for providing opinions, etc). The main policy objective in the area of civil procedural law is that borders between countries in the European Union should not constitute an obstacle either to the settlement of civil law matters or to initiating court proceedings, or to the enforcement of decisions in civil matters. With the Tampere conclusions and the Hague programme, major steps have been taken to reach this goal. However, the European Council notes that the effectiveness of Union instruments in this field still needs to be improved.

The European Council invites the Commission

— as a first step, to submit a report on the functioning of the present EU regime on civil procedural law across borders, and on the basis of that report put forward a proposal aimed at improving the consistency of existing Union legislation,

— to assess, also in the course of upcoming reviews of existing Regulations, the need to establish common minimum standards or standard rules of civil procedure for the cross-border execution of judgments and decisions on matters such as the service of documents, the taking of evidence, review procedures and enforcement, minimum standards in relation to the recognition of decisions on parental responsibility and, where appropriate, submit proposals on the issues,

— to continue the work on common conflict-of-law rules, where necessary.

3.4. The benefits for citizens of a European judicial area

3.4.1. *Providing easier access to justice*

Access to justice in the European judicial area must be made easier, particularly in cross-border proceedings. At the same time, efforts must continue to improve alternative methods of settling disputes, particularly in consumer law. Action is needed to help people overcome the language barriers that obstruct their access to justice.

The European Council considers that e-Justice presents an excellent opportunity to provide easier access to justice. The European e-Justice action plan, adopted at the end of November 2008, sets the framework for developing European e-Justice activities until the end of 2013. The European e-Justice portal will be a way of keeping people better informed of their rights and giving them access to a range of information and services on the various judicial systems. Better use should be made of videoconferencing, for example to spare victims the effort of needless travel and the stress of participating in court proceedings. In accordance with data protection rules, some national registers will be gradually interconnected (eg registers on insolvency, interpreters, translators and wills). Some existing databases may also be partially integrated into the portal (eg the European Business Register and the European Land Information Service). In the medium term, some European and national cross-border procedures could be dealt with on-line (eg the European payment order, the European small claims procedure and mediation). Furthermore, the use of electronic signatures should be promoted within the framework of the e-justice project.

The European Council invites the Council, the Commission and the Member States to

— create effective conditions to enable the parties to communicate with courts by electronic means in the context of legal proceedings. For that purpose, dynamic forms should be made available through the e-Justice portal as regards certain European procedures, such as the European order for payment procedure and the European small claims procedure. During this phase, electronic communication between judicial authorities should be improved decisively in the area of the application of e-Justice.

The European Council further encourages the EU institutions and the Member States to

— devote efforts to the full implementation of the e-Justice action plan. In that context, the European Commission is invited to put forward proposals within the framework of the financial perspectives for an adequate funding of e-Justice projects and in particular horizontal large-scale IT projects.

Certain formalities for the legalisation of documents also represent an obstacle or an excessive burden. Given the possibilities offered by the use of new technologies, including digital signatures, the EU should consider abolishing all formalities for the legalisation of documents between Member States. Where appropriate, thought should be given to the possibility of creating, in the long term, authentic European documents.

The European Council invites the Commission to

— examine the possibility of dispensing with the formalities for the legalisation of documents between Member States, and submit a proposal to that effect.

3.4.2.   Supporting economic activity

The European judicial area should serve to support economic activity in the single market.

The European Council invites the Commission to

— assess the need for, and the feasibility of, providing for certain provisional, including protective, measures at Union level, to prevent, eg the disappearance of assets before the enforcement of a claim,

— put forward appropriate proposals for improving the efficiency of enforcement of judgments in the EU regarding bank accounts and debtors' assets, based on the 2006 and 2008 Green Papers.

When devising measures of this kind, account should be taken on the impact they will have on the right to privacy and the right to the protection of citizens' personal data.

The European Council reaffirms that the common frame of reference for European contract law should be a non-binding set of fundamental principles, definitions and model rules to be used by the lawmakers at Union level to ensure greater coherence and quality in the lawmaking process. The Commission is invited to submit a proposal on a common frame of reference.

The current financial crisis has brought home the need to regulate financial markets and to prevent abuse. There is also a need to study further measures regarding business law, and to create a clear regulatory environment allowing small and medium business enterprises in particular to take full advantage of the internal market so that they can grow and operate across borders as they do in their domestic market. There is a need to explore whether common rules determining the law applicable to matters of company law, rules on insolvency for banks and transfer of claims could be devised. The issue of contractual law also needs to be examined further. The European Council invites the Commission to

— consider whether there is a need to take measures in these areas, and, where appropriate, to put forward proposals in this respect.

3.5. Increasing the EU's international presence in the legal field

3.5.1. Civil law

The European Council considers that clearly defining EU external interests and priorities in the area of judicial cooperation in civil matters is very important with a view to interacting with third countries in a secure legal environment.

The Lugano Convention is open to the accession of other States and it should be assessed, in cooperation with the other Contracting Parties, which third countries could be encouraged to accede to it.

The Union should use its membership of The Hague Conference to actively promote the widest possible accession to the most relevant Conventions and to offer as much assistance as possible to other States with a view to the proper implementation of the instruments. The European Council invites the Council, the Commission and the Member States to encourage all partner countries to accede to those Conventions which are of particular interest to the Union.

In cases where no legal framework is in place for relations between the EU and partner countries, and where the development of new multilateral cooperation is not possible from the Union's standpoint, the option of bilateral agreements should be explored, on a case-by-case basis.

The European Council invites the Council and the Commission to
— define a strategy in the area of civil law matters for the coming years which is coherent with overall EU external policy.

7. Europe in a globalised world — The external dimension of freedom, security and justice

The European Council emphasises the importance of the external dimension of the EU's policy in the area of freedom, security and justice and underlines the need for the increased integration of these policies into the general policies of the European Union. The external dimension is crucial to the successful implementation of the objectives of this programme and should in particular be fully coherent with all other aspects of EU foreign policy.

The European Union must continue to ensure effective implementation, and to conduct evaluations also in this area. All action should be based on transparency and accountability, in particular with regard to the financial instruments. ...

7.1. A reinforced external dimension

The European Council has decided that the following principles will continue to guide European Union action in external relations in the area of freedom, security and justice in the future:
— the Union has a single external relations policy;
— the Union and the Member States must work in partnership with third countries;
— the Union and the Member States will actively develop and promote European and international standards;

— the Union and the Member States will cooperate closely with their neighbours;
— the Member States will increase further the exchange of information between themselves and within the Union on multilateral and bilateral activities;
— the Union and the Member States must act with solidarity, coherence and complementarity;
— the Union will make full use of all ranges of instruments available to it;
— the Member States should coordinate with the Union so as to optimise the effective use of resources;
— the Union will engage in information, monitoring and evaluation, inter alia in collaboration with the European Parliament;
— the Union will work with a proactive approach in its external relations.

The European Council considers that the JLS policies should be well integrated into the general policies of the Union. The adoption of the Lisbon Treaty offers new possibilities for the European Union to act more efficiently in external relations. The new High Representative, who is also a Vice-President of the Commission, the European External Action Service and the Commission will ensure better coherence between traditional external policy instruments and internal instruments with significant external dimensions, such as freedom, security and justice. Consideration should be given to the added value that could be achieved by including specific JLS competence in EU delegations in strategic partner countries. Furthermore, the legal personality of the Union should enable the Union to act with increased strength in international organisations. …

The new basis under the Treaty for concluding international agreements will ensure that the Union can negotiate more effectively with key partners. The European Council intends to capitalise on all these new instruments to the fullest extent.

The European Council underscores the need for complementary between the EU and Member States' action. This will require a further commitment from the Union and the Member States. The European Council therefore asks the Commission to report on ways to ensure complementary by December 2011 at the latest.

7.2. Human rights

The Lisbon Treaty offers the Union new instruments as regards the protection of fundamental rights both internally and externally. The values of the Union should be promoted and strict compliance with and development of international law should be respected. The European Council calls for the establishment of a Human Rights Action Plan to promote its values in the external dimension of JLS policies. This Plan should be examined by the European Council and should take into account that internal and external aspects of Human Rights are interlinked, for instance as regards the principle of non-refoulement or the use of death penalty by partners that the Union cooperate with. The Plan should contain specific measures in the short, medium and long term, and designate who is responsible for carrying out the actions.

7.4. Agreements with third countries

The Lisbon Treaty provides for new and more efficient procedures for the conclusion of agreements with third countries. The European Council recommends that such agreements, in particular as regards judicial cooperation as well as in the field of civil law, should be considered to be used more frequently, while taking account of multilateral mechanisms. It notes however that Member States will maintain the option of entering into bilateral agreements which comply with Union law, and that a legal framework has been created for certain bilateral agreements in civil law as well.

Protection of personal data is a core activity of the Union. There is a need for a coherent legislative framework for the Union for personal data transfers to third countries for law enforcement. A framework model agreement consisting of commonly applicable core elements of data protection could be created.

7.5.   Geographical priorities and international organisations

EU action in external relations should focus on key partners, in particular:
— Candidate countries and countries with a European Union membership perspective for which the main objective would be to assist them in transposing the EU acquis,
— European neighbourhood countries, and other key partners with whom the EU should cooperate on all issues in the area of freedom, security and justice,
— EEA/Schengen states have a close relationship with the EU. This motivates closer cooperation, based on mutual trust and solidarity to enhance the positive effects of the internal market as well as to promote EU internal security,
— the United States of America, the Russian Federation and other strategic partners with which the EU should cooperate on all issues in the area of freedom, justice and security,
— other countries or regions of priority, in terms of their contribution to EU strategic or geographical priorities,
— International organisations such as the UN and the Council of Europe with whom the Union need to continue to work and within which the Union should coordinate its position.

In the Western Balkans, Stabilisation and Association Agreements are progressively entering into force and notable progress has been made in the area of visa policy, with visa facilitation and readmission agreements in place and a comprehensive visa liberalisation dialogue already achieved for some countries and still under way for others. Further efforts, including use of financial instruments, are needed to combat organised crime and corruption, to guarantee fundamental rights and to build administrative capacities in border management, law enforcement and the judiciary in order to make the European perspective a reality.

As regards the Union for the Mediterranean, it will be necessary to enhance the work started in the context of the Barcelona process and the Euro-Mediterranean Partnership, in particular regarding migration (maritime), border surveillance, preventing and fighting drug trafficking, civil protection, law enforcement and judicial cooperation. The European Council invites the Commission in cooperation with the High Representative to submit such a plan in 2010 and asks Coreper to prepare as soon as possible the decisions to be taken by the Council. The European Council will review the Plan by the end of 2012, and in particular to assess its impact on the ground…

Cooperation has been intensified with the USA in the past 10 years including on all matters relating to the area of freedom, security and justice. Regular Ministerial Troika and Senior officials' meetings are held under each Presidency. In line with what has been laid down in the 'Washington Statement' adopted at the Ministerial Troika meeting in October 2009, the dialogue should continue and be deepened.

Ongoing cooperation in the fight against terrorism and transnational crime, border security, visa policy, migration and judicial cooperation should be pursued. The agreement on the protection of personal data exchanged for law enforcement purposes needs to be negotiated and concluded rapidly. The EU and the USA will work together to complete visa-free travel between the US and the EU as soon as possible and increase security for travellers. Joint procedures should be set up for the implementation of the agreements on judicial cooperation, and regular consultations need to take place.

The Common Space for an area of freedom, security and justice and the new agreement currently under negotiation will provide the framework for intense and improved future cooperation with the Russian Federation. Building also on the outcomes of the bi-annual JLS Permanent Partnership Councils, the EU and Russia should continue to cooperate within the framework of the visa dialogue and on legal migration, while tackling illegal migration, enhance common fight against organised crime and particularly operational cooperation, and improve and intensify judicial cooperation. An agreement, which should satisfy high standards of data protection, should be made with Eurojust as soon as possible. A framework agreement on information exchange should be concluded in that context. The visa dialogue must continue. The visa facilitation and readmission agreement should be implemented fully...

The dialogues with China and India on counter-terrorism aspects should be broadened and cover other priority areas such as intellectual property rights, migration, including fight against illegal migration and judicial cooperation. When agreements on judicial cooperation are entered into, the Union will continue to require that the death penalty is an issue where no compromises can be made. The dialogue with India on migration should be intensified and cover all migration-related aspects. With regard to China, the dialogue on Human Rights must be continued. The dialogue with Brazil will have to become deeper and wider in the years to come. The Strategic Partnership and the Joint Action Plan should be implemented more efficiently and more specific measures should be considered.

7.6.   International organisations and promotion of European and international standards

The European Council reiterates its commitment to effective multilateralism that supplements the bilateral and regional partnership with third countries and regions.

The United Nations remains the most important international organisation for the Union. The Lisbon Treaty creates the basis for more coherent and efficient EU participation in the work of the UN and other international organisations.

The Union should continue to promote European and international standards and the ratification of international conventions, in particular those developed under the auspices of the United Nations and the Council of Europe.

The work of the Council of Europe is of particular importance. It is the hub of the European values of Democracy, Human Rights and the Rule of Law. The Union must continue to work together with the Council of Europe based on the Memorandum of Understanding signed in 2006 and support its important conventions such as the Trafficking Convention and the one on Protection of Children.

For law enforcement cooperation, Interpol is an important partner for the Union. Civil law cooperation is in particular made in the framework of the Hague Conference on Private International Law. The Union should continue to support the Conference and encourage its partners to ratify the conventions where the EU is or will become a Party or where all Member States are Parties.

The external dimension

A.1.   Treaty on the Functioning of the European Union

Article 2.   1.   When the Treaties confer on the Union exclusive competence in a specific area, only the Union may legislate and adopt legally binding acts, the Member States being able to do so themselves only if so empowered by the Union or for the implementation of Union acts.

2.   When the Treaties confer on the Union a competence shared with the Member States in a specific area, the Union and the Member States may legislate and adopt legally binding acts in that area. The Member States shall exercise their competence to the extent that the Union has not exercised its competence. The Member States shall again exercise their competence to the extent that the Union has decided to cease exercising its competence....

6.   The scope of and arrangements for exercising the Union's competences shall be determined by the provisions of the Treaties relating to each area.

Article 3.   2.   The Union shall also have exclusive competence for the conclusion of an international agreement when its conclusion is provided for in a legislative act of the Union or is necessary to enable the Union to exercise its internal competence, or in so far as its conclusion may affect common rules or alter their scope.

Article 4.   2.   Shared competence between the Union and the Member States applies in the following principal areas:...

(j)   area of freedom, security and justice...

Article 218 (ex Article 300 TEC).   1.   Without prejudice to the specific provisions laid down in Article 207, agreements between the Union and third countries or international organisations shall be negotiated and concluded in accordance with the following procedure.

2.   The Council shall authorise the opening of negotiations, adopt negotiating directives, authorise the signing of agreements and conclude them.

3.   The Commission, or the High Representative of the Union for Foreign Affairs and Security Policy where the agreement envisaged relates exclusively or principally to the common foreign and security policy, shall submit recommendations to the Council, which shall adopt a decision authorising the opening of negotiations and, depending on the subject of the agreement envisaged, nominating the Union negotiator or the head of the Union's negotiating team.

4. The Council may address directives to the negotiator and designate a special committee in consultation with which the negotiations must be conducted.

5. The Council, on a proposal by the negotiator, shall adopt a decision authorising the signing of the agreement and, if necessary, its provisional application before entry into force.

6. The Council, on a proposal by the negotiator, shall adopt a decision concluding the agreement. Except where agreements relate exclusively to the common foreign and security policy, the Council shall adopt the decision concluding the agreement:

(a) after obtaining the consent of the European Parliament in the following cases:

(i) association agreements;

(ii) agreement on Union accession to the European Convention for the Protection of Human Rights and Fundamental Freedoms;

(iii) agreements establishing a specific institutional framework by organising cooperation procedures;

(iv) agreements with important budgetary implications for the Union;

(v) agreements covering fields to which either the ordinary legislative procedure applies, or the special legislative procedure where consent by the European Parliament is required.

The European Parliament and the Council may, in an urgent situation, agree upon a time-limit for consent.

(b) after consulting the European Parliament in other cases. The European Parliament shall deliver its opinion within a time-limit which the Council may set depending on the urgency of the matter. In the absence of an opinion within that time-limit, the Council may act.

7. When concluding an agreement, the Council may, by way of derogation from paragraphs 5, 6 and 9, authorise the negotiator to approve on the Union's behalf modifications to the agreement where it provides for them to be adopted by a simplified procedure or by a body set up by the agreement. The Council may attach specific conditions to such authorisation.

8. The Council shall act by a qualified majority throughout the procedure.

However, it shall act unanimously when the agreement covers a field for which unanimity is required for the adoption of a Union act as well as for association agreements and the agreements referred to in Article 212 with the States which are candidates for accession. The Council shall also act unanimously for the agreement on accession of the Union to the European Convention for the Protection of Human Rights and Fundamental Freedoms; the decision concluding this agreement shall enter into force after it has been approved by the Member States in accordance with their respective constitutional requirements.

9. The Council, on a proposal from the Commission or the High Representative of the Union for Foreign Affairs and Security Policy, shall adopt a decision suspending application of an agreement and establishing the positions to be adopted on the Union's behalf in a body set up by an agreement, when that body is called upon to adopt acts having legal effects, with the exception of acts supplementing or amending the institutional framework of the agreement.

10. The European Parliament shall be immediately and fully informed at all stages of the procedure.

11. A Member State, the European Parliament, the Council or the Commission may obtain the opinion of the Court of Justice as to whether an agreement envisaged is compatible with the Treaties.

Where the opinion of the Court is adverse, the agreement envisaged may not enter into force unless it is amended or the Treaties are revised.

Article 351 (ex Article 307 TEC). — The rights and obligations arising from agreements concluded before 1 January 1958 or, for acceding States, before the date of their accession, between one or more Member States on the one hand, and one or more third countries on the other, shall not be affected by the provisions of the Treaties.

To the extent that such agreements are not compatible with the Treaties, the Member State or States concerned shall take all appropriate steps to eliminate the incompatibilities established. Member States shall, where necessary, assist each other to this end and shall, where appropriate, adopt a common attitude.

In applying the agreements referred to in the first paragraph, Member States shall take into account the fact that the advantages accorded under the Treaties by each Member State form an integral part of the establishment of the Union and are thereby inseparably linked with the creation of common institutions, the conferring of powers upon them and the granting of the same advantages by all the other Member States.

A.2.   Protocols to the Treaty on the European Union and to the Treaty on the Functioning of the European Union

Protocol (No 25) on the exercise of shared competence

The High Contracting Parties have agreed upon the following provisions, which shall be annexed to the Treaty on European Union and to the Treaty on the Functioning of the European Union

Sole Article: With reference to Article 2(2) of the Treaty on the Functioning of the European Union on shared competence, when the Union has taken action in a certain area, the scope of this exercise of competence only covers those elements governed by the Union act in question and therefore does not cover the whole area.

A.3.   Declarations annexed to the Final Act of the Intergovernmental Conference which adopted the Treaty of Lisbon, signed on 13 December 2007

Declaration in relation to the delimitation of competences (No 18)

The Conference underlines that, in accordance with the system of division of competences between the Union and the Member States as provided for in the Treaty on European Union and the Treaty on the Functioning of the European Union, competences not conferred upon the Union in the Treaties remain with the Member States.

When the Treaties confer on the Union a competence shared with the Member States in a specific area, the Member States shall exercise their competence to the extent that the Union has not exercised, or has decided to cease exercising, its competence. The latter situation arises when the relevant EU institutions decide to repeal a legislative act, in particular better to ensure constant respect for the principles of subsidiarity and proportionality. The Council may, at the initiative of one or several of its members (representatives of Member States) and in accordance with Article 241 of the Treaty on the Functioning of the European Union, request the Commission to submit proposals for repealing a legislative act. The Conference welcomes the Commission's declaration that it will devote particular attention to these requests.

Equally, the representatives of the governments of the Member States, meeting in an Intergovernmental Conference, in accordance with the ordinary revision procedure provided for in Article 48(2) to (5) of the Treaty on European Union, may decide to amend the Treaties upon which the Union is founded, including either to increase or to reduce the competences conferred on the Union in the said Treaties.

Declaration on Article 218 of the Treaty on the Functioning of the European Union concerning the negotiation and conclusion of international agreements by Member States relating to the area of freedom, security and justice (No 36)

The Conference confirms that Member States may negotiate and conclude agreements with third countries or international organisations in the areas covered by Chapters 3, 4 and 5 of Title V of Part Three in so far as such agreements comply with Union law.

B.1.   Council Regulation (EC) No 1346/2000 of 29 May 2000 on insolvency proceedings (OJ, L 160 of 30 June 2000): Article 44.3

See Chapter V, A.1.

B.2.   Declaration by the Council (OJ, C 183 of 30 June 2000)

See Chapter V, A.2.

C.1.   Council Regulation (EC) No 44/2001 of 22 December 2000 on jurisdiction and the recognition and enforcement of judgments in civil and commercial matters (OJ, L 12 of 16 January 2001): Articles 71–72

See Chapter IV, General provisions, A.1.

C.2.   Statements made at the meeting of the Council (JHA) of 14 December 2000 (Doc. Consilium No 14 139/00).

Joint Council and Commission statements. Statement on Articles 71 and 72 and on the negotiations within the Hague Conference on Private International Law.
   See Chapter IV, General provisions, A.2.

C.3.   Agreement between the European Community and the Kingdom of Denmark on jurisdiction and the recognition and enforcement of judgments in civil and commercial matters (OJ, L 299 of 16 November 2005)

See Chapter IV, General provisions, A.4.

C.4   Agreement between the European Community and the Kingdom of Denmark on jurisdiction and the recognition and enforcement of judgments in civil and commercial matters (OJ, L 149 of 12 June 2009)

See Chapter IV, General provisions, A.5.

C.5.   Convention on jurisdiction and the recognition and enforcement of judgments in civil and commercial matters (OJ, L 339 of 21 December 2007)

See Chapter IV, General provisions, B.4.

D.1.   Council Regulation (EC) No 2201/2003 of 27 November 2003 concerning jurisdiction and the recognition and enforcement of judgments in matrimonial matters and the matters of parental responsibility, repealing Regulation (EC) No 1347/2000 (OJ, L 388 of 23 December 2003): Articles 60–63

See Chapter XI, Matrimonial matters, A.1.

D.2. Statements and declarations made at the meeting of the Council (JHA) of 29 May 2000

1. Statement by the Council.
2. Statement by the Council.
3. Statement by the Commission on Article 16.
4. Declaration by the United Kingdom.
5. Statement by the United Kingdom.
6. Declaration by the United Kingdom.

See Chapter XI, Matrimonial matters, A.3.

E. Regulation (EC) No 805/2004 of the European Parliament and of the Council of 21 April 2004 creating a European Enforcement Order for uncontested claims (OJ, L 143 of 30 April 2004): Article 22

See Chapter IV, General provisions, C.

F. Regulation (EC) No 864/2007 of the European Parliament and of the Council of 11 July 2007 on the law applicable to non-contractual obligations (Rome II) (OJ, L 199 of 31 July 2007): Article 28

See Chapter VII, General provisions, A.1.

G. Regulation (EC) No 593/2008 of the European Parliament and of the Council of 17 June 2008 on the law applicable to contractual obligations (Rome I) (OJ, L 177 of 4 July 2008): Articles 25–26

See Chapter VI, General provisions, A.1.

H. The Hague Programme: strengthening freedom, security and justice in the European Union (OJ, C 53 of 3 March 2005): Points 3.4.1.-3.4.5

See in this Chapter, General provisions, E.

I.   Council of the European Union, Aspects of Judicial Cooperation in Civil Matters in the Framework of the Strategy for the External Dimension of JHA: Global Freedom, Security and Justice (Doc. Consilium No 8140/06 of 11 April 2006)

I.   Introduction

1.   In the Hague Programme the European Council considered the development of a coherent external dimension of the Union policy of freedom, security and justice as a growing priority and called for the development of a strategy reflecting the Union's special relations with third countries, groups of countries and regions, and focusing on the specific needs for JHA cooperation with them.

2.   As indicated in the Strategy for the External Dimension of the JHA, the development of an area of freedom, security and justice can only be successful if it is underpinned by a partnership with third countries on these issues, which includes strengthening the rule of law, and promoting the respect for human rights and international obligations.

3.   With regard to judicial cooperation in civil matters, the Hague Programme aims to ensure coherence between the EU and the international legal order. The Council and Commission Action Plan implementing the Hague Programme calls for the conclusion of a number of specific international agreements to that effect.

4.   The external dimension of judicial cooperation in civil matters has growing significance. On the one hand, international agreements with third countries are indispensable for the purpose of providing legal certainty and foreseeability for European citizens on a global scale. On the other hand, it is also important to safeguard the uniform application of Community law in international negotiations.

5.   The current document aims to set forth the general framework for the future strategy of the external dimension in the field of judicial cooperation in civil matters. It is not a strict legal framework but rather an evolving process of defining and achieving policy objectives in full conformity with the provisions of the EC Treaty.

II.   Cooperation with third countries in the field of judicial cooperation in civil matters

1.   Areas of cooperation

6.   Cooperation with third countries in the field of judicial cooperation in civil matters should focus on the areas covered by EC legislation.

7.   In particular jurisdiction, recognition and enforcement of decisions, applicable law, cross-border transmission of judicial and extra-judicial documents, taking of evidence and administrative cooperation between authorities involved in international legal aid could be identified as possible fields of cooperation (Article 65 of the EC Treaty).

2.   Method of work

a)   Principles

8.   To the greatest extent possible, cooperation in the field of judicial cooperation in civil law matters with third countries should follow the general framework for the relations between the EU and a particular third country. Account should be taken of the existing level of cooperation, of the legal framework and of reciprocal interest in deepening cooperation in the field of judicial cooperation in civil matters.

9.   It should also be noted that, depending on the status of the country with respect to the European Union (eg a possible candidate country or close economic ties), the objectives and the level of detail of such cooperation could vary significantly.

10.   Cooperation with third countries in the field of judicial cooperation in civil matters should also be undertaken where necessary, based on the mutual assessment of actual needs and shortcomings in practice.

11.   This general framework will be updated on a regular basis, depending on the work undertaken, progress achieved and the discussions held.

b)   Means of cooperation

12.   Accordingly, the means of cooperation employed with each particular country or a group of countries depend on the particular situation in question. Therefore there is no hierarchy between the means highlighted below and none of them should be excluded from the outset.

13.   Cooperation in the field of civil law could be carried out in at least three different manners:
—   in international negotiations at multilateral level;
—   in the form of bilateral agreements;
—   by exchange of best practices.

(I)   MULTILATERAL COOPERATION

14.   Having regard to the great number of international conventions in the fields outlined in para 7, it is clear that ensuring that the same legal framework applies to a large number of countries of different legal backgrounds as regards a specific field offers considerable benefits.

15.   Therefore, as far as appropriate and necessary, it would be useful to cooperate with third countries in the negotiations over multilateral conventions and in the implementation phase of these agreements.

16.   In particular, the work undertaken within the Hague Conference on Private International Law has provided for useful exchanges with third countries. With more than 60 member countries representing all continents and different legal traditions, the Hague Conference on Private International Law is an international organisation reinforcing legal certainty and security on a global scale in the area of judicial cooperation in civil matters.

17.   In addition, similar approach should be taken as regards other forums such as the Council of Europe, UNIDROIT, UNCITRAL, and others.

(II)   BILATERAL COOPERATION

18. In certain fields and with respect to some partners, it may be useful to proceed by way of concluding bilateral agreements between the EU and a respective third country in the field of judicial cooperation in civil matters.

19. This method offers more flexibility and enables tailor-made solutions in relations with some third countries as regards certain areas.

(III)   EXCHANGE OF BEST PRACTICES

20. Cooperation should in all cases, as appropriate, be supported by exchanges at a less formalised level, such as exchange of information, common training events, exchange of legal practitioners.

21. In particular, importance should be attached to electronic and web-based tools for developing cooperation in international legal cooperation. The success of the European Judicial Network in civil and commercial matters proves the viability of such solutions in the contemporary world.

3.   Target countries

a)   Acceding and candidate countries

22. The accession of Bulgaria and Romania is scheduled for 2007 or, at the latest by 2008. To facilitate the smooth integration of those countries into the European area of justice in civil matters, it is important to continue the ongoing dialogue and exchange of information within the existing forums at EU level as well as at international level.

23. Openness, information exchange and cooperation in international negotiations should be considered with regard to the current and future candidate countries on the basis of the Association Agreements, Accession Partnerships and other relevant instruments in the preaccession phase with regard to the objective of fully integrating the candidate countries into the area of justice from the moment of accession.

b)   Lugano States

24. Considering the particularly close relationship with the Lugano Member States (Iceland, Norway and Switzerland), judicial cooperation in civil matters with those countries should be reinforced. In particular, the following aspects should be taken into account in the planning of future work:

(i)   The first priority with regard to the Lugano States would be to conclude the new Lugano Convention. In view of the fact that the European Court of Justice has delivered an opinion defining the external competence of the EC in this field, this objective could be attained in the course of 2006.

(ii)   Preparatory work could be undertaken to consider extending the current Lugano system to other aspects of the area of justice. This would result in the creation of a parallel area of justice to that created by the EC rules in certain fields and would bring along benefits for the citizens in both EC and Lugano States.

c) European Neighbourhood Policy countries[2]

25. Considering the objectives of the European Neighbourhood Policy and the existing framework of cooperation the EU has established with each of these countries, closer cooperation in the field of judicial cooperation in civil matters should be envisaged with the countries falling under the European Neighbourhood Policy.

26. Having regard to the close ties of certain Member States with some of the EPN countries, cooperation should be reinforced, especially in the field of parental responsibility and child abduction. Attention should be given to the possibility of ratifying the existing Hague Conventions in this field. Regard should also be had to the facilitation of practical cooperation and contacts between legal practitioners, for example in the framework of the Malta process. If need be, cooperation could take the form of bilateral (mixed) agreements.

d) USA and Canada

27. The United States of America and Canada should be considered as privileged partners of the European Union. Cooperation in judicial cooperation in civil matters should take account of the following priorities:

(i)   reinforced dialogue in international negotiations, in particular in the framework of the Hague Conference on Private International Law;

(ii) closer contacts at the level of practitioners (judges, lawyers).

e) Russia

28. The bilateral basis for EU relations with Russia is the Partnership and Cooperation Agreement which came into force on 1 December 1997. In addition, a number of sectoral agreements exist.

29. Cooperation in the field of JHA was taken further by the long-term objective of establishing the Common Space on Freedom, Security and Justice between EU and Russia. To implement this objective, a Road Map has been prepared.

30. Cooperation with Russia in the field of judicial cooperation in civil matters should take into account the objectives defined in the Roadmap for the Common Space of Freedom, Security and Justice and the outcome of discussions of the Committee on Civil Law Matters (General questions) on this issue.

f) Other countries

31. In the longer term, cooperation frameworks in the field of judicial cooperation in civil law could be envisaged with other countries respecting the rule of law, independence of judiciary and other principles essential for the application of the principle of mutual recognition. In particular, such cooperation could be set up with countries which have close commercial ties with EU countries that should be reinforced by an appropriate legal framework.

---

[2] In alphabetical order: (a) in Europe: Belarus, Moldova, Ukraine; (b) in Asia: Armenia, Azerbaijan, Georgia, Israel, Jordan, Lebanon, the Palestinian Authority, Syria; (c) in Africa: Algeria, Egypt, Libya, Morocco, Tunisia.

32. As a first priority, cooperation should focus on the possibility of those countries acceding to certain key instruments of the Hague Conference on Private International Law.

4.   International forums

a)   The Hague Conference

33. As indicated above, the Hague Conference on Private International Law will continue to be an important forum for concluding agreements with third countries. The priorities of the EC in the immediate future in relations with the Hague Conference should be the following:
  (i)   to finalise the process for the accession of the EC to the Hague Conference;
  (ii) to examine whether it is in the interest of the EC to join those Hague Conventions in respect of which there is Community competence.

J.1.   Council Decision of 5 October 2006 on the accession of the Community to the Hague Conference on Private International Law (OJ, L 297 of 26 October 2006)

(1) The objective of the Hague Conference on Private International Law (HCCH) is to work for the progressive unification of the rules of private international law. The HCCH has to date adopted a substantial number of conventions in different fields of private international law.

(2) Since the entry into force of the Treaty of Amsterdam, the Community has competence to adopt measures in the field of judicial cooperation in civil matters having cross-border implications insofar as necessary for the proper functioning of the internal market. The Community has exerted this competence by adopting a number of instruments, many of which coincide, partially or fully, with the areas of work of the HCCH.

(3) It is essential that the Community be granted a status that corresponds to its new role as a major international player in the field of civil judicial cooperation and that it be able to exercise its external competence by participating as a full member in the negotiations of conventions by the HCCH in areas of its competence.

(4) By decision of 28 November 2002, the Council authorised the Commission to negotiate the conditions and modalities of Community accession to the HCCH.

(5) By a joint letter from the Commission and the Presidency to the HCCH of 19 December 2002, the Community applied to become a member of the HCCH, and requested the opening of negotiations.

(6) In April 2004, a Special Commission on General Affairs and Policy of the HCCH expressed the unanimous view that, as a matter of principle, the Community should become a Member of the HCCH and determined certain criteria and procedures for the modalities of its membership.

(7) In June 2005, the Diplomatic Conference of the HCCH adopted by consensus the amendments to the Statute of the HCCH (Statute) necessary to allow the accession of a Regional Economic Integration Organisation and the Members of the HCCH were

subsequently invited to cast their votes on the amendments, if possible within a period of nine months.

(8) The amendments to the Statute will enter into force three months after the Secretary-General of the HCCH has informed the Members that the required two-thirds majority for amending the Statute has been reached. Shortly after the entry into force, an extraordinary meeting of the Council on General Affairs and Policy will formally decide upon the Community's accession to the HCCH.

(9) The outcome of the negotiations on the revision of the Statute is satisfactory, taking into account the interests of the Community.

(10) Article 2A of the revised Statute entitles the Community, as a Regional Economic Integration Organisation, to become a Member of the HCCH.

(11) The Community should accede to the HCCH.

(12) In accordance with Article 3 of the Protocol on the position of the United Kingdom and Ireland annexed to the Treaty on the European Union and the Treaty establishing the European Community, the United Kingdom and Ireland are taking part in the adoption of this Decision.

(13) In accordance with Articles 1 and 2 of the Protocol on the position of Denmark annexed to the Treaty on the European Union and the Treaty establishing the European Community, Denmark does not take part in the adoption of this Decision and is not bound by it or subject to its application;

Sole Article

1.   The Community shall accede to the Hague Conference on Private International Law (HCCH) by means of the declaration of acceptance of the Statute of the HCCH (Statute), as set out in Annex I to this Decision, as soon as the HCCH has taken the formal decision to admit the Community as a Member.

2.   The Community shall also deposit a declaration of competence specifying the matters in respect of which competence has been transferred to it by its Member States, as set out in Annex II to this Decision, and a declaration on certain matters concerning the HCCH, as set out in Annex III to this Decision.

3.   The President of the Council is hereby authorised to carry out such procedures as may be necessary to give effect to paragraphs 1 and 2.

4.   The text of the Statute is attached to this Decision as Annex IV.

5.   For the purpose of this Decision the term 'Member State' shall mean Member States with the exception of Denmark.

J.2.   Declaration of competence of the European Community specifying the matters in respect of which competence has been transferred to it by its Member States (OJ, L 297 of 26 October 2006)

1.   This Declaration is given pursuant to Article 2A(3) of the Statute of the Hague Conference on Private International Law and specifies the matters in respect of which competence has been transferred to the European Community by its Member States.

2.   The European Community has internal competence to adopt general and specific measures relating to private international law in various fields in its Member

States. In respect of matters within the purview of the HCCH, the European Community notably has competence under Title IV of the EC Treaty to adopt measures in the field of judicial cooperation in civil matters having cross-border implications insofar as necessary for the proper functioning of the internal market (Articles 61(c) and 65 EC Treaty). Such measures include:

(a)   improving and simplifying the system for cross-border service of judicial and extrajudicial documents; cooperation in the taking of evidence; the recognition and enforcement of decisions in civil and commercial cases, including decisions in extrajudicial cases;

(b)   promoting the compatibility of the rules applicable in the Member States concerning the conflict of laws and of jurisdiction;

(c)   eliminating obstacles to the good functioning of civil proceedings, if necessary by promoting the compatibility of the rules on civil procedure applicable in the Member States.

3.   In areas which do not fall within its exclusive competence, the European Community shall take action, in accordance with the principle of subsidiarity, only if and insofar as the objectives of the proposed action cannot be sufficiently achieved by Member States and can therefore, by reason of the scale or effects of the proposed action, be better achieved by the European Community. Any action by the European Community shall not go beyond what is necessary to achieve the objectives.

4.   Furthermore, the European Community has competence in other fields which can be subject to conventions of the HCCH, as in the field of the internal market (Article 95 EC Treaty) or consumer protection (Article 153 EC Treaty).

5.   The European Community has made use of its competence by adopting a number of instruments under Article 61(c) of the EC Treaty, such as:

— Council Regulation (EC) No 1346/2000 of 29 May 2000 on insolvency proceedings;

— Council Regulation (EC) No 1348/2000 of 29 May 2000 on the service in the Member States of judicial and extrajudicial documents in civil or commercial matters;

— Council Regulation (EC) No 44/2001 of 22 December 2000 on jurisdiction, recognition and enforcement in civil and commercial matters;

— Council Regulation (EC) No 1206/2001 of 28 May 2001 on cooperation between the courts of the Member States in the taking of evidence in civil or commercial matters;

— Council Directive 2003/8/EC of 27 January 2003 to improve access to justice in cross-border disputes by establishing minimum common rules relating to legal aid for such disputes;

— Council Regulation (EC) No 2201/2003 of 27 November 2003 concerning jurisdiction and the recognition and enforcement of judgments in matrimonial matters and the matters of parental responsibility, repealing Regulation (EC) No 1347/2000, and

— Regulation (EC) No 805/2004 of the European Parliament and of the Council of 21 April 2004 creating a European Enforcement Order for uncontested claims.

Provisions on private international law can also be found in other Community legislation, notably in the area of consumer protection, insurance, financial services and intellectual property. Thus, the Community Directives affected by the Hague Convention on the Law Applicable to Certain Rights of Securities held with an Intermediary were adopted on the basis of Article 95 of the EC Treaty.

6.   Even if there is no explicit reference to external competence in the EC Treaty, it results from the jurisprudence of the Court of Justice of the European Communities that the provisions of the EC Treaty referred to above constitute legal bases not only for internal acts of the Community, but also for the conclusion of international agreements by the Community. The Community may conclude international agreements whenever the internal competence has already been used in order to adopt measures for implementing common policies, as listed above, or if international agreement is necessary to obtain one of the European Community's objectives.[3] The Community's external competence is exclusive to the extent to which an international agreement affects internal Community rules or alters their scope.[4] Where this is the case, it is not for the Member States but for the Community to enter into external undertakings with third States or International Organisations. An international agreement can fall entirely or only to some extent within exclusive Community competence.

7.   Community instruments are normally binding for all Member States. Concerning Title IV of the EC Treaty which comprises the legal basis for judicial cooperation in civil matters, a special regime applies to Denmark, Ireland and the United Kingdom. Measures taken under Title IV of the EC Treaty are not binding upon or applicable in Denmark. Ireland and the United Kingdom take part in legal instruments adopted under Title IV of the EC Treaty if they notify the Council to that effect. Ireland and the United Kingdom have decided to opt in on all measures listed at point 5 above.

8.   The extent of competence which the Member States have transferred to the European Community pursuant to the EC Treaty is, by its nature, liable to continuous development. The European Community and its Member States will ensure that any change in the Community's competences will be promptly notified to the Secretary-General of the HCCH as stipulated in Article 2A(4) of the Statute.

J.3.   Declaration by the Community on certain matters concerning the Hague Conference on Private International Law (OJ, L 297 of 26 October 2006)

The European Community endeavours to examine whether it is in its interest to join existing Hague Conventions in respect of which there is Community competence. Where this interest exists, the European Community, in cooperation with the HCCH, will make every effort to overcome the difficulties resulting from the absence of a clause providing for the accession of a Regional Economic Integration Organisation to those Conventions.

The European Community further endeavours to make it possible for representatives of the Permanent Bureau of the HCCH to take part in meetings of experts organised by the Commission of the European Communities where matters of interest to the HCCH are being discussed.

---

[3]   Opinion 1/76 of the Court of Justice, ECR 1977, p. 741; Opinion 2/91, ECR 1993, p. I-1061; Case 22/70 (AETR); *Commission v Council*, ECR 1971, p. 263; Case-C-467/98 (open skies), *Commission v Denmark*, ECR 2002, p. I-9519.

[4]   Case 22/70 ('AETR'), *Commission v Council*, Case-C-467/98 ('open skies'), *Commission v Denmark*.

J.4.   Statute of the Hague Conference on Private International Law (OJ, L 297 of 26 October 2006)

Article 1.   The purpose of the Hague Conference is to work for the progressive unification of the rules of private international law.

Article 3.   (1)   The Member States of the Conference may, at a meeting concerning general affairs and policy where the majority of Member States is present, by a majority of the votes cast, decide to admit also as a Member any Regional Economic Integration Organisation which has submitted an application for membership to the Secretary-General. References to Members under this Statute shall include such Member Organisations, except as otherwise expressly provided. The admission shall become effective upon the acceptance of the Statute by the Regional Economic Integration Organisation concerned.

(2)   To be eligible to apply for membership of the Conference, a Regional Economic Integration Organisation must be one constituted solely by sovereign States, and to which its Member States have transferred competence over a range of matters within the purview of the Conference, including the authority to make decisions binding on its Member States in respect of those matters.

(3)   Each Regional Economic Integration Organisation applying for membership shall, at the time of such application, submit a declaration of competence specifying the matters in respect of which competence has been transferred to it by its Member States.

(4)   Each Member Organisation and its Member States shall ensure that any change regarding the competence of the Member Organisation or in its membership shall be notified to the Secretary-General, who shall circulate such information to the other Members of the Conference.

(5)   Member States of the Member Organisation shall be presumed to retain competence over all matters in respect of which transfers of competence have not been specifically declared or notified.

(6)   Any Member of the Conference may request the Member Organisation and its Member States to provide information as to whether the Member Organisation has competence in respect of any specific question which is before the Conference. The Member Organisation and its Member States shall ensure that this information is provided on such request.

(7)   The Member Organisation shall exercise membership rights on an alternative basis with its Member States that are Members of the Conference, in the areas of their respective competences.

(8)   The Member Organisation may exercise on matters within its competence, in any meetings of the Conference in which it is entitled to participate, a number of votes equal to the number of its Member States which have transferred competence to the Member Organisation in respect of the matter in question, and which are entitled to vote in and have registered for such meetings. Whenever the Member Organisation exercises its right to vote, its Member States shall not exercise theirs, and conversely.

(9)   'Regional Economic Integration Organisation' means an international organisation that is constituted solely by sovereign States, and to which its Member States have transferred competence over a range of matters, including the authority to make decisions binding on its Member States in respect of those matters.

J.5.   European Parliament Resolution on the involvement of the European Parliament in the work of the Hague Conference following the accession of the Community (OJ, 305E of 4 December 2006)

The European Parliament,

— having regard to the proposal for a Council decision on the accession of the European Community to the Hague Conference on Private International Law,

— having regard to its position of 7 September 2006 on the proposal for a Council decision on the accession of the European Community to the Hague Conference on Private International Law,

— having regard to Rule 108 (5) of its Rules of Procedure,

A.   whereas the accession of the Community to the Hague Conference on Private International Law (CODIP) should improve consistency in the fields of international civil and commercial law and Community law and should considerably enhance the influence of the Community in this forum,

B.   whereas the CODIP conventions are an indispensable point of reference in civil and commercial law,

C.   whereas, ever since the Treaty of Amsterdam, the Community has had competence to adopt measures relating to judicial cooperation in civil matters which have cross-border implications in so far as necessary for the proper functioning of the internal market,

D.   whereas Parliament is involved as co-legislator in the adoption of such measures, where it is not simply consulted,

E.   whereas a number of instruments adopted or contemplated by the Community overlap with matters which have been dealt with or may in future be dealt with by the Hague Conference,

F.   whereas, furthermore, the Community will be asked to participate actively in setting the priorities of the CODIP and ensuring that they dovetail with the Hague programme on judicial cooperation, the action plan on financial services and the internal market strategy and, more generally, with the Commission's work programme,

G.   whereas the Commission will be required to consult Parliament on draft mandates for negotiation and the need for disconnection clauses,

H.   whereas there is therefore a need for Parliament to be closely involved with the proceedings of the Hague Conference and consulted on the outcome of its deliberations in order to secure more democratic scrutiny also of the Commission's participation in the Conference as sole representative of the Community as such, and a greater measure of transparency and openness for its proceedings, which are of considerable interest for citizens and practitioners;

1.   Calls on the Council and the Commission to ask Parliament to give its views on a case-by-case basis on the need for the Community to accede to the existing conventions which have been ratified by a significant number of Member States;

2.   Resolves to investigate fully with the Conference further modes of cooperation, and to take the lead in the founding of a 'parliamentary forum' with national parliamentarians to both follow and inform the work of the Conference;

3.   Calls on the Council and the Commission to propose suitable procedures so as to enable Parliament to play its proper role in the context of the Hague Conference on Private International Law;

4.   Instructs its President to forward this resolution to the Council, the Commission and the governments and parliaments of the Member States.

K.   Regulation (EC) No 662/2009 of the European Parliament and of the Council of 13 July 2009 establishing a procedure for the negotiation and conclusion of agreements between Member States and third countries on particular matters concerning the law applicable to contractual and non-contractual obligations (OJ, L 200 of 31 July 2009)

(1) Title IV of Part Three of the Treaty provides the legal basis for the adoption of Community legislation in the field of judicial cooperation in civil matters.

(2) Judicial cooperation in civil matters between Member States and third countries has traditionally been governed by agreements between Member States and third countries. Such agreements, of which there is a large number, often reflect special ties between a Member State and a third country and are intended to provide an adequate legal framework to meet specific needs of the parties concerned.

(3) Article 307 of the Treaty requires Member States to take all appropriate steps to eliminate any incompatibilities between the Community acquis and international agreements concluded between Member States and third countries. This may involve the need for the re-negotiation of such agreements.

(4) In order to provide an adequate legal framework to meet specific needs of a given Member State in its relations with a third country, there may also be a manifest need for the conclusion of new agreements with third countries relating to areas of civil justice that come within the purview of Title IV of Part Three of the Treaty.

(5) In its Opinion 1/03 of 7 February 2006 relating to the conclusion of the new Lugano Convention, the Court of Justice of the European Communities confirmed that the Community has acquired exclusive competence to conclude an international agreement like the Lugano Convention with third countries on matters affecting the rules laid down in Council Regulation (EC) No 44/2001 of 22 December 2000 on jurisdiction and the recognition and enforcement of judgments in civil and commercial matters (Brussels I).

(6) It is for the Community to conclude, pursuant to Article 300 of the Treaty, agreements between the Community and a third country on matters falling within the exclusive competence of the Community.

(7) Article 10 of the Treaty requires Member States to facilitate the achievement of the Community's tasks and to abstain from any measure which could jeopardise the attainment of the objectives of the Treaty. This duty of loyal cooperation is of general application and does not depend on whether or not the Community competence is exclusive.

(8) With regard to agreements with third countries on specific civil justice issues falling within the exclusive competence of the Community, a coherent and transparent procedure should be established to authorise a Member State to amend an existing agreement or to negotiate and conclude a new agreement, in particular where the Community itself has not indicated its intention to exercise its external competence to conclude an agreement by way of an already existing mandate of negotiation or an

envisaged mandate of negotiation. This procedure should be without prejudice to the exclusive competence of the Community and the provisions of Articles 300 and 307 of the Treaty. It should be regarded as an exceptional measure and should be limited in scope and in time.

(9) This Regulation should not apply if the Community has already concluded an agreement with the third country concerned on the same subject matter. Two agreements should be regarded as concerning the same subject matter only if, and to the extent that, they regulate in substance the same specific legal issues. Provisions simply stating a general intention to cooperate on such issues should not be regarded as concerning the same subject matter.

(10) Exceptionally, certain regional agreements between a few Member States and a few third countries, for example two or three, intended to address local situations and not open for accession to other States should also be covered by this Regulation.

(11) In order to ensure that an agreement envisaged by a Member State does not render Community law ineffective and does not undermine the proper functioning of the system established by that law, or undermine the Community's external relations policy as decided by the Community, the Member State concerned should be required to notify the Commission of its intentions with a view to obtaining an authorisation to open or continue formal negotiations on an agreement as well as to conclude an agreement. Such notification should be given by letter or by electronic means. It should contain all relevant information and documentation enabling the Commission to assess the expected impact on Community law of the outcome of the negotiations.

(12) It should be assessed whether there is sufficient Community interest in concluding a bilateral agreement between the Community and the third country concerned or, where appropriate, in replacing an existing bilateral agreement between a Member State and a third country with a Community agreement. To that end, all Member States should be informed of any notification received by the Commission concerning an agreement envisaged by a Member State in order to allow them to demonstrate their interest in joining the initiative of the notifying Member State. If, from this exchange of information, a sufficient Community interest were to emerge, the Commission should consider proposing a negotiating mandate with a view to the conclusion of an agreement between the Community and the third country concerned.

(13) If the Commission requests additional information from a Member State in connection with its assessment as to whether that Member State should be authorised to open negotiations with a third country, such a request should not affect the time limits within which the Commission is to give a reasoned decision on the application of that Member State.

(14) When authorising the opening of formal negotiations, the Commission should be able, if necessary, to propose negotiating guidelines or request the inclusion of particular clauses in the envisaged agreement. The Commission should be kept fully informed throughout the different stages of the negotiations as far as matters falling within the scope of this Regulation are concerned and should be allowed to participate as an observer in the negotiations as regards those matters.

(15) When notifying the Commission of their intention to enter into negotiations with a third country, Member States should only be required to inform the Commission of elements which are of relevance for the assessment to be made by the Commission. The authorisation by the Commission and any possible negotiating guidelines or, as the case

may be, the refusal by the Commission should concern only matters falling within the scope of this Regulation.

(16) All Member States should be informed of any notification to the Commission concerning envisaged or negotiated agreements and of any reasoned decision by the Commission under this Regulation. Such information should however fully comply with possible confidentiality requirements.

(17) The European Parliament, the Council and the Commission should ensure that any information identified as confidential is treated in accordance with Regulation (EC) No 1049/2001 of the European Parliament and of the Council of 30 May 2001 regarding public access to European Parliament, Council and Commission documents.

(18) Where the Commission, on the basis of its assessment, intends not to authorise the opening of formal negotiations or the conclusion of a negotiated agreement, it should, before giving its reasoned decision, give an opinion to the Member State concerned. In the case of refusal to authorise the conclusion of a negotiated agreement the opinion should also be submitted to the European Parliament and to the Council.

(19) In order to ensure that the negotiated agreement does not constitute an obstacle to the implementation of the Community's external policy on judicial cooperation in civil and commercial matters, the agreement should provide either for its full or partial denunciation in the event of the conclusion of a subsequent agreement between the Community or the Community and its Member States, on the one hand, and the same third country, on the other hand, on the same subject matter, or for a direct replacement of the relevant provisions of the agreement by the provisions of such subsequent agreement.

(20) Provision should be made for transitional measures to cover situations where, at the time of the entry into force of this Regulation, a Member State has already started the process of negotiating an agreement with a third country, or has completed the negotiations but has not yet expressed its consent to be bound by the agreement.

(21) In order to ensure that sufficient experience has been gained concerning the application of this Regulation, the Commission should submit a report on such application no earlier than eight years after the adoption of this Regulation. In that report, the Commission, exercising its prerogatives, should confirm the temporary nature of this Regulation or examine whether this Regulation should be replaced by a new Regulation covering the same subject matter or including also particular matters falling within the exclusive competence of the Community and governed by other Community instruments, as referred to in recital 5.

(22) If the report submitted by the Commission confirms the temporary nature of this Regulation, Member States should still be able, after the submission of the report, to notify the Commission of ongoing or already announced negotiations with a view to obtaining an authorisation to open formal negotiations.

(23) In accordance with the principle of proportionality, as set out in Article 5 of the Treaty, this Regulation does not go beyond what is necessary in order to achieve its objective.

(24) In accordance with Article 3 of the Protocol on the position of the United Kingdom and Ireland, annexed to the Treaty on European Union and to the Treaty establishing the European Community, the United Kingdom and Ireland have given notice of their wish to take part in the adoption and application of this Regulation.

(25) In accordance with Articles 1 and 2 of the Protocol on the position of Denmark,

annexed to the Treaty on European Union and to the Treaty establishing the European Community, Denmark is not taking part in the adoption of this Regulation and is not bound by it or subject to its application...

Article 1. Subject matter and scope. 1. This Regulation establishes a procedure to authorise a Member State to amend an existing agreement or to negotiate and conclude a new agreement with a third country, subject to the conditions laid down in this Regulation.

This procedure is without prejudice to the respective competencies of the Community and of the Member States.

2. This Regulation shall apply to agreements concerning particular matters falling, entirely or partly, within the scope of Regulation (EC) No 593/2008 of the European Parliament and of the Council of 17 June 2008 on the law applicable to contractual obligations (Rome I) and Regulation (EC) No 864/2007 of the European Parliament and of the Council of 11 July 2007 on the law applicable to non-contractual obligations (Rome II).

3. This Regulation shall not apply if the Community has already concluded an agreement with the third country concerned on the same subject matter.

Article 2. Definitions. 1. For the purposes of this Regulation, the term 'agreement' shall mean:

(a) a bilateral agreement between a Member State and a third country;

(b) a regional agreement between a limited number of Member States and of third countries neighbouring Member States which is intended to address local situations and which is not open for accession to other States.

2. In the context of regional agreements as referred to in paragraph 1(b), any reference in this Regulation to a Member State or a third country shall be read as referring to the Member States or the third countries concerned, respectively.

Article 3. Notification to the Commission. 1. Where a Member State intends to enter into negotiations in order to amend an existing agreement or to conclude a new agreement falling within the scope of this Regulation, it shall notify the Commission in writing of its intention at the earliest possible moment before the envisaged opening of formal negotiations.

2. The notification shall include, as appropriate, a copy of the existing agreement, the draft agreement or the draft proposal, and any other relevant documentation. The Member State shall describe the subject matter of the negotiations and specify the issues which are to be addressed in the envisaged agreement, or the provisions of the existing agreement which are to be amended. The Member State may provide any other additional information.

Article 4. Assessment by the Commission. 1. Upon receipt of the notification referred to in Article 3, the Commission shall assess whether the Member State may open formal negotiations.

2. In making that assessment, the Commission shall first check whether any relevant negotiating mandate with a view to concluding a Community agreement with the third country concerned is specifically envisaged within the next 24 months. If this is not the case, the Commission shall assess whether all of the following conditions are met:

(a) the Member State concerned has provided information showing that it has a specific interest in concluding the agreement due to economic, geographical, cultural, historical, social or political ties between the Member State and the third country concerned;

(b) on the basis of the information provided by the Member State, the envisaged agreement appears not to render Community law ineffective and not to undermine the proper functioning of the system established by that law; and

(c) the envisaged agreement would not undermine the object and purpose of the Community's external relations policy as decided by the Community.

3.   If the information provided by the Member State is not sufficient for the purposes of the assessment, the Commission may request additional information.

Article 5. Authorisation to open formal negotiations.   1.   If the envisaged agreement meets the conditions set out in Article 4(2), the Commission shall, within 90 days of receipt of the notification referred to in Article 3, give a reasoned decision on the application of the Member State authorising it to open formal negotiations on that agreement.

If necessary, the Commission may propose negotiating guidelines and may request the inclusion of particular clauses in the envisaged agreement.

2.   The envisaged agreement shall contain a clause providing for either:

(a) full or partial denunciation of the agreement in the event of the conclusion of a subsequent agreement between the Community or the Community and its Member States, on the one hand, and the same third country, on the other hand, on the same subject matter; or

(b) direct replacement of the relevant provisions of the agreement by the provisions of a subsequent agreement concluded between the Community or the Community and its Member States, on the one hand, and the same third country, on the other hand, on the same subject matter.

The clause referred to in point (a) of the first subparagraph should be worded along the following lines: '(name(s) of the Member State(s)) shall denounce this Agreement, in part or in full, if and when the European Community or the European Community and its Member States conclude an Agreement with (name(s) of the third country(ies)) on the same matters of civil justice as those governed by this Agreement'.

The clause referred to in point (b) of the first subparagraph should be worded along the following lines: 'This Agreement or certain provisions of this Agreement shall cease to be applicable on the day when an Agreement between the European Community or the European Community and its Member States, on the one hand, and (name(s) of the third country(ies)), on the other hand, has entered into force, in respect of the matters governed by the latter Agreement'.

Article 6. Refusal to authorise the opening of formal negotiations.   1.   If, on the basis of its assessment under Article 4, the Commission intends not to authorise the opening of formal negotiations on the envisaged agreement, it shall give an opinion to the Member State concerned within 90 days of receipt of the notification referred to in Article 3.

2.   Within 30 days of receipt of the opinion of the Commission, the Member State concerned may request the Commission to enter into discussions with it with a view to finding a solution.

3.   If the Member State concerned does not request the Commission to enter into discussions with it within the time limit provided for in paragraph 2, the Commission shall give a reasoned decision on the application of the Member State within 130 days of receipt of the notification referred to in Article 3.

4.   In the event of the discussions referred to in paragraph 2, the Commission shall give a reasoned decision on the application of the Member State within 30 days of the closure of the discussions.

Article 7. Participation of the Commission in the negotiations. — The Commission may participate as an observer in the negotiations between the Member State and the third country as far as matters falling within the scope of this Regulation are concerned. If the Commission does not participate as an observer, it shall be kept informed of the progress and results throughout the different stages of the negotiations.

Article 8. Authorisation to conclude the agreement.   1.   Before signing a negotiated agreement, the Member State concerned shall notify the outcome of the negotiations to the Commission and shall transmit to it the text of the agreement.

2.   Upon receipt of that notification the Commission shall assess whether the negotiated agreement:

(a)   meets the condition set out in Article 4(2)(b);

(b)   meets the condition set out in Article 4(2)(c), in so far as there are new and exceptional circumstances in relation to that condition; and

(c)   fulfils the requirement under Article 5(2).

3.   If the negotiated agreement fulfils the conditions and requirements referred to in paragraph 2, the Commission shall, within 90 days of receipt of the notification referred to in paragraph 1, give a reasoned decision on the application of the Member State authorising it to conclude that agreement.

Article 9. Refusal to authorise the conclusion of the agreement.   1.   If, on the basis of its assessment under Article 8(2), the Commission intends not to authorise the conclusion of the negotiated agreement, it shall give an opinion to the Member State concerned, as well as to the European Parliament and to the Council, within 90 days of receipt of the notification referred to in Article 8(1).

2.   Within 30 days of receipt of the opinion of the Commission, the Member State concerned may request the Commission to enter into discussions with it with a view to finding a solution.

3.   If the Member State concerned does not request the Commission to enter into discussions with it within the time limit provided for in paragraph 2, the Commission shall give a reasoned decision on the application of the Member State within 130 days of receipt of the notification referred to in Article 8(1).

4.   In the event of the discussions referred to in paragraph 2, the Commission shall give a reasoned decision on the application of the Member State within 30 days of the closure of the discussions.

5.   The Commission shall notify its decision to the European Parliament and to the Council within 30 days of the decision.

Article 10. Confidentiality. — When providing information to the Commission under Articles 3, 4(3) and 8, the Member State may indicate whether any of the information is to be regarded as confidential and whether the information provided can be shared with other Member States.

Article 11. Provision of information to the Member States. — The Commission shall send to the Member States the notifications received under Articles 3 and 8 and, if necessary, the accompanying documents, as well as all its reasoned decisions under Articles 5, 6, 8 and 9, subject to the confidentiality requirements.

Article 12. Transitional provisions.   1.   Where, at the time of entry into force of this Regulation, a Member State has already started the process of negotiating an agreement with a third country, Articles 3–11 shall apply.
Where the stage of the negotiations so permits, the Commission may propose negotiating guidelines or request the inclusion of particular clauses, as referred to in the second subparagraph of Article 5(1) and Article 5(2) respectively.
2.   Where, at the time of entry into force of this Regulation, a Member State has already completed the negotiations but has not yet concluded the agreement, Article 3, Article 8(2) to (4) and Article 9 shall apply.

Article 13. Review.   1.   No earlier than 13 July 2017 the Commission shall submit to the European Parliament, the Council and the European Economic and Social Committee a report on the application of this Regulation.
2.   That report shall either:
(a)   confirm that it is appropriate for this Regulation to expire on the date determined in accordance with Article 14(1); or
(b)   recommend that this Regulation be replaced as of that date by a new Regulation.
3.   If the report recommends a replacement of this Regulation as referred to in paragraph 2(b), it shall be accompanied by an appropriate legislative proposal.

Article 14. Expiry.   1.   This Regulation shall expire three years after the submission by the Commission of the report referred to in Article 13.
The period of three years referred to in the first subparagraph shall start to run on the first day of the month following the submission of the report to either the European Parliament or the Council, whichever is the later.
2.   Notwithstanding the expiry of this Regulation on the date determined in accordance with paragraph 1, all negotiations ongoing on that date which have been entered into by a Member State under this Regulation shall be allowed to continue and to be completed in accordance with this Regulation.

Article 15. Entry into force.   This Regulation shall enter into force on the 20th day following its publication in the Official Journal of the European Union.

L. Council Regulation (EC) No 664/2009 of 7 July 2009 establishing a procedure for the negotiation and conclusion of agreements between Member States and third countries concerning jurisdiction, recognition and enforcement of judgments and decisions in matrimonial matters, matters of parental responsibility and matters relating to maintenance obligations, and the law applicable to matters relating to maintenance obligations (OJ, L 200 of 31 July 2009)

(1) Title IV of Part Three of the Treaty provides the legal basis for the adoption of Community legislation in the field of judicial cooperation in civil matters.

(2) Judicial cooperation in civil matters between Member States and third countries has traditionally been governed by agreements between Member States and third countries. Such agreements, of which there is a large number, often reflect special ties between a Member State and a third country and are intended to provide an adequate legal framework to meet specific needs of the parties concerned.

(3) Article 307 of the Treaty requires Member States to take all appropriate steps to eliminate any incompatibilities between the Community acquis and international agreements concluded between Member States and third countries. This may involve the need for the renegotiation of such agreements.

(4) In order to provide an adequate legal framework to meet specific needs of a given Member State in its relations with a third country, there may also be a manifest need for the conclusion of new agreements with third countries relating to areas of civil justice that come within the purview of Title IV of Part Three of the Treaty.

(5) In its Opinion 1/03 of 7 February 2006 relating to the conclusion of the new Lugano Convention, the Court of Justice of the European Communities confirmed that the Community has acquired exclusive competence to conclude an international agreement like the Lugano Convention with third countries on matters affecting the rules laid down in Council Regulation (EC) No 44/2001 of 22 December 2000 on jurisdiction and the recognition and enforcement of judgments in civil and commercial matters (Brussels I).

(6) It is for the Community to conclude, pursuant to Article 300 of the Treaty, agreements between the Community and a third country on matters falling within the exclusive competence of the Community.

(7) Article 10 of the Treaty requires Member States to facilitate the achievement of the Community's tasks and to abstain from any measure which could jeopardise the attainment of the objectives of the Treaty. This duty of loyal cooperation is of general application and does not depend on whether or not the Community competence is exclusive.

(8) With regard to agreements with third countries on specific civil justice issues falling within the exclusive competence of the Community, a coherent and transparent procedure should be established to authorise a Member State to amend an existing agreement or to negotiate and conclude a new agreement, in particular where the Community itself has not indicated its intention to exercise its external competence to conclude an agreement by way of an already existing mandate of negotiation or an envisaged mandate of negotiation. This procedure should be without prejudice to the exclusive competence of the Community and the provisions of Articles 300 and 307 of the

Treaty. It should be regarded as an exceptional measure and should be limited in scope and in time.

(9) This Regulation should not apply if the Community has already concluded an agreement with the third country concerned on the same subject-matter. Two agreements should be regarded as concerning the same subject-matter only if, and to the extent that, they regulate in substance the same specific legal issues. Provisions simply stating a general intention to cooperate on such issues should not be regarded as concerning the same subject-matter.

(10) Certain regional agreements referred to in existing Community legal acts should also be covered by this Regulation.

(11) In order to ensure that an agreement envisaged by a Member State does not render Community law ineffective and does not undermine the proper functioning of the system established by that law, or undermine the Community's external relations policy as decided by the Community, the Member State concerned should be required to notify the Commission of its intentions with a view to obtaining an authorisation to open or continue formal negotiations on an agreement as well as to conclude an agreement. Such a notification should be given by letter or by electronic means. It should contain all relevant information and documentation enabling the Commission to assess the expected impact on Community law of the outcome of the negotiations.

(12) It should be assessed whether there is sufficient Community interest in concluding a bilateral agreement between the Community and the third country concerned or, where appropriate, in replacing an existing bilateral agreement between a Member State and a third country with a Community agreement. To that end, all Member States should be informed of any notification received by the Commission concerning an agreement envisaged by a Member State in order to allow them to demonstrate their interest in joining the initiative of the notifying Member State. If, from this exchange of information, a sufficient Community interest were to emerge, the Commission should consider proposing a negotiating mandate with a view to the conclusion of an agreement between the Community and the third country concerned.

(13) If the Commission requests additional information from a Member State in connection with its assessment as to whether that Member State should be authorised to open negotiations with a third country, such a request should not affect the time-limits within which the Commission is to give a reasoned decision on the application of that Member State.

(14) When authorising the opening of formal negotiations, the Commission should be able, if necessary, to propose negotiating guidelines or request the inclusion of particular clauses in the envisaged agreement. The Commission should be kept fully informed throughout the different stages of the negotiations as far as matters falling within the scope of this Regulation are concerned and should be allowed to participate as an observer in the negotiations as regards those matters.

(15) When notifying the Commission of their intention to enter into negotiations with a third country, Member States should only be required to inform the Commission of elements which are of relevance for the assessment to be made by the Commission. The authorisation by the Commission and any possible negotiating guidelines or, as the case may be, the refusal by the Commission should concern only matters falling within the scope of this Regulation.

(16)   All Member States should be informed of any notification to the Commission concerning envisaged or negotiated agreements and of any reasoned decision by the Commission under this Regulation. Such information should however fully comply with possible confidentiality requirements.

(17)   The European Parliament, the Council and the Commission should ensure that any information identified as confidential is treated in accordance with Regulation (EC) No 1049/2001 of the European Parliament and of the Council of 30 May 2001 regarding public access to European Parliament, Council and Commission documents.

(18)   Where the Commission, on the basis of its assessment, intends not to authorise the opening of formal negotiations or the conclusion of a negotiated agreement, it should, before giving its reasoned decision, give an opinion to the Member State concerned. In the case of refusal to authorise the conclusion of a negotiated agreement the opinion should also be submitted to the European Parliament and to the Council.

(19)   In order to ensure that the negotiated agreement does not constitute an obstacle to the implementation of the Community's external policy on judicial cooperation in civil and commercial matters, the agreement should provide either for its full or partial denunciation in the event of the conclusion of a subsequent agreement between the Community or the Community and its Member States, on the one hand, and the same third country, on the other hand, on the same subject-matter, or a direct replacement of the relevant provisions of the agreement by the provisions of such subsequent agreement.

(20)   Provision should be made for transitional measures to cover situations where, at the time of the entry into force of this Regulation, a Member State has already started the process of negotiating an agreement with a third country, or has completed the negotiations but has not yet expressed its consent to be bound by the agreement.

(21)   In order to ensure that sufficient experience has been gained concerning the application of this Regulation, the Commission should submit a report on such application no earlier than eight years after the adoption of this Regulation. In that report, the Commission, exercising its prerogatives, should confirm the temporary nature of this Regulation or examine whether this Regulation should be replaced by a new Regulation covering the same subject-matter or including also other matters falling within the exclusive competence of the Community and governed by other Community instruments.

(22)   If the report submitted by the Commission confirms the temporary nature of this Regulation, Member States should still be able, after the submission of the report, to notify the Commission of ongoing or already announced negotiations with a view to obtaining an authorisation to open formal negotiations.

(23)   In accordance with the principle of proportionality, as set out in Article 5 of the Treaty, this Regulation does not go beyond what is necessary in order to achieve its objective.

(24)   In accordance with Article 3 of the Protocol on the position of the United Kingdom and Ireland, annexed to the Treaty on European Union and to the Treaty establishing the European Community, the United Kingdom and Ireland have given notice of their wish to take part in the adoption and application of this Regulation.

(25)   In accordance with Articles 1 and 2 of the Protocol on the position of Denmark, annexed to the Treaty on European Union and to the Treaty establishing the European Community, Denmark is not taking part in the adoption of this Regulation and is not bound by it or subject to its application...

Article 1. Subject-matter and scope.   1.   This Regulation establishes a procedure to authorise a Member State to amend an existing agreement or to negotiate and conclude a new agreement with a third country, subject to the conditions laid down in this Regulation.

This procedure is without prejudice to the respective competencies of the Community and of the Member States.

2.   This Regulation shall apply to agreements concerning matters falling, entirely or partly, within the scope of Council Regulation (EC) No 2201/2003 of 27 November 2003 concerning jurisdiction and the recognition and enforcement of judgments in matrimonial matters and the matters of parental responsibility and Council Regulation (EC) No 4/2009 of 18 December 2008 on jurisdiction, applicable law, recognition and enforcement of decisions and cooperation in matters relating to maintenance obligations, to the extent that those matters fall within the exclusive competence of the Community.

3.   This Regulation shall not apply if the Community has already concluded an agreement with the third country concerned on the same subject-matter.

Article 2. Definitions.   1.   For the purposes of this Regulation, the term 'agreement' shall mean:

(a)   a bilateral agreement between a Member State and a third country;

(b)   the regional agreements referred to in Article 59(2)(a) of Regulation (EC) No 2201/2003, without prejudice to Article 59(2)(c) and Article 59(3) of that Regulation, and in Article 69(3) of Regulation (EC) No 4/2009.

2.   In the context of regional agreements as referred to in paragraph 1(b), any reference in this Regulation to a Member State or a third country shall be read as referring to the Member States or the third countries concerned, respectively.

Article 3. Notification to the Commission.   1.   Where a Member State intends to enter into negotiations in order to amend an existing agreement or to conclude a new agreement falling within the scope of this Regulation, it shall notify the Commission in writing of its intention at the earliest possible moment before the envisaged opening of formal negotiations.

2.   The notification shall include, as appropriate, a copy of the existing agreement, the draft agreement or the draft proposal, and any other relevant documentation. The Member State shall describe the subject-matter of the negotiations and specify the issues which are to be addressed in the envisaged agreement, or the provisions of the existing agreement which are to be amended. The Member State may provide any other additional information.

Article 4. Assessment by the Commission.   1.   Upon receipt of the notification referred to in Article 3, the Commission shall assess whether the Member State may open formal negotiations.

2.   In making that assessment, the Commission shall first check whether any relevant negotiating mandate with a view to concluding a Community agreement with the third country concerned is specifically envisaged within the next 24 months. If this is not the case, the Commission shall assess whether all of the following conditions are met:

(a) the Member State concerned has provided information showing that it has a specific interest in concluding the agreement due to economic, geographic, cultural, historical, social or political ties between the Member State and the third country concerned;

(b) on the basis of the information provided by the Member State, the envisaged agreement appears not to render Community law ineffective and not to undermine the proper functioning of the system established by that law; and

(c) the envisaged agreement would not undermine the object and purpose of the Community's external relations policy as decided by the Community.

3. If the information provided by the Member State is not sufficient for the purposes of the assessment, the Commission may request additional information.

Article 5. Authorisation to open formal negotiations.   1. If the envisaged agreement meets the conditions set out in Article 4(2), the Commission shall, within 90 days of receipt of the notification referred to in Article 3, give a reasoned decision on the application of the Member State authorising it to open formal negotiations on that agreement.

If necessary, the Commission may propose negotiating guidelines and may request the inclusion of particular clauses in the envisaged agreement.

2. The envisaged agreement shall contain a clause providing for either:

(a) full or partial denunciation of the agreement in the event of the conclusion of a subsequent agreement between the Community or the Community and its Member States, on the one hand, and the same third country, on the other hand, on the same subject-matter; or

(b) direct replacement of the relevant provisions of the agreement by the provisions of a subsequent agreement concluded between the Community or the Community and its Member States, on the one hand, and the same third country, on the other hand, on the same subject-matter.

The clause referred to in point (a) of the first subparagraph should be worded along the following lines: '(name(s) of the Member State(s)) shall denounce this Agreement, in part or in full, if and when the European Community or the European Community and its Member States conclude an Agreement with (name(s) of the third country(ies)) on the same matters of civil justice as those governed by this Agreement'.

The clause referred to in point (b) of the first subparagraph should be worded along the following lines: 'This Agreement or certain provisions of this Agreement shall cease to be applicable on the day when an Agreement between the European Community or the European Community and its Member States, on the one hand, and (name(s) of the third country(ies)), on the other hand, has entered into force, in respect of the matters governed by the latter Agreement'.

Article 6. Refusal to authorise the opening of formal negotiations.   1. If, on the basis of its assessment under Article 4, the Commission intends not to authorise the opening of formal negotiations on the envisaged agreement, it shall give an opinion to the Member State concerned within 90 days of receipt of the notification referred to in Article 3.

2. Within 30 days of receipt of the opinion of the Commission, the Member State concerned may request the Commission to enter into discussions with it with a view to finding a solution.

3.   If the Member State concerned does not request the Commission to enter into discussions with it within the time-limit provided for in paragraph 2, the Commission shall give a reasoned decision on the application of the Member State within 130 days of receipt of the notification referred to in Article 3.

4.   In the event of the discussions referred to in paragraph 2, the Commission shall give a reasoned decision on the application of the Member State within 30 days of the closure of the discussions.

Article 7. Participation of the Commission in the negotiations.   The Commission may participate as an observer in the negotiations between the Member State and the third country as far as matters falling within the scope of this Regulation are concerned. If the Commission does not participate as an observer, it shall be kept informed of the progress and results throughout the different stages of the negotiations.

Article 8. Authorisation to conclude the agreement   1.   Before signing a negotiated agreement, the Member State concerned shall notify the outcome of the negotiations to the Commission and shall transmit to it the text of the agreement.

2.   Upon receipt of that notification the Commission shall assess whether the negotiated agreement:

(a)   meets the condition set out in Article 4(2)(b);

(b)   meets the condition set out in Article 4(2)(c), in so far as there are new and exceptional circumstances in relation to that condition; and

(c)   fulfils the requirement under Article 5(2).

3.   If the negotiated agreement fulfils the conditions and requirements referred to in paragraph 2, the Commission shall, within 90 days of receipt of the notification referred to in paragraph 1, give a reasoned decision on the application of the Member State authorising it to conclude that agreement.

Article 9. Refusal to authorise the conclusion of the agreement   1.   If, on the basis of its assessment under Article 8(2), the Commission intends not to authorise the conclusion of the negotiated agreement, it shall give an opinion to the Member State concerned, as well as to the European Parliament and to the Council, within 90 days of receipt of the notification referred to in Article 8(1).

2.   Within 30 days of receipt of the opinion of the Commission, the Member State concerned may request the Commission to enter into discussions with it with a view to finding a solution.

3.   If the Member State concerned does not request the Commission to enter into discussions with it within the time limit provided for in paragraph 2, the Commission shall give a reasoned decision on the application of the Member State within 130 days of receipt of the notification referred to in Article 8(1).

4.   In the event of the discussions referred to in paragraph 2, the Commission shall give a reasoned decision on the application of the Member State within 30 days of the closure of the discussions.

5.   The Commission shall notify its decision to the European Parliament and to the Council within 30 days of the decision.

Article 10. Confidentiality.   When providing information to the Commission under Articles 3, 4(3) and 8, the Member State may indicate whether any of the information is to be regarded as confidential and whether the information provided can be shared with other Member States.

Article 11. Provision of information to the Member States.   The Commission shall send to the Member States the notifications received under Articles 3 and 8 and, if necessary, the accompanying documents, as well as all its reasoned decisions under Articles 5, 6, 8 and 9, subject to the confidentiality requirements.

Article 12. Transitional provisions   1.   Where, at the time of entry into force of this Regulation, a Member State has already started the process of negotiating an agreement with a third country, Articles 3 to 11 shall apply.

Where the stage of the negotiations so permits, the Commission may propose negotiating guidelines or request the inclusion of particular clauses, as referred to in the second subparagraph of Article 5(1) and Article 5(2) respectively.

2.   Where, at the time of entry into force of this Regulation, a Member State has already completed the negotiations but has not yet concluded the agreement, Article 3, Article 8(2) to (4) and Article 9 shall apply.

Article 13. Review   1.   No earlier than 13 July 2017 the Commission shall submit to the European Parliament, the Council and the European Economic and Social Committee a report on the application of this Regulation.

2.   That report shall either:

(a)   Confirm that it is appropriate for this Regulation to expire on the date determined in accordance with Article 14(1); or

(b)   recommend that this Regulation be replaced as of that date by a new Regulation.

3.   If the report recommends a replacement of this Regulation as referred to in paragraph 2(b), it shall be accompanied by an appropriate legislative proposal.

Article 14. Expiry   1.   This Regulation shall expire three years after the submission by the Commission of the report referred to in Article 13.

The period of three years referred to in the first subparagraph shall start to run on the first day of the month following the submission of the report to either the European Parliament or the Council, whichever is the later.

2.   Notwithstanding the expiry of this Regulation on the date determined in accordance with paragraph 1, all negotiations ongoing on that date which have been entered into by a Member State under this Regulation shall be allowed to continue and to be completed in accordance with this Regulation.

Article 15. Entry into force.   This Regulation shall enter into force on the 20th day following its publication in the Official Journal of the European Union.

M.   The Stockholm Programme — An open and secure Europe serving and protecting the citizens, adopted by the European Council on 10–11 December 2009 (Doc. Consilium No 17024/09): Part 7

See this Chapter, General provisions, F.

N.1.   Proposal for a Council Decision on the Conclusion by the European Community of the Agreement on the Accession of the European Community to the Convention concerning International Carriage by Rail (COTIF) of 9 May 1980, as amended by the Vilnius Protocol of 3 June 1999 (COM (2009) 441 of 31 August 2009)

(1)   The development of rail interoperability, both within the Community and between the Community and neighbouring countries, is a key component of the transport policy, targeted in particular at establishing a better balance between the various modes of transport.

(2)   The European Community has exclusive competence or shared competence with its Member States in the areas covered by the Convention concerning International Carriage by Rail (COTIF) of 9 May 1980, as amended by the Vilnius Protocol of 3 June 1999, hereinafter referred to as 'COTIF'.

(3)   The European Community's accession to COTIF for the purpose of exercising its competence is permitted by virtue of Article 38 of the COTIF as amended by the Vilnius Protocol.

(4)   On behalf of the Community, the Commission has negotiated an Agreement on the Accession of the European Community to COTIF with the Contracting Parties to COTIF.

(5)   The resolution of a number of conflicts between the provisions of certain Appendices of COTIF and Community law still pending, the European Community should, in connection with its accession to COTIF, make a declaration according to Article 42 of COTIF regarding the non-application of Appendices E, F and G of COTIF....

Article 1.   1.   The Agreement on the Accession of the European Community to the Convention concerning International Carriage by Rail (COTIF) of 9 May 1980, as amended by the Vilnius Protocol of 3 June 1999, is hereby approved on behalf of the Community, subject to the following conditions:

upon accession a declaration shall be made by the Community concerning the exercise of its competence,

upon accession a declaration shall be made by the Community concerning the non-application of Appendices E, F and G of COTIF.

2.   The text of the Agreement and the declarations referred to in paragraph 1 are attached as Annexes to this Decision.

Article 2. The President of the Council is hereby authorised to designate the person empowered to sign the Agreement in order to express the Community's consent to be bound thereby, to make the related declarations and to deposit the instrument of approval on the Community's behalf.

N.2. Agreement on the accession of the European Community to the Convention concerning International Carriage by Rail (COTIF) of 9 May 1980, as amended by the Vilnius Protocol of 3 June 1999

The Intergovernmental Organisation for International Carriage by Rail and the European Community,

Having regard to the Convention concerning International Carriage by Rail (COTIF) of 9 May 1980, as amended by the Vilnius Protocol of 3 June 1999, hereinafter referred to as 'the Convention', and in particular Article 38 of the said Convention,

Having regard to the responsibilities which the Treaty establishing the European Community confers on the European Community in certain areas covered by the Convention,

Whereas the Convention establishes an Intergovernmental Organisation for International Carriage by Rail (OTIF), the headquarters of which are at Bern;

Whereas the purpose of the European Community's accession to the Convention is to assist OTIF in pursuing its objective of promoting, improving and facilitating international rail transport in both technical and legal respects;

Whereas by virtue of Article 3 of the Convention, the obligations arising out of the Convention with regard to international cooperation do not take precedence, for Member States which are also Members of the European Communities or States party to the Agreement on the European Economic Area, over their obligations as Members of the European Communities or States party to the Agreement on the European Economic Area;

Whereas a disconnection clause is necessary for those parts of the Convention which fall within the competence of the European Community, in order to indicate that European Community Member States cannot invoke and apply the rights and obligations deriving from the Convention directly among themselves;

Whereas the Convention applies fully between the European Community and its Member States on the one hand, and the other Parties to the Convention, on the other;

Whereas the European Community's accession to the Convention requires the rules for applying the provisions of the Convention to the European Community and its Member States to be clearly established;

Whereas the conditions of the European Community's accession to the Convention must allow the Community to exercise within the Convention the competences conferred on it by its Member States,

Have agreed as follows:

Article 1. The European Community hereby accedes to the Convention under the terms and conditions laid down in this Agreement, in accordance with Article 38 of the Convention.

Article 2. Contracting Parties to the Convention which are Members of the European Community will, in their mutual relations, apply Community rules in so far as there are Community rules governing the particular subject concerned and applicable to the specific case, without prejudice to the object and purpose of the Convention and without prejudice to its full application with other Contracting Parties to the Convention.

Article 3. Subject to the provisions of this Agreement, provisions in the Convention shall be so interpreted as also to include the European Community, within the framework of its competence, and the various terms used to designate the Contracting Parties to the Convention and their representatives are to be understood accordingly.

Article 4. The European Community shall not contribute to the budget of OTIF and shall not take part in decisions concerning that budget.

Article 5. 1. Without prejudice to the exercise of its voting rights under Article 6, the European Community shall be entitled to be represented and involved in the work of all OTIF bodies in which any of its Member States is entitled to be represented as a Contracting Party, and where matters falling within its competence may be dealt with.
The European Community may not be a member of the Administrative Committee. It may be invited to participate in meetings of this Committee when the Committee wishes to consult it on matters of common interest that have been placed on the agenda.
2. The European Community will be represented by the European Commission. The European Commission may mandate one or more of the Member States of the Community to represent it.

Article 6. 1. For decisions in matters where the European Community has exclusive competence, the European Community will exercise the voting rights of its Member States under the Convention.
2. For decisions in matters where the European Community shares competence with its Member States, either the European Community or its Member States shall vote.
3. Subject to Article 26 paragraph 7 of the Convention, the European Community shall have a number of votes equal to that of its Members who are also Member States of OTIF. When the European Community votes, its Member States shall not vote.
4. The European Community shall, on a case-by-case basis, inform the other Contracting Parties to the Convention of the cases where, with regard to the various items on the agendas of the General Assembly and the other deliberating bodies, it will exercise the voting rights provided for in paragraphs 1 to 3 above. This obligation shall also apply when decisions are taken by correspondence. This information is to be provided early enough to the OTIF Secretary-General in order to allow its circulation together with meeting documents or a decision to be taken by correspondence.

Article 7. The scope of the competence of the Community shall be indicated in general terms in a written declaration made by the European Community at the time of the conclusion of this Agreement. This declaration may be modified as appropriate by notification from the European Community to OTIF. It shall not replace or in any way limit the matters that may be covered by the notifications of Community competence to be made prior to OTIF decision-making by means of formal voting or otherwise.

Article 8. Title V of the Convention shall apply to any dispute arising between the Contracting Parties to the present Accession Agreement in respect of the interpretation, application or implementation of this Agreement, including its existence, validity and termination.

Article 9. This Agreement shall enter into force on the first day of the first month following the signature of the agreement by the Contracting Parties. Article 34 paragraph 2 of the Convention shall not apply in this case.

Article 10. This Agreement shall remain in force for an indefinite period.

If all OTIF Member States which are Members of the European Community denounce the Convention, the notification of that denunciation, as well as of the denunciation of this Agreement, shall be considered to have been given by the European Community at the same time as the last Member State of the European Community to denounce the Convention notifies its denunciation under Article 41 of the Convention.

Article 11. Contracting Parties to the Convention other than Member States of the European Community which apply relevant European Community legislation as a result of their international agreements with the European Community may, with the acknowledgement of the Depositary of the Convention, enter individual declarations with regard to the preservation of their rights and obligations under their agreements with the European Community, COTIF and related regulations.

In witness whereof the undersigned Plenipotentiaries, having presented their Full Powers, found to be in due and proper form, have signed this Agreement.

N.3. Declaration by the European Community concerning the exercise of competence

In the rail sector, the European Community shares the competence with the Member States pursuant to Articles 70, 71, 80(1) and 156 of the EC Treaty.

Title V of the EC Treaty establishes the European Community's common transport policy and Title XV provides for the European Community's contribution to the establishment of and development of trans-European networks in the areas of transport.

More specifically, Article 71 of Title V of the EC Treaty provides that the European Community may adopt:

common rules applicable to international transport to or from the territory of a Member State or passing across the territory of one or more Member States;

the conditions under which non-resident carriers may operate transport services within a Member State;

measures to improve transport safety;

any other appropriate provisions.

With regard to Trans-European Networks, Article 155 of Title XV of the EC Treaty provides, more specifically, that the European Community:

shall establish a series of guidelines covering the objectives, priorities and broad lines of measures envisaged in the sphere of trans-European networks; these guidelines shall identify projects of common interest;

shall implement any measures that may prove necessary to ensure the interoperability of the networks, in particular in the field of technical standardisation;

may support projects of common interest supported by Member States, which are identified the framework of the guidelines referred to in the first indent, particularly through feasibility studies, loan guarantees or interest-rate subsidies; the Community may also contribute, through the Cohesion Fund, to the financing of specific projects in Member States in the area of transport infrastructure.

On the basis of these two provisions the European Community has adopted a substantial number of legal instruments applicable to rail transport.

Under European Community law, the European Community has acquired exclusive competence in matters of rail transport where the Convention concerning International Carriage by Rail (COTIF) of 9 May 1980, as amended by the Vilnius Protocol of 3 June 1999, hereinafter referred to as 'the Convention', or legal instruments adopted pursuant to it affect these existing Community rules.

For subject matters governed by the Convention in relation to which the European Community has exclusive competence, Member States of the European Community have no competence.

Where Community rules exist but are not affected by the Convention or legal instruments adopted pursuant to it, the European Community shares the competence on matters in relation to the Convention with Member States.

A list of the relevant Community instruments at the time of this agreement is contained in the Appendix. The scope of the Community competence arising out of these texts has to be assessed in relation to the specific provisions of each text, especially the extent to which these provisions establish common rules. Community competence is subject to continuous development. In the framework of the Treaty, the competent institutions may take decisions which determine the extent of the competence of the European Community. The European Community therefore reserves the right to amend this declaration accordingly, without this constituting a prerequisite for the exercise of its competence in matters covered by the Convention.

Appendix.   Community instruments relating to subjects dealt with by the Convention

To date, the Community has exercised its competence inter alia through the following Community instruments

Economic / Market Access Legislation

Regulation No 11, concerning the abolition of discrimination in transport rates and conditions, in implementation of Article 79(3) of the Treaty establishing the European Economic Community (OJ L532, 16.8.1960, p. 1121);

Council Directive 91/440/EEC of 29 July 1991 on the development of the Community's railways (OJ L237, 24.8.1991, p. 25);

Council Directive 95/18/EC of 19 June 1995 on the licensing of railway undertakings (OJ L143, 27.6.1995, p. 70);

Directive 2001/12/EC of the European Parliament and of the Council of 26 February 2001 on the development of the Community's railways (OJ L75, 15.3.2001, p. 1);

Directive 2001/13/EC of the European Parliament and of the Council of 26 February 2001 on the licensing of railway undertakings (OJ L75, 15.3.2001, p. 26);

Directive 2001/14/EC of the European Parliament and of the Council of 26 February 2001 on the allocation of railway infrastructure capacity and the levying of charges for the use of railway infrastructure and safety certification (OJ L75, 15.3.2001, p. 29);

Directive 2004/51/EC of the European Parliament and of the Council of 29 April 2004 amending Council Directive 91/440/EEC on the development of the Community's railways (OJ L164, 30.4.2004, p. 164–172 and OJ L220, 21.6.2004, p. 58–60);

Regulation (EC) No 1371/2007 of the European Parliament and of the Council of 23 October 2007 on rail passengers' rights and obligations (OJ L315, 3.12.2007, p. 14);

Directive 2007/58/EC of the European Parliament and of the Council of 23 October 2007 amending Council Directive 91/440/EEC on the development of the Community's railways and Directive 2001/14/EC on the allocation of railway infrastructure capacity and the levying of charges for the use of railway infrastructure (OJ L315, 3.12.2007, p. 44).

Interoperability and Safety Legislation

Council Directive 96/48/EC of 23 July 1996 on the interoperability of the trans-European high-speed rail system (OJ L235, 17.9.1996, p. 6);

Directive 2001/16/EC of the European Parliament and of the Council of 19 March 2001 on the interoperability of the trans-European conventional rail system (OJ L110, 20.4.2001, p. 1);

Council Directive 96/49/EC of 23 July 1996 on the approximation of the laws of the Member States with regard to the transport of dangerous goods by rail (OJ L235, 17.9.1996, p. 25);

Directive 2004/49/EC of the European Parliament and of the Council of 29 April 2004 on safety on the Community's railways and amending Council Directive 95/18/EC on the licensing of railway undertakings and Directive 2001/14/EC on the allocation of railway infrastructure capacity and the levying of charges for the use of railway infrastructure and safety certification (OJ L164, 30.4.2004, p 44–113 and OJ L220, 21.6.2004, p. 16–39);

Directive 2004/50/EC of the European Parliament and of the Council of 29 April 2004 amending Council Directive 96/48/EC on the interoperability of the trans-European high-speed rail system and Directive 2001/16/EC of the European Parliament and of the Council on the interoperability of the trans-European conventional rail system (OJ L164, 30.4.2004, p. 114–163 and OJ L220, 21.6.2004, p. 40–57);

Regulation (EC) No 881/2004 of the European Parliament and of the Council of 29 April 2004 establishing a European Railway Agency (OJL164, 30.4.2004, p. 1–43 and OJ L220, 21.6.2006, p. 3–14);

Directive 2007/59/EC of the European Parliament and of the Council of 23 October 2007 on the certification of train drivers operating locomotives and trains on the railway system in the Community (OJ L315, 3.12.2007, p. 51);

Directive 2008/57/EC of the European Parliament and of the Council of 17 June 2008 on the interoperability of the rail system within the Community (Recast) (OJ L191, 18.7.2008, p. 1);

Directive 2008/68/EC of the European Parliament and of the Council of 24 September 2008 on the inland transport of Dangerous Goods (OJ L260, 30.9.2008, p. 13);

Directive 2008/110/EC of the European Parliament and of the Council of 16 December 2008 amending Directive 2004/49/EC on safety on the Community's railways (Railway Safety Directive) (OJ L345, 23.12.2008, p. 62);

Regulation (EC) No 1335/2008 of the European Parliament and of the Council of 16 December 2008 amending Regulation (EC) No 881/2004 establishing a European Railway Agency (Agency Regulation) (OJ L354, 31.12.2008, p. 51).

Public Service Obligations

Regulation (EC) No 1370/2007 of the European Parliament and of the Council of 23 October 2007 on public passenger transport services by rail and by road and repealing Council Regulations (EEC) Nos 1191/69 and 1107/70 (OJ L315, 3.12.2007, p. 1).

N.4. Declaration by the European Community in accordance with Article 42 of COTIF

Pending the resolution of certain legal inconsistencies between Community legislation and certain rules of COTIF, the following appendices of COTIF will not be applied in their entirety by the European Community:

1.   The Uniform Rules concerning the Contract of Use of Infrastructure in International Rail Traffic (CUI — Appendix E to the Convention).

2.   The Uniform Rules concerning the Validation of Technical Standards and the Adoption of Uniform Technical Prescriptions applicable to Railway Material intended to be used in International Traffic (APTU — Appendix F to the Convention).

3.   The Uniform Rules concerning the Technical Admission of Railway Material used in International Traffic (ATMF — Appendix G to the Convention).

N.5. Internal Arrangements between the Council, the Member States and the Commission for the participation of the Community and its Member States in meetings held under the Convention concerning International Carriage by Rail 1999

Bearing in mind the requirement of unity of the international representation of the European Community and its Member States in accordance with the EC Treaty and the case law of the European Court of Justice also at the stage of implementation of international obligations;

The Council, the Member States and the Commission agree on the following internal arrangements:

1.   Nature and scope

1.1. This document sets out the internal arrangements between the Council, the Member States and the Commission in preparation for the meetings held under the Convention concerning international carriage by rail 1999, (hereinafter 'the Convention'). These internal arrangements will apply to all meetings organised by the Intergovernmental Organisation for International Carriage by Rail (OTIF) in respect of the application of the Convention.

2.   Division of tasks based on competence

2.1. On rail transport matters falling within the competence of Member States, the Presidency will convene on its own initiative or at the request of the Commission or a Member State coordination meetings of EU Member States' delegations before, during and after each meeting referred to in paragraph 1, aiming at elaborating coordinated positions. The Presidency will express these coordinated positions.

2.2. The Commission will express, on behalf of the Community, Community positions on matters falling within Community competence, in particular in relation to:

— Article 71 of Title V of the EC Treaty

— Article 155 of Title XV of the EC Treaty

— Any other matters falling exclusively or primarily within Community competence under Title V or XV of the EC Treaty,

— And in particular the Community instruments relating to subject matters dealt with by the Convention and detailed in the Appendix to Annex 2 of the Agreement on accession of the European Community to the Convention.

2.3. The Presidency and the Commission will agree on which of them will deliver any statement to be made on behalf of the Community and its Member States in cases where the respective competencies are inextricably linked. The Commission will present the common position when the preponderance of the matter concerned lies within the competence of the Community, and the Presidency will present the common position when the preponderance of the matter concerned lies within the competence of the Member States.

3.   Establishment of positions and coordination procedure

3.1. All positions of the Community and its Member States in OTIF meetings will be duly coordinated.

In matters falling under their competence Member States will aim at elaborating coordinated positions. Draft Statements on positions will be circulated among Member States beforehand.

Commission proposals for Community positions and for common positions between the Community and its Member States will be discussed in the appropriate Committee created by the relevant Community rail directives, namely,

— the Committee on the transport of dangerous goods for items covered by Appendix RID to the Convention; if these items affect rail interoperability, or the common safety approach developed under Directive 2004/49/EC, the Community position to be taken should be made in coordination with the Committee on rail interoperability and safety;

— the Committee on the development of the Community's railways for items covered by Appendices CIV, CIM, CUV, CUI to the Convention and for other systems of uniform law elaborated by the OTIF;

— the Committee on rail interoperability and safety for items covered by Appendices APTU and ATMF to the Convention;

The Commission and Member States will use their best endeavours in on the spot coordination meetings to establish an agreed position.

3.2. As far as work on the transport of dangerous goods is concerned, the European Community shall be represented on the RID Expert Committee by the European Commission, assisted for reasons of technical expertise, by experts from the Member States and / or the European Rail Agency or as the case may be, shall mandate Member States to represent it.

3.3. The Commission will notify the relevant committee of the items on each OTIF meeting agenda it deems requiring representations on behalf of the Community or the Community and its Member States.

3.4. If a vote is to be held on items on the agenda, the Commission will give its opinion as to whether the Community or the individual Member States should vote.

3.5. The exercise of responsibilities and arrangements in respect of representations and voting in relation to each item on the agenda that falls under exclusive Community competence will be decided in coordination meetings held by the committees detailed in paragraph 3.1.

3.6. If necessary, coordination meetings may also be held at the meeting venue.

4.   Speaking

4.1. In cases where the Presidency is not represented in meetings referred to in paragraph 1, the position of the Community and its Member States reached in the coordination process on matters covered by paragraph 2.1 and, as appropriate, in paragraph 2.3, is presented by the delegate of the Member State represented which comes first in the list of rotation for the EU Presidency.

5.   Voting

5.1. The Commission, on behalf of the European Community, will exercise the Community's voting rights on the basis of Community or common positions reached in the coordination process on matters referred to in paragraph 2.2, and, as appropriate, in paragraph 2.3.

It may be agreed that in cases where the Community is not represented by the Commission, the Presidency will exercise voting rights of the Community on those matters, on the basis of common positions.

5.2. The Member States will exercise their voting rights only on matters referred to in paragraph 2.1, and, as appropriate, in paragraph 2.3 on the basis of coordinated or common positions reached in the coordination process.

6.   Speaking and Voting in Cases of Disagreement

6.1. Where matters being discussed in any of the three committees detailed in paragraph 3.1 to above remain outstanding, those matters will be referred to the Permanent Representatives' Committee, without undue delay. In cases where the Commission and the Member States do not find an agreement on the matters, the Member States and the Commission will refrain from taking any position or casting any vote in a way that could damage the Community acquis.

6.2. The decisions referred to in the paragraph 6.1 do not affect the respective competence of the Community and its Member States.

O.   ECJ case-law

The ECJ has addressed the issue of the competence of the Community to stipulate treaties with third States several times, through judgments and opinions rendered pursuant to Article 300(6) EC, where it has specified the relevant scope and conditions. The first judgment was given on 31 March 1971 (case 22/70, *AETR*, Reports, 263), that concerns the competence of the Community to enter into international agreements in matters of transport, lacking any specific provision to this end in the EC Treaty. The ECJ stated that the Community was vested with such competence based on the theory of implied powers,

12-13/14-15. In the absence of specific provisions of the Treaty relating to the negotiation and conclusion of international agreements in the sphere of transport policy... one must turn to the general system of Community law in the sphere of relations with third countries. Article 210 provides that 'the Community shall have legal personality'. This provision, placed at the head of part six of the Treaty, devoted to 'general and final provisions', means that in its external relations the Community enjoys the capacity to establish contractual links with third countries over the whole field of objectives defined in part one of the Treaty, which part six supplements. To determine in a particular case the Community's authority to enter into international agreements, regard must be had to the whole scheme of the Treaty no less than to its substantive provisions.

16-17-18-19. Such authority arises not only from an express conferment by the Treaty — as is the case with Articles 113 and 114 for tariff and trade agreements and with Article 238 for association agreements — but may equally flow from other provisions of the Treaty and from measures adopted, within the framework of those provisions, by the Community institutions. In particular, each time the Community, with a view to implementing a common policy envisaged by the treaty, adopts provisions laying down common rules, whatever form these may take, the Member States no longer have the right, acting individually or even collectively, to undertake obligations with third countries which affect those rules. As and when such common rules come into being, the Community alone is in a position to assume and carry out contractual obligations towards third countries affecting the whole sphere of application of the Community legal system. With regard to the implementation of the provisions of the Treaty the system of internal Community measures may not therefore be separated from that of external relations.

20-21-22. Under Article 3(e), the adoption of a common policy in the sphere of transport is specially mentioned amongst the objectives of the Community. Under Article 5, the Member States are required on the one hand to take all appropriate measures to ensure fulfilment of the obligations arising out of the Treaty or resulting from action taken by the institutions and, on the other hand, to abstain from any measure which might jeopardise the attainment of the objectives of the Treaty. If these two provisions are read in conjunction, it follows that to the extent to which Community rules are promulgated for the attainment of the objectives of the Treaty, the Member States cannot, outside the framework of the Community institutions, assume obligations which might affect those rules or alter their scope.

In this case the ECJ stated that the Community was exclusively competent to enter into agreements with third countries, a least after the internal competence is exercised[5] (ie after the adoption of Regulation (EC) No 543/69 of 25 March 1969). However, given that the international negotiations was then rather advanced, the Council was justified in letting the Member States negotiate and conclude the European Agreement concerning the work of crews of vehicles engaged in international road transport, instead of activating the procedure established by Article 300 EC.

A few years later, in the *Kramer* case (14 July 1976, cases 3, 4 and 6/76, Reports, 1279), after referring to the *AETR* judgment the ECJ stated that

39   ...the Community not yet having fully exercised its functions in the matter, the answer which should be given to the questions asked is that at the time when the matters before the national courts arose, the Member States had the power to assume commitments, within the framework of the North-East Atlantic Fisheries Convention, in respect of the conservation of the biological resources of the sea, and that consequently they had the right to ensure the application of those commitments within the area of their jurisdiction.

40.   However, it should be stated first that this authority which the Member states have is only of a transitional nature and secondly that the Member States concerned are now bound by Community obligations in their negotiations within the framework of the Convention and of other comparable agreements.

44/45.   It follows from all these factors that Member States participating in the Convention and in other similar agreements are now not only under a duty not to enter into any commitment within the framework of those conventions which could hinder the Community in carrying out the tasks entrusted to it by Article 102 of the Act of accession, but also under a duty to proceed by common action within the Fisheries Commission. It further follows therefrom that as soon as the Community institutions have initiated the procedure for implementing the provisions of the said Article 102, and at the latest within the period laid down by that Article, those institutions and the Member States will be under a duty to use all the political and legal means at their disposal in order to ensure the participation of the Community in the Convention and in other similar agreements.

The ECJ then defined the time when the institutions must exercise the internal competence in order to invoke the external one (opinion No 1/76 of 26 April 1977, Reports, 741), and it stated that such competence exists

4.   ... in all cases in which internal power has already been used in order to adopt measures which come within the attainment of common policies. It is, however, not limited to that eventuality. Although the internal Community measures are only adopted when the international agreement is concluded and made enforceable, as is envisaged in the present case by the proposal for a regulation to be submitted to the Council by the Commission, the power to bind the Community vis-à-vis third countries nevertheless

---

[5]   See also opinion No 1/94 of 15 November 1994 (Reports, I-5267), paragraph 77, where the EJC stated that the external competence may also derive from the exercise of the internal competence ex Article 95 since 'the harmonization measures thus adopted may limit, or even remove, the freedom of the Member States to negotiate with non-member countries'.

flows by implication from the provisions of the Treaty creating the internal power and in so far as the participation of the Community in the international agreement is, as here, necessary for the attainment of one of the objectives of the Community.

Yet, in the more recent opinion No 2/92 of 24 March 1994 (Reports, I-521), the ECJ specified that the external competence may be exercised, and thus become exclusive, also lacking an internal act. However, this may happen when the conclusion of an international agreement is necessary in order to reach objectives of the Treaty that cannot be achieved by the adoption of autonomous provisions.

Some later cases have led the ECJ to define the borders between the competences of the Community and of Member States and to elaborate the distinction between exclusive and shared competence. In the opinion No 2/91 of 19 March 1993 (Reports, I-1061), concerning the ILO Convention No 170, the ECJ has stated that the Community ha exclusive competence with reference to Article 113 of the EC Treaty and to Article 102 of the Act of Accession, and that such competence excludes that the Member States might be vested with a parallel competence both at Community and international level (at paragraph 8). The same applies, according to the ECJ, when the Community competence derives from secondary EC legislation. The Member States' competence, though, is subject to restrictions also when the Community has not exercised the internal competence yet, since Article 10 EC obliges them to avoid entering into international agreements whose provisions may affect

11. ... rules already adopted in areas falling outside common policies or of altering their scope.

12. Finally, an agreement may be concluded in an area where competence is shared between the Community and the Member States. In such a case, negotiation and implementation of the agreement require joint action by the Community and the Member States.

18. For the purpose of determining whether this competence is exclusive in nature, it should be pointed out that the provisions of Convention No 170 are not of such a kind as to affect rules adopted pursuant to Article 118a. If, on the one hand, the Community decides to adopt rules which are less stringent than those set out in an ILO convention, Member States may, in accordance with Article 118a(3), adopt more stringent measures for the protection of working conditions or apply for that purpose the provisions of the relevant ILO convention. If, on the other hand, the Community decides to adopt more stringent measures than those provided for under an ILO convention, there is nothing to prevent the full application of Community law by the Member States under Article 19(8) of the ILO Constitution, which allows Members to adopt more stringent measures than those provided for in conventions or recommendations adopted by that organisation.

20. ... Difficulties... which might arise for the legislative function of the Community cannot constitute the basis for exclusive Community competence.

21. Nor, for the same reasons, can exclusive competence be founded on the Community provisions adopted on the basis of Article 100 of the Treaty... all of which lay down minimum requirements.

On the contrary, in case of directives aiming at granting a wider protection than that granted by ILO Convention No 170, Member States cannot undertake such commitments outside the framework of the Community institutions.

These principles have been confirmed in the '*Open Skies*' cases (eg 5 November 2002, Case C-467/98, *Commission v Denmark*, Reports, I-9519),[6] where the ECJ stated that

77. The Court has already held, in paragraphs 16 to 18 and 22 of the *AETR* judgment, that the Community's competence to conclude international agreements arises not only from an express conferment by the Treaty but may equally flow from other provisions of the Treaty and from measures adopted, within the framework of those provisions, by the Community institutions; that, in particular, each time the Community, with a view to implementing a common policy envisaged by the Treaty, adopts provisions laying down common rules, whatever form these may take, the Member States no longer have the right, acting individually or even collectively, to undertake obligations towards non-member countries which affect those rules or distort their scope; and that, as and when such common rules come into being, the Community alone is in a position to assume and carry out contractual obligations towards non-member countries affecting the whole sphere of application of the Community legal system.

78. Since those findings imply recognition of an exclusive external competence for the Community in consequence of the adoption of internal measures, it is appropriate to ask whether they also apply in the context of a provision such as Article 84(2) of the Treaty, which confers upon the Council the power to decide 'whether, to what extent and by what procedure appropriate provisions may be laid down' for air transport, including, therefore, for its external aspect.

79. If the Member States were free to enter into international commitments affecting the common rules adopted on the basis of Article 84(2) of the Treaty, that would jeopardise the attainment of the objective pursued by those rules and would thus prevent the Community from fulfilling its task in the defence of the common interest.

80. It follows that the findings of the Court in the *AETR* judgment also apply where, as in this case, the Council has adopted common rules on the basis of Article 84(2) of the Treaty.

81. It must next be determined under what circumstances the scope of the common rules may be affected or distorted by the international commitments at issue and, therefore, under what circumstances the Community acquires an external competence by reason of the exercise of its internal competence.

82. According to the Court's case-law, that is the case where the international commitments fall within the scope of the common rules (*AETR* judgment, paragraph 30), or in any event within an area which is already largely covered by such rules (Opinion 2/91, paragraph 25). In the latter case, the Court has held that Member States may not enter into international commitments outside the framework of the Community institutions, even if there is no contradiction between those commitments and the common rules (Opinion 2/91, paragraphs 25 and 26).

83. Thus it is that, whenever the Community has included in its internal legislative acts provisions relating to the treatment of nationals of non-member countries or expressly conferred on its institutions powers to negotiate with non-member countries, it

---

[6] On the same date other judgments have been adopted in the other 'Open Skies' cases, eg C-466/98, *Commission v United Kingdom* (Reports, I-9427), C-468/98, *Commission v Sweden* (Reports, I-9575), C-469/98, *Commission v Finland* (Reports, I-9627), C-471/98, *Commission v Belgium* (Reports, I-9797), C-476/98, *Commission v Germany* (Reports, I-9855). See further 2 June 2005, case C-266/03, *Commission v Luxembourg* (Reports, I-4805), specially at paras 87-90, and 14 July 2005, case C-433/03, *Commission v Germany* (Reports, I-6985), at paras 41–47.

acquires an exclusive external competence in the spheres covered by those acts (Opinion 1/94, paragraph 95; Opinion 2/92, paragraph 33).

84. The same applies, even in the absence of any express provision authorising its institutions to negotiate with non-member countries, where the Community has achieved complete harmonisation in a given area, because the common rules thus adopted could be affected within the meaning of the *AETR* judgment if the Member States retained freedom to negotiate with non-member countries (Opinion 1/94, paragraph 96; Opinion 2/92, paragraph 33).

In case of shared competences, in the opinion No 2/91 mentioned above, the ECJ has specified that

36. ... when it appears that the subject-matter of an agreement or contract falls in part within the competence of the Community and in part within that of the Member States, it is important to ensure that there is a close association between the institutions of the Community and the Member States both in the process of negotiation and conclusion and in the fulfilment of the obligations entered into ...

38. It is therefore for the Community institutions and the Member States to take all the measures necessary so as best to ensure such cooperation both in the procedure of submission to the competent authority and ratification of Convention No 170 and in the implementation of commitments resulting from that Convention.

When a Member State violates the duty to stipulate or adhere to a treaty deriving from a Community act, the Commission can start the proceedings under Article 226 EC.[7] According to the ECJ (19 March 2002, case C-13/00, *Commission v Ireland*, Reports, I-2943):

14. ... mixed agreements concluded by the Community, its Member States and non-member countries have the same status in the Community legal order as purely Community agreements, as these are provisions coming within the scope of Community competence.

15. From this the Court has concluded that, in ensuring respect for commitments arising from an agreement concluded by the Community institutions, the Member States fulfil, within the Community system, an obligation in relation to the Community, which has assumed responsibility for the due performance of the agreement.

20. It follows that the requirement of adherence to the Berne Convention [on literary and artistic work] which Article 5 of Protocol 28 to the EEA Agreement imposes on the Contracting Parties comes within the Community framework, given that it features in a mixed agreement concluded by the Community and its Member States and relates to an area covered in large measure by the Treaty. The Commission is thus competent to assess compliance with that requirement, subject to review by the Court.

In the most recent conventions concerning matters falling within the shared competence of the Community and the Member States, in order to facilitate the assessment by third countries of the respective competence, specific provisions impose a duty upon the regional organisations to inform on the scope of their competence in their instruments of accession and subsequently on any modification thereof. See, for example, Article 34 of

---

[7]   The same applies in case a Member State makes a proposal within an international organisation that may lead to adoption a binding act that will affect a Community act: ECJ, 12 February 2009, case C-45/07, *Commission v Greece*.

the Protocol of Cartagena on biosafety of 29 January 2000 and Article 18 of the Hague Convention on the law applicable to certain rights in respect of securities held through an intermediary of 5 July 2006.

The ECJ applied these general principles to the field of judicial cooperation in civil matters in its opinion No 1/03 of 7 February 2006 on the competence to conclude the new Lugano Convention on jurisdiction and the recognition and enforcement of judgments in civil and commercial matters (Reports, I-1145). In particular, the ECJ addressed the conditions upon which the exclusive Community competence is based and stated that

124. It should be noted in that context that the Community enjoys only conferred powers and that, accordingly, any competence, especially where it is exclusive and not expressly conferred by the Treaty, must have its basis in conclusions drawn from a specific analysis of the relationship between the agreement envisaged and the Community law in force and from which it is clear that the conclusion of such an agreement is capable of affecting the Community rules.

125. In certain cases, analysis and comparison of the areas covered both by the Community rules and by the agreement envisaged suffice to rule out any effect on the former.

126. However, it is not necessary for the areas covered by the international agreement and the Community legislation to coincide fully. Where the test of 'an area which is already covered to a large extent by Community rules' is to be applied, the assessment must be based not only on the scope of the rules in question but also on their nature and content. It is also necessary to take into account not only the current state of Community law in the area in question but also its future development, insofar as that is foreseeable at the time of that analysis.

127. That that assessment must include not only the extent of the area covered but also the nature and content of the Community rules is also clear from the Court's case-law referred to in paragraph 123 of the present opinion, stating that the fact that both the Community rules and the international agreement lay down minimum standards may justify the conclusion that the Community rules are not affected, even if the Community rules and the provisions of the agreement cover the same area.

128. In short, it is essential to ensure a uniform and consistent application of the Community rules and the proper functioning of the system which they establish in order to preserve the full effectiveness of Community law.

129. Furthermore, any initiative seeking to avoid contradictions between Community law and the agreement envisaged does not remove the obligation to determine, prior to the conclusion of the agreement, whether it is capable of affecting the Community rules.

130. In that regard, the existence in an agreement of a so-called 'disconnection clause' providing that the agreement does not affect the application by the Member States of the relevant provisions of Community law does not constitute a guarantee that the Community rules are not affected by the provisions of the agreement because their respective scopes are properly defined but, on the contrary, may provide an indication that those rules are affected. Such a mechanism seeking to prevent any conflict in the enforcement of the agreement is not in itself a decisive factor in resolving the question whether the Community has exclusive competence to conclude that agreement or whether competence belongs to the Member States; the answer to that question must be established before the agreement is concluded.

131. Lastly, the legal basis for the Community rules and more particularly the condition relating to the proper functioning of the internal market laid down in Article 65

EC are, in themselves, irrelevant in determining whether an international agreement affects Community rules: the legal basis of internal legislation is determined by its principal component, whereas the rule which may possibly be affected may be merely an ancillary component of that legislation. The purpose of the exclusive competence of the Community is primarily to preserve the effectiveness of Community law and the proper functioning of the systems established by its rules, independently of any limits laid down by the provision of the Treaty on which the institutions base the adoption of such rules.

132. If an international agreement contains provisions which presume a harmonisation of legislative or regulatory measures of the Member States in an area for which the Treaty excludes such harmonisation, the Community does not have the necessary competence to conclude that agreement. Those limits of the external competence of the Community concern the very existence of that competence and not whether or not it is exclusive.

133. It follows from all the foregoing that a comprehensive and detailed analysis must be carried out to determine whether the Community has the competence to conclude an international agreement and whether that competence is exclusive. In doing so, account must be taken not only of the area covered by the Community rules and by the provisions of the agreement envisaged, insofar as the latter are known, but also of the nature and content of those rules and those provisions, to ensure that the agreement is not capable of undermining the uniform and consistent application of the Community rules and the proper functioning of the system which they establish.

Competence of the Community to conclude the new Lugano Convention

134. The request for an opinion does not concern the actual existence of competence of the Community to conclude the agreement envisaged, but whether that competence is exclusive or shared. Suffice it to note in this regard that the Community has already adopted internal rules relating to jurisdiction and the recognition and enforcement of judgments in civil and commercial matters, whether in the form of Regulation No 44/2001, adopted on the basis of Articles 61(c) EC and 67(1) EC, or the specific provisions which appear in sectoral regulations, such as Title X of Regulation No 40/94 or Article 6 of Directive 96/71.

135. Regulation No 44/2001 was adopted to replace, as between the Member States apart from the Kingdom of Denmark, the Brussels Convention. It applies in civil and commercial matters, within the limits laid down by its scope as defined by Article 1 of that regulation. Since the purpose and the provisions of the regulation are largely reproduced in that Convention, reference will be made, so far as may be necessary, to the Court's interpretation of that Convention.

136. The purpose of the agreement envisaged is to replace the Lugano Convention, described as 'a parallel Convention to the …Brussels Convention' in the fifth recital to Regulation No 44/2001.

137. Whilst the text resulting from the revision of the two Conventions referred to above and the negotiating directives for the new Lugano Convention are known, it must be stressed that there is no certainty as to the final text which will be adopted.

138. Both Regulation No 44/2001 and the agreement envisaged essentially contain two parts. The first part of that agreement contains the rules on the jurisdiction of courts, such as those which are the subject of Chapter II of Regulation No 44/2001 and the specific provisions referred to in paragraph 134 of the present opinion. The second part contains the rules on the recognition and enforcement of judgments, such as those which are the subject of Chapter III of Regulation No 44/2001. Those two parts will be the subject of separate analysis.

The Rules on the jurisdiction of courts

139. The purpose of a rule of jurisdiction is to determine, in a given situation, which is the competent court to hear a dispute. In order to do so, the rule contains a test enabling the dispute to be 'linked' to the court which will be recognised as having jurisdiction. The linking factors vary, usually according to the subject-matter of the dispute. But they may also take account of the date when the action was brought, the particular characteristics of the claimant or defendant, or any other factor.

140. The variety of linking factors used by different legal systems generates conflicts between the rules of jurisdiction. These may be resolved by express provisions of the *lex fori* or by the application of general principles common to several legal systems. It may also happen that a law leaves to the applicant the choice between several courts whose jurisdiction is determined by several separate linking factors.

141. It follows from those factors that international provisions containing rules to resolve conflicts between different rules of jurisdiction drawn up by various legal systems using different linking factors may be a particularly complex system which, to be consistent, must be as comprehensive as possible. The smallest lacuna in those rules could give rise to the concurrent jurisdiction of several courts to resolve the same dispute, but also to a complete lack of judicial protection, since no court may have jurisdiction to decide such a dispute.

142. In international agreements concluded by the Member States or the Community with non-member countries those rules of conflict of jurisdiction necessarily establish criteria of jurisdiction for courts not only in non-member countries but also in the Member States and, consequently, cover matters governed by Regulation No 44/2001.

143. The purpose of that regulation, and more particularly Chapter II thereof, is to unify the rules on jurisdiction in civil and commercial matters, not only for intra-Community disputes but also for those which have an international element, with the objective of eliminating obstacles to the functioning of the internal market which may derive from disparities between national legislations on the subject (see the second recital in the preamble to Regulation No 44/2001 and, as regards the Brussels Convention, Case C-281/02 *Owusu* [2005] ECR I-1383, paragraph 34).

144. That regulation contains a set of rules forming a unified system which apply not only to relations between different Member States, since they concern both proceedings pending before the courts of different Member States and judgments delivered by the courts of a Member State for the purposes of their recognition or enforcement in another Member State, but also to relations between a Member State and a non-member country.

145. Ruling on the Brussels Convention, the Court has held in that connection that the application of the rules on jurisdiction requires an international element and that the international nature of the legal relationship at issue need not necessarily derive, for the purposes of the application of Article 2 of the Brussels Convention, from the involvement, because of the subject-matter of the proceedings or the respective domiciles of the parties, of a number of Contracting States. The involvement of a Contracting State and a non-Contracting State, for example because the claimant and defendant are domiciled in the first State and the events at issue occurred in the second, would also make the legal relationship at issue international in nature, as that situation may raise questions in the Contracting State relating to the determination of international jurisdiction, which is precisely one of the objectives of the Brussels Convention, according to the third recital in the preamble (*Owusu*, paragraphs 25 and 26).

146. The Court has further held that the rules of the Brussels Convention concerning exclusive jurisdiction or express prorogation of jurisdiction are also likely to apply to legal relationships involving only one Contracting State and one or more non-Contracting States (*Owusu*, paragraph 28). It has also held with regard to the Brussels Convention rules on *lis pendens* and related actions or recognition and enforcement, which concern proceedings pending before the courts of different Contracting States or judgments delivered by courts of a Contracting State with a view to recognition and enforcement thereof in another Contracting State, that the disputes with which such proceedings or decisions are concerned may be international, involving a Contracting State and a non-Contracting State, and allow recourse, on that ground, to the general rule of jurisdiction laid down by Article 2 of the Brussels Convention (*Owusu*, paragraph 29).

147. In that context, it must be noted that Regulation No 44/2001 contains provisions governing its relationship to other existing or future provisions of Community law. Thus Article 67 thereof provides that that regulation is without prejudice to the application of provisions governing jurisdiction and the enforcement of judgments in specific matters which are contained in Community instruments or in national legislation harmonised pursuant to such instruments. Article 71(1) also provides that that regulation is without prejudice to the application of any conventions with the same purpose as the preceding provisions to which the Member States are already parties. Article 71(2)(a) provides that that regulation is not to prevent a court of a Member State which is a party to such a convention from assuming jurisdiction in accordance with that Convention, even where the defendant is domiciled in another Member State not party thereto.

148. Given the uniform and coherent nature of the system of rules on conflict of jurisdiction established by Regulation No 44/2001, Article 4(1) thereof, which provides that 'if the defendant is not domiciled in a Member State, the jurisdiction of the courts of each Member State shall, subject to Articles 22 and 23, be determined by the law of that Member State', must be interpreted as meaning that it forms part of the system implemented by that regulation, since it resolves the situation envisaged by reference to the legislation of the Member State before whose court the matter is brought.

149. As regards that reference to the national legislation in question, even if it could provide the basis for competence on the part of the Member States to conclude an international agreement, it is clear that, on the basis of the wording of Article 4(1), the only criterion which may be used is that of the domicile of the defendant, provided that there is no basis for applying Articles 22 and 23 of the regulation.

150. Moreover, even if it complies with the rule laid down in Article 4(1) of Regulation No 44/2001, the agreement envisaged could still conflict with other provisions of that regulation. Thus, in the case of a legal person which is the defendant in proceedings and not domiciled in a Member State, that agreement could, by using the criterion of domicile of the defendant, conflict with the provisions of that regulation dealing with branches, agencies or other establishments lacking legal personality, such as Article 9(2) for disputes arising from insurance contracts, Article 15(2) for disputes arising from consumer contracts, or Article 18(2) for disputes arising from individual contracts of employment.

151. It is thus apparent from an analysis of Regulation No 44/2001 alone that, given the unified and coherent system of rules on jurisdiction for which it provides, any international agreement also establishing a unified system of rules on conflict of jurisdiction such as that established by that regulation is capable of affecting those rules

of jurisdiction. It is necessary however to continue the analysis by assessing the agreement envisaged in order to determine whether it supports that conclusion.

152. The purpose of the new Lugano Convention is the same as that of Regulation No 44/2001, but it has a wider territorial scope. Its provisions implement the same system as that of Regulation No 44/2001, in particular by using the same rules of jurisdiction, which, according to most of the governments which have submitted observations to the Court, ensures consistency between the two legal instruments and thus ensures that the Convention does not affect the Community rules.

153. However, whilst the fact that the purpose and wording of the Community rules and the provisions of the agreement envisaged are the same is a factor to be taken into account in determining whether that agreement affects those rules, that factor alone cannot demonstrate the absence of such an effect. As for the consistency arising from the application of the same rules of jurisdiction, this is not the same as the absence of such an effect since the application of a rule of jurisdiction laid down by the agreement envisaged may result in the choice of a court with jurisdiction other than that chosen pursuant to Regulation No 44/2001. Thus, where the new Lugano Convention contains articles identical to Articles 22 and 23 of Regulation No 44/2001 and leads on that basis to selection as the appropriate forum of a court of a non-member country which is a party to that Convention, where the defendant is domiciled in a Member State, in the absence of the Convention, that latter State would be the appropriate forum, whereas under the Convention it is the non-member country.

154. The new Lugano Convention contains a disconnection clause similar to that in Article 54B of the current Convention. However, as was noted in paragraph 130 of the present opinion, such a clause, the purpose of which is to prevent conflicts in the application of the two legal instruments, does not in itself provide an answer, before the agreement envisaged is even concluded, to the question whether the Community has exclusive competence to conclude that agreement. On the contrary, such a clause may provide an indication that that agreement may affect the Community rules.

155. Furthermore, as the Commission pointed out, a disconnection clause in an international agreement of private international law has a particular nature and is different from a classic disconnection clause. In the present case, the purpose is not to ensure that Regulation No 44/2001 is applied each time that that is possible, but rather to regulate in a consistent manner the relationship between that regulation and the new Lugano Convention.

156. Furthermore, the disconnection clause in Article 54B(1) of the Lugano Convention includes exceptions laid down in Article 54B(2) (a) and (b).

157. Thus, Article 54B(2) (a) of the Lugano Convention provides that the Convention applies in any event where the defendant is domiciled in the territory of a Contracting State which is not a member of the European Union. However, where for example the defendant is a legal person with a branch, agency or other establishment in a Member State, that provision may affect the application of Regulation No 44/2001, in particular Article 9(2), for proceedings concerning insurance contracts, Article 15(2) for proceedings concerning consumer contracts, or Article 18(2) for disputes concerning individual contracts of employment.

158. The same applies in respect of the two other exceptions to the disconnection clause laid down by the Lugano Convention, namely Article 54B(2) (a) *in fine*, where Articles 16 and 17 of the Convention, which relate to exclusive jurisdiction and the

prorogation of jurisdiction respectively, confer a jurisdiction on the courts of a Contracting State which is not a member of the European Union, and Article 54B(2) (b) in relation to *lis pendens* or related actions as provided for in Articles 21 and 22 of the Convention, when proceedings are instituted in a Contracting State which is not a member of the European Union and in a Contracting State which is a member of the European Union. The application of the Convention in the context of those exceptions may prevent the application of the rules of jurisdiction laid down by Regulation No 44/2001.

159. Some governments, in particular the Portuguese Government, argue that those few exceptions cannot negate the competence of the Member States to conclude the agreement envisaged since that competence must be determined by the main provisions of that agreement. Similarly, Ireland submits that it would be sufficient for the Community alone to negotiate the provision relating to those exceptions, with the Member States retaining competence to conclude the other provisions of that agreement.

160. However, it must be stressed that, as stated in paragraphs 151 to 153 of the present opinion, the main provisions of the agreement envisaged are capable of affecting the unified and coherent nature of the rules of jurisdiction laid down by Regulation No 44/2001. The exceptions to the disconnection clause and the need for a Community presence in the negotiations, envisaged by Ireland, are merely indications that the Community rules are affected in particular circumstances.

161. It follows from the analysis of the provisions of the new Lugano Convention relating to the rules on jurisdiction that those provisions affect the uniform and consistent application of the Community rules on jurisdiction and the proper functioning of the system established by those rules.

Rules on the recognition and enforcement of judgments in civil and commercial matters

162. Most of the governments which have submitted observations to the Court argue that the rules on the recognition and enforcement of judgments in civil and commercial matters constitute an area dissociable from that of the rules on jurisdiction, which justifies a separate analysis of the effect of the agreement envisaged on the Community rules. They submit in that regard that the scope of Regulation No 44/2001 is limited, since the recognition applies only to judgments delivered in other Member States, and that any agreement having a different scope, insofar as it concerns judgments external to the Community, is not capable of affecting the Community rules.

163. However, as other governments, the Parliament and the Commission submit, the rules of jurisdiction and those relating to the recognition and enforcement of judgments in Regulation No 44/2001 do not constitute distinct and autonomous systems but are closely linked. As the Commission noted at the hearing, the simplified mechanism of recognition and enforcement set out in Article 33(1) of that regulation, to the effect that a judgment given in a Member State is to be recognised in the other Member States without any special procedure being required and which leads in principle, pursuant to Article 35(3) of that regulation, to the lack of review of the jurisdiction of courts of the Member State of origin, rests on mutual trust between the Member States and, in particular, by that placed in the court of the State of origin by the court of the State in which enforcement is required, taking account in particular of the rules of direct jurisdiction set out in Chapter II of that regulation. As regards the Brussels Convention, the Report on the Convention submitted by Mr Jenard (OJ 1979 C 59, p. 1, at p. 46) stated as follows: 'The very strict rules of jurisdiction laid down in Title II, and the safeguards

granted in Article 20 to defendants who do not enter an appearance make it possible to dispense with any review, by the court in which recognition or enforcement is sought, of the jurisdiction of the court in which the original judgment was given.'

164. Several provisions of Regulation No 44/2001 confirm the link between the recognition and enforcement of judgments and the rules on jurisdiction. Thus, review of the jurisdiction of the court of origin is, exceptionally, maintained pursuant to Article 35(1) of the regulation where the provisions of that regulation concerning exclusive jurisdiction and jurisdiction in relation to insurance and consumer contracts are in question. Article 71(2)(b) and Article 72 of the Regulation also establish such a relationship between the rules on jurisdiction and those on the recognition and enforcement of those judgments.

165. Furthermore, Regulation No 44/2001 makes provision for conflicts which may arise between judgments delivered between the same parties by different courts. Thus, Article 34(3) states that a judgment is not to be recognised if it is irreconcilable with a judgment given in a dispute between the same parties in the Member State in which recognition is sought, whilst Article 34(4) provides that a judgment is not to be recognised if it is irreconcilable with an earlier judgment given in another Member State or in a third State involving the same cause of action and between the same parties, provided that the earlier judgment fulfils the conditions necessary for its recognition in the Member State in which recognition is sought.

166. Furthermore, as stated in paragraph 147 of the present opinion, Article 67 of that regulation governs the relationship of the system established by that regulation not only to the other existing and future provisions of Community law but also to the existing Conventions affecting the Community rules on recognition and enforcement, whether those Conventions contain rules on jurisdiction or provisions on the recognition and enforcement of judgments.

167. With regard to conventions to which the Member States are parties, referred to in Article 71 of Regulation No 44/001, the first paragraph of Article 71(2)(b) provides that 'judgments given in a Member State by a court in the exercise of jurisdiction provided for in a convention on a particular matter shall be recognised and enforced in the other Member States in accordance with this regulation'. The second paragraph of Article 71(2)(b) provides that 'where a convention on a particular matter to which both the Member State of origin and the Member State addressed are parties lays down conditions for the recognition or enforcement of judgments, those conditions shall apply'. Lastly, Article 72 provides that the regulation 'shall not affect agreements by which Member States undertook, prior to the entry into force of this regulation pursuant to Article 59 of the Brussels Convention, not to recognise judgments given, in particular in other Contracting States to that Convention, against defendants domiciled or habitually resident in a third country where, in cases provided for in Article 4 of that Convention, the judgment could only be founded on a ground of jurisdiction specified in the second paragraph of Article 3 of that Convention'.

168. It is thus apparent from an analysis of Regulation No 44/2001 alone that, because of the unified and coherent system which it establishes for the recognition and enforcement of judgments, an agreement such as that envisaged, whether it contains provisions on the jurisdiction of courts or on the recognition and enforcement of judgments, is capable of affecting those rules.

169. In the absence of the final text of the new Lugano Convention, the assessment

of any effect of that Convention on the Community rules is to be made having regard, by way of illustration, to the provisions of the current Lugano Convention.

170. The first paragraph of Article 26 of that Convention sets out the principle that a judgment given in a Contracting State is to be recognised in the other Contracting States without any special procedure being required. Such a principle affects the Community rules since it enlarges the scope of recognition of judicial decisions without any special procedure, thus increasing the number of cases in which judgments delivered by courts of countries not members of the Community whose jurisdiction does not arise from the application of the provisions of Regulation No 44/2001 will be recognised.

171. As regards the existence of a disconnection clause in the agreement envisaged, such as that in Article 54B(1) of the Lugano Convention, it follows from paragraphs 130 and 154 of the present opinion that its presence would not appear to alter that finding as regards the existence of exclusive competence on the part of the Community to conclude that agreement.

172. All those factors demonstrate that the Community rules on the recognition and enforcement of judgments are indissociable from those on the jurisdiction of courts, with which they form a unified and coherent system, and that the new Lugano Convention would affect the uniform and consistent application of the Community rules as regards both the jurisdiction of courts and the recognition and enforcement of judgments and the proper functioning of the unified system established by those rules.

173. It follows from all those considerations that the Community has exclusive competence to conclude the new Lugano Convention.

Finally, the ECJ addressed a specific question concerning the right of a Member State to make recourse to the means for the resolution of international disputes provided in international treaties rather than to Community procedures. In case C-459/03, *Commission v Ireland* (30 May 2006, Reports, I-4635), the Court has stated that the filing by a Member State of a claim with an arbitral tribunal against another Member State for an alleged violation of the United Nations Convention on the law of the sea infringes Article 10 EC. The ECJ further defined the scope of the competence transferred to the Community and stated that

104. ... the second sentence of the first paragraph of the second indent of point 2 of the Declaration of Community competence states, with regard to, inter alia, the provisions of the Convention relating to the prevention of marine pollution, that '[w]hen Community rules exist but are not affected, in particular in cases of Community provisions establishing only minimum standards, the Member States have competence, without prejudice to the competence of the Community to act in this field'.

105. Consequently, that declaration confirms that a transfer of areas of shared competence, in particular in regard to the prevention of marine pollution, took place within the framework of the Convention, and without any of the Community rules concerned being affected, within the terms of the principle set out in the *AETR* judgment.

106. However, that passage of the Declaration of Community competence makes the transfer of areas of shared competence subject to the existence of Community rules, even though it is not necessary that those rules be affected.

107. In the other cases, that is to say, those in which there are no Community rules, competence rests with the Member States, in accordance with the third sentence of the first paragraph of the second indent of point 2 of the Declaration of Community competence.

108. It follows that, within the specific context of the Convention, a finding that there has been a transfer to the Community of areas of shared competence is contingent on the existence of Community rules within the areas covered by the Convention provisions in issue, irrespective of what may otherwise be the scope and nature of those rules.

109. In this regard, the appendix to the Declaration of Community competence, while not exhaustive, constitutes a useful reference base.

110. It appears that the matters covered by the provisions of the Convention relied on by Ireland before the Arbitral Tribunal are very largely regulated by Community measures, several of which are mentioned expressly in the appendix to that declaration.

120. Those matters suffice to establish that the Convention provisions on the prevention of marine pollution relied on by Ireland, which clearly cover a significant part of the dispute relating to the MOX plant, come within the scope of Community competence which the Community has elected to exercise by becoming a party to the Convention.

121. It follows that the provisions of the Convention relied on by Ireland in the dispute relating to the MOX plant and submitted to the Arbitral Tribunal are rules which form part of the Community legal order. The Court therefore has jurisdiction to deal with disputes relating to the interpretation and application of those provisions and to assess a Member State's compliance with them (see, in that connection, Case C-13/00 *Commission v Ireland*, paragraph 20, and Case C-239/03 *Commission v France*, paragraph 31).

122. It is, however, necessary to determine whether this jurisdiction of the Court is exclusive, such as to preclude a dispute like that relating to the MOX plant being brought by a Member State before an arbitral tribunal established pursuant to Annex VII to the Convention.

123. The Court has already pointed out that an international agreement cannot affect the allocation of responsibilities defined in the Treaties and, consequently, the autonomy of the Community legal system, compliance with which the Court ensures under Article 220 EC. That exclusive jurisdiction of the Court is confirmed by Article 292 EC, by which Member States undertake not to submit a dispute concerning the interpretation or application of the EC Treaty to any method of settlement other than those provided for therein (see, to that effect, Opinion 1/91 [1991] ECR I-6079, paragraph 35, and Opinion 1/00 [2002] ECR I-3493, paragraphs 11 and 12).

124. It should be stated at the outset that the Convention precisely makes it possible to avoid such a breach of the Court's exclusive jurisdiction in such a way as to preserve the autonomy of the Community legal system.

125. It follows from Article 282 of the Convention that, as it provides for procedures resulting in binding decisions in respect of the resolution of disputes between Member States, the system for the resolution of disputes set out in the EC Treaty must in principle take precedence over that contained in Part XV of the Convention.

126. It has been established that the provisions of the Convention in issue in the dispute concerning the MOX plant come within the scope of Community competence which the Community exercised by acceding to the Convention, with the result that those provisions form an integral part of the Community legal order.

127. Consequently, the dispute in this case is indeed a dispute concerning the interpretation or application of the EC Treaty, within the terms of Article 292 EC.

128. Furthermore, as it is between two Member States in regard to an alleged failure to comply with Community-law obligations resulting from those provisions of the Convention, this dispute is clearly covered by one of the methods of dispute settlement

established by the EC Treaty within the terms of Article 292 EC, namely the procedure set out in Article 227 EC.

129. In addition, it is not open to dispute that proceedings such as those brought by Ireland before the Arbitral Tribunal fall to be described as a method of settlement of a dispute within the terms of Article 292 EC inasmuch as, under Article 296 of the Convention, the decisions delivered by such a tribunal are final and binding on the parties to the dispute.

130. Ireland contends, however, by way of alternative submission, that, if the Court were to conclude that the provisions of the Convention invoked before the Arbitral Tribunal form an integral part of Community law, that conclusion would also be unavoidable with regard to the provisions of the Convention dealing with dispute settlement. Consequently, it submits, the initiation of proceedings before an arbitral tribunal referred to in Article 287(1)(c) of the Convention constitutes a method of dispute settlement provided for in the EC Treaty, within the terms of Article 292 EC.

131. That argument must be rejected.

132. As has been pointed out in paragraph 123 of the present judgment, an international agreement such as the Convention cannot affect the exclusive jurisdiction of the Court in regard to the resolution of disputes between Member States concerning the interpretation and application of Community law. Furthermore, as indicated in paragraphs 124 and 125 of the present judgment, Article 282 of the Convention precisely makes it possible to avoid such a breach occurring, in such a way as to preserve the autonomy of the Community legal system.

More recently the ECJ addressed the issue of the extent of Community competence — and hence of its interpretative power — in case of a convention to which all the Member States are parties. The case concerned the interpretation of the 1929 Warsaw Convention for the Unification of Certain Rules Relating to International Carriage by Air, as amended by the four additional protocols signed at Montreal on 25 September 1975, that provides for a two-year limitation period for bringing a claim against the carrier (judgment 22 October 2009, case C-301/08, *Bogiatzi*). The ECJ stated that the Convention could not apply to intra-Community relations since it had been concluded prior to the entry into force of the EC Treaty and it declined jurisdiction to interpret the Convention for the following reasons:

22. In that connection, it must be stated at the outset that, pursuant to Article 234 EC, the Court has jurisdiction to give preliminary rulings concerning the interpretation of the EC Treaty and on the validity and interpretation of acts of the institutions of the Community.

23. According to settled case-law, an agreement concluded by the Council, in accordance with Articles 300 EC and 310 EC, is, as far as the Community is concerned, an act of one of the institutions of the Community, within the meaning of subparagraph (b) of the first paragraph of Article 234 EC. The provisions of such an agreement form an integral part of the Community legal order as from its entry into force and, within the framework of that order, the Court has jurisdiction to give preliminary rulings concerning the interpretation of such an agreement.

24. In the main proceedings, it is common ground that the Community is not a contracting party to the Warsaw Convention. Accordingly, the Court does not, in principle, have jurisdiction to interpret the provisions of that convention in preliminary ruling proceedings.

25. However, the Court has also held that, where and in so far as, pursuant to the Treaty, the Community has assumed the powers previously exercised by the Member States in the field to which an international convention applies and, therefore, its provisions have the effect of binding the Community, the Court has jurisdiction to interpret such a convention, even though it has not been ratified by the Community.

26. In the case in the main proceedings, it is common ground that all the Member States of the Community were parties to the Warsaw Convention at the material time.

27. It should therefore be considered whether, in that case, the Community has, pursuant to the Treaty, assumed the powers previously exercised by the Member States in the field to which the Warsaw Convention applies, a convention which covers all international carriage by air of persons, baggage and cargo.

28. At the material time, the Community had adopted, on the basis of Article 80(2) EC, three regulations in the field to which the Warsaw Convention applies.

29. First of all, mention should be made of Council Regulation (EEC) No 295/91 of 4 February 1991 establishing common rules for a denied-boarding compensation system in scheduled air transport. The purpose of that Regulation is limited however to establishing certain common minimum rules with respect to compensation from air carriers, applicable to passengers who are denied access to an overbooked scheduled flight. Unlike that regulation, which covers only denied boarding, the Warsaw Convention covers the liability of air carriers, including for flight delays.

30. Next, Council Regulation (EEC) No 2407/92 of 23 July 1992 on licensing of air carriers lays down, in Article 7, an obligation for air carriers to have civil liability insurance cover in case of accidents causing inter alia injury to passengers or damage to baggage. However, unlike the Warsaw Convention, the conditions for liability of the air carriers are not governed by that regulation.

31. Finally, Regulation No 2027/97 [on air carrier liability in the event of accidents], unlike the Warsaw Convention, covers only damage suffered as a result of death, wounding or other bodily injury, and not material damage to baggage and cargo.

32. It follows that the Community has not assumed all the powers previously exercised by the Member States in the field to which the Warsaw Convention applies.

33. In the absence of a full transfer of the powers previously exercised by the Member States to the Community, the latter cannot, simply because at the material time all those States were parties to the Warsaw Convention, be bound by the rules set out therein, which it has not itself approved.

34. In the light of the foregoing, the answer to the first question is that the Warsaw Convention does not form part of the rules of the Community legal order which the Court of Justice has jurisdiction to interpret under Article 234 EC.

II

Fundamental Rights, Public Policy and Overriding Mandatory Provisions

Fundamental rights

A.1. Treaty on the European Union

Article 6 (ex Article 6 TEU). 1. The Union recognises the rights, freedoms and principles set out in the Charter of Fundamental Rights of the European Union of 7 December 2000, as adapted at Strasbourg, on 12 December 2007, which shall have the same legal value as the Treaties.

The provisions of the Charter shall not extend in any way the competences of the Union as defined in the Treaties.

The rights, freedoms and principles in the Charter shall be interpreted in accordance with the general provisions in Title VII of the Charter governing its interpretation and application and with due regard to the explanations referred to in the Charter, that set out the sources of those provisions.

2. The Union shall accede to the European Convention for the Protection of Human Rights and Fundamental Freedoms. Such accession shall not affect the Union's competences as defined in the Treaties.

3. Fundamental rights, as guaranteed by the European Convention for the Protection of Human Rights and Fundamental Freedoms and as they result from the constitutional traditions common to the Member States, shall constitute general principles of the Union's law.

A.2. Treaty on the Functioning of the European Union

Article 8 (ex Article 3(2) TEC).   In all its activities, the Union shall aim to eliminate inequalities, and to promote equality, between men and women.

Article 18 (ex Article 12 TEC).   Within the scope of application of the Treaties, and without prejudice to any special provisions contained therein, any discrimination on grounds of nationality shall be prohibited.

The European Parliament and the Council, acting in accordance with the ordinary legislative procedure, may adopt rules designed to prohibit such discrimination.

Article 28 (ex Article 23 TEC).   1.   The Union shall comprise a customs union which shall cover all trade in goods and which shall involve the prohibition between Member States of customs duties on imports and exports and of all charges having equivalent effect, and the adoption of a common customs tariff in their relations with third countries.

2.   The provisions of Article 30 and of Chapter 2 of this Title shall apply to products originating in Member States and to products coming from third countries which are in free circulation in Member States.

Article 30 (ex Article 25 TEC).   Customs duties on imports and exports and charges having equivalent effect shall be prohibited between Member States. This prohibition shall also apply to customs duties of a fiscal nature.

Article 34 (ex Article 28 TEC).   Quantitative restrictions on imports and all measures having equivalent effect shall be prohibited between Member States.

Article 35 (ex Article 29 TEC).   Quantitative restrictions on exports, and all measures having equivalent effect, shall be prohibited between Member States.

Article 36 (ex Article 30 TEC).   The provisions of Articles 34 and 35 shall not preclude prohibitions or restrictions on imports, exports or goods in transit justified on grounds of public morality, public policy or public security; the protection of health and life of humans, animals or plants; the protection of national treasures possessing artistic, historic or archaeological value; or the protection of industrial and commercial property. Such prohibitions or restrictions shall not, however, constitute a means of arbitrary discrimination or a disguised restriction on trade between Member States.

Article 45 (ex Article 39 TEC).   1.   Freedom of movement for workers shall be secured within the Union.

2.   Such freedom of movement shall entail the abolition of any discrimination based on nationality between workers of the Member States as regards employment, remuneration and other conditions of work and employment.

3.   It shall entail the right, subject to limitations justified on grounds of public policy, public security or public health:

(a)   to accept offers of employment actually made;

(b)   to move freely within the territory of Member States for this purpose;

(c)   to stay in a Member State for the purpose of employment in accordance with the provisions governing the employment of nationals of that State laid down by law, regulation or administrative action;

(d)   to remain in the territory of a Member State after having been employed in that State, subject to conditions which shall be embodied in regulations to be drawn up by the Commission.

4.   The provisions of this Article shall not apply to employment in the public service.

Article 49 (ex Article 43 TEC).   Within the framework of the provisions set out below, restrictions on the freedom of establishment of nationals of a Member State in the territory of another Member State shall be prohibited. Such prohibition shall also apply to restrictions on the setting-up of agencies, branches or subsidiaries by nationals of any

Member State established in the territory of any Member State. Freedom of establishment shall include the right to take up and pursue activities as self-employed persons and to set up and manage undertakings, in particular companies or firms within the meaning of the second paragraph of Article 54, under the conditions laid down for its own nationals by the law of the country where such establishment is effected, subject to the provisions of the Chapter relating to capital.

Article 52 (ex Article 46 TEC).   1.   The provisions of this Chapter and measures taken in pursuance thereof shall not prejudice the applicability of provisions laid down by law, regulation or administrative action providing for special treatment for foreign nationals on grounds of public policy, public security or public health.

2.   The European Parliament and the Council shall, acting in accordance with the ordinary legislative procedure, issue directives for the coordination of the abovementioned provisions.

Article 54 (ex Article 48 TEC).   Companies or firms formed in accordance with the law of a Member State and having their registered office, central administration or principal place of business within the Union shall, for the purposes of this Chapter, be treated in the same way as natural persons who are nationals of Member States. 'Companies or firms' means companies or firms constituted under civil or commercial law, including cooperative societies, and other legal persons governed by public or private law, save for those which are non-profit-making.

Article 56 (ex Article 49 TEC).   Within the framework of the provisions set out below, restrictions on freedom to provide services within the Union shall be prohibited in respect of nationals of Member States who are established in a Member State other than that of the person for whom the services are intended.

The European Parliament and the Council, acting in accordance with the ordinary legislative procedure, may extend the provisions of the Chapter to nationals of a third country who provide services and who are established within the Union.

Article 57 (ex Article 50 TEC).   Services shall be considered to be 'services' within the meaning of the Treaties where they are normally provided for remuneration, in so far as they are not governed by the provisions relating to freedom of movement for goods, capital and persons.

'Services' shall in particular include:
(a)   activities of an industrial character;
(b)   activities of a commercial character;
(c)   activities of craftsmen;
(d)   activities of the professions.

Without prejudice to the provisions of the Chapter relating to the right of establishment, the person providing a service may, in order to do so, temporarily pursue his activity in the Member State where the service is provided, under the same conditions as are imposed by that State on its own nationals.

Article 58 (ex Article 51 TEC).   1.   Freedom to provide services in the field of transport shall be governed by the provisions of the Title relating to transport.

2.   The liberalisation of banking and insurance services connected with movements of capital shall be effected in step with the liberalisation of movement of capital.

Article 62 (ex Article 55 TEC).   The provisions of Articles 51 to 54 shall apply to the matters covered by this Chapter.

Article 63 (ex Article 56 TEC).   1.   Within the framework of the provisions set out in this Chapter, all restrictions on the movement of capital between Member States and between Member States and third countries shall be prohibited.
2.   Within the framework of the provisions set out in this Chapter, all restrictions on payments between Member States and between Member States and third countries shall be prohibited.

Article 64 (ex Article 57 TEC).   1.   The provisions of Article 63 shall be without prejudice to the application to third countries of any restrictions which exist on 31 December 1993 under national or Union law adopted in respect of the movement of capital to or from third countries involving direct investment — including in real estate — establishment, the provision of financial services or the admission of securities to capital markets. In respect of restrictions existing under national law in Bulgaria, Estonia and Hungary, the relevant date shall be 31 December 1999.
2.   Whilst endeavouring to achieve the objective of free movement of capital between Member States and third countries to the greatest extent possible and without prejudice to the other Chapters of the Treaties, the European Parliament and the Council, acting in accordance with the ordinary legislative procedure, shall adopt the measures on the movement of capital to or from third countries involving direct investment — including investment in real estate — establishment, the provision of financial services or the admission of securities to capital markets.
3.   Notwithstanding paragraph 2, only the Council, acting in accordance with a special legislative procedure, may unanimously, and after consulting the European Parliament, adopt measures which constitute a step backwards in Union law as regards the liberalisation of the movement of capital to or from third countries.

Article 65 (ex Article 58 TEC).   1.   The provisions of Article 63 shall be without prejudice to the right of Member States:
(a)   to apply the relevant provisions of their tax law which distinguish between taxpayers who are not in the same situation with regard to their place of residence or with regard to the place where their capital is invested;
(b)   to take all requisite measures to prevent infringements of national law and regulations, in particular in the field of taxation and the prudential supervision of financial institutions, or to lay down procedures for the declaration of capital movements for purposes of administrative or statistical information, or to take measures which are justified on grounds of public policy or public security.
2.   The provisions of this Chapter shall be without prejudice to the applicability of restrictions on the right of establishment which are compatible with the Treaties.
3.   The measures and procedures referred to in paragraphs 1 and 2 shall not constitute a means of arbitrary discrimination or a disguised restriction on the free movement of capital and payments as defined in Article 63.

4.   In the absence of measures pursuant to Article 64(3), the Commission or, in the absence of a Commission decision within three months from the request of the Member State concerned, the Council, may adopt a decision stating that restrictive tax measures adopted by a Member State concerning one or more third countries are to be considered compatible with the Treaties in so far as they are justified by one of the objectives of the Union and compatible with the proper functioning of the internal market. The Council shall act unanimously on application by a Member State.

Article 101 (ex Article 81 TEC).   1.   The following shall be prohibited as incompatible with the internal market: all agreements between undertakings, decisions by associations of undertakings and concerted practices which may affect trade between Member States and which have as their object or effect the prevention, restriction or distortion of competition within the internal market, and in particular those which:

(a)   directly or indirectly fix purchase or selling prices or any other trading conditions;

(b)   limit or control production, markets, technical development, or investment;

(c)   share markets or sources of supply;

(d)   apply dissimilar conditions to equivalent transactions with other trading parties, thereby placing them at a competitive disadvantage;

(e)   make the conclusion of contracts subject to acceptance by the other parties of supplementary obligations which, by their nature or according to commercial usage, have no connection with the subject of such contracts.

2.   Any agreements or decisions prohibited pursuant to this Article shall be automatically void.

3.   The provisions of paragraph 1 may, however, be declared inapplicable in the case of:

— any agreement or category of agreements between undertakings,

— any decision or category of decisions by associations of undertakings,

— any concerted practice or category of concerted practices,

which contributes to improving the production or distribution of goods or to promotingtechnical or economic progress, while allowing consumers a fair share of the resulting benefit, and which does not:

(a)   impose on the undertakings concerned restrictions which are not indispensable to the attainment of these objectives;

(b)   afford such undertakings the possibility of eliminating competition in respect of a substantial part of the products in question.

Article 102 (ex Article 82 TEC).   Any abuse by one or more undertakings of a dominant position within the internal market or in a substantial part of it shall be prohibited as incompatible with the internal market in so far as it may affect trade between Member States.

Such abuse may, in particular, consist in:

(a)   directly or indirectly imposing unfair purchase or selling prices or other unfair trading conditions;

(b)   limiting production, markets or technical development to the prejudice of consumers;

(c) applying dissimilar conditions to equivalent transactions with other trading parties, thereby placing them at a competitive disadvantage;

(d) making the conclusion of contracts subject to acceptance by the other parties of supplementary obligations which, by their nature or according to commercial usage, have no connection with the subject of such contracts.

Article 103 (ex Article 83 TEC).   1.   The appropriate regulations or directives to give effect to the principles set out in Articles 101 and 102 shall be laid down by the Council, on a proposal from the Commission and after consulting the European Parliament.

2.   The regulations or directives referred to in paragraph 1 shall be designed in particular:

(a) to ensure compliance with the prohibitions laid down in Article 101(1) and in Article 102 by making provision for fines and periodic penalty payments;

(b) to lay down detailed rules for the application of Article 101(3), taking into account the need to ensure effective supervision on the one hand, and to simplify administration to the greatest possible extent on the other;

(c) to define, if need be, in the various branches of the economy, the scope of the provisions of Articles 101 and 102;

(d) to define the respective functions of the Commission and of the Court of Justice of the European Union in applying the provisions laid down in this paragraph;

(e) to determine the relationship between national laws and the provisions contained in this Section or adopted pursuant to this Article.

Article 157 (ex Article 141 TEC).   1.   Each Member State shall ensure that the principle of equal pay for male and female workers for equal work or work of equal value is applied.

2.   For the purpose of this Article, 'pay' means the ordinary basic or minimum wage or salary and any other consideration, whether in cash or in kind, which the worker receives directly or indirectly, in respect of his employment, from his employer. Equal pay without discrimination based on sex means:

(a) that pay for the same work at piece rates shall be calculated on the basis of the same unit of measurement;

(b) that pay for work at time rates shall be the same for the same job.

3.   The European Parliament and the Council, acting in accordance with the ordinary legislative procedure, and after consulting the Economic and Social Committee, shall adopt measures to ensure the application of the principle of equal opportunities and equal treatment of men and women in matters of employment and occupation, including the principle of equal pay for equal work or work of equal value.

4.   With a view to ensuring full equality in practice between men and women in working life, the principle of equal treatment shall not prevent any Member State from maintaining or adopting measures providing for specific advantages in order to make it easier for the underrepresented sex to pursue a vocational activity or to prevent or compensate for disadvantages in professional careers.

B.   Joint Declaration by the European Parliament, the Council and the Commission (OJ, C 103 of 27 April 1977)

The European Parliament, the Council and the Commission,

Whereas the Treaties establishing the European Communities are based on the principle of respect for the law;

Whereas, as the Court of Justice has recognized, that law comprises, over and above the rules embodied in the treaties and secondary Community legislation, the general principles of law and in particular the fundamental rights, principles and rights on which the constitutional law of the Member States is based;

Whereas, in particular, all the Member States are Contracting Parties to the European Convention for the Protection of Human Rights and Fundamental Freedoms signed in Rome on 4 November 1950,

Have adopted the following declaration:

1.   The European Parliament, the Council and the Commission stress the prime importance they attach to the protection of fundamental rights, as derived in particular from the constitutions of the Member States and the European Convention for the Protection of Human Rights and Fundamental Freedoms.

2.   In the exercise of their powers and in pursuance of the aims of the European Communities they respect and will continue to respect these rights.

C.   Declaration against racism and xenophobia (OJ, C 158 of 25 June 1986)

The European Parliament, the Council, the Representatives of the member States, meeting with the Council, and the Commission:

Recognizing the existence and growth of xenophobic attitudes, movements and acts of violence in the Community which are often directed against immigrants;

Whereas the Community institutions attach prime importance to respect for fundamental rights, as solemnly proclaimed in the Joint Declaration of 5 April 1977, and to the principle of freedom of movement as laid down in the Treaty of Rome;

Whereas respect for human dignity and the elimination of forms of racial discrimination are part of the common cultural and legal heritage of all the Member States;

Mindful of the positive contribution which workers who have their origins in other Member States or in third countries have made, and can continue to make, to the development of the Member State in which they legally reside and of the resulting benefits for the Community as a whole,

1.   vigorously condemn all forms of intolerance, hostility and use of force against persons or groups of persons on the grounds of racial, religious, cultural, social or national differences;

2.   affirm their resolve to protect the individuality and dignity of every member of society and to reject any form of segregation of foreigners;

3.   look upon it as indispensable that all necessary steps be taken to guarantee that this joint resolve is carried through;

4.   are determined to pursue the endeavours already made to protect the individuality and dignity of every member of society and to reject any form of segregation of foreigners;

5.   stress the importance of adequate and objective information and of making all citizens aware of the dangers of racism and xenophobia, and the need to ensure that all acts or forms of discrimination are prevented or curbed.

D.   Council Directive 2000/43/EC of 29 June 2000 implementing the principle of equal treatment between persons irrespective of racial or ethnic origin (OJ, L 180 of 19 July 2000)

(1)   The Treaty on European Union marks a new stage in the process of creating an ever closer union among the peoples of Europe.

(2)   In accordance with Article 6 of the Treaty on European Union, the European Union is founded on the principles of liberty, democracy, respect for human rights and fundamental freedoms, and the rule of law, principles which are common to the Member States, and should respect fundamental rights as guaranteed by the European Convention for the protection of Human Rights and Fundamental Freedoms and as they result from the constitutional traditions common to the Member States, as general principles of Community Law.

(3)   The right to equality before the law and protection against discrimination for all persons constitutes a universal right recognised by the Universal Declaration of Human Rights, the United Nations Convention on the Elimination of all forms of Discrimination Against Women, the International Convention on the Elimination of all forms of Racial Discrimination and the United Nations Covenants on Civil and Political Rights and on Economic, Social and Cultural Rights and by the European Convention for the Protection of Human Rights and Fundamental Freedoms, to which all Member States are signatories.

(4)   It is important to respect such fundamental rights and freedoms, including the right to freedom of association. It is also important, in the context of the access to and provision of goods and services, to respect the protection of private and family life and transactions carried out in this context.

(5)   The European Parliament has adopted a number of Resolutions on the fight against racism in the European Union.

(6)   The European Union rejects theories which attempt to determine the existence of separate human races. The use of the term 'racial origin' in this Directive does not imply an acceptance of such theories.

(7)   The European Council in Tampere, on 15 and 16 October 1999, invited the Commission to come forward as soon as possible with proposals implementing Article 13 of the EC Treaty as regards the fight against racism and xenophobia.

(8)   The Employment Guidelines 2000 agreed by the European Council in Helsinki, on 10 and 11 December 1999, stress the need to foster conditions for a socially inclusive labour market by formulating a coherent set of policies aimed at combating discrimination against groups such as ethnic minorities.

(9)   Discrimination based on racial or ethnic origin may undermine the achievement of the objectives of the EC Treaty, in particular the attainment of a high level

of employment and of social protection, the raising of the standard of living and quality of life, economic and social cohesion and solidarity. It may also undermine the objective of developing the European Union as an area of freedom, security and justice.

(10) The Commission presented a communication on racism, xenophobia and anti-Semitism in December 1995.

(11) The Council adopted on 15 July 1996 Joint Action (96/443/JHA) concerning action to combat racism and xenophobia under which the Member States undertake to ensure effective judicial cooperation in respect of offences based on racist or xenophobic behaviour.

(12) To ensure the development of democratic and tolerant societies which allow the participation of all persons irrespective of racial or ethnic origin, specific action in the field of discrimination based on racial or ethnic origin should go beyond access to employed and self-employed activities and cover areas such as education, social protection including social security and healthcare, social advantages and access to and supply of goods and services.

(13) To this end, any direct or indirect discrimination based on racial or ethnic origin as regards the areas covered by this Directive should be prohibited throughout the Community. This prohibition of discrimination should also apply to nationals of third countries, but does not cover differences of treatment based on nationality and is without prejudice to provisions governing the entry and residence of third-country nationals and their access to employment and to occupation.

(14) In implementing the principle of equal treatment irrespective of racial or ethnic origin, the Community should, in accordance with Article 3(2) of the EC Treaty, aim to eliminate inequalities, and to promote equality between men and women, especially since women are often the victims of multiple discrimination.

(15) The appreciation of the facts from which it may be inferred that there has been direct or indirect discrimination is a matter for national judicial or other competent bodies, in accordance with rules of national law or practice. Such rules may provide in particular for indirect discrimination to be established by any means including on the basis of statistical evidence.

(16) It is important to protect all natural persons against discrimination on grounds of racial or ethnic origin. Member States should also provide, where appropriate and in accordance with their national traditions and practice, protection for legal persons where they suffer discrimination on grounds of the racial or ethnic origin of their members.

(17) The prohibition of discrimination should be without prejudice to the maintenance or adoption of measures intended to prevent or compensate for disadvantages suffered by a group of persons of a particular racial or ethnic origin, and such measures may permit organisations of persons of a particular racial or ethnic origin where their main object is the promotion of the special needs of those persons.

(18) In very limited circumstances, a difference of treatment may be justified where a characteristic related to racial or ethnic origin constitutes a genuine and determining occupational requirement, when the objective is legitimate and the requirement is proportionate. Such circumstances should be included in the information provided by the Member States to the Commission.

(19) Persons who have been subject to discrimination based on racial and ethnic origin should have adequate means of legal protection. To provide a more effective level of protection, associations or legal entities should also be empowered to engage, as the

Member States so determine, either on behalf or in support of any victim, in proceedings, without prejudice to national rules of procedure concerning representation and defence before the courts.

(20) The effective implementation of the principle of equality requires adequate judicial protection against victimisation.

(21) The rules on the burden of proof must be adapted when there is a prima facie case of discrimination and, for the principle of equal treatment to be applied effectively, the burden of proof must shift back to the respondent when evidence of such discrimination is brought.

(22) Member States need not apply the rules on the burden of proof to proceedings in which it is for the court or other competent body to investigate the facts of the case. The procedures thus referred to are those in which the plaintiff is not required to prove the facts, which it is for the court or competent body to investigate.

(23) Member States should promote dialogue between the social partners and with non-governmental organisations to address different forms of discrimination and to combat them.

(24) Protection against discrimination based on racial or ethnic origin would itself be strengthened by the existence of a body or bodies in each Member State, with competence to analyse the problems involved, to study possible solutions and to provide concrete assistance for the victims.

(25) This Directive lays down minimum requirements, thus giving the Member States the option of introducing or maintaining more favourable provisions. The implementation of this Directive should not serve to justify any regression in relation to the situation which already prevails in each Member State.

(26) Member States should provide for effective, proportionate and dissuasive sanctions in case of breaches of the obligations under this Directive.

(27) The Member States may entrust management and labour, at their joint request, with the implementation of this Directive as regards provisions falling within the scope of collective agreements, provided that the Member States take all the necessary steps to ensure that they can at all times guarantee the results imposed by this Directive.

(28) In accordance with the principles of subsidiarity and proportionality as set out in Article 5 of the EC Treaty, the objective of this Directive, namely ensuring a common high level of protection against discrimination in all the Member States, cannot be sufficiently achieved by the Member States and can therefore, by reason of the scale and impact of the proposed action, be better achieved by the Community. This Directive does not go beyond what is necessary in order to achieve those objectives...

Chapter I – General provisions

Article 1. Purpose.   The purpose of this Directive is to lay down a framework for combating discrimination on the grounds of racial or ethnic origin, with a view to putting into effect in the Member States the principle of equal treatment.

Article 2. Concept of discrimination.   1.   For the purposes of this Directive, the principle of equal treatment shall mean that there shall be no direct or indirect discrimination based on racial or ethnic origin.

2.   For the purposes of paragraph 1:

(a) direct discrimination shall be taken to occur where one person is treated less favourably than another is, has been or would be treated in a comparable situation on grounds of racial or ethnic origin;

(b) indirect discrimination shall be taken to occur where an apparently neutral provision, criterion or practice would put persons of a racial or ethnic origin at a particular disadvantage compared with other persons, unless that provision, criterion or practice is objectively justified by a legitimate aim and the means of achieving that aim are appropriate and necessary.

3. Harassment shall be deemed to be discrimination within the meaning of paragraph 1, when an unwanted conduct related to racial or ethnic origin takes place with the purpose or effect of violating the dignity of a person and of creating an intimidating, hostile, degrading, humiliating or offensive environment. In this context, the concept of harassment may be defined in accordance with the national laws and practice of the Member States.

4. An instruction to discriminate against persons on grounds of racial or ethnic origin shall be deemed to be discrimination within the meaning of paragraph 1.

Article 3. Scope. 1. Within the limits of the powers conferred upon the Community, this Directive shall apply to all persons, as regards both the public and private sectors, including public bodies, in relation to:

(a) conditions for access to employment, to self-employment and to occupation, including selection criteria and recruitment conditions, whatever the branch of activity and at all levels of the professional hierarchy, including promotion;

(b) access to all types and to all levels of vocational guidance, vocational training, advanced vocational training and retraining, including practical work experience;

(c) employment and working conditions, including dismissals and pay;

(d) membership of and involvement in an organisation of workers or employers, or any organisation whose members carry on a particular profession, including the benefits provided for by such organisations;

(e) social protection, including social security and healthcare;

(f) social advantages;

(g) education;

(h) access to and supply of goods and services which are available to the public, including housing.

2. This Directive does not cover difference of treatment based on nationality and is without prejudice to provisions and conditions relating to the entry into and residence of third-country nationals and stateless persons on the territory of Member States, and to any treatment which arises from the legal status of the third-country nationals and stateless persons concerned.

Article 4. Genuine and determining occupational requirements. Notwithstanding Article 2(1) and (2), Member States may provide that a difference of treatment which is based on a characteristic related to racial or ethnic origin shall not constitute discrimination where, by reason of the nature of the particular occupational activities concerned or of the context in which they are carried out, such a characteristic constitutes a genuine and determining occupational requirement, provided that the objective is legitimate and the requirement is proportionate.

Article 5. Positive action.   With a view to ensuring full equality in practice, the principle of equal treatment shall not prevent any Member State from maintaining or adopting specific measures to prevent or compensate for disadvantages linked to racial or ethnic origin.

Article 6. Minimum requirements.   1.   Member States may introduce or maintain provisions which are more favourable to the protection of the principle of equal treatment than those laid down in this Directive.

2.   The implementation of this Directive shall under no circumstances constitute grounds for a reduction in the level of protection against discrimination already afforded by Member States in the fields covered by this Directive.

Chapter II – Remedies and enforcement

Article 7. Defence of rights.   1.   Member States shall ensure that judicial and/or administrative procedures, including where they deem it appropriate conciliation procedures, for the enforcement of obligations under this Directive are available to all persons who consider themselves wronged by failure to apply the principle of equal treatment to them, even after the relationship in which the discrimination is alleged to have occurred has ended.

2.   Member States shall ensure that associations, organisations or other legal entities, which have, in accordance with the criteria laid down by their national law, a legitimate interest in ensuring that the provisions of this Directive are complied with, may engage, either on behalf or in support of the complainant, with his or her approval, in any judicial and/or administrative procedure provided for the enforcement of obligations under this Directive.

3.   Paragraphs 1 and 2 are without prejudice to national rules relating to time limits for bringing actions as regards the principle of equality of treatment.

Article 8. Burden of proof.   1.   Member States shall take such measures as are necessary, in accordance with their national judicial systems, to ensure that, when persons who consider themselves wronged because the principle of equal treatment has not been applied to them establish, before a court or other competent authority, facts from which it may be presumed that there has been direct or indirect discrimination, it shall be for the respondent to prove that there has been no breach of the principle of equal treatment.

2.   Paragraph 1 shall not prevent Member States from introducing rules of evidence which are more favourable to plaintiffs.

3.   Paragraph 1 shall not apply to criminal procedures.

4.   Paragraphs 1, 2 and 3 shall also apply to any proceedings brought in accordance with Article 7(2).

5.   Member States need not apply paragraph 1 to proceedings in which it is for the court or competent body to investigate the facts of the case.

Article 9. Victimisation.   Member States shall introduce into their national legal systems such measures as are necessary to protect individuals from any adverse treatment or adverse consequence as a reaction to a complaint or to proceedings aimed at enforcing compliance with the principle of equal treatment.

Article 10. Dissemination of information. Member States shall take care that the provisions adopted pursuant to this Directive, together with the relevant provisions already in force, are brought to the attention of the persons concerned by all appropriate means throughout their territory.

Article 11. Social dialogue.   1.   Member States shall, in accordance with national traditions and practice, take adequate measures to promote the social dialogue between the two sides of industry with a view to fostering equal treatment, including through the monitoring of workplace practices, collective agreements, codes of conduct, research or exchange of experiences and good practices.

2.   Where consistent with national traditions and practice, Member States shall encourage the two sides of the industry without prejudice to their autonomy to conclude, at the appropriate level, agreements laying down anti-discrimination rules in the fields referred to in Article 3 which fall within the scope of collective bargaining. These agreements shall respect the minimum requirements laid down by this Directive and the relevant national implementing measures.

Article 12. Dialogue with non-governmental organisations.   Member States shall encourage dialogue with appropriate non-governmental organisations which have, in accordance with their national law and practice, a legitimate interest in contributing to the fight against discrimination on grounds of racial and ethnic origin with a view to promoting the principle of equal treatment.

Chapter III – Bodies for the promotion of equal treatment

Article 13.   1.   Member States shall designate a body or bodies for the promotion of equal treatment of all persons without discrimination on the grounds of racial or ethnic origin. These bodies may form part of agencies charged at national level with the defence of human rights or the safeguard of individuals' rights.

2.   Member States shall ensure that the competences of these bodies include:

— without prejudice to the right of victims and of associations, organisations or other legal entities referred to in Article 7(2), providing independent assistance to victims of discrimination in pursuing their complaints about discrimination,

— conducting independent surveys concerning discrimination,

— publishing independent reports and making recommendations on any issue relating to such discrimination.

Chapter IV – Final provisions

Article 14. Compliance.   Member States shall take the necessary measures to ensure that:

(a) any laws, regulations and administrative provisions contrary to the principle of equal treatment are abolished;

(b) any provisions contrary to the principle of equal treatment which are included in individual or collective contracts or agreements, internal rules of undertakings, rules governing profit-making or non-profit-making associations, and rules governing the independent professions and workers' and employers' organisations, are or may be declared, null and void or are amended.

Article 15. Sanctions.   Member States shall lay down the rules on sanctions applicable to infringements of the national provisions adopted pursuant to this Directive and shall take all measures necessary to ensure that they are applied. The sanctions, which may comprise the payment of compensation to the victim, must be effective, proportionate and dissuasive. The Member States shall notify those provisions to the Commission by 19 July 2003 at the latest and shall notify it without delay of any subsequent amendment affecting them.

Article 16. Implementation.   Member States shall adopt the laws, regulations and administrative provisions necessary to comply with this Directive by 19 July 2003 or may entrust management and labour, at their joint request, with the implementation of this Directive as regards provisions falling within the scope of collective agreements. In such cases, Member States shall ensure that by 19 July 2003, management and labour introduce the necessary measures by agreement, Member States being required to take any necessary measures to enable them at any time to be in a position to guarantee the results imposed by this Directive. They shall forthwith inform the Commission thereof.

When Member States adopt these measures, they shall contain a reference to this Directive or be accompanied by such a reference on the occasion of their official publication. The methods of making such a reference shall be laid down by the Member States.

Article 17. Report.   1.   Member States shall communicate to the Commission by 19 July 2005, and every five years thereafter, all the information necessary for the Commission to draw up a report to the European Parliament and the Council on the application of this Directive.

2.   The Commission's report shall take into account, as appropriate, the views of the European Monitoring Centre on Racism and Xenophobia, as well as the viewpoints of the social partners and relevant non-governmental organisations. In accordance with the principle of gender mainstreaming, this report shall, inter alia, provide an assessment of the impact of the measures taken on women and men. In the light of the information received, this report shall include, if necessary, proposals to revise and update this Directive.

E.   Charter of Fundamental Rights of the European Union (OJ, C 303 of 14 December 2007)[1]

The European Parliament, the Council and the Commission solemnly proclaim the following text as the Charter of Fundamental Rights of the European Union.

---

[1]   On the application of the Charter, see Protocol (No 30) on the Application of the Charter of Fundamental Rights of the European Union to Poland and to the United Kingdom and Declaration by the Czech Republic annexed to the Final Act of the Intergovernmental Conference which adopted the Treaty of Lisbon (No 53), (OJ, C 115 of 9 May 2008). [Note of the Editor]

Preamble

The peoples of Europe, in creating an ever closer union among them, are resolved to share a peaceful future based on common values.

Conscious of its spiritual and moral heritage, the Union is founded on the indivisible, universal values of human dignity, freedom, equality and solidarity; it is based on the principles of democracy and the rule of law. It places the individual at the heart of its activities, by establishing the citizenship of the Union and by creating an area of freedom, security and justice.

The Union contributes to the preservation and to the development of these common values while respecting the diversity of the cultures and traditions of the peoples of Europe as well as the national identities of the Member States and the organisation of their public authorities at national, regional and local levels; it seeks to promote balanced and sustainable development and ensures free movement of persons, services, goods and capital, and the freedom of establishment.

To this end, it is necessary to strengthen the protection of fundamental rights in the light of changes in society, social progress and scientific and technological developments by making those rights more visible in a Charter.

This Charter reaffirms, with due regard for the powers and tasks of the Union and for the principle of subsidiarity, the rights as they result, in particular, from the constitutional traditions and international obligations common to the Member States, the European Convention for the Protection of Human Rights and Fundamental Freedoms, the Social Charters adopted by the Union and by the Council of Europe and the case-law of the Court of Justice of the European Union and of the European Court of Human Rights. In this context the Charter will be interpreted by the courts of the Union and the Member States with due regard to the explanations prepared under the authority of the Praesidium of the Convention which drafted the Charter and updated under the responsibility of the Praesidium of the European Convention.

Enjoyment of these rights entails responsibilities and duties with regard to other persons, to the human community and to future generations.

The Union therefore recognises the rights, freedoms and principles set out hereafter.

Title I — Dignity

Article 1. Human dignity. Human dignity is inviolable. It must be respected and protected.

Article 2. Right to life. 1. Everyone has the right to life.
2. No one shall be condemned to the death penalty, or executed.

Article 3. Right to the integrity of the person. 1. Everyone has the right to respect for his or her physical and mental integrity.
2. In the fields of medicine and biology, the following must be respected in particular:
(a) the free and informed consent of the person concerned, according to the procedures laid down by law;

(b) the prohibition of eugenic practices, in particular those aiming at the selection of persons;

(c) the prohibition on making the human body and its parts as such a source of financial gain; the prohibition of the reproductive cloning of human beings.

Article 4. Prohibition of torture and inhuman or degrading treatment or punishment.   No one shall be subjected to torture or to inhuman or degrading treatment or punishment.

Article 5. Prohibition of slavery and forced labour.   1.   No one shall be held in slavery or servitude.

2.   No one shall be required to perform forced or compulsory labour.

3.   Trafficking in human beings is prohibited.

Title II — Freedoms

Article 6. Right to liberty and security.   Everyone has the right to liberty and security of person.

Article 7. Respect for private and family life.   Everyone has the right to respect for his or her private and family life, home and communications.

Article 8. Protection of personal data.   1.   Everyone has the right to the protection of personal data concerning him or her.

2.   Such data must be processed fairly for specified purposes and on the basis of the consent of the person concerned or some other legitimate basis laid down by law. Everyone has the right of access to data which has been collected concerning him or her, and the right to have it rectified.

3.   Compliance with these rules shall be subject to control by an independent authority.

Article 9. Right to marry and right to found a family.   The right to marry and the right to found a family shall be guaranteed in accordance with the national laws governing the exercise of these rights.

Article 10. Freedom of thought, conscience and religion.   1.   Everyone has the right to freedom of thought, conscience and religion. This right includes freedom to change religion or belief and freedom, either alone or in community with others and in public or in private, to manifest religion or belief, in worship, teaching, practice and observance.

2.   The right to conscientious objection is recognised, in accordance with the national laws governing the exercise of this right.

Article 11. Freedom of expression and information.   1.   Everyone has the right to freedom of expression. This right shall include freedom to hold opinions and to receive and impart information and ideas without interference by public authority and regardless of frontiers.

2.   The freedom and pluralism of the media shall be respected.

Article 12. Freedom of assembly and of association.   1.   Everyone has the right to freedom of peaceful assembly and to freedom of association at all levels, in particular in political, trade union and civic matters, which implies the right of everyone to form and to join trade unions for the protection of his or her interests.

2.   Political parties at Union level contribute to expressing the political will of the citizens of the Union.

Article 13. Freedom of the arts and sciences.   The arts and scientific research shall be free of constraint. Academic freedom shall be respected.

Article 14. Right to education.   1.   Everyone has the right to education and to have access to vocational and continuing training.

2.   This right includes the possibility to receive free compulsory education.

3.   The freedom to found educational establishments with due respect for democratic principles and the right of parents to ensure the education and teaching of their children in conformity with their religious, philosophical and pedagogical convictions shall be respected, in accordance with the national laws governing the exercise of such freedom and right.

Article 15. Freedom to choose an occupation and right to engage in work.   1.   Everyone has the right to engage in work and to pursue a freely chosen or accepted occupation.

2.   Every citizen of the Union has the freedom to seek employment, to work, to exercise the right of establishment and to provide services in any Member State.

3.   Nationals of third countries who are authorised to work in the territories of the Member States are entitled to working conditions equivalent to those of citizens of the Union.

Article 16. Freedom to conduct a business.   The freedom to conduct a business in accordance with Union law and national laws and practices is recognised.

Article 17. Right to property.   1.   Everyone has the right to own, use, dispose of and bequeath his or her lawfully acquired possessions. No one may be deprived of his or her possessions, except in the public interest and in the cases and under the conditions provided for by law, subject to fair compensation being paid in good time for their loss. The use of property may be regulated by law in so far as is necessary for the general interest.

2.   Intellectual property shall be protected.

Article 18. Right to asylum.   The right to asylum shall be guaranteed with due respect for the rules of the Geneva Convention of 28 July 1951 and the Protocol of 31 January 1967 relating to the status of refugees and in accordance with the Treaty on European Union and the Treaty on the Functioning of the European Union (hereinafter referred to as 'the Treaties').

Article 19. Protection in the event of removal, expulsion or extradition.   1.   Collective expulsions are prohibited.

2.   No one may be removed, expelled or extradited to a State where there is a serious risk that he or she would be subjected to the death penalty, torture or other inhuman or degrading treatment or punishment.

Title III — Equality

Article 20. Equality before the law.   Everyone is equal before the law.

Article 21. Non-discrimination.   1.   Any discrimination based on any ground such as sex, race, colour, ethnic or social origin, genetic features, language, religion or belief, political or any other opinion, membership of a national minority, property, birth, disability, age or sexual orientation shall be prohibited.
2.   Within the scope of application of the Treaties and without prejudice to any of their specific provisions, any discrimination on grounds of nationality shall be prohibited.

Article 22. Cultural, religious and linguistic diversity.   The Union shall respect cultural, religious and linguistic diversity.

Article 23. Equality between women and men.   Equality between women and men must be ensured in all areas, including employment, work and pay.
The principle of equality shall not prevent the maintenance or adoption of measures providing for specific advantages in favour of the under-represented sex.

Article 24. The rights of the child.   1.   Children shall have the right to such protection and care as is necessary for their well-being. They may express their views freely. Such views shall be taken into consideration on matters which concern them in accordance with their age and maturity.
2.   In all actions relating to children, whether taken by public authorities or private institutions, the child's best interests must be a primary consideration.
3.   Every child shall have the right to maintain on a regular basis a personal relationship and direct contact with both his or her parents, unless that is contrary to his or her interests.

Article 25. The rights of the elderly.   The Union recognises and respects the rights of the elderly to lead a life of dignity and independence and to participate in social and cultural life.

Article 26. Integration of persons with disabilities.   The Union recognises and respects the right of persons with disabilities to benefit from measures designed to ensure their independence, social and occupational integration and participation in the life of the community.

Title IV — Solidarity

Article 27. Workers' right to information and consultation within the undertaking.   Workers or their representatives must, at the appropriate levels, be guaranteed information and consultation in good time in the cases and under the conditions provided for by Union law and national laws and practices.

Article 28. Right of collective bargaining and action.   Workers and employers, or their respective organisations, have, in accordance with Union law and national laws and practices, the right to negotiate and conclude collective agreements at the appropriate levels and, in cases of conflicts of interest, to take collective action to defend their interests, including strike action.

Article 29. Right of access to placement services.   Everyone has the right of access to a free placement service.

Article 30. Protection in the event of unjustified dismissal.   Every worker has the right to protection against unjustified dismissal, in accordance with Union law and national laws and practices.

Article 31. Fair and just working conditions.   1.   Every worker has the right to working conditions which respect his or her health, safety and dignity.
   2.   Every worker has the right to limitation of maximum working hours, to daily and weekly rest periods and to an annual period of paid leave.

Article 32. Prohibition of child labour and protection of young people at work.   The employment of children is prohibited. The minimum age of admission to employment may not be lower than the minimum school-leaving age, without prejudice to such rules as may be more favourable to young people and except for limited derogations.
   Young people admitted to work must have working conditions appropriate to their age and be protected against economic exploitation and any work likely to harm their safety, health or physical, mental, moral or social development or to interfere with their education.

Article 33. Family and professional life   1.   The family shall enjoy legal, economic and social protection.
   2.   To reconcile family and professional life, everyone shall have the right to protection from dismissal for a reason connected with maternity and the right to paid maternity leave and to parental leave following the birth or adoption of a child.

Article 34. Social security and social assistance.   1.   The Union recognises and respects the entitlement to social security benefits and social services providing protection in cases such as maternity, illness, industrial accidents, dependency or old age, and in the case of loss of employment, in accordance with the rules laid down by Union law and national laws and practices.

2.   Everyone residing and moving legally within the European Union is entitled to social security benefits and social advantages in accordance with Union law and national laws and practices.

3.   In order to combat social exclusion and poverty, the Union recognises and respects the right to social and housing assistance so as to ensure a decent existence for all those who lack sufficient resources, in accordance with the rules laid down by Union law and national laws and practices.

Article 35. Health care.   Everyone has the right of access to preventive health care and the right to benefit from medical treatment under the conditions established by national laws and practices. A high level of human health protection shall be ensured in the definition and implementation of all the Union's policies and activities.

Article 36. Access to services of general economic interest.   The Union recognises and respects access to services of general economic interest as provided for in national laws and practices, in accordance with the Treaties, in order to promote the social and territorial cohesion of the Union.

Article 37. Environmental protection.   A high level of environmental protection and the improvement of the quality of the environment must be integrated into the policies of the Union and ensured in accordance with the principle of sustainable development.

Article 38. Consumer protection.   Union policies shall ensure a high level of consumer protection.

Title V — Citizens' rights

Article 39. Right to vote and to stand as a candidate at elections to the European Parliament.   1.   Every citizen of the Union has the right to vote and to stand as a candidate at elections to the European Parliament in the Member State in which he or she resides, under the same conditions as nationals of that State.

2.   Members of the European Parliament shall be elected by direct universal suffrage in a free and secret ballot.

Article 40. Right to vote and to stand as a candidate at municipal elections.   Every citizen of the Union has the right to vote and to stand as a candidate at municipal elections in the Member State in which he or she resides under the same conditions as nationals of that State.

Article 41. Right to good administration.   1.   Every person has the right to have his or her affairs handled impartially, fairly and within a reasonable time by the institutions, bodies, offices and agencies of the Union.

2.   This right includes:

(a)   the right of every person to be heard, before any individual measure which would affect him or her adversely is taken;

(b)   the right of every person to have access to his or her file, while respecting the legitimate interests of confidentiality and of professional and business secrecy;

(c)   the obligation of the administration to give reasons for its decisions

3.   Every person has the right to have the Union make good any damage caused by its institutions or by its servants in the performance of their duties, in accordance with the general principles common to the laws of the Member States.

4.   Every person may write to the institutions of the Union in one of the languages of the Treaties and must have an answer in the same language.

Article 42. Right of access to documents.   Any citizen of the Union, and any natural or legal person residing or having its registered office in a Member State, has a right of access to documents of the institutions, bodies, officees and agencies of the Union, whatever their medium.

Article 43. European Ombudsman.   Any citizen of the Union and any natural or legal person residing or having its registered office in a Member State has the right to refer to the European Ombudsman cases of maladministration in the activities of the institutions, bodies, offices or agencies of the Union, with the exception of the Court of Justice of the European Union acting in its judicial role.

Article 44. Right to petition.   Any citizen of the Union and any natural or legal person residing or having its registered office in a Member State has the right to petition the European Parliament.

Article 45. Freedom of movement and of residence.   1.   Every citizen of the Union has the right to move and reside freely within the territory of the Member States.

2.   Freedom of movement and residence may be granted, in accordance with the Treaties, to nationals of third countries legally resident in the territory of a Member State.

Article 46. Diplomatic and consular protection.   Every citizen of the Union shall, in the territory of a third country in which the Member State of which he or she is a national is not represented, be entitled to protection by the diplomatic or consular authorities of any Member State, on the same conditions as the nationals of that Member State.

Title VI — Justice

Article 47. Right to an effective remedy and to a fair trial.[1] Everyone whose rights and freedoms guaranteed by the law of the Union are violated has the right to an effective remedy before a tribunal in compliance with the conditions laid down in this Article.

Everyone is entitled to a fair and public hearing within a reasonable time by an independent and impartial tribunal previously established by law. Everyone shall have the possibility of being advised, defended and represented.

Legal aid shall be made available to those who lack sufficient resources in so far as such aid is necessary to ensure effective access to justice.

Article 48. Presumption of innocence and right of defence.   1.   Everyone who has been charged shall be presumed innocent until proved guilty according to law.

2.   Respect for the rights of the defence of anyone who has been charged shall be guaranteed.

---

1   See CJ, judgment 22 December 2010, case C-279/09, *DEB*.

Article 49. Principles of legality and proportionality of criminal offences and penalties.   1.   No one shall be held guilty of any criminal offence on account of any act or omission which did not constitute a criminal offence under national law or international law at the time when it was committed. Nor shall a heavier penalty be imposed than the one that was applicable at the time the criminal offence was committed. If, subsequent to the commission of a criminal offence, the law provides for a lighter penalty, that penalty shall be applicable.

2.   This Article shall not prejudice the trial and punishment of any person for any act or omission which, at the time when it was committed, was criminal according to the general principles recognised by the community of nations.

3.   The severity of penalties must not be disproportionate to the criminal offence.

Article 50. Right not to be tried or punished twice in criminal proceedings for the same criminal offence.   No one shall be liable to be tried or punished again in criminal proceedings for an offence for which he or she has already been finally acquitted or convicted within the Union in accordance with the law.

Title VII — General provisions governing the interpretation and application of the Charter

Article 51. Field of application.   1.   The provisions of this Charter are addressed to the institutions, bodies, offices and agencies of the Union with due regard for the principle of subsidiarity and to the Member States only when they are implementing Union law. They shall therefore respect the rights, observe the principles and promote the application thereof in accordance with their respective powers and respecting the limits of the powers of the Union as conferred on it in the Treaties.

2.   The Charter does not extend the field of application of Union law beyond the powers of the Union or establish any new power or task for the Union, or modify powers and tasks as defined in the Treaties.

Article 52. Scope and interpretation of rights and principles.   1.   Any limitation on the exercise of the rights and freedoms recognised by this Charter must be provided for by law and respect the essence of those rights and freedoms. Subject to the principle of proportionality, limitations may be made only if they are necessary and genuinely meet objectives of general interest recognised by the Union or the need to protect the rights and freedoms of others.

2.   Rights recognised by this Charter for which provision is made in the Treaties shall be exercised under the conditions and within the limits defined by those Treaties.

3.   In so far as this Charter contains rights which correspond to rights guaranteed by the Convention for the Protection of Human Rights and Fundamental Freedoms, the meaning and scope of those rights shall be the same as those laid down by the said Convention. This provision shall not prevent Union law providing more extensive protection.

4.   In so far as this Charter recognises fundamental rights as they result from the constitutional traditions common to the Member States, those rights shall be interpreted in harmony with those traditions.

5.   The provisions of this Charter which contain principles may be implemented

by legislative and executive acts taken by institutions, bodies, offices and agencies of the Union, and by acts of Member States when they are implementing Union law, in the exercise of their respective powers. They shall be judicially cognisable only in the interpretation of such acts and in the ruling on their legality.

6.   Full account shall be taken of national laws and practices as specified in this Charter.

7.   The explanations drawn up as a way of providing guidance in the interpretation of this Charter shall be given due regard by the courts of the Union and of the Member States.

Article 53. Level of protection.   Nothing in this Charter shall be interpreted as restricting or adversely affecting human rights and fundamental freedoms as recognised, in their respective fields of application, by Union law and international law and by international agreements to which the Union or all the Member States are party, including the European Convention for the Protection of Human Rights and Fundamental Freedoms, and by the Member States' constitutions.

Article 54. Prohibition of abuse of rights.   Nothing in this Charter shall be interpreted as implying any right to engage in any activity or to perform any act aimed at the destruction of any of the rights and freedoms recognised in this Charter or at their limitation to a greater extent than is provided for herein.

F.   The Hague Programme: strengthening freedom, security and justice in the European Union (OJ, C 53 of 3 March 2005)

See Chapter I, General provisions, E.

G.   The Stockholm Programme — An open and secure Europe serving and protecting the citizens, adopted by the European Council on 10–11 December 2009 (Doc. Consilium No 17024/09): Parts 1.1, 2.1, 2.3.1, 7.2

See Chapter I, General provisions, F.

H.   ECJ case-law regarding the Charter and EU private international law provisions

In a case concerning the custody and return of children of an unmarried couple, with reference to the application of the principles of the Charter within the contest of Regulation No 2201/2003, in its judgment of 5 October 2010, case C-400/10 PPU, *McB*, the CJ stated that in the context of a case concerning the application of Regulation No 2201/2003 which involves reference to national law, the Charter should be taken into consideration solely for the purposes of interpreting Regulation No 2201/2003, and there should be no assessment of national law as such.

53. Moreover, it follows from Article 52(3) of the Charter that, in so far as the Charter contains rights which correspond to rights guaranteed by the ECHR, their meaning and scope are to be the same as those laid down by the ECHR. However, that provision does not preclude the grant of wider protection by European Union law. Under Article 7 of the Charter, '[e]veryone has the right to respect for his or her private and family life, home and communications'. The wording of Article 8(1) of the ECHR is identical to that of the said Article 7, except that it uses the expression 'correspondence' instead of 'communications'. That being so, it is clear that the said Article 7 contains rights corresponding to those guaranteed by Article 8(1) of the ECHR. Article 7 of the Charter must therefore be given the same meaning and the same scope as Article 8(1) of the ECHR, as interpreted by the case-law of the European Court of Human Rights.

54. The European Court of Human Rights has already considered a case in which the facts were comparable to those of the case in the main proceedings, where the child of an unmarried couple was taken to another State by its mother, who was the only person with parental responsibility for that child. In that regard, that court ruled, in essence, that national legislation granting, by operation of law, parental responsibility for such a child solely to the child's mother is not contrary to Article 8 of the ECHR, interpreted in the light of the 1980 Hague Convention, provided that it permits the child's father, not vested with parental responsibility, to ask the national court with jurisdiction to vary the award of that responsibility.

55. It follows that, for the purposes of applying Regulation No 2201/2003 in order to determine whether the removal of a child, taken to another Member State by its mother, is lawful, that child's natural father must have the right to apply to the national court with jurisdiction, before the removal, in order to request that rights of custody in respect of his child be awarded to him, which, in such a context, constitutes the very essence of the right of a natural father to a private and family life.

56. The European Court of Human Rights has also ruled that national legislation which does not allow the natural father any possibility of obtaining rights of custody in respect of his child in the absence of the mother's agreement constitutes unjustified discrimination against the father and is therefore a breach of Article 14 of the ECHR, taken together with Article 8 of the ECHR.

57. On the other hand, the fact that, unlike the mother, the natural father is not a person who automatically possesses rights of custody in respect of his child within the meaning of Article 2 of Regulation No 2201/2003 does not affect the essence of his right to private and family life, provided that the right described in paragraph 55 of this judgment is safeguarded.

58. That finding is not invalidated by the fact that, if steps are not taken by such a father in good time to obtain rights of custody, he finds himself unable, if the child is removed to another Member State by its mother, to obtain the return of that child to the Member State where the child previously had its habitual residence. Such a removal represents the legitimate exercise, by the mother with custody of the child, of her own right of freedom of movement, established in Article 20(2)(a) TFEU and Article 21(1) TFEU, and of her right to determine the child's place of residence, and that does not deprive the natural father of the possibility of exercising his right to submit an application to obtain rights of custody thereafter in respect of that child or rights of access to that child.

60. It must also be borne in mind that Article 7 of the Charter, mentioned by the referring court in its question, must be read in a way which respects the obligation to take into consideration the child's best interests, recognised in Article 24(2) of that Charter, and taking into account the fundamental right of a child to maintain on a regular basis personal relationships and direct contact with both of his or her parents, stated in Article 24(3). Moreover, it is apparent from recital 33 in the preamble to Regulation No 2201/2003 that that regulation recognises the fundamental rights and observes the principles of the Charter, while, in particular, seeking to ensure respect for the fundamental rights of the child as set out in Article 24 of the Charter. Accordingly, the provisions of that regulation cannot be interpreted in such a way that they disregard that fundamental right of the child, the respect for which undeniably merges into the best interests of the child.

62. It is necessary to take into account, in this regard, the great variety of extra-marital relationships and consequent parent-child relationships, a variety referred to by the referring court in its order for reference, which is reflected in the variation among Member States of the extent of parental responsibilities and their attribution. Accordingly, Article 24 of the Charter must be interpreted as not precluding a situation where, for the purposes of applying Regulation No 2201/2003, rights of custody are granted, as a general rule, exclusively to the mother and a natural father possesses rights of custody only as the result of a court judgment. Such a requirement enables the national court with jurisdiction to take a decision on custody of the child, and on rights of access to that child, while taking into account all the relevant facts, such as those mentioned by the referring court, and in particular the circumstances surrounding the birth of the child, the nature of the parents' relationship, the relationship of the child with each parent, and the capacity of each parent to take the responsibility of caring for the child. The taking into account of those facts is apt to protect the child's best interests, in accordance with Article 24(2) of the Charter.

Principle of non-discrimination on grounds of nationality

A.   Directive 2006/123/EC of the European Parliament and of the Council of 12 December 2006 on services in the internal market (OJ, L 376 of 27 December 2006)

Article 3. Relationship with other provisions of Community law.   2.   This Directive does not concern rules of private international law, in particular rules governing the law applicable to contractual and non contractual obligations, including those which guarantee that consumers benefit from the protection granted to them by the consumer protection rules laid down in the consumer legislation in force in their Member State …

Article 16. Freedom to provide services.   1.   Member States shall respect the right of providers to provide services in a Member State other than that in which they are established.

The Member State in which the service is provided shall ensure free access to and free exercise of a service activity within its territory.

Member States shall not make access to or exercise of a service activity in their territory subject to compliance with any requirements which do not respect the following principles:

(a) non-discrimination: the requirement may be neither directly nor indirectly discriminatory with regard to nationality or, in the case of legal persons, with regard to the Member State in which they are established;

(b) necessity: the requirement must be justified for reasons of public policy, public security, public health or the protection of the environment;

(c) proportionality: the requirement must be suitable for attaining the objective pursued, and must not go beyond what is necessary to attain that objective.

2.   Member States may not restrict the freedom to provide services in the case of a provider established in another Member State by imposing any of the following requirements:

(a) an obligation on the provider to have an establishment in their territory;

(b) an obligation on the provider to obtain an authorisation from their competent authorities including entry in a register or registration with a professional body or association in their territory, except where provided for in this Directive or other instruments of Community law;

(c) a ban on the provider setting up a certain form or type of infrastructure in their territory, including an office or chambers, which the provider needs in order to supply the services in question;

(d) the application of specific contractual arrangements between the provider and the recipient which prevent or restrict service provision by the self-employed;

(e) an obligation on the provider to possess an identity document issued by its competent authorities specific to the exercise of a service activity;

(f) requirements, except for those necessary for health and safety at work, which affect the use of equipment and material which are an integral part of the service provided;

(g) restrictions on the freedom to provide the services referred to in Article 19.

3.   The Member State to which the provider moves shall not be prevented from imposing requirements with regard to the provision of a service activity, where they are justified for reasons of public policy, public security, public health or the protection of the environment and in accordance with paragraph 1. Nor shall that Member State be prevented from applying, in accordance with Community law, its rules on employment conditions, including those laid down in collective agreements.

4.   By 28 December 2011 the Commission shall, after consultation of the Member States and the social partners at Community level, submit to the European Parliament and the Council a report on the application of this Article, in which it shall consider the need to propose harmonisation measures regarding service activities covered by this Directive.

Article 17. Additional derogations from the freedom to provide services.   Article 16 shall not apply to:

1) services of general economic interest which are provided in another Member State, *inter alia*:

(a) in the postal sector, services covered by Directive 97/67/EC of the European Parliament and of the Council of 15 December 1997 on common rules for the development of the internal market of Community postal services and the improvement of quality of service;

(b) in the electricity sector, services covered by Directive 2003/54/EC of the European Parliament and of the Council of 26 June 2003 concerning common rules for the internal market in electricity;

(c) in the gas sector, services covered by Directive 2003/55/EC of the European Parliament and of the Council of 26 June 2003 concerning common rules for the internal market in natural gas;

(d) water distribution and supply services and waste water services;

(e) treatment of waste;

2) matters covered by Directive 96/71/EC;

3) matters covered by Directive 95/46/EC of the European Parliament and of the Council of 24 October 1995 on the protection of individuals with regard to the processing of personal data and on the free movement of such data;

4) matters covered by Council Directive 77/249/EEC of 22 March 1977 to facilitate the effective exercise by lawyers of freedom to provide services;

5) the activity of judicial recovery of debts;

6) matters covered by Title II of Directive 2005/36/EC, as well as requirements in the Member State where the service is provided which reserve an activity to a particular profession;

7) matters covered by Regulation (EEC) No 1408/71;

8) as regards administrative formalities concerning the free movement of persons and their residence, matters covered by the provisions of Directive 2004/38/EC that lay down administrative formalities of the competent authorities of the Member State where the service is provided with which beneficiaries must comply;

9) as regards third country nationals who move to another Member State in the context of the provision of a service, the possibility for Member States to require visa or residence permits for third country nationals who are not covered by the mutual recognition regime provided for in Article 21 of the Convention implementing the Schengen Agreement of 14 June 1985 on the gradual abolition of checks at the common borders or the possibility to oblige third country nationals to report to the competent authorities of the Member State in which the service is provided on or after their entry;

10) as regards the shipment of waste, matters covered by Council Regulation (EEC) No 259/93 of 1 February 1993 on the supervision and control of shipments of waste within, into and out of the European Community;

11) copyright, neighbouring rights and rights covered by Council Directive 87/54/EEC of 16 December 1986 on the legal protection of topographies of semiconductor products and by Directive 96/9/EC of the European Parliament and of the Council of 11 March 1996 on the legal protection of databases, as well as industrial property rights;

12) acts requiring by law the involvement of a notary;

13) matters covered by Directive 2006/43/EC of the European Parliament and of the Council of 17 May 2006 on statutory audit of annual accounts and consolidated accounts;

14) the registration of vehicles leased in another Member State;

15) provisions regarding contractual and non-contractual obligations, including the form of contracts, determined pursuant to the rules of private international law.

Article 18. Case-by-case derogations.   1.   By way of derogation from Article 16, and in exceptional circumstances only, a Member State may, in respect of a provider established in another Member State, take measures relating to the safety of services …

3.   Paragraphs 1 and 2 shall be without prejudice to provisions, laid down in Community instruments, which guarantee the freedom to provide services or which allow derogations therefrom.

Article 20. Non-discrimination.   1.   Member States shall ensure that the recipient is not made subject to discriminatory requirements based on his nationality or place of residence.

2.   Member States shall ensure that the general conditions of access to a service, which are made available to the public at large by the provider, do not contain discriminatory provisions relating to the nationality or place of residence of the recipient, but without precluding the possibility of providing for differences in the conditions of access where those differences are directly justified by objective criteria.

B.   ECJ case-law

Over the years, on the basis of certain EC Treaty provisions the ECJ has identified within the EC legal system many fundamental principles, of which it has specified the relevant scope and meaning. They now consists of a well organised system of rules, strictly connected to one other, that sometimes operate at the same time, and are based on the four fundamental freedoms of the internal market. Among them, the principle of prohibition of discrimination on grounds of nationality takes the lead. The relevant provision is laid down as a general rule in Article 18 TFEU (former Article 12 EC) and it enjoys direct effects within the Member States, irrespective of any implementation at domestic level. Moreover, the scope of the principle has widened in order to embrace any discriminatory conditions, such as residence or origin. Since the *Sotgiu* judgment (12 February 1974, case 152/73, Reports, 153), the ECJ has stated that:

11.   The rules regarding equality of treatment, both in the treaty and in Article 7 of Regulation No 1612/68, forbid not only overt discrimination by reason of nationality but also all covert forms of discrimination which, by the application of other criteria of differentiation, lead in fact to the same result.

This interpretation, which is necessary to ensure the effective working of one of the fundamental principles of the community, is explicitly recognized by the fifth recital of the preamble to Regulation No 1612/68 which requires that equality of treatment of workers shall be ensured 'in fact and in law'.

It may therefore be that criteria such as place of origin or residence of a worker may, according to circumstances, be tantamount, as regards their practical effect, to discrimination on the grounds of nationality, such as is prohibited by the treaty and the regulation.

In the later *Cowan* judgment (2 February 1989, case 186/87, Reports, 195), the ECJ, dealing with a provision of the French Code of Criminal Procedure, has specified the scope of the principle of non-discrimination. Particularly, the national provision granted compensation for physical injury only to victims of French nationality, or to foreign nationals of a State which had entered into a reciprocal agreement with France, or to a person holding a residence permit. On this regard, the ECJ stated as follows:

10. By prohibiting 'any discrimination on grounds of nationality' Article 7 of the Treaty requires that persons in a situation governed by Community law be placed on a completely equal footing with nationals of the Member State. In so far as this principle is applicable it therefore precludes a Member State from making the grant of a right to such a person subject to the condition that he reside on the territory of that State — that condition is not imposed on the State's own nationals.

11. It should also be emphasized that the right to equal treatment is conferred directly by Community law and may not therefore be made subject to the issue of a certificate to that effect by the authorities of the relevant Member State.

12. Finally, it should be recalled, as the Court first stated in its judgment of 22 June 1972, case 1/72, *Frilli v Belgium*, Reports, 457, that the right to equal treatment laid down in Community law may not be made dependent on the existence of a reciprocal agreement between the relevant Member State and the country of which the person concerned is a national.

13. It follows that in so far as the prohibition of discrimination is applicable it precludes a Member State from making the award of a right to a person in a situation governed by Community law subject to the condition that he hold a residence permit or be a national of a country which has entered into a reciprocal agreement with that Member State.

As far as the scope of application of the prohibition of discrimination principle is concerned, the ECJ held that:

14. Under Article 7 of the Treaty the prohibition of discrimination applies 'within the scope of application of this Treaty' and 'without prejudice to any special provisions contained therein'. This latter expression refers particularly to other provisions of the Treaty in which the application of the general principle set out in that Article is given concrete form in respect of specific situations. Examples of that are the provisions concerning free movement of workers, the right of establishment and the freedom to provide services.

15. On that last point, in its judgment of 31 January 1984, joined cases 286/82 and 26/83, *Luisi and Carbone v Ministero del Tesoro*, Reports, 377, the Court held that the freedom to provide services includes the freedom for the recipients of services to go to another Member State in order to receive a service there, without being obstructed by restrictions, and that tourists, among others, must be regarded as recipients of services.

16. At the hearing the French Government submitted that as Community law now stands a recipient of services may not rely on the prohibition of discrimination to the extent that the national law at issue does not create any barrier to freedom of movement. A provision such as that at issue in the main proceedings, it says, imposes no restrictions in that respect. Furthermore, it concerns a right which is a manifestation of the principle of national solidarity. Such a right presupposes a closer bond with the State than that of a recipient of services, and for that reason it may be restricted to persons who are either nationals of that State or foreign nationals resident on the territory of that State.

17. That reasoning cannot be accepted. When Community law guarantees a natural person the freedom to go to another Member State the protection of that person

from harm in the Member State in question, on the same basis as that of nationals and persons residing there, is a corollary of that freedom of movement. It follows that the prohibition of discrimination is applicable to recipients of services within the meaning of the Treaty as regards protection against the risk of assault and the right to obtain financial compensation provided for by national law when that risk materializes. The fact that the compensation at issue is financed by the Public Treasury cannot alter the rules regarding the protection of the rights guaranteed by the Treaty.

18.   The French Government also submitted that compensation such as that at issue in the main proceedings is not subject to the prohibition of discrimination because it falls within the law of criminal procedure, which is not included within the scope of the Treaty.

19.   Although in principle criminal legislation and the rules of criminal procedure, among which the national provision in issue is to be found, are matters for which the Member States are responsible, the Court has consistently held that Community law sets certain limits to their power. Such legislative provisions may not discriminate against persons to whom Community law gives the right to equal treatment or restrict the fundamental freedoms guaranteed by Community law.

20.   In the light of all the foregoing the answer to the question submitted must be that the prohibition of discrimination laid down in particular in Article 7 of the EEC Treaty must be interpreted as meaning that in respect of persons whose freedom to travel to a Member State, in particular as recipients of services, is guaranteed by Community law that State may not make the award of State compensation for harm caused in that State to the victim of an assault resulting in physical injury subject to the condition that he hold a residence permit or be a national of a country which has entered into a reciprocal agreement with that Member State.

In a later case (judgment 30 April 1996, case C-214/94, *Boukhalfa*, Reports, I-2253), the ECJ had been asked to ascertain whether the applicability of the prohibition of discrimination based on nationality applies to a national of a Member State who is permanently resident in a non-member country, who is employed by another Member State in its embassy in that non-member country, and whose contract of employment is entered into and is permanently performed there. The ECJ gave an affirmative answer to above question, on the following grounds:

13.   It must be borne in mind that not only Article 48 of the Treaty but also regulations, as institutional acts adopted on the basis of the Treaty, apply in principle to the same geographical area as the Treaty itself.

14.   The geographical application of the Treaty is defined in Article 227. That Article does not, however, preclude Community rules from having effects outside the territory of the Community.

15.   The Court has consistently held that provisions of Community law may apply to professional activities pursued outside Community territory as long as the employment relationship retains a sufficiently close link with the Community. That principle must be deemed to extend also to cases in which there is a sufficiently close link between the employment relationship, on the one hand, and the law of a Member State and thus the relevant rules of Community law, on the other.

16.   In the present case, it is clear from the documents before the Court that the plaintiff's situation is subject to rules of German law in several respects. First, her

contract of employment was entered into in accordance with the law of the Member State which employs her and it is only pursuant to that law that it was stipulated that her conditions of employment were to be determined in accordance with Algerian law. Secondly, that contract contains a clause giving jurisdiction over any dispute between the parties concerning the contract to the courts in Bonn and, ultimately, Berlin. Thirdly, the plaintiff in the main proceedings is affiliated for pension purposes to the German State social security system and is subject, though to a limited extent, to German income tax.

17. In situations such as that of the plaintiff in the main proceedings, Community law and thus the prohibition of discrimination based on nationality contained in the abovementioned Community provisions are applicable to all aspects of the employment relationship which are governed by the law of a Member State.

18. The German Government maintains, however, that Ms Boukhalfa's conditions of employment are governed by Algerian law and that the abovementioned Community provisions prohibiting discrimination based on nationality are therefore inapplicable.

19. As has been pointed out in paragraph 16 above, however, it is only pursuant to Paragraph 33 of the GAD that Algerian law determines Ms Boukhalfa's conditions of employment and it is the compatibility of that paragraph with Community law which is in issue in the main proceedings.

20. The German Government further objects that, even before the contract was entered into, the plaintiff in the main proceedings was resident not in one of the Member States but in Algeria. The national court points out, moreover, that the contract of employment was entered into and is permanently performed in Algeria.

21. Those circumstances are not, however, such as to call into question the links with Community law noted above.

22. The answer to the national court' s question must therefore be that the prohibition of discrimination based on nationality, laid down in Article 48(2) of the Treaty and Article 7 (1) and (4) of Regulation No 1612/68, applies to a national of a Member State who is permanently resident in a non-member country, who is employed by another Member State in its embassy in that non-member country and whose contract of employment was entered into and is permanently performed there, as regards all aspects of the employment relationship which are governed by the legislation of the employing Member State.

In a later case, the ECJ ascertained the lawfulness of the obligation to lodge a sum of money as a security for the costs of the proceeding (so-called *cautio judicatum solvi*) within a proceeding brought before an Austrian Court, where the plaintiff was a national both of the United States of America and the United Kingdom, and resident in the United States of America (*Saldanha*, 2 October 1997, case C-122/96, Reports, I-5325; as regards issues related to dual nationality see Chapter III, Citizenship of the Member States, A). The ECJ, confirming its previous case-law, stated that the Austrian rule of procedure under discussion was not compatible with the EC Law on the grounds that it was conflicting with the prohibition of discrimination that applies to nationals of all Member States.

16. Since Article 6 of the Treaty produces effects within the area covered by the Treaty, it is necessary to consider next whether that Article applies to a provision in a Member State, such as that at issue in the main proceedings, which requires nationals of another Member State to provide security for costs where, in their capacity as shareholders,

they bring proceedings against a company established in that Member State, even though its own nationals are not subject to such a requirement.

17. In this connection, the Court has held, in case C-43/95, *Data Delecta and Forsberg v MSL Dynamics*, Reports, I-4661, paragraph 15, and in case C-323/95, *Hayes v Kronenberger*, Reports, I-1711, paragraph 17, that such a rule of domestic procedure falls within the scope of application of the Treaty within the meaning of the first paragraph of Article 6, where the main proceedings relate to the exercise of the fundamental freedoms guaranteed by Community law, such as, in those cases, proceedings to recover payment for the supply of goods.

19. It should be noted in this regard that, while a rule of procedure such as that at issue in the main proceedings is in principle a matter for which the Member States are responsible, the Court has consistently held that such a provision may not discriminate against persons to whom Community law gives the right to equal treatment or restrict the fundamental freedoms guaranteed by Community law.

20. In the abovementioned judgments in *Data Delecta and Forsberg*, paragraph 15, and *Hayes*, paragraph 17, the Court held that a rule of domestic procedure requiring for judicial proceedings, such as those at issue in those cases, the provision of security for costs was liable to have an effect, even though indirect, on trade in goods and services between Member States and therefore fell within the scope of application of the Treaty.

21. Without its being necessary to examine the argument of Hiross that, in view of the subject-matter of the dispute in the main proceedings, the contested rule cannot in this case restrict, even indirectly, any fundamental freedom guaranteed by Community law, it must be held that such a rule cannot, in any event, discriminate against persons on whom Community law confers the right to equal treatment.

22. The dispute in the main proceedings concerns the protection of interests relied on by a shareholder who is a national of one Member State against a company established in another Member State.

23. Article 54(3)(g) of the EC Treaty empowers the Council and the Commission, for the purpose of giving effect to the freedom of establishment, to coordinate to the necessary extent the safeguards which, for the protection of the interests of members and others, are required by Member States of companies or firms within the meaning of the second paragraph of Article 58 of the EC Treaty with a view to making such safeguards equivalent throughout the Community. It follows that rules which, in the area of company law, seek to protect the interests of shareholders come within the scope of the Treaty and are for that reason subject to the prohibition of all discrimination based on nationality.

24. If Community law thus prohibits all discrimination based on nationality in regard to the safeguards required, in the Member States, of companies or firms within the meaning of the second paragraph of Article 58 of the Treaty for the purpose of protecting the interests of shareholders, nationals of a Member State must also be in a position to seise the courts of another Member State of disputes to which their interests in companies there established may give rise, without being subject to discrimination vis-à-vis nationals of that State.

25. By prohibiting 'any discrimination on grounds of nationality', Article 6 of the Treaty requires, in the Member States, complete equality of treatment between persons in a situation governed by Community law and nationals of the Member State in question.

26. It is clear that a provision such as that at issue in the main proceedings amounts to direct discrimination on grounds of nationality. Under that provision, a Member State

does not require its own nationals to provide security, even if they are not resident and have no assets in that State.

29. Suffice it in this regard to point out that, even though the object of a provision such as that at issue in the main proceedings, namely that of ensuring enforcement of a decision on costs in favour of a defendant who has been successful in proceedings, is not as such contrary to Article 6 of the Treaty, the fact remains that that provision does not require Austrian nationals to provide security for costs, even if they are not resident and have no assets in Austria and are resident in a non-member country in which enforcement of a decision on costs in favour of a defendant is not guaranteed.

30. In those circumstances, the answer to the question submitted must be that the first paragraph of Article 6 of the Treaty must be construed as precluding a Member State from requiring provision of security for costs by a national of another Member State who is also a national of a non-member country, in which he is resident, where that national, who is not resident and has no assets in the first Member State, has brought proceedings before one of its civil courts in his capacity as a shareholder against a company established in that Member State, if such a requirement is not imposed on its own nationals who are not resident and have no assets there.

The ECJ did also address the issue of the applicability of the prohibition of discrimination in connection with private international law provisions which establish the nationality as a connecting factor (judgment 10 June 1999, case C-430/97, *Johannes*, Reports, I-3475; see Chapter XI, Matrimonial matters, B.3).

In *Tod's* (30 June 2005, case C-28/04, Reports, I-9843), the ECJ gave its ruling on the applicability of the prohibition of discrimination principle with reference to a national provision according to which the right of an author to claim in a Member State the copyright protection afforded by the law of such State is subject to a distinction based on the criterion of country of origin of the work. As a matter of fact, the enjoyment of the so-called twofold protection stated in the Berne Convention for the Protection of Literary and Artistic Works (which includes protection on designs, models and copyright) was not granted to the author of a work, whose country of origin was another Member State, which affords that work only protection under the law relating to designs. In considering whether the above rule was in compliance with the principle of non-discrimination, the ECJ held:

19. ... as the Court has consistently held, the rules regarding equality of treatment between nationals and non-nationals prohibit not only overt discrimination by reason of nationality but also all covert forms of discrimination which, by the application of other distinguishing criteria, lead to the same result.

24. The existence of a link between the country of origin of a work within the meaning of the Berne Convention, on the one hand, and the nationality of the author of that work, on the other, cannot be denied.

26. As regards published works, the country of origin is essentially, as Article 5(4)(a) of that convention indicates, the country where the work was first published. The author of a work first published in a Member State will, in the majority of cases, be a national of that State, whereas the author of a work published in another Member State will generally be a person who is not a national of the first Member State.

27. It follows that the application of rules such as those at issue in the main proceedings is liable to operate mainly to the detriment of nationals of other Member States and thus give rise to indirect discrimination on grounds of nationality.

28.   However, that finding is not sufficient under the Court's case-law to justify the conclusion that the rules at issue are incompatible with Article 12 EC. For that it would also be necessary for the application of those rules not to be justified by objective circumstances.

32.   As is apparent from Article 5(1) of the Berne Convention, the purpose of that convention is not to determine the applicable law on the protection of literary and artistic works, but to establish, as a general rule, a system of national treatment of the rights appertaining to such works.

33.   Article 2(7) of that convention contains, for its part, as the Commission rightly observes, a rule of reciprocity under which a country of the Union grants national treatment, that is to say, twofold protection, only if the country of origin of the work also does so.

34.   It should be recalled that it is settled case-law that implementation of the obligations imposed on Member States by the Treaty or secondary legislation cannot be made subject to a condition of reciprocity.

35.   Since no other objective circumstance capable of justifying rules, such as those at issue in the main proceedings has been relied on, those rules must be considered to constitute indirect discrimination on grounds of nationality prohibited by Article 12 EC.

It has to be remembered that both natural persons and companies benefit of the non-discrimination principle, as stated by the ECJ in *Factortame II* (judgment 25 July 1991, case C-221/89, Reports, I-3905; see also Chapter IX, General provision, Q). This case dealt with conditions stated by English law for the registration of vessels in the UK national register. Particularly, such registration was allowed upon condition that: the owners and the charterers, managers and operators of the vessel had to be UK nationals or companies incorporated under UK law, and that, in the latter case, at least 75 per cent of the shares in the company had to be owned by UK nationals or by companies fulfilling the same requirements, and 75 per cent of the directors of the company had to be UK nationals. The Court deemed above provisions in contrast to the EC law on the following grounds:

28.   The prohibition of discrimination on grounds of nationality, which is set out in particular, as regards the right of establishment, in Article 52 of the Treaty, is concerned with differences of treatment as between natural persons who are nationals of Member States and as between companies who are treated in the same way as such persons by virtue of Article 58.

29.   Consequently, in exercising its powers for the purposes of defining the conditions for the grant of its 'nationality' to a ship, each Member State must comply with the prohibition of discrimination against nationals of Member States on grounds of their nationality.

30.   It follows from the foregoing that a condition of the type at issue in the main proceedings which stipulates that where a vessel is owned or chartered by natural persons they must be of a particular nationality and where it is owned or chartered by a company the shareholders and directors must be of that nationality is contrary to Article 52 of the Treaty.

31.   Such a condition is also contrary to Article 221 of the Treaty, under which Member States must accord nationals of the other Member States the same treatment as their own nationals as regards participation in the capital of companies or firms within the meaning of Article 58.

32. As for the requirement for the owners, charterers, managers and operators of the vessel and, in the case of a company, the shareholders and directors to be resident and domiciled in the Member State in which the vessel is to be registered, it must be held that such a requirement, which is not justified by the rights and obligations created by the grant of a national flag to a vessel, results in discrimination on grounds of nationality. The great majority of nationals of the Member State in question are resident and domiciled in that State and therefore meet that requirement automatically, whereas nationals of other Member States would, in most cases, have to move their residence and domicile to that State in order to comply with the requirements of its legislation. It follows that such a requirement is contrary to Article 52.

Principle of equal treatment of men and women

A.   Council Directive 79/7/EEC of 19 December 1978 on the progressive implementation of the principle of equal treatment for men and women in matters of social security (OJ, L 6 of 10 January 1979) (Omissis)

B.   Council Directive 86/613/EEC of 11 December 1986 on the application of the principle of equal treatment between men and women engaged in an activity, including agriculture, in a self-employed capacity, and on the protection of self-employed women during pregnancy and motherhood (OJ, L 359 of 19 December 1986) (Omissis)[1]

C.   Council Directive 96/34/EC of 3 June 1996 on the framework agreement on parental leave concluded by UNICE, CEEP and the ETUC (OJ, L 145 of 19 June 1996) amended by the Council Directive 97/75/EC of 15 December 1997 (OJ, L 10 of 16 January 1998) (Omissis)

D.   Council Directive 2000/78/EC of 27 November 2000 establishing a general framework for equal treatment in employment and occupation (OJ, L 303 of 2 December 2000) (Omissis)

---

[1]   Directive 86/613/EEC shall be repealed, with effect from 5 August 2012, by Directive 2010/41/EU of the European Parliament and of the Council of 7 July 2010 on the application of the principle of equal treatment between men and women engaged in an activity in a self-employed capacity (OJ, L 180 of 15 July 2010).

E.   Directive 2006/54/EC of the European Parliament and of the Council of 5 July 2006 on the implementation of the principle of equal opportunities and equal treatment of men and women in matters of employment and occupation (recast) (OJ, L 204 of 26 July 2006) (Omissis)

F.   Council Regulation (EU) No 1259/2010 of 20 December 2010 implementing enhanced cooperation in the area of the law applicable to divorce and legal separation (Doc. Consilium No 17523/10): Recitals 16, 24-25, 30, Article 10

See Chapter XI, Matrimonial matters, B.2.

G.   ECJ case-law

Besides the principle of non-discrimination, the ECJ has affirmed other principles, pertaining to various areas such as the principle of equal treatment of men and women, laid down in ex Article 141 EC (former 119 and now 157 TFEU) as the right of the equal pay for male and female workers for equal work or work of equal value. This principle is deemed as a fundamental principle of the Union and enjoys direct effects within the Member States. Accordingly, in *Defrenne* (8 April 1976, case 43/75, Reports, 455), the ECJ has pointed out that:

7.   The question of the direct effect of Article 119 must be considered in the light of the nature of the principle of equal pay, the aim of this provision and its place in the scheme of the treaty.

8.   Article 119 pursues a double aim.

9.   First, in the light of the different stages of the development of social legislation in the various member States, the aim of Article 119 is to avoid a situation in which undertakings established in States which have actually implemented the principle of equal pay suffer a competitive disadvantage in intra-community competition as compared with undertakings established in states which have not yet eliminated discrimination against women workers as regards pay.

10.   Secondly, this provision forms part of the social objectives of the community, which is not merely an economic union, but is at the same time intended, by common action, to ensure social progress and seek the constant improvement of the living and working conditions of their peoples, as is emphasized by the preamble to the treaty.

11.   This aim is accentuated by the insertion of Article 119 into the body of a chapter devoted to social policy whose preliminary provision, Article 117, marks' the need to promote improved working conditions and an improved standard of living for workers, so as to make possible their harmonization while the improvement is being maintained.

12.   This double aim, which is at once economic and social, shows that the principle of equal pay forms part of the foundations of the community.

13.   Furthermore, this explains why the treaty has provided for the complete implementation of this principle by the end of the first stage of the transitional period.

14. Therefore, in interpreting this provision, it is impossible to base any argument on the dilatoriness and resistance which have delayed the actual implementation of this basic principle in certain member states.

15. In particular, since Article 119 appears in the context of the harmonization of working conditions while the improvement is being maintained, the objection that the terms of this Article may be observed in other ways than by raising the lowest salaries may be set aside.

16. Under the terms of the first paragraph of Article 119, the member states are bound to ensure and maintain 'the application of the principle that men and women should receive equal pay for equal work'.

17. The second and third paragraphs of the same Article add a certain number of details concerning the concepts of pay and work referred to in the first paragraph.

18. For the purposes of the implementation of these provisions a distinction must be drawn within the whole area of application of Article 119 between, first, direct and overt discrimination which may be identified solely with the aid of the criteria based on equal work and equal pay referred to by the Article in question and, secondly, indirect and disguised discrimination which can only be identified by reference to more explicit implementing provisions of a community or national character.

19. It is impossible not to recognize that the complete implementation of the aim pursued by Article 119, by means of the elimination of all discrimination, direct or indirect, between men and women workers, not only as regards individual undertakings but also entire branches of industry and even of the economic system as a whole, may in certain cases involve the elaboration of criteria whose implementation necessitates the taking of appropriate measures at community and national level.

20. This view is all the more essential in the light of the fact that the community measures on this question, to which reference will be made in answer to the second question, implement Article 119 from the point of view of extending the narrow criterion of 'equal work', in accordance in particular with the provisions of convention No 100 on equal pay concluded by the international labour organization in 1951, Article 2 of which establishes the principle of equal pay for work 'of equal value'.

21. Among the forms of direct discrimination which may be identified solely by reference to the criteria laid down by Article 119 must be included in particular those which have their origin in legislative provisions or in collective labour agreements and which may be detected on the basis of a purely legal analysis of the situation.

22. This applies even more in cases where men and women receive unequal pay for equal work carried out in the same establishment or service, whether public or private.

23. As is shown by the very findings of the judgment making the reference, in such a situation the court is in a position to establish all the facts which enable it to decide whether a woman worker is receiving lower pay than a male worker performing the same tasks.

24. In such situation, at least, Article 119 is directly applicable and may thus give rise to individual rights which the courts must protect.

25. Furthermore, as regards equal work, as a general rule, the national legislative provisions adopted for the implementation of the principle of equal pay as a rule merely reproduce the substance of the terms of Article 119 as regards the direct forms of discrimination.

26. Belgian legislation provides a particularly apposite illustration of this point, since Article 14 of royal decree No 40 of 24 October 1967 on the employment of women merely sets out the right of any female worker to institute proceedings before the relevant court for the application of the principle of equal pay set out in Article 119 and simply refers to that Article…

38. Furthermore it is not possible to sustain any objection that the application by national courts of the principle of equal pay would amount to modifying independent agreements concluded privately or in the sphere of industrial relations such as individual contracts and collective labour agreements.

39. In fact, since Article 119 is mandatory in nature, the prohibition on discrimination between men and women applies not only to the action of public authorities, but also extends to all agreements which are intended to regulate paid labour collectively, as well as to contracts between individuals.

Subsequently, in *Barber* (17 May 1990, case C-262/88, Reports, I-1889), the ECJ has specified the concept of remuneration holding, that comprises any other consideration provided by the employer to the worker upon termination of the employment relationship, apart from the circumstance that the worker receives it by reason of a contract of employment, pursuant to a statutory provision or by virtue of an ex gratia payment. The ECJ then has pointed out that:

32. …Article 119 prohibits any discrimination with regard to pay as between men and women, whatever the system which gives rise to such inequality. Accordingly, it is contrary to Article 119 to impose an age condition which differs according to sex in respect of pensions paid under a contracted-out scheme, even if the difference between the pensionable age for men and that for women is based on the one provided for by the national statutory scheme.

34. With regard to the means of verifying compliance with the principle of equal pay, it must be stated that if the national courts were under an obligation to make an assessment and a comparison of all the various types of consideration granted, according to the circumstances, to men and women, judicial review would be difficult and the effectiveness of Article 119 would be diminished as a result. It follows that genuine transparency, permitting an effective review, is assured only if the principle of equal pay applies to each of the elements of remuneration granted to men or women.

The principle of equal treatment of men and women has been clarified by the ECJ in the recent decision issued on the *K.B.* case (judgment 7 January 2004, case C-117/01, Reports, I-541). In particular, K.B was a woman who had shared for many years a domestic relationship with R, a person born a woman and registered as such in the UK Register of Births, who, following surgical gender reassignment, had become a man but had not, however, been able to amend his birth certificate to reflect this change officially. As a result, and contrary to their wishes, K.B. and R. had not been able to marry. This circumstance would imply that in case of pre-decease of one member of the couple, the surviving one would not have been able to receive a widower's pension, since that pension was payable only to a surviving spouse of a lawful marriage. Thus, in this case the discussion concerned the lawfulness in respect to ex Article 141 of the EC Treaty (former 119 EEC and now 157 TFEU) of a national provision which prevents a transsexual partner of a couple from gaining the social benefit of the survivor's pension. The ECJ, after recalling that the right for widows to receive a survivor's pension falls within the scope of Article 141 of the EC Treaty, ruled as follows:

28. The decision to restrict certain benefits to married couples while excluding all persons who live together without being married is either a matter for the legislature to decide or a matter for the national courts as to the interpretation of domestic legal rules, and individuals cannot claim that there is discrimination on grounds of sex, prohibited by Community law.

29. In this instance, such a requirement cannot be regarded per se as discriminatory on grounds of sex and, accordingly, as contrary to Article 141 EC or Directive 75/117, since for the purposes of awarding the survivor's pension it is irrelevant whether the claimant is a man or a woman.

30. However, in a situation such as that before the national court, there is inequality of treatment which, although it does not directly undermine enjoyment of a right protected by Community law, affects one of the conditions for the grant of that right. As the Advocate General noted in point 74 of his Opinion, the inequality of treatment does not relate to the award of a widower's pension but to a necessary precondition for the grant of such a pension: namely, the capacity to marry.

31. In the United Kingdom, by comparison with a heterosexual couple where neither partner's identity is the result of gender reassignment surgery and the couple are therefore able to marry and, as the case may be, have the benefit of a survivor's pension which forms part of the pay of one of them, a couple such as K.B. and R. are quite unable to satisfy the marriage requirement, as laid down by the *NHS Pension Scheme* for the purpose of the award of a survivor's pension.

32. The fact that it is impossible for them to marry is due to the fact, first, that the Matrimonial Causes Act 1973 deems a marriage void if the parties are not respectively male and female; second, that a person's sex is deemed to be that appearing on his or her birth certificate; and, third, that the Births and Deaths Registration Act does not allow for any alteration of the register of births, except in the case of clerical error or an error of fact.

33. The European Court of Human Rights has held that the fact that it is impossible for a transsexual to marry a person of the sex to which he or she belonged prior to gender reassignment surgery, which arises because, for the purposes of the registers of civil status, they belong to the same sex (United Kingdom legislation not admitting of legal recognition of transsexuals' new identity), was a breach of their right to marry under Article 12 of the ECHR (see Eur. Court H.R. judgments of 11 July 2002, *Goodwin v United Kingdom*, and *I v United Kingdom*, not yet published in the *Reports of Judgments and Decisions*, §§ 97 to104 and §§ 77 to84 respectively).

34. Legislation, such as that at issue in the main proceedings, which, in breach of the ECHR, prevents a couple such as K.B. and R. from fulfilling the marriage requirement which must be met for one of them to be able to benefit from part of the pay of the other must be regarded as being, in principle, incompatible with the requirements of Article 141 EC.

35. Since it is for the Member States to determine the conditions under which legal recognition is given to the change of gender of a person in R.'s situation — as the European Court of Human Rights has accepted (*Goodwin v United Kingdom*, § 103) — it is for the national court to determine whether in a case such as that in the main proceedings a person in K.B.'s situation can rely on Article 141 EC in order to gain recognition of her right to nominate her partner as the beneficiary of a survivor's pension.

36. It follows from the foregoing that Article 141 EC, in principle, precludes legislation, such as that at issue before the national court, which, in breach of the ECHR, prevents a couple such as K.B. and R. from fulfilling the marriage requirement which must be met for one of them to be able to benefit from part of the pay of the other. It is for the national court to determine whether in a case such as that in the main proceedings a person in K.B.'s situation can rely on Article 141 EC in order to gain recognition of her right to nominate her partner as the beneficiary of a survivor's pension.

Due process

A.   ECJ case-law

As regards procedural matters, it should be borne in mind the principle of due process and fair trial which has been recognised in various ECJ judgments in its activity of interpretation of Article 27(2) of the 1968 Brussels Convention, now replaced by Council Regulation (EC) No 44/2001 as hereinafter mentioned (see Chapter IV, General provisions, A.10). This principle has been recently re-affirmed in the *Krombach* judgment (28 March 2000, case C-7/98, Reports, I-1935) that deals with the concept of 'public policy' laid down in Article 27(1) of the 1968 Brussels Convention pursuant to which the contrast with public policy of a Member State is a ground to deny recognition and the enforcement in a Member State to a judgment issued in a different Member State. Following previous judgments, the ECJ confirmed that Article 27 should be interpreted in a strict manner and that the public-policy clause should be regarded as exceptional. The ECJ noted that:

22. It follows that, while the Contracting States in principle remain free, by virtue of the proviso in Article 27, point 1, of the Convention, to determine, according to their own conceptions, what public policy requires, the limits of that concept are a matter for interpretation of the Convention.

23. Consequently, while it is not for the Court to define the content of the public policy of a Contracting State, it is nonetheless required to review the limits within which the courts of a Contracting State may have recourse to that concept for the purpose of refusing recognition to a judgment emanating from a court in another Contracting State.

With specific regard to the due process, according to the ECJ

24. It should be noted in this regard that, since the Convention was concluded on the basis of Article 220 of the Treaty and within the framework which it defines, its provisions are linked to the Treaty.

25. The Court has consistently held that fundamental rights form an integral part of the general principles of law whose observance the Court ensures (see, in particular, opinion 2/94 of 28 March 1996, Reports, I-1759, paragraph 33). For that purpose, the Court draws inspiration from the constitutional traditions common to the Member States and from the guidelines supplied by international treaties for the protection of human rights on which the Member States have collaborated or of which they are signatories. In that regard, the European Convention for the Protection of Human Rights and Fundamental Freedoms (hereinafter the ECHR) has particular significance.

26. The Court has thus expressly recognised the general principle of Community law that everyone is entitled to fair legal process, which is inspired by those fundamental rights.

27. Article F(2) of the Treaty on European Union (after amendment, Article 6(2) EU) embodies that case-law. It provides: The Union shall respect fundamental rights, as guaranteed by the European Convention for the Protection of Human Rights and Fundamental Freedoms signed in Rome on 4 November 1950 and as they result from the constitutional traditions common to the Member States, as general principles of Community law.

31. Under the system of the [Brussels] Convention, with the exception of certain cases exhaustively listed in the first paragraph of Article 28... the court before which enforcement is sought cannot review the jurisdiction of the court of the State of origin. This fundamental principle, which is set out in the first phrase of the third paragraph of Article 28 of the Convention, is reinforced by the specific statement, in the second phrase of the same paragraph, that the test of public policy referred to in point 1 of Article 27 may not be applied to the rules relating to jurisdiction.

32. It follows that the public policy of the State in which enforcement is sought cannot be raised as a bar to recognition or enforcement of a judgment given in another Contracting State solely on the ground that the court of origin failed to comply with the rules of the Convention which relate to jurisdiction.

37. Recourse to the public-policy clause in Article 27, point 1, of the Convention can be envisaged only where recognition or enforcement of the judgment delivered in another Contracting State would be at variance to an unacceptable degree with the legal order of the State in which enforcement is sought in as much as it infringes a fundamental principle. In order for the prohibition of any review of the foreign judgment as to its substance to be observed, the infringement would have to constitute a manifest breach of a rule of law regarded as essential in the legal order of the State in which enforcement is sought or of a right recognised as being fundamental within that legal order.

38. With regard to the right to be defended, to which the question submitted to the Court refers, this occupies a prominent position in the organisation and conduct of a fair trial and is one of the fundamental rights deriving from the constitutional traditions common to the Member States.

39. More specifically still, the European Court of Human Rights has on several occasions ruled in cases relating to criminal proceedings that, although not absolute, the right of every person charged with an offence to be effectively defended by a lawyer, if need be one appointed by the court, is one of the fundamental elements in a fair trial and an accused person does not forfeit entitlement to such a right simply because he is not present at the hearing.

40. It follows from that case-law that a national court of a Contracting State is entitled to hold that a refusal to hear the defence of an accused person who is not present at the hearing constitutes a manifest breach of a fundamental right.

41. The national court is, however, unsure as to whether the court of the State in which enforcement is sought can take account, in relation to Article 27, point 1, of the Convention, of a breach of this nature having regard to the wording of Article II of the Protocol. That provision, which involves extending the scope of the Convention to the criminal field because of the consequences which a judgment of a criminal court may entail in civil and commercial matters, recognises the right to be defended without appearing in person before the criminal courts of a Contracting State for persons who

are not nationals of that State and who are domiciled in another Contracting State only in so far as they are being prosecuted for an offence committed unintentionally. This restriction has been construed as meaning that the Convention clearly seeks to deny the right to be defended without appearing in person to persons who are being prosecuted for offences which are sufficiently serious to justify this.

42. However, it follows from a line of case-law developed by the Court on the basis of the principles referred to in paragraphs 25 and 26 of the present judgment that observance of the right to a fair hearing is, in all proceedings initiated against a person which are liable to culminate in a measure adversely affecting that person, a fundamental principle of Community law which must be guaranteed even in the absence of any rules governing the proceedings in question.

43. The Court has also held that, even though the Convention is intended to secure the simplification of formalities governing the reciprocal recognition and enforcement of judgments of courts or tribunals, it is not permissible to achieve that aim by undermining the right to a fair hearing.

44. It follows from the foregoing developments in the case-law that recourse to the public-policy clause must be regarded as being possible in exceptional cases where the guarantees laid down in the legislation of the State of origin and in the Convention itself have been insufficient to protect the defendant from a manifest breach of his right to defend himself before the court of origin, as recognised by the ECHR. Consequently, Article II of the Protocol cannot be construed as precluding the court of the State in which enforcement is sought from being entitled to take account, in relation to public policy, as referred to in Article 27, point 1, of the Convention, of the fact that, in an action for damages based on an offence, the court of the State of origin refused to hear the defence of the accused person, who was being prosecuted for an intentional offence, solely on the ground that that person was not present at the hearing.

More recently the ECJ, in *Gambazzi* (2 April 2009, case C-394/07, Reports I-2563), observed that

26. In case C-7/98 *Krombach*, paragraph 23, the Court of Justice held that, while it is not for the Court to define the content of the public policy of a Contracting State, it is nonetheless required to review the limits within which the courts of a Contracting State may have recourse to that concept for the purpose of refusing recognition to a judgment emanating from a court in another Contracting State.

27. In that regard, the Court explained that recourse to a public policy clause can be envisaged only where recognition or enforcement of the judgment delivered in another Contracting State would be at variance to an unacceptable degree with the legal order of the State in which enforcement is sought in as much as it infringes a fundamental principle. The infringement would have to constitute a manifest breach of a rule of law regarded as essential in the legal order of the State in which enforcement is sought or of a right recognised as being fundamental within that legal order (*Krombach*, paragraph 37).

28. With regard to the exercise of the rights of the defence, to which the question submitted for a preliminary ruling refers, the Court has pointed out that this occupies a prominent position in the organisation and conduct of a fair trial and is one of the fundamental rights deriving from the constitutional traditions common to the Member States and from the international treaties for the protection of human rights on which the Member States have collaborated or of which they are signatories, among which the

European Convention for the Protection of Human Rights and Fundamental Freedoms, signed in Rome on 4 November 1950, is of particular importance (see, to that effect, *Krombach*, paragraphs 38 and 39).

29. It should, however, be borne in mind that fundamental rights, such as respect for the rights of the defence, do not constitute unfettered prerogatives and may be subject to restrictions. However, such restrictions must in fact correspond to the objectives of public interest pursued by the measure in question and must not constitute, with regard to the aim pursued, a manifest or disproportionate breach of the rights thus guaranteed.

30. The Government of the United Kingdom explained that the aim of the 'freezing', 'disclosure' and 'unless' orders is to ensure the fair and efficient administration of justice.

31. It must be conceded that such an objective is capable of justifying a restriction on the rights of the defence. As observed by the Italian and Greek Governments, the legal systems of most of the Member States provide for the imposition of sanctions on persons who, in civil proceedings, adopt delaying tactics which would ultimately lead to a denial of justice.

32. Such sanctions may not, however, be manifestly disproportionate to the aim pursued, which is to ensure the efficient conduct of proceedings in the interests of the sound administration of justice.

33. With regard to the sanction adopted in the main proceedings, the exclusion of Mr Gambazzi from any participation in the proceedings, that is, as the Advocate General stated in point 67 of her Opinion, the most serious restriction possible on the rights of the defence. Consequently, such a restriction must satisfy very exacting requirements if it is not to be regarded as a manifest and disproportionate infringement of those rights.

34. It is for the national court to assess, in the light of the specific circumstances of these proceedings, if that is the case.

35. In that context, the parties to the main proceedings refer to a judgment of 9 November 2004 of the Tribunal fédéral (Federal Supreme Court) (Switzerland) (case 4P082/2004). By that judgment, that court dismissed an appeal brought by CIBC and DaimlerChrysler against a decision of the Tribunale d'appello del cantone Ticino (Court of Appeal of the Canton of Ticino, Switzerland) which refused to recognise and enforce in Switzerland the High Court judgments against Mr Gambazzi on the basis of Article 27(1) of the Lugano Convention. The Tribunal fédéral held that Mr Gambazzi's exclusion from the High Court proceedings was not contrary to Swiss public policy, but considered that other circumstances, to which the national court did not refer in the present proceedings, nevertheless justified the application of the public policy clause.

36. In accordance with the declaration by the representatives of the Governments of the States signatories to the Lugano Convention which are members of the European Communities, it is appropriate that the Court pay due account to the principles contained in that Tribunal fédéral judgment and, in application of Article 1 of Protocol 2 on the uniform interpretation of that convention, the national court is to pay due account to those principles.

37. In that regard, it must be pointed out that the Tribunal fédéral refers, to give substance to the public policy clause, to the right to a fair trial and the right to be heard, principles to which the Court itself referred in *Krombach*, and to which it has drawn attention in paragraphs 27 and 28 of this judgment.

38. With regard to the specific assessment of the conflict with Swiss public policy carried out in the present case by the Tribunal fédéral in its abovementioned judgment,

it should be noted that that assessment cannot formally bind the national court. That is especially true in this case because the latter court must carry out its assessment with regard to Italian public policy.

39. In order to fulfil its task of interpretation described in paragraph 26 of the present judgment, it is however for the Court to explain the principles which it has defined by indicating the general criteria with regard to which the national court must carry out its assessment.

40. To that end, it must be stated that the question of the compatibility of the exclusion measure adopted by the court of the State of origin with public policy in the State in which enforcement is sought must be assessed having regard to the proceedings as a whole in the light of all the circumstances.

41. That means taking into account, in the present case, not only the circumstances in which, at the conclusion of the High Court proceedings, the decisions of that court — the enforcement of which is sought — were taken, but also the circumstances in which, at an earlier stage, the disclosure order and the unless order were adopted.

46. It must be underlined that verifying those points, to the extent that the sole purpose is to identify any manifest and disproportionate infringement of the right to be heard, does not mean reviewing the High Court's assessment of the merits, which would constitute a review as to the substance of the judgment expressly prohibited by Article 29 and the third paragraph of Article 34 of the Brussels Convention. The referring court must confine itself to identifying the legal remedies which were available to Mr Gambazzi and to verifying that they offered him the possibility of being heard, in compliance with the adversarial principle and the full exercise of the rights of defence.

Public policy, provisions which cannot be derogated from by agreement and overriding mandatory provisions of EU law

A.1.　Council Regulation (EC) No 2271/96 of 22 November 1996 protecting against the effects of the extra-territorial application of legislation adopted by a third country, and actions based thereon or resulting therefrom (OJ, L 309 of 29 November 1996)[1]

[1]　Whereas a third country has enacted certain laws, regulations, and other legislative instruments which purport to regulate activities of natural and legal persons under the jurisdiction of the Member State;

Whereas by their extra-territorial application such laws, regulations and other legislative instruments violate international law and impede the attainment of the aforementioned objectives;

[2] Whereas such laws, including regulations and other legislative instruments, and actions based thereon or resulting therefrom affect or are likely to affect the established

---

legal order and have adverse effects on the interests of the Community and the interests of natural and legal persons exercising rights under the Treaty establishing the European Community;

[3] Whereas, under these exceptional circumstances, it is necessary to take action at Community level to protect the established legal order, the interests of the Community and the interests of the said natural and legal persons, in particular by removing, neutralising, blocking or otherwise countering the effects of the foreign legislation concerned;

[4] Whereas the request to supply information under this Regulation does not preclude a Member State from requiring information of the same kind to be provided to the authorities of that State;

[5] Whereas the Council has adopted the Joint Action 96/668/CFSP of 22 November 1996 in order to ensure that the Member States take the necessary measures to protect those natural and legal persons whose interests are affected by the aforementioned laws and actions based thereon, insofar as those interests are not protected by this Regulation;...

Article 1. This Regulation provides protection against and counteracts the effects of the extra-territorial application of the laws specified in the Annex of this Regulation, including regulations and other legislative instruments, and of actions based thereon or resulting therefrom, where such application affects the interests of persons, referred to in Article 11, engaging in international trade and/or the movement of capital and related commercial activities between the Community and third countries.

Acting in accordance with the relevant provisions of the Treaty and notwithstanding the provisions of Article 7(c), the Council may add or delete laws to or from the Annex to this Regulation.

Article 4. No judgment of a court or tribunal and no decision of an administrative authority located outside the Community giving effect, directly or indirectly, to the laws specified in the Annex or to actions based thereon or resulting there from, shall be recognized or be enforceable in any manner.

Article 5. No person referred to in Article 11 shall comply, whether directly or through a subsidiary or other intermediary person, actively or by deliberate omission, with any requirement or prohibition, including requests of foreign courts, based on or resulting, directly or indirectly, from the laws specified in the Annex or from actions based thereon or resulting therefrom.

Persons may be authorized, in accordance with the procedures provided in Articles 7 and 8, to comply fully or partially to the extent that noncompliance would seriously damage their interests or those of the Community. The criteria for the application of this provision shall be established in accordance with the procedure set out in Article 8. When there is sufficient evidence that non-compliance would cause serious damage to a natural or legal person, the Commission shall expeditiously submit to the committee referred to in Article 8 a draft of the appropriate measures to be taken under the terms of the Regulation.

Article 6. Any person referred to in Article 11, who is engaging in an activity referred to in Article 1 shall be entitled to recover any damages, including legal costs, caused to that person by the application of the laws specified in the Annex or by actions based thereon or resulting therefrom.

Such recovery may be obtained from the natural or legal person or any other entity causing the damages or from any person acting on its behalf or intermediary.

The Brussels Convention of 27 September 1968 on jurisdiction and the enforcement of judgments in civil and commercial matters shall apply to proceedings brought and judgments given under this Article. Recovery may be obtained on the basis of the provisions of Sections 2 to 6 of Title II of that Convention, as well as, in accordance with Article 57 of that Convention, through judicial proceedings instituted in the Courts of any Member State where that person, entity, person acting on its behalf or intermediary holds assets.

Without prejudice to other means available and in accordance with applicable law, the recovery could take the form of seizure and sale of assets held by those persons, entities, persons acting on their behalf or intermediaries within the Community, including shares held in a legal person incorporated within the Community.

Article 11.   This Regulation shall apply to:

1.   any natural person being a resident in the Community[4] and a national of a Member State,

2.   any legal person incorporated within the Community,

3.   any natural or legal person referred to in Article 1(2) of Regulation (EEC) No 4055/86,

4.   any other natural person being a resident in the Community, unless that person is in the country of which he is a national,

5.   any other natural person within the Community, including its territorial waters and air space and in any aircraft or on any vessel under the jurisdiction or control of a Member State, acting in a professional capacity.

A.2. Joint Action of 22 November 1996 No 96/668/CFSP adopted by the Council on the basis of Articles J.3 and K.3 of the Treaty on European Union concerning measures protecting against the effects of the extra-territorial application of legislation adopted by a third country, and actions based thereon or resulting therefrom (OJ, L 309 of 29 November 1996)

Whereas a third country has enacted certain laws, regulations, and other legislative instruments which purport to regulate the activities of natural and legal persons under the jurisdiction of the Member States of the European Union;

Whereas by their extra-territorial application such laws, regulations and other legislative instruments violate international law;

Whereas such laws including regulations and other legislative instruments and actions based thereon or resulting therefrom affect or are likely to affect the established

---

[4]   [This footnote is published in the original numerical order as in OJ] For the purposes of this Regulation, being a resident in the Community means being legally established in the Community for a period of at least six months within the 12-month period immediately prior to the date on which, under this Regulation, an obligation arises or a right is exercised.

legal order and have adverse affects on the interests of the European Union, and the interests of the said natural and legal persons;

Whereas the Council has adopted Regulation (EC) No 2271/96 in order to protect the interests of the Community and of natural and legal persons exercising rights under the Treaty establishing the European Community;

Whereas, in these exceptional circumstances, the Member States should take the necessary measures in order to ensure protection for the interests of the said natural and legal persons in so far as such protection is not provided under Regulation (EC) No 2271/96;

Whereas this Joint Action and Regulation (EC) No 2271/96 constitute together an integrated system involving the Community and the Member States each in accordance with its own powers;

Article 1   Each Member State shall take the measures it deems necessary to protect the interests of any person referred to in Article 11 of Regulation (EC) No 2271/96 and affected by the extra-territorial application of laws including regulations and other legislative instruments referred to in Annex to Regulation (EC) No 2271/96, and actions based thereon or resulting therefrom, in so far as these interests are not protected under that Regulation.

Article 2   This Joint Action shall enter into force on the day of its adoption.

B.   Council Regulation (EC) No 2238/2003 of 15 December 2003 protecting against the effects of the application of the United States Anti-Dumping Act of 1916, and actions based thereon or resulting therefrom (OJ, L 333 of 20 December 2003)

(1)   The objectives of the Community include contributing to the harmonious development of world trade and to the progressive abolition of restrictions on international trade.

(2)   In the United States of America ('USA'), the Anti-Dumping Act of 1916[1] provides for civil and criminal proceedings and penalties against dumping of any articles when conducted with an intent to destroy or injure an industry in the USA, or to prevent the establishment of an industry in the USA, or to restrain or monopolise any part of trade and commerce in such articles in the USA.

(3)   On 26 September 2000, the Dispute Settlement Body of the World Trade Organisation (WTO), adopting the Appellate Body report[2] and the Panel report,[3]

as upheld by the Appellate Body report, found the Anti-Dumping Act of 1916 to be incompatible with the US obligations under the WTO agreements, notably by

---

[1]   [Footnotes are published in the original numerical order as in OJ] Enacted under the heading of 'unfair-competition' in Title VIII of the Revenue Act of 1916; Title VIII of that Act is codified at United States Code 71–74, cited as 15 USC § 72.

[2]   AB-2000-5 and AB-2000-6, 28 August 2000.

[3]   United States — Anti-Dumping Act of 1916, Panel report (WT/DS/136/R, 31 March 2000).

providing remedies against dumping, such as the imposition of treble damages, fines and imprisonment, none of which is permitted by the General Agreement on Tariffs and Trade 1994 ('GATT 1994') or by the Agreement on Implementation of Article VI of the General Agreement on Tariffs and Trade 1994 ('AD Agreement').

(4) The USA failed to comply with the Panel and Appellate Body recommendations and rulings within the time limit of 20 December 2001. As a result, the Community requested authorisation to suspend the application to the USA of its obligations under GATT 1994 and the AD Agreement.

(5) In February 2002, the Community agreed to suspend the arbitration on its request, on the express understanding that a bill was pending in the US Congress to repeal the Anti-Dumping Act of 1916 and to terminate the on-going cases before US Courts.

(6) The Anti-Dumping Act of 1916 has yet to be repealed, and claims brought under this Act are pending before US Courts against persons under the jurisdiction of the Member States.

(7) These judicial proceedings are causing substantial litigation costs and may ultimately result in a judgment awarding treble damages.

(8) By its maintenance and application, the Anti-Dumping Act of 1916 impedes the attainment of the aforementioned objectives, affects the established legal order and has adverse effects on the interests of the Community and the interests of natural and legal persons exercising rights under the Treaty

(9) Under these exceptional circumstances, it is necessary to take action at Community level to protect the interests of the natural and legal persons under the jurisdiction of the Member States, in particular by removing, neutralising, blocking or otherwise counteracting the effects of the Anti-Dumping Act of 1916,…

Article 1.   No judgment of a court or tribunal and no decision of an administrative authority located in the United States of America giving effect, directly or indirectly, to the Anti-Dumping Act of 1916 or to actions based thereon or resulting therefrom, shall be recognised or be enforceable in any manner.

Article 2.   1.   Any person referred to in Article 3 shall be entitled to recover any outlays, costs, damages and miscellaneous expenses incurred by him or her as a result of the application of the Anti-Dumping Act of 1916 or by actions based thereon or resulting therefrom.

2.   Recovery may be obtained as soon as an action under the Anti-Dumping Act of 1916 is commenced.

3.   Recovery may be obtained from the natural or legal person or any other entity that brought a claim under the Anti-Dumping Act of 1916 or from any person or entity related to that person or entity. Persons or entities shall be deemed to be related if:

(a)   they are officers or directors of one another's businesses;
(b)   they are legally recognised partners in business;
(c)   one of them controls directly or indirectly the other;
(d)   both of them are directly or indirectly controlled by a third person.

4.   Without prejudice to other means available and in accordance with applicable law, the recovery may take the form of seizure and sale of assets held by the defendant, including shares held in a legal person incorporated within the Community.

Article 3. The persons referred to in Article 2(1) shall be:

    (a) any natural person being a resident in the Community;

    (b) any legal person incorporated within the Community;

    (c) any natural or legal person referred to in Article 1(2) of Regulation (EEC) No 4055/86(4);

    (d) any other natural person acting in a professional capacity within the Community, including in territorial waters and air space and in any aircraft or on any vessel under the jurisdiction or control of a Member State.

For the purposes of point (a), 'being a resident in the Community' shall mean being legally established in the Community for a period of at least six months within the 12-month period immediately prior to the date on which, under this Regulation, an obligation arises or a right is exercised.

C. Council Regulation (EC) No 1/2003 of 16 December 2002 on the implementation of the rules on competition laid down in Articles 81 and 82 of the Treaty (OJ, L 1 of 4 January 2003)[1]

Article 16. Uniform application of Community competition law. 1. When national courts rule on agreements, decisions or practices under Article 81 or Article 82 of the Treaty which are already the subject of a Commission decision, they cannot take decisions running counter to the decision adopted by the Commission. They must also avoid giving decisions which would conflict with a decision contemplated by the Commission in proceedings it has initiated. To that effect, the national court may assess whether it is necessary to stay its proceedings. This obligation is without prejudice to the rights and obligations under Article 234 of the Treaty...

D. Regulation (EC) No 864/2007 of the European Parliament and of the Council of 11 July 2007 on the law applicable to non-contractual obligations (Rome II) (OJ, L 199 of 31 July 2007): Article 14(3)

See Chapter VII, A.1.

E. Regulation (EC) No 593/2008 of the European Parliament and of the Council of 17 June 2008 on the law applicable to contractual obligations (Rome I) (OJ, L 177 of 4 July 2008): Article 3(4)

See Chapter VI, General provisions, A.1.

---

[1] As finally amended by Regulation (EC) No 1419/2006 of 25 September 2006 (OJ, L 269 of 28 September 2006). [Note of the Editor]

F.   ECJ case-law

The ECJ held that Article 81 EC (now 101 TFEU), which safeguards competition, is a fundamental provision of EU public policy, whose breach can be opposed by national courts in order to refuse the recognition of arbitral award (judgment 1 June 1999, case C-126/97, *Eco Swiss*, Reports, I-3055):

36.   …according to Article 3(g) of the EC Treaty, Article 81 of the Treaty constitutes a fundamental provision which is essential for the accomplishment of the tasks entrusted to the Community and, in particular, for the functioning of the internal market. The importance of such a provision led the framers of the Treaty to provide expressly, in Article 81(2) of the Treaty, that any agreements or decisions prohibited pursuant to that article are to be automatically void.

37.   It follows that where its domestic rules of procedure require a national court to grant an application for annulment of an arbitration award where such an application is founded on failure to observe national rules of public policy, it must also grant such an application where it is founded on failure to comply with the prohibition laid down in Article 81(1) of the Treaty.

38.   That conclusion is not affected by the fact that the New York Convention of 10 June 1958 on the Recognition and Enforcement of Foreign Arbitral Awards, which has been ratified by all the Member States, provides that recognition and enforcement of an arbitration award may be refused only on certain specific grounds, namely where the award does not fall within the terms of the submission to arbitration or goes beyond its scope, where the award is not binding on the parties or where recognition or enforcement of the award would be contrary to the public policy of the country where such recognition and enforcement are sought (Articles V(1)(c) and (e) and II(b) of the New York Convention).

39.   For the reasons stated in paragraph 36 above, the provisions of Article 81 of the Treaty may be regarded as a matter of public policy within the meaning of the New York Convention.

40.   Lastly, it should be recalled that, as explained in paragraph 34 above, arbitrators, unlike national courts and tribunals, are not in a position to request this Court to give a preliminary ruling on questions of interpretation of Community law. However, it is manifestly in the interest of the Community legal order that, in order to forestall differences of interpretation, every Community provision should be given a uniform interpretation, irrespective of the circumstances in which it is to be applied. It follows that, in the circumstances of the present case, unlike *Van Schijndel and Van Veen*, Community law requires that questions concerning the interpretation of the prohibition laid down in Article 81(1) of the Treaty should be open to examination by national courts when asked to determine the validity of an arbitration award and that it should be possible for those questions to be referred, if necessary, to the Court of Justice for a preliminary ruling.

41.   The answer to be given to the second question must therefore be that a national court to which application is made for annulment of an arbitration award must grant that application if it considers that the award in question is in fact contrary to Article 81 of the Treaty, where its domestic rules of procedure require it to grant an application for annulment founded on failure to observe national rules of public policy.

In the more recent decision issued in *Manfredi* (judgment 13 July 2006, joined cases C-295/04 to C-298/04, Reports, I-6619), the ECJ has reaffirmed that:

31. Moreover, it should be recalled that Articles 81 EC and 82 EC are a matter of public policy which must be automatically applied by national courts.

Even before the adoption of Regulation No 1/2003, the ECJ, in *Masterfoods* (14 December 2000, case C-344/98, Reports, I-11369), inferred from the nature of Articles 81 and 82 EC (now Articles 101 and 102 TFEU) that:

57. When the outcome of the dispute before the national court depends on the validity of the Commission decision, it follows from the obligation of sincere cooperation that the national court should, in order to avoid reaching a decision that runs counter to that of the Commission, stay its proceedings pending final judgment in the action for annulment by the Community Courts, unless it considers that, in the circumstances of the case, a reference to the Court of Justice for a preliminary ruling on the validity of the Commission decision is warranted.

The principles expressed in above-mentioned *Eco Swiss* case are recalled and clarified in *Mostaza Claro* (26 October 2006, case C-168/05, Reports, I-10421), with reference to Article 6 of Directive 93/13/EEC of 5 April 1993 on unfair terms in consumer contracts.

36. The importance of consumer protection has in particular led the Community legislature to lay down, in Article 6(1) of the Directive, that unfair terms used in a contract concluded with a consumer by a seller or supplier 'shall… not be binding on the consumer'. This is a mandatory provision which, taking into account the weaker position of one of the parties to the contract, aims to replace the formal balance which the latter establishes between the rights and obligations of the parties with an effective balance which re-establishes equality between them.

37. Moreover, as the aim of the Directive is to strengthen consumer protection, it constitutes, according to Article 3(1)(t) EC, a measure which is essential to the accomplishment of the tasks entrusted to the Community and, in particular, to raising the standard of living and the quality of life in its territory (see, by analogy, concerning Article 81 EC, *Eco Swiss*, paragraph 36).

38. The nature and importance of the public interest underlying the protection which the Directive confers on consumers justify, moreover, the national court being required to assess of its own motion whether a contractual term is unfair, compensating in this way for the imbalance which exists between the consumer and the seller or supplier.

39. Having regard to the foregoing, the answer to the question referred must be that the Directive must be interpreted as meaning that a national court seised of an action for annulment of an arbitration award must determine whether the arbitration agreement is void and annul that award where that agreement contains an unfair term, even though the consumer has not pleaded that invalidity in the course of the arbitration proceedings, but only in that of the action for annulment.

The ECJ confirmed this approach and clarified the nature of Directive 93/13/EEC in *Asturcom Telecomunicaciones* (6 October 2009, case C-40/08, Reports, I-9579), where it ruled that

52. … [i]n view of the nature and importance of the public interest underlying the protection which Directive 93/13 confers on consumers, Article 6 of the Directive must be regarded as a provision of equal standing to national rules which rank, within the domestic legal system, as rules of public policy.

53. It follows from this that, inasmuch as the national court or tribunal seised of an action for enforcement of a final arbitration award is required, in accordance with domestic rules of procedure, to assess of its own motion whether an arbitration clause is in conflict with domestic rules of public policy, it is also obliged to assess of its own motion whether that clause is unfair in the light of Article 6 of that Directive, where it has available to it the legal and factual elements necessary for that task.

54. The national court or tribunal is also under such an obligation where, under the domestic legal system, it has a discretion whether to consider of its own motion whether such a clause is in conflict with national rules of public policy.

Not every breach of the EC rules on the fundamental freedoms justifies recourse to public policy in order to refuse recognition or enforcement of a foreign judgment or an arbitral award. In *Renault* (11 May 2000, case C-38/98, Reports, I-2973), which refers extensively to *Krombach*, the ECJ has stated:

31. In this case, what has led the court of the State in which enforcement was sought to question the compatibility of the foreign judgment with public policy in its own State is the possibility that the court of the State of origin erred in applying certain rules of Community law. The court of the State in which enforcement was sought is in doubt as to the compatibility with the principles of free movement of goods and freedom of competition of recognition by the court of the State of origin of the existence of an intellectual property right in body parts for cars enabling the holder to prohibit traders in another Contracting State from manufacturing, selling, transporting, importing or exporting such body parts in that Contracting State.

32. The fact that the alleged error concerns rules of Community law does not alter the conditions for being able to rely on the clause on public policy. It is for the national court to ensure with equal diligence the protection of rights established in national law and rights conferred by Community law.

33. The court of the State in which enforcement is sought cannot, without undermining the aim of the Convention, refuse recognition of a decision emanating from another Contracting State solely on the ground that it considers that national or Community law was misapplied in that decision. On the contrary, it must be considered whether, in such cases, the system of legal remedies in each Contracting State, together with the preliminary ruling procedure provided for in Article 177 of the Treaty, affords a sufficient guarantee to individuals.

34. Since an error of law such as that alleged in the main proceedings does not constitute a manifest breach of a rule of law regarded as essential in the legal order of the State in which enforcement is sought, the reply to the third question must be that Article 27, point 1, of the Convention must be interpreted as meaning that a judgment of a court or tribunal of a Contracting State recognising the existence of an intellectual property right in body parts for cars, and conferring on the holder of that right protection by enabling him to prevent third parties trading in another Contracting State from manufacturing, selling, transporting, importing or exporting in that Contracting State such body parts, cannot be considered to be contrary to public policy.

More recently the ECJ affirmed the existence of overriding mandatory provisions of the EU, which must be applied even when the law governing a contract is the law of a third country. In *Boukhalfa*, the ECJ affirmed that the non-discrimination principle applies also when a national of a Member State is employed by the embassy of another Member State under a contract subject to the law of a non Member State where the activity is carried out. In *Ingmar* (9 November 2000, case C-381/98, Reports, I-9305), the ECJ held that Articles 17 and 18 of Directive No 86/653/EEC on the coordination of the laws of the Member States relating to self-employed commercial agents, which guarantee certain rights to commercial agents after termination of agency contracts, must be applied where the commercial agent carried on his activity in a Member State, although the principal is established in a non-member country and a clause of the contract stipulates that the contract is to be governed by the law of that country.

15. The parties to the main proceedings, the United Kingdom and German Governments and the Commission agree that the freedom of contracting parties to choose the system of law by which they wish their contractual relations to be governed is a basic tenet of private international law and that that freedom is removed only by rules that are mandatory.

16. However, their submissions differ as to the conditions which a legal rule must satisfy in order to be classified as a mandatory rule for the purposes of private international law.

17. Eaton contends that such mandatory rules can arise only in extremely limited circumstances and that, in the present case, there is no reason to apply the Directive, which is intended to harmonise the domestic laws of the Member States, to parties established outside the European Union.

18. Ingmar, the United Kingdom Government and the Commission submit that the question of the territorial scope of the Directive is a question of Community law. In their submission, the objectives pursued by the Directive require that its provisions be applied to all commercial agents established in a Member State, irrespective of the nationality or the place of establishment of their principal.

19. According to the German Government, in the absence of any express provision in the Directive as regards its territorial scope, it is for the court of a Member State seised of a dispute concerning a commercial agent's entitlement to indemnity or compensation to examine the question whether the applicable national rules are to be regarded as mandatory rules for the purposes of private international law.

20. In that respect, it should be borne in mind, first, that the Directive is designed to protect commercial agents, as defined in the Directive.

21. The purpose of Articles 17 to 19 of the Directive, in particular, is to protect the commercial agent after termination of the contract. The regime established by the Directive for that purpose is mandatory in nature. Article 17 requires Member States to put in place a mechanism for providing reparation to the commercial agent after termination of the contract. Admittedly, that article allows the Member States to choose between indemnification and compensation for damage. However, Articles 17 and 18 prescribe a precise framework within which the Member States may exercise their discretion as to the choice of methods for calculating the indemnity or compensation to be granted.

22. The mandatory nature of those articles is confirmed by the fact that, under Article 19 of the Directive, the parties may not derogate from them to the detriment of the commercial agent before the contract expires. It is also borne out by the fact that, with regard to the United Kingdom, Article 22 of the Directive provides for the immediate application of the national provisions implementing the Directive to contracts in operation.

23.   Second, it should be borne in mind that, as is apparent from the second recital in the preamble to the Directive, the harmonising measures laid down by the Directive are intended, inter alia, to eliminate restrictions on the carrying-on of the activities of commercial agents, to make the conditions of competition within the Community uniform and to increase the security of commercial transactions.

24.   The purpose of the regime established in Articles 17 to 19 of the Directive is thus to protect, for all commercial agents, freedom of establishment and the operation of undistorted competition in the internal market. Those provisions must therefore be observed throughout the Community if those Treaty objectives are to be attained.

25.   It must therefore be held that it is essential for the Community legal order that a principal established in a non-member country, whose commercial agent carries on his activity within the Community, cannot evade those provisions by the simple expedient of a choice-of-law clause. The purpose served by the provisions in question requires that they be applied where the situation is closely connected with the Community, in particular where the commercial agent carries on his activity in the territory of a Member State, irrespective of the law by which the parties intended the contract to be governed.

Public policy of Member States

A.   Council Regulation (EC) No 1346/2000 of 29 May 2000 on insolvency proceedings (OJ, L 160 of 30 June 2000): Article 26

See Chapter V, A.1.

B.   Council Regulation (EC) No 44/2001 of 22 December 2000 on jurisdiction and the recognition and enforcement of judgments in civil and commercial matters (OJ, L 12 of 16 January 2001): Articles 34–35, 57

See Chapter IV, General provisions, A.1.

C.1.   Council Regulation (EC) No 2201/2003 of 27 November 2003 concerning jurisdiction and the recognition and enforcement of judgments in matrimonial matters and the matters of parental responsibility, repealing Regulation (EC) No 1347/2000 (OJ, L 338 of 23 December 2003): Articles 22(a), 23(a), 24

See Chapter XI, Matrimonial matters, A.1.

C.2.   Proposal for a Council Regulation amending Regulation (EC) No 2201/2003 as regards jurisdiction and introducing rules concerning applicable law in matrimonial matters (COM (2006) 399 fin. of 17 July 2006): Article 1(7)

See Chapter XI, Matrimonial matters, A.6.

D.   Regulation (EC) No 864/2007 of the European Parliament and of the Council of 11 July 2007 on the law applicable to non-contractual obligations (Rome II) (OJ, L 199 of 31 July 2007): Recital 32, Article 26

See Chapter VII, A.1.

E.   Regulation (EC) No 593/2008 of the European Parliament and of the Council of 17 June 2008 on the law applicable to contractual obligations (Rome I) (OJ, L 177 of 4 July 2008): Article 21

See Chapter VI, General provisions, A.1.

F.   Council Regulation (EC) No 4/2009 of 18 December 2008 on jurisdiction, applicable law, recognition and enforcement of decisions and cooperation in matters relating to maintenance obligations (OJ, L 7 of 10 January 2009): Article 24(a)

See Chapter XI, Maintenance obligations, A.1

G.   Council Regulation (EU) 1259/2010 of 20 December 2010 implementing enhanced cooperation in the area of the law applicable to divorce and legal separation (Doc. Consilium No 17523/10) : Recitals 24-25, Article 12

See Chapter XI, Matrimonial matters, B.2.

H.   Proposal for a Regulation of the European Parliament and of the Council on jurisdiction, applicable law, recognition and enforcement of decisions and authentic instruments in matters of succession and the creation of a European Certificate of Succession (COM (2009) 154 of 14 October 2009): Recital 24, Articles 27, 30, 34–35

See Chapter XII, A.

I.   ECJ case-law

In addition to the statements made in *Krombach* about the contents and scope of public policy of a Member State in relation to the recognition of judgments, it has to be borne in mind that EU rules establishing freedom of movement for persons, freedom of establishment, freedom to provide services and capitals, and competition, apply directly within the Member States and limit the application of domestic public policy to which Member States can make recourse only in very exceptional cases. For example, in *Bouchereau* (27 October 1977, case 30/77, Reports, 1999) the ECJ stated:

33. ... the concept of public policy in the context of the community and where, in particular, it is used as a justification for derogating from the fundamental principle of freedom of movement for workers, must be interpreted strictly, so that its scope cannot be determined unilaterally by each member state without being subject to control by the institutions of the community.

34. ... the particular circumstances justifying recourse to the concept of public policy may vary from one country to another and from one period to another and it is therefore necessary in this matter to allow the competent national authorities an area of discretion within the limits imposed by the treaty and the provisions adopted for its implementation.

35. In so far as it may justify certain restrictions on the free movement of persons subject to community law, recourse by a national authority to the concept of public policy presupposes, in any event, the existence, in addition to the perturbation of the social order which any infringement of the law involves, of a genuine and sufficiently serious threat to the requirements of public policy affecting one of the fundamental interests of society.

However, according to the ECJ (judgment 14 October 2004, case C-36/02, *Omega*, Reports, I-9609)

30. ... the possibility of a Member State relying on a derogation laid down by the Treaty does not prevent judicial review of measures applying that derogation. In addition, the concept of 'public policy' in the Community context, particularly as justification for a derogation from the fundamental principle of the freedom to provide services, must be interpreted strictly, so that its scope cannot be determined unilaterally by each Member State without any control by the Community institutions. Thus, public policy may be relied on only if there is a genuine and sufficiently serious threat to a fundamental interest of society.

In *Arblade* (23 November 1999, joined cases C-369/96 to C-376/96, Reports, I-8453), the ECJ has pointed out that national public order legislation comprises

30. ... national provisions compliance with which has been deemed to be so crucial for the protection of the political, social or economic order in the Member State concerned as to require compliance therewith by all persons present on the national territory of that Member State and all legal relationships within that State.

31. The fact that national rules are categorised as public-order legislation does not mean that they are exempt from compliance with the provisions of the Treaty; if it did, the primacy and uniform application of Community law would be undermined.

The considerations underlying such national legislation can be taken into account by Community law only in terms of the exceptions to Community freedoms expressly provided for by the Treaty and, where appropriate, on the ground that they constitute overriding reasons relating to the public interest.

34. Even if there is no harmonisation in the field, the freedom to provide services, as one of the fundamental principles of the Treaty, may be restricted only by rules justified by overriding requirements relating to the public interest and applicable to all persons and undertakings operating in the territory of the State where the service is provided, in so far as that interest is not safeguarded by the rules to which the provider of such a service is subject in the Member State where he is established...

35. The application of national rules to providers of services established in other Member States must be appropriate for securing the attainment of the objective which they pursue and must not go beyond what is necessary in order to attain it...

36. The overriding reasons relating to the public interest which have been acknowledged by the Court include the protection of workers...

37. By contrast, considerations of a purely administrative nature cannot justify derogation by a Member State from the rules of Community law, especially where the derogation in question amounts to preventing or restricting the exercise of one of the fundamental freedoms of Community law...

Concerning the nature of public policy provisions of EU directives after implementation in the Member States, see also ECJ, judgment 6 October 2009, case C-40/08, *Asturcom Telecomunicaciones* (in this Chapter, Public policy of EU law, F).

III

Citizenship of the Union, Citizenship of the Member States and Dual Nationality

Citizenship of the Union

A.1. Treaty on the European Union

Article 9. In all its activities, the Union shall observe the principle of the equality of its citizens, who shall receive equal attention from its institutions, bodies, offices and agencies. Every national of a Member State shall be a citizen of the Union. Citizenship of the Union shall be additional to national citizenship and shall not replace it.

A.2. Treaty on the Functioning of the European Union

Article 20 (ex Article 17 TEC). 1. Citizenship of the Union is hereby established. Every person holding the nationality of a Member State shall be a citizen of the Union. Citizenship of the Union shall be additional to and not replace national citizenship.
  2. Citizens of the Union shall enjoy the rights and be subject to the duties provided for in the Treaties. They shall have, inter alia:
  (a) the right to move and reside freely within the territory of the Member States;
  (b) the right to vote and to stand as candidates in elections to the European Parliament and in municipal elections in their Member State of residence, under the same conditions as nationals of that State;
  (c) the right to enjoy, in the territory of a third country in which the Member State of which they are nationals is not represented, the protection of the diplomatic and consular authorities of any Member State on the same conditions as the nationals of that State;
  (d) the right to petition the European Parliament, to apply to the European Ombudsman, and to address the institutions and advisory bodies of the Union in any of the Treaty languages and to obtain a reply in the same language.
  These rights shall be exercised in accordance with the conditions and limits defined by the Treaties and by the measures adopted thereunder.

Article 21 (ex Article 18 TEC). 1. Every citizen of the Union shall have the right to move and reside freely within the territory of the Member States, subject to the limitations and conditions laid down in the Treaties and by the measures adopted to give them effect.

2.   If action by the Union should prove necessary to attain this objective and the Treaties have not provided the necessary powers, the European Parliament and the Council, acting in accordance with the ordinary legislative procedure, may adopt provisions with a view to facilitating the exercise of the rights referred to in paragraph 1.

3.   For the same purposes as those referred to in paragraph 1 and if the Treaties have not provided the necessary powers, the Council, acting in accordance with a special legislative procedure, may adopt measures concerning social security or social protection. The Council shall act unanimously after consulting the European Parliament.

Article 22 (ex Article 19 TEC).   1.   Every citizen of the Union residing in a Member State of which he is not a national shall have the right to vote and to stand as a candidate at municipal elections in the Member State in which he resides, under the same conditions as nationals of that State. This right shall be exercised subject to detailed arrangements adopted by the Council, acting unanimously in accordance with a special legislative procedure and after consulting the European Parliament; these arrangements may provide for derogations where warranted by problems specific to a Member State.

2.   Without prejudice to Article 223(1) and to the provisions adopted for its implementation, every citizen of the Union residing in a Member State of which he is not a national shall have the right to vote and to stand as a candidate in elections to the European Parliament in the Member State in which he resides, under the same conditions as nationals of that State. This right shall be exercised subject to detailed arrangements adopted by the Council, acting unanimously in accordance with a special legislative procedure and after consulting the European Parliament; these arrangements may provide for derogations where warranted by problems specific to a Member State.

Article 23 (ex Article 20 TEC).   Every citizen of the Union shall, in the territory of a third country in which the Member State of which he is a national is not represented, be entitled to protection by the diplomatic or consular authorities of any Member State, on the same conditions as the nationals of that State. Member States shall adopt the necessary provisions and start the international negotiations required to secure this protection.

The Council, acting in accordance with a special legislative procedure and after consulting the European Parliament, may adopt directives establishing the coordination and cooperation measures necessary to facilitate such protection.

Article 24 (ex Article 21 TEC).   The European Parliament and the Council, acting by means of regulations in accordance with the ordinary legislative procedure, shall adopt the provisions for the procedures and conditions required for a citizens' initiative within the meaning of Article 11 of the Treaty on European Union, including the minimum number of Member States from which such citizens must come.

Every citizen of the Union shall have the right to petition the European Parliament in accordance with Article 227.

Every citizen of the Union may apply to the Ombudsman established in accordance with Article 228.

Every citizen of the Union may write to any of the institutions, bodies, offices or agencies referred to I this Article or in Article 13 of the Treaty on European Union in one of the languages mentioned in Article 55(1) of the Treaty on European Union and have an answer in the same language.

Article 25 (ex Article 22 TEC).   The Commission shall report to the European Parliament, to the Council and to the Economic and Social Committee every three years on the application of the provisions of this Part. This report shall take account of the development of the Union.

On this basis, and without prejudice to the other provisions of the Treaties, the Council, acting unanimously in accordance with a special legislative procedure and after obtaining the consent of the European Parliament, may adopt provisions to strengthen or to add to the rights listed in Article 20(2).

These provisions shall enter into force after their approval by the Member States in accordance with their respective constitutional requirements.

B.   The Hague Programme: strengthening freedom, security and justice in the European Union (OJ, C 53 of 3 March 2005): Point III(1) (1).

See Chapter I, General provisions, E.

C.   The Stockholm Programme — An open and secure Europe serving and protecting the citizens, adopted by the European Council on 10–11 December 2009 (Doc. Consilium 17024/09): Parts 1 and 2.

See Chapter I, General provisions, F.

D.   Charter of Fundamental Rights of the European Union (OJ, C 303 of 14 December 2007): Articles 39–46.

See Chapter II, Fundamental rights, E.

E.   ECJ case-law

Upon requests by national courts the ECJ has interpreted the scope of the citizenship of the Union several times. In the *Grzelczyk* case, for example (20 September 2001, case C-184/99, Reports, I-6193), concerning the right of a student, national of a Member State, to obtain an allowance that under Belgian law was granted only to Belgian student, the Court stated that

29. … The fact that Mr Grzelczyk is not of Belgian nationality is the only bar to [the minimex] being granted to him. It is not therefore in dispute that the case is one of discrimination solely on the ground of nationality.

30. Within the sphere of application of the Treaty, such discrimination is, in principle, prohibited by Article 6. In the present case, Article 6 must be read in conjunction with

the provisions of the Treaty concerning citizenship of the Union in order to determine its sphere of application.

31.   Union citizenship is destined to be the fundamental status of nationals of the Member States, enabling those who find themselves in the same situation to enjoy the same treatment in law irrespective of their nationality, subject to such exceptions as are expressly provided for.

32.   As the Court held in paragraph 63 of its judgment in *Martínez Sala*, a citizen of the European Union, lawfully resident in the territory of a host Member State, can rely on Article 6 of the Treaty in all situations which fall within the scope *ratione materiae* of Community law.

33.   Those situations include those involving the exercise of the fundamental freedoms guaranteed by the Treaty and those involving the exercise of the right to move and reside freely in another Member State, as conferred by Article 8a of the Treaty.

In the later *Baumbast* decision (17 September 2002, case C-413/99, Reports, I-7091), the Court specified that

80.   According to settled case-law, the right of nationals of one Member State to enter the territory of another Member State and to reside there constitutes a right conferred directly by the EC Treaty or, depending on the case, by the provisions adopted to implement it.

81.   Although, before the Treaty on European Union entered into force, the Court had held that that right of residence, conferred directly by the EC Treaty, was subject to the condition that the person concerned was carrying on an economic activity within the meaning of Articles 48, 52 or 59 of the EC Treaty (now, after amendment, Articles 39 EC, 43 EC and 49 EC), it is none the less the case that, since then, Union citizenship has been introduced into the EC Treaty and Article 18(1) EC has conferred a right, for every citizen, to move and reside freely within the territory of the Member States.

82.   Under Article 17(1) EC, every person holding the nationality of a Member State is to be a citizen of the Union. Union citizenship is destined to be the fundamental status of nationals of the Member States.

83.   Moreover, the Treaty on European Union does not require that citizens of the Union pursue a professional or trade activity, whether as an employed or self-employed person, in order to enjoy the rights provided in Part Two of the EC Treaty, on citizenship of the Union. Furthermore, there is nothing in the text of that Treaty to permit the conclusion that citizens of the Union who have established themselves in another Member State in order to carry on an activity as an employed person there are deprived, where that activity comes to an end, of the rights which are conferred on them by the EC Treaty by virtue of that citizenship.

84.   As regards, in particular, the right to reside within the territory of the Member States under Article 18(1) EC, that right is conferred directly on every citizen of the Union by a clear and precise provision of the EC Treaty. Purely as a national of a Member State, and consequently a citizen of the Union, Mr Baumbast therefore has the right to rely on Article 18(1) EC.

85.   Admittedly, that right for citizens of the Union to reside within the territory of another Member State is conferred subject to the limitations and conditions laid down by the EC Treaty and by the measures adopted to give it effect.

86.   However, the application of the limitations and conditions acknowledged in Article 18(1) EC in respect of the exercise of that right of residence is subject to judicial

review. Consequently, any limitations and conditions imposed on that right do not prevent the provisions of Article 18(1) EC from conferring on individuals rights which are enforceable by them and which the national courts must protect.

The ECJ confirmed that the citizenship of the Union plays a crucial role in *D'Hoop* (11 July 2002, case C-224/98, Reports, I-6191), on a dispute concerning the right to tideover allowances that a Member State law granted only to its nationals on condition that they had completed their secondary education in an educational establishment in its territory. According to the Court:

28. Union citizenship is destined to be the fundamental status of nationals of the Member States, enabling those who find themselves in the same situation to enjoy within the scope *ratione materiae* of the Treaty the same treatment in law irrespective of their nationality, subject to such exceptions as are expressly provided for.

29. The situations falling within the scope of Community law include those involving the exercise of the fundamental freedoms guaranteed by the Treaty, in particular those involving the freedom to move and reside within the territory of the Member States, as conferred by Article 8(a) of the EC Treaty (now, after amendment, Article 18 EC).

30. In that a citizen of the Union must be granted in all Member States the same treatment in law as that accorded to the nationals of those Member States who find themselves in the same situation, it would be incompatible with the right of freedom of movement were a citizen, in the Member State of which he is a national, to receive treatment less favourable than he would enjoy if he had not availed himself of the opportunities offered by the Treaty in relation to freedom of movement.

31. Those opportunities could not be fully effective if a national of a Member State could be deterred from availing himself of them by obstacles raised on his return to his country of origin by legislation penalising the fact that he has used them.

Notwithstanding the fact that the Member State has the right to require that there is a real link between the applicant and the geographic employment market concerned,

39. ... a single condition concerning the place where the diploma of completion of secondary education was obtained is too general and exclusive in nature. It unduly favours an element which is not necessarily representative of the real and effective degree of connection between the applicant for the tideover allowance and the geographic employment market, to the exclusion of all other representative elements. It therefore goes beyond what is necessary to attain the objective pursued

Along these lines two more recent decisions are worth full consideration. The first one (23 March 2004, case C-138/02, *Collins*, Reports, I-2703) concerned the refusal by the United Kingdom to grant a dual U.S. and Irish national the jobseeker's allowance provided for by domestic law on the ground that he was not habitually resident in the UK. According to the Court, the right to equal treatment — established by Article 48(2) (now 45(2) TFEU) read in conjunction with Articles 6 and 8 (now 18 and 20 TFEU) — does not preclude national legislation which makes entitlement to a jobseeker's allowance conditional on a residence requirement, in so far as that requirement may be justified on the basis of objective considerations that are independent of the nationality of the persons concerned and proportionate to the legitimate aim of the national provisions. Indeed,

61. As the Court has held on a number of occasions, citizens of the Union lawfully resident in the territory of a host Member State can rely on Article 6 of the Treaty in all

situations which fall within the scope *ratione materiae* of Community law. Citizenship of the Union is destined to be the fundamental status of nationals of the Member States, enabling those who find themselves in the same situation to enjoy the same treatment in law irrespective of their nationality, subject to such exceptions as are expressly provided for.

The second judgment (29 April 2004, case C-224/02, *Pusa*, Reports, I-5763) concerned the calculation of the amount in which the Finnish mutual association of cooperative banks was to be authorised to carry out an attachment on the pension which the claimant — a Finnish national that had moved to Spain upon retirement — received in Finland. Following the calculation made by the association the claimant would be left with only a monthly disposable sum less than that which he would have received had he continued to reside in Finland. According to the ECJ:

16. As may be seen from the Court's case-law, Union citizenship is destined to be the fundamental status of nationals of the Member States, enabling those who find themselves in the same situation to enjoy within the scope *ratione materiae* of the Treaty the same treatment in law irrespective of their nationality, subject to such exceptions as are expressly provided for.

17. The situations falling within the scope of Community law include those involving the exercise of the fundamental freedoms guaranteed by the Treaty, in particular those involving the freedom to move and reside within the territory of the Member States, as conferred by Article 18 EC.

18. In that a citizen of the Union must be granted in all Member States the same treatment in law as that accorded to the nationals of those Member States who find themselves in the same situation, it would be incompatible with the right of freedom of movement were a citizen, in the Member State of which he is a national, to receive treatment less favourable than he would enjoy if he had not availed himself of the opportunities offered by the Treaty in relation to freedom of movement.

19. Those opportunities could not be fully effective if a national of a Member State could be deterred from availing himself of them by obstacles raised to his residence in the host Member State by legislation of his State of origin penalising the fact that he has used them.

20. National legislation which places at a disadvantage certain of its nationals simply because they have exercised their freedom to move and to reside in another Member State would give rise to inequality of treatment, contrary to the principles which underpin the status of citizen of the Union, that is, the guarantee of the same treatment in law in the exercise of the citizen's freedom to move. Such legislation could be justified only if it were based on objective considerations independent of the nationality of the persons concerned and proportionate to the legitimate aim of the national provisions

Citizenship of the Member States, dual nationality and European Union law

A.   ECJ case-law

Many countries provide for specific legal rules concerning the acquisition of their nationality and the solution of positive and negative conflicts of nationalities, ie cases where an individual possesses the nationality of more than one State or does not possess any nationality. The TEU and the TFEU do not provide for any rule addressing the acquisition of the citizenship of the Union, and Article 20 TFEU refers to this end to national legislations of the Member States.

The ECJ was requested to address the issue of the relevant criteria that should apply in order to establish if an individual is a national of a Member State and the relevant rules that should apply in case of dual nationality, both when an individual holds the nationality of a Member State and a third country and when he holds the nationality of two Member States.

As concerns the former case, in the famous *Micheletti* judgment (7 July 1992, case C-369/90, Reports, I-4239), the ECJ has clearly stated that

10. Under international law, it is for each Member State, having due regard to Community law, to lay down the conditions for the acquisition and loss of nationality.

This statement has provided the basis for numerous judgments in this field, that have addressed various important issues. In the *Kaur* judgment (20 February 2001, case C-192/99, Reports, I-1237) the ECJ had to assess a situation arising under UK law, which provided for various categories of British subjects, but only some of them had the right to enter and remain in the UK. The dispute concerned a British Overseas Citizen, who had re-applied for leave to remain in the country and had stated that she wished to periodically to travel to other Member States in order to make purchases of goods and services and, if necessary, to work there. The application having been rejected, the ECJ was requested to assess whether Ms Kaur had to be considered a national of a Member State. It is important to notice that when acceding the Community the UK had lodged a declaration annexed to the Final Act to the Accession Treaty, whereby it defined the notion of 'national' for the purposes of the application of Community law. The 1972 declaration had been replaced by a new declaration in 1982, in view of the entry into force of the British Nationality Act 1981, that provided:

As to the United Kingdom of Great Britain and Northern Ireland, the terms 'nationals', 'nationals of Member States' or 'nationals of Member States and overseas countries and territories', wherever used in the Treaty establishing the European Economic Community, the Treaty establishing the European Atomic Energy Community or the Treaty establishing the European Coal and Steel Community or in any of the Community acts deriving from those Treaties, are to be understood to refer to:

(a) British citizens;

(b) Persons who are British subjects by virtue of Part IV of the British Nationality Act (1981) and who have the right of abode in the United Kingdom and are therefore exempt from United Kingdom immigration control;

(c) British Dependent Territories citizens who acquire their citizenship from a connection with Gibraltar.

The ECJ stated that in order to assess the nationality of Ms Kaur the declarations had to be given full consideration for the interpretation of the Treaty and thus she did not qualify as a national of a Member State under Community law:

21. The United Kingdom has defined those rights in its domestic legislation, in particular in the Immigration Act 1971, which became applicable from 1 January 1973 — the same date as that on which the Treaty on the Accession of the United Kingdom entered into force. That national legislation reserved the right of abode within the territory of the United Kingdom to those citizens who had the closest connections to that State.

22. When it acceded to the European Communities, the United Kingdom notified the other Contracting Parties, by means of its 1972 Declaration, of the categories of citizens to be regarded as its nationals for the purposes of Community law by designating, in substance, those entitled to the right of residence in the territory of the United Kingdom within the meaning of the Immigration Act 1971 and citizens having a specified connection with Gibraltar.

23. Although unilateral, this declaration annexed to the Final Act was intended to clarify an issue of particular importance for the other Contracting Parties, namely delimiting the scope *ratione personae* of the Community provisions which were the subject of the Accession Treaty. It was intended to define the United Kingdom nationals who would benefit from those provisions and, in particular, from the provisions relating to the free movement of persons. The other Contracting Parties were fully aware of its content and the conditions of accession were determined on that basis.

24. It follows that the 1972 Declaration must be taken into consideration as an instrument relating to the Treaty for the purpose of its interpretation and, more particularly, for determining the scope of the Treaty *ratione personae.*

25. Furthermore, adoption of that declaration did not have the effect of depriving any person who did not satisfy the definition of a national of the United Kingdom of rights to which that person might be entitled under Community law. The consequence was rather that such rights never arose in the first place for such a person.

26. It is common ground that the 1982 Declaration was an adaptation of the 1972 Declaration necessitated by the adoption, in 1981, of a new Nationality Act, that it substantially designated the same categories of persons as the 1972 Declaration and that, as such, it did not alter Ms Kaur's situation as regards Community law. Furthermore, it has not been challenged by the other Member States.

27. The answer to be given to Questions 1(1)(a) and (b) must therefore be that, in order to determine whether a person is a national of the United Kingdom of Great Britain and Northern Ireland for the purposes of Community law, it is necessary to refer to the 1982 Declaration which replaced the 1972 Declaration.

The Court fully relied upon the domestic law of the Member States in the *Chen* case as well (19 October 2004, case C-200/02, Reports, I-9925), where it recognised the rights related to the citizenship of the Union also to a baby, born in Northern Ireland of a Chinese mother. The baby had acquired Irish nationality by birth pursuant to the Irish legislation applicable at that time. It was common ground that the mother had taken up residence in Northern Ireland in order to enable the child to acquire Irish nationality and, consequently, to enable her to acquire the right to reside, should the occasion arise, with her child in the United Kingdom. The Secretary of State for the Home Department's had refused to grant a long-term residence permit and the mother had appealed this decision. The ECJ stated that

19. The situation of a national of a Member State who was born in the host Member State and has not made use of the right to freedom of movement cannot, for that reason alone, be assimilated to a purely internal situation, thereby depriving that national of the benefit in the host Member State of the provisions of Community law on freedom of movement and of residence.

20. Moreover, … a young child can take advantage of the rights of free movement and residence guaranteed by Community law. The capacity of a national of a Member State to be the holder of rights guaranteed by the Treaty and by secondary law on the free

movement of persons cannot be made conditional upon the attainment by the person concerned of the age prescribed for the acquisition of legal capacity to exercise those rights personally. Moreover, as the Advocate General made clear in points 47 to 52 of his Opinion, it does not follow either from the terms of, or from the aims pursued by, Articles 18 EC and 49 EC and Directives 73/148 and 90/364 that the enjoyment of the rights with which those provisions are concerned should be made conditional upon the attainment of a minimum age.

36. It is true that Mrs Chen admits that the purpose of her stay in the United Kingdom was to create a situation in which the child she was expecting would be able to acquire the nationality of another Member State in order thereafter to secure for her child and for herself a long-term right to reside in the United Kingdom.

37. Nevertheless, under international law, it is for each Member State, having due regard to Community law, to lay down the conditions for the acquisition and loss of nationality.

38. None of the parties that submitted observations to the Court has questioned either the legality, or the fact, of Catherine's acquisition of Irish nationality.

39. Moreover, it is not permissible for a Member State to restrict the effects of the grant of the nationality of another Member State by imposing an additional condition for recognition of that nationality with a view to the exercise of the fundamental freedoms provided for in the Treaty.

40. However, that would be precisely what would happen if the United Kingdom were entitled to refuse nationals of other Member States, such as Catherine, the benefit of a fundamental freedom upheld by Community law merely because their nationality of a Member State was in fact acquired solely in order to secure a right of residence under Community law for a national of a non-member country.

41. Accordingly, in circumstances like those of the main proceedings, Article 18 EC and Directive 90/364 confer on a young minor who is a national of a Member State, is covered by appropriate sickness insurance and is in the care of a parent who is a third-country national having sufficient resources for that minor not to become a burden on the public finances of the host Member State, a right to reside for an indefinite period in that State.

The ECJ relied upon the national provisions of the Member States also as concerns dual nationality, but it applied them within the framework of Community law.

The *Airola* case, for example (20 February 1975, case 21/74, Reports, 221), concerned the interpretation of the condition of 'nationality' laid down in Article 4(a) of Annex VII of the Staff Regulations, whereby an expatriation allowance was paid to officials who 'are not and have never been nationals of the State in whose European territory the place where they are employed is situated'. The official at stake was the wife of an Italian citizen and she had acquired the Italian nationality against her will, through the automatic operation of a provision of Italian law. Upon the appeal against the decision of the Commission to withdraw the expatriation allowance originally granted, the ECJ ruled that

5. On the question of nationality, the provisions of national legislations are not uniform; some laws, particularly those of recent date, provide that a foreign wife does not automatically acquire the nationality of her husband, whereas, under other legislations, it is still provided that, as was once the common rule, the nationality of a married woman depends upon that of her husband.

6. In accordance with the general pattern of Article 4 of Annex VII this provision

adopts the official's habitual residence before he entered the service as the paramount consideration in determining entitlement to an expatriation allowance.

7.   The official's nationality is regarded as being only a subsidiary consideration, ie as serving to define the effect of the length of such residence outside the territory in which the place where he is employed is situated.

8.   The object of the expatriation allowance is to compensate officials for the extra expense and inconvenience of taking up employment with the Community and being thereby obliged to change their residence.

9.   Though 'expatriation' is a subjective state conditioned by the official's assimilation into new surroundings, the Staff Regulations of officials cannot treat officials differently in this respect according to whether they are of the male or of the female sex since, in either case, payment of the expatriation allowance must be determined by considerations which are uniform and disregard the difference in sex.

10.   The concept of 'nationals' contained in Article 4(a) must therefore be interpreted in such a way as to avoid any unwarranted difference of treatment as between male and female officials who are, in fact, placed in comparable situations.

11.   Such unwarranted difference of treatment between female officials and officials of the male sex would result from an interpretation of the concept of 'nationals' referred to above as also embracing the nationality which was imposed by law on an official of the female sex by virtue of her marriage, and which she was unable to renounce.

12.   It is therefore necessary to define the concept of an official's present or previous nationality under Article 4(a) of Annex VII as excluding nationality imposed by law on a female official upon her marriage with a national of another State, when she has no possibility of renouncing it.

13.   In the present case the applicant, on her marriage, had the nationality of her husband conferred on her without the right to renounce it but by an express declaration she retained her Belgian nationality of origin.

14.   Consequently, in applying the provision in question, the applicant's Italian nationality has not to be taken into account.

On the contrary, in the *Van den Broeck* judgment on the same day (case 37/74, Reports, 235), the Court ruled that Article 4(a) of the Staff Regulations applies when the official — having the possibility to renounce a nationality automatically acquired by marriage — does not prevails herself of such possibility. The ECJ later confirmed this approach rejecting the claim lodged by a British official that had acquired the Belgian nationality by marriage and had not renounced it, even though she could have rendered an explicit declaration to this end under Belgian law. In the *Devred, née Kenny-Levick* judgment (14 December 1979, case 257/78, Reports, 3767), the Court referred to the *Airola* case and stated that

12.   ... In fact where the person concerned was able to renounce the nationality which causes her to lose the benefit of the expatriation allowance, there is no reason associated with the purposes for which that allowance was granted for disregarding the fact that, by an act of her own volition subsequent to, but distinct from, her marriage, the official decided to assume the nationality of the place in which she is employed.

13.   Secondly, the applicant claims that when, as a result of her marriage, a female official, whilst acquiring a new nationality, retains her nationality of origin and the latter entitled her to the expatriation allowance, the nationality of origin should be considered

as the preponderant nationality, thus justifying continuance of the expatriation allowance, or in any event that that is the solution to be adopted when the nationality of origin appears in fact to be the 'effective' nationality compared with the nationality acquired by marriage.

14. The concept of effective nationality is used mainly in private international law in order to resolve positive conflicts of nationality. The concept cannot be transferred to a quite different sphere from that for which it was developed, specifically the scope of the staff regulations for officials of the Communities, in order to determine entitlement to receive the expatriation allowance, when, apart from the exception expressly provided for in Article 4(1)(b), an official who has the nationality of the place in which he is employed is not entitled to that allowance.

15. Moreover, even if the applicant's point of view were to be adopted, it should be observed that she has failed to show that she is considered in Great Britain as a 'patrial', whereas under the declaration made by the Government of the United Kingdom of Great Britain and Northern Ireland on the definition of the term 'nationals' annexed to the Final Act of 22 January 1972 on the Accession to the European Communities of the new Member States, the term 'national' is to be understood, as far as the United Kingdom is concerned, to refer only to patrials and to Gibraltarians.

In another case the Court had been requested to address the issue of the compliance with Community law of a bilateral convention for the avoidance of double taxation that provided for different rules in the case of frontier workers, who were to be taxed in their State of residence where they worked in the private sector, while were to be taxed in the paying State if they worked in the public sector. This latter rules, however, where the remuneration was paid to persons having the nationality of the State of residence without being at the same time nationals of the paying State; in such cases, the remuneration was taxable only in the State in which such persons were resident. The case had been brought before a French court by a couple residing in France, close to the German border (12 May 1998, case C-336/96, *Gilly*, Reports, I-2793). The wife, a German national who had acquired French nationality by marriage, taught in a State school in Germany and in accordance with the Convention the remuneration she received in Germany was taxed both in this country, because she was a German national, and in France. When France expressed the view that Mrs Gilly had not exercised in France the rights conferred upon her by Article 48 of the Treaty, since she worked in her State of origin, the ECJ rejected this argument stating that

21. It need merely be pointed out here that Mrs Gilly has acquired French nationality by her marriage and works in Germany whilst residing in France. She must therefore be considered in France as a worker exercising her right to freedom of movement, as guaranteed by the Treaty, in order to work in a Member State other than that in which she resides. The circumstance that she has retained the nationality of the State in which she is employed in no way affects the fact that, for the French authorities, she is a French national working in another Member State

As anticipated above, the leading case on matters of dual nationality is the *Micheletti* case, that concerned an Argentine and Italian dual national who had obtained by the Spanish authorities the recognition of his university degree in dentistry under a cultural cooperation agreement between Spain and Argentina. Afterwards he had applied to the Spanish authorities for a temporary Community residence card, submitting for that purpose a valid Italian passport issued by an Italian Consulate in Argentina and before the expiry of that period, had applied for a permanent residence card as a Community national in order to set up as a dentist in Spain. That application and a subsequent administrative appeal were dismissed on the basis of Article 9 of the Spanish Civil Code, according to which, in cases of dual nationality where neither nationality is Spanish, the nationality corresponding to the habitual residence of the person concerned before his arrival in Spain is to take precedence, ie Argentine nationality in the case at stake. The ECJ has stated that this provision could not apply:

8.   The national court's question seeks essentially to determine whether the provisions of Community law concerning freedom of establishment preclude a Member State from denying a national of another Member State who possesses at the same time the nationality of a non-member country entitlement to that freedom on the ground that the law of the host State deems him to be a national of the non-member country.

9.   In answering that question, it must be borne in mind that Article 52 of the Treaty grants freedom of establishment to persons who are 'nationals of a Member State'.

10.   Under international law, it is for each Member State, having due regard to Community law, to lay down the conditions for the acquisition and loss of nationality. However, it is not permissible for the legislation of a Member State to restrict the effects of the grant of the nationality of another Member State by imposing an additional condition for recognition of that nationality with a view to the exercise of the fundamental freedoms provided for in the Treaty.

11.   Consequently, it is not permissible to interpret Article 52 of the Treaty to the effect that, where a national of a Member State is also a national of a non-member country, the other Member States may make recognition of the status of Community national subject to a condition such as the habitual residence of the person concerned in the territory of the first Member State.

12.   That conclusion is reinforced by the fact that the consequence of allowing such a possibility would be that the class of persons to whom the Community rules on freedom of establishment were applied might vary from one Member State to another.

13.   In keeping with that interpretation, Directive 73/148 provides that Member States are to grant to the persons referred to in Article 1 the right to enter their territory merely on production of a valid identity card or passport (Article 3) and are to issue a residence card or permit to such persons, and to those mentioned in Article 4, upon production, in particular, of the document with which they entered their territory (Article 6).

14.   Thus, once the persons concerned have produced one of the documents mentioned in Directive 73/148 in order to establish their status as nationals of a Member State, the other Member States are not entitled to challenge that status on the ground that the persons concerned might also have the nationality of a non-member country which, under the legislation of the host Member State, overrides that of the Member State.

15.   The answer to the question submitted must therefore be that the provisions of Community law on freedom of establishment preclude a Member State from denying a national of another Member State who possesses at the same time the nationality of a non-member country entitlement to that freedom on the ground that the law of the host State deems him to be a national of the non-member country.

More recently, the *Garcia Avello* judgment (2 October 2003, case C-148/02, Reports, I-11613, also at Chapter XI, Right to name, A) concerned the case of the children of Spanish and Belgian couple, who had both nationalities and resided in Belgium, and had been denied by the Belgian authorities the right to adopt as family name the first surname of the father followed by that of the mother, as provided by Spanish law, under which they had been registered at the Spanish consulate. According to the ECJ:

25. Although, as Community law stands at present, the rules governing a person's surname are matters coming within the competence of the Member States, the latter must none the less, when exercising that competence, comply with Community law, in particular the Treaty provisions on the freedom of every citizen of the Union to move and reside in the territory of the Member States.

26. Citizenship of the Union, established by Article 17 EC, is not, however, intended to extend the scope *ratione materiae* of the Treaty also to internal situations which have no link with Community law.

27. Such a link with Community law does, however, exist in regard to persons in a situation such as that of the children of Mr Garcia Avello, who are nationals of one Member State lawfully resident in the territory of another Member State.

28. That conclusion cannot be invalidated by the fact that the children involved in the main proceedings also have the nationality of the Member State in which they have been resident since their birth and which, according to the authorities of that State, is by virtue of that fact the only nationality recognised by the latter. It is not permissible for a Member State to restrict the effects of the grant of the nationality of another Member State by imposing an additional condition for recognition of that nationality with a view to the exercise of the fundamental freedoms provided for in the Treaty. Furthermore, Article 3 of the Hague Convention, on which the Kingdom of Belgium relies in recognising only the nationality of the forum where there are several nationalities, one of which is Belgian, does not impose an obligation but simply provides an option for the contracting parties to give priority to that nationality over any other.

29. That being so, the children of the applicant in the main proceedings may rely on the right set out in Article 12 EC not to suffer discrimination on grounds of nationality in regard to the rules governing their surname.

The ECJ thus solved the case through the rules on free movement, without addressing the issue of the law applicable to the name of an individual from the point of view of private international law. Positive conflicts between the nationality of two Member States came before the ECJ more recently in a case concerning the application of Regulation (EC) No 2201/2003 on jurisdiction and the recognition and enforcement of judgments in matrimonial matters and in matters of parental responsibility for children of both spouses (Brussels IIa, see Chapter XI). The case concerned the divorce of a dual Hungarian and French couple, that had been declared by a Hungarian judgment, whose recognition was challenged in France (16 July 2009, case C-168/08, *Hadadi*, also at Chapter XI, Matrimonial matters, A. 5). According to the prevailing French academic writing and case-law, in case of conflicting nationalities if one of the spouses holds the nationality of the State of the court seised, it will prevail. Lacking any specific provision in the Brussels IIa Regulation, the ECJ stated that

38. According to settled case-law, it follows from the need for uniform application of Community law and from the principle of equality that the terms of a provision of Community law which makes no express reference to the law of the Member States for the purpose of determining its meaning and scope must normally be given an autonomous and uniform interpretation throughout the Community, having regard to the context of the provision and the objective pursued by the legislation in question.

39. In that regard, it should be pointed out that Article 3(1) of Regulation No 2201/2003 does not make any express reference to the law of the Member States for the purpose of determining the exact scope of the 'nationality' ground of jurisdiction.

40. Moreover, Regulation No 2201/2003 does not appear, at least in principle, to make a distinction according to whether a person holds one or, as the case may be, several nationalities.

41. Accordingly, where the spouses have the same dual nationality, the court seised cannot overlook the fact that the individuals concerned hold the nationality of another Member State, with the result that persons with the same dual nationality are treated as if they had only the nationality of the Member State of the court seised. That would have the effect of precluding such persons, in the context of the transitional rule of recognition referred to in Article 64(4) of Regulation No 2201/2003, from relying on Article 3(1)(b) of that Regulation before a court of the Member State addressed in order to establish the jurisdiction of the courts of another Member State, even though those persons hold the nationality of the latter State.

42. On the contrary, in the context of Article 64(4) of the Regulation, where the spouses hold both the nationality of the Member State of the court seised and that of the same other Member State, that court must take into account the fact that the courts of that other Member State could, since the persons concerned hold the nationality of the latter State, properly have been seised of the case under Article 3(1)(b) of Regulation No 2201/2003.

43. Consequently, the answer to the first question is that, where the court of the Member State addressed must verify, pursuant to Article 64(4) of Regulation No 2201/2003, whether the court of the Member State of origin of a judgment would have had jurisdiction under Article 3(1)(b) of that Regulation, the latter provision precludes the court of the Member State addressed from regarding spouses who each hold the nationality both of that State and of the Member State of origin as nationals only of the Member State addressed. That court must, on the contrary, take into account the fact that the spouses also hold the nationality of the Member State of origin and that, therefore, the courts of the latter could have had jurisdiction to hear the case.

44. By its second and third questions, which it is appropriate to examine together, the referring court asks, in essence, whether Article 3(1)(b) of Regulation No 2201/2003 must be interpreted as meaning that, in order to determine the court which has jurisdiction in respect of the divorce of persons having the same dual nationality, only the nationality of the Member State with which those persons have the closest links — the 'most effective' nationality — is to be taken into account, so that the courts of that State alone have jurisdiction on the basis of nationality (second question), or whether, on the contrary, both nationalities are to be taken into account, so that the courts of those two Member States can have jurisdiction on that basis, allowing the persons concerned to choose the Member State in which to bring proceedings (third question).

47. In that regard, it should be noted at the outset that, according to recital 1 in the preamble to Regulation No 2201/2003, that Regulation is to contribute to creating an area of freedom, security and justice, in which the free movement of persons is ensured. To that end, Chapters II and III of the Regulation lay down rules on jurisdiction and on recognition and enforcement of judgments concerning the dissolution of matrimonial ties.

48. In that context, Article 3(1)(a) and (b) of Regulation No 2201/2003 provides for a number of grounds of jurisdiction, without establishing any hierarchy. All the objective grounds set out in Article 3(1) are alternatives. Taking into account that Regulation's purpose of ensuring legal certainty, Article 6 thereof provides, in substance, that the grounds of jurisdiction contained in Articles 3 to 5 of the Regulation are exclusive in nature.

49. It follows that the system of jurisdiction established by Regulation No 2201/2003 concerning the dissolution of matrimonial ties is not intended to preclude the courts of several States from having jurisdiction. Rather, the coexistence of several courts having jurisdiction is expressly provided for, without any hierarchy being established between them.

50. In that regard, while the grounds of jurisdiction listed in Article 3(1)(a) of that Regulation are based in various respects on the habitual residence of the spouses, that in Article 3(1)(b) is 'the nationality of both spouses or, in the case of the United Kingdom and Ireland, the "domicile" of both spouses'. Thus, except in relation to the latter two Member States, the courts of the other Member States of which the spouses hold the nationality have jurisdiction in proceedings relating to the dissolution of matrimonial ties.

51. However, there is nothing in the wording of Article 3(1)(b) to suggest that only the 'effective' nationality can be taken into account in applying that provision. Article 3(1) (b), inasmuch as it makes nationality a ground of jurisdiction, endorses a link that is unambiguous and easy to apply. It does not provide for any other criterion relating to nationality such as, for example, how effective it is.

52. Moreover, no basis can be found in the objectives of that provision or in the context of which it forms part for an interpretation according to which only an 'effective' nationality can be taken into consideration for the purposes of Article 3(1) of Regulation No 2201/2003.

53. First, such an interpretation would restrict individuals' choice of the court having jurisdiction, particularly in cases where the right to freedom of movement for persons had been exercised.

54. In particular, since habitual residence would be an essential consideration for the purpose of determining the most effective nationality, the grounds of jurisdiction provided for in Article 3(1)(a) and (b) of Regulation No 2201/2203 would frequently overlap. On the facts, that would amount to establishing, with regard to persons holding a number of nationalities, a hierarchy between the grounds of jurisdiction laid down in Article 3(1), for which there is no basis in the wording of that paragraph. By contrast, a couple holding only the nationality of one Member State would always be able to seise the courts of that State, even if they had not had their habitual residence in that Member State for many years and even if they had few real links with that State.

55. Secondly, in the light of the imprecise nature of the concept of 'effective nationality', a whole set of factors would have to be taken into consideration, not always leading to a clear result. The need to check the links between the spouses and their respective nationalities would make verification of jurisdiction more onerous and thus be at odds with the objective of facilitating the application of Regulation No 2201/2003 by the use of a simple and unambiguous connecting factor.

56. It is true that, pursuant to Article 3(1)(b) of Regulation No 2201/2003, the courts of a number of Member States can have jurisdiction where the individuals in

question hold several nationalities. However ... were the courts of several Member States to be seised pursuant to that provision, the conflict of jurisdiction could be resolved by applying the rule laid down in Article 19(1) of that Regulation.

57.   Finally, it should be acknowledged that Regulation No 2201/2003, in so far as it regulates only jurisdiction but does not lay down conflict rules determining the substantive law to be applied, might indeed ... induce spouses to rush into seising one of the courts having jurisdiction in order to secure the advantages of the substantive divorce law applicable under the private international law rules used by the court seised. However ... such a fact cannot, by itself, mean that the seising of a court having jurisdiction under Article 3(1)(b) of that Regulation may be regarded as an abuse. As paragraphs 49 to 52 of the present judgment make clear, seising the courts of a Member State of which both spouses hold the nationality, even in the absence of any other link with that Member State, is not contrary to the objectives pursued by that provision.

58.   In those circumstances, the answer to the second and third questions referred must be that, where spouses each hold the nationality of the same two Member States, Article 3(1)(b) of Regulation No 2201/2003 precludes the jurisdiction of the courts of one of those Member States from being rejected on the ground that the applicant does not put forward other links with that State. On the contrary, the courts of those Member States of which the spouses hold the nationality have jurisdiction under that provision and the spouses may seise the court of the Member State of their choice.

In the *Saldanha* judgment (2 October 1997, case C-122/96, Reports, I-5325, also at Chapter II, Principle of non-discrimination, B), the ECJ addressed also the issue of the application to a dual US and UK citizen living in the US of an Austrian provision of law imposing to foreign nationals who are plaintiffs in proceedings brought before Austrian courts the duty to lodge a security on cost for the proceedings (cautio judicatum solvi), except where otherwise provided by international treaty or convention. That obligation does not apply, however, where the plaintiff is normally resident in Austria or a judicial decision ordering the plaintiff to indemnify the defendant for his legal costs is enforceable in the State in which the plaintiff is normally resident. Such security is contrary to the principle of equality of treatment under EU law, but the proceedings had started in Austria shortly before its accession to the Community and in any case it would have been legitimate vis-à-vis a non-EU national, and even so more lacking a convention between Austria and the US on the enforcement of decisions on legal costs. Moreover, the 1931 Convention on legal assistance between Austria and the United Kingdom did not apply, since it limited the exemption from the obligation to provide such security to persons domiciled in one of the two Contracting Parties, nor did the 1988 Lugano Convention on jurisdiction and the enforcement of judgments in civil and commercial matters, that bound these two countries at the time, as Austrian law made its application subject to the possibility of enforcement in State of residence of the plaintiff, ie the US. The ECJ declared that Article 6 of the Treaty (now Article 18 TFEU) was immediately applicable and binding on Austria from the date of its accession, with the result that it applied to the future effects of situations arising prior to that new Member State's accession to the Communities and, referring to *Micheletti*, stated that

15.   ... the mere fact that a national of a Member State is also a national of a non-member country, in which he is resident, does not deprive him of the right, as a national of

that Member State, to rely on the prohibition of discrimination on grounds of nationality enshrined in the first paragraph of Article 6.

Finally, in the *Rottmann* case (2 March 2010, C-135/08), the Court had been asked to state whether Community law precludes the legal consequence of the loss of Union citizenship (and of the associated rights and fundamental freedoms) resulting from the fact that a revocation, lawful as such under national (German) law, of a naturalisation as a national of a Member State (Germany) acquired by intentional deception has the effect, in combination with the national law on nationality of another Member State (Austria) — as with the claimant in the present case because of the non-revival of the original Austrian nationality — that statelessness supervenes. The Court ruled that it is not contrary to EU law for a Member State to withdraw from a citizen of the Union the nationality of that State acquired by naturalisation when that nationality was obtained by deception, on condition that the decision to withdraw observes the principle of proportionality, on the following grounds:

48. The proviso that due regard must be had to European Union law does not compromise the principle of international law previously recognised by the Court... that the Member States have the power to lay down the conditions for the acquisition and loss of nationality, but rather enshrines the principle that, in respect of citizens of the Union, the exercise of that power, in so far as it affects the rights conferred and protected by the legal order of the Union, as is in particular the case of a decision withdrawing naturalisation such as that at issue in the main proceedings, is amenable to judicial review carried out in the light of European Union law.

49. Unlike the applicant in the case giving rise to the judgment in *Kaur* who, not meeting the definition of a national of the United Kingdom of Great Britain and Northern Ireland, could not be deprived of the rights deriving from the status of citizen of the Union, Dr Rottmann has unquestionably held Austrian and then German nationality and has, in consequence, enjoyed that status and the rights attaching thereto.

50. Nevertheless... if a decision withdrawing naturalisation such as that at issue in the main proceedings is based on the deception practised by the person concerned in connection with the procedure for acquisition of the nationality in question, such a decision could be compatible with European Union law.

51. A decision withdrawing naturalisation because of deception corresponds to a reason relating to the public interest. In this regard, it is legitimate for a Member State to wish to protect the special relationship of solidarity and good faith between it and its nationals and also the reciprocity of rights and duties, which form the bedrock of the bond of nationality.

52. That conclusion relating to the legitimacy, in principle, of a decision withdrawing naturalisation adopted in circumstances such as those in the main proceedings is borne out by the relevant provisions of the Convention on the reduction of statelessness. Article 8(2) thereof provides that a person may be deprived of the nationality of a Contracting State if he has acquired that nationality by means of misrepresentation or by any other act of fraud. Likewise, Article 7(1) and (3) of the European Convention on nationality does not prohibit a State Party from depriving a person of his nationality, even if he thus becomes stateless, when that nationality was acquired by means of fraudulent conduct, false information or concealment of any relevant fact attributable to that person.

53. That conclusion is, moreover, in keeping with the general principle of international law that no one is arbitrarily to be deprived of his nationality, that principle being reproduced in Article 15(2) of the Universal Declaration of Human Rights and in Article 4(c) of the European Convention on nationality. When a State deprives a person of his nationality because of his acts of deception, legally established, that deprivation cannot be considered to be an arbitrary act.

54. Those considerations on the legitimacy, in principle, of a decision withdrawing naturalisation on account of deception remain, in theory, valid when the consequence of that withdrawal is that the person in question loses, in addition to the nationality of the Member State of naturalisation, citizenship of the Union.

55. In such a case, it is, however, for the national court to ascertain whether the withdrawal decision at issue in the main proceedings observes the principle of proportionality so far as concerns the consequences it entails for the situation of the person concerned in the light of European Union law, in addition, where appropriate, to examination of the proportionality of the decision in the light of national law.

56. Having regard to the importance which primary law attaches to the status of citizen of the Union, when examining a decision withdrawing naturalisation it is necessary, therefore, to take into account the consequences that the decision entails for the person concerned and, if relevant, for the members of his family with regard to the loss of the rights enjoyed by every citizen of the Union. In this respect it is necessary to establish, in particular, whether that loss is justified in relation to the gravity of the offence committed by that person, to the lapse of time between the naturalisation decision and the withdrawal decision and to whether it is possible for that person to recover his original nationality.

57. With regard, in particular, to that last aspect, a Member State whose nationality has been acquired by deception cannot be considered bound, pursuant to Article 17 EC, to refrain from withdrawing naturalisation merely because the person concerned has not recovered the nationality of his Member State of origin.

58. It is, nevertheless, for the national court to determine whether, before such a decision withdrawing naturalisation takes effect, having regard to all the relevant circumstances, observance of the principle of proportionality requires the person concerned to be afforded a reasonable period of time in order to try to recover the nationality of his Member State of origin....

62. It is to be borne in mind, in these proceedings for a preliminary ruling, that the principles stemming from this judgment with regard to the powers of the Member States in the sphere of nationality, and also their duty to exercise those powers having due regard to European Union law, apply both to the Member State of naturalisation and to the Member State of the original nationality.

IV

Jurisdiction, Recognition and Enforcement of Judgments in Civil and Commercial Matters

General provisions

A.1. Council Regulation (EC) No 44/2001 of 22 December 2000 on jurisdiction and the recognition and enforcement of judgments in civil and commercial matters (OJ, L 12 of 16 January 2001)[1]

(1) The Community has set itself the objective of maintaining and developing an area of freedom, security and justice, in which the free movement of persons is ensured. In order to establish progressively such an area, the Community should adopt, amongst other things, the measures relating to judicial cooperation in civil matters which are necessary for the sound operation of the internal market.

(2) Certain differences between national rules governing jurisdiction and recognition of judgments hamper the sound operation of the internal market. Provisions to unify the rules of conflict of jurisdiction in civil and commercial matters and to simplify the formalities with a view to rapid and simple recognition and enforcement of judgments from Member States bound by this Regulation are essential.

(3) This area is within the field of judicial cooperation in civil matters within the meaning of Article 65 of the Treaty.

(4) In accordance with the principles of subsidiarity and proportionality as set out in Article 5 of the Treaty, the objectives of this Regulation cannot be sufficiently achieved by the Member States and can therefore be better achieved by the Community. This Regulation confines itself to the minimum required in order to achieve those objectives and does not go beyond what is necessary for that purpose.

(5) On 27 September 1968 the Member States, acting under Article 293, fourth indent, of the Treaty, concluded the Brussels Convention on Jurisdiction and the Enforcement of Judgments in Civil and Commercial Matters, as amended by Conventions on the Accession of the New Member States to that Convention (hereinafter referred to as the 'Brussels Convention'). On 16 September 1988 Member States and EFTA States concluded the Lugano Convention on Jurisdiction and the Enforcement of Judgments

---

[1] So-called 'Brussels I' Regulation. As finally amended by Commission Regulation (EC) No 280/2009 (OJ, L 93 of 7 April 2009). The provisions of the 2007 Lugano Convention that are different from the corresponding articles of Regulation (EC) No 44/2001 are published in the footnotes. The final provisions of the 2007 Lugano Convention are published in this Chapter, General provisions, B.4. [Note of the Editor]

in Civil and Commercial Matters, which is a parallel Convention to the 1968 Brussels Convention. Work has been undertaken for the revision of those Conventions, and the Council has approved the content of the revised texts. Continuity in the results achieved in that revision should be ensured.

(6)   In order to attain the objective of free movement of judgments in civil and commercial matters, it is necessary and appropriate that the rules governing jurisdiction and the recognition and enforcement of judgments be governed by a Community legal instrument which is binding and directly applicable.

(7)   The scope of this Regulation must cover all the main civil and commercial matters apart from certain well-defined matters.

(8)   There must be a link between proceedings to which this Regulation applies and the territory of the Member States bound by this Regulation. Accordingly common rules on jurisdiction should, in principle, apply when the defendant is domiciled in one of those Member States.

(9)   A defendant not domiciled in a Member State is in general subject to national rules of jurisdiction applicable in the territory of the Member State of the court seised, and a defendant domiciled in a Member State not bound by this Regulation must remain subject to the Brussels Convention.

(10) For the purposes of the free movement of judgments, judgments given in a Member State bound by this Regulation should be recognised and enforced in another Member State bound by this Regulation, even if the judgment debtor is domiciled in a third State.

(11) The rules of jurisdiction must be highly predictable and founded on the principle that jurisdiction is generally based on the defendant's domicile and jurisdiction must always be available on this ground save in a few well-defined situations in which the subjectmatter of the litigation or the autonomy of the parties warrants a different linking factor. The domicile of a legal person must be defined autonomously so as to make the common rules more transparent and avoid conflicts of jurisdiction.

(12) In addition to the defendant's domicile, there should be alternative grounds of jurisdiction based on a close link between the court and the action or in order to facilitate the sound administration of justice.

(13) In relation to insurance, consumer contracts and employment, the weaker party should be protected by rules of jurisdiction more favourable to his interests than the general rules provide for.

(14) The autonomy of the parties to a contract, other than an insurance, consumer or employment contract, where only limited autonomy to determine the courts having jurisdiction is allowed, must be respected subject to the exclusive grounds of jurisdiction laid down in this Regulation.

(15) In the interests of the harmonious administration of justice it is necessary to minimise the possibility of concurrent proceedings and to ensure that irreconcilable judgments will not be given in two Member States. There must be a clear and effective mechanism for resolving cases of *lis pendens* and related actions and for obviating problems flowing from national differences as to the determination of the time when a case is regarded as pending. For the purposes of this Regulation that time should be defined autonomously.

(16) Mutual trust in the administration of justice in the Community justifies judgments given in a Member State being recognised automatically without the need for any procedure except in cases of dispute.

(17) By virtue of the same principle of mutual trust, the procedure for making enforceable in one Member State a judgment given in another must be efficient and rapid. To that end, the declaration that a judgment is enforceable should be issued virtually automatically after purely formal checks of the documents supplied, without there being any possibility for the court to raise of its own motion any of the grounds for non-enforcement provided for by this Regulation.

(18) However, respect for the rights of the defence means that the defendant should be able to appeal in an adversarial procedure, against the declaration of enforceability, if he considers one of the grounds for non-enforcement to be present. Redress procedures should also be available to the claimant where his application for a declaration of enforceability has been rejected.

(19) Continuity between the Brussels Convention and this Regulation should be ensured, and transitional provisions should be laid down to that end. The same need for continuity applies as regards the interpretation of the Brussels Convention by the Court of Justice of the European Communities and the 1971 Protocol should remain applicable also to cases already pending when this Regulation enters into force.

(20) The United Kingdom and Ireland, in accordance with Article 3 of the Protocol on the position of the United Kingdom and Ireland annexed to the Treaty on European Union and to the Treaty establishing the European Community, have given notice of their wish to take part in the adoption and application of this Regulation.

(21) Denmark, in accordance with Articles 1 and 2 of the Protocol on the position of Denmark annexed to the Treaty on European Union and to the Treaty establishing the European Community, is not participating in the adoption of this Regulation, and is therefore not bound by it nor subject to its application.

(22) Since the Brussels Convention remains in force in relations between Denmark and the Member States that are bound by this Regulation, both the Convention and the 1971 Protocol continue to apply between Denmark and the Member States bound by this Regulation.

(23) The Brussels Convention also continues to apply to the territories of the Member States which fall within the territorial scope of that Convention and which are excluded from this Regulation pursuant to Article 299 of the Treaty.

(24) Likewise for the sake of consistency, this Regulation should not affect rules governing jurisdiction and the recognition of judgments contained in specific Community instruments.

(25) Respect for international commitments entered into by the Member States means that this Regulation should not affect conventions relating to specific matters to which the Member States are parties.

(26) The necessary flexibility should be provided for in the basic rules of this Regulation in order to take account of the specific procedural rules of certain Member States. Certain provisions of the Protocol annexed to the Brussels Convention should accordingly be incorporated in this Regulation.

(27) In order to allow a harmonious transition in certain areas which were the subject of special provisions in the Protocol annexed to the Brussels Convention, this Regulation lays down, for a transitional period, provisions taking into consideration the specific situation in certain Member States.

(28) No later than five years after entry into force of this Regulation the Commission will present a report on its application and, if need be, submit proposals for adaptations.

(29) The Commission will have to adjust Annexes I to IV on the rules of national jurisdiction, the courts or competent authorities and redress procedures available on the basis of the amendments forwarded by the Member State concerned; amendments made to Annexes V and VI should be adopted in accordance with Council Decision 1999/468/EC of 28 June 1999 laying down the procedures for the exercise of implementing poker conferred on the Commission;

Chapter I — Scope

Article 1.[2]   1.   This Regulation shall apply in civil and commercial matters whatever the nature of the court or tribunal. It shall not extend, in particular, to revenue, customs or administrative matters.

   2.   The Regulation shall not apply to:

   (a)   the *status* or legal capacity of natural persons, rights in property arising out of a matrimonial relationship, wills and succession;[3]

   (b)   bankruptcy, proceedings relating to the winding-up of insolvent companies or other legal persons, judicial arrangements, compositions and analogous proceedings;

   (c)   social security;

   (d)   arbitration.

   3.   In this Regulation, the term 'Member State' shall mean Member States with the exception of Denmark.

Chapter II — Jurisdiction

Section 1 — General provisions

Article 2.   1.   Subject to this Regulation, persons domiciled in a Member State shall, whatever their nationality, be sued in the courts of that Member State.

   2.   Persons who are not nationals of the Member State in which they are domiciled shall be governed by the rules of jurisdiction applicable to nationals of that State.

Article 3.   1.   Persons domiciled in a Member State may be sued in the courts of another Member State only by virtue of the rules set out in Sections 2 to 7 of this Chapter.

   2.   In particular the rules of national jurisdiction set out in Annex I shall not be applicable as against them.

Article 4.   1.   If the defendant is not domiciled in a Member State, the jurisdiction of the courts of each Member State shall, subject to Articles 22 and 23, be determined by the law of that Member State.

---

[2]   *Article 1(3), Lugano Convention.*

In this Convention, the term 'State bound by this Convention' shall mean any State that is a Contracting Party to this Convention or a Member State of the European Community. It may also mean the European Community.

[3]   After the entry into force of Council Regulation (EC) No 4/2009 of 18 December 2008 on jurisdiction, applicable law, recognition and enforcement of decisions and cooperation in matters relating to maintenance obligations (OJ, L 7 of 10 January 2009, Chapter XI, Maintenance obligations, A.1), Regulation (EC) No 44/2001 will not apply in matters relating to maintenance. [Note of the Editor]

2.   As against such a defendant, any person domiciled in a Member State may, whatever his nationality, avail himself in that State of the rules of jurisdiction there in force, and in particular those specified in Annex I, in the same way as the nationals of that State.

Section 2 — Special jurisdiction

Article 5.   A person domiciled in a Member State may, in another Member State, be sued:

1.   (a) in matters relating to a contract, in the courts for the place of performance of the obligation in question;

(b)   for the purpose of this provision and unless otherwise agreed, the place of performance of the obligation in question shall be:

—   in the case of the sale of goods, the place in a Member State where, under the contract, the goods were delivered or should have been delivered;

—   in the case of the provision of services, the place in a Member State where, under the contract, the services were provided or should have been provided;

(c)   if subparagraph (b) does not apply then subparagraph (a) applies;

2.   [4,5]

3.   in matters relating to tort, delict or quasi-delict, in the courts for the place where the harmful event occurred or may occur;

4.   as regards a civil claim for damages or restitution which is based on an act giving rise to criminal proceedings, in the court seised of those proceedings, to the extent that that court has jurisdiction under its own law to entertain civil proceedings;

5.   as regards a dispute arising out of the operations of a branch, agency or other establishment, in the courts for the place in which the branch, agency or other establishment is situated;

6.   as settlor, trustee or beneficiary of a trust created by the operation of a statute, or by a written instrument, or created orally and evidenced in writing, in the courts of the Member State in which the trust is domiciled;

7.   as regards a dispute concerning the payment of remuneration claimed in respect of the salvage of a cargo or freight, in the court under the authority of which the cargo or freight in question:

(a)   has been arrested to secure such payment, or

(b)   could have been so arrested, but bail or other security has been given;

provided that this provision shall apply only if it is claimed that the defendant has an interest in the cargo or freight or had such an interest at the time of salvage.

---

[4]   Article 5(2), *Lugano Convention.*
In matters relating to maintenance:
(a)   in the courts for the place where the maintenance creditor is domiciled or habitually resident; or
(b)   in the court which, according to its own law, has jurisdiction to entertain proceedings concerning the status of a person if the matter relating to maintenance is ancillary to those proceedings, unless that jurisdiction is based solely on the nationality of one of the parties; or
(c)   in the court which, according to its own law, has jurisdiction to entertain proceedings concerning parental responsibility, if the matter relating to maintenance is ancillary to those proceedings, unless that jurisdiction is based solely on the nationality of one of the parties.
[5]   Article 5(2) of Regulation (EC) No 44/2001 has been repealed by Regulation (EC) No 4/2009. See fn 3.
[Note of the Editor]

Article 6.   A person domiciled in a Member State may also be sued:

1.   where he is one of a number of defendants, in the courts for the place where any one of them is domiciled, provided the claims are so closely connected that it is expedient to hear and determine them together to avoid the risk of irreconcilable judgments resulting from separate proceedings;

2.   as a third party in an action on a warranty or guarantee or in any other third party proceedings, in the court seised of the original proceedings, unless these were instituted solely with the object of removing him from the jurisdiction of the court which would be competent in his case;

3.   on a counter-claim arising from the same contract or facts on which the original claim was based, in the court in which the original claim is pending;

4.   in matters relating to a contract, if the action may be combined with an action against the same defendant in matters relating to rights *in rem* in immovable property, in the court of the Member State in which the property is situated.

Article 7.   Where by virtue of this Regulation a court of a Member State has jurisdiction in actions relating to liability from the use or operation of a ship, that court, or any other court substituted for this purpose by the internal law of that Member State, shall also have jurisdiction over claims for limitation of such liability.

Section 3 — Jurisdiction in matters relating to insurance

Article 8.   In matters relating to insurance, jurisdiction shall be determined by this Section, without prejudice to Article 4 and point 5 of Article 5.

Article 9.   1.   An insurer domiciled in a Member State may be sued:

(a)   in the courts of the Member State where he is domiciled, or

(b)   in another Member State, in the case of actions brought by the policyholder, the insured or a beneficiary, in the courts for the place where the plaintiff is domiciled,

(c)   if he is a co-insurer, in the courts of a Member State in which proceedings are brought against the leading insurer.

2.   An insurer who is not domiciled in a Member State but has a branch, agency or other establishment in one of the Member States shall, in disputes arising out of the operations of the branch, agency or establishment, be deemed to be domiciled in that Member State.

Article 10.   In respect of liability insurance or insurance of immovable property, the insurer may in addition be sued in the courts for the place where the harmful event occurred. The same applies if movable and immovable property are covered by the same insurance policy and both are adversely affected by the same contingency.

Article 11.   1.   In respect of liability insurance, the insurer may also, if the law of the court permits it, be joined in proceedings which the injured party has brought against the insured.

2.   Articles 8, 9 and 10 shall apply to actions brought by the injured party directly against the insurer, where such direct actions are permitted.

3.   If the law governing such direct actions provides that the policyholder or the insured may be joined as a party to the action, the same court shall have jurisdiction over them.

Article 12.   1.   Without prejudice to Article 11(3), an insurer may bring proceedings only in the courts of the Member State in which the defendant is domiciled, irrespective of whether he is the policyholder, the insured or a beneficiary.

2.   The provisions of this Section shall not affect the right to bring a counter-claim in the court in which, in accordance with this Section, the original claim is pending.

Article 13.   The provisions of this Section may be departed from only by an agreement:

1.   which is entered into after the dispute has arisen, or

2.   which allows the policyholder, the insured or a beneficiary to bring proceedings in courts other than those indicated in this Section, or

3.   which is concluded between a policyholder and an insurer, both of whom are at the time of conclusion of the contract domiciled or habitually resident in the same Member State, and which has the effect of conferring jurisdiction on the courts of that State even if the harmful event were to occur abroad, provided that such an agreement is not contrary to the law of that State, or

4.   which is concluded with a policyholder who is not domiciled in a Member State, except in so far as the insurance is compulsory or relates to immovable property in a Member State, or

5.   which relates to a contract of insurance in so far as it covers one or more of the risks set out in Article 14.

Article 14.   The following are the risks referred to in Article 13(5):

1.   any loss of or damage to:

(a)   seagoing ships, installations situated offshore or on the high seas, or aircraft, arising from perils which relate to their use for commercial purposes;

(b)   goods in transit other than passengers' baggage where the transit consists of or includes carriage by such ships or aircraft;

2.   any liability, other than for bodily injury to passengers or loss of or damage to their baggage:

(a)   arising out of the use or operation of ships, installations or aircraft as referred to in point 1(a) in so far as, in respect of the latter, the law of the Member State in which such aircraft are registered does not prohibit agreements on jurisdiction regarding insurance of such risks;

(b)   for loss or damage caused by goods in transit as described in point 1(b);

3.   any financial loss connected with the use or operation of ships, installations or aircraft as referred to in point 1(a), in particular loss of freight or charter-hire;

4.   any risk or interest connected with any of those referred to in points 1 to 3;

5.   notwithstanding points 1 to 4, all 'large risks' as defined in Council Directive 73/239/EEC, as amended by Council Directives 88/357/EEC and 90/618/EEC, as they may be amended.[6]

Section 4 — Jurisdiction over consumer contracts

Article 15.   1.   In matters relating to a contract concluded by a person, the consumer, for a purpose which can be regarded as being outside his trade or profession, jurisdiction shall be determined by this Section, without prejudice to Article 4 and point 5 of Article 5, if:

---

[6]   [Note of the Editor] The First Council Directive 73/239/EEC of 24 July 1973 on the coordination of laws, regulations and administrative provisions relating to the taking-up and pursuit of the business of direct insurance other than life assurance (OJ, L 228 of 16 August 1973, amended by Council Directive 2006/101/EC of 20 November 2006, in OJ, L 363 of 20 December 2006), at last has been repealed by Directive 2009/138/EC of the European Parliament and of the Council of 25 November 2009 on the taking-up and pursuit of the business of Insurance and Reinsurance (Solvency II) (OJ, L 335 of 17 December 2009, in this book, Chapter IX, General provisions, N). Pursuant to Article 13(27) of Directive 2009/138 'Large risks' means:
(i)   risks classified under classes 4, 5, 6, 7, 11 and 12 of point A of the Annex:
(ii)   risks classified under classes 14 and 15 of point A of the Annex I, where the policy-holder is engaged professionally in an industrial or commercial activity or in one of the liberal professions, and the risks relate to such activity:
(iii)   risks classified under classes 3, 8, 9, 10, 13 and 16 of point A of the Annex I in so far as the policy-holder exceeds the limits of at least two of the following three criteria:
—   a balance-sheet total of EUR 6,2 million;
—   a net turnover, within the meaning of Fourth Council Directive 78/660/EEC of 25 July 1978 based on Article 54(3)(g) of the Treaty on the annual accounts of certain types of companies, of EUR 12,8 million;
—   an average number of 250 employees during the financial year.
If the policy-holder belongs to a group of undertakings for which consolidated accounts within the meaning of Directive83/349/EEC are drawn up, the criteria set out in point (c) of the first subparagraph shall be applied on the basis of the consolidated accounts.
Member States may add to the category referred to in point (c) of the first subparagraph the risks insured by professional associations, joint ventures or temporary groupings.
Annex I
A. Classification of risks according to classes of insurance
3. *Land vehicles* (other than railway rolling stock): All damage to or loss of land motor vehicles; land vehicles other than motor vehicles;
4. *Railway rolling stock*: All damage to or loss of railway rolling stock;
5. *Aircraft*: All damage to or loss of aircraft;
6. *Ships (sea, lake and river and canal vessels)*: All damage to or loss of river and canal vessels; lake vessels; sea vessels;
7. *Goods in transit (including merchandise, baggage, and all other goods)*: All damage to or loss of goods in transit or baggage, irrespective of the form of transport;
8. *Fire and natural forces*: All damage to or loss of property (other than property included in classes 3, 4, 5, 6 and 7) due to fire; explosion; storm; natural forces other than storm; nuclear energy; land subsidence;
9. *Other damage to property*: All damage to or loss of property (other than property included in classes 3, 4, 5, 6 and 7) due to hail or frost, and any event such as theft, other than that included in class 8;
10. *Motor vehicle liability*: All liability arising out of the use of motor vehicles operating on the land (including carrier's liability);
11. *Aircraft liability*: All liability arising out of the use of aircraft (including carrier's liability);
12. *Liability for ships (sea, lake and river and canal vessels)*:All liability arising out of the use of ships, vessels or boats on the sea, lakes, rivers or canals (including carrier's liability);
13. *General liability*: All liability other than those referred to in classes 10, 11 and 12;
14. *Credit*: insolvency (general); export credit; instalment credit; mortgages; agricultural credit;
15. *Suretyship*: suretyship (direct); suretyship (indirect);
16. *Miscellaneous financial loss*: employment risks; insufficiency of income (general); bad weather; loss of benefits; continuing general expenses; unforeseen trading expenses; loss of market value; loss of rent or revenue; other indirect trading loss; other non-trading financial loss; other forms of financial loss.

(a)   it is a contract for the sale of goods on instalment credit terms; or

(b)   it is a contract for a loan repayable by instalments, or for any other form of credit, made to finance the sale of goods; or

(c)   in all other cases, the contract has been concluded with a person who pursues commercial or professional activities in the Member State of the consumer's domicile or, by any means, directs such activities to that Member State or to several States including that Member State, and the contract falls within the scope of such activities.

2.   Where a consumer enters into a contract with a party who is not domiciled in the Member State but has a branch, agency or other establishment in one of the Member States, that party shall, in disputes arising out of the operations of the branch, agency or establishment, be deemed to be domiciled in that State.

3.   This Section shall not apply to a contract of transport other than a contract which, for an inclusive price, provides for a combination of travel and accommodation.

Article 16.   1.   A consumer may bring proceedings against the other party to a contract either in the courts of the Member State in which that party is domiciled or in the courts for the place where the consumer is domiciled.

2.   Proceedings may be brought against a consumer by the other party to the contract only in the courts of the Member State in which the consumer is domiciled.

3.   This Article shall not affect the right to bring a counter-claim in the court in which, in accordance with this Section, the original claim is pending.

Article 17.   The provisions of this Section may be departed from only by an agreement:

1.   which is entered into after the dispute has arisen; or

2.   which allows the consumer to bring proceedings in courts other than those indicated in this Section; or

3.   which is entered into by the consumer and the other party to the contract, both of whom are at the time of conclusion of the contract domiciled or habitually resident in the same Member State, and which confers jurisdiction on the courts of that Member State, provided that such an agreement is not contrary to the law of that Member State.

Section 5 — Jurisdiction over individual contracts of employment

Article 18.   1.   In matters relating to individual contracts of employment, jurisdiction shall be determined by this Section, without prejudice to Article 4 and point 5 of Article 5.

2.   Where an employee enters into an individual contract of employment with an employer who is not domiciled in a Member State but has a branch, agency or other establishment in one of the Member States, the employer shall, in disputes arising out of the operations of the branch, agency or establishment, be deemed to be domiciled in that Member State.

Article 19.   An employer domiciled in a Member State may be sued:

1.   in the courts of the Member State where he is domiciled; or

2.   in another Member State:

(a) in the courts for the place where the employee habitually carries out his work or in the courts for the last place where he did so, or

(b) if the employee does not or did not habitually carry out his work in any one country, in the courts for the place where the business which engaged the employee is or was situated.

Article 20. 1. An employer may bring proceedings only in the courts of the Member State in which the employee is domiciled.

2. The provisions of this Section shall not affect the right to bring a counter-claim in the court in which, in accordance with this Section, the original claim is pending.

Article 21. The provisions of this Section may be departed from only by an agreement on jurisdiction:

1. which is entered into after the dispute has arisen; or

2. which allows the employee to bring proceedings in courts other than those indicated in this Section.

Section 6 — Exclusive jurisdiction

Article 22. The following courts shall have exclusive jurisdiction, regardless of domicile:

1. in proceedings which have as their object rights *in rem* in immovable property or tenancies of immovable property, the courts of the Member State in which the property is situated.

However, in proceedings which have as their object tenancies of immovable property concluded for temporary private use for a maximum period of six consecutive months, the courts of the Member State in which the defendant is domiciled shall also have jurisdiction, provided that the tenant is a natural person and that the landlord and the tenant are domiciled in the same Member State;

2. in proceedings which have as their object the validity of the constitution, the nullity or the dissolution of companies or other legal persons or associations of natural or legal persons, or of the validity of the decisions of their organs, the courts of the Member State in which the company, legal person or association has its seat. In order to determine that seat, the court shall apply its rules of private international law;

3. in proceedings which have as their object the validity of entries in public registers, the courts of the Member State in which the register is kept;

4. in proceedings concerned with the registration or validity of patents, trade marks, designs, or other similar rights required to be deposited or registered, the courts of the Member State in which the deposit or has been applied for, has taken place or is under the terms of a Community instrument or an international convention deemed to have taken place;

Without prejudice to the jurisdiction of the European Patent Office under the Convention on the Grant of European Patents, signed at Munich on 5 October 1973, the courts of each Member State shall have exclusive jurisdiction, regardless of domicile, in proceedings concerned with the registration or validity of any European patent granted for that State;[7]

5.   in proceedings concerned with the enforcement of judgments, the courts of the Member State in which the judgment has been or is to be enforced.

Section 7 — Prorogation of jurisdiction

Article 23.   1.   If the parties, one or more of whom is domiciled in a Member State, have agreed that a court or the courts of a Member State are to have jurisdiction to settle any disputes which have arisen or which may arise in connection with a particular legal relationship, that court or those courts shall have jurisdiction. Such jurisdiction shall be exclusive unless the parties have agreed otherwise. Such an agreement conferring jurisdiction shall be either:

(a)   in writing or evidenced in writing; or

(b)   in a form which accords with practices which the parties have established between themselves; or

(c)   in international trade or commerce, in a form which accords with a usage of which the parties are or ought to have been aware and which in such trade or commerce is widely known to, and regularly observed by, parties to contracts of the type involved in the particular trade or commerce concerned.

2.   Any communication by electronic means which provides a durable record of the agreement shall be equivalent to 'writing'.

3.   Where such an agreement is concluded by parties, none of whom is domiciled in a Member State, the courts of other Member States shall have no jurisdiction over their disputes unless the court or courts chosen have declined jurisdiction.

4.   The court or courts of a Member State on which a trust instrument has conferred jurisdiction shall have exclusive jurisdiction in any proceedings brought against a settlor, trustee or beneficiary, if relations between these persons or their rights or obligations under the trust are involved.

5.   Agreements or provisions of a trust instrument conferring jurisdiction shall have no legal force if they are contrary to Articles 13, 17 or 21, or if the courts whose jurisdiction they purport to exclude have exclusive jurisdiction by virtue of Article 22.

Article 24.   Apart from jurisdiction derived from other provisions of this Regulation, a court of a Member State before which a defendant enters an appearance shall have jurisdiction. This rule shall not apply where appearance was entered to contest the jurisdiction, or where another court has exclusive jurisdiction by virtue of Article 22.

---

[7]   Article 22(4), *Lugano Convention.*

In proceedings concerned with the registration or validity of patents, trade marks, designs, or other similar rights required to be deposited or registered, irrespective of whether the issue is raised by way of an action or as a defence, the courts of the State bound by this Convention in which the deposit or registration has been applied for, has taken place or is, under the terms of a Community instrument or an international convention, deemed to have taken place.

Without prejudice to the jurisdiction of the European Patent Office under the Convention on the grant of European patents, signed at Munich on 5 October 1973, the courts of each State bound by this Convention shall have exclusive jurisdiction, regardless of domicile, in proceedings concerned with the registration or validity of any European patent granted for that State irrespective of whether the issue is raised by way of an action or as a defence.

Section 8 — Examination as to jurisdiction and admissibility

Article 25.   Where a court of a Member State is seised of a claim which is principally concerned with a matter over which the courts of another Member State have exclusive jurisdiction by virtue of Article 22, it shall declare of its own motion that it has no jurisdiction.

Article 26.[8]   1.   Where a defendant domiciled in one Member State is sued in a court of another Member State and does not enter an appearance, the court shall declare of its own motion that it has no jurisdiction unless its jurisdiction is derived from the provisions of this Regulation.

2.   The court shall stay the proceedings so long as it is not shown that the defendant has been able to receive the document instituting the proceedings or an equivalent document in sufficient time to enable him to arrange for his defence, or that all necessary steps have been taken to this end.

3.   Article 19 of Council Regulation (EC) No 1348/2000 of 29 May 2000 on the service in the Member States of judicial and extrajudicial documents in civil or commercial matters shall apply instead of the provisions of paragraph 2 if the document instituting the proceedings or an equivalent document had to be transmitted from one Member State to another pursuant to this Regulation.

4.   Where the provisions of Regulation (EC) No 1348/2000 are not applicable, Article 15 of the Hague Convention of 15 November 1965 on the Service Abroad of Judicial and Extrajudicial Documents in Civil or Commercial Matters shall apply if the document instituting the proceedings or an equivalent document had to be transmitted pursuant to that Convention.

Section 9 — Lis pendens – related actions

Article 27.   1.   Where proceedings involving the same cause of action and between the same parties are brought in the courts of different Member States, any court other than the court first seised shall of its own motion stay its proceedings until such time as the jurisdiction of the court first seised is established.

2.   Where the jurisdiction of the court first seised is established, any court other than the court first seised shall decline jurisdiction in favour of that court.

Article 28.   1.   Where related actions are pending in the courts of different Member States, any court other than the court first seised may stay its proceedings.

---

[8]   Article 26(3) and (4), *Lugano Convention.*
Instead of the provisions of Art 15, para 2 of the Hague Convention of 15 November 1965 on the Service Abroad of Judicial and Extrajudicial Documents in Civil and Commercial matters shall apply if the document instituting the proceedings or an equivalent document had to be transmitted pursuant to that Convention.
Member States of the European Community bound by Council Regulation (EC) No 1348/2000 of 29 May 2000 or by the Agreement between the European Community and the Kingdom of Denmark on the service of judicial and extrajudicial documents in civil or commercial matters, signed at Brussels on 19 October 2005, shall apply in their mutual relations the provision in Article 19 of that Regulation if the document instituting the proceedings or an equivalent document had to be transmitted pursuant to that Regulation or that Agreement.

2.   Where these actions are pending at first instance, any court other than the court first seised may also, on the application of one of the parties, decline jurisdiction if the court first seised has jurisdiction over the actions in question and its law permits the consolidation thereof.

3.   For the purposes of this Article, actions are deemed to be related where they are so closely connected that it is expedient to hear and determine them together to avoid the risk of irreconcilable judgments resulting from separate proceedings.

Article 29.   Where actions come within the exclusive jurisdiction of several courts, any court other than the court first seised shall decline jurisdiction in favour of that court.

Article 30.   For the purposes of this Section, a court shall be deemed to be seised:

1.   at the time when the document instituting the proceedings or an equivalent document is lodged with the court, provided that the plaintiff has not subsequently failed to take the steps he was required to take to have service effected on the defendant, or

2.   if the document has to be served before being lodged with the court, at the time when it is received by the authority responsible for service, provided that the plaintiff has not subsequently failed to take the steps he was required to take to have the document lodged with the court.

Section 10 — Provisional, including protective, measures

Article 31.   Application may be made to the courts of a Member State for such provisional, including protective, measures as may be available under the law of that State, even if, under this Regulation, the courts of another Member State have jurisdiction as to the substance of the matter.

Chapter III – Recognition and enforcement

Article 32.   For the purposes of this Regulation, 'judgment' means any judgment given by a court or tribunal of a Member State, whatever the judgment may be called, including a decree, order, decision or writ of execution, as well as the determination of costs or expenses by an officer of the court.

Section 1 — Recognition

Article 33.   1.   A judgment given in a Member State shall be recognised in the other Member States without any special procedure being required.

2.   Any interested party who raises the recognition of a judgment as the principal issue in a dispute may, in accordance with the procedures provided for in Sections 2 and 3 of this Chapter, apply for a decision that the judgment be recognised.

3.   If the outcome of proceedings in a court of a Member State depends on the determination of an incidental question of recognition that court shall have jurisdiction over that question.

Article 34.   A judgment shall not be recognised:

1.   if such recognition is manifestly contrary to public policy in the Member State in which recognition is sought;

2.   where it was given in default of appearance, if the defendant was not served with the document which instituted the proceedings or with an equivalent document in sufficient time and in such a way as to enable him to arrange for his defence, unless the defendant failed to commence proceedings to challenge the judgment when it was possible for him to do so;

3.   if it is irreconcilable with a judgment given in a dispute between the same parties in the Member State in which recognition is sought;

4.   if it is irreconcilable with an earlier judgment given in another Member State or in a third State involving the same cause of action and between the same parties, provided that the earlier judgment fulfils the conditions necessary for its recognition in the Member State addressed.

Article 35.[9]   1.   Moreover, a judgment shall not be recognised if it conflicts with Sections 3, 4 or 6 of Chapter II, or in a case provided for in Article 72.

2.   In its examination of the grounds of jurisdiction referred to in the foregoing paragraph, the court or authority applied to shall be bound by the findings of fact on which the court of the Member State of origin based its jurisdiction.

3.   Subject to the paragraph 1, the jurisdiction of the court of the Member State of origin may not be reviewed. The test of public policy referred to in point 1 of Article 34 may not be applied to the rules relating to jurisdiction.

Article 36.   Under no circumstances may a foreign judgment be reviewed as to its substance.

Article 37.   1.   A court of a Member State in which recognition is sought of a judgment given in another Member State may stay the proceedings if an ordinary appeal against the judgment has been lodged.

2.   A court of a Member State in which recognition is sought of a judgment given in Ireland or the United Kingdom may stay the proceedings if enforcement is suspended in the State of origin, by reason of an appeal.

Section 2 — Enforcement

Article 38.   1.   A judgment given in a Member State and enforceable in that State shall be enforced in another Member State when, on the application of any interested party, it has been declared enforceable there.

2.   However, in the United Kingdom, such a judgment shall be enforced in England and Wales, in Scotland, or in Northern Ireland when, on the application of any interested party, it has been registered for enforcement in that part of the United Kingdom.

---

[9]   Article 35(1), *Lugano Convention*.
Moreover, a judgment shall not be recognised if it conflicts with Sections 3, 4 or 6 of Title II, or in a case provided for in Article 68. A judgment may furthermore be refused recognition in any case provided for in Articles 64(3) or 67(4).

Article 39. 1 The application shall be submitted to the court or competent authority indicated in the list in Annex II.

2. The local jurisdiction shall be determined by reference to the place of domicile of the party against whom enforcement is sought, or to the place of enforcement.

Article 40. 1. The procedure for making the application shall be governed by the law of the Member State in which enforcement is sought.

2. The applicant must give an address for service of process within the area of jurisdiction of the court applied to. However, if the law of the Member State in which enforcement is sought does not provide for the furnishing of such an address, the applicant shall appoint a representative *ad litem*.

3. The documents referred to in Article 53 shall be attached to the application.

Article 41. The judgment shall be declared enforceable immediately on completion of the formalities in Article 53 without any review under Articles 34 and 35. The party against whom enforcement is sought shall not at this stage of the proceedings be entitled to make any submissions on the application.

Article 42. 1. The decision on the application for a declaration of enforceability shall forthwith be brought to the notice of the applicant in accordance with the procedure laid down by the law of the Member State in which enforcement is sought.

2. The declaration of enforceability shall be served on the party against whom enforcement is sought, accompanied by the judgment, if not already served on that party.

Article 43. 1. The decision on the application for a declaration of enforceability may be appealed against by either party.

2. The appeal is to be lodged with the court indicated in the list in Annex III.

3. The appeal shall be dealt with in accordance with the rules governing procedure in contradictory matters.

4. If the party against whom enforcement is sought fails to appear before the appellate court in proceedings concerning an appeal brought by the applicant, Article 26(2) to (4) shall apply even where the party against whom enforcement is sought is not domiciled in any of the Member States.

5. An appeal against the declaration of enforceability is to be lodged within one month of service thereof. If the party against whom enforcement is sought is domiciled in a Member State other than that in which the declaration of enforceability was given, the time for appealing shall be two months and shall run from the date of service, either on him in person or at his residence. No extension of time may be granted on account of distance.

Article 44. The judgment given on the appeal may be contested only by the appeal referred to in Annex IV.

Article 45. 1. The court with which an appeal is lodged under Article 43 or Article 44 shall refuse or revoke a declaration of enforceability only on one of the grounds specified in Articles 34 and 35. It shall give its decision without delay.

2.   Under no circumstances may the foreign judgment be reviewed as to its substance.

Article 46.   1.   The court with which an appeal is lodged under Article 43 or Article 44 may, on the application of the party against whom enforcement is sought, stay the proceedings if an ordinary appeal has been lodged against the judgment in the Member State of origin or if the time for such an appeal has not yet expired; in the latter case, the court may specify the time within which such an appeal is to be lodged.

2.   Where the judgment was given in Ireland or the United Kingdom, any form of appeal available in the Member State of origin shall be treated as an ordinary appeal for the purposes of paragraph 1.

3.   The court may also make enforcement conditional on the provision of such security as it shall determine.

Article 47.   1.   When a judgment must be recognised in accordance with this Regulation, nothing shall prevent the applicant from availing himself of provisional, including protective, measures in accordance with the law of the Member State requested without a declaration of enforceability under Article 41 being required.

2.   The declaration of enforceability shall carry with it the power to proceed to any protective measures.

3.   During the time specified for an appeal pursuant to Article 43(5) against the declaration of enforceability and until any such appeal has been determined, no measures of enforcement may be taken other than protective measures against the property of the party against whom enforcement is sought.

Article 48.   1.   Where a foreign judgment has been given in respect of several matters and the declaration of enforceability cannot be given for all of them, the court or competent authority shall give it for one or more of them.

2.   An applicant may request a declaration of enforceability limited to parts of a judgment.

Article 49.   A foreign judgment which orders a periodic payment by way of a penalty shall be enforceable in the Member State in which enforcement is sought only if the amount of the payment has been finally determined by the courts of the Member State of origin.

Article 50.[10]   An applicant who, in the Member State of origin has benefited from complete or partial legal aid or exemption from costs or expenses, shall be entitled, in the procedure provided for in this Section, to benefit from the most favourable legal aid or the most extensive exemption from costs or expenses provided for by the law of the Member State addressed.

---

[10]   Article 50(2), *Lugano Convention.*
   However, an applicant who requests the enforcement of a decision given by an administrative authority in Denmark, in Iceland or in Norway in respect of maintenance may, in the State addressed, claim the benefits referred to in paragraph 1 if he presents a statement from the Danish, Icelandic, or Norwegian Ministry of Justice to the effect that he fulfils the economic requirements to qualify for the grant of complete or partial legal aid or exemption from costs or expenses.

Article 51. No security, bond or deposit, however described, shall be required of a party who in one Member State applies for enforcement of a judgment given in another Member State on the ground that he is a foreign national or that he is not domiciled or resident in the State in which enforcement is sought.

Article 52. In proceedings for the issue of a declaration of enforceability, no charge, duty or fee calculated by reference to the value of the matter at issue may be levied in the Member State in which enforcement is sought.

Section 3 — Common provisions

Article 53. 1. A party seeking recognition or applying for a declaration of enforceability shall produce a copy of the judgment which satisfies the conditions necessary to establish its authenticity.

2. A party applying for a declaration of enforceability shall also produce the certificate referred to in Article 54, without prejudice to Article 55.

Article 54. The court or competent authority of a Member State where a judgment was given shall issue, at the request of any interested party, a certificate using the standard form in Annex 5 to this Regulation.

Article 55. 1. If the certificate referred to in Article 54 is not produced, the court or competent authority may specify a time for its production or accept an equivalent document or, if it considers that it has sufficient information before it, dispense with its production.

2. If the court or competent authority so requires, a translation of the documents shall be produced. The translation shall be certified by a person qualified to do so in one of the Member States.

Article 56. No legalisation or other similar formality shall be required in respect of the documents referred to in Article 53 or Article 55(2), or in respect of a document appointing a representative *ad litem*.

Chapter IV — Authentic instruments and court settlements

Article 57. 1. A document which has been formally drawn up or registered as an authentic instrument and is enforceable in one Member State shall, in another Member State, be declared enforceable there, on application made in accordance with the procedures provided for in Articles 38, *et seq*. The court with which an appeal is lodged under Article 43 or Article 44 shall refuse or revoke a declaration of enforceability only if enforcement of the instrument is manifestly contrary to public policy in the Member State addressed.

2. [11]

3. The instrument produced must satisfy the conditions necessary to establish its authenticity in the Member State of origin.

---

[11] Article 57(2) of Regulation (EC) No 44/2001 has been repealed by Regulation (EC) No 4/2009. See fn 3. [Note of the Editor]

4.   Section 3 of Chapter III shall apply as appropriate. The competent authority of a Member State where an authentic instrument was drawn up or registered shall issue, at the request of any interested party, a certificate using the standard form in Annex VI to this Regulation.

Article 58.   A settlement which has been approved by a court in the course of proceedings and is enforceable in the Member State in which it was concluded shall be enforceable in the State addressed under the same conditions as authentic instruments. The court or competent authority of a Member State where a court settlement was approved shall issue, at the request of any interested party, a certificate using the standard form in Annex V to this Regulation.

Chapter V — General provisions

Article 59.   1.   In order to determine whether a party is domiciled in the Member State whose courts are seised of a matter, the court shall apply its internal law.
2.   If a party is not domiciled in the Member State whose courts are seised of the matter, then, in order to determine whether the party is domiciled in another Member State, the court shall apply the law of that Member State.

Article 60.   1.   For the purposes of this Regulation, a company or other legal person or association of natural or legal persons is domiciled at the place where it has its:
    (a) statutory seat, or
    (b) central administration, or
    (c) principal place of business.
2.   For the purposes of the United Kingdom and Ireland 'statutory seat' means the registered office or, where there is no such office anywhere, the place of incorporation or, where there is no such place anywhere, the place under the law of which the formation took place.
3.   In order to determine whether a trust is domiciled in the Member State whose courts are seised of the matter, the court shall apply its rules of private international law.

Article 61.   Without prejudice to any more favourable provisions of national laws, persons domiciled in a Member State who are being prosecuted in the criminal courts of another Member State of which they are not nationals for an offence which was not intentionally committed may be defended by persons qualified to do so, even if they do not appear in person. However, the court seised of the matter may order appearance in person; in the case of failure to appear, a judgment given in the civil action without the person concerned having had the opportunity to arrange for his defence need not be recognised or enforced in the other Member States.

Article 62.[12] In Sweden, in summary proceedings concerning orders to pay (betalningsföreläggande) and assistance (handräckning), the expression 'court' includes the 'Swedish enforcement service' (kronofogdemyndighet).

Article 63. 1.   A person domiciled in the territory of the Grand Duchy of Luxembourg and sued in the court of another Member State pursuant to Article 5(1) may refuse to submit to the jurisdiction of that court if the final place of delivery of the goods or provision of the services is in Luxembourg.

2.   Where, under paragraph 1, the final place of delivery of the goods or provision of the services is in Luxembourg, any agreement conferring jurisdiction must, in order to be valid, be accepted in writing or evidenced in writing within the meaning of Article 23(1)(a).

3.   The provisions of this Article shall not apply to contracts for the provision of financial services.

4.   The provisions of this Article shall apply for a period of six years from entry into force of this Regulation.

Article 64. 1.   In proceedings involving a dispute between the master and a member of the crew of a seagoing ship registered in Greece or in Portugal, concerning remuneration or other conditions of service, a court in a Member State shall establish whether the diplomatic or consular officer responsible for the ship has been notified of the dispute. It may act as soon as that officer has been notified.

2.   The provisions of this Article shall apply for a period of six years from entry into force of this Regulation.

Article 65. 1.   The jurisdiction specified in Article 6(2) and Article 11 in actions on a warranty of guarantee or in any other third party proceedings may not be resorted to Germany, Austria and Hungary. Any person domiciled in another Member State may be sued in the courts:

(a)   of Germany, pursuant to Articles 68 and 72 to 74 of the Code of Civil Procedure (*Zivilprozessordnung*) concerning third–party notices:

(b)   of Austria, pursuant to Article 21 of the Code of Civil Procedure (*Zivilprozessordnung*) concerning third–party notices:

(c)   of Hungary, pursuant to Articles 58 to 60 of the Code of Civil Procedure (*Polgári perrendtartás*) concerning third–party notices.

2.   Judgments given in other Member States by virtue of Article 6(2), or Article 11 shall be recognised and enforced in Germany, Austria and Hungary in accordance with Chapter III. Any effects which judgments given in these States may have on third parties by application of the provisions in paragraph 1 shall also be recognised in the other Member States.

---

[12]   In the Lugano Convention there are no provisions corresponding to Articles 62–65 of Regulation (EC) No 44/2001.

Article 62, Lugano Convention.
For the purposes of this Convention, the expression 'court' shall include any authorities designated by a State bound by this Convention as having jurisdiction in the matters falling within the scope of this Convention.

Chapter VI — Transitional provisions

Article 66.[13]   1.   This Regulation shall apply only to legal proceedings instituted and to documents formally drawn up or registered as authentic instruments after the entry into force thereof.

2.   However, if the proceedings in the Member State of origin were instituted before the entry into force of this Regulation, judgments given after that date shall be recognised and enforced in accordance with Chapter III,

(a)   if the proceedings in the Member State of origin were instituted after the entry into force of the Brussels or the Lugano Convention both in the Member State or origin and in the Member State addressed;

(b)   in all other cases, if jurisdiction was founded upon rules which accorded with those provided for either in Chapter II or in a convention concluded between the Member State of origin and the Member State addressed which was in force when the proceedings were instituted.

Chapter VII — Relations with other instruments

Article 67.[14]   This Regulation shall not prejudice the application of provisions governing jurisdiction and the recognition and enforcement of judgments in specific matters which

---

[13]   *Article 63, Lugano Convention.*
    1. This Convention shall apply only to legal proceedings instituted and to documents formally drawn up or registered as authentic instruments after its entry into force in the State of origin and, where recognition or enforcement of a judgment or authentic instruments is sought, in the State addressed.
    2. However, if the proceedings in the State of origin were instituted before the entry into force of this Convention, judgments given after that date shall be recognised and enforced in accordance with Title III:
    (a) if the proceedings in the State of origin were instituted after the entry into force of the Lugano Convention of 16 September 1988 both in the State of origin and in the State addressed;
    (b) in all other cases, if jurisdiction was founded upon rules which accorded with those provided for either in Title II or in a convention concluded between the State of origin and the State addressed which was in force when the proceedings were instituted.
[14]   *Article 64, Lugano Convention.*
    1. This Convention shall not prejudice the application by the Member States of the European Community of the Council Regulation (EC) No 44/2001 on jurisdiction and the recognition and enforcement of judgments in civil and commercial matters, as well as any amendments thereof, of the Convention on Jurisdiction and the Enforcement of Judgments in Civil and Commercial Matters, signed at Brussels on 27 September 1968, and of the Protocol on interpretation of that Convention by the Court of Justice of the European Communities, signed at Luxembourg on 3 June 1971, as amended by the Conventions of Accession to the said Convention and the said Protocol by the States acceding to the European Communities, as well as of the Agreement between the European Community and the Kingdom of Denmark on jurisdiction and the recognition and enforcement of judgments in civil and commercial matters, signed at Brussels on 19 October 2005.
    2. However, this Convention shall in any event be applied:
    (a) in matters of jurisdiction, where the defendant is domiciled in the territory of a State where this Convention but not an instrument referred to in paragraph 1 of this Article applies, or where Articles 22 or 23 of this Convention confer jurisdiction on the courts of such a State;
    (b) in relation to *lis pendens* or to related actions as provided for in Articles 27 and 28, when proceedings are instituted in a State where the Convention but not an instrument referred to in paragraph 1 of this Article applies and in a State where this Convention as well as an instrument referred to in paragraph 1 of this Article apply;
    (c) in matters of recognition and enforcement, where either the State of origin or the State addressed is not applying an instrument referred to in paragraph 1 of this Article.
    3. In addition to the grounds provided for in Title III, recognition or enforcement may be refused if the ground of jurisdiction on which the judgment has been based differs from that resulting from this Convention and recognition or enforcement is sought against a party who is domiciled in a State where this Convention but not an instrument referred to in paragraph 1 of this Article applies, unless the judgment may otherwise be recognised or enforced under any rule of law in the State addressed.

are contained in Community instruments or in national legislation harmonised pursuant to such instruments.

Article 68. 1. This Regulation shall, as between the Member States, supersede the Brussels Convention, except as regards the territories of the Member States which fall within the territorial scope of that Convention and which are excluded from this Regulation pursuant to Article 299 of the Treaty.

2. In so far as this Regulation replaces the provisions of the Brussels Convention between Member States, any reference to the Convention shall be understood as a reference to this Regulation.

Article 69.[15] Subject to Article 66(2) and Article 70, this Regulation shall, as between Member States, supersede the following conventions and treaty concluded between two or more of them:

— the Convention between Belgium and France on Jurisdiction and the Validity and Enforcement of Judgments, Arbitration Awards and Authentic Instruments, signed at Paris on 8 July 1899;

— the Convention between Belgium and the Netherlands on Jurisdiction, Bankruptcy, and the Validity and Enforcement of Judgments, Arbitration Awards and Authentic Instruments, signed at Brussels on 28 March 1925;

— the Convention between France and Italy on the Enforcement of Judgments in Civil and Commercial Matters, signed at Rome on 3 June 1930;

— the Convention between the United Kingdom and the French Republic providing for the reciprocal enforcement of judgments in civil and commercial matters, with Protocol, signed at Paris on 18 January 1934;

— the Convention between the United Kingdom and the Kingdom of Belgium providing for the reciprocal enforcement of judgments in civil and commercial matters, with Protocol, signed at Brussels on 2 May 1934;

— the Convention between Germany and Italy on the Recognition and Enforcement of Judgments in Civil and Commercial Matters, signed at Rome on 9 March 1936;

— the Convention between Belgium and Austria on the Reciprocal Recognition and Enforcement of Judgments and Authentic Instruments relating to Maintenance Obligations, signed at Vienna on 25 October 1957;

— the Convention between Germany and Belgium on the Mutual Recognition and Enforcement of Judgments, Arbitration Awards and Authentic Instruments in Civil and Commercial Matters, signed at Bonn on 30 June 1958;

— the Convention between the Netherlands and Italy on the Recognition and Enforcement of Judgments in Civil and Commercial Matters, signed at Rome on 17 April 1959;

— the Convention between Germany and Austria on the Reciprocal Recognition and Enforcement of Judgments, Settlements and Authentic Instruments in Civil and Commercial Matters, signed at Vienna on 6 June 1959;

---

[15] *Article 65, Lugano Convention.*
Subject to the provisions of Articles 63(2), 66 and 67, this Convention shall, as between the States bound by this Convention, supersede the conventions concluded between two or more of them that cover the same matters as those to which this Convention applies. In particular, the conventions mentioned in Annex VII shall be superseded.

—   the Convention between Belgium and Austria on the Reciprocal Recognition and Enforcement of Judgments, Arbitral Awards and Authentic Instruments in Civil and Commercial Matters, signed at Vienna on 16 June 1959;

—   the Convention between the United Kingdom and the Federal Republic of Germany for the reciprocal recognition and enforcement of judgments in civil and commercial matters, signed at Bonn on 14 July 1960;

—   the Convention between the United Kingdom and Austria providing for the reciprocal recognition and enforcement of judgments in civil and commercial matters, signed at Vienna on 14 July 1961, with amending Protocol signed at London on 6 March 1970;

—   the Convention between Greece and Germany for the Reciprocal Recognition and Enforcement of Judgments, Settlements and Authentic Instruments in Civil and Commercial Matters, signed in Athens on 4 November 1961;

—   the Convention between Belgium and Italy on the Recognition and Enforcement of Judgments and other Enforceable Instruments in Civil and Commercial Matters, signed at Rome on 6 April 1962;

—   the Convention between the Netherlands and Germany on the Mutual Recognition and Enforcement of Judgments and Other Enforceable Instruments in Civil and Commercial Matters, signed at The Hague on 30 August 1962;

—   the Convention between the Netherlands and Austria on the Reciprocal Recognition and Enforcement of Judgments and Authentic Instruments in Civil and Commercial Matters, signed at The Hague on 6 February 1963;

—   the Convention between the United Kingdom and the Republic of Italy for the reciprocal recognition and enforcement of judgments in civil and commercial matters, signed at Rome on 7 February 1964, with amending Protocol signed at Rome on 14 July 1970;

—   the Convention between France and Austria on the Recognition and Enforcement of Judgments and Authentic Instruments in Civil and Commercial Matters, signed at Vienna on 15 July 1966;

—   the Convention between the United Kingdom and the Kingdom of the Netherlands providing for the reciprocal recognition and enforcement of judgments in civil matters, signed at The Hague on 17 November 1967;

—   the Convention between Spain and France on the Recognition and Enforcement of Arbitration Awards in Civil and Commercial Matters, signed at Paris on 28 May 1969;

—   the Convention between Luxembourg and Austria on the Recognition and Enforcement of Judgments and Authentic Instruments in Civil and Commercial Matters, signed at Luxembourg on 29 July 1971;

—   the Convention between Italy and Austria on the Recognition and Enforcement of Judgments in Civil and Commercial Matters, of Judicial Settlements and of Authentic Instruments, signed at Rome on 16 November 1971;

—   the Convention between Spain and Italy regarding Legal Aid and the Recognition and Enforcement of Judgments in Civil and Commercial Matters, signed at Madrid on 22 May 1973;

—   the Convention between Finland, Iceland, Norway, Sweden and Denmark on the Recognition and Enforcement of Judgments in Civil Matters, signed at Copenhagen on 11 October 1977;

—   the Convention between Austria and Sweden on the Recognition and Enforcement of Judgments in Civil Matters, signed at Stockholm on 16 September 1982;

—   the Convention between Spain and the Federal Republic of Germany on the Recognition and Enforcement of Judgments, Settlements and Enforceable Authentic Instruments in Civil and Commercial Matters, signed at Bonn on 14 November 1983;

—   the Convention between Austria and Spain on the Recognition and Enforcement of Judgments, Settlements and Enforceable Authentic Instruments in Civil and Commercial Matters, signed at Vienna on 17 February 1984;

—   the Convention between Finland and Austria on the Recognition and Enforcement of Judgments in Civil Matters, signed at Vienna on 17 November 1986;

—   the Treaty between Belgium, the Netherlands and Luxembourg in Jurisdiction, Bankruptcy, and the Validity and Enforcement of Judgments, Arbitration Awards and Authentic Instruments, signed at Brussels on 24 November 1961, in so far as it is in force;

—   the Convention between the Czechoslovak Republic and Portugal on the Recognition and Enforcement of Court Decisions, signed at Lisbon on 23 November 1927, still in force between the Czech Republic and Portugal;

—   the Convention between the Federative People's Republic of Yugoslavia and the Republic of Austria on Mutual Judicial Cooperation, signed at Vienna on 16 December 1954;

—   the Convention between the Polish People's Republic and the Hungarian People's Republic on the Legal Assistance in Civil, Family and Criminal Matters, signed at Budapest on 6 March 1959;

—   the Convention between the Federative People's Republic of Yugoslavia and the Kingdom of Greece on the Mutual Recognition and Enforcement of Judgments, signed at Athens on 18 June 1959;

—   the Convention between the Polish People's Republic and the Federative People's Republic of Yugoslavia on the Legal Assistance in Civil and Criminal Matters, signed at Warsaw on 6 February 1960, now in force between Poland and Slovenia;

—   the Agreement between the Federative People's Republic of Yugoslavia and the Republic of Austria on the Mutual Recognition and Enforcement of Arbitral Awards and Arbitral Settlements in Commercial Matters, signed at Belgrade on 18 March 1960;

—   the Agreement between the Federative People's Republic of Yugoslavia and the Republic of Austria on the Mutual Recognition and Enforcement of Decisions in Alimony Matters, signed at Vienna on 10 October 1961;

—   the Convention between Poland and Austria on Mutual Relations in Civil Matters and on Documents, signed at Vienna on 11 December 1963;

—   the Treaty between the Czechoslovak Socialist Republic and the Socialist Federative Republic of Yugoslavia on Settlement of Legal Relations in Civil, Family and Criminal Matters, signed at Belgrade on 20 January 1964, still in force between the Czech Republic, Slovakia and Slovenia;

—   the Convention between Poland and France on Applicable Law, Jurisdiction and the Enforcement of Judgments in the field of Personal and Family Law, concluded in Warsaw on 5 April 1967;

—   the Convention between the Governments of Yugoslavia and France on the Recognition and Enforcement of Judgments in Civil and Commercial Matters, signed at Paris on 18 May 1971;

— the Convention between the Federative Socialist Republic of Yugoslavia and the Kingdom of Belgium on the Recognition and Enforcement of Court Decisions in Alimony Matters, signed at Belgrade on 12 December 1973;

— the Convention between Hungary and Greece on Legal Assistance in Civil and Criminal Matters, signed at Budapest on 8 October 1979;

— the Convention between Poland and Greece on Legal Assistance in Civil and Criminal Matters, signed at Athens on 24 October 1979;

— the Convention between Hungary and France on Legal Assistance in Civil and Family Law, on the Recognition and Enforcement of Decisions and on Legal Assistance in Criminal Matters and on Extradition, signed at Budapest on 31 July 1980;

— the Treaty between the Czechoslovak Socialist Republic and the Hellenic Republic on Legal Aid in Civil and Criminal Matters, signed at Athens on 22 October 1980, still in force between the Czech Republic, Slovakia and Greece;

— the Convention between the Republic of Cyprus and the Hungarian People's Republic on Legal Assistance in Civil and Criminal Matters, signed at Nicosia on 30 November 1981;

— the Treaty between the Czechoslovak Socialistic Republic and the Republic of Cyprus on Legal Aid in Civil and Criminal Matters, signed at Nicosia on 23 April 1982, still in force between the Czech Republic, Slovakia and Cyprus;

— the Agreement between the Republic of Cyprus and the Republic of Greece on Legal Cooperation in Matters of Civil, Family, Commercial and Criminal Law, signed at Nicosia on 5 March 1984;

— the Treaty between the Government of the Czechoslovak Socialist Republic and the Government of the Republic of France on Legal Aid and the Recognition and Enforcement of Judgments in Civil, Family and Commercial Matters, signed at Paris on 10 May 1984, still in force between the Czech Republic, Slovakia and France;

— the Agreement between the Republic of Cyprus and the Socialist Federal Republic of Yugoslavia on Legal Assistance in Civil and Criminal Matters, signed at Nicosia on 19 September 1984, now in force between Cyprus and Slovenia;

— the Treaty between the Czechoslovak Socialist Republic and the Italian Republic on Legal Aid in Civil and Criminal Matters, signed at Prague on 6 December 1985, still in force between the Czech Republic, Slovakia and Italy;

— the Treaty between the Czechoslovak Socialist Republic and the Kingdom of Spain on Legal Aid, Recognition and Enforcement of Court Decisions in Civil Matters, signed at Madrid on 4 May 1987, still in force between the Czech Republic, Slovakia and Spain;

— the Treaty between the Czechoslovak Socialist Republic and the Polish People's Republic on Legal Aid and Settlement of Legal Relations in Civil, Family, Labour and Criminal Matters, signed at Warsaw on 21 December 1987, still in force between the Czech Republic, Slovakia and Poland;

— the Treaty between the Czechoslovak Socialist Republic and the Hungarian People's Republic on Legal Aid and Settlement of Legal Relations in Civil, Family and Criminal Matters, signed at Bratislava on 28 March 1989, still in force between the Czech Republic, Slovakia and Hungary;

— the Convention between Poland and Italy on Judicial Assistance and the Recognition and Enforcement of Judgments in Civil Matters, signed at Warsaw on 28 April 1989;

— the Treaty between the Czech Republic and the Slovak Republic on Legal Aid provided by Judicial Bodies and on Settlements of Certain Legal Relations in Civil and Criminal Matters, signed at Prague on 29 October 1992;

— the Agreement between the Republic of Latvia, the Republic of Estonia and the Republic of Lithuania on Legal Assistance and Legal Relationships, signed at Tallinn on 11 November 1992;

— the Agreement between the Republic of Poland and the Republic of Lithuania on Legal Assistance and Legal Relations in Civil, Family, Labour and Criminal Matters, signed in Warsaw on 26 January 1993;

— the Agreement between the Republic of Latvia and the Republic of Poland on Legal Assistance and Legal Relationships in Civil, Family, Labour and Criminal Matters, signed at Riga on 23 February 1994;

— the Agreement between the Republic of Cyprus and the Republic of Poland on Legal Cooperation in Civil and Criminal Matters, signed at Nicosia on 14 November 1996, and

— the Agreement between Estonia and Poland on Granting Legal Assistance and Legal Relations on Civil, Labour and Criminal Matters, signed at Tallinn on 27 November 1998;

— the Convention between Bulgaria and Belgium on certain Judicial Matters, signed at Sofia on 2 July 1930;

— the Agreement between the People's Republic of Bulgaria and the Federative People's Republic of Yugoslavia on Mutual Legal Assistance, signed at Sofia on 23 March 1956, still in force between Bulgaria and Slovenia;

— the Treaty between the People's Republic of Romania and the People's Republic of Hungary on Legal Assistance in Civil, Family and Criminal Matters, signed at Bucharest on 7 October 1958;

— the Treaty between the People's Republic of Romania and the Czechoslovak Republic on Legal Assistance in Civil, Family and Criminal Matters, signed at Prague on 25 October 1958, still in force between Romania and Slovakia;

— the Agreement between the People's Republic of Bulgaria and the Romanian People's Republic on Legal Assistance in Civil, Family and Criminal Matters, signed at Sofia on 3 December 1958;

— the Treaty between the People's Republic of Romania and the Federal People's Republic of Yugoslavia on Legal Assistance, signed at Belgrade on 18 October 1960 and its Protocol, still in force between Romania and Slovenia;

— the Agreement between the People's Republic of Bulgaria and the Polish People's Republic on Legal Assistance and Legal Relations in Civil, Family and Criminal Matters, signed at Warsaw on 4 December 1961;

— the Convention between the Socialist Republic of Romania and the Republic of Austria on Legal Assistance in Civil and Family law and the Validity and Service of Documents and its annexed Protocol, signed at Vienna on 17 November 1965;

— the Agreement between the People's Republic of Bulgaria and the Hungarian People's Republic on Legal Assistance in Civil, Family and Criminal Matters, signed at Sofia on 16 May 1966;

— the Convention between the Socialist Republic of Romania and the Hellenic Republic on Legal Assistance in Civil and Criminal Matters and its Protocol, signed at Bucharest on 19 October 1972;

— the Convention between the Socialist Republic of Romania and the Italian Republic on Judicial Assistance in Civil and Criminal Matters, signed at Bucharest on 11 November 1972;

— the Convention between the Socialist Republic of Romania and the French Republic on Legal Assistance in Civil and Commercial Matters, signed at Paris on 5 November 1974;

— the Convention between the Socialist Republic of Romania and the Kingdom of Belgium on Legal Assistance in Civil and Commercial Matters, signed at Bucharest on 30 October 1975;

— the Agreement between the People's Republic of Bulgaria and the Hellenic Republic on Legal Assistance in Civil and Criminal Matters, signed at Athens on 10 April 1976;

— the Agreement between the People's Republic of Bulgaria and the Czechoslovak Socialist Republic on Legal Assistance and Settlement of Relations in Civil, Family and Criminal Matters, signed at Sofia on 25 November 1976;

— the Convention between the Socialist Republic of Romania and the United Kingdom of Great Britain and Northern Ireland on Legal Assistance in Civil and Commercial Matters, signed at London on 15 June 1978;

— the Additional Protocol to the Convention between the Socialist Republic of Romania and the Kingdom of Belgium on Legal Assistance Civil and Commercial Matters, signed at Bucharest on 30 October 1979;

— the Convention between the Socialist Republic of Romania and the Kingdom of Belgium on Recognition and Enforcement of Decisions in Alimony Obligations, signed at Bucharest on 30 October 1979;

— the Convention between the Socialist Republic of Romania and the Kingdom of Belgium on Recognition and Enforcement of Divorce Decisions, signed at Bucharest on 6 November 1980;

— the Agreement between the People's Republic of Bulgaria and the Republic of Cyprus on Legal Assistance in Civil and Criminal Matters, signed at Nicosia on 29 April 1983;

— the Agreement between the Government of the People's Republic of Bulgaria and the Government of the French Republic on Mutual Legal Assistance in Civil Matters, signed at Sofia on 18 January 1989;

— the Agreement between the People's Republic of Bulgaria and the Italian Republic on Legal Assistance and Enforcement of Decisions in Civil Matters, signed at Rome on 18 May 1990;

— the Agreement between the Republic of Bulgaria and the Kingdom of Spain on Mutual Legal Assistance in Civil Matters, signed at Sofia on 23 May 1993;

— the Treaty between Romania and the Czech Republic on Judicial Assistance in Civil Matters, signed at Bucharest on 11 July 1994;

— the Convention between Romania and the Kingdom of Spain on Jurisdiction, Recognition and Enforcement of Decisions in Civil and Commercial Matters, signed at Bucharest on 17 November 1997;

— the Convention between Romania and the Kingdom of Spain — complementary to the Hague Convention relating to civil procedure law (Hague, 1 March 1954), signed at Bucharest on 17 November 1997;

—   the Treaty between Romania and the Republic of Poland on Legal Assistance and Legal Relations in Civil Cases, signed at Bucharest on 15 May 1999.

Article 70.[16]   1.   The Treaty and the Conventions referred to in Article 69 shall continue to have effect in relation to matters to which this Regulation does not apply.

2.   They shall continue to have effect in respect of judgments given and documents formally drawn up or registered as authentic instruments before the entry into force of this Regulation.

Article 71.[17]   1.   This Regulation shall not affect any conventions to which the Member States are parties and which in relation to particular matters, govern jurisdiction or the recognition or enforcement of judgments.

2.   With a view to its uniform interpretation, paragraph 1 shall be applied in the following manner:

(a)   this Regulation shall not prevent a court of a Member State, which is a party to a convention on a particular matter, from assuming jurisdiction in accordance with that convention, even where the defendant is domiciled in another Member State which is not a party to that convention. The court hearing the action shall, in any event, apply Article 26 of this Regulation;

(b)   judgments given in a Member State by a court in the exercise of jurisdiction provided for in a convention on a particular matter shall be recognised and enforced in the other Member States in accordance with this Regulation.

Where a convention on a particular matter to which both the Member State of origin and the Member State addressed are parties lays down conditions for the recognition or enforcement of judgments, those conditions shall apply. In any event, the provisions of this

---

[16]   *Article 66, Lugano Convention.*

1.   The conventions referred to in Article 65 shall continue to have effect in relation to matters to which this Convention does not apply.

2.   They shall continue to have effect in respect of judgments given and documents formally drawn up or registered as authentic instruments before the entry into force of this Convention.

[17]   *Article 67, Lugano Convention.*

1.   This Convention shall not affect any conventions by which the Contracting Parties and/or the States bound by this Convention are bound and which in relation to particular matters, govern jurisdiction or the recognition or enforcement of judgments. Without prejudice to obligations resulting from other agreements between certain Contracting Parties, this Convention shall not prevent Contracting Parties from entering into such conventions.

2.   This Convention shall not prevent a court of a State bound by this Convention and by a convention on a particular matter from assuming jurisdiction in accordance with that convention, even where the defendant is domiciled in another State bound by this Convention which is not a party to that convention. The court hearing the action shall, in any event, apply Article 26 of this Convention.

3.   Judgments given in a State bound by this Convention by a court in the exercise of jurisdiction provided for in a convention on a particular matter shall be recognised and enforced in the other States bound by this Convention in accordance with Title III of this Convention.

4.   In addition to the grounds provided for in Title III, recognition or enforcement may be refused if the State addressed is not bound by the convention on a particular matter and the person against whom recognition or enforcement is sought is domiciled in that State, or, if the State addressed is a Member State of the European Community and in respect of conventions which would have to be concluded by the European Community, in any of its Member States, unless the judgment may otherwise be recognised or enforced under any rule of law in the State addressed.

5.   Where a convention on a particular matter to which both the State of origin and the State addressed are parties lays down conditions for the recognition or enforcement of judgments, those conditions shall apply. In any event, the provisions of this Convention which concern the procedures for recognition and enforcement of judgments may be applied.

Regulation which concern the procedure for recognition and enforcement of judgments may be applied.

Article 72.[18]   This Regulation shall not affect agreements by which Member States undertook, prior to the entry into force of this Regulation pursuant to Article 59 of the Brussels Convention, not to recognise judgments given, in particular in other Contracting States to that Convention, against defendants domiciled or habitually resident in a third country where, in cases provided for in Article 4 of that Convention, the judgment could only be founded on a ground of jurisdiction specified in the second paragraph of Article 3 of that Convention.

Chapter VIII — Final provisions

Article 73.   No later than five years after the entry into force of this Regulation, the Commission shall present to the European Parliament, the Council and the Economic and Social Committee a report on the application of this Regulation. The report shall be accompanied, if need be, by proposals for adaptations to this Regulation.

Article 74.   1.   The Member States shall notify the Commission of the texts amending the lists set out in Annexes I to IV. The Commission shall adapt the Annexes concerned accordingly.

2.   The updating or technical adjustments of the forms, specimens of which appear in Annexes V and VI, shall be adopted by the Commission. Those measures, designed to amend non-essential elements of this Regulation, shall be adopted in accordance with the regulatory procedure with scrutiny referred to in Article 75(2).

Article 75.   1.   The Commission shall be assisted by a committee.

2.   Where reference is made to this paragraph, Article 5a(1) to (4) and Article 7 of Decision 1999/468/EC shall apply, having regard to the provisions of Article 8 thereof.

Article 76.   This Regulation shall enter into force on l March 2002.

This Regulation is binding in its entirety and directly applicable in the Member States in accordance with the Treaty establishing the European Community.

---

[18] *Article 68, Lugano Convention.*

1. This Convention shall not affect agreements by which States bound by this Convention undertook, prior to the entry into force of this Convention, not to recognise judgments given in other States bound by this Convention against defendants domiciled or habitually resident in a third State where, in cases provided for in Article 4, the judgment could only be founded on a ground of jurisdiction as specified in Article 3(2). Without prejudice to obligations resulting from other agreements between certain Contracting Parties, this Convention shall not prevent Contracting Parties from entering into such conventions.

2. However, a Contracting Party may not assume an obligation towards a third State not to recognise a judgment given in another State bound by this Convention by a court basing its jurisdiction on the presence within that State of property belonging to the defendant, or the seizure by the plaintiff of property situated there:

(a) if the action is brought to assert or declare proprietary or possessory rights in that property, seeks to obtain authority to dispose of it, or arises from another issue relating to such property; or

(b) if the property constitutes the security for a debt which is the subject-matter of the action.

Annex I[19]

Rules of jurisdiction referred to in Article 3(2) and Article 4(2):
— in Belgium: Articles 5 through 14 of the Law of 16 July 2004 on private international law;
— in Bulgaria: Article 4(1)(2) of the International Private Law Code;
— in the Czech Republic: Article 86 of Act No 99/1963 Coll, the Code of Civil Procedure (*občanský soudní řád*), as amended;
— in Germany: Article 23 of the code of civil procedure (*Zivilprozeßordnung*);
— in Estonia: Article 86 of the Code of Civil Procedure (*tsiviilkohtumenetluse seadustik*);
— in Greece: Article 40 of the code of civil procedure (*Κώδικας Πολιτικής Δικονομίας*);
— in France: Articles 14 and 15 of the civil code (*Code civil*);
— in Ireland: the rules which enable jurisdiction to be founded on the document instituting the proceedings having been served on the defendant during his temporary presence in Ireland;
— in Italy: Articles 3 and 4 law 218 of 31 May 1995;
— in Cyprus: Section 21(2) of the Courts of Justice Law No 14 of 1960, as amended;
— in Latvia: section 27 and paragraphs 3, 5, 6 and 9 of Section 28 of the Civil Procedure Law (*Civilprocesa likums*);
— in Lithuania: Article 31 of the Code of Civil Procedure (*Civilinio proceso kodeksas*);
— in Luxembourg: Articles 14 and 15 of the civil code (*Code civil*);
— in Hungary: Article 57 of Law Decree No 13 of 1979 on International Private Law (*a nemzetközi magánjogról szóló 1979. évi 13. törvényerejű rendelet*);
— in Malta: Articles 742, 743 and 744 of the Code of Organisation and Civil Procedure — Cap. 12 (*Kodiċi ta' Organizzazzjoni u Proċedura Ċivili — Kap. 12*) and Article 549 of the Commercial Code — Cap. 13 (*Kodiċi tal-kummerċ — Kap. 13*);
— in Austria: Article 99 of the Law on court Jurisdiction (*Jurisdiktionsnorm*);
— in Poland: Article 1103 paragraph 4 of the Code of—Civil Procedure (*Kodeks postępowania cywilnego*);
— in Portugal: Article 65(1a) of the Code of Civil Procedure (*Código de Processo Civil*), in so far as it may encompass exorbitant grounds of jurisdiction, such as the courts of the place in which the branch, agency or other establishment (if located in Portugal) when the central administration (if located in foreign state) is the party served, and Article 10 of the Code of Labour Procedure (*Código de Processo do Trabalho*), in so far as it may encompass exorbitant grounds of jurisdiction, such as the courts of the place where

---

[19] Annex I to the Lugano Convention provides as follows:
– in Denmark: Article 246(2) and (3) of the Administration of Justice Act (Lov om rettens pleje),
– in Iceland: Article 32 paragraph 4 of the Civil Proceedings Act (Lög um meðferð einkamála nr. 91/1991),
– in Norway: Section 4-3(2) second sentence of the Dispute Act (tvisteloven),
– in Switzerland: le for du lieu du séquestre/Gerichtsstand des Arrestortes/foro del luogo del sequestro within the meaning of Article 4 of the loi fédérale sur le droit international privé/Bundesgesetz über das internationale Privatrecht/legge federale sul diritto internazionale privato.

the plaintiff is domiciled in proceedings relating to individual contracts of employment brought by the employee against the employer,

— in Romania: Articles 148–157 of Law No 105/1992 on Private International Law Relations;

— in Slovenia: Article 48(2) of the Private International Law and Procedure Act (*Zakon o medarodnem zasebnem pravu in postopku*) in relation to Article 47(2) of Civil Procedure Act (*Zakon o pravdnem postopku*) and Article 58 of the Private International Law and Procedure Act (*Zakon o medarodnem zasebnem pravu in postopku*) in relation to Article 59 of Civil Procedure Act (*Zakon o pravdnem postopku*);

— in Slovakia: Articles 37 to 37(e) of Act No 97/1963 on Private International Law and the Rules of Procedure relating thereto;

— in Finland: paragraphs 1 and 2 of Section 18(1) of Chapter 10 of the Code of Judicial Procedure (*oikeudenkäymiskaari/rättegångsbalken*;

— in Sweden: the first sentence of the first paragraph of Section 3 of Chapter 10 of the Code of Judicial Procedure (*rättegångsbalken*);

— in the United Kingdom: the rules which enable jurisdiction to be founded on:

(a)   the document instituting the proceedings having been served on the defendant during his temporary presence in the United Kingdom; or

(b)   the presence within the United Kingdom of property belonging to the defendant; or

(c)   the seizure by the plaintiff of property situated in the United Kingdom.

Annex II[20]

The courts or competent authorities to which the application referred to in Article 39 may be submitted are the following:

— in Belgium, the '*tribunal de première instance*' or '*rechtbank van eerste aanleg*' or '*erstinstanzliches Gericht*',

— in Bulgaria, the '*окръжния съд*',

— in the Czech Republic, the '*okresní soud*' or '*soudní exekutor*',

— in Germany:

(a)   the presiding judge of a chamber of the '*Landgericht*';

(b)   a notary in a procedure of declaration of enforceability of an authentic instrument;

— in Estonia, the '*maakohus*' (county court);

— in Greece, the '*Μονομελές Πρωτοδικείο*';

---

[20] Annex II to the Lugano Comvention provides as follows:
– in Denmark: the 'byret',
– in Iceland: the 'héraðsdómur',
– in Norway: the 'tingrett',
– in Switzerland:
(a) in respect of judgments ordering the payment of a sum of money, the 'juge de la mainlevée'/ 'Rechtsö ffnungsrichter'/'giudice competente a pronunciare sul rigetto dell'opposizione', within the framework of the procedure governed by Arts 80 and 81 of the loi fédérale sur la poursuite pour dettes et la faillite/ Bundesgesetz über Schuldbetreibung und Konkurs/legge federale sulla esecuzione e sul fallimento,
(b) in respect of judgments ordering a performance other than the payment of a sum of money, the 'juge cantonal d'exequatur' compétent/zuständiger 'kantonaler Vollstreckungsrichter'/'giudice cantonale' competente a pronunciare l'exequatur.

— in Spain, the '*Juzgado de Primera Instancia*';

— in France:

(a)   the '*greffier en chef du tribunal de grande instance*';

(b)   the '*président de la chambre départementale des notaires*' in the case of application for a declaration of enforceability of a notarial authentic instrument;

— in Ireland, the '*High Court*';

— in Italy, the '*corte d'appello*',

— in Cyprus, the 'Επαρχιακό Δικαστήριο' or in the case of a maintenance judgment the 'Οικογενειακό Δικαστήριο';

— in Latvia, the '*rajona (pilsētas) tiesa*',

— in Lithuania, the '*Lietuvos apeliacinis teismas*',

— in Luxembourg, the presiding judge of the '*tribunal d'arrondissement*',

— in Hungary, the '*megyei bíróság székhelyén működő helyi bíróság*', and in Budapest the '*Budai Központi Kerületi Bíróság*',

— in Malta, the '*Prim Awla tal-Qorti Ċivili*', or '*Qorti tal-Maġistrati ta Għawdex fil-ġurisdizzjoni superjuri tagħha*', or, in the case of a maintenance judgment, the '*Reġistratur tal-Qorti*', on transmission by the '*Ministru responsabbli għall-Ġustizzja*',

— in the Netherlands, the '*voorzieningenrechter van de rechtbank*',

— in Austria, the '*Bezirksgericht*';

— in Poland, the '*sąd okręgowy*',

— in Portugal, the '*Tribunal de Comarca*',

— in Romania, the '*Tribunal*';

— in Slovenia, the '*okrožno sodišče*',

— in Slovakia, '*okresný súd*',

— in Finland, the '*käräjäoikeus/tingsrätt*',

— in Sweden, the '*Svea hovrätt*',

— in the United Kingdom:

(a)   in England and Wales, the '*High Court of Justice*', or in the case of a maintenance judgment to the '*Magistrates Court*', on transmission by the Secretary of State;

(b)   in Scotland, the '*Court of Session*', or in the case of a maintenance judgment to the '*Sheriff Court*' on transmission by the Scottish Ministers;

(c)   in Northern Ireland, the '*High Court of Justice*', or in the case of a maintenance judgment to the '*Magistrates Court*' on transmission by the Secretary of State;

(d)   in Gibraltar, the '*Supreme Court of Gibraltar*', or in the case of a maintenance judgment, the '*Magistrates Court*' on transmission by the Attorney General of Gibraltar.

Annex III[21]

The courts with which appeals referred to in Article 43(2) may be lodged are the following:

---

[21]   Annex III to the Lugano Convention provides as follows:
  – in Denmark: the 'landsret',
  – in Iceland: the 'héraðsdómur',
  – in Norway: the 'lagmannsrett',
  – in Switzerland: the 'tribunal cantonal/Kantonsgericht/tribunale cantonale'.

— in Belgium;
(a)   as regards appeal by the defendant, the 'tribunal de première instance' or 'rechtbank van eerste aanleg' or 'erstinstanzliche Gericht';
(b)   as regards appeal by the applicant: the 'Cour d'appel' or 'hof van beroep';
— in Bulgaria, the 'Апелативен съд — София',
— in the Czech Republic, the court of appeal through the district court;
— in Germany, the 'Oberlandesgericht';
— in Estonia, the 'ringkonnakohus';
— in Greece the 'Εφετείο';
— in Spain, the 'Juzgado de Primera Instancia' which issued the contested decision, with the appeal to be solved by the 'Audiencia Provincial';
— in France:
(a)   the 'cour d'appel' on decisions allowing the application;
(b)   the presiding judge of the 'tribunal de grande instance', on decisions rejecting the application;
— in Ireland, the 'High Court';
— in Iceland, the 'heradsdomur';
— in Italy, the 'corte d'appello',
— in Cyprus, the 'Επαρχιακό Δικαστήριο' or in the case of a maintenance judgment the 'Οικογενειακό Δικαστήριο';
— in Latvia, the 'Apgabaltiesa' via the 'rajona (pilsētas) tiesa',
— in Lithuania, the 'Lietuvos apeliacinis teismas',
— in Luxembourg, the 'Cour supérieure de justice' sitting as a court of civil appeal;
— in Hungary, the local court situated at the seat of the county court (in Budapest, the Central District Court of Buda); the appeal is adjudicated by the county court (in Budapest, the Capital Court);
— in Malta, the 'Qorti ta' l-Appell' in accordance with the procedure laid down for appeals in the 'Kodiċi ta' Organizzazzjoni u Proċedura Ċivili – Kap.12' or in the case of a maintenance judgment by 'ċitazzjoni' before the 'Prim' Awla tal-Qorti ivili jew il-Qorti tal-Maġistrati ta' Għawdex fil-ġurisdizzjoni superjuri tagħha';
— in the Netherlands, the 'rechtbank';
— in Austria, the 'Landesgericht via the Bezirksgericht',
— in Poland, the 'sąd apelacyjny' via the 'sąd okręgowy',
— in Portugal, the 'Tribunal da Relação' is the competent court. The appeals are launched, in accordance with the national law in force, by way of a request addressed to the court which issued the contested decision;
— in Romania, the 'Curte de Apel',
— in Slovenia, the 'okrožno sodišče',
— in Slovakia, the court of appeal through the district court whose decision is being appealed;
— in Finland, the 'hovioikeus/hovrätt',
— in Sweden, the 'Svea hovrätt',
— in the United Kingdom:
(a)   in England and Wales, the '*High Court of Justice*', or in the case of a maintenance judgment the '*Magistrates' Court*';

(b)   in Scotland, the '*Court of Session*', or in the case of a maintenance judgment the '*Sheriff Court*';

(c)   in Northern Ireland, the '*High Court of Justice*', or in the case of a maintenance judgment the '*Magistrates' Court*';

(d)   in Gibraltar, the '*Supreme Court of Gibraltar*', or in the case of a maintenance judgment, the '*Magistrates' Court*'.

Annex IV[22]

The appeals which may be lodged pursuant to Article 44 are the following:
— in Belgium, Greece, Spain, France, Italy, Luxembourg and the Netherlands, an appeal in cassation,
— in Bulgaria, '*обжалване пред Върховния касационен съд*',
— in the Czech Republic, a '*dovolání*' and a '*žaloba pro zmatečnost*',
— in Germany, a '*Rechtsbeschwerde*',
— in Estonia, a '*kassatsioonikaebus*',
— in Ireland, an appeal on a point of law to the Supreme Court,
— in Iceland, an appeal to the '*Hæstiréttur*',
— in Cyprus, an appeal to the Supreme Court,
— in Latvia, an appeal to the '*Augstākās tiesas Senāts*' via the '*Apgabaltiesa*',
— in Lithuania, an appeal to the '*Lietuvos Aukščiausiasis Teismas*',
— in Hungary, '*felülvizsgálati kérelem*',
— in Malta, no further appeal lies to any other court; in the case of a maintenance judgment the '*Qorti ta' l-Appell*' in accordance with the procedure laid down for appeal in the '*kodiċi ta Organizzazzjoni u Procedura Ċivili — Kap. 12*',
— in Austria, a '*Revisionsrekurs*',
— in Poland, '*skarga kasacyjna*',
— in Portugal, an appeal on a point of law,
— in Romania, a '*contestatie in anulare*' or a '*revizuire*';
— in Slovenia, an appeal to the '*Vrhovno sodišče Republike Slovenije*',
— in Slovakia, the '*dovolanie*',
— in Finland, an appeal to the '*korkein oikeus/högsta domstolen*',
— in Sweden, an appeal to the '*Högsta domstolen*',
— in the United Kingdom, a single further appeal on a point of law.

---

[22]   Annex 4 to the Lugano Convention provides as follows:
– in Denmark: an appeal to the 'højesteret', with the leave of the 'Procesbevillingsnævnet',
– in Iceland: an appeal to the 'Hæstiréttur',
– in Norway: an appeal to the 'Høyesterett',
– in Switzerland: a 'recours devant le Tribunal fédéral'/'Beschwerde beim Bundesgericht'/'ricorso davanti al Tribunale federale'.

A.2. Statements made at the meeting of the Council (JHA) of 14 December 2000 (Doc. Consilium No 14139/00)

1. Joint Council and Commission statements

a) Statement on Articles 71 and 72 and on the negotiations within the framework of the Hague Conference on Private International Law

1.   It follows from Article 4 in conjunction with Chapter III of the Regulation that, where a court in a Member State delivers a judgment which is founded on a ground of jurisdiction drawn from that Member State's national law, against a defendant who is not domiciled in the territory of a Member State, that judgment will be recognised and enforced in the other Member States, pursuant to the Regulation.

In some cases this rule may be disadvantageous to persons who are not domiciled in the territory of a Member State. In the Brussels Convention of 27 September 1968, this situation was mitigated by Article 59, which allowed Contracting States to conclude agreements with third States not to recognise judgments founded on certain grounds of jurisdiction drawn from national law.

The Council and the Commission will pay particular attention to the possibility of engaging in negotiations with a view to the conclusion of international agreements that would mitigate the consequences of Chapter III of the Regulation for persons domiciled in third States, in respect of judgments founded on certain national grounds of jurisdiction.

2.   Pursuant to Article 57 thereof, the Brussels Convention of 27 September 1968 did not affect conventions governing jurisdiction or the recognition or enforcement of judgments in relation to particular matters.

Since it may sometimes be useful to draw up specific rules on particular matters, the Council and the Commission will pay particular attention to the possibility of engaging in negotiations with a view to the conclusion of international agreements in some of these areas.

3.   The Regulation is a response to the objective of progressively establishing an area of freedom, security and justice, laid down in Title IV of Part Three of the Treaty establishing the European Community. The Council and the Commission hold that establishing this area within Europe should not rule out the possibility of concluding international agreements of broader geographical scope with third States or international organisations which might allow the creation of a global or regional legal environment conducive to the circulation of judgments in civil and commercial matters.

In this connection, the Council and the Commission consider it essential that special importance be accorded to the work of the Hague Conference on Private International Law. In particular, there is a need to pursue efforts within that framework to bring negotiations for a convention on jurisdiction and foreign judgments in civil and commercial matters to a conclusion within a reasonable period of time.

4.   Work on drawing up the Hague convention on jurisdiction and foreign judgments in civil and commercial matters began several years ago; it has so far been the Member States which have conducted the negotiations. In order that negotiation of this convention can continue after the Regulation has been adopted, the Council and the Commission have agreed on the following working method.

This method, which is quite without prejudice to the scope of the Community's external powers, is designed to ensure the continuity of the current negotiations, while making sure that Community positions are consistent and that Member States take an effective part in the negotiations.

That working method is as follows:

—   The Community negotiating directives, laid down in advance by the Council, may be adjusted and added to in the course of negotiations, in the light of developments. To that end, coordination meetings will be held whenever necessary; they will be convened by the Presidency-in-Office of the Council, at the suggestion of a Member State or of the Commission.

—   The Presidency–in–Office of the Council and the Commission will state the Community positions contained in the negotiating directives; to that end, they may submit drafting proposals. Member States may express their own views, as long as these are not incompatible with the negotiating directives laid down by the Council. They may make suggestions and reply to suggestions submitted by other States in the course of negotiation. Written suggestions from Member States will be forwarded to the Presidency-in-Office of the Council and to the Commission in advance.

—   Should a serious difficulty arise, owing to a disagreement or to the need to take a new approach which departs from the Community negotiating directives, the matter will be referred to the Council.

The Council and the Commission will consider the results of this working method at the close of the negotiations.

5.   With reference to the case law of the Court of Justice of the European Communities, the Council and the Commission consider that the Regulation does not prevent a Member State from concluding agreements with third States on matters covered by the Regulation, where the latter is unaffected by those agreements.

b)   Statement on Articles 15 and 73

1.   The Council and the Commission are aware that the development of electronic commerce in the information society facilitates the economic growth of undertakings. Community law is an essential if citizens, economic operators and consumers are to benefit from the possibilities afforded by electronic commerce.

They consider that the development of new distance marketing techniques based on the use of the Internet depends in part on the mutual confidence which may grow up between undertakings and consumers. One of the major elements in this confidence is the opportunity offered to consumers by Article 16 of the Regulation to bring possible disputes before the courts of the Member States in which they reside, where the contract concluded by the consumer is covered by Article 15 of the Regulation.

The Council and the Commission point out in this connection that for Article 15(1)(c) to be applicable it is not sufficient for an undertaking to target its activities at the Member State of the consumer's residence, or at a number of Member States including that Member State; a contract must also be concluded within the framework of its activities. This provision relates to a number of marketing methods, including contracts concluded at a distance through the Internet.

In this context, the Council and the Commission stress that the mere fact that an Internet site is accessible is not sufficient for Article 15 to be applicable, although a factor will be that this Internet site solicits the conclusion of distance contracts and that a contract has actually been concluded at a distance, by whatever means. In this respect, the language or currency which a website uses does not constitute a relevant factor.

2.   The Council and the Commission take the view that in general it is in the interest of consumers and undertakings to try to settle their disputes amicably before resorting to the courts. The Council and the Commission stress in this connection that the purpose of the Regulation, and in particular of Articles 15 and 17 thereof, is not to prohibit the parties from making use of alternative methods of dispute settlement.

The Council and the Commission accordingly wish to reiterate how important it is that work on alternative methods of dispute settlement in civil and commercial matters should continue at European Community level, in keeping with the Council's conclusions of 29 May 2000.

They are aware of the great significance of this work and stress the useful complementary role represented by alternative methods of dispute settlement in civil and commercial matters, in particular with regard to electronic commerce.

3.   Pursuant to Article 73 of the Regulation, the Commission is to submit a report on the application of the Regulation, accompanied, if need be, by proposals for adaptations, to the European Parliament, the Council and the Economic and Social Committee.

The Council and the Commission consider that in preparing the report especial attention should be paid to the application of the provisions of the Regulation relating to consumers and small and medium–sized undertakings, in particular with respect to electronic commerce. For this purpose, the Commission will, where appropriate, propose amendments to the Regulation before the expiry of the period referred to in Article 73 of the Regulation.

2.   Joint statement by the Grand Duchy of Luxembourg and the Commission

The Government of the Grand Duchy of Luxembourg undertakes to use its best endeavours, during the period provided for in Article 63(4), to prepare business circles in the Grand Duchy of Luxembourg to adjust to the new situation resulting from Article 5, point (1), and Article 23 of the Regulation.

The Commission undertakes to devote special attention to developments in Luxembourg in its report on application of the Regulation, provided for in Article 73. In the light of this report the Commission will take the necessary initiatives to enable the Council to take a decision within the time limit provided for in Article 63(4).

3.   Statement by the United Kingdom

In accordance with arrangements notified in Council document 7998/00 of 19 April 2000, where decisions of a Gibraltar court are to be directly enforced by a court or other enforcement authority in another Member State under the relevant provisions of this Regulation, the documents containing such decisions of the Gibraltar court will be certified as authentic by the United Kingdom/Gibraltar Liaison Unit for EU Affairs of the Foreign and Commonwealth Office based in London ('the Unit'). To this effect the Gibraltar court will make the necessary request to the Unit. The certification will take the form of a note.

A.3. Council Decision 2006/325/EC of 27 April 2006 concerning the conclusion of the Agreement between the European Community and the Kingdom of Denmark on jurisdiction and the recognition and enforcement of judgments in civil and commercial matters (OJ, L 120 of 5 May 2006)[1]

(1)   In accordance with Articles 1 and 2 of the Protocol on the position of Denmark annexed to the Treaty on European Union and the Treaty establishing the European Community, Denmark is not bound by the provisions of Council Regulation (EC) No 44/2001 of 22 December 2000 on jurisdiction and the recognition and enforcement of judgments in civil and commercial matters, nor subject to their application.

(2)   The Commission has negotiated an Agreement between the European Community and the Kingdom of Denmark extending to Denmark the provisions of Regulation (EC) No 44/2001.

(3)   The Agreement was signed, on behalf of the European Community, on 19 October 2005, subject to its possible conclusion at a later date, in accordance with Council Decision 2005/790/EC of 20 September 2005.

(4)   In accordance with Article 3 of the Protocol on the position of the United Kingdom and Ireland annexed to the Treaty on European Union and the Treaty establishing the European Community, the United Kingdom and Ireland are taking part in the adoption and application of this Decision.

(5)   In accordance with Articles 1 and 2 of the Protocol on the position of Denmark, Denmark is not taking part in the adoption of this Decision and is not bound by it or subject to its application.

(6)   The Agreement should be approved;

Article 1.   The Agreement between the European Community and the Kingdom of Denmark on jurisdiction and the recognition and enforcement of judgments in civil and commercial matters is hereby approved on behalf of the Community.

Article 1a.   1.   For the purpose of applying Article 5(2) of the Agreement, the Commission shall assess, before taking a decision expressing the Community's agreement, whether the international agreement envisaged by Denmark would not render the Agreement ineffective and would not undermine the proper functioning of the system established by its rules.

2.   The Commission shall take a reasoned decision within 90 days of being informed by Denmark of Denmark's intention to enter into the international agreement in question.

If the international agreement in question meets the conditions referred to in paragraph 1, the decision by the Commission shall express the Community's agreement within the meaning of Article 5(2) of the Agreement.

---

[1]   Text as amended by Council Decision 2009/942/EC (OJ, L 331 of 16 December 2009). [Note of the Editor]

Article 1b.   The Commission shall inform the Member States of the international agreements which Denmark has been authorised to conclude in accordance with Article 1a.

Article 2.   The President of the Council is hereby authorised to designate the person empowered to make the notification provided for in Article 12(2) of the Agreement.

A.4.   Agreement between the European Community and the Kingdom of Denmark on jurisdiction and the recognition and enforcement of judgments in civil and commercial matters (OJ, L 299 of 16 November 2005)[1]

Whereas on 27 September 1968 the Member States, acting under Article 293, fourth indent, of the Treaty establishing the European Community, concluded the Brussels Convention on Jurisdiction and the Enforcement of Judgments in Civil and Commercial Matters (the Brussels Convention), as amended by Conventions on the Accession of the new Member States to that Convention. On 16 September 1988 the Member States and the EFTA States concluded the Convention on Jurisdiction and the Enforcement of Judgments in Civil and Commercial Matters (the Lugano Convention), which is a parallel Convention to the Brussels Convention,

Whereas the main content of the Brussels Convention has been taken over in Council Regulation (EC) No 44/2001 of 22 December 2000 on jurisdiction and the recognition and enforcement of judgments in civil and commercial matters (the Brussels I Regulation),

Referring to the Protocol on the position of Denmark annexed to the Treaty on European Union and to the Treaty establishing the European Community (the Protocol on the position of Denmark) pursuant to which the Brussels I Regulation shall not be binding upon or applicable in Denmark,

Stressing that a solution to the unsatisfactory legal situation arising from differences in applicable rules on jurisdiction, recognition and enforcement of judgments within the Community must be found,

Desiring that the provisions of the Brussels I Regulation, future amendments thereto and the implementing measures relating to it should under international law apply to the relations between the Community and Denmark being a Member State with a special position with respect to Title IV of the Treaty establishing the European Community,

Stressing that continuity between the Brussels Convention and this Agreement should be ensured, and that transitional provisions as in the Brussels I Regulation should be applied to this Agreement as well. The same need for continuity applies as regards the interpretation of the Brussels Convention by the Court of Justice of the European Communities and the 1971 Protocol should remain applicable also to cases already pending when this Agreement enters into force,

Stressing that the Brussels Convention also continues to apply to the territories of the Member States which fall within the territorial scope of that Convention and which are excluded from this Agreement,

---

[1]   The Agreement has entered into force on 1 July 2007. [Note of the Editor]

Stressing the importance of proper coordination between the Community and Denmark with regard to the negotiation and conclusion of international agreements that may affect or alter the scope of the Brussels I Regulation,

Stressing that Denmark should seek to join international agreements entered into by the Community where Danish participation in such agreements is relevant for the coherent application of the Brussels I Regulation and this Agreement,

Stating that the Court of Justice of the European Communities should have jurisdiction in order to secure the uniform application and interpretation of this Agreement including the provisions of the Brussels I Regulation and any implementing Community measures forming part of this Agreement,

Referring to the jurisdiction conferred to the Court of Justice of the European Communities pursuant to Article 68(1) of the Treaty establishing the European Community to give rulings on preliminary questions relating to the validity and interpretation of acts of the institutions of the Community based on Title IV of the Treaty, including the validity and interpretation of this Agreement, and to the circumstance that this provision shall not be binding upon or applicable in Denmark, as results from the Protocol on the position of Denmark,

Considering that the Court of Justice of the European Communities should have jurisdiction under the same conditions to give preliminary rulings on questions concerning the validity and interpretation of this Agreement which are raised by a Danish court or tribunal, and that Danish courts and tribunals should therefore request preliminary rulings under the same conditions as courts and tribunals of other Member States in respect of the interpretation of the Brussels I Regulation and its implementing measures,

Referring to the provision that, pursuant to Article 68(3) of the Treaty establishing the European Community, the Council of the European Union, the European Commission and the Member States may request the Court of Justice of the European Communities to give a ruling on the interpretation of acts of the institutions of the Community based on Title IV of the Treaty, including the interpretation of this Agreement, and the circumstance that this provision shall not be binding upon or applicable in Denmark, as results from the Protocol on the position of Denmark,

Considering that Denmark should, under the same conditions as other Member States in respect of the Brussels I Regulation and its implementing measures, be accorded the possibility to request the Court of Justice of the European Communities to give rulings on questions relating to the interpretation of this Agreement,

Stressing that under Danish law the courts in Denmark should, when interpreting this Agreement including the provisions of the Brussels I Regulation and any implementing Community measures forming part of this Agreement, take due account of the rulings contained in the case law of the Court of Justice of the European Communities and of the courts of the Member States of the European Communities in respect of provisions of the Brussels Convention, the Brussels I Regulation and any implementing Community measures,

Considering that it should be possible to request the Court of Justice of the European Communities to rule on questions relating to compliance with obligations under this Agreement pursuant to the provisions of the Treaty establishing the European Community governing proceedings before the Court,

Whereas, by virtue of Article 300(7) of the Treaty establishing the European Community, this Agreement binds Member States; it is therefore appropriate that Denmark, in the case of non-compliance by a Member State, should be able to seize the Commission as guardian of the Treaty,

Article 1. Aim.   1.   The aim of this Agreement is to apply the provisions of the Brussels I Regulation and its implementing measures to the relations between the Community and Denmark, in accordance with Article 2(1) of this Agreement.

2.   It is the objective of the Contracting Parties to arrive at a uniform application and interpretation of the provisions of the Brussels I Regulation and its implementing measures in all Member States.

3.   The provisions of Articles 3(1), 4(1) and 5(1) of this Agreement result from the Protocol on the position of Denmark.

Article 2. Jurisdiction and the recognition and enforcement of judgments in civil and commercial matters.   1.   The provisions of the Brussels I Regulation, which is annexed to this Agreement and forms part thereof, together with its implementing measures adopted pursuant to Article 74(2) of the Regulation and, in respect of implementing measures adopted after the entry into force of this Agreement, implemented by Denmark as referred to in Article 4 of this Agreement, and the measures adopted pursuant to Article 74(1) of the Regulation, shall under international law apply to the relations between the Community and Denmark.

2.   However, for the purposes of this Agreement, the application of the provisions of that Regulation shall be modified as follows:

(a)   Article 1(3) shall not apply.

(b)   Article 50 shall be supplemented by the following paragraph (as paragraph 2):
"2. However, an applicant who requests the enforcement of a decision given by an administrative authority in Denmark in respect of a maintenance order may, in the Member State addressed, claim the benefits referred to in the first paragraph if he presents a statement from the Danish Ministry of Justice to the effect that he fulfils the financial requirements to qualify for the grant of complete or partial legal aid or exemption from costs or expenses".

(c)   Article 62 shall be supplemented by the following paragraph (as paragraph 2):
"2. In matters relating to maintenance, the expression 'court' includes the Danish administrative authorities".

(d)   Article 64 shall apply to seagoing ships registered in Denmark as well as in Greece and Portugal.

(e)   The date of entry into force of this Agreement shall apply instead of the date of entry into force of the Regulation as referred to in Articles 70(2), 72 and 76 thereof.

(f)   The transitional provisions of this Agreement shall apply instead of Article 66 of the Regulation.

(g)   In Annex I the following shall be added: 'in Denmark: Articles 246(2) and (3) of the Administration of Justice Act (*lov om rettens pleje*)'.

(h)   In Annex II the following shall be added: 'in Denmark, the "*byret*" '.

(i)   In Annex III the following shall be added: 'in Denmark, the "*landsret*" '.

(j)   In Annex IV the following shall be added: 'in Denmark, an appeal to the "*Højesteret*" with leave from the "*Procesbevillingsnævnet*" '.

Article 3. Amendments to the Brussels I Regulation. 1.   Denmark shall not take part in the adoption of amendments to the Brussels I Regulation and no such amendments shall be binding upon or applicable in Denmark.

2.   Whenever amendments to the Regulation are adopted Denmark shall notify the Commission of its decision whether or not to implement the content of such amendments. Notification shall be given at the time of the adoption of the amendments or within 30 days thereafter.

3.   If Denmark decides that it will implement the content of the amendments the notification shall indicate whether implementation can take place administratively or requires parliamentary approval.

4.   If the notification indicates that implementation can take place administratively the notification shall, moreover, state that all necessary administrative measures enter into force on the date of entry into force of the amendments to the Regulation or have entered into force on the date of the notification, whichever date is the latest.

5.   If the notification indicates that implementation requires parliamentary approval in Denmark, the following rules shall apply:

(a)   Legislative measures in Denmark shall enter into force on the date of entry into force of the amendments to the Regulation or within 6 months after the notification, whichever date is the latest;

(b)   Denmark shall notify the Commission of the date upon which the implementing legislative measures enter into force.

6.   A Danish notification that the content of the amendments has been implemented in Denmark, in accordance with paragraphs 4 and 5, creates mutual obligations under international law between Denmark and the Community. The amendments to the Regulation shall then constitute amendments to this Agreement and shall be considered annexed hereto.

7.   In cases where:

(a)   Denmark notifies its decision not to implement the content of the amendments; or

(b)   Denmark does not make a notification within the 30-day time-limit set out in paragraph 2; or

(c)   Legislative measures in Denmark do not enter into force within the time-limits set out in paragraph 5, this Agreement shall be considered terminated unless the parties decide otherwise within 90 days or, in the situation referred to under (c), legislative measures in Denmark enter into force within the same period. Termination shall take effect three months after the expiry of the 90-day period.

8.   Legal proceedings instituted and documents formally drawn up or registered as authentic instruments before the date of termination of the Agreement as set out in paragraph 7 are not affected hereby.

Article 4. Implementing measures. 1.   Denmark shall not take part in the adoption of opinions by the Committee referred to in Article 75 of the Brussels I Regulation. Implementing measures adopted pursuant to Article 74(2) of that Regulation shall not be binding upon and shall not be applicable in Denmark.

2.   Whenever implementing measures are adopted pursuant to Article 74(2) of the Regulation, the implementing measures shall be communicated to Denmark. Denmark shall notify the Commission of its decision whether or not to implement the content of

the implementing measures. Notification shall be given upon receipt of the implementing measures or within 30 days thereafter.

3.   The notification shall state that all necessary administrative measures in Denmark enter into force on the date of entry into force of the implementing measures or have entered into force on the date of the notification, whichever date is the latest.

4.   A Danish notification that the content of the implementing measures has been implemented in Denmark creates mutual obligations under international law between Denmark and the Community. The implementing measures will then form part of this Agreement.

5.   In cases where:

(a)   Denmark notifies its decision not to implement the content of the implementing measures; or

(b)   Denmark does not make a notification within the 30-day time-limit set out in paragraph 2, this Agreement shall be considered terminated unless the parties decide otherwise within 90 days. Termination shall take effect three months after the expiry of the 90-day period.

6.   Legal proceedings instituted and documents formally drawn up or registered as authentic instruments before the date of termination of the Agreement as set out in paragraph 5 are not affected hereby.

7.   If in exceptional cases the implementation requires parliamentary approval in Denmark, the Danish notification under paragraph 2 shall indicate this and the provisions of Articles 3(5) to (8) shall apply.

8.   Denmark shall notify the Commission of texts amending the items set out in Articles 2(2)(g) to (j) of this Agreement. The Commission shall adapt Articles 2(2)(g) to (j) accordingly.

Article 5. International agreements which affect the Brussels I Regulation.   1.   International agreements entered into by the Community based on the rules of the Brussels I Regulation shall not be binding upon and shall not be applicable in Denmark.

2.   Denmark will abstain from entering into international agreements which may affect or alter the scope of the Brussels I Regulation as annexed to this Agreement unless it is done in agreement with the Community and satisfactory arrangements have been made with regard to the relationship between this Agreement and the international agreement in question.

3.   When negotiating international agreements that may affect or alter the scope of the Brussels I Regulation as annexed to this Agreement, Denmark will coordinate its position with the Community and will abstain from any actions that would jeopardise the objectives of a Community position within its sphere of competence in such negotiations.

Article 6. Jurisdiction of the Court of Justice of the European Communities in relation to the interpretation of the Agreement.   1.   Where a question on the validity or interpretation of this Agreement is raised in a case pending before a Danish court or tribunal, that court or tribunal shall request the Court of Justice to give a ruling thereon whenever under the same circumstances a court or tribunal of another Member State of the European Union would be required to do so in respect of the Brussels I Regulation and its implementing measures referred to in Article 2(1) of this Agreement.

2. Under Danish law, the courts in Denmark shall, when interpreting this Agreement, take due account of the rulings contained in the case law of the Court of Justice in respect of provisions of the Brussels Convention, the Brussels I Regulation and any implementing Community measures.

3. Denmark may, like the Council, the Commission and any Member State, request the Court of Justice to give a ruling on a question of interpretation of this Agreement. The ruling given by the Court of Justice in response to such a request shall not apply to judgments of courts or tribunals of the Member States which have become *res judicata*.

4. Denmark shall be entitled to submit observations to the Court of Justice in cases where a question has been referred to it by a court or tribunal of a Member State for a preliminary ruling concerning the interpretation of any provision referred to in Article 2(1).

5. The Protocol on the Statute of the Court of Justice of the European Communities and its Rules of Procedure shall apply.

6. If the provisions of the Treaty establishing the European Community regarding rulings by the Court of Justice are amended with consequences for rulings in respect of the Brussels I Regulation, Denmark may notify the Commission of its decision not to apply the amendments in respect of this Agreement. Notification shall be given at the time of the entry into force of the amendments or within 60 days thereafter.

In such a case this Agreement shall be considered terminated. Termination shall take effect three months after the notification.

7. Legal proceedings instituted and documents formally drawn up or registered as authentic instruments before the date of termination of the Agreement as set out in paragraph 6 are not affected hereby.

Article 7. Jurisdiction of the Court of Justice of the European Communities in relation to compliance with the Agreement. 1. The Commission may bring before the Court of Justice cases against Denmark concerning non-compliance with any obligation under this Agreement.

2. Denmark may bring a complaint before the Commission as to the non-compliance by a Member State of its obligations under this Agreement.

3. The relevant provisions of the Treaty establishing the European Community governing proceedings before the Court of Justice as well as the Protocol on the Statute of the Court of Justice of the European Communities and its Rules of Procedure shall apply.

Article 8. Territorial application. 1. This Agreement shall apply to the territories referred to in Article 299 of the Treaty establishing the European Community.

2. If the Community decides to extend the application of the Brussels I Regulation to territories currently governed by the Brussels Convention, the Community and Denmark shall cooperate in order to ensure that such an application also extends to Denmark.

Article 9. Transitional provisions. 1. This Agreement shall apply only to legal proceedings instituted and to documents formally drawn up or registered as authentic instruments after the entry into force thereof.

2.   However, if the proceedings in the Member State of origin were instituted before the entry into force of this Agreement, judgments given after that date shall be recognised and enforced in accordance with this Agreement;

(a)   if the proceedings in the Member State of origin were instituted after the entry into force of the Brussels or the Lugano Convention both in the Member State of origin and in the Member State addressed;

(b)   in all other cases, if jurisdiction was founded upon rules which accorded with those provided for either in this Agreement or in a convention concluded between the Member State of origin and the Member State addressed which was in force when the proceedings were instituted.

Article 10. Relationship to the Brussels I Regulation.   1.   This Agreement shall not prejudice the application by the Member States of the Community other than Denmark of the Brussels I Regulation.

2.   However, this Agreement shall in any event be applied:

(a)   in matters of jurisdiction, where the defendant is domiciled in Denmark, or where Articles 22 or 23 of the Regulation, applicable to the relations between the Community and Denmark by virtue of Article 2 of this Agreement, confer jurisdiction on the courts of Denmark;

(b)   in relation to a *lis pendens* or to related actions as provided for in Articles 27 and 28 of the Brussels I Regulation, applicable to the relations between the Community and Denmark by virtue of Article 2 of this Agreement, when proceedings are instituted in a Member State other than Denmark and in Denmark;

(c)   in matters of recognition and enforcement, where Denmark is either the State of origin or the State addressed.

Article 11. Termination of the agreement.   1.   This Agreement shall terminate if Denmark informs the other Member States that it no longer wishes to avail itself of the provisions of Part I of the Protocol on the position of Denmark, in accordance with Article 7 of that Protocol.

2.   This Agreement may be terminated by either Contracting Party giving notice to the other Contracting Party. Termination shall be effective six months after the date of such notice.

3.   Legal proceedings instituted and documents formally drawn up or registered as authentic instruments before the date of termination of the Agreement as set out in paragraph 1 or 2 are not affected hereby.

Article 12. Entry into force.   1.   The Agreement shall be adopted by the Contracting Parties in accordance with their respective procedures.

2.   The Agreement shall enter into force on the first day of the sixth month following the notification by the Contracting Parties of the completion of their respective procedures required for this purpose.

Article 13. Authenticity of texts.   This Agreement is drawn up in duplicate in the Czech, Danish, Dutch, English, Estonian, Finnish, French, German, Greek, Hungarian, Italian, Latvian, Lithuanian, Maltese, Polish, Portuguese, Slovene, Slovak, Spanish and Swedish languages, each of these texts being equally authentic.

A.5. Agreement between the European Community and the Kingdom of Denmark on jurisdiction and the recognition and enforcement of judgments in civil and commercial matters (OJ, L 149 of 12 June 2009)

According to Article 3(2) of the Agreement of 19 October 2005 between the European Community and the Kingdom of Denmark on jurisdiction and the recognition and enforcement of judgments in civil and commercial matters (hereafter the Agreement), concluded by Council Decision 2006/325/EC, whenever amendments to Council Regulation (EC) No 44/2001 of 22 December 2000 on jurisdiction and the recognition and enforcement of judgments in civil and commercial matters are adopted, Denmark shall notify the Commission of its decision whether or not to implement the content of such amendments.

Council Regulation (EC) No 4/2009 on jurisdiction, applicable law, recognition and enforcement of decisions and cooperation in matters relating to maintenance obligations was adopted on 18 December 2008. Article 68 of Regulation (EC) No 4/2009 provides that subject to transitional provisions in Article 75(2) of Regulation (EC) No 4/2009, Regulation (EC) No 4/2009 shall modify Regulation (EC) No 44/2001 by replacing provisions of that Regulation applicable to matters relating to maintenance obligations.

In accordance with Article 3(2) of the Agreement, Denmark has by letter of 14 January 2009 notified the Commission of its decision to implement the contents of Regulation (EC) No 4/2009 to the extent that this Regulation amends Regulation (EC) No 44/2001. This means that the provisions of Regulation (EC) No 4/2009 on jurisdiction, applicable law, recognition and enforcement of decisions and cooperation in matters relating to maintenance obligations will be applied to relations between the Community and Denmark with the exception of the provisions in Chapters III and VII. The provisions in Article 2 and Chapter IX of Regulation (EC) No 4/2009, however, are applicable only to the extent that they relate to jurisdiction, recognition, enforceability and enforcement of judgments, and access to justice.

In accordance with Article 3(6) of the Agreement, the Danish notification creates mutual obligations between Denmark and the Community. Thus, Regulation (EC) No 4/2009 constitutes an amendment to the Agreement to the extent that it amends Regulation (EC) No 44/2001 and is considered annexed thereto.

With reference to Articles 3(3) and (4) of the Agreement, implementation of the above-mentioned provisions of Regulation (EC) No 4/2009 in Denmark can take place administratively under Section 9 of the Danish Law No 1563 of 20 December 2006 on the Brussels I Regulation and therefore does not require the Folketing's approval. The necessary administrative measures entered into force on the date of entry into force of Regulation (EC) No 4/2009 on 30 January 2009.

A.6.   Council Regulation (EC) No 1346/2000 of 29 May 2000 on insolvency proceedings (OJ, L 160 of 30 June 2000): Recital 7, Article 25

See Chapter V, A.1.

A.7.   Council Regulation (EC) No 2201/2003 of 27 November 2003 concerning jurisdiction and the recognition and enforcement of judgments in matrimonial matters and the matters of parental responsibility, repealing Regulation (EC) No 1347/2000 (OJ, L 338 of 23 December 2003): Recitals 9, 11

See Chapter XI, Matrimonial matters, A.1.

A.8.   Council Regulation (EC) No 4/2009 of 18 December 2008 on jurisdiction, applicable law, recognition and enforcement of decisions and cooperation in matters relating to maintenance obligations (OJ, L 7 of 10 January 2009): Recitals 9–10, 15–16, 26, Articles 3–43, 68, 75

See Chapter XI, Maintenance obligations, A.1.

A.9.   Council Regulation (EC) No 2271/96 of 22 November 1996 protecting against the effects of the extra-territorial application of legislation adopted by a third country, and actions based thereon or resulting therefrom (OJ, L 309 of 29 November 1996): Article 6

See Chapter II, Public policy of the EU, A.1.

A.10.   Commission decision on general implementing provisions concerning persons to be treated as dependent children (Article 2(4) of Annex VII to the Staff Regulations) (C (2004) 1364 of 15 April 2004): Article 3

See Chapter XI, Maintenance obligations, D.

A.11. Proposal for a Regulation of the European Parliament and of the Council on jurisdiction, applicable law, recognition and enforcement of decisions and authentic instruments in matters of succession and the creation of a European Certificate of Succession (COM (2009) 154 of 14 October 2009): Recitals 4, 11–16, 25–26, Articles 3–15, 29–35

See Chapter XII, A.

A.12. Proposal for a regulation of the European Parliament and of the Council on jurisdiction and the recognition and enforcement of judgments in civil and commercial matters (recast) (COM (2010) 748 of 14 December 2010)

(1)   Council Regulation (EC) No 44/2001 of 22 December 2000 on jurisdiction and the recognition and enforcement of judgments in civil and commercial matters has been amended several times. Since further amendments are to be made, it should be recast in the interests of clarity.

(2)   The Union has set itself the objective of maintaining and developing an area of freedom, security and justice, facilitating access to justice, in particular through the principle of mutual recognition of judicial and extra-judicial decisions in civil matters. In order to establish progressively such an area, the Union should adopt, amongst other things, the measures relating to judicial cooperation in civil matters, particularly when necessary for the proper functioning of the internal market.

(3)   Certain differences between national rules governing jurisdiction and recognition of judgments hamper the sound operation of the internal market. Provisions to unify the rules of conflict of jurisdiction in civil and commercial matters and to ensure rapid and simple recognition and enforcement of judgments from Member States bound by this Regulation are essential.

(4)   This area is within the field of judicial cooperation in civil matters within the meaning of Article 81 of the Treaty on the Functioning of the European Union.

(5)   In order to attain the objective of free movement of judgments in civil and commercial matters, it is necessary and appropriate that the rules governing jurisdiction and the recognition and enforcement of judgments be governed by a legal instrument of the Union which is binding and directly applicable.

(6)   Since the objective of this Regulation cannot be sufficiently achieved by the Member States and can be better achieved at Union level, the Union may adopt measures in accordance with the principle of subsidiarity as set out in Article 5 of the Treaty on European Union. In accordance with the principle of proportionality, as set out in that Article, this Regulation does not go beyond what is necessary in order to achieve that objective.

(7)   On 27 September 1968 the Member States, acting under Article 293, fourth indent, of the Treaty establishing the European Community, concluded the Brussels Convention on Jurisdiction and the Enforcement of Judgments in Civil and Commercial

Matters, as amended by Conventions on the Accession of the New Member States to that Convention (hereinafter referred to as the 'Brussels Convention'). On 16 September 1988 Member States and EFTA States concluded the Lugano Convention on Jurisdiction and the Enforcement of Judgments in Civil and Commercial Matters, which is a parallel Convention to the 1968 Brussels Convention.

(8)   On 22 December 2000, the Council adopted Regulation (EC) No 44/2001 on jurisdiction and the recognition and enforcement of judgment in civil and commercial matters, which replaced the Brussels Convention insofar as Union territory is concerned as between all Member States except Denmark. By Council Decision 2006/325/EC of 27 April 2006, the Union concluded an agreement with Denmark ensuring the application of the provisions of Regulation No 44/2001 in Denmark. The 1988 Lugano Convention was revised by the Lugano Convention on Jurisdiction and the Recognition and Enforcement of Judgments in Civil and Commercial Matters, concluded on 30 October 2007 by the Union, Denmark and EFTA states. Continuity in the interpretation of these Conventions and this Regulation should be ensured.

(9)   On 21 April 2009, the Commission adopted a report on the application of Regulation (EC) No 44/2001. The report concluded that, in general, the operation of the Regulation is satisfactory, but that it is desirable to improve the application of certain of its provisions, further facilitate the free circulation of judgments, and further enhance access to justice.

(10) The scope of this Regulation should cover all the main civil and commercial matters apart from certain well-defined matters. In light of the adoption of Council Regulation (EC) No 4/2009 of 18 December 2008 on jurisdiction, applicable law, recognition and enforcement of decisions and cooperation in matters relating to maintenance obligations, these matters should be excluded from the scope of this Regulation.

(11) This Regulation does not apply to arbitration, save in the limited case provided for therein. In particular, it does not apply to the form, existence, validity or effects of arbitration agreements, the powers of the arbitrators, the procedure before arbitral tribunals, and the validity, annulment, and recognition and enforcement of arbitral awards.

(12) The rules of jurisdiction should be highly predictable and founded on the principle that jurisdiction is generally based on the defendant's domicile and jurisdiction should always be available on this ground save in a few well-defined situations in which the subject-matter of the litigation or the autonomy of the parties warrants a different linking factor. The domicile of a legal person must be defined autonomously so as to make the common rules more transparent and avoid conflicts of jurisdiction.

(13) In addition to the defendant's domicile, there should be alternative grounds of jurisdiction based on a close link between the court and the action or in order to facilitate the sound administration of justice. The existence of a close link should ensure legal certainty avoiding that the defendant is sued before a court of a Member State which was not reasonably foreseeable for him. This is important, particularly in disputes concerning non-contractual obligations arising out of violations of privacy and rights relating to personality, including defamation.

(14) In relation to insurance, consumer contracts and employment, the weaker party should be protected by rules of jurisdiction more favourable to his interests than the general rules provide for.

(15) The autonomy of the parties to a contract, other than an insurance, consumer or employment contract, where only limited autonomy to determine the courts having jurisdiction is allowed, must be respected subject to the exclusive grounds of jurisdiction laid down in this Regulation.

(16) In order to promote the interests of claimants and defendants and promote the proper administration of justice within the Union, the circumstance that the defendant is domiciled in a third State should no longer entail the non-application of certain Union rules on jurisdiction, and there should no longer be any referral to national law.

(17) This Regulation should therefore establish a complete set of rules on international jurisdiction of the courts in the Member States. The existing rules on jurisdiction ensure a close link between proceedings to which this Regulation applies and the territory of the Member States which justifies their extension to defendants wherever they are domiciled. In addition, this Regulation should determine the cases in which a court in a Member State may exercise subsidiary jurisdiction.

(18) In the interests of the harmonious administration of justice it is necessary to minimise the possibility of concurrent proceedings and to ensure that irreconcilable judgments will not be given in two Member States. There must be a clear and effective mechanism for resolving cases of *lis pendens* and related actions and for obviating problems flowing from national differences as to the determination of the time when a case is regarded as pending. For the purposes of this Regulation that time should be defined autonomously.

(19) The effectiveness of choice of court agreements should be improved in order to give full effect to the will of the parties and avoid abusive litigation tactics. This Regulation should therefore grant priority to the court designated in the agreement to decide on its jurisdiction, regardless of whether it is first or second seised.

(20) The effectiveness of arbitration agreements should also be improved in order to give full effect to the will of the parties. This should be the case, in particular, where the agreed or designated seat of an arbitration is in a Member State. This Regulation should therefore contain special rules aimed at avoiding parallel proceedings and abusive litigation tactics in those circumstances. The seat of the arbitration should refer to the seat selected by the parties or the seat designated by an arbitral tribunal, by an arbitral institution or by any other authority directly or indirectly chosen by the parties.

(21) A flexible mechanism should exist allowing the courts in the Member States to take into account proceedings pending before the courts of third States, considering in particular the proper administration of justice and whether or not any third State judgment is capable of recognition and enforcement in that Member State.

(22) The notion of provisional, including protective measures should be clarified. They should include, in particular, protective orders aimed at obtaining information or preserving evidence, thus covering search and seizure orders as referred to in Article 6 and 7 of Directive 2004/48/EC of the European Parliament and of the Council of 29 April 2004 on the enforcement of intellectual property rights. They should not include measures which are not of a protective nature, such as measures ordering the hearing of a witness for the purpose of enabling the applicant to decide whether to bring a case.

(23) Mutual trust in the administration of justice in the Union and the aim of making crossborder litigation less time consuming and costly justify the abolition of the existing intermediate measures to be taken prior to enforcement in the Member State in which enforcement is sought. As a result, a judgment given by the courts of a Member

State should, for enforcement purposes, be treated as if it had been delivered in the Member State in which enforcement is sought. However, in the light of the divergences between Member States' systems and the particular sensitivity of matters relating to defamation and compensation obtained in collective proceedings, the current procedure for recognition and enforcement should be maintained for the time being for judgments given on such matters, pending further developments of the law in this area. The scope of the specific provision relating to defamation should correspond to the scope of the exclusion of this matter in Regulation (EC) No 864/2007 of the European Parliament and of the Council of 11 July 2007 on the law applicable to non-contractual obligations (Rome II) and should be interpreted in the same way. The provisions abolishing intermediate enforcement measures should be extended to judgments ordering compensation in collective proceedings in the event of adoption of measures for the harmonisation or approximation of the procedural rules applicable to such proceedings. Such an extension should be without prejudice to the possibility for the Commission to propose the abolition of intermediate measures for collective damages proceedings even in the absence of such harmonisation or approximation measures, in the light of evidence regarding the efficiency and acceptability of such a development in the European judicial order.

(24) The abolition of intermediate measures should be accompanied by necessary safeguards aimed in particular at ensuring full respect of the rights of the defence and fair trial, as established in Article 47 of the Charter of Fundamental Rights of the European Union. This requires putting in place, at the stage of enforcement, extraordinary remedies for the benefit of defendants who did not enter an appearance as a result of a lack of notice or who otherwise suffered procedural defects in the proceedings before the court of origin which may amount to an infringement of Article 47 of the Charter.

(25) The removal of intermediate measures requires an adaptation of the free circulation of provisional, including protective measures. Where such measures are ordered by a court having jurisdiction as to the substance of a dispute, their free circulation should be ensured. Where, however, such measures are adopted by a court not having jurisdiction as to the substance, the effect of such measures should be confined to the territory of that Member State. Furthermore, the free circulation of measures ordered *ex parte* should be allowed if accompanied by appropriate safeguards.

(26) Continuity between the Brussels Convention and this Regulation should be ensured, and transitional provisions should be laid down to that end. The same need for continuity applies as regards the interpretation of the Brussels Convention and the Regulations replacing it by the Court of Justice of the European Union

(27) This Regulation should ensure full respect for fundamental rights as set out in the Charter of Fundamental Rights of the European Union, in particular the right to an effective remedy and the right to a fair trial guaranteed in Article 47 of the Charter. Nothing in this Regulation should affect the freedom of expression and information (Article 11), the right to private and family life (Article 7), nor the right of workers and employers, or their respective organisations, in accordance with Union law and national law and practices, to negotiate and conclude collective agreements at the appropriate levels and, in cases of conflicts of interest, to take collective action to defend their interests, including strike action (Article 28).

(28) The United Kingdom and Ireland, in accordance with Article 3 of the Protocol on the position of the United Kingdom and Ireland in respect of the Area of Freedom, Security and Justice, annexed to the Treaty on European Union and to the Treaty on

the Functioning of the European Union, took part in the adoption and application of Regulation (EC) No 44/2001. In accordance with Articles 1 and 2 of the Protocol on the position of the United Kingdom and Ireland annexed to the Treaty on European Union and the Treaty on the Functioning of the European Union, [the United Kingdom and Ireland have notified their wish to participate in the adoption and application of this Regulation]/[without prejudice to Article 4 of the Protocol, the United Kingdom and Ireland will not participate in the adoption of this Regulation and will not be bound by it or be subject to its application].

(29) Denmark, in accordance with Articles 1 and 2 of the Protocol on the position of Denmark annexed to the Treaty on European Union and to the Treaty on the Functioning of the European Union, is not taking part in the adoption of this Regulation, and is therefore not bound by it nor subject to its application, without prejudice of the possibility for Denmark of applying the amendments to Regulation (EC) No 44/2001 pursuant to Article 3 of the Agreement between the European Community and the Kingdom of Denmark on jurisdiction and the recognition and enforcement of judgments in civil and commercial matters done on 19 October 2005.

(30) The Brussels Convention continues to apply to the territories of the Member States which fall within the territorial scope of that Convention and which are excluded from this Regulation pursuant to Article 355 of the Treaty on the Functioning of the European Union.

(31) Likewise for the sake of consistency, this Regulation should not affect rules governing jurisdiction and the recognition of judgments contained in specific instruments of the Union.

(32) Respect for international commitments entered into by the Member States means that this Regulation should not affect conventions relating to specific matters to which the Member States are parties.

(33) The Commission should be empowered to adopt delegated acts in accordance with Article 290 of the Treaty on the Functioning of the European Union for the purpose of adjusting Annexes I, II, V, VI and VII. ...

Chapter I — Scope and definitions

Article 1.   1.   This Regulation shall apply in civil and commercial matters whatever the nature of the court or tribunal. It shall not extend, in particular, to revenue, customs or administrative matters.

2.   This Regulation shall not apply to:

(a)   the status or legal capacity of natural persons, rights in property arising out of a matrimonial relationship, wills and succession;

(b)   bankruptcy, proceedings relating to the winding-up of insolvent companies or other legal persons, judicial arrangements, compositions and analogous proceedings;

(c)   social security;

(d)   arbitration, save as provided for in Articles 29, paragraph 4 and 33, paragraph 3;

(e)   maintenance obligations arising from a family relationship, parentage, marriage or affinity.

3.   In this Regulation, the term 'Member State' shall mean Member States with the exception of Denmark.

Article 2.   For the purposes of this Regulation,:

(a)   'judgment' means any judgment given by a court or tribunal of a Member State, whatever the judgment may be called, including the determination of costs or expenses by an officer of the court.

For the purposes of Chapter III, the term 'judgment' includes provisional, including protective measures ordered by a court which by virtue of this Regulation has jurisdiction as to the substance of the matter. It also includes measures ordered without the defendant being summoned to appear and which are intended to be enforced without prior service of the defendant if the defendant has the right to challenge the measure subsequently under the national law of the Member State of origin;

(b)   'provisional, including protective measures' shall include protective orders aimed at obtaining information and evidence;

(c)   'court' shall include any authorities designated by a Member State as having jurisdiction in the matters falling within the scope of this Regulation;

(d)   'court settlement´ means a settlement which has been approved by a court or concluded before a court in the course of proceedings;

(e)   'authentic instrument' means a document which has been formally drawn up or registered as an authentic instrument in the Member State of origin and the authenticity of which:

(i)   relates to the signature and the content of the instrument, and

(ii)   has been established by a public authority or other authority empowered for that purpose.

(f)   'Member State of origin´ means the Member State in which, as the case may be, the judgment has been given, the court settlement has been approved or concluded, or the authentic instrument has been established;

(g)   'Member State of enforcement´ means the Member State in which the enforcement of the judgment, the court settlement or the authentic instrument is sought;

(h)   'court of origin´ means the court which has given the judgment to be recognised and enforced.

Chapter II — Jurisdiction

Section 1 — General provisions

Article 3.   1.   Subject to this Regulation, persons domiciled in a Member State shall, whatever their nationality, be sued in the courts of that Member State.

2.   Persons who are not nationals of the Member State in which they are domiciled shall be governed by the rules of jurisdiction applicable to nationals of that State.

Article 4.   1.   Persons domiciled in a Member State may be sued in the courts of another Member State only by virtue of the rules set out in Sections 2 to 7 of this Chapter.

2.   Persons not domiciled in any of the Member States may be sued in the courts of a Member State only by virtue of the rules set out in Sections 2 to 8 of this Chapter.

Section 2 — Special jurisdiction

Article 5.   The following courts shall have jurisdiction: 1.   (a)   in matters relating to a contract, the courts for the place of performance of the obligation in question;
(b)   for the purpose of this provision and unless otherwise agreed, the place of performance of the obligation in question shall be:
–   in the case of the sale of goods, the place in a Member State where, under the contract, the goods were delivered or should have been delivered,
–   in the case of the provision of services, the place in a Member State where, under the contract, the services were provided or should have been provided,
(c)   if subparagraph point (b) does not apply then subparagraph point (a) applies;
2.   in matters relating to tort, *delict* or *quasi-delict*, the courts for the place where the harmful event occurred or may occur;
3.   as regards *rights in rem* or possession in moveable property, the courts for the place where the property is situated;
4.   as regards a civil claim for damages or restitution which is based on an act giving rise to criminal proceedings, the court seised of those proceedings, to the extent that that court has jurisdiction under its own law to entertain civil proceedings;
5.   as regards a dispute arising out of the operations of a branch, agency or other establishment, the courts for the place in which the branch, agency or other establishment is situated;
6.   as settlor, trustee or beneficiary of a trust created by the operation of a statute, or by a written instrument, or created orally and evidenced in writing, the courts of the Member State in which the trust is domiciled;
7.   as regards a dispute concerning the payment of remuneration claimed in respect of the salvage of a cargo or freight, the court under the authority of which the cargo or freight in question:
(a)   has been arrested to secure such payment, or
(b)   could have been so arrested, but bail or other security has been given;
provided that this provision shall apply only if it is claimed that the defendant has an interest in the cargo or freight or had such an interest at the time of salvage.

Article 6.   A person may also be sued: 1.   where he is domiciled in a Member State and is one of a number of defendants, in the courts for the place where any one of them is domiciled, provided the claims are so closely connected that it is expedient to hear and determine them together to avoid the risk of irreconcilable judgments resulting from separate proceedings;
2.   as a third party in an action on a warranty or guarantee or in any other third party proceedings, in the court seised of the original proceedings, unless these were instituted solely with the object of removing him from the jurisdiction of the court which would be competent in his case;
3.   on a counter-claim arising from the same contract or facts on which the original claim was based, in the court in which the original claim is pending;
4.   in matters relating to a contract, if the action may be combined with an action against the same defendant in matters relating to rights *in rem* in immovable property, in the court of the Member State in which the property is situated.

Article 7.   Where by virtue of this Regulation a court of a Member State has jurisdiction in actions relating to liability from the use or operation of a ship, that court, or any other court substituted for this purpose by the internal law of that Member State, shall also have jurisdiction over claims for limitation of such liability.

Section 3 — Jurisdiction in matters relating to insurance

Article 8.   In matters relating to insurance, jurisdiction shall be determined by this Section, without prejudice to point 5 of Article 5.

Article 9.   1.   An insurer may be sued:
     (a)   in the courts of the Member State where he is domiciled, or
     (b)   in another Member State, in the case of actions brought by the policyholder, the insured or a beneficiary, in the courts for the place where the plaintiff is domiciled,
     (c)   if he is a co-insurer, in the courts of a Member State in which proceedings are brought against the leading insurer.
     2.   An insurer who is not domiciled in a Member State but has a branch, agency or other establishment in one of the Member States shall, in disputes arising out of the operations of the branch, agency or establishment, be deemed to be domiciled in that Member State.

Article 10.   In respect of liability insurance or insurance of immovable property, the insurer may in addition be sued in the courts for the place where the harmful event occurred. The same applies if movable and immovable property are covered by the same insurance policy and both are adversely affected by the same contingency.

Article 11.   1.   In respect of liability insurance, the insurer may also, if the law of the court permits it, be joined in proceedings which the injured party has brought against the insured.
     2.   Articles 8, 9 and 10 shall apply to actions brought by the injured party directly against the insurer, where such direct actions are permitted.
     3.   If the law governing such direct actions provides that the policyholder or the insured may be joined as a party to the action, the same court shall have jurisdiction over them.

Article 12.   1.   Without prejudice to Article 11(3), an insurer may bring proceedings only in the courts of the Member State in which the defendant is domiciled, irrespective of whether he is the policyholder, the insured or a beneficiary.
     2.   The provisions of this Section shall not affect the right to bring a counter-claim in the court in which, in accordance with this Section, the original claim is pending.

Article 13.   The provisions of this Section may be departed from only by an agreement:
     1.   which is entered into after the dispute has arisen, or
     2.   which allows the policyholder, the insured or a beneficiary to bring proceedings in courts other than those indicated in this Section, or
     3.   which is concluded between a policyholder and an insurer, both of whom are at the time of conclusion of the contract domiciled or habitually resident in the same

Member State, and which has the effect of conferring jurisdiction on the courts of that State even if the harmful event were to occur abroad, provided that such an agreement is not contrary to the law of that State, or

4. which is concluded with a policyholder who is not domiciled in a Member State, except in so far as the insurance is compulsory or relates to immovable property in a Member State, or

5. which relates to a contract of insurance in so far as it covers one or more of the risks set out in Article 14.

Article 14. The following are the risks referred to in Article 13(5):

1. any loss of or damage to:

(a) seagoing ships, installations situated offshore or on the high seas, or aircraft, arising from perils which relate to their use for commercial purposes;

(b) goods in transit other than passengers' baggage where the transit consists of or includes carriage by such ships or aircraft;

2. any liability, other than for bodily injury to passengers or loss of or damage to their baggage:

(a) arising out of the use or operation of ships, installations or aircraft as referred to in point 1(a) in so far as, in respect of the latter, the law of the Member State in which such aircraft are registered does not prohibit agreements on jurisdiction regarding insurance of such risks;

(b) for loss or damage caused by goods in transit as described in point 1(b);

3. any financial loss connected with the use or operation of ships, installations or aircraft as referred to in point 1(a), in particular loss of freight or charter-hire;

4. any risk or interest connected with any of those referred to in points 1 to 3;

5. notwithstanding points 1 to 4, all 'large risks' as defined in Directive 2009/138/EC of the European Parliament and of the Council.

Section 4 — Jurisdiction over consumer contracts

Article 15. 1. In matters relating to a contract concluded by a person, the consumer, for a purpose which can be regarded as being outside his trade or profession, jurisdiction shall be determined by this Section, without prejudice to point 5 of Article 5, if:

(a) it is a contract for the sale of goods on instalment credit terms; or

(b) it is a contract for a loan repayable by instalments, or for any other form of credit, made to finance the sale of goods; or

(c) in all other cases, the contract has been concluded with a person who pursues commercial or professional activities in the Member State of the consumer's domicile or, by any means, directs such activities to that Member State or to several States including that Member State, and the contract falls within the scope of such activities.

2. Where a consumer enters into a contract with a party who is not domiciled in the Member State but has a branch, agency or other establishment in one of the Member States, that party shall, in disputes arising out of the operations of the branch, agency or establishment, be deemed to be domiciled in that State.

3. This Section shall not apply to a contract of transport other than a contract which, for an inclusive price, provides for a combination of travel and accommodation.

Article 16.   1.   A consumer may bring proceedings against the other party to a contract either in the courts of the Member State in which that party is domiciled or in the courts for the place where the consumer is domiciled.

2.   Proceedings may be brought against a consumer by the other party to the contract only in the courts of the Member State in which the consumer is domiciled.

3.   This Article shall not affect the right to bring a counter-claim in the court in which, in accordance with this Section, the original claim is pending.

Article 17.   The provisions of this Section may be departed from only by an agreement: 1.   which is entered into after the dispute has arisen; or

2.   which allows the consumer to bring proceedings in courts other than those indicated in this Section; or

3.   which is entered into by the consumer and the other party to the contract, both of whom are at the time of conclusion of the contract domiciled or habitually resident in the same Member State, and which confers jurisdiction on the courts of that Member State, provided that such an agreement is not contrary to the law of that Member State.

Section 5 — Jurisdiction over individual contracts of employment

Article 18.   1.   In matters relating to individual contracts of employment, jurisdiction shall be determined by this Section, without prejudice to point 5 of Article 5 and Article 6(1).

2.   Where an employee enters into an individual contract of employment with an employer who is not domiciled in a Member State but has a branch, agency or other establishment in one of the Member States, the employer shall, in disputes arising out of the operations of the branch, agency or establishment, be deemed to be domiciled in that Member State.

Article 19.   An employer may be sued:

1.   in the courts of the Member State where he is domiciled; or

2.   in another Member State:

(a)   in the courts for the place where or from where the employee habitually carries out his work or in the courts for the last place where he did so, or

(b)   if the employee does not or did not habitually carry out his work in any one country, in the courts for the place where the business which engaged the employee is or was situated.

Article 20.   1.   An employer may bring proceedings only in the courts of the Member State in which the employee is domiciled.

2.   The provisions of this Section shall not affect the right to bring a counter-claim in the court in which, in accordance with this Section, the original claim is pending.

Article 21.   The provisions of this Section may be departed from only by an agreement: 1.   which is entered into after the dispute has arisen; or

2.   which allows the employee to bring proceedings in courts other than those indicated in this Section.

Section 6 — Exclusive jurisdiction

Article 22. The following courts shall have exclusive jurisdiction:

1. in proceedings which have as their object rights in rem in immovable property or tenancies of immovable property, the courts of the Member State in which the property is situated. However:

(a) in proceedings which have as their object tenancies of immovable property concluded for temporary private use for a maximum period of six consecutive months, the courts of the Member State in which the defendant is domiciled shall also have jurisdiction, provided that the tenant is a natural person and that the landlord and the tenant are domiciled in the same Member State, either at the moment of conclusion of the agreement or at the moment of the institution of proceedings;

(b) in agreements concerning tenancies of premises for professional use, parties may agree that a court or the courts of a Member State are to have jurisdiction in accordance with Article 23;

2. in proceedings which have as their object the validity of the constitution, the nullity or the dissolution of companies or other legal persons or associations of natural or legal persons, or of the validity of the decisions of their organs, the courts of the Member State in which the company, legal person or association has its seat. In order to determine that seat, the court shall apply its rules of private international law;

3. in proceedings which have as their object the validity of entries in public registers, the courts of the Member State in which the register is kept;

4. in proceedings concerned with the registration or validity of patents, trade marks, designs, or other similar rights required to be deposited or registered, irrespective of whether the issue is raised by way of an action or as a defence, the courts of the Member State in which the deposit or registration has been applied for, has taken place or is under the terms of an instrument of the Union or an international convention deemed to have taken place.

Without prejudice to the jurisdiction of the European Patent Office under the Convention on the Grant of European Patents, signed at Munich on 5 October 1973, the courts of each Member State shall have exclusive jurisdiction, regardless of domicile, in proceedings concerned with the registration or validity of any European patent granted for that State;

5. in proceedings concerned with the enforcement of judgments, the courts of the Member State in which the judgment has been or is to be enforced.

Section 7 — Prorogation of jurisdiction

Article 23. 1. If the parties have agreed that a court or the courts of a Member State are to have jurisdiction to settle any disputes which have arisen or which may arise in connection with a particular legal relationship, that court or those courts shall have jurisdiction, unless the agreement is null and void as to its substance under the law of that Member State. Such jurisdiction shall be exclusive unless the parties have agreed otherwise. Such an agreement conferring jurisdiction shall be either:

(a) in writing or evidenced in writing; or

(b) in a form which accords with practices which the parties have established between themselves; or

(c)   in international trade or commerce, in a form which accords with a usage of which the parties are or ought to have been aware and which in such trade or commerce is widely known to, and regularly observed by, parties to contracts of the type involved in the particular trade or commerce concerned.

2.   Any communication by electronic means which provides a durable record of the agreement shall be equivalent to 'writing'.

3.   The court or courts of a Member State on which a trust instrument has conferred jurisdiction shall have exclusive jurisdiction in any proceedings brought against a settlor, trustee or beneficiary, if relations between these persons or their rights or obligations under the trust are involved.

4.   Agreements or provisions of a trust instrument conferring jurisdiction shall have no legal force if they are contrary to Articles 13, 17 or 21, or if the courts whose jurisdiction they purport to exclude have exclusive jurisdiction by virtue of Article 22.

Article 24.   1.   Apart from jurisdiction derived from other provisions of this Regulation, a court of a Member State before which a defendant enters an appearance shall have jurisdiction. This rule shall not apply where appearance was entered to contest the jurisdiction, or where another court has exclusive jurisdiction by virtue of Article 22.

2.   In matters referred to in Sections 3, 4, and 5 of this Chapter, the document instituting proceedings or the equivalent document must contain information for the defendant on his right to contest the jurisdiction of the court and the consequences of entering an appearance. Before assuming jurisdiction on the basis of this Article, the court shall ensure that such information was provided to the defendant .

Section 8 — Subsidiary jurisdiction and forum necessitatis

Article 25.   Where no court of a Member State has jurisdiction in accordance with Articles 2 to24, jurisdiction shall lie with the courts of the Member State where property belonging to the defendant is located, provided that

(a)   the value of the property is not disproportionate to the value of the claim; and

(b)   the dispute has a sufficient connection with the Member State of the court seised.

Article 26.   Where no court of a Member State has jurisdiction under this Regulation, the courts of a Member State may, on an exceptional basis, hear the case if the right to a fair trial or the right to access to justice so requires, in particular:

(a)   if proceedings cannot reasonably be brought or conducted or would be impossible in a third State with which the dispute is closely connected; or

(b)   if a judgment given on the claim in a third State would not be entitled to recognition and enforcement in the Member State of the court seised under the law of that State and such recognition and enforcement is necessary to ensure that the rights of the claimant are satisfied;

and the dispute has a sufficient connection with the Member State of the court seised.

Section 9 — Examination as to jurisdiction and admissibility

Article 27.   Where a court of a Member State is seised of a claim which is principally concerned with a matter over which it has no jurisdiction under this Regulation, it shall declare of its own motion that it has no jurisdiction.

Article 28.   1.   Where a defendant is sued in a court of a Member State and does not enter an appearance, the court shall stay the proceedings so long as it is not shown that the defendant has been able to receive the document instituting the proceedings or an equivalent document in sufficient time to enable him to arrange for his defence, or that all necessary steps have been taken to this end.

2.   Article 19, paragraphs 1, 2, and 3 Regulation (EC) No 1393/2007 of the European Parliament and of the Council shall apply instead of the provisions of paragraph 2 if the document instituting the proceedings or an equivalent document had to be transmitted from one Member State to another pursuant to this Regulation.

3.   Where the provisions of Regulation (EC) No 1393/2007 are not applicable, Article 15 of the Hague Convention of 15 November 1965 on the Service Abroad of Judicial and Extrajudicial Documents in Civil or Commercial Matters shall apply if the document instituting the proceedings or an equivalent document had to be transmitted pursuant to that Convention.

Section 10 — Lis pendens — Related actions

Article 29.   1.   Without prejudice to Article 32(2), where proceedings involving the same cause of action and between the same parties are brought in the courts of different Member States, any court other than the court first seised shall of its own motion stay its proceedings until such time as the jurisdiction of the court first seised is established.

2.   In cases referred to in paragraph 1, the court first seised shall establish its jurisdiction within six months except where exceptional circumstances make this impossible. Upon request by any other court seised of the dispute, the court first seised shall inform that court of the date on which it was seised and of whether it has established jurisdiction over the dispute or, failing that, of the estimated time for establishing jurisdiction.

3.   Where the jurisdiction of the court first seised is established, any court other than the court first seised shall decline jurisdiction in favour of that court.

4.   Where the agreed or designated seat of an arbitration is in a Member State, the courts of another Member State whose jurisdiction is contested on the basis of an arbitration agreement shall stay proceedings once the courts of the Member State where the seat of the arbitration is located or the arbitral tribunal have been seised of proceedings to determine, as their main object or as an incidental question, the existence, validity or effects of that arbitration agreement.

This paragraph does not prevent the court whose jurisdiction is contested from declining jurisdiction in the situation referred to above if its national law so prescribes.

Where the existence, validity or effects of the arbitration agreement are established, the court seised shall decline jurisdiction.

This paragraph does not apply in disputes concerning matters referred to in Sections 3, 4, and 5 of Chapter II.

Article 30.   1.   Where related actions are pending in the courts of different Member States, any court other than the court first seised may stay its proceedings.

2.   Where the action in the court first seised is pending at first instance, any other court than the court first seised may also, on the application of one of the parties, decline jurisdiction if the court first seised has jurisdiction over the actions in question and its law permits the consolidation thereof.

3.   For the purposes of this Article, actions are deemed to be related where they are so closely connected that it is expedient to hear and determine them together to avoid the risk of irreconcilable judgments resulting from separate proceedings.

Article 31.   If proceedings as to the substance are pending before a court of a Member State and the courts of another Member State are seised with an application for provisional, including protective measures, the courts concerned shall cooperate in order to ensure proper coordination between the proceedings as to the substance and the provisional relief.

In particular, the court seised with an application for provisional, including protective measures shall seek information from the other court on all relevant circumstances of the case, such as the urgency of the measure sought or any refusal of a similar measure by the court seised as to the substance.

Article 32.   1.   Where actions come within the exclusive jurisdiction of several courts, any court other than the court first seised shall decline jurisdiction in favour of that court.

2.   With the exception of agreements governed by Sections 3, 4 and 5 of this Chapter, where an agreement referred to in Article 23 confers exclusive jurisdiction to a court or the courts of a Member State, the courts of other Member States shall have no jurisdiction over the dispute until such time as the court or courts designated in the agreement decline their jurisdiction.

Article 33.   1.   For the purposes of this Section, a court shall be deemed to be seised:

(a)   at the time when the document instituting the proceedings or an equivalent document is lodged with the court, provided that the plaintiff has not subsequently failed to take the steps he was required to take to have service effected on the defendant, or

(b)   if the document has to be served before being lodged with the court, at the time when it is received by the authority responsible for service, provided that the plaintiff has not subsequently failed to take the steps he was required to take to have the document lodged with the court.

The authority responsible for service referred to in point (b) shall be the first authority receiving the documents to be served.

2.   The courts and authorities responsible for service referred to in paragraph 1 shall note, as applicable, the date and time of lodging of the document instituting proceedings or of receipt of the documents to be served.

3.   For the purposes of this Section, an arbitral tribunal is deemed to be seised when a party has nominated an arbitrator or when a party has requested the support of an institution, authority or a court for the tribunal's constitution

Article 34. 1. Notwithstanding the rules in Articles 3 to 7, if proceedings in relation to the same cause of action and between the same parties are pending before the courts of a third State at a time when a court in a Member State is seised, that court may stay its proceedings if:

(a) the court of the third State was seised first in time;

(b) it may be expected that the court in the third State will, within a reasonable time, render a judgment that will be capable of recognition and, where applicable, enforcement in that Member State; and

(c) the court is satisfied that it is necessary for the proper administration of justice to do so.

2. During the period of the stay, the party who has seised the court in the Member State shall not lose the benefit of interruption of prescription or limitation periods provided for under the law of that Member State.

3. The court may discharge the stay at any time upon application by either party or of its own motion if one of the following conditions is met:

(a) the proceedings in the court of the third State are themselves stayed or are discontinued;

(b) it appears to the court that the proceedings in the court of the third State are unlikely to be concluded within a reasonable time;

(c) discharge of the stay is required for the proper administration of justice.

4. The court shall dismiss the proceedings upon application by either party or of its own motion if the proceedings in the court of the third State are concluded and have resulted in a judgment enforceable in that State, or capable of recognition and, where applicable, enforcement in the Member State.

Section 11 — Provisional, including protective, measures

Article 35. Where the courts of a Member State have jurisdiction as to the substance of a matter, those courts shall have jurisdiction to issue provisional, including protective measures as may be available under the law of that State.

Article 36. Application may be made to the courts of a Member State for such provisional, including protective, measures as may be available under the law of that State, even if the courts of another State or an arbitral tribunal have jurisdiction as to the substance of the matter.

Chapter III — Recognition, enforceability and enforcement

Article 37. 1. This Chapter shall govern the recognition, enforceability and enforcement of judgments falling within the scope of this Regulation.

2. Section 1 shall apply to all judgments with the exception of those referred to in paragraph 3.

3. Section 2 shall apply to judgments given in another Member State

(a) concerning non-contractual obligations arising out of violations of privacy and rights relating to personality, including defamation, and

(b) in proceedings which concern the compensation of harm caused by unlawful business practices to a multitude of injured parties and which are brought by

    i.   a state body,

    ii.   a non-profit making organisation whose main purpose and activity is to represent and defend the interests of groups of natural or legal persons, other than by, on a commercial basis, providing them with legal advice or representing them in court, or

    iii.   a group of more than twelve claimants.

    4.   Without prejudice to the competence of the Commission to propose at any time the extension of the rules of Section 1 to judgments falling within the scope of paragraph 3(b) in view of the state of convergence of national laws and of the development of Union law, three years after the entry into force of this Regulation, or earlier in case the Commission proposes further harmonisation, the Commission shall submit to the European Parliament, the Council and the European Economic and Social Committee a report reviewing the continuing need to maintain the procedure for recognition and enforcement for judgments given in matters referred to in paragraph 3(b).

Section 1 — Judgments for which no declaration of enforceability is required

Subsection 1 — Abolition of exequatur

Article 38.   1.   Subject to the provisions of this Chapter, a judgment given in a Member State shall be recognised in the other Member States without any special procedure being required and without any possibility of opposing its recognition.

    2.   A judgment given in one Member State which is enforceable in that State shall be enforceable in another Member State without the need for a declaration of enforceability.

Article 39.   1.   A party who wishes to invoke in another Member State a judgment recognised pursuant to Article 38 (1) shall produce a copy of the judgment which satisfies the conditions necessary to establish its authenticity.

    2.   The court before which the recognised judgment is invoked may, where necessary, ask the party invoking it to produce a certificate issued by the court of origin using the form set out in Annex I and to provide a transliteration or a translation of the contents of the form in accordance with Article 69.

    The court of origin shall also issue such a certificate at the request of any interested party.

    3.   The court before which the recognised judgment is invoked may suspend its proceedings, in whole or in part, if the judgment is challenged in the Member State of origin or in the event of an application for a review pursuant to Articles 45 or 46.

Subsection 2 — Enforcement

Article 40.   An enforceable judgment shall carry with it by operation of law the power to proceed to any protective measures which exist under the law of the Member State of enforcement.

Article 41.   1.   Subject to the provisions of this Chapter, the procedure for the enforcement of judgments given in another Member State shall be governed by the law of the Member State of enforcement. A judgment given in a Member State which is enforceable in the Member State of enforcement shall be enforced there under the same conditions as a judgment given in that Member State.

2.   Notwithstanding paragraph 1, the grounds of refusal or suspension of enforcement under the law of the Member State of enforcement shall not apply in so far as they concern situations referred to in Articles 43 to 46.

Article 42.   1.   For the purposes of enforcement in another Member State of a judgment other than those referred to in paragraph 2 , the applicant shall provide the competent enforcement authorities with:

(a)   a copy of the judgment which satisfies the conditions necessary to establish its authenticity; and

(b)   the certificate in the form set out in Annex I issued by the court of origin, certifying that the judgment is enforceable and, containing, where appropriate, an extract of the judgment as well as relevant information on the recoverable costs of the proceedings and the calculation of interest.

2.   For the purposes of enforcement in another Member State of a judgment ordering a provisional, including protective measure, the applicant shall provide the competent enforcement authorities with

(a)   a copy of the judgment which satisfies the conditions necessary to establish its authenticity; and

(b)   the certificate in the form set out in Annex I issued by the court of origin, containing a description of the measure and certifying

(i)   that the court has jurisdiction as to the substance of the matter; and

(ii)   where the measure is ordered without the defendant being summoned to appear and is intended to be enforced without prior service of the defendant, that the defendant has the right to challenge the measure under the law of the Member State of origin.

3.   The competent authority may, where necessary, request a transliteration or a translation of the content of the form referred to in point (b) of paragraphs 1 and 2 above in accordance with Article 69.

4.   The competent authorities may not require the applicant to provide a translation of the judgment. However, a translation may be required if the enforcement of the judgment is challenged and a translation appears necessary.

Article 43.   The competent authority in the Member State of enforcement shall, on application by the defendant, refuse, either wholly or in part, the enforcement of the judgment if

(a)   it is irreconcilable with a judgment given in a dispute between the same parties in the Member State of enforcement;

(b)   it is irreconcilable with an earlier judgment given in another Member State or in a third State involving the same cause of action and between the same parties provided that the earlier judgment fulfils the conditions necessary for its recognition in the Member State of enforcement.

Article 44.   1.   In the event of an application for a review pursuant to Article 45 or Article 46, the competent authority in the Member State of enforcement may, on application by the defendant:

(a)　limit the enforcement proceedings to protective measures;

(b)　make enforcement conditional on the provision of such security as it shall determine; or

(c)　suspend, either wholly or in part, the enforcement of the judgment.

2.　The competent authority shall, on application by the defendant, suspend the enforcement of the judgment where the enforceability of that judgment is suspended in the Member State of origin.

3.　Where a protective measure was ordered without the defendant having been summoned to appear and enforced without prior service of the defendant, the competent authority may, on application by the defendant, suspend the enforcement if the defendant has challenged the measure in the Member State of origin.

Subsection 3 — Common provisions

Article 45.　1.　A defendant who did not enter an appearance in the Member State of origin shall have the right to apply for a review of the judgment before the competent court of that Member State where:

(a)　he was not served with the document instituting the proceedings or an equivalent document in sufficient time and in such a way as to enable him to arrange for his defence; or

(b)　he was prevented from contesting the claim by reason of force majeure or due to extraordinary circumstances without any fault on his part;

unless he failed to challenge the judgment when it was possible for him to do so.

2.　The application shall be submitted using the form set out in Annex II.

3.　The application may be submitted directly to the court in the Member State of origin which is competent for the review pursuant to this Article. The application may also be submitted to the competent court of the Member State of enforcement which will without undue delay transfer the application to the competent court in the Member State of origin using the means of communication as notified pursuant to Article 87 point b.

4.　The application for a review shall be made promptly, in any event within 45 days from the day the defendant was effectively acquainted with the contents of the judgment and was able to react. Where the defendant applies for a review in the context of enforcement proceedings, the time period shall run at the latest from the date of the first enforcement measure having the effect of making his property non-disposable in whole or in part. The application shall be deemed to be made when it is received by either of the courts referred to in paragraph 3.

5.　If the application for a review is manifestly unfounded, the court shall dismiss the application immediately and in any event within 30 days from the receipt of the application. In such case, the judgment shall remain in force.

If the court decides that a review is justified on one of the grounds laid down in paragraph 1, the judgment shall be null and void. However, the party who obtained the judgment before the court of origin shall not lose the benefits of the interruption of prescription or limitation periods acquired in the initial proceedings.

6.　This provision shall apply instead of Article 19, paragraph 4 of Regulation (EC) No 1393/2007, if the document instituting the proceedings or an equivalent document had to be transmitted from one Member State to another pursuant to that Regulation.

Article 46. 1. In cases other than those covered by Article 45, a party shall have the right to apply for a refusal of recognition or enforcement of a judgment where such recognition or enforcement would not be permitted by the fundamental principles underlying the right to a fair trial.

2. The application shall be brought before the court of the Member State of enforcement, listed in Annex III. The local jurisdiction shall be determined by reference to the place of domicile of the party against whom recognition or enforcement is sought or to the place of enforcement.

3. The procedure for making the application shall be governed by the law of the Member State of enforcement.

4. If the application is manifestly unfounded, the court shall dismiss the application immediately and in any event within 30 days from the receipt of the application.

5. If the court decides that the application is justified, recognition or enforcement of the judgment shall be refused.

6. The judgment given in accordance with this Article may be contested only by the appeal referred to in Annex IV.

7. The court seised of an application in accordance with this Article may stay the proceedings if an ordinary appeal has been lodged against the judgment in the Member State of origin or if the time for such an appeal has not yet expired. Where the time for such an appeal has not yet expired, the court may specify the time within which such an appeal is to be lodged.

8. The unsuccessful party shall bear the costs of the proceedings under this Article, including the legal costs of the other party.

Section 2 — Judgments for which a declaration of enforceability is required on a transitional basis

Article 47. 1. A judgment given in a Member State concerning matters referred to in Article 37(3) shall be recognised in the other Member States without any special procedure being required.

2. Any interested party who raises the recognition of a judgment as the principal issue in a dispute may, in accordance with the procedures provided for in Articles 50 to 63, apply for a decision that the judgment be recognised.

3. If the outcome of proceedings in a court of a Member State depends on the determination of an incidental question of recognition that court shall have jurisdiction over that question.

Article 48. A judgment shall not be recognised:

1. if such recognition is manifestly contrary to public policy (*ordre public*) in the Member State in which recognition is sought;

2. where it was given in default of appearance, if the defendant was not served with the document which instituted the proceedings or with an equivalent document in sufficient time and in such a way as to enable him to arrange for his defence, unless the defendant failed to commence proceedings to challenge the judgment when it was possible for him to do so;

3. if it is irreconcilable with a judgment given in a dispute between the same parties in the Member State in which recognition is sought;

4.   if it is irreconcilable with an earlier judgment given in another Member State or in a third State involving the same cause of action and between the same parties, provided that the earlier judgment fulfils the conditions necessary for its recognition in the Member State in which recognition is sought.

Article 49.   1.   A court of a Member State in which recognition is sought of a judgment given in another Member State shall stay the proceedings if the enforceability of the decision is suspended in the Member State of origin by reason of an appeal.

Article 50.   A judgment given in a Member State and enforceable in that State shall be enforceable in the other Member States when, on the application of any interested party, it has been declared enforceable there in accordance with the procedure provided for in Articles 51 to 63.

Article 51.   1.   The application for a declaration of enforceability shall be submitted to the court or competent authority of the Member State of enforcement notified by that Member State to the Commission in accordance with Article 87 point d.
2.   The local jurisdiction shall be determined by reference to the place of domicile of the party against whom enforcement is sought, or to the place of enforcement.

Article 52.   1.   The procedure for making the application for a declaration of enforceability shall be governed by the law of the Member State of enforcement.
2.   The application shall be accompanied by the following documents:
(a)   a copy of the judgment which satisfies the conditions necessary to establish its authenticity
(b)   the certificate issued by the court or competent authority of the Member State of origin using the form set out in Annex VI, without prejudice to Article 53.

Article 53.   1.   If the certificate referred to in Article 52(2)(b) is not produced, the court or competent authority may specify a time for its production or accept an equivalent document or, if it considers that it has sufficient information before it, dispense with its production.
2.   In the situation referred to in paragraph 1, if the court or competent authority so requires, a translation of the documents shall be produced.

Article 54.   The judgment shall be declared enforceable without any review under Article 48 immediately on completion of the formalities in Article 52. The party against whom enforcement is sought shall not at this stage of the proceedings be entitled to make any submissions on the application.

Article 55.   1.   The decision on the application for a declaration of enforceability shall forthwith be brought to the notice of the applicant in accordance with the procedure laid down by the law of the Member State of enforcement.
2.   The declaration of enforceability shall be served on the party against whom enforcement is sought, accompanied by the judgment, if not already served on that party.

Article 56.   1.   The decision on the application for a declaration of enforceability may be appealed against by either party.

2.   The appeal is to be lodged with the court of the Member State of enforcement notified by that Member State to the Commission in accordance with Article 87 point e.

3.   The appeal shall be dealt with in accordance with the rules governing procedure in contradictory matters.

4.   If the party against whom enforcement is sought fails to appear before the appellate court in proceedings concerning an appeal brought by the applicant, Article 28 shall apply even where the party against whom enforcement is sought is not domiciled in any of the Member States.

5.   An appeal against the declaration of enforceability is to be lodged within 30 days of service thereof. If the party against whom enforcement is sought is domiciled in a Member State other than that in which the declaration of enforceability was given, the time for appealing shall be 45 days and shall run from the date of service, either on him in person or at his residence. No extension of time may be granted on account of distance.

Article 57.   The judgment given on the appeal may be contested only by the procedure notified by the Member State concerned to the Commission in accordance with Article 87 point f.

Article 58.   1.   The court with which an appeal is lodged under Article 56 or Article 57 shall refuse or revoke a declaration of enforceability only on one of the grounds specified in Article 48. It shall give its decision without delay.

2.   Subject to Article 56 (4), the court seised of an appeal under Article 56 shall give its decision within 90 days from the date it was seised, except where exceptional circumstances make this impossible.

3. The court seised of an appeal under Article 57 shall give its decision without delay.

Article 59.   1. The court with which an appeal is lodged under Article 56 or Article 57 shall, on the application of the party against whom enforcement is sought, stay the proceedings if the enforceability of the decision is suspended in the Member State of origin by reason of an appeal.

2.   The court may also make enforcement conditional on the provision of such security as it shall determine.

Article 60.   1.   When a judgment must be recognised in accordance with this Section, nothing shall prevent the applicant from availing himself of provisional, including protective, measures in accordance with the law of the Member State of enforcement without a declaration of enforceability under Article 54 being required.

2.   The declaration of enforceability shall carry with it by operation of law the power to proceed to any protective measures.

3.   During the time specified for an appeal pursuant to Article 56(5) against the declaration of enforceability and until any such appeal has been determined, no measures of enforcement may be taken other than protective measures against the property of the party against whom enforcement is sought.

Article 61. 1. Where a judgment has been given in respect of several matters and the declaration of enforceability cannot be given for all of them, the court or competent authority shall give it for one or more of them.

2. An applicant may request a declaration of enforceability limited to parts of a judgment.

Article 62. An applicant who, in the Member State of origin has benefited from complete or partial legal aid or exemption from costs or expenses, shall be entitled, in any proceedings for a declaration of enforceability, to benefit from the most favourable legal aid or the most extensive exemption from costs or expenses provided for by the law of the Member State of enforcement.

Article 63. In proceedings for the issue of a declaration of enforceability, no charge, duty or fee calculated by reference to the value of the matter at issue may be levied in the Member State of enforcement.

Section 3 — Common provisions

Article 64. Under no circumstances may a judgment given in a Member State be reviewed as to its substance in the Member State in which recognition, enforceability or enforcement is sought.

Article 65. The party seeking the recognition, enforceability or enforcement of a judgment given in another Member State shall not be required to have a postal address or an authorised representative in the Member State of enforcement.

Article 66. If a judgment contains a measure or an order which is not known in the Member State of enforcement, the competent authority in that Member State shall, to the extent possible, adapt the measure or order to one known under its own law which has equivalent effects attached to it and pursues similar aims and interests.

Article 67. A judgment given in a Member State which orders a payment by way of a penalty shall be enforceable in the Member State of enforcement in accordance with Sections 1 or 2, as the case may be. The competent court or authority in the Member State of enforcement shall determine the amount of the payment if that amount has not been finally determined by the courts of the Member State of origin.

Article 68. No security, bond or deposit, however described, shall be required of a party who in one Member State applies for enforcement of a judgment given in another Member State on the ground that he is a foreign national or that he is not domiciled or resident in the Member State of enforcement.

Article 69. 1. When a transliteration or translation is required under this Regulation, such transliteration or translation shall be into the official language of the Member State concerned or, where there are several official languages in that Member State, into the official language or one of the official languages of court proceedings of the place where a recognised judgment is invoked or an application is made, in accordance with the law of that Member State.

2.   For the purposes of the forms referred to in Articles 39 and 42, transliterations or translations may also be into any other official language or languages of the institutions of the Union that the Member State concerned has indicated it can accept.

3.   Any translation made under this Regulation shall be done by a person qualified to do translations in one of the Member States.

Chapter IV — Authentic instruments and court settlements

Article 70.   1.   An authentic instrument which is enforceable in one Member State shall be enforced in the other Member States in the same way as judgments in accordance with Sections 1 or 2 of Chapter III respectively.

2.   The instrument produced must satisfy the conditions necessary to establish its authenticity in the Member State of origin. The competent authority of the Member State of origin shall issue, at the request of any interested party, the certificate in the form set out in Annex V and VII, as the case may be, containing a summary of the enforceable obligation contained in the instrument.

3.   The provisions of Section 1 or 2 of Chapter III, respectively, shall apply as appropriate.

Article 71.   A court settlement which is enforceable in the Member State of origin shall be enforced in the other Member States under the same conditions as authentic instruments. The competent court or authority of the Member State of origin shall issue, at the request of any interested party, the certificate in the form set out in Annex V, containing a summary of the agreement between the parties.

Chapter V — General provisions

Article 72.   No legalisation or other similar formality shall be required in the context of this Regulation.

Article 73.   1.   In order to determine whether a party is domiciled in the Member State whose courts are seised of a matter, the court shall apply its internal law.

2.   If a party is not domiciled in the Member State whose courts are seised of the matter, then, in order to determine whether the party is domiciled in another Member State, the court shall apply the law of that Member State

Article 74.   1.   For the purposes of this Regulation, a company or other legal person or association of natural or legal persons is domiciled at the place where it has its:
   (a)   statutory seat, or
   (b)   central administration, or
   (c)   principal place of business.

2.   For the purposes of the United Kingdom and Ireland 'statutory seat' means the registered office or, where there is no such office anywhere, the place of incorporation or, where there is no such place anywhere, the place under the law of which the formation took place.

3.   In order to determine whether a trust is domiciled in the Member State whose courts are seised of the matter, the court shall apply its rules of private international law.

Article 75.   Without prejudice to any more favourable provisions of national laws, persons domiciled in a Member State who are being prosecuted in the criminal courts of another Member State of which they are not nationals for an offence which was not intentionally committed may be defended by persons qualified to do so, even if they do not appear in person. However, the court seised of the matter may order appearance in person; in the case of failure to appear, a judgment given in the civil action without the person concerned having had the opportunity to arrange for his defence need not be recognised or enforced in the other Member States.

Article 76.   1.   The jurisdiction specified in Article 6(2) and Article 11 in actions on a warranty or guarantee or in any other third party proceedings may be resorted to in the Member States referred to in Annex VIII only insofar as permitted under national law. A person may be sued in the courts of those Member States pursuant to the rules referred to in Annex VIII on third party notice, without prejudice to Articles 22 and 23.

The court having jurisdiction pursuant to this Article shall decide on the admissibility of the third party notice.

2.   Judgments given in other Member States by virtue of Article 6(2) or Article 11 shall be recognised and enforced in the Member States referred to in Annex VIII in accordance with Chapter III. Any effects which judgments given in these States may have on third parties by application of the provisions in paragraph 1 shall also be recognised in the other Member States.

Chapter VI — Transitional provisions

Article 77.   1.   This Regulation shall apply only to legal proceedings instituted and to documents formally drawn up or registered as authentic instruments as of the date of entry into application thereof.

2.   Legal proceedings instituted and documents formally drawn up or registered as authentic instruments prior to the date of entry into application of this Regulation shall be governed by Chapter III, Sections 2 and 3.

Chapter VII — Relations with other instruments

Article 78.   This Regulation shall not prejudice the application of provisions governing jurisdiction and the recognition and enforcement of judgments in specific matters which are contained in instruments of the Union or in national legislation harmonised pursuant to such instruments.

Article 79.   1.   This Regulation shall, as between the Member States, supersede the Brussels Convention, except as regards the territories of the Member States which fall within the territorial scope of that Convention and which are excluded from this Regulation pursuant to Article 355 of the Treaty.

2.   In so far as this Regulation replaces the provisions of the Brussels Convention between Member States, any reference to the Convention shall be understood as a reference to this Regulation.

Article 80. Subject to Articles 81 and 82 , this Regulation shall, as between Member States, supersede the conventions that cover the same matters as those to which this Regulation applies. In particular, the conventions mentioned in Annex IX shall be superseded.

Article 81. 1. The conventions referred to in Article 80 shall continue to have effect in relation to matters to which this Regulation does not apply.
2. They shall continue to have effect in respect of judgments given and documents formally drawn up or registered as authentic instruments before 1 March 2002.

Article 82. 1. This Regulation shall not affect any conventions to which the Member States are parties and which in relation to particular matters, govern jurisdiction or the recognition or enforcement of judgments.
2. With a view to its uniform interpretation, paragraph 1 shall be applied in the following manner:
(a) this Regulation shall not prevent a court of a Member State, which is a party to a convention on a particular matter, from assuming jurisdiction in accordance with that convention, even where the defendant is domiciled in another Member State which is not a party to that convention. The court hearing the action shall, in any event, apply Article 28 of this Regulation;
(b) judgments given in a Member State by a court in the exercise of jurisdiction provided for in a convention on a particular matter shall be recognised and enforced in the other Member States in accordance with this Regulation.
Where a convention on a particular matter to which both the Member State of origin and the Member State addressed are parties lays down conditions for the recognition or enforcement of judgments, those conditions shall apply. In any event, the provisions of this Regulation which concern the procedure for recognition and enforcement of judgments may be applied.

Article 83. This Regulation shall not affect agreements by which Member States undertook, prior to the entry into force of this Regulation pursuant to Article 59 of the Brussels Convention, not to recognise judgments given, in particular in other Contracting States to that Convention, against defendants domiciled or habitually resident in a third country where, in cases provided for in Article 4 of that Convention, the judgment could only be founded on a ground of jurisdiction specified in the second paragraph of Article 3 of that Convention.

Article 84. This Regulation shall not affect the application of the Convention on jurisdiction and the recognition and enforcement of judgments in civil and commercial matters, signed on 30 October 2007 in Lugano.

Chapter VIII — Final provisions

Article 85. This Regulation shall not affect the right of workers and employers, or their respective organisations, to engage in collective action to protect their interests, in particular the right or freedom to strike or to take other actions, in accordance with Union law and national law and practices.

Article 86. The Member States shall provide within the framework of the European Judicial Network in civil and commercial matters established by Decision 2001/470/ EC28, as amended by Decision 568/2009 with a view to making it available to the public, a description of national rules and procedures concerning enforcement, including authorities competent for enforcement, information on any limitations on enforcement, in particular debtor protection rules and limitation or prescription periods.

Member States shall keep this information permanently updated.

Article 87. By .... [1 year before the entry into force of the Regulation], the Member States shall communicate to the Commission

(a)   the courts competent for the review in the Member State of origin pursuant to Article 45(3);

(b)   the means of communication accepted in the Member State of origin for receiving applications for the review pursuant to Article 45;

(c)   the courts competent in the Member State of enforcement to which the application for a review may be submitted in accordance with Article 45(3);

(d)   the courts to which the application for a declaration of enforceability has to be submitted pursuant to Article 51 (1);

(e)   the courts with which an appeal against the decision on the application for a declaration of enforceability is to be lodged pursuant to Article 56 (2);

(f)   the courts with which a further appeal is to be lodged pursuant to Article 57;

(g)   the languages accepted for translations of the forms as referred to in Article 69.

The Commission shall make the information publicly available through any appropriate means, in particular through the European Judicial Network in civil and commercial matters established by Decision 2001/470.

Article 88. 1.   The Member States shall notify the Commission of the texts amending the lists set out in Annexes III, IV and IX, as well as of any withdrawals or technical amendments of the provisions listed in Annex VIII. The Commission shall adapt the Annexes concerned accordingly.

2.   The Commission may adopt, by means of delegated acts in accordance with Articles 90 to 92 amendments to Annexes I, II, V, VI and VII.

Article 89. 1.   The powers to adopt the delegated acts referred to in Article 88 (2) shall be conferred on the Commission for an indeterminate period of time.

2.   As soon as it adopts a delegated act, the Commission shall notify it simultaneously to the European Parliament and to the Council.

3.   The powers to adopt delegated acts are conferred on the Commission subject to the conditions laid down in Articles 90 and 91.

Article 90. 1.   The delegation of power referred to in Article 88 (2) may be revoked at any time by the European Parliament or by the Council.

2.   The institution which has commenced an internal procedure for deciding whether to revoke the delegation of power shall endeavour to inform the other institution and the Commission within a reasonable time before the final decision is taken, indicating the delegated powers which could be subject to revocation and possible reasons for a revocation.

3.   The decision of revocation shall put an end to the delegation of the powers specified in that decision. It shall take effect immediately or at a later date specified therein. It shall not affect the validity of the delegated acts already in force. It shall be published in the Official Journal of the European Union.

Article 91.   1.   The European Parliament and the Council may object to the delegated act within a period of two months from the date of notification. At the initiative of the European Parliament or the Council this period shall be extended by two months.
    2.   If, on expiry of that period, neither the European Parliament nor the Council has objected to the delegated act it shall be published in the *Official Journal of the European Union* and shall enter into force at the date stated therein.
    The delegated act may be published in the *Official Journal of the European Union* and enter into force before the expiry of that period if the European Parliament and the Council have both informed the Commission of their intention not to raise objections.
    3.   If the European Parliament or the Council objects to a delegated act, it shall not enter into force. The institution which objects shall state the reasons for objecting to the delegated act.

Article 92.   1.   This Regulation shall repeal Regulation (EC) No 44/2001. References to the repealed Regulation shall be construed as references to this Regulation and shall be read in accordance with the correlation table in Annex X.
    2.   Except with respect to judgments referred to in Article 37(3), this Regulation shall replace Regulation (EC) No 805/2004 of the European Parliament and of the Council of 21 April 2004 creating a European Enforcement Order for uncontested claims.

Article 93.   This Regulation shall enter into force on the twentieth day following that of its publication in the *Official Journal of the European Union.*
    This Regulation shall be binding in its entirety and directly applicable in all Member States.
    It shall apply from [24 months after entry into force], with the exception of Article 87, which shall apply from [12 months after entry into force].

A.13   ECJ case-law regarding Regulation (EC) No 44/2001

Article 1(1)

ECJ, 14 October 1976, case 29/76, LTU

In the interpretation of the concept 'civil and commercial matters' for the purposes of the application of the 1968 Brussels Convention, in particular Title III thereof, reference must not be made to the law of one of the States concerned but, first, to the objectives and scheme of the Convention and, secondly, to the general principles which stem from the corpus of the national legal systems.
    A judgment given in an action between a public authority and a person governed by private law, in which the public authority has acted in the exercise of its powers, is excluded from the area of application of the Convention.

ECJ, 14 July 1977, joined cases 9/77 and 10/77, Bavaria

The first paragraph of Article 56 of the 1968 Brussels Convention does not prevent a bilateral agreement such as the German–Belgian Convention, which is the fifth to be listed in Article 55, from continuing to have effect in relation to judgments which do not fall under the second paragraph of Article 1 of the Convention first abovementioned, but to which nevertheless that Convention does not apply.

ECJ, 16 December 1980, case 814/79, Netherlands State

The concept of 'civil and commercial matters' within the meaning of the first paragraph of Article 1 of the 1968 Brussels Convention does not include actions such as that referred to by the national court brought by the agent responsible for administering public waterways against the person having liability in law in order to recover the costs incurred in the removal of a wreck carried out by or at the instigation of the administering agent in the exercise of its public authority.

ECJ, 21 April 1993, case C-172/91, Sonntag

'Civil matters' within the meaning of the first sentence of the first paragraph of Article 1 of the 1968 Brussels Convention cover an action for compensation for damage brought before a criminal court against a teacher in a State school who, during a school trip, caused injury to a pupil through a culpable and unlawful breach of his duties of supervision; this is so even where cover is provided under a social insurance scheme governed by public law.

ECJ, 14 November 2002, case C-271/00, Baten

The first paragraph of Article 1 of the 1968 Brussels Convention must be interpreted as meaning that the concept of 'civil matters' encompasses an action under a right of recourse whereby a public body seeks from a person governed by private law recovery of sums paid by it by way of social assistance to the divorced spouse and the child of that person, provided that the basis and the detailed rules relating to the bringing of that action are governed by the rules of the ordinary law in regard to maintenance obligations. Where the action under a right of recourse is founded on provisions by which the legislature conferred on the public body a prerogative of its own, that action cannot be regarded as being brought in 'civil matters'.

ECJ, 15 May 2003, case C-266/01, Pres. foncière Tiard

'Civil and commercial matters', within the meaning of the first sentence of Article 1 of the 1968 Brussels Convention, covers a claim by which a contracting State seeks to enforce against a person governed by private law a private-law guarantee contract which was concluded in order to enable a third person to supply a guarantee required and defined by that State, in so far as the legal relationship between the creditor and the guarantor, under the guarantee contract, does not entail the exercise by the State of powers going beyond those existing under the rules applicable to relations between private individuals.

'Customs matters', within the meaning of the second sentence of that provision, does not cover a claim by which a contracting State seeks to enforce a guarantee contract intended to guarantee the payment of a customs debt, where the legal relationship between the State and the guarantor, under that contract, does not entail the exercise by the State of powers going beyond those existing under the rules applicable to relations between private individuals, even if the guarantor may raise pleas in defence which necessitate an investigation into the existence and content of the customs debt.

ECJ, 15 February 2007, case C-292/05, Lechoritou

On a proper construction of the first sentence of the first paragraph of Article 1 of the 1968 Brussels Convention, 'civil matters' within the meaning of that provision does not cover a legal action brought by natural persons in a Contracting State against another Contracting State for compensation in respect of the loss or damage suffered by the successors of the victims of acts perpetrated by armed forces in the course of warfare in the territory of the first State.

Article 1(2)(a) [ex 1(2)(1)]

ECJ, 27 March 1979, case 143/78, de Cavel

Judicial decisions authorising provisional protective measures — such as the placing under seal or the freezing of the assets of the spouses — in the course of proceedings for divorce do not fall within the scope of the 1968 Brussels Convention as defined in Article 1 thereof if those measures concern or are closely connected with either questions of the status of the persons involved in the divorce proceedings or proprietary legal relations resulting directly from the matrimonial relationship or the dissolution thereof.

ECJ, 6 March 1980, case 120/79, de Cavel

The 1968 Brussels Convention is applicable, on the one hand, to the enforcement of an interlocutory order made by a French court in divorce proceedings whereby one of the parties to the proceedings is awarded a monthly maintenance allowance and, on the other hand, to an interim compensation payment, payable monthly, awarded to one of the parties by a French divorce judgment pursuant to Article 270 *et seq* of the French civil code.

ECJ, 31 March 1982, case 25/81, C.H.W.

An application for provisional measures to secure the delivery up of a document in order to prevent it from being used as evidence in an action concerning a husband's management of his wife's property does not fall within the scope of the 1968 Brussels Convention if such management is closely connected with the proprietary relationship resulting directly from the marriage bond.

ECJ, 27 February 1997, case C-220/95, van den Boogaard

A decision rendered in divorce proceedings ordering payment of a lump sum and transfer of ownership in certain property by one party to his or her former spouse must be regarded as relating to maintenance and therefore as falling within the scope of the 1968 Brussels Convention, if its purpose is to ensure the former spouse's maintenance. The fact that in its decision the court of origin disregarded a marriage contract is of no account in this regard.

Article 1(2)(b) [ex 1(2)(2)]

ECJ, 22 February 1979, case 133/78, Gourdain

As far as concerns bankruptcy, proceedings relating to the winding-up of insolvent companies or other legal persons, judicial arrangements, compositions and analogous proceedings, according to the various laws of the Contracting Parties relating to debtors who have declared themselves unable to meet their liabilities, insolvency or the collapse of the debtor's creditworthiness, which involve the intervention of the courts culminating in the compulsory 'liquidation des biens' in the interest of the general body of creditors of the person, firm or company, or at least in supervision by the courts, it is necessary, if decisions relating to bankruptcy and winding-up are to be excluded from the scope of the convention, that they must derive directly from the bankruptcy or winding-up and be closely connected with the proceedings for the 'liquidation des biens' or the 'reglement judiciaire'.
　　A decision such as that of a French civil court based on article 99 of the French law No 67–563 of 15 July 1967, ordering the de facto manager of a legal person to pay a certain sum into the assets of a company must be considered as given in the context of bankruptcy, proceedings relating to the winding-up of insolvent companies or other legal persons or analogous proceedings within the meaning of subparagraph 2 of the second paragraph of Article 1 of the 1968 Brussels Convention.

ECJ, 2 July 2009, case C-111/08, SCT Industri

The exception provided for in Article 1(2)(b) of Regulation No 44/2001 must be interpreted as applying to a judgment of a court of Member State A regarding registration of ownership of shares in a company having its registered office in Member State A, according to which the transfer of those shares was to be regarded as invalid on the ground that the court of Member State A did not recognise the powers of a liquidator from a Member State B in the context of insolvency proceedings conducted and closed in Member State B.

ECJ, 10 September 2009, case C-292/08, German Graphics

Article 25(2) of Regulation No 1346/2000 on insolvency proceedings must be interpreted as meaning that the words 'provided that that Convention is applicable' imply that, before it can be concluded that the recognition and enforcement provisions of Regulation No 44/2001 are applicable to judgments other than those referred to in Article 25(1) of Regulation No 1346/2000, it is necessary to determine whether such judgments fall outside the material scope of Regulation No 44/2001.

The exception provided for in Article 1(2)(b) of Regulation No 44/2001, read in conjunction with Article 7(1) of Regulation No 1346/2000, must be interpreted, account being taken of the provisions of Article 4(2)(b) of the latter regulation, as meaning that it does not apply to an action brought by a seller based on a reservation of title against a purchaser who is insolvent, where the asset covered by the reservation of title is situated in the Member State of the opening of those proceedings at the time of opening of those proceedings against that purchaser.

Article 1(2)(c) [ex 1(2)(3)]

ECJ, 14 November 2002, case C-271/00, Baten

Point 3 of the second paragraph of Article 1 of the 1968 Brussels Convention must be interpreted as meaning that the concept of 'social security' does not encompass the action under a right of recourse by which a public body seeks from a person governed by private law recovery in accordance with the rules of the ordinary law of sums paid by it by way of social assistance to the divorced spouse and the child of that person.

Article 1(2)(d) [ex 1(2)(4)]

ECJ, 17 November 1998, case C-391/95, Van Uden

Where the parties have validly excluded the jurisdiction of the courts in a dispute arising under a contract and have referred that dispute to arbitration, no provisional or protective measures may be ordered on the basis of Article 5(1) of the 1968 Brussels Convention.

ECJ, 25 July 1991, case C-190/89, Marc Rich

Article 1(4) of the 1968 Brussels Convention must be interpreted as meaning that the exclusion provided for therein extends to litigation pending before a national court concerning the appointment of an arbitrator, even if the existence or validity of an arbitration agreement is a preliminary issue in that litigation.

ECJ, 10 February 2009, case C-185/07, West Tankers

It is incompatible with Regulation No 44/2001 for a court of a Member State to make an order to restrain a person from commencing or continuing proceedings before the courts of another Member State on the ground that such proceedings would be contrary to an arbitration agreement.

Article 2

ECJ, 15 February 1989, case 32/88, Six Constructions

Where, in the case of a contract of employment, the obligation of the employee to carry out the agreed work was performed and has to be performed outside the territory of the Contracting States, Article 5(1) of the 1968 Brussels Convention is not applicable; in such a case jurisdiction is to be determined on the basis of the place of the defendant's domicile in accordance with Article 2 of the Convention.

ECJ, 19 February 2002, case C-256/00, Besix

The special jurisdictional rule in matters relating to a contract, laid down in Article 5(1) of the 1968 Brussels Convention, is not applicable where, as in the present case, the place of performance of the obligation in question cannot be determined because it consists in an undertaking not to do something which is not subject to any geographical limit and is therefore characterised by a multiplicity of places for its performance. In such a case, jurisdiction can be determined only by application of the general criterion laid down in the first paragraph of Article 2 of the Convention.

ECJ, 1 March 2005, case C-281/02, Owuzu

The 1968 Brussels Convention precludes a court of a Contracting State from declining the jurisdiction conferred on it by Article 2 of that Convention on the ground that a court of a non-Contracting State would be a more appropriate forum for the trial of the action even if the jurisdiction of no other Contracting State is in issue or the proceedings have no connecting factors to any other Contracting State.

Article 5(1)

ECJ, 6 October 1976, case 12/76, Industrie Tessili Italiana Como

The 'place of performance of the obligation in question' within the meaning of Article 5(1) of the 1968 Brussels Convention is to be determined in accordance with the law which governs the obligations in question according to the rules of conflict of laws of the court before which the matter is brought.

ECJ, 6 October 1976, case 14/76, de Bloos

In disputes in which the grantee of an exclusive sales concession is charging the grantor with having infringed the exclusive concession, the word 'obligation' contained in Article 5(1) of the 1968 Brussels Convention refers to the contractual obligation forming the basis of the legal proceedings, namely the obligation of the grantor which corresponds to the contractual right relied upon by the grantee in support of the application.

In disputes concerning the consequences of the infringement by the grantor of a contract conferring an exclusive concession, such as the payment of damages or the dissolution of the contract, the obligation to which reference must be made for the purposes of applying Article 5(1) of the Convention is that which the contract imposes on the grantor and the non-performance of which is relied upon by the grantee in support of the application for damages or for the dissolution of the contract.

In the case of actions for payment of compensation by way of damages, it is for the national court to ascertain whether, under the law applicable to the contract, an independent contractual obligation or an obligation replacing the unperformed contractual obligation is involved.

ECJ, 17 January 1980, case 56/79, Zelger

If the place of performance of a contractual obligation has been specified by the parties in a clause which is valid according to the national law applicable to the contract, the court for that place has jurisdiction to take cognisance of disputes relating to that obligation under Article 5(1) of the 1968 Brussels Convention, irrespective of whether the formal conditions provided for under article 17 have been observed.

ECJ, 4 March 1982, case 38/81, Effer

The plaintiff may invoke the jurisdiction of the courts of the place of performance in accordance with article 5(1) of the 1968 Brussels Convention even when the existence of the contract on which the claim is based is in dispute between the parties.

ECJ, 22 March 1983, case 34/82, Martin Peters Bauunternehmung

Obligations in regard to the payment of a sum of money which have their basis in the relationship existing between an association and its members by virtue of membership are 'matters relating to a contract' within the meaning of article 5(1) of the 1968 Brussels Convention.

It makes no difference in that regard whether the obligations in question arise simply from the act of becoming a member or from that act in conjunction with one or more decisions made by organs of the association.

ECJ, 15 January 1987, case 266/85, Shenavai

For the purposes of determining the place of performance within the meaning of Article 5(1) of the 1968 Brussels Convention, the obligation to be taken into consideration in a dispute concerning proceedings for the recovery of fees commenced by an architect commissioned to draw up plans for the building of houses is the contractual obligation which forms the actual basis of legal proceedings.

ECJ, 8 March 1988, case 9/87, Arcado

Proceedings relating to the wrongful repudiation of an independent commercial agency agreement and the payment of commission due under such an agreement are proceedings in matters relating to a contract within the meaning of Article 5(1) of the 1968 Brussels Convention.

ECJ, 15 May 1990, case C-365/88, Kongress Agentur Hagen

Where a defendant domiciled in a Contracting State is sued in a court of another Contracting State pursuant to Article 5(1) of the 1968 Brussels Convention, that court also has jurisdiction by virtue of Article 6(2) of the Convention to entertain an action on a warranty or guarantee brought against a person domiciled in a Contracting State other than that of the court seised of the original proceedings.

ECJ, 17 June 1992, case C-26/91, Handte

Article 5(1) of the 1968 Brussels Convention is to be understood as meaning that it does not apply to an action between a sub-buyer of goods and the manufacturer, who is not the seller, relating to defects in those goods or to their unsuitability for their intended purpose.

ECJ, 29 June 1994, case C-288/92, Custom-Made

Article 5(1) of the 1968 Brussels Convention must be interpreted as meaning that, in the case of a demand for payment made by a supplier to his customer under a contract of manufacture and supply, the place of performance of the obligation to pay the price is to be determined pursuant to the substantive law governing the obligation in dispute under the conflicts rules of the court seised, even where those rules refer to the application to the contract of provisions such as those of the Uniform Law on the International Sale of Goods, annexed to the Hague Convention of 1 July 1964.

ECJ, 9 January 1997, case C-383/95, Rutten

Article 5(1) of the 1968 Brussels Convention must be interpreted as meaning that where, in the performance of a contract of employment, an employee carries out his work in several Contracting States, the place where he habitually carries out his work, within the meaning of that provision, is the place where he has established the effective centre of his working activities. When identifying that place, it is necessary to take into account the fact that the employee spends most of his working time in one of the Contracting States in which he has an office where he organises his activities for his employer and to which he returns after each business trip abroad.

ECJ, 20 February 1997, case C-106/95, Mainschiffahrts -Genossenschaft

The 1968 Brussels Convention must be interpreted as meaning that an oral agreement on the place of performance which is designed not to determine the place where the person liable is actually to perform the obligations incumbent upon him, but solely to establish that the courts for a particular place have jurisdiction, is not governed by Article 5(1) of the Convention, but by Article 17, and is valid only if the requirements set out therein are complied with.

ECJ, 27 October 1998, case C-51/97, Réunion européenne

An action by which the consignee of goods found to be damaged on completion of a transport operation by sea and then by land, or by which his insurer who has been subrogated to his rights after compensating him, seeks redress for the damage suffered, relying on the bill of lading covering the maritime transport, not against the person who issued that document on his headed paper but against the person whom the plaintiff considered to be the actual maritime carrier, falls within the scope not of matters relating to a contract within the meaning of Article 5(1) of the 1968 Brussels Convention, but of matters relating to tort, delict or quasi-delict within the meaning of Article 5(3) of that Convention.

ECJ, 17 November 1998, case C-391/95, Van Uden

On a proper construction of Article 5(1) of 1968 Brussels Convention, the court which has jurisdiction by virtue of that provision also has jurisdiction to order provisional or protective measures, without that jurisdiction being subject to any further conditions.

Where the parties have validly excluded the jurisdiction of the courts in a dispute arising under a contract and have referred that dispute to arbitration, no provisional or protective measures may be ordered on the basis of Article 5(1) of the Convention.

ECJ, 5 October 1999, case C-420/97, Leathertex

On a proper construction of Article 5(1) of the 1968 Brussels Convention, the same court does not have jurisdiction to hear the whole of an action founded on two obligations of equal rank arising from the same contract when, according to the conflict rules of the State where that court is situated, one of those obligations is to be performed in that State and the other in another Contracting State.

ECJ, 19 February 2002, case C-256/00, Besix

The special jurisdictional rule in matters relating to a contract, laid down in Article 5(1) of the 1968 Brussels Convention, is not applicable where, as in the present case, the place of performance of the obligation in question cannot be determined because it consists in an undertaking not to do something which is not subject to any geographical limit and is therefore characterised by a multiplicity of places for its performance. In such a case, jurisdiction can be determined only by application of the general criterion laid down in the first paragraph of Article 2 of that Convention.

ECJ, 17 September 2002, case C-334/00, Fonderie Officine Meccaniche Tacconi

In circumstances such as those of the main proceedings, characterised by the absence of obligations freely assumed by one party towards another on the occasion of negotiations with a view to the formation of a contract and by a possible breach of rules of law, in particular the rule which requires the parties to act in good faith in such negotiations, an action founded on the pre-contractual liability of the defendant is a matter relating to tort, delict or quasi-delict within the meaning of Article 5(3) of the 1968 Brussels Convention.

ECJ, 5 February 2004, case C-265/02, Frahuil

Article 5(1) of the 1968 Brussels Convention must be interpreted as meaning that matters relating to a contract do not cover the obligation which a guarantor who paid customs duties under a guarantee obtained by the forwarding agent seeks to enforce in legal proceedings by way of subrogation to the rights of the customs authorities and by way of recourse against the owner of the goods, if the latter, who was not a party to the contract of guarantee, did not authorise the conclusion of that contract.

ECJ, 20 January 2005, case C-27/02, Engler

Legal proceedings by which a consumer seeks an order, under the law of the Contracting State in which he is domiciled, that a mail order company established in another Contracting State award a prize ostensibly won by him is contractual in nature for the purpose of Article 5(1) of the 1968 Brussels Convention, provided that, first, that company, with the intention of inducing the consumer to enter a contract, addresses to him in person a letter of such a kind as to give the impression that a prize will be awarded to him if he returns the 'payment notice' attached to the letter and, second, he accepts the conditions laid down by the vendor and does in fact claim payment of the prize announced.

On the other hand, even though the letter also contains a catalogue advertising goods for that company and a request for a 'trial without obligation', the fact that the award of the prize does not depend on an order for goods and that the consumer has not, in fact, placed such an order has no bearing on that interpretation.

ECJ, 3 May 2007, case C-386/05, Color Drack

The first indent of Article 5(1)(b) of Regulation No 44/2001 must be interpreted as applying where there are several places of delivery within a single Member State. In such a case, the court having jurisdiction to hear all the claims based on the contract for the sale of goods is that for the principal place of delivery, which must be determined on the basis of economic criteria. In the absence of determining factors for establishing the principal place of delivery, the plaintiff may sue the defendant in the court for the place of delivery of its choice

ECJ, 23 April 2009, case C-533/07, Falco Privatstiftung

The second indent of Article 5(1)(b) of Regulation No 44/2001 is to be interpreted to the effect that a contract under which the owner of an intellectual property right grants its contractual partner the right to use that right in return for remuneration is not a contract for the provision of services within the meaning of that provision.

In order to determine, under Article 5(1)(a) of Regulation No 44/2001, the court having jurisdiction over an application for remuneration owed pursuant to a contract under which the owner of an intellectual property right grants to its contractual partner the right to use that right, reference must continue to be made to the principles which result from the case-law of the Court of Justice on Article 5(1) of the 1968 Brussels Convention.

ECJ, 9 July 2009, case C-204/08, Rehder

The second indent of Article 5(1)(b) of Regulation No 44/2001 must be interpreted as meaning that, in the case of air transport of passengers from one Member State to another Member State, carried out on the basis of a contract with only one airline, which is the operating carrier, the court having jurisdiction to deal with a claim for compensation founded on that transport contract and on Regulation No 261/2004 establishing common rules on compensation and assistance to passengers in the event of denied boarding and of cancellation or long delay of flights, and repealing Regulation No 295/91, is that, at the applicant's choice, which has territorial jurisdiction over the place of departure or place of arrival of the aircraft, as those places are agreed in that contract.

CJ, 25 February 2010, case C-381/08, Car Trim

Article 5(1)(b) of Regulation No 44/2001 must be interpreted as meaning that where the purpose of contracts is the supply of goods to be manufactured or produced and, even though the purchaser has specified certain requirements with regard to the provision, fabrication and delivery of the components to be produced, the purchaser has not supplied the materials and the supplier is responsible for the quality of the goods and their compliance with the contract, those contracts must be classified as a 'sale of goods' within the meaning of the first indent of Article 5(1)(b) of that regulation.

The first indent of Article 5(1)(b) of Regulation No 44/2001 must be interpreted as meaning that, in the case of a sale involving carriage of goods, the place where, under the contract, the goods sold were delivered or should have been delivered must be determined on the basis of the provisions of that contract. Where it is impossible to determine the place of delivery on that basis, without reference to the substantive law applicable to the contract, that place is the place where the physical transfer of the goods took place, as a result of which the purchaser obtained, or should have obtained, actual power of disposal over those goods at the final destination of the sales transaction.

CJ, 11 March 2010, case C-19/09, Wood Floor Solutions

The second indent of Article 5(1)(b) of Regulation No 44/2001 must be interpreted as meaning that that provision is applicable in the case where services are provided in several Member States.

The second indent of Article 5(1)(b) of Regulation No 44/2001 must be interpreted as meaning that where services are provided in several Member States, the court which has jurisdiction to hear and determine all the claims arising from the contract is the court in whose jurisdiction the place of the main provision of services is situated. For a commercial agency contract, that place is the place of the main provision of services by the agent, as it appears from the provisions of the contract or, in the absence of such provisions, the actual performance of that contract or, where it cannot be established on that basis, the place where the agent is domiciled.

Article 5(2)

ECJ, 27 February 1997, case C-220/95, van den Boogaard

A decision rendered in divorce proceedings ordering payment of a lump sum and transfer of ownership in certain property by one party to his or her former spouse must be regarded as relating to maintenance and therefore as falling within the scope of the 1968 Brussels Convention, if its purpose is to ensure the former spouse's maintenance. The fact that in its decision the court of origin disregarded a marriage contract is of no account in this regard.

ECJ, 20 March 1997, case C-295/95, Farrell

The first limb of Article 5(2) of the 1968 Brussels Convention must be interpreted as meaning that the term 'maintenance creditor' covers any person applying for maintenance, including a person bringing a maintenance action for the first time.

ECJ, 15 January 2004, case C-433/01, Freistaat Bayern

Article 5(2) of the 1968 Brussels Convention must be interpreted as meaning that it cannot be relied on by a public body which seeks, in an action for recovery, reimbursement of sums paid under public law by way of an education grant to a maintenance creditor, to whose rights it is subrogated against the maintenance debtor.

Article 5(3)

ECJ, 30 November 1976, case 21/76, Mines de Potasse d'Alsace

Where the place of the happening of the event which may give rise to liability in tort, delict or quasidelict and the place where that event results in damage are not identical, the expression 'place where the harmful event occurred', in Article 5(3) of the 1968 Brussels Convention, must be understood as being intended to cover both the place where the damage occurred and the place of the event giving rise to it.

The result is that the defendant may be sued, at the option of the plaintiff, either in the courts for the place where the damage occurred or in the courts for the place of the event which gives rise to and is at the origin of that damage.

ECJ, 27 September 1988, case 189/87, Kalfelis

The term 'matters relating to tort, delict or quasi-delict' used in Article 5(3) of the 1968 Brussels Convention must be regarded as an independent concept covering all actions which seek to establish the liability of a defendant and which are not related to a 'contract' within the meaning of Article 5(1).

A court which has jurisdiction under Article 5(3) over an action in so far as it is based on tort or delict does not have jurisdiction over that action in so far as it is not so based.

ECJ, 11 January 1990, case C-220/88, Dumez

The rule on jurisdiction laid down in Article 5(3) of the 1968 Brussels Convention cannot be interpreted as permitting a plaintiff pleading damage which he claims to be the consequence of the harm suffered by other persons who were direct victims of the harmful act to bring proceedings against the perpetrator of that act in the courts of the place in which he himself ascertained the damage to his assets.

ECJ, 26 March 1992, case C-261/90, Reichert

An action provided for by national law, such as the action paulienne in French law, whereby a creditor seeks to obtain the revocation in regard to him of a transfer of rights *in rem* in immovable property by his debtor in a way which the creditor regards as being in fraud of his rights does not come within the scope of Articles 5(3), 16(5) or 24 of the 1968 Brussels Convention.

ECJ, 7 March 1995, case C-68/93, Fiona Shevill

On a proper construction of the expression 'place where the harmful event occurred' in Article 5(3) of the 1968 Brussels Convention, the victim of a libel by a newspaper article distributed in several Contracting States may bring an action for damages against the publisher either before the courts of the Contracting State of the place where the publisher of the defamatory publication is established, which have jurisdiction to award damages for all the harm caused by the defamation, or before the courts of each Contracting State in which the publication was distributed and where the victim claims to have suffered injury to his reputation, which have jurisdiction to rule solely in respect of the harm caused in the State of the court seised.

The criteria for assessing whether the event in question is harmful and the evidence required of the existence and extent of the harm alleged by the victim of the defamation are not governed by the Convention but by the substantive law determined by the national conflict of laws rules of the court seised, provided that the effectiveness of the Convention is not thereby impaired.

ECJ, 19 September 1995, case C-364/93, Marinari

The term 'place where the harmful event occurred' in Article 5(3) of the 1968 Brussels Convention does not, on a proper interpretation, cover the place where the victim claims to have suffered financial damage following upon initial damage arising and suffered by him in another Contracting State.

ECJ, 27 October 1998, case C-51/97, Réunion européenne

The place where the consignee of the goods, on completion of a transport operation by sea and then by land, merely discovered the existence of the damage to the goods delivered to him cannot serve to determine the 'place where the harmful event occurred' within the meaning of Article 5(3) of the 1968 Brussels Convention, as interpreted by the Court.

ECJ, 17 September 2002, case C-334/00, Fonderie Officine Meccaniche Tacconi

In circumstances such as those of the main proceedings, characterised by the absence of obligations freely assumed by one party towards another on the occasion of negotiations with a view to the formation of a contract and by a possible breach of rules of law, in particular the rule which requires the parties to act in good faith in such negotiations, an action founded on the pre-contractual liability of the defendant is a matter relating to tort, delict or quasi-delict within the meaning of Article 5(3) of the 1968 Brussels Convention.

ECJ, 1 October 2002, case C-167/00, Henkel

The rules on jurisdiction laid down in the 1968 Brussels Convention must be interpreted as meaning that a preventive action brought by a consumer protection organisation for the purpose of preventing a trader from using terms considered to be unfair in contracts with private individuals is a matter relating to tort, delict or quasi-delict within the meaning of Article 5(3) of the Convention.

ECJ, 5 February 2004, case C-18/02, DFDS Torline

Article 5(3) of the 1968 Brussels Convention must be interpreted as meaning that a case concerning the legality of industrial action, in respect of which exclusive jurisdiction belongs, in accordance with the law of the Contracting State concerned, to a court other than the court which has jurisdiction to try the claims for compensation for the damage caused by that industrial action, falls within the definition of tort, delict or quasi-delict.

For the application of Article 5(3) of the Convention to a situation such as that in the dispute in the main proceedings, it is sufficient that that industrial action is a necessary precondition of sympathy action which may result in harm.

The application of Article 5(3) of the Convention is not affected by the fact that the implementation of industrial action was suspended by the party giving notice pending a ruling on its legality.

In circumstances such as those in the main proceedings, Article 5(3) must be interpreted as meaning that the damage resulting from industrial action taken by a trade union in a Contracting State to which a ship registered in another Contracting State sails must not necessarily be regarded as having occurred in the flag State, with the result that the shipowner can bring an action for damages against that trade union in the flag State.

ECJ, 10 June 2004, case C-168/02, Kronhofer

Article 5(3) of the 1968 Brussels Convention must be interpreted as meaning that the expression 'place where the harmful event occurred' does not refer to the place where the claimant is domiciled or where 'his assets are concentrated' by reason only of the fact that he has suffered financial damage there resulting from the loss of part of his assets which arose and was incurred in another Contracting State.

CFI, Order 5 September 2007, case T-295/05, Document Security Systems

The action for patent infringement lodged against the ECB before the Court of First Instance is inadmissible since no provision of the Treaty confers it such competence, that belongs exclusively to national courts.

ECJ, 16 July 2009, case C-189/08, Zuid-Chemie

Article 5(3) of Regulation No 44/2001 must be interpreted as meaning that, in the context of a dispute such as that in the main proceedings, the words 'place where the harmful event occurred' designate the place where the initial damage occurred as a result of the normal use of the product for the purpose for which it was intended.

Article 5(5)

ECJ, 6 October 1976, case 14/76, de Bloos

When the grantee of an exclusive sales concession is not subject either to the control or to the direction of the grantor, he cannot be regarded as being at the head of a branch, agency or other establishment of the grantor within the meaning of article 5(5) of the 1968 Brussels Convention.

ECJ, 22 November 1978, case 33/78, Somafer

The need to ensure legal certainty and equality of rights and obligations for the parties as regards the power to derogate from the general jurisdiction of Article 2 requires an independent interpretation, common to all the Contracting States, of the concepts in Article 5(5) of the 1968 Brussels Convention.

The concept of branch, agency or other establishment implies a place of business which has the appearance of permanency, such as the extension of a parent body, has a management and is materially equipped to negotiate business with third parties so that the latter, although knowing that there will if necessary be a legal link with the parent body, the head office of which is abroad, do not have to deal directly with such parent body but may transact business at the place of business constituting the extension.

The concept of 'operations' comprises:

—   actions relating to rights and contractual or non-contractual obligations concerning the management properly so-called of the agency, branch or other establishment itself such as those concerning the situation of the building where such entity is established or the local engagement of staff to work there;

—   actions relating to undertakings which have been entered into at the above-mentioned place of business in the name of the parent body and which must be performed in the Contracting State where the place of business is established and also actions concerning non-contractual obligations arising from the activities in which the branch, agency or other establishment within the above defined meaning, has engaged at the place in which it is established on behalf of the parent body.

It is in each case for the court before which the matter comes to find the facts whereon it may be established that an effective place of business exists and to determine the legal position by reference to the concept of 'operations' as above defined.

ECJ, 18 March 1981, case 139/80, Blanckaert & Willelms

An independent commercial agent who merely negotiates business (Handelsvertreter (Vermittlungsvertreter)), in as much as his legal status leaves him basically free to arrange his own work and decide what proportion of his time to devote to the interests of the undertaking which he agrees to represent and whom that undertaking may not prevent from representing at the same time several firms competing in the same manufacturing or marketing sector, and who, moreover, merely transmits orders to the parent undertaking without being involved in either their terms or their execution, does not have the character of a branch, agency or other establishment within the meaning of Article 5(5) of the 1968 Brussels Convention.

ECJ, 9 December 1987, case 218/86, SAR Schotte

Article 5(5) of the 1968 Brussels Convention must be interpreted as applying to a case in which a legal entity established in a Contracting State maintains no dependent branch, agency or other establishment in another Contracting State but nevertheless pursues its activities there through an independent company with the same name and identical management which negotiates and conducts business in its name and which it uses as an extension of itself.

ECJ, 6 April 1995, case C-439/93, Lloyd's Register

A branch, agency or other ancillary establishment within the meaning of Article 5(5) of the 1968 Brussels Convention is an entity capable of being the principal, or even exclusive, interlocutor for third parties in the negotiation of contracts.

There does not necessarily have to be a close link between the entity with which a customer conducts negotiations and places an order and the place where the order will be performed. Accordingly, undertakings may form part of the operations of an ancillary establishment within the meaning of Article 5(5) of the Convention even though they are to be performed outside the Contracting State where it is situated, possibly by another ancillary establishment.

The expression 'dispute arising out of the operations of a branch, agency or other establishment' in Article 5(5) of the Convention, does not presuppose that the undertakings in question entered into by the branch in the name of its parent body are to be performed in the Contracting State in which the branch is established.

Article 6(1)

ECJ, 27 September 1988, case 189/87, Kalfelis

For Article 6(1) of the 1968 Brussels Convention to apply there must exist between the various actions brought by the same plaintiff against different defendants a connection of such a kind that it is expedient to determine the actions together in order to avoid the risk of irreconcilable judgments resulting from separate proceedings.

ECJ, 27 October 1998, case C-51/97, Réunion européenne

Article 6(1) of the 1968 Brussels Convention must be interpreted as meaning that a defendant domiciled in a Contracting State cannot be sued in another Contracting State before a court seised of an action against a co-defendant not domiciled in a Contracting State on the ground that the dispute is indivisible rather than merely displaying a connection.

ECJ, 13 July 2006, case C-539/03, Roche

Article 6(1) of the 1968 Brussels Convention must be interpreted as meaning that it does not apply in European patent infringement proceedings involving a number of companies established in various Contracting States in respect of acts committed in one or more of those States even where those companies, which belong to the same group, may have acted in an identical or similar manner in accordance with a common policy elaborated by one of them.

ECJ, 11 October 2007, case C-98/06, Freeport

Article 6(1) of Regulation No 44/2001 is to be interpreted as meaning that the fact that claims brought against a number of defendants have different legal bases does not preclude application of that provision.

Article 6(1) of Regulation No 44/2001 applies where claims brought against different defendants are connected when the proceedings are instituted, that is to say, where it is expedient to hear and determine them together to avoid the risk of irreconcilable judgments resulting from separate proceedings, without there being any further need to establish separately that the claims were not brought with the sole object of ousting the jurisdiction of the courts of the Member State where one of the defendants is domiciled.

ECJ, 22 May 2008, case C-462/06, Glaxosmith

The rule of special jurisdiction provided for in Article 6(1) of Regulation No 44/2001 cannot be applied to a dispute falling under Section 5 of Chapter II of that Regulation concerning the jurisdiction rules applicable to individual contracts of employment.

Article 6(2)

ECJ, 15 May 1990, case C-365/88, Kongress Agentur Hagen

Where a defendant domiciled in a Contracting State is sued in a court of another Contracting State pursuant to Article 5(1) of the 1968 Brussels Convention, that court also has jurisdiction by virtue of Article 6(2) of the Convention to entertain an action on a warranty or guarantee brought against a person domiciled in a Contracting State other than that of the court seised of the original proceedings.

Article 6(2) must be interpreted as meaning that it does not require the national court to accede to the request for leave to bring an action on a warranty or guarantee and that the national court may apply the procedural rules of its national law in order to determine whether that action is admissible, provided that the effectiveness of the Convention in that regard is not impaired and, in particular, that leave to bring the action on the warranty or guarantee is not refused on the ground that the third party resides or is domiciled in a Contracting State other than that of the court seised of the original proceedings.

ECJ, 26 May 2005, case C-77/04, GIE Réunion européenne

Article 6(2) of the 1968 Brussels Convention is applicable to third-party proceedings between insurers based on multiple insurance, in so far as there is a sufficient connection between the original proceedings and the third-party proceedings to support the conclusion that the choice of forum does not amount to an abuse.

Article 6(3)

ECJ, 13 July 1995, case C-341/93, Danvaern

Article 6(3) of the 1968 Brussels Convention applies only to claims by defendants which seek the pronouncement of a separate judgment or decree. It does not apply to the situation where a defendant raises, as a pure defence, a claim which he allegedly has against the plaintiff. The defences which may be raised and the conditions under which they may be raised are governed by national law.

Articles 8–14 [ex 7–12a]

ECJ, 13 July 2000, case C-412/98, Group Josi

Title II of the 1968 Brussels Convention is in principle applicable where the defendant has its domicile or seat in a Contracting State, even if the plaintiff is domiciled in a non-member country. It would be otherwise only in exceptional cases where an express provision of that Convention provides that the application of the rule of jurisdiction which it sets out is dependent on the plaintiff's domicile being in a Contracting State.

The rules of special jurisdiction in matters relating to insurance set out in Articles 7 to 12a of that Convention do not cover disputes between a reinsurer and a reinsured in connection with a reinsurance contract.

ECJ, 12 May 2005, case C-112/03, SFI Peloux

A jurisdiction clause conforming with Article 12(3) of the 1968 Brussels Convention cannot be relied on against a beneficiary under that contract who has not expressly subscribed to that clause and is domiciled in a Contracting State other than that of the policy-holder and the insurer.

ECJ, 26 May 2005, case C-77/04, GIE Réunion européenne

Third-party proceedings between insurers based on multiple insurance are not subject to the provisions of Section 3 of Title II of the 1968 Brussels Convention.

ECJ, 13 December 2007, case C-463/06, FBTO Schadeverzekeringen

The reference in Article 11(2) of Regulation No 44/2001 to Article 9(1)(b) of that Regulation is to be interpreted as meaning that the injured party may bring an action directly against the insurer before the courts for the place in a Member State where that injured party is domiciled, provided that such a direct action is permitted and the insurer is domiciled in a Member State.

ECJ, 17 September 2009, case C-347/08, Voralberg Gebietskrankenkasse

The reference in Article 11(2) of Regulation No 44/2001 to Article 9(1)(b) thereof must be interpreted as meaning that a social security institution, acting as the statutory assignee of the rights of the directly injured party in a motor accident, may not bring an action directly in the courts of its Member State of establishment against the insurer of the person allegedly responsible for the accident, where that insurer is established in another Member State.

CJ, 20 May 2010, case C-111/09, ČPP

Article 24 of Regulation No 44/2001 must be interpreted as meaning that the court seised, where the rules in Section 3 of Chapter II of the Regulation were not complied with, must declare itself to have jurisdiction where the defendant enters an appearance and does not contest that court's jurisdiction, since entering an appearance in that way amounts to a tacit prorogation of jurisdiction.

Articles 15–17 [ex 13–15]

ECJ, 21 June 1978, case 150/77, Bertrand

The concept of the sale of goods on instalment credit terms within the meaning of Article 13 of the 1968 Brussels Convention is not to be understood to extend to the sale of a machine which one company agrees to make to another company on the basis of a price to be paid by way of bills of exchange spread over a period.

ECJ, 19 January 1993, case C-89/91, Shearson Lehmann Hutton

Article 13 of the 1968 Brussels Convention is to be interpreted as meaning that a plaintiff who is acting in pursuance of his trade or professional activity and who is not, therefore, himself a consumer party to one of the contracts listed in the first paragraph of that provision, may not enjoy the benefit of the rules of special jurisdiction laid down by the Convention concerning consumer contracts.

ECJ, 15 September 1994, case C-318/93, Brenner and Noller

The courts of the State in which the consumer is domiciled have jurisdiction in proceedings under the second alternative in the first paragraph of Article 14 of the 1968 Brussels Convention if the other party to the contract is domiciled in a Contracting State or is deemed under the second paragraph of Article 13 of that Convention to be so domiciled.

ECJ, 3 July 1997, case C-269/95, Benincasa

The first paragraph of Article 13 and the first paragraph of Article 14 of the 1968 Brussels Convention must be interpreted as meaning that a plaintiff who has concluded a contract with a view to pursuing a trade or profession, not at the present time but in the future, may not be regarded as a consumer.

ECJ, 27 April 1999, case C-99/96, Mietz

Article 13, first paragraph, point 1, of the 1968 Brussels Convention must be construed as not applying to a contract between two parties having the following characteristics, that is to say, a contract:
    —   relating to the manufacture by the first contracting party of goods corresponding to a standard model, to which certain alterations have been made;
    —   by which the first contracting party has undertaken to transfer the property in those goods to the second contracting party, who has undertaken, by way of consideration, to pay the price in several instalments; and
    —   in which provision is made for the final instalment to be paid before possession of the goods is transferred definitively to the second contracting party.
    It is in this regard irrelevant that the contracting parties have described their contract as a 'contract of sale'. A contract having the characteristics mentioned above is however to be classified as a contract for the supply of services or of goods within the meaning of Article 13, first paragraph, point 3, of the 1968 Brussels Convention. It is for the national court, should the need arise, to determine whether the particular case before it involves a supply of services or a supply of goods.

ECJ, 1 October 2002, case C-167/00, Henkel

The rules on jurisdiction laid down in the 1968 Brussels Convention must be interpreted as meaning that a preventive action brought by a consumer protection organisation for the purpose of preventing a trader from using terms considered to be unfair in contracts with private individuals is a matter relating to tort, delict or quasi-delict within the meaning of Article 5(3) of the Convention.

ECJ, 11 July 2002, case C-96/00, Gabriel

The jurisdiction rules set out in the 1968 Brussels Convention are to be construed as meaning that judicial proceedings by which a consumer seeks an order, in the Contracting State in which he is domiciled and pursuant to that State's legislation, requiring a mail-order company established in another Contracting State to pay him a financial benefit in circumstances where that company had sent to that consumer in person a letter likely to create the impression that a prize would be awarded to him on condition that he ordered goods to a specified amount, and where that consumer actually placed such an order in the State of his domicile without, however, obtaining payment of that financial benefit, are contractual in nature in the sense contemplated in Article 13, first paragraph, point 3, of that Convention.

ECJ, 20 January 2005, case C-464/01, Gruber

The rules of jurisdiction laid down by the 1968 Brussels Convention must be interpreted as follows:
    —   a person who concludes a contract for goods intended for purposes which are in part within and in part outside his trade or profession may not rely on the special rules of jurisdiction laid down in Articles 13 to 15 of the Convention, unless the trade or

professional purpose is so limited as to be negligible in the overall context of the supply, the fact that the private element is predominant being irrelevant in that respect;

— it is for the court seised to decide whether the contract at issue was concluded in order to satisfy, to a non-negligible extent, needs of the business of the person concerned or whether, on the contrary, the trade or professional purpose was negligible;

— to that end, that court must take account of all the relevant factual evidence objectively contained in the file. On the other hand, it must not take account of facts or circumstances of which the other party to the contract may have been aware when the contract was concluded, unless the person who claims the capacity of consumer behaved in such a way as to give the other party to the contract the legitimate impression that he was acting for the purposes of his business.

ECJ, 20 January 2005, case C-27/02, Engler

The rules of jurisdiction of the must be interpreted in the following way:

— legal proceedings by which a consumer seeks an order, under the law of the Contracting State in which he is domiciled, that a mail order company established in another Contracting State award a prize ostensibly won by him is contractual in nature for the purpose of Article 5(1) of that Convention, provided that, first, that company, with the intention of inducing the consumer to enter a contract, addresses to him in person a letter of such a kind as to give the impression that a prize will be awarded to him if he returns the 'payment notice' attached to the letter and, second, he accepts the conditions laid down by the vendor and does in fact claim payment of the prize announced;

— on the other hand, even though the letter also contains a catalogue advertising goods for that company and a request for a 'trial without obligation', the fact that the award of the prize does not depend on an order for goods and that the consumer has not, in fact, placed such an order has no bearing on that interpretation.

ECJ, 14 May 2009, case C-180/06, Ilsinger

In a situation such as that at issue in the main proceedings, in which a consumer seeks, in accordance with the legislation of the Member State in which he is domiciled and before the court for the place in which he resides, an order requiring a mail-order company established in another Member State to pay a prize which that consumer has apparently won, and

— where that company, with the aim of encouraging that consumer to conclude a contract, sent a letter addressed to him personally of such a kind as to give him the impression that he would be awarded a prize if he requested payment by returning the 'prize claim certificate' attached to that letter;

— but without the award of that prize depending on an order for goods offered for sale by that company or on a trial order, the rules on jurisdiction laid down by Regulation No 44/2001 must be interpreted as follows:

— such legal proceedings brought by the consumer are covered by Article 15(1) (c) of that Regulation, on condition that the professional vendor has undertaken in law to pay that prize to the consumer;

— where that condition has not been fulfilled, such proceedings are covered by Article 15(1)(c) of Regulation No 44/2001 only if the consumer has in fact placed an order with that professional vendor.

CJ, 7 December 2010, joined cases C-585/08 and C-144/09, Pammer,

A contract concerning a voyage by freighter, such as that at issue in the main proceedings in Case C-585/08, is a contract of transport which, for an inclusive price, provides for a combination of travel and accommodation within the meaning of Article 15(3) of Council Regulation (EC) No 44/2001.

In order to determine whether a trader whose activity is presented on its website or on that of an intermediary can be considered to be 'directing' its activity to the Member State of the consumer's domicile, within the meaning of Article 15(1)(c) of Regulation No 44/2001, it should be ascertained whether, before the conclusion of any contract with the consumer, it is apparent from those websites and the trader's overall activity that the trader was envisaging doing business with consumers domiciled in one or more Member States, including the Member State of that consumer's domicile, in the sense that it was minded to conclude a contract with them.

The following matters, the list of which is not exhaustive, are capable of constituting evidence from which it may be concluded that the trader's activity is directed to the Member State of the consumer's domicile, namely the international nature of the activity, mention of itineraries from other Member States for going to the place where the trader is established, use of a language or a currency other than the language or currency generally used in the Member State in which the trader is established with the possibility of making and confirming the reservation in that other language, mention of telephone numbers with an international code, outlay of expenditure on an internet referencing service in order to facilitate access to the trader's site or that of its intermediary by consumers domiciled in other Member States, use of a top-level domain name other than that of the Member State in which the trader is established, and mention of an international clientele composed of customers domiciled in various Member States. It is for the national courts to ascertain whether such evidence exists.

On the other hand, the mere accessibility of the trader's or the intermediary's website in the Member State in which the consumer is domiciled is insufficient. The same is true of mention of an email address and of other contact details, or of use of a language or a currency which are the language and/or currency generally used in the Member State in which the trader is established.

Articles 18–21 [Ex 5(1) and 17 as concerns employment contracts][1]

ECJ, 15 February 1989, case 32/88, Six Constructions

Where, in the case of a contract of employment, the obligation of the employee to carry out the agreed work was performed and has to be performed outside the territory of the

---

[1]   The provisions of Regulation No 44/2001 on employment contracts supersede the ECJ judgment 26 May 1982, case 133/81, *Ivenel* ('The obligation to be taken into account for the purposes of the application of article 5(1) of the 1968 Brussels Convention in the case of claims based on different obligations arising under contract of employment as a representative binding a worker to an undertaking is the obligation which characterizes the contract') as well as partially the judgment 15 February 1989, case 32/88, *Six Constructions* ('Article 5(1) of the 1968 Brussels Convention must be interpreted as meaning that, as regards contracts of employment, the obligation to be taken into consideration is that which characterizes such contracts, in particular the obligation to carry out the agreed work'). [Note of the Editor]

Contracting States, Article 5(1) of the 1968 Brussels Convention is not applicable; in such a case jurisdiction is to be determined on the basis of the place of the defendant's domicile in accordance with Article 2 of the Convention.

ECJ, 13 July 1993, case C-125/92, Mulox

Article 5(1) of the 1968 Brussels Convention must be interpreted as meaning that, in the case of a contract of employment in pursuance of which the employee performs his work in more than one Contracting State, the place of performance of the obligation characterising the contract, within the meaning of that provision, is the place where or from which the employee principally discharges his obligations towards his employer.

ECJ, 27 February 2002, case C-37/00, Weber

Work carried out by an employee on fixed or floating installations positioned on or above the part of the continental shelf adjacent to a Contracting State, in the context of the prospecting and/or exploitation of its natural resources, is to be regarded as work carried out in the territory of that State for the purposes of applying Article 5(1) of the 1968 Brussels Convention.

    Article 5(1) of the Convention must be interpreted as meaning that where an employee performs the obligations arising under his contract of employment in several Contracting States the place where he habitually works, within the meaning of that provision, is the place where, or from which, taking account of all the circumstances of the case, he in fact performs the essential part of his duties vis-a-vis his employer.

    In the case of a contract of employment under which an employee performs for his employer the same activities in more than one Contracting State, it is necessary, in principle, to take account of the whole of the duration of the employment relationship in order to identify the place where the employee habitually works, within the meaning of Article 5(1).

    Failing other criteria, that will be the place where the employee has worked the longest.

    It will only be otherwise if, in light of the facts of the case, the subject-matter of the dispute is more closely connected with a different place of work, which would, in that case, be the relevant place for the purposes of applying Article 5(1) of the Convention.

    In the event that the criteria laid down by the Court of Justice do not enable the national court to identify the habitual place of work, as referred to in Article 5(1) of the Convention, the employee will have the choice of suing his employer either in the courts for the place where the business which engaged him is situated, or in the courts of the Contracting State in whose territory the employer is domiciled.

    National law applicable to the main dispute has no bearing on the interpretation of the concept of the place where an employee habitually works, within the meaning of Article 5(1) of the Convention.

ECJ, 10 April 2003, case C-437/00, Pugliese

Article 5(1) of the 1968 Brussels Convention must be interpreted as meaning that, in a dispute between an employee and a first employer, the place where the employee performs his obligations to a second employer can be regarded as the place where he habitually carries out his work when the first employer, with respect to whom the employee's contractual obligations are suspended, has, at the time of the conclusion of the second contract of employment, an interest in the performance of the service by the employee to the second employer in a place decided on by the latter. The existence of such an interest must be determined on a comprehensive basis, taking into consideration all the circumstances of the case.

Article 5(1) of the 1968 Brussels Convention must be interpreted as meaning that, in matters relating to contracts of employment, the place where the employee carries out his work is the only place of performance of an obligation which can be taken into consideration in order to determine which court has jurisdiction.

ECJ, 22 May 2008, case C-462/06, Glaxosmith

The rule of special jurisdiction provided for in Article 6(1) of Regulation No 44/2001 cannot be applied to a dispute falling under Section 5 of Chapter II of that Regulation concerning the jurisdiction rules applicable to individual contracts of employment.

Article 22(1) [ex 16(1)]

ECJ, 14 December 1977, case 73/77, Sanders

The concept of 'matters relating to tenancies of immovable property' within the context of Article 16 of the 1968 Brussels Convention must not be interpreted as including an agreement to rent under a usufructuary lease a retail business ('verpachting van een winkelbedrijf') carried on in immovable property rented from a third person by the lessor.

The fact that there is a dispute as to the existence of the agreement which forms the subject of the action does not affect the reply given as regards the applicability of Article 16 of the Convention.

ECJ, 15 January 1985, case 241/83, Rösler

Article 16(1) of the 1968 Brussels Convention applies to all lettings of immovable property, even for a short term and even where they relate only to the use and occupation of a holiday home.

All disputes concerning the obligations of the landlord or of the tenant under a tenancy, in particular those concerning the existence of tenancies or the interpretation of the terms thereof, their duration, the giving up of possession to the landlord, the repairing of damage caused by the tenant or the recovery of rent and of incidental charges payable by the tenant, such as charges for the consumption of water, gas and electricity, fall within the exclusive jurisdiction conferred by article 16(1) of the Convention on the courts of the State in which the property is situated. On the other hand, disputes which are only indirectly related to the use of the property let, such as those concerning the loss of holiday enjoyment and travel expenses, do not fall within the exclusive jurisdiction conferred by that Article.

ECJ, 6 July 1988, case 158/87, Scherrens

Article 16(1) of the 1968 Brussels Convention must be interpreted as meaning that, in a dispute as to the existence of a lease relating to immovable property situated in two Contracting States, exclusive jurisdiction over the immovable property situated in each contracting State is held by the courts of that State.

ECJ, 26 February 1992, case C-280/90, Hacker

Article 16(1) of the 1968 Brussels Convention is to be interpreted as not applying to a contract concluded in a Contracting State whereby a business organising travel with its seat in that State undertakes to procure for a client domiciled in the same State the use for several weeks of holiday accommodation not owned by it in another Contracting State, and to book the travel arrangements.

ECJ, 17 May 1994, case C-294/92, Webb

An action for a declaration that a person holds immovable property as trustee and for an order requiring that person to execute such documents as should be required to vest the legal ownership in the plaintiff does not constitute an action *in rem* within the meaning of Article 16(1) of the 1968 Brussels Convention.

ECJ, 9 June 1994, case C-292/93, Lieber

A claim for compensation for use of a dwelling after the annulment of a transfer of ownership is not included in the matters governed by Article 16(1) of the 1968 Brussels Convention.

ECJ, 27 January 2000, case C-8/98, Dansommer

The rule laid down in Article 16(1)(a) of the 1968 Brussels Convention conferring exclusive jurisdiction in proceedings having as their object tenancies of immovable property is applicable to an action for damages for taking poor care of premises and causing damage to accommodation which a private individual had rented for a few weeks' holiday, even where the action is not brought directly by the owner of the property but by a professional tour operator from whom the person in question had rented the accommodation and who has brought legal proceedings after being subrogated to the rights of the owner of the property.

The ancillary clauses relating to insurance in the event of cancellation and to guarantee of repayment of the price paid by the client, which are contained in the general terms and conditions of the contract concluded between that organiser and the tenant, and which do not form the subject of the dispute in the main proceedings, do not affect the nature of the tenancy as a tenancy of immovable property within the meaning of that provision of the Convention.

ECJ, Order 5 April 2001, case C-518/99, Gaillard

An action for rescission of a contract for the sale of land and consequential damages is not within the scope of the rules on exclusive jurisdiction in proceedings which have as their object rights *in rem* in immovable property under Article 16(1) of the 1968 Brussels Convention.

ECJ, 13 October 2005, case C-73/04, Klein and Klein

On a proper construction of Article 16(1)(a) of the 1968 Brussels Convention, that Article does not apply to a club membership contract which, in return for a membership fee which represents the major part of the total price, allows members to acquire a right to use on a time-share basis immoveable property of a specified type in a specified location and provides for the affiliation of members to a service which enables them to exchange their right of use.

ECJ, 18 May 2006, case C-343/04, CEZ

Article 16(1)(a) of the 1968 Brussels Convention must be interpreted as meaning that an action which, like that brought under Paragraph 364(2) of the Allgemeines Bürgerliches Gesetzbuch (Austrian Civil Code) in the main proceedings, seeks to prevent a nuisance affecting or likely to affect land belonging to the applicant, caused by ionising radiation emanating from a nuclear power station situated on the territory of a neighbouring State to that in which the land is situated, does not fall within the scope of that provision.

Article 22(2) [ex 16(2)]

ECJ, 2 October 2008, case C-372/07, Hassett and Doherty

Point 2 of Article 22 of Regulation No 44/2001 is to be interpreted as meaning that proceedings, such as those at issue before the referring court, in the context of which one of the parties alleges that a decision adopted by an organ of a company has infringed rights that it claims under that company's Articles of Association, do not concern the validity of the decisions of the organs of a company within the meaning of that provision.

Article 22(4) [ex 16(4)]

ECJ, 15 November 1983, case 288/82, Duijnstee

The term 'proceedings concerned with the registration or validity of patents' contained in Article 16(4) must be regarded as an independent concept intended to have uniform application in all the Contracting States.

The term 'proceedings concerned with the registration or validity of patents' does not include a dispute between an employee for whose invention a patent has been applied for or obtained and his employer, where the dispute relates to their respective rights in that patent arising out of the contract of employment.

ECJ, 13 July 2006, case C-4/03, GAT

Article 16(4) of the 1968 Brussels Convention is to be interpreted as meaning that the rule of exclusive jurisdiction laid down therein concerns all proceedings relating to the registration or validity of a patent, irrespective of whether the issue is raised by way of an action or a plea in objection.

CFI, Order 5 September 2007, case T-295/05, Document Security Systems

The action for patent infringement lodges against the ECB before the Court of First Instance is inadmissible since no provision of the Treaty confers it such competence, that belongs exclusively to national courts. Moreover, as stated by the ECJ in the GAT case, the issue of the validity of the patent is often decisive within the action for infringement and it falls within the exclusive jurisdiction — pursuant to Article 22 of Regulation No 44/2001 — of the courts of the Member State in which registration has taken place.

Article 22(5) [ex 16(5)]

ECJ, 4 July 1985, case 220/84, AS-Autoteile Service

Applications to oppose enforcement, as provided for under paragraph 767 of the German code of civil procedure, fall, as such, within the jurisdiction provision contained in Article 16(5) of the Convention; that provision does not however make it possible, in an application to oppose enforcement made to the courts of the Contracting State in which enforcement is to take place, to plead a set-off between the right whose enforcement is being sought and a claim over which the courts of that State would have no jurisdiction if it were raised independently.

ECJ, 26 March 1992, case C-261/90, Reichert

An action provided for by national law, such as the action paulienne in French law, whereby a creditor seeks to obtain the revocation in regard to him of a transfer of rights *in rem* in immovable property by his debtor in a way which the creditor regards as being in fraud of his rights does not come within the scope of Articles 5(3), 16(5) or 24 of the 1968 Brussels Convention.

Article 23 [ex 17]

ECJ, 14 December 1976, case 24/76, Estasis Salotti

Where a clause conferring jurisdiction is included among the general conditions of sale of one of the parties, printed on the back of a contract, the requirement of a writing under the first paragraph of Article 17 of the 1968 Brussels Convention is fulfilled only if the contract signed by both parties contains an express reference to those general conditions.

In the case of a contract concluded by reference to earlier offers, which were themselves made with reference to the general conditions of one of the parties including a clause conferring jurisdiction, the requirement of a writing under the first paragraph of Article 17 of the Convention is satisfied only if the reference is express and can therefore be checked by a party exercising reasonable care.

ECJ, 14 December 1976, case 25/76, Galeries Segoura

In the case of an orally concluded contract, the requirements of the first paragraph of Article 17 of the 1968 Brussels Convention as to form are satisfied only if the vendor's confirmation in writing accompanied by notification of the general conditions of sale has been accepted in writing by the purchaser.

    The fact that the purchaser does not raise any objections against a confirmation issued unilaterally by the other party does not amount to acceptance on his part of the clause conferring jurisdiction unless the oral agreement comes within the framework of a continuing trading relationship between the parties which is based on the general conditions of one of them, and those conditions contain a clause conferring jurisdiction.

ECJ, 9 November 1978, case 23/78, Meeth

The first paragraph of Article 17 of the 1968 Brussels Convention cannot be interpreted as prohibiting an agreement under which the two parties to a contract for sale, who are domiciled in different States, can be sued only in the courts of their respective States.

    Where there is a clause conferring jurisdiction such as that described in the reply to the first question the first paragraph of Article 17 of the Convention cannot be interpreted as prohibiting the court before which a dispute has been brought in pursuance of such a clause from taking into account a set-off connected with the legal relationship in dispute.

ECJ, 13 November 1979, case 25/79, Sanicentral

Articles 17 and 54 of the 1968 Brussels Convention must be interpreted to mean that, in judicial proceedings instituted after the coming into force of the Convention, clauses conferring jurisdiction included in contracts of employment concluded prior to that date must be considered valid even in cases in which they would have been regarded as void under the national law in force at the time when the contract was entered into.

ECJ, 17 January 1980, case 56/79, Zelger

If the place of performance of a contractual obligation has been specified by the parties in a clause which is valid according to the national law applicable to the contract, the court for that place has jurisdiction to take cognisance of disputes relating to that obligation under Article 5(1) of the 1968 Brussels Convention, irrespective of whether the formal conditions provided for under Article 17 have been observed.

ECJ, 6 May 1980, case 784/79, Porta-Leasing

The second paragraph of Article I of the Protocol annexed to the 1968 Brussels Convention must be interpreted as meaning that a clause conferring jurisdiction within the meaning of that provision may not be considered to have been expressly and specifically agreed to by a person domiciled in Luxembourg unless that clause, besides being in writing as required by Article 17 of the Convention, is mentioned in a provision specially and exclusively meant for this purpose and specifically signed by the party domiciled in Luxembourg; in this respect the signing of the contract as a whole does not in itself suffice. It is not however necessary for that clause to be mentioned in a document separate from the one which constitutes the written instrument of the contract.

ECJ, 24 June 1981, case 150/80, Elefanten Schuh

Article 18 of the 1968 Brussels Convention applies even where the parties have by agreement designated a court which is to have jurisdiction within the meaning of Article 17 of the Convention.

Article 17 of the Convention must be interpreted as meaning that the legislation of a Contracting State may not allow the validity of an agreement conferring jurisdiction to be called in question solely on the ground that the language used is not that prescribed by that legislation.

ECJ, 14 July 1983, case 201/82, Gerling Konzern

The first paragraph of Article 17 of the 1968 Brussels Convention must be interpreted as meaning that where a contract of insurance, entered into between an insurer and a policy-holder and stipulated by the latter to be for his benefit and to ensure for the benefit of third parties to such a contract, contains a clause conferring jurisdiction relating to proceedings which might be brought by such third parties, the latter, even if they have not expressly signed the said clause, may rely upon it provided that, as between the insurer and the policy-holder, the condition as to writing laid down by Article 17 of the Convention has been satisfied and provided that the consent of the insurer in that respect has been clearly manifested.

ECJ, 19 June 1984, case 71/83, Tilly Russ

A jurisdiction clause contained in the printed conditions on a bill of lading satisfies the conditions laid down by Article 17 of the 1968 Brussels Convention:

— if the agreement of both parties to the conditions containing that clause has been expressed in writing, or

— if the jurisdiction clause has been the subject-matter of a prior oral agreement between the parties expressly relating to that clause, in which case the bill of lading, signed by the carrier, must be regarded as confirmation in writing of the oral agreement, or

— if the bill of lading comes within the framework of a continuing business relationship between the parties, in so far as it is thereby established that that relationship is governed by general conditions containing the jurisdiction clause.

As regards the relationship between the carrier and a third party holding the bill of lading, the conditions laid down by Article 17 of the Convention are satisfied if the jurisdiction clause has been adjudged valid as between the carrier and the shipper and if, by virtue of the relevant national law, the third party, upon acquiring the bill of lading, succeeded to the shipper's rights and obligations.

ECJ, 7 March 1985, case 48/84, Spitzley

The court of a Contracting State before which the applicant, without raising any objection as to the court's jurisdiction, enters an appearance in proceedings relating to a claim for a set-off which is not based on the same contract or subject-matter as the claims in his application and in respect of which there is a valid agreement conferring exclusive jurisdiction on the courts of another Contracting State within the meaning of Article 17 of the 1968 Brussels Convention has jurisdiction by virtue of Article 18 of the Convention.

ECJ, 11 July 1985, case 221/84, Berghöfer

The first paragraph of Article 17 of the 1968 Brussels Convention must be interpreted as meaning that the formal requirements therein laid down are satisfied if it is established that jurisdiction was conferred by express oral agreement, that written confirmation of that agreement by one of the parties was received by the other and that the latter raised no objection.

ECJ, 11 November 1986, case 313/85, Iveco Fiat

Article 17 of the 1968 Brussels Convention must be interpreted as meaning that where a written agreement containing a jurisdiction clause and stipulating that an agreement can be renewed only in writing has expired but has continued to serve as the legal basis for the contractual relations between the parties, the jurisdiction clause satisfies the formal requirements in Article 17 if, under the law applicable, the parties could validly renew the original agreement otherwise than in writing, or if, conversely, one of the parties has confirmed in writing either the jurisdiction clause or the set of terms which has been tacitly renewed and of which the jurisdiction clause forms part, without any objection from the other party to whom such confirmation has been notified.

ECJ, 10 March 1992, case C-214/89, Powell Duffryn

A clause contained in the statutes of a company limited by shares and adopted in accordance with the provisions of the applicable national law and those statutes themselves conferring jurisdiction on a court of a Contracting State to settle disputes between that company and its shareholders constitutes an agreement conferring jurisdiction within the meaning of Article 17 of the 1968 Brussels Convention.

Irrespective of how shares are acquired, the formal requirements laid down in Article 17 must be considered to be complied with in regard to any shareholder if the clause conferring jurisdiction is contained in the statutes of the company and those statutes are lodged in a place to which the shareholder may have access or are contained in a public register.

The requirement that a dispute arise in connection with a particular legal relationship within the meaning of Article 17 is satisfied if the clause conferring jurisdiction contained in the statutes of a company may be interpreted as referring to the disputes between the company and its shareholders as such.

It is for the national court to interpret the clause conferring jurisdiction invoked before it in order to determine which disputes fall within its scope.

ECJ, 17 November 1998, case C-391/95, Van Uden

Where the parties have validly excluded the jurisdiction of the courts in a dispute arising under a contract and have referred that dispute to arbitration, no provisional or protective measures may be ordered on the basis of Article 5(1) of the 1968 Brussels Convention.

ECJ, 20 February 1997, case C-106/95, Mainschiffahrts-Genossenschaft

The third hypothesis in the second sentence of the first paragraph of Article 17 of the 1968 Brussels Convention must be interpreted as meaning that, under a contract concluded orally in international trade or commerce, an agreement conferring jurisdiction will be deemed to have been validly concluded under that provision by virtue of the fact that one party to the contract did not react to a commercial letter of confirmation sent to it by the other party to the contract or repeatedly paid invoices without objection where those documents contained a pre-printed reference to the courts having jurisdiction, provided that such conduct is consistent with a practice in force in the field of international trade or commerce in which the parties in question operate and the latter are aware or ought to have been aware of the practice in question. It is for the national court to determine whether such a practice exists and whether the parties to the contract were aware of it. A practice exists in a branch of international trade or commerce in particular where a particular course of conduct is generally followed by contracting parties operating in that branch when they conclude contracts of a particular type. The fact that the contracting parties were aware of that practice is made out in particular where they had previously had trade or commercial relations between themselves or with other parties operating in the branch of trade or commerce in question or where, in that branch, a particular course of conduct is generally and regularly followed when concluding a certain type of contract, with the result that it may be regarded as being a consolidated practice.

The Convention must be interpreted as meaning that an oral agreement on the place of performance which is designed not to determine the place where the person liable is actually to perform the obligations incumbent upon him, but solely to establish that the courts for a particular place have jurisdiction, is not governed by Article 5(1) of the Convention, but by Article 17, and is valid only if the requirements set out therein are complied with.

ECJ, 16 March 1999, case C-159/97, Trasporti Castelletti

The third case mentioned in the second sentence of the first paragraph of Article 17 of the 1968 Brussels Convention is to be interpreted as follows:
— the contracting parties' consent to the jurisdiction clause is presumed to exist where their conduct is consistent with a usage which governs the area of international trade or commerce in which they operate and of which they are, or ought to have been, aware.
— the existence of a usage, which must be determined in relation to the branch of trade or commerce in which the parties to the contract operate, is established where a particular course of conduct is generally and regularly followed by operators in that branch when concluding contracts of a particular type.

—   it is not necessary for such a course of conduct to be established in specific countries or, in particular, in all the Contracting States.

—   a specific form of publicity cannot be required in all cases.

The fact that a course of conduct amounting to a usage is challenged before the courts is not sufficient to cause the conduct no longer to constitute a usage.

The specific requirements covered by the expression 'form which accords' must be assessed solely in the light of the commercial usages of the branch of international trade or commerce concerned, without taking into account any particular requirements which national provisions might lay down.

Awareness of the usage must be assessed with respect to the original parties to the agreement conferring jurisdiction, their nationality being irrelevant in this regard. Awareness of the usage will be established when, regardless of any specific form of publicity, in the branch of trade or commerce in which the parties operate a particular course of conduct is generally and regularly followed in the conclusion of a particular type of contract, so that it may be regarded as an established usage.

The choice of court in a jurisdiction clause may be assessed only in the light of considerations connected with the requirements laid down in Article 17 of the Convention. Considerations about the links between the court designated and the relationship at issue, about the validity of the clause, or about the substantive rules of liability applicable before the chosen court are unconnected with those requirements.

ECJ, 9 November 2000, case C-387/98, Coreck Maritime

The first paragraph of Article 17 of the 1968 Brussels Convention must be interpreted as follows.

It does not require that a jurisdiction clause be formulated in such a way that the competent court can be determined on its wording alone. It is sufficient that the clause state the objective factors on the basis of which the parties have agreed to choose a court or the courts to which they wish to submit disputes which have arisen or which may arise between them. Those factors, which must be sufficiently precise to enable the court seised to ascertain whether it has jurisdiction, may, where appropriate, be determined by the particular circumstances of the case.

It applies only if, first, at least one of the parties to the original contract is domiciled in a Contracting State and, secondly, the parties agree to submit any disputes before a court or the courts of a Contracting State.

A jurisdiction clause agreed between a carrier and a shipper which appears in a bill of lading is enforceable against a third party bearer of the bill of lading if he succeeded to the rights and obligations of the shipper under the applicable national law when he acquired the bill of lading. If he did not, it must be ascertained whether he accepted that clause having regard to the requirements laid down in the first paragraph of Article 17 of the Convention, as amended.

ECJ, 3 July 1997, case C-269/95, Benincasa

The courts of a Contracting State which have been designated in a jurisdiction clause validly concluded under the first paragraph of Article 17 of the 1968 Brussels Convention also have exclusive jurisdiction where the action seeks in particular a declaration that the contract containing that clause is void.

ECJ, 9 December 2003, case C-116/02, Gasser

Article 21 of the 1968 Brussels Convention must be interpreted as meaning that a court second seised whose jurisdiction has been claimed under an agreement conferring jurisdiction must nevertheless stay proceedings until the court first seised has declared that it has no jurisdiction.

Article 24 [ex 18]

ECJ, 24 June 1981, case 150/80, Elefanten Schuh

Article 18 of the 1968 Brussels Convention applies even where the parties have by agreement designated a court which is to have jurisdiction within the meaning of Article 17 of the Convention.

      Article 18 of the Convention must be interpreted as meaning that the rule on jurisdiction which that provision lays down does not apply where the defendant not only contests the court's jurisdiction but also makes submissions on the substance of the action, provided that, if the challenge to jurisdiction is not preliminary to any defence as to the substance, it does not occur after the making of the submissions which under national procedural law are considered to be the first defence addressed to the court seised.

ECJ, 7 March 1985, case 48/84, Spitzley

The court of a Contracting State before which the applicant, without raising any objection as to the court's jurisdiction, enters an appearance in proceedings relating to a claim for a set-off which is not based on the same contract or subject-matter as the claims in his application and in respect of which there is a valid agreement conferring exclusive jurisdiction on the courts of another Contracting State within the meaning of Article 17 of the 1968 Brussels Convention has jurisdiction by virtue of Article 18 of the Convention.

CJ, 20 May 2010, case C-111/09, ČPP

Article 24 of Regulation No 44/2001 must be interpreted as meaning that the court seised, where the rules in Section 3 of Chapter II of the Regulation were not complied with, must declare itself to have jurisdiction where the defendant enters an appearance and does not contest that court's jurisdiction, since entering an appearance in that way amounts to a tacit prorogation of jurisdiction.

Article 25 [ex 19]

ECJ, 15 November 1983, case 288/82, Duijnstee

Article 19 of the 1968 Brussels Convention requires the national court to declare of its own motion that it has no jurisdiction whenever it finds that a court of another Contracting State has exclusive jurisdiction under Article 16 of the Convention, even in an appeal in cassation where the national rules of procedure limit the court's reviewal to the grounds raised by the parties.

Article 26 [ex 20]

ECJ, 28 October 2004, case C-148/03, Nürnberger Allgemeine Vers

Article 57(2)(a) of the 1968 Brussels Convention should be interpreted as meaning that the court of a Contracting State in which a defendant domiciled in another Contracting State is sued may derive its jurisdiction from a specialised convention to which the first State is a party as well and which contains specific rules on jurisdiction, even where the defendant, in the course of the proceedings in question, submits no pleas on the merits.

Article 27 [ex 21]

ECJ, 7 June 1984, case 129/83, Zelger

Article 21 of the 1968 Brussels Convention must be interpreted as meaning that the court 'first seised' is the one before which the requirements for proceedings to become definitively pending are first fulfilled, such requirements to be determined in accordance with the national law of each of the courts concerned.

ECJ, 8 December 1987, case 144/86, Gubisch

The concept of lis pendens pursuant to Article 21 of the 1968 Brussels Convention covers a case where a party brings an action before a court in a Contracting State for the rescission or discharge of an international sales contract whilst an action by the other party to enforce the same contract is pending before a court in another contracting state.

ECJ, 27 June 1991, case C-351/89, Overseas Union

Article 21 of the 1968 Brussels Convention must be interpreted as applying irrespective of the domicile of the parties to the two sets of proceedings.

Without prejudice to the case where the court second seised has exclusive jurisdiction under the Convention and in particular under Article 16 thereof, Article 21 of the Convention must be interpreted as meaning that, where the jurisdiction of the court first seised is contested, the court second seised may, if it does not decline jurisdiction, only stay the proceedings and may not itself examine the jurisdiction of the court first seised.

ECJ, 20 January 1994, case C-129/92, Owens Bank

The 1968 Brussels Convention, in particular Articles 21, 22 and 23, does not apply to proceedings, or issues arising in proceedings, in Contracting States concerning the recognition and enforcement of judgments given in civil and commercial matters in non-contracting States.

ECJ, 6 December 1994, case C-406/92, Tatry

On a proper construction of Article 21 of the 1968 Brussels Convention, where two actions involve the same cause of action and some but not all of the parties to the second action are the same as the parties to the action commenced earlier in another Contracting State, the second court seised is required to decline jurisdiction only to the extent to which the parties to the proceedings before it are also parties to the action previously commenced; it does not prevent the proceedings from continuing between the other parties.

On a proper construction of Article 21 of the Convention, an action seeking to have the defendant held liable for causing loss and ordered to pay damages has the same cause of action and the same object as earlier proceedings brought by that defendant seeking a declaration that he is not liable for that loss.

A subsequent action does not cease to have the same cause of action and the same object and to be between the same parties as a previous action where the latter, brought by the owner of a ship before a court of a Contracting State, is an action *in personam* for a declaration that that owner is not liable for alleged damage to cargo transported by his ship, whereas the subsequent action has been brought by the owner of the cargo before a court of another Contracting State by way of an action *in rem* concerning an arrested ship, and has subsequently continued both *in rem* and *in personam*, or solely *in personam*, according to the distinctions drawn by the national law of that other Contracting State.

ECJ, 9 October 1997, case C-163/95, von Horn

Article 29(1) of the Convention of 26 May 1989 on the Accession of the Kingdom of Spain and the Portuguese Republic to the 1968 Brussels Convention must be interpreted as meaning that where proceedings involving the same cause of action and between the same parties are pending in two different Contracting States, the first proceedings having been brought before the date of entry into force of the Brussels Convention between those States and the second proceedings after that date, the court second seised must apply Article 21 of the latter Convention if the court first seised has assumed jurisdiction on the basis of a rule which accords with the provisions of Title II of that Convention or with the provisions of a convention which was in force between the two States concerned when the proceedings were instituted, and must do so provisionally if the court first seised has not yet ruled on whether it has jurisdiction. On the other hand, the court second seised must not apply Article 21 of the 1968 Brussels Convention if the court first seised has assumed jurisdiction on the basis of a rule which does not accord with the provisions of Title II of that Convention or with the provisions of a convention which was in force between those two States when the proceedings were instituted.

ECJ, 19 May 1998, case C-351/96, Drouot assurances

Article 21 of the 1968 Brussels Convention is not applicable in the case of two actions for contribution to general average, one brought by the insurer of the hull of a vessel which has foundered against the owner and the insurer of the cargo which the vessel was carrying when it sank, the other brought by the latter two parties against the owner and the charterer of the vessel, unless it is established that, with regard to the subject-matter of the two disputes, the interests of the insurer of the hull of the vessel are identical to and indissociable from those of its insured, the owner and the charterer of that vessel.

ECJ, 8 May 2003, case C-111/01, Gantner

Article 21 of the 1968 Brussels Convention must be construed as meaning that, in order to determine whether two claims brought between the same parties before the courts of different Contracting States have the same subject-matter, account should be taken only of the claims of the respective applicants, to the exclusion of the defence submissions raised by a defendant.

ECJ, 9 December 2003, case C-116/02, Gasser

Article 21 of the 1968 Brussels Convention must be interpreted as meaning that a court second seised whose jurisdiction has been claimed under an agreement conferring jurisdiction must nevertheless stay proceedings until the court first seised has declared that it has no jurisdiction.

Article 21 of the Brussels Convention must be interpreted as meaning that it cannot be derogated from where, in general, the duration of proceedings before the courts of the Contracting State in which the court first seised is established is excessively long.

ECJ, 14 October 2004, case C-39/02, Maersk Olie & Gas

An application to a court of a Contracting State by a shipowner for the establishment of a liability limitation fund, in which the potential victim of the damage is indicated, and an action for damages brought before a court of another Contracting State by that victim against the shipowner do not create a situation of *lis pendens* within the terms of Article 21 of the 1968 Brussels Convention.

A decision ordering the establishment of a liability limitation fund, such as that in the main proceedings in the present case, is a judgment within the terms of Article 25 of the Convention.

A decision to establish a liability limitation fund, in the absence of prior service on the claimant concerned, and even where the latter has appealed against that decision in order to challenge the jurisdiction of the court which delivered it, cannot be refused recognition in another Contracting State pursuant to Article 27(2) of the Convention, on condition that it was duly served on or notified to the defendant in good time.

Article 28 [ex 22]

ECJ, 24 June 1981, case 150/80, Elefanten Schuh

Article 22 of the 1968 Brussels Convention applies only where related actions are brought before courts of two or more Contracting States.

ECJ, 20 January 1994, case C-129/92, Owens Bank

The Brussels Convention, in particular Articles 21, 22 and 23, does not apply to proceedings, or issues arising in proceedings, in Contracting States concerning the recognition and enforcement of judgments given in civil and commercial matters in non-contracting States.

ECJ, 6 December 1994, case C-406/92, Tatry

On a proper construction of Article 22 of the 1968 Brussels Convention, it is sufficient, in order to establish the necessary relationship between, on the one hand, an action brought in a Contracting State by one group of cargo owners against a shipowner seeking damages for harm caused to part of the cargo carried in bulk under separate but identical contracts, and, on the other, an action in damages brought in another Contracting State against the same shipowner by the owners of another part of the cargo shipped under the same conditions and under contracts which are separate from but identical to those between the first group and the shipowner, that separate trial and judgment would involve the risk of conflicting decisions, without necessarily involving the risk of giving rise to mutually exclusive legal consequences.

Article 29 [ex 23]

ECJ, 20 January 1994, case C-129/92, Owens Bank

The 1968 Brussels Convention, in particular Articles 21, 22 and 23, does not apply to proceedings, or issues arising in proceedings, in Contracting States concerning the recognition and enforcement of judgments given in civil and commercial matters in non-contracting States.

Article 31 [ex 24]

ECJ, 6 March 1980, case 120/79, de Cavel

The 1968 Brussels Convention is applicable, on the one hand, to the enforcement of an interlocutory order made by a French court in divorce proceedings whereby one of the parties to the proceedings is awarded a monthly maintenance allowance and, on the other hand, to an interim compensation payment, payable monthly, awarded to one of the parties by a French divorce judgment pursuant to article 270 *et seq* of the French civil code.

ECJ, 31 March 1982, case 25/81, C.H.W.

Article 24 of the 1968 Brussels Convention may not be relied on to bring within the scope of the convention provisional or protective measures relating to matters which are excluded from it.

ECJ, 26 March 1992, case C-261/90, Reichert

An action provided for by national law, such as the action paulienne in French law, whereby a creditor seeks to obtain the revocation in regard to him of a transfer of rights *in rem* in immovable property by his debtor in a way which the creditor regards as being in fraud of his rights does not come within the scope of Articles 5(3), 16(5) or 24 of the 1968 Brussels Convention.

ECJ, 10 February 1994, case C-398/92, Mund & Fester

Article 7 of the EEC Treaty, read in conjunction with Article 220 of the Treaty and the 1968 Brussels Convention, precludes a national provision of civil procedure which, in the case of a judgment to be enforced within national territory, authorises seizure only on the ground that it is probable that enforcement will otherwise be made impossible or substantially more difficult, but, in the case of a judgment to be enforced in another Member State, authorises seizure simply on the ground that enforcement is to take place abroad.

ECJ, 17 November 1998, case C-391/95, Van Uden

On a proper construction of Article 5(1) of the 1968 Brussels Convention, the court which has jurisdiction by virtue of that provision also has jurisdiction to order provisional or protective measures, without that jurisdiction being subject to any further conditions.

Where the parties have validly excluded the jurisdiction of the courts in a dispute arising under a contract and have referred that dispute to arbitration, no provisional or protective measures may be ordered on the basis of Article 5(1) of the Convention.

Where the subject-matter of an application for provisional measures relates to a question falling within the scope *ratione materiae* of the 1968 Brussels Convention, the Convention is applicable and Article 24 thereof may confer jurisdiction on the court hearing that application even where proceedings have already been, or may be, commenced on the substance of the case and even where those proceedings are to be conducted before arbitrators.

On a proper construction, the granting of provisional or protective measures on the basis of Article 24 of the Convention is conditional on, inter alia, the existence of a real connecting link between the subject-matter of the measures sought and the territorial jurisdiction of the Contracting State of the court before which those measures are sought.

Interim payment of a contractual consideration does not constitute a provisional measure within the meaning of Article 24 of the Convention unless, first, repayment to the defendant of the sum awarded is guaranteed if the plaintiff is unsuccessful as regards the substance of his claim and, second, the measure sought relates only to specific assets of the defendant located or to be located within the confines of the territorial jurisdiction of the court to which application is made.

ECJ, 27 April 1999, case C-99/96, Mietz

A judgment ordering interim payment of contractual consideration, delivered at the end of a procedure such as that provided for under Articles 289 to 297 of the Netherlands Code of Civil Procedure by a court not having jurisdiction under the 1968 Brussels Convention as to the substance of the matter is not a provisional measure capable of being granted under Article 24 of the Convention unless, first, repayment to the defendant of the sum awarded is guaranteed if the plaintiff is unsuccessful as regards the substance of his claim and, second, the measure ordered relates only to specific assets of the defendant located or to be located within the confines of the territorial jurisdiction of the court to which application is made.

ECJ, 27 April 2004, case C-159/02, Turner

The 1968 Brussels Convention is to be interpreted as precluding the grant of an injunction whereby a court of a Contracting State prohibits a party to proceedings pending before it from commencing or continuing legal proceedings before a court of another Contracting State, even where that party is acting in bad faith with a view to frustrating the existing proceedings.

ECJ, judgment 28 April 2005, case C-104/03, St Paul Dairy

Article 24 of the 1968 Brussels Convention must be interpreted as meaning that a measure ordering the hearing of a witness for the purpose of enabling the applicant to decide whether to bring a case, determine whether it would be well-founded and assess the relevance of evidence which might be adduced in that regard is not covered by the notion of 'provisional, including protective, measures'.

ECJ, 10 February 2009, case C-185/07, West Tankers

It is incompatible with Regulation No 44/2001 for a court of a Member State to make an order to restrain a person from commencing or continuing proceedings before the courts of another Member State on the ground that such proceedings would be contrary to an arbitration agreement.

Article 32 [ex 25]

ECJ, 14 October 2004, case C-39/02, Maersk Olie & Gas

A decision ordering the establishment of a liability limitation fund, such as that in the main proceedings in the present case, is a judgment within the terms of Article 25 of the 1968 Brussels Convention.

   In fact, while it is true that, according to settled case-law, the Convention is concerned essentially with judicial decisions which, before their recognition and enforcement are sought in a State other than the State of origin, have been, or have been capable of being, the subject in that State of origin, and under various procedures, of an inquiry in contested proceedings, it must be stated clearly that, even if it was taken at the conclusion of an initial phase of the proceedings in which both parties were not heard, the order of the Netherlands court could have been the subject of submissions by both parties before the issue of its recognition or its enforcement pursuant to the Convention came to be addressed.

   It is thus evident from the case-file that such an order does not have any effect in law prior to being notified to claimants, who may then assert their rights before the court which has made the order by challenging both the right of the debtor to benefit from a limitation of liability and the amount of that limitation. Claimants may, in addition, lodge an appeal against that order challenging the jurisdiction of the court which adopted it — as indeed happened in the main proceedings in the present case.

Article 33 [ex 26]

ECJ, 30 November 1976, case 42/76, de Wolf

The provisions of the 1968 Brussels Convention prevent a party who has obtained a judgment in his favour in a Contracting State, being a judgment for which an order for enforcement under Article 31 of the Convention may issue in another Contracting State, from making an application to a court in that other State for a judgment against the other party in the same terms as the judgment delivered in the first State.

ECJ, 21 May 1980, case 125/79, Denilauler

Judicial decisions authorising provisional or protective measures, which are delivered without the party against which they are directed having been summoned to appear and which are intended to be enforced without prior service do not come within the system of recognition and enforcement provided for by Title III of the 1968 Brussels Convention.

ECJ, 4 February 1988, case 145/86, Hoffmann

A foreign judgment which has been recognised by virtue of Article 26 of the 1968 Brussels Convention must in principle have the same effects in the State in which enforcement is sought as it does in the State in which the judgment was given.

Article 34(1) [ex 27(1)]

ECJ, 28 March 2000, case C-7/98, Krombach

The court of the State in which enforcement is sought cannot, with respect to a defendant domiciled in that State, take account, for the purposes of the public-policy clause in Article 27(1) of the 1968 Brussels Convention, of the fact, without more, that the court of the State of origin based its jurisdiction on the nationality of the victim of an offence.

The court of the State in which enforcement is sought can, with respect to a defendant domiciled in that State and prosecuted for an intentional offence, take account, in relation to the public-policy clause in Article 27(1) of that Convention, of the fact that the court of the State of origin refused to allow that person to have his defence presented unless he appeared in person.

ECJ, 2 April 2009, case C-394/07, Gambazzi

Article 27(1) of the 1968 Brussels Convention is to be interpreted as follows: 'The court of the State in which enforcement is sought may take into account, with regard to the public policy clause referred to in that Article, the fact that the court of the State of origin ruled on the applicant's claims without hearing the defendant, who entered appearance before it but who was excluded from the proceedings by order on the ground that he had not complied with the obligations imposed by an order made earlier in the same proceedings, if, following a comprehensive assessment of the proceedings and in the light of all the circumstances, it appears to it that that exclusion measure constituted a manifest and disproportionate infringement of the defendant's right to be heard'.

ECJ, 28 April 2009, case C-420/07, Apostolides

The fact that a judgment given by the courts of a Member State concerning land situated in an area of that State over which its Government does not exercise effective control, cannot, as a practical matter, be enforced where the land is situated does not constitute a ground for refusal of recognition or enforcement under Article 34(1) of Regulation No 44/2001 and it does not mean that such a judgment is unenforceable for the purposes of Article 38(1) of the Regulation.

Article 34(2) [ex 27(2)]

ECJ, 16 June 1981, case 166/80, Klomps

The words 'the document which instituted the proceedings' cover any document, such as the order for payment (Zahlungsbefehl) in German law, service of which enables the plaintiff, under the law of the State of the court in which the judgment was given to obtain, in default of appropriate action taken by the defendant, a decision capable of being recognised and enforced under the provisions of the Convention.

A decision such as the enforcement order (Vollstreckungsbefehl) in German law, which is issued after service of the order for payment has been effected and which is enforceable under the Convention, is not covered by the words 'the document which instituted the proceedings'.

In order to determine whether the defendant has been enabled to arrange for his defence as required by Article 27(2), the court in which enforcement is sought must take account only of the time, such as that allowed under German law for submitting an objection (Widerspruch) to the order for payment, available to the defendant for the purposes of preventing the issue of a judgment in default which is enforceable under the Convention.

Article 27(2) remains applicable where the defendant has lodged an objection against the decision given in default and a court of the State in which the judgment was given has held the objection to be inadmissible on the ground that the time for lodging an objection has expired.

Even if a court of the State in which the judgment was given has held, in separate adversary proceedings, that service was duly effected article 27(2) still requires the court in which enforcement is sought to examine whether service was effected in sufficient time to enable the defendant to arrange for his defence.

The court in which enforcement is sought may as a general rule confine itself to examining whether the period, reckoned from the date on which service was duly effected, allowed the defendant sufficient time for his defence. It must, however, consider whether, in a particular case, there are exceptional circumstances such as the fact that, although service was duly effected, it was inadequate for the purposes of causing that time to begin to run.

Article 52 of the Convention and the fact that the court of the State in which enforcement is sought concluded that under the law of that State the defendant was habitually resident within its territory at the date of service of the document which instituted the proceedings do not affect the replies given above.

ECJ, 15 July 1982, case 228/81, Pendy Plastic Products

The court of the State in which enforcement is sought may, if it considers that the conditions laid down by article 27(2) of the 1968 Brussels Convention are fulfilled, refuse to grant recognition and enforcement of a judgment, even though the court of the State in which the judgment was given regarded it as proven, in accordance with the third paragraph of Article 20 of that Convention in conjunction with Article 15 of the Hague Convention of 15 November 1965, that the defendant, who failed to enter an appearance, had an opportunity to receive service of the document instituting the proceedings in sufficient time to enable him to make arrangements for his defence.

ECJ, 11 June 1985, case 49/84, Debaecker and Plouvier

The requirement, laid down in article 27(2) of the 1968 Brussels Convention, that service of the document which instituted the proceedings should have been effected in sufficient time is applicable where service was effected within a period prescribed by the court of the State in which the judgment was given or where the defendant resided, exclusively or otherwise, within the jurisdiction of that court or in the same country as that court.

In examining whether service was effected in sufficient time, the court in which enforcement is sought may take account of exceptional circumstances which arose after service was duly effected.

The fact that the plaintiff was apprised of the defendant's new address, after service was effected, and the fact that the defendant was responsible for the failure of the duly served document to reach him are matters which the court in which enforcement is sought may take into account in assessing whether service was effected in sufficient time.

ECJ, 3 July 1990, case C-305/88, Isabelle Lancray

Article 27(2) of the 1968 Brussels Convention is to be interpreted as meaning that a judgment given in default of appearance may not be recognised where the document instituting the proceedings was not served on the defendant in due form, even though it was served in sufficient time to enable him to arrange for his defence.

Article 27(2) of the Convention is to be interpreted as meaning that questions concerning the curing of defective service are governed by the law of the State in which judgment was given, including any relevant international agreements

ECJ, 12 November 1992, case C-123/91, Minalmet

Article 27(2) of the 1968 Brussels Convention must be interpreted as precluding a judgment given in default of appearance in one Contracting State from being recognised in another Contracting State where the defendant was not duly served with the document which instituted the proceedings, even if he subsequently became aware of the judgment which was given and did not avail himself of the legal remedies provided for under the procedure of the State where the judgment was delivered.

ECJ, 21 April 1993, case C-172/91, Sonntag

Non-recognition of a judgment for the reasons set out in Article 27(2) of the 1968 Brussels Convention is possible only where the defendant was in default of appearance in the original proceedings. Consequently, that provision may not be relied upon where the defendant appeared. A defendant is deemed to have appeared for the purposes of Article 27(2) of the Convention where, in connection with a claim for compensation joined to criminal proceedings, he answered at the trial, through counsel of his own choice, to the criminal charges but did not express a view on the civil claim, on which oral argument was also submitted in the presence of his counsel.

ECJ, 13 July 1995, case C-474/93, Hengst

The *decreto ingiuntivo* within the meaning of Book IV of the Italian Code of Civil Procedure (Articles 633–656), together with the application instituting the proceedings, must be regarded as 'the document which instituted proceedings or… an equivalent document' within the meaning of Article 27(2) of the 1968 Brussels Convention.

ECJ, 10 October 1996, case C-78/95, Hendrikman

Article 27(2) of the 1968 Brussels Convention applies to judgments given against a defendant who was not duly served with, or notified of, the document instituting proceedings in sufficient time and who was not validly represented during those proceedings, albeit the judgments given were not given in default of appearance because someone purporting to represent the defendant appeared before the court first seised.

ECJ, 14 October 2004, case C-39/02, Maersk Olie & Gas

A decision to establish a liability limitation fund, in the absence of prior service on the claimant concerned, and even where the latter has appealed against that decision in order to challenge the jurisdiction of the court which delivered it, cannot be refused recognition in another Contracting State pursuant to Article 27(2) of the 1968 Brussels Convention, on condition that it was duly served on or notified to the defendant in good time.

ECJ, 13 October 2005, case C-522/03, Scania

Article 27 of the 1968 Brussels Convention and the first paragraph of Article IV of the Protocol annexed to it must be interpreted as meaning that, where a relevant international convention is applicable between the State in which the judgment is given and the State in which recognition is sought, the question whether the document instituting the proceedings was duly served on a defendant in default of appearance must be determined in the light of the provisions of that convention, without prejudice to the use of direct transmission between public officers, where the State in which recognition is sought has not officially objected, in accordance with the second paragraph of Article IV of the Protocol.

ECJ, 14 December 2006, case C-283/05, ASML Netherlands

Article 34(2) of Regulation No 44/2001 is to be interpreted as meaning that it is 'possible' for a defendant to bring proceedings to challenge a default judgment against him only if he was in fact acquainted with its contents, because it was served on him in sufficient time to enable him to arrange for his defence before the courts of the State in which the judgment was given.

ECJ, 28 April 2009, case C-420/07, Apostolides

The recognition or enforcement of a default judgment cannot be refused under Article 34(2) of Regulation No 44/2001 where the defendant was able to commence proceedings to challenge the default judgment and those proceedings enabled him to argue that he had not been served with the document which instituted the proceedings or with the equivalent document in sufficient time and in such a way as to enable him to arrange for his defence.

Article 34(3) [ex 27(3)]

ECJ, 4 February 1988, case 145/86, Hoffmann

A foreign judgment ordering a person to make maintenance payments to his spouse by virtue of his conjugal obligations to support her is irreconcilable within the meaning of Article 27(3) of the 1968 Brussels Convention with a national judgment pronouncing the divorce of the spouses.

ECJ, 2 June 1994, case C-414/92, Solo Kleinmotoren

Article 27(3) of the 1968 Brussels Convention is to be interpreted as meaning that an enforceable settlement reached before a court of the State in which recognition is sought in order to settle legal proceedings which are in progress does not constitute a 'judgment', within the meaning of that provision, 'given in a dispute between the same parties in the State in which recognition is sought' which, under the Convention, may preclude recognition and enforcement of a judgment given in another Contracting State.

ECJ, 6 June 2002, case C-80/00, Italian Leather

On a proper construction of Article 27(3) of the 1968 Brussels Convention, a foreign decision on interim measures ordering an obligor not to carry out certain acts is irreconcilable with a decision on interim measures refusing to grant such an order in a dispute between the same parties in the State where recognition is sought.

Where a court of the State in which recognition is sought finds that a judgment of a court of another Contracting State is irreconcilable with a judgment given by a court of the former State in a dispute between the same parties, it is required to refuse to recognise the foreign judgment.

Article 35 [ex 28]

ECJ, 28 April 2009, case C-420/07, Apostolides

Article 35(1) of Regulation No 44/2001 does not authorise the court of a Member State to refuse recognition or enforcement of a judgment given by the courts of another Member State concerning land situated in an area of the latter State over which its Government does not exercise effective control.

CJ, 20 May 2010, case C-111/09, ČPP

Article 24 of Regulation No 44/2001 must be interpreted as meaning that the court seised, where the rules in Section 3 of Chapter II of the Regulation were not complied with, must declare itself to have jurisdiction where the defendant enters an appearance and does not contest that court's jurisdiction, since entering an appearance in that way amounts to a tacit prorogation of jurisdiction.

Article 37 [ex 30]

ECJ, 22 November 1977, case 43/77, Industrial Diamond Supplies

The expression 'ordinary appeal' within the meaning of Articles 30 and 38 of the 1968 Brussels Convention must be defined solely within the framework of the system of the Convention itself and not according to the law either of the State in which the judgment was given or of the State in which recognition of enforcement of that judgment is sought.

Within the meaning of Articles 30 and 38 of the Convention, any appeal which is such that it may result in the annulment or the amendment of the judgment which is the subject-matter of the procedure for recognition or enforcement under the Convention and the lodging of which is bound, in the State in which the judgment was given, to a period which is laid down by the law and starts to run by virtue of that same judgment constitutes an 'ordinary appeal' which has been lodged or may be lodged against a foreign judgment.

Article 38 [ex 31]

ECJ, 30 November 1976, case 42/76, de Wolf

The provisions of the 1968 Brussels Convention prevent a party who has obtained a judgment in his favour in a Contracting State, being a judgment for which an order for enforcement under Article 31 of the Convention may issue in another Contracting State, from making an application to a court in that other State for a judgment against the other party in the same terms as the judgment delivered in the first State.

ECJ, 4 February 1988, case 145/86, Hoffmann

A foreign judgment whose enforcement has been ordered in a Contracting State pursuant to Article 31 of the 1968 Brussels Convention and which remains enforceable in the State in which it was given must not continue to be enforced in the State where enforcement is sought when, under the law of the latter State, it ceases to be enforceable for reasons which lie outside the scope of the Convention.

ECJ, 29 April 1999, case C-267/97, Coursier

The term 'enforceable' in the first paragraph of Article 31 of the 1968 Brussels Convention is to be interpreted as referring solely to the enforceability, in formal terms, of foreign decisions and not to the circumstances in which such decisions may be executed in the State of origin. It is for the court of the State in which enforcement is sought, in appeal proceedings brought under Article 36 of the Convention, to determine, in accordance with its domestic law including the rules of private international law, the legal effects of a decision given in the State of origin in relation to a court-supervised liquidation.

ECJ, 28 April 2009, case C-420/07, Apostolides

The fact that a judgment given by the courts of a Member State concerning land situated in an area of that State over which its Government does not exercise effective control, cannot, as a practical matter, be enforced where the land is situated does not constitute a ground for refusal of recognition or enforcement under Article 34(1) of Regulation No 44/2001 and it does not mean that such a judgment is unenforceable for the purposes of Article 38(1) of the Regulation.

Article 40 [ex 33]

ECJ, 10 July 1986, case 198/85, Carron

The second paragraph of Article 33 of the 1968 Brussels Convention must be interpreted as meaning that the obligation to give an address for service of process laid down in that provision must be fulfilled in conformity with the rules laid down by the law of the State in which enforcement is sought, and if that law is silent as to the time at which that formality must be observed, no later than the date on which the decision authorising enforcement is served.

The consequences of a failure to comply with the rules on the furnishing of an address for service are, by virtue of Article 33 of the Convention, governed by the law of the State in which enforcement is sought, provided that the aims of the Convention are respected.

Article 42 [ex 36]

ECJ, 16 February 2006, case C-3/05, Verdoliva

Article 36 of the 1968 Brussels Convention is to be interpreted as requiring due service of the decision authorising enforcement in accordance with the procedural rules of the Contracting State in which enforcement is sought, and therefore, in cases of failure of, or defective, service of the decision authorising enforcement, the mere fact that the party against whom enforcement is sought has notice of that decision is not sufficient to cause time to run for the purposes of the time-limit fixed in that Article.

Article 43 [ex 36, 37 (1) and 40]

ECJ, 12 July 1984, case 178/83, Firma P.

The court hearing an appeal by the party seeking enforcement is required to hear the party against whom enforcement is sought, pursuant to the first sentence of the second paragraph of Article 40 of the 1968 Brussels Convention, even though the application for an enforcement order was dismissed simply because documents were not produced at the appropriate time and the enforcement order is applied for in a State which is not the state of residence of the party against whom enforcement is sought.

ECJ, 2 July 1985, case 148/84, Deutsche Genossenschaftsbank

Article 36 of the 1968 Brussels Convention excludes any procedure whereby interested third parties may challenge an enforcement order, even where such a procedure is available to third parties under the domestic law of the State in which the enforcement order is granted.

ECJ, 3 October 1985, case 119/84, Capelloni and Aquilini

A party who has obtained authorisation for enforcement may proceed with the protective measures referred to in Article 39 until the expiry of the period prescribed in Article 36 for lodging an appeal and, if such an appeal is lodged, until a decision is given thereon.

ECJ, 4 February 1988, case 145/86, Hoffmann

Article 36 of the 1968 Brussels Convention must be interpreted as meaning that a party who has not appealed against the enforcement order referred to in that provision is thereafter precluded, at the stage of the execution of the judgment, from relying on a valid ground which he could have pleaded in such an appeal against the enforcement order, and that that rule must be applied of their own motion by the courts of the State in which enforcement is sought. However, that rule does not apply when it has the result of obliging the national court to make the effects of a national judgment which lies outside the scope of the Convention conditional on its recognition in the State in which the foreign judgment whose enforcement is at issue was given.

ECJ, 23 April 2009, case C-167/08, Draka NK Cables

Article 43(1) of Regulation No 44/2001 must be interpreted as meaning that a creditor of a debtor cannot lodge an appeal against a decision on a request for a declaration of enforceability if he has not formally appeared as a party in the proceedings in which another creditor of that debtor applied for that declaration of enforceability.

Article 44 [ex 37(2)]

ECJ, 27 November 1984, case 258/83, Calzaturificio Brennero

The second paragraph of Article 37 of the 1968 Brussels Convention must be interpreted as meaning that an appeal in cassation and, in the Federal Republic of Germany, a Rechtsbeschwerde may be lodged only against the judgment given on the appeal.

ECJ, 4 October 1991, case C-183/90, van Dalfsen

The second paragraph of Article 37 of the 1968 Brussels Convention is to be interpreted as meaning that a decision taken under Article 38 of the Convention by which the court with which an appeal has been lodged against an order for the enforcement of a judgment given in another Contracting State has refused to stay the proceedings and has ordered the party to whom the enforcement order was granted to provide security does not constitute a 'judgment given on the appeal' within the meaning of the second paragraph of Article 37 of the Convention and may not, therefore, be contested by an appeal in cassation or similar form of appeal. The position is the same where the decision taken under Article 38 of the Convention and the 'judgment given on the appeal' within the meaning of the second paragraph of Article 37 of the Convention are given in a single judgment.

The first paragraph of Article 38 of the Convention is to be interpreted as meaning that a court with which an appeal is lodged against an order for the enforcement of a judgment given in another Contracting State may take into consideration, in a decision concerning an application for the proceedings to be stayed under that paragraph, only such submissions as the appellant was unable to make before the court of the State in which the judgment was given.

ECJ, 21 April 1993, case C-172/91, Sonntag

Article 37(2) of the 1968 Brussels Convention must be interpreted as precluding any appeal by interested third parties against a judgment given on an appeal under Article 36 of the Convention, even where the domestic law of the State in which enforcement is sought confers on such third parties a right of appeal.

ECJ, 11 August 1995, case C-432/93, SISRO

Article 37(2) and the first paragraph of Article 38 of the 1968 Brussels Convention are to be interpreted as meaning that a decision by which a court of a Contracting State, seised of an appeal against authorisation to enforce an enforceable judgment of a court in another Contracting State, refuses a stay or lifts a stay previously ordered cannot be contested by an appeal in cassation or similar form of appeal limited to the examination of points of law only. Moreover, the court seised of such an appeal on a point of law under Article 37(2) of the Convention does not have jurisdiction to impose or reimpose such a stay.

Article 46 [ex 38]

ECJ, 22 November 1977, case 43/77, Industrial Diamond Supplies

The expression 'ordinary appeal' within the meaning of Articles 30 and 38 of the 1968 Brussels Convention must be defined solely within the framework of the system of the Convention itself and not according to the law either of the State in which the judgment was given or of the State in which recognition of enforcement of that judgment is sought.

Within the meaning of Articles 30 and 38 of the Convention, any appeal which is such that it may result in the annulment or the amendment of the judgment which is the subject-matter of the procedure for recognition or enforcement under the Convention and the lodging of which is bound, in the State in which the judgment was given, to a period which is laid down by the law and starts to run by virtue of that same judgment constitutes an 'ordinary appeal' which has been lodged or may be lodged against a foreign judgment.

ECJ, 27 November 1984, case 258/83, Calzaturificio Brennero

The second paragraph of Article 38 of the 1968 Brussels Convention must be interpreted as meaning that a court with which an appeal has been lodged against a decision authorising enforcement, given pursuant to the Convention, may make enforcement conditional on the provision of security only when it gives judgment on the appeal.

ECJ, 4 October 1991, case C-183/90, van Dalfsen

The second paragraph of Article 37 of the 1968 Brussels Convention is to be interpreted as meaning that a decision taken under Article 38 of the Convention by which the court with which an appeal has been lodged against an order for the enforcement of a judgment given in another Contracting State has refused to stay the proceedings and has ordered the party to whom the enforcement order was granted to provide security does not constitute a 'judgment given on the appeal' within the meaning of the second paragraph of Article 37 of the Convention and may not, therefore, be contested by an appeal in cassation or similar form of appeal. The position is the same where the decision taken under Article 38 of the Convention and the 'judgment given on the appeal' within the meaning of the second paragraph of Article 37 of the Convention are given in a single judgment.

The first paragraph of Article 38 of the Convention is to be interpreted as meaning that a court with which an appeal is lodged against an order for the enforcement of a judgment given in another Contracting State may take into consideration, in a decision concerning an application for the proceedings to be stayed under that paragraph, only such submissions as the appellant was unable to make before the court of the State in which the judgment was given.

ECJ, 11 August 1995, case C-432/93, SISRO

Article 37(2) and the first paragraph of Article 38 of the 1968 Brussels Convention are to be interpreted as meaning that a decision by which a court of a Contracting State, seised of an appeal against authorisation to enforce an enforceable judgment of a court in another

Contracting State, refuses a stay or lifts a stay previously ordered cannot be contested by an appeal in cassation or similar form of appeal limited to the examination of points of law only. Moreover, the court seised of such an appeal on a point of law under Article 37(2) of the Convention does not have jurisdiction to impose or reimpose such a stay.

Article 47 [ex 39]

ECJ, 3 October 1985, case 119/84, Capelloni and Aquilini

By virtue of Article 39 of the Convention, a party who has applied for and obtained authorisation for enforcement may, within the period mentioned in that Article, proceed directly with protective measures against the property of the party against whom enforcement is sought and is under no obligation to obtain specific authorisation.

A party who has obtained authorisation for enforcement may proceed with the protective measures referred to in Article 39 until the expiry of the period prescribed in Article 36 for lodging an appeal and, if such an appeal is lodged, until a decision is given thereon.

A party who has proceeded with the protective measures referred to in Article 39 of the Convention is under no obligation to obtain, in respect of those measures, any confirmatory judgment required by the national law of the court in question.

Article 47 of the Convention

ECJ, 14 March 1996, case C-275/94, van der Linden

Article 47(1) of the 1968 Brussels Convention is to be interpreted as meaning that, where the domestic procedural rules so permit, proof of service of the judgment may be produced after the application has been made, in particular during the course of appeal proceedings subsequently brought by the party against whom enforcement is sought, provided that that party is given a reasonable period of time in which to satisfy the judgment voluntarily and that the party seeking enforcement bears all costs unnecessarily incurred.

Article 57 [ex 50]

ECJ, 17 June 1999, case C-260/97, Unibank

An acknowledgment of indebtedness enforceable under the law of the State of origin whose authenticity has not been established by a public authority or other authority empowered for that purpose by that State does not constitute an authentic instrument within the meaning of Article 50 of the 1968 Brussels Convention.

Article 61 [ex II of the Protocol annexed]

ECJ, 26 May 1981, case 157/80, Rinkau

The expression 'an offence which was not intentionally committed' within the meaning of Article II of the Protocol annexed to the 1968 Brussels Convention should be understood as meaning any offence the legal definition of which does not require, either expressly or as appears from the nature of the offence defined, the existence of intent on the part of the accused to commit the punishable act or omission.

The accused's right to be defended without appearing in person, granted by Article II of the Protocol annexed to the Convention, applies in all criminal proceedings concerning offences which were not intentionally committed, in which the accused's liability at civil law, arising from the elements of the offence for which he is being prosecuted, is in question or on which such liability might subsequently be based.

Article 66 [ex 54]

ECJ, 13 November 1979, case 25/79, Sanicentral

Articles 17 and 54 of the 1968 Brussels Convention must be interpreted to mean that, in judicial proceedings instituted after the coming into force of the Convention, clauses conferring jurisdiction included in contracts of employment concluded prior to that date must be considered valid even in cases in which they would have been regarded as void under the national law in force at the time when the contract was entered into.

Article 68

ECJ, 28 April 2009, case C-420/07, Apostolides

The suspension of the application of the *acquis communautaire* in those areas of the Republic of Cyprus in which the Government of that Member State does not exercise effective control, provided for by Article 1(1) of Protocol No 10 on Cyprus to the Act concerning the conditions of accession [to the European Union] of the Czech Republic, the Republic of Estonia, the Republic of Cyprus, the Republic of Latvia, the Republic of Lithuania, the Republic of Hungary, the Republic of Malta, the Republic of Poland, the Republic of Slovenia and the Slovak Republic and the adjustments to the Treaties on which the European Union is founded, does not preclude the application of Regulation No 44/2001 of 22 December 2000 on jurisdiction and the recognition and enforcement of judgments in civil and commercial matters to a judgment which is given by a Cypriot court sitting in the area of the island effectively controlled by the Cypriot Government, but concerns land situated in areas not so controlled.

Articles 69–70 [ex 55–56]

ECJ, 14 July 1977, joined cases 9/77 and 10/77, Bavaria

The first paragraph of Article 56 of the 1968 Brussels Convention does not prevent a bilateral agreement such as the German-Belgian Convention, which is the fifth to be listed in Article 55, from continuing to have effect in relation to judgments which do not fall under the second paragraph of Article 1 of the Convention first abovementioned, but to which nevertheless that Convention does not apply.

Article 71 [ex 57]

ECJ, 6 December 1994, case C-406/92, Tatry

On a proper construction, Article 57 of the 1968 Brussels Convention means that, where a Contracting State is also a contracting party to another convention on a specific matter containing rules on jurisdiction, that specialised convention precludes the application of the provisions of the Brussels Convention only in cases governed by the specialised convention and not in those to which it does not apply.

ECJ, 28 October 2004, case C-148/03, Nürnberger Allgemeine Vers

Article 57(2)(a) of the 1968 Brussels Convention should be interpreted as meaning that the court of a Contracting State in which a defendant domiciled in another Contracting State is sued may derive its jurisdiction from a specialised convention to which the first State is a party as well and which contains specific rules on jurisdiction, even where the defendant, in the course of the proceedings in question, submits no pleas on the merits.

CJ, 4 May 2010, case C-533/08, TNT Express

Article 71 of Regulation No 44/2001 must be interpreted as meaning that, in a case such as the main proceedings, the rules governing jurisdiction, recognition and enforcement that are laid down by a convention on a particular matter, such as the *lis pendens* rule set out in Article 31(2) of the Convention on the Contract for the International Carriage of Goods by Road, signed at Geneva on 19 May 1956, as amended by the Protocol signed at Geneva on 5 July 1978, and the rule relating to enforceability set out in Article 31(3) of that convention, apply provided that they are highly predictable, facilitate the sound administration of justice and enable the risk of concurrent proceedings to be minimised and that they ensure, under conditions at least as favourable as those provided for by the regulation, the free movement of judgments in civil and commercial matters and mutual trust in the administration of justice in the European Union (*favor executionis*).

 The Court of Justice of the European Union does not have jurisdiction to interpret Article 31 of the Convention on the Contract for the International Carriage of Goods by Road, as amended.

B.1.   Council Decision 2009/430/EC of 27 November 2008 concerning the conclusion of the Convention on jurisdiction and the recognition and enforcement of judgments in civil and commercial matters (OJ, L 147 of 10 June 2009)

 (1)   On 16 September 1988, the Member States of the European Communities signed an international agreement with the Republic of Iceland, the Kingdom of Norway and the Swiss Confederation on jurisdiction and the enforcement of judgments in civil and commercial matters (the Lugano Convention), thereby extending to Iceland, Norway,

and Switzerland the application of the rules of the Convention of 27 September 1968 on the same subject matter (the Brussels Convention).

(2)   Negotiations concerning a revision of the Brussels Convention and the Lugano Convention were undertaken during the years 1998–99 within the framework of an ad hoc Working Party enlarged with Iceland, Norway and Switzerland. These negotiations led to the adoption of a text of a draft convention prepared by the Working Party, which was confirmed by the Council at its meeting on 27 and 28 May 1999.

(3)   Subsequent negotiations within the Council on the basis of this text led to the adoption of Council Regulation (EC) No 44/2001 of 22 December 2000 on jurisdiction and the recognition and enforcement of judgments in civil and commercial matters, which modernised the rules of the Brussels Convention and made the system of recognition and enforcement swifter and more efficient.

(4)   In the light of the parallelism between the Brussels and the Lugano Convention regimes on jurisdiction and on recognition and enforcement of judgments in civil and commercial matters, the rules of the Lugano Convention should be aligned with the rules of Regulation (EC) No 44/2001 in order to achieve the same level of circulation of judgments between the EU Member States and the EFTA States concerned.

(5)   In accordance with the Protocol on the position of Denmark, annexed to the Treaty on European Union and to the Treaty establishing the European Community, Denmark does not take part in the application of measures pursuant to Title IV of the Treaty establishing the European Community. In order for the rules of the Lugano Convention to apply to Denmark, Denmark should therefore participate as a Contracting Party to a new convention covering the same subject matter.

(6)   By Decision of 27 September 2002, the Council authorised the Commission to negotiate with a view to the adoption of a new Lugano Convention on jurisdiction and the recognition and enforcement of judgments in civil and commercial matters.

(7)   The Commission negotiated such a convention, on behalf of the Community, with Iceland, Norway, Switzerland and Denmark. This Convention was signed, on behalf of the Community, on 30 October 2007 in accordance with Council Decision 2007/712/EC, subject to its conclusion at a later date.

(8)   At the time of the adoption of Decision 2007/712/EC the Council agreed to examine in the framework of the discussions on the conclusion of the new Lugano Convention the possibility of making a declaration in accordance with Article II(2) of Protocol 1 to the Convention. The Community should make such a declaration at the time of conclusion of the Convention.

(9)   During the negotiations of the Convention the Community committed itself to making a declaration, at the time of ratification of the Convention, to the effect that when amending Regulation (EC) No 44/2001 the Community would clarify the scope of Article 22(4) of the said Regulation with a view to taking into account the relevant case law of the Court of Justice of the European Communities with respect to proceedings concerned with the registration or validity of intellectual property rights, thereby ensuring its parallelism with Article 22(4) of the Convention. In this context, regard should be had to the results of the evaluation of the application of Regulation (EC) No 44/2001.

(10) In accordance with Article 3 of the Protocol on the position of the United Kingdom and Ireland, annexed to the Treaty on European Union and to the Treaty establishing the European Community, the United Kingdom and Ireland are taking part in the adoption and application of this Decision.

(11) In accordance with Articles 1 and 2 of the Protocol on the position of Denmark, Denmark does not take part in the adoption of this Decision and is not bound by it or subject to its application.

(12) The Convention should now be concluded.

Article 1.   The conclusion of the Convention on jurisdiction and the recognition and enforcement of judgments in civil and commercial matters, which will replace the Lugano Convention of 16 September 1988, is hereby approved on behalf of the Community.

When depositing its instrument of ratification, the Community shall make the declarations set out in Annexes I and II to this Decision.

The text of the Convention is attached to this Decision.

Article 2.   The President of the Council is hereby authorised to designate the person(s) empowered to deposit on behalf of the Community the instrument of ratification in accordance with Article 69(2) of the Convention.

B.2.   Declaration by the European Community (OJ, L 147 of 10 June 2009)

The European Community hereby declares that, when amending Council Regulation (EC) No 44/2001 on jurisdiction, recognition and enforcement of judgments in civil and commercial matters, it intends to clarify the scope of Article 22(4) of the said Regulation with a view to taking into account the relevant case law of the Court of Justice of the European Communities with respect to proceedings concerned with the registration or validity of intellectual property rights, thereby ensuring its parallelism with Article 22(4) of the Convention while taking into account the results of the evaluation of the application of Regulation (EC) No 44/2001.

B.3.   Declaration by the European Community in accordance with Article II(2) of Protocol 1 to the Convention (OJ, L 147 of 10 June 2009)

The European Community declares that proceedings referred to in Articles 6(2) and 11 may not be resorted to in the following Member States: Estonia, Latvia, Lithuania, Poland and Slovenia in addition to the three already mentioned in Annex IX to the Convention.

In accordance with Article 77(2) of the Convention the Standing Committee set up by Article 4 of Protocol 2 to the Convention should therefore as soon as the Convention enters into force be requested to amend Annex IX to the Convention as follows:

'Annex IX

The States and the rules referred to in Article II of Protocol 1 are the following:
—   Germany: Articles 68, 72, 73 and 74 of the code of civil procedure (Zivilprozessordnung) concerning third-party notices,
—   Estonia: Articles 214(3) and (4) and Article 216 of the Code of Civil Procedure (tsiviilkohtumenetluse seadustik) concerning third-party notices,
—   Latvia: Articles 78, 79, 80 and 81 of the Civil Procedure Law (Civilprocesa likums) concerning third-party notices,
—   Lithuania: Article 47 of the Code of Civil Procedure (Civilinio proceso kodeksas),
—   Hungary: Articles 58 to 60 of the Code of Civil Procedure (Polgári perrendtartás) concerning third-party notices,
—   Austria: Article 21 of the code of civil procedure (Zivilprozessordnung) concerning third-party notices,
—   Poland: Articles 84 and 85 of the Code of Civil Procedure (Kodeks postępowania cywilnego) concerning third-party notices (przypozwanie),
—   Slovenia: Article 204 of the Civil Procedure Act (Zakon o pravdnem postopku) concerning third-party notices,
—   Switzerland, with respect to those cantons whose applicable code of civil procedure does not provide for the jurisdiction referred to in Articles 6(2) and 11 of the Convention: the appropriate provisions concerning third-party notices (*litis denuntiatio*) of the applicable code of civil procedure.'

B.4.   Convention on jurisdiction and the recognition and enforcement of judgments in civil and commercial matters (OJ, L 147 of 10 June 2009)[1]

Article 69.   1.   The Convention shall be open for signature by the European Community, Denmark, and States which, at the time of the opening for signature, are Members of the European Free Trade Association.
2.   This Convention shall be subject to ratification by the Signatories. The instruments of ratification shall be deposited with the Swiss Federal Council, which shall act as Depositary of this Convention.
3.   At the time of the ratification, the Contracting Parties may submit declarations in accordance with Articles I, II and III of Protocol 1.
4.   The Convention shall enter into force on the first day of the sixth month following the date on which the European Community and a Member of the European Free Trade Association deposit their instruments of ratification.

---

[1]   Only the final provisions (Title VIII) of the Lugano Convention, with Protocols, are published here. Annexes and other provisions are published as footnotes to the text of Regulation (EC) No 44/2001, in this Chapter, General provisions, A.1, in so far as they differ from the provisions of the latter. The Explanatory report by professor F Pocar is published in OJ, C 319 of 23 December 2009. The Convention has entered into force on 1 January 2010 for the European Union, Denmark and Norway (OJ, L 140 of 8 June 2010) and it will entry into force in the relationships with Switzerland on 1 January 2011. [Note of the Editor]

5.   The Convention shall enter into force in relation to any other Party on the first day of the third month following the deposit of its instrument of ratification.

6.   Without prejudice to Article 3(3) of Protocol 2, this Convention shall replace the Convention on jurisdiction and the enforcement of judgments in civil and commercial matters done at Lugano on 16 September 1988 as of the date of its entry into force in accordance with paragraphs 4 and 5 above. Any reference to the 1988 Lugano Convention in other instruments shall be understood as a reference to this Convention.

7.   In so far as the relations between the Member States of the European Community and the non–European territories referred to in Article 70(1)(b) are concerned, this Convention shall replace the Convention on Jurisdiction and the Enforcement of Judgments in Civil and Commercial Matters, signed at Brussels on 27 September 1968, and of the Protocol on interpretation of that Convention by the Court of Justice of the European Communities, signed at Luxembourg on 3 June 1971, as amended by the Conventions of Accession to the said Convention and the said Protocol by the States acceding to the European Communities, as of the date of the entry into force of this Convention with respect to these territories in accordance with Article 73(2).

Article 70.   1.   After entering into force this Convention shall be open for accession by:

(a)   the States which, after the opening of this Convention for signature, become Members of the European Free Trade Association, under the conditions laid down in Article 71;

(b)   Member States of the European Community acting on behalf of certain non-European territories that are part of the territory of that Member State or for whose external relations that Member State is responsible, under the conditions laid down in Article 71;

(c)   any other State, under the conditions laid down in Article 72.

2.   States referred to in paragraph 1, which wish to become a Contracting Party to this Convention, shall address their application to the Depositary. The application, including the information referred to in Articles 71 and 72 shall be accompanied by a translation into English and French.

Article 71.   1.   Any State referred to in Articles 70(1)(a) and (b) wishing to become a Contracting Party to this Convention:

(a)   shall communicate the information required for the application of this Convention;

(b)   may submit declarations in accordance with Articles I and III of Protocol 1.

2. The Depositary shall transmit any information received pursuant to paragraph 1 to the other Contracting Parties prior to the deposit of the instrument of accession by the State concerned.

Article 72.   1.   Any State referred to in Article 70(1)(c) wishing to become a Contracting Party to this Convention:

(a)   shall communicate the information required for the application of this Convention;

(b)   may submit declarations in accordance with Articles I and III of Protocol 1; and

(c)   shall provide the Depositary with information on, in particular:

(1) their judicial system, including information on the appointment and independence of judges;

(2) their internal law concerning civil procedure and enforcement of judgments; and

(3) their private international law relating to civil procedure.

2. The Depositary shall transmit any information received pursuant to paragraph 1 to the other Contracting Parties prior to inviting the State concerned to accede in accordance with paragraph 3 of this Article.

3. Without prejudice to paragraph 4, the Depositary shall invite the State concerned to accede only if it has obtained the unanimous agreement of the Contracting Parties. The Contracting Parties shall endeavour to give their consent at the latest within one year after the invitation by the Depositary.

4. The Convention shall enter into force only in relations between the acceding State and the Contracting Parties which have not made any objections to the accession before the first day of the third month following the deposit of the instrument of accession.

Article 73. 1. The instruments of accession shall be deposited with the Depositary.

2. In respect of an acceding State referred to in Article 70, the Convention shall enter into force on the first day of the third month following the deposit of its instrument of accession. As of that moment, the acceding State shall be considered a Contracting Party to the Convention.

3. Any Contracting Party may submit to the Depositary a text of this Convention in the language or languages of the Contracting Party concerned, which shall be authentic if so agreed by the Contracting Parties in accordance with Article 4 of Protocol 2.

Article 74. 1. This Convention is concluded for an unlimited period.

2. Any Contracting Party may, at any time, denounce the Convention by sending a notification to the Depositary.

3. The denunciation shall take effect at the end of the calendar year following the expiry of a period of six months from the date of receipt by the Depositary of the notification of denunciation.

Article 75. The following are annexed to this Convention:
— a Protocol 1, on certain questions of jurisdiction, procedure and enforcement;
— a Protocol 2, on the uniform interpretation of this Convention and on the Standing Committee;
— a Protocol 3, on the application of Article 67 of this Convention;
— Annexes I through IV and Annex VII, with information related to the application of this Convention;
— Annexes V and VI, containing the certificates referred to in Articles 54, 58 and 57 of this Convention;
— Annex VIII, containing the authentic languages referred to in Article 79 of this Convention, and
— Annex IX, concerning the application of Article II of Protocol 1.

These Protocols and Annexes shall form an integral part of this Convention.

Article 76. Without prejudice to Article 77, any Contracting Party may request the revision of this Convention. To that end, the Depositary shall convene the Standing Committee as laid down in Article 4 of Protocol 2.

Article 77. 1. The Contracting Parties shall communicate to the Depositary the text of any provisions of the laws which amend the lists set out in Annexes I through IV as well as any deletions in or additions to the list set out in Annex VII and the date of their entry into force. Such communication shall be made within reasonable time before the entry into force and be accompanied by a translation into English and French. The Depositary shall adapt the Annexes concerned accordingly, after having consulted the Standing Committee in accordance with Article 4 of Protocol 2. For that purpose, the Contracting Parties shall provide a translation of the adaptations into their languages.

2. Any amendment of Annexes V through VI and VIII through IX to this Convention shall be adopted by the Standing Committee in accordance with Article 4 of Protocol 2.

Article 78. 1. The Depositary shall notify the Contracting Parties of:
(a) the deposit of each instrument of ratification or accession:
(b) the dates of entry into force of this Convention in respect of the Contracting Parties;
(c) any declaration received pursuant to Articles I to IV of Protocol 1;
(d) any communication made pursuant to Article 74(2), Article 77(1) and paragraph 4 of Protocol 3.

2. The notifications will be accompanied by translations into English and French.

Protocol 1 on certain questions of jurisdiction, procedure and enforcement

Article I. 1. Judicial and extrajudicial documents drawn up in one State bound by this Convention which have to be served on persons in another State bound by this Convention shall be transmitted in accordance with the procedures laid down in the conventions and agreements applicable between these States.

2. Unless the Contracting Party on whose territory service is to take place objects by declaration to the Depositary, such documents may also be sent by the appropriate public officers of the State in which the document has been drawn up directly to the appropriate public officers of the State in which the addressee is to be found. In this case the officer of the State of origin shall send a copy of the document to the officer of the State applied to who is competent to forward it to the addressee. The document shall be forwarded in the manner specified by the law of the State applied to. The forwarding shall be recorded by a certificate sent directly to the officer of the State of origin.

3. Member States of the European Community bound by Council Regulation (EC) No 1348/2000 of 29 May 2000 or by the Agreement between the European Community and the Kingdom of Denmark on the service of judicial and extrajudicial documents in civil or commercial matters, signed at Brussels on 19 October 2005, shall apply in their mutual relations that Regulation and that Agreement.

Article II. 1. The jurisdiction specified in Articles 6(2) and 11 in actions on a warranty or guarantee or in any other third party proceedings may not be fully resorted to in the

States bound by this Convention referred to in Annex IX. Any person domiciled in another State bound by this Convention may be sued in the courts of these States pursuant to the rules referred to in Annex IX.

2.   At the time of ratification the European Community may declare that proceedings referred to in Articles 6(2) and 11 may not be resorted to in some other Member States and provide information on the rules that shall apply.

3.   Judgments given in the other States bound by this Convention by virtue of Article 6(2) or Article 11 shall be recognised and enforced in the States mentioned in paragraphs 1 and 2 in accordance with Title III. Any effects which judgments given in these States may have on third parties by application of the provisions in paragraphs 1 and 2 shall also be recognised in the other States bound by this Convention.

Article III.   1.   Switzerland reserves the right to declare upon ratification that it will not apply the following part of the provision in Article 34(2): 'unless the defendant failed to commence proceedings to challenge the judgment when it was possible for him to do so'.

If Switzerland makes such declaration, the other Contracting Parties shall apply the same reservation in respect of judgments rendered by the courts of Switzerland.

2.   Contracting Parties may, in respect of judgments rendered in an acceding State referred to in Article 70(1)(c), by declaration reserve:

(a)   the right mentioned in paragraph 1; and

(b)   the right of an authority mentioned in Article 39, notwithstanding the provisions of Article 41, to examine of its own motion whether any of the grounds for refusal of recognition and enforcement of a judgment is present or not.

3.   If a Contracting Party has made such a reservation towards an acceding State as referred to in paragraph 2, this acceding State may by declaration reserve the same right in respect of judgments rendered by the courts of that Contracting Party.

4.   Except for the reservation mentioned in paragraph 1, the declarations are valid for periods of five years and are renewable at the end of such periods. The Contracting Party shall notify a renewal of a declaration referred to under paragraph 2 not later than six months prior to the end of such period. An acceding State may only renew its declaration made under paragraph 3 after renewal of the respective declaration under paragraph 2.

Article IV.   The declarations referred to in this Protocol may be withdrawn at any time by notification to the Depositary. The notification shall be accompanied by a translation into English and French. The Contracting Parties provide for translations into their languages. Any such withdrawal shall take effect as of the first day of the third month following that notification.

Protocol 2 on the uniform interpretation of the Convention and on the Standing Committee

Considering the substantial link between this Convention, the 1988 Lugano Convention, and the instruments referred to in Article 64(1) of this Convention,

Considering that the Court of Justice of the European Communities has jurisdiction to give rulings on the interpretation of the provisions of the instruments referred to in Article 64(1) of this Convention,

Considering that this Convention becomes part of Community rules and that therefore the Court of Justice of the European Communities has jurisdiction to give rulings on the interpretation of the provisions of this Convention as regards the application by the courts of the Member States of the European Community,

Being aware of the rulings delivered by the Court of Justice of the European Communities on the interpretation of the instruments referred to in Article 64(1) of this Convention up to the time of signature of this Convention, and of the rulings delivered by the courts of the Contracting Parties to the 1988 Lugano Convention on the latter Convention up to the time of signature of this Convention,

Considering that the parallel revision of both the 1988 Lugano and Brussels Conventions, which led to the conclusion of a revised text for these Conventions, was substantially based on the above-mentioned rulings on the 1968 Brussels and the 1988 Lugano Conventions,

Considering that the revised text of the Brussels Convention has been incorporated, after the entry into force of the Amsterdam Treaty, into Regulation (EC) No 44/2001,

Considering that this revised text also constituted the basis for the text of this Convention,

Desiring to prevent, in full deference to the independence of the courts, divergent interpretations and to arrive at an interpretation as uniform as possible of the provisions of this Convention and of those of the Regulation (EC) No 44/2001 which are substantially reproduced in this Convention and of other instruments referred to in Article 64(1) of this Convention.

Article 1.   1.   Any court applying and interpreting this Convention shall pay due account to the principles laid down by any relevant decision concerning the provision(s) concerned or any similar provision(s) of the 1988 Lugano Convention and the instruments referred to in Article 64(1) of the Convention rendered by the courts of the States bound by this Convention and by the Court of Justice of the European Communities.

2.   For the courts of Member States of the European Community, the obligation laid down in paragraph 1 shall apply without prejudice to their obligations in relation to the Court of Justice of the European Communities resulting from the Treaty establishing the European Community or from the Agreement between the European Community and the Kingdom of Denmark on jurisdiction and the recognition and enforcement of judgments in civil and commercial matters, signed at Brussels on 19 October 2005.

Article 2.   Any State bound by this Convention and which is not a Member State of the European Community is entitled to submit statements of case or written observations, in accordance with Article 23 of the Protocol on the Statute of the Court of Justice of the European Communities, where a court or tribunal of a Member State of the European Community refers to the Court of Justice for a preliminary ruling a question on the interpretation of this Convention or of the instruments referred to in Article 64(1) of this Convention.

Article 3.   1.   The Commission of the European Communities shall set up a system of exchange of information concerning relevant judgments delivered pursuant to this Convention as well as relevant judgments under the 1988 Lugano Convention and the instruments referred to in Article 64(1) of this Convention. This system shall be accessible to the public and contain judgments delivered by the courts of last instance and of the Court of Justice of the European Communities as well as judgments of particular importance which have become final and have been delivered pursuant to this Convention, the 1988 Lugano Convention, and the instruments referred to in Article 64(1) of this Convention. The judgments shall be classified and provided with an abstract.

The system shall comprise the transmission to the Commission by the competent authorities of the States bound by this Convention of judgments as referred to above delivered by the courts of these States.

2.   A selection of cases of particular interest for the proper functioning of the Convention will be made by the Registrar of the Court of Justice of the European Communities, who shall present the selected case law at the meeting of experts in accordance with Article 5 of this Protocol.

3.   Until the European Communities have set up the system pursuant to paragraph 1, the Court of Justice of the European Communities shall maintain the system for the exchange of information established by Protocol 2 of the 1988 Lugano Convention for judgments delivered under this Convention and the 1988 Lugano Convention.

Article 4.   1.   A Standing Committee shall be set up, composed of the representatives of the Contracting Parties.

2.   At the request of a Contracting Party, the Depositary of the Convention shall convene meetings of the Committee for the purpose of:

—   a consultation on the relationship between this Convention and other international instruments;

—   a consultation on the application of Article 67, including intended accessions to instruments on particular matters according to Article 67(1), and proposed legislation according to Protocol 3;

—   the consideration of the accession of new States. In particular, the Committee may ask acceding States referred to in Article 70(1)(c) questions about their judicial systems and the implementation of the Convention. The Committee may also consider possible adaptations to the Convention necessary for its application in the acceding States;

—   the acceptance of new authentic language versions pursuant to Article 73(3) of this Convention and the necessary amendments to Annex VIII;

—   a consultation on a revision of the Convention pursuant to Article 76;

—   a consultation on amendments to Annexes I through IV and Annex VII pursuant to Article 77(1);

—   the adoption of amendments to Annexes V and VI pursuant to Article 77(2);

—   a withdrawal of the reservations and declarations made by the Contracting Parties pursuant to Protocol 1 and necessary amendments to Annex IX.

3.   The Committee shall establish the procedural rules concerning its functioning and decision–making. These rules shall provide for the possibility to consult and decide by written procedure.

Article 5.   1.   The Depositary may convene, whenever necessary, a meeting of experts to exchange views on the functioning of the Convention, in particular on the development of the case-law and new legislation that may influence the application of the Convention.

2.   This meeting shall be composed of experts of the Contracting Parties, of the States bound by this Convention, of the Court of Justice of the European Communities,

and of the European Free Trade Association. It shall be open to any other experts whose presence is deemed appropriate.

3.   Any problems arising on the functioning of the Convention may be referred to the Standing Committee referred to in Article 4 of this Protocol for further action.

Protocol 3 on the application of Article 67 of the Convention

1.   For the purposes of the Convention, provisions which, in relation to particular matters, govern jurisdiction or the recognition or enforcement of judgments and which are or will be contained in acts of the institutions of the European Communities shall be treated in the same way as the conventions referred to in Article 67(1).

2.   If one of the Contracting Parties is of the opinion that a provision contained in a proposed act of the institutions of the European Communities is incompatible with the Convention, the Contracting Parties shall promptly consider amending the Convention pursuant to Article 76, without prejudice to the procedure established by Protocol 2.

3.   Where a Contracting Party or several Parties together incorporate some or all of the provisions contained in acts of the institutions of the European Community referred to in paragraph 1 into national law, then these provisions of national law shall be treated in the same way as the conventions referred to in Article 67(1).

4.   The Contracting Parties shall communicate to the Depositary the text of the provisions mentioned in paragraph 3. Such communication shall be accompanied by a translation into English and French.

B.5.   Statements made at the meeting of the Council (LSA) of 24 September 1996 (Doc. Consilium No 10048/96 ADD. 1): Statement 2(a)

See Chapter VI, Employment and agency, B.2.

B.6.   ECJ case-law regarding the Lugano Convention

ECJ, opinion 7 February 2006, n. 1/03: points 134–173

See Chapter I, The external dimension, O.

ECJ, 2 April 2009, case C–394/07, Gambazzi

See Chapter II, Due process, A.

C. Regulation (EC) No 805/2004 of the European Parliament and of the Council of 21 April 2004 creating a European Enforcement Order for uncontested claims (OJ, L 143 of 30 April 2004)[1]

(1) The Community has set itself the objective of maintaining and developing an area of freedom, security and justice, in which the free movement of persons is ensured. To this end, the Community is to adopt, inter alia, measures in the field of judicial cooperation in civil matters that are necessary for the proper functioning of the internal market.

(2) On 3 December 1998, the Council adopted an Action Plan of the Council and the Commission on how best to implement the provisions of the Treaty of Amsterdam on an area of freedom, security and justice (the Vienna Action Plan).

(3) The European Council meeting in Tampere on 15 and 16 October 1999 endorsed the principle of mutual recognition of judicial decisions as the cornerstone for the creation of a genuine judicial area.

(4) On 30 November 2000, the Council adopted a programme of measures for implementation of the principle of mutual recognition of decisions in civil and commercial matters. This programme includes in its first stage the abolition of *exequatur*, that is to say, the creation of a European Enforcement Order for uncontested claims.

(5) The concept of 'uncontested claims' should cover all situations in which a creditor, given the verified absence of any dispute by the debtor as to the nature or extent of a pecuniary claim, has obtained either a court decision against that debtor or an enforceable document that requires the debtor's express consent, be it a court settlement or an authentic instrument.

(6) The absence of objections from the debtor as stipulated in Article 3(1)(b) can take the shape of default of appearance at a court hearing or of failure to comply with an invitation by the court to give written notice of an intention to defend the case.

(7) This Regulation should apply to judgments, court settlements and authentic instruments on uncontested claims and to decisions delivered following challenges to judgments, court settlements and authentic instruments certified as European Enforcement Orders.

(8) In its Tampere conclusions, the European Council considered that access to enforcement in a Member State other than that in which the judgment has been given should be accelerated and simplified by dispensing with any intermediate measures to be taken prior to enforcement in the Member State in which enforcement is sought. A judgment that has been certified as a European Enforcement Order by the court of origin should, for enforcement purposes, be treated as if it had been delivered in the Member State in which enforcement is sought. In the United Kingdom, for example, the registration of a certified foreign judgment will therefore follow the same rules as the registration of a judgment from another part of the United Kingdom and is not to imply a review as to the substance of the foreign judgment. Arrangements for the enforcement of judgments should continue to be governed by national law.

(9) Such a procedure should offer significant advantages as compared with the *exequatur* procedure provided for in Council Regulation (EC) No 44/2001 of 22 December

---

[1] As finally amended by Regulation (EC) No 1103/2008 (OJ, L 304 of 14 November 2008). The Annexes to the Regulation are not published. [Note of the Editor]

2000 on jurisdiction and the recognition and enforcement of judgments in civil and commercial matters, in that there is no need for approval by the judiciary in a second Member State with the delays and expenses that this entails.

(10) Where a court in a Member State has given judgment on an uncontested claim in the absence of participation of the debtor in the proceedings, the abolition of any checks in the Member State of enforcement is inextricably linked to and dependent upon the existence of a sufficient guarantee of observance of the rights of the defence.

(11) This Regulation seeks to promote the fundamental rights and takes into account the principles recognised in particular by the Charter of Fundamental Rights of the European Union. In particular, it seeks to ensure full respect for the right to a fair trial as recognised in Article 47 of the Charter.

(12) Minimum standards should be established for the proceedings leading to the judgment in order to ensure that the debtor is informed about the court action against him, the requirements for his active participation in the proceedings to contest the claim and the consequences of his non-participation in sufficient time and in such a way as to enable him to arrange for his defence.

(13) Due to differences between the Member States as regards the rules of civil procedure and especially those governing the service of documents, it is necessary to lay down a specific and detailed definition of those minimum standards. In particular, any method of service that is based on a legal fiction as regards the fulfilment of those minimum standards cannot be considered sufficient for the certification of a judgment as a European Enforcement Order.

(14) All the methods of service listed in Articles 13 and 14 are characterised by either full certainty (Article 13) or a very high degree of likelihood (Article 14) that the document served has reached its addressee. In the second category, a judgment should only be certified as a European Enforcement Order if the Member State of origin has an appropriate mechanism in place enabling the debtor to apply for a full review of the judgment under the conditions set out in Article 19 in those exceptional cases where, in spite of compliance with Article 14, the document has not reached the addressee.

(15) Personal service on certain persons other than the debtor himself pursuant to Articles 14(1)(a) and (b) should be understood to meet the requirements of those provisions only if those persons actually accepted/received the document in question.

(16) Article 15 should apply to situations where the debtor cannot represent himself in court, as in the case of a legal person, and where a person to represent him is determined by law as well as situations where the debtor has authorised another person, in particular a lawyer, to represent him in the specific court proceedings at issue.

(17) The courts competent for scrutinising full compliance with the minimum procedural standards should, if satisfied, issue a standardised European Enforcement Order certificate that makes that scrutiny and its result transparent.

(18) Mutual trust in the administration of justice in the Member States justifies the assessment by the court of one Member State that all conditions for certification as a European Enforcement Order are fulfilled to enable a judgment to be enforced in all other Member States without judicial review of the proper application of the minimum procedural standards in the Member State where the judgment is to be enforced.

(19) This Regulation does not imply an obligation for the Member States to adapt their national legislation to the minimum procedural standards set out herein. It provides an incentive to that end by making available a more efficient and rapid enforceability of judgments in other Member States only if those minimum standards are met.

(20) Application for certification as a European Enforcement Order for uncontested claims should be optional for the creditor, who may instead choose the system of recognition and enforcement under Regulation (EC) No 44/2001 or other Community instruments.

(21) When a document has to be sent from one Member State to another for service there, this Regulation and in particular the rules on service set out herein should apply together with Council Regulation (EC) No 1348/2000 of 29 May 2000 on the service in the Member States of judicial and extrajudicial documents in civil or commercial matters (1), and in particular Article 14 thereof in conjunction with Member States declarations made under Article 23 thereof.

(22) Since the objectives of the proposed action cannot be sufficiently achieved by the Member States and can therefore, by reason of the scale or effects of the action, be better achieved at Community level, the Community may adopt measures, in accordance with the principle of subsidiarity as set out in Article 5 of the Treaty. In accordance with the principle of proportionality, as set out in that Article, this Regulation does not go beyond what is necessary in order to achieve those objectives.

(23) The measures necessary for the implementation of this Regulation should be adopted in accordance with Council Decision the exercise of implementing powers conferred on the Commission.

(24) In accordance with Article 3 of the Protocol on the position of the United Kingdom and Ireland annexed to the Treaty on European Union and the Treaty establishing the European Community, the United Kingdom and Ireland have notified their wish to take part in the adoption and application of this Regulation.

(25) In accordance with Articles 1 and 2 of the Protocol on the position of Denmark annexed to the Treaty on European Union and the Treaty establishing the European Community, Denmark does not take part in the adoption of this Regulation, and is therefore not bound by it or subject to its application.

(26) Pursuant to the second indent of Article 67(5) of the Treaty, the codecision procedure is applicable from 1 February 2003 for the measures laid down in this Regulation;

Chapter I — Subject matter, scope and definitions

Article 1. Subject matter. The purpose of this Regulation is to create a European Enforcement Order for uncontested claims to permit, by laying down minimum standards, the free circulation of judgments, court settlements and authentic instruments throughout all Member States without any intermediate proceedings needing to be brought in the Member State of enforcement prior to recognition and enforcement.

Article 2. Scope. 1. This Regulation shall apply in civil and commercial matters, whatever the nature of the court or tribunal. It shall not extend, in particular, to revenue, customs or administrative matters or the liability of the State for acts and omissions in the exercise of State authority (*acta iure imperii*).

2. This Regulation shall not apply to:

(a) the status or legal capacity of natural persons, rights in property arising out of a matrimonial relationship, wills and succession;

(b)   bankruptcy, proceedings relating to the winding-up of insolvent companies or other legal persons, judicial arrangements, compositions and analogous proceedings;

(c)   social security;

(d)   arbitration.

3.   In this Regulation, the term 'Member State' shall mean Member States with the exception of Denmark.

Article 3. Enforcement titles to be certified as a European Enforcement Order.   1.   This Regulation shall apply to judgments, court settlements and authentic instruments on uncontested claims.

A claim shall be regarded as uncontested if:

(a)   the debtor has expressly agreed to it by admission or by means of a settlement which has been approved by a court or concluded before a court in the course of proceedings; or

(b)   the debtor has never objected to it, in compliance with the relevant procedural requirements under the law of the Member State of origin, in the course of the court proceedings; or

(c)   the debtor has not appeared or been represented at a court hearing regarding that claim after having initially objected to the claim in the course of the court proceedings, provided that such conduct amounts to a tacit admission of the claim or of the facts alleged by the creditor under the law of the Member State of origin; or

(d)   the debtor has expressly agreed to it in an authentic instrument.

2.   This Regulation shall also apply to decisions delivered following challenges to judgments, court settlements or authentic instruments certified as European Enforcement Orders.

Article 4. Definitions.   For the purposes of this Regulation, the following definitions shall apply:

1.   'judgment': any judgment given by a court or tribunal of a Member State, whatever the judgment may be called, including a decree, order, decision or writ of execution, as well as the determination of costs or expenses by an officer of the court;

2.   'claim': a claim for payment of a specific sum of money that has fallen due or for which the due date is indicated in the judgment, court settlement or authentic instrument;

3.   'authentic instrument':

(a)   a document which has been formally drawn up or registered as an authentic instrument, and the authenticity of which:

(i)   relates to the signature and the content of the instrument; and

(ii)   has been established by a public authority or other authority empowered for that purpose by the Member State in which it originates; or

(b)   an arrangement relating to maintenance obligations concluded with administrative authorities or authenticated by them;

4.   'Member State of origin': the Member State in which the judgment has been given, the court settlement has been approved or concluded or the authentic instrument has been drawn up or registered, and is to be certified as a European Enforcement Order;

5.   'Member State of enforcement': the Member State in which enforcement of the judgment, court settlement or authentic instrument certified as a European Enforcement Order is sought;

6.   'court of origin': the court or tribunal seised of the proceedings at the time of fulfilment of the conditions set out in Article 3(1)(a), (b) or (c);

7.   in Sweden, in summary proceedings concerning orders to pay (*betalningsföreläggande*), the expression 'court' includes the Swedish enforcement service (*kronofogdemyndighet*).

Chapter II — European Enforcement Order

Article 5. Abolition of exequatur.   A judgment which has been certified as a European Enforcement Order in the Member State of origin shall be recognised and enforced in the other Member States without the need for a declaration of enforceability and without any possibility of opposing its recognition.

Article 6. Requirements for certification as a European Enforcement Order.   1.   A judgment on an uncontested claim delivered in a Member State shall, upon application at any time to the court of origin, be certified as a European Enforcement Order if:

(a)   the judgment is enforceable in the Member State of origin; and

(b)   the judgment does not conflict with the rules on jurisdiction as laid down in sections 3 and 6 of Chapter II of Regulation (EC) No 44/2001; and

(c)   the court proceedings in the Member State of origin met the requirements as set out in Chapter III where a claim is uncontested within the meaning of Article 3(1)(b) or (c); and

(d)   the judgment was given in the Member State of the debtor's domicile within the meaning of Article 59 of Regulation (EC) No 44/2001, in cases where

—   a claim is uncontested within the meaning of Article 3(1)(b) or (c); and

—   it relates to a contract concluded by a person, the consumer, for a purpose which can be regarded as being outside his trade or profession; and

—   the debtor is the consumer.

2.   Where a judgment certified as a European Enforcement Order has ceased to be enforceable or its enforceability has been suspended or limited, a certificate indicating the lack or limitation of enforceability shall, upon application at any time to the court of origin, be issued, using the standard form in Annex IV.

3.   Without prejudice to Article 12(2), where a decision has been delivered following a challenge to a judgment certified as a European Enforcement Order in accordance with paragraph 1 of this Article, a replacement certificate shall, upon application at any time, be issued, using the standard form in Annex V, if that decision on the challenge is enforceable in the Member State of origin.

Article 7. Costs related to court proceedings.   Where a judgment includes an enforceable decision on the amount of costs related to the court proceedings, including the interest rates, it shall be certified as a European Enforcement Order also with regard to the costs unless the debtor has specifically objected to his obligation to bear such costs in the course of the court proceedings, in accordance with the law of the Member State of origin.

Article 8. Partial European Enforcement Order certificate.   If only parts of the judgment meet the requirements of this Regulation, a partial European Enforcement Order certificate shall be issued for those parts.

Article 9. Issue of the European Enforcement Order certificate.   1.   The European Enforcement Order certificate shall be issued using the standard form in Annex I.

2.   The European Enforcement Order certificate shall be issued in the language of the judgment.

Article 10. Rectification or withdrawal of the European Enforcement Order certificate.   1.   The European Enforcement Order certificate shall, upon application to the court of origin, be

(a)   rectified where, due to a material error, there is a discrepancy between the judgment and the certificate;

(b)   withdrawn where it was clearly wrongly granted, having regard to the requirements laid down in this Regulation.

2.   The law of the Member State of origin shall apply to the rectification or withdrawal of the European Enforcement Order certificate.

3.   An application for the rectification or withdrawal of a European Enforcement Order certificate may be made using the standard form in Annex VI.

4.   No appeal shall lie against the issuing of a European Enforcement Order certificate.

Article 11. Effect of the European Enforcement Order certificate.   The European Enforcement Order certificate shall take effect only within the limits of the enforceability of the judgment.

Chapter III — Minimum Standards for Uncontested Claims Procedures

Article 12. Scope of application of minimum standards.   1.   A judgment on a claim that is uncontested within the meaning of Article 3(1)(b) or (c) can be certified as a European Enforcement Order only if the court proceedings in the Member State of origin met the procedural requirements as set out in this Chapter.

2.   The same requirements shall apply to the issuing of a European Enforcement Order certificate or a replacement certificate within the meaning of Article 6(3) for a decision following a challenge to a judgment where, at the time of that decision, the conditions of Article 3(1)(b) or (c) are fulfilled.

Article 13. Service with proof of receipt by the debtor.   1.   The document instituting the proceedings or an equivalent document may have been served on the debtor by one of the following methods:

(a)   personal service attested by an acknowledgement of receipt, including the date of receipt, which is signed by the debtor;

(b)   personal service attested by a document signed by the competent person who effected the service stating that the debtor has received the document or refused to receive it without any legal justification, and the date of the service;

(c)   postal service attested by an acknowledgement of receipt including the date of receipt, which is signed and returned by the debtor;

(d)   service by electronic means such as fax or e-mail, attested by an acknowledgement of receipt including the date of receipt, which is signed and returned by the debtor.

2.   Any summons to a court hearing may have been served on the debtor in compliance with paragraph 1 or orally in a previous court hearing on the same claim and stated in the minutes of that previous court hearing.

Article 14. Service without proof of receipt by the debtor.   1.   Service of the document instituting the proceedings or an equivalent document and any summons to a court hearing on the debtor may also have been effected by one of the following methods:
(a)   personal service at the debtor's personal address on persons who are living in the same household as the debtor or are employed there;
(b)   in the case of a self-employed debtor or a legal person, personal service at the debtor's business premises on persons who are employed by the debtor;
(c)   deposit of the document in the debtor's mailbox;
(d)   deposit of the document at a post office or with competent public authorities and the placing in the debtor's mailbox of written notification of that deposit, provided that the written notification clearly states the character of the document as a court document or the legal effect of the notification as effecting service and setting in motion the running of time for the purposes of time limits;
(e)   postal service without proof pursuant to paragraph 3 where the debtor has his address in the Member State of origin;
(f)   electronic means attested by an automatic confirmation of delivery, provided that the debtor has expressly accepted this method of service in advance.
2.   For the purposes of this Regulation, service under paragraph 1 is not admissible if the debtor's address is not known with certainty.
3.   Service pursuant to paragraph 1, (a) to (d), shall be attested by:
(a)   a document signed by the competent person who effected the service, indicating:
(i) the method of service used; and
(ii) the date of service; and
(iii) where the document has been served on a person other than the debtor, the name of that person and his relation to the debtor, or
(b)   an acknowledgement of receipt by the person served, for the purposes of paragraph 1(a) and (b).

Article 15. Service on the debtor's representatives.   Service pursuant to Articles 13 or 14 may also have been effected on a debtor's representative.

Article 16. Provision to the debtor of due information about the claim.   In order to ensure that the debtor was provided with due information about the claim, the document instituting the proceedings or the equivalent document must have contained the following:
(a)   the names and the addresses of the parties;
(b)   the amount of the claim;
(c)   if interest on the claim is sought, the interest rate and the period for which interest is sought unless statutory interest is automatically added to the principal under the law of the Member State of origin;
(d)   a statement of the reason for the claim.

Article 17. Provision to the debtor of due information about the procedural steps necessary to contest the claim.   The following must have been clearly stated in or together with the document instituting the proceedings, the equivalent document or any summons to a court hearing:

(a)   the procedural requirements for contesting the claim, including the time limit for contesting the claim in writing or the time for the court hearing, as applicable, the name and the address of the institution to which to respond or before which to appear, as applicable, and whether it is mandatory to be represented by a lawyer;

(b)   the consequences of an absence of objection or default of appearance, in particular, where applicable, the possibility that a judgment may be given or enforced against the debtor and the liability for costs related to the court proceedings.

Article 18. Cure of non-compliance with minimum standards.   1.   If the proceedings in the Member State of origin did not meet the procedural requirements as set out in Articles 13 to 17, such noncompliance shall be cured and a judgment may be certified as a European Enforcement Order if:

(a)   the judgment has been served on the debtor in compliance with the requirements pursuant to Article 13 or Article 14; and

(b)   it was possible for the debtor to challenge the judgment by means of a full review and the debtor has been duly informed in or together with the judgment about the procedural requirements for such a challenge, including the name and address of the institution with which it must be lodged and, where applicable, the time limit for so doing; and

(c)   the debtor has failed to challenge the judgment in compliance with the relevant procedural requirements.

2.   If the proceedings in the Member State of origin did not comply with the procedural requirements as set out in Article 13 or Article 14, non-compliance shall be cured if it is proved by the conduct of the debtor in the court proceedings that he has personally received the document to be served in sufficient time to arrange for his defence.

Article 19. Minimum standards for review in exceptional cases.   1.   Further to Articles 13 to 18, a judgment can only be certified as a European Enforcement Order if the debtor is entitled, under the law of the Member State of origin, to apply for a review of the judgment where:

(a)   (i)   the document instituting the proceedings or an equivalent document or, where applicable, the summons to a court hearing, was served by one of the methods provided for in Article 14; and

(ii)   service was not effected in sufficient time to enable him to arrange for his defence, without any fault on his part; or

(b)   the debtor was prevented from objecting to the claim by reason of force majeure, or due to extraordinary circumstances without any fault on his part, provided in either case that he acts promptly.

2.   This Article is without prejudice to the possibility for Member States to grant access to a review of the judgment under more generous conditions than those mentioned in paragraph 1.

Chapter IV — Enforcement

Article 20. Enforcement procedure. 1. Without prejudice to the provisions of this Chapter, the enforcement procedures shall be governed by the law of the Member State of enforcement. A judgment certified as a European Enforcement Order shall be enforced under the same conditions as a judgment handed down in the Member State of enforcement.

2. The creditor shall be required to provide the competent enforcement authorities of the Member State of enforcement with:

(a) a copy of the judgment which satisfies the conditions necessary to establish its authenticity; and

(b) a copy of the European Enforcement Order certificate which satisfies the conditions necessary to establish its authenticity; and

(c) where necessary, a transcription of the European Enforcement Order certificate or a translation thereof into the official language of the Member State of enforcement or, if there are several official languages in that Member State, the official language or one of the official languages of court proceedings of the place where enforcement is sought, in conformity with the law of that Member State, or into another language that the Member State of enforcement has indicated it can accept. Each Member State may indicate the official language or languages of the institutions of the European Community other than its own which it can accept for the completion of the certificate. The translation shall be certified by a person qualified to do so in one of the Member States.

3. No security, bond or deposit, however described, shall be required of a party who in one Member State applies for enforcement of a judgment certified as a European Enforcement Order in another Member State on the ground that he is a foreign national or that he is not domiciled or resident in the Member State of enforcement.

Article 21. Refusal of enforcement. 1. Enforcement shall, upon application by the debtor, be refused by competent court in the Member State of enforcement if the judgment certified as a European Enforcement Order is irreconcilable with an earlier judgment given in any Member State or in a third country, provided that:

(a) the earlier judgment involved the same cause of action and was between the same parties; and

(b) the earlier judgment was given in the Member State of enforcement or fulfils the conditions necessary for its recognition in the Member State of enforcement; and

(c) the irreconcilability was not and could not have been raised as an objection in the court proceedings in the Member State of origin.

2. Under no circumstances may the judgment or its certification as a European Enforcement Order be reviewed as to their substance in the Member State of enforcement.

Article 22. Agreements with third countries. This Regulation shall not affect agreements by which Member States undertook, prior to the entry into force of Regulation (EC) No 44/2001, pursuant to Article 59 of the Brussels Convention on jurisdiction and the enforcement of judgments in civil and commercial matters, not to recognise judgments given, in particular in other Contracting States to that Convention, against defendants domiciled or habitually resident in a third country where, in cases provided for in Article 4 of that Convention, the judgment could only be founded on a ground of jurisdiction specified in the second paragraph of Article 3 of that Convention.

Article 23. Stay or limitation of enforcement. – Where the debtor has
—   challenged a judgment certified as a European Enforcement Order, including an application for review within the meaning of Article 19, or
—   applied for the rectification or withdrawal of a European Enforcement Order certificate in accordance with Article 10, the competent court or authority in the Member State of enforcement may, upon application by the debtor:
    (a)   limit the enforcement proceedings to protective measures; or
    (b)   make enforcement conditional on the provision of such security as it shall determine; or
    (c)   under exceptional circumstances, stay the enforcement proceedings.

Chapter V — Court settlements and authentic instruments

Article 24. Court settlements.   1.   A settlement concerning a claim within the meaning of Article 4(2) which has been approved by a court or concluded before a court in the course of proceedings and is enforceable in the Member State in which it was approved or concluded shall, upon application to the court that approved it or before which it was concluded, be certified as a European Enforcement Order using the standard form in Annex II.
    2.   A settlement which has been certified as a European Enforcement Order in the Member State of origin shall be enforced in the other Member States without the need for a declaration of enforceability and without any possibility of opposing its enforceability.
    3.   The provisions of Chapter II, with the exception of Articles 5, 6(1) and 9(1), and of Chapter IV, with the exception of Articles 21(1) and 22, shall apply as appropriate.

Article 25. Authentic instruments.   1.   An authentic instrument concerning a claim within the meaning of Article 4(2) which is enforceable in one Member State shall, upon application to the authority designated by the Member State of origin, be certified as a European Enforcement Order, using the standard form in Annex III.
    2.   An authentic instrument which has been certified as a European Enforcement Order in the Member State of origin shall be enforced in the other Member States without the need for a declaration of enforceability and without any possibility of opposing its enforceability.
    3.   The provisions of Chapter II, with the exception of Articles 5, 6(1) and 9(1), and of Chapter IV, with the exception of Articles 21(1) and 22, shall apply as appropriate.

Chapter VI — Transitional provision

Article 26. Transitional provision.   This Regulation shall apply only to judgments given, to court settlements approved or concluded and to documents formally drawn up or registered as authentic instruments after the entry into force of this Regulation.

Chapter VII — Relationship with other Community instruments

Article 27. Relationship with Regulation (EC) No 44/2001. This Regulation shall not affect the possibility of seeking recognition and enforcement, in accordance with Regulation (EC) No 44/2001, of a judgment, a court settlement or an authentic instrument on an uncontested claim.

Article 28. Relationship with Regulation (EC) No 1348/2000. This Regulation shall not affect the application of Regulation (EC) No 1348/2000.

Chapter VIII — General and final provisions

Article 29. Information on enforcement procedures and authorities. The Member States shall cooperate to provide the general public and professional circles with information on:

(a)   the methods and procedures of enforcement in the Member States; and

(b)   the competent authorities for enforcement in the Member States, in particular via the European Judicial Network in civil and commercial matters established in accordance with Decision 2001/470/EC.

Article 30. Information relating to redress procedures, languages and authorities.   1.   The Member States shall notify the Commission of:

(a)   the procedures for rectification and withdrawal referred to in Article 10(2) and for review referred to in Article 19(1);

(b)   the languages accepted pursuant to Article 20(2)(c);

(c)   the lists of the authorities referred to in Article 25; and any subsequent changes thereof.

2.   The Commission shall make the information notified in accordance with paragraph 1 publicly available through publication in the *Official Journal of the European Union* and through any other appropriate means.

Article 31. Amendments to the Annexes. The Commission shall amend the standard forms set out in the Annexes. Those measures, designed to amend non-essential elements of this Regulation, shall be adopted in accordance with the regulatory procedure with scrutiny referred to in Article 32(2).

Article 32. Committee.   1.   The Commission shall be assisted by the committee referred to in Article 75 of Regulation (EC) No 44/2001.

2.   Where reference is made to this paragraph, Article 5a(1) to (4) and Article 7 of Decision 1999/468/EC shall apply, having regard to the provisions of Article 8 thereof.

Article 33. Entry into force. This Regulation shall enter into force on 21 January 2005. It shall apply from 21 October 2005, with the exception of Articles 30, 31 and 32, which shall apply from 21 January 2005.

D.   Regulation (EC) No 1896/2006 of the European Parliament and of the Council of 12 December 2006 creating a European order for payment procedure (OJ, L 399 of 30 December 2006)[1]

(1)   The Community has set itself the objective of maintaining and developing an area of freedom, security and justice in which the free movement of persons is ensured. For the gradual establishment of such an area, the Community is to adopt, inter alia, measures in the field of judicial cooperation in civil matters having cross-border implications and needed for the proper functioning of the internal market.

(2)   According to Article 65(c) of the Treaty, these measures are to include measures eliminating obstacles to the good functioning of civil proceedings, if necessary by promoting the compatibility of the rules on civil procedure applicable in the Member States.

(3)   The European Council meeting in Tampere on 15 and 16 October 1999 invited the Council and the Commission to prepare new legislation on issues that are instrumental to smooth judicial cooperation and to enhanced access to law and specifically made reference, in that context, to orders for money payment.

(4)   On 30 November 2000, the Council adopted a joint Commission and Council programme of measures for implementation of the principle of mutual recognition of decisions in civil and commercial matters. The programme envisages the possibility of a specific, uniform or harmonised procedure laid down within the Community to obtain a judicial decision in specific areas including that of uncontested claims. This was taken forward by the Hague Programme, adopted by the European Council on 5 November 2004, which called for work to be actively pursued on the European order for payment.

(5)   The Commission adopted a Green Paper on a European order for payment procedure and on measures to simplify and speed up small claims litigation on 20 December 2002. The Green Paper launched consultations on the possible objectives and features of a uniform or harmonised European procedure for the recovery of uncontested claims.

(6)   The swift and efficient recovery of outstanding debts over which no legal controversy exists is of paramount importance for economic operators in the European Union, as late payments constitute a major reason for insolvency threatening the survival of businesses, particularly small and medium-sized enterprises, and resulting in numerous job losses.

(7)   All Member States are trying to tackle the issue of mass recovery of uncontested claims, in the majority of States by means of a simplified order for payment procedure, but both the content of national legislation and the performance of domestic procedures vary substantially. Furthermore, the procedures currently in existence are frequently either inadmissible or impracticable in cross-border cases.

(8)   The resulting impediments to access to efficient justice in crossborder cases and the distortion of competition within the internal market due to imbalances in the functioning of procedural means afforded to creditors in different Member States necessitate Community legislation guaranteeing a level playing field for creditors and debtors throughout the European Union.

---

[1]   The Annexes to the Regulation are not published. [Note of the Editor]

(9) The purpose of this Regulation is to simplify, speed up and reduce the costs of litigation in cross-border cases concerning uncontested pecuniary claims by creating a European order for payment procedure, and to permit the free circulation of European orders for payment throughout the Member States by laying down minimum standards, compliance with which renders unnecessary any intermediate proceedings in the Member State of enforcement prior to recognition and enforcement.

(10) The procedure established by this Regulation should serve as an additional and optional means for the claimant, who remains free to resort to a procedure provided for by national law. Accordingly, this Regulation neither replaces nor harmonises the existing mechanisms for the recovery of uncontested claims under national law.

(11) The procedure should be based, to the largest extent possible, on the use of standard forms in any communication between the court and the parties in order to facilitate its administration and enable the use of automatic data processing.

(12) When deciding which courts are to have jurisdiction to issue a European order for payment, Member States should take due account of the need to ensure access to justice.

(13) In the application for a European order for payment, the claimant should be obliged to provide information that is sufficient to clearly identify and support the claim in order to place the defendant in a position to make a well-informed choice either to oppose the claim or to leave it uncontested.

(14) In that context, it should be compulsory for the claimant to include a description of evidence supporting the claim. For that purpose the application form should include as exhaustive a list as possible of types of evidence that are usually produced in support of pecuniary claims.

(15) The lodging of an application for a European order for payment should entail the payment of any applicable court fees.

(16) The court should examine the application, including the issue of jurisdiction and the description of evidence, on the basis of the information provided in the application form. This would allow the court to examine prima facie the merits of the claim and inter alia to exclude clearly unfounded claims or inadmissible applications. The examination should not need to be carried out by a judge.

(17) There is to be no right of appeal against the rejection of the application. This does not preclude, however, a possible review of the decision rejecting the application at the same level of jurisdiction in accordance with national law.

(18) The European order for payment should apprise the defendant of his options to pay the amount awarded to the claimant or to send a statement of opposition within a time limit of 30 days if he wishes to contest the claim. In addition to being provided with full information concerning the claim as supplied by the claimant, the defendant should be advised of the legal significance of the European order for payment and in particular of the consequences of leaving the claim uncontested.

(19) Due to differences between Member States' rules of civil procedure and especially those governing the service of documents, it is necessary to lay down a specific and detailed definition of minimum standards that should apply in the context of the European order for payment procedure. In particular, as regards the fulfilment of those standards, any method based on legal fiction should not be considered sufficient for the service of the European order for payment.

(20) All the methods of service listed in Articles 13 and 14 are characterised by either complete certainty (Article 13) or a very high degree of likelihood (Article 14) that the document served has reached its addressee.

(21) Personal service on certain persons other than the defendant himself pursuant to Article 14(1)(a) and (b) should be deemed to meet the requirements of those provisions only if those persons actually accepted/received the European order for payment.

(22) Article 15 should apply to situations where the defendant cannot represent himself in court, as in the case of a legal person, and where a person authorised to represent him is determined by law, as well as to situations where the defendant has authorised another person, in particular a lawyer, to represent him in the specific court proceedings at issue.

(23) The defendant may submit his statement of opposition using the standard form set out in this Regulation. However, the courts should take into account any other written form of opposition if it is expressed in a clear manner.

(24) A statement of opposition filed within the time limit should terminate the European order for payment procedure and should lead to an automatic transfer of the case to ordinary civil proceedings unless the claimant has explicitly requested that the proceedings be terminated in that event. For the purposes of this Regulation the concept of ordinary civil proceedings should not necessarily be interpreted within the meaning of national law.

(25) After the expiry of the time limit for submitting the statement of opposition, in certain exceptional cases the defendant should be entitled to apply for a review of the European order for payment. Review in exceptional cases should not mean that the defendant is given a second opportunity to oppose the claim. During the review procedure the merits of the claim should not be evaluated beyond the grounds resulting from the exceptional circumstances invoked by the defendant. The other exceptional circumstances could include a situation where the European order for payment was based on false information provided in the application form.

(26) Court fees covered by Article 25 should not include for example lawyers' fees or costs of service of documents by an entity other than a court.

(27) A European order for payment issued in one Member State which has become enforceable should be regarded for the purposes of enforcement as if it had been issued in the Member State in which enforcement is sought. Mutual trust in the administration of justice in the Member States justifies the assessment by the court of one Member State that all conditions for issuing a European order for payment are fulfilled to enable the order to be enforced in all other Member States without judicial review of the proper application of minimum procedural standards in the Member State where the order is to be enforced. Without prejudice to the provisions of this Regulation, in particular the minimum standards laid down in Article 22(1) and (2) and Article 23, the procedures for the enforcement of the European order for payment should continue to be governed by national law.

(28) For the purposes of calculating time limits, Regulation (EEC, Euratom) No 1182/71 of the Council of 3 June 1971 determining the rules applicable to periods, dates and time limits should apply. The defendant should be advised of this and should be informed that account will be taken of the public holidays of the Member State in which the court issuing the European order for payment is situated.

(29) Since the objective of this Regulation, namely to establish a uniform rapid and efficient mechanism for the recovery of uncontested pecuniary claims throughout the European Union, cannot be sufficiently achieved by the Member States and can therefore, by reason of the scale and effects of the Regulation, be better achieved at Community level, the Community may adopt measures in accordance with the principle of subsidiarity as set out in Article 5 of the Treaty. In accordance with the principle of proportionality as set out in that Article, this Regulation does not go beyond what is necessary in order to achieve that objective.

(30) The measures necessary for the implementation of this Regulation should be adopted in accordance with Council Decision 1999/468/EC of 28 June 1999 laying down the procedures for the exercise of implementing powers conferred on the Commission.

(31) The United Kingdom and Ireland, in accordance with Article 3 of the Protocol on the position of the United Kingdom and Ireland annexed to the Treaty on European Union and the Treaty establishing the European Community, have given notice of their wish to take part in the adoption and application of this Regulation.

(32) In accordance with Articles 1 and 2 of the Protocol on the position of Denmark annexed to the Treaty on European Union and the Treaty establishing the European Community, Denmark does not take part in the adoption of this Regulation, and is not bound by it or subject to its application.

Article 1. Subject matter.   1.   The purpose of this Regulation is:

(a)   to simplify, speed up and reduce the costs of litigation in crossborder cases concerning uncontested pecuniary claims by creating a European order for payment procedure; and

(b)   to permit the free circulation of European orders for payment throughout the Member States by laying down minimum standards, compliance with which renders unnecessary any intermediate proceedings in the Member State of enforcement prior to recognition and enforcement.

2.   This Regulation shall not prevent a claimant from pursuing a claim within the meaning of Article 4 by making use of another procedure available under the law of a Member State or under Community law.

Article 2. Scope.   1.   This Regulation shall apply to civil and commercial matters in cross-border cases, whatever the nature of the court or tribunal. It shall not extend, in particular, to revenue, customs or administrative matters or the liability of the State for acts and omissions in the exercise of State authority (*acta iure imperii*).

2.   This Regulation shall not apply to:

(a)   rights in property arising out of a matrimonial relationship, wills and succession;

(b)   bankruptcy, proceedings relating to the winding–up of insolvent companies or other legal persons, judicial arrangements, compositions and analogous proceedings;

(c)   social security;

(d)   claims arising from non-contractual obligations, unless:

(i)   they have been the subject of an agreement between the parties or there has been an admission of debt, or

(ii)   they relate to liquidated debts arising from joint ownership of property.

3.   In this Regulation, the term 'Member State' shall mean Member States with the exception of Denmark.

Article 3. Cross-border cases.   1.   For the purposes of this Regulation, a cross-border case is one in which at least one of the parties is domiciled or habitually resident in a Member State other than the Member State of the court seised.

2.   Domicile shall be determined in accordance with Articles 59 and 60 of Council Regulation (EC) No 44/2001 of 22 December 2000 on jurisdiction and the recognition and enforcement of judgments in civil and commercial matters.

3.   The relevant moment for determining whether there is a crossborder case shall be the time when the application for a European order for payment is submitted in accordance with this Regulation.

Article 4. European order for payment procedure.   The European order for payment procedure shall be established for the collection of pecuniary claims for a specific amount that have fallen due at the time when the application for a European order for payment is submitted.

Article 5. Definitions.   For the purposes of this Regulation, the following definitions shall apply:

(1)   'Member State of origin' means the Member State in which a European order for payment is issued;

(2)   'Member State of enforcement' means the Member State in which enforcement of a European order for payment is sought;

(3)   'court' means any authority in a Member State with competence regarding European orders for payment or any other related matters;

(4)   'court of origin' means the court which issues a European order for payment.

Article 6. Jurisdiction.   1.   For the purposes of applying this Regulation, jurisdiction shall be determined in accordance with the relevant rules of Community law, in particular Regulation (EC) No 44/2001.

2.   However, if the claim relates to a contract concluded by a person, the consumer, for a purpose which can be regarded as being outside his trade or profession, and if the defendant is the consumer, only the courts in the Member State in which the defendant is domiciled, within the meaning of Article 59 of Regulation (EC) No 44/2001, shall have jurisdiction.

Article 7. Application for a European order for payment.   1.   An application for a European order for payment shall be made using standard form A as set out in Annex I.

2.   The application shall state:

(a)   the names and addresses of the parties, and, where applicable, their representatives, and of the court to which the application is made;

(b)   the amount of the claim, including the principal and, where applicable, interest, contractual penalties and costs;

(c)   if interest on the claim is demanded, the interest rate and the period of time for which that interest is demanded unless statutory interest is automatically added to the principal under the law of the Member State of origin;

(d)   the cause of the action, including a description of the circumstances invoked as the basis of the claim and, where applicable, of the interest demanded;

(e)   a description of evidence supporting the claim;

(f)   the grounds for jurisdiction; and

(g)   the cross-border nature of the case within the meaning of Article 3.

3.   In the application, the claimant shall declare that the information provided is true to the best of his knowledge and belief and shall acknowledge that any deliberate false statement could lead to appropriate penalties under the law of the Member State of origin.

4.   In an Appendix to the application the claimant may indicate to the court that he opposes a transfer to ordinary civil proceedings within the meaning of Article 17 in the event of opposition by the defendant. This does not prevent the claimant from informing the court thereof subsequently, but in any event before the order is issued.

5.   The application shall be submitted in paper form or by any other means of communication, including electronic, accepted by the Member State of origin and available to the court of origin.

6.   The application shall be signed by the claimant or, where applicable, by his representative. Where the application is submitted in electronic form in accordance with paragraph 5, it shall be signed in accordance with Article 2(2) of Directive 1999/93/EC of the European Parliament and of the Council of 13 December 1999 on a Community framework for electronic signatures. The signature shall be recognised in the Member State of origin and may not be made subject to additional requirements.

However, such electronic signature shall not be required if and to the extent that an alternative electronic communications system exists in the courts of the Member State of origin which is available to a certain group of pre-registered authenticated users and which permits the identification of those users in a secure manner. Member States shall inform the Commission of such communications systems.

Article 8. Examination of the application. — The court seised of an application for a European order for payment shall examine, as soon as possible and on the basis of the application form, whether the requirements set out in Articles 2, 3, 4, 6 and 7 are met and whether the claim appears to be founded. This examination may take the form of an automated procedure.

Article 9. Completion and rectification.   1.   If the requirements set out in Article 7 are not met and unless the claim is clearly unfounded or the application is inadmissible, the court shall give the claimant the opportunity to complete or rectify the application. The court shall use standard form B as set out in Annex II.

2.   Where the court requests the claimant to complete or rectify the application, it shall specify a time limit it deems appropriate in the circumstances. The court may at its discretion extend that time limit.

Article 10. Modification of the application.   1.   If the requirements referred to in Article 8 are met for only part of the claim, the court shall inform the claimant to that effect, using standard form C as set out in Annex III. The claimant shall be invited to accept or refuse a proposal for a European order for payment for the amount specified by the court and shall be informed of the consequences of his decision. The claimant shall reply by returning standard form C sent by the court within a time limit specified by the court in accordance with Article 9(2).

2.   If the claimant accepts the court's proposal, the court shall issue a European order for payment, in accordance with Article 12, for that part of the claim accepted by the claimant. The consequences with respect to the remaining part of the initial claim shall be governed by national law.

3.   If the claimant fails to send his reply within the time limit specified by the court or refuses the court's proposal, the court shall reject the application for a European order for payment in its entirety.

Article 11. Rejection of the application.   1.   The court shall reject the application if:

(a)   the requirements set out in Articles 2, 3, 4, 6 and 7 are not met; or

(b)   the claim is clearly unfounded; or

(c)   the claimant fails to send his reply within the time limit specified by the court under Article 9(2); or

(d)   the claimant fails to send his reply within the time limit specified by the court or refuses the court's proposal, in accordance with Article 10.

The claimant shall be informed of the grounds for the rejection by means of standard form D as set out in Annex IV.

2.   There shall be no right of appeal against the rejection of the application.

3.   The rejection of the application shall not prevent the claimant from pursuing the claim by means of a new application for a European order for payment or of any other procedure available under the law of a Member State.

Article 12. Issue of a European order for payment.   1.   If the requirements referred to in Article 8 are met, the court shall issue, as soon as possible and normally within 30 days of the lodging of the application, a European order for payment using standard form E as set out in Annex V. The 30-day period shall not include the time taken by the claimant to complete, rectify or modify the application.

2.   The European order for payment shall be issued together with a copy of the application form. It shall not comprise the information provided by the claimant in Appendices 1 and 2 to form A.

3.   In the European order for payment, the defendant shall be advised of his options to:

(a)   pay the amount indicated in the order to the claimant; or

(b)   oppose the order by lodging with the court of origin a statement of opposition, to be sent within 30 days of service of the order on him.

4.   In the European order for payment, the defendant shall be informed that:

(a)   the order was issued solely on the basis of the information which was provided by the claimant and was not verified by the court;

(b)   the order will become enforceable unless a statement of opposition has been lodged with the court in accordance with Article 16;

(c)   where a statement of opposition is lodged, the proceedings shall continue before the competent courts of the Member State of origin in accordance with the rules of ordinary civil procedure unless the claimant has explicitly requested that the proceedings be terminated in that event.

5.   The court shall ensure that the order is served on the defendant in accordance with national law by a method that shall meet the minimum standards laid down in Articles 13, 14 and 15.

Article 13. Service with proof of receipt by the defendant.   The European order for payment may be served on the defendant in accordance with the national law of the State in which the service is to be effected, by one of the following methods:
(a)   personal service attested by an acknowledgement of receipt, including the date of receipt, which is signed by the defendant;
(b)   personal service attested by a document signed by the competent person who effected the service stating that the defendant has received the document or refused to receive it without any legal justification, and the date of service;
(c)   postal service attested by an acknowledgement of receipt, including the date of receipt, which is signed and returned by the defendant;
(d)   service by electronic means such as fax or e-mail, attested by an acknowledgement of receipt, including the date of receipt, which is signed and returned by the defendant.

Article 14. Service without proof of receipt by the defendant.   1.   The European order for payment may also be served on the defendant in accordance with the national law of the State in which service is to be effected, by one of the following methods:
(a)   personal service at the defendant's personal address on persons who are living in the same household as the defendant or are employed there;
(b)   in the case of a self-employed defendant or a legal person, personal service at the defendant's business premises on persons who are employed by the defendant;
(c)   deposit of the order in the defendant's mailbox;
(d)   deposit of the order at a post office or with competent public authorities and the placing in the defendant's mailbox of written notification of that deposit, provided that the written notification clearly states the character of the document as a court document or the legal effect of the notification as effecting service and setting in motion the running of time for the purposes of time limits;
(e)   postal service without proof pursuant to paragraph 3 where the defendant has his address in the Member State of origin;
(f)   electronic means attested by an automatic confirmation of delivery, provided that the defendant has expressly accepted this method of service in advance.
2.   For the purposes of this Regulation, service under paragraph 1 is not admissible if the defendant's address is not known with certainty.
3.   Service pursuant to paragraph 1(a), (b), (c) and (d) shall be attested by:
(a)   a document signed by the competent person who effected the service, indicating:
(i)   the method of service used; and
(ii)   the date of service; and
(iii)   where the order has been served on a person other than the defendant, the name of that person and his relation to the defendant; or
(b)   an acknowledgement of receipt by the person served, for the purposes of paragraphs (1)(a) and (b).

Article 15. Service on a representative.   Service pursuant to Articles 13 or 14 may also be effected on a defendant's representative.

Article 16. Opposition to the European order for payment.   1.   The defendant may lodge a statement of opposition to the European order for payment with the court of origin using standard form F as set out in Annex VI, which shall be supplied to him together with the European order for payment.

2.   The statement of opposition shall be sent within 30 days of service of the order on the defendant.

3.   The defendant shall indicate in the statement of opposition that he contests the claim, without having to specify the reasons for this.

4.   The statement of opposition shall be submitted in paper form or by any other means of communication, including electronic, accepted by the Member State of origin and available to the court of origin.

5.   The statement of opposition shall be signed by the defendant or, where applicable, by his representative. Where the statement of opposition is submitted in electronic form in accordance with paragraph 4, it shall be signed in accordance with Article 2(2) of Directive 1999/93/EC. The signature shall be recognised in the Member State of origin and may not be made subject to additional requirements. However, such electronic signature shall not be required if and to the extent that an alternative electronic communications system exists in the courts of the Member State of origin which is available to a certain group of pre-registered authenticated users and which permits the identification of those users in a secure manner. Member States shall inform the Commission of such communications systems.

Article 17. Effects of the lodging of a statement of opposition.   1.   If a statement of opposition is entered within the time limit laid down in Article 16(2), the proceedings shall continue before the competent courts of the Member State of origin in accordance with the rules of ordinary civil procedure unless the claimant has explicitly requested that the proceedings be terminated in that event. Where the claimant has pursued his claim through the European order for payment procedure, nothing under national law shall prejudice his position in subsequent ordinary civil proceedings.

2.   The transfer to ordinary civil proceedings within the meaning of paragraph 1 shall be governed by the law of the Member State of origin.

3.   The claimant shall be informed whether the defendant has lodged a statement of opposition and of any transfer to ordinary civil proceedings.

Article 18. Enforceability.   1.   If within the time limit laid down in Article 16(2), taking into account an appropriate period of time to allow a statement to arrive, no statement of opposition has been lodged with the court of origin, the court of origin shall without delay declare the European order for payment enforceable using standard form G as set out in Annex VII. The court shall verify the date of service.

2.   Without prejudice to paragraph 1, the formal requirements for enforceability shall be governed by the law of the Member State of origin.

3.   The court shall send the enforceable European order for payment to the claimant.

Article 19. Abolition of exequatur. A European order for payment which has become enforceable in the Member State of origin shall be recognised and enforced in the other Member States without the need for a declaration of enforceability and without any possibility of opposing its recognition.

Article 20. Review in exceptional cases. 1. After the expiry of the time limit laid down in Article 16(2) the defendant shall be entitled to apply for a review of the European order for payment before the competent court in the Member State of origin where:
(a) (i) the order for payment was served by one of the methods provided for in Article 14, and
(ii) service was not effected in sufficient time to enable him to arrange for his defence, without any fault on his part, or
(b) the defendant was prevented from objecting to the claim by reason of force majeure or due to extraordinary circumstances without any fault on his part, provided in either case that he acts promptly.
2. After expiry of the time limit laid down in Article 16(2) the defendant shall also be entitled to apply for a review of the European order for payment before the competent court in the Member State of origin where the order for payment was clearly wrongly issued, having regard to the requirements laid down in this Regulation, or due to other exceptional circumstances.
3. If the court rejects the defendant's application on the basis that none of the grounds for review referred to in paragraphs 1 and 2 apply, the European order for payment shall remain in force. If the court decides that the review is justified for one of the reasons laid down in paragraphs 1 and 2, the European order for payment shall be null and void.

Article 21. Enforcement. 1. Without prejudice to the provisions of this Regulation, enforcement procedures shall be governed by the law of the Member State of enforcement. A European order for payment which has become enforceable shall be enforced under the same conditions as an enforceable decision issued in the Member State of enforcement.
2. For enforcement in another Member State, the claimant shall provide the competent enforcement authorities of that Member State with:
(a) a copy of the European order for payment, as declared enforceable by the court of origin, which satisfies the conditions necessary to establish its authenticity; and
(b) where necessary, a translation of the European order for payment into the official language of the Member State of enforcement or, if there are several official languages in that Member State, the official language or one of the official languages of court proceedings of the place where enforcement is sought, in conformity with the law of that Member State, or into another language that the Member State of enforcement has indicated it can accept. Each Member State may indicate the official language or languages of the institutions of the European Union other than its own which it can accept for the European order for payment. The translation shall be certified by a person qualified to do so in one of the Member States.
3. No security, bond or deposit, however described, shall be required of a claimant who in one Member State applies for enforcement of a European order for payment issued in another Member State on the ground that he is a foreign national or that he is not domiciled or resident in the Member State of enforcement.

Article 22. Refusal of enforcement.　1.　Enforcement shall, upon application by the defendant, be refused by the competent court in the Member State of enforcement if the European order for payment is irreconcilable with an earlier decision or order previously given in any Member State or in a third country, provided that:

(a)　the earlier decision or order involved the same cause of action between the same parties; and

(b)　the earlier decision or order fulfils the conditions necessary for its recognition in the Member State of enforcement; and

(c)　the irreconcilability could not have been raised as an objection in the court proceedings in the Member State of origin.

2.　Enforcement shall, upon application, also be refused if and to the extent that the defendant has paid the claimant the amount awarded in the European order for payment.

3.　Under no circumstances may the European order for payment be reviewed as to its substance in the Member State of enforcement.

Article 23. Stay or limitation of enforcement.　Where the defendant has applied for a review in accordance with Article 20, the competent court in the Member State of enforcement may, upon application by the defendant:

(a)　limit the enforcement proceedings to protective measures; or

(b)　make enforcement conditional on the provision of such security as it shall determine; or

(c)　under exceptional circumstances, stay the enforcement proceedings.

Article 24. Legal representation.　Representation by a lawyer or another legal professional shall not be mandatory:

(a) for the claimant in respect of the application for a European order for payment;

(b) for the defendant in respect of the statement of opposition to a European order for payment.

Article 25. Court fees.　1.　The combined court fees of a European order for payment procedure and of the ordinary civil proceedings that ensue in the event of a statement of opposition to a European order for payment in a Member State shall not exceed the court fees of ordinary civil proceedings without a preceding European order for payment procedure in that Member State.

2.　For the purposes of this Regulation, court fees shall comprise fees and charges to be paid to the court, the amount of which is fixed in accordance with national law.

Article 26. Relationship with national procedural law.　All procedural issues not specifically dealt with in this Regulation shall be governed by national law.

Article 27. Relationship with Regulation (EC) No 1348/2000.　This Regulation shall not affect the application of Council Regulation (EC) No 1348/2000 of 29 May 2000 on the service in the Member States of judicial and extrajudicial documents in civil and commercial matters.

Article 28. Information relating to service costs and enforcement.   Member States shall cooperate to provide the general public and professional circles with information on:
(a)   costs of service of documents; and
(b)   which authorities have competence with respect to enforcement for the purposes of applying Articles 21, 22 and 23, in particular via the European Judicial Network in civil and commercial matters established in accordance with Council Decision 2001/470/EC.

Article 29. Information relating to jurisdiction, review procedures, means of communication and languages.   1.   By 12 June 2008, Member States shall communicate to the Commission:
(a)   which courts have jurisdiction to issue a European order for payment;
(b)   the review procedure and the competent courts for the purposes of the application of Article 20;
(c)   the means of communication accepted for the purposes of the European order for payment procedure and available to the courts;
(d)   languages accepted pursuant to Article 21(2)(b). Member States shall apprise the Commission of any subsequent changes to this information.
2.   The Commission shall make the information notified in accordance with paragraph 1 publicly available through publication in the *Official Journal of the European Union* and through any other appropriate means.

Article 30. Amendments to the Annexes.   The standard forms set out in the Annexes shall be updated or technically adjusted, ensuring full conformity with the provisions of this Regulation, in accordance with the procedure referred to in Article 31(2).

Article 31. Committee.   1.   The Commission shall be assisted by the committee established by Article 75 of Regulation (EC) No 44/2001.
2.   Where reference is made to this paragraph, Article 5a (1)–(4) and Article 7 of Decision 1999/468/EC shall apply, having regard to the provisions of Article 8 thereof.
3.   The Committee shall adopt its Rules of Procedure.

Article 32. Review.   By 12 December 2013, the Commission shall present to the European Parliament, the Council and the European Economic and Social Committee a detailed report reviewing the operation of the European order for payment procedure. That report shall contain an assessment of the procedure as it has operated and an extended impact assessment for each Member State.
To that end, and in order to ensure that best practice in the European Union is duly taken into account and reflects the principles of better legislation, Member States shall provide the Commission with information relating to the cross-border operation of the European order for payment. This information shall cover court fees, speed of the procedure, efficiency, ease of use and the internal payment order procedures of the Member States.
The Commission's report shall be accompanied, if appropriate, by proposals for adaptation.

Article 33. Entry into force.   This Regulation shall enter into force on the day following the date of its publication in the *Official Journal of the European Union.*

It shall apply from 12 December 2008, with the exception of Articles 28, 29, 30 and 31 which shall apply from 12 June 2008.

E. Regulation (EC) No 861/2007 of the European Parliament and of the Council of 11 July 2007 establishing a European Small Claims Procedure (OJ, L 199 of 31 July 2007)[1]

(1)   The Community has set itself the objective of maintaining and developing an area of freedom, security and justice in which the free movement of persons is ensured. For the gradual establishment of such an area, the Community is to adopt, inter alia, measures in the field of judicial cooperation in civil matters having cross-border implications and needed for the proper functioning of the internal market.

(2)   According to Article 65(c) of the Treaty, those measures are to include those eliminating obstacles to the good functioning of civil proceedings, if necessary by promoting the compatibility of the rules on civil procedure applicable in the Member States.

(3)   In this respect, the Community has, among other measures, already adopted Council Regulation (EC) No 1348/2000 of 29 May 2000 on the service in the Member States of judicial and extrajudicial documents in civil or commercial matters, Council Regulation (EC) No 44/2001 of 22 December 2000 on jurisdiction and the recognition and enforcement of judgments in civil and commercial matters, Council Decision 2001/470/EC of 28 May 2001 establishing a European Judicial Network in civil and commercial matters, Regulation (EC) No 805/2004 of the European Parliament and of the Council of 21 April 2004 creating a European Enforcement Order for uncontested claims and Regulation (EC) No 1896/2006 of the European Parliament and of the Council of 12 December 2006 creating a European order for payment procedure.

(4)   The European Council meeting in Tampere on 15 and 16 October 1999 invited the Council and the Commission to establish common procedural rules for simplified and accelerated cross-border litigation on small consumer and commercial claims.

(5)   On 30 November 2000, the Council adopted a joint programme of the Commission and the Council of measures for the implementation of the principle of mutual recognition of decisions in civil and commercial matters.[8]

The programme refers to simplifying and speeding up the settlement of cross-border litigation on small claims. This was taken forward by the Hague Programme,[9] adopted by the European Council on 5 November 2004, which called for work on small claims to be actively pursued.

(6)   On 20 December 2002, the Commission adopted a Green Paper on a European order for payment procedure and on measures to simplify and speed up small claims litigation. The Green Paper launched a consultation on measures concerning the simplification and the speeding up of small claims litigation.

(7)   Many Member States have introduced simplified civil procedures for small claims since costs, delays and complexities connected with litigation do not necessarily

---

[1]   The Annexes to the Regulation are not published. [Note of the Editor]
[8]   [Footnotes are published in the original numerical order as in OJ] OJ, C 12 of 15 January 2001, 1.
[9]   OJ, C 53 of 3 March 2005, 1.

decrease proportionally with the value of the claim. The obstacles to obtaining a fast and inexpensive judgment are exacerbated in cross-border cases. It is therefore necessary to establish a European procedure for small claims (European Small Claims Procedure). The objective of such a procedure should be to facilitate access to justice. The distortion of competition within the internal market due to imbalances with regard to the functioning of the procedural means afforded to creditors in different Member States entails the need for Community legislation that guarantees a level playing-field for creditors and debtors throughout the European Union. It should be necessary to have regard to the principles of simplicity, speed and proportionality when setting the costs of dealing with a claim under the European Small Claims Procedure. It is appropriate that details of the costs to be charged be made public, and that the means of setting any such costs be transparent.

(8)   The European Small Claims Procedure should simplify and speed up litigation concerning small claims in cross-border cases, whilst reducing costs, by offering an optional tool in addition to the possibilities existing under the laws of the Member States, which will remain unaffected. This Regulation should also make it simpler to obtain the recognition and enforcement of a judgment given in the European Small Claims Procedure in another Member State.

(9)   This Regulation seeks to promote fundamental rights and takes into account, in particular, the principles recognised by the Charter of Fundamental Rights of the European Union. The court or tribunal should respect the right to a fair trial and the principle of an adversarial process, in particular when deciding on the necessity of an oral hearing and on the means of taking evidence and the extent to which evidence is to be taken.

(10) For the purposes of facilitating calculation of the value of a claim, all interest, expenses and disbursements should be disregarded. This should affect neither the power of the court or tribunal to award these in its judgment nor the national rules on the calculation of interest.

(11) In order to facilitate the commencement of the European Small Claims Procedure, the claimant should make an application by filling in a standard claim form and lodging it with the court or tribunal. The claim form should be submitted only to a court or tribunal that has jurisdiction.

(12) The claim form should be accompanied, where appropriate, by any relevant supporting documents. However, this does not prevent the claimant from submitting, where appropriate, further evidence during the procedure. The same principle should apply to the response by the defendant.

(13) The concepts of 'clearly unfounded' in the context of the dismissal of a claim and of 'inadmissible' in the context of the dismissal of an application should be determined in accordance with national law.

(14) The European Small Claims Procedure should be a written procedure, unless an oral hearing is considered necessary by the court or tribunal or a party so requests. The court or tribunal may refuse such a request. Such refusal may not be contested separately.

(15) The parties should not be obliged to be represented by a lawyer or another legal professional.

(16) The concept of 'counterclaim' should be interpreted within the meaning of Article 6(3) of Regulation (EC) No 44/2001 as arising from the same contract or facts on which the original claim was based. Articles 2 and 4 as well as Articles 5(3), (4) and (5) should apply, *mutatis mutandis*, to counterclaims.

(17) In cases where the defendant invokes a right of set-off during the proceedings, such claim should not constitute a counterclaim for the purposes of this Regulation. Therefore, the defendant should not be obliged to use standard Form A, as set out in Annex I, for invoking such a right.

(18) The Member State addressed for the purposes of the application of Article 6 is the Member State where service is to be effected or to where the document is to be dispatched. In order to reduce costs and delays, documents should be served on the parties primarily by postal service attested by an acknowledgment of receipt, including the date of receipt.

(19) A party may refuse to accept a document at the time of service or by returning the document within one week if it is not written in, or accompanied by a translation into, the official language of the Member State addressed (or, if there are several official languages in that Member State, the official language or one of the official languages of the place where service is to be effected or to where the document is to be dispatched) or a language which the addressee understands.

(20) In the context of oral hearings and the taking of evidence, the Member States should encourage the use of modern communication technology subject to the national law of the Member State where the court or tribunal is situated. The court or tribunal should use the simplest and least costly method of taking evidence.

(21) The practical assistance to be made available to the parties should include technical information concerning the availability and the filling in of the forms.

(22) The information about procedural questions can also be given by the court or tribunal staff in accordance with national law.

(23) As the objective of this Regulation is to simplify and speed up litigation concerning small claims in cross-border cases, the court or tribunal should act as soon as possible even when this Regulation does not prescribe any time limit for a specific phase of the procedure.

(24) For the purposes of calculating time limits as provided for in this Regulation, Regulation (EEC, Euratom) No 1182/71 of the Council of 3 June 1971 determining the rules applicable to periods, dates and time limits should apply.

(25) In order to speed up the recovery of small claims, the judgment should be enforceable notwithstanding any possible appeal and without the condition of the provision of a security except as provided for in this Regulation.

(26) Any reference in this Regulation to an appeal should include any possible means of appeal available under national law.

(27) The court or tribunal must include a person qualified to serve as a judge in accordance with national law.

(28) Whenever the court or tribunal is required to set a time limit, the party concerned should be informed of the consequences of not complying with it.

(29) The unsuccessful party should bear the costs of the proceedings. The costs of the proceedings should be determined in accordance with national law. Having regard to the objectives of simplicity and cost–effectiveness, the court or tribunal should order that an unsuccessful party be obliged to pay only the costs of the proceedings, including for example any costs resulting from the fact that the other party was represented by a lawyer or another legal professional, or any costs arising from the service or translation of documents, which are proportionate to the value of the claim or which were necessarily incurred.

(30) In order to facilitate recognition and enforcement, a judgment given in a Member State in the European Small Claims Procedure should be recognised and enforceable in another Member State without the need for a declaration of enforceability and without any possibility of opposing its recognition.

(31) There should be minimum standards for the review of a judgment in situations where the defendant was not able to contest the claim.

(32) Having regard to the objectives of simplicity and cost-effectiveness, the party seeking enforcement shall not be required to have an authorised representative or a postal address in the Member State of enforcement, other than with agents having competence for the enforcement procedure in accordance with the national law of that Member State.

(33) Chapter III of this Regulation should also apply to the determination of costs and expenses made by officers of the court or tribunal due to a judgment given pursuant to the procedure specified in this Regulation.

(34) The measures necessary for the implementation of this Regulation should be adopted in accordance with Council Decision 1999/468/EC of 28 June 1999 laying down the procedures for the exercise of implementing powers conferred on the Commission.

(35) In particular, power should be conferred on the Commission to adopt measures necessary to update or make technical amendments to the forms set out in the Annexes. Since those measures are of general scope and are designed to amend non-essential elements of this Regulation and/or to supplement this Regulation by the addition of new non-essential elements, they should be adopted in accordance with the regulatory procedure with scrutiny provided for in Article 5a of Decision 1999/468/EC.

(36) Since the objectives of this Regulation, namely, the establishment of a procedure to simplify and speed up litigation concerning small claims in cross-border cases, and to reduce costs, cannot be sufficiently achieved by the Member States and can therefore, by reason of the scale and effects of this Regulation, be better achieved at Community level, the Community may adopt measures in accordance with the principle of subsidiarity as set out in Article 5 of the Treaty. In accordance with the principle of proportionality, as set out in that Article, this Regulation does not go beyond what is necessary to achieve those objectives.

(37) In accordance with Article 3 of the Protocol on the position of the United Kingdom and Ireland annexed to the Treaty on European Union and to the Treaty establishing the European Community, the United Kingdom and Ireland have given notice of their wish to take part in the adoption and application of this Regulation.

(38) In accordance with Articles 1 and 2 of the Protocol on the position of Denmark annexed to the Treaty on European Union and to the Treaty establishing the European Community, Denmark does not take part in the adoption of this Regulation and is not bound by it or subject to its application.

Chapter I — Subject matter and scope

Article 1. Subject matter. This Regulation establishes a European procedure for small claims (hereinafter referred to as the 'European Small Claims Procedure'), intended to simplify and speed up litigation concerning small claims in cross-border cases, and to reduce costs. The European Small Claims Procedure shall be available to litigants as an alternative to the procedures existing under the laws of the Member States.

This Regulation also eliminates the intermediate proceedings necessary to enable recognition and enforcement, in other Member States, of judgments given in one Member State in the European Small Claims Procedure.

Article 2. Scope.   1.   This Regulation shall apply, in cross-border cases, to civil and commercial matters, whatever the nature of the court or tribunal, where the value of a claim does not exceed EUR 2000 at the time when the claim form is received by the court or tribunal with jurisdiction, excluding all interest, expenses and disbursements. It shall not extend, in particular, to revenue, customs or administrative matters or to the liability of the State for acts and omissions in the exercise of State authority (*acta jure imperii*).

2.   This Regulation shall not apply to matters concerning:

(a)   the *status* or legal capacity of natural persons;

(b)   rights in property arising out of a matrimonial relationship, maintenance obligations, wills and succession;

(c)   bankruptcy, proceedings relating to the winding-up of insolvent companies or other legal persons, judicial arrangements, compositions and analogous proceedings;

(d)   social security;

(e)   arbitration;

(f)   employment law;

(g)   tenancies of immovable property, with the exception of actions on monetary claims; or

(h)   violations of privacy and of rights relating to personality, including defamation.

3.   In this Regulation, the term 'Member State' shall mean Member States with the exception of Denmark.

Article 3. Cross-border cases.   1.   For the purposes of this Regulation, a cross-border case is one in which at least one of the parties is domiciled or habitually resident in a Member State other than the Member State of the court or tribunal seised.

2.   Domicile shall be determined in accordance with Articles 59 and 60 of Regulation (EC) No 44/2001.

3.   The relevant moment for determining whether there is a cross-border case is the date on which the claim form is received by the court or tribunal with jurisdiction.

Chapter II — The European Small Claims Procedure

Article 4. Commencement of the Procedure.   1.   The claimant shall commence the European Small Claims Procedure by filling in standard claim Form A, as set out in Annex I, and lodging it with the court or tribunal with jurisdiction directly, by post or by any other means of communication, such as fax or e-mail, acceptable to the Member State in which the procedure is commenced. The claim form shall include a description of evidence supporting the claim and be accompanied, where appropriate, by any relevant supporting documents.

2.   Member States shall inform the Commission which means of communication are acceptable to them. The Commission shall make such information publicly available.

3.   Where a claim is outside the scope of this Regulation, the court or tribunal shall inform the claimant to that effect. Unless the claimant withdraws the claim, the court or

tribunal shall proceed with it in accordance with the relevant procedural law applicable in the Member State in which the procedure is conducted.

4.   Where the court or tribunal considers the information provided by the claimant to be inadequate or insufficiently clear or if the claim form is not filled in properly, it shall, unless the claim appears to be clearly unfounded or the application inadmissible, give the claimant the opportunity to complete or rectify the claim form or to supply supplementary information or documents or to withdraw the claim, within such period as it specifies. The court or tribunal shall use standard Form B, as set out in Annex II, for this purpose.

Where the claim appears to be clearly unfounded or the application inadmissible or where the claimant fails to complete or rectify the claim form within the time specified, the application shall be dismissed.

5.   Member States shall ensure that the claim form is available at all courts and tribunals at which the European Small Claims Procedure can be commenced.

Article 5. Conduct of the Procedure.   1.   The European Small Claims Procedure shall be a written procedure. The court or tribunal shall hold an oral hearing if it considers this to be necessary or if a party so requests. The court or tribunal may refuse such a request if it considers that with regard to the circumstances of the case, an oral hearing is obviously not necessary for the fair conduct of the proceedings. The reasons for refusal shall be given in writing. The refusal may not be contested separately.

2.   After receiving the properly filled in claim form, the court or tribunal shall fill in Part I of the standard answer Form C, as set out in Annex III. A copy of the claim form, and, where applicable, of the supporting documents, together with the answer form thus filled in, shall be served on the defendant in accordance with Article 13. These documents shall be dispatched within 14 days of receiving the properly filled in claim form.

3.   The defendant shall submit his response within 30 days of service of the claim form and answer form, by filling in Part II of standard answer Form C, accompanied, where appropriate, by any relevant supporting documents, and returning it to the court or tribunal, or in any other appropriate way not using the answer form.

4.   Within 14 days of receipt of the response from the defendant, the court or tribunal shall dispatch a copy thereof, together with any relevant supporting documents to the claimant.

5.   If, in his response, the defendant claims that the value of a non-monetary claim exceeds the limit set out in Article 2(1), the court or tribunal shall decide within 30 days of dispatching the response to the claimant, whether the claim is within the scope of this Regulation. Such decision may not be contested separately.

6.   Any counterclaim, to be submitted using standard Form A, and any relevant supporting documents shall be served on the claimant in accordance with Article 13. Those documents shall be dispatched within 14 days of receipt.

The claimant shall have 30 days from service to respond to any counterclaim.

7.   If the counterclaim exceeds the limit set out in Article 2(1), the claim and counterclaim shall not proceed in the European Small Claims Procedure but shall be dealt with in accordance with the relevant procedural law applicable in the Member State in which the procedure is conducted.

Articles 2 and 4 as well as paragraphs 3, 4 and 5 of this Article shall apply, *mutatis mutandis*, to counterclaims.

Article 6. Languages.   1.   The claim form, the response, any counterclaim, any response to a counterclaim and any description of relevant supporting documents shall be submitted in the language or one of the languages of the court or tribunal.

2.   If any other document received by the court or tribunal is not in the language in which the proceedings are conducted, the court or tribunal may require a translation of that document only if the translation appears to be necessary for giving the judgment.

3.   Where a party has refused to accept a document because it is not in either of the following languages:

(a)   the official language of the Member State addressed, or, if there are several official languages in that Member State, the official language or one of the official languages of the place where service is to be effected or to where the document is to be dispatched; or

(b)   a language which the addressee understands, the court or tribunal shall so inform the other party with a view to that party providing a translation of the document.

Article 7. Conclusion of the Procedure.   1.   Within 30 days of receipt of the response from the defendant or the claimant within the time limits laid down in Article 5(3) or (6), the court or tribunal shall give a judgment, or:

(a)   demand further details concerning the claim from the parties within a specified period of time, not exceeding 30 days;

(b)   take evidence in accordance with Article 9; or

(c)   summon the parties to an oral hearing to be held within 30 days of the summons.

2.   The court or tribunal shall give the judgment either within 30 days of any oral hearing or after having received all information necessary for giving the judgment. The judgment shall be served on the parties in accordance with Article 13.

3.   If the court or tribunal has not received an answer from the relevant party within the time limits laid down in Article 5(3) or (6), it shall give a judgment on the claim or counterclaim.

Article 8. Oral hearing.   The court or tribunal may hold an oral hearing through video conference or other communication technology if the technical means are available.

Article 9. Taking of evidence.   1.   The court or tribunal shall determine the means of taking evidence and the extent of the evidence necessary for its judgment under the rules applicable to the admissibility of evidence. The court or tribunal may admit the taking of evidence through written statements of witnesses, experts or parties. It may also admit the taking of evidence through video conference or other communication technology if the technical means are available.

2.   The court or tribunal may take expert evidence or oral testimony only if it is necessary for giving the judgment. In making its decision, the court or tribunal shall take costs into account.

3.   The court or tribunal shall use the simplest and least burdensome method of taking evidence.

Article 10. Representation of parties.   Representation by a lawyer or another legal professional shall not be mandatory.

Article 11. Assistance for the parties.   The Member States shall ensure that the parties can receive practical assistance in filling in the forms.

Article 12. Remit of the court or tribunal.   1.   The court or tribunal shall not require the parties to make any legal assessment of the claim.

2.   If necessary, the court or tribunal shall inform the parties about procedural questions.

3.   Whenever appropriate, the court or tribunal shall seek to reach a settlement between the parties.

Article 13. Service of documents.   1.   Documents shall be served by postal service attested by an acknowledgement of receipt including the date of receipt.

2.   If service in accordance with paragraph 1 is not possible, service may be effected by any of the methods provided for in Articles 13 or 14 of Regulation (EC) No 805/2004.

Article 14. Time limits.   1.   Where the court or tribunal sets a time limit, the party concerned shall be informed of the consequences of not complying with it.

2.   The court or tribunal may extend the time limits provided for in Article 4(4), Article 5(3) and (6) and Article 7(1), in exceptional circumstances, if necessary in order to safeguard the rights of the parties.

3.   If, in exceptional circumstances, it is not possible for the court or tribunal to respect the time limits provided for in Article 5(2) to (6) and Article 7, it shall take the steps required by those provisions as soon as possible.

Article 15. Enforceability of the judgment.   1.   The judgment shall be enforceable notwithstanding any possible appeal. The provision of a security shall not be required.

2.   Article 23 shall also apply in the event that the judgment is to be enforced in the Member State where the judgment was given.

Article 16. Costs.   The unsuccessful party shall bear the costs of the proceedings. However, the court or tribunal shall not award costs to the successful party to the extent that they were unnecessarily incurred or are disproportionate to the claim.

Article 17. Appeal.   1.   Member States shall inform the Commission whether an appeal is available under their procedural law against a judgment given in the European Small Claims Procedure and within what time limit such appeal shall be lodged. The Commission shall make that information publicly available.

2.   Article 16 shall apply to any appeal.

Article 18. Minimum standards for review of the judgment.   1.   The defendant shall be entitled to apply for a review of the judgment given in the European Small Claims Procedure before the court or tribunal with jurisdiction of the Member State where the judgment was given where:

   (a)   (i)   the claim form or the summons to an oral hearing were served by a method without proof of receipt by him personally, as provided for in Article 14 of Regulation (EC) No 805/2004; and

(ii) service was not effected in sufficient time to enable him to arrange for his defence without any fault on his part, or

(b) the defendant was prevented from objecting to the claim by reason of *force majeure*, or due to extraordinary circumstances without any fault on his part, provided in either case that he acts promptly.

2. If the court or tribunal rejects the review on the basis that none of the grounds referred to in paragraph 1 apply, the judgment shall remain in force. If the court or tribunal decides that the review is justified for one of the reasons laid down in paragraph 1, the judgment given in the European Small Claims Procedure shall be null and void.

Article 19. Applicable procedural law.   Subject to the provisions of this Regulation, the European Small Claims Procedure shall be governed by the procedural law of the Member State in which the procedure is conducted.

Chapter III — Recognition and enforcement in another Member State

Article 20. Recognition and enforcement.   1.   A judgment given in a Member State in the European Small Claims Procedure shall be recognised and enforced in another Member State without the need for a declaration of enforceability and without any possibility of opposing its recognition.

2. At the request of one of the parties, the court or tribunal shall issue a certificate concerning a judgment in the European Small Claims Procedure using standard Form D, as set out in Annex IV, at no extra cost.

Article 21. Enforcement procedure.   1.   Without prejudice to the provisions of this Chapter, the enforcement procedures shall be governed by the law of the Member State of enforcement.

Any judgment given in the European Small Claims Procedure shall be enforced under the same conditions as a judgment given in the Member State of enforcement.

2. The party seeking enforcement shall produce:

(a) a copy of the judgment which satisfies the conditions necessary to establish its authenticity; and

(b) a copy of the certificate referred to in Article 20(2) and, where necessary, the translation thereof into the official language of the Member State of enforcement or, if there are several official languages in that Member State, the official language or one of the official languages of court or tribunal proceedings of the place where enforcement is sought in conformity with the law of that Member State, or into another language that the Member State of enforcement has indicated it can accept. Each Member State may indicate the official language or languages of the institutions of the European Union other than its own which it can accept for the European Small Claims Procedure. The content of Form D shall be translated by a person qualified to make translations in one of the Member States.

3. The party seeking the enforcement of a judgment given in the European Small Claims Procedure in another Member State shall not be required to have:

(a) an authorised representative; or

(b) a postal address in the Member State of enforcement, other than with agents having competence for the enforcement procedure.

4.   No security, bond or deposit, however described, shall be required of a party who in one Member State applies for enforcement of a judgment given in the European Small Claims Procedure in another Member State on the ground that he is a foreign national or that he is not domiciled or resident in the Member State of enforcement.

Article 22. Refusal of enforcement.   1.   Enforcement shall, upon application by the person against whom enforcement is sought, be refused by the court or tribunal with jurisdiction in the Member State of enforcement if the judgment given in the European Small Claims Procedure is irreconcilable with an earlier judgment given in any Member State or in a third country, provided that:
    (a)   the earlier judgment involved the same cause of action and was between the same parties;
    (b)   the earlier judgment was given in the Member State of enforcement or fulfils the conditions necessary for its recognition in the Member State of enforcement; and
    (c)   the irreconcilability was not and could not have been raised as an objection in the court or tribunal proceedings in the Member State where the judgment in the European Small Claims Procedure was given.
    2.   Under no circumstances may a judgment given in the European Small Claims Procedure be reviewed as to its substance in the Member State of enforcement.

Article 23. Stay or limitation of enforcement.   Where a party has challenged a judgment given in the European Small Claims Procedure or where such a challenge is still possible, or where a party has made an application for review within the meaning of Article 18, the court or tribunal with jurisdiction or the competent authority in the Member State of enforcement may, upon application by the party against whom enforcement is sought:
    (a)   limit the enforcement proceedings to protective measures;
    (b)   make enforcement conditional on the provision of such security as it shall determine; or
    (c)   under exceptional circumstances, stay the enforcement proceedings.

Chapter IV — Final provisions

Article 24. Information.   The Member States shall cooperate to provide the general public and professional circles with information on the European Small Claims Procedure, including costs, in particular by way of the European Judicial Network in Civil and Commercial Matters established in accordance with Decision 2001/470/EC.

Article 25. Information relating to jurisdiction, means of communication and appeals.   1.   By 1 January 2008 the Member States shall communicate to the Commission:
    (a)   which courts or tribunals have jurisdiction to give a judgment in the European Small Claims Procedure;
    (b)   which means of communication are accepted for the purposes of the European Small Claims Procedure and available to the courts or tribunals in accordance with Article 4(1);
    (c)   whether an appeal is available under their procedural law in accordance with Article 17 and with which court or tribunal this may be lodged;
    (d)   which languages are accepted pursuant to Article 21(2)(b); and

(e)   which authorities have competence with respect to enforcement and which authorities have competence for the purposes of the application of Article 23.

Member States shall apprise the Commission of any subsequent changes to this information.

2.   The Commission shall make the information notified in accordance with paragraph 1 publicly available through publication in the Official Journal of the European Union and through any other appropriate means.

Article 26. Implementing measures.   The measures designed to amend non-essential elements of this Regulation, including by supplementing it, relating to updates or technical amendments to the forms in the Annexes shall be adopted in accordance with the regulatory procedure with scrutiny referred to in Article 27(2).

Article 27. Committee.   1.   The Commission shall be assisted by a Committee.
2.   Where reference is made to this paragraph, Article 5a(1) to (4), and Article 7 of Decision 1999/468/EC shall apply, having regard to the provisions of Article 8 thereof.

Article 28. Review.   By 1 January 2014, the Commission shall present to the European Parliament, the Council and the European Economic and Social Committee a detailed report reviewing the operation of the European Small Claims Procedure, including the limit of the value of the claim referred to in Article 2(1). That report shall contain an assessment of the procedure as it has operated and an extended impact assessment for each Member State. To that end and in order to ensure that best practice in the European Union is duly taken into account and reflects the principles of better legislation, Member States shall provide the Commission with information relating to the cross-border operation of the European Small Claims Procedure. This information shall cover court fees, speed of the procedure, efficiency, ease of use and the internal small claims procedures of the Member States. The Commission's report shall be accompanied, if appropriate, by proposals for adaptation.

Article 29. Entry into force.   This Regulation shall enter into force on the day following its publication in the Official Journal of the European Union.

It shall apply from 1 January 2009, with the exception of Article 25, which shall apply from 1 January 2008.

F.   Council Framework Decision 2003/577/JHA of 22 July 2003 on the execution in the European Union of orders freezing property or evidence (OJ, L 196 of 2 August 2003)[1]

(1)   The European Council, meeting in Tampere on 15 and 16 October 1999, endorsed the principle of mutual recognition, which should become the cornerstone of judicial cooperation in both civil and criminal matters within the Union.

(2)   The principle of mutual recognition should also apply to pre-trial orders, in particular to those which would enable competent judicial authorities quickly to secure evidence and to seize property which are easily movable.

---

[1]   The Annex to the Decision is not published. [Note of the Editor]

(3) On 29 November 2000 the Council, in accordance with the Tampere conclusions, adopted a programme of measures to implement the principle of mutual recognition in criminal matters, giving first priority (measures 6 and 7) to the adoption of an instrument applying the principle of mutual recognition to the freezing of evidence and property.

(4) Cooperation between Member States, based on the principle of mutual recognition and immediate execution of judicial decisions, presupposes confidence that the decisions to be recognised and enforced will always be taken in compliance with the principles of legality, subsidiarity and proportionality.

(5) Rights granted to the parties or bona fide interested third parties should be preserved.

(6) This Framework Decision respects the fundamental rights and observes the principles recognised by Article 6 of the Treaty and reflected by the Charter of Fundamental Rights of the European Union, notably Chapter VI thereof. Nothing in this Framework Decision may be interpreted as prohibiting refusal to freeze property for which a freezing order has been issued when there are reasons to believe, on the basis of objective elements, that the freezing order is issued for the purpose of prosecuting or punishing a person on account of his or her sex, race, religion, ethnic origin, nationality, language, political opinions or sexual orientation, or that that person's position may be prejudiced for any of these reasons.

This Framework Decision does not prevent any Member State from applying its constitutional rules relating to due process, freedom of association, freedom of the press and freedom of expression in other media.

Title I — Scope

Article 1. Objective. The purpose of the Framework Decision is to establish the rules under which a Member State shall recognise and execute in its territory a freezing order issued by a judicial authority of another Member State in the framework of criminal proceedings. It shall not have the effect of amending the obligation to respect the fundamental rights and fundamental legal principles as enshrined in Article 6 of the Treaty.

Article 2. Definitions. For the purposes of this Framework Decision:

(a) 'issuing State' shall mean the Member State in which a judicial authority, as defined in the national law of the issuing State, has made, validated or in any way confirmed a freezing order in the framework of criminal proceedings;

(b) 'executing State' shall mean the Member State in whose territory the property or evidence is located;

(c) 'freezing order' property that could be subject to confiscation or evidence;

(d) 'property' includes property of any description, whether corporeal or incorporeal, movable or immovable, and legal documents and instruments evidencing title to or interest in such property, which the competent judicial authority in the issuing State considers:

— is the proceeds of an offence referred to in Article 3, or equivalent to either the full value or part of the value of such proceeds, or

— constitutes the instrumentalities or the objects of such an offence;

(e)   'evidence' shall mean objects, documents or data which could be produced as evidence in criminal proceedings concerning an offence referred to in Article 3.

Article 3. Offences.   1.   This Framework Decision applies to freezing orders issued for purposes of:
    (a)   securing evidence, or
    (b)   subsequent confiscation of property.
    2.   The following offences, as they are defined by the law of the issuing State, and if they are punishable in the issuing State by a custodial sentence of a maximum period of at least three years shall not be subject to verification of the double criminality of the act:
    —   participation in a criminal organisation;
    —   terrorism;
    —   trafficking in human beings;
    —   sexual exploitation of children and child pornography;
    —   illicit trafficking in narcotic drugs and psychotropic substances;
    —   illicit trafficking in weapons, munitions and explosives;
    —   corruption;
    —   fraud, including that affecting the financial interests of the European Communities within the meaning of the Convention of 26 July 1995 on the Protection of the European Communities' Financial Interests;
    —   laundering of the proceeds of crime;
    —   counterfeiting currency, including of the euro;
    —   computer-related crime;
    —   environmental crime, including illicit trafficking in endangered animal species and in endangered plant species and varieties;
    —   facilitation of unauthorised entry and residence;
    —   murder, grievous bodily injury;
    —   illicit trade in human organs and tissue;
    —   kidnapping, illegal restraint and hostage-taking;
    —   racism and xenophobia;
    —   organised or armed robbery;
    —   illicit trafficking in cultural goods, including antiques and works of art;
    —   swindling;
    —   racketeering and extortion;
    —   counterfeiting and piracy of products;
    —   forgery of administrative documents and trafficking therein;
    —   forgery of means of payment;
    —   illicit trafficking in hormonal substances and other growth promoters;
    —   illicit trafficking in nuclear or radioactive materials;
    —   trafficking in stolen vehicles;
    —   rape;
    —   arson;
    —   crimes within the jurisdiction of the International Criminal Tribunal;
    —   unlawful seizure of aircraft/ships;
    —   sabotage.
    3.   The Council may decide, at any time, acting unanimously after consultation of the European Parliament under the conditions laid down in Article 39(1) of the Treaty,

to add other categories of offence to the list contained in paragraph 2. The Council shall examine, in the light of the report submitted by the Commission pursuant to Article 14 of this Framework Decision, whether the list should be extended or amended.

4. For cases not covered by paragraph 2, the executing State may subject the recognition and enforcement of a freezing order made for purposes referred to in paragraph 1(a) to the condition that the acts for which the order was issued constitute an offence under the laws of that State, whatever the constituent elements or however described under the law of the issuing State.

For cases not covered by paragraph 2, the executing State may subject the recognition and enforcement of a freezing order made for purposes referred to in paragraph 1(b) to the condition that the acts for which the order was issued constitute an offence which, under the laws of that State, allows for such freezing, whatever the constituent elements or however described under the law of the issuing State.

Title II — Procedure for executing freezing orders

Article 4. Transmission of freezing orders. 1. A freezing order within the meaning of this Framework Decision, together with the certificate provided for in Article 9, shall be transmitted by the judicial authority which issued it directly to the competent judicial authority for execution by any means capable of producing a written record under conditions allowing the executing State to establish authenticity.

2. The United Kingdom and Ireland, respectively, may, before the date referred to in Article 14(1), state in a declaration that the freezing order together with the certificate must be sent via a central authority or authorities specified by it in the declaration. Any such declaration may be modified by a further declaration or withdrawn any time. Any declaration or withdrawal shall be deposited with the General Secretariat of the Council and notified to the Commission. These Member States may at any time by a further declaration limit the scope of such a declaration for the purpose of giving greater effect to paragraph 1. They shall do so when the provisions on mutual assistance of the Convention implementing the Schengen Agreement are put into effect for them.

3. If the competent judicial authority for execution is unknown, the judicial authority in the issuing State shall make all necessary inquiries, including via the contact points of the European Judicial Network, in order to obtain the information from the executing State.

4. When the judicial authority in the executing State which receives a freezing order has no jurisdiction to recognise it and take the necessary measures for its execution, it shall, ex officio, transmit the freezing order to the competent judicial authority for execution and shall so inform the judicial authority in the issuing State which issued it.

Article 5. Recognition and immediate execution. 1. The competent judicial authorities of the executing State shall recognise a freezing order, transmitted in accordance with Article 4, without any further formality being required and shall forthwith take the necessary measures for its immediate execution in the same way as for a freezing order made by an authority of the executing State, unless that authority decides to invoke one of the grounds for non-recognition or non-execution provided for in Article 7 or one of the grounds for postponement provided for in Article 8.

Whenever it is necessary to ensure that the evidence taken is valid and provided that such formalities and procedures are not contrary to the fundamental principles of law in the executing State, the judicial authority of the executing State shall also observe the formalities and procedures expressly indicated by the competent judicial authority of the issuing State in the execution of the freezing order.

A report on the execution of the freezing order shall be made forthwith to the competent authority in the issuing State by any means capable of producing a written record.

2.   Any additional coercive measures rendered necessary by the freezing order shall be taken in accordance with the applicable procedural rules of the executing State.

3.   The competent judicial authorities of the executing State shall decide and communicate the decision on a freezing order as soon as possible and, whenever practicable, within 24 hours of receipt of the freezing order.

Article 6. Duration of the freezing.   1.   The property shall remain frozen in the executing State until that State has responded definitively to any request made under Articles 10(1) (a) or (b).

2.   However, after consulting the issuing State, the executing State may in accordance with its national law and practices lay down appropriate conditions in the light of the circumstances of the case in order to limit the period for which the property will be frozen. If, in accordance with those conditions, it envisages lifting the measure, it shall inform the issuing State, which shall be given the opportunity to submit its comments.

3.   The judicial authorities of the issuing State shall forthwith notify the judicial authorities of the executing State that the freezing order has been lifted. In these circumstances it shall be the responsibility of the executing State to lift the measure as soon as possible.

Article 7. Grounds for non-recognition or non-execution.   1.   The competent judicial authorities of the executing State may refuse to recognise or execute the freezing order only if:

(a)   the certificate provided for in Article 9 is not produced, is incomplete or manifestly does not correspond to the freezing order;

(b)   there is an immunity or privilege under the law of the executing State which makes it impossible to execute the freezing order;

(c)   it is instantly clear from the information provided in the certificate that rendering judicial assistance pursuant to Article 10 for the offence in respect of which the freezing order has been made, would infringe the *ne bis in idem* principle;

(d)   if, in one of the cases referred to in Article 3(4), the act on which the freezing order is based does not constitute an offence under the law of the executing State; however, in relation to taxes or duties, customs and exchange, execution of the freezing order may not be refused on the ground that the law of the executing State does not impose the same kind of tax or duty or does not contain a tax, duty, customs and exchange regulation of the same kind as the law of the issuing State.

2.   In case of paragraph 1(a), the competent judicial authority may:

(a)   specify a deadline for its presentation, completion or correction; or

(b)   accept an equivalent document; or

(c)   exempt the issuing judicial authority from the requirement if it considers that the information provided is sufficient.

3.   Any decision to refuse recognition or execution shall be taken and notified forthwith to the competent judicial authorities of the issuing State by any means capable of producing a written record.

4.   In case it is in practice impossible to execute the freezing order for the reason that the property or evidence have disappeared, have been destroyed, cannot be found in the location indicated in the certificate or the location of the property or evidence has not been indicated in a sufficiently precise manner, even after consultation with the issuing State, the competent judicial authorities of the issuing State shall likewise be notified forthwith.

Article 8. Grounds for postponement of execution.   1.   The competent judicial authority of the executing State may postpone the execution of a freezing order transmitted in accordance with Article 4:

(a)   where its execution might damage an ongoing criminal investigation, until such time as it deems reasonable;

(b)   where the property or evidence concerned have already been subjected to a freezing order in criminal proceedings, and until that freezing order is lifted;

(c)   where, in the case of an order freezing property in criminal proceedings with a view to its subsequent confiscation, that property is already subject to an order made in the course of other proceedings in the executing State and until that order is lifted. However, this point shall only apply where such an order would have priority over subsequent national freezing orders in criminal proceedings under national law.

2.   A report on the postponement of the execution of the freezing order, including the grounds for the postponement and, if possible, the expected duration of the postponement, shall be made forthwith to the competent authority in the issuing State by any means capable of producing a written record.

3.   As soon as the ground for postponement has ceased to exist, the competent judicial authority of the executing State shall forthwith take the necessary measures for the execution of the freezing order and inform the competent authority in the issuing State thereof by any means capable of producing a written record.

4.   The competent judicial authority of the executing State shall inform the competent authority of the issuing State about any other restraint measure to which the property concerned may be subjected.

Article 9. Certificate.   1.   The certificate, the standard form for which is given in the Annex, shall be signed, and its contents certified as accurate, by the competent judicial authority in the issuing State that ordered the measure.

2.   The certificate must be translated into the official language or one of the official languages of the executing State.

3.   Any Member State may, either when this Framework Decision is adopted or at a later date, state in a declaration deposited with the General Secretariat of the Council that it will accept a translation in one or more other official languages of the institutions of the European Communities.

Article 10. Subsequent treatment of the frozen property.   1.   The transmission referred to in Article 4:

(a)   shall be accompanied by a request for the evidence to be transferred to the issuing State; or

(b)   shall be accompanied by a request for confiscation requiring either enforcement of a confiscation order that has been issued in the issuing State or confiscation in the executing State and subsequent enforcement of any such order; or

(c)   shall contain an instruction in the certificate that the property shall remain in the executing State pending a request referred to in (a) or (b). The issuing State shall indicate in the certificate the (estimated) date for submission of this request. Article 6(2) shall apply.

2.   Requests referred to in paragraph 1(a) and (b) shall be submitted by the issuing State and processed by the executing State in accordance with the rules applicable to mutual assistance in criminal matters and the rules applicable to international cooperation relating to confiscation.

3.   However, by way of derogation from the rules on mutual assistance referred to in paragraph 2, the executing State may not refuse requests referred to under paragraph 1(a) on grounds of absence of double criminality, where the requests concern the offences referred to in Article 3(2) and those offences are punishable in the issuing State by a prison sentence of at least three years.

Article 11. Legal remedies.   1.   Member States shall put in place the necessary arrangements to ensure that any interested party, including bona fide third parties, have legal remedies without suspensive effect against a freezing order executed pursuant to Article 5, in order to preserve their legitimate interests; the action shall be brought before a court in the issuing State or in the executing State in accordance with the national law of each.

2.   The substantive reasons for issuing the freezing order can be challenged only in an action brought before a court in the issuing State.

3.   If the action is brought in the executing State, the judicial authority of the issuing State shall be informed thereof and of the grounds of the action, so that it can submit the arguments that it deems necessary. It shall be informed of the outcome of the action.

4.   The issuing and executing States shall take the necessary measures to facilitate the exercise of the right to bring an action mentioned in paragraph 1, in particular by providing adequate information to interested parties.

5.   The issuing State shall ensure that any time limits for bringing an action mentioned in paragraph 1 are applied in a way that guarantees the possibility of an effective legal remedy for the interested parties.

Article 12. Reimbursement.   1.   Without prejudice to Article 11(2), where the executing State under its law is responsible for injury caused to one of the parties mentioned in Article 11 by the execution of a freezing order transmitted to it pursuant to Article 4, the issuing State shall reimburse to the executing State any sums paid in damages by virtue of that responsibility to the said party except if, and to the extent that, the injury or any part of it is exclusively due to the conduct of the executing State.

2.   Paragraph 1 is without prejudice to the national law of the Member States on claims by natural or legal persons for compensation of damage.

Title III — Final provisions

Article 13. Territorial application.　This Framework Decision shall apply to Gibraltar.

Article 14. Implementation.　1.　Member States shall take the necessary measures to comply with the provisions of this Framework Decision before 2 August 2005.

　　2.　By the same date Member States shall transmit to the General Secretariat of the Council and to the Commission the text of the provisions transposing into their national law the obligations imposed on them under this Framework Decision. On the basis of a report established using this information and a written report by the Commission, the Council shall, before 2 August 2006, assess the extent to which Member States have complied with the provisions of this Framework Decision.

　　3.　The General Secretariat of the Council shall notify Member States and the Commission of the declarations made pursuant to Article 9(3).

Article 15. Entry into force.　This Framework Decision shall enter into force on the day of its publication in the Official Journal of the European Union.

G.　Council Regulation (EC) No 2238/2003 of 15 December 2003 protecting against the effects of the application of the United States Anti-Dumping Act of 1916, and actions based thereon or resulting therefrom (OJ, L 333 of 20 December 2003): Recitals 1–9, Article 1

See Chapter II, Public policy of the EU, B.

H.　Council Framework Decision 2005/214/JHA of 24 February 2005 on the application of the principle of mutual recognition to financial penalties (OJ, L 76 of 22 March 2005)

Article 1. Definitions.
　　(b)　'financial penalty' shall mean the obligation to pay:
　　(i)　a sum of money on conviction of an offence imposed in a decision;
　　(ii)　compensation imposed in the same decision for the benefit of victims, where the victim may not be a civil party to the proceedings and the court is acting in the exercise of its criminal jurisdiction;
　　(iii)　a sum of money in respect of the costs of court or administrative proceedings leading to the decision;
　　(iv)　a sum of money to a public fund or a victim support organisation, imposed in the same decision.
　　A financial penalty shall not include:
　　—　orders for the confiscation of instrumentalities or proceeds of crime;
　　—　orders that have a civil nature and arise out of a claim for damages and restitution and which are enforceable in accordance with Council Regulation (EC) No

44/2001 of 22 December 2000 on jurisdiction and the recognition and enforcement of judgments in civil and commercial matters.

I.   Directive 2000/35/EC of the European Parliament and of the Council of 29 June 2000 on combating late payment in commercial transactions (OJ, L 200 of 8 August 2000)

Article 4. Retention of title.   1.   Member States shall provide in conformity with the applicable national provisions designated by private international law that the seller retains title to goods until they are fully paid for if a retention of title clause has been expressly agreed between the buyer and the seller before the delivery of the goods.

Article 5. Recovery procedures for unchallenged claims.   1.   Member States shall ensure that an enforceable title can be obtained, irrespective of the amount of the debt, normally within 90 calendar days of the lodging of the creditor's action or application at the court or other competent authority, provided that the debt or aspects of the procedure are not disputed. This duty shall be carried out by Member States in conformity with their respective national legislation, regulations and administrative provisions.

2.   The respective national legislation, regulations and administrative provisions shall apply the same conditions for all creditors who are established in the European Community.

3.   The 90 calendar day period referred to in paragraph 1 shall not include the following:

(a)   periods for service of documents;

(b)   any delays caused by the creditor, such as periods devoted to correcting applications.

4.   This Article shall be without prejudice to the provisions of the Brussels Convention on jurisdiction and enforcement of judgments in civil and commercial matters.

L.   Directive 2008/52/EC of the European Parliament and of the Council of 21 May 2008 on certain aspects of mediation in civil and commercial matters (OJ, L 136 of 24 May 2008)[1]

(1)   The Community has set itself the objective of maintaining and developing an area of freedom, security and justice, in which the free movement of persons is ensured. To that end, the Community has to adopt, inter alia, measures in the field of judicial cooperation in civil matters that are necessary for the proper functioning of the internal market.

(2)   The principle of access to justice is fundamental and, with a view to facilitating better access to justice, the European Council at its meeting in Tampere on 15 and 16 October 1999 called for alternative, extra-judicial procedures to be created by the

---

[1]   [Footnotes are published in the original numerical order as in OJ]

Member States.

(3) In May 2000 the Council adopted Conclusions on alternative methods of settling disputes under civil and commercial law, stating that the establishment of basic principles in this area is an essential step towards enabling the appropriate development and operation of extrajudicial procedures for the settlement of disputes in civil and commercial matters so as to simplify and improve access to justice.

(4) In April 2002 the Commission presented a Green Paper on alternative dispute resolution in civil and commercial law, taking stock of the existing situation as concerns alternative dispute resolution methods in the European Union and initiating widespread consultations with Member States and interested parties on possible measures to promote the use of mediation.

(5) The objective of securing better access to justice, as part of the policy of the European Union to establish an area of freedom, security and justice, should encompass access to judicial as well as extrajudicial dispute resolution methods. This Directive should contribute to the proper functioning of the internal market, in particular as concerns the availability of mediation services.

(6) Mediation can provide a cost-effective and quick extrajudicial resolution of disputes in civil and commercial matters through processes tailored to the needs of the parties. Agreements resulting from mediation are more likely to be complied with voluntarily and are more likely to preserve an amicable and sustainable relationship between the parties. These benefits become even more pronounced in situations displaying cross-border elements.

(7) In order to promote further the use of mediation and ensure that parties having recourse to mediation can rely on a predictable legal framework, it is necessary to introduce framework legislation addressing, in particular, key aspects of civil procedure.

(8) The provisions of this Directive should apply only to mediation in cross-border disputes, but nothing should prevent Member States from applying such provisions also to internal mediation processes.

(9) This Directive should not in any way prevent the use of modern communication technologies in the mediation process.

(10) This Directive should apply to processes whereby two or more parties to a cross-border dispute attempt by themselves, on a voluntary basis, to reach an amicable agreement on the settlement of their dispute with the assistance of a mediator. It should apply in civil and commercial matters. However, it should not apply to rights and obligations on which the parties are not free to decide themselves under the relevant applicable law. Such rights and obligations are particularly frequent in family law and employment law.

(11) This Directive should not apply to pre-contractual negotiations or to processes of an adjudicatory nature such as certain judicial conciliation schemes, consumer complaint schemes, arbitration and expert determination or to processes administered by persons or bodies issuing a formal recommendation, whether or not it be legally binding as to the resolution of the dispute.

(12) This Directive should apply to cases where a court refers parties to mediation or in which national law prescribes mediation. Furthermore, in so far as a judge may act as a mediator under national law, this Directive should also apply to mediation conducted by a judge who is not responsible for any judicial proceedings relating to the matter or matters in dispute. This Directive should not, however, extend to attempts made by the

court or judge seised to settle a dispute in the context of judicial proceedings concerning the dispute in question or to cases in which the court or judge seised requests assistance or advice from a competent person.

(13) The mediation provided for in this Directive should be a voluntary process in the sense that the parties are themselves in charge of the process and may organise it as they wish and terminate it at any time. However, it should be possible under national law for the courts to set time–limits for a mediation process. Moreover, the courts should be able to draw the parties' attention to the possibility of mediation whenever this is appropriate.

(14) Nothing in this Directive should prejudice national legislation making the use of mediation compulsory or subject to incentives or sanctions provided that such legislation does not prevent parties from exercising their right of access to the judicial system. Nor should anything in this Directive prejudice existing self-regulating mediation systems in so far as these deal with aspects which are not covered by this Directive.

(15) In order to provide legal certainty, this Directive should indicate which date should be relevant for determining whether or not a dispute which the parties attempt to settle through mediation is a cross-border dispute. In the absence of a written agreement, the parties should be deemed to agree to use mediation at the point in time when they take specific action to start the mediation process.

(16) To ensure the necessary mutual trust with respect to confidentiality, effect on limitation and prescription periods, and recognition and enforcement of agreements resulting from mediation, Member States should encourage, by any means they consider appropriate, the training of mediators and the introduction of effective quality control mechanisms concerning the provision of mediation services.

(17) Member States should define such mechanisms, which may include having recourse to market–based solutions, and should not be required to provide any funding in that respect. The mechanisms should aim at preserving the flexibility of the mediation process and the autonomy of the parties, and at ensuring that mediation is conducted in an effective, impartial and competent way. Mediators should be made aware of the existence of the European Code of Conduct for Mediators which should also be made available to the general public on the Internet.

(18) In the field of consumer protection, the Commission has adopted a Recommendation[5] establishing minimum quality criteria which out-of-court bodies involved in the consensual resolution of consumer disputes should offer to their users. Any mediators or organisations coming within the scope of that Recommendation should be encouraged to respect its principles. In order to facilitate the dissemination of information concerning such bodies, the Commission should set up a database of out-of-court schemes which Member States consider as respecting the principles of that Recommendation.

(19) Mediation should not be regarded as a poorer alternative to judicial proceedings in the sense that compliance with agreements resulting from mediation would depend on the goodwill of the parties. Member States should therefore ensure that the parties to a written agreement resulting from mediation can have the content of their agreement made enforceable. It should only be possible for a Member State to refuse to

---

5   Commission Recommendation 2001/310/EC of 4 April 2001 on the principles for out-of-court bodies involved in the consensual resolution of consumer disputes (OJ, L 109 of 19 April 2001, 56).

make an agreement enforceable if the content is contrary to its law, including its private international law, or if its law does not provide for the enforceability of the content of the specific agreement. This could be the case if the obligation specified in the agreement was by its nature unenforceable.

(20) The content of an agreement resulting from mediation which has been made enforceable in a Member State should be recognised and declared enforceable in the other Member States in accordance with applicable Community or national law. This could, for example, be on the basis of Council Regulation (EC) No 44/2001 of 22 December 2000 on jurisdiction and the recognition and enforcement of judgments in civil and commercial matters or Council Regulation (EC) No 2201/2003 of 27 November 2003 concerning jurisdiction and the recognition and enforcement of judgments in matrimonial matters and the matters of parental responsibility.

(21) Regulation (EC) No 2201/2003 specifically provides that, in order to be enforceable in another Member State, agreements between the parties have to be enforceable in the Member State in which they were concluded. Consequently, if the content of an agreement resulting from mediation in a family law matter is not enforceable in the Member State where the agreement was concluded and where the request for enforceability is made, this Directive should not encourage the parties to circumvent the law of that Member State by having their agreement made enforceable in another Member State.

(22) This Directive should not affect the rules in the Member States concerning enforcement of agreements resulting from mediation.

(23) Confidentiality in the mediation process is important and this Directive should therefore provide for a minimum degree of compatibility of civil procedural rules with regard to how to protect the confidentiality of mediation in any subsequent civil and commercial judicial proceedings or arbitration.

(24) In order to encourage the parties to use mediation, Member States should ensure that their rules on limitation and prescription periods do not prevent the parties from going to court or to arbitration if their mediation attempt fails. Member States should make sure that this result is achieved even though this Directive does not harmonise national rules on limitation and prescription periods. Provisions on limitation and prescription periods in international agreements as implemented in the Member States, for instance in the area of transport law, should not be affected by this Directive.

(25) Member States should encourage the provision of information to the general public on how to contact mediators and organisations providing mediation services. They should also encourage legal practitioners to inform their clients of the possibility of mediation.

(26) In accordance with point 34 of the Interinstitutional agreement on better law-making,[6] Member States are encouraged to draw up, for themselves and in the interests of the Community, their own tables illustrating, as far as possible, the correlation between this Directive and the transposition measures, and to make them public.

---

[6]   OJ, C 321of 31 December 2003, 1.

(27) This Directive seeks to promote the fundamental rights, and takes into account the principles, recognised in particular by the Charter of Fundamental Rights of the European Union.

(28) Since the objective of this Directive cannot be sufficiently achieved by the Member States and can therefore, by reason of the scale or effects of the action, be better achieved at Community level, the Community may adopt measures in accordance with the principle of subsidiarity as set out in Article 5 of the Treaty. In accordance with the principle of proportionality, as set out in that Article, this Directive does not go beyond what is necessary in order to achieve that objective.

(29) In accordance with Article 3 of the Protocol on the position of the United Kingdom and Ireland, annexed to the Treaty on European Union and to the Treaty establishing the European Community, the United Kingdom and Ireland have given notice of their wish to take part in the adoption and application of this Directive.

(30) In accordance with Articles 1 and 2 of the Protocol on the position of Denmark, annexed to the Treaty on European Union and to the Treaty establishing the European Community, Denmark does not take part in the adoption of this Directive and is not bound by it or subject to its application.

Article 1. Objective and scope.   1.   The objective of this Directive is to facilitate access to alternative dispute resolution and to promote the amicable settlement of disputes by encouraging the use of mediation and by ensuring a balanced relationship between mediation and judicial proceedings.

2.   This Directive shall apply, in cross-border disputes, to civil and commercial matters except as regards rights and obligations which are not at the parties' disposal under the relevant applicable law. It shall not extend, in particular, to revenue, customs or administrative matters or to the liability of the State for acts and omissions in the exercise of State authority (*acta iure imperii*).

3.   In this Directive, the term 'Member State' shall mean Member States with the exception of Denmark.

Article 2. Cross-border disputes.   1.   For the purposes of this Directive a cross-border dispute shall be one in which at least one of the parties is domiciled or habitually resident in a Member State other than that of any other party on the date on which:
   (a)   the parties agree to use mediation after the dispute has arisen;
   (b)   mediation is ordered by a court;
   (c)   an obligation to use mediation arises under national law; or
   (d)   for the purposes of Article 5 an invitation is made to the parties.

2.   Notwithstanding paragraph 1, for the purposes of Articles 7 and 8 a cross-border dispute shall also be one in which judicial proceedings or arbitration following mediation between the parties are initiated in a Member State other than that in which the parties were domiciled or habitually resident on the date referred to in paragraphs 1(a), (b) or (c).

3.   For the purposes of paragraphs 1 and 2, domicile shall be determined in accordance with Articles 59 and 60 of Regulation (EC) No 44/2001.

Article 3. Definitions.   For the purposes of this Directive the following definitions shall apply:

(a)   'Mediation' means a structured process, however named or referred to, whereby two or more parties to a dispute attempt by themselves, on a voluntary basis, to reach an agreement on the settlement of their dispute with the assistance of a mediator. This process may be initiated by the parties or suggested or ordered by a court or prescribed by the law of a Member State.

It includes mediation conducted by a judge who is not responsible for any judicial proceedings concerning the dispute in question. It excludes attempts made by the court or the judge seised to settle a dispute in the course of judicial proceedings concerning the dispute in question.

(b)   'Mediator' means any third person who is asked to conduct a mediation in an effective, impartial and competent way, regardless of the denomination or profession of that third person in the Member State concerned and of the way in which the third person has been appointed or requested to conduct the mediation.

Article 4. Ensuring the quality of mediation.   1.   Member States shall encourage, by any means which they consider appropriate, the development of, and adherence to, voluntary codes of conduct by mediators and organisations providing mediation services, as well as other effective quality control mechanisms concerning the provision of mediation services.

2.   Member States shall encourage the initial and further training of mediators in order to ensure that the mediation is conducted in an effective, impartial and competent way in relation to the parties.

Article 5. Recourse to mediation.   1.   A court before which an action is brought may, when appropriate and having regard to all the circumstances of the case, invite the parties to use mediation in order to settle the dispute. The court may also invite the parties to attend an information session on the use of mediation if such sessions are held and are easily available.

2.   This Directive is without prejudice to national legislation making the use of mediation compulsory or subject to incentives or sanctions, whether before or after judicial proceedings have started, provided that such legislation does not prevent the parties from exercising their right of access to the judicial system.

Article 6. Enforceability of agreements resulting from mediation.   1.   Member States shall ensure that it is possible for the parties, or for one of them with the explicit consent of the others, to request that the content of a written agreement resulting from mediation be made enforceable. The content of such an agreement shall be made enforceable unless, in the case in question, either the content of that agreement is contrary to the law of the Member State where the request is made or the law of that Member State does not provide for its enforceability.

2.   The content of the agreement may be made enforceable by a court or other competent authority in a judgment or decision or in an authentic instrument in accordance with the law of the Member State where the request is made.

3.   Member States shall inform the Commission of the courts or other authorities competent to receive requests in accordance with paragraphs 1 and 2.

4.   Nothing in this Article shall affect the rules applicable to the recognition and enforcement in another Member State of an agreement made enforceable in accordance with paragraph 1.

Article 7. Confidentiality of mediation.   1.   Given that mediation is intended to take place in a manner which respects confidentiality, Member States shall ensure that, unless the parties agree otherwise, neither mediators nor those involved in the administration of the mediation process shall be compelled to give evidence in civil and commercial judicial proceedings or arbitration regarding information arising out of or in connection with a mediation process, except:

(a)   where this is necessary for overriding considerations of public policy of the Member State concerned, in particular when required to ensure the protection of the best interests of children or to prevent harm to the physical or psychological integrity of a person; or

(b)   where disclosure of the content of the agreement resulting from mediation is necessary in order to implement or enforce that agreement.

2.   Nothing in paragraph 1 shall preclude Member States from enacting stricter measures to protect the confidentiality of mediation.

Article 8. Effect of mediation on limitation and prescription periods.   1.   Member States shall ensure that parties who choose mediation in an attempt to settle a dispute are not subsequently prevented from initiating judicial proceedings or arbitration in relation to that dispute by the expiry of limitation or prescription periods during the mediation process.

2.   Paragraph 1 shall be without prejudice to provisions on limitation or prescription periods in international agreements to which Member States are party.

Article 9. Information for the general public.   Member States shall encourage, by any means which they consider appropriate, the availability to the general public, in particular on the Internet, of information on how to contact mediators and organisations providing mediation services.

Article 10. Information on competent courts and authorities.   The Commission shall make publicly available, by any appropriate means, information on the competent courts or authorities communicated by the Member States pursuant to Article 6(3).

Article 11. Review.   Not later than 21 May 2016, the Commission shall submit to the European Parliament, the Council and the European Economic and Social Committee a report on the application of this Directive. The report shall consider the development of mediation throughout the European Union and the impact of this Directive in the Member States. If necessary, the report shall be accompanied by proposals to adapt this Directive.

Article 12. Transposition.   1.   Member States shall bring into force the laws, regulations, and administrative provisions necessary to comply with this Directive before 21 May 2011, with the exception of Article 10, for which the date of compliance shall be 21 November 2010 at the latest. They shall forthwith inform the Commission thereof.

When they are adopted by Member States, these measures shall contain a reference to this Directive or shall be accompanied by such reference on the occasion of their official publication. The methods of making such reference shall be laid down by Member States.

2.   Member States shall communicate to the Commission the text of the main provisions of national law which they adopt in the field covered by this Directive.

Article 13. Entry into force.   This Directive shall enter into force on the 20th day following its publication in the Official Journal of the European Union.

Article 14. Addressees.   This Directive is addressed to the Member States.

M.   Green paper on improving the efficiency of the enforcement of judgments in the European Union: the attachment of bank accounts (COM(2006) 618 final of 24 October 2006)

1.1.   *Shortcomings of the current situation*

Enforcement law has often been termed the 'Achilles' heel' of the European Civil Judicial Area. While a number of Community instruments provide for the jurisdiction of the courts, the procedure to have judgments recognised and declared enforceable and mechanisms for cooperation of courts in civil procedures, no legislative proposal has yet been made for actual measures of enforcement. To date, execution on a court order after it has been declared enforceable in another Member State remains entirely a matter of national law. Current fragmentation of national rules on enforcement severely hampers cross-border debt collection. Creditors seeking to enforce an order in another Member State are confronted with different legal systems, procedural requirements and language barriers which entail additional costs and delays in the enforcement procedure. In practice, a creditor seeking to recover a monetary claim in Europe will most commonly try to do so by obtaining an attachment [1] of his debtor's bank account(s). Such procedures exist in most Member States and, if working efficiently, can be a powerful weapon against recalcitrant or fraudulent debtors. However, while debtors are today able to move their monies almost instantaneously, out of accounts known to their creditors into other accounts in the same or another Member State creditors are not able to block these monies with the same swiftness. Under existing Community instruments, it is not possible to obtain a bank attachment which can be enforced throughout the European Union. Notably, the Regulation 44/2001 (Brussels I) does not ensure that a protective remedy such as a banking seizure obtained *ex parte* is recognised and enforced in a Member State other than the one where it was issued. [3] The Commission already noted the difficulties of cross-border debt recovery in its 1998 Communication 'Towards greater efficiency in obtaining and enforcing judgments in the European Union'. [4] In view of the diversity of Member States' legislation and the complexity of the subject, it proposed to confine reflection

---

[1]   [Footnotes are published in the original numerical order as in OJ] Note on the terminology: The term 'attachment' in this Green Paper denotes a procedure which attaches or freezes a debtor's moveable property which is in the hands of a third party and prevents the third party from giving up possession of the property.

[3]   ECJ judgment of 21 May 1980 in case C-125/79 (*Denilauler*).

[4]   Commission communication to the Council and the European Parliament (OJ, C 33 of 31 January 1998, 3).

initially to the problem of banking seizures.[5] Two years later, the Programme on Mutual Recognition called upon the Commission to improve attachment measures concerning banks.[6] In 2002, the Commission issued an invitation to tender for a study *on making more efficient the enforcement of judicial decisions within the European Union*. The study's report analyses the situation in the then 15 Member States and proposed several measures to improve the enforcement of judicial decisions in the European Union, notably the creation of a European order for the attachment of bank accounts, a European protective order to the same effect and a number of measures enhancing the transparency of the debtor's assets.[7] The latter issue will be dealt with in a Green Paper to be published in 2007. The problems of cross-border debt recovery risk constituting an obstacle to the free circulation of payment orders within the European Union and an impediment for the proper functioning of the Internal Market. Late payment and non-payment jeopardises the interests of businesses and consumers alike. The differences in the efficiency of debt-recovery within the European Union also risk distorting competition among businesses operating in Member States as between efficient systems of enforcing payment orders and those where this is not the case. Community action on this subject therefore needs to be considered.

3.5. Jurisdictional Issues

Since in most Member States courts deciding the main proceedings have competence for protective measures, it could be argued that a court which has jurisdiction on the merits under the relevant rules of Community law should be competent also for a protective order under the European system. In addition to the court which has jurisdiction in the principal action, the attachment order could be granted by the courts of the Member State of the defendant's domicile, if different; and/or the courts of any Member State in which a bank account against which an attachment is to be used, is located. Given that the aim of the European instrument would be to remedy the current situation in which the creditor has to go to the Member State where the account is situated, there might be a case for enabling the creditor to choose between the different fora mentioned above.

5.1. Implementation

Once an attachment order has been issued by a court in a Member State, the question arises how it should be implemented. Given the need to act swiftly and the purely protective nature of the instrument, it is suggested that an attachment should take effect directly throughout the European Union without any intermediary procedure (like a declaration of enforceability) in the Member State requested being required. The ways of transmitting the attachment from the issuing court to the bank holding the account to be seized will need to be considered. The procedure has to balance the creditor's interest to effect a speedy transmission with the interests of the debtor and the bank to minimise unjustified

---

[5]   Cf Communication (Fn 1), 14 s.

[6]   Programme of measures for implementation of the principle of mutual recognition of decisions in civil and commercial matters, OJ, C 12 of 15 January 2001, 1.

[7]   Study No. JAI/A3/2002/02. The final report is available at://ec.europa.eu/justice-home/doc-centre/civil/studies/doc-civil-studies-en.htm.

seizures. The cross-border transmission of documents is governed by Regulation 1348/2000 which provides for the direct transmission of an attachment order from the court to the bank by postal services. While this method already allows for a relatively rapid service of judicial decisions, additional consideration should be given to the question whether the use of electronic communication can be used to further speed up the transmission process. In order to achieve the policy objective to render the freezing of accounts more efficacious, it is suggested that a bank attachment should operate electronically at all or most of the stages of the procedure, i.e. from the court granting it to the bank holding the account. It would need to be assessed which mechanisms will have to be devised to provide for an appropriate degree of security in the transmission process and whether the use of an electronic signature would suffice to certify the identity and competence of the issuing authority and guarantee the accuracy of the data transmitted. It would also have to be considered which time limit the bank would have to respect in order to implement the attachment, i.e. whether the account would be blocked immediately upon receipt or within a specified time period following receipt of the attachment by the bank, and how transactions should be treated that have been initiated before the service of the attachment order was effected on the bank. The banks should be required to inform the competent enforcement authority whether the attachment has 'caught' any funds standing to the credit of the debtor in the account(s) seized. Ideally, this information would also be transmitted electronically. In this context, consideration will have to be given as to how an appropriate level of data protection and banking secrecy can be guaranteed in this process.

5.4. 'Transformation' into an executory measure

A creditor who has blocked his debtor's account by means of an attachment order might eventually obtain an order in the principle action that is enforceable in the Member State where the account is situated, whether by a declaration of enforceability under Regulation 44/2001 or by providing a certificate issued under the rules of the new European procedures for small or uncontested claims. This creditor will want to have the seized funds transferred to his own account or receive the money by other means. It will need to be considered how an attachment can in this case be transformed into an executory measure effecting the transfer of the amount seized to the creditor.

N.1.   Council Decision 2009/397/EC of 26 February 2009 on the signing on behalf of the European Community of the Convention on Choice of Court Agreements (OJ, L 133 of 29 May 2009)

(1)   The Community is working towards the establishment of a common judicial area based on the principle of mutual recognition of judicial decisions.

(2)   The Convention on Choice of Court Agreements concluded on 30 June 2005 under The Hague Conference on Private International Law, (hereinafter referred to as the Convention) makes a valuable contribution to promoting party autonomy in international commercial transactions and increasing the predictability of judicial solutions in such transactions.

(3)   The Convention affects Community secondary legislation on jurisdiction based on choice by the parties and the recognition and enforcement of the resulting judgments, in particular Council Regulation (EC) 44/2001 of 22 December 2000 on jurisdiction and the recognition and enforcement of judgments in civil and commercial matters.

(4)   The Community has exclusive competence in all matters governed by the Convention.

(5)   Article 30 of the Convention allows the Community to sign, accept, approve or accede to the Convention.

(6)   The United Kingdom and Ireland are taking part in the adoption and application of this Decision.

(7)   In accordance with Articles 1 and 2 of the Protocol on the position of Denmark annexed to the Treaty on European Union and the Treaty establishing the European Community, Denmark is not taking part in the adoption of this Decision and is not bound by it nor subject to its application.

(8)   The Convention should be signed and the attached declaration be approved,

Article 1.   The signing of the Convention on Choice of Court Agreements concluded at The Hague on 30 June 2005 is hereby approved on behalf of the European Community, subject to the conclusion of the Convention at a later date.

The text of the Convention is attached to this Decision as Annex I.

Article 2.   The President of the Council is hereby authorised to designate the person(s) empowered to sign the Convention on behalf of the Community and to make the declaration set out in Annex II to this Decision.

N.2.   Convention on choice of court agreements (OJ, L 133 of 29 May 2009)[1]

Chapter I — Scope and definitions

Article 1. Scope.   1.   This Convention shall apply in international cases to exclusive choice of court agreements concluded in civil or commercial matters.

2.   For the purposes of Chapter II, a case is international unless the parties are resident in the same Contracting State and the relationship of the parties and all other elements relevant to the dispute, regardless of the location of the chosen court, are connected only with that State.

3.   For the purposes of Chapter III, a case is international where recognition or enforcement of a foreign judgment is sought.

Article 2. Exclusions from scope.   1.   This Convention shall not apply to exclusive choice of court agreements:

(a)   to which a natural person acting primarily for personal, family or household purposes (a consumer) is a party;

---

[1]   Not yet in force as of 30 November 2010. [Note of the Editor]

(b)   relating to contracts of employment, including collective agreements.

2.   This Convention shall not apply to the following matters:

(a)   the *status* and legal capacity of natural persons;

(b)   maintenance obligations;

(c)   other family law matters, including matrimonial property regimes and other rights or obligations arising out of marriage or similar relationships;

(d)   wills and succession;

(e)   insolvency, composition and analogous matters;

(f)   the carriage of passengers and goods;

(g)   marine pollution, limitation of liability for maritime claims, general average, and emergency towage and salvage;

(h)   anti-trust (competition) matters;

(i)   liability for nuclear damage;

(j)   claims for personal injury brought by or on behalf of natural persons;

(k)   tort or delict claims for damage to tangible property that do not arise from a contractual relationship;

(l)   rights *in rem* in immovable property, and tenancies of immovable property;

(m)   the validity, nullity, or dissolution of legal persons, and the validity of decisions of their organs;

(n)   the validity of intellectual property rights other than copyright and related rights;

(o)   infringement of intellectual property rights other than copyright and related rights, except where infringement proceedings are brought for breach of a contract between the parties relating to such rights, or could have been brought for breach of that contract;

(p)   the validity of entries in public registers.

3.   Notwithstanding paragraph 2, proceedings are not excluded from the scope of this Convention where a matter excluded under that paragraph arises merely as a preliminary question and not as an object of the proceedings. In particular, the mere fact that a matter excluded under paragraph 2 arises by way of defence does not exclude proceedings from the Convention, if that matter is not an object of the proceedings.

4.   This Convention shall not apply to arbitration and related proceedings.

5.   Proceedings are not excluded from the scope of this Convention by the mere fact that a State, including a government, a governmental agency or any person acting for a State, is a party thereto.

6.   Nothing in this Convention shall affect privileges and immunities of States or of international organisations, in respect of themselves and of their property.

Article 3. Exclusive choice of court agreements.   For the purposes of this Convention:

(a)   'exclusive choice of court agreement' means an agreement concluded by two or more parties that meets the requirements of paragraph (c) and designates, for the purpose of deciding disputes which have arisen or may arise in connection with a particular legal relationship, the courts of one Contracting State or one or more specific courts of one Contracting State to the exclusion of the jurisdiction of any other courts;

(b)   a choice of court agreement which designates the courts of one Contracting State or one or more specific courts of one Contracting State shall be deemed to be exclusive unless the parties have expressly provided otherwise;

(c)   an exclusive choice of court agreement must be concluded or documented:

(i)   in writing; or

(ii)   by any other means of communication which renders information accessible so as to be usable for subsequent reference;

(d)   an exclusive choice of court agreement that forms part of a contract shall be treated as an agreement independent of the other terms of the contract. The validity of the exclusive choice of court agreement cannot be contested solely on the ground that the contract is not valid.

Article 4. Other definitions.   1.   In this Convention, 'judgment' means any decision on the merits given by a court, whatever it may be called, including a decree or order, and a determination of costs or expenses by the court (including an officer of the court), provided that the determination relates to a decision on the merits which may be recognised or enforced under this Convention. An interim measure of protection is not a judgment.

2.   For the purposes of this Convention, an entity or person other than a natural person shall be considered to be resident in the State:

(a)   where it has its statutory seat;

(b)   under whose law it was incorporated or formed;

(c)   where it has its central administration; or

(d)   where it has its principal place of business.

Chapter II — Jurisdiction

Article 5. Jurisdiction of the chosen court.   1.   The court or courts of a Contracting State designated in an exclusive choice of court agreement shall have jurisdiction to decide a dispute to which the agreement applies, unless the agreement is null and void under the law of that State.

2.   A court that has jurisdiction under paragraph 1 shall not decline to exercise jurisdiction on the ground that the dispute should be decided in a court of another State.

3.   The preceding paragraphs shall not affect rules:

(a)   on jurisdiction related to subject matter or to the value of the claim;

(b)   on the internal allocation of jurisdiction among the courts of a Contracting State. However, where the chosen court has discretion as to whether to transfer a case, due consideration should be given to the choice of the parties.

Article 6. Obligations of a court not chosen.   A court of a Contracting State other than that of the chosen court shall suspend or dismiss proceedings to which an exclusive choice of court agreement applies unless:

(a)   the agreement is null and void under the law of the State of the chosen court;

(b)   a party lacked the capacity to conclude the agreement under the law of the State of the court seised;

(c)   giving effect to the agreement would lead to a manifest injustice or would be manifestly contrary to the public policy of the State of the court seised;

(d)   for exceptional reasons beyond the control of the parties, the agreement cannot reasonably be performed; or

(e)   the chosen court has decided not to hear the case.

Article 7. Interim measures of protection. Interim measures of protection are not governed by this Convention. This Convention neither requires nor precludes the grant, refusal or termination of interim measures of protection by a court of a Contracting State and does not affect whether or not a party may request or a court should grant, refuse or terminate such measures.

Chapter III — Recognition and enforcement

Article 8. Recognition and enforcement. 1. A judgment given by a court of a Contracting State designated in an exclusive choice of court agreement shall be recognised and enforced in other Contracting States in accordance with this Chapter. Recognition or enforcement may be refused only on the grounds specified in this Convention.

    2. Without prejudice to such review as is necessary for the application of the provisions of this Chapter, there shall be no review of the merits of the judgment given by the court of origin. The court addressed shall be bound by the findings of fact on which the court of origin based its jurisdiction, unless the judgment was given by default.

    3. A judgment shall be recognised only if it has effect in the State of origin, and shall be enforced only if it is enforceable in the State of origin.

    4. Recognition or enforcement may be postponed or refused if the judgment is the subject of review in the State of origin or if the time limit for seeking ordinary review has not expired. A refusal does not prevent a subsequent application for recognition or enforcement of the judgment.

    5. This Article shall also apply to a judgment given by a court of a Contracting State pursuant to a transfer of the case from the chosen court in that Contracting State as permitted by Article 5(3). However, where the chosen court had discretion as to whether to transfer the case to another court, recognition or enforcement of the judgment may be refused against a party who objected to the transfer in a timely manner in the State of origin.

Article 9. Refusal of recognition or enforcement. Recognition or enforcement may be refused if:

    (a) the agreement was null and void under the law of the State of the chosen court, unless the chosen court has determined that the agreement is valid;

    (b) a party lacked the capacity to conclude the agreement under the law of the requested State;

    (c) the document which instituted the proceedings or an equivalent document, including the essential elements of the claim:

    (i) was not notified to the defendant in sufficient time and in such a way as to enable him to arrange for his defence, unless the defendant entered an appearance and presented his case without contesting notification in the court of origin, provided that the law of the State of origin permitted notification to be contested; or

    (ii) was notified to the defendant in the requested State in a manner that is incompatible with fundamental principles of the requested State concerning service of documents;

    (d) the judgment was obtained by fraud in connection with a matter of procedure;

    (e) recognition or enforcement would be manifestly incompatible with the public policy of the requested State, including situations where the specific proceedings leading to the judgment were incompatible with fundamental principles of procedural fairness of that State;

(f)   the judgment is inconsistent with a judgment given in the requested State in a dispute between the same parties; or

(g)   the judgment is inconsistent with an earlier judgment given in another State between the same parties on the same cause of action, provided that the earlier judgment fulfils the conditions necessary for its recognition in the requested State.

Article 10. Preliminary questions.   1.   Where a matter excluded under Article 2(2), or under Article 21, arose as a preliminary question, the ruling on that question shall not be recognised or enforced under this Convention.

2.   Recognition or enforcement of a judgment may be refused if, and to the extent that, the judgment was based on a ruling on a matter excluded under Article 2(2).

3.   However, in the case of a ruling on the validity of an intellectual property right other than copyright or a related right, recognition or enforcement of a judgment may be refused or postponed under the preceding paragraph only where:

(a)   that ruling is inconsistent with a judgment or a decision of a competent authority on that matter given in the State under the law of which the intellectual property right arose; or

(b)   proceedings concerning the validity of the intellectual property right are pending in that State.

4.   Recognition or enforcement of a judgment may be refused if, and to the extent that, the judgment was based on a ruling on a matter excluded pursuant to a declaration made by the requested State under Article 21.

Article 11. Damages.   1.   Recognition or enforcement of a judgment may be refused if, and to the extent that, the judgment awards damages, including exemplary or punitive damages, that do not compensate a party for actual loss or harm suffered.

2.   The court addressed shall take into account whether and to what extent the damages awarded by the court of origin serve to cover costs and expenses relating to the proceedings.

Article 12. Judicial settlements (transactions judiciaries).   Judicial settlements (transactions judiciaires) which a court of a Contracting State designated in an exclusive choice of court agreement has approved, or which have been concluded before that court in the course of proceedings, and which are enforceable in the same manner as a judgment in the State of origin, shall be enforced under this Convention in the same manner as a judgment.

Article 13. Documents to be produced.   1.   The party seeking recognition or applying for enforcement shall produce:

(a)   a complete and certified copy of the judgment;

(b)   the exclusive choice of court agreement, a certified copy thereof, or other evidence of its existence;

(c)   if the judgment was given by default, the original or a certified copy of a document establishing that the document which instituted the proceedings or an equivalent document was notified to the defaulting party;

(d)   any documents necessary to establish that the judgment has effect or, where applicable, is enforceable in the State of origin;

(e)   in the case referred to in Article 12, a certificate of a court of the State of origin that the judicial settlement or a part of it is enforceable in the same manner as a judgment in the State of origin.

2.   If the terms of the judgment do not permit the court addressed to verify whether the conditions of this Chapter have been complied with, that court may require any necessary documents.

3.   An application for recognition or enforcement may be accompanied by a document, issued by a court (including an officer of the court) of the State of origin, in the form recommended and published by the Hague Conference on Private International Law.

4.   If the documents referred to in this Article are not in an official language of the requested State, they shall be accompanied by a certified translation into an official language, unless the law of the requested State provides otherwise.

Article 14. Procedure.   The procedure for recognition, declaration of enforceability or registration for enforcement, and the enforcement of the judgment, are governed by the law of the requested State unless this Convention provides otherwise. The court addressed shall act expeditiously.

Article 15. Severability.   Recognition or enforcement of a severable part of a judgment shall be granted where recognition or enforcement of that part is applied for, or only part of the judgment is capable of being recognised or enforced under this Convention.

Chapter IV — General clauses

Article 16. Transitional provisions.   1.   This Convention shall apply to exclusive choice of court agreements concluded after its entry into force for the State of the chosen court.

2.   This Convention shall not apply to proceedings instituted before its entry into force for the State of the court seised.

Article 17. Contracts of insurance and reinsurance.   1.   Proceedings under a contract of insurance or reinsurance are not excluded from the scope of this Convention on the ground that the contract of insurance or reinsurance relates to a matter to which this Convention does not apply.

2.   Recognition and enforcement of a judgment in respect of liability under the terms of a contract of insurance or reinsurance may not be limited or refused on the ground that the liability under that contract includes liability to indemnify the insured or reinsured in respect of:

(a)   a matter to which this Convention does not apply; or

(b)   an award of damages to which Article 11 might apply.

Article 18. No legalization.   All documents forwarded or delivered under this Convention shall be exempt from legalisation or any analogous formality, including an Apostille.

Article 19. Declarations limiting jurisdiction.   A State may declare that its courts may refuse to determine disputes to which an exclusive choice of court agreement applies if, except for the location of the chosen court, there is no connection between that State and the parties or the dispute.

Article 20. Declarations limiting recognition and enforcement.   A State may declare that its courts may refuse to recognise or enforce a judgment given by a court of another Contracting State if the parties were resident in the requested State, and the relationship of the parties and all other elements relevant to the dispute, other than the location of the chosen court, were connected only with the requested State.

Article 21. Declarations with respect to specific matters.   1.   Where a State has a strong interest in not applying this Convention to a specific matter, that State may declare that it will not apply the Convention to that matter. The State making such a declaration shall ensure that the declaration is no broader than necessary and that the specific matter excluded is clearly and precisely defined.

2.   With regard to that matter, the Convention shall not apply:

(a)   in the Contracting State that made the declaration;

(b)   in other Contracting States, where an exclusive choice of court agreement designates the courts, or one or more specific courts, of the State that made the declaration.

Article 22. Reciprocal declarations on non-exclusive choice of court agreements.   1.   A Contracting State may declare that its courts will recognise and enforce judgments given by courts of other Contracting States designated in a choice of court agreement concluded by two or more parties that meets the requirements of Article 3(c), and designates, for the purpose of deciding disputes which have arisen or may arise in connection with a particular legal relationship, a court or courts of one or more Contracting States (a non-exclusive choice of court agreement).

2.   Where recognition or enforcement of a judgment given in a Contracting State that has made such a declaration is sought in another Contracting State that has made such a declaration, the judgment shall be recognised and enforced under this Convention, if:

(a)   the court of origin was designated in a non-exclusive choice of court agreement;

(b)   there exists neither a judgment given by any other court before which proceedings could be brought in accordance with the non-exclusive choice of court agreement, nor a proceeding pending between the same parties in any other such court on the same cause of action; and

(c)   the court of origin was the court first seised.

Article 23. Uniform interpretation.   In the interpretation of this Convention, regard shall be had to its international character and to the need to promote uniformity in its application.

Article 24. Review of operation of the Convention.   The Secretary General of the Hague Conference on Private International Law shall at regular intervals make arrangements for:

(a)   review of the operation of this Convention, including any declarations; and

(b)   consideration of whether any amendments to this Convention are desirable.

Article 25. Non-unified legal systems.   1.   In relation to a Contracting State in which two or more systems of law apply in different territorial units with regard to any matter dealt with in this Convention:

(a)   any reference to the law or procedure of a State shall be construed as referring, where appropriate, to the law or procedure in force in the relevant territorial unit;

(b)   any reference to residence in a State shall be construed as referring, where appropriate, to residence in the relevant territorial unit;

(c)   any reference to the court or courts of a State shall be construed as referring, where appropriate, to the court or courts in the relevant territorial unit;

(d)   any reference to a connection with a State shall be construed as referring, where appropriate, to a connection with the relevant territorial unit.

2.   Notwithstanding the preceding paragraph, a Contracting State with two or more territorial units in which different systems of law apply shall not be bound to apply this Convention to situations which involve solely such different territorial units.

3.   A court in a territorial unit of a Contracting State with two or more territorial units in which different systems of law apply shall not be bound to recognise or enforce a judgment from another Contracting State solely because the judgment has been recognised or enforced in another territorial unit of the same Contracting State under this Convention.

4.   This Article shall not apply to a Regional Economic Integration Organisation.

Article 26. Relationship with other international instruments.   1. This Convention shall be interpreted so far as possible to be compatible with other treaties in force for Contracting States, whether concluded before or after this Convention.

2.   This Convention shall not affect the application by a Contracting State of a treaty, whether concluded before or after this Convention, in cases where none of the parties is resident in a Contracting State that is not a Party to the treaty.

3.   This Convention shall not affect the application by a Contracting State of a treaty that was concluded before this Convention entered into force for that Contracting State, if applying this Convention would be inconsistent with the obligations of that Contracting State to any non–Contracting State. This paragraph shall also apply to treaties that revise or replace a treaty concluded before this Convention entered into force for that Contracting State, except to the extent that the revision or replacement creates new inconsistencies with this Convention.

4.   This Convention shall not affect the application by a Contracting State of a treaty, whether concluded before or after this Convention, for the purposes of obtaining recognition or enforcement of a judgment given by a court of a Contracting State that is also a Party to that treaty. However, the judgment shall not be recognised or enforced to a lesser extent than under this Convention.

5.   This Convention shall not affect the application by a Contracting State of a treaty which, in relation to a specific matter, governs jurisdiction or the recognition or enforcement of judgments, even if concluded after this Convention and even if all States concerned are Parties to this Convention. This paragraph shall apply only if the Contracting State has made a declaration in respect of the treaty under this paragraph. In

the case of such a declaration, other Contracting States shall not be obliged to apply this Convention to that specific matter to the extent of any inconsistency, where an exclusive choice of court agreement designates the courts, or one or more specific courts, of the Contracting State that made the declaration.

6.   This Convention shall not affect the application of the rules of a Regional Economic Integration Organisation that is a Party to this Convention, whether adopted before or after this Convention:

(a)   where none of the parties is resident in a Contracting State that is not a Member State of the Regional Economic Integration Organisation;

(b)   as concerns the recognition or enforcement of judgments as between Member States of the Regional Economic Integration Organisation.

Chapter V — Final clauses

Article 27. Signature, ratification, acceptance, approval or accession.   1.   This Convention is open for signature by all States.

2.   This Convention is subject to ratification, acceptance or approval by the signatory States.

3.   This Convention is open for accession by all States.

4.   Instruments of ratification, acceptance, approval or accession shall be deposited with the Ministry of Foreign Affairs of the Kingdom of the Netherlands, depositary of the Convention.

Article 28. Declarations with respect to non-unified legal systems.   1.   If a State has two or more territorial units in which different systems of law apply in relation to matters dealt with in this Convention, it may at the time of signature, ratification, acceptance, approval or accession declare that the Convention shall extend to all its territorial units or only to one or more of them and may modify this declaration by submitting another declaration at any time.

2.   A declaration shall be notified to the depositary and shall state expressly the territorial units to which the Convention applies.

3.   If a State makes no declaration under this Article, the Convention shall extend to all territorial units of that State.

4.   This Article shall not apply to a Regional Economic Integration Organisation.

Article 29. Regional Economic Integration Organisations.   1.   A Regional Economic Integration Organisation which is constituted solely by sovereign States and has competence over some or all of the matters governed by this Convention may similarly sign, accept, approve or accede to this Convention. The Regional Economic Integration Organisation shall in that case have the rights and obligations of a Contracting State, to the extent that the Organisation has competence over matters governed by this Convention.

2.   The Regional Economic Integration Organisation shall, at the time of signature, acceptance, approval or accession, notify the depositary in writing of the matters governed by this Convention in respect of which competence has been transferred to that Organisation by its Member States. The Organisation shall promptly notify the depositary in writing of any changes to its competence as specified in the most recent notice given under this paragraph.

3. For the purposes of the entry into force of this Convention, any instrument deposited by a Regional Economic Integration Organisation shall not be counted unless the Regional Economic Integration Organisation declares in accordance with Article 30 that its Member States will not be Parties to this Convention.

4. Any reference to a 'Contracting State' or 'State' in this Convention shall apply equally, where appropriate, to a Regional Economic Integration Organisation that is a Party to it.

Article 30. Accession by a Regional Economic Integration Organisation without its Member States. 1. At the time of signature, acceptance, approval or accession, a Regional Economic Integration Organisation may declare that it exercises competence over all the matters governed by this Convention and that its Member States will not be Parties to this Convention but shall be bound by virtue of the signature, acceptance, approval or accession of the Organisation.

2. In the event that a declaration is made by a Regional Economic Integration Organisation in accordance with paragraph 1, any reference to a 'Contracting State' or 'State' in this Convention shall apply equally, where appropriate, to the Member States of the Organisation.

Article 31. Entry into force. 1. This Convention shall enter into force on the first day of the month following the expiration of three months after the deposit of the second instrument of ratification, acceptance, approval or accession referred to in Article 27.

2. Thereafter this Convention shall enter into force:

(a) for each State or Regional Economic Integration Organisation subsequently ratifying, accepting, approving or acceding to it, on the first day of the month following the expiration of three months after the deposit of its instrument of ratification, acceptance, approval or accession;

(b) for a territorial unit to which this Convention has been extended in accordance with Article 28(1), on the first day of the month following the expiration of three months after the notification of the declaration referred to in that Article.

Article 32. Declarations. 1. Declarations referred to in Articles 19, 20, 21, 22 and 26 may be made upon signature, ratification, acceptance, approval or accession or at any time thereafter, and may be modified or withdrawn at any time.

2. Declarations, modifications and withdrawals shall be notified to the depositary.

3. A declaration made at the time of signature, ratification, acceptance, approval or accession shall take effect simultaneously with the entry into force of this Convention for the State concerned.

4. A declaration made at a subsequent time, and any modification or withdrawal of a declaration, shall take effect on the first day of the month following the expiration of three months after the date on which the notification is received by the depositary.

5. A declaration under Articles 19, 20, 21 and 26 shall not apply to exclusive choice of court agreements concluded before it takes effect.

Article 33. Denunciation. 1. This Convention may be denounced by notification in writing to the depositary. The denunciation may be limited to certain territorial units of a non-unified legal system to which this Convention applies.

2.   The denunciation shall take effect on the first day of the month following the expiration of 12 months after the date on which the notification is received by the depositary. Where a longer period for the denunciation to take effect is specified in the notification, the denunciation shall take effect upon the expiration of such longer period after the date on which the notification is received by the depositary.

Article 34. Notifications by the depositary.   The depositary shall notify the Members of the Hague Conference on Private International Law, and other States and Regional Economic Integration Organisations which have signed, ratified, accepted, approved or acceded in accordance with Articles 27, 29 and 30 of the following:

(a)   the signatures, ratifications, acceptances, approvals and accessions referred to in Articles 27, 29 and 30;

(b)   the date on which this Convention enters into force in accordance with Article 31;

(c)   the notifications, declarations, modifications and withdrawals of declarations referred to in Articles 19, 20, 21, 22, 26, 28, 29 and 30;

(d)   the denunciations referred to in Article 33.

N.3.   Declaration by the European Community in accordance with Article 30 of the Convention on Choice of Court Agreements (OJ, L 133 of 29 May 2009)

The European Community declares, in accordance with Article 30 of the Convention on Choice of Court Agreements, that it exercises competence over all the matters governed by this Convention. Its Member States will not sign, ratify, accept or approve the Convention, but shall be bound by the Convention by virtue of its conclusion by the European Community.

For the purpose of this declaration, the term "European Community" does not include Denmark by virtue of Articles 1 and 2 of the Protocol on the position of Denmark annexed to the Treaty on European Union and the Treaty establishing the European Community.

O.   Convention on the international recovery of child support and other forms of family maintenance: Articles 1-3, 18-34, 36-37

See Chapter XI, Maintenance obligations, H.2.

Employment

A.   Directive 96/71/EC of the European Parliament and of the Council of 16 December 1996 concerning the posting of workers in the framework of the provision of services (OJ, L 18 of 21 January 1997): Article 6

See Chapter VI, Employment and agency, B.1.

Consumers

A.   Regulation (EC) No 2006/2004 of the European Parliament and of the Council of 27 October 2004 on cooperation between national authorities responsible for the enforcement of consumer protection laws (the Regulation on consumer protection cooperation) (OJ, L 364 of 9 December 2004)[1]

(2)   Existing national enforcement arrangements for the laws that protect consumers' interests are not adapted to the challenges of enforcement in the internal market and effective and efficient enforcement cooperation in these cases is not currently possible. These difficulties give rise to barriers to cooperation between public enforcement authorities to detect, investigate and bring about the cessation or prohibition of intra–Community infringements of the laws that protect consumers' interests. The resulting lack of effective enforcement in cross-border cases enables sellers and suppliers to evade enforcement attempts by relocating within the Community. This gives rise to a distortion of competition for law-abiding sellers and suppliers operating either domestically or cross-border. The difficulties of enforcement in cross-border cases also undermine the confidence of consumers in taking up cross-border offers and hence their confidence in the internal market.

(3)   It is therefore appropriate to facilitate cooperation between public authorities responsible for enforcement of the laws that protect consumers' interests in dealing with intra-Community infringements, and to contribute to the smooth functioning of the internal market, the quality and consistency of enforcement of the laws that protect consumers' interests and the monitoring of the protection of consumers' economic interests.

Article 2. Scope. ...   2.   This Regulation shall be without prejudice to the Community rules on private international law, in particular rules related to court jurisdiction and applicable law.

3.   This Regulation shall be without prejudice to the application in the Member States of measures relating to judicial cooperation in criminal and civil matters, in particular the operation of the European Judicial Network.

---

[1]   As finally amended by Directive 2007/65/EC (O.J., L 332 of 18 December 2007). [Note of the Editor]

4.   This Regulation shall be without prejudice to the fulfilment by the Member States of any additional obligations in relation to mutual assistance on the protection of the collective economic interests of consumers, including in criminal matters, ensuing from other legal acts, including bilateral or multilateral agreements.

5.   This Regulation shall be without prejudice to Directive 98/27/EC of the European Parliament and of the Council of 19 May 1998 on injunctions for the protection of consumers' interests.

6.   This Regulation shall be without prejudice to Community law relating to the internal market, in particular those provisions concerning the free movement of goods and services.

B.   Directive 2009/22/EC of the European Parliament and of the Council of 23 April 2009 on injunctions for the protection of consumers' interests (Codified version) (OJ, L 110 of 1 May 2009): Recital 7

See Chapter VII, E.

Carriage

A.1.   Council Decision 2001/539/EC of 5 April 2001 on the conclusion by the European Community of the Convention for the Unification of Certain Rules for International Carriage by Air (the Montreal Convention) (OJ, L 194 of 18 July 2001)

(1)   It is beneficial for European Community air carriers to operate under uniform and clear rules regarding their liability for damage and that such rules should be the same as those applicable to carriers from third countries.

(2)   The Community took part in the International Diplomatic Conference on air law convened in Montreal from 10 to 28 May 1999, which resulted in the adoption of the Convention for the unification of certain rules for international carriage by air (the Montreal Convention), and it signed the said Convention on 9 December 1999.

(3)   Regional Economic Integration Organisations which have competence in respect of certain matters governed by the Montreal Convention may be parties to it.

(4)   The Community and its Member States share competence in the matters covered by the Montreal Convention and it is therefore necessary for them simultaneously to ratify it in order to guarantee uniform and complete application of its provisions within the European Union,

Article 1. The Convention for the Unification of Certain Rules for International Carriage by Air (the Montreal Convention) is hereby approved on behalf of the European Community.

The text of the Convention is attached to this Decision.

Article 2. – The President of the Council shall deposit, on behalf of the European Community, the instrument provided for in Article 53(3) of the Montreal Convention with the International Civil Aviation Organisation, together with the Declaration of Competence.

The instrument shall be deposited simultaneously with the instruments of ratification of all the Member States.

A.2.   Convention for the Unification of Certain Rules for International Carriage by Air (the Montreal Convention) (OJ, L 194 of 18 July 2001)[1]

Article 1. Scope of application.   This Convention applies to all international carriage of persons, baggage or cargo performed by aircraft for reward. It applies equally to gratuitous carriage by aircraft performed by an air transport undertaking.

2.   For the purposes of this Convention, the expression international carriage means any carriage in which, according to the agreement between the parties, the place of departure and the place of destination, whether or not there be a break in the carriage or a transhipment, are situated either within the territories of two States Parties, or within the territory of a single State Party if there is an agreed stopping place within the territory of another State, even if that State is not a State Party. Carriage between two points within the territory of a single State Party without an agreed stopping place within the territory of another State is not international carriage for the purposes of this Convention.

3.   Carriage to be performed by several successive carriers is deemed, for the purposes of this Convention, to be one undivided carriage if it has been regarded by the parties as a single operation, whether it has been agreed upon under the form of a single contract or of a series of contracts, and it does not lose its international character merely because one contract or a series of contracts is to be performed entirely within the territory of the same State.

4.   This Convention applies also to carriage as set out in Chapter V, subject to the terms contained therein.

Article 2. Carriage performed by State and carriage of postal items.   1.   This Convention applies to carriage performed by the State or by legally constituted public bodies provided it falls within the conditions laid down in Article 1.

2.   In the carriage of postal items, the carrier shall be liable only to the relevant postal administration in accordance with the rules applicable to the relationship between the carriers and the postal administrations.

3.   Except as provided in paragraph 2 of this Article, the provisions of this Convention shall not apply to the carriage of postal items.

---

[1]   The Convention entered into force for the European Union on 28 June 2004. On the same date it entered into force for Austria, Belgium, Denmark, Finland, France, Germany, Ireland, Italy, Luxembourg, Netherlands, Spain, Sweden and United Kingdom. Moreover, the Convention is in force for the following Member States: Bulgaria (9 January 2004); Cyprus, Czech Republic, Estonia, Greece, Portugal, Romania, Slovakia, Slovenia (4 November 2003); Hungary (7 January 2005); Latvia (15 February 2005); Lithuania (29 January 2005); Malta (4 July 2004); Poland (18 March 2006). [Note of the Editor]

Article 29. Basis of claims.   In the carriage of passengers, baggage and cargo, any action for damages, however founded, whether under this Convention or in contract or in tort or otherwise, can only be brought subject to the conditions and such limits of liability as are set out in this Convention without prejudice to the question as to who are the persons who have the right to bring suit and what are their respective rights. In any such action, punitive, exemplary or any other non-compensatory damages shall not be recoverable.

Article 33. Jurisdiction.   1.   An action for damages must be brought, at the option of the plaintiff, in the territory of one of the States Parties, either before the court of the domicile of the carrier or of its principal place of business, or where it has a place of business through which the contract has been made or before the court at the place of destination.

2.   In respect of damage resulting from the death or injury of a passenger, an action may be brought before one of the courts mentioned in paragraph 1 of this Article, or in the territory of a State Party in which at the time of the accident the passenger has his or her principal and permanent residence and to or from which the carrier operates services for the carriage of passengers by air, either on its own aircraft, or on another carrier's aircraft pursuant to a commercial agreement, and in which that carrier conducts its business of carriage of passengers by air from premises leased or owned by the carrier itself or by another carrier with which it has a commercial agreement.

3.   For the purposes of paragraph 2,

(a)   "commercial agreement" means an agreement, other than an agency agreement, made between carriers and relating to the provision of their joint services for carriage of passengers by air;

(b)   "principal and permanent residence" means the one fixed and permanent abode of the passenger at the time of the accident. The nationality of the passenger shall not be the determining factor in this regard.

4.   Questions of procedure shall be governed by the law of the court seised of the case.

Article 34. Arbitration.   1.   Subject to the provisions of this Article, the parties to the contract of carriage for cargo may stipulate that any dispute relating to the liability of the carrier under this Convention shall be settled by arbitration. Such agreement shall be in writing.

2.   The arbitration proceedings shall, at the option of the claimant, take place within one of the jurisdictions referred to in Article 33.

3.   The arbitrator or arbitration tribunal shall apply the provisions of this Convention.

4.   The provisions of paragraphs 2 and 3 of this Article shall be deemed to be part of every arbitration clause or agreement, and any term of such clause or agreement which is inconsistent therewith shall be null and void.

Article 35. Limitation of actions.   1.   The right to damages shall be extinguished if an action is not brought within a period of two years, reckoned from the date of arrival at the destination, or from the date on which the aircraft ought to have arrived, or from the date on which the carriage stopped.

2.   The method of calculating that period shall be determined by the law of the court seised of the case.

Article 45. Addressee of claims.   In relation to the carriage performed by the actual carrier, an action for damages may be brought, at the option of the plaintiff, against that carrier or the contracting carrier, or against both together or separately. If the action is brought against only one of those carriers, that carrier shall have the right to require the other carrier to be joined in the proceedings, the procedure and effects being governed by the law of the court seised of the case.

Article 46. Additional jurisdiction.   Any action for damages contemplated in Article 45 must be brought, at the option of the plaintiff, in the territory of one of the States Parties, either before a court in which an action may be brought against the contracting carrier, as provided in Article 33, or before the court having jurisdiction at the place where the actual carrier has its domicile or its principal place of business.

Article 47. Invalidity of contractual provisions.   Any contractual provision tending to relieve the contracting carrier or the actual carrier of liability under this Chapter or to fix a lower limit than that which is applicable according to this Chapter shall be null and void, but the nullity of any such provision does not involve the nullity of the whole contract, which shall remain subject to the provisions of this Chapter.

Article 49. Mandatory application.   Any clause contained in the contract of carriage and all special agreements entered into before the damage occurred by which the parties purport to infringe the rules laid down by this Convention, whether by deciding the law to be applied, or by altering the rules as to jurisdiction, shall be null and void.

A.3.   ECJ case-law regarding the Montreal Convention

The *Rehder* case (9 July 2009, case C-204/08, Reports 2009, not yet reported) concerned the issue of whether the claim concerning the right to compensation pursuant to Article 7(1) of Regulation (EC) No 261/2004 falls within the competence established at Article 33(1) of the Montreal Convention. The Court so stated:

26.   Before examining the questions referred by the Bundesgerichtshof, it should be noted, as a preliminary point, that some of the observations submitted to the Court raised the question of the applicability, in a situation such as that which arises in the main proceedings, of Article 33 of the Montreal Convention for the purpose of determining which court has jurisdiction.

27.   In that regard, the right which the applicant in the main proceedings relies on in the present case, which is based on Article 7 of Regulation No 261/2004, is a passenger's right to a standardised and lump-sum payment following the cancellation of a flight, a right which is independent of compensation for damage in the context of Article 19 of the Montreal Convention. The rights based respectively on those provisions of Regulation No 261/2004 and of the Montreal Convention accordingly fall within different regulatory frameworks.

28.   It follows that, since it was introduced on the basis of Regulation No 261/2004 alone, the claim in the main proceedings must be examined in the light of Regulation No 44/2001.

B.1.   Proposal for a Council Decision concerning the conclusion by the European Community of the Protocol of 2002 to the Athens Convention Relating to the Carriage of Passengers and their Luggage by Sea, 1974 (COM (2003) 375 final of 24 June 2003, OJ, C 76 of 25 March 2004)[1]

3)   Articles 10 and 11 of the Protocol regulate matters which affect Community rules as laid down in Regulation 44/2001 on jurisdiction and the recognition and enforcement of judgments in civil and commercial matters. Member States are therefore prevented from assuming obligations with third countries relating to those matters, outside the Community institutions.

Article 1.   The Protocol of 2002 to the Athens Convention Relating to the Carriage of Passengers and their Luggage by Sea, 1974, (the 'Athens Protocol') is hereby approved on behalf of the Community. The text of the Protocol is reproduced in Annex 1 to this Decision.

B.2.   Protocol of 2002 to the Athens Convention Relating to the Carriage of Passengers and their Luggage by Sea, 1974 (OJ, C 76 of 25 March 2004)

Article 10.   Article 17 of the Convention is replaced by the following text:

Article 17. Competent jurisdiction.   1.   An action arising under Articles 3 and 4 of this Convention shall, at the option of the claimant, be brought before one of the courts listed below, provided that the court is located in a State Party to this Convention, and subject to the domestic law of each State Party governing proper venue within those States with multiple possible forums:

(a)   the court of the State of permanent residence or principal place of business of the defendant, or

(b)   the court of the State of departure or that of the destination according to the contract of carriage, or

(c)   the court of the State of the domicile or permanent residence of the claimant, if the defendant has a place of business and is subject to jurisdiction in that State, or

(d)   the court of the State where the contract of carriage was made, if the defendant has a place of business and is subject to jurisdiction in that State.

---

[1]   This proposal has been amended by COM(2010)686 of 30 November 2010.

2.   Actions under Article 4bis of this Convention shall, at the option of the claimant, be brought before one of the courts where action could be brought against the carrier or performing carrier according to paragraph 1.

3.   After the occurrence of the incident which has caused the damage, the parties may agree that the claim for damages shall be submitted to any jurisdiction or to arbitration.

Article 11.   The following text is added as Article 17bis of the Convention:

Article 17bis. Recognition and enforcement.   1.   Any judgment given by a court with jurisdiction in accordance with Article 17 which is enforceable in the State of origin where it is no longer subject to ordinary forms of review, shall be recognised in any State Party, except

(a)   where the judgment was obtained by fraud; or

(b)   where the defendant was not given reasonable notice and a fair opportunity to present the case.

2.   A judgment recognised under paragraph 1 shall be enforceable in each State Party as soon as the formalities required in that State have been complied with. The formalities shall not permit the merits of the case to be re-opened.

3.   A State Party to this Protocol may apply other rules for the recognition and enforcement of judgments, provided that their effect is to ensure that judgments are recognised and enforced at least to the same extent as under paragraphs 1 and 2.

C.1.   Convention concerning International Carriage by Rail (COTIF) of 9 May 1980 in the version of the Protocol of Modification of 3 June 1999: Article 12

See Chapter VI, Carriage, D.1.

C.2.   Uniform Rules concerning the Contract of International Carriage of Passengers by Rail (CIV – Appendix A to the Convention): Articles 57, 63

See Chapter VI, Carriage, D.2.

C.3.   Uniform Rules concerning the Contract of International Carriage of Goods by Rail (CIM – Appendix B to the Convention): Articles 46, 51

See Chapter VI, Carriage, D.3.

C.4.   Uniform Rules concerning Contracts of Use of Vehicles in International Rail Traffic (CUV – Appendix D to the Convention): Article 11

See Chapter VI, Carriage, D.4.

C.5.   Uniform Rules concerning the Contract of Use of Infrastructure in International Rail Traffic (CUI – Appendix E to the Convention): Article 24

See Chapter VI, Carriage, D.5.

Transfer of personal data

A.   Commission Decision 2001/497/EC of 15 June 2001 on standard contractual clauses for the transfer of personal data to third countries, under Directive 95/46/EC (OJ, L 181 of 4 July 2001): Recital 21, Clause 7

See Chapter XI, Right to protection of personal data, A.2.

B.   Commission Decision 2010/87/EU of 5 February 2010 on standard contractual clauses for the transfer of personal data to processors established in third countries under Directive 95/46/EC of the European Parliament and of the Council (OJ, L 39 of 12 February 2010): Recital 21, Clause 7

See Chapter XI, Right to protection of personal data, A.3.

Cultural goods

A.   Council Directive 93/7/EEC of 15 March 1993 on the return of cultural objects unlawfully removed from the territory of a Member State (OJ, L 74 of 27 March 1993): Articles 1-2, 5

See Chapter VIII, Rights on cultural goods, B.

IP rights

A.   Council Regulation (EC) No 2100/94 of 27 July 1994 on Community plant variety rights (OJ, L 227 of 1 September 1994): Articles 24, 67, 72-74, 86, 101-107

See Chapter VIII, IP rights, A.

B.   Council Regulation (EC) No 6/2002 of 12 December 2001 on Community designs (OJ, L 3 of 5 January 2002): Articles 30, 55, 60-61, 71, 79-87, 89-95

See Chapter VIII, IP rights, B.

C.   Council Regulation (EC) No 207/2009 of 26 February 2009 on the Community trade mark (OJ, L 78 of 24 March 2009): Recitals 16-17, Articles 20, 65, 86, 94-109, 118, 130-135

See Chapter VIII, IP rights, C.

D.   Commission Regulation (EC) No 874/2004 of 28 April 2004 laying down public policy rules concerning the implementation and functions of the .eu Top Level Domain and the principles governing registration (OJ, L 162 of 30 April 2004): Recitals 5, 16-17, Articles 5, 18

See Chapter VIII, IP rights, D.2.

E.   Directive 2004/48/EC of the European Parliament and of the Council of 29 April 2004 on the enforcement of intellectual property rights (OJ, L 157 of 30 April 2004): Recital 11

See Chapter VIII, IP rights, F.

F.1.   Proposal for a Council Regulation on the European Union patent (Doc. Consilium No 16113/09 of 27 November 2009): Recital 7.

See Chapter VIII, IP rights, I.1.

F.2.   Draft Agreement on the European and Community Patents Court and Draft Statute (Doc. Consilium No 7928/09 of 23 March 2009): Articles 15-17, 34(a)-35(b), 37-39, 41, 45, 48, 56.

See Chapter VIII, IP rights, I.2.

Environmental damages

A.   Directive 2004/35/EC of the European Parliament and of the Council of 21 April 2004 on environmental liability with regard to the prevention and remedying of environmental damage (OJ, L 143 of 30 April 2004)[1]

(10)   Express account should be taken of the Euratom Treaty and relevant international conventions and of Community legislation regulating more comprehensively and more stringently the operation of any of the activities falling under the scope of this Directive. This Directive, which does not provide for additional rules of conflict of laws when it specifies the powers of the competent authorities, is without prejudice to the rules on international jurisdiction of courts as provided, inter alia, in Council Regulation (EC) No 44/2001 of 22 December 2000 on jurisdiction and the recognition and enforcement of judgments in civil and commercial matters. This Directive should not apply to activities the main purpose of which is to serve national defence or international security.

Article 3. Scope.   1.   This Directive shall apply to:
    (a)   environmental damage caused by any of the occupational activities listed in Annex III, and to any imminent threat of such damage occurring by reason of any of those activities;
    (b)   damage to protected species and natural habitats caused by any occupational activities other than those listed in Annex III, and to any imminent threat of such damage occurring by reason of any of those activities, whenever the operator has been at fault or negligent.
    2.   This Directive shall apply without prejudice to more stringent Community legislation regulating the operation of any of the activities falling within the scope of this Directive and without prejudice to Community legislation containing rules on conflicts of jurisdiction.

---

[1]   As finally amended by Directive 2009/31/EC (O.J., L 140 of 5 June 2009). [Note of the Editor]

3. Without prejudice to relevant national legislation, this Directive shall not give private parties a right of compensation as a consequence of environmental damage or of an imminent threat of such damage.

B.1. Council Decision 2002/762/EC of 19 September 2002 authorising the Member States, in the interest of the Community, to sign, ratify or accede to the International Convention on Civil Liability for Bunker Oil Pollution Damage, 2001 (the Bunkers Convention) (OJ, L 256 of 25 September 2002)

(1) The International Convention on Civil Liability for Bunker Oil Pollution Damage, 2001 (hereinafter referred to as the Bunkers Convention) was adopted on 23 March 2001 with the aim of ensuring adequate, prompt and effective compensation of persons who suffer damage caused by spills of oil, when carried as fuel in ships' bunkers. The Bunkers Convention fills a significant gap in the international regulation of marine pollution liability.

(2) Articles 9 and 10 of the Bunkers Convention affect Community secondary legislation on jurisdiction and the recognition and enforcement of judgments, as laid down in Council Regulation (EC) No 44/2001 of 22 December 2000 on jurisdiction and the recognition and enforcement of judgments in civil and commercial matters.

(3) The Community therefore has sole competence in relation to Articles 9 and 10 of the Bunkers Convention inasmuch as those Articles affect the rules laid down in Regulation (EC) No 44/2001. The Member States retain their competence for matters covered by that Convention which do not affect Community law.

(4) Pursuant to the Bunkers Convention, only sovereign States may be party to it; there are no plans, in the short term, to reopen negotiations for the purpose of taking into account Community competence for the matter. It is not therefore possible for the Community to sign, ratify or accede to the Bunkers Convention at present, nor is there any prospect that it will be able do so in the near future.

(5) The Bunkers Convention is particularly important, given the interests of the Community and its Member States, because it makes for improved victim protection under international rules on marine pollution liability, in keeping with the 1982 United Nations Convention on the Law of the Sea.

(6) The substantive rules of the system established by the Bunkers Convention fall under the national competence of Member States and only the provisions of jurisdiction and the recognition and enforcement of the judgments are matters covered by exclusive Community competence. Given the subject matters and the aim of the Bunkers Convention, acceptance of the provisions of that Convention which come under Community competence cannot be dissociated from the provisions which come under the competence of the Member States.

(7) The Council should therefore authorise the Member States to sign, ratify or accede to the Bunkers Convention in the interest of the Community, under the conditions set out in this Decision.

(8) Member States should make efforts to sign the Bunkers Convention before 30 September 2002 and should finalise, within a reasonable time, their procedures

for ratification of, or accession to, that Convention in the interest of the Community. Member States should exchange information on the state of their ratification or accession procedures in order to prepare the deposit of their instruments of ratification of, or accession to, the Convention.

(9) The United Kingdom and Ireland are taking part in the adoption and application of this Decision.

(10) In accordance with Articles 1 and 2 of the Protocol on the position of Denmark annexed to the Treaty on European Union and to the Treaty establishing the European Community, Denmark is not taking part in the adoption of this Decision, and is not bound by it or subject to its application,

Article 1. 1. Without prejudice to existing Community competence in the matter, the Council hereby authorises the Member States to sign, ratify or accede to the Bunkers Convention in the interest of the Community, subject to the conditions set out in the following Articles.

2. The text of the Bunkers Convention is attached to this Decision.

3. In this Decision, the term "Member State" shall mean all Member States with the exception of Denmark.

Article 2. When signing, ratifying or acceding to the Bunkers Convention, Member States shall make the following declaration: "Judgments on matters covered by the Convention shall, when given by a court of (...[3]), be recognised and enforced in (...[4]) according to the relevant internal Community rules on the subject".[5]

Article 3. 1. Member States shall make efforts to sign the Bunkers Convention before 30 September 2002.

2. Member States shall take the necessary steps to deposit the instruments of ratification of, or accession to, the Bunkers Convention within a reasonable time with the Secretary–General of the International Maritime Organisation and, if possible, before 30 June 2006.

3. Member States shall inform the Council and the Commission, before 30 June 2004, of the prospective date of finalisation of their ratification or accession procedures.

4. Member Sates shall seek to exchange information on the state of their ratification or accession proceedings.

Article 4. When signing, ratifying or acceding to the Bunkers Convention, Member States shall inform the Secretary–General of the International Maritime Organisation in writing that such signing, ratification or accession has taken place in accordance with this Decision.

Article 5. Member States shall, at the earliest opportunity, use their best endeavours to ensure that the Bunkers Convention is amended to allow the Community to become a contracting party to it.

---

[3] [Footnotes are published in the original numerical order as in O.J.] All the Member States to which this Decision is applicable except the Member State making the declaration and Denmark.

[4] Member State making the declaration.

[5] At present, these rules are laid down in Regulation (EC) No 44/2001.

This Decision is addressed to the Member States in accordance with the Treaty establishing the European Community.

B.2.   International Convention on Civil Liability for Bunker Oil Pollution Damage, 2001 (the Bunkers Convention) (OJ, L 256 of 25 September 2002)

Article 1. Definitions.   For the purposes of this Convention:

1.   "ship" means any seagoing vessel and seaborne craft, of any type whatsoever,

2.   "person" means any individual or partnership or any public or private body, whether corporate or not, including a State or any of its constituent subdivisions,

3.   "shipowner" means the owner, including the registered owner, bareboat charterer, manager and operator of the ship,

4.   "registered owner" means the person or persons registered as the owner of the ship or, in the absence of registration, the person or persons owning the ship. However, in the case of a ship owned by a State and operated by a company which in that State is registered as the ship's operator, "registered owner" shall mean such company,

5.   "bunker oil" means any hydrocarbon mineral oil, including lubricating oil, used or intended to be used for the operation or propulsion of the ship, and any residues of such oil,

6.   "Civil Liability Convention" means the International Convention on Civil Liability for Oil Pollution Damage, 1992, as amended,

7.   "preventive measures" means any reasonable measures taken by any person after an incident has occurred to prevent or minimise pollution damage,

8.   "incident" means any occurrence or series of occurrences having the same origin, which causes pollution damage or creates a grave and imminent threat of causing such damage,

9.   "pollution damage" means:

(a)   loss or damage caused outside the ship by contamination resulting from the escape or discharge of bunker oil from the ship, wherever such escape or discharge may occur, provided that compensation for impairment of the environment other than loss of profit from such impairment shall be limited to costs of reasonable measures of reinstatement actually undertaken or to be undertaken, and

(b)   the costs of preventive measures and further loss or damage caused by preventive measures,

10.   "State of the ship's registry" means, in relation to a registered ship, the State of registration of the ship and, in relation to an unregistered ship, the State whose flag the ship is entitled to fly,

11.   "gross tonnage" means gross tonnage calculated in accordance with the tonnage measurement regulations contained in Annex 1 of the International Convention on Tonnage Measurement of Ships, 1969,

12.   "Organisation" means the International Maritime Organisation,

13.   "Secretary-General" means the Secretary-General of the Organisation.

Article 2. Scope of application.   This Convention shall apply exclusively:

(a)   to pollution damage caused:

(i)   in the territory, including the territorial sea, of a State Party, and

(ii)   in the exclusive economic zone of a State Party, established in accordance with international law, or, if a State Party has not established such a zone, in an area beyond and adjacent to the territorial sea of that State determined by that State in accordance with international law and extending not more than 200 nautical miles from the baselines from which the breadth of its territorial sea is measured;

(b)   to preventive measures, wherever taken, to prevent or minimise such damage.

Article 3. Liability of the shipowner.   1.   Except as provided in paragraphs 3 and 4, the shipowner at the time of an incident shall be liable for pollution damage caused by any bunker oil on board or originating from the ship, provided that, if an incident consists of a series of occurrences having the same origin, the liability shall attach to the shipowner at the time of the first of such occurrences.

2.   Where more than one person is liable in accordance with paragraph 1, their liability shall be joint and several.

3.   No liability for pollution damage shall attach to the shipowner if the shipowner proves that:

(a)   the damage resulted from an act of war, hostilities, civil war, insurrection or a natural phenomenon of an exceptional, inevitable and irresistible character; or

(b)   the damage was wholly caused by an act or omission done with the intent to cause damage by a third party; or

(c)   the damage was wholly caused by the negligence or other wrongful act of any Government or other authority responsible for the maintenance of lights or other navigational aids in the exercise of that function.

4.   If the shipowner proves that the pollution damage resulted wholly or partially either from an act or omission done with intent to cause damage by the person who suffered the damage or from the negligence of that person, the shipowner may be exonerated wholly or partially from liability to such person.

5.   No claim for compensation for pollution damage shall be made against the shipowner otherwise than in accordance with this Convention.

6.   Nothing in this Convention shall prejudice any right of recourse of the shipowner which exists independently of this Convention.

Article 4. Exclusions.   1.   This Convention shall not apply to pollution damage as defined in the Civil Liability Convention, whether or not compensation is payable in respect of it under that Convention.

2.   Except as provided in paragraph 3, the provisions of this Convention shall not apply to warships, naval auxiliary or other ships owned or operated by a State and used, for the time being, only on Government non–commercial service.

3.   A State Party may decide to apply this Convention to its warships or other ships described in paragraph 2, in which case it shall notify the Secretary–General thereof specifying the terms and conditions of such application.

4.   With respect to ships owned by a State Party and used for commercial purposes, each State shall be subject to suit in the jurisdictions set forth in Article 9 and shall waive all defences based on its status as a sovereign State.

Article 9. Jurisdiction. 1. Where an incident has caused pollution damage in the territory, including the territorial sea, or in an area referred to in Article 2(a)(ii) of one or more States Parties, or preventive measures have been taken to prevent or minimise pollution damage in such territory, including the territorial sea, or in such area, actions for compensation against the shipowner, insurer or other person providing security for the shipowner's liability may be brought only in the courts of any such States Parties.

2. Reasonable notice of any action taken under paragraph 1 shall be given to each defendant.

3. Each State Party shall ensure that its courts have jurisdiction to entertain actions for compensation under this Convention.

Article 10. Recognition and enforcement. 1. Any judgement given by a court with jurisdiction in accordance with Article 9 which is enforceable in the State of origin where it is no longer subject to ordinary forms of review, shall be recognised in any State Party, except:

(a) where the judgement was obtained by fraud; or

(b) where the defendant was not given reasonable notice and a fair opportunity to present his or her case.

2. A judgement recognised under paragraph 1 shall be enforceable in each State Party as soon as the formalities required in that State have been complied with. The formalities shall not permit the merits of the case to be reopened.

Article 11. Supersession clause. This Convention shall supersede any Convention in force or open for signature, ratification or accession at the date on which this Convention is opened for signature, but only to the extent that such Convention would be in conflict with it; however, nothing in this Article shall affect the obligations of States Parties to States not party to this Convention arising under such Convention.

C.1. Council Decision 2002/971/EC of 18 November 2002 authorising the Member States, in the interest of the Community, to ratify or accede to the International Convention on Liability and Compensation for Damage in Connection with the Carriage of Hazardous and Noxious Substances by Sea, 1996 (the HNS Convention) (OJ, L 337 of 13 December 2002)

(1) The International Convention on Liability and Compensation for Damage in Connection with the Carriage of Hazardous and Noxious Substances by Sea, 1996 (hereinafter referred to as the 'HNS Convention') is aimed at ensuring adequate, prompt, and effective compensation of persons who suffer damage caused by spills of hazardous and noxious substances, when carried by sea. The HNS Convention fills a significant gap in the International regulation of marine pollution liability.

(2) Articles 38, 39 and 40 of the HNS Convention affect Community secondary legislation on jurisdiction and the recognition and enforcement of judgments, as laid down in Council Regulation (EC) No 44/2001 of 22 December 2000 on jurisdiction and the recognition and enforcement of judgments in civil and commercial matters.

(3)   The Community therefore has sole competence in relation to Articles 38, 39 and 40 of the HNS Convention inasmuch as that Convention affects the rules laid down in Regulation (EC) No 44/2001. The Member States retain their competence for matters covered by that Convention which do not affect Community law.

(4)   Pursuant to the HNS Convention, only sovereign States may be party toit; there are noplans, in the short term, to reopen negotiations for the purpose of taking into account Community competence for the matter. It is not therefore possible for the Community to ratify or accede to the HNS Convention at present, nor is there any prospect that it will be able todosoin the near future.

(5)   The HNS Convention is particularly important, given the interests of the Community and its Member States, because it makes for improved victim protection under international rules on marine pollution liability, in keeping with the 1982 United Nations Convention on the Law of the Sea.

(6)   The substantive rules of the system established by the HNS Convention fall under the national competence of Member States and only the provisions of jurisdiction and the recognition and enforcement of the judgments are matters covered by exclusive Community competence. Given the subject matters and the aim of the HNS Convention, acceptance of the provisions of that Convention which come under Community competence cannot be dissociated from the provisions which come under the competence of the Member States.

(7)   The Council should therefore authorise the Member States to ratify or accede to the HNS Convention in the interest of the Community, under the conditions set out in this Decision.

(8)   Member States should finalise, within a reasonable time, their procedures for ratification of, or accession to, the HNS Convention in the interest of the Community. Member States should exchange information on the state of their ratification or accession procedures in order to prepare the deposit of their instruments of ratification of, or accession to, the Convention.

(9)   The United Kingdom and Ireland are taking part in the adoption and application of this Decision.

(10)   In accordance with Articles 1 and 2 of the Protocol on the position of Denmark annexed to the Treaty on European Union and to the Treaty establishing the European Community, Denmark is not taking part in the adoption of this Decision, and is not bound by it or subject toits application,

Article 1.   1.   Without prejudice to existing European Community competence in the matter, the Council hereby authorises the Member States to ratify or accede to the HNS Convention in the interest of the Community, subject to the conditions set out in the following Articles.

2.   The text of the HNS Convention is attached to this Decision.

3.   In this Decision, the term 'Member State' shall mean all Member States with the exception of Denmark.

Article 2.   When ratifying or acceding to the HNS Convention, Member States shall make the following declaration: 'Judgments on matters covered by the Convention shall, when given by a court of (...[4]), be recognised and enforced in (...[5]) according to the relevant internal Community rules on the subject.'[6]

Article 3.   1.   Member States shall take the necessary steps todepo sit the instruments of ratification of, or accession to, the HNS Convention within a reasonable time with the Secretary– General of the International Maritime Organisation and, if possible, before 30 June 2006.

2.   Member States shall inform the Council and the Commission, before 30 June 2004, of the prospective date of finalisation of their ratification or accession procedures.

3.   Member Sates shall seek to exchange information on the state of their ratification or accession procedures.

Article 4.   When ratifying or acceding to the HNS Convention, Member States shall inform the Secretary–General of the International Maritime Organisation in writing that such ratification or accession has taken place in accordance with this Decision.

Article 5.   Member States shall, at the earliest opportunity, use their best endeavours to ensure that the HNS Convention is amended

C.2.   International Convention on liability and compensation for damage in connection with the carriage of hazardous and noxious substances by sea, 1996 (HNS Convention) (OJ, L 337 of 13 December 2002)

Chapter I — General provisions – definitions

Article 1.   For the purposes of this Convention:

1.   'Ship' means any seagoing vessel and seaborne craft, of any type whatsoever.

2.   'Person' means any individual or partnership or any public or private body, whether corporate or not, including a State or any of its constituent subdivisions.

3.   'Owner' means the person or persons registered as the owner of the ship or, in the absence of registration, the person or persons owning the ship. However, in the case of a ship owned by a State and operated by a company which in that State is registered as the ship's operator, 'owner' shall mean such company.

4.   'Receiver' means either:

(a)   the person who physically receives contributing cargo discharged in the ports and terminals of a State Party; provided that if at the time of receipt the person who physically receives the cargo acts as an agent for another who is subject to the jurisdiction of any State Party, then the principal shall be deemed to be the receiver, if the agent discloses the principal to the HNS Fund; or

---

[4]   [Footnotes are published in the original numerical order as in O.J.] All the Member States to which this Decision is applicable except the Member State making the declaration and Denmark.

[5]   Member State making the declaration.

[6]   At present, these rules are laid down in Regulation (EC) No 44/2001.

(b)   the person in the State Party who in accordance with the national law of that State Party is deemed to be the receiver of contributing cargo discharged in the ports and terminals of a State Party, provided that the total contributing cargo received according to such national law is substantially the same as that which would have been received under (a).

5.   'Hazardous and noxious substances' (HNS) means:

(a)   any substances, materials and articles carried on board a ship as cargo, referred to in (i) to (vii) below:

(i) oils carried in bulk listed in Appendix I to Annex I to the International Convention for the Prevention of Pollution from Ships, 1973, as modified by the Protocol of 1978 relating thereto, as amended;

(ii) noxious liquid substances carried in bulk referred to in Appendix II to Annex II to the International Convention for the Prevention of Pollution from Ships, 1973, as modified by the Protocol of 1978 relating thereto, as amended, and those substances and mixtures provisionally categorised as falling in pollution category A, B, C or D in accordance with Regulation 3(4) of the said Annex II;

(iii) dangerous liquid substances carried in bulk listed in Chapter 17 of the International Code for the Construction and Equipment of Ships Carrying Dangerous Chemicals in Bulk, 1983, as amended, and the dangerous products for which the preliminary suitable conditions for the carriage have been prescribed by the Administration and port administrations involved in accordance with paragraph 1.1.3 of the Code;

(iv) dangerous, hazardous and harmful substances, materials and articles in packaged form covered by the International Maritime Dangerous Goods Code, as amended;

(v) liquefied gases as listed in Chapter 19 of the International Code for the Construction and Equipment of Ships carrying Liquefied Gases in Bulk, 1983, as amended, and the products for which preliminary suitable conditions for the carriage have been prescribed by the Administration and port administrations involved in accordance with paragraph 1.1.6 of the Code;

(vi) liquid substances carried in bulk with a flashpoint not exceeding 60 °C (measured by a closed cup test);

(vii) solid bulk materials possessing chemical hazards covered by Appendix B of the Code of Safe Practice for Solid Bulk Cargoes, as amended, to the extent that these substances are also subject to the provisions of the International Maritime Dangerous Goods Code when carried in packaged form; and

(b)   residues from the previous carriage in bulk of substances referred to in (a)(i) to (iii) and (v) to (vii) above.

6.   'Damage' means:

(a)   loss of life or personal injury on board or outside the ship carrying the hazardous and noxious substances caused by those substances;

(b)   loss of or damage to property outside the ship carrying the hazardous and noxious substances caused by those substances;

(c)   loss or damage by contamination of the environment caused by the hazardous and noxious substances, provided that compensation for impairment of the environment other than loss of profit from such impairment shall be limited to costs of reasonable measures of reinstatement actually undertaken or to be undertaken; and

(d)   the costs of preventive measures and further loss or damage caused by preventive measures.

Where it is not reasonably possible to separate damage caused by the hazardous and noxious substances from that caused by other factors, all such damage shall be deemed to be caused by the hazardous and noxious substances except if, and to the extent that, the damage caused by other factors is damage of a type referred to in Article 4(3).

In this paragraph, 'caused by those substances' means caused by the hazardous or noxious nature of the substances.

7.   'Preventive measures' means any reasonable measures taken by any person after an incident has occurred to prevent or minimise damage.

8.   'Incident' means any occurrence or series of occurrences having the same origin, which causes damage or creates a grave and imminent threat of causing damage.

9.   'Carriage by sea' means the period from the time when the hazardous and noxious substances enter any part of the ship's equipment, on loading, to the time they cease to be present in any part of the ship's equipment, on discharge. If no ship's equipment is used, the period begins and ends respectively when the hazardous and noxious substances cross the ship's rail.

10.   'Contributing cargo' means any hazardous and noxious substances which are carried by sea as cargo to a port or terminal in the territory of a State Party and discharged in that State. Cargo in transit which is transferred directly, or through a port or terminal, from one ship to another, either wholly or in part, in the course of carriage from the port or terminal of original loading to the port or terminal of final destination shall be considered as contributing cargo only in respect of receipt at the final destination.

11.   The 'HNS Fund' means the International Hazardous and Noxious Substances Fund established under Article 13.

12.   'Unit of account' means the Special Drawing Right as defined by the International Monetary Fund.

13.   'State of the ship's registry' means in relation to a registered ship the State of registration of the ship, and in relation to an unregistered ship the State whose flag the ship is entitled tofly.

14.   'Terminal' means any site for the storage of hazardous and noxious substances received from waterborne transportation, including any facility situated off–shore and linked by pipeline or otherwise to such site.

15.   'Director' means the Director of the HNS Fund.

16.   'Organisation' means the International Maritime Organisation.

17.   'Secretary-General' means the Secretary-General of the Organisation.

Annexes

Article 2.   The Annexes to this Convention shall constitute an integral part of this Convention

Scope of application

Article 3.   The Annexes to this shall apply exclusively:

(a)   to any damage caused in the territory, including the territorial sea, of a State Party;

(b)   to damage by contamination of the environment caused in the exclusive economic zone of a State Party, established in accordance with international law, or, if a State Party has not established such a zone, in an area beyond and adjacent to the territorial sea of that State determined by that State in accordance with international law and extending not more than 200 nautical miles from the baselines from which the breadth of its territorial sea is measured;

(c)   to damage, other than damage by contamination of the environment, caused outside the territory, including the territorial sea, of any State, if this damage has been caused by a substance carried on board a ship registered in a State Party or, in the case of an unregistered ship, on board a ship entitled to fly the flag of a State Party; and

(d)   to preventive measures, wherever taken.

Article 4.   1.   This Convention shall apply to claims, other than claims arising out of any contract for the carriage of goods and passengers, for damage arising from the carriage of hazardous and noxious substances by sea.

2.   This Convention shall not apply to the extent that its provisions are incompatible with those of the applicable law relating to workers' compensation or social security schemes.

3.   This Convention shall not apply:

(a)   to pollution damage as defined in the International Convention on Civil Liability for Oil Pollution Damage, 1969, as amended, whether or not compensation is payable in respect of it under that Convention; and

(b)   to damage caused by a radioactive material of class 7 either in the International Maritime Dangerous Goods Code, as amended, or in appendix B of the Code of Safe Practice for Solid Bulk Cargoes, as amended.

4.   Except as provided in paragraph 5, the provisions of this Convention shall not apply to warships, naval auxiliary or other ships owned or operated by a State and used, for the time being, only on Government non–commercial service.

5.   A State Party may decide to apply this Convention to its warships or other vessels described in paragraph 4, in which case it shall notify the Secretary–General thereof specifying the terms and conditions of such application.

6.   With respect to ships owned by a State Party and used for commercial purposes, each State shall be subject to suit in the jurisdictions set forth in Article 38 and shall waive all defences based on its status as a sovereign State.

Article 5.   1.   A State may, at the time of ratification, acceptance, approval of, or accession to, this Convention, or any time thereafter, declare that this Convention does not apply to ships:

(a)   which do not exceed 200 gross tonnage; and

(b)   which carry hazardous and noxious substances only in packaged form; and

(c)   while they are engaged on voyages between ports or facilities of that State.

2.   Where two neighbouring States agree that this Convention does not apply also to ships which are covered by paragraph 1(a) and (b) while engaged on voyages between ports or facilities of those States, the States concerned may declare that the exclusion from the application of this Convention declared under paragraph 1 covers also ships referred to in this paragraph.

3.   Any State which has made the declaration under paragraph 1 or 2 may withdraw such declaration at any time.

4.   A declaration made under paragraph 1 or 2, and the withdrawal of the declaration made under paragraph 3, shall be deposited with the Secretary-General who shall, after the entry into force of this communicate it to the Director.

5.   Where a State has made a declaration under paragraph 1 or 2 and has not withdrawn it, hazardous and noxious substances carried on board ships covered by that paragraph shall not be considered to be contributing cargo for the purpose of application of Articles 18, 20, Article 21(5) and Article 43.

6.   The HNS Fund is not liable to pay compensation for damage caused by substances carried by a ship to which the Convention does not apply pursuant to a declaration made under paragraph 1 or 2, to the extent that:

(a)   the damage as defined in Article 1, paragraph 6(a), (b) or (c) was caused in:

(i)   the territory, including the territorial sea, of the State which has made the declaration, or in the case of neighbouring States which have made a declaration under paragraph 2, of either of them; or

(ii)   the exclusive economic zone, or area mentioned in Article 3(b), of the State or States referred to in (i);

(b)   the damage includes measures taken toprevent or minimise such damage.

Chapter II — Liability – Liability of the owner

Article 7.   1.   Except as provided in paragraphs 2 and 3, the owner at the time of an incident shall be liable for damage caused by any hazardous and noxious substances in connection with their carriage by sea on board the ship, provided that if an incident consists of a series of occurrences having the same origin the liability shall attach to the owner at the time of the first of such occurrences.

2.   No liability shall attach to the owner if the owner proves that:

(a)   the damage resulted from an act of war, hostilities, civil war, insurrection or a natural phenomenon of an exceptional, inevitable and irresistible character; or

(b)   the damage was wholly caused by an act or omission done with the intent to cause damage by a third party; or

(c)   the damage was wholly caused by the negligence or other wrongful act of any Government or other authority responsible for the maintenance of lights or other navigational aids in the exercise of that function; or

(d)   the failure of the shipper or any other person to furnish information concerning the hazardous and noxious nature of the substances shipped either

(i)   has caused the damage, wholly or partly; or

(ii)   has led the owner not to obtain insurance in accordance with Article 12;

provided that neither the owner nor its servants or agents knew or ought reasonably to have known of the hazardous and noxious nature of the substances shipped.

3.   If the owner proves that the damage resulted wholly or partly either from an act or omission done with intent to cause damage by the person who suffered the damage or from the negligence of that person, the owner may be exonerated wholly or partially from liability to such person.

4.   No claim for compensation for damage shall be made against the owner otherwise than in accordance with this.

5.   Subject to paragraph 6, no claim for compensation for damage under this Convention or otherwise may be made against:

(a)   the servants or agents of the owner or the members of the crew;

(b)   the pilot or any other person who, without being a member of the crew, performs services for the ship;

(c)   any charterer (howsoever described, including a bareboat charterer), manager or operator of the ship;

(d)   any person performing salvage operations with the consent of the owner or on the instructions of a competent public authority;

(e)   any person taking preventive measures; and

(f)   the servants or agents of persons mentioned in (c), (d) and (e);

unless the damage resulted from their personal act or omission, committed with the intent to cause such damage, or recklessly and with knowledge that such damage would probably result.

6.   Nothing in this Convention shall prejudice any existing right of recourse of the owner against any third party, including, but not limited to, the shipper or the receiver of the substance causing the damage, or the persons indicated in paragraph 5.

Incidents involving two or more ships

Article 8.   1.   Whenever damage has resulted from an incident involving two or more ships each of which is carrying hazardous and noxious substances, each owner, unless exonerated under Article 7, shall be liable for the damage. The owners shall be jointly and severally liable for all such damage which is not reasonably separable.

2.   However, owners shall be entitled to the limits of liability applicable to each of them under Article 9.

3.   Nothing in this Article shall prejudice any right of recourse of an owner against any other owner.

Jurisdiction in respect of action against the owner

Article 38.   1.   Where an incident has caused damage in the territory, including the territorial sea or in an area referred to in Article 3(b), of one or more States Parties, or preventive measures have been taken to prevent or minimise damage in such territory including the territorial sea or in such area, actions for compensation may be brought against the owner or other person providing financial security for the owner's liability only in the courts of any such States Parties.

2.   Where an incident has caused damage exclusively outside the territory, including the territorial sea, of any State and either the conditions for application of this Convention set out in Article 3(c) have been fulfilled or preventive measures to prevent or minimise such damage have been taken, actions for compensation may be brought against the owner or other person providing financial security for the owner's liability only in the courts of:

(a)   the State Party where the ship is registered or, in the case of an unregistered ship, the State Party whose flag the ship is entitled to fly; or

(b)   the State Party where the owner has habitual residence or where the principal place of business of the owner is established; or

(c)   the State Party where a fund has been constituted in accordance with Article 9(3).

3.   Reasonable notice of any action taken under paragraph 1 or 2 shall be given to the defendant.

4.   Each State Party shall ensure that its courts have jurisdiction to entertain actions for compensation under this Convention.

5.   After a fund under Article 9 has been constituted by the owner or by the insurer or other person providing financial security in accordance with Article 12, the courts of the State in which such fund is constituted shall have exclusive jurisdiction to determine all matters relating to the apportionment and distribution of the fund.

Jurisdiction in respect of action against the HNS Fund or taken by the HNS Fund

Article 39.   1.   Subject to the subsequent provisions of this Article, any action against the HNS Fund for compensation under Article 14 shall be brought only before a court having jurisdiction under Article 38 in respect of actions against the owner who is liable for damage caused by the relevant incident or before a court in a State Party which would have been competent if an owner had been liable.

2.   In the event that the ship carrying the hazardous or noxious substances which caused the damage has not been identified, the provisions of Article 38(1), shall apply *mutatis mutandis* to actions against the HNS Fund.

3.   Each State Party shall ensure that its courts have jurisdiction to entertain such actions against the HNS Fund as are referred to in paragraph 1.

4.   Where an action for compensation for damage has been brought before a court against the owner or the owner's guarantor, such court shall have exclusive jurisdiction over any action against the HNS Fund for compensation under the provisions of Article 14 in respect of the same damage.

5.   Each State Party shall ensure that the HNS Fund shall have the right to intervene as a party to any legal proceedings instituted in accordance with this Convention before a competent court of that State against the owner or the owner's guarantor.

6.   Except as otherwise provided in paragraph 7, the HNS Fund shall not be bound by any judgement or decision in proceedings to which it has not been a party or by any settlement to which it is not a party.

7.   Without prejudice to the provisions of paragraph 5, where an action under this Convention for compensation for damage has been brought against an owner or the owner's guarantor before a competent court in a State Party, each party to the proceedings shall be entitled under the national law of that State to notify the HNS Fund of the proceedings. Where such notification has been made in accordance with the formalities required by the law of the court seised and in such time and in such a manner that the HNS Fund has in fact been in a position effectively to intervene as a party to the proceedings, any judgement rendered by the court in such proceedings shall, after it has become final and enforceable in the State where the judgement was given, become binding upon the HNS Fund in the sense that the facts and findings in that judgement may not be disputed by the HNS Fund even if the HNS Fund has not actually intervened in the proceedings.

Recognition and enforcement

Article 40.   1.   Any judgement given by a court with jurisdiction in accordance with Article 38, which is enforceable in the State of origin where it is no longer subject to ordinary forms of review, shall be recognised in any State Party, except:

(a)   where the judgement was obtained by fraud; or

(b)   where the defendant was not given reasonable notice and a fair opportunity to present the case.

2.   A judgement recognised under paragraph 1 shall be enforceable in each State Party as soon as the formalities required in that State have been complied with. The formalities shall not permit the merits of the case to be re-opened.

3.   Subject to any decision concerning the distribution referred to in Article 14(6), any judgement given against the HNS Fund by a court having jurisdiction in accordance with Article 39(1) and (3) shall, when it has become enforceable in the State of origin and is in that State no longer subject to ordinary forms of review, be recognised and enforceable in each State Party.

Supersession clause

Article 42.   This Convention shall supersede any convention in force or open for signature, ratification or accession at the date on which this Convention is opened for signature, but only to the extent that such convention would be in conflict with it; however, nothing in this Article shall affect the obligations of States Parties to States not party to this Convention arising under such convention.

D.1.   Council Decision 2004/246/EC of 2 March 2004 authorising the Member States to sign, ratify or accede to, in the interest of the European Community, the Protocol of 2003 to the International Convention on the Establishment of an International Fund for Compensation for Oil Pollution Damage, 1992, and authorising Austria and Luxembourg, in the interest of the European Community, to accede to the underlying instruments (OJ, L 78 of 16 March 2004)[1]

(1)   The Protocol to the International Convention on the Establishment of an International Fund for Compensation for Oil Pollution Damage, 1992, (hereinafter the Supplementary Fund Protocol), is aimed at ensuring adequate, prompt, and effective compensation of persons who suffer damage caused by oil spills caused by tankers. By significantly raising the limits of compensation available in the present international system, the Supplementary Fund Protocol addresses one of the most significant shortcomings in the international regulation of oil pollution liability.

---

[1]   As finally amended by Decision 2004/664 (OJ, L 303 of 30 September 2004). [Note of the Editor]

(2)   Articles 7 and 8 of the Supplementary Fund Protocol affect Community legislation on jurisdiction and the recognition and enforcement of judgments, as laid down in Council Regulation (EC) No 44/2001 of 22 December 2000 on jurisdiction and the recognition and enforcement of judgments in civil and commercial matters.

(3)   The Community has exclusive competence in relation to Articles 7 and 8 of the Protocol, insofar as those Articles affect the rules laid down in Regulation (EC) No 44/2001. The Member States retain their competence for matters covered by the Protocol which do not affect Community law.

(6)   The United Kingdom and Ireland are bound by Regulation (EC) No 44/2001 and are therefore taking part in the adoption and application of this Decision.

(7)   In accordance with Articles 1 and 2 of the Protocol on the position of Denmark annexed to the Treaty on European Union and to the Treaty establishing the European Community, Denmark is not taking part in the adoption of this Decision, and is not bound by it or subject to its application.

(8)   Only Contracting Parties to the underlying instruments may become Contracting Parties to the Supplementary Fund Protocol. Austria and Luxembourg are not currently parties to the underlying instruments. Since the underlying instruments contain provisions affecting Regulation (EC) No 44/2001, Austria and Luxembourg should also be authorised to accede to these instruments.

Article 1.   1.   The Member States are hereby authorised to sign, ratify or accede to, in the interest of the European Community, the Protocol of 2003 to the International Convention on the Establishment of an International Fund for Compensation for Oil Pollution Damage, 1992, (the Supplementary Fund Protocol) subject to the conditions set out in the following Articles.

2.   Furthermore, the Czech Republic, Estonia, Luxembourg, Hungary, Austria and Slovakia are hereby authorised to accede to the underlying instruments.

3.   The text of the Supplementary Fund Protocol is attached in Annex I to this Decision. The text of the underlying instruments is attached in Annexes II and III to this Decision.

4.   In this Decision, the term "underlying instruments" shall mean the Protocol of 1992 to amend the International Convention on Civil Liability for Oil Pollution Damage, 1969 and the Protocol of 1992 to amend the International Convention on the Establishment of an International Fund for Compensation for Oil Pollution Damage, 1971.

5.   In this Decision, "Member State" means all the Member States with the exception of Denmark.

D.2. Protocol of 2003 to the International Convention on the Establishment of an International Fund for Compensation for Oil Pollution Damage, 1992 (OJ, L 78 of 16 March 2004)

Article 7.   1.   The provisions of Article 7(1), (2), (4), (5) and (6) of the 1992 Fund Convention[1] shall apply to actions for compensation brought against the Supplementary Fund in accordance with Article 4(1) of this Protocol.

2.   Where an action for compensation for pollution damage has been brought before a court competent under Article IX[2] of the 1992 Liability Convention against the owner of a ship or his guarantor, such court shall have exclusive jurisdictional competence over any action against the Supplementary Fund for compensation under the provisions of Article 4 of this Protocol in respect of the same damage. However, where an action for compensation for pollution damage under the 1992 Liability Convention has been brought before a court in a Contracting State to the 1992 Liability Convention but not to this Protocol, any action against the Supplementary Fund under Article 4 of this Protocol shall at the option of the claimant be brought either before a court of the State where the Supplementary Fund has its headquarters or before any court of a Contracting State to this Protocol competent under Article IX of the 1992 Liability Convention.

3.   Notwithstanding paragraph 1, where an action for compensation for pollution damage against the 1992 Fund has been brought before a court in a Contracting State to the 1992 Fund Convention but not to this Protocol, any related action against the

---

[1]   *Article 7*, International Convention on the Establishment of an International Fund for Compensation for Oil Pollution Damage 1992: 1. Subject to the subsequent provisions of this Article, any action against the Fund for compensation under Article 4 of this Convention shall be brought only before a court competent under Article IX of the 1992 Liability Convention in respect of actions against the owner who is or who would, but for the provisions of Article III, paragraph 2, of that Convention, have been liable for pollution damage caused by the relevant incident.

2. Each Contracting State shall ensure that its courts possess the necessary jurisdiction to entertain such actions against the Fund as are referred to in paragraph 1.

4. Each Contracting State shall ensure that the Fund shall have the right to intervene as a party to any legal proceedings instituted in accordance with Article IX of the 1992 Liability Convention before a competent court of that State against the owner of a ship or his guarantor.

5. Except as otherwise provided in paragraph 6, the Fund shall not be bound by any judgment or decision in proceedings to which it has not been a party or by any settlement to which it is not a party.

6. Without prejudice to the provisions of paragraph 4, where an action under the 1992 Liability Convention for compensation for pollution damage has been brought against an owner or his guarantor before a competent court in a Contracting State, each party to the proceedings shall be entitled under the national law of that State to notify the Fund of the proceedings. Where such notification has been made in accordance with the formalities required by the law of the court seized and in such time and in such a manner that the Fund has in fact been in a position effectively to intervene as a party to the proceedings, any judgment rendered by the court in such proceedings shall, after it has become final and enforceable in the State where the judgment was given, become binding upon the Fund in the sense that the facts and findings in that judgment may not be disputed by the Fund even if the Fund has not actually intervened in the proceedings.

[2]   *Article IX*, CLC Convention 1992: 1. Where an incident has caused pollution damage in the territory, including the territorial sea or an area referred to in Article II, of one or more Contracting States or preventive measures have been taken to prevent or minimize pollution damage in such territory including the territorial sea or area, actions for compensation may only be brought in the Courts of any such Contracting State or States. Reasonable notice of any such action shall be given to the defendant.

2. Each Contracting State shall ensure that its Courts possess the necessary jurisdiction to entertain such actions for compensation.

3. After the fund has been constituted in accordance with Article V the Courts of the State in which the fund is constituted shall be exclusively competent to determine all matters relating to the apportionment and distribution of the fund. [Note of the Editor]

Supplementary Fund shall, at the option of the claimant, be brought either before a court of the State where the Supplementary Fund has its headquarters or before any court of a Contracting State competent under paragraph 1.

Article 8.   1.   Subject to any decision concerning the distribution referred to in Article 4(3) of this Protocol, any judgment given against the Supplementary Fund by a court having jurisdiction in accordance with Article 7 of this Protocol, shall, when it has become enforceable in the State of origin and is in that State no longer subject to ordinary forms of review, be recognised and enforceable in each Contracting State on the same conditions as are prescribed in Article X[3] of the 1992 Liability Convention.

2.   A Contracting State may apply other rules for the recognition and enforcement of judgments, provided that their effect is to ensure that judgments are recognised and enforced at least to the same extent as under paragraph 1.

Article 9.   1.   The Supplementary Fund shall, in respect of any amount of compensation for pollution damage paid by the Supplementary Fund in accordance with Article 4(1), of this Protocol, acquire by subrogation the rights that the person so compensated may enjoy under the 1992 Liability Convention against the owner or his guarantor.

2.   The Supplementary Fund shall acquire by subrogation the rights that the person compensated by it may enjoy under the 1992 Fund Convention against the 1992 Fund.

3.   Nothing in this Protocol shall prejudice any right of recourse or subrogation of the Supplementary Fund against persons other than those referred to in the preceding paragraphs. In any event the right of the Supplementary Fund to subrogation against such person shall not be less favourable than that of an insurer of the person to whom compensation has been paid.

4.   Without prejudice to any other rights of subrogation or recourse against the Supplementary Fund which may exist, a Contracting State or agency thereof which has paid compensation for pollution damage in accordance with provisions of national law shall acquire by subrogation the rights which the person so compensated would have enjoyed under this Protocol.

---

[3]   *Article X,* CLC Convention 1992: 1. Any judgment given by a Court with jurisdiction in accordance with Article IX which is enforceable in the State of origin where it is no longer subject to ordinary forms of review, shall be recognized in any Contracting State, except:

(a) where the judgment was obtained by fraud; or

(b) where the defendant was not given reasonable notice and a fair opportunity to present his case.

2. A judgment recognized under paragraph 1 of this Article shall be enforceable in each Contracting State as soon as the formalities required in that State have been complied with. The formalities shall not permit the merits of the case to be re-opened. [Note of the Editor]

D.3. Protocol of 1992 to amend the International Convention on the Establishment of an International Fund for Compensation for Oil Pollution Damage of 1971 (OJ, L 78 of 16 March 2004)

Article 8.   Article IX of the 1969 Liability Convention is amended as follows:
paragraph 1 is replaced by the following:
"1. Where an incident has caused pollution damage in the territory, including the territorial sea or an area referred to in Article II, of one or more Contracting States or preventive measures have been taken to prevent or minimize pollution damage in such territory including the territorial sea or area, actions for compensation may only be brought in the Courts of any such Contracting State or States. Reasonable notice of any such action shall be given to the defendant."

E.1.   Council Decision 2004/294/EC of 8 March 2004 authorising the Member States which are Contracting Parties to the Paris Convention of 29 July 1960 on Third Party Liability in the Field of Nuclear Energy to ratify, in the interest of the European Community, the Protocol amending that Convention, or to accede to it (OJ, L 97 of 8 March 2004)

(4)   The Community has exclusive jurisdiction with regard to amending Article 13 of the Paris Convention where such amendment would affect the rules laid down in Council Regulation (EC) No 44/2001 of 22 December 2000 on jurisdiction and the recognition and enforcement of judgments in civil and commercial matters. The Member States retain their jurisdiction for matters covered by the Protocol which do not affect Community law. Given the subject matter and the aim of the Protocol of amendment, acceptance of the provisions of the Protocol which come under Community jurisdiction cannot be dissociated from the provisions which come under the jurisdiction of the Member States.

(5)   The Protocol of amendment to the Paris Convention is particularly important, in the light of the interests of the Community and its Member States, because it improves compensation for damage caused by nuclear accidents.

(6)   The Protocol was signed by the Member States which are Contracting Parties to the Paris Convention, on behalf of the European Community, on 12 February 2004, subject to its possible conclusion at a later date, in accordance with Council Decision 2003/882/EC.

(7)   The Paris Convention and its Protocol of amendment are not open to participation by regional organisations. As a result, the Community is not in a position to sign or ratify the Protocol, or to accede to it. Under these circumstances, it is justified, on a very exceptional basis, that the Member States ratify or accede to the Protocol in the interest of the Community.

(8)   However, three of the Member States, namely Austria, Ireland and Luxembourg, are not Parties to the Paris Convention. Given that the Protocol amends the Paris

Convention, that Regulation (EC) No 44/2001 authorises the Member States bound by that Convention to continue to apply the rules on jurisdiction provided for in it and that the Protocol does not substantially amend the rules on jurisdiction of the Convention, it is objectively justified that this Decision should be addressed only to those Member States that are Parties to the Paris Convention. Accordingly, Austria, Ireland and Luxembourg will continue to base themselves on the Community rules contained in Regulation (EC) No 44/2001 and to apply them in the area covered by the Paris Convention and by the Protocol amending that Convention.

(11) The United Kingdom and Ireland are bound by Council Regulation (EC) No 44/2001 and are therefore taking part in the adoption of this Decision.

(12) In accordance with Articles 1 and 2 of the Protocol on the position of Denmark annexed to the Treaty on European Union and to the Treaty establishing the European Community, Denmark does not take part in the adoption of this Decision, and is not bound by it or subject to its application,

Article 1. 1. Without prejudice to the Community's powers, the Member States which are currently Contracting Parties to the Paris Convention shall ratify the Protocol amending the Paris Convention, or accede to it, in the interest of the European Community. Such ratification or accession shall be without prejudice to the position of Austria, Ireland and Luxembourg.

2. The text of the Protocol amending the Paris Convention is attached to this Decision.

3. For the purposes of this Decision, the term "Member State" shall mean all Member States with the exception of Austria, Denmark, Ireland and Luxembourg.

E.2. Protocol to amend the Convention on Third Party Liability in the Field of Nuclear Energy of 29 July 1960, as amended by the Additional Protocol of 28 January 1964 and by the Protocol of 16 November 1982 (OJ, L 97 of 8 March 2004)

M. Article 13 shall be replaced by the following:

"Article 13: (a) Except as otherwise provided in this Article, jurisdiction over actions under Articles 3, 4 and 6(a) shall lie only with the courts of the Contracting Party in whose territory the nuclear incident occurred.

(b) Where a nuclear incident occurs within the area of the exclusive economic zone of a Contracting Party or, if such a zone has not been established, in an area not exceeding the limits of an exclusive economic zone were one to be established, jurisdiction over actions concerning nuclear damage from that nuclear incident shall, for the purposes of this Convention, lie only with the courts of that Party, provided that the Contracting Party concerned has notified the Secretary–General of the Organisation of such area prior to the nuclear incident. Nothing in this paragraph shall be interpreted as permitting the exercise of jurisdiction or the delimitation of a maritime zone in a manner which is contrary to the international law of the sea.

(c)   Where a nuclear incident occurs outside the territory of the Contracting Parties, or where it occurs within an area in respect of which no notification has been given pursuant to paragraph (b) of this Article, or where the place of the nuclear incident cannot be determined with certainty, jurisdiction over such actions shall lie with the courts of the Contracting Party in whose territory the nuclear installation of the operator liable is situated.

(d)   Where a nuclear incident occurs in an area in respect of which the circumstances of Article 17(d) apply, jurisdiction shall lie with the courts determined, at the request of a Contracting Party concerned, by the Tribunal referred to in Article 17 as being the courts of that Contracting Party which is most closely related to and affected by the consequences of the incident.

(e)   The exercise of jurisdiction under this Article as well as the notification of an area made pursuant to paragraph (b) of this Article shall not create any right or obligation or set a precedent with respect to the delimitation of maritime areas between States with opposite or adjacent coasts.

(f)   Where jurisdiction would lie with the courts of more than one Contracting Party by virtue of paragraph (a), (b) or (c) of this Article, jurisdiction shall lie,

(i)   if the nuclear incident occurred partly outside the territory of any Contracting Party and partly in the territory of a single Contracting Party, with the courts of that Contracting Party; and

(ii)   in any other case, with the courts determined, at the request of a Contracting Party concerned, by the Tribunal referred to in Article 17 as being the courts of that Contracting Party which is most closely related to and affected by the consequences of the incident.

(g)   The Contracting Party whose courts have jurisdiction shall ensure that in relation to actions for compensation of nuclear damage:

(i)   any State may bring an action on behalf of persons who have suffered nuclear damage, who are nationals of that State or have their domicile or residence in its territory, and who have consented thereto; and

(ii)   any person may bring an action to enforce rights under this Convention acquired by subrogation or assignment.

(h)   The Contracting Party whose courts have jurisdiction under this Convention shall ensure that only one of its courts shall be competent to rule on compensation for nuclear damage arising from any one nuclear incident, the criteria for such selection being determined by the national legislation of such Contracting Party.

(i)   Judgements entered by the competent court under this Article after trial, or by default, shall, when they have become enforceable under the law applied by that court, become enforceable in the territory of any of the other Contracting Parties as soon as the formalities required by the Contracting Party concerned have been complied with. The merits of the case shall not be the subject of further proceedings. The foregoing provisions shall not apply to interim judgements.

(j)   If an action is brought against a Contracting Party under this Convention, such Contracting Party may not, except in respect of measures of execution, invoke any jurisdictional immunities before the court competent in accordance with this Article."

N.   Paragraph (b) of Article 14 shall be replaced by the following:

"(b) 'National law' and 'national legislation' mean the law or the national legislation of the court having jurisdiction under this Convention over claims arising out of a nuclear incident, excluding the rules on conflict of laws relating to such claims. That law or legislation shall apply to all matters both substantive and procedural not specifically governed by this Convention."

F.1.   Proposal for a Council Decision concerning conclusion on behalf of the European Community of a Framework Agreement on a Multilateral Nuclear Environmental Programme in the Russian Federation and of the Protocol on Claims, Legal Proceedings and Indemnification to the Framework Agreement on a Multilateral Nuclear Environmental Programme in the Russian Federation (COM (2006) 665 final of 8 November 2006)

Article 1.   1.   The Framework Agreement on a Multilateral Nuclear Environmental Programme in the Russian Federation and the additional Protocol on Claims, Legal Proceedings and Indemnification to the Framework Agreement on a Multilateral Nuclear Environmental Programme in the Russian Federation are hereby concluded on behalf of the European Community.

2.   The text of the Framework Agreement and the additional Protocol are attached to this decision.

F.2.   Framework agreement on a Multilateral Nuclear Environmental Programme in the Russian Federation

Article 7. Claims, legal proceedings and indemnification.   1.   This Agreement is supplemented by a Protocol containing provisions on claims, legal proceedings and indemnification in respect of claims against Contributors and their personnel or contractors, subcontractors, consultants, suppliers or subsuppliers of equipment, goods and services at any tier and their personnel, for any loss or damage of whatsoever nature arising from activities undertaken pursuant to this Agreement.

2.   The Protocol and its Annex shall not apply to any Party that does not become a party to the Protocol.

3.   Any Party that does not become a party to the Protocol may conclude with the Russian Party a separate agreement covering claims, legal proceedings and indemnification in respect of claims for any loss or damage of whatsoever nature arising from activities undertaken pursuant to this Agreement.

474 Jurisdiction, Recognition & Enforcement of Judgments in Civil & Commercial Matters

F.3. Protocol on Claims, Legal Proceedings and Indemnification to the Framework Agreement on a Multilateral Nuclear Environmental Programme in the Russian Federation

Article 1.   1.   The definitions contained in Article 2 of the Agreement shall apply to this Protocol as fully and effectively as if they were set forth in full herein.

2.   For the purposes of this Protocol, the following terms shall have the following meanings:

Nuclear Incident: Any occurrence or series of occurrences having the same origin which causes Nuclear Damage.

Nuclear Damage: (i) loss of life, any personal injury or any loss of, or damage to, property which arises out of or results from the radioactive properties or a combination of radioactive properties with toxic, explosive or other hazardous properties of nuclear fuel or radioactive products or waste in, or of nuclear material coming from, originating in, or sent to, a nuclear installation;

(ii)   any other loss or damage so arising or resulting if and to the extent that the law of the competent court so provides; and

(iii)   if the law of the State in which the nuclear installation of the liable operator is situated so provides, loss of life, any personal injury or any loss of, or damage to, property which arises out of or results from other ionising radiation emitted by any other source of radiation inside a nuclear installation.

3.   For the purposes of this Protocol, whenever both nuclear damage and damage other than nuclear damage have been caused by a nuclear incident, or jointly by a nuclear incident and one or more other occurrences, such other damage shall, to the extent that it is not reasonably separable from the nuclear damage, be deemed, for the purposes of this Protocol, to be nuclear damage caused by that nuclear incident.

Article 2.   1.   With the exception of claims for injury or damage against individuals arising from omissions or acts of such individuals done with intent to cause injury or damage, the Russian Party shall bring no claims or legal proceedings of any kind against the Contributors and their personnel or contractors, subcontractors, consultants, suppliers or subsuppliers of equipment, goods or services at any tier and their personnel, for any loss or damage of whatsoever nature, including but not limited to personal injury, loss of life, direct, indirect and consequential damage to property owned by the Russian Federation arising from activities undertaken pursuant to the Agreement. This paragraph shall not apply to the enforcement of the express provisions of a contract.

2   With the exception of claims for nuclear damage against individuals arising from omissions or acts of such individuals done with intent to cause damage, the Russian Party shall provide for the adequate legal defence of and indemnify, and shall bring no claims or legal proceedings against the Contributors and their personnel, or any contractors, subcontractors, consultants, suppliers, or subsuppliers of equipment, goods or services at any tier and their personnel in connection with third-party claims, in any court or forum, arising from activities undertaken pursuant to the Agreement, for nuclear damage occurring within or outside the territory of the Russian Federation, that results from a nuclear incident occurring within the territory of the Russian Federation.

3.   Upon request by a Party, the Russian Party or its authorised representative shall issue an indemnity confirmation letter to any contractor, subcontractor, consultant,

supplier or subsupplier confirming the provisions of this Protocol. A standard form of such Indemnity Confirmation Letter is enclosed as an integral part of this Protocol.

4.   The Parties may consult as appropriate, on claims and proceedings under this Article.

5.   Any payments related to the indemnification in paragraph 2 of this Article shall be made promptly and shall be freely transferable to the beneficiary in its national currency.

6.   Contributors, contractors, subcontractors, consultants, suppliers or subsuppliers of equipment, goods or services at any tier and their personnel may refer any dispute concerning the implementation of obligations under this Article to arbitration in accordance with UNCITRAL Arbitration Rules, if such dispute has not been resolved amicably within 90 days of its submission to the Russian Party. Any arbitration award shall be final and binding on the parties to the dispute.

7.   Nothing in this Article shall be construed as acknowledging the jurisdiction of any court or forum outside the Russian Federation over third-party claims to which paragraph 2 of this Article applies, except as provided for in paragraph 6 of this Article and in any other case where the Russian Federation has pledged itself to acknowledge and execute a legal decision on the basis of provisions of international agreements.

8.   Nothing in this Article shall be construed as waiving the immunity of the Parties with respect to potential third–party claims that may be brought against any of them.

Interests in goods and equipment

A.1.   Council Decision 2009/370/EC of 6 April 2009 on the accession of the European Community to the Convention on international interests in mobile equipment and its Protocol on matters specific to aircraft equipment, adopted jointly in Cape Town on 16 November 2001 (OJ, L 121 of 15 May 2009): Recitals 5, 9, Articles 1–3

See Chapter VIII, Interests in goods and equipment, A.1.

A.2.   General declarations concerning the competence of the European Community to be made by the Community at the time of accession to the Convention on international interests in mobile equipment (Cape Town Convention) and the Protocol on matters specific to aircraft equipment (Aircraft Protocol), adopted jointly in Cape Town on 16 November 2001 (OJ, L 121 of 15 May 2009): Paragraphs 5–6

See Chapter VIII, Interests in goods and equipment, A.2.

A.3.   Declarations to be made by the European Community at the time of accession to the Convention on international interests in mobile equipment (Cape Town Convention) and the Protocol on matters specific to aircraft equipment (Aircraft Protocol) concerning certain provisions and measures contained therein (OJ, L 121 of 15 May 2009)

See Chapter VIII, Interests in goods and equipment, A.3.

A.4.   Convention on international interests in mobile equipment (OJ, L 121 of 15 May 2009): Articles 42–45, 53, 55-56

See Chapter VIII, Interests in goods and equipment, A.4.

A.5.   Protocol to the Convention on international interests in mobile equipment on matters specific to aircraft equipment (OJ, L 121 of 15 May 2009): Articles XXI-XXII, XXX(1), XXX(5), XXXI-XXXII

See Chapter VIII, Interests in goods and equipment, A.5.

A.6.   Council Decision 2009/940/EC on the signing by the European Community of the Protocol to the Convention on International Interests in Mobile Equipment on Matters Specific to Railway Rolling Stock, adopted in Luxembourg on 23 February 2007 (OJ, L 331 of 16 December 2009): Recital 6

See Chapter VIII, Interests in goods and equipment, A.6.

A.7.   Declaration to be made pursuant to Article XXII(2) concerning the competence of the European Community over matters governed by the Protocol to the Convention on International Interests in Mobile Equipment on Matters Specific to Railway Rolling Stock (the 'Rail Protocol'), adopted in Luxembourg on 23 February 2007, in respect of which the Member States have transferred their competence to the Community (OJ, L 331 of 16 December 2009): Paragraph 5

See Chapter VIII, Interests in goods and equipment, A.7.

A.8. Luxembourg protocol to the convention on international interests in mobile equipment on matters specific to railway rolling stock (OJ, L 331 of 16 December 2009): Articles VIII(3), XVIII, XXVII(2), XXIX(1)

See Chapter VIII, Interests in goods and equipment, A.8.

Social security

A. Regulation (EC) No 987/2009 of the European Parliament and of the Council of 16 September 2009 laying down the procedure for implementing Regulation (EC) No 883/2004 on the coordination of social security systems (OJ, L 284 of 30 October 2009): Recital 20

See Chapter X, A.2.

Other relevant instruments[30]

A. Commission Interpretative Communication – Freedom to Provide Services and the Interest of the General Good in the Second Banking Directive (OJ, C 209 of 10 July 1997)

See Chapter IX, General provisions, O.

B. Commission Interpretative Communication – Freedom to provide services and the general good in the insurance sector (OJ, C 43 of 16 February 2000)

See Chapter IX, General provisions, P.

---

[30] Together with EC acts and ECJ decisions there are a number of other useful instruments adopted by the Community institutions in other fields of activity that may come into consideration for the interpretation of the former. They mainly relate to the assessment of the localisation of the activity of undertakings for purposes of exercising the freedom of establishment or freedom to provide services or of applying the rules on competition. [Note of the Editor]

C.   Commission notice — Guidelines on Vertical Restraints (OJ, C 130 of 19 May 2010)

(51) There are four exceptions to the hardcore restriction in Article 4(b) of the Block Exemption Regulation. The first exception in Article 4(b)(i) allows a supplier to restrict active sales by a buyer party to the agreement to a territory or a customer group which has been allocated exclusively to another buyer or which the supplier has reserved to itself. A territory or customer group is exclusively allocated when the supplier agrees to sell its product only to one distributor for distribution in a particular territory or to a particular customer group and the exclusive distributor is protected against active selling into its territory or to its customer group by all the other buyers of the supplier within the Union, irrespective of sales by the supplier. The supplier is allowed to combine the allocation of an exclusive territory and an exclusive customer group by for instance appointing an exclusive distributor for a particular customer group in a certain territory. Such protection of exclusively allocated territories or customer groups must, however, permit passive sales to such territories or customer groups. For the application of Article 4(b) of the Block Exemption Regulation, the Commission interprets "active" and "passive" sales as follows:

—   "Active" sales mean actively approaching individual customers by for instance direct mail, including the sending of unsolicited e-mails, or visits; or actively approaching a specific customer group or customers in a specific territory through advertisement in media, on the internet or other promotions specifically targeted at that customer group or targeted at customers in that territory. Advertisement or promotion that is only attractive for the buyer if it (also) reaches a specific group of customers or customers in a specific territory, is considered active selling to that customer group or customers in that territory.

—   "Passive" sales mean responding to unsolicited requests from individual customers including delivery of goods or services to such customers. General advertising or promotion that reaches customers in other distributors' (exclusive) territories or customer groups but which is a reasonable way to reach customers outside those territories or customer groups, for instance to reach customers in one's own territory, are considered passive selling. General advertising or promotion is considered a reasonable way to reach such customers if it would be attractive for the buyer to undertake these investments also if they would not reach customers in other distributors' (exclusive) territories or customer groups.

(52) The internet is a powerful tool to reach a greater number and variety of customers than by more traditional sales methods, which explains why certain restrictions on the use of the internet are dealt with as (re)sales restrictions. In principle, every distributor must be allowed to use the internet to sell products. In general, where a distributor uses a website to sell products that is considered a form of passive selling, since it is a reasonable way to allow customers to reach the distributor. The use of a website may have effects that extend beyond the distributor's own territory and customer group; however, such effects result from the technology allowing easy access from everywhere. If a customer visits the web site of a distributor and contacts the distributor and if such contact leads to a sale, including delivery, then that is considered passive selling. The same is true if a customer opts to be kept (automatically) informed by the distributor and it leads to a sale. Offering different language options on the website does not, of itself, change the passive character of such selling. The Commission thus regards the following as examples of hardcore restrictions of passive selling given the capability of these restrictions to limit the distributor's access to a greater number and variety of customers:

(a) an agreement that the (exclusive) distributor shall prevent customers located in another (exclusive) territory from viewing its website or shall automatically re-rout its customers to the manufacturer's or other (exclusive) distributors' websites. This does not exclude an agreement that the distributor's website shall also offer a number of links to websites of other distributors and/or the supplier;

(b) an agreement that the (exclusive) distributor shall terminate consumers' transactions over the internet once their credit card data reveal an address that is not within the distributor's (exclusive) territory;

(c) an agreement that the distributor shall limit its proportion of overall sales made over the internet. This does not exclude the supplier requiring, without limiting the online sales of the distributor, that the buyer sells at least a certain absolute amount (in value or volume) of the products offline to ensure an efficient operation of its brick and mortar shop (physical point of sales), nor does it preclude the supplier from making sure that the online activity of the distributor remains consistent with the supplier's distribution model (see paragraphs (54) and (56)). This absolute amount of required offline sales can be the same for all buyers, or determined individually for each buyer on the basis of objective criteria, such as the buyer's size in the network or its geographic location;

(d) an agreement that the distributor shall pay a higher price for products intended to be resold by the distributor online than for products intended to be resold offline. This does not exclude the supplier agreeing with the buyer a fixed fee (that is, not a variable fee where the sum increases with the realised offline turnover as this would amount indirectly to dual pricing) to support the latter's offline or online sales efforts.

D. Commission Notice on the co-operation between the Commission and the courts of the EU Member States in the application of Articles 81 and 82 EC (OJ, C 101 of 27 April 2004): Points 2–3

See Chapter VII, M.

E. Directive 2000/31/EC of the European Parliament and of the Council of 8 June 2000 on certain legal aspects of information society services, in particular electronic commerce, in the Internal Market (Directive on electronic commerce) (OJ, L 178 of 17 July 2000): Recital 19, Article 1(4)

See Chapter IX, General provisions, D.

F. Directive 2009/103/EC of the European Parliament and of the Council of 16 September 2009 relating to insurance against civil liability in respect of the use of motor vehicles, and the enforcement of the obligation to insure against such liability (codified version) (OJ, L 263 of 7 October 2009): Recitals 32, 35, 37-38, Articles 1, 21(6)

See Chapter VII, H.

V

Insolvency Proceedings

A.1. Council Regulation (EC) No 1346/2000 of 29 May 2000 on insolvency proceedings (OJ, L 160 of 30 June 2000)[1]

(1) The European Union has set out the aim of establishing an area of freedom, security and justice.

(2) The proper functioning of the internal market requires that cross-border insolvency proceedings should operate efficiently and effectively and this Regulation needs to be adopted in order to achieve this objective which comes within the scope of judicial cooperation in civil matters within the meaning of Article 65 of the Treaty.

(3) The activities of undertakings have more and more cross-border effects and are therefore increasingly being regulated by Community law. While the insolvency of such undertakings also affects the proper functioning of the internal market, there is a need for a Community act requiring coordination of the measures to be taken regarding an insolvent debtor's assets.

(4) It is necessary for the proper functioning of the internal market to avoid incentives for the parties to transfer assets or judicial proceedings from one Member State to another, seeking to obtain a more favourable legal position (forum shopping).

(5) These objectives cannot be achieved to a sufficient degree at national level and action at Community level is therefore justified.

(6) In accordance with the principle of proportionality this Regulation should be confined to provisions governing jurisdiction for opening insolvency proceedings and judgments which are delivered directly on the basis of the insolvency proceedings and are closely connected with such proceedings. In addition, this Regulation should contain provisions regarding the recognition of those judgments and the applicable law which also satisfy that principle.

(7) Insolvency proceedings relating to the winding-up of insolvent companies or other legal persons, judicial arrangements, compositions and analogous proceedings are excluded from the scope of the 1968 Brussels Convention on Jurisdiction and the Enforcement of Judgments in Civil and Commercial Matters, as amended by the Conventions on Accession to this Convention.

(8) In order to achieve the aim of improving the efficiency and effectiveness of insolvency proceedings having cross-border effects, it is necessary, and appropriate, that the provisions on jurisdiction, recognition and applicable law in this area should

---

[1] As finally amended by Implementing Regulation of the Council (EU) No 210/2010 of 25 February 2010 (OJ, L 65 of 13 March 2010). The Convention of 1995, which preceded the Regulation but has never entered into force was accompanied by an explanatory report by M Virgós and E Schmit, which has not been published in the OJ, but it is reproduced in G Moss, IF Fletcher, S Isaacs (eds), *The EC Regulation on Insolvency Proceedings. A Commentary and Annotated Guide*, 2nd ed., (Oxford, 2009), 381 *et seq*. [Note of the Editor]

be contained in a Community law measure which is binding and directly applicable in Member States.

(9)   This Regulation should apply to insolvency proceedings, whether the debtor is a natural person or a legal person, a trader or an individual. The insolvency proceedings to which this Regulation applies are listed in the Annexes. Insolvency proceedings concerning insurance undertakings, credit institutions, investment undertakings holding funds or securities for third parties and collective investment undertakings should be excluded from the scope of this Regulation. Such undertakings should not be covered by this Regulation since they are subject to special arrangements and, to some extent, the national supervisory authorities have extremely wide-ranging powers of intervention.

(10)   Insolvency proceedings do not necessarily involve the intervention of a judicial authority; the expression 'court' in this Regulation should be given a broad meaning and include a person or body empowered by national law to open insolvency proceedings. In order for this Regulation to apply, proceedings (comprising acts and formalities set down in-law) should not only have to comply with the provisions of this Regulation, but they should also be officially recognised and legally effective in the Member State in which the insolvency proceedings are opened and should be collective insolvency proceedings which entail the partial or total divestment of the debtor and the appointment of a liquidator.

(11)   This Regulation acknowledges the fact that as a result of widely differing substantive laws it is not practical to introduce insolvency proceedings with universal scope in the entire Community. The application without exception of the law of the State of opening of proceedings would, against this background, frequently lead to difficulties. This applies, for example, to the widely differing laws on security interests to be found in the Community. Furthermore, the preferential rights enjoyed by some creditors in the insolvency proceedings are, in some cases, completely different. This Regulation should take account of this in two different ways. On the one hand, provision should be made for special rules on applicable law in the case of particularly significant rights and legal relationships (e.g. rights in rem and contracts of employment). On the other hand, national proceedings covering only assets situated in the State of opening should also be allowed alongside main insolvency proceedings with universal scope.

(12)   This Regulation enables the main insolvency proceedings to be opened in the Member State where the debtor has the centre of his main interests. These proceedings have universal scope and aim at encompassing all the debtor's assets. To protect the diversity of interests, this Regulation permits secondary proceedings to be opened to run in parallel with the main proceedings. Secondary proceedings may be opened in the Member State where the debtor has an establishment. The effects of secondary proceedings are limited to the assets located in that State. Mandatory rules of coordination with the main proceedings satisfy the need for unity in the Community.

(13)   The 'centre of main interests' should correspond to the place where the debtor conducts the administration of his interests on a regular basis and is therefore ascertainable by third parties.

(14)   This Regulation applies only to proceedings where the centre of the debtor's main interests is located in the Community.

(15)   The rules of jurisdiction set out in this Regulation establish only international jurisdiction, that is to say, they designate the Member State the courts of which may open insolvency proceedings. Territorial jurisdiction within that Member State must be established by the national law of the Member State concerned.

(16) The court having jurisdiction to open the main insolvency proceedings should be enabled to order provisional and protective measures from the time of the request to open proceedings. Preservation measures both prior to and after the commencement of the insolvency proceedings are very important to guarantee the effectiveness of the insolvency proceedings. In that connection this Regulation should afford different possibilities. On the one hand, the court competent for the main insolvency proceedings should be able also to order provisional protective measures covering assets situated in the territory of other Member States. On the other hand, a liquidator temporarily appointed prior to the opening of the main insolvency proceedings should be able, in the Member States in which an establishment belonging to the debtor is to be found, to apply for the preservation measures which are possible under the law of those States.

(17) Prior to the opening of the main insolvency proceedings, the right to request the opening of insolvency proceedings in the Member State where the debtor has an establishment should be limited to local creditors and creditors of the local establishment or to cases where main proceedings cannot be opened under the law of the Member State where the debtor has the centre of his main interest. The reason for this restriction is that cases where territorial insolvency proceedings are requested before the main insolvency proceedings are intended to be limited to what is absolutely necessary. If the main insolvency proceedings are opened, the territorial proceedings become secondary.

(18) Following the opening of the main insolvency proceedings, the right to request the opening of insolvency proceedings in a Member State where the debtor has an establishment is not restricted by this Regulation. The liquidator in the main proceedings or any other person empowered under the national law of that Member State may request the opening of secondary insolvency proceedings.

(19) Secondary insolvency proceedings may serve different purposes, besides the protection of local interests. Cases may arise where the estate of the debtor is too complex to administer as a unit or where differences in the legal systems concerned are so great that difficulties may arise from the extension of effects deriving from the law of the State of the opening to the other States where the assets are located. For this reason the liquidator in the main proceedings may request the opening of secondary proceedings when the efficient administration of the estate so requires.

(20) Main insolvency proceedings and secondary proceedings can, however, contribute to the effective realisation of the total assets only if all the concurrent proceedings pending are coordinated. The main condition here is that the various liquidators must cooperate closely, in particular by exchanging a sufficient amount of information. In order to ensure the dominant role of the main insolvency proceedings, the liquidator in such proceedings should be given several possibilities for intervening in secondary insolvency proceedings which are pending at the same time. For example, he should be able to propose a restructuring plan or composition or apply for realisation of the assets in the secondary insolvency proceedings to be suspended.

(21) Every creditor, who has his habitual residence, domicile or registered office in the Community, should have the right to lodge his claims in each of the insolvency proceedings pending in the Community relating to the debtor's assets. This should also apply to tax authorities and social insurance institutions. However, in order to ensure equal treatment of creditors, the distribution of proceeds must be coordinated. Every creditor should be able to keep what he has received in the course of insolvency proceedings but should be entitled only to participate in the distribution of total assets in

other proceedings if creditors with the same standing have obtained the same proportion of their claims.

(22) This Regulation should provide for immediate recognition of judgments concerning the opening, conduct and closure of insolvency proceedings which come within its scope and of judgments handed down in direct connection with such insolvency proceedings. Automatic recognition should therefore mean that the effects attributed to the proceedings by the law of the State in which the proceedings were opened extend to all other Member States. Recognition of judgments delivered by the courts of the Member States should be based on the principle of mutual trust. To that end, grounds for non-recognition should be reduced to the minimum necessary. This is also the basis on which any dispute should be resolved where the courts of two Member States both claim competence to open the main insolvency proceedings. The decision of the first court to open proceedings should be recognised in the other Member States without those Member States having the power to scrutinise the court's decision.

(23) This Regulation should set out, for the matters covered by it, uniform rules on conflict of laws which replace, within their scope of application, national rules of private international law. Unless otherwise stated, the law of the Member State of the opening of the proceedings should be applicable (*lex concursus*). This rule on conflict of laws should be valid both for the main proceedings and for local proceedings; the *lex concursus* determines all the effects of the insolvency proceedings, both procedural and substantive, on the persons and legal relations concerned. It governs all the conditions for the opening, conduct and closure of the insolvency proceedings.

(24) Automatic recognition of insolvency proceedings to which the law of the opening State normally applies may interfere with the rules under which transactions are carried out in other Member States. To protect legitimate expectations and the certainty of transactions in Member States other than that in which proceedings are opened, provisions should be made for a number of exceptions to the general rule.

(25) There is a particular need for a special reference diverging from the law of the opening State in the case of rights in rem, since these are of considerable importance for the granting of credit. The basis, validity and extent of such a right in rem should therefore normally be determined according to the *lex situs* and not be affected by the opening of insolvency proceedings. The proprietor of the right in rem should therefore be able to continue to assert his right to segregation or separate settlement of the collateral security. Where assets are subject to rights in rem under the *lex situs* in one Member State but the main proceedings are being carried out in another Member State, the liquidator in the main proceedings should be able to request the opening of secondary proceedings in the jurisdiction where the rights in rem arise if the debtor has an establishment there. If a secondary proceeding is not opened, the surplus on sale of the asset covered by rights in rem must be paid to the liquidator in the main proceedings.

(26) If a set-off is not permitted under the law of the opening State, a creditor should nevertheless be entitled to the set-off if it is possible under the law applicable to the claim of the insolvent debtor. In this way, set-off will acquire a kind of guarantee function based on legal provisions on which the creditor concerned can rely at the time when the claim arises.

(27) There is also a need for special protection in the case of payment systems and financial markets. This applies for example to the position-closing agreements and netting agreements to be found in such systems as well as to the sale of securities and to the

guarantees provided for such transactions as governed in particular by Directive 98/26/EC of the European Parliament and of the Council of 19 May 1998 on settlement finality in payment and securities settlement systems. For such transactions, the only law which is material should thus be that applicable to the system or market concerned. This provision is intended to prevent the possibility of mechanisms for the payment and settlement of transactions provided for in the payment and set-off systems or on the regulated financial markets of the Member States being altered in the case of insolvency of a business partner. Directive 98/26/EC contains special provisions which should take precedence over the general rules in this Regulation.

(28) In order to protect employees and jobs, the effects of insolvency proceedings on the continuation or termination of employment and on the rights and obligations of all parties to such employment must be determined by the law applicable to the agreement in accordance with the general rules on conflict of law. Any other insolvency-law questions, such as whether the employees' claims are protected by preferential rights and what status such preferential rights may have, should be determined by the law of the opening State.

(29) For business considerations, the main content of the decision opening the proceedings should be published in the other Member States at the request of the liquidator. If there is an establishment in the Member State concerned, there may be a requirement that publication is compulsory. In neither case, however, should publication be a prior condition for recognition of the foreign proceedings.

(30) It may be the case that some of the persons concerned are not in fact aware that proceedings have been opened and act in good faith in a way that conflicts with the new situation. In order to protect such persons who make a payment to the debtor because they are unaware that foreign proceedings have been opened when they should in fact have made the payment to the foreign liquidator, it should be provided that such a payment is to have a debt-discharging effect.

(31) This Regulation should include Annexes relating to the organisation of insolvency proceedings. As these Annexes relate exclusively to the legislation of Member States, there are specific and substantiated reasons for the Council to reserve the right to amend these Annexes in order to take account of an amendments to the domestic law of the Member States.

(32) The United Kingdom and Ireland, in accordance with Article 3 of the Protocol on the position of the United Kingdom and Ireland annexed to the Treaty on European Union and the Treaty establishing the European Community, have given notice of their wish to take part in the adoption and application of this Regulation.

(33) Denmark, in accordance with Articles 1 and 2 of the Protocol on the position of Denmark annexed to the Treaty on European Union and the Treaty establishing the European Community, is not participating in the adoption of this Regulation, and is therefore not bound by it nor subject to its application ...

Chapter I — General provisions

Article 1. Scope.   1.   This Regulation shall apply to collective insolvency proceedings which entail the partial or total divestment of a debtor and the appointment of a liquidator.

2.   This Regulation shall not apply to insolvency proceedings concerning insurance undertakings, credit institutions, investment undertakings which provide services

involving the holding of funds or securities for third parties, or to collective investment undertakings.

Article 2. Definitions.   For the purposes of this Regulation:

(a) 'insolvency proceedings' shall mean the collective proceedings referred to in Article 1(1). These proceedings are listed in Annex A;

(b) 'liquidator' shall mean any person or body whose function is to administer or liquidate assets of which the debtor has been divested or to supervise the administration of his affairs. Those persons and bodies are listed in Annex C;

(c) 'winding-up proceedings' shall mean insolvency proceedings within the meaning of point (a) involving realising the assets of the debtor, including where the proceedings have been closed by a composition or other measure terminating the insolvency, or closed by reason of the insufficiency of the assets. Those proceedings are listed in Annex B;

(d) 'court' shall mean the judicial body or any other competent body of a Member State empowered to open insolvency proceedings or to take decisions in the course of such proceedings;

(e) 'judgment' in relation to the opening of insolvency proceedings or the appointment of a liquidator shall include the decision of any court empowered to open such proceedings or to appoint a liquidator;

(f) 'the time of the opening of proceedings' shall mean the time at which the judgment opening proceedings becomes effective, whether it is a final judgment or not;

(g) 'the Member State in which assets are situated' shall mean, in the case of:

— tangible property, the Member State within the territory of which the property is situated;

— property and rights ownership of or entitlement to which must be entered in a public register, the Member State under the authority of which the register is kept;

— claims, the Member State within the territory of which the third party required to meet them has the centre of his main interests, as determined in Article 3(1);

(h) 'establishment' shall mean any place of operations where the debtor carries out a non-transitory economic activity with human means and goods.

Article 3. International jurisdiction.   1.   The courts of the Member State within the territory of which the centre of a debtor's main interests is situated shall have jurisdiction to open insolvency proceedings. In the case of a company or legal person, the place of the registered office shall be presumed to be the centre of its main interests in the absence of proof to the contrary.

2.   Where the centre of a debtor's main interests is situated within the territory of a Member State, the courts of another Member State shall have jurisdiction to open insolvency proceedings against that debtor only if he possesses an establishment within the territory of that other Member State. The effects of those proceedings shall be restricted to the assets of the debtor situated in the territory of the latter Member State.

3.   Where insolvency proceedings have been opened under paragraph 1, any proceedings opened subsequently under paragraph 2 shall be secondary proceedings. These latter proceedings must be winding-up proceedings.

4.   Territorial insolvency proceedings referred to in paragraph 2 may be opened prior to the opening of main insolvency proceedings in accordance with paragraph 1 only:

(a) where insolvency proceedings under paragraph 1 cannot be opened because of the conditions laid down by the law of the Member State within the territory of which the centre of the debtor's main interests is situated; or

(b) where the opening of territorial insolvency proceedings is requested by a creditor who has his domicile, habitual residence or registered office in the Member State within the territory of which the establishment is situated, or whose claim arises from the operation of that establishment.

Article 4. Law applicable.   1.   Save as otherwise provided in this Regulation, the law applicable to insolvency proceedings and their effects shall be that of the Member State within the territory of which such proceedings are opened, hereafter referred to as the 'State of the opening of proceedings'.

2.   The law of the State of the opening of proceedings shall determine the conditions for the opening of those proceedings, their conduct and their closure. It shall determine in particular:

(a)   against which debtors insolvency proceedings may be brought on account of their capacity;

(b)   the assets which form part of the estate and the treatment of assets acquired by or devolving on the debtor after the opening of the insolvency proceedings;

(c)   the respective powers of the debtor and the liquidator;

(d)   the conditions under which set-offs may be invoked;

(e)   the effects of insolvency proceedings on current contracts to which the debtor is party;

(f)   the effects of the insolvency proceedings on proceedings brought by individual creditors, with the exception of lawsuits pending;

(g)   the claims which are to be lodged against the debtor's estate and the treatment of claims arising after the opening of insolvency proceedings;

(h)   the rules governing the lodging, verification and admission of claims;

(i)   the rules governing the distribution of proceeds from the realisation of assets, the ranking of claims and the rights of creditors who have obtained partial satisfaction after the opening of insolvency proceedings by virtue of a right in rem or through a set-off;

(j)   the conditions for and the effects of closure of insolvency proceedings, in particular by composition;

(k)   creditors' rights after the closure of insolvency proceedings;

(l)   who is to bear the costs and expenses incurred in the insolvency proceedings;

(m) the rules relating to the voidness, voidability or unenforceability of legal acts detrimental to all the creditors.

Article 5. Third parties' rights in rem.   1.   The opening of insolvency proceedings shall not affect the rights in rem of creditors or third parties in respect of tangible or intangible, moveable or immoveable assets — both specific assets and collections of indefinite assets as a whole which change from time to time — belonging to the debtor which are situated within the territory of another Member State at the time of the opening of proceedings.

2.   The rights referred to in paragraph 1 shall in particular mean:

(a)   the right to dispose of assets or have them disposed of and to obtain satisfaction from the proceeds of or income from those assets, in particular by virtue of a lien or a mortgage;

(b)   the exclusive right to have a claim met, in particular a right guaranteed by a lien in respect of the claim or by assignment of the claim by way of a guarantee;

(c)   the right to demand the assets from, and/or to require restitution by, anyone having possession or use of them contrary to the wishes of the party so entitled;

(d)   a right in rem to the beneficial use of assets.

3.   The right, recorded in a public register and enforceable against third parties, under which a right in rem within the meaning of paragraph 1 may be obtained, shall be considered a right in rem.

4.   Paragraph 1 shall not preclude actions for voidness, voidability or unenforceability as referred to in Article 4(2)(m).

Article 6. Set-off.   1.   The opening of insolvency proceedings shall not affect the right of creditors to demand the set-off of their claims against the claims of the debtor, where such a set-off is permitted by the law applicable to the insolvent debtor's claim.

2.   Paragraph 1 shall not preclude actions for voidness, voidability or unenforceability as referred to in Article 4(2)(m).

Article 7. Reservation of title.   1.   The opening of insolvency proceedings against the purchaser of an asset shall not affect the seller's rights based on a reservation of title where at the time of the opening of proceedings the asset is situated within the territory of a Member State other than the State of opening of proceedings.

2.   The opening of insolvency proceedings against the seller of an asset, after delivery of the asset, shall not constitute grounds for rescinding or terminating the sale and shall not prevent the purchaser from acquiring title where at the time of the opening of proceedings the asset sold is situated within the territory of a Member State other than the State of the opening of proceedings.

3.   Paragraphs 1 and 2 shall not preclude actions for voidness, voidability or unenforceability as referred to in Article 4(2)(m).

Article 8. Contracts relating to immoveable property.   The effects of insolvency proceedings on a contract conferring the right to acquire or make use of immoveable property shall be governed solely by the law of the Member State within the territory of which the immoveable property is situated.

Article 9. Payment systems and financial markets.   1.   Without prejudice to Article 5, the effects of insolvency proceedings on the rights and obligations of the parties to a payment or settlement system or to a financial market shall be governed solely by the law of the Member State applicable to that system or market.

2.   Paragraph 1 shall not preclude any action for voidness, voidability or unenforceability which may be taken to set aside payments or transactions under the law applicable to the relevant payment system or financial market.

Article 10. Contracts of employment. The effects of insolvency proceedings on employment contracts and relationships shall be governed solely by the law of the Member State applicable to the contract of employment.

Article 11. Effects on rights subject to registration. The effects of insolvency proceedings on the rights of the debtor in immoveable property, a ship or an aircraft subject to registration in a public register shall be determined by the law of the Member State under the authority of which the register is kept.

Article 12. Community patents and trade marks. For the purposes of this Regulation, a Community patent, a Community trade mark or any other similar right established by Community law may be included only in the proceedings referred to in Article 3(1).

Article 13. Detrimental acts. Article 4(2)(m) shall not apply where the person who benefited from an act detrimental to all the creditors provides proof that:
— the said act is subject to the law of a Member State other than that of the State of the opening of proceedings, and
— that law does not allow any means of challenging that act in the relevant case.

Article 14. Protection of third-party purchasers. Where, by an act concluded after the opening of insolvency proceedings, the debtor disposes, for consideration, of:
— an immoveable asset, or
— a ship or an aircraft subject to registration in a public register, or
— securities whose existence presupposes registration in a register laid down by law, the validity of that act shall be governed by the law of the State within the territory of which the immoveable asset is situated or under the authority of which the register is kept.

Article 15. Effects of insolvency proceedings on lawsuits pending. The effects of insolvency proceedings on a lawsuit pending concerning an asset or a right of which the debtor has been divested shall be governed solely by the law of the Member State in which that lawsuit is pending.

Chapter II — Recognition of insolvency proceedings

Article 16. Principle. 1. Any judgment opening insolvency proceedings handed down by a court of a Member State which has jurisdiction pursuant to Article 3 shall be recognised in all the other Member States from the time that it becomes effective in the State of the opening of proceedings.

This rule shall also apply where, on account of his capacity, insolvency proceedings cannot be brought against the debtor in other Member States.

2. Recognition of the proceedings referred to in Article 3(1) shall not preclude the opening of the proceedings referred to in Article 3(2) by a court in another Member State. The latter proceedings shall be secondary insolvency proceedings within the meaning of Chapter III.

Article 17. Effects of recognition.   1.   The judgment opening the proceedings referred to in Article 3(1) shall, with no further formalities, produce the same effects in any other Member State as under this law of the State of the opening of proceedings, unless this Regulation provides otherwise and as long as no proceedings referred to in Article 3(2) are opened in that other Member State.

2.   The effects of the proceedings referred to in Article 3(2) may not be challenged in other Member States. Any restriction of the creditors' rights, in particular a stay or discharge, shall produce effects vis-à-vis assets situated within the territory of another Member State only in the case of those creditors who have given their consent.

Article 18. Powers of the liquidator.   1.   The liquidator appointed by a court which has jurisdiction pursuant to Article 3(1) may exercise all the powers conferred on him by the law of the State of the opening of proceedings in another Member State, as long as no other insolvency proceedings have been opened there nor any preservation measure to the contrary has been taken there further to a request for the opening of insolvency proceedings in that State. He may in particular remove the debtor's assets from the territory of the Member State in which they are situated, subject to Articles 5 and 7.

2.   The liquidator appointed by a court which has jurisdiction pursuant to Article 3(2) may in any other Member State claim through the courts or out of court that moveable property was removed from the territory of the State of the opening of proceedings to the territory of that other Member State after the opening of the insolvency proceedings. He may also bring any action to set aside which is in the interests of the creditors.

3.   In exercising his powers, the liquidator shall comply with the law of the Member State within the territory of which he intends to take action, in particular with regard to procedures for the realisation of assets. Those powers may not include coercive measures or the right to rule on legal proceedings or disputes.

Article 19. Proof of the liquidator's appointment.   The liquidator's appointment shall be evidenced by a certified copy of the original decision appointing him or by any other certificate issued by the court which has jurisdiction.

A translation into the official language or one of the official languages of the Member State within the territory of which he intends to act may be required. No legalisation or other similar formality shall be required.

Article 20. Return and imputation.   1.   A creditor who, after the opening of the proceedings referred to in Article 3(1) obtains by any means, in particular through enforcement, total or partial satisfaction of his claim on the assets belonging to the debtor situated within the territory of another Member State, shall return what he has obtained to the liquidator, subject to Articles 5 and 7.

2.   In order to ensure equal treatment of creditors a creditor who has, in the course of insolvency proceedings, obtained a dividend on his claim shall share in distributions made in other proceedings only where creditors of the same ranking or category have, in those other proceedings, obtained an equivalent dividend.

Article 21. Publication.   1.   The liquidator may request that notice of the judgment opening insolvency proceedings and, where appropriate, the decision appointing him, be published in any other Member State in accordance with the publication procedures provided for in that State. Such publication shall also specify the liquidator appointed and whether the jurisdiction rule applied is that pursuant to Article 3(1) or Article 3(2).

2.   However, any Member State within the territory of which the debtor has an establishment may require mandatory publication. In such cases, the liquidator or any authority empowered to that effect in the Member State where the proceedings referred to in Article 3(1) are opened shall take all necessary measures to ensure such publication.

Article 22. Registration in a public register.   1.   The liquidator may request that the judgment opening the proceedings referred to in Article 3(1) be registered in the land register, the trade register and any other public register kept in the other Member States.

2.   However, any Member State may require mandatory registration. In such cases, the liquidator or any authority empowered to that effect in the Member State where the proceedings referred to in Article 3(1) have been opened shall take all necessary measures to ensure such registration.

Article 23. Costs.   The costs of the publication and registration provided for in Articles 21 and 22 shall be regarded as costs and expenses incurred in the proceedings.

Article 24. Honouring of an obligation to a debtor.   1.   Where an obligation has been honoured in a Member State for the benefit of a debtor who is subject to insolvency proceedings opened in another Member State, when it should have been honoured for the benefit of the liquidator in those proceedings, the person honouring the obligation shall be deemed to have discharged it if he was unaware of the opening of proceedings.

2.   Where such an obligation is honoured before the publication provided for in Article 21 has been effected, the person honouring the obligation shall be presumed, in the absence of proof to the contrary, to have been unaware of the opening of insolvency proceedings; where the obligation is honoured after such publication has been effected, the person honouring the obligation shall be presumed, in the absence of proof to the contrary, to have been aware of the opening of proceedings.

Article 25. Recognition and enforceability of other judgments.   1.   Judgments handed down by a court whose judgment concerning the opening of proceedings is recognised in accordance with Article 16 and which concern the course and closure of insolvency proceedings, and compositions approved by that court shall also be recognised with no further formalities. Such judgments shall be enforced in accordance with Articles 31 to 51, with the exception of Article 34(2), of the Brussels Convention on Jurisdiction and the Enforcement of Judgments in Civil and Commercial Matters, as amended by the Conventions of Accession to this Convention.

The first subparagraph shall also apply to judgments deriving directly from the insolvency proceedings and which are closely linked with them, even if they were handed down by another court.

The first subparagraph shall also apply to judgments relating to preservation measures taken after the request for the opening of insolvency proceedings.

2.   The recognition and enforcement of judgments other than those referred to in paragraph 1 shall be governed by the Convention referred to in paragraph 1, provided that that Convention is applicable.

3.   The Member States shall not be obliged to recognise or enforce a judgment referred to in paragraph 1 which might result in a limitation of personal freedom or postal secrecy.

Article 26. Public policy.   Any Member State may refuse to recognise insolvency proceedings opened in another Member State or to enforce a judgment handed down in the context of such proceedings where the effects of such recognition or enforcement would be manifestly contrary to that State's public policy, in particular its fundamental principles or the constitutional rights and liberties of the individual.

Chapter III — Secondary insolvency proceedings

Article 27. Opening of proceedings.   The opening of the proceedings referred to in Article 3(1) by a court of a Member State and which is recognised in another Member State (main proceedings) shall permit the opening in that other Member State, a court of which has jurisdiction pursuant to Article 3(2), of secondary insolvency proceedings without the debtor's insolvency being examined in that other State. These latter proceedings must be among the proceedings listed in Annex B. Their effects shall be restricted to the assets of the debtor situated within the territory of that other Member State.

Article 28. Applicable law.   Save as otherwise provided in this Regulation, the law applicable to secondary proceedings shall be that of the Member State within the territory of which the secondary proceedings are opened.

Article 29. Right to request the opening of proceedings.   The opening of secondary proceedings may be requested by:
    (a)   the liquidator in the main proceedings;
    (b)   any other person or authority empowered to request the opening of insolvency proceedings under the law of the Member State within the territory of which the opening of secondary proceedings is requested.

Article 30. Advance payment of costs and expenses.   Where the law of the Member State in which the opening of secondary proceedings is requested requires that the debtor's assets be sufficient to cover in whole or in part the costs and expenses of the proceedings, the court may, when it receives such a request, require the applicant to make an advance payment of costs or to provide appropriate security.

Article 31. Duty to cooperate and communicate information.   1.   Subject to the rules restricting the communication of information, the liquidator in the main proceedings and the liquidators in the secondary proceedings shall be duty bound to communicate information to each other. They shall immediately communicate any information which may be relevant to the other proceedings, in particular the progress made in lodging and verifying claims and all measures aimed at terminating the proceedings.
    2.   Subject to the rules applicable to each of the proceedings, the liquidator in the main proceedings and the liquidators in the secondary proceedings shall be duty bound to cooperate with each other.

3.   The liquidator in the secondary proceedings shall give the liquidator in the main proceedings an early opportunity of submitting proposals on the liquidation or use of the assets in the secondary proceedings.

Article 32. Exercise of creditors' rights.   1.   Any creditor may lodge his claim in the main proceedings and in any secondary proceedings.

2.   The liquidators in the main and any secondary proceedings shall lodge in other proceedings claims which have already been lodged in the proceedings for which they were appointed, provided that the interests of creditors in the latter proceedings are served thereby, subject to the right of creditors to oppose that or to withdraw the lodgement of their claims where the law applicable so provides.

3.   The liquidator in the main or secondary proceedings shall be empowered to participate in other proceedings on the same basis as a creditor, in particular by attending creditors' meetings.

Article 33. Stay of liquidation.   1.   The court, which opened the secondary proceedings, shall stay the process of liquidation in whole or in part on receipt of a request from the liquidator in the main proceedings, provided that in that event it may require the liquidator in the main proceedings to take any suitable measure to guarantee the interests of the creditors in the secondary proceedings and of individual classes of creditors. Such a request from the liquidator may be rejected only if it is manifestly of no interest to the creditors in the main proceedings. Such a stay of the process of liquidation may be ordered for up to three months. It may be continued or renewed for similar periods.

2.   The court referred to in paragraph 1 shall terminate the stay of the process of liquidation
   —   at the request of the liquidator in the main proceedings;
   —   of its own motion, at the request of a creditor or at the request of the liquidator in the secondary proceedings if that measure no longer appears justified, in particular, by the interests of creditors in the main proceedings or in the secondary proceedings.

Article 34. Measures ending secondary insolvency proceedings.   1.   Where the law applicable to secondary proceedings allows for such proceedings to be closed without liquidation by a rescue plan, a composition or a comparable measure, the liquidator in the main proceedings shall be empowered to propose such a measure himself.

Closure of the secondary proceedings by a measure referred to in the first subparagraph shall not become final without the consent of the liquidator in the main proceedings; failing his agreement, however, it may become final if the financial interests of the creditors in the main proceedings are not affected by the measure proposed.

2.   Any restriction of creditors' rights arising from a measure referred to in paragraph 1 which is proposed in secondary proceedings, such as a stay of payment or discharge of debt, may not have effect in respect of the debtor's assets not covered by those proceedings without the consent of all the creditors having an interest.

3.   During a stay of the process of liquidation ordered pursuant to Article 33, only the liquidator in the main proceedings or the debtor, with the former's consent, may propose measures laid down in paragraph 1 of this Article in the secondary proceedings; no other proposal for such a measure shall be put to the vote or approved.

Article 35. Assets remaining in the secondary proceedings.   If by the liquidation of assets in the secondary proceedings it is possible to meet all claims allowed under those proceedings, the liquidator appointed in those proceedings shall immediately transfer any assets remaining to the liquidator in the main proceedings.

Article 36. Subsequent opening of the main proceedings.   Where the proceedings referred to in Article 3(1) are opened following the opening of the proceedings referred to in Article 3(2) in another Member State, Articles 31 to 35 shall apply to those opened first, in so far as the progress of those proceedings so permits.

Article 37. Conversion of earlier proceedings.   The liquidator in the main proceedings may request that proceedings listed in Annex A previously opened in another Member State be converted into winding-up proceedings if this proves to be in the interests of the creditors in the main proceedings.

   The court with jurisdiction under Article 3(2) shall order conversion into one of the proceedings listed in Annex B.

Article 38. Preservation measures.   Where the court of a Member State which has jurisdiction pursuant to Article 3(1) appoints a temporary administrator in order to ensure the preservation of the debtor's assets, that temporary administrator shall be empowered to request any measures to secure and preserve any of the debtor's assets situated in another Member State, provided for under the law of that State, for the period between the request for the opening of insolvency proceedings and the judgment opening the proceedings.

Chapter IV — Provision of information for creditors and lodgement of their claims

Article 39. Right to lodge claims.   Any creditor who has his habitual residence, domicile or registered office in a Member State other than the State of the opening of proceedings, including the tax authorities and social security authorities of Member States, shall have the right to lodge claims in the insolvency proceedings in writing.

Article 40. Duty to inform creditors.   1.   As soon as insolvency proceedings are opened in a Member State, the court of that State having jurisdiction or the liquidator appointed by it shall immediately inform known creditors who have their habitual residences, domiciles or registered offices in the other Member States.

   2.   That information, provided by an individual notice, shall in particular include time limits, the penalties laid down in regard to those time limits, the body or authority empowered to accept the lodgement of claims and the other measures laid down. Such notice shall also indicate whether creditors whose claims are preferential or secured in rem need lodge their claims.

Article 41. Content of the lodgement of a claim.   A creditor shall send copies of supporting documents, if any, and shall indicate the nature of the claim, the date on which it arose and its amount, as well as whether he alleges preference, security in rem or a reservation of title in respect of the claim and what assets are covered by the guarantee he is invoking.

Article 42. Languages. 1. The information provided for in Article 40 shall be provided in the official language or one of the official languages of the State of the opening of proceedings. For that purpose a form shall be used bearing the heading 'Invitation to lodge a claim. Time limits to be observed' in all the official languages of the institutions of the European Union.

2. Any creditor who has his habitual residence, domicile or registered office in a Member State other than the State of the opening of proceedings may lodge his claim in the official language or one of the official languages of that other State. In that event, however, the lodgement of his claim shall bear the heading 'Lodgement of claim' in the official language or one of the official languages of the State of the opening of proceedings. In addition, he may be required to provide a translation into the official language or one of the official languages of the State of the opening of proceedings.

Chapter V — Transitional and final provisions

Article 43. Applicability in time. The provisions of this Regulation shall apply only to insolvency proceedings opened after its entry into force. Acts done by a debtor before the entry into force of this Regulation shall continue to be governed by the law which was applicable to them at the time they were done.

Article 44. Relationship to Conventions. 1. After its entry into force, this Regulation replaces, in respect of the matters referred to therein, in the relations between Member States, the Conventions concluded between two or more Member States, in particular:

(a) the Convention between Belgium and France on Jurisdiction and the Validity and Enforcement of Judgments, Arbitration Awards and Authentic Instruments, signed at Paris on 8 July 1899;

(b) the Convention between Belgium and Austria on Bankruptcy, Winding-up, Arrangements, Compositions and Suspension of Payments (with Additional Protocol of 13 June 1973), signed at Brussels on 16 July 1969;

(c) the Convention between Belgium and the Netherlands on Territorial Jurisdiction, Bankruptcy and the Validity and Enforcement of Judgments, Arbitration Awards and Authentic Instruments, signed at Brussels on 28 March 1925;

(d) the Treaty between Germany and Austria on Bankruptcy, Winding-up, Arrangements and Compositions, signed at Vienna on 25 May 1979;

(e) the Convention between France and Austria on Jurisdiction, Recognition and Enforcement of Judgments on Bankruptcy, signed at Vienna on 27 February 1979;

(f) the Convention between France and Italy on the Enforcement of Judgments in Civil and Commercial Matters, signed at Rome on 3 June 1930;

(g) the Convention between Italy and Austria on Bankruptcy, Winding-up, Arrangements and Compositions, signed at Rome on 12 July 1977;

(h) the Convention between the Kingdom of the Netherlands and the Federal Republic of Germany on the Mutual Recognition and Enforcement of Judgments and other Enforceable Instruments in Civil and Commercial Matters, signed at The Hague on 30 August 1962;

(i) the Convention between the United Kingdom and the Kingdom of Belgium providing for the Reciprocal Enforcement of Judgments in Civil and Commercial Matters, with Protocol, signed at Brussels on 2 May 1934;

(j)   the Convention between Denmark, Finland, Norway, Sweden and Iceland on Bankruptcy, signed at Copenhagen on 7 November 1933;

(k)   the European Convention on Certain International Aspects of Bankruptcy, signed at Istanbul on 5 June 1990;

(l)   the Convention between the Federative People's Republic of Yugoslavia and the Kingdom of Greece on the Mutual Recognition and Enforcement of Judgments, signed at Athens on 18 June 1959;

(m)   the Agreement between the Federative People's Republic of Yugoslavia and the Republic of Austria on the Mutual Recognition and Enforcement of Arbitral Awards and Arbitral Settlements in Commercial Matters, signed at Belgrade on 18 March 1960;

(n)   the Convention between the Federative People's Republic of Yugoslavia and the Republic of Italy on Mutual Judicial Cooperation in Civil and Administrative Matters, signed at Rome on 3 December 1960;

(o)   the Agreement between the Socialist Federative Republic of Yugoslavia and the Kingdom of Belgium on Judicial Cooperation in Civil and Commercial Matters, signed at Belgrade on 24 September 1971;

(p)   the Convention between the Governments of Yugoslavia and France on the Recognition and Enforcement of Judgments in Civil and Commercial Matters, signed at Paris on 18 May 1971;

(q)   the Agreement between the Czechoslovak Socialist Republic and the Hellenic Republic on Legal Aid in Civil and Criminal Matters, signed at Athens on 22 October 1980, still in force between the Czech Republic and Greece;

(r)   the Agreement between the Czechoslovak Socialist Republic and the Republic of Cyprus on Legal Aid in Civil and Criminal Matters, signed at Nicosia on 23 April 1982, still in force between the Czech Republic and Cyprus;

(s)   the Treaty between the Government of the Czechoslovak Socialist Republic and the Government of the Republic of France on Legal Aid and the Recognition and Enforcement of Judgments in Civil, Family and Commercial Matters, signed at Paris on 10 May 1984, still in force between the Czech Republic and France;

(t)   the Treaty between the Czechoslovak Socialist Republic and the Italian Republic on Legal Aid in Civil and Criminal Matters, signed at Prague on 6 December 1985, still in force between the Czech Republic and Italy;

(u)   the Agreement between the Republic of Latvia, the Republic of Estonia and the Republic of Lithuania on Legal Assistance and Legal Relationships, signed at Tallinn on 11 November 1992;

(v)   the Agreement between Estonia and Poland on Granting Legal Aid and Legal Relations on Civil, Labour and Criminal Matters, signed at Tallinn on 27 November 1998;

(w)   the Agreement between the Republic of Lithuania and the Republic of Poland on Legal Assistance and Legal Relations in Civil, Family, Labour and Criminal Matters, signed in Warsaw on 26 January 1993;

(x)   the Convention between Socialist Republic of Romania and the Hellenic Republic on legal assistance in civil and criminal matters and its Protocol, signed at Bucharest on 19 October 1972;

(y)   the Convention between Socialist Republic of Romania and the French Republic on legal assistance in civil and commercial matters, signed at Paris on 5 November 1974;

(z)   the Agreement between the People's Republic of Bulgaria and the Hellenic Republic on Legal Assistance in Civil and Criminal Matters, signed at Athens on 10 April 1976;

(aa) the Agreement between the People's Republic of Bulgaria and the Republic of Cyprus on Legal Assistance in Civil and Criminal Matters, signed at Nicosia on 29 April 1983;

(ab) the Agreement between the Government of the People's Republic of Bulgaria and the Government of the French Republic on Mutual Legal Assistance in Civil Matters, signed at Sofia on 18 January 1989;

(ac) the Treaty between Romania and the Czech Republic on judicial assistance in civil matters, signed at Bucharest on 11 July 1994;

(ad) the Treaty between Romania and Poland on legal assistance and legal relations in civil cases, signed at Bucharest on 15 May 1999.

2.   The Conventions referred to in paragraph 1 shall continue to have effect with regard to proceedings opened before the entry into force of this Regulation.

3.   This Regulation shall not apply:

(a) in any Member State, to the extent that it is irreconcilable with the obligations arising in relation to bankruptcy from a convention concluded by that State with one or more third countries before the entry into force of this Regulation;

(b) in the United Kingdom of Great Britain and Northern Ireland, to the extent that is irreconcilable with the obligations arising in relation to bankruptcy and the winding-up of insolvent companies from any arrangements with the Commonwealth existing at the time this Regulation enters into force.

Article 45. Amendment of the Annexes.   The Council, acting by qualified majority on the initiative of one of its members or on a proposal from the Commission, may amend the Annexes.

Article 46. Reports.   No later than 1 June 2012, and every five years thereafter, the Commission shall present to the European Parliament, the Council and the Economic and Social Committee a report on the application of this Regulation. The report shall be accompanied if need be by a proposal for adaptation of this Regulation.

Article 47. Entry into force.   This Regulation shall enter into force on 31 May 2002.

Annex A

Insolvency proceedings referred to in Article 2(a)

BELGIË/BELGIQUE
— Het faillissement/La faillite
— De gerechtelijke reorganisatie door een collectief akkoord/La réorganisation judiciaire par accord collectif
— De gerechtelijke reorganisatie door overdracht onder gerechtlijk gezag/La réorganisation judiciaire par transfert sous autorité de justice
— De collectieve schuldenregeling/Le règlement collectif de dettes
— De vrijwillige vereffening/La liquidation volontaire
— De gerechtelijke vereffening/La liquidation judiciaire
— De voorlopige ontneming van beheer, bepaald in artikel 8 van de faillissementswet/Le dessaisissement provisoire, visé à l'article 8 de la loi sur les faillites

БЪЛГАРИЯ
— Производство по несъстоятелност

ČESKÁ REPUBLIKA
— Konkurz
— Reorganizace
— Oddlužení

DEUTSCHLAND
— Das Konkursverfahren
— Das gerichtliche Vergleichsverfahren
— Das Gesamtvollstreckungsverfahren
— Das Insolvenzverfahren

EESTI
— Pankrotimenetlus

ΕΛΛΑΔΑ
— Η πτώχευση
— Η ειδική εκκαθάριση
— Η προσωρινή διαχείριση εταιρείας. Η διοίκηση και διαχείριση των πιστωτών
— Η υπαγωγή επιχείρησης υπό επίτροπο με σκοπό τη σύναψη συμβιβασμού με τους πιστωτές

ESPAÑA
— Concurso

FRANCE
— Sauvegarde
— Redressement judiciaire
— Liquidation judiciaire

IRELAND
— Compulsory winding-up by the court
— Bankruptcy
— The administration in bankruptcy of the estate of persons dying insolvent
— Winding-up in bankruptcy of partnerships
— Creditors' voluntary winding-up (with confirmation of a court)
— Arrangements under the control of the court which involve the vesting of all or part of the property of the debtor in the official assignee for realisation and distribution
— Company examinership

ITALIA
— Fallimento
— Concordato preventivo
— Liquidazione coatta amministrativa
— Amministrazione straordinaria

ΚΥΠΡΟΣ
— Υποχρεωτική εκκαθάριση από το Δικαστήριο
— Εκούσια εκκαθάριση από πιστωτές κατόπιν Δικαστικού Διατάγματος
— Εκούσια εκκαθάριση από μέλη
— Εκκαθάριση με την εποπτεία του Δικαστηρίου
— Πτώχευση κατόπιν Δικαστικού Διατάγματος
— Διαχείριση της περιουσίας προσώπων που απεβίωσαν αφερέγγυα

LATVIJA
— Tiesiskās aizsardzības process
— Sanācija juridiskās personas maksātnespējas procesā
— Izlīgums juridiskās personas maksātnespējas procesā
— Izlīgums fiziskās personas maksātnespējas procesā
— Bankrota procedūra juridiskās personas maksātnespējas procesā
— Bankrota procedūra fiziskās personas maksātnespējas procesā

LIETUVA
— įmonės restruktūrizavimo byla
— įmonės bankroto byla
— įmonės bankroto procesas ne teismo tvarka

LUXEMBOURG
— Faillite
— Gestion contrôlée
— Concordat préventif de faillite (par abandon d'actif)
— Régime spécial de liquidation du notariat

MAGYARORSZÁG
— Csődeljárás
— Felszámolási eljárás

MALTA
— Xoljiment
— Amministrazzjoni
— Stralċ volontarju mill-membri jew mill-kredituri
— Stralċ mill-Qorti
— Falliment f'każ ta' negozjant

NEDERLAND
— Het faillissement
— De surséance van betaling
— De schuldsaneringsregeling natuurlijke personen

ÖSTERREICH
— Das Konkursverfahren
— Das Ausgleichsverfahren

POLSKA
— Postępowanie upadłościowe
— Postępowanie układowe
— Upadłość obejmująca likwidację
— Upadłość z możliwością zawarcia układu

PORTUGAL
— Processo de insolvência
— Processo de falência
— Processos especiais de recuperação de empresa, ou seja:
— Concordata
— Reconstituição empresarial
— Reestruturação financeira
— Gestão controlada

ROMÂNIA
— procedura insolvenţei
— reorganizarea judiciară
— procedura falimentului

SLOVENIJA
— Stečajni postopek
— Skrajšani stečajni postopek
— Postopek prisilne poravnave
— Prisilna poravnava v stečaju

SLOVENSKO
— Konkurzné konanie
— Reštrukturalizačné konanie

SUOMI/FINLAND
— Konkurssi/konkurs
— Yrityssaneeraus/företagssanering

SVERIGE
— Konkurs
— Företagsrekonstruktion

UNITED KINGDOM
— Winding-up by or subject to the supervision of the court
— Creditors' voluntary winding-up (with confirmation by the court)
— Administration, including appointments made by filing prescribed documents with the court
— Voluntary arrangements under insolvency legislation
— Bankruptcy or sequestration

Annex B

Winding-up proceedings referred to in Article 2(c)

BELGIË/BELGIQUE
— Het faillissement/La faillite
— De vrijwillige vereffening/La liquidation volontaire
— De gerechtelijke vereffening/La liquidation judiciaire
— De gerechtelijke reorganisatie door overdracht onder gerechtelijk gezag/La réorganisation judiciaire par transfert sous autorité de justice

БЪЛГАРИЯ
— Производство по несъстоятелност

ČESKÁ REPUBLIKA
— Konkurz

DEUTSCHLAND
— Das Konkursverfahren
— Das Gesamtvollstreckungsverfahren
— Das Insolvenzverfahren

EESTI
— Pankrotimenetlus

ΕΛΛΑΔΑ
— Η πτώχευση
— Η ειδική εκκαθάριση

ESPAÑA
— Concurso

FRANCE
— Liquidation judiciaire

IRELAND
— Compulsory winding-up
— Bankruptcy
— The administration in bankruptcy of the estate of persons dying insolvent
— Winding-up in bankruptcy of partnerships
— Creditors' voluntary winding-up (with confirmation of a court)
— Arrangements under the control of the court which involve the vesting of all or part of the property of the debtor in the official assignee for realisation and distribution

ITALIA
— Fallimento
— Concordato preventivo con cessione dei beni
— Liquidazione coatta amministrativa
— Amministrazione straordinaria con programma di cessione dei complessi aziendali
— Amministrazione straordinaria con programma di ristrutturazione di cui sia parte integrante un concordato con cessione dei beni

ΚΥΠΡΟΣ
— Υποχρεωτική εκκαθάριση από το Δικαστήριο
— Εκκαθάριση με την εποπτεία του Δικαστηρίου
— Εκούσια εκκαθάριση από πιστωτές (με την επικύρωση του Δικαστηρίου)
— Πτώχευση
— Διαχείριση της περιουσίας προσώπων που απεβίωσαν αφερέγγυα

LATVIJA
— Bankrota procedūra juridiskās personas maksātnespējas procesā
— Bankrota procedūra fiziskās personas maksātnespējas procesā

LIETUVA
— įmonės bankroto byla
— įmonės bankroto procesas ne teismo tvarka

LUXEMBOURG
— Faillite
— Régime spécial de liquidation du notariat

MAGYARORSZÁG
— Felszámolási eljárás

MALTA
— Stralċ volontarju
— Stralċ mill-Qorti
— Falliment inkluż il-ħruġ ta' mandat ta' qbid mill-Kuratur f'każ ta' negozjant fallut

NEDERLAND
— Het faillissement
— De schuldsaneringsregeling natuurlijke personen

ÖSTERREICH
— Das Konkursverfahren

POLSKA
— Postępowanie upadłościowe
— Upadłość obejmująca likwidację

PORTUGAL
 — Processo de insolvência
 — Processo de falência

ROMÂNIA
 — procedura falimentului

SLOVENIJA
 — Stečajni postopek
 — Skrajšani stečajni postopek

SLOVENSKO
 — Konkurzné konanie

SUOMI/FINLAND
 — Konkurssi/konkurs

SVERIGE
 — Konkurs

UNITED KINGDOM
 — Winding-up by or subject to the supervision of the court
 — Winding-up through administration, including appointments made by filing prescribed documents with the court
 — Creditors' voluntary winding-up (with confirmation by the court)
 — Bankruptcy or sequestration

Annex C

Liquidators referred to in Article 2(b)

BELGIË/BELGIQUE
 — De curator/Le curateur
 — De gedelegeerd rechter/Le juge-délégué
 — De gerechtsmandataris/Le mandataire de justice
 — De schuldbemiddelaar/Le médiateur de dettes
 — De vereffenaar/Le liquidateur
 — De voorlopige bewindvoerder/L'administrateur provisoire

БЪЛГАРИЯ
 — Назначен предварително временен синдик
 — Временен синдик
 — (Постоянен) синдик
 — Служебен синдик

ČESKÁ REPUBLIKA
— Insolvenční správce
— Předběžný insolvenční správce
— Oddělený insolvenční správce
— Zvláštní insolvenční správce
— Zástupce insolvenčního správce

DEUTSCHLAND
— Konkursverwalter
— Vergleichsverwalter
— Sachverwalter (nach der Vergleichsordnung)
— Verwalter
— Insolvenzverwalter
— Sachverwalter (nach der Insolvenzordnung)
— Treuhänder
— Vorläufiger Insolvenzverwalter

EESTI
— Pankrotihaldur
— Ajutine pankrotihaldur
— Usaldusisik

ΕΛΛΑΔΑ
— Ο σύνδικος
— Ο προσωρινός διαχειριστής. Η διοικούσα επιτροπή των πιστωτών
— Ο ειδικός εκκαθαριστής
— Ο επίτροπος

ESPAÑA
— Administradores concursales

FRANCE
— Mandataire judiciaire
— Liquidateur
— Administrateur judiciaire
— Commissaire à l'exécution du plan

IRELAND
— Liquidator
— Official assignee
— Trustee in bankruptcy
— Provisional liquidator
— Examiner

ITALIA
— Curatore
— Commissario giudiziale

— Commissario straordinario
— Commissario liquidatore
— Liquidatore giudiziale

ΚΥΠΡΟΣ

— Εκκαθαριστής και Προσωρινός Εκκαθαριστής
— Επίσημος Παραλήπτης
— Διαχειριστής της Πτώχευσης
— Εξεταστής

LATVIJA

— Maksātnespējas procesa administrators

LIETUVA

— Bankrutuojančių įmonių administratorius
— Restruktūrizuojamų įmonių administratorius

LUXEMBOURG

— Le curateur
— Le commissaire
— Le liquidateur
— Le conseil de gérance de la section d'assainissement du notariat

MAGYARORSZÁG

— Vagyonfelügyelő
— Felszámoló

MALTA

— Amministratur Proviżorju
— Riċevitur Uffiċjali
— Stralċjarju
— Manager Speċjali
— Kuraturi f'każ ta' proċeduri ta' falliment

NEDERLAND

— De curator in het faillissement
— De bewindvoerder in de surséance van betaling
— De bewindvoerder in de schuldsaneringsregeling natuurlijke personen

ÖSTERREICH

— Masseverwalter
— Ausgleichsverwalter
— Sachverwalter
— Treuhänder
— Besondere Verwalter
— Konkursgericht

POLSKA
— Syndyk
— Nadzorca sądowy
— Zarządca

PORTUGAL
— Administrador da insolvência
— Gestor judicial
— Liquidatário judicial
— Comissão de credores

ROMÂNIA
— practician în insolvenţă
— administrator judiciar
— lichidator

SLOVENIJA
— Upravitelj prisilne poravnave
— Stečajni upravitelj
— Sodišče, pristojno za postopek prisilne poravnave
— Sodišče, pristojno za stečajni postopek

SLOVENSKO
— Predbežný správca
— Správca

SUOMI/FINLAND
— Pesänhoitaja/boförvaltare
— Selvittäjä/utredare

SVERIGE
— Förvaltare
— Rekonstruktör

UNITED KINGDOM
— Liquidator
— Supervisor of a voluntary arrangement
— Administrator
— Official receiver
— Trustee
— Provisional liquidator
— Judicial factor

A.2. Declaration by the Council (OJ, C 183 of 30 June 2000)

Regulation (EC) No 1346/2000 shall not prevent a Member State from concluding agreements with non-Member States, which cover the same matter as this Regulation, where the agreement in question does not affect this Regulation.

A.3. Declaration by Portugal concerning the application of Articles 26 and 37 of Council Regulation (EC) No 1346/2000 of 29 May 2000 on insolvency proceedings (OJ, C 183 of 30 June 2000)

Article 37 of Council Regulation (EC) No 1346/2000 of 29 May 2000 on insolvency proceedings, which mentions the possibility of converting territorial proceedings opened prior to the main proceedings into winding-up proceedings, should be interpreted as meaning that such conversion does not exclude judicial appreciation of the state of the local proceedings (as is the case in Article 36) or of the application of the interests of public policy as provided for in Article 26.

A.4. Form for lodgement of claim

1. Personal data

....

2. Information about your claim
— Nature:
— Date:
— Amount: .... euro

Please supply copies of supporting documents

3. In respect of this claim, do you allege:

☐ Any preference

☐ Any security in rem

☐ Any reservation of title

Please cross the relevant box and give below a description of assets that are covered by the guarantee: ....

Done at ...., date ....

Signature ....

A.5.   Information notice 'Invitation to lodge a claim. Time limits to be observed'

This information notice is to be filled in and sent by the court or the liquidator to each creditor, immediately after the opening of the insolvency proceedings

1.   Information about the debtor

....

2.   Information about proceedings for the lodgement of claims
     —   Time limits:
     —   Penalties in regard to time limits:
     —   Body or authority empowered to accept the lodgement of claims:
     —   Other requirements:

3.   Information about certain categories of claims

Creditors whose claims are preferential or secured in rem:

☐   need lodge their claims

☐   are exempted to do so

Done at ...., date ....

Signature and/or stamp ....

A.6.   ECJ case-law regarding Regulation (EC) No 1346/2000

Article 1

ECJ, 17 March 2005, case C-294/02, AMI Semiconductor

The aim of Regulation No 1346/2000 is, as is clear in particular from recitals 2, 3, 4 and 8 in its preamble, to ensure the efficiency and proper coordination of insolvency proceedings within the European Union and thus to ensure equal distribution of available assets amongst all the creditors. The Community institutions would enjoy an unjustifiable advantage over the other creditors if they were allowed to pursue their claims in proceedings brought before the Community judicature when any action before national courts was impossible.

Article 3

ECJ, 17 January 2006, case C-1/04, Staubitz-Schreiber

Article 3(1) of Regulation No 1346/2000 must be interpreted as meaning that the court of the Member State within the territory of which the centre of the debtor's main interests is situated at the time when the debtor lodges the request to open insolvency proceedings retains jurisdiction to open those proceedings if the debtor moves the centre of his main interests to the territory of another Member State after lodging the request but before the proceedings are opened.

ECJ, 2 May 2006, case C-341/04, Eurofood

Where a debtor is a subsidiary company whose registered office and that of its parent company are situated in two different Member States, the presumption laid down in the second sentence of Article 3(1) of Regulation No 1346/2000, whereby the centre of main interests of that subsidiary is situated in the Member State where its registered office is situated, can be rebutted only if factors which are both objective and ascertainable by third parties enable it to be established that an actual situation exists which is different from that which location at that registered office is deemed to reflect. That could be so in particular in the case of a company not carrying out any business in the territory of the Member State in which its registered office is situated. By contrast, where a company carries on its business in the territory of the Member State where its registered office is situated, the mere fact that its economic choices are or can be controlled by a parent company in another Member State is not enough to rebut the presumption laid down by that Regulation.

ECJ, 12 February 2009, case C-339/07, Deko Marty

Article 3(1) of Regulation No 1346/2000 must be interpreted as meaning that the courts of the Member State within the territory of which insolvency proceedings have been opened have jurisdiction to decide an action to set a transaction aside by virtue of insolvency that is brought against a person whose registered office is in another Member State.

CJ, 21 January 2010, case C-444/07, MG Probud Gdynia

Regulation No 1346/2000, in particular Articles 3, 4, 16, 17 and 25, must be interpreted as meaning that, in a case such as that in the main action, after the main insolvency proceedings have been opened in a Member State the competent authorities of another Member State, in which no secondary insolvency proceedings have been opened, are required, subject to the grounds for refusal derived from Articles 25(3) and 26 of that Regulation, to recognise and enforce all judgments relating to the main insolvency proceedings and, therefore, are not entitled to order, pursuant to the legislation of that other Member State, enforcement measures relating to the assets of the debtor declared insolvent that are situated in its territory when the legislation of the State of the opening of proceedings does not so permit and the conditions to which application of Articles 5 and 10 of the Regulation is subject are not met.

Article 4

ECJ, 17 March 2005, case C-294/02, AMI Semiconductor

It appears that in the procedural laws of most of the Member States a creditor is not entitled to pursue his claims before the courts on an individual basis against a person who is the subject of insolvency proceedings but is required to observe the specific rules of the applicable procedure and that, if he fails to observe those rules, his action will be inadmissible. Moreover, the Member States are required, on a mutual basis, to respect proceedings commenced in any one of them. That is clear from Article 4(2)(f) of Regulation No 1346/2000 according to which the law governing the effects of insolvency proceedings brought by individual creditors is that of the State in which they were opened.

Article 7

ECJ, 10 September 2009, case C-292/08, German Graphics

The exception provided for in Article 1(2)(b) of Regulation No 44/2001, read in conjunction with Article 7(1) of Regulation No 1346/2000, must be interpreted, account being taken of the provisions of Article 4(2)(b) of the latter Regulation, as meaning that it does not apply to an action brought by a seller based on a reservation of title against a purchaser who is insolvent, where the asset covered by the reservation of title is situated in the Member State of the opening of those proceedings at the time of opening of those proceedings against that purchaser.

CJ, 21 January 2010, case C-444/07, MG Probud Gdynia

Regulation No 1346/2000, in particular Articles 3, 4, 16, 17 and 25, must be interpreted as meaning that, in a case such as that in the main action, after the main insolvency proceedings have been opened in a Member State the competent authorities of another Member State, in which no secondary insolvency proceedings have been opened, are required, subject to the grounds for refusal derived from Articles 25(3) and 26 of that Regulation, to recognise and enforce all judgments relating to the main insolvency proceedings and, therefore, are not entitled to order, pursuant to the legislation of that other Member State, enforcement measures relating to the assets of the debtor declared insolvent that are situated in its territory when the legislation of the State of the opening of proceedings does not so permit and the conditions to which application of Articles 5 and 10 of the Regulation is subject are not met.

Article 16

ECJ, 17 March 2005, case C-294/02, AMI Semiconductor

By virtue of Articles 16 and 17 of Regulation No 1346/2000, the opening of insolvency proceedings in a Member State is to be recognised in all the other Member States and is to produce the effects attributed thereto by the law of the State in which the proceedings are opened.

ECJ, 2 May 2006, case C-341/04, Eurofood

On a proper interpretation of the first subparagraph of Article 16(1) of Regulation No 1346/2000, the main insolvency proceedings opened by a court of a Member State must be recognised by the courts of the other Member States, without the latter being able to review the jurisdiction of the court of the opening State.

On a proper interpretation of the first subparagraph of Article 16(1) of the Regulation, a decision to open insolvency proceedings for the purposes of that provision is a decision handed down by a court of a Member State to which application for such a decision has been made, based on the debtor's insolvency and seeking the opening of proceedings referred to in Annex A to the Regulation, where that decision involves the divestment of the debtor and the appointment of a liquidator referred to in Annex C to the Regulation. Such divestment implies that the debtor loses the powers of management that he has over his assets.

CJ, 21 January 2010, case C-444/07, MG Probud Gdynia

Regulation No 1346/2000, in particular Articles 3, 4, 16, 17 and 25, must be interpreted as meaning that, in a case such as that in the main action, after the main insolvency proceedings have been opened in a Member State the competent authorities of another Member State, in which no secondary insolvency proceedings have been opened, are required, subject to the grounds for refusal derived from Articles 25(3) and 26 of that Regulation, to recognise and enforce all judgments relating to the main insolvency proceedings and, therefore, are not entitled to order, pursuant to the legislation of that other Member State, enforcement measures relating to the assets of the debtor declared insolvent that are situated in its territory when the legislation of the State of the opening of proceedings does not so permit and the conditions to which application of Articles 5 and 10 of the Regulation is subject are not met.

Article 17

ECJ, 17 March 2005, case C-294/02, AMI Semiconductor

By virtue of Articles 16 and 17 of Regulation No 1346/2000, the opening of insolvency proceedings in a Member State is to be recognised in all the other Member States and is to produce the effects attributed thereto by the law of the State in which the proceedings are opened.

The Commission may not invoke Article 40 of Regulation No 1346/2000 by referring to the period of two-and-a-half months which had elapsed between the opening of the insolvency proceedings, on 10 July 2002, and the giving of notice thereof on 23 September 2002, in order to oppose the application of the Regulation to this case. First, pursuant to Article 17(1) of the Regulation, the opening of insolvency proceedings takes effect in the other Member States without the need for any notice to be given under Article 40. Second, even if the notice given to the Commission might be regarded as belated, Regulation No 1346/2000 does not provide for such belatedness to have any repercussions on recognition of the proceedings in other Member States, subject to possible entitlement to compensation for harm caused by late notification.

CJ, 21 January 2010, case C-444/07, MG Probud Gdynia

Regulation No 1346/2000, in particular Articles 3, 4, 16, 17 and 25, must be interpreted as meaning that, in a case such as that in the main action, after the main insolvency proceedings have been opened in a Member State the competent authorities of another Member State, in which no secondary insolvency proceedings have been opened, are required, subject to the grounds for refusal derived from Articles 25(3) and 26 of that Regulation, to recognise and enforce all judgments relating to the main insolvency proceedings and, therefore, are not entitled to order, pursuant to the legislation of that other Member State, enforcement measures relating to the assets of the debtor declared insolvent that are situated in its territory when the legislation of the State of the opening of proceedings does not so permit and the conditions to which application of Articles 5 and 10 of the Regulation is subject are not met.

Article 25

ECJ, 10 September 2009, case C-292/08, German Graphics

Article 25(2) of Regulation No 1346/2000 must be interpreted as meaning that the words 'provided that that Convention is applicable' imply that, before it can be concluded that the recognition and enforcement provisions of Regulation No 44/2001 are applicable to judgments other than those referred to in Article 25(1) of Regulation No 1346/2000, it is necessary to determine whether such judgments fall outside the material scope of Regulation No 44/2001.

CJ, 21 January 2010, case C-444/07, MG Probud Gdynia

Regulation No 1346/2000, in particular Articles 3, 4, 16, 17 and 25, must be interpreted as meaning that, in a case such as that in the main action, after the main insolvency proceedings have been opened in a Member State the competent authorities of another Member State, in which no secondary insolvency proceedings have been opened, are required, subject to the grounds for refusal derived from Articles 25(3) and 26 of that Regulation, to recognise and enforce all judgments relating to the main insolvency proceedings and, therefore, are not entitled to order, pursuant to the legislation of that other Member State, enforcement measures relating to the assets of the debtor declared insolvent that are situated in its territory when the legislation of the State of the opening of proceedings does not so permit and the conditions to which application of Articles 5 and 10 of the Regulation is subject are not met.

Article 26

ECJ, 2 May 2006, case C-341/04, Eurofood

On a proper interpretation of Article 26 of Regulation No 1346/2000, a Member State may refuse to recognise insolvency proceedings opened in another Member State where the decision to open the proceedings was taken in flagrant breach of the fundamental right to be heard, which a person concerned by such proceedings enjoys.

Article 40

ECJ, 17 March 2005, case C-294/02, AMI Semiconductor

The Commission may not invoke Article 40 of Regulation No 1346/2000 by referring to the period of two-and-a-half months which had elapsed between the opening of the insolvency proceedings, on 10 July 2002, and the giving of notice thereof on 23 September 2002, in order to oppose the application of the Regulation to this case. First, pursuant to Article 17(1) of the Regulation, the opening of insolvency proceedings takes effect in the other Member States without the need for any notice to be given under Article 40. Second, even if the notice given to the Commission might be regarded as belated, Regulation No 1346/2000 does not provide for such belatedness to have any repercussions on recognition of the proceedings in other Member States, subject to possible entitlement to compensation for harm caused by late notification.

Article 43

ECJ, 17 January 2006, case C-1/04, Staubitz-Schreiber

The first sentence of Article 43 of Regulation No 1346/2000 lays down the principle governing the temporal conditions for application of that Regulation. That provision must be interpreted as applying if no judgment opening insolvency proceedings has been delivered before its entry into force on 31 May 2002, even if the request to open proceedings was lodged prior to that date.

ECJ, 12 February 2009, case C-339/07, Deko Marty

Article 3(1) of Regulation No 1346/2000 must be interpreted as meaning that the courts of the Member State within the territory of which insolvency proceedings have been opened have jurisdiction to decide an action to set a transaction aside by virtue of insolvency that is brought against a person whose registered office is in another Member State.

B. Directive 2001/24/EC of the European Parliament and of the Council of 4 April 2001 on the reorganisation and winding up of credit institutions (OJ, L 125 of 5 May 2001)

(1)   In accordance with the objectives of the Treaty, the harmonious and balanced development of economic activities throughout the Community should be promoted through the elimination of any obstacles to the freedom of establishment and the freedom to provide services within the Community.

(2)   At the same time as those obstacles are eliminated, consideration should be given to the situation which might arise if a credit institution runs into difficulties, particularly where that institution has branches in other Member States.

(3)   This Directive forms part of the Community legislative framework set up by Directive 2000/12/EC of the European Parliament and of the Council of 20 March 2000 relating to the taking up and pursuit of the business of credit institutions. It follows therefrom that, while they are in operation, a credit institution and its branches form a single entity subject to the supervision of the competent authorities of the State where authorisation valid throughout the Community was granted.

(4)   It would be particularly undesirable to relinquish such unity between an institution and its branches where it is necessary to adopt reorganisation measures or open winding-up proceedings.

(5)   The adoption of Directive 94/19/EC of the European Parliament and of the Council of 30 May 1994 on deposit-guarantee schemes, which introduced the principle of compulsory membership by credit institutions of a guarantee scheme in their home Member State, brings out even more clearly the need for mutual recognition of reorganisation measures and winding-up proceedings.

(6)   The administrative or judicial authorities of the home Member State must have sole power to decide upon and to implement the reorganisation measures provided for in the law and practices in force in that Member State. Owing to the difficulty of harmonising Member States' laws and practices, it is necessary to establish mutual recognition by the Member States of the measures taken by each of them to restore to viability the credit institutions which it has authorised.

(7)   It is essential to guarantee that the reorganisation measures adopted by the administrative or judicial authorities of the home Member State and the measures adopted by persons or bodies appointed by those authorities to administer those reorganisation measures, including measures involving the possibility of a suspension of payments, suspension of enforcement measures or reduction of claims and any other measure which could affect third parties' existing rights, are effective in all Member States.

(8)   Certain measures, in particular those affecting the functioning of the internal structure of credit institutions or managers' or shareholders' rights, need not be covered by this Directive to be effective in Member States insofar as, pursuant to the rules of private international law, the applicable law is that of the home State.

(9)   Certain measures, in particular those connected with the continued fulfilment of conditions of authorisation, are already the subject of mutual recognition pursuant to Directive 2000/12/EC insofar as they do not affect the rights of third parties existing before their adoption.

(10) Persons participating in the operation of the internal structures of credit institutions as well as managers and shareholders of such institutions, considered in those capacities, are not to be regarded as third parties for the purposes of this Directive.

(11) It is necessary to notify third parties of the implementation of reorganisation measures in Member States where branches are situated when such measures could hinder the exercise of some of their rights.

(12) The principle of equal treatment between creditors, as regards the opportunities open to them to take action, requires the administrative or judicial authorities of the home Member State to adopt such measures as are necessary for the creditors in the host Member State to be able to exercise their rights to take action within the time limit laid down.

(13) There must be some coordination of the role of the administrative or judicial authorities in reorganisation measures and winding-up proceedings for branches of credit institutions having head offices outside the Community and situated in different Member States.

(14) In the absence of reorganisation measures, or in the event of such measures failing, the credit institutions in difficulty must be wound up. Provision should be made in such cases for mutual recognition of winding-up proceedings and of their effects in the Community.

(15) The important role played by the competent authorities of the home Member State before winding-up proceedings are opened may continue during the process of winding up so that these proceedings can be properly carried out.

(16) Equal treatment of creditors requires that the credit institution is wound up according to the principles of unity and universality, which require the administrative or judicial authorities of the home Member State to have sole jurisdiction and their decisions to be recognised and to be capable of producing in all the other Member States, without any formality, the effects ascribed to them by the law of the home Member State, except where this Directive provides otherwise.

(17) The exemption concerning the effects of reorganisation measures and winding-up proceedings on certain contracts and rights is limited to those effects and does not cover other questions concerning reorganisation measures and winding-up proceedings such as the lodging, verification, admission and ranking of claims concerning those contracts and rights and the rules governing the distribution of the proceeds of the realisation of the assets, which are governed by the law of the home Member State.

(18) Voluntary winding up is possible when a credit institution is solvent. The administrative or judicial authorities of the home Member State may nevertheless, where appropriate, decide on a reorganisation measure or winding-up proceedings, even after voluntary winding up has commenced.

(19) Withdrawal of authorisation to pursue the business of banking is one of the consequences which winding up a credit institution necessarily entails. Withdrawal should not, however, prevent certain activities of the institution from continuing insofar as is necessary or appropriate for the purposes of winding up. Such a continuation of activity may nonetheless be made subject by the home Member State to the consent of, and supervision by, its competent authorities.

(20) Provision of information to known creditors on an individual basis is as essential as publication to enable them, where necessary, to lodge their claims or submit observations relating to their claims within the prescribed time limits. This should take

place without discrimination against creditors domiciled in a Member State other than the home Member State, based on their place of residence or the nature of their claims. Creditors must be kept regularly informed in an appropriate manner throughout winding-up proceedings.

(21) For the sole purpose of applying the provisions of this Directive to reorganisation measures and winding-up proceedings involving branches located in the Community of a credit institution of which the head office is situated in a third country, the definitions of 'home Member State', 'competent authorities' and 'administrative or judicial authorities' should be those of the Member State in which the branch is located.

(22) Where a credit institution which has its head office outside the Community possesses branches in more than one Member State, each branch should receive individual treatment in regard to the application of this Directive. In such a case, the administrative or judicial authorities and the competent authorities as well as the administrators and liquidators should endeavour to coordinate their activities.

(23) Although it is important to follow the principle that the law of the home Member State determines all the effects of reorganisation measures or winding-up proceedings, both procedural and substantive, it is also necessary to bear in mind that those effects may conflict with the rules normally applicable in the context of the economic and financial activity of the credit institution in question and its branches in other Member States. In some cases reference to the law of another Member State represents an unavoidable qualification of the principle that the law of the home Member State is to apply.

(24) That qualification is especially necessary to protect employees having a contract of employment with a credit institution, ensure the security of transactions in respect of certain types of property and protect the integrity of regulated markets functioning in accordance with the law of a Member State on which financial instruments are traded.

(25) Transactions carried out in the framework of a payment and settlement system are covered by Directive 98/26/EC of the European Parliament and of the Council of 19 May 1998 on settlement finality in payment and securities settlement systems.

(26) The adoption of this Directive does not call into question the provisions of Directive 98/26/EC according to which insolvency proceedings must not have any effect on the enforceability of orders validly entered into a system, or on collateral provided for a system.

(27) Some reorganisation measures or winding-up proceedings involve the appointment of a person to administer them. The recognition of his appointment and his powers in all other Member States is therefore an essential factor in the implementation of decisions taken in the home Member State. However, the limits within which he may exercise his powers when he acts outside the home Member State should be specified.

(28) Creditors who have entered into contracts with a credit institution before a reorganisation measure is adopted or winding-up proceedings are opened should be protected against provisions relating to voidness, voidability or unenforceability laid down in the law of the home Member State, where the beneficiary of the transaction produces evidence that in the law applicable to that transaction there is no available means of contesting the act concerned in the case in point.

(29) The confidence of third-party purchasers in the content of the registers or accounts regarding certain assets entered in those registers or accounts and by extension of the purchasers of immovable property should be safeguarded, even after winding-up proceedings have been opened or a reorganisation measure adopted. The only means of

safeguarding that confidence is to make the validity of the purchase subject to the law of the place where the immovable asset is situated or of the State under whose authority the register or account is kept.

(30) The effects of reorganisation measures or winding-up proceedings on a lawsuit pending are governed by the law of the Member State in which the lawsuit is pending, by way of exception to the application of the *lex concursus*. The effects of those measures and procedures on individual enforcement actions arising from such lawsuits are governed by the legislation of the home Member State, in accordance with the general rule established by this Directive.

(31) Provision should be made for the administrative or judicial authorities in the home Member State to notify immediately the competent authorities of the host Member State of the adoption of any reorganisation measure or the opening of any winding-up proceedings, if possible before the adoption of the measure or the opening of the proceedings, or, if not, immediately afterwards.

(32) Professional secrecy as defined in Article 30 of Directive 2000/12/EC is an essential factor in all information or consultation procedures. For that reason it should be respected by all the administrative authorities taking part in such procedures, whereas the judicial authorities remain, in this respect, subject to the national provisions relating to them...

Title I — Scope and definitions

Article 1. Scope. 1. This Directive shall apply to credit institutions and their branches set up in Member States other than those in which they have their head offices, as defined in points (1) and (3) of Article 1 of Directive 2000/12/EC, subject to the conditions and exemptions laid down in Article 2(3) of that Directive.

2. The provisions of this Directive concerning the branches of a credit institution having a head office outside the Community shall apply only where that institution has branches in at least two Member States of the Community.

Article 2. Definitions. For the purposes of this Directive:
— 'home Member State' shall mean the Member State of origin within the meaning of Article 1, point (6) of Directive 2000/12/EC;
— 'host Member State' shall mean the host Member State within the meaning of Article 1, point (7) of Directive 2000/12/EC;
— 'branch' shall mean a branch within the meaning of Article 1, point (3) of Directive 2000/12/EC;
— 'competent authorities' shall mean the competent authorities within the meaning of Article 1, point (4) of Directive 2000/12/EC;
— 'administrator' shall mean any person or body appointed by the administrative or judicial authorities whose task is to administer reorganisation measures;
— 'administrative or judicial authorities' shall mean such administrative or judicial authorities of the Member States as are competent for the purposes of reorganisation measures or winding-up proceedings;
— 'reorganisation measures' shall mean measures which are intended to preserve or restore the financial situation of a credit institution and which could affect third

parties' preexisting rights, including measures involving the possibility of a suspension of payments, suspension of enforcement measures or reduction of claims;

— 'liquidator' shall mean any person or body appointed by the administrative or judicial authorities whose task is to administer winding-up proceedings;

— 'winding-up proceedings' shall mean collective proceedings opened and monitored by the administrative or judicial authorities of a Member State with the aim of realising assets under the supervision of those authorities, including where the proceedings are terminated by a composition or other, similar measure;

— 'regulated market' shall mean a regulated market within the meaning of Article 1, point (13) of Directive 93/22/EEC;

— 'instruments' shall mean all the instruments referred to in Section B of the Annex to Directive 93/22/EEC.

Title II — Reorganisation measures

A.   Credit institutions having their head offices within the Community

Article 3. Adoption of reorganisation measures — applicable law.   1.   The administrative or judicial authorities of the home Member State shall alone be empowered to decide on the implementation of one or more reorganisation measures in a credit institution, including branches established in other Member States.

2.   The reorganisation measures shall be applied in accordance with the laws, regulations and procedures applicable in the home Member State, unless otherwise provided in this Directive.

They shall be fully effective in accordance with the legislation of that Member State throughout the Community without any further formalities, including as against third parties in other Member States, even where the rules of the host Member State applicable to them do not provide for such measures or make their implementation subject to conditions which are not fulfilled.

The reorganisation measures shall be effective throughout the Community once they become effective in the Member State where they have been taken.

Article 4. Information for the competent authorities of the host Member State.   The administrative or judicial authorities of the home Member State shall without delay inform, by any available means, the competent authorities of the host Member State of their decision to adopt any reorganisation measure, including the practical effects which such a measure may have, if possible before it is adopted or otherwise immediately thereafter. Information shall be communicated by the competent authorities of the home Member State.

Article 5. Information for the supervisory authorities of the home Member State.   Where the administrative or judicial authorities of the host Member State deem it necessary to implement within their territory one or more reorganisation measures, they shall inform the competent authorities of the home Member State accordingly. Information shall be communicated by the host Member State's competent authorities.

Article 6. Publication.   1.   Where implementation of the reorganisation measures decided on pursuant to Article 3(1) and (2) is likely to affect the rights of third parties in a host Member State and where an appeal may be brought in the home Member State against the decision ordering the measure, the administrative or judicial authorities of the home Member State, the administrator or any person empowered to do so in the home Member State shall publish an extract from the decision in the *Official Journal of the European Communities* and in two national newspapers in each host Member State, in order in particular to facilitate the exercise of the right of appeal in good time.

2.   The extract from the decision provided for in paragraph 1 shall be forwarded at the earliest opportunity, by the most appropriate route, to the Office for Official Publications of the European Communities and to the two national newspapers in each host Member State.

3.   The Office for Official Publications of the European Communities shall publish the extract at the latest within twelve days of its dispatch.

4.   The extract from the decision to be published shall specify, in the official language or languages of the Member States concerned, in particular the purpose and legal basis of the decision taken, the time limits for lodging appeals, specifically a clearly understandable indication of the date of expiry of the time limits, and the full address of the authorities or court competent to hear an appeal.

5.   The reorganisation measures shall apply irrespective of the measures prescribed in paragraphs 1 to 3 and shall be fully effective as against creditors, unless the administrative or judicial authorities of the home Member State or the law of that State governing such measures provide otherwise.

Article 7. Duty to inform known creditors and right to lodge claims.   1.   Where the legislation of the home Member State requires lodgement of a claim with a view to its recognition or provides for compulsory notification of the measure to creditors who have their domiciles, normal places of residence or head offices in that State, the administrative or judicial authorities of the home Member State or the administrator shall also inform known creditors who have their domiciles, normal places of residence or head offices in other Member States, in accordance with the procedures laid down in Articles 14 and 17(1).

2.   Where the legislation of the home Member State provides for the right of creditors who have their domiciles, normal places of residence or head offices in that State to lodge claims or to submit observations concerning their claims, creditors who have their domiciles, normal places of residence or head offices in other Member States shall also have that right in accordance with the procedures laid down in Article 16 and Article 17(2).

B.   Credit institutions having their head offices outside the Community

Article 8. Branches of third-country credit institutions.   1.   The administrative or judicial authorities of the host Member State of a branch of a credit institution having its head office outside the Community shall without delay inform, by any available means, the competent authorities of the other host Member States in which the institution has set up branches which are included on the list referred to in Article 11 of Directive 2000/12/EC and published each year in the *Official Journal of the European Communities,* of their decision to adopt any reorganisation measure, including the practical effects which that measure may have, if possible before it is adopted or otherwise immediately thereafter.

Information shall be communicated by the competent authorities of the host Member State whose administrative or judicial authorities decide to apply the measure.

2.   The administrative or judicial authorities referred to in paragraph 1 shall endeavour to coordinate their actions.

Title III — Winding-up proceedings

A.   Credit institutions having their head offices within the Community

Article 9. Opening of winding-up proceedings — Information to be communicated to other competent authorities.   1.   The administrative or judicial authorities of the home Member State which are responsible for winding up shall alone be empowered to decide on the opening of winding-up proceedings concerning a credit institution, including branches established in other Member States.

A decision to open winding-up proceedings taken by the administrative or judicial authority of the home Member State shall be recognised, without further formality, within the territory of all other Member States and shall be effective there when the decision is effective in the Member State in which the proceedings are opened.

2.   The administrative or judicial authorities of the home Member State shall without delay inform, by any available means, the competent authorities of the host Member State of their decision to open winding-up proceedings, including the practical effects which such proceedings may have, if possible before they open or otherwise immediately thereafter. Information shall be communicated by the competent authorities of the home Member State.

Article 10. Law applicable.   1.   A credit institution shall be wound up in accordance with the laws, regulations and procedures applicable in its home Member State insofar as this Directive does not provide otherwise.

2.   The law of the home Member State shall determine in particular:

(a)   the goods subject to administration and the treatment of goods acquired by the credit institution after the opening of winding-up proceedings;

(b)   the respective powers of the credit institution and the liquidator;

(c)   the conditions under which set-offs may be invoked;

(d)   the effects of winding-up proceedings on current contracts to which the credit institution is party;

(e)   the effects of winding-up proceedings on proceedings brought by individual creditors, with the exception of lawsuits pending, as provided for in Article 32;

(f)   the claims which are to be lodged against the credit institution and the treatment of claims arising after the opening of winding-up proceedings;

(g)   the rules governing the lodging, verification and admission of claims;

(h)   the rules governing the distribution of the proceeds of the realisation of assets, the ranking of claims and the rights of creditors who have obtained partial satisfaction after the opening of insolvency proceedings by virtue of a right *in re* or through a set-off;

(i)   the conditions for, and the effects of, the closure of insolvency proceedings, in particular by composition;

(j)   creditors' rights after the closure of winding-up proceedings;

(k)   who is to bear the costs and expenses incurred in the winding-up proceedings;

(l)   the rules relating to the voidness, voidability or unenforceability of legal acts detrimental to all the creditors.

Article 11. Consultation of competent authorities before voluntary winding up.   1.   The competent authorities of the home Member State shall be consulted in the most appropriate form before any voluntary winding-up decision is taken by the governing bodies of a credit institution.

2.   The voluntary winding up of a credit institution shall not preclude the adoption of a reorganisation measure or the opening of winding-up proceedings.

Article 12. Withdrawal of a credit institution's authorisation.   1.   Where the opening of winding-up proceedings is decided on in respect of a credit institution in the absence, or following the failure, of reorganisation measures, the authorisation of the institution shall be withdrawn in accordance with, in particular, the procedure laid down in Article 22(9) of Directive 2000/12/EC.

2.   The withdrawal of authorisation provided for in paragraph 1 shall not prevent the person or persons entrusted with the winding up from carrying on some of the credit institution's activities insofar as that is necessary or appropriate for the purposes of winding up.

The home Member State may provide that such activities shall be carried on with the consent, and under the supervision, of the competent authorities of that Member State.

Article 13. Publication.   The liquidators or any administrative or judicial authority shall announce the decision to open winding-up proceedings through publication of an extract from the winding-up decision in the *Official Journal of the European Communities* and at least two national newspapers in each of the host Member States.

Article 14. Provision of information to known creditors.   1.   When winding-up proceedings are opened, the administrative or judicial authority of the home Member State or the liquidator shall without delay individually inform known creditors who have their domiciles, normal places of residence or head offices in other Member States, except in cases where the legislation of the home State does not require lodgement of the claim with a view to its recognition.

2.   That information, provided by the dispatch of a notice, shall in particular deal with time limits, the penalties laid down in regard to those time limits, the body or authority empowered to accept the lodgement of claims or observations relating to claims and the other measures laid down. Such a notice shall also indicate whether creditors whose claims are preferential or secured *in re* need lodge their claims.

Article 15. Honouring of obligations.   Where an obligation has been honoured for the benefit of a credit institution which is not a legal person and which is the subject of winding-up proceedings opened in another Member State, when it should have been honoured for the benefit of the liquidator in those proceedings, the person honouring the obligation shall be deemed to have discharged it if he was unaware of the opening of proceedings. Where such an obligation is honoured before the publication provided for in Article 13 has been effected, the person honouring the obligation shall be presumed, in the absence of proof to the contrary, to have been unaware of the opening of winding-up proceedings;

where the obligation is honoured after the publication provided for in Article 13 has been effected, the person honouring the obligation shall be presumed, in the absence of proof to the contrary, to have been aware of the opening of proceedings.

Article 16. Right to lodge claims.   1.   Any creditor who has his domicile, normal place of residence or head office in a Member State other than the home Member State, including Member States' public authorities, shall have the right to lodge claims or to submit written observations relating to claims.

2.   The claims of all creditors whose domiciles, normal places of residence or head offices are in Member States other than the home Member State shall be treated in the same way and accorded the same ranking as claims of an equivalent nature which may be lodged by creditors having their domiciles, normal places of residence, or head offices in the home Member State.

3.   Except in cases where the law of the home Member State provides for the submission of observations relating to claims, a creditor shall send copies of supporting documents, if any, and shall indicate the nature of the claim, the date on which it arose and its amount, as well as whether he alleges preference, security *in re* or reservation of title in respect of the claim and what assets are covered by his security.

Article 17. Languages.   1.   The information provided for in Articles 13 and 14 shall be provided in the official language or one of the official languages of the home Member State. For that purpose a form shall be used bearing, in all the official languages of the European Union, the heading 'Invitation to lodge a claim. Time limits to be observed' or, where the law of the home Member State provides for the submission of observations relating to claims, the heading 'Invitation to submit observations relating to a claim. Time limits to be observed'.

2.   Any creditor who has his domicile, normal place of residence or head office in a Member State other than the home Member State may lodge his claim or submit observations relating to his claim in the official language or one of the official languages of that other Member State. In that event, however, the lodgement of his claim or the submission of observations on his claim shall bear the heading 'Lodgement of claim' or 'Submission of observations relating to claims' in the official language or one of the official languages of the home Member State. In addition, he may be required to provide a translation into that language of the lodgement of claim or submission of observations relating to claims.

Article 18. Regular provision of information to creditors.   Liquidators shall keep creditors regularly informed, in an appropriate manner, particularly with regard to progress in the winding up.

B.   Credit institutions the head offices of which are outside the Community

Article 19. Branches of third-country credit institutions.   1.   The administrative or judicial authorities of the host Member State of the branch of a credit institution the head office of which is outside the Community shall without delay inform, by any available means, the competent authorities of the other host Member States in which the credit institution has set up branches on the list referred to in Article 11 of Directive 2000/12/EC and published each year in the *Official Journal of the European Communities*, of their decision to open winding-up proceedings, including the practical effects which these proceedings may have, if possible before they open or otherwise immediately thereafter.

Information shall be communicated by the competent authorities of the first abovementioned host Member State.

2. Administrative or judicial authorities which decide to open proceedings to wind up a branch of a credit institution the head office of which is outside the Community shall inform the competent authorities of the other host Member States that winding-up proceedings have been opened and authorisation withdrawn.

Information shall be communicated by the competent authorities in the host Member State which has decided to open the proceedings.

3. The administrative or judicial authorities referred to in paragraph 1 shall endeavour to coordinate their actions.

Any liquidators shall likewise endeavour to coordinate their actions.

Title IV — Provisions common to reorganisation measures and winding-up proceedings

Article 20. Effects on certain contracts and rights. The effects of a reorganisation measure or the opening of winding-up proceedings on:

(a) employment contracts and relationships shall be governed solely by the law of the Member State applicable to the employment contract;

(b) a contract conferring the right to make use of or acquire immovable property shall be governed solely by the law of the Member State within the territory of which the immovable property is situated. That law shall determine whether property is movable or immovable;

(c) rights in respect of immovable property, a ship or an aircraft subject to registration in a public register shall be governed solely by the law of the Member State under the authority of which the register is kept.

Article 21. Third parties' rights in re. 1. The adoption of reorganisation measures or the opening of winding-up proceedings shall not affect the rights *in re* of creditors or third parties in respect of tangible or intangible, movable or immovable assets — both specific assets and collections of indefinite assets as a whole which change from time to time — belonging to the credit institution which are situated within the territory of another Member State at the time of the adoption of such measures or the opening of such proceedings.

2. The rights referred to in paragraph 1 shall in particular mean:

(a) the right to dispose of assets or have them disposed of and to obtain satisfaction from the proceeds of or income from those assets, in particular by virtue of a lien or a mortgage;

(b) the exclusive right to have a claim met, in particular a right guaranteed by a lien in respect of the claim or by assignment of the claim by way of a guarantee;

(c) the right to demand the assets from, and/or to require restitution by, anyone having possession or use of them contrary to the wishes of the party so entitled;

(d) a right *in re* to the beneficial use of assets.

3. The right, recorded in a public register and enforceable against third parties, under which a right *in re* within the meaning of paragraph 1 may be obtained, shall be considered a right *in re*.

4.   Paragraph 1 shall not preclude the actions for voidness, voidability or unenforceability laid down in Article 10(2)(l).

Article 22. Reservation of title.   1.   The adoption of reorganisation measures or the opening of winding-up proceedings concerning a credit institution purchasing an asset shall not affect the seller's rights based on a reservation of title where at the time of the adoption of such measures or opening of such proceedings the asset is situated within the territory of a Member State other than the State in which the said measures were adopted or the said proceedings were opened.

2.   The adoption of reorganisation measures or the opening of winding-up proceedings concerning a credit institution selling an asset, after delivery of the asset, shall not constitute grounds for rescinding or terminating the sale and shall not prevent the purchaser from acquiring title where at the time of the adoption of such measures or the opening of such proceedings the asset sold is situated within the territory of a Member State other than the State in which such measures were adopted or such proceedings were opened.

3.   Paragraphs 1 and 2 shall not preclude the actions for voidness, voidability or unenforceability laid down in Article 10(2)(l).

Article 23. Set-off.   1.   The adoption of reorganisation measures or the opening of winding-up proceedings shall not affect the right of creditors to demand the set-off of their claims against the claims of the credit institution, where such a set-off is permitted by the law applicable to the credit institution's claim.

2.   Paragraph 1 shall not preclude the actions for voidness, voidability or unenforceability laid down in Article 10(2)(l).

Article 24. Lex rei sitae.   The enforcement of proprietary rights in instruments or other rights in such instruments the existence or transfer of which presupposes their recording in a register, an account or a centralised deposit system held or located in a Member State shall be governed by the law of the Member State where the register, account, or centralised deposit system in which those rights are recorded is held or located.

Article 25. Netting agreements.   Netting agreements shall be governed solely by the law of the contract which governs such agreements.

Article 26. Repurchase agreements.   Without prejudice to Article 24, repurchase agreements shall be governed solely by the law of the contract which governs such agreements.

Article 27. Regulated markets.   Without prejudice to Article 24, transactions carried out in the context of a regulated market shall be governed solely by the law of the contract which governs such transactions.

Article 28. Proof of liquidators' appointment.   1.   The administrator or liquidator's appointment shall be evidenced by a certified copy of the original decision appointing him or by any other certificate issued by the administrative or judicial authority of the home Member State.

A translation into the official language or one of the official languages of the Member State within the territory of which the administrator or liquidator wishes to act may be required. No legalisation or other similar formality shall be required.

2.   Administrators and liquidators shall be entitled to exercise within the territory of all the Member States all the powers which they are entitled to exercise within the territory of the home Member State. They may also appoint persons to assist or, where appropriate, represent them in the course of the reorganisation measure or winding-up proceedings, in particular in host Member States and, specifically, in order to help overcome any difficulties encountered by creditors in the host Member State.

3.   In exercising his powers, an administrator or liquidator shall comply with the law of the Member States within the territory of which he wishes to take action, in particular with regard to procedures for the realisation of assets and the provision of information to employees. Those powers may not include the use of force or the right to rule on legal proceedings or disputes.

Article 29. Registration in a public register.   1.   The administrator, liquidator or any administrative or judicial authority of the home Member State may request that a reorganisation measure or the decision to open winding-up proceedings be registered in the land register, the trade register and any other public register kept in the other Member States.

A Member State may, however, prescribe mandatory registration. In that event, the person or authority referred to in the preceding subparagraph shall take all the measures necessary to ensure such registration.

2.   The costs of registration shall be regarded as costs and expenses incurred in the proceedings.

Article 30. Detrimental acts.   1.   Article 10 shall not apply as regards the rules relating to the voidness, voidability or unenforceability of legal acts detrimental to the creditors as a whole, where the beneficiary of these acts provides proof that:

— the act detrimental to the creditors as a whole is subject to the law of a Member State other than the home Member State, and

— that law does not allow any means of challenging that act in the case in point.

2.   Where a reorganisation measure decided on by a judicial authority provides for rules relating to the voidness, voidability or unenforceability of legal acts detrimental to the creditors as a whole performed before adoption of the measure, Article 3(2) shall not apply in the cases provided for in paragraph 1 of this Article.

Article 31. Protection of third parties.   Where, by an act concluded after the adoption of a reorganisation measure or the opening of winding-up proceedings, a credit institution disposes, for consideration, of:

— an immovable asset;

— a ship or an aircraft subject to registration in a public register, or

— instruments or rights in such instruments the existence or transfer of which presupposes their being recorded in a register, an account or a centralised deposit system held or located in a Member State,

the validity of that act shall be governed by the law of the Member State within the territory of which the immovable asset is situated or under the authority of which that register, account or deposit system is kept.

Article 32. Lawsuits pending.   The effects of reorganisation measures or winding-up proceedings on a pending lawsuit concerning an asset or a right of which the credit institution has been divested shall be governed solely by the law of the Member State in which the lawsuit is pending.

Article 33. Professional secrecy.   All persons required to receive or divulge information in connection with the information or consultation procedures laid down in Articles 4, 5, 8, 9, 11 and 19 shall be bound by professional secrecy, in accordance with the rules and conditions laid down in Article 30 of Directive 2000/12/EC, with the exception of any judicial authorities to which existing national provisions apply.

Title V — Final provisions

Article 34. Implementation.   1.   Member States shall bring into force the laws, regulations and administrative provisions necessary to comply with this Directive on 5 May 2004. They shall forthwith inform the Commission thereof.

National provisions adopted in application of this Directive shall apply only to reorganisation measures or winding-up proceedings adopted or opened after the date referred to in the first subparagraph. Measures adopted or proceedings opened before that date shall continue to be governed by the law that was applicable to them at the time of adoption or opening.

2.   When Member States adopt these measures, they shall contain a reference to this Directive or shall be accompanied by such reference on the occasion of their official publication. The methods of making such reference shall be laid down by Member States.

3.   Member States shall communicate to the Commission the texts of the main provisions of national law which they adopt in the field governed by this Directive. ...

C.   Directive 2009/138/EC of the European Parliament and of the Council of 25 November 2009 on the taking-up and pursuit of the business of Insurance and Reinsurance (Solvency II) (recast) (OJ, L 335 of 17 December 2009)[1]

(105)   All policy holders and beneficiaries should receive equal treatment regardless of their nationality or place of residence. For this purpose, each Member State should ensure that all measures taken by a supervisory authority on the basis of that supervisory authority's national mandate are not regarded as contrary to the interests of that Member

---

[1] This Directive will replace Directive 2001/17/EC of the European Parliament and of the Council of 19 March 2001 on the reorganisation and winding-up of insurance undertakings (OJ, L 110 of 20 April 2001), starting from 1 November 2012. The relevant provisions of the latter are reported below. For the provisions of this Directive concerning the law applicable to insurance contracts and company law see Chapters VI, Insurance contracts, B, and IX, General provisions, N.

State or of policy holders and beneficiaries in that Member State. In all situations of settling of claims and winding-up, assets should be distributed on an equitable basis to all relevant policy holders, regardless of their nationality or place of residence.

Title I — Scope and definitions

Article 1. Scope.   1.   This Directive applies to reorganisation measures and winding-up proceedings concerning insurance undertakings.

2.   This Directive also applies, to the extent provided for in Article 30, to reorganisation measures and winding-up proceedings concerning branches in the territory of the Community of insurance undertakings having their head office outside the Community.

Article 2. Definitions.   For the purpose of this Directive:

(a)   'insurance undertaking' means an undertaking which has received official authorisation in accordance with Article 6 of Directive 73/239/EEC or Article 6 of Directive 79/267/EEC;

(b)   'branch' means any permanent presence of an insurance undertaking in the territory of a Member State other than the home Member State which carries out insurance business;

(c)   'reorganisation measures' means measures involving any intervention by administrative bodies or judicial authorities which are intended to preserve or restore the financial situation of an insurance undertaking and which affect pre-existing rights of parties other than the insurance undertaking itself, including but not limited to measures involving the possibility of a suspension of payments, suspension of enforcement measures or reduction of claims;

(d)   'winding-up proceedings' means collective proceedings involving realising the assets of an insurance undertaking and distributing the proceeds among the creditors, shareholders or members as appropriate, which necessarily involve any intervention by the administrative or the judicial authorities of a Member State, including where the collective proceedings are terminated by a composition or other analogous measure, whether or not they are founded on insolvency or are voluntary or compulsory;

(e)   'home Member State' means the Member State in which an insurance undertaking has been authorised in accordance with Article 6 of Directive 73/239/EEC or Article 6 of Directive 79/267/EEC;

(f)   'host Member State' means the Member State other than the home Member State in which an insurance undertaking has a branch;

(g)   'competent authorities' means the administrative or judicial authorities of the Member States which are competent for the purposes of the reorganisation measures or the winding-up proceedings;

(h)   'supervisory authorities' means the competent authorities within the meaning of Article 1(k) of Directive 92/49/EEC and of Article 1(l) of Directive 92/96/EEC;

(i)   'administrator' means any person or body appointed by the competent authorities for the purpose of administering reorganisation measures;

(j)   'liquidator' means any person or body appointed by the competent authorities or by the governing bodies of an insurance undertaking, as appropriate, for the purpose of administering winding-up proceedings;

(k)   'insurance claims' means any amount which is owed by an insurance undertaking to insured persons, policy holders, beneficiaries or to any injured party having direct right of action against the insurance undertaking and which arises from an insurance contract or from any operation provided for in Article 1(2) and (3), of Directive 79/267/EEC in direct insurance business, including amounts set aside for the aforementioned persons, when some elements of the debt are not yet known. The premiums owed by an insurance undertaking as a result of the non-conclusion or cancellation of these insurance contracts and operations in accordance with the law applicable to such contracts or operations before the opening of the winding-up proceedings shall also be considered insurance claims.

Title II — Reorganisation measures

Article 3. Scope.   This Title applies to the reorganisation measures defined in Article 2(c).

Article 4. Adoption of reorganisation measures — Applicable law.   1.   Only the competent authorities of the home Member State shall be entitled to decide on the reorganisation measures with respect to an insurance undertaking, including its branches in other Member States. The reorganisation measures shall not preclude the opening of winding-up proceedings by the home Member State.

2.   The reorganisation measures shall be governed by the laws, regulations and procedures applicable in the home Member State, unless otherwise provided in Articles 19 to 26.

3.   The reorganisation measures shall be fully effective throughout the Community in accordance with the

(116)   Insurance and reinsurance undertakings which are part of a group, the head of which is outside the Community should be subject to equivalent and appropriate group supervisory arrangements. It is therefore necessary to provide for transparency of rules

---

legislation of the home Member State without any further formalities, including against third parties in other Member States, even if the legislation of those other Member States does not provide for such reorganisation measures or alternatively makes their implementation subject to conditions which are not fulfilled.

4.   The reorganisation measures shall be effective throughout the Community once they become effective in the Member State where they have been taken.

Article 5. Information to the supervisory authorities.   The competent authorities of the home Member State shall inform as a matter of urgency the home Member State's supervisory authorities of their decision on any reorganisation measure, where possible before the adoption of such a measure and failing that immediately thereafter. The supervisory authorities of the home Member State shall inform as a matter of urgency the supervisory authorities of all other Member States of the decision to adopt reorganisation measures including the possible practical effects of such measures.

Article 6. Publication.   1.   Where an appeal is possible in the home Member State against a reorganisation measure, the competent authorities of the home Member State, the administrator or any person entitled to do so in the home Member State shall make public its decision on a reorganisation measure in accordance with the publication procedures provided for in the home Member State and, furthermore, publish in the *Official Journal of the European Communities* at the earliest opportunity an extract from the document establishing the reorganisation measure. The supervisory authorities of all the other Member States which have been informed of the decision on a reorganisation measure pursuant to Article 5 may ensure the publication of such decision within their territory in the manner they consider appropriate.

2.   The publications provided for in paragraph 1 shall also specify the competent authority of the home Member State, the applicable law as provided in Article 4(2) and the administrator appointed, if any. They shall be carried out in the official language or in one of the official languages of the Member State in which the information is published.

3.   The reorganisation measures shall apply regardless of the provisions concerning publication set out in paragraphs 1 and 2 and shall be fully effective as against creditors, unless the competent authorities of the home Member State or the law of that State provide otherwise.

4.   When reorganisation measures affect exclusively the rights of shareholders, members or employees of an insurance undertaking, considered in those capacities, this Article shall not apply unless the law applicable to these reorganisation measures provides otherwise. The competent authorities shall determine the manner in which the interested parties affected by such reorganisation measures shall be informed in accordance with the relevant legislation.

Article 7. Information to known creditors — Right to lodge claims.   1.   Where the legislation of the home Member State requires lodgement of a claim with a view to its recognition or provides for compulsory notification of a reorganisation measure to creditors who have their normal place of residence, domicile or head office in that State, the competent authorities of the home Member State or the administrator shall also inform known creditors who have their normal place of residence, domicile or head office in another Member State, in accordance with the procedures laid down in Articles 15 and 17(1).

2.   Where the legislation of the home Member State provides for the right of creditors who have their normal place of residence, domicile or head office in that State to lodge claims or to submit observations concerning their claims, creditors who have their normal place of residence, domicile or head office in another Member State shall have the same right to lodge claims or submit observations in accordance with the procedures laid down in Articles 16 and 17(2).

Title III — Winding-up proceedings

Article 8. Opening of winding-up proceedings — Information to the supervisory authorities.   1.   Only the competent authorities of the home Member State shall be entitled to take a decision concerning the opening of winding-up proceedings with regard to an insurance undertaking, including its branches in other Member States. This decision may be taken in the absence, or following the adoption, of reorganisation measures.

2.   A decision adopted according to the home Member State's legislation concerning the opening of winding-up proceedings of an insurance undertaking, including its branches in other Member States, shall be recognised without further formality within the territory of all other Member States and shall be effective there as soon as the decision is effective in the Member State in which the proceedings are opened.

and exchange of information with third-country authorities in all relevant circumstances. In order to ensure a harmonised approach to the determination and assessment of equivalence of third-country insurance and reinsurance supervision, provision should be

---

3. The supervisory authorities of the home Member State shall be informed as a matter of urgency of the decision to open winding-up proceedings, if possible before the proceedings are opened and failing that immediately thereafter. The supervisory authorities of the home Member State shall inform as a matter of urgency the supervisory authorities of all other Member States of the decision to open winding-up proceedings including the possible practical effects of such proceedings.

Article 9. Applicable law. 1. The decision to open winding-up proceedings with regard to an insurance under-taking, the winding-up proceedings and their effects shall be governed by the laws, regulations and administrative provisions applicable in its home Member State unless otherwise provided in Articles 19 to 26.

2. The law of the home Member State shall determine in particular:

(a) the assets which form part of the estate and the treatment of assets acquired by, or devolving on, the insurance undertaking after the opening of the winding-up proceedings;

(b) the respective powers of the insurance undertaking and the liquidator;

(c) the conditions under which set-off may be invoked;

(d) the effects of the winding-up proceedings on current contracts to which the insurance undertaking is party;

(e) the effects of the winding-up proceedings on proceedings brought by individual creditors, with the exception of lawsuits pending as provided for in Article 26;

(f) the claims which are to be lodged against the insurance undertaking's estate and the treatment of claims arising after the opening of winding-up proceedings;

(g) the rules governing the lodging, verification and admission of claims;

(h) the rules governing the distribution of proceeds from the realisation of assets, the ranking of claims, and the rights of creditors who have obtained partial satisfaction after the opening of winding-up proceedings by virtue of a right in rem or through a set-off;

(i) the conditions for and the effects of closure of winding-up proceedings, in particular by composition;

(j) creditors' rights after the closure of winding-up proceedings;

(k) who is to bear the cost and expenses incurred in the winding-up proceedings;

(l) the rules relating to the voidness, voidability or unenforceability of legal acts detrimental to all the creditors.

Article 10. Treatment of insurance claims. 1. Member States shall ensure that insurance claims take precedence over other claims on the insurance undertaking according to one or both of the following methods:

(a) insurance claims shall, with respect to assets representing the technical provisions, take absolute precedence over any other claim on the insurance undertaking;

(b) insurance claims shall, with respect to the whole of the insurance undertaking's assets, take precedence over any other claim on the insurance undertaking with the only possible exception of:

(i) claims by employees arising from employment contracts and employment relationships,

(ii) claims by public bodies on taxes,

(iii) claims by social security systems,

(iv) claims on assets subject to rights in rem.

2. Without prejudice to paragraph 1, Member States may provide that the whole or a part of the expenses arising from the winding-up procedure, as defined by their national legislation, shall take precedence over insurance claims.

3. Member States which have opted for the method provided for in paragraph 1(a) shall require that insurance undertakings establish and keep up to date a special register in line with the provisions set out in the Annex.

Article 11. Subrogation to a guarantee scheme. The home Member State may provide that, where the rights of insurance creditors have been subrogated to a guarantee scheme established in that Member State, claims by that scheme shall not benefit from the provisions of Article 10(1).

Article 12. Representation of preferential claims by assets. By way of derogation from Article 18 of Directive 73/239/EEC and Article 21 of Directive 79/267/EEC, Member States which apply the method set out in Article 10(1)(b) of this Directive shall require every insurance undertaking to represent, at any moment and inde-pendently from a possible winding-up, the claims which may take precedence over insurance claims pursuant to Article 10(1)(b) and which are registered in the insurance undertaking's accounts, by assets mentioned in Article 21 of Directive 92/49/EEC and Article 21 of Directive 92/96/EEC.

made for the Commission to make a binding decision regarding the equivalence of third-country solvency regimes. For third countries regarding which no decision has been made by the Commission the assessment of equivalence should be made by the group supervisor after consulting the other relevant supervisory authorities.

Article 13. Withdrawal of the authorisation.   1.   Where the opening of winding-up proceedings is decided in respect of an insurance undertaking, the authorisation of the insurance undertaking shall be withdrawn, except to the extent necessary for the purposes of paragraph 2, in accordance with the procedure laid down in Article 22 of Directive 73/239/EEC and Article 26 of Directive 79/267/EEC, if the authorisation has not been previously withdrawn.

   2.   The withdrawal of authorisation pursuant to paragraph 1 shall not prevent the liquidator or any other person entrusted by the competent authorities from carrying on some of the insurance undertakings' activities in so far as that is necessary or appropriate for the purposes of winding-up. The home Member State may provide that such activities shall be carried on with the consent and under the supervision of the supervisory authorities of the home Member State.

Article 14. Publication.   1.   The competent authority, the liquidator or any person appointed for that purpose by the competent authority shall publish the decision to open winding-up proceedings in accordance with the publication procedures provided for in the home Member State and also publish an extract from the winding-up decision in the *Official Journal of the European Communities*. The supervisory authorities of all the other Member States which have been informed of the decision to open winding-up proceedings in accordance with Article 8(3) may ensure the publication of such decision within their territories in the manner they consider appropriate.

2.   The publication of the decision to open winding-up proceedings provided for in paragraph 1 shall also specify the competent authority of the home Member State, the applicable law and the liquidator appointed. It shall be in the official language or in one of the official languages of the Member State in which the information is published.

Article 15. Information to known creditors.   1.   When winding-up proceedings are opened, the competent authorities of the home Member State, the liquidator or any person appointed for that purpose by the competent authorities shall without delay individually inform by written notice each known creditor who has his normal place of residence, domicile or head office in another Member State thereof.

   2.   The notice referred to in paragraph 1 shall in particular deal with time limits, the penalties laid down with regard to those time limits, the body or authority empowered to accept the lodgement of claims or observations relating to claims and the other measures laid down. The notice shall also indicate whether creditors whose claims are preferential or secured in rem need to lodge their claims. In the case of insurance claims, the notice shall further indicate the general effects of the winding-up proceedings on the insurance contracts, in particular, the date on which the insurance contracts or the operations will cease to produce effects and the rights and duties of insured persons with regard to the contract or operation.

Article 16. Right to lodge claims.   1.   Any creditor who has his normal place of residence, domicile or head office in a Member State other than the home Member State, including Member States' public authorities, shall have the right to lodge claims or to submit written observations relating to claims.

   2.   The claims of all creditors who have their normal place of residence, domicile or head office in a Member State other than the home Member State, including the aforementioned authorities, shall be treated in the same way and accorded the same ranking as claims of an equivalent nature lodgeable by creditors who have their normal place of residence, domicile or head office in the home Member State.

   3.   Except in cases where the law of the home Member State allows otherwise, a creditor shall send copies of supporting documents, if any, and shall indicate the nature of the claim, the date on which it arose and the amount, whether he alleges preference, security in rem or reservation of title in respect of the claim and what assets are covered by his security. The precedence granted to insurance claims by Article 10 need not be indicated.

Article 17. Languages and form.   1.   The information in the notice referred to in Article 15 shall be provided in the official language or one of the official languages of the home Member State. For that purpose a form shall be used bearing the heading 'Invitation to lodge a claim; time limits to be observed' or, where the law of the home Member State provides for the submission of observations relating to claims, 'Invitation to submit observations relating to a claim; time limits to be observed', in all the official languages of the European Union.

   However, where a known creditor is a holder of an insurance claim, the information in the notice referred to in Article 15 shall be provided in the official language or one of the official languages of the Member State in which the creditor has his normal place of residence, domicile or head office.

(117)   Since national legislation concerning reorganisation measures and winding-up proceedings is not harmonised, it is appropriate, in the framework of the internal market, to ensure the mutual recognition of reorganisation measures and winding-up legislation of the Member States concerning insurance undertakings, as well as the

---

2.   Any creditor who has his normal place of residence, domicile or head office in a Member State other than the home Member State may lodge his claim or submit observations relating to his claim in the official language or one of the official languages of that other Member State. However, in that event the lodgement of his claim or the submission of observations on his claim, as appropriate, shall bear the heading 'Lodgement of claim' or 'Submission of observations relating to claims', as appropriate, in the official language or one of the official languages of the home Member State.

Article 18. Regular information to the creditors.   1.   Liquidators shall keep creditors regularly informed, in an appropriate manner, in particular regarding the progress of the winding-up.
2.   The supervisory authorities of the Member States may request information on developments in the winding-up procedure from the supervisory authorities of the home Member State.

Title IV — Provision common to reorganisation measures and winding-up proceedings

Article 19. Effects on certain contracts and rights.   By way of derogation from Articles 4 and 9, the effects of the opening of reorganisation measures or of winding-up proceedings on the contracts and rights specified below shall be governed by the following rules:
   (a)   employment contracts and employment relationships shall be governed solely by the law of the Member State applicable to the employment contract or employment relationship;
   (b)   a contract conferring the right to make use of or acquire immovable property shall be governed solely by the law of the Member State in whose territory the immovable property is situated;
   (c)   rights of the insurance undertaking with respect to immovable property, a ship or an aircraft subject to registration in a public register shall be governed by the law of the Member State under whose authority the register is kept.

Article 20. Third parties' rights in rem.   1.   The opening of reorganisation measures or winding-up proceedings shall not affect the rights in rem of creditors or third parties in respect of tangible or intangible, movable or im-movable assets — both specific assets and collections of indefinite assets as a whole which change from time to time — belonging to the insurance undertaking which are situated within the territory of another Member State at the time of the opening of such measures or proceedings.
2.   The rights referred to in paragraph 1 shall in particular mean:
   (a)   the right to dispose of assets or have them disposed of and to obtain satisfaction from the proceeds of or income from those assets, in particular by virtue of a lien or a mortgage;
   (b)   the exclusive right to have a claim met, in particular a right guaranteed by a lien in respect of the claim or by assignment of the claim by way of a guarantee;
   (c)   the right to demand the assets from, and/or to require restitution by, anyone having possession or use of them contrary to the wishes of the party so entitled;
   (d)   a right in rem to the beneficial use of assets.
3.   The right, recorded in a public register and enforceable against third parties, under which a right in rem within the meaning of paragraph 1 may be obtained, shall be considered a right in rem.
4.   Paragraph 1 shall not preclude actions for voidness, voidability or unenforceability referred to in Article 9(2)(l).

Article 21. Reservation of title.   1.   The opening of reorganisation measures or winding-up proceedings against an insurance undertaking purchasing an asset shall not affect the seller's rights based on a reservation of title where at the time of the opening of such measures or proceedings the asset is situated within the territory of a Member State other than the State in which such measures or proceedings were opened.
2.   The opening of reorganisation measures or winding-up proceedings against an insurance undertaking selling an asset, after delivery of the asset, shall not constitute grounds for rescinding or terminating the sale and shall not prevent the purchaser from acquiring title where at the time of the opening of such measures or proceedings the asset sold is situated within the territory of a Member State other than the State in which such measures or proceedings were opened.
3.   Paragraphs 1 and 2 shall not preclude actions for voidness, voidability or unenforceability referred to in Article 9(2)(l).

necessary cooperation, taking into account the need for unity, universality, coordination and publicity for such measures and the equivalent treatment and protection of insurance creditors.

Article 22. Set-off.   1. The opening of reorganisation measures or winding-up proceedings shall not affect the right of creditors to demand the set-off of their claims against the claims of the insurance undertaking, where such a set-off is permitted by the law applicable to the insurance undertaking's claim.

2.   Paragraph 1 shall not preclude actions for voidness, voidability or unenforceability referred to in Article 9(2)(l).

Article 23. Regulated markets.   1.   Without prejudice to Article 20 the effects of a reorganisation measure or the opening of winding-up proceedings on the rights and obligations of the parties to a regulated market shall be governed solely by the law applicable to that market.

2.   Paragraph 1 shall not preclude any action for voidness, voidability, or unenforceability referred to in Article 9(2)(l) which may be taken to set aside payments or transactions under the law applicable to that market.

Article 24. Detrimental acts.   Article 9(2)(l) shall not apply, where a person who has benefited from a legal act detrimental to all the creditors provides proof that:

(a) the said act is subject to the law of a Member State other than the home Member State, and

(b) that law does not allow any means of challenging that act in the relevant case.

Article 25. Protection of third-party purchasers.   Where, by an act concluded after the adoption of a reorganisation measure or the opening of winding-up proceedings, an insurance undertaking disposes, for a consideration, of:

(a)   an immovable asset,

(b)   a ship or an aircraft subject to registration in a public register, or

(c)   transferable or other securities whose existence or transfer presupposes entry in a register or account laid down by law or which are placed in a central deposit system governed by the law of a Member State, the validity of that act shall be governed by the law of the Member State within whose territory the immovable asset is situated or under whose authority the register, account or system is kept.

Article 26. Lawsuits pending.   The effects of reorganisation measures or winding-up proceedings on a pending lawsuit concerning an asset or a right of which the insurance undertaking has been divested shall be governed solely by the law of the Member State in which the lawsuit is pending.

Article 27. Administrators and liquidators.   1.   The administrator's or liquidator's appointment shall be evidenced by a certified copy of the original decision appointing him or by any other certificate issued by the competent authorities of the home Member State.

A translation into the official language or one of the official languages of the Member State within the territory of which the administrator or liquidator wishes to act may be required. No legalisation or other similar formality shall be required.

2.   Administrators and liquidators shall be entitled to exercise within the territory of all the Member States all the powers which they are entitled to exercise within the territory of the home Member State. Persons to assist or, where appropriate, represent administrators and liquidators may be appointed, according to the home Member State's legislation, in the course of the reorganisation measure or winding-up proceedings, in particular in host Member States and, specifically, in order to help overcome any difficulties encountered by creditors in the host Member State.

3.   In exercising his powers according to the home Member State's legislation, an administrator or liquidator shall comply with the law of the Member States within whose territory he wishes to take action, in particular with regard to procedures for the realisation of assets and the informing of employees. Those powers may not include the use of force or the right to rule on legal proceedings or disputes.

Article 28. Registration in a public register.   1.   The administrator, liquidator or any other authority or person duly empowered in the home Member State may request that a reorganisation measure or the decision to open winding-up proceedings be registered in the land register, the trade register and any other public register kept in the other Member States.

However, if a Member State prescribes mandatory registration, the authority or person referred to in subparagraph 1 shall take all the measures necessary to ensure such registration.

2.   The costs of registration shall be regarded as costs and expenses incurred in the proceedings.

(118)   It should be ensured that reorganisation measures which were adopted by the competent authority of a Member State in order to preserve or restore the financial soundness of an insurance undertaking and to prevent as far as possible a winding-up situation, produce full effects throughout the Community. However, the effects of any such reorganisation measures as well as winding-up proceedings vis-à-vis third countries should not be affected.

(119)   A distinction should be made between the competent authorities for the purposes of reorganisation measures and winding-up proceedings and the supervisory authorities of the insurance undertakings.

(120)   The definition of a branch for insolvency purposes, should, in accordance with existing insolvency principles, take account of the single legal personality of the insurance undertaking. However, the legislation of the home Member State should determine the manner in which the assets and liabilities held by independent persons who have a permanent authority to act as agent for an insurance undertaking are to be treated in the winding-up of that insurance undertaking.

(121)   Conditions should be laid down under which winding-up proceedings which, without being founded on insolvency, involve a priority order for the payment of insurance claims, fall within the scope of this Directive. Claims by the employees of an insurance undertaking arising from employment contracts and employment relationships should be capable of being subrogated to a national wage guarantee scheme. Such

---

Article 29. Professional secrecy.   All persons required to receive or divulge information in connection with the procedures of communication laid down in Articles 5, 8 and 30 shall be bound by professional secrecy, in the same manner as laid down in Article 16 of Directive 92/49/EEC and Article 15 of Directive 92/96/EEC, with the exception of any judicial authorities to which existing national provisions apply.

Article 30. Branches of third country insurance undertakings.   1.   Notwithstanding the definitions laid down in Article 2(e), (f) and (g) and for the purpose of applying the provisions of this Directive to the reorganisation measures and winding-up proceedings concerning a branch situated in a Member State of an insurance undertaking whose head office is located outside the Community:

(a)   'home Member State' means the Member State in which the branch has been granted authorisation according to Article 23 of Directive 73/239/EEC and Article 27 of Directive 79/267/EEC, and

(b)   'supervisory authorities' and 'competent authorities' mean such authorities of the Member State in which the branch was authorised.

2.   When an insurance undertaking whose head office is outside the Community has branches established in more than one Member State, each branch shall be treated independently with regard to the application of this Directive. The competent authorities and the supervisory authorities of these Member States shall endeavour to coordinate their actions. Any administrators or liquidators shall likewise endeavour to coordinate their actions.

Article 31. Implementation of this Directive.   1.   Member States shall bring into force the laws, regulations and administrative provisions necessary to comply with this Directive before 20 April 2003. They shall forthwith inform the Commission thereof.

When Member States adopt these measures, they shall contain a reference to this Directive or shall be accompanied by such reference on the occasion of their official publication. The methods of making such reference shall be laid down by Member States.

2.   National provisions adopted in application of this Directive shall apply only to reorganisation measures or winding-up proceedings adopted or opened after the date referred to in paragraph 1. Reorganisation measures adopted or winding up proceedings opened before that date shall continue to be governed by the law that was applicable to them at the time of adoption or opening.

3.   Member States shall communicate to the Commission the text of the main provisions of domestic law which they adopt in the field governed by this Directive.

subrogated claims should benefit from the treatment determined by the law of the home Member State (lex concursus).

(122)   Reorganisation measures do not preclude the opening of winding-up proceedings. Winding-up proceedings should therefore be able to be opened in the absence of, or following, the adoption of reorganisation measures and they may terminate with composition or other analogous measures, including reorganisation measures.

(123)   Only the competent authorities of the home Member State should be empowered to take decisions on winding-up proceedings concerning insurance undertakings. The decisions should produce their effects throughout the Community and should be recognised by all Member States. The decisions should be published in accordance with the procedures of the home Member State and in the *Official Journal of the European Union*. Information should also be made available to known creditors who are resident in the Community, who should have the right to lodge claims and submit observations.

(124)   All the assets and liabilities of the insurance undertaking should be taken into consideration in the winding-up proceedings.

(125)   All the conditions for the opening, conduct and closure of winding-up proceedings should be governed by the law of the home Member State.

(126)   In order to ensure coordinated action amongst the Member States the supervisory authorities of the home Member State and those of all the other Member States should be informed as a matter of urgency of the opening of winding-up proceedings.

(127)   It is of utmost importance that insured persons, policy holders, beneficiaries and any injured party having a direct right of action against the insurance undertaking on a claim arising from insurance operations be protected in winding-up proceedings, it being understood that such protection does not include claims which arise not from obligations under insurance contracts or insurance operations but from civil liability caused by an agent in negotiations for which, according to the law applicable to the insurance contract or operation, the agent is not responsible under such insurance contract or operation. In order to achieve that objective, Member States should be provided with a choice between equivalent methods to ensure special treatment for insurance creditors, none of those methods impeding a Member State from establishing a ranking between different categories of insurance claim. Furthermore, an appropriate balance should be ensured between the protection of insurance creditors and other privileged creditors protected under the legislation of the Member State concerned.

(128)   The opening of winding-up proceedings should involve the withdrawal of the authorisation to conduct business granted to the insurance undertaking unless this has already occurred.

(129)   Creditors should have the right to lodge claims or to submit written observations in winding-up proceedings. Claims by creditors resident in a Member State other than the home Member State should be treated in the same way as equivalent claims in the home Member State without discrimination on grounds of nationality or residence.

(130)   In order to protect legitimate expectations and the certainty of certain transactions in Member States other than the home Member State, it is necessary to determine the law applicable to the effects of reorganisation measures and winding-up proceedings on pending lawsuits and on individual enforcement actions arising from lawsuits.

Title I — General rules on the taking-up and pursuit of direct insurance and reinsurance activities

Chapter I — Subject matter, scope and definitions

Section 1 — Subject matter and scope

Article 1. Subject matter.   This Directive lays down rules concerning the following: ...
    (3) the reorganisation and winding-up of direct insurance undertakings.

Chapter VIII — Right of establishment and freedom to provide services

Section 5 — Treatment of contracts of branches in winding-up proceedings

Article 160. Winding-up of insurance undertakings.   Where an insurance undertaking is wound up, commitments arising out of contracts underwritten through a branch or under the freedom to provide services shall be met in the same way as those arising out of the other insurance contracts of that undertaking, without distinction as to nationality as far as the persons insured and the beneficiaries are concerned.

Article 161. Winding-up of reinsurance undertakings.   Where a reinsurance undertaking is wound up, commitments arising out of contracts underwritten through a branch or under the freedom to provide services shall be met in the same way as those arising out of the other reinsurance contracts of that undertaking.

Title IV — Reorganisation and winding-up of insurance undertakings

Chapter I — Scope and definitions

Article 267. Scope of this Title.   This Title shall apply to reorganisation measures and winding-up proceedings concerning the following:
    (a) insurance undertakings;
    (b) branches situated in the territory of the Community of third-country insurance undertakings.

Article 268. Definitions.   1.   For the purpose of this Title the following definitions shall apply:
    (a) 'competent authorities' means the administrative or judicial authorities of the Member States which are competent for the purposes of the reorganisation measures or the winding-up proceedings;
    (b) 'branch' means a permanent presence of an insurance undertaking in the territory of a Member State other than the home Member State which pursues insurance activities;
    (c) 'reorganisation measures' means measures involving any intervention by the competent authorities which are intended to preserve or restore the financial situation of an insurance undertaking and which affect pre-existing rights of parties other than the

insurance undertaking itself, including but not limited to measures involving the possibility of a suspension of payments, suspension of enforcement measures or reduction of claims;

(d) 'winding-up proceedings' means collective proceedings involving the realisation of the assets of an insurance undertaking and the distribution of the proceeds among the creditors, shareholders or members as appropriate, which necessarily involve any intervention by the competent authorities, including where the collective proceedings are terminated by a composition or other analogous measure, whether or not they are founded on insolvency or are voluntary or compulsory;

(e) 'administrator' means a person or body appointed by the competent authorities for the purpose of administering reorganisation measures;

(f) 'liquidator' means a person or body appointed by the competent authorities or by the governing bodies of an insurance undertaking for the purpose of administering winding-up proceedings;

(g) 'insurance claim' means an amount which is owed by an insurance undertaking to insured persons, policy holders, beneficiaries or to any injured party having direct right of action against the insurance undertaking and which arises from an insurance contract or from any operation provided for in Article 2(3)(b) and (c) in direct insurance business, including an amount set aside for those persons, when some elements of the debt are not yet known.

The premium owed by an insurance undertaking as a result of the non-conclusion or cancellation of an insurance contract or operation referred to in point (g) of the first subparagraph in accordance with the law applicable to such a contract or operation before the opening of the winding-up proceedings shall also be considered an insurance claim.

2.   For the purpose of applying this Title to reorganisation measures and winding-up proceedings concerning a branch situated in a Member State of a third-country insurance undertaking the following definitions shall apply:

(a) 'home Member State' means the Member State in which the branch was granted authorisation in accordance with Articles 145 to 149;

(b) 'supervisory authorities' means the supervisory authorities of the home Member State;

(c) 'competent authorities' means the competent authorities of the home Member State.

Chapter II — Reorganisation measures

Article 269. Adoption of reorganisation measures applicable law.   1.   Only the competent authorities of the home Member State shall be entitled to decide on the reorganisation measures with respect to an insurance undertaking, including its branches.

2.   The reorganisation measures shall not preclude the opening of winding-up proceedings by the home Member State.

3.   The reorganisation measures shall be governed by the laws, regulations and procedures applicable in the home Member State, unless otherwise provided in Articles 285 to 292.

4.   Reorganisation measures taken in accordance with the legislation of the home Member State shall be fully effective throughout the Community without any further formalities, including against third parties in other Member States, even where the legislation of those other Member States does not provide for such reorganisation

measures or alternatively makes their implementation subject to conditions which are not fulfilled.

5. The reorganisation measures shall be effective throughout the Community once they become effective in the home Member State.

Article 270. Information to the supervisory authorities. The competent authorities of the home Member State shall inform as a matter of urgency the supervisory authorities of that Member State of their decision on any reorganisation measure, where possible before the adoption of such a measure and failing that immediately thereafter.

The supervisory authorities of the home Member State shall inform as a matter of urgency the supervisory authorities of all other Member States of the decision to adopt reorganisation measures including the possible practical effects of such measures.

Article 271. Publication of decisions on reorganisation measures. 1. Where an appeal is possible in the home Member State against a reorganisation measure, the competent authorities of the home Member State, the administrator or any person entitled to do so in the home Member State shall make public the decision on a reorganisation measure in accordance with the publication procedures provided for in the home Member State and, furthermore, publish in the *Official Journal of the European Union* at the earliest opportunity an extract from the document establishing the reorganisation measure.

The supervisory authorities of the other Member States which have been informed of the decision on a reorganisation measure pursuant to Article 270 may ensure the publication of such decision within their territory in the manner they consider appropriate.

2. The publications provided for in paragraph 1 shall specify the competent authority of the home Member State, the applicable law as provided in Article 269(3) and the administrator appointed, if any. They shall be made in the official language or in one of the official languages of the Member State in which the information is published.

3. The reorganisation measures shall apply regardless of the provisions concerning publication set out in paragraphs 1 and 2 and shall be fully effective as against creditors, unless the competent authorities of the home Member State or the law of that Member State provide otherwise.

4. Where reorganisation measures affect exclusively the rights of shareholders, members or employees of an insurance undertaking, considered in those capacities, paragraphs 1, 2 and 3 shall not apply unless the law applicable to the reorganisation measures provides otherwise.

The competent authorities shall determine the manner in which the parties referred to in the first subparagraph are to be informed in accordance with the applicable law.

Article 272. Information to known creditors right to lodge claims. 1. Where the law of the home Member State requires a claim to be lodged in order for it to be recognised or provides for compulsory notification of a reorganisation measure to creditors whose habitual residence, domicile or head office is situated in that Member State, the competent authorities of the home Member State or the administrator shall also inform known creditors whose habitual residence, domicile or head office is situated in another Member State, in accordance with Article 281 and Article 283(1).

2.   Where the law of the home Member State provides for the right of creditors whose habitual residence, domicile or head office is situated in that Member State to lodge claims or to submit observations concerning their claims, creditors whose habitual residence, domicile or head office is situated in another Member State shall have the same right in accordance with Article 282 and Article 283(2).

Chapter III — Winding-up proceedings

Article 273. Opening of winding-up proceedings information to the supervisory authorities.   1.   Only the competent authorities of the home Member State shall be entitled to take a decision concerning the opening of winding-up proceedings with regard to an insurance undertaking, including its branches in other Member States. This decision may be taken in the absence, or following the adoption, of reorganisation measures.

2.   A decision concerning the opening of winding-up proceedings of an insurance undertaking, including its branches in other Member States, adopted in accordance with the legislation of the home Member State shall be recognised without further formality throughout the Community and shall be effective there as soon as the decision is effective in the Member State in which the proceedings are opened.

3.   The competent authorities of the home Member State shall inform as a matter of urgency the supervisory authorities of that Member State of the decision to open winding-up proceedings, where possible before the proceedings are opened and failing that immediately thereafter.

The supervisory authorities of the home Member State shall inform as a matter of urgency the supervisory authorities of all other Member States of the decision to open winding-up proceedings including the possible practical effects of such proceedings.

Article 274. Applicable law.   1.   The decision to open winding-up proceedings with regard to an insurance undertaking, the winding-up proceedings and their effects shall be governed by the law applicable in the home Member State unless otherwise provided in Articles 285 to 292.

2.   The law of the home Member State shall determine at least the following:

(a)   the assets which form part of the estate and the treatment of assets acquired by, or devolving to, the insurance undertaking after the opening of the winding-up proceedings;

(b)   the respective powers of the insurance undertaking and the liquidator;

(c)   the conditions under which set-off may be invoked;

(d)   the effects of the winding-up proceedings on current contracts to which the insurance undertaking is party;

(e)   the effects of the winding-up proceedings on proceedings brought by individual creditors, with the exception of lawsuits pending referred to in Article 292;

(f)   the claims which are to be lodged against the estate of the insurance undertaking and the treatment of claims arising after the opening of winding-up proceedings;

(g)   the rules governing the lodging, verification and admission of claims;

(h)   the rules governing the distribution of proceeds from the realisation of assets, the ranking of claims, and the rights of creditors who have obtained partial satisfaction after the opening of winding-up proceedings by virtue of a right in rem or through a set-off;

(i)   the conditions for and the effects of closure of winding-up proceedings, in particular by composition;

(j)   rights of the creditors after the closure of winding-up proceedings;

(k) the party who is to bear the cost and expenses incurred in the winding-up proceedings; and

(l)   the rules relating to the nullity, voidability or unenforceability of legal acts detrimental to all the creditors.

Article 275. Treatment of insurance claims.   1.   Member States shall ensure that insurance claims take precedence over other claims against the insurance undertaking in one or both of the following ways:

(a) with regard to assets representing the technical provisions, insurance claims shall take absolute precedence over any other claim on the insurance undertaking; or

(b) with regard to the whole of the assets of the insurance undertaking, insurance claims shall take precedence over any other claim on the insurance undertaking with the only possible exception of the following:

(i)   claims by employees arising from employment contracts and employment relationships;

(ii) claims by public bodies on taxes;

(iii) claims by social security systems;

(iv) claims on assets subject to rights in rem.

2.   Without prejudice to paragraph 1, Member States may provide that the whole or part of the expenses arising from the winding-up procedure, as determined by their national law, shall take precedence over insurance claims.

3.   Member States which have chosen the option provided for in paragraph 1(a) shall require insurance undertakings to establish and keep up to date a special register in accordance with Article 276.

Article 276. Special register.   1.   Every insurance undertaking shall keep at its head office a special register of the assets used to cover the technical provisions calculated and invested in accordance with the law of the home Member State.

2.   Where an insurance undertaking carries on both life and non-life insurance activities, it shall keep at its head office separate registers for each type of business.

However, where a Member State authorises insurance undertakings to cover life and the risks listed in classes 1 and 2 of Part A of Annex I, it may provide that those insurance undertakings must keep a single register for the whole of their activities.

3.   The total value of the assets entered, valued in accordance with the law applicable in the home Member State, shall at no time be less than the value of the technical provisions.

4.   Where an asset entered in the register is subject to a right in rem in favour of a creditor or a third party, with the result that part of the value of the asset is not available for the purpose of covering commitments, that fact shall be recorded in the register and the amount not available shall not be included in the total value referred to in paragraph 3.

5.   The treatment of an asset in the case of the winding-up of the insurance undertaking with respect to the option provided for in Article 275(1)(a) shall be determined by the legislation of the home Member State, except where Articles 286, 287 or 288 apply to that asset where:

(a) the asset used to cover technical provisions is subject to a right in rem in favour of a creditor or a third party, without meeting the conditions set out in paragraph 4;

(b)   such an asset is subject to a reservation of title in favour of a creditor or of a third party; or

(c)   a creditor has a right to demand the set-off of his claim against the claim of the insurance undertaking.

6.   Once winding-up proceedings have been opened, the composition of the assets entered in the register in accordance with paragraphs 1 to 5 shall not be changed and no alteration other than the correction of purely clerical errors shall be made in the registers, except with the authorisation of the competent authority.

However, the liquidators shall add to those assets the yield therefrom and the value of the pure premiums received in respect of the class of insurance concerned between the opening of the winding-up proceedings and the time of payment of the insurance claims or until any transfer of portfolio is effected.

7.   Where the product of the realisation of assets is less than their estimated value in the registers, the liquidators shall justify this to the supervisory authorities of the home Member States.

Article 277. Subrogation to a guarantee scheme.   The home Member State may provide that, where the rights of insurance creditors have been subrogated to a guarantee scheme established in that Member State, claims by that scheme shall not benefit from the provisions of Article 275(1).

Article 278. Representation of preferential claims by assets.   Member States which choose the option set out in Article 275(1)(b) shall require every insurance undertaking to ensure that the claims which may take precedence over insurance claims pursuant to Article 275(1)(b) and which are registered in the insurance undertaking's accounts are represented, at any moment and independently of a possible winding-up, by assets.

Article 279. Withdrawal of the authorisation.   1.   Where the opening of winding-up proceedings is decided in respect of an insurance undertaking, the authorisation of that undertaking shall be withdrawn in accordance with the procedure laid down in Article 144, except to the extent necessary for the purposes of paragraph 2.

2.   The withdrawal of authorisation pursuant to paragraph 1 shall not prevent the liquidator or any other person appointed by the competent authorities from pursuing some of the activities of the insurance undertaking in so far as that is necessary or appropriate for the purposes of winding-up.

The home Member State may provide that such activities shall be pursued with the consent and under the supervision of the supervisory authorities of that Member State.

Article 280. Publication of decisions on winding-up proceedings.   1.   The competent authority, the liquidator or any person appointed for that purpose by the competent authority shall publish the decision to open winding-up proceedings in accordance with the publication procedures provided for in the home Member State and also publish an extract from the winding-up decision in the *Official Journal of the European Union.*

The supervisory authorities of all other Member States which have been informed of the decision to open winding-up proceedings in accordance with Article 273(3) may ensure the publication of such decision within their territories in the manner they consider appropriate.

2.   The publication referred to in paragraph 1 shall specify the competent authority of the home Member State, the applicable law and the liquidator appointed. It shall be in the official language or in one of the official languages of the Member State in which the information is published.

Article 281. Information to known creditors.   1.   When winding-up proceedings are opened, the competent authorities of the home Member State, the liquidator or any person appointed for that purpose by the competent authorities shall without delay individually inform by written notice each known creditor whose habitual residence, domicile or head office is situated in another Member State.

2.   The notice referred to in paragraph 1 shall cover time-limits, the sanctions laid down with regard to those time-limits, the body or authority empowered to accept the lodging of claims or observations relating to claims and any other measures.

The notice shall also indicate whether creditors whose claims are preferential or secured in rem need to lodge their claims.

In the case of insurance claims, the notice shall further indicate the general effects of the winding-up proceedings on the insurance contracts, in particular, the date on which the insurance contracts or the operations will cease to produce effects and the rights and duties of insured persons with regard to the contract or operation.

Article 282. Right to lodge claims.   1.   Any creditor, including public authorities of Member States, whose habitual residence, domicile or head office is situated in a Member State other than the home Member State shall have the right to lodge claims or to submit written observations relating to claims.

2.   The claims of all creditors referred to in paragraph 1 shall be treated in the same way and given the same ranking as claims of an equivalent nature which may be lodged by creditors whose habitual residence, domicile or head office is situated in the home Member State. Competent authorities shall therefore operate without discrimination at Community level.

3.   Except in cases where the law of the home Member State otherwise allows, a creditor shall send to the competent authority copies of any supporting documents and shall indicate the following:

(a)   the nature and the amount of the claim;

(b)   the date on which the claim arose;

(c)   whether he alleges preference, security in rem or reservation of title in respect of the claim;

(d)   where appropriate, what assets are covered by his security.

The precedence granted to insurance claims by Article 275 need not be indicated.

Article 283. Languages and form.   1.   The information in the notice referred to in Article 281(1) shall be provided in the official language or one of the official languages of the home Member State.

For that purpose a form shall be used bearing either of the following headings in all the official languages of the European Union:

(a) 'Invitation to lodge a claim; time-limits to be observed'; or

(b) where the law of the home Member State provides for the submission of observations relating to claims, 'Invitation to submit observations relating to a claim; time-limits to be observed'.

However, where a known creditor is the holder of an insurance claim, the information in the notice referred to in Article 281(1) shall be provided in the official language or one of the official languages of the Member State in which the habitual residence, domicile or head office of the creditor is situated.

2.   Creditors whose habitual residence, domicile or head office is situated in a Member State other than the home Member State may lodge their claims or submit observations relating to claims in the official language or one of the official languages of that other Member State. However, in that case, the lodging of their claims or the submission of observations on their claims, as appropriate, shall bear the heading 'Lodgement of claim' or 'Submission of observations relating to claims', as appropriate, in the official language or in one of the official languages of the home Member State.

Article 284. Regular information to the creditors.   1.   Liquidators shall, in an appropriate manner, keep creditors regularly informed on the progress of the winding-up.

2.   The supervisory authorities of the Member States may request information on developments in the winding-up procedure from the supervisory authorities of the home Member State.

Chapter IV — Common provisions

Article 285. Effects on certain contracts and rights.   By way of derogation from Articles 269 and 274, the effects of the opening of reorganisation measures or of winding-up proceedings shall be governed as follows:

(a)   in regard to employment contracts and employment relationships, exclusively by the law of the Member State applicable to the employment contract or employment relationship;

(b)   in regard to contracts conferring the right to make use of or acquire immovable property, exclusively by the law of the Member State where the immovable property is situated; and

(c)   in regard to rights of the insurance undertaking with respect to immovable property, a ship or an aircraft subject to registration in a public register, exclusively by the law of the Member State under the authority of which the register is kept.

Article 286. Rights in rem of third parties.   1.   The opening of reorganisation measures or winding-up proceedings shall not affect the rights in rem of creditors or third parties in respect of tangible or intangible, movable or immovable assets — both specific assets and collections of indefinite assets as a whole which change from time to time — which belong to the insurance undertaking and which are situated within the territory of another Member State at the time of the opening of such measures or proceedings.

2.   The rights referred to in paragraph 1 shall include at least:

(a)   the right to dispose of assets or have them disposed of and to obtain satisfaction from the proceeds of or income from those assets, in particular by virtue of a lien or a mortgage;

(b) the exclusive right to have a claim met, in particular a right guaranteed by a lien in respect of the claim or by assignment of the claim by way of a guarantee;

(c) the right to demand the assets from or to require restitution by anyone having possession or use of them contrary to the wishes of the party so entitled;

(d) a right to the beneficial use of assets.

3. The right, recorded in a public register and enforceable against third parties, under which a right in rem within the meaning of paragraph 1 may be obtained, shall be considered to be a right in rem.

4. Paragraph 1 shall not preclude actions for nullity, voidability or unenforceability referred to in Article 274(2)(l).

Article 287. Reservation of title. 1. The opening of reorganisation measures or winding-up proceedings against an insurance undertaking purchasing an asset shall not affect the rights of a seller which are based on a reservation of title where at the time of the opening of such measures or proceedings the asset is situated within the territory of a Member State other than that in which such measures or proceedings were opened.

2. The opening, after delivery of the asset, of reorganisation measures or winding-up proceedings against an insurance undertaking which is selling an asset shall not constitute grounds for rescinding or terminating the sale and shall not prevent the purchaser from acquiring title where at the time of the opening of such measures or proceedings the asset sold is situated within the territory of a Member State other than that in which such measures or proceedings were opened.

3. Paragraphs 1 and 2 shall not preclude actions for nullity, voidability or unenforceability referred to in Article 274(2)(l).

Article 288. Set-off. 1. The opening of reorganisation measures or winding-up proceedings shall not affect the right of creditors to demand the set-off of their claims against the claims of the insurance undertaking, where such a set-off is permitted by the law applicable to the claim of the insurance undertaking.

2. Paragraph 1 shall not preclude actions for nullity, voidability or unenforceability referred to in Article 274(2)(l).

Article 289. Regulated markets. 1. Without prejudice to Article 286 the effects of a reorganisation measure or the opening of winding-up proceedings on the rights and obligations of the parties to a regulated market shall be governed solely by the law applicable to that market.

2. Paragraph 1 shall not preclude actions for nullity, voidability, or unenforceability referred to in Article 274(2)(l) which may be taken to set aside payments or transactions under the law applicable to that market.

Article 290. Detrimental acts. Article 274(2)(l) shall not apply where a person who has benefited from a legal act which is detrimental to all the creditors provides proof of that act being subject to the law of a Member State other than the home Member State, and proof that that law does not allow any means of challenging that act in the relevant case.

Article 291. Protection of third-party purchasers.   The following law shall be applicable where, by an act concluded after the adoption of a reorganisation measure or the opening of winding-up proceedings, an insurance undertaking disposes, for consideration, of any of the following:

(a)   in regard to immovable assets, the law of the Member State where the immovable property is situated;

(b)   in regard to ships or aircraft subject to registration in a public register, the law of the Member State under the authority of which the register is kept;

(c)   in regard to transferable or other securities, the existence or transfer of which presupposes entry in a register or account laid down by law or which are placed in a central deposit system governed by the law of a Member State, the law of the Member State under the authority of which the register, account or system is kept.

Article 292. Lawsuits pending.   The effects of reorganisation measures or winding-up proceedings on a pending lawsuit concerning an asset or a right of which the insurance undertaking has been divested shall be governed solely by the law of the Member State in which the lawsuit is pending.

Article 293. Administrators and liquidators.   1.   The appointment of the administrator or the liquidator shall be evidenced by a certified copy of the original decision of appointment or by any other certificate issued by the competent authorities of the home Member State.

The Member State in which the administrator or liquidator wishes to act may require a translation into the official language or one of the official languages of that Member State. No formal authentication of that translation or other similar formality shall be required.

2.   Administrators and liquidators shall be entitled to exercise within the territory of all the Member States all the powers which they are entitled to exercise within the territory of the home Member State.

Persons to assist or represent administrators and liquidators may be appointed, in accordance with the law of the home Member State, in the course of the reorganisation measure or winding-up proceedings, in particular in host Member States and, specifically, in order to help overcome any difficulties encountered by creditors in that State.

3.   In exercising their powers according to the law of the home Member State, administrators or liquidators shall comply with the law of the Member States within which they wish to take action, in particular with regard to procedures for the realisation of assets and the informing of employees.

Those powers shall not include the use of force or the right to rule on legal proceedings or disputes.

Article 294. Registration in a public register.   1.   The administrator, liquidator or any other authority or person duly empowered in the home Member State may request that a reorganisation measure or the decision to open winding-up proceedings be registered in any relevant public register kept in the other Member States.

However, where a Member State provides for mandatory registration, the authority or person referred to in the first subparagraph shall take all the measures necessary to ensure such registration.

2.   The costs of registration shall be regarded as costs and expenses incurred in the proceedings.

Article 295. Professional secrecy.   All persons required to receive or divulge information in connection with the procedures laid down in Articles 270, 273 and 296 shall be bound by the provisions on professional secrecy, as laid down in Articles 64 to 69, with the exception of any judicial authorities to which existing national provisions apply.

Article 296. Treatment of branches of third-country insurance undertakings.   Where a third-country insurance undertaking has branches established in more than one Member State, each branch shall be treated independently with regard to the application of this Title.

   The competent authorities and the supervisory authorities of those Member States shall endeavour to coordinate their actions.

   Any administrators or liquidators shall likewise endeavour to coordinate their actions.

D.   Council Regulation (EEC) No 2137/85 of 25 July 1985 on the European Economic Interest Grouping (EEIG) (OJ, L 199 of 31 July 1985): Articles 35–36

See Chapter IX, Supranational legal entities, A.

E.   Council Regulation (EC) No 2157/2001 of 8 October 2001 on the Statute for a European company (SE) (OJ, L 294 of 10 November 2001): Articles 8, 63–65

See Chapter IX, Supranational legal entities, B.1.

F.   Council Regulation (EC) No 1435/2003 of 22 July 2003 on the Statute for a European Cooperative Society (SCE) (OJ, L 207 of 18 August 2003): Articles 72–75

See Chapter IX, Supranational legal entities, C.1.

G.   Proposal for a Council Regulation on the statute for a European private company (COM (2008) 396 final of 25 June 2008): Recital 6, Articles 35, 40

See Chapter IX, Supranational legal entities, D.

H.   Directive 2008/94/EC of the European Parliament and of the Council of 22 October 2008 on the protection of employees in the event of the insolvency of their employer (Codified version) (OJ, L 283 of 28 October 2008)

(4)   In order to ensure equitable protection for the employees concerned, the state of insolvency should be defined in the light of the legislative trends in the Member States and that concept should also include insolvency proceedings other than liquidation. In this context, Member States should, in order to determine the liability of the guarantee institution, be able to lay down that where an insolvency situation results in several insolvency proceedings, the situation is to be treated as a single insolvency procedure.

Article 1.   1.   This Directive shall apply to employees' claims arising from contracts of employment or employment relationships and existing against employers who are in a state of insolvency within the meaning of Article 2(1). ...

Article 2.   1.   For the purposes of this Directive, an employer shall be deemed to be in a state of insolvency where a request has been made for the opening of collective proceedings based on insolvency of the employer, as provided for under the laws, regulations and administrative provisions of a Member State, and involving the partial or total divestment of the employer's assets and the appointment of a liquidator or a person performing a similar task, and the authority which is competent pursuant to the said provisions has:

(a)   either decided to open the proceedings; or

(b)   established that the employer's undertaking or business has been definitively closed down and that the available assets are insufficient to warrant the opening of the proceedings. ...

4.   This Directive does not prevent Member States from extending employee protection to other situations of insolvency, for example where payments have been de facto stopped on a permanent basis, established by proceedings different from those mentioned in paragraph 1 as provided for under national law.

Such procedures shall not however create a guarantee obligation for the institutions of the other Member States in the cases referred to in Chapter IV.

Article 9.   1.   If an undertaking with activities in the territories of at least two Member States is in a state of insolvency within the meaning of Article 2(l), the institution responsible for meeting employees' outstanding claims shall be that in the Member State in whose territory they work or habitually work.

2.   The extent of employees' rights shall be determined by the law governing the competent guarantee institution.

3.   Member States shall take the measures necessary to ensure that, in the cases referred to in paragraph 1 of this Article, decisions taken in the context of insolvency proceedings referred to in Article 2(1), which have been requested in another Member State, are taken into account when determining the employer's state of insolvency within the meaning of this Directive.

Article 10. 1. For the purposes of implementing Article 9, Member States shall make provision for the sharing of relevant information between their competent administrative authorities and/or the guarantee institutions mentioned in the first paragraph of Article 3, making it possible in particular to inform the guarantee institution responsible for meeting the employees' outstanding claims.

2. Member States shall notify the Commission and the other Member States of the contact details of their competent administrative authorities and/or guarantee institutions. The Commission shall make that information publicly accessible.

I. Directive 98/26/EC of the European Parliament and of the Council of 19 May 1998 on settlement finality in payment and securities settlement systems (OJ, L 166 of 11 June 1998)[1]

(1) Whereas the Lamfalussy report of 1990 to the Governors of the central banks of the Group of Ten Countries demonstrated the important systemic risk inherent in payment systems which operate on the basis of several legal types of payment netting, in particular multilateral netting; whereas the reduction of legal risks associated with participation in real time gross settlement systems is of paramount importance, given the increasing development of these systems;

(2) Whereas it is also of the utmost importance to reduce the risk associated with participation in securities settlement systems, in particular where there is a close connection between such systems and payment systems;

(3) Whereas this Directive aims at contributing to the efficient and cost-effective operation of cross-border payment and securities settlement arrangements in the Community, which reinforces the freedom of movement of capital in the internal market; whereas this Directive thereby follows up the progress made towards completion of the internal market, in particular towards the freedom to provide services and liberalisation of capital movements, with a view to the realisation of Economic and Monetary Union;

(4) Whereas it is desirable that the laws of the Member States should aim to minimise the disruption to a system caused by insolvency proceedings against a participant in that system;

(5) Whereas a proposal for a Directive on the reorganisation and winding-up of credit institutions submitted in 1985 and amended on 8 February 1988 is still pending before the Council; whereas the Convention on Insolvency Proceedings drawn up on 23 November 1995 by the Member States meeting within the Council explicitly excludes insurance undertakings, credit institutions and investment firms;

(6) Whereas this Directive is intended to cover payment and securities settlement systems of a domestic as well as of a cross-border nature; whereas the Directive is applicable to Community systems and to collateral security constituted by their participants, be they Community or third country participants, in connection with participation in these systems;

---

[1] As amended by Directive 2009/44/EC of the European Parliament and of the Council of 6 May 2009 (OJ, L 146 of 10 June 2009).

(7)   Whereas Member States may apply the provisions of this Directive to their domestic institutions which participate directly in third country systems and to collateral security provided in connection with participation in such systems;

(8) $(-)^2$

(9)   Whereas the reduction of systemic risk requires in particular the finality of settlement and the enforceability of collateral security; whereas collateral security is meant to comprise all means provided by a participant to the other participants in the payment and/or securities settlement systems to secure rights and obligations in connection with that system, including repurchase agreements, statutory liens and fiduciary transfers; whereas regulation in national law of the kind of collateral security which can be used should not be affected by the definition of collateral security in this Directive;

(10)   Whereas this Directive, by covering collateral security provided in connection with operations of the central banks of the Member States functioning as central banks, including monetary policy operations, assists the European Monetary Institute in its task of promoting the efficiency of cross-border payments with a view to the preparation of the third stage of Economic and Monetary Union and thereby contributes to developing the necessary legal framework in which the future European central bank may develop its policy;

(11)   Whereas transfer orders and their netting should be legally enforceable under all Member States' jurisdictions and binding on third parties;

(12)   Whereas rules on finality of netting should not prevent systems testing, before the netting takes place, whether orders that have entered the system comply with the rules of that system and allow the settlement of that system to take place;

(13)   Whereas nothing in this Directive should prevent a participant or a third party from exercising any right or claim resulting from the underlying transaction which they may have in law to recovery or restitution in respect of a transfer order which has entered a system, e.g. in case of fraud or technical error, as long as this leads neither to the unwinding of netting nor to the revocation of the transfer order in the system;

(14)   Whereas it is necessary to ensure that transfer orders cannot be revoked after a moment defined by the rules of the system;

(14a)   Whereas national competent authorities or supervisors should ensure that the operators of the systems establishing the interoperable systems have agreed to the extent possible on common rules on the moment of entry into the interoperable systems. National competent authorities or supervisors should ensure that the rules on the moment of entry into an interoperable system are coordinated insofar as possible and necessary in order to avoid legal uncertainty in the event of default of a participating system;

(15)   Whereas it is necessary that a Member State should immediately notify other Member States of the opening of insolvency proceedings against a participant in the system;

(16)   Whereas insolvency proceedings should not have a retroactive effect on the rights and obligations of participants in a system;

---

² This Recital has been deleted by the aforesaid Directive 2009/44/EC of the European Parliament and of the Council of 6 May 2009.

(17) Whereas, in the event of insolvency proceedings against a participant in a system, this Directive furthermore aims at determining which insolvency law is applicable to the rights and obligations of that participant in connection with its participation in a system;

(18) Whereas collateral security should be insulated from the effects of the insolvency law applicable to the insolvent participant;

(19) Whereas the provisions of Article 9(2) should only apply to a register, account or centralized deposit system which evidences the existence of proprietary rights in or for the delivery or transfer of the securities concerned;

(20) Whereas the provisions of Article 9(2) are intended to ensure that if the participant, the central bank of a Member State or the future European central bank has a valid and effective collateral security as determined under the law of the Member State where the relevant register, account or centralized deposit system is located, then the validity and enforceability of that collateral security as against that system (and the operator thereof) and against any other person claiming directly or indirectly through it, should be determined solely under the law of that Member State;

(21) Whereas the provisions of Article 9(2) are not intended to prejudice the operation and effect of the law of the Member State under which the securities are constituted or of the law of the Member State where the securities may otherwise be located (including, without limitation, the law concerning the creation, ownership or transfer of such securities or of rights in such securities) and should not be interpreted to mean that any such collateral security will be directly enforceable or be capable of being recognised in any such Member State otherwise than in accordance with the law of that Member State;

(22) Whereas it is desirable that Member States endeavour to establish sufficient links between all the securities settlement systems covered by this Directive with a view towards promoting maximum transparency and legal certainty of transactions relating to securities;

(22a) Whereas in the case of interoperable systems, a lack of coordination as to which rules apply on the moment of entry and irrevocability may expose participants in one system, or even the system operator itself, to the spill-over effects of a default in another system. In order to limit systemic risk, it is desirable to provide that system operators of interoperable systems coordinate the rules on the moment of entry and irrevocability in the systems they operate;

(23) Whereas the adoption of this Directive constitutes the most appropriate way of realising the above-mentioned objectives and does not go beyond what is necessary to achieve them …

Section I — Scope and definitions

Article 1.   The provisions of this Directive shall apply to:

(a)   any system as defined in Article 2(a), governed by the law of a Member State and operating in any currency, the euro or in various currencies which the system converts one against another;

(b)   any participant in such a system;

(c)   collateral security provided in connection with:

—   participation in a system, or

— operations of the central banks of the Member States or the European Central Bank in the context of their function as central banks.

Article 2.   For the purpose of this Directive:

(a) 'system' shall mean a formal arrangement

— between three or more participants, excluding the system operator of that system, a possible settlement agent, a possible central counterparty, a possible clearing house or a possible indirect participant, with common rules and standardised arrangements for the clearing, whether or not through a central counterparty, or execution of transfer orders between the participants

— governed by the law of a Member State chosen by the participants; the participants may, however, only choose the law of a Member State in which at least one of them has its head office, and

— designated, without prejudice to other more stringent conditions of general application laid down by national law, as a system and notified to the Commission by the Member State whose law is applicable, after that Member State is satisfied as to the adequacy of the rules of the system.

Subject to the conditions in the first subparagraph, a Member State may designate as a system such a formal arrangement whose business consists of the execution of transfer orders as defined in the second indent of (i) and which to a limited extent executes orders relating to other financial instruments, when that Member State considers that such a designation is warranted on grounds of systemic risk.

A Member State may also on a case-by-case basis designate as a system such a formal arrangement between two participants, without counting a possible settlement agent, a possible central counterparty, a possible clearing house or a possible indirect participant, when that Member State considers that such a designation is warranted on grounds of systemic risk.

An arrangement entered into between interoperable systems shall not constitute a system:

(b) 'institution' shall mean:

— a credit institution as defined in Article 4(1) of Directive 2006/48/EC of the European Parliament and of the Council of 14 June 2006 relating to the taking up and pursuit of the business of credit institutions (recast) including the institutions listed in Article 2 of that Directive,

— an investment firm as defined in Article 4(1)(1) of Directive 2004/39/EC of the European Parliament and of the Council of 21 April 2004 on markets in financial instruments, excluding the institutions set out in Article 2(1) thereof,

— public authorities and publicly guaranteed undertakings, or

— any undertaking whose head office is outside the Community and whose functions correspond to those of the Community credit institutions or investment firms as defined in the first and second indent,

which participates in a system and which is responsible for discharging the financial obligations arising from transfer orders within that system.

If a system is supervised in accordance with national legislation and only executes transfer orders as defined in the second indent of (i), as well as payments resulting from such orders, a Member State may decide that undertakings which participate in such a system and which have responsibility for discharging the financial obligations arising from transfer orders within this system, can be considered institutions, provided that at least three participants of this system are covered by the categories referred to in the first subparagraph and that such a decision is warranted on grounds of systemic risk;

(c) 'central counterparty' shall mean an entity which is interposed between the institutions in a system and which acts as the exclusive counterparty of these institutions with regard to their transfer orders;

(d) 'settlement agent' shall mean an entity providing to institutions and/or a central counterparty participating in systems, settlement accounts through which transfer orders within such systems are settled and, as the case may be, extending credit to those institutions and/or central counterparties for settlement purposes;

(e) 'clearing house' shall mean an entity responsible for the calculation of the net positions of institutions, a possible central counterparty and/or a possible settlement agent;

(f) 'participant' shall mean an institution, a central counterparty, a settlement agent, a clearing house or a system operator.

According to the rules of the system, the same participant may act as a central counterparty, a settlement agent or a clearing house or carry out part or all of these tasks.

A Member State may decide that, for the purposes of this Directive, an indirect participant may be considered a participant if that is justified on the grounds of systemic risk. Where an indirect participant is considered to be a participant on grounds of systemic risk, this does not limit the responsibility of the participant through which the indirect participant passes transfer orders to the system:

(g) 'indirect participant' shall mean an institution, a central counterparty, a settlement agent, a clearing house or a system operator with a contractual relationship with a participant in a system executing transfer orders which enables the indirect participant to pass transfer orders through the system, provided that the indirect participant is known to the system operator;

(h) 'securities' shall mean all instruments referred to in section C of Annex I to Directive 2004/39/EC;

(i) 'transfer order' shall mean:

— any instruction by a participant to place at the disposal of a recipient an amount of money by means of a book entry on the accounts of a credit institution, a central bank, a central counterparty or a settlement agent, or any instruction which results in the assumption or discharge of a payment obligation as defined by the rules of the system, or

— an instruction by a participant to transfer the title to, or interest in, a security or securities by means of a book entry on a register, or otherwise;

(j) 'insolvency proceedings' shall mean any collective measure provided for in the law of a Member State, or a third country, either to wind up the participant or to reorganise it, where such measure involves the suspending of, or imposing limitations on, transfers or payments;

(k) 'netting' shall mean the conversion into one net claim or one net obligation of claims and obligations resulting from transfer orders which a participant or participants either issue to, or receive from, one or more other participants with the result that only a net claim can be demanded or a net obligation be owed;

(l) 'settlement account' shall mean an account at a central bank, a settlement agent or a central counterparty used to hold funds or securities and to settle transactions between participants in a system;

(m) 'collateral security' shall mean all realisable assets, including, without limitations, financial collateral referred to in Article 1(4)(a) of Directive 2002/47/EC of the European Parliament and of the Council of 6 June 2002 on financial collateral arrangements, provided under a pledge (including money provided under a pledge), a repurchase or similar agreement, or otherwise, for the purpose of securing rights and obligations potentially arising in connection with a system, or provided to central banks of the Member States or to the European Central Bank;

(n) 'business day' shall cover both day and night-time settlements and shall encompass all events happening during the business cycle of a system;

(o) 'interoperable systems' shall mean two or more systems whose system operators have entered into an arrangement with one another that involves cross-system execution of transfer orders;

(p) 'system operator' shall mean the entity or entities legally responsible for the operation of a system. A system operator may also act as a settlement agent, central counterparty or clearing house.

Section II — Netting and transfer orders

Article 3.   1.   Transfer orders and netting shall be legally enforceable and binding on third parties even in the event of insolvency proceedings against a participant, provided that transfer orders were entered into the system before the moment of opening of such insolvency proceedings as defined in Article 6(1). This shall apply even in the event of insolvency proceedings against a participant (in the system concerned or in an interoperable system) or against the system operator of an interoperable system which is not a participant.

Where transfer orders are entered into a system after the moment of opening of insolvency proceedings and are carried out within the business day, as defined by the rules of the system, during which the opening of such proceedings occur, they shall be legally enforceable and binding on third parties only if the system operator can prove that, at the time that such transfer orders become irrevocable, it was neither aware, nor should have been aware, of the opening of such proceedings.

2.   No law, regulation, rule or practice on the setting aside of contracts and transactions concluded before the moment of opening of insolvency proceedings, as defined in Article 6(1) shall lead to the unwinding of a netting.

3.   The moment of entry of a transfer order into a system shall be defined by the rules of that system. If there are conditions laid down in the national law governing the system as to the moment of entry, the rules of that system must be in accordance with such conditions.

4.   In the case of interoperable systems, each system determines in its own rules the moment of entry into its system, in such a way as to ensure, to the extent possible, that the rules of all interoperable systems concerned are coordinated in this regard. Unless expressly provided for by the rules of all the systems that are party to the interoperable systems, one system's rules on the moment of entry shall not be affected by any rules of the other systems with which it is interoperable.

Article 4.   Member States may provide that the opening of insolvency proceedings against a participant or a system operator of an interoperable system shall not prevent funds or securities available on the settlement account of that participant from being used to fulfil that participants obligations in the system or in an interoperable system on the business day of the opening of the insolvency proceedings. Member States may also provide that such a participant's credit facility connected to the system be used against available, existing collateral security to fulfil that participant's obligations in the system or in an interoperable system.

Article 5.   A transfer order may not be revoked by a participant in a system, nor by a third party, from the moment defined by the rules of that system.

In the case of interoperable systems, each system determines in its own rules the moment of irrevocability, in such a way as to ensure, to the extent possible that the rules of all interoperable systems concerned are coordinated in this regard. Unless expressly provided for by the rules of all the systems that are party to the interoperable systems, one system's rules on the moment of irrevocability shall not be affected by any rules of the other systems with which it is interoperable.

Section III — Provisions concerning insolvency proceedings

Article 6.   1.   For the purpose of this Directive, the moment of opening of insolvency proceedings shall be the moment when the relevant judicial or administrative authority handed down its decision.

2.   When a decision has been taken in accordance with paragraph 1, the relevant judicial or administrative authority shall immediately notify that decision to the appropriate authority chosen by its Member State.

3.   The Member State referred to in paragraph 2 shall immediately notify other Member States.

Article 7.   Insolvency proceedings shall not have retroactive effects on the rights and obligations of a participant arising from, or in connection with, its participation in a system before the moment of opening of such proceedings as defined in Article 6(1). This shall apply, *inter alia*, as regards the rights and obligations of a participant in an interoperable system, or of a system operator of an interoperable system which is not a participant.

Article 8.   In the event of insolvency proceedings being opened against a participant in a system, the rights and obligations arising from, or in connection with, the participation of that participant shall be determined by the law governing that system.

Section IV — Insulation of the rights of holders of collateral security from the effects of the insolvency of the provider

Article 9.   1.   The rights of a system operator or of a participant to collateral security provided to them in connection with a system or any interoperable system, and the rights of central banks of the Member States or the European Central Bank to collateral security provided to them, shall not be affected by insolvency proceedings against:
  (a)   the participant (in the system concerned or in an interoperable system);
  (b)   the system operator of an interoperable system which is not a participant;

(c)   a counterparty to central banks of the Member States or the European Central Bank; or

(d)   any third party which provided the collateral security.

Such collateral security may be realised for the satisfaction of those rights.

2.   Where securities including rights in securities are provided as collateral security to participants, system operators or to central banks of the Member States or the European Central Bank as described in paragraph 1, and their right or that of any nominee, agent or third party acting on their behalf with respect to the securities is legally recorded on a register, account or centralised deposit system located in a Member State, the determination of the rights of such entities as holders of collateral security in relation to those securities shall be governed by the law of that Member State.

Section V — Final provisions

Article 10.   1.   Member States shall specify the systems, and the respective system operators, which are to be included in the scope of this Directive and shall notify them to the Commission and inform the Commission of the authorities they have chosen in accordance with Article 6(2).

The system operator shall indicate to the Member State whose law is applicable the participants in the system, including any possible indirect participants, as well as any change in them.

In addition to the indication provided for in the second subparagraph, Member States may impose supervision or authorisation requirements on systems which fall under their jurisdiction.

An institution shall, on request, inform anyone with a legitimate interest of the systems in which it participates and provide information about the main rules governing the functioning of those systems.

2.   A system designated prior to the entry into force of national provisions implementing Directive 2009/44/EC of the European Parliament and of the Council of 6 May 2009 amending Directive 98/26/EC on settlement finality in payment and securities settlement systems and Directive 2002/47/EC on financial collateral arrangements as regards linked systems and credit claims shall continue to be designated for the purposes of this Directive.

A transfer order which enters a system before the entry into force of national provisions implementing Directive 2009/44/EC, but is settled thereafter shall be deemed to be a transfer order for the purposes of this Directive.

Article 11.   1.   Member States shall bring into force the laws, regulations and administrative provisions necessary to comply with this Directive before 11 December 1999. They shall forthwith inform the Commission thereof.

When Member States adopt these measures, they shall contain a reference to this Directive or shall be accompanied by such reference on the occasion of their official publication. The methods of making such a reference shall be laid down by the Member States.

2.   Member States shall communicate to the Commission the text of the provisions of domestic law which they adopt in the field governed by this Directive. In this Communication, Member States shall provide a table of correspondence showing

the national provisions which exist or are introduced in respect of each Article of this Directive.

Article 12.   No later than three years after the date mentioned in Article 11(1), the Commission shall present a report to the European Parliament and the Council on the application of this Directive, accompanied where appropriate by proposals for its revision. ...

J.1.   Directive 2002/47/EC of the European Parliament and of the Council of 6 June 2002 on financial collateral arrangements (OJ, L 168 of 27 June 2002): Recitals 5–6, Articles 1–2, 8–9

See Chapter VIII, Rights on financial instruments, C.1.

J.2.   Statement of the Council's reasons attached to the Common Position (EC) No 32/2002 adopted by the Council on 5 March 2002 (OJ, C 119 E of 22 May 2002): Points III.8-III.9

See Chapter VIII, Rights on financial instruments, C.2.

K.   Council Regulation (EC) No 2100/94 of 27 July 1994 on Community plant variety rights (OJ, L 227 of 1 September 1994): Article 25

See Chapter VIII, IP rights, A.

L.   Council Regulation (EC) No 6/2002 of 12 December 2001 on Community designs (OJ, L 3 of 5 January 2002): Articles 31, 33

See Chapter VIII, IP rights, B.

M.   Council Regulation (EC) No 207/2009 of 26 February 2009 on the Community trade mark (codified version) (OJ, L 78 of 24 March 2009): Articles 21, 23

See Chapter VIII, IP rights, C.

N.   Proposal for a Council Regulation on the European Union patent (Doc. Consilium No 16113/09 of 27 November 2009): Article 18

See Chapter VIII, IP rights, I.1.

O.1.   Council Decision 2009/370/EC of 6 April 2009 on the accession of the European Community to the Convention on international interests in mobile equipment and its Protocol on matters specific to aircraft equipment, adopted jointly in Cape Town on 16 November 2001 (OJ, L 121 of 15 May 2009): Recitals 5, 10

See Chapter VIII, Interests in goods and equipment, A.1.

O.2.   General declarations concerning the competence of the European Community to be made by the Community at the time of accession to the Convention on international interests in mobile equipment (Cape Town Convention) and the Protocol on matters specific to aircraft equipment (Aircraft Protocol), adopted jointly in Cape Town on 16 November 2001 (OJ, L 121 of 15 May 2009): Paragraphs 5–6

See Chapter VIII, Interests in goods and equipment, A.2.

O.3.   Convention on international interests in mobile equipment (OJ, L 121 of 15 May 2009): Articles 30, 37, 45

See Chapter VIII, Interests in goods and equipment, A.4.

O.4.   Protocol to the Convention on international interests in mobile equipment on matters specific to aircraft equipment (OJ, L 121 of 15 May 2009): Articles XI–XII, XXX

See Chapter VIII, Interests in goods and equipment, A.5.

O.5.   Council Decision 2009/940/EC of 30 November 2009 on the signing by the European Community of the Protocol to the Convention on International Interests in Mobile Equipment on Matters Specific to Railway Rolling Stock, adopted in Luxembourg on 23 February 2007 (OJ, L 331 of 16 December 2009): Recital 6

See Chapter VIII, Interests in goods and equipment, A.6.

O.6.   Declaration to be made pursuant to Article XXII(2) concerning the competence of the European Community over matters governed by the Protocol to the Convention on International Interests in Mobile Equipment on Matters Specific to Railway Rolling Stock (the 'Rail Protocol'), adopted in Luxembourg on 23 February 2007, in respect of which the Member States have transferred their competence to the Community (OJ, L 331 of 16 December 2009): Paragraph 5

See Chapter VIII, Interests in goods and equipment, A.7.

O.7.   Luxembourg Protocol to the Convention on International Interests in Mobile Equipment on Matters Specific to Railway Rolling Stock (OJ, L 331 of 16 December 2009): Articles III, IX–X, XXVII

See Chapter VIII, Interests in goods and equipment, A.8.

VI

Law Applicable to Contractual Obligations

General provisions

A.1.   Regulation (EC) No 593/2008 of the European Parliament and of the Council of 17 June 2008 on the law applicable to contractual obligations (Rome I) (OJ, L 177 of 4 July 2008)[*]

(1)   The Community has set itself the objective of maintaining and developing an area of freedom, security and justice. For the progressive establishment of such an area, the Community is to adopt measures relating to judicial cooperation in civil matters with a cross-border impact to the extent necessary for the proper functioning of the internal market.

(2)   According to Article 65, point (b) of the Treaty, these measures are to include those promoting the compatibility of the rules applicable in the Member States concerning the conflict of laws and of jurisdiction.

(3)   The European Council meeting in Tampere on 15 and 16 October 1999 endorsed the principle of mutual recognition of judgments and other decisions of judicial authorities as the cornerstone of judicial cooperation in civil matters and invited the Council and the Commission to adopt a programme of measures to implement that principle.

(4)   On 30 November 2000 the Council adopted a joint Commission and Council programme of measures for implementation of the principle of mutual recognition of decisions in civil and commercial matters. The programme identifies measures relating to the harmonisation of conflict-of-law rules as those facilitating the mutual recognition of judgments.

(5)   The Hague Programme, adopted by the European Council on 5 November 2004, called for work to be pursued actively on the conflict-of-law rules regarding contractual obligations (Rome I).

(6)   The proper functioning of the internal market creates a need, in order to improve the predictability of the outcome of litigation, certainty as to the law applicable and the free movement of judgments, for the conflict-of-law rules in the Member States to designate the same national law irrespective of the country of the court in which an action is brought.

---

[*]   The list of the conventions notified by the Member States under Article 26(1) of the Regulation is published in OJ, C 343 of 17 December 2010.

(7)   The substantive scope and the provisions of this Regulation should be consistent with Council Regulation (EC) No 44/2001 of 22 December 2000 on jurisdiction and the recognition and enforcement of judgments in civil and commercial matters (Brussels I) and Regulation (EC) No 864/2007 of the European Parliament and of the Council of 11 July 2007 on the law applicable to non-contractual obligations (Rome II).

(8)   Family relationships should cover parentage, marriage, affinity and collateral relatives. The reference in Article 1(2) to relationships having comparable effects to marriage and other family relationships should be interpreted in accordance with the law of the Member State in which the court is seised.

(9)   Obligations under bills of exchange, cheques and promissory notes and other negotiable instruments should also cover bills of lading to the extent that the obligations under the bill of lading arise out of its negotiable character.

(10)   Obligations arising out of dealings prior to the conclusion of the contract are covered by Article 12 of Regulation (EC) No 864/2007. Such obligations should therefore be excluded from the scope of this Regulation.

(11)   The parties' freedom to choose the applicable law should be one of the cornerstones of the system of conflict-of-law rules in matters of contractual obligations.

(12)   An agreement between the parties to confer on one or more courts or tribunals of a Member State exclusive jurisdiction to determine disputes under the contract should be one of the factors to be taken into account in determining whether a choice of law has been clearly demonstrated.

(13)   This Regulation does not preclude parties from incorporating by reference into their contract a non-State body of law or an international convention.

(14)   Should the Community adopt, in an appropriate legal instrument, rules of substantive contract law, including standard terms and conditions, such instrument may provide that the parties may choose to apply those rules.

(15)   Where a choice of law is made and all other elements relevant to the situation are located in a country other than the country whose law has been chosen, the choice of law should not prejudice the application of provisions of the law of that country which cannot be derogated from by agreement. This rule should apply whether or not the choice of law was accompanied by a choice of court or tribunal. Whereas no substantial change is intended as compared with Article 3(3) of the 1980 Convention on the Law Applicable to Contractual Obligations (the Rome Convention), the wording of this Regulation is aligned as far as possible with Article 14 of Regulation (EC) No 864/2007.

(16)   To contribute to the general objective of this Regulation, legal certainty in the European judicial area, the conflict-of-law rules should be highly foreseeable. The courts should, however, retain a degree of discretion to determine the law that is most closely connected to the situation.

(17)   As far as the applicable law in the absence of choice is concerned, the concept of 'provision of services' and 'sale of goods' should be interpreted in the same way as when applying Article 5 of Regulation (EC) No 44/2001 in so far as sale of goods and provision of services are covered by that Regulation. Although franchise and distribution contracts are contracts for services, they are the subject of specific rules.

(18)   As far as the applicable law in the absence of choice is concerned, multilateral systems should be those in which trading is conducted, such as regulated markets and multilateral trading facilities as referred to in Article 4 of Directive 2004/39/EC of

the European Parliament and of the Council of 21 April 2004 on markets in financial instruments, regardless of whether or not they rely on a central counterparty.

(19) Where there has been no choice of law, the applicable law should be determined in accordance with the rule specified for the particular type of contract. Where the contract cannot be categorised as being one of the specified types or where its elements fall within more than one of the specified types, it should be governed by the law of the country where the party required to effect the characteristic performance of the contract has his habitual residence. In the case of a contract consisting of a bundle of rights and obligations capable of being categorised as falling within more than one of the specified types of contract, the characteristic performance of the contract should be determined having regard to its centre of gravity.

(20) Where the contract is manifestly more closely connected with a country other than that indicated in Article 4(1) or (2), an escape clause should provide that the law of that other country is to apply. In order to determine that country, account should be taken, inter alia, of whether the contract in question has a very close relationship with another contract or contracts.

(21) In the absence of choice, where the applicable law cannot be determined either on the basis of the fact that the contract can be categorised as one of the specified types or as being the law of the country of habitual residence of the party required to effect the characteristic performance of the contract, the contract should be governed by the law of the country with which it is most closely connected. In order to determine that country, account should be taken, inter alia, of whether the contract in question has a very close relationship with another contract or contracts.

(22) As regards the interpretation of contracts for the carriage of goods, no change in substance is intended with respect to Article 4(4), third sentence, of the Rome Convention. Consequently, single-voyage charter parties and other contracts the main purpose of which is the carriage of goods should be treated as contracts for the carriage of goods. For the purposes of this Regulation, the term 'consignor' should refer to any person who enters into a contract of carriage with the carrier and the term 'the carrier' should refer to the party to the contract who undertakes to carry the goods, whether or not he performs the carriage himself.

(23) As regards contracts concluded with parties regarded as being weaker, those parties should be protected by conflict-of-law rules that are more favourable to their interests than the general rules.

(24) With more specific reference to consumer contracts, the conflict-of-law rule should make it possible to cut the cost of settling disputes concerning what are commonly relatively small claims and to take account of the development of distance-selling techniques. Consistency with Regulation (EC) No 44/2001 requires both that there be a reference to the concept of directed activity as a condition for applying the consumer protection rule and that the concept be interpreted harmoniously in Regulation (EC) No 44/2001 and this Regulation, bearing in mind that a joint declaration by the Council and the Commission on Article 15 of Regulation (EC) No 44/2001 states that 'for Article 15(1) (c) to be applicable it is not sufficient for an undertaking to target its activities at the Member State of the consumer's residence, or at a number of Member States including that Member State; a contract must also be concluded within the framework of its activities'. The declaration also states that 'the mere fact that an Internet site is accessible

is not sufficient for Article 15 to be applicable, although a factor will be that this Internet site solicits the conclusion of distance contracts and that a contract has actually been concluded at a distance, by whatever means. In this respect, the language or currency which a website uses does not constitute a relevant factor.'.

(25) Consumers should be protected by such rules of the country of their habitual residence that cannot be derogated from by agreement, provided that the consumer contract has been concluded as a result of the professional pursuing his commercial or professional activities in that particular country. The same protection should be guaranteed if the professional, while not pursuing his commercial or professional activities in the country where the consumer has his habitual residence, directs his activities by any means to that country or to several countries, including that country, and the contract is concluded as a result of such activities.

(26) For the purposes of this Regulation, financial services such as investment services and activities and ancillary services provided by a professional to a consumer, as referred to in sections A and B of Annex I to Directive 2004/39/EC, and contracts for the sale of units in collective investment undertakings, whether or not covered by Council Directive 85/611/EEC of 20 December 1985 on the coordination of laws, regulations and administrative provisions relating to undertakings for collective investment in transferable securities (UCITS), should be subject to Article 6 of this Regulation. Consequently, when a reference is made to terms and conditions governing the issuance or offer to the public of transferable securities or to the subscription and redemption of units in collective investment undertakings, that reference should include all aspects binding the issuer or the offeror to the consumer, but should not include those aspects involving the provision of financial services.

(27) Various exceptions should be made to the general conflict-of-law rule for consumer contracts. Under one such exception the general rule should not apply to contracts relating to rights *in rem* in immovable property or tenancies of such property unless the contract relates to the right to use immovable property on a timeshare basis within the meaning of Directive 94/47/EC of the European Parliament and of the Council of 26 October 1994 on the protection of purchasers in respect of certain aspects of contracts relating to the purchase of the right to use immovable properties on a timeshare basis.

(28) It is important to ensure that rights and obligations which constitute a financial instrument are not covered by the general rule applicable to consumer contracts, as that could lead to different laws being applicable to each of the instruments issued, therefore changing their nature and preventing their fungible trading and offering. Likewise, whenever such instruments are issued or offered, the contractual relationship established between the issuer or the offeror and the consumer should not necessarily be subject to the mandatory application of the law of the country of habitual residence of the consumer, as there is a need to ensure uniformity in the terms and conditions of an issuance or an offer. The same rationale should apply with regard to the multilateral systems covered by Article 4(1)(h), in respect of which it should be ensured that the law of the country of habitual residence of the consumer will not interfere with the rules applicable to contracts concluded within those systems or with the operator of such systems.

(29) For the purposes of this Regulation, references to rights and obligations constituting the terms and conditions governing the issuance, offers to the public or public take-over bids of transferable securities and references to the subscription and redemption

of units in collective investment undertakings should include the terms governing, inter alia, the allocation of securities or units, rights in the event of over-subscription, withdrawal rights and similar matters in the context of the offer as well as those matters referred to in Articles 10, 11, 12 and 13, thus ensuring that all relevant contractual aspects of an offer binding the issuer or the offeror to the consumer are governed by a single law.

(30) For the purposes of this Regulation, financial instruments and transferable securities are those instruments referred to in Article 4 of Directive 2004/39/EC.

(31) Nothing in this Regulation should prejudice the operation of a formal arrangement designated as a system under Article 2(a) of Directive 98/26/EC of the European Parliament and of the Council of 19 May 1998 on settlement finality in payment and securities settlement systems.

(32) Owing to the particular nature of contracts of carriage and insurance contracts, specific provisions should ensure an adequate level of protection of passengers and policy holders. Therefore, Article 6 should not apply in the context of those particular contracts.

(33) Where an insurance contract not covering a large risk covers more than one risk, at least one of which is situated in a Member State and at least one of which is situated in a third country, the special rules on insurance contracts in this Regulation should apply only to the risk or risks situated in the relevant Member State or Member States.

(34) The rule on individual employment contracts should not prejudice the application of the overriding mandatory provisions of the country to which a worker is posted in accordance with Directive 96/71/EC of the European Parliament and of the Council of 16 December 1996 concerning the posting of workers in the framework of the provision of services.

(35) Employees should not be deprived of the protection afforded to them by provisions which cannot be derogated from by agreement or which can only be derogated from to their benefit.

(36) As regards individual employment contracts, work carried out in another country should be regarded as temporary if the employee is expected to resume working in the country of origin after carrying out his tasks abroad. The conclusion of a new contract of employment with the original employer or an employer belonging to the same group of companies as the original employer should not preclude the employee from being regarded as carrying out his work in another country temporarily.

(37) Considerations of public interest justify giving the courts of the Member States the possibility, in exceptional circumstances, of applying exceptions based on public policy and overriding mandatory provisions. The concept of 'overriding mandatory provisions' should be distinguished from the expression 'provisions which cannot be derogated from by agreement' and should be construed more restrictively.

(38) In the context of voluntary assignment, the term "relationship" should make it clear that Article 14(1) also applies to the property aspects of an assignment, as between assignor and assignee, in legal orders where such aspects are treated separately from the aspects under the law of obligations. However, the term 'relationship' should not be understood as relating to any relationship that may exist between assignor and assignee. In particular, it should not cover preliminary questions as regards a voluntary assignment or a contractual subrogation. The term should be strictly limited to the aspects which are directly relevant to the voluntary assignment or contractual subrogation in question.

(39) For the sake of legal certainty there should be a clear definition of habitual residence, in particular for companies and other bodies, corporate or unincorporated. Unlike Article 60(1) of Regulation (EC) No 44/2001, which establishes three criteria, the conflict-of-law rule should proceed on the basis of a single criterion; otherwise, the parties would be unable to foresee the law applicable to their situation.

(40) A situation where conflict-of-law rules are dispersed among several instruments and where there are differences between those rules should be avoided. This Regulation, however, should not exclude the possibility of inclusion of conflict-of-law rules relating to contractual obligations in provisions of Community law with regard to particular matters.

This Regulation should not prejudice the application of other instruments laying down provisions designed to contribute to the proper functioning of the internal market in so far as they cannot be applied in conjunction with the law designated by the rules of this Regulation. The application of provisions of the applicable law designated by the rules of this Regulation should not restrict the free movement of goods and services as regulated by Community instruments, such as Directive 2000/31/EC of the European Parliament and of the Council of 8 June 2000 on certain legal aspects of information society services, in particular electronic commerce, in the Internal Market (Directive on electronic commerce).

(41) Respect for international commitments entered into by the Member States means that this Regulation should not affect international conventions to which one or more Member States are parties at the time when this Regulation is adopted. To make the rules more accessible, the Commission should publish the list of the relevant conventions in the Official Journal of the European Union on the basis of information supplied by the Member States.

(42) The Commission will make a proposal to the European Parliament and to the Council concerning the procedures and conditions according to which Member States would be entitled to negotiate and conclude, on their own behalf, agreements with third countries in individual and exceptional cases, concerning sectoral matters and containing provisions on the law applicable to contractual obligations.

(43) Since the objective of this Regulation cannot be sufficiently achieved by the Member States and can therefore, by reason of the scale and effects of this Regulation, be better achieved at Community level, the Community may adopt measures, in accordance with the principle of subsidiarity as set out in Article 5 of the Treaty. In accordance with the principle of proportionality, as set out in that Article, this Regulation does not go beyond what is necessary to attain its objective.

(44) In accordance with Article 3 of the Protocol on the position of the United Kingdom and Ireland, annexed to the Treaty on European Union and to the Treaty establishing the European Community, Ireland has notified its wish to take part in the adoption and application of the present Regulation.

(45) In accordance with Articles 1 and 2 of the Protocol on the position of the United Kingdom and Ireland, annexed to the Treaty on European Union and to the Treaty establishing the European Community, and without prejudice to Article 4 of the said Protocol, the United Kingdom is not taking part in the adoption of this Regulation and is not bound by it or subject to its application.[1]

---

[1]   The Council (JHA) of 24–25 July 2008 took notice of the express will of the United Kingdom to be bound by this Regulation (Doc. Consilium No 11653/08). See Commission Decision 2009/26/EC of 22 December 2008, OJ, L 10 of *15 January 2009*. [Note of the Editor]

(46) In accordance with Articles 1 and 2 of the Protocol on the position of Denmark, annexed to the Treaty on European Union and to the Treaty establishing the European Community, Denmark is not taking part in the adoption of this Regulation and is not bound by it or subject to its application,

Chapter I — Scope

Article 1. Material scope. 1. This Regulation shall apply, in situations involving a conflict of laws, to contractual obligations in civil and commercial matters.

It shall not apply, in particular, to revenue, customs or administrative matters.

2. The following shall be excluded from the scope of this Regulation:

(a) questions involving the status or legal capacity of natural persons, without prejudice to Article 13;

(b) obligations arising out of family relationships and relationships deemed by the law applicable to such relationships to have comparable effects, including maintenance obligations;

(c) obligations arising out of matrimonial property regimes, property regimes of relationships deemed by the law applicable to such relationships to have comparable effects to marriage, and wills and succession;

(d) obligations arising under bills of exchange, cheques and promissory notes and other negotiable instruments to the extent that the obligations under such other negotiable instruments arise out of their negotiable character;

(e) arbitration agreements and agreements on the choice of court;

(f) questions governed by the law of companies and other bodies, corporate or unincorporated, such as the creation, by registration or otherwise, legal capacity, internal organisation or winding-up of companies and other bodies, corporate or unincorporated, and the personal liability of officers and members as such for the obligations of the company or body;

(g) the question whether an agent is able to bind a principal, or an organ to bind a company or other body corporate or unincorporated, in relation to a third party;

(h) the constitution of trusts and the relationship between settlors, trustees and beneficiaries;

(i) obligations arising out of dealings prior to the conclusion of a contract;

(j) insurance contracts arising out of operations carried out by organizations other than undertakings referred to in Article 2 of Directive 2002/83/EC of the European Parliament and of the Council of 5 November 2002 concerning life assurance the object of which is to provide benefits for employed or self-employed persons belonging to an undertaking or group of undertakings, or to a trade or group of trades, in the event of death or survival or of discontinuance or curtailment of activity, or of sickness related to work or accidents at work.

3. This Regulation shall not apply to evidence and procedure, without prejudice to Article 18.

4. In this Regulation, the term 'Member State' shall mean Member States to which this Regulation applies. However, in Article 3(4) and Article 7 the term shall mean all the Member States.

Article 2. Universal application. Any law specified by this Regulation shall be applied whether or not it is the law of a Member State.

Chapter II — Uniform rules

Article 3. Freedom of choice. 1. A contract shall be governed by the law chosen by the parties. The choice shall be made expressly or clearly demonstrated by the terms of the contract or the circumstances of the case. By their choice the parties can select the law applicable to the whole or to part only of the contract.

2. The parties may at any time agree to subject the contract to a law other than that which previously governed it, whether as a result of an earlier choice made under this Article or of other provisions of this Regulation. Any change in the law to be applied that is made after the conclusion of the contract shall not prejudice its formal validity under Article 11 or adversely affect the rights of third parties.

3. Where all other elements relevant to the situation at the time of the choice are located in a country other than the country whose law has been chosen, the choice of the parties shall not prejudice the application of provisions of the law of that other country which cannot be derogated from by agreement.

4. Where all other elements relevant to the situation at the time of the choice are located in one or more Member States, the parties' choice of applicable law other than that of a Member State shall not prejudice the application of provisions of Community law, where appropriate as implemented in the Member State of the forum, which cannot be derogated from by agreement.

5. The existence and validity of the consent of the parties as to the choice of the applicable law shall be determined in accordance with the provisions of Articles 10, 11 and 13.

Article 4. Applicable law in the absence of choice. 1. To the extent that the law applicable to the contract has not been chosen in accordance with Article 3 and without prejudice to Articles 5 to 8, the law governing the contract shall be determined as follows:

(a) a contract for the sale of goods shall be governed by the law of the country where the seller has his habitual residence;

(b) a contract for the provision of services shall be governed by the law of the country where the service provider has his habitual residence;

(c) a contract relating to a right *in rem* in immovable property or to a tenancy of immovable property shall be governed by the law of the country where the property is situated;

(d) notwithstanding point (c), a tenancy of immovable property concluded for temporary private use for a period of no more than six consecutive months shall be governed by the law of the country where the landlord has his habitual residence, provided that the tenant is a natural person and has his habitual residence in the same country;

(e) a franchise contract shall be governed by the law of the country where the franchisee has his habitual residence;

(f) a distribution contract shall be governed by the law of the country where the distributor has his habitual residence;

(g) a contract for the sale of goods by auction shall be governed by the law of the country where the auction takes place, if such a place can be determined;

(h)   a contract concluded within a multilateral system which brings together or facilitates the bringing together of multiple third-party buying and selling interests in financial instruments, as defined by Article 4(1), point (17) of Directive 2004/39/EC, in accordance with non-discretionary rules and governed by a single law, shall be governed by that law.

2.   Where the contract is not covered by paragraph 1 or where the elements of the contract would be covered by more than one of points (a) to (h) of paragraph 1, the contract shall be governed by the law of the country where the party required to effect the characteristic performance of the contract has his habitual residence.

3.   Where it is clear from all the circumstances of the case that the contract is manifestly more closely connected with a country other than that indicated in paragraphs 1 or 2, the law of that other country shall apply.

4.   Where the law applicable cannot be determined pursuant to paragraphs 1 or 2, the contract shall be governed by the law of the country with which it is most closely connected.

Article 5. Contracts of carriage.   1.   To the extent that the law applicable to a contract for the carriage of goods has not been chosen in accordance with Article 3, the law applicable shall be the law of the country of habitual residence of the carrier, provided that the place of receipt or the place of delivery or the habitual residence of the consignor is also situated in that country. If those requirements are not met, the law of the country where the place of delivery as agreed by the parties is situated shall apply.

2.   To the extent that the law applicable to a contract for the carriage of passengers has not been chosen by the parties in accordance with the second subparagraph, the law applicable shall be the law of the country where the passenger has his habitual residence, provided that either the place of departure or the place of destination is situated in that country. If these requirements are not met, the law of the country where the carrier has his habitual residence shall apply.

The parties may choose as the law applicable to a contract for the carriage of passengers in accordance with Article 3 only the law of the country where:

(a)   the passenger has his habitual residence; or
(b)   the carrier has his habitual residence; or
(c)   the carrier has his place of central administration; or
(d)   the place of departure is situated; or
(e)   the place of destination is situated.

3.   Where it is clear from all the circumstances of the case that the contract, in the absence of a choice of law, is manifestly more closely connected with a country other than that indicated in paragraphs 1 or 2, the law of that other country shall apply.

Article 6. Consumer contracts.   1.   Without prejudice to Articles 5 and 7, a contract concluded by a natural person for a purpose which can be regarded as being outside his trade or profession (the consumer) with another person acting in the exercise of his trade or profession (the professional) shall be governed by the law of the country where the consumer has his habitual residence, provided that the professional:

(a)   pursues his commercial or professional activities in the country where the consumer has his habitual residence, or

(b)   by any means, directs such activities to that country or to several countries including that country, and the contract falls within the scope of such activities.

2.   Notwithstanding paragraph 1, the parties may choose the law applicable to a contract which fulfils the requirements of paragraph 1, in accordance with Article 3. Such a choice may not, however, have the result of depriving the consumer of the protection afforded to him by provisions that cannot be derogated from by agreement by virtue of the law which, in the absence of choice, would have been applicable on the basis of paragraph 1.

3.   If the requirements in points (a) or (b) of paragraph 1 are not fulfilled, the law applicable to a contract between a consumer and a professional shall be determined pursuant to Articles 3 and 4.

4.   Paragraphs 1 and 2 shall not apply to:

(a)   a contract for the supply of services where the services are to be supplied to the consumer exclusively in a country other than that in which he has his habitual residence;

(b)   a contract of carriage other than a contract relating to package travel within the meaning of Council Directive 90/314/EEC of 13 June 1990 on package travel, package holidays and package tours;

(c)   a contract relating to a right in rem in immovable property or a tenancy of immovable property other than a contract relating to the right to use immovable properties on a timeshare basis within the meaning of Directive 94/47/EC;

(d)   rights and obligations which constitute a financial instrument and rights and obligations constituting the terms and conditions governing the issuance or offer to the public and public take-over bids of transferable securities, and the subscription and redemption of units in collective investment undertakings in so far as these activities do not constitute provision of a financial service;

(e)   a contract concluded within the type of system falling within the scope of Article 4(1)(h).

Article 7. Insurance contracts.   1.   This Article shall apply to contracts referred to in paragraph 2, whether or not the risk covered is situated in a Member State, and to all other insurance contracts covering risks situated inside the territory of the Member States. It shall not apply to reinsurance contracts.

2.   An insurance contract covering a large risk as defined in Article 5(d) of the First Council Directive 73/239/EEC of 24 July 1973 on the coordination of laws, regulations and administrative provisions relating to the taking-up and pursuit of the business of direct insurance other than life assurance shall be governed by the law chosen by the parties in accordance with Article 3 of this Regulation.

To the extent that the applicable law has not been chosen by the parties, the insurance contract shall be governed by the law of the country where the insurer has his habitual residence. Where it is clear from all the circumstances of the case that the contract is manifestly more closely connected with another country, the law of that other country shall apply.

3.   In the case of an insurance contract other than a contract falling within paragraph 2, only the following laws may be chosen by the parties in accordance with Article 3:

(a)   the law of any Member State where the risk is situated at the time of conclusion of the contract;

(b)   the law of the country where the policy holder has his habitual residence;

(c)   in the case of life assurance, the law of the Member State of which the policy holder is a national;

(d)   for insurance contracts covering risks limited to events occurring in one Member State other than the Member State where the risk is situated, the law of that Member State;

(e)   where the policy holder of a contract falling under this paragraph pursues a commercial or industrial activity or a liberal profession and the insurance contract covers two or more risks which relate to those activities and are situated in different Member States, the law of any of the Member States concerned or the law of the country of habitual residence of the policy holder.

Where, in the cases set out in points (a), (b) or (e), the Member States referred to grant greater freedom of choice of the law applicable to the insurance contract, the parties may take advantage of that freedom.

To the extent that the law applicable has not been chosen by the parties in accordance with this paragraph, such a contract shall be governed by the law of the Member State in which the risk is situated at the time of conclusion of the contract.

4.   The following additional rules shall apply to insurance contracts covering risks for which a Member State imposes an obligation to take out insurance:

(a)   the insurance contract shall not satisfy the obligation to take out insurance unless it complies with the specific provisions relating to that insurance laid down by the Member State that imposes the obligation. Where the law of the Member State in which the risk is situated and the law of the Member State imposing the obligation to take out insurance contradict each other, the latter shall prevail;

(b)   by way of derogation from paragraphs 2 and 3, a Member State may lay down that the insurance contract shall be governed by the law of the Member State that imposes the obligation to take out insurance.

5.   For the purposes of paragraph 3, third subparagraph, and paragraph 4, where the contract covers risks situated in more than one Member State, the contract shall be considered as constituting several contracts each relating to only one Member State.

6.   For the purposes of this Article, the country in which the risk is situated shall be determined in accordance with Article 2(d) of the Second Council Directive 88/357/EEC of 22 June 1988 on the coordination of laws, regulations and administrative provisions relating to direct insurance other than life assurance and laying down provisions to facilitate the effective exercise of freedom to provide services and, in the case of life assurance, the country in which the risk is situated shall be the country of the commitment within the meaning of Article 1(1)(g) of Directive 2002/83/EC.

Article 8. Individual employment contracts.   1.   An individual employment contract shall be governed by the law chosen by the parties in accordance with Article 3. Such a choice of law may not, however, have the result of depriving the employee of the protection afforded to him by provisions that cannot be derogated from by agreement under the law that, in the absence of choice, would have been applicable pursuant to paragraphs 2, 3 and 4 of this Article.

2.   To the extent that the law applicable to the individual employment contract has not been chosen by the parties, the contract shall be governed by the law of the

country in which or, failing that, from which the employee habitually carries out his work in performance of the contract. The country where the work is habitually carried out shall not be deemed to have changed if he is temporarily employed in another country.

3.   Where the law applicable cannot be determined pursuant to paragraph 2, the contract shall be governed by the law of the country where the place of business through which the employee was engaged is situated.

4.   Where it appears from the circumstances as a whole that the contract is more closely connected with a country other than that indicated in paragraphs 2 or 3, the law of that other country shall apply.

Article 9. Overriding mandatory provisions.   1.   Overriding mandatory provisions are provisions the respect for which is regarded as crucial by a country for safeguarding its public interests, such as its political, social or economic organization, to such an extent that they are applicable to any situation falling within their scope, irrespective of the law otherwise applicable to the contract under this Regulation.

2.   Nothing in this Regulation shall restrict the application of the overriding mandatory provisions of the law of the forum.

3.   Effect may be given to the overriding mandatory provisions of the law of the country where the obligations arising out of the contract have to be or have been performed, in so far as those overriding mandatory provisions render the performance of the contract unlawful. In considering whether to give effect to those provisions, regard shall be had to their nature and purpose and to the consequences of their application or non-application.

Article 10. Consent and material validity.   1.   The existence and validity of a contract, or of any term of a contract, shall be determined by the law which would govern it under this Regulation if the contract or term were valid.

2.   Nevertheless, a party, in order to establish that he did not consent, may rely upon the law of the country in which he has his habitual residence if it appears from the circumstances that it would not be reasonable to determine the effect of his conduct in accordance with the law specified in paragraph 1.

Article 11. Formal validity.   1.   A contract concluded between persons who, or whose agents, are in the same country at the time of its conclusion is formally valid if it satisfies the formal requirements of the law which governs it in substance under this Regulation or of the law of the country where it is concluded.

2.   A contract concluded between persons who, or whose agents, are in different countries at the time of its conclusion is formally valid if it satisfies the formal requirements of the law which governs it in substance under this Regulation, or of the law of either of the countries where either of the parties or their agent is present at the time of conclusion, or of the law of the country where either of the parties had his habitual residence at that time.

3.   A unilateral act intended to have legal effect relating to an existing or contemplated contract is formally valid if it satisfies the formal requirements of the law which governs or would govern the contract in substance under this Regulation, or of the law of the country where the act was done, or of the law of the country where the person by whom it was done had his habitual residence at that time.

4.   Paragraphs 1, 2 and 3 of this Article shall not apply to contracts that fall within the scope of Article 6. The form of such contracts shall be governed by the law of the country where the consumer has his habitual residence.

5.   Notwithstanding paragraphs 1 to 4, a contract the subject matter of which is a right *in rem* in immovable property or a tenancy of immovable property shall be subject to the requirements of form of the law of the country where the property is situated if by that law:

(a)   those requirements are imposed irrespective of the country where the contract is concluded and irrespective of the law governing the contract; and

(b)   those requirements cannot be derogated from by agreement.

Article 12. Scope of the law applicable.   1.   The law applicable to a contract by virtue of this Regulation shall govern in particular:

(a)   interpretation;

(b)   performance;

(c)   within the limits of the powers conferred on the court by its procedural law, the consequences of a total or partial breach of obligations, including the assessment of damages in so far as it is governed by rules of law;

(d)   the various ways of extinguishing obligations, and prescription and limitation of actions;

(e)   the consequences of nullity of the contract.

2.   In relation to the manner of performance and the steps to be taken in the event of defective performance, regard shall be had to the law of the country in which performance takes place.

Article 13. Incapacity.   In a contract concluded between persons who are in the same country, a natural person who would have capacity under the law of that country may invoke his incapacity resulting from the law of another country, only if the other party to the contract was aware of that incapacity at the time of the conclusion of the contract or was not aware thereof as a result of negligence.

Article 14. Voluntary assignment and contractual subrogation.   1.   The relationship between assignor and assignee under a voluntary assignment or contractual subrogation of a claim against another person (the debtor) shall be governed by the law that applies to the contract between the assignor and assignee under this Regulation.

2.   The law governing the assigned or subrogated claim shall determine its assignability, the relationship between the assignee and the debtor, the conditions under which the assignment or subrogation can be invoked against the debtor and whether the debtor's obligations have been discharged.

3.   The concept of assignment in this Article includes outright transfers of claims, transfers of claims by way of security and pledges or other security rights over claims.

Article 15. Legal subrogation.   Where a person (the creditor) has a contractual claim against another (the debtor) and a third person has a duty to satisfy the creditor, or has in fact satisfied the creditor in discharge of that duty, the law which governs the third person's duty to satisfy the creditor shall determine whether and to what extent the third person is entitled to exercise against the debtor the rights which the creditor had against the debtor under the law governing their relationship.

Article 16. Multiple liability.   If a creditor has a claim against several debtors who are liable for the same claim, and one of the debtors has already satisfied the claim in whole or in part, the law governing the debtor's obligation towards the creditor also governs the debtor's right to claim recourse from the other debtors. The other debtors may rely on the defences they had against the creditor to the extent allowed by the law governing their obligations towards the creditor.

Article 17. Set-off.   Where the right to set-off is not agreed by the parties, set-off shall be governed by the law applicable to the claim against which the right to set-off is asserted.

Article 18. Burden of proof.   1.   The law governing a contractual obligation under this Regulation shall apply to the extent that, in matters of contractual obligations, it contains rules which raise presumptions of law or determine the burden of proof.
    2.   A contract or an act intended to have legal effect may be proved by any mode of proof recognized by the law of the forum or by any of the laws referred to in Article 11 under which that contract or act is formally valid, provided that such mode of proof can be administered by the forum.

Chapter III — Other provisions

Article 19. Habitual residence.   1.   For the purposes of this Regulation, the habitual residence of companies and other bodies, corporate or unincorporated, shall be the place of central administration.
    The habitual residence of a natural person acting in the course of his business activity shall be his principal place of business.
    2.   Where the contract is concluded in the course of the operations of a branch, agency or any other establishment, or if, under the contract, performance is the responsibility of such a branch, agency or establishment, the place where the branch, agency or any other establishment is located shall be treated as the place of habitual residence.
    3.   For the purposes of determining the habitual residence, the relevant point in time shall be the time of the conclusion of the contract.

Article 20. Exclusion of renvoi.   The application of the law of any country specified by this Regulation means the application of the rules of law in force in that country other than its rules of private international law, unless provided otherwise in this Regulation.

Article 21. Public policy of the forum.   The application of a provision of the law of any country specified by this Regulation may be refused only if such application is manifestly incompatible with the public policy (ordre public) of the forum.

Article 22. States with more than one legal system.   1.   Where a State comprises several territorial units, each of which has its own rules of law in respect of contractual obligations, each territorial unit shall be considered as a country for the purposes of identifying the law applicable under this Regulation.
    2.   A Member State where different territorial units have their own rules of law in respect of contractual obligations shall not be required to apply this Regulation to conflicts solely between the laws of such units.

Article 23. Relationship with other provisions of Community law.   With the exception of Article 7, this Regulation shall not prejudice the application of provisions of Community law which, in relation to particular matters, lay down conflict-of-law rules relating to contractual obligations.

Article 24. Relationship with the Rome Convention.   1.   This Regulation shall replace the Rome Convention in the Member States, except as regards the territories of the Member States which fall within the territorial scope of that Convention and to which this Regulation does not apply pursuant to Article 299 of the Treaty.
2.   In so far as this Regulation replaces the provisions of the Rome Convention, any reference to that Convention shall be understood as a reference to this Regulation.

Article 25. Relationship with existing international conventions.   1.   This Regulation shall not prejudice the application of international conventions to which one or more Member States are parties at the time when this Regulation is adopted and which lay down conflict-of-law rules relating to contractual obligations.
2.   However, this Regulation shall, as between Member States, take precedence over conventions concluded exclusively between two or more of them in so far as such conventions concern matters governed by this Regulation.

Article 26. List of Conventions.   1.   By 17 June 2009, Member States shall notify the Commission of the conventions referred to in Article 25(1). After that date, Member States shall notify the Commission of all denunciations of such conventions.
2.   Within six months of receipt of the notifications referred to in paragraph 1, the Commission shall publish in the Official Journal of the European Union:
    (a)   a list of the conventions referred to in paragraph 1;
    (b)   the denunciations referred to in paragraph 1.

Article 27. Review clause.   1.   By 17 June 2013, the Commission shall submit to the European Parliament, the Council and the European Economic and Social Committee a report on the application of this Regulation. If appropriate, the report shall be accompanied by proposals to amend this Regulation. The report shall include:
    (a)   a study on the law applicable to insurance contracts and an assessment of the impact of the provisions to be introduced, if any; and
    (b)   an evaluation on the application of Article 6, in particular as regards the coherence of Community law in the field of consumer protection.
2.   By 17 June 2010, the Commission shall submit to the European Parliament, the Council and the European Economic and Social Committee a report on the question of the effectiveness of an assignment or subrogation of a claim against third parties and the priority of the assigned or subrogated claim over a right of another person. The report shall be accompanied, if appropriate, by a proposal to amend this Regulation and an assessment of the impact of the provisions to be introduced.

Article 28. Application in time.   This Regulation shall apply to contracts concluded as from 17 December 2009.[2]

---

[2]   This article was subject to corrigendum (OJ, L 309 of 24 November 2009).

Chapter IV — Final provisions

Article 29. Entry into force and application.   This Regulation shall enter into force on the 20th day following its publication in the Official Journal of the European Union.

It shall apply from 17 December 2009 except for Article 26 which shall apply from 17 June 2009.

This Regulation shall be binding in its entirety and directly applicable in the Member States in accordance with the Treaty establishing the European Community.

A.2.   Statements made at the meeting of the Council (JHA) of 5–6 June 2008 (Doc. Consilium No 10383/08 Add. 1)

1.   Statement by the Council and the Commission re the law applicable to insurance contracts

The Council and the Commission note that the rules contained in Article 7 essentially reflect the legal situation as regards applicable law as presently included in the insurance Directives. Any future substantive revision of the present regime should take place in the context of the review clause of this Regulation.

2.   Statement by the French delegation re Article 6 of Rome I on the law applicable to consumers

In view of the importance of conflict-of-law rules in international private law, and in order to achieve the objective, laid down in Article 153 of the EC Treaty, of ensuring a high level of consumer protection within the Community, France wishes to state that, in the revision of Regulation (EC) No 44/2001 on jurisdiction and the recognition and enforcement of judgments in civil and commercial matters, the provisions relating to jurisdiction (section 4 of Brussels I) must be consistent with Article 6 of the Regulation applicable to contractual obligations (Rome I), concerning the law applicable to consumer contracts.

A.3.   Proposal for a Regulation of the European Parliament and of the Council on jurisdiction, applicable law, recognition and enforcement of decisions and authentic instruments in matters of succession and the creation of a European Certificate of Succession (COM (2009) 154 of 14 October 2009): Recital 9

See Chapter XII, A.

B.1.   Convention on the law applicable to contractual obligations, opened for signature in Rome on 19 June 1980[*,1]

The High Contracting Parties to the Treaty establishing the European Economic Community,

Anxious to continue in the field of private international law the work of unification of law which has already been done within the Community, in particular in the field of jurisdiction and enforcement of judgments,

Wishing to establish uniform rules concerning the law applicable to contractual obligations,

Have agreed as follows:

Title I — Scope of the Convention

Article 1. Scope of the Convention.   1.   The rules of this Convention shall apply to contractual obligations in any situation involving a choice between the laws of different countries.

2.   They shall not apply to:

(a)   questions involving the status or legal capacity of natural persons, without prejudice to Article 11;

(b)   contractual obligations relating to:

— wills and succession;

— rights in property arising out of a matrimonial relationship;

— rights and duties arising out of a family relationship, parentage, marriage or affinity, including maintenance obligations in respect of children who are not legitimate;

(c)   obligations arising under bills of exchange, cheques and promissory notes and other negotiable instruments to the extent that the obligations under such other negotiable instruments arise out of their negotiable character;

(d)   arbitration agreements and agreements on the choice of court;

(e)   questions governed by the law of companies and other bodies corporate or unincorporate such as the creation, by registration or otherwise, legal capacity, internal organisation or winding up of companies and other bodies corporate or unincorporate and the personal liability of officers and members as such for the obligations of the company or body;

(f)   the question whether an agent is able to bind a principal, or an organ to bind a company or body corporate or unincorporate, to a third party;

---

[*]   The Convention entered into force internationally on 1 April 1991. It was accompanied by an explanatory report by professors M Giuliano and P Lagarde (OJ, C 282 of 31 October 1980). The following footnotes are published in OJ, C 334 of 30 December 2005.

[1]   Text as amended by the Convention of 10 April 1984 on the accession of the Hellenic Republic — hereafter referred to as the '1984 Accession Convention' –, by the Convention of 18 May 1992 on the accession of the Kingdom of Spain and the Portuguese Republic — hereafter referred to as the '1992 Accession Convention' –, by the Convention of 29 November 1996 on the accession of the Republic of Austria, the Republic of Finland and the Kingdom of Sweden — hereafter referred to as the '1996 Accession Convention' — and by the Convention of 14 April 2005 on the accession of the Czech Republic, the Republic of Estonia, the Republic of Cyprus, the Republic of Latvia, the Republic of Lithuania, the Republic of Hungary, the Republic of Malta, the Republic of Poland, the Republic of Slovenia and the Slovak Republic — hereafter referred to as the '2005 Accession Convention.'

(g)   the constitution of trusts and the relationship between settlors, trustees and beneficiaries;

(h)   evidence and procedure, without prejudice to Article 14.

3.   The rules of this Convention do not apply to contracts of insurance which cover risks situated in the territories of the Member States of the European Economic Community. In order to determine whether a risk is situated in those territories the court shall apply its internal law.

4.   The preceding paragraph does not apply to contracts of re-insurance.

Article 2. Application of law of non-contracting States.   Any law specified by this Convention shall be applied whether or not it is the law of a Contracting State.

Title II — Uniform rules

Article 3. Freedom of choice.   1.   A contract shall be governed by the law chosen by the parties. The choice must be expressed or demonstrated with reasonable certainty by the terms of the contract or the circumstances of the case. By their choice the parties can select the law applicable to the whole or a part only of the contract.

2.   The parties may at any time agree to subject the contract to a law other than that which previously governed it, whether as a result of an earlier choice under this Article or of other provisions of this Convention. Any variation by the parties of the law to be applied made after the conclusion of the contract shall not prejudice its formal validity under Article 9 or adversely affect the rights of third parties.

3.   The fact that the parties have chosen a foreign law, whether or not accompanied by the choice of a foreign tribunal, shall not, where all the other elements relevant to the situation at the time of the choice are connected with one country only, prejudice the application of rules of the law at the country which cannot be derogated from by contract, hereinafter called 'mandatory rules'.

4.   The existence and validity of the consent of the parties as to the choice of the applicable law shall be determined in accordance with the provisions of Articles 8, 9 and 11.

Article 4. Applicable law in the absence of choice.   1.   To the extent that the law applicable to the contract has not been chosen in accordance with Article 3, the contract shall be governed by the law of the country with which it is most closely connected. Nevertheless, a separable part of the contract which has a closer connection with another country may by way of exception be governed by the law of that other country.

2.   Subject to the provisions of paragraph 5 of this Article, it shall be presumed that the contract is most closely connected with the country where the party who is to effect the performance which is characteristic of the contract has, at the time of conclusion of the contract, his habitual residence, or, in the case of a body corporate or unincorporate, its central administration. However, if the contract is entered into in the course of that party's trade or profession, that country shall be the country in which the principal place of business is situated or, where under the terms of the contract the performance is to be effected through a place of business other than the principal place of business, the country in which that other place of business is situated.

3. Notwithstanding the provisions of paragraph 2 of this Article, to the extent that the subject matter of the contract is a right in immovable property or a right to use immovable property it shall be presumed that the contract is most closely connected with the country where the immovable property is situated.

4. A contract for the carriage of goods shall not be subject to the presumption in paragraph 2. In such a contract if the country in which, at the time the contract is concluded, the carrier has his principal place of business is also the country in which the place of loading or the place of discharge or the principal place of business of the consignor is situated, it shall be presumed that the contract is most closely connected with that country. In applying this paragraph single voyage charter-parties and other contracts the main purpose of which is the carriage of goods shall be treated as contracts for the carriage of goods.

5. Paragraph 2 shall not apply if the characteristic performance cannot be determined, and the presumptions in paragraphs 2, 3 and 4 shall be disregarded if it appears from the circumstances as a whole that the contract is more closely connected with another country.

Article 5. Certain consumer contracts. 1. This Article applies to a contract the object of which is the supply of goods or services to a person ('the consumer') for a purpose which can be regarded as being outside his trade or profession, or a contract for the provision of credit for that object.

2. Notwithstanding the provisions of Article 3, a choice of law made by the parties shall not have the result of depriving the consumer of the protection afforded to him by the mandatory rules of the law of the country in which he has his habitual residence:

— if in that country the conclusion of the contract was preceded by a specific invitation addressed to him or by advertising, and he had taken in that country all the steps necessary on his part for the conclusion of the contract, or

— if the other party or his agent received the consumer's order in that country, or

— if the contract is for the sale of goods and the consumer travelled from that country to another country and there gave his order, provided that the consumer's journey was arranged by the seller for the purpose of inducing the consumer to buy.

3. Notwithstanding the provisions of Article 4, a contract to which this Article applies shall, in the absence of choice in accordance with Article 3, be governed by the law of the country in which the consumer has his habitual residence if it is entered into in the circumstances described in paragraph 2 of this Article.

4. This Article shall not apply to:

(a) a contract of carriage;

(b) a contract for the supply of services where the services are to be supplied to the consumer exclusively in a country other than that in which he has his habitual residence.

5. Notwithstanding the provisions of paragraph 4, this Article shall apply to a contract which, for an inclusive price, provides for a combination of travel and accommodation.

Article 6. Individual employment contracts. 1. Notwithstanding the provisions of Article 3, in a contract of employment a choice of law made by the parties shall not have the result of depriving the employee of the protection afforded to him by the mandatory rules of the law which would be applicable under paragraph 2 in the absence of choice.

2.   Notwithstanding the provisions of Article 4, a contract of employment shall, in the absence of choice in accordance with Article 3, be governed:

(a)   by the law of the country in which the employee habitually carries out his work in performance of the contract, even if he is temporarily employed in another country; or

(b)   if the employee does not habitually carry out his work in any one country, by the law of the country in which the place of business through which he was engaged is situated;

unless it appears from the circumstances as a whole that the contract is more closely connected with another country, in which case the contract shall be governed by the law of that country.

Article 7. Mandatory rules.   1.   When applying under this Convention the law of a country, effect may be given to the mandatory rules of the law of another country with which the situation has a close connection, if and in so far as, under the law of the latter country, those rules must be applied whatever the law applicable to the contract. In considering whether to give effect to these mandatory rules, regard shall be had to their nature and purpose and to the consequences of their application or non-application.

2.   Nothing in this Convention shall restrict the application of the rules of the law of the forum in a situation where they are mandatory irrespective of the law otherwise applicable to the contract.

Article 8. Material validity.   1.   The existence and validity of a contract, or of any term of a contract, shall be determined by the law which would govern it under this Convention if the contract or term were valid.

2.   Nevertheless a party may rely upon the law of the country in which he has his habitual residence to establish that he did not consent if it appears from the circumstances that it would not be reasonable to determine the effect of his conduct in accordance with the law specified in the preceding paragraph.

Article 9. Formal validity.   1.   A contract concluded between persons who are in the same country is formally valid if it satisfies the formal requirements of the law which governs it under this Convention or of the law of the country where it is concluded.

2.   A contract concluded between persons who are in different countries is formally valid if it satisfies the formal requirements of the law which governs it under this Convention or of the law of one of those countries.

3.   Where a contract is concluded by an agent, the country in which the agent acts is the relevant country for the purposes of paragraphs 1 and 2.

4.   An act intended to have legal effect relating to an existing or contemplated contract is formally valid if it satisfies the formal requirements of the law which under this Convention governs or would govern the contract or of the law of the country where the act was done.

5.   The provisions of the preceding paragraphs shall not apply to a contract to which Article 5 applies, concluded in the circumstances described in paragraph 2 of Article 5. The formal validity of such a contract is governed by the law of the country in which the consumer has his habitual residence.

6.   Notwithstanding paragraphs 1 to 4 of this Article, a contract the subject matter of which is a right in immovable property or a right to use immovable property shall be subject to the mandatory requirements of form of the law of the country where the property is situated if by that law those requirements are imposed irrespective of the country where the contract is concluded and irrespective of the law governing the contract.

Article 10. Scope of applicable law.   1.   The law applicable to a contract by virtue of Articles 3 to 6 and 12 of this Convention shall govern in particular:
    (a)   interpretation;
    (b)   performance;
    (c)   within the limits of the powers conferred on the court by its procedural law, the consequences of breach, including the assessment of damages in so far as it is governed by rules of law;
    (d)   the various ways of extinguishing obligations, and prescription and limitation of actions;
    (e)   the consequences of nullity of the contract.
    2.   In relation to the manner of performance and the steps to be taken in the event of defective performance regard shall be had to the law of the country in which performance takes place.

Article 11. Incapacity.   In a contract concluded between persons who are in the same country, a natural person who would have capacity under the law of that country may invoke his incapacity resulting from another law only if the other party to the contract was aware of this incapacity at the time of the conclusion of the contract or was not aware thereof as a result of negligence.

Article 12. Voluntary assignment.   1.   The mutual obligations of assignor and assignee under a voluntary assignment of a right against another person ('the debtor') shall be governed by the law which under this Convention applies to the contract between the assignor and assignee.
    2.   The law governing the right to which the assignment relates shall determine its assignability, the relationship between the assignee and the debtor, the conditions under which the assignment can be invoked against the debtor and any question whether the debtor's obligations have been discharged.

Article 13. Subrogation.   1.   Where a person ('the creditor') has a contractual claim upon another ('the debtor'), and a third person has a duty to satisfy the creditor, or has in fact satisfied the creditor in discharge of that duty, the law which governs the third person's duty to satisfy the creditor shall determine whether the third person is entitled to exercise against the debtor the rights which the creditor had against the debtor under the law governing their relationship and, if so, whether he may do so in full or only to a limited extent.
    2.   The same rule applies where several persons are subject to the same contractual claim and one of them has satisfied the creditor.

Article 14. *Burden of proof, etc.*   1.   The law governing the contract under this Convention applies to the extent that it contains, in the law of contract, rules which raise presumptions of law or determine the burden of proof.

   2.   A contract or an act intended to have legal effect may be proved by any mode of proof recognised by the law of the forum or by any of the laws referred to in Article 9 under which that contract or act is formally valid, provided that such mode of proof can be administered by the forum.

Article 15. *Exclusion of renvoi.*   The application of the law of any country specified by this Convention means the application of the rules of law in force in that country other than its rules of private international law.

Article 16. *'Ordre public'.*   The application of a rule of the law of any country specified by this Convention may be refused only if such application is manifestly incompatible with the public policy ('ordre public') of the forum.

Article 17. *No retrospective effect.*   This Convention shall apply in a Contracting State to contracts made after the date on which this Convention has entered into force with respect to that State.

Article 18. *Uniform interpretation.*   In the interpretation and application of the preceding uniform rules, regard shall be had to their international character and to the desirability of achieving uniformity in their interpretation and application.

Article 19. *States with more than one legal system.*   1.   Where a State comprises several territorial units each of which has its own rules of law in respect of contractual obligations, each territorial unit shall be considered as a country for the purposes of identifying the law applicable under this Convention.

   2.   A State within which different territorial units have their own rules of law in respect of contractual obligations shall not be bound to apply this Convention to conflicts solely between the laws of such units.

Article 20. *Precedence of Community law.*   This Convention shall not affect the application of provisions which, in relation to particular matters, lay down choice of law rules relating to contractual obligations and which are or will be contained in acts of the institutions of the European Communities or in national laws harmonised in implementation of such acts.

Article 21. *Relationship with other conventions.*   This Convention shall not prejudice the application of international conventions to which a Contracting State is, or becomes, a party.

Article 22. *Reservations.*   1.   Any Contracting State may, at the time of signature, ratification, acceptance or approval, reserve the right not to apply:

    (a)   the provisions of Article 7(1);
    (b)   the provisions of Article 10(1) (e).
    2.[2]

    3.   Any Contracting State may at any time withdraw a reservation which it has made; the reservation shall cease to have effect on the first day of the third calendar month after notification of the withdrawal.

Title III — Final provisions

Article 23.   1.   If, after the date on which this Convention has entered into force for a Contracting State, that State wishes to adopt any new choice of law rule in regard to any particular category of contract within the scope of this Convention, it shall communicate its intention to the other signatory States through the Secretary-General of the Council of the European Communities.

    2.   Any signatory State may, within six months from the date of the communication made to the Secretary-General, request him to arrange consultations between signatory States in order to reach agreement (…). [3]

    3.   If no signatory State has requested consultations within this period or if within two years following the communication made to the Secretary-General no agreement is reached in the course of consultations, the Contracting State concerned may amend its law in the manner indicated. The measures taken by that State shall be brought to the knowledge of the other signatory States through the Secretary-General of the Council of the European Communities.

Article 24.   1.   If, after the date on which this Convention has entered into force with respect to a Contracting State, that State wishes to become a party to a multilateral convention whose principal aim or one of whose principal aims is to lay down rules of private international law concerning any of the matters governed by this Convention, the procedure set out in Article 23 shall apply. However, the period of two years, referred to in paragraph 3 of that Article, shall be reduced to one year.

    2.   The procedure referred to in the preceding paragraph need not be followed if a Contracting State or one of the European Communities is already a party to the multilateral convention, or if its object is to revise a convention to which the State concerned is already a party, or if it is a convention concluded within the framework of the Treaties establishing the European Communities.

Article 25.   If a Contracting State considers that the unification achieved by this Convention is prejudiced by the conclusion of agreements not covered by Article 24(1), that State may request the Secretary-General of the Council of the European Communities to arrange consultations between the signatory States of this Convention.

---

[2]   Paragraph deleted by Article 2(1) of the 1992 Accession Convention.
[3]   Phrase deleted by the 1992 Accession Convention.

Article 26. Any Contracting State may request the revision of this Convention. In this event a revision conference shall be convened by the President of the Council of the European Communities.

Article 27.[4]

Article 28. 1. This Convention shall be open from 19 June 1980 for signature by the States party to the Treaty establishing the European Economic Community.

    2. This Convention shall be subject to ratification, acceptance or approval by the signatory States. The instruments of ratification, acceptance or approval shall be deposited with the Secretary-General of the Council of the European Communities.[5]

Article 29.[6] 1. This Convention shall enter into force on the first day of the third month following the deposit of the seventh instrument of ratification, acceptance or approval.

---

   [4] Article deleted by Article 2(1) of the 1992 Accession Convention.
   [5] Ratification of the Accession Conventions is governed by the following provisions of those Conventions:
- as regards the 1984 Accession Convention, by Article 3 of that Convention, which reads as follows:
- 'Article 3. – This Convention shall be ratified by signatory States. The instruments of ratification shall be deposited with the Secretary-General of the Council of the European Communities.',
- as regards the 1992 Accession Convention, by Article 4 of that Convention, which reads as follows:
- 'Article 4. – This Convention shall be ratified by signatory States. The instruments of ratification shall be deposited with the Secretary-General of the Council of the European Communities.',
- as regards the 1996 Accession Convention, by Article 5 of that Convention, which reads as follows:
- 'Article 5. – This Convention shall be ratified by signatory States. The instruments of ratification shall be deposited with the Secretary-General of the Council of the European Union.',
- as regards the 2005 Accession Convention, by Article 4 of the Convention, which reads as follows:
- 'Article 4. – This Convention shall be ratified by signatory States. The instruments of ratification shall be deposited with the Secretary-General of the Council of the European Union.'.

   [6] The entry into force of the Accession Conventions is governed by the following provisions of those Conventions:
- as regards the 1984 Accession Convention, by Article 4 of that Convention, which reads as follows:

'Article 4. — This Convention shall enter into force, as between the States which have ratified it, on the first day of the third month following the deposit of the last instrument of ratification by the Hellenic Republic and seven States which have ratified the Convention on the law applicable to contractual obligations.

This Convention shall enter into force for each Contracting State which subsequently ratifies it on the first day of the third month following the deposit of its instrument of ratification.',
- as regards the 1992 Accession Convention, by Article 5 of that Convention, which reads as follows:

'Article 5. — This Convention shall enter into force, as between the States which have ratified it, on the first day of the third month following the deposit of the last instrument of ratification by the Kingdom of Spain or the Portuguese Republic and by one State which has ratified the Convention on the law applicable to contractual obligations.

This Convention shall enter into force for each Contracting State which subsequently ratifies it on the first day of the third month following the deposit of its instrument of ratification.',
- as regards the 1996 Accession Convention, by Article 6 of that Convention, which reads as follows:

'Article 6. –1. This Convention shall enter into force, as between the States which have ratified it, on the first day of the third month following the deposit of the last instrument of ratification by the Republic of Austria, the Republic of Finland or the Kingdom of Sweden and by one Contracting State which has ratified the Convention on the law applicable to contractual obligations.

   2. This Convention shall enter into force for each Contracting State which subsequently ratifies it on the first day of the third month following the deposit of its instrument of ratification.',
- as regards the 2005 Accession Convention, by Article 5 of the Convention, which reads as follows:

'Article 5. –1. This Convention shall enter into force between the States which have ratified it, on the first day of the third month following the deposit of the second instrument of ratification.'

   2. Thereafter, this Convention shall enter into force, for each signatory State which subsequently ratifies it, on the first day of the third month following the deposit of its instrument of ratification.

2.   This Convention shall enter into force for each signatory State ratifying, accepting or approving at a later date on the first day of the third month following the deposit of its instrument of ratification, acceptance or approval.

Article 30.   1.   This Convention shall remain in force for 10 years from the date of its entry into force in accordance with Article 29(1), even for States for which it enters into force at a later date.

2.   If there has been no denunciation it shall be renewed tacitly every five years.

3.   A Contracting State which wishes to denounce shall, not less than six months before the expiration of the period of 10 or five years, as the case may be, give notice to the Secretary-General of the Council of the European Communities.[7]

4.   The denunciation shall have effect only in relation to the State which has notified it. The Convention will remain in force as between all other Contracting States.

Article 31[8]   The Secretary-General of the Council of the European Communities shall notify the States party to the Treaty establishing the European Economic Community of:
  (a)   the signatures;
  (b)   deposit of each instrument of ratification, acceptance or approval;
  (c)   the date of entry into force of this Convention;
  (d)   communications made in pursuance of Articles 23, 24, 25, 26 and 30[9];
  (e)   the reservations and withdrawals of reservations referred to in Article 22.

Article 32.   The Protocol annexed to this Convention shall form an integral part thereof.

---

[7]   Phrase deleted by the 1992 Accession Convention.

[8]   Notification concerning the Accession Conventions is governed by the following provisions of those Conventions:
  •   as regards the 1984 Accession Convention, by Article 5 of that Convention, which reads as follows:
'Article 5. — The Secretary-General of the Council of the European Communities shall notify the signatory States of:
  (a) the deposit of each instrument of ratification;
  (b) the dates of entry into force of this Convention for the Contracting States.'
  •   as regards the 1992 Accession Convention, by Article 6 of that Convention, which reads as follows:
'Article 6. — The Secretary-General of the Council of the European Communities shall notify the signatory States of:
  (a) the deposit of each instrument of ratification;
  (b) the dates of entry into force of this Convention for the Contracting States.'
  •   as regards the 1996 Accession Convention, by Article 7 of that Convention, which reads as follows:
'Article 7. — The Secretary-General of the Council of the European Union shall notify the signatory States of:
  (a) the deposit of each instrument of ratification;
  (b) the dates of entry into force of this Convention for the Contracting States.'
  •   as regards the 2005 Accession Convention, by Article 6 of the Convention, which reads as follows:
'Article 6. — The Secretary-General of the Council of the European Communities shall notify the signatory States of:
  (a) the deposit of each instrument of ratification;
  (b) the dates of entry into force of this Convention for the Contracting States.'
[9]   Point (d) as amended by the 1992 Accession Convention.

Article 33.[10] This Convention, drawn up in a single original in the Danish, Dutch, English, French, German, Irish and Italian languages, these texts being equally authentic, shall be

---

[10] An indication of the authentic texts of the Accession Convention is to be found in the following provisions:

• as regards the 1984 Accession Convention, in Articles 2 and 6 of that Convention, which reads as follows:

'*Article 2.* — The Secretary-General of the Council of the European Communities shall transmit a certified copy of the Convention on the law applicable to contractual obligations in the Danish, Dutch, English, French, German, Irish and Italian languages to the Government of the Hellenic Republic.

The text of the Convention on the law applicable to contractual obligations in the Greek language is annexed hereto. The text in the Greek language shall be authentic under the same conditions as the other texts of the Convention on the law applicable to contractual obligations.'

'*Article 6.* – This Convention, drawn up in a single original in the Danish, Dutch, English, French, German, Greek, Irish and Italian languages, all eight texts being equally authentic, shall be deposited in the archives of the General Secretariat of the Council of the European Communities. The Secretary-General shall transmit a certified copy to the government of each Signatory State.'

• as regards the 1992 Accession Convention, in Articles 3 and 7 of that Convention, which reads as follows:

'*Article 3.* — 1. The Secretary-General of the Council of the European Communities shall transmit a certified copy of the Convention on the law applicable to contractual obligations in the Danish, Dutch, English, French, German, Greek, Irish and Italian languages to the Governments of the Kingdom of Spain and the Portuguese Republic.

2.   The text of the Convention on the law applicable to contractual obligations in the Portuguese and Spanish languages is set out in Annexes I and II to this Convention. The texts drawn up in the Portuguese and Spanish languages shall be authentic under the same conditions as the other texts of the Convention on the law applicable to contractual obligations.'

'*Article 7.* – This Convention, drawn up in a single original in the Danish, Dutch, English, French, German, Greek, Irish, Italian, Portuguese and Spanish languages, all ten texts being equally authentic, shall be deposited in the archives of the General Secretariat of the Council of the European Communities. The Secretary-General shall transmit a certified copy to the government of each Signatory State.'

• as regards the 1996 Accession Convention, in Articles 4 and 8 of that Convention, which read as follows:

'*Article 4.* — 1. The Secretary-General of the Council of the European Union shall transmit a certified copy of the Convention of 1980, the Convention of 1984, the First Protocol of 1988, the Second Protocol of 1988 and the Convention of 1992 in the Danish, Dutch, English, French, German, Greek, Irish, Italian, Spanish and Portuguese languages to the Governments of the Republic of Austria, the Republic of Finland and the Kingdom of Sweden.

2. The text of the Convention of 1980, the Convention of 1984, the First Protocol of 1988, the Second Protocol of 1988 and the Convention of 1992 in the Finnish and Swedish languages shall be authentic under the same conditions as the other texts of the Convention of 1980, the Convention of 1984, the First Protocol of 1988, the Second Protocol of 1988 and the Convention of 1992.'

'*Article 8.* – This Convention, drawn up in a single original in the Danish, Dutch, English, Finnish, French, German, Greek, Irish, Italian, Portuguese, Spanish and Swedish languages, all twelve texts being equally authentic, shall be deposited in the archives of the General Secretariat of the Council of the European Union. The Secretary-General shall transmit a certified copy to the government of each Signatory State.'

• as regards the 2005 Accession Convention, in Articles 3 and 7 of that Convention, which reads as follows:

'*Article 3.* —   1.   The Secretary-General of the Council of the European Union shall transmit a certified copy of the Convention of 1980, the Convention of 1984, the First Protocol of 1988, the Second Protocol of 1988, the Convention of 1992 and the Convention of 1996 in the Danish, Dutch, English, Finnish, French, German, Greek, Irish, Italian, Portuguese, Spanish and Swedish languages to the Governments of the Czech Republic, the Republic of Estonia, the Republic of Cyprus, the Republic of Latvia, the Republic of Lithuania, the Republic of Hungary, the Republic of Malta, the Republic of Poland, the Republic of Slovenia and the Slovak Republic.

2.   The text of the Convention of 1980, the Convention of 1984, the First Protocol of 1988, the Second Protocol of 1988, the Convention of 1992 and the Convention of 1996 in the Czech, Estonian, Hungarian, Latvian, Lithuanian, Maltese, Polish, Slovakian and Slovenian languages shall be authentic under the same conditions as the other texts of the Convention of 1980, the Convention of 1984, the First Protocol of 1988, the Second Protocol of 1988, the Convention of 1992 and the Convention of 1996.'

'*Article 7.* — This Convention, drawn up in a single original in the Czech, Danish, Dutch, English, Estonian, Finnish, French, German, Greek, Hungarian, Irish, Italian, Latvian, Lithuanian, Maltese, Polish, Portuguese, Slovakian, Slovenian, Spanish and Swedish languages, all twenty-one texts being equally authentic, shall be deposited in the archives of the General Secretariat of the Council of the European Union. The Secretary-General shall transmit a certified copy to the Government of each Signatory State.'

deposited in the archives of the Secretariat of the Council of the European Communities. The Secretary-General shall transmit a certified copy thereof to the Government of each Signatory State.

Protocol.[11]

The High Contracting Parties have agreed upon the following provision which shall be annexed to the Convention:

'Notwithstanding the provisions of the Convention, Denmark, Sweden and Finland may retain national provisions concerning the law applicable to questions relating to the carriage of goods by sea and may amend such provisions without following the procedure provided for in Article 23 of the Convention of Rome. The national provisions applicable in this respect are the following:

— in Denmark, paragraphs 252 and 321 (3) and (4) of the 'Sølov' (maritime law),
— in Sweden, Chapter 13, Articles 2(1) and (2), and Chapter 14, Article 1(3), of 'sjölagen' (maritime law),
— in Finland, Chapter 13, Articles 2(1) and (2), and Chapter 14, Article 1(3), of 'merilaki'/'sjölagen' (maritime law).'

Joint declaration

At the time of the signature of the Convention on the law applicable to contractual obligations, the Governments of the Kingdom of Belgium, the Kingdom of Denmark, the Federal Republic of Germany, the French Republic, Ireland, the Italian Republic, the Grand Duchy of Luxembourg, the Kingdom of the Netherlands and the United Kingdom of Great Britain and Northern Ireland:

I.   anxious to avoid, as far as possible, dispersion of choice of law rules among several instruments and differences between these rules, express the wish that the institutions of the European Communities, in the exercise of their powers under the Treaties by which they were established, will, where the need arises, endeavour to adopt choice of law rules which are as far as possible consistent with those of this Convention;

II. declare their intention as from the date of signature of this Convention until becoming bound by Article 24, to consult with each other if any one of the signatory States wishes to become a party to any convention to which the procedure referred to in Article 24 would apply;

III. having regard to the contribution of the Convention on the law applicable to contractual obligations to the unification of choice of law rules within the European Communities, express the view that any State which becomes a member of the European Communities should accede to this Convention.

---

[11]   Text as amended by the 1996 Accession Convention.

Joint declaration

The Governments of the Kingdom of Belgium, the Kingdom of Denmark, the Federal Republic of Germany, the French Republic, Ireland, the Italian Republic, the Grand Duchy of Luxembourg, the Kingdom of the Netherlands and the United Kingdom of Great Britain and Northern Ireland,

On signing the Convention on the law applicable to contractual obligations;

Desiring to ensure that the Convention is applied as effectively as possible;

Anxious to prevent differences of interpretation of the Convention from impairing its unifying effect;

Declare themselves ready:

    1.   to examine the possibility of conferring jurisdiction in certain matters on the Court of Justice of the European Communities and, if necessary, to negotiate an agreement to this effect;

    2.   to arrange meetings at regular intervals between their representatives.

B.2.   First Protocol on the interpretation by the Court of Justice of the European Communities of the convention on the law applicable to contractual obligations, opened for signature in Rome on 19 June 1980[1]

The High Contracting Parties to the Treaty establishing the European Economic Community,

Having regard to the Joint Declaration annexed to the Convention on the law applicable to contractual obligations, opened for signature in Rome on 19 June 1980,

Have decided to conclude a Protocol conferring jurisdiction on the Court of Justice of the European Communities to interpret that Convention, and to this end have designated as their Plenipotentiaries: (*Omissis*)

Who, meeting within the Council of the European Communities, having exchanged their full powers, found in good and due form,

Have greed as follows:

Article 1.   The Court of Justice of the European Communities shall have jurisdiction to give rulings on the interpretation of:

    (a) the Convention on the law applicable to contractual obligations, opened for signature in Rome on 19 June 1980, hereinafter referred to as 'the Rome Convention';

---

[1]   The First and the Second Protocol entered into force on 1 August 2004. The text published above is a non-official consolidated text as amended by the Accession Conventions, based on the last official codified text (OJ, C 334 of 30 December 2005) and by Council Decision of 8 November 2007 concerning the accession of the Republic of Bulgaria and of Romania to the Convention (OJ, L 347 of 29 December 2007).

    (b) the Convention on accession to the Rome Convention by the States which have become Members of the European Communities since the date on which it was opened for signature;

    (c) this Protocol.

Article 2.   Any of the courts referred to below may request the Court of Justice to give a preliminary ruling on a question raised in a case pending before it and concerning interpretation of the provisions contained in the instruments referred to in Article 1 if that court considers that a decision on the question is necessary to enable it to give judgment:

    (a) — . in Belgium: 'la Cour de cassation' ('het Hof van Cassatie') and 'le Conseil d'État' ('de Raad van State'),

— in the Czech Republic: 'Nejvyšší soud České republiky' and 'Nejvyšší správní soud',

— in Bulgaria: Върховен касационен съд et Върховен административен съд,

— in Denmark: 'Højesteret',

— in the Federal Republic of Germany: 'die obersten Gerichtshöfe des Bundes',

— in Estonia: 'Riigikohus',

— in Greece: Τα ανώτατα Δικαστήρια,

— in Spain: 'el Tribunal Supremo',

— in France: 'la Cour de cassation' and 'le Conseil d'État',

— in Ireland: the Supreme Court,

— in Italy: 'la Corte suprema di cassazione' and 'il Consiglio di Stato',

— in Cyprus: 'Ανώτατο Δικαστήριο',

— in Latvia: 'Augstākās Tiesas Senāts',

— in Lithuania: 'Lietuvos Aukščiausiasis Teismas' and 'Lietuvos vyriausiasis administracinis teismas',

— in Luxembourg: 'la Cour Supérieure de Justice' when sitting as 'Cour de cassation',

— in Hungary: 'Legfelsõbb Bíróság',

— in Malta: 'Qorti ta' l-Appell',

— in the Netherlands: 'de Hoge Raad',

— in Austria: the 'Oberste Gerichtshof', the 'Verwaltungsgerichtshof' and the 'Verfassungsgerichtshof',

— in Poland: 'Sąd Najwyższy' and 'Naczelny Sąd Administracyjny',

— in Portugal: 'o Supremo Tribunal de Justiça' and 'o Supremo Tribunal Administrativo',

— in Romania: Înalta Curte de Casație și Justiție;

— in Slovenia: 'Ustavno sodišče Republike Slovenije', 'Vrhovno sodišče Republike Slovenije',

— in Slovakia: 'Najvyšší súd Slovenskej republiky',

— in Finland: 'korkein oikeus/högsta domstolen', 'korkein hallinto-oikeus/ högsta förvaltningsdomstolen', 'markkinatuomioistuin/marknadsdomstolen' and 'työtuomioistuin/arbetsdomstolen',

— in Sweden: 'Högsta domstolen', 'Regeringsrätten', 'Arbetsdomstolen' and 'Marknadsdomstolen',

— in the United Kingdom: the House of Lords and other courts from which no further appeal is possible;

    (b) the courts of the Contracting States when acting as appeal courts.

Article 3.   1.   The competent authority of a Contracting State may request the Court of Justice to give a ruling on a question of interpretation of the provisions contained in the instruments referred to in Article 1 if judgments given by courts of that State conflict with the interpretation given either by the Court of Justice or in a judgment of one of the courts of another Contracting State referred to in Article 2. The provisions of this paragraph shall apply only to judgments which have become res judicata.

2.   The interpretation given by the Court of Justice in response to such a request shall not affect the judgments which gave rise to the request for interpretation.

3.   The Procurators-General of the Supreme Courts of Appeal of the Contracting States, or any other authority designated by a Contracting State, shall be entitled to request the Court of Justice for a ruling on interpretation in accordance with paragraph 1.

4.   The Registrar of the Court of Justice shall give notice of 4. The Registrar of the Court of Justice shall give notice of the request to the Contracting States, to the Commission and to the Council of the European Communities; they shall then be entitled within two months of the notification to submit statements of case or written observations to the Court.

5.   No fees shall be levied or any costs or expenses awarded in respect of the proceedings provided for in this Article.

Article 4.   1.   Except where this Protocol otherwise provides, the provisions of the Treaty establishing the European Economic Community and those of the Protocol on the Statute of the Court of Justice annexed thereto, which are applicable when the Court is requested to give a preliminary ruling, shall also apply to any proceedings for the interpretation of the instruments referred to in Article 1.

2.   The Rules of Procedure of the Court of Justice shall, if necessary, be adjusted and supplemented in accordance with Article 188 of the Treaty establishing the European Economic Community.

Article 5.   This Protocol shall be subject to ratification by the Signatory States. The instruments of ratification shall be deposited with the Secretary-General of the Council of the European Communities.

Article 6.   1.   To enter into force, this Protocol must be ratified by seven States in respect of which the Rome Convention is in force. This Protocol shall enter into force on the first day of the third month following the deposit of the instrument of ratification by the last such State to take this step. If, however, the Second Protocol conferring on the Court of Justice of the European Communities certain powers to interpret the Convention on the law applicable to contractual obligations, opened for signature in Rome on 19 June 1980, concluded in Brussels on 19 December 1988 (1), enters into force on a later date, this Protocol shall enter into force on the date of entry into force of the Second Protocol.

2.   Any ratification subsequent to the entry into force of this Protocol shall take effect on the first day of the third month following the deposit of the instrument of ratification, provided that the ratification, acceptance or approval of the Rome Convention by the State in question has become effective.

Article 7.   The Secretary-General of the Council of the European Communities shall notify the Signatory States of:

(a) the deposit of each instrument of ratification;
(b) the date of entry into force of this Protocol;
(c) any designation communicated pursuant to Article 3(3);
(d) any communication made pursuant to Article 8.

Article 8.   The Contracting States shall communicate to the Secretary-General of the Council of the European Communities the texts of any provisions of their laws which necessitate an amendment to the list of courts in Article 2(a).

Article 9.   This Protocol shall have effect for as long as the Rome Convention remains in force under the conditions laid down in Article 30 of that Convention.

Article 10.   Any Contracting State may request the revision of this Protocol. In this event, a revision conference shall be convened by the President of the Council of the European Communities.

Article 11.   This Protocol, drawn up in a single original in the Danish, Dutch, English, French, German, Greek, Irish, Italian, Portuguese and Spanish languages, all 10 texts being equally authentic, shall be deposited in the archives of the General Secretariat of the Council of the European Communities. The Secretary-General shall transmit a certified copy to the Government of each Signatory State.

Joint declaration

The Governments of the Kingdom of Belgium, the Kingdom of Denmark, the Federal Republic of Germany, the Hellenic Republic, the Kingdom of Spain, the French Republic, Ireland, the Italian Republic, the Grand Duchy of Luxembourg, the Kingdom of the Netherlands, the Portuguese Republic and the United Kingdom of Great Britain and Northern Ireland,

On signing the First Protocol on the interpretation by the Court of Justice of the European Communities of the Convention on the law applicable to contractual obligations, opened for signature in Rome on 19 June 1980,

Desiring to ensure that the Convention is applied as effectively and as uniformly as possible,

Declare themselves ready to organize, in cooperation with the Court of Justice of the European Communities, an exchange of information on judgments which have become *res judicata* and have been handed down pursuant to the Convention on the law applicable to contractual obligations by the courts referred to in Article 2 of the said Protocol. The exchange of information will comprise:

    —   the forwarding to the Court of Justice by the competent national authorities of judgments handed down by the courts referred to in Article 2(a) and significant judgments handed down by the courts referred to in Article 2(b);

    —   the classification and the documentary exploitation of these judgments by the Court of Justice including, as far as necessary, the drawing up of abstracts and translations, and the publication of judgments of particular importance;

—   the communication by the Court of Justice of the documentary material to the competent national authorities of the States parties to the Protocol and to the Commission and the Council of the European Communities.

B.3.   Second Protocol conferring on the Court of Justice of the European Communities certain powers to interpret the Convention on the law applicable to contractual obligations, opened for signature in Rome on 19 June 1980[1]

The High Contracting Parties to the Treaty establishing the European Economic Community,

Whereas the Convention on the law applicable to contractual obligations, opened for signature in Rome on 19 June 1980, hereinafter referred to as 'the Rome Convention', will enter into force after the deposit of the seventh instrument of ratification, acceptance or approval;

Whereas the uniform application of the rules laid down in the Rome Convention requires that machinery to ensure uniform interpretation be set up and whereas to that end appropriate powers should be conferred upon the Court of Justice of the European Communities, even before the Rome Convention enters into force with respect to all the Member States of the European Economic Community,

Have decided to conclude this Protocol and to this end have designated as their Plenipotentiaries: (*Omissis*)

Who, meeting within the Council of the European Communities, having exchanged their full powers, found in good and due form,

Have agreed as follows:

Article 1.   1.   The Court of Justice of the European Communities shall, with respect to the Rome Convention, have the jurisdiction conferred upon it by the First Protocol on the interpretation by the Court of Justice of the European Communities of the Convention on the law applicable to contractual obligations, opened for signature in Rome on 19 June 1980, concluded in Brussels on 19 December 1988. The Protocol on the Statute of the Court of Justice of the European Communities and the Rules of Procedure of the Court of Justice shall apply.

2.   The Rules of Procedure of the Court of Justice shall be adapted and supplemented as necessary in accordance with Article 188 of the Treaty establishing the European Economic Community.

---

[1]   The First and the Second Protocol entered into force on 1 August 2004. The text published above is a non-official consolidated text as amended by the Accession Conventions, based on the last official codified text (OJ, C 334 of 30 December 2005) and by Council Decision of 8 November 2007 concerning the accession of the Republic of Bulgaria and of Romania to the Convention (OJ, L 347 of 29 December 2007).

Article 2.   This Protocol shall be subject to ratification by the Signatory States. The instruments of ratification shall be deposited with the Secretary-General of the Council of the European Communities.

Article 3.   This Protocol shall enter into force on the first day of the third month following the deposit of the instrument of ratification of the last Signatory State to complete that formality.

Article 4.   This Protocol, drawn up in a single original in the Danish, Dutch, English, French, German, Greek, Irish, Italian, Portuguese and Spanish languages, all 10 texts being equally authentic, shall be deposited in the archives of the General Secretariat of the Council of the European Communities. The Secretary-General shall transmit a certified copy to the Government of each signatory.

B.4.   Commission Opinion of 17 March 1980 concerning the draft convention on the law applicable to contractual obligations (OJ, L 94 of 11 April 1980)

I.   The Convention on the law applicable to contractual obligations was prepared between 1969 and 1979 by experts from the Governments of the Member States and from the Commission of the European Communities in consultation with the Council and the Commission. It is to be signed in 1980 by the plenipotentiaries of the Member States meeting within the Council.

The draft is the first step towards unification and codification of general rules of conflict in the field of civil law in the Community. Unification will make it easier to determine the law applicable and will increase legal certainty. It should also ensure that all courts in the Community always apply the same substantive law to the same matter in dispute between the same parties. Where the parties are free to choose between courts in different Member States, their choice should not influence the law applicable to the action, and this should operate to prevent forum shopping. The Convention is a logical complement to the Convention of 27 September 1968 on jurisdiction and the enforcement of judgments in civil and commercial matters (the Judgments Convention) and to the Convention of Accession of 9 October 1978 of the Kingdom of Denmark, of Ireland and of the United Kingdom of Great Britain and Northern Ireland to the Convention of 27 September 1968.

II.   The Convention has a very wide scope of application in view of the fact that the courts of the Contracting States will always have to apply it whenever they have to decide what substantive law is applicable in an individual case, whether the choice is between the laws of several Contracting States or of several non-contracting States or of both Contracting and non-contracting States.

The uniform conflict rules created by the Convention cover in principle all types of contract. They are supplemented by special rules of conflict for certain types of contract which are contained in the Convention itself, eg the rules relating to contracts of carriage, or which have been adopted, or will later be adopted in Community legal instruments or in bilateral or multilateral international treaties.

The content of the Convention takes full account of the legal principles prevailing in the Member States. It has regard to developments which have taken place in case-law, legal theory and law reform in the Contracting States and outside them.

The basic rule is that the parties may themselves select the substantive law applicable to their contract except where all the elements relevant to the situation are connected with one country only. In that case, the fact that a foreign law has been chosen will not result in the exclusion of the mandatory rules of the law of that country.

If the parties have not made a choice of law, the contract is as a general rule governed by the law of the country with which it is most closely connected. There is a rebuttable presumption that this is the country where the party who is to perform the obligation which is characteristic of the contract has, at the time of conclusion of the contract, his habitual residence or, in the case of a legal person, its central administration.

III.   The Commission welcomes the proposed unification of rules in the field of private international law and endorses the principles embodied in the Convention. It regrets, however, the fact that it has not been possible in this Convention, which is the first on private international law, to cover non-contractual obligations as well. Cases will in fact frequently occur where not only contractual but also non-contractual claims form the subject-matter of the same action. Other cases will turn on the question whether a claim is to be considered as contractual or non-contractual (delictual or quasi-delictual). The application of the Convention in its present form may therefore result in the situation in which if an action is brought in one Contracting State it will be decided in accordance with the rules contained in the Convention, whereas if it is brought in another Contracting State it will be decided in accordance with the conflicts rules of the lex fori which have not yet been unified. This shortcoming is, however, not so serious that the Commission would wish to oppose signature of the Convention as it stands.

IV.   Much more important, however, is the fact that in a number of respects the Convention does not fully succeed in creating a set of rules common to all the Member States:

1.   Entry into force in all Member States is not guaranteed. Five ratifications will be sufficient for it to enter into force (Article 28).

2.   It has not been concluded for an unlimited period. Its duration may be restricted to 10 years by denunciation (Article 29).

3.   Uniform interpretation of the Convention is likewise not guaranteed since the Member States have so far been unable to agree on the incorporation in the Convention, or in a Protocol corresponding to the Protocol of 3 June 1971 on the interpretation of the Judgments Convention, of a provision based on Article 177 of the EEC Treaty. The inclusion of such a provision would confer jurisdiction on the Court of Justice of the European Communities to give preliminary rulings concerning the interpretation of the Convention.

The defects mentioned at 1 and 2 above might have the effect of preventing the creation and maintenance of a unified juridical area within the Community. They are both fundamental defects, as a result of which the Convention cannot contribute, or can contribute only temporarily, to the functioning of the common market. Another consequence is that the rights and obligations of nationals of the Member States in intra-Community and international trade and legal transactions will continue to be dissimilar. Forum shopping will still be possible. The Convention no longer has any semblance of being a 'Community convention'. The close connection with the Judgments Convention does in fact require that the territorial scope of both conventions be the same.

The Convention will likewise have to be applicable in all Member States if uniform interpretation by the Court of Justice is to be guaranteed. It is of course not inconceivable, nor impossible, that the Court would interpret legal instruments that are in force only in some Member States. Nevertheless, the Community's supreme judicial authority should be able, when interpreting a rule of law, to take into account the legal position in all Member States. It is debatable whether this is still possible where a rule does not apply in all those States.

Above all, however, the absence of provisions guaranteeing uniform interpretation and conferring jurisdiction for that purpose on the Court of Justice is a totally unacceptable omission in a set of legal rules which aim among other things at uniform application and development of the uniform rules now prepared. It is precisely because of its numerous framework provisions and the imprecision of many of the legal concepts employed that this Convention needs to be interpreted in a uniform manner. Past experience with other conventions has shown that, without the intervention of the Court of Justice, the same text is inevitably interpreted after a short space of time in different ways by the courts of the individual Contracting States.

The Commission has therefore repeatedly stated through its representatives that it considers the insertion of a provision based on Article 177 of the EEC Treaty to be necessary in order to guarantee uniformity of interpretation and application from the moment the Convention enters into force.

The Commission would be willing to accept that the matter be dealt with by means of a Protocol on interpretation, along the lines of the Protocol dated 3 June 1971, so that at least some national courts are empowered, or are placed under the obligation, to refer questions of interpretation to the Court of Justice for a preliminary ruling.

The Commission would not consider it satisfactory, however, that no obligation to refer to the Court of Justice be placed on national courts from whose judgments no further appeal lies under national law ; nor would it be satisfactory that those courts be allowed discretion to determine whether they refer questions of interpretation to the Court of Justice. Consistency of case-law and uniform application of the law cannot be achieved in all Contracting States unless those courts are bound to refer to the Court of Justice. This is the only way of ensuring that the law contained in the Convention, which is a law common to all the Contracting States, is not fragmented as a result of divergent interpretation by the national courts. A restriction of the jurisdiction of the Court of Justice to the giving of rulings on questions of interpretation 'in the interests of the law', which have no effect on the judgments which gave rise to the reference to the Court, would, in the Commission's opinion, be completely inadequate.

V.   For these reasons, the Commission delivers the following opinion pursuant to the Treaty establishing the European Economic Community, and in particular the second indent of Article 155 thereof:

1. The Commission favours the signature and ratification of the Convention on the law applicable to contractual obligations by all Member States of the European Communities, on condition that the Governments of the Member States at least express their willingness in a joint declaration made at the time of signature of the Convention to negotiate forthwith a Protocol conferring on the Court of Justice of the European Communities powers which guarantee the uniform interpretation and application of the Convention in all Member States.

2.   In the absence of such a declaration, the Commission will feel free to propose that the Council adopt a legal instrument based on the EEC Treaty to attain the desired unification of private international law and thereby eliminate the defects mentioned at IV above.

3.   This opinion is addressed to the Member States.

B.5. Commission Recommendation of 15 January 1985 concerning the Convention of 19 June 1980 on the law applicable to contractual obligations (OJ, L 44 of 14 February 1985)

I.   The Convention on the law applicable to contractual obligations, opened for signature in Rome on 19 June 1980, has been signed by all 10 Member States of the Community: it was signed on 19 June 1980 by Belgium, the Federal Republic of Germany, France, Ireland, Italy, Luxembourg and the Netherlands, on 10 March 1981 by Denmark and on 7 December 1981 by the United Kingdom; on 10 April 1984, the representatives of the Governments of the Member States signed the Convention on the accession of the Hellenic Republic to the Convention on the law applicable to contractual obligations.

The Convention is the first step towards unification and codification of general rules of conflict in the field of civil law in the Community. Unification will make it easier to determine the law applicable and will increase legal certainty. It should also ensure that all courts in the Community always apply the same substantive law to the same matter in dispute between the same parties. Where the parties are free to choose between courts in different Member States, their choice should not prejudice the question of the substantive law in accordance with which the action is to be judged. The aim, therefore, is to prevent forum shopping. The Convention is thus a logical complement to the legal unification process begun with the Convention of 27 September 1968 on jurisdiction and the enforcement of judgments in civil and commercial matters (the Judgments Convention).

II.   The Convention creates uniform conflict rules for contractual obligations within the Community. Its provisions have the character of unified law. This can be seen from the preamble, which expresses the wish of the Member States 'to continue in the field of private international law the work of unification of law which has already been done within the Community, in particular in the field of jurisdiction and enforcement of judgments' and 'to establish uniform rules concerning the law applicable to contractual obligations'.

Title II of the Convention accordingly bears the heading 'Uniform rules'. Article 25 of the Convention provides for consultations between the signatory States in cases where a Contracting State considers that 'the unification achieved by this Convention is prejudiced by the conclusion of other agreements'. The Joint Declaration of 19 June 1980 annexed to the Convention also states that differences of interpretation of the Convention should not be allowed to impair its unifying effect. It may be inferred from this that all the Contracting States have an obligation to incorporate the Convention into national law in a manner which is in line with the character of the Convention as a common source of law, embodying unified rules.

Uniform interpretation is possible only if the courts of the Contracting States can acknowledge and apply the provisions of the Convention as rules common to all the Contracting States. In the Commission's view, the Contracting States are obliged to give effect to the Convention in such a way as to ensure that this is possible. If the Convention could be referred to indirectly for interpretative purposes only in cases where the interpretation of the law implementing it was doubtful, this would contradict the character of the Convention as an instrument embodying unified rules.

Giving effect to the Convention in the Federal Republic of Germany, if carried out, as planned, in accordance with Article 1(2) of the draft Law on the Convention on the law applicable to contractual obligations (Entwurf des Gesetzes zum EuIPRUE, Bundestag publication 10/503) would prevent direct application of the provisions contained in Articles 1 to 21 of the Convention. Furthermore, if the incorporation of these Community provisions into the Law introducing the Civil Code (Einfuehrungsgesetz zum Buergerlichen Gesetzbuch) were effected with amendments, omissions and adjustments to the logical arrangement of that introductory Law, this would undo a set of rules that was uniform and common to all the Member States of the Community. Under Article 36 of the draft Law on the Convention, the German courts are to take account of the international character of the provisions corresponding to the Convention. Article 36 of the draft Law is modelled on Article 18 of the Convention and reads as follows:

> '*Article 36. Uniform interpretation.* In the interpretation and application of the provisions of this chapter relating to contractual obligations, regard shall be had to the international character of the rules and to the desirability of achieving uniformity in their interpretation and application in the Contracting States which are parties to the Convention of 19 June 1980 on the Law applicable to contractual obligations (BGBL. .... II p. ....).'

Article 36 of the draft Law does not allow performance of the obligations arising from Articles 1 to 21 of the Convention, Articles whose direct application is precluded by Article 1(2) of the draft Law.

A number of provisions contained in Articles 1 to 21 of the Convention are not included in the draft Law, eg Article 1(1) and (2)(a), (b), (d), (g) and (h) (Scope), Article 20 (Precedence of Community law) and Article 21 (Relationship with other conventions).

Some of the provisions of the Convention which have been incorporated into the draft Law have been redrafted or changed in substance. The provisions subject to such changes are, in particular, Article 13 'Subrogation' (Article 33(3) EGBGB-E), Article 15 'Exclusion of renvoi' (Articles 3 and 4 of the draft Law), Article 16 'Ordre public' (Article 6 of the draft Law) and Article 19 'States with more than one legal system' (Article 4(3) of the draft Law).

In general terms, comprehension and interpretation of the Convention are made more difficult because its provisions are divided up among various sections of the draft Law.

Even scrupulous application of Article 36 of the draft Law would not allow the desired goal of legal clarity and legal certainty through legal uniformity to be achieved. On the contrary, the work of the courts would be made more difficult, because they would have to compare texts which differed from one another in form and substance and would have to decide which provisions of national law corresponded to the Convention, in order, where necessary, to refer matters to the Court of Justice of the European Communities for interpretation.

The systematization aimed at in incorporating the Convention into the draft Law would, in its proposed form, result not only in a formal modification of the uniform law common to all the Member States of the Community, but also in a substantive change in that uniform law.

The manner in which implementation of the Convention is envisaged would render practically nugatory the jurisdiction of the European Court in respect of the Federal Republic of Germany. This would be contrary to the obligation accepted correspondingly by the Federal Republic of Germany in the Joint Declaration on the Convention on the law applicable to contractual obligations opened for signature in Rome on 19 June 1980 'to examine the possibility of conferring jurisdiction in certain matters on the Court of Justice of the European Communities and, if necessary, to negotiate an agreement to this effect'.

Since the agreed aim in the signing of the Convention by all the Member States of the Community was to achieve unification in an important area of private international law, it is essential that the codification, arrangement and drafting of its provisions for the purposes of national law should also respect the limits necessarily imposed by such unification. Each Member State must refrain from all measures which might jeopardise achievement of the stated aims of the Convention, and should introduce only those measures which are best suited to achieving such goals.

III.   For these reasons, the Commission delivers the following recommendation pursuant to the Treaty establishing the European Economic Community, and in particular the second indent of Article 155 thereof:

1.   The Commission recommends that the Federal Republic of Germany should make full use of all the scope afforded by its constitution in order to ensure that:

(a)   its courts can resort directly to the wording of the Convention on the law applicable to contractual obligations;

(b)   changes in the content, formulation and order of the provisions of the Convention on the law applicable to contractual obligations and omissions and adaptations of those provisions are avoided in giving effect to the Convention under national law.

2.   This recommendation is addressed to the Federal Republic of Germany.

B.6.   ECJ case-law regarding the 1980 Rome Convention

Article 4

ECJ, 6 October 2009, case C-133/08, Intercontainer Interfrigo

The last sentence of Article 4(4) of the 1980 Rome Convention must be interpreted as meaning that the connecting criterion provided for in the second sentence of Article 4(4) applies to a charter-party, other than a single voyage charter-party, only when the main purpose of the contract is not merely to make available a means of transport, but the actual carriage of goods.

The second sentence of Article 4(1) of the Convention must be interpreted as meaning that a part of a contract may be governed by a law other than that applied to the rest of the contract only where the object of that part is independent.

Where the connecting criterion applied to a charter-party is that set out in Article 4(4) of the Convention, that criterion must be applied to the whole of the contract, unless the part of the contract relating to carriage is independent of the rest of the contract.

Article 4(5) of the Convention must be construed as meaning that, where it is clear from the circumstances as a whole that the contract is more closely connected with a country other than that determined on the basis of one of the criteria set out in Articles 4(2) to 4 of the Convention, it is for the court to disregard those criteria and apply the law of the country with which the contract is most closely connected.

Article 5

See ECJ, judgment 9 September 2004, case C-70/03, *Commission v Spain*, in this Chapter, Consumer contracts, O.

Article 6

ECJ, 26 May 1982, case 133/81, Ivenel

Article 6 of the 1980 Rome Convention provides that a contract of employment is to be governed, in the absence of choice of the applicable law, by the law of the country in which the employee habitually carries out his work in performance of the contract unless it appears from the circumstances as a whole that the contract is more closely connected with another country. The experts' report on the Convention explains in that respect that the adopting of a special conflict rule in relation to contracts of employment was intended to provide an appropriate arrangement for matters in which the interests of one of the contracting parties were not the same as those of the other and to secure thereby adequate protection for the party who from the socio-economic point of view was to be regarded as the weaker in the contractual relationship.

In interpreting Article 5(1) of the 1968 Brussels Convention in the case of a contract of employment the close connection between the dispute and the competent court lies particularly in the law applicable to the contract; according to the trend in the conflict rules in regard to this matter that law is determined by the obligation characterising the contract in question and is normally the obligation to carry out work.

C.   Other Relevant Instruments

1.   Commission Communication - Freedom to Provide Services and the Interest of the General Good in the Second Banking Directive' (OJ, C 209 of 10 July 1997).

See Chapter IX, General provisions, O.

2.   Commission Communication - Freedom to provide services and the general good in the insurance sector' (OJ, C 43 of 16 February 2000).

See Chapter IX, General provisions, P.

3.　Commission notice – Guidelines on Vertical Restraints (OJ, C 130 of 19 May 2010): Paragraphs 51, 52.

See Chapter IV, Other relevant instruments, C.

4.　Directive 2000/31/EC of the European Parliament and of the Council of 8 June 2000 on certain legal aspects of information society services, in particular electronic commerce, in the Internal Market ('Directive on electronic commerce') (OJ, L 178 of 17 July 2000): Recital 19, Article 1(4)

See Chapter IX, General provisions, D.

D.　Regulation (EC) No 662/2009 of the European Parliament and of the Council of 13 July 2009 establishing a procedure for the negotiation and conclusion of agreements between Member States and third countries on particular matters concerning the law applicable to contractual and noncontractual obligations (OJ, L 200 of 31 July 2009)

See Chapter I, The external dimension, K.

E.　ECJ case-law on the law applicable to contractual obligations

While the ECJ has been requested by national courts to interpret the 1980 Rome Convention only recently (see above in this Chapter, General provisions, A.8), it tackled several issues concerning the law applicable to contractual obligations in relation to contracts concluded by the Community. Disputes concerning thereto must be decided according to the law governing the contract as per Article 340(1) TFEU (ex Article 288(1) TEC). In a case concerning the alleged non-performance of a public works contract concluded by the Commission with an undertaking, whose general conditions designated Belgian law as the applicable law, the ECJ (26 November 1985, case 318/81, *Commission v CO.DE.MI.*, Reports, 3693) stated that

　　20. ... Article 2 of each contract expressly states that all the provisions of the conditions are an integral part of the contract. Article 17 of the conditions, according to which the contract is governed by Belgian law, unless otherwise provided in the special terms and conditions, is therefore itself an integral part of the contract. The special terms and conditions, that is to say the two contracts in question, contain no express derogation from Article 17. Neither the simple fact that the two contracts contain certain references to provisions of the Italian civil code nor an alleged general attitude of the parties can prevail over the clear words of Article 17 and permit the inference that the parties displayed an intention to apply Italian law. That conclusion is all the more compelling inasmuch as the references in the contracts to Articles 1341 and 1664 of the Italian civil code are merely intended to prevent disputes over the validity of certain clauses of the contracts. Those

references are thus simply a precaution against possible disputes and are not intended to call in question the determination of the law applicable to the contracts as laid down in Article 17 of the conditions.

21. Furthermore, in the circumstances of this case the place of conclusion of the contract can have no effect on the determination of the applicable law. Contractual provisions expressing the common intention of the parties must take precedence over any other criterion which might be used only where the contract is silent on a particular point.

22. The Court concludes that in accordance with Article 17 of the conditions, and in the absence of any express derogation in the special terms and conditions, the contracts at issue are governed by Belgian law.

A second case concerns the legality of the set-off between a claim subject to Belgian law and a claim subject to EC law, the ECJ (10 July 2003, case C-87/01 P, *Commission v CCRE*, Reports, I-7617) stated that

61. In so far as it extinguishes two obligations simultaneously, an out-of-court set-off between claims governed by two separate legal orders can take effect only in so far as it satisfies the requirements of both legal orders concerned. More specifically, any set-off of that nature makes it necessary to ensure, as regards each of the claims concerned, that the conditions relating to set-off provided for in the relevant legal order are not disregarded.

62. In that regard, it is immaterial that, in the present case, one of the legal orders concerned is the Community legal order and the other the legal order of one of the Member States. In particular, the fact that both legal orders are equally competent to govern any set-off cannot be called in question on the basis of considerations linked with the primacy of Community law. It must be emphasised that the fact that the MED URBS contracts are subject to Belgian law is the consequence of the free choice of the parties, a choice expressed in compliance with the Treaties, which provide that a Community institution may subject its contractual relations to the law of a Member State.

The ECJ addressed also certain issues concerning the law applicable to interests and their rate in relation to a contract. In case C-127/03 (8 July 2004, *Commission v Trendsoft*) the ECJ decided that, in the absence of a different choice by the parties, the law applicable is the same law that governs the contract and it stated that

31. In the absence of contractual interest, and given that the contract is governed by the law of Ireland, section 22(1) of the Courts Act, 1981, must be applied, which provides that where in any proceedings a court orders the payment by any person of a sum of money (which expression includes in this section damages), the judge concerned may, if he thinks fit, also order the payment of interest at the rate per annum standing specified for the time being in section 26 of the Debtors (Ireland) Act, 1840. That interest relates to the whole or any part of the principal sum and is in respect of the whole or any part of the period between the date when the cause of action accrued and the date of the judgment.

In a later judgment (12 May 2005, case C-315/03, *Commission v Huthamaki Dourdan*), the ECJ touched upon the nature of the rules that apply to the calculation of interests and declared that they pertain to the merits of the case rather than to the procedure and consequently they are governed by the law applicable to the contract at the time of its signature (paras 52–53).

Employment and agency*

A. Council Directive 91/533/EEC of 14 October 1991 on an employer's obligation to inform employees of the conditions applicable to the contract or employment relationship (OJ, L 288 of 18 October 1991)

...

Whereas the development, in the Member States, of new forms of work has led to an increase in the number of types of employment relationship;

Whereas, faced with this development, certain Member States have considered it necessary to subject employment relationships to formal requirements; whereas these provisions are designed to provide employees with improved protection against possible infringements of their rights and to create greater transparency on the labour market;

Whereas the relevant legislation of the Member States differs considerably on such fundamental points as the requirement to inform employees in writing of the main terms of the contract or employment relationship;

Whereas differences in the legislation of Member States may have a direct effect on the operation of the common market;

Whereas Article 117 of the Treaty provides for the Member States to agree upon the need to promote improved working conditions and an improved standard of living for workers, so as to make possible their harmonization while the improvement is being maintained;

Whereas point 9 of the Community Charter of Fundamental Social Rights for Workers, adopted at the Strasbourg European Council on 9 December 1989 by the Heads of State and Government of 11 Member States, states:

'The conditions of employment of every worker of the European Community shall be stipulated in laws, a collective agreement or a contract of employment, according to arrangements applying in each country.';

Whereas it is necessary to establish at Community level the general requirement that every employee must be provided with a document containing information on the essential elements of his contract or employment relationship;

---

* On the law applicable to employment contracts see also Article 8 of Regulation (EC) No 593/08 (Rome I) and Article 6 of the 1980 Rome Convention, above in this Chapter, General provisions, A.1 and A.3. Apart from the acts published in this section, numerous directives provide for rules aiming at granting a certain level of protection to employees, that rule on their scope of application. See, for example, Council Directive 1999/63/EC of 21 June 1999 concerning the Agreement on the organisation of working time of seafarers (OJ, L 167 of 2 July 1999), Council Directive 2001/23/EC of 12 March 2001 on the approximation of the laws of the Member States relating to the safeguarding of employees' rights in the event of transfers of undertakings, businesses or parts of undertakings or businesses (OJ, L 82 of 22 March 2001), and Directive 2003/88/EC of the European Parliament and of the Council of 4 November 2003 concerning certain aspects of the organisation of working time (OJ, L 299 of 18 November 2003).

Whereas, in view of the need to maintain a certain degree of flexibility in employment relationships, Member States should be able to exclude certain limited cases of employment relationship from this Directive's scope of application…

Article 1. Scope.   1.   This Directive shall apply to every paid employee having a contract or employment relationship defined by the law in force in a Member State and/or governed by the law in force in a Member State.

2.   Member States may provide that this Directive shall not apply to employees having a contract or employment relationship:

(a)   —   with a total duration not exceeding one month, and/or

—   with a working week not exceeding eight hours; or

(b)   of a casual and/or specific nature provided, in these cases, that its non-application is justified by objective considerations.

Article 2. Obligation to provide information.   An employer shall be obliged to notify an employee to whom this Directive applies, hereinafter referred to as 'the employee', of the essential aspects of the contract or employment relationship.…

Article 4. Expatriate employees.   1.   Where an employee is required to work in a country or countries other than the Member State whose law and/or practice governs the contract or employment relationship, the document(s) referred to in Article 3 must be in his/her possession before his/her departure and must include at least the following additional information:

(a)   the duration of the employment abroad;

(b)   the currency to be used for the payment of remuneration;

(c)   where appropriate, the benefits in cash or kind attendant on the employment abroad;

(d)   where appropriate, the conditions governing the employee's repatriation.

2.   The information referred to in paragraph 1(b) and (c) may, where appropriate, be given in the form of a reference to the laws, regulations and administrative or statutory provisions or collective agreements governing those particular points.

3.   Paragraphs 1 and 2 shall not apply if the duration of the employment outside the country whose law and/or practice governs the contract or employment relationship is one month or less.

Article 6.   Form and proof of the existence of a contract or employment relationship and procedural rules.   This Directive shall be without prejudice to national law and practice concerning:

—   the form of the contract or employment relationship;

—   proof as regards the existence and content of a contract or employment relationship;

—   the relevant procedural rules.

Article 7. More favourable provisions. This Directive shall not affect Member States' prerogative to apply or to introduce laws, regulations or administrative provisions which are more favourable to employees or to encourage or permit the application of agreements which are more favourable to employees....

B.1.   Directive 96/71/EC of the European Parliament and of the Council of 16 December 1996 concerning the posting of workers in the framework of the provision of services (OJ, L 18 of 21 January 1997)

(1)   Whereas, pursuant to Article 3(c) of the Treaty, the abolition, as between Member States, of obstacles to the free movement of persons and services constitutes one of the objectives of the Community;

(2)   Whereas, for the provision of services, any restrictions based on nationality or residence requirements are prohibited under the Treaty with effect from the end of the transitional period;

(3)   Whereas the completion of the internal market offers a dynamic environment for the transnational provision of services, prompting a growing number of undertakings to post employees abroad temporarily to perform work in the territory of a Member State other than the State in which they are habitually employed;

(4)   Whereas the provision of services may take the form either of performance of work by an undertaking on its account and under its direction, under a contract concluded between that undertaking and the party for whom the services are intended, or of the hiring-out of workers for use by an undertaking in the framework of a public or a private contract;

(5)   Whereas any such promotion of the transnational provision of services requires a climate of fair competition and measures guaranteeing respect for the rights of workers;

(6)   Whereas the transnationalization of the employment relationship raises problems with regard to the legislation applicable to the employment relationship; whereas it is in the interests of the parties to lay down the terms and conditions governing the employment relationship envisaged;

(7)   Whereas the Rome Convention of 19 June 1980 on the law applicable to contractual obligations, signed by 12 Member States, entered into force on 1 April 1991 in the majority of Member States;

(8)   Whereas Article 3 of that Convention provides, as a general rule, for the free choice of law made by the parties; whereas, in the absence of choice, the contract is to be governed, according to Article 6(2), by the law of the country, in which the employee habitually carries out his work in performance of the contract, even if he is temporarily employed in another country, or, if the employee does not habitually carry out his work in any one country, by the law of the country in which the place of business through which he was engaged is situated, unless it appears from the circumstances as a whole that the contract is more closely connected with another country, in which case the contract is to be governed by the law of that country;

(9) Whereas, according to Article 6(1) of the said Convention, the choice of law made by the parties is not to have the result of depriving the employee of the protection afforded to him by the mandatory rules of the law which would be applicable under paragraph 2 of that Article in the absence of choice;

(10) Whereas Article 7 of the said Convention lays down, subject to certain conditions, that effect may be given, concurrently with the law declared applicable, to the mandatory rules of the law of another country, in particular the law of the Member State within whose territory the worker is temporarily posted;

(11) Whereas, according to the principle of precedence of Community law laid down in its Article 20, the said Convention does not affect the application of provisions which, in relation to a particular matter, lay down choice-of-law rules relating to contractual obligations and which are or will be contained in acts of the institutions of the European Communities or in national laws harmonised in implementation of such acts;

(12) Whereas Community law does not preclude Member States from applying their legislation, or collective agreements entered into by employers and labour, to any person who is employed, even temporarily, within their territory, although his employer is established in another Member State; whereas Community law does not forbid Member States to guarantee the observance of those rules by the appropriate means;

(13) Whereas the laws of the Member States must be coordinated in order to lay down a nucleus of mandatory rules for minimum protection to be observed in the host country by employers who post workers to perform temporary work in the territory of a Member State where the services are provided; whereas such coordination can be achieved only by means of Community law;

(14) Whereas a 'hard core' of clearly defined protective rules should be observed by the provider of the services notwithstanding the duration of the worker's posting;

(15) Whereas it should be laid down that, in certain clearly defined cases of assembly and/or installation of goods, the provisions on minimum rates of pay and minimum paid annual holidays do not apply;

(16) Whereas there should also be some flexibility in application of the provisions concerning minimum rates of pay and the minimum length of paid annual holidays; whereas, when the length of the posting is not more than one month, Member States may, under certain conditions, derogate from the provisions concerning minimum rates of pay or provide for the possibility of derogation by means of collective agreements; whereas, where the amount of work to be done is not significant, Member States may derogate from the provisions concerning minimum rates of pay and the minimum length of paid annual holidays;

(17) Whereas the mandatory rules for minimum protection in force in the host country must not prevent the application of terms and conditions of employment which are more favourable to workers;

(18) Whereas the principle that undertakings established outside the Community must not receive more favourable treatment than undertakings established in the territory of a Member State should be upheld;

(19) Whereas, without prejudice to other provisions of Community law, this Directive does not entail the obligation to give legal recognition to the existence of temporary employment undertakings, nor does it prejudice the application by Member States of their laws concerning the hiring-out of workers and temporary employment

undertakings to undertakings not established in their territory but operating therein in the framework of the provision of services;

(20) Whereas this Directive does not affect either the agreements concluded by the Community with third countries or the laws of Member States concerning the access to their territory of third-country providers of services; whereas this Directive is also without prejudice to national laws relating to the entry, residence and access to employment of third-country workers;

(21) Whereas Council Regulation (EEC) No 1408/71 of 14 June 1971 on the application of social security schemes to employed persons and their families moving within the Community lays down the provisions applicable with regard to social security benefits and contributions;

(22) Whereas this Directive is without prejudice to the law of the Member States concerning collective action to defend the interests of trades and professions;

(23) Whereas competent bodies in different Member States must cooperate with each other in the application of this Directive; whereas Member States must provide for appropriate remedies in the event of failure to comply with this Directive;

(24) Whereas it is necessary to guarantee proper application of this Directive and to that end to make provision for close collaboration between the Commission and the Member States;

(25) Whereas five years after adoption of this Directive at the latest the Commission must review the detailed rules for implementing this Directive with a view to proposing, where appropriate, the necessary amendments…

Article 1. Scope.   1.   This Directive shall apply to undertakings established in a Member State which, in the framework of the transnational provision of services, post workers, in accordance with paragraph 3, to the territory of a Member State.

2.   This Directive shall not apply to merchant navy undertakings as regards seagoing personnel.

3.   This Directive shall apply to the extent that the undertakings referred to in paragraph 1 take one of the following transnational measures:

(a)   post workers to the territory of a Member State on their account and under their direction, under a contract concluded between the undertaking making the posting and the party for whom the services are intended, operating in that Member State, provided there is an employment relationship between the undertaking making the posting and the worker during the period of posting; or

(b)   post workers to an establishment or to an undertaking owned by the group in the territory of a Member State, provided there is an employment relationship between the undertaking making the posting and the worker during the period of posting; or

(c)   being a temporary employment undertaking or placement agency, hire out a worker to a user undertaking established or operating in the territory of a Member State, provided there is an employment relationship between the temporary employment undertaking or placement agency and the worker during the period of posting.

4.   Undertakings established in a non-member State must not be given more favourable treatment than undertakings established in a Member State.

Article 2. Definition. 1. For the purposes of this Directive, 'posted worker' means a worker who, for a limited period, carries out his work in the territory of a Member State other than the State in which he normally works.

2. For the purposes of this Directive, the definition of a worker is that which applies in the law of the Member State to whose territory the worker is posted.

Article 3. Terms and conditions of employment. 1. Member States shall ensure that, whatever the law applicable to the employment relationship, the undertakings referred to in Article 1(1) guarantee workers posted to their territory the terms and conditions of employment covering the following matters which, in the Member State where the work is carried out, are laid down:

— by law, regulation or administrative provision, and/or

— by collective agreements or arbitration awards which have been declared universally applicable within the meaning of paragraph 8, insofar as they concern the activities referred to in the Annex:

(a) maximum work periods and minimum rest periods;

(b) minimum paid annual holidays;

(c) the minimum rates of pay, including overtime rates; this point does not apply to supplementary occupational retirement pension schemes;

(d) the conditions of hiring-out of workers, in particular the supply of workers by temporary employment undertakings;

(e) health, safety and hygiene at work;

(f) protective measures with regard to the terms and conditions of employment of pregnant women or women who have recently given birth, of children and of young people;

(g) equality of treatment between men and women and other provisions on non-discrimination.

For the purposes of this Directive, the concept of minimum rates of pay referred to in paragraph 1(c) is defined by the national law and/or practice of the Member State to whose territory the worker is posted.

2. In the case of initial assembly and/or first installation of goods where this is an integral part of a contract for the supply of goods and necessary for taking the goods supplied into use and carried out by the skilled and/or specialist workers of the supplying undertaking, the first subparagraph of paragraph 1(b) and (c) shall not apply, if the period of posting does not exceed eight days.

This provision shall not apply to activities in the field of building work listed in the Annex.

3. Member States may, after consulting employers and labour, in accordance with the traditions and practices of each Member State, decide not to apply the first subparagraph of paragraph 1(c) in the cases referred to in Article 1(3)(a) and (b) when the length of the posting does not exceed one month.

4. Member States may, in accordance with national laws and/or practices, provide that exemptions may be made from the first subparagraph of paragraph 1(c) in the cases referred to in Article 1(3)(a) and (b) and from a decision by a Member State within the meaning of paragraph 3 of this Article, by means of collective agreements within the meaning of paragraph 8 of this Article, concerning one or more sectors of activity, where the length of the posting does not exceed one month.

5.   Member States may provide for exemptions to be granted from the first subparagraph of paragraph 1(b) and (c) in the cases referred to in Article 1(3)(a) and (b) on the grounds that the amount of work to be done is not significant.

Member States availing themselves of the option referred to in the first subparagraph shall lay down the criteria which the work to be performed must meet in order to be considered as 'non-significant'.

6.   The length of the posting shall be calculated on the basis of a reference period of one year from the beginning of the posting.

For the purpose of such calculations, account shall be taken of any previous periods for which the post has been filled by a posted worker.

7.   Paragraphs 1 to 6 shall not prevent application of terms and conditions of employment which are more favourable to workers.

Allowances specific to the posting shall be considered to be part of the minimum wage, unless they are paid in reimbursement of expenditure actually incurred on account of the posting, such as expenditure on travel, board and lodging.

8.   'Collective agreements or arbitration awards which have been declared universally applicable' means collective agreements or arbitration awards which must be observed by all undertakings in the geographical area and in the profession or industry concerned.

In the absence of a system for declaring collective agreements or arbitration awards to be of universal application within the meaning of the first subparagraph, Member States may, if they so decide, base themselves on:

— collective agreements or arbitration awards which are generally applicable to all similar undertakings in the geographical area and in the profession or industry concerned, and/or

— collective agreements which have been concluded by the most representative employers' and labour organizations at national level and which are applied throughout national territory, provided that their application to the undertakings referred to in Article 1(1) ensures equality of treatment on matters listed in the first subparagraph of paragraph 1 of this Article between those undertakings and the other undertakings referred to in this subparagraph which are in a similar position.

Equality of treatment, within the meaning of this Article, shall be deemed to exist where national undertakings in a similar position:

— are subject, in the place in question or in the sector concerned, to the same obligations as posting undertakings as regards the matters listed in the first subparagraph of paragraph 1, and

— are required to fulfil such obligations with the same effects.

9.   Member States may provide that the undertakings referred to in Article 1(1) must guarantee workers referred to in Article 1(3)(c) the terms and conditions which apply to temporary workers in the Member State where the work is carried out.

10.   This Directive shall not preclude the application by Member States, in compliance with the Treaty, to national undertakings and to the undertakings of other States, on a basis of equality of treatment, of:

— terms and conditions of employment on matters other than those referred to in the first subparagraph of paragraph 1 in the case of public policy provisions;

—   terms and conditions of employment laid down in the collective agreements or arbitration awards within the meaning of paragraph 8 and concerning activities other than those referred to in the Annex.

Article 4. Cooperation on information.   1.   For the purposes of implementing this Directive, Member States shall, in accordance with national legislation and/or practice, designate one or more liaison offices or one or more competent national bodies.

2.   Member States shall make provision for cooperation between the public authorities which, in accordance with national legislation, are responsible for monitoring the terms and conditions of employment referred to in Article 3. Such cooperation shall in particular consist in replying to reasoned requests from those authorities for information on the transnational hiring-out of workers, including manifest abuses or possible cases of unlawful transnational activities.

The Commission and the public authorities referred to in the first subparagraph shall cooperate closely in order to examine any difficulties which might arise in the application of Article 3(10).

Mutual administrative assistance shall be provided free of charge.

3.   Each Member State shall take the appropriate measures to make the information on the terms and conditions of employment referred to in Article 3 generally available.

4.   Each Member State shall notify the other Member States and the Commission of the liaison offices and/or competent bodies referred to in paragraph 1.

Article 5. Measures.   Member States shall take appropriate measures in the event of failure to comply with this Directive.

They shall in particular ensure that adequate procedures are available to workers and/or their representatives for the enforcement of obligations under this Directive.

Article 6. Jurisdiction.   In order to enforce the right to the terms and conditions of employment guaranteed in Article 3, judicial proceedings may be instituted in the Member State in whose territory the worker is or was posted, without prejudice, where applicable, to the right, under existing international conventions on jurisdiction, to institute proceedings in another State.

Annex

The activities mentioned in Article 3(1), second indent, include all building work relating to the construction, repair, upkeep, alteration or demolition of buildings, and in particular the following work:
    1.   excavation
    2.   earthmoving
    3.   actual building work
    4.   assembly and dismantling of prefabricated elements
    5.   fitting out or installation
    6.   alterations
    7.   renovation
    8.   repairs
    9.   dismantling

10. demolition
11. maintenance
12. upkeep, painting and cleaning work
13. improvements.

B.2. Statements made at the meeting of the Council (LSA) of 24 September 1996 (Doc. Consilium No 10048/96 ADD. 1)

1. Statements by the Council and the Commission

a) Re the Directive as a whole (Statement No 1)

This Directive is without prejudice to Regulation (EEC) No 1408/71 (Social security for migrant workers).

b) Re Article 1(3)(a) (Statement No 3)

The provisions of Article 1(3)(a) cover posting situations which meet the following conditions:
— the transnational provision of services by an undertaking on its own account and under its direction under a contract concluded between the undertaking and the party for whom the services are intended;
— posting as part of such provision of services.

Therefore, if the above conditions are not met, the following situations do not fall within the scope of Article 1(3)(a):
—   that of a worker who is normally employed in the territory of two or more Member States and who forms part of the mobile staff of an undertaking engaged in operating professionally on its own account international passenger or goods transport services by rail, road, air or water;
—   that of a worker forming part of the travelling staff of a press, radio/television or entertainment business engaged temporarily on its own account in its field of activities in the territory of another Member State.

c) Re Article 1(3)(c) (Statement No 4)

1. The provisions referred to do not, as regards Member States the legislation of which makes no provision for temporary employment or prohibits the placement of workers with user undertakings, entail any obligation to make provision for that type of employment or to authorize such placement.

2. The provisions referred to do not preclude application by the Member States of their rules on temporary employment or on the placement of workers with user undertakings to undertakings not established in their territory and operating there within the framework of the provision of services within the meaning of the Treaty.

d)   Re points (b) and (c) of the first subparagraph of Article 3(1) (Statement No 7)

Points (b) and (c) cover national social fund ('Sozialkassen') benefit scheme contributions and benefits, governed by collective agreements or legal provisions, provided that they do not come within the sphere of social security.

e)   Re the first indent of Article 3(10) (Statement No 10)

The expression 'public policy provisions' should be construed as covering those mandatory rules from which there can be no derogation and which, by their nature and objective, meet the imperative requirements of the public interest. These may include, in particular, the prohibition of forced labour or the involvement of public authorities in monitoring compliance with legislation on working conditions.

2.   Statement by the Council

a)   Re Article 6 (Statement No 13)

The Council notes that the Member States declare themselves willing to maintain the homogeneity of the legal system created by the Lugano Convention of 16 September 1988 on Jurisdiction and the Enforcement of Judgments in Civil and Commercial Matters and to begin negotiations with the EFTA Member States as soon as possible in order to conclude with them, before the date on which this Directive must be transposed into national law, an agreement stipulating that, insofar as it recognizes jurisdiction other than that resulting from the jurisdiction arrangements in the said Convention, Article 6 of the Directive also applies to undertakings established in an EFTA State.
   The Commission took note of this statement.

B.3.   Communication from the Commission 'The implementation of Directive 96/71/EC in the Member States' (COM (2003) 458 of 25 July 2003)

2.   Directive 96/71/EC — Its context in Community law, its key content and its added value

2.1.   The context of the Directive

With the achievement of the single market, in particular as regards freedom to supply services between Member States, a new form of worker mobility has emerged, quite distinct from the mobility of migrant workers explicitly addressed in the EC Treaty and in secondary legislation concerning the free movement of workers. The dynamic environment created by the single market, with its economic freedoms, is encouraging undertakings to develop their transnational activities and increasingly to provide transnational services. The situation of employees posted temporarily to another Member State to perform work under a service contract on behalf of their employer has raised all sorts of legal questions.

As these are transnational situations, questions often arise as to which law is applicable to the employment relationship. On this subject, the Convention of Rome of 19 June 1980 on the law applicable to contractual obligations provides, as a general rule, for freedom of choice as regards the law applicable by the parties. In the absence of choice, the employment contract is governed, pursuant to Article 6(2), by the law of the country in which the employee habitually carries out his work, even if he is temporarily employed in another country. If the employee does not habitually carry out his work in any one country, the law applicable is that of the country in which the place of business through which he was engaged is situated, unless it appears from the circumstances as a whole that the contract is more closely connected with another country. According to Article 6(1) of the Convention, the choice of law made by the parties must not have the result of depriving the employee of the protection afforded to him by the mandatory rules of the law which would be applicable under paragraph 2 of that Article in the absence of choice. Article 7 provides that, under certain conditions, effect may be given, concurrently with the law declared applicable, to the mandatory rules of the law of another country, in particular those of the Member State within whose territory the worker is temporarily posted.

As regards posted workers within the context of the EC Treaty, the Court of Justice has been requested on several occasions to clarify their situation in the context of the freedom to supply services as referred to in Article 49 of the Treaty. In a number of cases the Court of Justice has taken the opportunity to develop criteria, first and foremost to distinguish between freedom to supply services and freedom of movement of workers. On this point, the Court has emphasised that — unlike migrant workers — posted workers who are sent to another country to perform a service return to their country of origin after completing their mission, without at any time joining the labour market of the host Member State. Given this specific situation, the rules of primary and secondary Community law devised for migrant workers would not therefore resolve the specific problems of posting. In particular, as regards the employment conditions applicable during the period of posting, the Court has recognised that Community law does not preclude Member States from extending their legislation, or collective labour agreements entered into by both sides of industry, to any person who is employed, even temporarily, within their territory, no matter in which country the employer is established, on condition that the rules of the EC Treaty, and in particular Article 49 are complied with.[1]

In order to facilitate the free movement of services it was deemed necessary and advisable to coordinate the laws of the Member States affected by this Court of Justice case law and thus lay down, at Community level, a nucleus of mandatory minimum protection rules to be observed in the host country by employers who post workers to perform temporary work in the territory of the Member State where the services are provided. Directive 96/71/EC concerning the posting of workers, which is based on Articles 47 (ex 57), paragraph 2 and 55 (ex 66) of the EC Treaty establishes this Community catalogue of minimum rules deemed mandatory. This Directive takes account of the specific situation of posted workers and ties in with the legal context outlined above.

It should be stressed that the Directive's scope does not extend to social security; the provisions applicable with regard to benefits and social security contributions are those laid down by Council Regulation (EEC) No 1408/71 of 14 June 1971.

---

[1] Judgment of 3 February 1982, cases 62/81 and 63/81, *Seco and Desquenne*, point 14, Reports, 223; judgment of 27 March 1990, C-113/89, *Rush Portuguesa*, point 18, Reports, I-1417.

2.2.   The key content of the Directive

The Directive applies to undertakings which post workers to work temporarily in a Member State other than the State whose laws govern the employment relationship. It covers three transnational posting situations, namely:

—   posting under a contract concluded between the undertaking making the posting and the party for whom the services are intended;

—   posting to an establishment or an undertaking owned by the group;

—   posting by a temporary employment undertaking to a user undertaking operating in a Member State other than that of the undertaking making the posting, with the proviso, in all three situations, that there is an employment relationship between the undertaking making the posting and the posted worker.

Undertakings established in a non-member State must not be given more favourable treatment than undertakings established in a Member State. In this context, Recital 20 of the Directive indicates that the Directive does not affect either the agreements concluded by the Community with third countries or the laws of Member States concerning the access to their territory of third-country providers of services. The Directive is also without prejudice to national laws relating to the entry, residence and access to employment of third-country workers.

Whatever the law applicable to the employment relationship, the Directive seeks to guarantee that posted workers will enjoy the application of certain minimum protective provisions in force in the Member State to which they are posted. To this end, Article 3(1) of the Directive lays down the mandatory rules to be observed by employers during the period of posting in regard to the following issues: maximum work periods and minimum rest periods; minimum paid annual holidays; minimum rates of pay; the conditions of hiring-out of workers, in particular the supply of workers by temporary employment undertakings; health, safety and hygiene at work; and protective measures with regard to the terms and conditions of employment of pregnant women or women who have recently given birth, of children and of young people. These rules must be laid down by the legislations of the host country and/or by collective agreements or arbitration awards which have been declared universally acceptable in the case of activities in the building work sector, while Member States are left the choice of imposing such rules laid down by collective agreements in the case of activities other than building work. They may also, in compliance with the Treaty, impose the application of terms and conditions of employment on matters other than those referred to in the Directive in the case of public policy provisions.

For the purposes of implementing the Directive, Member States must designate liaison offices and make provision for administrative cooperation regarding the provision of information. The Directive also contains a jurisdiction clause which states that judicial proceedings may be instituted in the Member State in whose territory the worker is or was posted, without prejudice to the right, under existing international conventions on jurisdiction, to institute proceedings in another State.

2.3.   The added value of the Directive

2.3.1.   *What does this Directive add as regards private international Law?*

2.3.1.1.   THE ROME CONVENTION

The Rome Convention lays down the general criteria for determining the law applicable to contractual obligations. It also permits the judge — exceptionally — to set aside the law that would normally be applicable to the contract and instead apply the mandatory rules within the meaning of private international law ['règles impératives', also known in French as 'lois d'application immédiate' or 'lois de police'] that obtain at the place where the work is carried out (Article 7). These mandatory rules are not defined by the Rome Convention. Directive 96/71 designates at Community level mandatory rules within the meaning of Article 7 of the Rome Convention in transnational posting situations. These rules thus constitute a nucleus of minimum protection for posted workers, while respecting the principle of equality of treatment between national and non-national providers of services (Article 49 of the EC Treaty) and between national and non-national workers.

The choice-of-law rules provided for by the Rome Convention for determining the law applicable offer a general legal framework, whereas the Directive specifically concerns the situation of posted workers and is thus able to refine this legal framework.

The Directive in no way seeks to amend the law applicable to the employment contract, but it lays down a number of mandatory rules to be observed during the period of posting in the host Member State, 'whatever the law applicable to the employment relationship'.

2.3.1.2.   JURISDICTION

Council Regulation (EC) No 44/2001 of 22 December 2000 on jurisdiction and the recognition and enforcement of judgments in civil and commercial matters establishes Community rules on jurisdiction and the recognition of judgments in civil and commercial matters. With regard to individual employment contracts, Article 19 of this Regulation provides that an employer domiciled in a Member State may be sued in the courts of the Member State where he is domiciled, or in another Member State in the courts for the place where the employee habitually carries out his work or in the courts for the last place where he habitually carried out his work. This rule thus introduces, in the worker's favour, an exemption from the general principle that judicial proceedings against persons domiciled in the territory of a Member State must be instituted in that same Member State.

Article 6 of Directive 96/71/EC adds to these rules, in favour of posted workers employed temporarily in another Member State, a new specific jurisdiction clause tailored to the specific situation in which posted workers find themselves. In order to allow the right to the terms and conditions of employment guaranteed in Article 3 of the Directive to be enforced, Article 6 provides that judicial proceedings may be instituted in the Member State in whose territory the worker is or was posted.

This clause constitutes a provision governing a specific matter, as authorised by Article 67 of Regulation 44/2001, and is without prejudice to the right to institute judicial proceedings in another State pursuant to the above-mentioned provisions of the Regulation or pursuant to international conventions on the subject of jurisdiction.

2.3.1.3.   WHAT DOES THIS DIRECTIVE ADD AS REGARDS THE COURT'S CASE LAW?

The Court of Justice has held that Community law does not preclude Member States from extending their legislation, or collective labour agreements entered into by both sides of industry, to any person who is employed, even temporarily, within their territory, no matter in which country the employer is established. This case law thus makes it possible for Member States to extend, in compliance with the Treaty, certain rules to employees posted on their territory, whereas the Directive makes it obligatory to guarantee that certain mandatory rules concerning the terms and conditions of employment of posted workers are observed.

In addition, the case law does not specify the legislative provisions or collective labour agreements in question. The Directive therefore seeks to coordinate Member States' laws with a view to compiling a list of the mandatory rules which undertakings posting workers temporarily to another country must observe in the host country. It does not harmonise the material content of the rules categorised as 'mandatory', but it identifies them and makes them binding on undertakings posting workers to a Member State other than the State in whose territory these workers habitually work....

4.   Assessment of the situation

4.1.   Transposition of the Directive in the Member States

According to studies by independent experts, transposition of the Directive by the Member States has, generally speaking, been satisfactory. However, the Commission would like to mention three categories of transposition problems encountered in certain Member States.

4.1.1.   THE METHOD

The Commission considers that the method used in the two countries which have not adopted a specific transposal instrument [Ireland and United Kingdom] needs to be assessed in the light of the criteria established by the Court of Justice in cases C-365/93[2] and C-144/99.[3] In these two cases the Court pointed out that it is settled law that 'whilst legislative action on the part of each Member State is not necessarily required in order to implement a directive, it is essential for national law to guarantee that the national authorities will effectively apply the directive in full, that the legal position under national law should be sufficiently precise and clear and that individuals are made fully aware of their rights and, where appropriate, may rely on them before the national courts.' The Court added that this last condition is of particular importance where the directive in question is intended to accord rights to nationals of other Member States (*Commission v Greece*, case 365/93, point 9 and *Commission v The Netherlands*, case 144/99, point 18).

---

[2]   Judgment of 23 March 1995, *Commission v Greece*, Reports, I-499, point 9.
[3]   Judgment of 10 May 2001, *Commission v Kingdom of the Netherlands*, Reports, I-3541, point 17.

It should be pointed out that in these two countries, the posting situations covered and the rights deriving from the provisions of the Directive are not clearly defined and the jurisdiction clause contained in Article 6 of the Directive has not been implemented.

Insofar as the absence of identification of 'mandatory rules' is to be interpreted as meaning that the totality of the legislation in the field of labour law applies to posting situations, it should be pointed out that the Directive in no way permits Member States to extend all their legislative provisions and/or collective agreements governing terms and conditions of employment to workers posted on their territory, and that the application of such rules must be in compliance with the EC Treaty, in particular Article 49. As regards the matters covered, the Directive lays down a catalogue of mandatory rules (listed in Article 3) applicable to posted workers, to which Member States may add only public policy provisions in the international context (see below).

4.1.2.   THE NATURE OF THE STANDARDS APPLICABLE

According to Article 3(1) of the Directive, Member States must ensure that undertakings covered by the Directive guarantee workers posted to their territory the terms and conditions of employment established by law, regulation or administrative provision and/or by universally applicable collective agreements or arbitration awards. Thus, the Directive first determines the nature of the standards which Member States must apply, and then the content of these standards.

4.1.2.1.   *Collective agreements*

Not all the transposing legislation has addressed the question of determining the collective agreements applicable to posting situations. The Commission intends to look into this more closely and examine the criteria used for determining the collective agreements applicable to national undertakings on the one hand and undertakings from other countries on the other. As the Court of Justice emphasised in the joined cases C-49/98, C-50/98, C-52/98 to C-54/98 and C-68/98 to C-71/98,[4] these criteria may have different practical consequences in the case of 'mixed' businesses, ie businesses which carry out activities in a variety of sectors.

Collective agreements as referred to in Article 3(1) of the Directive must, for the purposes of implementation of the Directive, be declared universally applicable within the meaning of Article 3(8). The first subparagraph of Article 3(8) of the Directive refers to *erga omnes* collective agreements, which must be observed by all undertakings in the geographical area and in the profession or industry concerned in order to guarantee equality of treatment between domestic undertakings and undertakings established in another Member State providing services in the territory of a Member State.

In the absence of a system for declaring collective agreements to be of universal application, the second subparagraph of Article 3(8) offers Member States options designed to guarantee equality of treatment. The group of experts which prepared the transposal of the Directive was of the opinion that if Member States, in the absence of a system for declaring collective agreements or arbitration awards to be of universal application,

---

4   Judgment of 25 October 2001, '*Finalarte*', Reports, I-7831, points 76–83.

decide to base themselves on the two other categories of collective agreements referred to in Article 3(8), ie generally applicable collective agreements or collective agreements concluded by the most representative employers' and labour organisations, they must make explicit mention thereof in their legislation implementing the posted workers Directive. If their implementing legislation makes no reference to this effect, Member States may not oblige undertakings established in another Member State which post workers to their territory to observe the collective agreements referred to in the second subparagraph of Article 3(8).

Since no Member State's transposing legislation makes any mention of the options offered by the second subparagraph of Article 3(8), the Commission concludes that those Member States which do not have collective agreements declared to be universally applicable within the meaning of the first subparagraph of Article 3(8) of the Directive do not apply the terms and conditions of employment laid down in collective agreements to workers posted on their territory. In these countries, therefore, only the terms and conditions of employment laid down in legislative provisions apply to workers posted on their territory.

4.1.2.2. The nature of the legislative standards applicable concerning matters other than those explicitly referred to in the Directive

The first indent of the first subparagraph of Article 3(10) stipulates that the Directive shall not preclude the application by Member States, in compliance with the Treaty, to national undertakings and to the undertakings of other States, on a basis of equality of treatment, of terms and conditions of employment on matters other than those referred to in the first subparagraph of paragraph 1 in the case of public policy provisions.

As regards the meaning of public policy provisions, the Commission would point out that, at the time of adoption of the Directive, the Council and the Commission stated (Statement 10) that 'the expression "public policy provisions" should be construed as covering those mandatory rules from which there can be no derogation and which, by their nature and objective, meet the imperative requirements of the public interest. These may include, in particular, the prohibition of forced labour or the involvement of public authorities in monitoring compliance with legislation on working conditions'. As explicitly stated in Article 3(10), the application of public policy provisions has to be carried out in compliance with the Treaty and on a basis of equality of treatment.

The Commission considers that the first indent of Article 3(10) has to be interpreted bearing in mind the objective of facilitating the free movement of services within the Community. Thus, the Directive lays down a nucleus of minimum rules for the protection of the rights of workers in the host State, with which undertakings posting workers must comply. Member States are not free to impose all their mandatory labour law provisions on service providers established in another Member State. They must comply with the rules of the EC Treaty, and in particular Article 49, as interpreted by the Court of Justice (cf the *Portugaia Construções*[5] and *Mazzoleni*[6] judgments).

---

[5] Judgment of 24 January 2002, case 164/99.
[6] Judgment of 15 March 2001, case 165/98, Reports, I-2189.

The concept of public policy within the meaning of Directive 96/71/EC must be interpreted in the light of the case law of the Court, which has ruled on this concept on several occasions. The case law, while not giving a precise definition of the concept of public policy, which appears, inter alia, in Articles 46 and 56 of the EC Treaty, recognises that this concept may vary from one country to another and from one period to another,[7] thus leaving the national authorities an area of discretion within the limits imposed by the Treaty. However, the Court has ruled that the concept of public policy must be interpreted strictly[8] and should not be determined unilaterally by each Member State. It has ruled that recourse to the concept of public policy must be justified on overriding general interest grounds,[9] must presuppose the existence of a genuine and sufficiently serious threat affecting one of the fundamental interests of society[10] and must be in conformity with the general principles of law, in particular fundamental rights and the general principle of freedom of expression.

As regards the classification of the national provisions at issue as public-order legislation, the Court of Justice ruled, in its judgment in the joined cases C-369/96 and C-376/96,[11] that 'the term must be understood as applying to national provisions compliance with which has been deemed to be so crucial for the protection of the political, social or economic order in the Member State concerned as to require compliance therewith by all persons present on the national territory of that Member State and all legal relationships within that State.'

To illustrate the difference between domestic public policy provisions on the one hand and public policy provisions and mandatory provisions ['lois de police'] in the international context on the other, we can cite the example of the rules concerning dismissal, which in some countries are domestic public order provisions. These are national mandatory rules from which the parties may not derogate by contract, and which are intended to protect a 'weak' party (the worker). In these countries, any contract between an employer and employee in which the employee waived his rights to redundancy pay or agreed to shorter than normal periods of notice without compensation would be null and void in regard to national contract law. However, these same rules are not considered to be international public policy provisions or mandatory rules within the meaning of Article 7 of the Rome Convention, which would apply whatever the law applicable to the contract. Accordingly, when the employment contract is validly subject to a foreign law, the domestic public policy provisions regarding dismissal do not apply automatically.

Some of the provisions of the Rome Convention might offer Member States valuable guidance in the application of Article 3(10) of the posted workers Directive. For example, pursuant to Article 10 of the Convention the consequences of breach of a contractual obligation are governed by the law applicable to the contract by virtue of Articles 3 to 6 and Article 12 of the Convention: in posting situations this will normally be the law of the home State. This confirms that the rules of the host State concerning the consequences of breach of an employment contract (eg termination of the employment contract) could not be applied under Article 3(10) of the Directive.

---

[7] Judgment of 27 October 1977, case 30/77, Reports, 1999.
[8] Judgment of 18 June 1991, case C-260/89, Reports, I-2925.
[9] Judgment of 14 November 1995, case 484/93, Reports, I-3955.
[10] Judgment of 27 October 1977, case 30/77, Reports, 1999.
[11] Judgment of the Court of 23 November 1999, *Jean Claude Arblade v Bernard Leloup*, point 30, Reports, I-8453.

Finally, the group of experts which prepared the transposal of the Directive considered that the concept of 'public policy provisions' referred to in Article 3(10) covers provisions concerning fundamental rights and freedoms as laid down by the law of the Member State concerned and/or by international law, such as freedom of association and collective bargaining, prohibition of forced labour, the principle of non-discrimination and elimination of exploitative forms of child labour,[12] data protection and the right to privacy.

Consequently, Member States whose transposing legislation obliges foreign undertakings, during the period of posting, to comply with the labour law of the host country in its totality, are clearly exceeding the framework established by the Community legislation. Other Member States which, in their transposing legislation, explicitly add to the list of mandatory rules their own domestic public policy provisions, must also revise their legislation in the light of the above.

B.4.   Communication from the Commission 'Guidance on the posting of workers in the framework of the provision of services' (COM (2006) 159 of 4 April 2006)

1.   *Purpose of this Communication*

Article 49 of the EC Treaty (hereinafter known as 'EC') establishes the principle that Member States should ensure the freedom to provide services within the Community. This fundamental freedom includes the right of a service provider established in a Member State to temporarily post workers to another Member State in order to provide a service. Under the case law, the free provision of services, a fundamental principle of the Treaty, may only be restricted by rules justified on one of the grounds listed in Article 46 EC and by overriding reasons based on the general interest, in accordance with the principles of non-discrimination and proportionality.

Directive 96/71/EC (hereinafter known as 'the Directive') identifies the mandatory rules in force in the host country that are to be applied to posted workers by establishing a hard core of terms and conditions of work and employment and making them binding on undertakings posting workers to a Member State other than the State in whose territory these workers habitually work. The Directive has a clear social objective: that posted workers are guaranteed during the period of posting the respect by their employer of certain protective rules of the Member State to which they are posted. These rules include in particular:

— maximum work periods and minimum rest periods;
— minimum paid annual holidays;
— minimum rates of pay;
— the conditions of hiring-out of workers, in particular the supply of workers by temporary employment undertakings;

---

[12] The right to organise and collective bargaining are dealt with in ILO Conventions 87 and 98. Conventions 29 and 105 cover the prohibition of forced labour, while Convention 111 establishes the principle of non-discrimination. Convention 182 covers the worst forms of child labour.

— health, safety and hygiene at work;

— protective measures with regard to the terms and conditions of employment of pregnant women or women who have recently given birth, of children and of young people.

Member States have a legal obligation to adopt the rules necessary to comply with the Directive, to take the appropriate measures in the event of failure to comply with those rules and to ensure that workers and/or their representatives have appropriate measures available to enforce the obligations defined in the Directive, as well as to make provision for cooperation between the public authorities.

The aim of the Directive is to reconcile companies' rights to provide transnational services under Article 49 EC, on the one hand, and the rights of workers temporarily posted abroad to provide them, on the other.

Following the adoption by the European Parliament on 16 February 2006 of a legislative resolution on the proposal for a directive on services in the internal market, the Commission presented an amended proposal, in which Articles 24 and 25 of the initial proposal setting out specific provisions on the posting of workers are deleted. In these Articles, the Commission proposed the scrapping of certain administrative obligations concerning the posting of workers, accompanied by measures to reinforce administrative cooperation between Member States.

The Commission undertook to draw up guidelines to clarify the prevailing Community law on the administrative procedures dealt with in Articles 24 and 25. This Communication tells the Member States how to observe the Community acquis as interpreted by the European Court of Justice with reference to Article 49 EC and how to achieve the results required by the Directive in a more effective manner. The evidence gathered in the Commission's report SEC (2006) 439, which is annexed to the present Communication, shows that there is considerable scope for improving access to information, administrative cooperation and monitoring of compliance, inter alia by identifying and disseminating best practices.

This Communication does not affect the Commission's prerogative provided for under the Treaty to ensure Member States' compliance with Community law, nor does it affect general rules on visa requirements.

2. Guidance: control measures

In its case law,[1] the Court accepted that Member States could verify that no abuses of the freedom to provide services had taken place, for example the use of workers from third countries on the labour market of the host Member State. It also accepted the justification for the inspection measures necessary to monitor the observance of obligations justified under the general interest. However, the Commission would like to point out that, when performing inspections as part of the implementation of the Directive, Member States must abide by Article 49 EC and refrain from creating or upholding unjustified and disproportionate restrictions to the free provision of services within the Community. The Court has underlined several times that these inspections must be suitable for achieving

---

[1]   Case C-113/89, *Rush Portuguesa Lda v Office national d'immigration*, judgment of 27 March 1990, para 17, and joint cases C-369/96 and 376/96 (*Public Prosecutor v Jean-Claude Arblade et al.*), judgment of 23 November 1999, para 62.

the objectives pursued without restricting this freedom any more than necessary,[2] in accordance with the principle of proportionality.

2.1. General application measures

Of the measures implemented by certain Member States, the following urgently require clarification on the basis of the case law of the Court of Justice based on Article 49 EC:
—   the requirement to have a representative on the territory of the host Member State;
—   the requirement to obtain authorisation from the competent authorities of the host Member State or to be registered with them, or any other equivalent obligation;
—   the requirement to make a declaration;
—   the requirement to keep and maintain social documents on the territory of the host country and/or under the conditions which apply in its territory.

a)   The requirement to have a representative established on the territory of the host Member State

The Court[3] described the requirement to have a subsidiary on the national territory as constituting 'the very negation of the free provision of services'. An obligation on the service provider to appoint a representative domiciled in a particular Member State in order to offer services there would appear to be incompatible with Article 49 EC, being similar to the requirement to elect domicile with an approved agent, which has already been declared unlawful by the Court.[4]

In the judgment Arblade *et al*,[5] the Court ruled that the obligation to have available and keep certain documents at the domicile of a natural person resident in the host Member State, who would hold them as the employer's appointed agent or proxy, even after the employer has stopped employing workers in that State, could only be admissible if the national authorities were not able to effectively perform their control duties effectively in the absence of such an obligation. This case law must be interpreted on a case-by-case basis, but it can be considered that, to fulfil this role, the appointment of a person from among the posted workers, for example a foreman, to act as the link between the foreign company and the labour inspectorate, should be sufficient.

Conclusion: Pursuant to current case law, it must be concluded that the requirement made by a Member State that companies posting workers on its territory must have a representative domiciled in that host Member State is disproportionate for monitoring the working conditions of these workers. The appointment of a person from among the posted workers, for example a foreman, to act as the link between the foreign company the labour inspectorate, should suffice.

---

[2]   See, in this context, the judgments *Commission v Luxembourg*, case C-445/03, judgment of 21 October 2004, para 40 and *Commission v Germany*, C-224/04, judgment of 19 January 2006, para 36.
[3]   Case C-279/00 (*Commission v Republic of Italy*), judgment of 7 February 2002, para 18.
[4]   See, in this context, for example, the Court's judgment of 6 March 2003 in case C-478/01, para 19.
[5]   See footnote 1, para 76.

b)   *The requirement to obtain authorisation from the competent authorities of the host Member State or to be registered with them, or any other equivalent obligation*

According to the established case law of the Court of Justice, national rules which stipulate that the provision of services on national territory by a company established in another Member State is subject, as a general rule and for all activities, to obtaining an administrative authorisation, constitute a restriction of the free provision of services within the meaning of Article 49 EC (see, in particular, the Vander Elst judgment[6]).

There are certain activities whose exercise is regulated in the Member States by legal or regulatory provisions including a specific authorisation system for each activity. For example, many Member States insist that temporary employment agents must be properly authorised, so as to ensure that they have sufficient guarantees to perform this work.

The host Member State is entitled to require prior authorisation only for the performance of certain activities, whatever the posting situation, on condition that this can be justified by overriding reasons based on the general interest, is proportionate and is compatible with the relevant provisions of the Treaty concerning the free provision of services. This requirement must take into account the controls and monitoring already carried out in the Member State of origin.

Conclusion: Pursuant to current case law, it must be concluded that any rules which make the posting of workers subject to systematic prior control, including by way of compulsory and systematic prior authorisation or registration, would be disproportionate.

c)   *Requirement to make a declaration*

Almost half the Member States require service providers which post workers to their territory to submit a prior declaration to their authorities.[7] The purpose of such declarations would appear to be, on the one hand, to enable the national authorities to verify the information on the posting of workers obtained during in situ checks and, on the other, to help the labour inspectorates to conduct risk assessments in order to target their checks at situations or companies which are at high risk.

At this stage, the Court has not delivered any judgments relating specifically to the admissibility of an obligation to make a declaration concerning the posting of workers. In the case *Commission v Luxembourg*,[8] in which a posted worker who was a national of a third country was required to have a work permit in order to provide services, the Court declared that 'a measure which would be just as effective whilst being less restrictive than the measures at issue here would be an obligation imposed on a service-providing undertaking to report beforehand to the local authorities on the presence of one or more deployed workers, the anticipated duration of their presence and the provision or provisions of services justifying the deployment. It would enable those authorities to monitor compliance with Luxembourg social welfare legislation during the deployment while at the same time taking account of the obligations by which the undertaking is

---

[6]   Case C-43/93 (*Raymond Vander Elst v Office des migrations internationals*), judgment of 9 August 1994.
[7]   The Member States in question are: Austria, Belgium, Germany, Spain, France, Greece, Luxembourg, Hungary, Latvia, Malta, Netherlands and Portugal. Slovenia and the Czech Republic impose a similar obligation on the recipients of the services.
[8]   See footnote 2, para 31.

already bound under the social welfare legislation applicable in the Member State of origin'.

As regards the posting of workers who are nationals of a third country by a Community service provider, the Court concluded in its judgment in the case Commission v Federal Republic of Germany,[9] that 'as the Advocate General observed in point 27 of his Opinion, a requirement that the service provider furnishes a simple prior declaration certifying that the situation of the workers concerned is lawful (…) in the Member State where that provider employs them, would give the national authorities, in a less restrictive but as effective a manner as checks in advance of posting, a guarantee that those workers' situation is lawful and that they are carrying on their main activity in the Member State where the service provider is established. Such a requirement would enable the national authorities to check that information subsequently and to take the necessary measures if those workers' situation was not regular'.

Under this case law of the Court, a declaration is deemed to be a measure which is just as effective as and less restrictive than a prior authorisation when it comes to ensuring that Member States are informed at all times about the presence of posted workers from third countries on their territory.

The Member States must refrain from using declarations for purposes other than for providing information, such as for checking or registering companies which provide services, which would amount to a system of authorisation.

Conclusion: On the basis of existing case law, the Commission considers that the host Member State, in order to be able to monitor compliance with the conditions of employment laid down in the Directive, should be able to demand, in accordance with the principle of proportionality, that the service provider submit a declaration, by the time the work starts, at the latest, which contains information on the workers who have been posted, the type of service they will provide, where, and how long the work will take. The declaration could mention that posted workers from third countries are in a lawful situation in the country in which the service provider is established, including with regard to the visa requirements, and legally employed in that country.

d)   The requirement to keep and maintain social documents on the territory of the host country and/or under the conditions which apply in its territory

The Court of Justice has expressed its opinion on the obligation to keep and store social security documents on posted workers in the host Member State.

In its judgment in the case concerning Arblade *et al*,[10] the Court pointed out that the effective protection of workers, particularly as regards health and safety matters and working hours, could require that certain documents be kept in an accessible and clearly identified place in the territory of the host Member State, so that they were available to the authorities of that State responsible for carrying out checks, 'particularly where there exists no organised system for cooperation or exchanges of information between Member States as provided for in Article 4 of Directive 96/71/EC'.

However, in the same judgment, the Court explained that, before imposing an obligation of this kind on a service provider, the competent authorities in the host

---

[9] See footnote 2, para 41.
[10] See footnote 1, para 61.

country would have to verify that the social protection of the workers concerned was not sufficiently safeguarded by the production, within a reasonable time, of the documents kept in the Member State of establishment.[11] In the Finalarte cases,[12] the Court accepted that businesses established outside the host Member State could be required to provide more information than businesses established in that State, to the extent that this difference in treatment could be attributed to objective differences between those businesses and businesses established in the host Member State.

However, the Court also said that it was necessary to check whether the information provided in the documents required under the legislation of the Member State of establishment were sufficient as a whole to enable the checks needed in the host Member State to be carried out.[13]

Since the period for transposing the Directive came to an end in 1999, and since a system of cooperation on information pursuant to Article 4 has been gradually put in place, the Member States have had less scope to demand that certain social documents be kept in the State to which workers have been posted. However, the Commission takes the view that the host Member State could still demand that certain documents which have to be generated and held in situ are kept in the workplace, such as records on actual hours worked or documents on conditions of health and safety in the workplace. In order that the authorities in the host Member State can monitor conditions of employment in accordance with the Directive, they are allowed to require the service provider to produce documents which are considered necessary for carrying out these checks within a reasonable period of time.

However, it is not acceptable for the host Member State to demand that a second set of documents which comply with its own legislation be provided simply because the documents which comply with the legislation of the Member State of establishment exhibit certain differences in terms of form and content. Nor is it acceptable for the host Member State to require that social security documents be provided as they are the subject of a specific procedure in the country of origin, pursuant to Regulation (EEC) No 1408/71. However, the Court of Justice recognised in the cases concerning Arblade *et al*[14] that 'the items of information respectively required by the rules of the Member State of establishment and by those of the host Member State (…) may differ to such an extent that the monitoring required under the rules of the host Member State cannot be carried out on the basis of documents kept in accordance with the rules of the Member State of establishment'.

Conclusion: On the basis of the aforementioned case law, it must be concluded that, in order to be able to monitor compliance with the conditions of employment laid down in the Directive, the host Member State must be able to demand, in accordance with the principle of proportionality, that documents be kept in the workplace which are, by their nature, created there, such as time sheets or documents on conditions of health and safety in the workplace. The host Member State cannot demand a second set of documents if the documents required under the legislation of the Member State of establishment, taken as

---

[11] See footnote 1, para 65.
[12] Joined Cases C-49/98, 50/98, 52/98, 54/98, 68/98 and 71/98 (*Finalarte Sociedade de Construção Civil Lda v Urlaubs-und Lohnausgleichskasse der Bauwirtschaft and others*), judgment of 25 October 2001, paras 69–74.
[13] See footnote 1, paras 64–65.
[14] See footnote 1, para 63.

a whole, already provide sufficient information, to allow the host Member State to carry out the checks required.

2.2.   Measures which apply to posted workers who are nationals of third countries

In the existing case law on the freedom to provide services in accordance with Article 49 EC (see, for example, the judgments in the Vander Elst[15] and Commission v Luxembourg cases[16]), the Court took the view that workers who were regularly and habitually employed by a service provider established in a Member State (country of origin) could be posted to another Member State (host country) without being subject in the latter State to administrative formalities, such as the obligation to obtain a work permit.

The Court also held that a number of additional conditions which certain Member States imposed with regard to the posting of workers from third countries were excessive. In the case *Commission v Germany*,[17] the Court held that German legislation ran counter to Article 49 EC by requiring nationals of third countries posted to Germany by a company established in another Member State to have been employed by that company for at least a year in order to be eligible for a residence visa. In this case, the Court confirmed its judgment in the case Commission v Luxembourg,[18] in which it concluded that legislation requiring posted workers to have been employed for at least six months before being posted went beyond what was required for the objective of the social welfare protection of workers who were nationals of a third country and therefore was not justified. In the latter judgment, the Court also censured the requirement concerning contracts of employment of indefinite duration.

Conclusion: On the basis of existing case law, it must be concluded that the host Member State may not impose administrative formalities or additional conditions on posted workers from third countries when they are lawfully employed by a service provider established in another Member State, without prejudice to the right of the host Member State to check that these conditions are complied with in the Member State where the service provider is established....

B.5.   Directive 2006/123/EC of the European Parliament and of the Council of 12 December 2006 on services in the internal market (OJ, L 376 of 27 December 2006): Article 17(2)

See Chapter II, Principle of non-discrimination, A.

---

[15] See footnote 6.
[16] See footnote 2.
[17] See footnote 2.
[18] See footnote 2.

B.6.   ECJ case-law

Well before the adoption of Directive 96/71/EC the ECJ had indicated the guiding principles to determine which rules of the host country can apply to the posted worker. In particular, with reference to the application of Luxembourg law that required an employer established in another Member State and temporarily carrying out work in Luxembourg using posted workers to pay social security contributions, the ECJ (3 February 1982, joined cases 62 and 63/81, *Seco*, Reports, 223) had stated that

10.   ... legislation which requires employers to pay in respect of their workers social security contributions not related to any social security benefit for those workers, who are moreover exempt from insurance in the Member State in which the service is provided and remain compulsorily affiliated, for the duration of the work carried out, to the social security scheme of the Member State in which their employer is established, may not reasonably be considered justified on account of the general interest in providing workers with social security.

12.   ... A Member State's power to control the employment of nationals from a non-Member Country may not be used in order to impose a discriminatory burden on an undertaking from another Member State enjoying the freedom under Articles 59 and 60 of the Treaty to provide services

unless they are justified under Community law. According to the ECJ:

14.   it is well-established that Community law does not preclude Member States from applying their legislation, or collective labour agreements entered into by both sides of industry relating to minimum wages, to any person who is employed, even temporarily, within their territory, no matter in which country the employer is established, just as Community law does not prohibit Member States from enforcing those rules by appropriate means. However, it is not possible to describe as an appropriate means any rule or practice which imposes a general requirement to pay social security contributions, or other such charges affecting the freedom to provide services, on all persons providing services who are established in other Member States and employ workers who are nationals of non-Member countries, irrespective of whether those persons have complied with the legislation on minimum wages in the Member State in which the services are provided, because such a general measure is by its nature unlikely to make employers comply with that legislation or to be of any benefit whatsoever to the workers in question.

In the *Rush Portuguesa* case (27 March 1990, case C-113/89, Reports, I-1417) the ECJ dealt with the applicability of French law on matters related to the recruitment of manpower in situ and the obtaining of work permits for the posted Portuguese work force and it pointed out that

17.   ... Member States must... be able to ascertain whether a Portuguese undertaking engaged in construction or public works is not availing itself of the freedom to provide services for another purpose, for example that of bringing his workers for the purposes of placing workers or making them available in breach of Article 216 of the Act of Accession. However, such checks must observe the limits imposed by Community law and in particular those stemming from the freedom to provide services which cannot be rendered illusory and whose exercise may not be made subject to the discretion of the authorities.

18.   Finally, it should be stated, in response to the concern expressed in this connection by the French Government, that Community law does not preclude Member States from extending their legislation, or collective labour agreements entered into by both sides of industry, to any person who is employed, even temporarily, within their territory, no matter in which country the employer is established; nor does Community law prohibit Member States from enforcing those rules by appropriate means.

19.   ... Articles 59 and 60 of the EEC Treaty and Articles 215 and 216 of the Act of Accession of the Kingdom of Spain and the Portuguese Republic must be interpreted as meaning that an undertaking established in Portugal providing services in the construction and public works sector in another Member State may move with its own labour force which it brings from Portugal for the duration of the works in question. In such a case, the authorities of the Member State in whose territory the works are to be carried out may not impose on the supplier of services conditions relating to the recruitment of manpower in situ or the obtaining of work permits for the Portuguese work force.

On the basis of these principles, in the *Vander Elst* case (9 August 1994, case C-43/93, Reports, I-3803) concerning the application of French law to non-EU workers employed by a Belgian undertaking under a contract governed by Belgian law and temporarily transferred to France in order to provide services, the ECJ stated that

25.   ... irrespective of the possibility of applying national rules of public policy governing the various aspects of the employment relationship to workers sent temporarily to France, the application of the Belgian system in any event excludes any substantial risk of workers being exploited or of competition between undertakings being distorted.

In the following *Arblade* case (23 November 1999, joined cases C-369/96 and C-376/96, Reports, I-8453), to which Directive 96/71/EC did not apply, the ECJ addressed the issue of whether and to what extent the host State may impose its rules thus hindering the exercise of Community freedoms:

41.   ... Community law does not preclude Member States from extending their legislation, or collective labour agreements entered into by both sides of industry, relating to minimum wages, to any person who is employed, even temporarily, within their territory, regardless of the country in which the employer is established, and, moreover, that Community law does not prohibit Member States from enforcing those rules by appropriate means.

42.   It follows that the provisions of a Member State's legislation or collective labour agreements which guarantee minimum wages may in principle be applied to employers providing services within the territory of that State, regardless of the country in which the employer is established.

43.   However, in order for infringement of the provisions in question to justify the criminal prosecution of an employer established in another Member State, those provisions must be sufficiently precise and accessible that they do not render it impossible or excessively difficult in practice for such an employer to determine the obligations with which he is required to comply. It is for the competent authority — in the present case, the Belgian Social Law Inspectorate -, when laying an information before the criminal courts, to state unequivocally the obligations with which the employer is accused of having failed to comply.

44.   Thus, it is for the national court to determine, in the light of those considerations, which of the relevant provisions of its national law are applicable to an

employer established in another Member State and, where appropriate, the amount of the minimum wage prescribed by them.

50.   National rules which require an employer, as a provider of services within the meaning of the Treaty, to pay employers' contributions to the host Member State's fund, in addition to those which he has already paid to the fund of the Member State in which he is established, constitute a restriction on freedom to provide services. Such an obligation gives rise to additional expenses and administrative and economic burdens for undertakings established in another Member State, with the result that such undertakings are not on an equal footing, from the standpoint of competition, with employers established in the host Member State, and may thus be deterred from providing services in the host Member State.

51.   It must be acknowledged that the public interest relating to the social protection of workers in the construction industry and the monitoring of compliance with the relevant rules may constitute an overriding requirement justifying the imposition on an employer established in another Member State who provides services in the host Member State of obligations capable of constituting restrictions on freedom to provide services. However, that is not the case where the workers employed by the employer in question are temporarily engaged in carrying out works in the host Member State and enjoy the same protection, or essentially similar protection, by virtue of the obligations to which the employer is already subject in the Member State in which he is established.

52.   Moreover, an obligation requiring a provider of services to pay employers' contributions to the host Member State's fund cannot be justified where those contributions confer no social advantage on the workers in question

After the implementation of Directive 96/71/EC the ECJ tackled also the issue of the application of the host country's rules on minimum remuneration to the employees of an undertaking established in a frontier region of another Member State who are required to carry out, on a part-time basis and for brief periods, a part of their work in the territory of the former State (15 March 2001, case C-165/98, *Mazzoleni*, Reports, I-2189), as follows:

34.   ... even if it be accepted that the rules of the host Member State imposing a minimum wage have the legitimate objective of protecting workers, the national authorities of that State must, before applying them to a service provider established in an adjacent region of another Member State, consider whether the application of those rules is necessary and proportionate for the purpose of protecting the workers concerned.

35.   The host Member State's objective of ensuring the same level of welfare protection for the employees of such service providers as that applicable in its territory to workers in the same sector may be regarded as attained if all the workers concerned enjoy an equivalent position overall in relation to remuneration, taxation and social security contributions in the host Member State and in the Member State of establishment.

36.   Furthermore, application of the host Member State's national rules on minimum wages to service providers established in a frontier region of a Member State other than the host Member State may result, first, in an additional, disproportionate administrative burden including, in certain cases, the calculation, hour-by-hour, of the appropriate remuneration for each employee according to whether he has, in the course of his work, crossed the frontier of another Member State and, second, in the payment of different levels of wages to employees who are all attached to the same operational base and carry out identical work. That last consequence might, in its turn, result in tension between employees and even threaten the cohesion of the collective labour agreements that are applicable in the Member State of establishment.

37.   In a case such as that at issue in the main proceedings, it is therefore incumbent on the competent authorities of the host Member State, for the purpose of determining whether application of its rules imposing a minimum wage is necessary and proportionate, to evaluate all the relevant factors.

38.   That evaluation means, first, that they must take account, in particular, of the duration of the provision of services, of their predictability, and of whether the employees have actually been sent to work in the host Member State or continue to be attached to the operational base of their employer in the Member State in which it is established.

39.   Second, in order to ensure that the protection enjoyed by employees in the Member State of establishment is equivalent, they must, in particular, take account of factors related to the amount of remuneration and the work-period to which it relates, as well as the level of social security contributions and the impact of taxation.

In the later *Portugaia Construções* case (24 January 2002, case C-164/99, Reports, I-787), dealing again with the application of the rules on minimum wage of the host State, the ECJ stated that

19.   ... it is clear from settled case-law that, where such domestic legislation is applicable to all persons and undertakings operating in the territory of the Member State in which the service is provided, it may be justified where it meets overriding requirements relating to the public interest in so far as that interest is not safeguarded by the rules to which the provider of such a service is subject in the Member State in which he is established and in so far as it is appropriate for securing the attainment of the objective which it pursues and does not go beyond what is necessary in order to attain it.

22.   In other words, it may be acknowledged that, in principle, the application by the host Member State of its minimum-wage legislation to providers of services established in another Member State pursues an objective of public interest, namely the protection of employees.

23.   However, there may be circumstances in which the application of such rules would not be in conformity with Articles 59 and 60 of the Treaty.

24.   It is therefore for the national authorities or, as the case may be, the courts of the host Member State, before applying the minimum-wage legislation to service providers established in another Member State, to determine whether that legislation does indeed pursue an objective of public interest and by appropriate means.

In a dispute concerning the correct implementation of Article 3(1)(c) of Directive 96/71/EC in Germany, whose legislation did not recognise as constituent elements of the minimum wage all of the allowances and supplements paid by employers in other Member States to their employees in the construction industry posted to Germany (14 April 2005, case C-341/02, *Commission v Germany*, Reports, I-2733), the ECJ explained how the comparison between the minimum wage established by the rules of the host country and the wage actually paid under the law of the country where the employer is established should be carried out:

29.   It is necessary, first, to point out that the parties are in agreement that, in accordance with Article 3(1)(c) and 3(7), second subparagraph, of Directive 96/71, account need not be taken, as component elements of the minimum wage, of payment for overtime, contributions to supplementary occupational retirement pension schemes, the amounts paid in respect of reimbursement of expenses actually incurred by reason of the posting and, finally, flat-rate sums calculated on a basis other than that of the hourly rate. It is the gross amounts of wages that must be taken into account.

30.   Next ... account [is] to be taken, in the monitoring of the payment of the minimum wage, of all additional payments made by employers established in another Member State, in so far as the relationship between the service provided by the worker and the consideration which he receives in return is not altered in a manner detrimental to the worker.

31.   The German Government also states in its defence that it envisages supplementing the wording of the explanatory notes in order to recognise bonuses in respect of the 13th and 14th salary months as being constituent elements of the minimum wage, on condition that they are paid regularly, proportionately, effectively and irrevocably during the period for which the worker is posted to Germany and that they are made available to the worker on the date on which they are supposed to fall due.

38.   Finally, it is necessary to analyse the main question which remains in dispute as to whether the allowances and supplements paid by an employer which, according to the German Government, alter the balance between the service provided by the worker, on the one hand, and the consideration which he receives in return, on the other, have to be treated as constituent elements of the minimum wage. In issue here, in particular, are quality bonuses and bonuses for dirty, heavy or dangerous work.

39.   Contrary to what the Commission submits, allowances and supplements which are not defined as being constituent elements of the minimum wage by the legislation or national practice of the Member State to the territory of which the worker is posted, and which alter the relationship between the service provided by the worker, on the one hand, and the consideration which he receives in return, on the other, cannot, under the provisions of Directive 96/71, be treated as being elements of that kind.

40.   It is entirely normal that, if an employer requires a worker to carry out additional work or to work under particular conditions, compensation must be provided to the worker for that additional service without its being taken into account for the purpose of calculating the minimum wage.

A further case concerned the implementation by the host country of procedural rules granting the respect of the provisions on the minimum wage, as established by Article 5 of the Directive, and in particular the application of the German provisions whereby, when subcontracting the conduct of building work to another undertaking, a building contractor becomes liable, in the same way as a guarantor who has waived the defence of prior recourse, for the obligation on that undertaking or that undertaking's subcontractors to pay the minimum wage to a worker or to pay contributions to a joint scheme for parties to a collective agreement. In the case at stake the guarantor was a German undertaking that had subcontracted certain building work to a Portuguese undertaking which had carried out the work through some posted workers (12 October 2004, case C-60/03, *Wolff&Müller*, Reports, I-9553). The ECJ held as follows:

34.   It is further clear from settled case-law that, where legislation such as Paragraph 1a of the AEntG, on the supposition that it constitutes a restriction on freedom to provide services, is applicable to all persons and undertakings operating in the territory of the Member State in which the service is provided, it may be justified where it meets overriding requirements relating to the public interest in so far as that interest is not safeguarded by the rules to which the provider of such a service is subject in the Member State in which he is established and in so far as it is appropriate for securing the attainment of the objective which it pursues and does not go beyond what is necessary in order to attain it.

35. Overriding reasons relating to the public interest which have been recognised by the Court include the protection of workers.

36. However, although it may be acknowledged that, in principle, the application by the host Member State of its minimum-wage legislation to providers of services established in another Member State pursues an objective of public interest, namely the protection of employees, the same is true in principle of measures adopted by the host Member State and intended to reinforce the procedural arrangements enabling a posted worker usefully to assert his right to a minimum rate of pay.

37. In fact, if entitlement to minimum rates of pay constitutes a feature of worker protection, procedural arrangements ensuring observance of that right, such as the liability of the guarantor in the main proceedings, must likewise be regarded as being such as to ensure that protection.

38. … it is for that court to verify whether, on an objective view, the legislation at issue in the main proceedings secures the protection of posted workers. It is necessary to determine whether those rules confer a genuine benefit on the workers concerned, which significantly augments their social protection. In this context, the stated intention of the legislature may lead to a more careful assessment of the alleged benefits conferred on workers by the measures which it has adopted.

A further case concerned the applicability of German rules concerning the paid leave funds scheme established to finance holiday entitlement for construction workers to workers posted in Germany by undertakings established in other Member States (25 October 2001, joined cases C-49/98, C-50/98, C-52/98 to C-54/98 and C-68/98 to C-71/98, *Finalarte*, Reports, I-7831). The ECJ stated that

53. Articles 59 and 60 of the Treaty do not preclude a Member State from imposing national rules, such as those laid down by the first sentence of Paragraph 1(3) of the AEntG guaranteeing entitlement to paid leave for posted workers, on a business established in another Member State which provides services in the first Member State by posting workers for that purpose, on the twofold condition that: (i) the workers do not enjoy an essentially similar level of protection under the law of the Member State where their employer is established, so that the application of the national rules of the first Member State confers a genuine benefit on the workers concerned, which significantly adds to their social protection, and (ii) the application of those rules by the first Member State is proportionate to the public interest objective pursued.

75. … it is for the national court to determine the type of information that the German authorities may reasonably require of providers of services established outside the Federal Republic of Germany, having regard to the principle of proportionality. For this purpose, the national court should consider whether the objective differences between the position of businesses established in Germany and that of businesses established outside Germany objectively require the additional information required of the latter.

83. … Articles 59 and 60 of the Treaty preclude the application of a Member State's scheme for paid leave to all businesses established in other Member States providing services to the construction industry in the first Member State where businesses established in the first Member State, only part of whose activities are carried out in that industry, are not all subject to that scheme in respect of their workers engaged in that industry.

The ECJ further declared that certain Luxembourg rules that imposed on a service provider established in another Member State posting workers in Luxembourg the requirement of an individual work permit or a collective work permit subject to the existence of a contract of indefinite duration and previous employment with the same service provider for a period of at least six months, and to the provision of a bank guarantee, were contrary to Community law (21 October 2004, case C-445/03, *Commission v Luxembourg*, Reports, I-10191):

> 32.   ... making the granting of a collective work permit subject to the requirement that an employment contract of indefinite duration must have been in existence between the workers and their undertaking of origin for at least six months before their deployment to Luxembourg goes beyond what is required for the objective of social welfare protection as a necessary condition for providing services through the deployment of workers who are nationals of non-member countries.
>
> 33.   As correctly pointed out by the Commission, that requirement is liable to make considerably more complicated the deployment in Luxembourg of workers who are nationals of non-member countries for the purposes of providing services in sectors where, due to the particular features of the activity in question, frequent use is made of short-term and service-specific contracts. It should be borne in mind in this regard that, according to the information provided by the Luxembourg Government, the national legislation governing employment contracts authorises the use of such contracts for the hiring of Community workers for certain types of tasks.
>
> 38.   It should in this regard be borne in mind that, although the desire to avoid disturbances on the labour market is undoubtedly an overriding reason of general interest, workers employed by an undertaking established in a Member State and who are deployed to another Member State for the purposes of providing services there do not purport to gain access to the labour market of that second State, as they return to their country of origin or residence after the completion of their work.
>
> 47.   The obligation to provide, for the purposes of obtaining a work permit, a bank guarantee to cover costs in the event of repatriation of the worker at the end of his deployment is an excessive burden for service-providing undertakings, having regard to the objective pursued. As stated by the Advocate General at point 56 of his Opinion, it is perfectly possible to envisage measures more in keeping with the freedom to provide services than the general obligation to provide a prior guarantee, such as an order to pay costs actually incurred due to repatriation.

Luxembourg law came under scrutiny also in respect to certain rules that the legislature had described as mandatory provisions falling under national public policy pursuant to Article 3(10) of Directive 96/71/EC and that imposed a number of conditions on the posting of workers by undertakings established in other Member States when providing services in Luxembourg (19 June 2008, case C-319/06, *Commission v Luxembourg*). Recalling its prior judgments, the ECJ stated that

> 27.   ... under the first indent of Article 3(10) of Directive 96/71 it is open to Member States, in compliance with the EC Treaty, to apply, in a non-discriminatory manner, to undertakings which post workers to their territory terms and conditions of employment on matters other than those referred to the first subparagraph of Article 3(1), in the case of public policy provisions.
>
> 29.   In that connection, it must be recalled that the classification of national provisions by a Member State as public-order legislation applies to national provisions compliance with which has been deemed to be so crucial for the protection of the political, social or economic order in the Member State concerned as to require compliance

therewith by all persons present on the national territory of that Member State and all legal relationships within that State.

30. Therefore, contrary to the Grand Duchy of Luxembourg's submissions, the public policy exception is a derogation from the fundamental principle of freedom to provide services which must be interpreted strictly, the scope of which cannot be determined unilaterally by the Member States.

31. In the context of Directive 96/71, the first indent of Article 3(10), constitutes a derogation from the principle that the matters with respect to which the host Member State may apply its legislation to undertakings which post workers to its territory are set out in an exhaustive list in the first subparagraph of Article 3(1) thereof. The first indent of Article 3(10) must therefore be interpreted strictly.

32. Moreover, Declaration No 10 which, as the Advocate General rightly pointed out in point 45 of her Opinion, may be relied on in support of an interpretation of the first indent of Article 3(10) of Directive 96/71, states that the expression 'public policy provisions' is to be construed as covering those mandatory rules from which there can be no derogation and which, by their nature and objective, meet the imperative requirements of the public interest.

33. In any event, Article 3(10) of Directive 96/71 provides that availing themselves of the option for which it provides does not exempt the Member States from complying with their obligations under the EC Treaty and, in particular, those relating to the freedom to provide services, the promotion of which is referred to in recital 5 of the preamble to the directive.

The ECJ also tackled the issue of the legality under Directive 96/71/EC of a collective action through blockading taken by Swedish trade unions in order to induce a Latvian undertaking, posting workers in Sweden, to sign and apply the collective agreement for the building sector establishing more favourable conditions than those established by Swedish law (18 December 2007, case C-341/05, *Laval*, Reports, I-11767). The ECJ stated that

71. a Member State in which the minimum rates of pay are not determined in accordance with one of the means provided for in Article 3(1) and (8) of Directive 96/71 is not entitled, pursuant to that directive, to impose on undertakings established in other Member States, in the framework of the transnational provision of services, negotiation at the place of work, on a case-by-case basis, having regard to the qualifications and tasks of the employees, so that the undertakings concerned may ascertain the wages which they are to pay their posted workers.

80. ... Article 3(7) of Directive 96/71 cannot be interpreted as allowing the host Member State to make the provision of services in its territory conditional on the observance of terms and conditions of employment which go beyond the mandatory rules for minimum protection. As regards the matters referred to in Article 3(1), first subparagraph, (a) to (g), Directive 96/71 expressly lays down the degree of protection for workers of undertakings established in other Member States who are posted to the territory of the host Member State which the latter State is entitled to require those undertakings to observe. Moreover, such an interpretation would amount to depriving the directive of its effectiveness.

81. Therefore — without prejudice to the right of undertakings established in other Member States to sign of their own accord a collective labour agreement in the host Member State, in particular in the context of a commitment made to their own posted

staff, the terms of which might be more favourable — the level of protection which must be guaranteed to workers posted to the territory of the host Member State is limited, in principle, to that provided for in Article 3(1), first subparagraph, (a) to (g) of Directive 96/71, unless, pursuant to the law or collective agreements in the Member State of origin, those workers already enjoy more favourable terms and conditions of employment as regards the matters referred to in that provision.

82.   Moreover, it must be pointed out that, pursuant to the first indent of Article 3(10) of Directive 96/71, Member States may apply terms and conditions of employment on matters other than those specifically referred to in Article 3(1), first subparagraph, (a) to (g), in compliance with the Treaty and, in the case of public policy provisions, on a basis of equality of treatment, to national undertakings and to the undertakings of other Member States.

107.   ... in principle, blockading action by a trade union of the host Member State which is aimed at ensuring that workers posted in the framework of a transnational provision of services have their terms and conditions of employment fixed at a certain level, falls within the objective of protecting workers.

108.   However, as regards the specific obligations, linked to signature of the collective agreement for the building sector, which the trade unions seek to impose on undertakings established in other Member States by way of collective action such as that at issue in the case in the main proceedings, the obstacle which that collective action forms cannot be justified with regard to such an objective. In addition to what is set out in paragraphs 81 and 83 of the present judgment, with regard to workers posted in the framework of a transnational provision of services, their employer is required, as a result of the coordination achieved by Directive 96/71, to observe a nucleus of mandatory rules for minimum protection in the host Member State.

109.   Finally, as regards the negotiations on pay which the trade unions seek to impose, by way of collective action such as that at issue in the main proceedings, on undertakings, established in another Member State which post workers temporarily to their territory, it must be emphasised that Community law certainly does not prohibit Member States from requiring such undertakings to comply with their rules on minimum pay by appropriate means.

110.   However, collective action such as that at issue in the main proceedings cannot be justified in the light of the public interest objective referred to in paragraph 102 of the present judgment, where the negotiations on pay, which that action seeks to require an undertaking established in another Member State to enter into, form part of a national context characterised by a lack of provisions, of any kind, which are sufficiently precise and accessible that they do not render it impossible or excessively difficult in practice for such an undertaking to determine the obligations with which it is required to comply as regards minimum pay.

The ECJ dealt also with the more general issue of the legality under Community law of a collective action initiated by a trade union against an undertaking in order to induce that undertaking to enter into a collective agreement, the terms of which were liable to deter it from exercising freedom of establishment (11 December 2007, case C-438/05, *Viking*, Reports, I-10779). According to the ECJ:

72.   In the present case, first, it cannot be disputed that collective action, such as that envisaged by FSU has the effect of making less attractive, or even pointless, as the national court has pointed out, Viking's exercise of its right to freedom of establishment, inasmuch

as such action prevents both Viking and its subsidiary, Viking Eesti, from enjoying the same treatment in the host Member State as other economic operators established in that State.

73. Secondly, collective action taken in order to implement ITF's policy of combating the use of flags of convenience, which seeks, primarily, as is apparent from ITF's observations, to prevent shipowners from registering their vessels in a State other than that of which the beneficial owners of those vessels are nationals, must be considered to be at least liable to restrict Viking's exercise of its right of freedom of establishment.

74. It follows that collective action such as that at issue in the main proceedings constitutes a restriction on freedom of establishment within the meaning of Article 43 EC.

C.1. Council Directive 86/653/EEC of 18 December 1986 on the coordination of the laws of the Member States relating to self-employed commercial agents (OJ, L 382 of 31 December 1986)

Whereas the restrictions on the freedom of establishment and the freedom to provide services in respect of activities of intermediaries in commerce, industry and small craft industries were abolished by Directive 64/224/EEC:

Whereas the differences in national laws concerning commercial representation substantially affect the conditions of competition and the carrying-on of that activity within the Community and are detrimental both to the protection available to commercial agents vis-à-vis their principals and to the security of commercial transactions; whereas moreover those differences are such as to inhibit substantially the conclusion and operation of commercial representation contracts where principal and commercial agents are established in different Member States:

Whereas trade in goods between Member States should be carried on under conditions which are similar to those of a single market, and this necessitates approximation of the legal systems of the Member States to the extent required for the proper functioning of the common market; whereas in this regard the rules concerning conflict of laws do not, in the matter of commercial representation, remove the inconsistencies referred to above, nor would they even if they were made uniform, and accordingly the proposed harmonization is necessary notwithstanding the existence of those rules:

Whereas in this regard the legal relationship between commercial agent and principal must be given priority:

Whereas it is appropriate to be guided by the principles of Article 117 of the Treaty and to maintain improvements already made, when harmonizing the laws of the Member States relating to commercial agents:

Whereas additional transitional periods should be allowed for certain Member States which have to make a particular effort to adapt their regulations, especially those concerning indemnity for termination of contract between the principal and the commercial agent, to the requirements of this Directive …

Chapter 1 — Scope

Article 1. 1. The harmonization measures prescribed by this Directive shall apply to the laws, regulations and administrative provisions of the Member States governing the relations between commercial agents and their principals.

2. For the purposes of this Directive, 'commercial agent' shall mean a self-employed intermediary who has continuing authority to negotiate the sale or the purchase of goods on behalf of another person, hereinafter called the 'principal', or to negotiate and conclude such transactions on behalf of and in the name of that principal.

3. A commercial agent shall be understood within the meaning of this Directive as not including in particular:

— a person who, in his capacity as an officer, is empowered to enter into commitments binding on a company or association;

— a partner who is lawfully authorized to enter into commitments binding on his partners;

— a receiver, a receiver and manager, a liquidator or a trustee in bankruptcy.

Article 2. 1. This Directive shall not apply to:

— commercial agents whose activities are unpaid:

— commercial agents when they operate on commodity exchanges or in the commodity market, or

— the body known is the Crown Agents for Overseas Governments and Administrations, as set up under the Crown Agents Act 1979 in the United Kingdom, or its subsidiaries.

2. Each of the Member States shall have the right to provide that the Directive shall not apply to those persons whose activities as commercial agents are considered secondary by the law of that Member State.

Chapter II — Rights and obligations

Article 3. 1. In performing has activities a commercial agent must look after his principal's interests and act dutifully and in good faith.

2. In particular, a commercial agent must:

(a) make proper efforts to negotiate and, where appropriate, conclude the transactions he is instructed to take care of;

(b) communicate to his principal all the necessary information available to him;

(c) comply with reasonable instructions given by his principal.

Article 4. 1. In his relations with his commercial agent a principal must act dutifully and in good faith.

2. A principal must in particular:

(a) provide his commercial agent with the necessary documentation relating to the goods concerned;

(b) obtain for his commercial agent the information necessary for the performance of the agency contract, and in particular notify the commercial agent within a reasonable period once he anticipates that the volume of commercial transactions will be significantly lower than that which the commercial agent could normally have expected.

3.   A principal must, in addition, inform the commercial agent within a reasonable period of his acceptance, refusal, and of any non-execution of a commercial transaction which the commercial agent has procured for the principal.

Article 5.   The parties may not derogate from the provisions of Articles 3 and 4.

Chapter III — Remuneration

Article 6.   1.   In the absence of any agreement on this matter between the parties, and without prejudice to the application of the compulsory provisions of the Member States concerning the level of remuneration, a commercial agent shall be entitled to the remuneration that commercial agents appointed for the goods forming the subject of his agency contract are customarily allowed in the place where he carries on his activities. If there is no such customary practice a commercial agent shall be entitled to reasonable remuneration taking into account all the aspects of the transaction.

2.   Any part of the remuneration which varies with the number or value of business transactions shall be deemed to be commission within the meaning of this Directive.

3.   Articles 7 to 12 shall not apply if the commercial agent is not remunerated wholly or in part by commission.

Article 7.   1.   A commercial agent shall be entitled to commission on commercial transactions concluded during the period covered by the agency contract:

(a)   where the transaction has been concluded as a result of his action; or

(b)   where the transaction is concluded with a third party whom he has previously acquired as a customer for transactions of the same kind.

2.   A commercial agent shall also be entitled to commission on transactions concluded during the period covered by the agency contract:

— either where he is entrusted with a specific geographical area or group of customers;

— or where he has an exclusive right to a specific geographical area or group of customers, and where the transaction has been entered into with a customer belonging to that area or group.

Member States shall include in their legislation one of the possibilities referred to in the above two indents.

Article 8.   A commercial agent shall be entitled to commission on commercial transactions concluded after the agency contract has terminated:

(a)   if the transaction is mainly attributable to the commercial agent's efforts during the period covered by the agency contract and if the transaction was entered into within a reasonable period after that contract terminated; or

(b)   if, in accordance with the conditions mentioned in Article 7, the order of the third party reached the principal or the commercial agent before the agency contract terminated.

Article 9.   A commercial agent shall not be entitled to the commission referred to in Article 7, if that commission is payable, pursuant to Article 8, to the previous commercial agent, unless it is equitable because of the circumstances for the commission to be shared between the commercial agents.

Article 10.   1.   The commission shall become due as soon as and to the extent that one of the following circumstances obtains:
(a)   the principal has executed the transaction; or
(b)   the principal should, according to his agreement with the third party, have executed the transaction; or
(c)   the third party has executed the transaction.
2.   The commission shall become due at the latest when the third party has executed his part of the transaction or should have done so if the principal had executed his part of the transaction, as he should have.
3.   The commission shall be paid not later than on the last day of the month following the quarter in which it became due.
4.   Agreements to derogate from paragraphs 2 and 3 to the detriment of the commercial agent shall not be permitted.

Article 11.   1.   The right to commission can be extinguished only if and to the extent that:
—   it is established that the contract between the third party and the principal will not be executed, and
—   that face is due to a reason for which the principal is not to blame.
2.   Any commission which the commercial agent has already received shall be refunded if the right to it is extinguished.
3.   Agreements to derogate from paragraph 1 to the detriment of the commercial agent shall not be permitted.

Article 12.   1.   The principal shall supply his commercial agent with a statement of the commission due, not later than the last day of the month following the quarter in which the commission has become due. This statement shall set out the main components used in calculating the amount of commission.
2.   A commercial agent shall be entitled to demand that he be provided with all the information, and in particular an extract from the books, which is available to his principal and which he needs in order to check the amount of the commission due to him.
3.   Agreements to derogate from paragraphs 1 and 2 to the detriment of the commercial agent shall not be permitted.
4.   This Directive shall not conflict with the internal provisions of Member States which recognize the right of a commercial agent to inspect a principal's books.

Chapter IV — Conclusion and termination of the agency contract

Article 13.   1.   Each party shall be entitled to receive from the other on request a signed written document setting out the terms of the agency contract including any terms subsequently agreed. Waiver of this right shall not be permitted.
2.   Notwithstanding paragraph 1 a Member State may provide that an agency contract shall not be valid unless evidenced in writing.

Article 14.   An agency contract for a fixed period which continues to be performed by both parties after that period has expired shall be deemed to be converted into an agency contract for an indefinite period.

Article 15.   1.   Where an agency contract is concluded for an indefinite period either party may terminate it by notice.

2.   The period of notice shall be one month for the first year of the contract, two months for the second year commenced, and three months for the third year commenced and subsequent years. The parties may not agree on shorter periods of notice.

3.   Member States may fix the period of notice at four months for the fourth year of the contract, five months for the fifth year and six months for the sixth and subsequent years. They may decide that the parties may not agree to shorter periods.

4.   If the parties agree on longer periods than those laid down in paragraphs 2 and 3, the period of notice to be observed by the principal must not be shorter than that to be observed by the commercial agent.

5.   Unless otherwise agreed by the parties, the end of the period of notice must coincide with the end of a calendar month.

6.   The provision of this Article shall apply to an agency contract for a fixed period where it is converted under Article 14 into an agency contract for an indefinite period, subject to the proviso that the earlier fixed period must be taken into account in the calculation of the period of notice.

Article 16.   Nothing in this Directive shall affect the application of the law of the Member States where the latter provides for the immediate termination of the agency contract:
    (a)   because of the failure of one party to carry out all or part of his obligations;
    (b)   where exceptional circumstances arise.

Article 17.   1.   Member States shall take the measures necessary to ensure that the commercial agent is, after termination of the agency contract, indemnified in accordance with paragraph 2 or compensated for damage in accordance with paragraph 3.

2.   (a)   The commercial agent shall be entitled to an indemnity if and to the extent that:
—   he has brought the principal new customers or has significantly increased the volume of business with existing customers and the principal continues to derive substantial benefits from the business with such customers, and
—   the payment of this indemnity is equitable having regard to all the circumstances and, in particular, the commission lost by the commercial agent on the business transacted with such customers. Member States may provide for such circumstances also to include the application or otherwise of a restraint of trade clause, within the meaning of Article 20;

(b)   The amount of the indemnity may not exceed a figure equivalent to an indemnity for one year calculated from the commercial agent's average annual remuneration over the preceding five years and if the contract goes back less than five years the indemnity shall be calculated on the average for the period in question;

(c)   The grant of such an indemnity shall not prevent the commercial agent from seeking damages.

3.   The commercial agent shall be entitled to compensation for the damage he suffers as a result of the termination of his relations with the principal.

Such damage shall be deemed to occur particularly when the termination takes place in circumstances:

—   depriving the commercial agent of the commission which proper performance of the agency contract would have procured him whilst providing the principal with substantial benefits linked to the commercial agent's activities;

—   and/or which have not enabled the commercial agent to amortize the costs and expenses that he had incurred for the performance of the agency contract on the principal's advice.

4.   Entitlement to the indemnity as provided for in paragraph 2 or to compensation for damage as provided for under paragraph 3, shall also arise where the agency contract is terminated as a result of the commercial agent's death.

5.   The commercial agent shall lose his entitlement to the indemnity in the instances provided for in paragraph 2 or to compensation for damage in the instances provided for in paragraph 3, if within one year following termination of the contract he has not notified the principal that he intends pursuing his entitlement.

6.   The Commission shall submit to the Council, within eight years following the date of notification of this Directive, a report on the implementation of this Article, and shall if necessary submit to it proposals for amendments.

Article 18.   The indemnity or compensation referred to in Article 17 shall not be payable:

(a)   where the principal has terminated the agency contract because of default attributable to the commercial agent which would justify immediate termination of the agency contract under national law;

(b)   where the commercial agent has terminated the agency contract, unless such termination is justified by circumstances attributable to the principal or on grounds of age, infirmity or illness of the commercial agent in consequence of which he cannot reasonably be required to continue his activities;

(c)   where, with the agreement of the principal, the commercial agent assigns his rights and duties under the agency contract to another person.

Article 19.   The parties may not derogate from Articles 17 and 18 to the detriment of the commercial agent before the agency contract expires.

Article 20.   1.   For the purposes of this Directive an agreement restricting the business activities of a commercial agent following termination of the agency contract is hereinafter referred to as a restraint of trade clause.

2.   A restraint of trade clause shall be valid only if and to the extent that:

(a)   it is concluded in writing; and

(b)   it relates to the geographical area or the group of customers and the geographical area entrusted to the commercial agent and to the kind of goods covered by his agency under the contract.

3.   A restraint of trade clause shall be valid for not more than two years after termination of the agency contract.

4.   This Article shall not affect provisions of national law which impose other restrictions on the validity or enforceability of restraint of trade clauses or which enable the courts to reduce the obligations on the parties resulting from such an agreement.

Chapter V — General and final provisions

Article 21. Nothing in this Directive shall require a Member State to provide for the disclosure of information where such disclosure would be contrary to public policy.

C.2. ECJ case-law

Judgment 9 November 2000, case C-381/98, *Ingmar*, Reports, I-9305.
    See Chapter II, Public policy of the EU, F.

Consumer contracts*

A. Council Directive 93/13/EEC of 5 April 1993 on unfair terms in consumer contracts (OJ, L 95 of 21 April 1993)

Whereas, in particular, the laws of Member States relating to unfair terms in consumer contracts show marked divergences;

Whereas it is the responsibility of the Member States to ensure that contracts concluded with consumers do not contain unfair terms;

Whereas, generally speaking, consumers do not know the rules of law which, in Member States other than their own, govern contracts for the sale of goods or services; whereas this lack of awareness may deter them from direct transactions for the purchase of goods or services in another Member State;

Whereas, in order to facilitate the establishment of the internal market and to safeguard the citizen in his role as consumer when acquiring goods and services under contracts which are governed by the laws of Member States other than his own, it is essential to remove unfair terms from those contracts;

Whereas sellers of goods and suppliers of services will thereby be helped in their task of selling goods and supplying services, both at home and throughout the internal market; whereas competition will thus be stimulated, so contributing to increased choice for Community citizens as consumers...

---

* See also Article 6 of Regulation (EC) No 593/08 on the law applicable to contractual obligations (Rome I) and Article 5 of the Rome Convention, above, in this Chapter, General provisions, A.1 and A.3. Cf also the Communication of the Commission "European Contract Law and the revision of the acquis: the way forward (COM (2004) 651 of 11 October 2004) and the Green Paper on the revision of the Consumer Acquis (OJ, C 61 of 15 March 2007).

Whereas more effective protection of the consumer can be achieved by adopting uniform rules of law in the matter of unfair terms; whereas those rules should apply to all contracts concluded between sellers or suppliers and consumers; whereas as a result inter alia contracts relating to employment, contracts relating to succession rights, contracts relating to rights under family law and contracts relating to the incorporation and organization of companies or partnership agreements must be excluded from this Directive...

Whereas the statutory or regulatory provisions of the Member States which directly or indirectly determine the terms of consumer contracts are presumed not to contain unfair terms; whereas, therefore, it does not appear to be necessary to subject the terms which reflect mandatory statutory or regulatory provisions and the principles or provisions of international conventions to which the Member States or the Community are party; whereas in that respect the wording 'mandatory statutory or regulatory provisions' in Article 1 (2) also covers rules which, according to the law, shall apply between the contracting parties provided that no other arrangements have been established...

Whereas there is a risk that, in certain cases, the consumer may be deprived of protection under this Directive by designating the law of a non-Member country as the law applicable to the contract; whereas provisions should therefore be included in this Directive designed to avert this risk...

Article 1.   1.   The purpose of this Directive is to approximate the laws, regulations and administrative provisions of the Member States relating to unfair terms in contracts concluded between a seller or supplier and a consumer.
    2.   The contractual terms which reflect mandatory statutory or regulatory provisions and the provisions or principles of international conventions to which the Member States or the Community are party, particularly in the transport area, shall not be subject to the provisions of this Directive.

Article 2.   For the purposes of this Directive:
    (a)   'unfair terms' means the contractual terms defined in Article 3;
    (b)   'consumer' means any natural person who, in contracts covered by this Directive, is acting for purposes which are outside his trade, business or profession;
    (c)   'seller or supplier' means any natural or legal person who, in contracts covered by this Directive, is acting for purposes relating to his trade, business or profession, whether publicly owned or privately owned.

Article 3.   1.   A contractual term which has not been individually negotiated shall be regarded as unfair if, contrary to the requirement of good faith, it causes a significant imbalance in the parties' rights and obligations arising under the contract, to the detriment of the consumer.
    2.   A term shall always be regarded as not individually negotiated where it has been drafted in advance and the consumer has therefore not been able to influence the substance of the term, particularly in the context of a pre-formulated standard contract.
The fact that certain aspects of a term or one specific term have been individually negotiated shall not exclude the application of this Article to the rest of a contract if an overall assessment of the contract indicates that it is nevertheless a pre-formulated standard contract.

Where any seller or supplier claims that a standard term has been individually negotiated, the burden of proof in this respect shall be incumbent on him.

    3.   The Annex shall contain an indicative and non-exhaustive list of the terms which may be regarded as unfair.

Article 6.   1.   Member States shall lay down that unfair terms used in a contract concluded with a consumer by a seller or supplier shall, as provided for under their national law, not be binding on the consumer and that the contract shall continue to bind the parties upon those terms if it is capable of continuing in existence without the unfair terms.

    2.   Member States shall take the necessary measures to ensure that the consumer does not lose the protection granted by this Directive by virtue of the choice of the law of a non-Member country as the law applicable to the contract if the latter has a close connection with the territory of the Member States.

Article 8.   Member States may adopt or retain the most stringent provisions compatible with the Treaty in the area covered by this Directive, to ensure a maximum degree of protection for the consumer.

ANNEX

Terms referred to in Article 3(3):

1.   Terms which have the object or effect of:

    (a)   excluding or limiting the legal liability of a seller or supplier in the event of the death of a consumer or personal injury to the latter resulting from an act or omission of that seller or supplier;

    (b)   inappropriately excluding or limiting the legal rights of the consumer vis-à-vis the seller or supplier or another party in the event of total or partial non-performance or inadequate performance by the seller or supplier of any of the contractual obligations, including the option of offsetting a debt owed to the seller or supplier against any claim which the consumer may have against him;

    (c)   making an agreement binding on the consumer whereas provision of services by the seller or supplier is subject to a condition whose realization depends on his own will alone;

    (d)   permitting the seller or supplier to retain sums paid by the consumer where the latter decides not to conclude or perform the contract, without providing for the consumer to receive compensation of an equivalent amount from the seller or supplier where the latter is the party cancelling the contract;

    (e)   requiring any consumer who fails to fulfil his obligation to pay a disproportionately high sum in compensation;

    (f)   authorizing the seller or supplier to dissolve the contract on a discretionary basis where the same facility is not granted to the consumer, or permitting the seller or supplier to retain the sums paid for services not yet supplied by him where it is the seller or supplier himself who dissolves the contract;

    (g)   enabling the seller or supplier to terminate a contract of indeterminate duration without reasonable notice except where there are serious grounds for doing so;

(h)   automatically extending a contract of fixed duration where the consumer does not indicate otherwise, when the deadline fixed for the consumer to express this desire not to extend the contract is unreasonably early;

(i)   irrevocably binding the consumer to terms with which he had no real opportunity of becoming acquainted before the conclusion of the contract;

(j)   enabling the seller or supplier to alter the terms of the contract unilaterally without a valid reason which is specified in the contract;

(k)   enabling the seller or supplier to alter unilaterally without a valid reason any characteristics of the product or service to be provided;

(l)   providing for the price of goods to be determined at the time of delivery or allowing a seller of goods or supplier of services to increase their price without in both cases giving the consumer the corresponding right to cancel the contract if the final price is too high in relation to the price agreed when the contract was concluded;

(m)   giving the seller or supplier the right to determine whether the goods or services supplied are in conformity with the contract, or giving him the exclusive right to interpret any term of the contract;

(n)   limiting the seller's or supplier's obligation to respect commitments undertaken by his agents or making his commitments subject to compliance with a particular formality;

(o)   obliging the consumer to fulfil all his obligations where the seller or supplier does not perform his;

(p)   giving the seller or supplier the possibility of transferring his rights and obligations under the contract, where this may serve to reduce the guarantees for the consumer, without the latter's agreement;

(q)   excluding or hindering the consumer's right to take legal action or exercise any other legal remedy, particularly by requiring the consumer to take disputes exclusively to arbitration not covered by legal provisions, unduly restricting the evidence available to him or imposing on him a burden of proof which, according to the applicable law, should lie with another party to the contract.

2.   Scope of subparagraphs (g), (j) and (l)

(a)   Subparagraph (g) is without hindrance to terms by which a supplier of financial services reserves the right to terminate unilaterally a contract of indeterminate duration without notice where there is a valid reason, provided that the supplier is required to inform the other contracting party or parties thereof immediately.

(b)   Subparagraph (j) is without hindrance to terms under which a supplier of financial services reserves the right to alter the rate of interest payable by the consumer or due to the latter, or the amount of other charges for financial services without notice where there is a valid reason, provided that the supplier is required to inform the other contracting party or parties thereof at the earliest opportunity and that the latter are free to dissolve the contract immediately.

Subparagraph (j) is also without hindrance to terms under which a seller or supplier reserves the right to alter unilaterally the conditions of a contract of indeterminate duration, provided that he is required to inform the consumer with reasonable notice and that the consumer is free to dissolve the contract.

(c)   Subparagraphs (g), (j) and (l) do not apply to:

— transactions in transferable securities, financial instruments and other products or services where the price is linked to fluctuations in a stock exchange quotation or index or a financial market rate that the seller or supplier does not control;

— contracts for the purchase or sale of foreign currency, traveller's cheques or international money orders denominated in foreign currency;

(d)   Subparagraph (l) is without hindrance to price-indexation clauses, where lawful, provided that the method by which prices vary is explicitly described.

B.   Directive 97/7/EC of the European Parliament and of the Council of 20 May 1997 on the protection of consumers in respect of distance contracts (OJ, L 144 of 4 June 1994)[1]

(1)   Whereas, in connection with the attainment of the aims of the internal market, measures must be taken for the gradual consolidation of that market;

(2)   Whereas the free movement of goods and services affects not only the business sector but also private individuals; whereas it means that consumers should be able to have access to the goods and services of another Member State on the same terms as the population of that State;

(23)   Whereas there is a risk that, in certain cases, the consumer may be deprived of protection under this Directive through the designation of the law of a non-member country as the law applicable to the contract; whereas provisions should therefore be included in this Directive to avert that risk;

Article 1. Object.   The object of this Directive is to approximate the laws, regulations and administrative provisions of the Member States concerning distance contracts between consumers and suppliers.

Article 2. Definitions.   For the purposes of this Directive:
(1)   'distance contract' means any contract concerning goods or services concluded between a supplier and a consumer under an organized distance sales or service-provision scheme run by the supplier, who, for the purpose of the contract, makes exclusive use of one or more means of distance communication up to and including the moment at which the contract is concluded;

(2)   'consumer' means any natural person who, in contracts covered by this Directive, is acting for purposes which are outside his trade, business or profession;

(3)   'supplier' means any natural or legal person who, in contracts covered by this Directive, is acting in his commercial or professional capacity;

(4)   'means of distance communication' means any means which, without the simultaneous physical presence of the supplier and the consumer, may be used for the conclusion of a contract between those parties. An indicative list of the means covered by this Directive is contained in Annex I;

---

[1]   As finally amended by Directive 2007/64/EC of the European Council and of the Council of 13 November 2007 (OJ, L 319 of 5 December 2007).

(5)   'operator of a means of communication' means any public or private natural or legal person whose trade, business or profession involves making one or more means of distance communication available to suppliers.

Article 3. Exemptions.   1.   This Directive shall not apply to contracts:
—   relating to financial services, a non-exhaustive list of which is given in Annex II;
—   concluded by means of automatic vending machines or automated commercial premises;
—   concluded with telecommunications operators through the use of public payphones;
—   concluded for the construction and sale of immovable property or relating to other immovable property rights, except for rental;
—   concluded at an auction.
2.   Articles 4, 5, 6 and 7(1) shall not apply:
—   to contracts for the supply of foodstuffs, beverages or other goods intended for everyday consumption supplied to the home of the consumer, to his residence or to his workplace by regular roundsmen;
—   to contracts for the provision of accommodation, transport, catering or leisure services, where the supplier undertakes, when the contract is concluded, to provide these services on a specific date or within a specific period; exceptionally, in the case of outdoor leisure events, the supplier can reserve the right not to apply Article 7(2) in specific circumstances.

Article 12. Binding nature.   1.   The consumer may not waive the rights conferred on him by the transposition of this Directive into national law.
2.   Member States shall take the measures needed to ensure that the consumer does not lose the protection granted by this Directive by virtue of the choice of the law of a non-member country as the law applicable to the contract if the latter has close connection with the territory of one or more Member States.

Article 13. Community rules.   1.   The provisions of this Directive shall apply insofar as there are no particular provisions in rules of Community law governing certain types of distance contracts in their entirety.
2.   Where specific Community rules contain provisions governing only certain aspects of the supply of goods or provision of services, those provisions, rather than the provisions of this Directive, shall apply to these specific aspects of the distance contracts.

Article 14. Minimal clause.   Member States may introduce or maintain, in the area covered by this Directive, more stringent provisions compatible with the Treaty, to ensure a higher level of consumer protection. Such provisions shall, where appropriate, include a ban, in the general interest, on the marketing of certain goods or services, particularly medicinal products, within their territory by means of distance contracts, with due regard for the Treaty.

C. Directive 1999/44/EC of the European Parliament and of the Council of 25 May 1999 on certain aspects of the sale of consumer goods and associated guarantees (OJ, L 171 of 7 July 1999)

(1)   Whereas Article 153(1) and (3) of the Treaty provides that the Community should contribute to the achievement of a high level of consumer protection by the measures it adopts pursuant to Article 95 thereof;

(2)   Whereas the internal market comprises an area without internal frontiers in which the free movement of goods, persons, services and capital is guaranteed; whereas free movement of goods concerns not only transactions by persons acting in the course of a business but also transactions by private individuals; whereas it implies that consumers resident in one Member State should be free to purchase goods in the territory of another Member State on the basis of a uniform minimum set of fair rules governing the sale of consumer goods;

(3)   Whereas the laws of the Member States concerning the sale of consumer goods are somewhat disparate, with the result that national consumer goods markets differ from one another and that competition between sellers may be distorted;

(22)   Whereas the parties may not, by common consent, restrict or waive the rights granted to consumers, since otherwise the legal protection afforded would be thwarted; whereas this principle should apply also to clauses which imply that the consumer was aware of any lack of conformity of the consumer goods existing at the time the contract was concluded; whereas the protection granted to consumers under this Directive should not be reduced on the grounds that the law of a non-member State has been chosen as being applicable to the contract;

Article 1. Scope and definitions.   1.   The purpose of this Directive is the approximation of the laws, regulations and administrative provisions of the Member States on certain aspects of the sale of consumer goods and associated guarantees in order to ensure a uniform minimum level of consumer protection in the context of the internal market.

2.   For the purposes of this Directive:

(a)   consumer: shall mean any natural person who, in the contracts covered by this Directive, is acting for purposes which are not related to his trade, business or profession;

(b)   consumer goods: shall mean any tangible movable item, with the exception of:

—   goods sold by way of execution or otherwise by authority of law;

—   water and gas where they are not put up for sale in a limited volume or set quantity;

—   electricity;

(c)   seller: shall mean any natural or legal person who, under a contract, sells consumer goods in the course of his trade, business or profession;

(d)   producer: shall mean the manufacturer of consumer goods, the importer of consumer goods into the territory of the Community or any person purporting to be a producer by placing his name, trade mark or other distinctive sign on the consumer goods;

(e)   guarantee: shall mean any undertaking by a seller or producer to the consumer, given without extra charge, to reimburse the price paid or to replace, repair or handle consumer goods in any way if they do not meet the specifications set out in the guarantee statement or in the relevant advertising;

(f)   repair: shall mean, in the event of lack of conformity, bringing consumer goods into conformity with the contract of sale.

3.   Member States may provide that the expression 'consumer goods' does not cover second-hand goods sold at public auction where consumers have the opportunity of attending the sale in person.

4.   Contracts for the supply of consumer goods to be manufactured or produced shall also be deemed contracts of sale for the purpose of this Directive.

Article 7. Binding nature.   1.   Any contractual terms or agreements concluded with the seller before the lack of conformity is brought to the seller's attention which directly or indirectly waive or restrict the rights resulting from this Directive shall, as provided for by national law, not be binding on the consumer.

Member States may provide that, in the case of second-hand goods, the seller and consumer may agree contractual terms or agreements which have a shorter time period for the liability of the seller than that set down in Article 5(1). Such period may not be less than one year.

2.   Member States shall take the necessary measures to ensure that consumers are not deprived of the protection afforded by this Directive as a result of opting for the law of a non-member State as the law applicable to the contract where the contract has a close connection with the territory of the Member States.

Article 8. National law and minimum protection.   1.   The rights resulting from this Directive shall be exercised without prejudice to other rights which the consumer may invoke under the national rules governing contractual or non-contractual liability.

2.   Member States may adopt or maintain in force more stringent provisions, compatible with the Treaty in the field covered by this Directive, to ensure a higher level of consumer protection.

D.   Directive 2000/31/EC of the European Parliament and of the Council of 8 June 2000 on certain legal aspects of information society services, in particular electronic commerce, in the Internal Market (Directive on electronic commerce) (OJ, L 178 of 17 July 2000): Recitals 11, 55–56, Article 3(3)

See Chapter IX, General provisions, D.

E.   Directive 2002/65/EC of the European Parliament and of the Council of 23 September 2002 concerning the distance marketing of consumer financial services and amending Council Directive 90/619/EEC and Directives 97/7/EC and 98/27/EC (OJ, L 271 of 9 October 2002)[1]

...

(2)   Both for consumers and suppliers of financial services, the distance marketing of financial services will constitute one of the main tangible results of the completion of the internal market.

(3)   Within the framework of the internal market, it is in the interest of consumers to have access without discrimination to the widest possible range of financial services available in the Community so that they can choose those that are best suited to their needs. In order to safeguard freedom of choice, which is an essential consumer right, a high degree of consumer protection is required in order to enhance consumer confidence in distance selling.

(4)   It is essential to the smooth operation of the internal market for consumers to be able to negotiate and conclude contracts with a supplier established in other Member States, regardless of whether the supplier is also established in the Member State in which the consumer resides.

(5)   Because of their intangible nature, financial services are particularly suited to distance selling and the establishment of a legal framework governing the distance marketing of financial services should increase consumer confidence in the use of new techniques for the distance marketing of financial services, such as electronic commerce.

(6)   This Directive should be applied in conformity with the Treaty and with secondary law, including Directive 2000/31/EC on electronic commerce, the latter being applicable solely to the transactions which it covers.

(7)   This Directive aims to achieve the objectives set forth above without prejudice to Community or national law governing freedom to provide services or, where applicable, host Member State control and/or authorisation or supervision systems in the Member States where this is compatible with Community legislation.

(8)   Moreover, this Directive, and in particular its provisions relating to information about any contractual clause on law applicable to the contract and/or on the competent court does not affect the applicability to the distance marketing of consumer financial services of Council Regulation (EC) No 44/2001 of 22 December 2000 on jurisdiction and the recognition and enforcement of judgements in civil and commercial matters or of the 1980 Rome Convention on the law applicable to contractual obligations.

(13)   A high level of consumer protection should be guaranteed by this Directive, with a view to ensuring the free movement of financial services. Member States should not be able to adopt provisions other than those laid down in this Directive in the fields it harmonises, unless otherwise specifically indicated in it....

---

[1]   As finally amended by Directive 2007/64/EC of the European Council and of the Council of 13 November 2007 (OJ, L 319 of 5 December 2007).

Article 1. Object and scope.   1.   The object of this Directive is to approximate the laws, regulations and administrative provisions of the Member States concerning the distance marketing of consumer financial services.

2.   In the case of contracts for financial services comprising an initial service agreement followed by successive operations or a series of separate operations of the same nature performed over time, the provisions of this Directive shall apply only to the initial agreement.

In case there is no initial service agreement but the successive operations or the separate operations of the same nature performed over time are performed between the same contractual parties, Articles 3 and 4 apply only when the first operation is performed. Where, however, no operation of the same nature is performed for more than one year, the next operation will be deemed to be the first in a new series of operations and, accordingly, Articles 3 and 4 shall apply.

Article 2. Definitions.   For the purposes of this Directive:

(a)   'distance contract' means any contract concerning financial services concluded between a supplier and a consumer under an organised distance sales or service-provision scheme run by the supplier, who, for the purpose of that contract, makes exclusive use of one or more means of distance communication up to and including the time at which the contract is concluded;

(b)   'financial service' means any service of a banking, credit, insurance, personal pension, investment or payment nature;

(c)   'supplier' means any natural or legal person, public or private, who, acting in his commercial or professional capacity, is the contractual provider of services subject to distance contracts;

(d)   'consumer' means any natural person who, in distance contracts covered by this Directive, is acting for purposes which are outside his trade, business or profession;

(e)   'means of distance communication' refers to any means which, without the simultaneous physical presence of the supplier and the consumer, may be used for the distance marketing of a service between those parties;

(f)   'durable medium' means any instrument which enables the consumer to store information addressed personally to him in a way accessible for future reference for a period of time adequate for the purposes of the information and which allows the unchanged reproduction of the information stored;

(g)   'operator or supplier of a means of distance communication' means any public or private, natural or legal person whose trade, business or profession involves making one or more means of distance communication available to suppliers.

Article 3. Information to the consumer prior to the conclusion of the distance contract.   1.   In good time before the consumer is bound by any distance contract or offer, he shall be provided with the following information concerning …

(3)   the distance contract …

(e)   the Member State or States whose laws are taken by the supplier as a basis for the establishment of relations with the consumer prior to the conclusion of the distance contract;

(f)   any contractual clause on law applicable to the distance contract and/or on competent court;

4.   Information on contractual obligations, to be communicated to the consumer during the pre-contractual phase, shall be in conformity with the contractual obligations which would result from the law presumed to be applicable to the distance contract if the latter were concluded.

Article 12. *Imperative nature of this Directive's provisions.*   1.   Consumers may not waive the rights conferred on them by this Directive.
   2.   Member States shall take the measures needed to ensure that the consumer does not lose the protection granted by this Directive by virtue of the choice of the law of a non-member country as the law applicable to the contract, if this contract has a close link with the territory of one or more Member States.

F.   Regulation (EC) No 2006/2004 of the European Parliament and of the Council of 27 October 2004 on cooperation between national authorities responsible for the enforcement of consumer protection laws (OJ, L 364 of 9 December 2004): Article 2(2)

See Chapter IV, Consumers, A.

G.   Directive 2008/48/EC of the European Parliament and of the Council of 23 April 2008 on credit agreements for consumers and repealing Council Directive 87/102/EEC (OJ, L 133 of 22 May 2008)

(1)   Council Directive 87/102/EEC of 22 December 1986 for the approximation of the laws, regulations and administrative provisions of the Member States concerning consumer credit [3] lays down rules at Community level concerning consumer credit agreements.
   (2) In 1995, the Commission presented a report on the operation of Directive 87/102/EEC and undertook a broad consultation of the interested parties. In 1997, the Commission presented a summary report of reactions to the 1995 report. A second report was produced in 1996 on the operation of Directive 87/102/EEC.
   (3) Those reports and consultations revealed substantial differences between the laws of the various Member States in the field of credit for natural persons in general and consumer credit in particular. An analysis of the national laws transposing Directive 87/102/EEC shows that Member States use a variety of consumer protection mechanisms, in addition to Directive 87/102/EEC, on account of differences in the legal or economic situation at national level.
   (4)   The de facto and de jure situation resulting from those national differences in some cases leads to distortions of competition among creditors in the Community and creates obstacles to the internal market where Member States have adopted different mandatory provisions more stringent than those provided for in Directive 87/102/EEC.

It restricts consumers' ability to make direct use of the gradually increasing availability of cross-border credit. Those distortions and restrictions may in turn have consequences in terms of the demand for goods and services.

(9)   Full harmonisation is necessary in order to ensure that all consumers in the Community enjoy a high and equivalent level of protection of their interests and to create a genuine internal market. Member States should therefore not be allowed to maintain or introduce national provisions other than those laid down in this Directive. However, such restriction should only apply where there are provisions harmonised in this Directive. Where no such harmonised provisions exist, Member States should remain free to maintain or introduce national legislation. Accordingly, Member States may, for instance, maintain or introduce national provisions on joint and several liability of the seller or the service provider and the creditor. Another example of this possibility for Member States could be the maintenance or introduction of national provisions on the cancellation of a contract for the sale of goods or supply of services if the consumer exercises his right of withdrawal from the credit agreement. In this respect Member States, in the case of open-end credit agreements, should be allowed to fix a minimum period needing to elapse between the time when the creditor asks for reimbursement and the day on which the credit has to be reimbursed. ...

(37)   In the case of linked credit agreements, a relationship of interdependence exists between the purchase of goods or services and the credit agreement concluded for that purpose. Therefore, where the consumer exercises his right of withdrawal in respect of the purchase agreement, based on Community law, he should no longer be bound by the linked credit agreement. This should not affect national law applicable to linked credit agreements in cases where a purchase agreement has been voided or where the consumer has exercised his right of withdrawal based on national law. Nor should this affect the rights of consumers granted by national provisions according to which no commitment may be entered into between the consumer and a supplier of goods or services, nor any payment made between those persons, as long as the consumer has not signed the credit agreement to finance the purchase of the goods or services....

Article 1. Subject matter.   The purpose of this Directive is to harmonise certain aspects of the laws, regulations and administrative provisions of the Member States concerning agreements covering credit for consumers.

Article 2. Scope.   1.   This Directive shall apply to credit agreements.

2.   This Directive shall not apply to the following:

(a)   credit agreements which are secured either by a mortgage or by another comparable security commonly used in a Member State on immovable property or secured by a right related to immovable property;

(b)   credit agreements the purpose of which is to acquire or retain property rights in land or in an existing or projected building;

(c)   credit agreements involving a total amount of credit less than EUR 200 or more than EUR 75000;

(d)   hiring or leasing agreements where an obligation to purchase the object of the agreement is not laid down either by the agreement itself or by any separate agreement; such an obligation shall be deemed to exist if it is so decided unilaterally by the creditor;

(e)   credit agreements in the form of an overdraft facility and where the credit has to be repaid within one month;

(f)   credit agreements where the credit is granted free of interest and without any other charges and credit agreements under the terms of which the credit has to be repaid within three months and only insignificant charges are payable;

(g)   credit agreements where the credit is granted by an employer to his employees as a secondary activity free of interest or at annual percentage rates of charge lower than those prevailing on the market and which are not offered to the public generally;

(h)   credit agreements which are concluded with investment firms as defined in Article 4(1) of Directive 2004/39/EC of the European Parliament and of the Council of 21 April 2004 on markets in financial instruments [9] or with credit institutions as defined in Article 4 of Directive 2006/48/EC for the purposes of allowing an investor to carry out a transaction relating to one or more of the instruments listed in Section C of Annex I to Directive 2004/39/EC, where the investment firm or credit institution granting the credit is involved in such transaction;

(i)   credit agreements which are the outcome of a settlement reached in court or before another statutory authority;

(j)   credit agreements which relate to the deferred payment, free of charge, of an existing debt;

(k)   credit agreements upon the conclusion of which the consumer is requested to deposit an item as security in the creditor's safe-keeping and where the liability of the consumer is strictly limited to that pledged item;

(l)   credit agreements which relate to loans granted to a restricted public under a statutory provision with a general interest purpose, and at lower interest rates than those prevailing on the market or free of interest or on other terms which are more favourable to the consumer than those prevailing on the market and at interest rates not higher than those prevailing on the market.

3.   In the case of credit agreements in the form of an overdraft facility and where the credit has to be repaid on demand or within three months, only Articles 1 to 3, Article 4(1), Article 4(2)(a) to (c), Article 4(4), Articles 6 to 9, Article 10(1), Article 10(4), Article 10(5), Articles 12, 15, 17 and Articles 19 to 32 shall apply.

4.   In the case of credit agreements in the form of overrunning, only Articles 1 to 3, 18, 20 and 22 to 32 shall apply.

5.   Member States may determine that only Articles 1 to 4, 6, 7 and 9, Article 10(1), points (a) to (h) and (l) of Article 10(2), Article 10(4) and Articles 11, 13 and 16 to 32 shall apply to credit agreements which are concluded by an organisation which:

(a)   is established for the mutual benefit of its members;

(b)   does not make profits for any other person than its members;

(c)   fulfils a social purpose required by domestic legislation;

(d)   receives and manages the savings of, and provides sources of credit to, its members only; and

(e)   provides credit on the basis of an annual percentage rate of charge which is lower than that prevailing on the market or subject to a ceiling laid down by national law, and whose membership is restricted to persons residing or employed in a particular location or employees and retired employees of a particular employer, or to persons meeting other qualifications laid down under national law as the basis for the existence of a common bond between the members.

Member States may exempt from the application of this Directive credit agreements concluded by such an organisation where the total value of all existing credit agreements entered into by the organisation is insignificant in relation to the total value of all existing credit agreements in the Member State in which the organisation is based and the total value of all existing credit agreements entered into by all such organisations in the Member State is less than 1% of the total value of all existing credit agreements entered into in that Member State.

Member States shall each year review whether the conditions for the application of any such exemption continue to exist and shall take action to withdraw the exemption where they consider that the conditions are no longer met.

6.   Member States may determine that only Articles 1 to 4, 6, 7, 9, Article 10(1), points (a) to (i), (l) and (r) of Article 10(2), Article 10(4), Articles 11, 13, 16 and Articles 18 to 32 shall apply to credit agreements which provide for arrangements to be agreed by the creditor and the consumer in respect of deferred payment or repayment methods, where the consumer is already in default on the initial credit agreement and where:

(a)   such arrangements would be likely to avert the possibility of legal proceedings concerning such default; and

(b)   the consumer would not thereby be subject to terms less favourable than those laid down in the initial credit agreement.

However, if the credit agreement falls within the scope of paragraph 3, only the provisions of that paragraph shall apply.

Article 3. Definitions.   For the purposes of this Directive, the following definitions shall apply:

(a)   'consumer' means a natural person who, in transactions covered by this Directive, is acting for purposes which are outside his trade, business or profession;

(b)   'creditor' means a natural or legal person who grants or promises to grant credit in the course of his trade, business or profession;

(c)   'credit agreement' means an agreement whereby a creditor grants or promises to grant to a consumer credit in the form of a deferred payment, loan or other similar financial accommodation, except for agreements for the provision on a continuing basis of services or for the supply of goods of the same kind, where the consumer pays for such services or goods for the duration of their provision by means of instalments;

(d)   'overdraft facility' means an explicit credit agreement whereby a creditor makes available to a consumer funds which exceed the current balance in the consumer's current account;

(e)   'overrunning' means a tacitly accepted overdraft whereby a creditor makes available to a consumer funds which exceed the current balance in the consumer's current account or the agreed overdraft facility;

(f)   'credit intermediary' means a natural or legal person who is not acting as a creditor and who, in the course of his trade, business or profession, for a fee, which may take a pecuniary form or any other agreed form of financial consideration:

(i)   presents or offers credit agreements to consumers;

(ii)   assists consumers by undertaking preparatory work in respect of credit agreements other than as referred to in (i); or

(iii)   concludes credit agreements with consumers on behalf of the creditor;

(g)   'total cost of the credit to the consumer' means all the costs, including interest, commissions, taxes and any other kind of fees which the consumer is required to pay in connection with the credit agreement and which are known to the creditor, except for notarial costs; costs in respect of ancillary services relating to the credit agreement, in particular insurance premiums, are also included if, in addition, the conclusion of a service contract is compulsory in order to obtain the credit or to obtain it on the terms and conditions marketed;

(h)   'total amount payable by the consumer' means the sum of the total amount of the credit and the total cost of the credit to the consumer;

(i)   'annual percentage rate of charge' means the total cost of the credit to the consumer, expressed as an annual percentage of the total amount of credit, where applicable including the costs referred to in Article 19(2);

(j)   'borrowing rate' means the interest rate expressed as a fixed or variable percentage applied on an annual basis to the amount of credit drawn down;

(k)   'fixed borrowing rate' means that the creditor and the consumer agree in the credit agreement on one borrowing rate for the entire duration of the credit agreement or on several borrowing rates for partial periods using exclusively a fixed specific percentage. If not all borrowing rates are determined in the credit agreement, the borrowing rate shall be deemed to be fixed only for the partial periods for which the borrowing rates are determined exclusively by a fixed specific percentage agreed on the conclusion of the credit agreement;

(l)   'total amount of credit' means the ceiling or the total sums made available under a credit agreement;

(m)   'durable medium' means any instrument which enables the consumer to store information addressed personally to him in a way accessible for future reference for a period of time adequate for the purposes of the information and which allows the unchanged reproduction of the information stored;

(n)   'linked credit agreement' means a credit agreement where

(i)   the credit in question serves exclusively to finance an agreement for the supply of specific goods or the provision of a specific service, and

(ii)   those two agreements form, from an objective point of view, a commercial unit; a commercial unit shall be deemed to exist where the supplier or service provider himself finances the credit for the consumer or, if it is financed by a third party, where the creditor uses the services of the supplier or service provider in connection with the conclusion or preparation of the credit agreement, or where the specific goods or the provision of a specific service are explicitly specified in the credit agreement.

Article 22. Harmonisation and imperative nature of this Directive.   1.   Insofar as this Directive contains harmonised provisions, Member States may not maintain or introduce in their national law provisions diverging from those laid down in this Directive.

2.   Member States shall ensure that consumers may not waive the rights conferred on them by the provisions of national law implementing or corresponding to this Directive.

3.   Member States shall further ensure that the provisions they adopt in implementation of this Directive cannot be circumvented as a result of the way in which agreements are formulated, in particular by integrating drawdowns or credit agreements

falling within the scope of this Directive into credit agreements the character or purpose of which would make it possible to avoid its application.

4.   Member States shall take the necessary measures to ensure that consumers do not lose the protection granted by this Directive by virtue of the choice of the law of a third country as the law applicable to the credit agreement, if the credit agreement has a close link with the territory of one or more Member States.

H.   Directive 2008/122/EC of the European Parliament and of the Council of 14 January 2009 on the protection of consumers in respect of certain aspects of timeshare, long-term holiday product, resale and exchange contracts (OJ, L 33 of 3 February 2009)[1]

(1)   Since the adoption of Directive 94/47/EC of the European Parliament and of the Council of 26 October 1994 on the protection of purchasers in respect of certain aspects of contracts relating to the purchase of the right to use immovable properties on a timeshare basis, timeshare has evolved and new holiday products similar to it have appeared on the market. These new holiday products and certain transactions related to timeshare, such as resale contracts and exchange contracts, are not covered by Directive 94/47/EC. In addition, experience with the application of Directive 94/47/EC has shown that some subjects already covered need to be updated or clarified, in order to prevent the development of products aiming at circumventing this Directive.

(2)   The existing regulatory gaps create appreciable distortions of competition and cause serious problems for consumers, thus hindering the smooth functioning of the internal market. Directive 94/47/EC should therefore be replaced by a new up-to-date directive. Since tourism plays an increasingly important role in the economies of the Member States, greater growth and productivity in the timeshare and long-term holiday product industries should be encouraged by adopting certain common rules.

(3)   In order to enhance legal certainty and fully achieve the benefits of the internal market for consumers and businesses, the relevant laws of the Member States need to be approximated further. Therefore, certain aspects of the marketing, sale and resale of timeshares and long-term holiday products as well as the exchange of rights deriving from timeshare contracts should be fully harmonised. Member States should not be allowed to maintain or introduce in their national legislation provisions diverging from those laid down in this Directive. Where no such harmonised provisions exist, Member States should remain free to maintain or introduce national legislation in conformity with Community law. Thus, Member States should, for instance, be able to maintain or introduce provisions on the effects of exercising the right of withdrawal in legal relationships falling outside the scope of this Directive or provisions according to which no commitment may be entered into between a consumer and a trader of a timeshare or

---

[1]   This directive repeals Directive 94/47/EC (Article 18). References to the repealed Directive shall be construed as references to this Directive and shall be read in accordance with the correlation table in Annex VI.

long-term holiday product, nor any payment made between those persons, as long as the consumer has not signed a credit agreement to finance the purchase of those services.

(4) This Directive should be without prejudice to the application by Member States, in accordance with Community law, of the provisions of this Directive to areas not within its scope. Member States could therefore maintain or introduce national legislation corresponding to the provisions of this Directive or certain of its provisions in relation to transactions that fall outside the scope of this Directive....

(17) Consumers should not be deprived of the protection granted by this Directive where the law applicable to the contract is that of a Member State. The law applicable to a contract should be determined in accordance with the Community rules on private international law, in particular Regulation (EC) No 593/2008 of the European Parliament and of the Council of 17 June 2008 on the law applicable to contractual obligations (Rome I). Under that Regulation, the law of a third country may be applicable, in particular where consumers are targeted by traders whilst on holiday in a country other than their country of residence. Given that such commercial practices are common in the area covered by this Directive and that the contracts involve considerable amounts of money, an additional safeguard should be provided in certain specific situations, in particular where the courts of any Member State have jurisdiction over the contract, to ensure that the consumer is not deprived of the protection granted by this Directive. This concept reflects the particular needs of consumer protection arising from the typical complexity, long-term nature and financial relevance of the contracts falling within the scope of this Directive.

(18) It should be determined in accordance with Council Regulation (EC) No 44/2001 of 22 December 2000 on jurisdiction and the recognition and enforcement of judgments in civil and commercial matters which courts have jurisdiction in proceedings *which have as their object matters covered by this Directive.*

Article 1. Purpose and scope. 1. The purpose of this Directive is to contribute to the proper functioning of the internal market and to achieve a high level of consumer protection, by approximating the laws, regulations and administrative provisions of the Member States in respect of certain aspects of the marketing, sale and resale of timeshares and long-term holiday products as well as exchange contracts.

2. This Directive applies to trader-to-consumer transactions.

This Directive is without prejudice to national legislation which:

(a) provides for general contract law remedies;

(b) relates to the registration of immovable or movable property and conveyance of immovable property;

(c) relates to conditions of establishment or authorisation regimes or licensing requirements; and

(d) relates to the determination of the legal nature of the rights which are the subject of the contracts covered by this Directive.

Article 2. Definitions. 1. For the purposes of this Directive, the following definitions shall apply:

(a) 'timeshare contract' means a contract of a duration of more than one year under which a consumer, for consideration, acquires the right to use one or more overnight accommodation for more than one period of occupation;

(b) 'long-term holiday product contract' means a contract of a duration of more than one year under which a consumer, for consideration, acquires primarily the right to obtain discounts or other benefits in respect of accommodation, in isolation or together with travel or other services;

(c) 'resale contract' means a contract under which a trader, for consideration, assists a consumer to sell or buy a timeshare or a long-term holiday product;

(d) 'exchange contract' means a contract under which a consumer, for consideration, joins an exchange system which allows that consumer access to overnight accommodation or other services in exchange for granting to other persons temporary access to the benefits of the rights deriving from that consumer's timeshare contract;

(e) 'trader' means a natural or legal person who is acting for purposes relating to that person's trade, business, craft or profession and anyone acting in the name of or on behalf of a trader;

(f) 'consumer' means a natural person who is acting for purposes which are outside that person's trade, business, craft or profession;

(g) 'ancillary contract' means a contract under which the consumer acquires services which are related to a timeshare contract or long-term holiday product contract and which are provided by the trader or a third party on the basis of an arrangement between that third party and the trader;

(h) 'durable medium' means any instrument which enables the consumer or the trader to store information addressed personally to him in a way which is accessible for future reference for a period of time adequate for the purposes of the information and which allows the unchanged reproduction of the information stored;

(i) 'code of conduct' means an agreement or set of rules not imposed by law, regulation or administrative provision of a Member State which defines the behaviour of traders who undertake to be bound by the code in relation to one or more particular commercial practices or business sectors;

(j) 'code owner' means any entity, including a trader or group of traders, which is responsible for the formulation and revision of a code of conduct and/or for monitoring compliance with the code by those who have undertaken to be bound by it.

2. In calculating the duration of a timeshare contract or a long-term holiday product contract, as defined in points (a) and (b) of paragraph 1 respectively, any provision in the contract allowing for tacit renewal or prolongation shall be taken into account.

Article 12. Imperative nature of the Directive and application in international cases. 1. Member States shall ensure that, where the law applicable to the contract is the law of a Member State, consumers may not waive the rights conferred on them by this Directive.

2. Where the applicable law is that of a third country, consumers shall not be deprived of the protection granted by this Directive, as implemented in the Member State of the forum if:

— any of the immovable properties concerned is situated within the territory of a Member State, or;

— in the case of a contract not directly related to immovable property, the trader pursues commercial or professional activities in a Member State or, by any means, directs such activities to a Member State and the contract falls within the scope of such activities.

I.   Directive 2009/22/EC of the European Parliament and of the Council of 23 April 2009 on injunctions for the protection of consumers' interests (Codified version) (OJ, L 110 of 1 May 2009): Recital 7, Article 2(2)

See Chapter VII, E.

J.   Commission Recommendation of 30 July 1997 concerning transactions by electronic payment instruments and in particular the relationship between issuer and holder (OJ, L 208 of 2 August 1997)

(8)   Whereas this recommendation seeks to ensure a high level of consumer protection in the field of electronic payment instruments...

Article 3. Minimum information contained in the terms and conditions governing the issuing and use of an electronic payment instrument.   1.   Upon signature of the contract or in any event in good time prior to delivering an electronic payment instrument, the issuer communicates to the holder the contractual terms and conditions (hereinafter referred to as 'the terms') governing the issue and use of that electronic payment instrument. The terms indicate the law applicable to the contract.

2.   The terms are set out in writing, including where appropriate by electronic means, in easily understandable words and in a readily comprehensive form, and are available at least in the official language or languages of the Member State in which the electronic payment instrument is offered.

K.   Commission Communication - Freedom to Provide Services and the Interest of the General Good in the Second Banking Directive (OJ, C 209 of 10 July 1997)

See Chapter IX, General provisions, O.

L.   Commission Interpretative Communication - Freedom to provide services and the general good in the insurance sector (OJ, C 43 of 16 February 2000)

See Chapter IX, General provisions, P.

M.   Proposal for a Directive of the European Parliament and of the Council on consumer rights (COM (2008) 614 of 8 October 2008)

(1)   Council Directive 85/577/EEC of 20 December 1985 to protect the consumer in respect of contracts negotiated away from business premises, Council Directive 93/13/EEC of 5 April 1993 on unfair terms in consumer contracts, Directive 97/7/EC of the European Parliament and of the Council of 20 May 1997 on the protection of consumers in respect of distance contracts, Directive 1999/44/EC of the European Parliament and of the Council of 25 May 1999 on certain aspects of the sale of consumer goods and associated guarantees, lay down a number of contractual rights for consumers.

(2)   Those Directives have been reviewed in the light of experience with a view to simplifying and updating the applicable rules, removing inconsistencies and closing unwanted gaps in the rules. That review has shown that it is appropriate to replace those four Directives by this single Directive. This Directive should accordingly lay down standard rules for the common aspects and move away from the minimum harmonisation approach in the former Directives under which Member States could maintain or adopt stricter national rules.

(8)   Full harmonisation of some key regulatory aspects will considerably increase legal certainty for both consumers and business. Both consumers and business will be able to rely on a single regulatory framework based on clearly defined legal concepts regulating certain aspects of business-to-consumer contracts across the Community. The effect will be to eliminate the barriers stemming from the fragmentation of the rules and to complete the internal market in this area. These barriers can only be eliminated by establishing uniform rules at Community level. Furthermore consumers will enjoy a high common level of protection across the Community.

(9)   The field harmonised by this Directive should cover certain aspects of business to consumer contracts. These are rules on information to be provided before conclusion and during performance of the contract, the right of withdrawal for distance and off-premises contracts, consumer rights specific to contracts of sale and unfair contract terms in consumer contracts.

(10)   The provisions of this Directive should be without prejudice to Regulation (EC) No 593/2008 of the European Parliament and of the Council applicable to contractual obligations (Rome I).

(11)   The existing Community legislation on consumer financial services contains numerous rules on consumer protection. For this reason the provisions of this Directive cover contracts relating to financial services only insofar as this is necessary to fill the regulatory gaps.

(59)   The consumer should not be deprived of the protection granted by this Directive. Where the law applicable to the contract is that of a third country, Regulation (EC) No 593/2008 of the European Parliament and of the Council on the law applicable to contractual obligations (Rome I) should apply, in order to determine whether the consumer retains the protection granted by this Directive.

Article 1. Subject matter.   The purpose of this Directive is to contribute to the proper functioning of the internal market and achieve a high level of consumer protection by approximating certain aspects of the laws, regulations and administrative provisions of the Member States concerning contracts between consumers and traders.

Article 2. Definitions. For the purpose of this Directive, the following definitions shall apply: (1) 'consumer' means any natural person who, in contracts covered by this Directive, is acting for purposes which are outside his trade, business, craft or profession;

(2) 'trader' means any natural or legal person who, in contracts covered by this Directive, is acting for purposes relating to his trade, business, craft or profession and anyone acting in the name of or on behalf of a trader;

(3) 'sales contract' means any contract for the sale of goods by the trader to the consumer including any mixed-purpose contract having as its object both goods and services;

(4) 'goods' means any tangible movable item, with the exception of:

(a) goods sold by way of execution or otherwise by authority of law,

(b) water and gas where they are not put up for sale in a limited volume or set quantity,

(c) electricity;

(5) 'service contract' means any contract other than a sales contract whereby a service is provided by the trader to the consumer;

(6) 'distance contract' means any sales or service contract where the trader, for the conclusion of the contract, makes exclusive use of one or more means of distance communication;

(7) 'means of distance communication' means any means which, without the simultaneous physical presence of the trader and the consumer, may be used for the conclusion of a contract between those parties;

(8) 'off-premises contract' means:

(a) any sales or service contract concluded away from business premises with the simultaneous physical presence of the trader and the consumer or any sales or service contract for which an offer was made by the consumer in the same circumstances, or

(b) any sales or service contract concluded on business premises but negotiated away from business premises, with the simultaneous physical presence of the trader and the consumer.

(9) 'business premises' means:

(a) any immovable or movable retail premises, including seasonal retail premises, where the trader carries on his activity on a permanent basis, or

(b) market stalls and fair stands where the trader carries on his activity on a regular or temporary basis;

(10) 'durable medium' means any instrument which enables the consumer or the trader to store information addressed personally to him in a way accessible for future reference for a period of time adequate for the purposes of the information and which allows the unchanged reproduction of the information stored;

(11) 'order form' means an instrument setting out the contract terms, to be signed by the consumer with a view to concluding an off-premises contract;

(12) 'product' means any good or service including immoveable property, rights and obligations;

(13) 'financial service' means any service of a banking, credit, insurance, personal pension, investment or payment nature;

(14) 'professional diligence' means the standard of special skill and care which a trader may reasonably be expected to exercise towards consumers, commensurate with honest market practice and/or the general principle of good faith in the trader's field of activity;

(15) 'auction' means a method of sale where goods or services are offered by the trader through a competitive bidding procedure which may include the use of means of distance communication and where the highest bidder is bound to purchase the goods or the services. A transaction concluded on the basis of a fixed-price offer, despite the option given to the consumer to conclude it through a bidding procedure is not an auction;

(16) 'public auction' means a method of sale where goods are offered by the trader to consumers, who attend or are given the possibility to attend the auction in person, through a competitive bidding procedure run by an auctioneer and where the highest bidder is bound to purchase the goods;

(17) 'producer' means the manufacturer of goods, the importer of goods into the territory of the Community or any person purporting to be a producer by placing his name, trade mark or other distinctive sign on the goods;

(18) 'commercial guarantee' means any undertaking by the trader or producer (the 'guarantor') to the consumer to reimburse the price paid or to replace, repair or service goods in any way if they do not meet the specifications set out in the guarantee statement or in the relevant advertising available at the time of, or before the conclusion of the contract;

(19) 'intermediary' means a trader who concludes the contract in the name of or on behalf of the consumer;

(20) 'ancillary contract' means a contract by which the consumer acquires goods or services related to a distance contract or an off-premises contract and these goods or services are provided by the trader or a third party on the basis of an arrangement between that third party and the trader.

Article 3. Scope.   1.   This Directive shall apply, under the conditions and to the extent set out in its provisions, to sales and service contracts concluded between the trader and the consumer.

2.   This Directive shall only apply to financial services as regards certain off-premises contracts as provided for by Articles 8 to 20, unfair contract terms as provided for by Articles 30 to 39 and general provisions as provided for by Articles 40 to 46, read in conjunction with Article 4 on full harmonisation.

3.   Only Articles 30 to 39 on consumer rights concerning unfair contract terms, read in conjunction with Article 4 on full harmonisation, shall apply to contracts which fall within the scope of Directive 94/47/EC of the European Parliament and of the Council and of Council Directive 90/314/EEC.

4.   Articles 5, 7, 9 and 11 shall be without prejudice to the provisions concerning information requirements contained in Directive 2006/123/EC of the European Parliament and of the Council and Directive 2000/31/EC of the European Parliament and of the Council.

Article 4. Full harmonisation.   Member States may not maintain or introduce, in their national law, provisions diverging from those laid down in this Directive, including more or less stringent provisions to ensure a different level of consumer protection.

Article 43. Imperative nature of the Directive.   If the law applicable to the contract is the law of a Member State, consumers may not waive the rights conferred on them by this Directive.

N.   Green Paper. Mortgage Credit in the EU (COM (2005) 327 of 19 July 2005)

Introduction

1.   This Green Paper is the central part of the process to assess the merits of Commission intervention in the EU residential mortgage credit markets. Another key aspect of this assessment process is a Commission funded study on the costs and benefits of further integration of these markets....

2.   Consideration of intervention in the EU mortgage credit markets is a key aspect of the Commission's commitment to meeting the 'Lisbon' objectives aimed at enhancing EU competitiveness. It forms a very important element of the Commission's policy for the integration of financial services in general and retail financial services in particular. A more efficient and competitive mortgage credit market that could result through greater integration could contribute to the growth of the EU economy. It has the potential to facilitate labour mobility and to enable EU consumers to maximise their ability to tap into their housing assets, where appropriate, to facilitate future long-term security in the face of an increasing aging population.

iii.   Legal issues

Applicable law

50.   The 1980 Rome Convention, which governs the determination of the law applicable to contracts including mortgage credits, is currently undergoing a revision process in order to transform it into an EU Regulation. The Commission considers it advisable and consistent to address all issues of applicable law, including the law applicable to mortgage credit contracts, within the context of this process.

51.   As of today, at least three potential solutions have been identified within this process:

52.   Provide for a specific regime for the law applicable to consumer mortgage credit contracts in the future Regulation. This could consist of aligning the law applicable to the mortgage credit contract with the law applicable to the collateral contract.

53.   Continue to subject mortgage credit contracts to the general principles which, in the Rome Convention as it stands, would mean essentially that parties can freely decide on the law applicable to their contract, subject to the application — under some conditions — of the mandatory rules of the consumer's country of residence.

54.   Exclude the application to a consumer mortgage credit contract of the consumer's mandatory protection rules, provided that some conditions are met, for example that there is a high level of consumer protection in place at EU level.

55.   On the law applicable to the collateral, the Commission sees a priori no reason to depart from the well-established principle that the law of the country in which the property is situated applies.

Annex II — Text of Forum Group report recommendations

Legal issues

19. The Commission should ensure that the applicable (substantive) law for the mortgage deed and any related security agreement is the law of the Member State where the property is located (lex rei sitae).

20. Industry Representatives advocate that the Commission should ensure that the applicable law for the mortgage loan contract is defined by a general conflict of law rule based upon the principle of free choice. The Rome Convention should be amended accordingly, provided that certain essential standards are met. Member States should no longer be able to seek to impose any additional national consumer protection rules to cross-border mortgage loan contracts. For further details see Recommendations 13–18 on Consumer Confidence.

21. Consumer Representatives do not agree with Recommendation 20 that the applicable law for the mortgage loan contract should be defined by a general conflict of law rule based on the principle of free choice and accordingly reject the proposal for such an amendment of the Rome Convention. Instead they recommend the retention of the specific rules on consumer protections contained within the Rome Convention and advocate the additional protection described in Recommendations 8–12 on Consumer Confidence.

O.   ECJ case-law

The ECJ was asked by the Commission to assess the correct implementation of Articles 5 and 6(2) of Directive 93/13/EC on unfair terms in consumer contracts in Spain (9 September 2004, case C-70/03, *Commission v Spain*, Reports, I-7999). The Directive had been transposed into the Spanish legal system by Law 7/1998 on general terms in contracts, amending Law 26/1984 providing for consumer protection. Article 10a(3) of the latter provided that 'The rules on protection of consumers against unfair terms shall be applicable, irrespective of the law chosen by the parties to govern the contract, under the terms and conditions provided for in Article 5 of the Rome Convention on the law applicable to contractual obligations', while Article 3(2) of the former stated that 'Without prejudice to the provisions of international treaties and agreements, [this law] shall also apply to contracts subject to foreign law when the party agreeing to be bound thereby has given such consent on Spanish territory and is habitually resident there'. The ECJ stated that these provisions were not in compliance with the Directive for the following reasons:

30. As is clear from the sixth recital in its preamble, the Directive is intended 'to safeguard the citizen in his role as consumer when acquiring goods and services under contracts which are governed by the laws of Member States other than his own'. Article 6(2) of the Directive gives effect thereto. As is clear from the 22nd recital of the preamble to Directive 93/13, that provision seeks to avert the risk that, in certain cases, the consumer may be deprived of Community protection by the designation of the law of a non-Member country as the law applicable to the contract. For that purpose, it provides that the protection granted by the Directive to consumers in contractual relationships

within the Community is to be maintained for contractual relationships involving non-Member countries, as long as the contract has close ties with the territory of the Member States.

31.   Under Article 1(1) and Article 3(1) of the Directive, the substantive scope of the protection granted by it covers terms not individually negotiated in all contracts concluded between a seller or supplier and a consumer. It is true that, as the Commission rightly maintains, Article 10a of amended Law 26/1984 is more restricted in its scope since it applies only to the types of contracts referred to in Article 5(1)(4) and (5) of the Rome Convention. However, as the Spanish Government contends, that lacuna is supplied by Article 3(2) of Law 7/1998, which applies to all contracts concluded, without individual negotiation, on the basis of general conditions.

32.   As regards ties with the Community, Article 6(2) of the Directive merely states that the contract is to have 'a close connection with the territory of the Member States'. That general expression seeks to make it possible to take account of various ties depending on the circumstances of the case.

33.   Although concrete effect may be given to the deliberately vague term 'close connection' chosen by the Community legislature by means of presumptions, it cannot, on the other hand, be circumscribed by a combination of predetermined criteria for ties such as the cumulative conditions as to residence and conclusion of the contract referred to in Article 5 of the Rome Convention.

34.   By referring to the latter provision, expressly as regards Article 10a of amended Law 26/1984 and, by implication, as regards Article 3(2) of Law 7/1998, the provisions of the Spanish legal system supposedly transposing Article 6(2) of the Directive thus introduce a restriction incompatible with the level of protection laid down therein.

Insurance contracts*

A.   Directive 2009/103/EC of the European Parliament and of the Council of 16 September 2009 relating to insurance against civil liability in respect of the use of motor vehicles, and the enforcement of the obligation to insure against such liability (OJ, L 263 of 7 October 2009): Recital 35

See Chapter VII, H.

---

*   See also Article 7 of Regulation (EC) No 593/08 on the law applicable to contractual obligations (Rome I) above, in this Chapter, General provisions, A.1.

B.   Directive 2009/138/EC of the European Parliament and of the Council of 25 November 2009 on the taking-up and pursuit of the business of insurance and reinsurance (Solvency II) (recast) (OJ, L 335 of 17 December 2009)[1]

(88)   Those Member States not subject to the application of Regulation (EC) No 593/2008 of the European Parliament and of the Council of 17 June 2008 on the law applicable to contractual obligations (Rome I) should, in accordance with this Directive, apply the provisions of that Regulation in order to determine the law applicable to contracts of insurance falling within the scope of Article 7 of that Regulation.

Title II — Specific provisions for insurance and reinsurance

Chapter I — Applicable law and conditions of direct insurance contracts

Section 1 — Applicable law

Article 178. Applicable Law.   Any Member State not subject to the application of Regulation (EC) No 593/2008 shall apply the provisions of that Regulation in order to determine the law applicable to insurance contracts falling within the scope of Article 7 of that Regulation.

Section 3 — General Good

Article 180. General good.   Neither the Member State in which a risk is situated nor the Member State of the commitment shall prevent a policy holder from concluding a contract with an insurance undertaking authorised under the conditions of Article 14 as long as that conclusion of contract does not conflict with legal provisions protecting the general good in the Member State in which the risk is situated or in the Member State of the commitment.

Section 5 — Information for Policy Holders

SUBSECTION 1 — NON-LIFE INSURANCE

Article 183. General information for policy holders.   1.   Before a non-life insurance contract is concluded the non-life insurance undertaking shall inform the policy holder of the following:

(a)   the law applicable to the contract, where the parties do not have a free choice;

(b)   the fact that the parties are free to choose the law applicable and the law the insurer proposes to choose....

2.   The obligations referred to in paragraph 1 shall apply only where the policy holder is a natural person.

---

[1]   For the provisions concerning the insolvency of insurance undertakings and freedom of establishment see Chapters V, C, and IX, General provisions, N.

3.   The detailed rules for implementing paragraphs 1 and 2 shall be laid down by the Member State in which the risk is situated.

SUBSECTION 2 — LIFE INSURANCE

Article 185. Information for policy holders.   1.   Before the life insurance contract is concluded, at least the information set out in paragraphs 2 to 4 shall be communicated to the policy holder.
2.   The following information about the life insurance undertaking shall be communicated:...
(m)   the law applicable to the contract where the parties do not have a free choice or, where the parties are free to choose the law applicable, the law the life insurance undertaking proposes to choose....
5.   The policy holder shall be kept informed throughout the term of the contract of any change concerning the following information:
(c)   all the information listed in points (d) to (j) of paragraph 3 in the event of a change in the policy conditions or amendment of the law applicable to the contract...
6.   The information referred to in paragraphs 2 to 5 shall be provided in a clear and accurate manner, in writing, in an official language of the Member State of the commitment
However, such information may be in another language if the policy holder so requests and the law of the Member State so permits or the policy holder is free to choose the law applicable.
8.   The detailed rules for implementing paragraphs 1 to 7 shall be laid down by the Member State of the commitment.

Article 186. Cancellation period.   1.   Member States shall provide for policy holders who conclude individual life insurance contracts to have a period of between 14 and 30 days from the time when they were informed that the contract had been concluded within which to cancel the contract.
The giving of notice of cancellation by the policy holders shall have the effect of releasing them from any future obligation arising from the contract.
The other legal effects and the conditions of cancellation shall be determined by the law applicable to the contract, notably as regards the arrangements for informing the policy holder that the contract has been concluded.
2.   The Member States may opt not to apply paragraph 1 in the following cases:
(a)   where a contract has a duration of six months or less;
(b)   where, because of the status of the policy holder or the circumstances in which the contract is concluded, the policy holder does not need special protection.
Where Member States make use of the option set out in the first subparagraph they shall specify that fact in their law.

C.   Commission Communication - Freedom to provide services and the general good in the insurance sector (OJ, C 43 of 16 February 2000)

See Chapter IX, General provisions, P.

Sale*

A.   Directive 2000/35/EC of the European Parliament and of the Council of 29 June 2000 on combating late payment in commercial transactions (OJ, L 200 of 8 August 2000): Article 4(1)

See Chapter IV, General provisions, I.

B.   Convention on international interests in mobile equipment (OJ, L 121 of 15 May 2009): Article 41

See Chapter VIII, Interests in goods and equipment, A.4.

C.   ECJ case-law

In a case concerning the implementation of Directive 2000/35 in Italy, where the law provided that a retention of title clause had to be confirmed on individual invoices for successive supplies bearing a specific date prior to any attachment procedure and entered in the accounting records in order for it to be enforceable against third party creditors of the buyer, the ECJ (judgment 26 October 2006, case C-302/05, *Commission v Italy*, Reports, I-10597) stated that

27.   ... the reference to national provisions designated by private international law in Article 4(1) of Directive 2000/35 is directed at conditions of validity for retention of title clauses.

28.   According to that provision, read in conjunction with recital 21 in the preamble to Directive 2000/35, the Community legislature considered it desirable to ensure that creditors are in a position to exercise a retention of title on a non-discriminatory basis throughout the Community if the retention of title clause is valid under the applicable national provisions designated by private international law. The availability of such

---

*   See also Article 6 of Regulation (EC) No 593/08 on the law applicable to contractual obligations (Rome I) and Article 5 of the Rome Convention, above, in this Chapter, General provisions, A.1 and A.3. Cf also the Communication of the Commission "European Contract Law and the revision of the acquis: the way forward (*COM* (2004) 651 of 11 October 2004) and the Green Paper on the revision of the Consumer Acquis (OJ, C 61 of 15 March 2007).

a clause to creditors may be considered to be a specific contribution to combating late payments in commercial transactions.

29.   In view of the wording of Article 4(1) of Directive 2000/35 and the purpose of that directive, it cannot be inferred from that provision that it is intended to affect any rules other than those which expressly provide, firstly, that it is possible for the seller and the buyer expressly to agree a retention of title clause before the goods are delivered and, secondly, that it is possible for the seller to retain title to the goods until they have been paid for in full.

30.   Accordingly, the rules in question in the present case, which concern the enforceability of retention of title clauses against third parties, whose rights are not affected by Directive 2000/35, are still governed exclusively by the national legal orders of the Member States.

Carriage*

A.   Regulation (EC) No 2027/97 of the Council of 9 October 1997 on air carrier liability in respect of the carriage of passengers and their baggage by air (OJ, L 285 of 17 October 1997)[1]

(1)   Whereas, in the framework of the common transport policy, it is necessary to improve the level of protection of passengers involved in air accidents;

(2) Whereas the rules on liability in the event of accidents are governed by the Convention for the Unification of Certain Rules Relating to International Carriage by Air, signed at Warsaw on 12 October 1929, or that Convention as amended at The Hague on 28 September 1955 and the Convention done at Guadalajara on 18 September 1961, whichever may be applicable each being hereinafter referred to, as applicable, as the 'Warsaw Convention'; whereas the Warsaw Convention is applied worldwide for the benefit of both passengers and air carriers;

(3) Whereas the limit set on liability by the Warsaw Convention is too low by today's economic and social standards and often leads to lengthy legal actions which damage the image of air transport; whereas as a result Member States have variously increased the liability limit, thereby leading to different terms and conditions of carriage in the internal aviation market;

(4) Whereas in addition the Warsaw Convention applies only to international transport; whereas, in the internal aviation market, the distinction between national and international transport has been eliminated; whereas it is therefore appropriate to have the same level and nature of liability in both national and international transport;

(5) Whereas a full review and revision of the Warsaw Convention is long overdue and would represent, in the long term, a more uniform and applicable response, at an international level, to the issue of air carrier liability in the event of accidents; whereas

---

*   See also Article 5 of Regulation (EC) No 593/08 on the law applicable to contractual obligations (Rome I), in this chapter, General provisions, A.1.

[1]   As amended by Regulation (EC) No 889/2002 of the European Parliament and of the Council of 13 May 2002 (OJ, L 140 of 30 May 2002).

efforts to increase the limits of liability imposed in the Warsaw Convention should continue through negotiation at multilateral level;

(6) Whereas, in compliance with the principle of subsidiarity, action at Community level is desirable in order to achieve harmonization in the field of air carrier liability and could serve as a guideline for improved passenger protection on a global scale;

(7) Whereas it is appropriate to remove all monetary limits of liability within the meaning of Article 22(1) of the Warsaw Convention or any other legal or contractual limits, in accordance with present trends at international level...

Article 1.   This Regulation implements the relevant provisions of the Montreal Convention in respect of the carriage of passengers and their baggage by air and lays down certain supplementary provisions. It also extends the application of these provisions to carriage by air within a single Member State.

Article 2.   1.   For the purpose of this Regulation:

(a)   'air carrier' shall mean an air transport undertaking with a valid operating licence;

(b)   'Community air carrier' shall mean an air carrier with a valid operating licence granted by a Member State in accordance with the provisions of Regulation (EEC) No 2407/92;

(c)   'person entitled to compensation' shall mean a passenger or any person entitled to claim in respect of that passenger, in accordance with applicable law;

(d)   'baggage', unless otherwise specified, shall mean both checked and unchecked baggage with the meaning of Article 17(4) of the Montreal Convention;

(e)   'SDR' shall mean a special drawing right as defined by the International Monetary Fund;

(f)   'Warsaw Convention' shall mean the Convention for the Unification of Certain Rules Relating to International Carriage by Air, signed at Warsaw on 12 October 1929, or the Warsaw Convention as amended at The Hague on 28 September 1955 and the Convention supplementary to the Warsaw Convention done at Guadalajara on 18 September 1961;

(g)   'Montreal Convention' shall mean the 'Convention for the Unification of Certain Rules Relating to International Carriage by Air', signed at Montreal on 28 May 1999.

2.   Concepts contained in this Regulation which are not defined in paragraph 1 shall be equivalent to those used in the Montreal Convention.

Article 3.   1.   The liability of a Community air carrier in respect of passengers and their baggage shall be governed by all provisions of the Montreal Convention relevant to such liability.

2.   The obligation of insurance set out in Article 7 of Regulation (EEC) No 2407/92 as far as it relates to liability for passengers shall be understood as requiring that a Community air carrier shall be insured up to a level that is adequate to ensure that all persons entitled to compensation receive the full amount to which they are entitled in accordance with this Regulation.[2]

---

[2]   These articles were amended by Regulation (EC) No 889/2002 of the European Parliament and of the Council of 13 May 2002 amending Council Regulation (EC) No 2027/97 on air carrier liability in the event of accidents (OJ, L 140 of 30 May 2002)

B. Regulation (EC) No 261/2004 of the European Parliament and of the Council of 11 February 2004 establishing common rules on compensation and assistance to passengers in the event of denied boarding and of cancellation or long delay of flights, and repealing Regulation (EEC) No 295/91 (OJ, L 46 of 17 February 2004)

(8)   This Regulation should not restrict the rights of the operating air carrier to seek compensation from any person, including third parties, in accordance with the law applicable....

Article 1. Subject.   1.   This Regulation establishes, under the conditions specified herein, minimum rights for passengers when:
    (a)   they are denied boarding against their will;
    (b)   their flight is cancelled;
    (c)   their flight is delayed.
    2.   Application of this Regulation to Gibraltar airport is understood to be without prejudice to the respective legal positions of the Kingdom of Spain and the United Kingdom with regard to the dispute over sovereignty over the territory in which the airport is situated.
    3.   Application of this Regulation to Gibraltar airport shall be suspended until the arrangements in the Joint Declaration made by the Foreign Ministers of the Kingdom of Spain and the United Kingdom on 2 December 1987 enter into operation. The Governments of Spain and the United Kingdom will inform the Council of such date of entry into operation.

Article 2. Definitions.   For the purposes of this Regulation:
    (a)   'air carrier' means an air transport undertaking with a valid operating licence;
    (b)   'operating air carrier' means an air carrier that performs or intends to perform a flight under a contract with a passenger or on behalf of another person, legal or natural, having a contract with that passenger;
    (c)   'Community carrier' means an air carrier with a valid operating licence granted by a Member State in accordance with the provisions of Council Regulation (EEC) No 2407/92 of 23 July 1992 on licensing of air carriers (5);
    (d)   'tour operator' means, with the exception of an air carrier, an organiser within the meaning of Article 2, point 2, of Council Directive 90/314/EEC of 13 June 1990 on package travel, package holidays and package tours (6);
    (e)   'package' means those services defined in Article 2, point 1, of Directive 90/314/EEC;
    (f)   'ticket' means a valid document giving entitlement to transport, or something equivalent in paperless form, including electronic form, issued or authorized by the air carrier or its authorized agent;
    (g)   'reservation' means the fact that the passenger has a ticket, or other proof, which indicates that the reservation has been accepted and registered by the air carrier or tour operator;

(h) 'final destination' means the destination on the ticket presented at the check-in counter or, in the case of directly connecting flights, the destination of the last flight; alternative connecting flights available shall not be taken into account if the original planned arrival time is respected;

(i) 'person with reduced mobility' means any person whose mobility is reduced when using transport because of any physical disability (sensory or locomotory, permanent or temporary), intellectual impairment, age or any other cause of disability, and whose situation needs special attention and adaptation to the person's needs of the services made available to all passengers;

(j) 'denied boarding' means a refusal to carry passengers on a flight, although they have presented themselves for boarding under the conditions laid down in Article 3(2), except where there are reasonable grounds to deny them boarding, such as reasons of health, safety or security, or inadequate travel documentation;

(k) 'volunteer' means a person who has presented himself for boarding under the conditions laid down in Article 3(2) and responds positively to the air carrier's call for passengers prepared to surrender their reservation in exchange for benefits.

(l) 'cancellation' means the non-operation of a flight which was previously planned and on which at least one place was reserved.

Article 3. Scope.   1.   This Regulation shall apply:

(a)   to passengers departing from an airport located in the territory of a Member State to which the Treaty applies;

(b)   to passengers departing from an airport located in a third country to an airport situated in the territory of a Member State to which the Treaty applies, unless they received benefits or compensation and were given assistance in that third country, if the operating air carrier of the flight concerned is a Community carrier.

2.   Paragraph 1 shall apply on the condition that passengers:

(a)   have a confirmed reservation on the flight concerned and, except in the case of cancellation referred to in Article 5, present themselves for check-in;

—   as stipulated and at the time indicated in advance and in writing (including by electronic means) by the air carrier, the tour operator or an authorised travel agent, or, if no time is indicated;

—   not later than 45 minutes before the published departure time; or

(b)   have been transferred by an air carrier or tour operator from the flight for which they held a reservation to another flight, irrespective of the reason.

3.   This Regulation shall not apply to passengers travelling free of charge or at a reduced fare not available directly or indirectly to the public. However, it shall apply to passengers having tickets issued under a frequent flyer programme or other commercial programme by an air carrier or tour operator.

4.   This Regulation shall only apply to passengers transported by motorised fixed wing aircraft.

5.   This Regulation shall apply to any operating air carrier providing transport to passengers covered by paragraphs 1 and 2. Where an operating air carrier which has no contract with the passenger performs obligations under this Regulation, it shall be regarded as doing so on behalf of the person having a contract with that passenger.

6.   This Regulation shall not affect the rights of passengers under Directive 90/314/EEC. This Regulation shall not apply in cases where a package tour is cancelled for reasons other than cancellation of the flight.

Article 13. Right of redress.   In cases where an operating air carrier pays compensation or meets the other obligations incumbent on it under this Regulation, no provision of this Regulation may be interpreted as restricting its right to seek compensation from any person, including third parties, in accordance with the law applicable. In particular, this Regulation shall in no way restrict the operating air carrier's right to seek reimbursement from a tour operator or another person with whom the operating air carrier has a contract. Similarly, no provision of this Regulation may be interpreted as restricting the right of a tour operator or a third party, other than a passenger, with whom an operating air carrier has a contract, to seek reimbursement or compensation from the operating air carrier in accordance with applicable relevant laws.

Article 15. Exclusion of waiver.   1.   Obligations vis-à-vis passengers pursuant to this Regulation may not be limited or waived, notably by a derogation or restrictive clause in the contract of carriage.
  2.   If, nevertheless, such a derogation or restrictive clause is applied in respect of a passenger, or if the passenger is not correctly informed of his rights and for that reason has accepted compensation which is inferior to that provided for in this Regulation, the passenger shall still be entitled to take the necessary proceedings before the competent courts or bodies in order to obtain additional compensation.

C.   Convention for the Unification of Certain Rules for International Carriage by Air (the Montreal Convention) (OJ, L 194 of 18 July 2001): Articles 47, 49

See Chapter IV, Carriage, A.2.

D.1.   Convention concerning International Carriage by Rail (COTIF) of 9 May 1980 in the version of the Protocol of Modification of 3 June 1999

Title I — General provisions

Article 1. Intergovernmental Organisation.   § 1.   The Parties to this Convention shall constitute, as Member States, the Intergovernmental Organisation for International Carriage by Rail (OTIF), hereinafter called 'the Organisation'....

Article 2. Aim of the Organisation.   §1.   The aim of the Organisation shall be to promote, improve and facilitate, in all respects, international traffic by rail, in particular by

(a)   establishing systems of uniform law in the following fields of law:

1.   contract of international carriage of passengers and goods in international through traffic by rail, including complementary carriage by other modes of transport subject to a single contract;

2.   contract of use of wagons as means of transport in international rail traffic;

3.   contract of use of infrastructure in international rail traffic;

4.   carriage of dangerous goods in international rail traffic;

(b)   contributing to the removal, in the shortest time possible, of obstacles to the crossing of frontiers in international rail traffic, while taking into account special public interests, to the extent that the causes of these obstacles are within the responsibility of States;

(c)   contributing to interoperability and technical harmonisation in the railway field by the validation of technical standards and the adoption of uniform technical prescriptions;

(d)   establishing a uniform procedure for the technical admission of railway material intended for use in international traffic;

(e)   keeping a watch on the application of all the rules and recommendations established within the Organisation;

(f)   developing the systems of uniform law, rules and procedures referred to in letters a) to e) taking account of legal, economic and technical developments.

§2.   The Organisation may

(a)   within the framework of the aim referred to in § 1, elaborate other systems of uniform law;

(b)   constitute a framework within which the Member States can elaborate other international conventions aiming to promote, improve and facilitate international rail traffic.

Article 3. International cooperation.   §1.   The Member States undertake to concentrate their international cooperation in the railway field, in principle, within the framework of the Organisation, and this to the extent that there exists a coherence in the tasks which are attributed to it in accordance with Articles 2 and 4. To attain this objective, the Member States will adopt all measures necessary and useful in order that the international multilateral conventions and agreements in force to which they are contracting parties should be adapted, to the extent that these conventions and agreements concern international cooperation in the railway field and attribute competences to other intergovernmental or non-governmental organisations which cut across the tasks attributed to the Organisation.

§2.   The obligations resulting from § 1 for the Member States, which are at the same time Members of the European Communities or States parties to the European Economic Area Agreement, shall not prevail over their obligations as members of the European Communities or States parties to the European Economic Area Agreement.

Article 6. Uniform Rules.   §1.   So far as declarations are not made in accordance with Article 42 § 1, first sentence, international rail traffic and admission of railway material to use in international traffic shall be governed by:

(a)   the 'Uniform Rules concerning the Contract of International Carriage of Passengers by Rail (CIV)', forming Appendix A to the Convention;

(b)   the 'Uniform Rules concerning the Contract of International Carriage of Goods by Rail (CIM)', forming Appendix B to the Convention;

(c)   the 'Regulation concerning the International Carriage of Dangerous Goods by Rail (RID)', forming Appendix C to the Convention;

(d)   the 'Uniform Rules concerning Contracts of Use of Vehicles in International Rail Traffic (CUV)', forming Appendix D to the Convention;

(e)   the 'Uniform Rules concerning the Contract of Use of Infrastructure in International Rail Traffic (CUI)', forming Appendix E to the Convention;

(f)   the 'Uniform Rules concerning the Validation of Technical Standards and the Adoption of Uniform Technical Prescriptions applicable to Railway Material intended to be used in International Traffic (APTU)', forming Appendix F to the Convention;

(g)   the 'Uniform Rules concerning Technical Admission of Railway Material used in International Traffic (ATMF)', forming Appendix G to the Convention;

(h)   other systems of uniform law elaborated by the Organisation pursuant to Article 2 § 2, letter (a), also forming Appendices to the Convention.

§2.   The Uniform Rules, the Regulation and the systems listed in §1, including their Annexes, shall form an integral part of the Convention.

Article 7. Definition of the expression 'Convention'.   In the following provisions the expression 'Convention' covers the Convention itself, the Protocol referred to in article 1 § 4 and the Appendices referred to in Article 6, including their Annexes.

Title II — Common provisions

Article 8. National law.   §1.   When interpreting and applying the Convention, its character of international law and the necessity to promote uniformity shall be taken into account.

§2.   In the absence of provisions in the Convention, national law shall apply.

§3.   'National law' means the law of the State in which the person entitled asserts his rights, including the rules relating to conflict of laws.

Article 12. Execution of judgments. Attachment.   § 1.   Judgments pronounced by the competent court or tribunal pursuant to the provisions of the Convention after trial or by default shall, when they have become enforceable under the law applied by that court or tribunal, become enforceable in each of the other Member States on completion of the formalities required in the State where enforcement is to take place. The merits of the case shall not be subject to review. These provisions shall apply also to judicial settlements.

§2.   § 1 shall apply neither to judgments which are provisionally enforceable, nor to awards of damages in addition to costs against a plaintiff who fails in his action.

§3.   Debts arising from a transport operation subject to the CIV Uniform Rules or the CIM Uniform Rules, owed to one transport undertaking by another transport undertaking not under the jurisdiction of the same Member State, may only be attached under a judgment given by the judicial authority of the Member State which has jurisdiction over the undertaking entitled to payment of the debt sought to be attached.

§4.   Debts arising from a contract subject to the CUV Uniform Rules or the CUI Uniform Rules may only be attached under a judgment given by the judicial authority of the Member State which has jurisdiction over the undertaking entitled to payment of the debts sought to be attached.

§5.   Railway vehicles may only be seized on a territory other than that of the Member State in which the keeper has its registered office, under a judgment given by the judicial authority of that State. The term 'keeper' means the person who, being the owner or having the right to dispose of it, exploits the railway vehicle economically in a permanent manner as a means of transport.

D.2.   Uniform Rules concerning the Contract of International Carriage of Passengers by Rail (CIV — Appendix A to the Convention)

Article 1. Scope.   §1.   These Uniform Rules shall apply to every contract of carriage of passengers by rail for reward or free of charge, when the place of departure and the place of destination are situated in two different Member States, irrespective of the domicile or the place of business and the nationality of the parties to the contract of carriage.

§2.   When international carriage being the subject of a single contract includes carriage by road or inland waterway in internal traffic of a Member State as a supplement to transfrontier carriage by rail, these Uniform Rules shall apply.

§3.   When international carriage being the subject of a single contract of carriage includes carriage by sea or transfrontier carriage by inland waterway as a supplement to carriage by rail, these Uniform Rules shall apply if the carriage by sea or inland waterway is performed on services included in the lists of services provided for in Article 24 §1 of the Convention.

§4.   These Uniform Rules shall also apply, as far as the liability of the carrier in case of death of, or personal injury to, passengers is concerned, to persons accompanying a consignment whose carriage is effected in accordance with the CIM Uniform Rules.

§5.   These Uniform Rules shall not apply to carriage performed between stations situated on the territory of neighbouring States, when the infrastructure of these stations is managed by one or more infrastructure managers subject to only one of those States.

§6.   Any State which is a party to a convention concerning international through carriage of passengers by rail comparable with these Uniform Rules may, when it makes an application for accession to the Convention, declare that it will apply these Uniform Rules only to carriage performed on a part of the railway infrastructure situated on its territory. This part of the railway infrastructure must be precisely defined and connected to the railway infrastructure of a Member State. When a State has made the above-mentioned declaration, these Uniform Rules shall apply only on the condition

(a)   that the place of departure or of destination, as well as the route designated in the contract of carriage, is situated on the specified infrastructure or

(b)   that the specified infrastructure connects the infrastructure of two Member States and that it has been designated in the contract of carriage as a route for transit carriage.

§7.   A State which has made a reservation in accordance with § 6 may withdraw it at any time by notification to the Depositary. This withdrawal shall take effect one month after the day on which the Depositary notifies it to the Member States. The declaration shall cease to have effect when the convention referred to in § 6, first sentence, ceases to be in force for that State.

Article 3. Definitions.   For purposes of these Uniform Rules, the term

(a)   'carrier' means the contractual carrier with whom the passenger has concluded the contract of carriage pursuant to these Uniform Rules, or a successive carrier who is liable on the basis of this contract;

(b)   'substitute carrier' means a carrier, who has not concluded the contract of carriage with the passenger, but to whom the carrier referred to in letter (a) has entrusted, in whole or in part, the performance of the carriage by rail;

(c)   'General Conditions of Carriage' means the conditions of the carrier in the form of general conditions or tariffs legally in force in each Member State and which have become, by the conclusion of the contract of carriage, an integral part of it;

(d)   'vehicle' means a motor vehicle or a trailer carried on the occasion of the carriage of passengers.

Article 4. Derogations.   §1.   The Member States may conclude agreements which provide for derogations from these Uniform Rules for carriage performed exclusively between two stations on either side of the frontier, when there is no other station between them.

§2.   For carriage performed between two Member States, passing through a State which is not a Member State, the States concerned may conclude agreements which derogate from these Uniform Rules.

§3.   Subject to other provisions of public international law, two or more Member States may set between themselves conditions under which carriers are subject to the obligation to carry passengers, luggage, animals and vehicles in traffic between those States.

§4.   Agreements referred to in §§ 1 to 3 as well as their coming into force shall be notified to the Intergovernmental Organisation for International Carriage by Rail. The Secretary-General of the Organisation shall notify the Member States and interested undertakings of this.

Article 5. Mandatory law.   Unless provided otherwise in these Uniform Rules, any stipulation which, directly or indirectly, would derogate from these Uniform Rules shall be null and void. The nullity of such a stipulation shall not involve the nullity of the other provisions of the contract of carriage. Nevertheless, a carrier may assume a liability greater and obligations more burdensome than those provided for in these Uniform Rules.

Article 57. Forum.   §1.   Actions based on these Uniform Rules may be brought before the courts or tribunals of Member States designated by agreement between the parties or before the courts or tribunals of the Member State on whose territory the defendant has his domicile or habitual residence, his principal place of business or the branch or agency which concluded the contract of carriage. Other courts or tribunals may not be seized.

§2.   Where an action based on these Uniform Rules is pending before a court or tribunal competent pursuant to §1, or where in such litigation a judgment has been delivered by such a court or tribunal, no new action may be brought between the same parties on the same grounds unless the judgment of the court or tribunal before which the first action was brought is not enforceable in the State in which the new action is brought.

Article 62. Right of recourse.   §1.   A carrier who has paid compensation pursuant to these Uniform Rules shall have a right of recourse against the carriers who have taken part in the carriage in accordance with the following provisions:

  (a)   the carrier who has caused the loss or damage shall be solely liable for it;

  (b)   when the loss or damage has been caused by several carriers, each shall be liable for the loss or damage he has caused; if such distinction is impossible, the compensation shall be apportioned between them in accordance with letter c);

  (c)   if it cannot be proved which of the carriers has caused the loss or damage, the compensation shall be apportioned between all the carriers who have taken part in the carriage, except those who prove that the loss or damage was not caused by them; such apportionment shall be in proportion to their respective shares of the carriage charge.

  §2.   In the case of insolvency of any one of these carriers, the unpaid share due from him shall be apportioned among all the other carriers who have taken part in the carriage, in proportion to their respective shares of the carriage charge.

Article 63. Procedure for recourse.   §1.   The validity of the payment made by the carrier exercising a right of recourse pursuant to Article 62 may not be disputed by the carrier against whom the right to recourse is exercised, when compensation has been determined by a court or tribunal and when the latter carrier, duly served with notice of the proceedings, has been afforded an opportunity to intervene in the proceedings. The court or tribunal seized of the principal action shall determine what time shall be allowed for such notification of the proceedings and for intervention in the proceedings.

  §2.   A carrier exercising his right of recourse must present his claim in one and the same proceedings against all the carriers with whom he has not reached a settlement, failing which he shall lose his right of recourse in the case of those against whom he has not taken proceedings.

  §3.   The court or tribunal shall give its decision in one and the same judgment on all recourse claims brought before it.

  §4.   The carrier wishing to enforce his right of recourse may bring his action in the courts or tribunals of the State on the territory of which one of the carriers participating in the carriage has his principal place of business, or the branch or agency which concluded the contract of carriage.

  §5.   When the action must be brought against several carriers, the plaintiff carrier shall be entitled to choose the court or tribunal in which he will bring the proceedings from among those having competence pursuant to §4.

  §6.   Recourse proceedings may not be joined with proceedings for compensation taken by the person entitled under the contract of carriage.

D.3.   Uniform Rules concerning the Contract of International Carriage of Goods by Rail (CIM — Appendix B to the Convention)

Article 1. Scope.   §1.   These Uniform Rules shall apply to every contract of carriage of goods by rail for reward when the place of taking over of the goods and the place designated for delivery are situated in two different Member States, irrespective of the place of business and the nationality of the parties to the contract of carriage.

§2.   These Uniform Rules shall apply also to contracts of carriage of goods by rail for reward, when the place of taking over of the goods and the place designated for delivery are situated in two different States, of which at least one is a Member State and the parties to the contract agree that the contract is subject to these Uniform Rules.

§3.   When international carriage being the subject of a single contract includes carriage by road or inland waterway in internal traffic of a Member State as a supplement to transfrontier carriage by rail, these Uniform Rules shall apply.

§4.   When international carriage being the subject of a single contract of carriage includes carriage by sea or transfrontier carriage by inland waterway as a supplement to carriage by rail, these Uniform Rules shall apply if the carriage by sea or inland waterway is performed on services included in the list of services provided for in Article 24 §1 of the Convention.

§5.   These Uniform Rules shall not apply to carriage performed between stations situated on the territory of neighbouring States, when the infrastructure of these stations is managed by one or more infrastructure managers subject to only one of those States.

§6.   Any State which is a party to a convention concerning international through carriage of goods by rail comparable with these Uniform Rules may, when it makes an application for accession to the Convention, declare that it will apply these Uniform Rules only to carriage performed on part of the railway infrastructure situated on its territory. This part of the railway infrastructure must be precisely defined and connected to the railway infrastructure of a Member State. When a State has made the above-mentioned declaration, these Uniform Rules shall apply only on the condition

(a)   that the place of taking over of the goods or the place designated for delivery, as well as the route designated in the contract of carriage, is situated on the specified infrastructure or

(b)   that the specified infrastructure connects the infrastructure of two Member States and that it has been designated in the contract of carriage as a route for transit carriage.

§7.   A State which has made a reservation in accordance with §6 may withdraw it at any time by notification to the Depositary. This withdrawal shall take effect one month after the day on which the Depositary notifies it to the Member States. The declaration shall cease to have effect when the convention referred to in §6, first sentence, ceases to be in force for that State.

Article 2. Prescriptions of public law.   Carriage to which these Uniform Rules apply shall remain subject to the prescriptions of public law, in particular the prescriptions relating to the carriage of dangerous goods as well as the prescriptions of customs law and those relating to the protection of animals.

Article 3. Definitions.   For purposes of these Uniform Rules the term

(a)   'carrier' means the contractual carrier with whom the consignor has concluded the contract of carriage pursuant to these Uniform Rules, or a subsequent carrier who is liable on the basis of this contract;

(b)   'substitute carrier' means a carrier, who has not concluded the contract of carriage with the consignor, but to whom the carrier referred to in letter a) has entrusted, in whole or in part, the performance of the carriage by rail;

(c)   'General Conditions of Carriage' means the conditions of the carrier in the form of general conditions or tariffs legally in force in each Member State and which have become, by the conclusion of the contract of carriage, an integral part of it;

(d)   'intermodal transport unit' means a container, swap body, semi-trailer or other comparable loading unit used in intermodal transport.

Article 4. Derogations.   §1.   Member States may conclude agreements which provide for derogations from these Uniform Rules for carriage performed exclusively between two stations on either side of the frontier, when there is no other station between them.

§2.   For carriage performed between two Member States, passing through a State which is not a Member State, the States concerned may conclude agreements which derogate from these Uniform Rules.

§3.   Agreements referred to in §§ 1 and 2 as well as their coming into force shall be notified to the Intergovernmental Organisation for International Carriage by Rail. The Secretary-General of the Organisation shall inform the Member States and interested undertakings of these notifications.

Article 5. Mandatory law.   Unless provided otherwise in these Uniform Rules, any stipulation which, directly or indirectly, would derogate from these Uniform Rules shall be null and void. The nullity of such a stipulation shall not involve the nullity of the other provisions of the contract of carriage. Nevertheless, a carrier may assume a liability greater and obligations more burdensome than those provided for in these Uniform Rules.

Article 46. Forum.   §1.   Actions based on these Uniform Rules may be brought before the courts or tribunals of Member States designated by agreement between the parties or before the courts or tribunals of a State on whose territory

(a)   the defendant has his domicile or habitual residence, his principal place of business or the branch or agency which concluded the contract of carriage, or

(b)   the place where the goods were taken over by the carrier or the place designated for delivery is situated.

Other courts or tribunals may not be seized.

§2.   Where an action based on these Uniform Rules is pending before a court or tribunal competent pursuant to §1, or where in such litigation a judgment has been delivered by such a court or tribunal, no new action may be brought between the same parties on the same grounds unless the judgment of the court or tribunal before which the first action was brought is not enforceable in the State in which the new action is brought.

Article 48. Limitation of actions.   §1.   The period of limitation for an action arising from the contract of carriage shall be one year. Nevertheless, the period of limitation shall be two years in the case of an action

(a)   to recover a cash on delivery payment collected by the carrier from the consignee;

(b)   to recover the proceeds of a sale effected by the carrier;

(c)   for loss or damage resulting from an act or omission done with intent to cause such loss or damage, or recklessly and with knowledge that such loss or damage would probably result;

d)   based on one of the contracts of carriage prior to the reconsignment in the case provided for in Article 28.

2.   The period of limitation shall run for actions

a)   for compensation for total loss, from the thirtieth day after expiry of the transit period;

b)   for compensation for partial loss, damage or exceeding of the transit period, from the day when delivery took place;

c)   in all other cases, from the day when the right of action may be exercised.

The day indicated for the commencement of the period of limitation shall not be included in the period.

§3.   The period of limitation shall be suspended by a claim in writing in accordance with Article 43 until the day that the carrier rejects the claim by notification in writing and returns the documents submitted with it. If part of the claim is admitted, the period of limitation shall start to run again in respect of the part of the claim still in dispute. The burden of proof of receipt of the claim or of the reply and of the return of the documents shall lie on the party who relies on those facts. The period of limitation shall not be suspended by further claims having the same object.

§4.   A right of action which has become time-barred may not be exercised further, even by way of counter-claim or relied upon by way of exception.

§5.   Otherwise, the suspension and interruption of periods of limitation shall be governed by national law.

Article 50. Right of recourse.   §1.   A carrier who has paid compensation pursuant to these Uniform Rules shall have a right of recourse against the carriers who have taken part in the carriage in accordance with the following provisions:

(a)   the carrier who has caused the loss or damage shall be solely liable for it;

(b)   when the loss or damage has been caused by several carriers, each shall be liable for the loss or damage he has caused; if such distinction is impossible, the compensation shall be apportioned between them in accordance with letter c);

(c)   if it cannot be proved which of the carriers has caused the loss or damage, the compensation shall be apportioned between all the carriers who have taken part in the carriage, except those who prove that the loss or damage was not caused by them; such apportionment shall be in proportion to their respective shares of the carriage charge.

§2.   In the case of insolvency of any one of these carriers, the unpaid share due from him shall be apportioned among all the other carriers who have taken part in the carriage, in proportion to their respective shares of the carriage charge.

Article 51. Procedure for recourse.   §1.   The validity of the payment made by the carrier exercising a right of recourse pursuant to Article 50 may not be disputed by the carrier against whom the right of recourse is exercised, when compensation has been determined by a court or tribunal and when the latter carrier, duly served with notice of the proceedings, has been afforded an opportunity to intervene in the proceedings. The court or tribunal seized of the principal action shall determine what time shall be allowed for such notification of the proceedings and for intervention in the proceedings.

§2.   A carrier exercising his right of recourse must make his claim in one and the same proceedings against all the carriers with whom he has not reached a settlement, failing which he shall lose his right of recourse in the case of those against whom he has not taken proceedings.

§3.   The court or tribunal must give its decision in one and the same judgment on all recourse claims brought before it.

§4.   The carrier wishing to enforce his right of recourse may bring his action in the courts or tribunals of the State on the territory of which one of the carriers participating in the carriage has his principal place of business, or the branch or agency which concluded the contract of carriage.

§5.   When the action must be brought against several carriers, the plaintiff carrier shall be entitled to choose the court or tribunal in which he will bring the proceedings from among those having competence pursuant to §4.

§6.   Recourse proceedings may not be joined with proceedings for compensation taken by the person entitled under the contract of carriage.

D.4.   Uniform Rules concerning Contracts of Use of Vehicles in International Rail Traffic (CUV — Appendix D to the Convention)

Article 1. Scope.   These Uniform Rules shall apply to bi- or multilateral contracts concerning the use of railway vehicles as means of transport for carriage in accordance with the CIV Uniform Rules and in accordance with the CIM Uniform Rules.

Article 2. Definitions.   For the purposes of these Uniform Rules the term

(a)   'rail transport undertaking' means a private or public undertaking which is authorised to carry persons or goods and which ensures traction;

(b)   'vehicle' means a vehicle, suitable to circulate on its own wheels on railway lines, not provided with a means of traction;

(c)   'keeper' means the person who, being the owner or having the right to dispose of it, exploits a vehicle economically in a permanent manner as a means of transport;

(d)   'home station' means the place mentioned on the vehicle and to which the vehicle may or must be sent back in accordance with the conditions of the contract of use.

Article 11. Forum.   §1.   Actions based on a contract concluded in accordance with these Uniform Rules may be brought before the courts or tribunals designated by agreement between the parties to the contract.

§2.   Unless the parties otherwise agree, the competent courts or tribunals shall be those of the Member State where the defendant has his place of business. If the defendant has no place of business in a Member State, the competent courts or tribunals shall be those of the Member State where the loss or damage occurred.

D.5. Uniform Rules concerning the Contract of Use of Infrastructure in International Rail Traffic (CUI — Appendix E to the Convention)

Article 1. Scope. §1. These Uniform Rules shall apply to any contract of use of railway infrastructure for the purposes of international carriage within the meaning of the CIV Uniform Rules and the CIM Uniform Rules. They shall apply regardless of the place of business and the nationality of the contracting parties. These Uniform Rules shall apply even when the railway infrastructure is managed or used by States or by governmental institutions or organisations.

§2. Subject to Article 21, these Uniform Rules shall not apply to other legal relations, such as in particular

(a) the liability of the carrier or the manager to their servants or other persons whose services they make use of to accomplish their tasks;

(b) the liability to each other of the carrier or the manager of the one part and third parties of the other part.

Article 3. Definitions. For the purposes of these Uniform Rules, the term

(a) 'railway infrastructure' means all the railway lines and fixed installations, so far as these are necessary for the circulation of railway vehicles and the safety of traffic;

(b) 'manager' means the person who makes railway infrastructure available;

(c) 'carrier' means the person who carries persons or goods by rail in international traffic under the CIV Uniform Rules or the CIM Uniform Rules;

(d) 'auxiliary' means the servants or other persons whose services the carrier or the manager makes use of for the performance of the contract when these servants or other persons are acting within the scope of their functions;

(e) 'third party' means any person other than the manager, the carrier and their auxiliaries;

(f) 'licence' means the authorization, in accordance with the laws and prescriptions of the State in which the carrier has the place of business of his principal activity, to carry on the activity of carrier by rail;

(g) 'safety certificate' means the document attesting, in accordance with the laws and prescriptions of the State in which the infrastructure being used is situated, that so far as concerns the carrier,

— the internal organisation of the undertaking as well as

— the personnel to be employed and the vehicles to be used on the infrastructure,

meet the requirements imposed in respect of safety in order to ensure a service without danger on that infrastructure.

Article 4. Mandatory law. Unless provided otherwise in these Uniform Rules, any stipulation which, directly or indirectly, would derogate from these Uniform Rules, shall be null and void. The nullity of such a stipulation shall not involve the nullity of other provisions of the contract. Nevertheless, the parties to the contract may assume a liability greater and obligations more burdensome than those provided for in these Uniform Rules or fix a maximum amount of compensation for loss of or damage to property.

Article 24. Forum.   §1. Actions based on these Uniform Rules may be brought before the courts or tribunals of the Member States designated by agreement between the parties to the contract.

§2.   Unless the parties to the contract otherwise agree, the competent courts or tribunals shall be those of the Member State where the manager has his place of business.

Article 25. Limitation of actions.   §1.   The period of limitation for actions based on these Uniform Rules shall be three years.

§2.   The period of limitation shall run from the day when the loss or damage occurred.

§3.   In case of death of persons, the period of limitation shall be three years from the day after the day the death occurred, but not exceeding five years from the day after the day of the accident.

§4.   A recourse action by a person held liable may be brought even after the expiration of the limitation period provided for in §1, if it is brought within the period allowed by the law of the State where the proceedings are brought. However, the period allowed shall be not less than ninety days from the day when the person bringing the recourse action has settled the claim or has been served with notice of the proceedings against himself.

§5.   The period of limitation shall be suspended when the parties agree a conciliation procedure or when they seize the Arbitration Tribunal provided for in Title V of the Convention.

§6.   Otherwise, suspension and interruption of the limitation period shall be governed by national law.

Transfer of personal data

A.   Directive 2006/123/EC of the European Parliament and of the Council of 12 December 2006 on services in the internal market (OJ, L 376 of 27 December 2006): Article 17(3)

See Chapter II, Principle of non-discrimination, A.

B.1. Commission Decision 2001/497/EC of 15 June 2001 on standard contractual clauses for the transfer of personal data to third countries, under Directive 95/46/EC (OJ, L 181 of 4 July 2001)

See Chapter XI, Right to protection of personal data, A.2.

B.2. Commission Decision 2010/87/EU of 5 February 2010 on standard contractual clauses for the transfer of personal data to processors established in third countries under Directive 95/46/EC of the European Parliament and of the Council (OJ, L 39 of 12 February 2010)

See Chapter XI, Right to protection of personal data, A.3.

Contracts concerning IP rights

A.   Council Regulation (EC) No 2100/94 of 27 July 1994 on Community plant variety rights (OJ, L 227 of 1 September 1994): Article 33

See Chapter VIII, IP rights, A.

B.   Council Regulation (EC) No 207/2009 of 26 February 2009 on the Community trade mark (codified version) (OJ, L 78 of 24 March 2009): Articles 17, 118

See Chapter VIII, IP rights, C.

C.   Commission Regulation (EC) No 874/2004 of 28 April 2004 laying down public policy rules concerning the implementation and functions of the .eu Top Level Domain and the principles governing registration (OJ, L 162 of 30 April 2004): Recital 5, Article 5(1)

See Chapter VIII, IP rights, D.2.

D.   Proposal for a Council Regulation on the European Union patent: Articles 14–15

See Chapter VIII, IP rights, I.1.

Contracts concerning interests in goods and equipment

A.1.   Council Decision 2009/370/EC of 6 April 2009 on the accession of the European Community to the Convention on international interests in mobile equipment and its Protocol on matters specific to aircraft equipment, adopted jointly in Cape Town on 16 November 2001 (OJ, L 121 of 15 May 2009): Recital 5, 11–12; Articles 1–3

See Chapter VIII, Interests in goods and equipment, A.1.

A.2.   General declarations concerning the competence of the European Community to be made by the Community at the time of accession to the Convention on international interests in mobile equipment (Cape Town Convention) and the Protocol on matters specific to aircraft equipment (Aircraft Protocol), adopted jointly in Cape Town on 16 November 2001 (OJ, L 121 of 15 May 2009)

I.   Declaration made pursuant to Article 48(2) concerning the competence of the European Community over matters governed by the Convention on international interests in mobile equipment (Cape Town Convention) in respect of which the Member States have transferred their competence to the Community: paragraph 5.

See Chapter VIII, Interests in goods and equipment, A.2.

A.3.   Convention on international interests in mobile equipment (OJ, L 121 of 15 May 2009): Articles 2(4), 5(2)-(4), 29, 31(3), 36, 38(1), 41

See Chapter VIII, Interests in goods and equipment, A.4.

A.4.   Protocol to the Convention on international interests in mobile equipment on matters specific to aircraft equipment (OJ, L 121 of 15 May 2009): Article VIII

See Chapter VIII, Interests in goods and equipment, A.5.

A.5.   Council Decision 2009/940/EC on the signing by the European Community of the Protocol to the Convention on International Interests in Mobile Equipment on Matters Specific to Railway Rolling Stock, Adopted in Luxembourg on 23 February 2007 (OJ, L 331 of 16 December 2009): Recital 6

See Chapter VIII, Interests in goods and equipment, A.6.

A.6.   Declaration to be made pursuant to Article XXII(2) concerning the competence of the European Community over matters governed by the Protocol to the Convention on International Interests in Mobile Equipment on Matters Specific to Railway Rolling Stock (the 'Rail Protocol'), adopted in Luxembourg on 23 February 2007, in respect of which the Member States have transferred their competence to the Community (OJ, L 331 of 16 December 2009): paragraph 5

See Chapter VIII, Interests in goods and equipment, A.7.

A.7.   Luxembourg Protocol to the Convention on international interests in mobile equipment on matters specific to railway rolling stock (OJ, L 331 of 16 December 2009): Articles VI, XIX, XX, XXVII(1)

See Chapter VIII, Interests in goods and equipment, A.8.

Financial collateral arrangements

A.   Directive 2002/47/EC of the European Parliament and of the Council of 6 June 2002 on financial collateral arrangements (OJ, L 168 of 27 June 2002)

See Chapter VIII, Rights on financial instruments, C.1.

B.   Statement of the Council's reasons attached to the Common Position (EC) No 32/2002 of 5 March 2002 adopted by the Council (OJ, C 119 E of 22 May 2002)

See Chapter VIII, Rights on financial instruments, C.2.

Transactions on regulated markets

A.   Directive 2004/39/EC of the European Parliament and of the Council of 21 April 2004 on markets in financial instruments amending Council Directives 85/611/EEC and 93/6/EEC and Directive 2000/12/EC of the European Parliament and of the Council and repealing Council Directive 93/22/EEC (OJ, L 145 of 30 April 2004): Article 36(4)

See Chapter IX, General provisions, H.

VII

Law Applicable to Non-Contractual Obligations

A.1.   Regulation (EC) No 864/2007 of the European Parliament and of the Council of 11 July 2007 on the law applicable to non-contractual obligations (Rome II) (OJ, L 199 of 31 July 2007)*

(1)   The Community has set itself the objective of maintaining and developing an area of freedom, security and justice. For the progressive establishment of such an area, the Community is to adopt measures relating to judicial cooperation in civil matters with a cross-border impact to the extent necessary for the proper functioning of the internal market.

(2)   According to Article 65(b) of the Treaty, these measures are to include those promoting the compatibility of the rules applicable in the Member States concerning the conflict of laws and of jurisdiction.

(3)   The European Council meeting in Tampere on 15 and 16 October 1999 endorsed the principle of mutual recognition of judgments and other decisions of judicial authorities as the cornerstone of judicial cooperation in civil matters and invited the Council and the Commission to adopt a programme of measures to implement the principle of mutual recognition.

(4)   On 30 November 2000, the Council adopted a joint Commission and Council programme of measures for implementation of the principle of mutual recognition of decisions in civil and commercial matters. The programme identifies measures relating to the harmonisation of conflict-of-law rules as those facilitating the mutual recognition of judgments.

(5)   The Hague Programme, adopted by the European Council on 5 November 2004, called for work to be pursued actively on the rules of conflict of laws regarding non-contractual obligations (Rome II).

(6)   The proper functioning of the internal market creates a need, in order to improve the predictability of the outcome of litigation, certainty as to the law applicable and the free movement of judgments, for the conflict-of-law rules in the Member States to designate the same national law irrespective of the country of the court in which an action is brought.

(7)   The substantive scope and the provisions of this Regulation should be consistent with Council Regulation (EC) No 44/2001 of 22 December 2000 on jurisdiction and the

---

* The list of the conventions notified by the Member States under Article 29(1) of the Regulation is published in OJ, C 343 of 17 December 2010.

recognition and enforcement of judgments in civil and commercial matters (Brussels I) and the instruments dealing with the law applicable to contractual obligations.

(8)   This Regulation should apply irrespective of the nature of the court or tribunal seised.

(9)   Claims arising out of *acta iure imperii* should include claims against officials who act on behalf of the State and liability for acts of public authorities, including liability of publicly appointed office-holders. Therefore, these matters should be excluded from the scope of this Regulation.

(10)   Family relationships should cover parentage, marriage, affinity and collateral relatives. The reference in Article 1(2) to relationships having comparable effects to marriage and other family relationships should be interpreted in accordance with the law of the Member State in which the court is seised.

(11)   The concept of a non-contractual obligation varies from one Member State to another. Therefore for the purposes of this Regulation non-contractual obligation should be understood as an autonomous concept. The conflict-of-law rules set out in this Regulation should also cover non-contractual obligations arising out of strict liability.

(12)   The law applicable should also govern the question of the capacity to incur liability in tort/delict.

(13)   Uniform rules applied irrespective of the law they designate may avert the risk of distortions of competition between Community litigants.

(14)   The requirement of legal certainty and the need to do justice in individual cases are essential elements of an area of justice. This Regulation provides for the connecting factors which are the most appropriate to achieve these objectives. Therefore, this Regulation provides for a general rule but also for specific rules and, in certain provisions, for an 'escape clause' which allows a departure from these rules where it is clear from all the circumstances of the case that the tort/delict is manifestly more closely connected with another country. This set of rules thus creates a flexible framework of conflict-of-law rules. Equally, it enables the court seised to treat individual cases in an appropriate manner.

(15)   The principle of the *lex loci delicti commissi* is the basic solution for non-contractual obligations in virtually all the Member States, but the practical application of the principle where the component factors of the case are spread over several countries varies. This situation engenders uncertainty as to the law applicable.

(16)   Uniform rules should enhance the foreseeability of court decisions and ensure a reasonable balance between the interests of the person claimed to be liable and the person who has sustained damage. A connection with the country where the direct damage occurred (*lex loci damni*) strikes a fair balance between the interests of the person claimed to be liable and the person sustaining the damage, and also reflects the modern approach to civil liability and the development of systems of strict liability.

(17)   The law applicable should be determined on the basis of where the damage occurs, regardless of the country or countries in which the indirect consequences could occur. Accordingly, in cases of personal injury or damage to property, the country in which the damage occurs should be the country where the injury was sustained or the property was damaged respectively.

(18)   The general rule in this Regulation should be the *lex loci damni* provided for in Article 4(1). Article 4(2) should be seen as an exception to this general principle, creating

a special connection where the parties have their habitual residence in the same country. Article 4(3) should be understood as an 'escape clause' from Articles 4(1) and (2), where it is clear from all the circumstances of the case that the tort/delict is manifestly more closely connected with another country.

(19) Specific rules should be laid down for special torts/delicts where the general rule does not allow a reasonable balance to be struck between the interests at stake.

(20) The conflict-of-law rule in matters of product liability should meet the objectives of fairly spreading the risks inherent in a modern high-technology society, protecting consumers' health, stimulating innovation, securing undistorted competition and facilitating trade. Creation of a cascade system of connecting factors, together with a foreseeability clause, is a balanced solution in regard to these objectives. The first element to be taken into account is the law of the country in which the person sustaining the damage had his or her habitual residence when the damage occurred, if the product was marketed in that country. The other elements of the cascade are triggered if the product was not marketed in that country, without prejudice to Article 4(2) and to the possibility of a manifestly closer connection to another country.

(21) The special rule in Article 6 is not an exception to the general rule in Article 4(1) but rather a clarification of it. In matters of unfair competition, the conflict-of-law rule should protect competitors, consumers and the general public and ensure that the market economy functions properly. The connection to the law of the country where competitive relations or the collective interests of consumers are, or are likely to be, affected generally satisfies these objectives.

(22) The non-contractual obligations arising out of restrictions of competition in Article 6(3) should cover infringements of both national and Community competition law. The law applicable to such non-contractual obligations should be the law of the country where the market is, or is likely to be, affected. In cases where the market is, or is likely to be, affected in more than one country, the claimant should be able in certain circumstances to choose to base his or her claim on the law of the court seised.

(23) For the purposes of this Regulation, the concept of restriction of competition should cover prohibitions on agreements between undertakings, decisions by associations of undertakings and concerted practices which have as their object or effect the prevention, restriction or distortion of competition within a Member State or within the internal market, as well as prohibitions on the abuse of a dominant position within a Member State or within the internal market, where such agreements, decisions, concerted practices or abuses are prohibited by Articles 81 and 82 of the Treaty or by the law of a Member State.

(24) 'Environmental damage' should be understood as meaning adverse change in a natural resource, such as water, land or air, impairment of a function performed by that resource for the benefit of another natural resource or the public, or impairment of the variability among living organisms.

(25) Regarding environmental damage, Article 174 of the Treaty, which provides that there should be a high level of protection based on the precautionary principle and the principle that preventive action should be taken, the principle of priority for corrective action at source and the principle that the polluter pays, fully justifies the use of the principle of discriminating in favour of the person sustaining the damage. The question of when the person seeking compensation can make the choice of the law applicable

should be determined in accordance with the law of the Member State in which the court is seised.

(26) Regarding infringements of intellectual property rights, the universally acknowledged principle of the *lex loci protectionis* should be preserved. For the purposes of this Regulation, the term 'intellectual property rights' should be interpreted as meaning, for instance, copyright, related rights, the *sui generis* right for the protection of databases and industrial property rights.

(27) The exact concept of industrial action, such as strike action or lock–out, varies from one Member State to another and is governed by each Member State's internal rules. Therefore, this Regulation assumes as a general principle that the law of the country where the industrial action was taken should apply, with the aim of protecting the rights and obligations of workers and employers.

(28) The special rule on industrial action in Article 9 is without prejudice to the conditions relating to the exercise of such action in accordance with national law and without prejudice to the legal *status* of trade unions or of the representative organisations of workers as provided for in the law of the Member States.

(29) Provision should be made for special rules where damage is caused by an act other than a tort/delict, such as unjust enrichment, *negotiorum gestio* and *culpa in contrahendo*.

(30) *Culpa in contrahendo* for the purposes of this Regulation is an autonomous concept and should not necessarily be interpreted within the meaning of national law. It should include the violation of the duty of disclosure and the breakdown of contractual negotiations. Article 12 covers only non-contractual obligations presenting a direct link with the dealings prior to the conclusion of a contract. This means that if, while a contract is being negotiated, a person suffers personal injury, Article 4 or other relevant provisions of this Regulation should apply.

(31) To respect the principle of party autonomy and to enhance legal certainty, the parties should be allowed to make a choice as to the law applicable to a non-contractual obligation. This choice should be expressed or demonstrated with reasonable certainty by the circumstances of the case. Where establishing the existence of the agreement, the court has to respect the intentions of the parties. Protection should be given to weaker parties by imposing certain conditions on the choice.

(32) Considerations of public interest justify giving the courts of the Member States the possibility, in exceptional circumstances, of applying exceptions based on public policy and overriding mandatory provisions. In particular, the application of a provision of the law designated by this Regulation which would have the effect of causing non-compensatory exemplary or punitive damages of an excessive nature to be awarded may, depending on the circumstances of the case and the legal order of the Member State of the court seised, be regarded as being contrary to the public policy (ordre public) of the forum.

(33) According to the current national rules on compensation awarded to victims of road traffic accidents, when quantifying damages for personal injury in cases in which the accident takes place in a State other than that of the habitual residence of the victim, the court seised should take into account all the relevant actual circumstances of the specific victim, including in particular the actual losses and costs of after-care and medical attention.

(34) In order to strike a reasonable balance between the parties, account must be taken, in so far as appropriate, of the rules of safety and conduct in operation in the country in which the harmful act was committed, even where the non-contractual obligation is governed by the law of another country. The term 'rules of safety and conduct' should be interpreted as referring to all regulations having any relation to safety and conduct, including, for example, road safety rules in the case of an accident.

(35) A situation where conflict-of-law rules are dispersed among several instruments and where there are differences between those rules should be avoided. This Regulation, however, does not exclude the possibility of inclusion of conflict-of-law rules relating to non-contractual obligations in provisions of Community law with regard to particular matters. This Regulation should not prejudice the application of other instruments laying down provisions designed to contribute to the proper functioning of the internal market in so far as they cannot be applied in conjunction with the law designated by the rules of this Regulation. The application of provisions of the applicable law designated by the rules of this Regulation should not restrict the free movement of goods and services as regulated by Community instruments, such as Directive 2000/31/EC of the European Parliament and of the Council of 8 June 2000 on certain legal aspects of information society services, in particular electronic commerce, in the Internal Market (Directive on electronic commerce).

(36) Respect for international commitments entered into by the Member States means that this Regulation should not affect international conventions to which one or more Member States are parties at the time this Regulation is adopted. To make the rules more accessible, the Commission should publish the list of the relevant conventions in the *Official Journal of the European Union* on the basis of information supplied by the Member States.

(37) The Commission will make a proposal to the European Parliament and the Council concerning the procedures and conditions according to which Member States would be entitled to negotiate and conclude on their own behalf agreements with third countries in individual and exceptional cases, concerning sectoral matters, containing provisions on the law applicable to non-contractual obligations.

(38) Since the objective of this Regulation cannot be sufficiently achieved by the Member States, and can therefore, by reason of the scale and effects of this Regulation, be better achieved at Community level, the Community may adopt measures, in accordance with the principle of subsidiarity set out in Article 5 of the Treaty. In accordance with the principle of proportionality set out in that Article, this Regulation does not go beyond what is necessary to attain that objective.

(39) In accordance with Article 3 of the Protocol on the position of the United Kingdom and Ireland annexed to the Treaty on European Union and to the Treaty establishing the European Community, the United Kingdom and Ireland are taking part in the adoption and application of this Regulation.

(40) In accordance with Articles 1 and 2 of the Protocol on the position of Denmark, annexed to the Treaty on European Union and to the Treaty establishing the European Community, Denmark does not take part in the adoption of this Regulation, and is not bound by it or subject to its application;

Chapter I – Scope

Article 1. Scope.   1.   This Regulation shall apply, in situations involving a conflict of laws, to non-contractual obligations in civil and commercial matters. It shall not apply, in particular, to revenue, customs or administrative matters or to the liability of the State for acts and omissions in the exercise of State authority (*acta iure imperii*).

2.   The following shall be excluded from the scope of this Regulation:

(a)   non-contractual obligations arising out of family relationships and relationships deemed by the law applicable to such relationships to have comparable effects, including maintenance obligations;

(b)   non-contractual obligations arising out of matrimonial property regimes, property regimes of relationships deemed by the law applicable to such relationships to have comparable effects to marriage, and wills and succession;

(c)   non-contractual obligations arising under bills of exchange, cheques and promissory notes and other negotiable instruments to the extent that the obligations under such other negotiable instruments arise out of their negotiable character;

(d)   non-contractual obligations arising out of the law of companies and other bodies corporate or unincorporated regarding matters such as the creation, by registration or otherwise, legal capacity, internal organisation or winding–up of companies and other bodies corporate or unincorporated, the personal liability of officers and members as such for the obligations of the company or body and the personal liability of auditors to a company or to its members in the statutory audits of accounting documents;

(e)   non-contractual obligations arising out of the relations between the settlors, trustees and beneficiaries of a trust created voluntarily;

(f)   non-contractual obligations arising out of nuclear damage;

(g)   non-contractual obligations arising out of violations of privacy and rights relating to personality, including defamation.

3.   This Regulation shall not apply to evidence and procedure, without prejudice to Articles 21 and 22.

4.   For the purposes of this Regulation, 'Member State' shall mean any Member State other than Denmark.

Article 2. Non-contractual obligations.   1.   For the purposes of this Regulation, damage shall cover any consequence arising out of tort/delict, unjust enrichment, *negotiorum gestio* or *culpa in contrahendo*.

2.   This Regulation shall apply also to non-contractual obligations that are likely to arise.

3.   Any reference in this Regulation to:

(a)   an event giving rise to damage shall include events giving rise to damage that are likely to occur; and

(b)   damage shall include damage that is likely to occur.

Article 3. Universal application.   Any law specified by this Regulation shall be applied whether or not it is the law of a Member State.

Chapter II – Torts/Delicts

Article 4. General rule.   1.   Unless otherwise provided for in this Regulation, the law applicable to a non-contractual obligation arising out of a tort/delict shall be the law of the country in which the damage occurs irrespective of the country in which the event giving rise to the damage occurred and irrespective of the country or countries in which the indirect consequences of that event occur.

2.   However, where the person claimed to be liable and the person sustaining damage both have their habitual residence in the same country at the time when the damage occurs, the law of that country shall apply.

3.   Where it is clear from all the circumstances of the case that the tort/delict is manifestly more closely connected with a country other than that indicated in paragraphs 1 or 2, the law of that other country shall apply. A manifestly closer connection with another country might be based in particular on a pre-existing relationship between the parties, such as a contract, that is closely connected with the tort/delict in question.

Article 5. Product liability.   1.   Without prejudice to Article 4(2), the law applicable to a non-contractual obligation arising out of damage caused by a product shall be:

(a)   the law of the country in which the person sustaining the damage had his or her habitual residence when the damage occurred, if the product was marketed in that country; or, failing that,

(b)   the law of the country in which the product was acquired, if the product was marketed in that country; or, failing that,

(c)   the law of the country in which the damage occurred, if the product was marketed in that country.

However, the law applicable shall be the law of the country in which the person claimed to be liable is habitually resident if he or she could not reasonably foresee the marketing of the product, or a product of the same type, in the country the law of which is applicable under (a), (b) or (c).

2.   Where it is clear from all the circumstances of the case that the tort/delict is manifestly more closely connected with a country other than that indicated in paragraph 1, the law of that other country shall apply. A manifestly closer connection with another country might be based in particular on a pre-existing relationship between the parties, such as a contract, that is closely connected with the tort/delict in question.

Article 6. Unfair competition and acts restricting free competition.   1.   The law applicable to a non-contractual obligation arising out of an act of unfair competition shall be the law of the country where competitive relations or the collective interests of consumers are, or are likely to be, affected.

2.   Where an act of unfair competition affects exclusively the interests of a specific competitor, Article 4 shall apply.

3.   (a)   The law applicable to a non-contractual obligation arising out of a restriction of competition shall be the law of the country where the market is, or is likely to be, affected.

(b)   When the market is, or is likely to be, affected in more than one country, the person seeking compensation for damage who sues in the court of the domicile of the defendant, may instead choose to base his or her claim on the law of the court seised, provided that the market in that Member State is amongst those directly and substantially affected by the restriction of competition out of which the non-contractual obligation on which the claim is based arises; where the claimant sues, in accordance with the applicable rules on jurisdiction, more than one defendant in that court, he or she can only choose to base his or her claim on the law of that court if the restriction of competition on which the claim against each of these defendants relies directly and substantially affects also the market in the Member State of that court.

4.   The law applicable under this Article may not be derogated from by an agreement pursuant to Article 14.

Article 7. Environmental damage.   The law applicable to a non-contractual obligation arising out of environmental damage or damage sustained by persons or property as a result of such damage shall be the law determined pursuant to Article 4(1), unless the person seeking compensation for damage chooses to base his or her claim on the law of the country in which the event giving rise to the damage occurred.

Article 8. Infringement of intellectual property rights.   1.   The law applicable to a non-contractual obligation arising from an infringement of an intellectual property right shall be the law of the country for which protection is claimed.

2.   In the case of a non-contractual obligation arising from an infringement of a unitary Community intellectual property right, the law applicable shall, for any question that is not governed by the relevant Community instrument, be the law of the country in which the act of infringement was committed.

3.   The law applicable under this Article may not be derogated from by an agreement pursuant to Article 14.

Article 9. Industrial action.   Without prejudice to Article 4(2), the law applicable to a non-contractual obligation in respect of the liability of a person in the capacity of a worker or an employer or the organisations representing their professional interests for damages caused by an industrial action, pending or carried out, shall be the law of the country where the action is to be, or has been, taken.

Chapter III – Unjust Enrichment, Negotiorum Gestio and Culpa In Contrahendo

Article 10. Unjust enrichment.   1.   If a non-contractual obligation arising out of unjust enrichment, including payment of amounts wrongly received, concerns a relationship existing between the parties, such as one arising out of a contract or a tort/delict, that is closely connected with that unjust enrichment, it shall be governed by the law that governs that relationship.

2.   Where the law applicable cannot be determined on the basis of paragraph 1 and the parties have their habitual residence in the same country when the event giving rise to unjust enrichment occurs, the law of that country shall apply.

3.   Where the law applicable cannot be determined on the basis of paragraphs 1 or 2, it shall be the law of the country in which the unjust enrichment took place.

4.   Where it is clear from all the circumstances of the case that the non-contractual obligation arising out of unjust enrichment is manifestly more closely connected with a country other than that indicated in paragraphs 1, 2 and 3, the law of that other country shall apply.

Article 11. Negotiorum gestio.   1.   If a non-contractual obligation arising out of an act performed without due authority in connection with the affairs of another person concerns a relationship existing between the parties, such as one arising out of a contract or a tort/delict, that is closely connected with that non-contractual obligation, it shall be governed by the law that governs that relationship.

2.   Where the law applicable cannot be determined on the basis of paragraph 1, and the parties have their habitual residence in the same country when the event giving rise to the damage occurs, the law of that country shall apply.

3.   Where the law applicable cannot be determined on the basis of paragraphs 1 or 2, it shall be the law of the country in which the act was performed.

4.   Where it is clear from all the circumstances of the case that the non-contractual obligation arising out of an act performed without due authority in connection with the affairs of another person is manifestly more closely connected with a country other than that indicated in paragraphs 1, 2 and 3, the law of that other country shall apply.

Article 12. Culpa in contrahendo.   1.   The law applicable to a non-contractual obligation arising out of dealings prior to the conclusion of a contract, regardless of whether the contract was actually concluded or not, shall be the law that applies to the contract or that would have been applicable to it had it been entered into.

2.   Where the law applicable cannot be determined on the basis of paragraph 1, it shall be:

(a)   the law of the country in which the damage occurs, irrespective of the country in which the event giving rise to the damage occurred and irrespective of the country or countries in which the indirect consequences of that event occurred; or

(b)   where the parties have their habitual residence in the same country at the time when the event giving rise to the damage occurs, the law of that country; or

(c)   where it is clear from all the circumstances of the case that the non-contractual obligation arising out of dealings prior to the conclusion of a contract is manifestly more closely connected with a country other than that indicated in points (a) and (b), the law of that other country.

Article 13. Applicability of Article 8.   For the purposes of this Chapter, Article 8 shall apply to non-contractual obligations arising from an infringement of an intellectual property right.

Chapter IV – Freedom of choice

Article 14. Freedom of choice.   1.   The parties may agree to submit non-contractual obligations to the law of their choice:

(a)   by an agreement entered into after the event giving rise to the damage occurred; or

(b)   where all the parties are pursuing a commercial activity, also by an agreement freely negotiated before the event giving rise to the damage occurred.

The choice shall be expressed or demonstrated with reasonable certainty by the circumstances of the case and shall not prejudice the rights of third parties.

2.   Where all the elements relevant to the situation at the time when the event giving rise to the damage occurs are located in a country other than the country whose law

has been chosen, the choice of the parties shall not prejudice the application of provisions of the law of that other country which cannot be derogated from by agreement.

3.   Where all the elements relevant to the situation at the time when the event giving rise to the damage occurs are located in one or more of the Member States, the parties' choice of the law applicable other than that of a Member State shall not prejudice the application of provisions of Community law, where appropriate as implemented in the Member State of the forum, which cannot be derogated from by agreement.

Chapter V – Common rules

Article 15. Scope of the law applicable.   The law applicable to non-contractual obligations under this Regulation shall govern in particular:

(a)   the basis and extent of liability, including the determination of persons who may be held liable for acts performed by them;

(b)   the grounds for exemption from liability, any limitation of liability and any division of liability;

(c)   the existence, the nature and the assessment of damage or the remedy claimed;

(d)   within the limits of powers conferred on the court by its procedural law, the measures which a court may take to prevent or terminate injury or damage or to ensure the provision of compensation;

(e)   the question whether a right to claim damages or a remedy may be transferred, including by inheritance;

(f)   persons entitled to compensation for damage sustained personally;

(g)   liability for the acts of another person;

(h)   the manner in which an obligation may be extinguished and rules of prescription and limitation, including rules relating to the commencement, interruption and suspension of a period of prescription or limitation.

Article 16. Overriding mandatory provisions.   Nothing in this Regulation shall restrict the application of the provisions of the law of the forum in a situation where they are mandatory irrespective of the law otherwise applicable to the non-contractual obligation.

Article 17. Rules of safety and conduct.   In assessing the conduct of the person claimed to be liable, account shall be taken, as a matter of fact and in so far as is appropriate, of the rules of safety and conduct which were in force at the place and time of the event giving rise to the liability.

Article 18. Direct action against the insurer of the person liable.   The person having suffered damage may bring his or her claim directly against the insurer of the person liable to provide compensation if the law applicable to the non-contractual obligation or the law applicable to the insurance contract so provides.

Article 19. Subrogation.   Where a person (the creditor) has a non-contractual claim upon another (the debtor), and a third person has a duty to satisfy the creditor, or has in fact satisfied the creditor in discharge of that duty, the law which governs the third person's duty to satisfy the creditor shall determine whether, and the extent to which, the third person is entitled to exercise against the debtor the rights which the creditor had against the debtor under the law governing their relationship.

Article 20. Multiple liability. If a creditor has a claim against several debtors who are liable for the same claim, and one of the debtors has already satisfied the claim in whole or in part, the question of that debtor's right to demand compensation from the other debtors shall be governed by the law applicable to that debtor's non-contractual obligation towards the creditor.

Article 21. Formal validity. A unilateral act intended to have legal effect and relating to a non-contractual obligation shall be formally valid if it satisfies the formal requirements of the law governing the non-contractual obligation in question or the law of the country in which the act is performed.

Article 22. Burden of proof. 1. The law governing a non-contractual obligation under this Regulation shall apply to the extent that, in matters of non-contractual obligations, it contains rules which raise presumptions of law or determine the burden of proof.

2. Acts intended to have legal effect may be proved by any mode of proof recognised by the law of the forum or by any of the laws referred to in Article 21 under which that act is formally valid, provided that such mode of proof can be administered by the forum.

Chapter VI – Other provisions

Article 23. Habitual residence. 1. For the purposes of this Regulation, the habitual residence of companies and other bodies, corporate or unincorporated, shall be the place of central administration.Where the event giving rise to the damage occurs, or the damage arises, in the course of operation of a branch, agency or any other establishment, the place where the branch, agency or any other establishment is located shall be treated as the place of habitual residence.

2. For the purposes of this Regulation, the habitual residence of a natural person acting in the course of his or her business activity shall be his or her principal place of business.

Article 24. Exclusion of renvoi. The application of the law of any country specified by this Regulation means the application of the rules of law in force in that country other than its rules of private international law.

Article 25. States with more than one legal system. 1. Where a State comprises several territorial units, each of which has its own rules of law in respect of non-contractual obligations, each territorial unit shall be considered as a country for the purposes of identifying the law applicable under this Regulation.

2. A Member State within which different territorial units have their own rules of law in respect of non-contractual obligations shall not be required to apply this Regulation to conflicts solely between the laws of such units.

Article 26. Public policy of the forum. The application of a provision of the law of any country specified by this Regulation may be refused only if such application is manifestly incompatible with the public policy (*ordre public*) of the forum.

Article 27. Relationship with other provisions of Community law.   This Regulation shall not prejudice the application of provisions of Community law which, in relation to particular matters, lay down conflict-of-law rules relating to non-contractual obligations.

Article 28. Relationship with existing international conventions.   1.   This Regulation shall not prejudice the application of international conventions to which one or more Member States are parties at the time when this Regulation is adopted and which lay down conflict-of-law rules relating to non-contractual obligations.

    2.   However, this Regulation shall, as between Member States, take precedence over conventions concluded exclusively between two or more of them in so far as such conventions concern matters governed by this Regulation.

Chapter VII — Final provisions

Article 29. List of conventions.   1.   By 11 July 2008, Member States shall notify the Commission of the conventions referred to in Article 28(1). After that date, Member States shall notify the Commission of all denunciations of such conventions.

    2.   The Commission shall publish in the Official Journal of the European Union within six months of receipt:

    (i)   a list of the conventions referred to in paragraph 1;

    (ii)   the denunciations referred to in paragraph 1.

Article 30. Review clause.   1.   Not later than 20 August 2011, the Commission shall submit to the European Parliament, the Council and the European Economic and Social Committee a report on the application of this Regulation. If necessary, the report shall be accompanied by proposals to adapt this Regulation. The report shall include:

    (i)   a study on the effects of the way in which foreign law is treated in the different jurisdictions and on the extent to which courts in the Member States apply foreign law in practice pursuant to this Regulation;

    (ii)   a study on the effects of Article 28 of this Regulation with respect to the Hague Convention of 4 May 1971 on the law applicable to traffic accidents.

    2.   Not later than 31 December 2008, the Commission shall submit to the European Parliament, the Council and the European Economic and Social Committee a study on the situation in the field of the law applicable to non-contractual obligations arising out of violations of privacy and rights relating to personality, taking into account rules relating to freedom of the press and freedom of expression in the media, and conflict-of-law issues related to Directive 95/46/EC of the European Parliament and of the Council of 24 October 1995 on the protection of individuals with regard to the processing of personal data and on the free movement of such data.

Article 31. Application in time.   This Regulation shall apply to events giving rise to damage which occur after its entry into force.

Article 32. Date of application.   This Regulation shall apply from 11 January 2009, except for Article 29, which shall apply from 11 July 2008.

    This Regulation shall be binding in its entirety and directly applicable in the Member States in accordance with the Treaty establishing the European Community.

A.2.   Commission Statements (OJ, L 199 of 31 July 2007)

1.   Commission Statement on the review clause (Article 30)

The Commission, following the invitation by the European Parliament and the Council in the frame of Article 30 of the 'Rome II' Regulation, will submit, not later than December 2008, a study on the situation in the field of the law applicable to non-contractual obligations arising out of violations of privacy and rights relating to personality. The Commission will take into consideration all aspects of the situation and take appropriate measures if necessary.

2.   Commission Statement on road accidents

The Commission, being aware of the different practices followed in the Member States as regards the level of compensation awarded to victims of road traffic accidents, is prepared to examine the specific problems resulting for EU residents involved in road traffic accidents in a Member State other than the Member State of their habitual residence. To that end the Commission will make available to the European Parliament and to the Council, before the end of 2008, a study on all options, including insurance aspects, for improving the position of cross–border victims, which would pave the way for a Green Paper.

3.   Commission Statement on the treatment of foreign law

The Commission, being aware of the different practices followed in the Member States as regards the treatment of foreign law, will publish at the latest four years after the entry into force of the 'Rome II' Regulation and in any event as soon as it is available a horizontal study on the application of foreign law in civil and commercial matters by the courts of the Member States, having regard to the aims of the Hague Programme. It is also prepared to take appropriate measures if necessary.

B.1.   Council Regulation (EC) No 2100/94 of 27 July 1994 on Community plant variety rights (OJ, L 227 of 1 September 1994): Articles 33, 94, 97, 107

See Chapter VIII, IP rights, A.

B.2.   Council Regulation (EC) No 207/2009 of 26 February 2009 on the Community trade mark (OJ, L 78 of 24 March 2009): Articles 14, 101, 110, 118

See Chapter VIII, IP rights, C.

B.3.   Directive 2004/48/EC of the European Parliament and of the Council of 29 April 2004 in the enforcement of intellectual property rights (OJ, L 157 of 30 April 2004): Recital 11

See Chapter VIII, IP rights, F.

C.   Council Framework Decision 2005/214/JHA of 24 February 2005 on the application of the principle of mutual recognition to financial penalties (OJ, L 76 of 22 March 2005): Article 1(b)

See Chapter IV, General provisions, H.

D.   Council Directive 84/450/EEC of 10 September 1984 concerning misleading and comparative advertising (OJ, L 250 of 19 September 1984)[1]

(1)   Whereas the laws against misleading advertising now in force in the Member States differ widely; whereas, since advertising reaches beyond the frontiers of individual Member States, it has a direct effect on the establishment and the functioning of the common market;

(2)   Whereas misleading advertising can lead to distortion of competition within the common market;

(3)   Whereas advertising, whether or not it induces a contract, affects the economic welfare of consumers;

(4)   Whereas misleading advertising may cause a consumer to take decisions prejudicial to him when acquiring goods or other property, or using services, and the differences between the laws of the Member States not only lead, in many cases, to inadequate levels of consumer protection, but also hinder the execution of advertising campaigns beyond national boundaries and thus affect the free circulation of goods and provision of services;

(6)   Whereas it is in the interest of the public in general, as well as that of consumers and all those who, in competition with one another, carry on a trade, business, craft or profession, in the common market, to harmonise in the first instance national provisions against misleading advertising and that, at a second stage, unfair advertising and, as far as necessary, comparative advertising should be dealt with, on the basis of appropriate Commission proposals;

(7)   Whereas minimum and objective criteria for determining whether advertising is misleading should be established for this purpose;

Article 1. The purpose of this Directive is to protect traders against misleading advertising and the unfair consequences thereof and to lay down the conditions under which comparative advertising is permitted.

---

[1]   As finally amended by Directive 2005/29/EC (OJ, L 149 of 11 June 2005). [Note of the Editor]

Article 7. 1. This Directive shall not preclude Member States from retaining or adopting provisions with a view to ensuring more extensive protection, with regard to misleading advertising, for traders and competitors.

2. Paragraph 1 shall not apply to comparative advertising as far as the comparison is concerned.

3. The provisions of this Directive shall apply without prejudice to Community provisions on advertising for specific products and/or services or to restrictions or prohibitions on advertising in particular media.

4. The provisions of this Directive concerning comparative advertising shall not oblige Member States which, in compliance with the provisions of the Treaty, maintain or introduce advertising bans regarding certain goods or services, whether imposed directly or by a body or organisation responsible, under the law of the Member States, for regulating the exercise of a commercial, industrial, craft or professional activity, to permit comparative advertising regarding those goods or services. Where these bans are limited to particular media, the Directive shall apply to the media not covered by these bans.

5. Nothing in this Directive shall prevent Member States from, in compliance with the provisions of the Treaty, maintaining or introducing bans or limitations on the use of comparisons in the advertising of professional services, whether imposed directly or by a body or organisation responsible, under the law of the Member States, for regulating the exercise of a professional activity.

E. Directive 2009/22/EC of the European Parliament and of the Council of 23 April 2009 on injunctions for the protection of consumers' interests (Codified version) (OJ, L 110 of 1 May 2009)

(1) Directive 98/27/EC of the European Parliament and of the Council of 19 May 1998 on injunctions for the protection of consumers' interests has been substantially amended several times. In the interests of clarity and rationality the said Directive should be Codified.

(2) Certain Directives, listed in Annex I to this Directive, lay down rules with regard to the protection of consumers' interests.

(3) Current mechanisms available for ensuring compliance with those Directives, both at national and at Community level, do not always allow infringements harmful to the collective interests of consumers to be terminated in good time. Collective interests means interests which do not include the cumulation of interests of individuals who have been harmed by an infringement. This is without prejudice to individual actions brought by individuals who have been harmed by an infringement.

(4) As far as the purpose of bringing about the cessation of practices that are unlawful under the national provisions applicable is concerned, the effectiveness of national measures transposing the Directives in question, including protective measures that go beyond the level required by those Directives, provided they are compatible with the Treaty and allowed by those Directives, may be thwarted where those practices produce effects in a Member State other than that in which they originate.

(5) Those difficulties can disrupt the smooth functioning of the internal market, their consequence being that it is sufficient to move the source of an unlawful practice

to another country in order to place it out of reach of all forms of enforcement. This constitutes a distortion of competition.

(6)   Those difficulties are likely to diminish consumer confidence in the internal market and may limit the scope for action by organisations representing the collective interests of consumers or independent public bodies responsible for protecting the collective interests of consumers, adversely affected by practices that infringe Community law.

(7)   Those practices often extend beyond the frontiers between the Member States. There is an urgent need for some degree of approximation of national provisions designed to enjoin the cessation of the unlawful practices irrespective of the Member State in which the unlawful practice has produced its effects. With regard to jurisdiction, this is without prejudice to the rules of private international law and the Conventions in force between Member States, while respecting the general obligations of the Member States deriving from the Treaty, in particular those related to the smooth functioning of the internal market.

Article 1. Scope.   1.   The purpose of this Directive is to approximate the laws, regulations and administrative provisions of the Member States relating to actions for an injunction referred to in Article 2 aimed at the protection of the collective interests of consumers included in the Directives listed in Annex I, with a view to ensuring the smooth functioning of the internal market.

2.   For the purposes of this Directive, an infringement means any act contrary to the Directives listed in Annex I as transposed into the internal legal order of the Member States which harms the collective interests referred to in paragraph 1.

Article 2. Actions for an injunction.   1.   Member States shall designate the courts or administrative authorities competent to rule on proceedings commenced by qualified entities within the meaning of Article 3 seeking:

(a)   an order with all due expediency, where appropriate by way of summary procedure, requiring the cessation or prohibition of any infringement;

(b)   where appropriate, measures such as the publication of the decision, in full or in part, in such form as deemed adequate and/or the publication of a corrective statement with a view to eliminating the continuing effects of the infringement;

(c)   in so far as the legal system of the Member State concerned so permits, an order against the losing defendant for payments into the public purse or to any beneficiary designated in or under national legislation, in the event of failure to comply with the decision within a time limit specified by the courts or administrative authorities, of a fixed amount for each day's delay or any other amount provided for in national legislation, with a view to ensuring compliance with the decisions.

2.   This Directive shall be without prejudice to the rules of private international law with respect to the applicable law, that is, normally, either the law of the Member State where the infringement originated or the law of the Member State where the infringement has its effects.

Annex I

List of Directives referred to in Article 1[1]

1.   Council Directive 85/577/EEC of 20 December 1985 to protect the consumer in respect of contracts negotiated away from business premises (OJ, L 372 of 31 December 1985, 31).

2.   Council Directive 87/102/EEC of 22 December 1986 for the approximation of the laws, regulations and administrative provisions of the Member States concerning consumer credit (OJ, L 42 of 12 February 1987, 48).[2]

3.   Council Directive 89/552/EEC of 3 October 1989 on the coordination of certain provisions laid down by law, regulation or administrative action in Member States concerning the pursuit of television broadcasting activities: Articles 10 to 21 (OJ, L 298 of 17 October 1989, 23).

4.   Council Directive 90/314/EEC of 13 June 1990 on package travel, package holidays and package tours (OJ, L 158 of 23 June 1990, 59).

5.   Council Directive 93/13/EEC of 5 April 1993 on unfair terms in consumer contracts (OJ, L 95 of 21 April 1993, 29).

6.   Directive 97/7/EC of the European Parliament and of the Council of 20 May 1997 on the protection of consumers in respect of distance contracts (OJ, L 144 of 4 June 1997, 19).

7.   Directive 1999/44/EC of the European Parliament and of the Council of 25 May 1999 on certain aspects of the sale of consumer goods and associated guarantees (OJ, L 171 of 7 July 1999, 12).

8.   Directive 2000/31/EC of the European Parliament and of the Council of 8 June 2000 on certain legal aspects on information society services, in particular electronic commerce, in the internal market (Directive on electronic commerce) (OJ, L 178 of 17 July 2000, 1).

9.   Directive 2001/83/EC of the European Parliament and of the Council of 6 November 2001 on the Community code relating to medicinal products for human use: Articles 86 to 100 (OJ, L 311 of 28 November 2001, 67).

10.   Directive 2002/65/EC of the European Parliament and of the Council of 23 September 2002 concerning the distance marketing of consumer financial services (OJ, L 271 of 9 October 2002, 16).

11.   Directive 2005/29/EC of the European Parliament and of the Council of 11 May 2005 concerning unfair business–to–consumer commercial practices in the internal market (OJ, L 149 of 11 June 2005, 22).

12.   Directive 2006/123/EC of the European Parliament and of the Council of 12 December 2006 on services in the internal market (OJ, L 376 of 27 December 2006, 36).

13.   Directive 2008/122/EC of the European Parliament and of the Council of 14 January 2009 on the protection of consumers in respect of certain aspects of timeshare, long-term holiday product, resale and exchange contracts (OJ, L 33 of 3 February 2009, 10).

---

[1]   [Footnotes are published in the original numerical order as in OJ] The Directives referred to in points 5, 6, 9 and 11 contain specific provisions concerning injunctions.

[2]   The said Directive was repealed and replaced, with effect from 12 May 2010, by Directive 2008/48/EC (OJ, L 133 of 22 May 2008, 66).

F.   Directive 2004/35/EC of the European Parliament and of the Council of 21 April 2004 on environmental liability with regard to the prevention and remedying of environmental damage (OJ, L 143 of 30 April 2004): Recital 10, Article 3

See Chapter IV, Environmental damages, A.

G.   Council Directive 2004/80/EC of 29 April 2004 relating to compensation to crime victims (OJ, L 261 of 6 August 2004): Articles 1–2

See Chapter XIII, Compensation to crime victims, B.

H.   Directive 2009/103/EC of the European Parliament and of the Council of 16 September 2009 relating to insurance against civil liability in respect of the use of motor vehicles, and the enforcement of the obligation to insure against such liability (codified version) (OJ, L 263 of 7 October 2009)

(22)   Personal injuries and damage to property suffered by pedestrians, cyclists and other non-motorised road users, who are usually the weakest party in an accident, should be covered by the compulsory insurance of the vehicle involved in the accident where they are entitled to compensation under national civil law. This provision does not prejudge the issue of civil liability, or the level of awards of damages in respect of a given accident, under national legislation.

(32) Under Article 11(2) read in conjunction with Article 9(1)(b) of Council Regulation (EC) No 44/2001 of 22 December 2000 on jurisdiction and the recognition and enforcement of judgments in civil and commercial matters, injured parties may bring legal proceedings against the civil liability insurance provider in the Member State in which they are domiciled.

(35) This system of having claims representatives in the injured party's Member State of residence affects neither the substantive law to be applied in each individual case nor the matter of jurisdiction.

(37) It should be provided that the Member State where the insurance undertaking is authorised should require that undertaking to appoint claims representatives resident or established in the other Member States to collect all necessary information in relation to claims resulting from such accidents and to take appropriate action to settle the claims on behalf and for the account of the insurance undertaking, including the payment of compensation. Claims representatives should have sufficient powers to represent the insurance undertaking in relation to persons suffering damage from such accidents, and also to represent the insurance undertaking before national authorities including, where necessary, before the courts, in so far as this is compatible with the rules of private international law on the conferral of jurisdiction.

(38) The activities of the claims representative are not sufficient in order to confer jurisdiction on the courts in the injured party's Member State of residence if the rules of private international law on the conferral of jurisdiction do not so provide.

(46) Certain information provided, such as the name and address of the owner or usual driver of the vehicle and the number of the insurance policy or the registration number of the vehicle, constitutes personal data within the meaning of Directive 95/46/ EC of the European Parliament and of the Council of 24 October 1995 on the protection of individuals with regard to the processing of personal data and on the free movement of such data. The processing of such data which is required for the purposes of this Directive should therefore comply with the national measures taken pursuant to Directive 95/46/ EC. The name and address of the usual driver should be communicated only if national legislation provides for such communication.

Article 1. Definitions. For the purposes of this Directive: 1. 'vehicle' means any motor vehicle intended for travel on land and propelled by mechanical power, but not running on rails, and any trailer, whether or not coupled;

2. 'injured party' means any person entitled to compensation in respect of any loss or injury caused by vehicles;

3. 'national insurers' bureau' means a professional organisation which is constituted in accordance with Recommendation No 5 adopted on 25 January 1949 by the Road Transport Sub-Committee of the Inland Transport Committee of the United Nations Economic Commission for Europe and which groups together insurance undertakings which, in a State, are authorised to conduct the business of motor vehicle insurance against civil liability;

4. 'territory in which the vehicle is normally based' means:

(a) the territory of the State of which the vehicle bears a registration plate, irrespective of whether the plate is permanent or temporary; or

(b) in cases where no registration is required for a type of vehicle but the vehicle bears an insurance plate, or a distinguishing sign analogous to the registration plate, the territory of the State in which the insurance plate or the sign is issued; or

(c) in cases where neither a registration plate nor an insurance plate nor a distinguishing sign is required for certain types of vehicle, the territory of the State in which the person who has custody of the vehicle is permanently resident; or

(d) in cases where the vehicle does not bear any registration plate or bears a registration plate which does not correspond or no longer corresponds to the vehicle and has been involved in an accident, the territory of the State in which the accident took place, for the purpose of settling the claim as provided for in the first indent of Article 2(a) or in Article 10;

5. 'green card' means an international certificate of insurance issued on behalf of a national bureau in accordance with Recommendation No 5 adopted on 25 January 1949 by the Road Transport Sub-committee of the Inland Transport Committee of the United Nations Economic Commission for Europe;

6. 'insurance undertaking' means an undertaking which has received its official authorisation in accordance with Article 6 or Article 23(2) of Directive 73/239/EEC;

7. 'establishment' means the head office, agency or branch of an insurance undertaking as defined in Article 2(c) of Second Council Directive 88/357/EEC of 22 June 1988 on the coordination of laws, regulations and administrative provisions relating to

direct insurance other than life assurance and laying down provisions to facilitate the effective exercise of freedom to provide services.

Article 2. Scope. The provisions of Articles 4, 6, 7 and 8 shall apply to vehicles normally based on the territory of one of the Member States:

(a) after an agreement has been concluded between the national insurers' bureaux under the terms of which each national bureau guarantees the settlement, in accordance with the provisions of national law on compulsory insurance, of claims in respect of accidents occurring in its territory, caused by vehicles normally based in the territory of another Member State, whether or not such vehicles are insured;

(b) from the date fixed by the Commission, upon its having ascertained in close cooperation with the Member States that such an agreement has been concluded;

(c) for the duration of that agreement.

Article 3. Compulsory insurance of vehicles. Each Member State shall, subject to Article 5, take all appropriate measures to ensure that civil liability in respect of the use of vehicles normally based in its territory is covered by insurance.

The extent of the liability covered and the terms and conditions of the cover shall be determined on the basis of the measures referred to in the first paragraph.

Each Member State shall take all appropriate measures to ensure that the contract of insurance also covers:

(a) according to the law in force in other Member States, any loss or injury which is caused in the territory of those States;

(b) any loss or injury suffered by nationals of Member States during a direct journey between two territories in which the Treaty is in force, if there is no national insurers' bureau responsible for the territory which is being crossed; in such a case, the loss or injury shall be covered in accordance with the national laws on compulsory insurance in force in the Member State in whose territory the vehicle is normally based.

The insurance referred to in the first paragraph shall cover compulsorily both damage to property and personal injuries.

Article 18. Direct right of action. Member States shall ensure that any party injured as a result of an accident caused by a vehicle covered by insurance as referred to in Article 3 enjoys a direct right of action against the insurance undertaking covering the person responsible against civil liability.

Article 20. Special provisions concerning compensation for injured parties following an accident in a Member State other than that of their residence. 1. The object of Articles 20 to 26 is to lay down special provisions applicable to injured parties entitled to compensation in respect of any loss or injury resulting from accidents occurring in a Member State other than the Member State of residence of the injured party which are caused by the use of vehicles insured and normally based in a Member State.

Without prejudice to the legislation of third countries on civil liability and private international law, these provisions shall also apply to injured parties resident in a Member State and entitled to compensation in respect of any loss or injury resulting from accidents occurring in third countries whose national insurer's bureaux have joined the green card system whenever such accidents are caused by the use of vehicles insured and normally based in a Member State.

2.   Articles 21 and 24 shall apply only in the case of accidents caused by the use of a vehicle:

(a)   insured through an establishment in a Member State other than the State of residence of the injured party; and

(b)   normally based in a Member State other than the State of residence of the injured party.

Article 21. Claims representatives. 1.   Each Member State shall take all measures necessary to ensure that all insurance undertakings covering the risks classified in class 10 of point A of the Annex to Directive 73/239/EEC, other than carrier's liability, appoint a claims representative in each Member State other than that in which they have received their official authorisation.

The claims representative shall be responsible for handling and settling claims arising from an accident in the cases referred to in Article 20(1).

The claims representative shall be resident or established in the Member State where he is appointed.

2.   The choice of its claims representative shall be at the discretion of the insurance undertaking.The Member States may not restrict this freedom of choice.

3.   The claims representative may act for one or more insurance undertakings.

4.   The claims representative shall, in relation to such claims, collect all information necessary in connection with the settlement of the claims and shall take the measures necessary to negotiate a settlement of claims.

The requirement of appointing a claims representative shall not preclude the right of the injured party or his insurance undertaking to institute proceedings directly against the person who caused the accident or his insurance undertaking.

5.   Claims representatives shall possess sufficient powers to represent the insurance undertaking in relation to injured parties in the cases referred to in Article 20(1) and to meet their claims in full.

They must be capable of examining cases in the official language(s) of the Member State of residence of the injured party.

6.   The appointment of a claims representative shall not in itself constitute the opening of a branch within the meaning of Article 1(b) of Directive 92/49/EEC and the claims representative shall not be regarded as an establishment within the meaning of Article 2(c) of Directive 88/357/EEC or an establishment within the meaning of Regulation (EC) No 44/2001.

Article 23. Information centres. 6.   The processing of personal data resulting from paragraphs 1 to 5 must be carried out in accordance with national measures taken pursuant to Directive 95/46/EC.

Article 25. Compensation. 1.   If it is impossible to identify the vehicle or if, within two months of the date of the accident, it is impossible to identify the insurance undertaking, the injured party may apply for compensation from the compensation body in the Member State where he resides. The compensation shall be provided in accordance with the provisions of Articles 9 and 10. The compensation body shall then have a claim, on the conditions laid down in Article 24(2):

(a)   where the insurance undertaking cannot be identified: against the guarantee fund in the Member State where the vehicle is normally based;

(b)   in the case of an unidentified vehicle: against the guarantee fund in the Member State in which the accident took place;

(c)   in the case of a third-country vehicle: against the guarantee fund in the Member State in which the accident took place.

2.   This Article shall apply to accidents caused by third-country vehicles covered by Articles 7 and 8.

Article 28. National provisions.   1.   Member States may, in accordance with the Treaty, maintain or bring into force provisions which are more favourable to injured parties than the provisions needed to comply with this Directive.

2.   Member States shall communicate to the Commission the text of the main provisions of domestic law which they adopt in the field governed by this Directive.

I.   Regulation (EC) No 261/2004 of the European Parliament and of the Council of 11 February 2004 establishing common rules on compensation and assistance to passengers in the event of denied boarding and of cancellation or long delay of flights, and repealing Regulation (EEC) No 295/91 (OJ, L 46 of 17 February 2004): Recital 8, Articles 1(1), 3, 13, 15

See Chapter VI, Carriage, B.

L.   Regulation (EC) No 883/2004 of the European Parliament and of the Council of 29 April 2004 on the coordination of social security systems (OJ, L 166 of 30 April 2004): Article 85

See Chapter X, A.1.

M.   Commission Notice on the cooperation between the Commission and the courts of the EU Member States in the application of Articles 81 and 82 EC (OJ, C 101 of 27 April 2004)

I.   The scope of the notice

1.   The present notice addresses the cooperation between the Commission and the courts of the EU Member States, when the latter apply Articles 81 and 82 EC. For the purpose of this notice, the 'courts of the EU Member States' (hereinafter 'national courts') are those courts and tribunals within an EU, Member State that can apply Articles 81 and 82 EC and

that are authorised to ask a preliminary question to the Court of Justice of the European Communities pursuant to Article 234 EC.

2.   The national courts may be called upon to apply Articles 81 or 82 EC in lawsuits between private parties, such as actions relating to contracts or actions for damages. They may also act as public enforcer or as review court. A national court may indeed be designated as a competition authority of a Member State (hereinafter 'the national competition authority') pursuant to Article 35(1) of Regulation (EC) No 1/2003 (hereinafter 'the regulation'). In that case, the cooperation between the national courts and the Commission is not only covered by the present notice, but also by the notice on the cooperation within the network of competition authorities.

II.   *The application of EC competition rules by national courts*

A.   The competence of national courts to apply EC competition rules

3.   To the extent that national courts have jurisdiction to deal with a case, they have the power to apply Articles 81 and 82 EC. Moreover, it should be remembered that Articles 81 and 82 EC are a matter of public policy and are essential to the accomplishment of the tasks entrusted to the Community, and, in particular, for the functioning of the internal market. According to the Court of Justice, where, by virtue of domestic law, national courts must raise of their own motion points of law based on binding domestic rules which have not been raised by the parties, such an obligation also exists where binding Community rules, such as the EC competition rules, are concerned. The position is the same if domestic law confers on national courts a discretion to apply of their own motion binding rules of law: national courts must apply the EC competition rules, even when the party with an interest in application of those provisions has not relied on them, where domestic law allows such application by the national court. However, Community law does not require national courts to raise of their own motion an issue concerning the breach of provisions of Community law where examination of that issue would oblige them to abandon the passive role assigned to them by going beyond the ambit of the dispute defined by the parties themselves and relying on facts and circumstances other than those on which the party with an interest in application of those provisions bases his claim.

4.   Depending on the functions attributed to them under national law, national courts may be called upon to apply Articles 81 and 82 EC in administrative, civil or criminal proceedings. In particular, where a natural or legal person asks the national court to safeguard his individual rights, national courts play a specific role in the enforcement of Articles 81 and 82 EC, which is different from the enforcement in the public interest by the Commission or by national competition authorities. Indeed, national courts can give effect to Articles 81 and 82 EC by finding contracts to be void or by awards of damages.

5.   National courts can apply Articles 81 and 82 EC, without it being necessary to apply national competition law in parallel. However, where a national court applies national competition law to agreements, decisions by associations of undertakings or concerted practices which may affect trade between Member States within the meaning of Article 81(1) EC or to any abuse prohibited by Article 82 EC, they also have to apply EC competition rules to those agreements, decisions or practices.

6.   The regulation does not only empower the national courts to apply EC competition law. The parallel application of national competition law to agreements,

decisions of associations of undertakings and concerted practices which affect trade between Member States may not lead to a different outcome from that of EC competition law. Article 3(2) of the regulation provides that agreements, decisions or concerted practices which do not infringe Article 81(1) EC or which fulfill the conditions of Article 81(3) EC cannot be prohibited either under national competition law. On the other hand, the Court of Justice has ruled that agreements, decisions or concerted practices that violate Article 81(1) and do not fulfill the conditions of Article 81(3) EC cannot be upheld under national law. As to the parallel application of national competition law and Article 82 EC in the case of unilateral conduct, Article 3 of the regulation does not provide for a similar convergence obligation. However, in case of conflicting provisions, the general principle of primacy of Community law requires national courts to disapply any provision of national law which contravenes a Community rule, regardless of whether that national law provision was adopted before or after the Community rule.

7.   Apart from the application of Articles 81 and 82 EC, national courts are also competent to apply acts adopted by EU institutions in accordance with the EC Treaty or in accordance with the measures adopted to give the Treaty effect, to the extent that these acts have direct effect. National courts may thus have to enforce Commission decisions or regulations applying Article 81(3) EC to certain categories of agreements, decisions or concerted practices. When applying these EC competition rules, national courts act within the framework of Community law and are consequently bound to observe the general principles of Community law.

8.   The application of Articles 81 and 82 EC by national courts often depends on complex economic and legal assessments. When applying EC competition rules, national courts are bound by the case law of the Community courts as well as by Commission regulations applying Article 81(3) EC to certain categories of agreements, decisions or concerted practices. Furthermore, the application of Articles 81 and 82 EC by the Commission in a specific case binds the national courts when they apply EC competition rules in the same case in parallel with or subsequent to the Commission. Finally, and without prejudice to the ultimate interpretation of the EC Treaty by the Court of Justice, national courts may find guidance in Commission regulations and decisions which present elements of analogy with the case they are dealing with, as well as in Commission notices and guidelines relating to the application of Articles 81 and 82 EC and in the annual report on competition policy.

B.   Procedural aspects of the application of EC competition rules by national courts

9.   The procedural conditions for the enforcement of EC competition rules by national courts and the sanctions they can impose in case of an infringement of those rules, are largely covered by national law. However, to some extent, Community law also determines the conditions in which EC competition rules are enforced. Those Community law provisions may provide for the faculty of national courts to avail themselves of certain instruments, e.g. to ask for the Commission's opinion on questions concerning the application of EC competition rules or they may create rules that have an obligatory impact on proceedings before them, e.g. allowing the Commission and national competition authorities to submit written observations. These Community law provisions prevail over national rules. Therefore, national courts have to set aside national rules which, if applied, would conflict with these Community law provisions. Where such Community

law provisions are directly applicable, they are a direct source of rights and duties for all those affected, and must be fully and uniformly applied in all the Member States from the date of their entry into force.

10. In the absence of Community law provisions on procedures and sanctions related to the enforcement of EC competition rules by national courts, the latter apply national procedural law and – to the extent that they are competent to do so — impose sanctions provided for under national law. However, the application of these national provisions must be compatible with the general principles of Community law. In this regard, it is useful to recall the case law of the Court of Justice, according to which:

(a) where there is an infringement of Community law, national law must provide for sanctions which are effective, proportionate and dissuasive;

(b) where the infringement of Community law causes harm to an individual, the latter should under certain conditions be able to ask the national court for damages;

(c) the rules on procedures and sanctions which national courts apply to enforce Community law

— must not make such enforcement excessively difficult or practically impossible (the principle of effectiveness) and they

— must not be less favourable than the rules applicable to the enforcement of equivalent national law (the principle of equivalence).

On the basis of the principle of primacy of Community law, a national court may not apply national rules that are incompatible with these principles.

N. Written question E-2647/02 of 20 September 2002 to the Commission and Commission's answer of 11 October 2002. Uniform application of standards (OJ, C 28 E of 6 February 2003)

Subject: Uniform application of standards

Is the Commission aware that machinery certified in one Member State (e.g. Italy) as being in conformity with CEN standard, and purchased on that basis by a company in another Member State (e.g. the UK), sometimes fails inspections by the authorities in the Member State of purchase, who have a different interpretation of CEN rules?

Does the Commission realise that, in such circumstances, the company in question has no recourse against the manufacturer, as the latter points out that he has due certification that CEN standards have been met?

Has the Commission conducted any studies as to the uniform application of standards across the EU and the problems that arise from different interpretations by various national authorities thereof?

Does the Commission have any suggestions as to what a company should do if it is victim of such a situation as described above?

Answer given by Mr Liikanen on behalf of the Commission

Machinery placed on the market in the European Economic Area (EEA) must comply with the essential health and safety requirements of the Machinery Directive.[1] Application of the technical specifications of harmonised European standards remains voluntary. However, machinery manufactured according to these specifications is, as a rule, presumed to comply with the requirements of the Directive covered by the standards.

The Commission is particularly concerned to develop consistent application of the essential requirements. Within the Working Group of the Machinery Directive, Member States and the Commission seek to reach common interpretation. A group has also been set up to develop administrative cooperation between national authorities in matters of market surveillance. For machinery subject to type-examination before being placed on the market, the Notified Bodies concerned meet regularly to coordinate their activity and formulate common answers to questions of interpretation of the Directive and of harmonised standards.

Member States have the duty to ensure that machinery placed on the market does not endanger the health or safety of persons and, to this end, they carry out appropriate surveillance of machinery placed on the market. It may occur that, despite application of a harmonised European standard, the market surveillance authorities of a Member State find that a given model of machinery is not in compliance with the requirements of the Directive and is liable to endanger the health and safety of persons.

In practice, the matter is often raised with the manufacturer concerned and measures to bring the machinery into conformity are agreed between the manufacturer and the national authorities. This should enable a company which has purchased items of such machinery to have it brought into conformity by the manufacturer.

If such a case reveals a shortcoming in a harmonised standard, this should be drawn to the attention of the relevant national and European standardisation bodies. If necessary, the national authorities shall bring the matter before the Technical Standards and Regulations Committee,[2] following the procedure laid down in Article 6(1) of the Machinery Directive. The Commission will then decide whether to withdraw the references of the standard concerned from the Official Journal and mandate the standardisation organisation to amend the standard as necessary.

When they ascertain that a machine is liable to endanger the health or safety of persons and a voluntary solution is not found, the national authorities can decide to order withdrawal of the unsafe machinery from the market, following the safeguard procedure laid down in Article 7 of the Machinery Directive. The Member State must inform the Commission of any such measure, indicating whether the nonconformity results from failure to satisfy the essential health and safety requirements, from incorrect application of a harmonised standard or from shortcomings in the standard itself.

After consulting interested parties, the Commission decides whether the measure taken by the national authorities is justified. If a harmonised standard proves deficient,

---

[1]   [Footnotes are published in the original numerical order as in OJ] Directive 98/37/EC of the Parliament and of the Council of 22 June 1998 on the approximation of the laws of the Member States relating to machinery, OJ, L 207 of 23 July 1998.

[2]   Set up under Arts 5 and 6 of Directive 98/34/EC of the Parliament and of the Council of 22 June 1998 laying down a procedure for the provision of information in the field of technical standards and regulations, OJ, L 204 of 21 July 1998.

the references of the standard are withdrawn from the Official Journal and a mandate is given to the relevant European standardisation body to amend the standard as necessary.

The possibility of redress open to a company that has purchased machinery subject to such a safeguard measure depends on the legal provisions in force in the Member State concerned.

O.   Protocol of 2003 to the International Convention on the Establishment of an International Fund for Compensation for Oil Pollution Damage, 1992 (OJ, L 78 of 16 March 2004): Article 9

See Chapter IV, Environmental damages, D.2.

P.   Regulation (EC) No 662/2009 of the European Parliament and of the Council of 13 July 2009 establishing a procedure for the negotiation and conclusion of agreements between Member States and third countries on particular matters concerning the law applicable to contractual and non-contractual obligations (OJ, L 200 of 31 July 2009)

See Chapter I, The external dimension, K.

Q.   ECJ case-law on the law applicable to non-contractual obligations

In the *Kordel* case (21 September 1999, case C-397/96, Reports, I-5959) the ECJ addressed the issue of the law applicable to non-contractual liability and the subrogation of an institution responsible for benefit to the right enjoyed by the victim, considering Article 93(1)(a) of Regulation (EEC) No 1408/71 of 14 June 1971 on the application of social security schemes to employed persons, to self-employed persons and to members of their families moving within the Community, as amended and updated by Regulation (EEC) No 2001/83 of 2 June 1983. This Article provides: 'If a person receives benefits under the legislation of one Member State in respect of an injury resulting from an occurrence in the territory of another State. Any rights of the institution responsible for benefits against a third party bound to compensate for the injury shall be governed by the following rules: a) where the institution responsible for benefit is, by virtue of the legislation which it administers, subrogated to the rights which the recipient has against the third party, such subrogation shall be recognised by each Member State'. This question was raised in a proceedings between a social security institution and two German citizens and a German insurance company, concerning the recovery of sums paid by the security institution on the death of one of its insured in an accident occurred in Germany. The Court ruled that the legislation of the Member State to which the institution belongs, providing for the subrogation, had to be applied according to the following grounds:

13.   By these questions, which it is appropriate to examine together, the national court is essentially asking the Court to interpret Article 93(1)(a) of the Regulation so that it may ascertain whether, and to what extent, subrogation of a social security institution within the meaning of the Regulation to the rights which an injured party, or those entitled under such a party, have against the person responsible for causing, in another Member State, an injury which gave rise to the payment by that institution of social security benefits, is to be determined in accordance with the law of the Member State to which the institution belongs, and whether the extent of the rights so subrogated is also to be determined in accordance with that law. More specifically, the national court asks whether it is necessary to apply the legislative provisions of the Member State to which the institution responsible for benefits belongs which, like Article 4 of the Grand–Ducal Regulation, would result in the exclusion or limitation of the subrogation of that institution to the beneficiary's rights or the exclusion or limitation of the assertion of those rights by that institution before the courts of the Member State where the injury occurred.

14.   In order to give an answer that may be of assistance to the national court, it is appropriate to consider in turn the rights enjoyed by the victim of the accident, or those entitled under him, the possibility of subrogation of the institution responsible for benefits to those rights and the extent of such subrogation, and lastly, any limitations which the legislation of the Member State to which the institution belongs imposes upon the exercise of rights to which that institution is subrogated.

15.   As regards, first of all, the rights of the victim, or those entitled under him, against the person who caused the injury, Article 93(1)(a) of the Regulation is intended only to ensure that any right of action which an institution responsible for benefits may enjoy by virtue of the legislation which it administers is recognised by the other Member States. That provision does not purport to alter the applicable rules for determining whether and to what extent non-contractual liability on the part of the third party who caused the injury is to be incurred. The third party's liability continues to be governed by the substantive rules which are normally to be applied by the national court before which proceedings are brought by the victim or those entitled under him, that is to say, in principle, the legislation of the Member State in whose territory the injury was sustained.

16.   It follows that the rights that the victim or those entitled under him have against the person who caused the injury and the requirements to be satisfied to enable an action in damages to be brought before the courts of the Member State where the injury was sustained must be determined in accordance with the law of that State, including any applicable rules of private international law.

17.   It is to such rights alone, thus determined, that the institution responsible for benefits can be subrogated. Subrogation such as that provided for in Article 93(1)(a) of the Regulation cannot have the effect of creating additional rights for the recipient of the benefits against third parties.

18.   Next, as regards the subrogation of the institution responsible for benefits to the rights of those entitled under the victim, the referring court states that, under German law, a social insurance institution is subrogated to the rights of such persons against a liable third party only to the extent that they were entitled to demand maintenance from the person who was killed. However, the referring court does not make it clear whether, under German law, it is only if the survivors of the victim of a fatal accident had been entitled to demand maintenance from him that they have a right of action against a

liable third party or whether, on the contrary, the rule in question applies only to the subrogation of the institution responsible for benefits.

19.   If German law makes any right of action of a victim's survivors against the liable third party subject to the existence, for their benefit, of a present or future obligation of the victim, if in life, to pay them maintenance, such a rule, which governs the very principle of the survivors' right of action, would, in accordance with the principles outlined in paragraphs 15 to 17 of this judgment, have the effect of depriving the survivors, if they had no right to maintenance, of any right to which the institution responsible for benefits could have been subrogated.

20.   Nor does the referring court make it clear whether, under German law, it is necessary for the victim to have been paying maintenance immediately before his death to those who claim a right of action, or whether it was sufficient for those persons to have been entitled, in the future, to demand the payment of maintenance. On this point, it is sufficient to point out that it is not necessarily the national law of the court before which the action is brought that determines the nature and extent of the victim's obligation towards his survivors in the matter of maintenance. The rules of private international law may designate the law of another jurisdiction as being applicable.

21.   In so far as the rule of German law mentioned by the referring court affects only the subrogation of the institution responsible for benefits to the rights of recipients of benefits, it should be recalled that Article 93(1)(a) of the Regulation provides that each Member State is to recognise the subrogation of the institution responsible for benefits to the rights which the recipient of the benefits has against the third party bound to compensate for the injury, where that institution is so subrogated under the legislation of the Member State to which it belongs.

22.   That provision is thus to be regarded as a conflict-of-laws rule which requires the national court hearing an action for compensation brought against the party liable for the injury to apply the law of the Member State to which the institution responsible belongs, not only to determine whether that institution is subrogated by law to the rights of the injured party or those entitled under him, but also to determine the nature and extent of the claims to which the institution responsible for benefits is subrogated.

23.   It follows that the institution responsible for benefits which is subrogated, and the national courts of each Member State, are bound by the legislation of the Member State to which the institution belongs, provided always that the exercise of the right to subrogation provided for by that legislation cannot exceed the rights that the victim, or those entitled under him, have against the person who caused the injury.

24.   Finally, on the question whether the rights of the Pension Fund must be determined by reference to Article 4 of the Grand–Ducal Regulation, the Pension Fund disputes that the application of that provision has any relevance to the main proceedings.

25.   In this connection, suffice it to recall that, according to settled case-law, it is not for the Court, in proceedings under Article 177 of the Treaty, to interpret national law or assess its effects.

26.   It is for the court hearing the action to identify and apply the relevant provisions of the legislation of the Member State to which the institution responsible for benefits belongs, even if those provisions exclude or limit the subrogation of such an institution to the rights of the recipient of the benefits against the person who caused the injury, or exclude or limit the exercise of those rights by the institution so subrogated.

27.   In those circumstances, the questions referred to the Court must be answered as follows:

—   on a proper construction of Article 93(1)(a) of the Regulation, where an injury has been sustained in the territory of a Member State and has given rise to the payment of social security benefits to the victim or those entitled under him by a social security institution (within the meaning of the Regulation) of another Member State, the rights of the victim, or those entitled under him, against the person who caused the injury and to which that institution may be subrogated, and the requirements which must be satisfied to enable an action in damages to be brought before the courts of the Member State where the injury was sustained, are to be determined in accordance with the law of that State, including any applicable rules of private international law;

—   on a proper construction of Article 93(1)(a) of the Regulation, the subrogation of a social security institution (within the meaning of the Regulation) governed by the law of a Member State to the rights of the victim or those entitled under him against a person who, in the territory of another Member State, caused an injury which gave rise to the payment by that institution of social security benefits, and the extent of the rights to which that institution is subrogated, are to be determined in accordance with the law of the Member State to which the institution belongs, provided always that the exercise of the right to subrogation provided for by that law cannot exceed the rights, under the law of the Member State where the injury was sustained, of the victim, or those entitled under him, against the person who caused the injury;

—   it is for the court hearing the action to identify and apply the relevant provisions of the legislation of the Member State to which the institution responsible for benefits belongs, even if those provisions exclude or limit the subrogation of such an institution to the rights of the recipient of the benefits against the person who caused the injury, or exclude or limit the exercise of those rights by the institution so subrogated.

Recently, in the *Clinique La Ramée* case (9 September 2004, case C-397/02, Reports, I-7947) the Court ruled in the same way about the European Communities' right to be subrogated to the rights of the victim, official of the Council, against a third party liable, pursuant to Article 85(a) on the European Communities' Staff Regulations (No 259/68), as follows:

15.   In that regard, it must be borne in mind that the subrogation provided for by Article 85a of the Staff Regulations is subrogation by operation of law. It takes place, within the limits of the obligations devolving upon the Communities under the provisions of the Staff Regulations, upon the occurrence of the harmful event for which a third party is liable.

16.   However, Article 85a(1) of the Staff Regulations states that the Communities stand subrogated 'to the rights, including rights of action, of the victim or of those entitled under him against the third party'. As the Advocate General observed in paragraph 26 of his Opinion, it follows clearly from that phrase that the Communities do not have greater rights against the third party than the victim or those entitled under him.

17.   In that context, it must be noted that the purpose of Article 85a of the Staff Regulations is not to alter the national rules applicable for determining whether and to what extent there is liability on the part of the third party who caused the injury. That third party's liability remains subject to the substantive rules which are normally to be applied by the national court before which the victim's proceedings are brought, that is to say, in principle, the legislation of the Member State in whose territory the injury

has occurred (see, in respect of the subrogation of social security bodies under Council Regulation (EEC) No 1408/71 of 14 June 1971 on the application of social security schemes to employed persons and their families moving within the Community, in its version amended and updated by Council Regulation (EEC) No 2001/83 of 2 June 1983 (OJ 1983 L 230, p. 6), Case C-428/92 *DAK*, *ECR*, I-2259, paragraph 21).

18. It follows that if the national law on liability applicable to this case excludes a survivor's pension, such as that provided for by Articles 79 and 79(a) of the Staff Regulations, from the scope of the compensation obligation of the perpetrator of a wrongful act, the Communities cannot obtain reimbursement of the sums corresponding to that survivor's pension by means of the subrogation under Article 85a of the Staff Regulations.

In the *Shevill* case (7 March 1995, case C-68/93, Reports, I-415, see also Chapter IV, General provisions, A.13, under Article 5(3)) the Court has considered whether the national court is required to follow specific rules different from those laid down by its national law, in relation to the criteria for assessing whether the event in question is harmful and to the evidence required of the existence and extent of the harm alleged by the victim. The question arisen was about which law applied to the assessment of the damages incurred by a United Kingdom citizen, libelled by a French newspaper article, who had brought an action for damages before the English court, having jurisdiction to award damages for harm caused by the publication of a defamatory newspaper pursuant to Article 5(3) of the Brussels Convention. The Court stated that:

37. In the area of non-contractual liability, the context in which the questions referred have arisen, the sole object of the Convention is to determine which court or courts have jurisdiction to hear the dispute by reference to the place or places where an event considered harmful occurred.

38. It does not, however, specify the circumstances in which the event giving rise to the harm may be considered to be harmful to the victim, or the evidence which the plaintiff must adduce before the court seised to enable it to rule on the merits of the case.

39. Those questions must therefore be settled solely by the national court seised, applying the substantive law determined by its national conflict of laws rules, provided that the effectiveness of the Convention is not thereby impaired.

40. The fact that under the national law applicable to the main proceedings damage is presumed in libel actions, so that the plaintiff does not have to adduce evidence of the existence and extent of that damage, does not therefore preclude the application of Article 5(3) of the Convention in determining which courts have territorial jurisdiction to hear the action for damages for harm caused by an international libel through the press.

41. The answer to the referring court must accordingly be that the criteria for assessing whether the event in question is harmful and the evidence required of the existence and extent of the harm alleged by the victim of the defamation are not governed by the Convention but by the substantive law determined by the national conflict of laws rules of the court seised, provided that the effectiveness of the Convention is not thereby impaired.

In a following case, *Manfredi* (13 July 2006, joined cases C-295/04 to C-298/04, Reports, I-6619; see also Chapter II, Public policy of EU law, F), the Court clarified which criteria apply for determining the extent of the damages. The Court was asked whether the award of the damages for harm caused by a practice prohibited under Article 81 EC would be exemplar or not. The Court so answered:

90.   As was pointed out in paragraph 60 of this judgment, the full effectiveness of Article 81 EC and, in particular, the practical effect of the prohibition laid down in Article 81(1) EC would be put at risk if it were not open to any individual to claim damages for loss caused to him by a contract or by conduct liable to restrict or distort competition.

91.   Indeed, the existence of such a right strengthens the working of the Community competition rules and discourages agreements or practices, frequently covert, which are liable to restrict or distort competition. From that point of view, actions for damages before the national courts can make a significant contribution to the maintenance of effective competition in the Community.

92.   As to the award of damages and the possibility of an award of punitive damages, in the absence of Community rules governing the matter, it is for the domestic legal system of each Member State to set the criteria for determining the extent of the damages, provided that the principles of equivalence and effectiveness are observed.

93.   In that respect, first, in accordance with the principle of equivalence, it must be possible to award particular damages, such as exemplary or punitive damages, pursuant to actions founded on the Community competition rules, if such damages may be awarded pursuant to similar actions founded on domestic law.

94.   However, it is settled case-law that Community law does not prevent national courts from taking steps to ensure that the protection of the rights guaranteed by Community law does not entail the unjust enrichment of those who enjoy them.

95.   Secondly, it follows from the principle of effectiveness and the right of any individual to seek compensation for loss caused by a contract or by conduct liable to restrict or distort competition that injured persons must be able to seek compensation not only for actual loss (*damnum emergens*) but also for loss of profit (*lucrum cessans*) plus interest.

96.   Total exclusion of loss of profit as a head of damage for which compensation may be awarded cannot be accepted in the case of a breach of Community law since, especially in the context of economic or commercial litigation, such a total exclusion of loss of profit would be such as to make reparation of damage practically impossible.

97.   As to the payment of interest, the Court pointed out in paragraph 31 of Case C-271/91 Marshall that an award made in accordance with the applicable national rules constitutes an essential component of compensation.

98.   It follows that the answer to the fourth question in Cases C-295/04 to C-297/04 and the fifth question in Case C–298/04 must be that, in the absence of Community rules governing that field, it is for the domestic legal system of each Member State to set the criteria for determining the extent of the damages for harm caused by an agreement or practice prohibited under Article 81 EC, provided that the principles of equivalence and effectiveness are observed.

99.   Therefore, first, in accordance with the principle of equivalence, if it is possible to award specific damages, such as exemplary or punitive damages, in domestic actions similar to actions founded on the Community competition rules, it must also be possible to award such damages in actions founded on Community rules. However, Community law does not prevent national courts from taking steps to ensure that the protection of the rights guaranteed by Community law does not entail the unjust enrichment of those who enjoy them.

100. Secondly, it follows from the principle of effectiveness and the right of individuals to seek compensation for loss caused by a contract or by conduct liable to restrict or distort competition that injured persons must be able to seek compensation not only for actual loss (damnum emergens) but also for loss of profit (*lucrum cessans*) plus interest.

VIII

Law Applicable to Rights *in Rem*, Securities and IP Rights

Rights on cultural goods

A. Council Regulation (EC) No 116/2009 of 18 December 2008 on the export of cultural goods (Codified version) (OJ, L 39 of 10 February 2009)

Article 1. Definition. Without prejudice to Member States' powers under Article 30 of the Treaty, the term 'cultural goods' shall refer, for the purposes of this Regulation, to the items listed in Annex I.

Article 2. Export licence. 1. The export of cultural goods outside the customs territory of the Community shall be subject to the presentation of an export licence. ...

4. Without prejudice to the provisions of paragraphs 1, 2 and 3, direct export from the customs territory of the Community of national treasures having artistic, historic or archaeological value which are not cultural goods within the meaning of this Regulation is subject to the national law of the Member State of export.

Article 3. Competent authorities.[1] 1. Member States shall furnish the Commission with a list of the authorities empowered to issue export licences for cultural goods.

2. The Commission shall publish a list of the authorities and any amendment to that list in the 'C' series of the *Official Journal of the European Union*.

Article 6. Administrative cooperation. ... In addition to the cooperation provided for under the first paragraph, Member States shall take all necessary steps to establish, in the context of their mutual relations, cooperation between the customs authorities and the competent authorities referred to in Article 4 of Directive 93/7/EEC.

---

[1] The list of the authorities set forth by Article 3 is published in OJ, C 164 of 16 July 2009. [Note of the Editor]

Annex I *

Categories of cultural objects covered by Article 1

A. 1.   Archaeological objects more than 100 years old which are the products of:
— excavations and finds on land or under water
— archaeological sites
— archaeological collections

2.   Elements forming an integral part of artistic, historical or religious monuments which have been dismembered, of an age exceeding 100 years

3.   Pictures and paintings, other than those included in categories 4 or 5, executed entirely by hand in any medium and on any material[1]

4.   Watercolours, gouaches and pastels executed entirely by hand on any material[1]

5.   Mosaics in any material executed entirely by hand, other than those falling in categories 1 or 2, and drawings in any medium executed entirely by hand on any material[1]

6.   Original engravings, prints, serigraphs and lithographs with their respective plates and original posters[1]

7.   Original sculptures or statuary and copies produced by the same process as the original,[1] other than those in category

8.   Photographs, films and negatives thereof[1]

9.   Incunabula and manuscripts, including maps and musical scores, singly or in collections[1]

10.   Books more than 100 years old, singly or in collections

11.   Printed maps more than 200 years old

12.   Archives, and any elements thereof, of any kind or any medium which are more than 50 years old

13.   (a)   Collections[2] and specimens from zoological, botanical, mineralogical or anatomical collections;

(b)   Collections[2] of historical, palaeontological, ethnographic or numismatic interest

14.   Means of transport more than 75 years old

15.   Any other antique items not included in categories A.1 to A.14

(a)   between 50 and 100 years old
toys, games
glassware articles of goldsmiths' or silversmiths' wares
furniture
optical, photographic or cinematographic apparatus
musical instruments

---

*   The two following footnotes are published in the original numerical order as in the OJ.
[1]   Which are more than 50 years old and do not belong to their originators.
[2]   As defined by the Court of Justice in its judgment in Case 252/84, as follows: 'Collectors' pieces within the meaning of heading No 97.05 of the Common Customs Tariff are articles which possess the requisite characteristics for inclusion in a collection, that is to say, articles which are relatively rare, are not normally used for their original purpose, are the subject of special transactions outside the normal trade in similar utility articles and are of high value'.

clocks and watches and parts thereof
articles of wood
pottery
tapestries
carpets
wallpaper
arms

(b)   more than 100 years old

The cultural objects in categories A.1 to A.15 are covered by this Regulation only if their value corresponds to, or exceeds, the financial thresholds under B.

B.   Financial thresholds applicable to certain categories under A (in euro)

Value:

Whatever the value
— 1   (Archaeological objects)
— 2   (Dismembered monuments)
— 9   (Incunabula and manuscripts)
— 12 (Archives)

15000
— 5   (Mosaics and drawings)
— 6   (Engravings)
— 8   (Photographs)
— 11 (Printed maps)

30000
— 4 (Watercolours, gouaches and pastels)

50000
— 7   (Statuary)
— 10 (Books)
— 13 (Collections)
— 14 (Means of transport)
— 15 (Any other object)

150000
— 3 (Pictures)

The assessment of whether or not the conditions relating to financial value are fulfilled must be made when an application for an export licence is submitted. The financial value is that of the cultural object in the Member State referred to in Article 2(2).

For the Member States which do not have the euro as their currency, the values expressed in euro in Annex I shall be converted and expressed in national currencies at the rate of exchange on 31 December 2001 published in the *Official Journal of the European Communities*.[3] This countervalue in national currencies shall be reviewed every two years with effect from 31 December 2001. Calculation of this countervalue shall be based on the average daily value of those currencies, expressed in euro, during the 24 months ending on the last day of August preceding the revision which takes effect on 31 December. This method of calculation shall be reviewed, on a proposal from the Commission, by the

---

[3]   The countervalue in national currencies of the values expressed in euro is published in OJ, C 262 of 4 November 2009. [Note of the Editor]

Advisory Committee on Cultural Goods, in principle two years after the first application. For each revision, the values expressed in euro and their countervalues in national currency shall be published periodically in the *Official Journal of the European Union* in the first days of the month of November preceding the date on which the revision takes effect.

B.   Council Directive 93/7/EEC of 15 March 1993 of 15 March 1993 on the return of cultural objects unlawfully removed from the territory of a Member State (OJ, L 74 of 27 March 1993)[1]

Whereas Article 8a of the Treaty provides for the establishment, not later than 1 January 1993, of the internal market, which is to comprise an area without internal frontiers in which the free movement of goods, persons, services and capital is ensured in accordance with the provisions of the Treaty;

Whereas, under the terms and within the limits of Article 36 of the Treaty, Member States will, after 1992, retain the right to define their national treasures and to take the necessary measures to protect them in this area without internal frontiers;

Whereas arrangements should therefore be introduced enabling Member States to secure the return to their territory of cultural objects which are classified as national treasures within the meaning of the said Article 36 and have been removed from their territory in breach of the abovementioned national measures or of Council Regulation (EEC) No 3911/92 of 9 December 1992 on the export of cultural goods; whereas the implementation of these arrangements should be as simple and efficient as possible; whereas, to facilitate cooperation with regard to return, the scope of the arrangements should be confined to items belonging to common categories of cultural object; whereas the Annex to this Directive is consequently not intended to define objects which rank as 'national treasures' within the meaning of the said Article 36, but merely categories of object which may be classified as such and may accordingly be covered by the return procedure introduced by this Directive;

Whereas cultural objects classified as national treasures and forming an integral part of public collections or inventories of ecclesiastical institutions but which do not fall within these common categories should also be covered by this Directive;

Whereas administrative cooperation should be established between Member States as regards their national treasures, in close liaison with their cooperation in the field of stolen works of art and involving in particular the recording, with Interpol and other qualified bodies issuing similar lists, of lost, stolen or illegally removed cultural objects forming part of their national treasures and their public collections;

Whereas the procedure introduced by this Directive is a first step in establishing cooperation between Member States in this field in the context of the internal market;

---

[1]   As finally modified by Directive 2001/38/EC of the European Parliament and of the Council of 5 June 2001 (OJ, L 187 of 10 July 2001). The categories listed in the Annex are similar to the ones listed in the Annex to Council Regulation (EC) No 116/2009. The list of central authorities set forth by Article 3 is published in OJ, C 94 of 23 April 2009. The countervalue in national currencies of the values expressed in euro is published in OJ, C 262 of 4 November 2009. [Note of the Editor]

whereas the aim is mutual recognition of the relevant national laws; whereas provision should therefore be made, in particular, for the Commission to be assisted by an advisory committee; ...

Article 1. For the purposes of this Directive: 1. 'Cultural object' shall mean an object which:

— is classified, before or after its unlawful removal from the territory of a Member State, among the 'national treasures possessing artistic, historic or archaeological value' under national legislation or administrative procedures within the meaning of Article 36 of the Treaty, and

— belongs to one of the categories listed in the Annex or does not belong to one of these categories but forms an integral part of;

— public collections listed in the inventories of museums, archives or libraries' conservation collection.

For the purposes of this Directive, 'public collections' shall mean collections which are the property of a Member State, local or regional authority within a Member States or an institution situated in the territory of a Member State and defined as public in accordance with the legislation of that Member State, such institution being the property of, or significantly financed by, that Member State or a local or regional authority:

— the inventories of ecclesiastical institutions.

2. 'Unlawfully removed from the territory of a Member State' shall mean:

— removed from the territory of a Member State in breach of its rules on the protection of national treasures or in breach of Regulation (EEC) No 3911/92, or

— not returned at the end of a period of lawful temporary removal or any breach of another condition governing such temporary removal.

3. 'Requesting Member State' shall mean the Member State from whose territory the cultural object has been unlawfully removed.

4. 'Requested Member State' shall mean the Member State in whose territory a cultural object unlawfully removed from the territory of another Member State is located.

5. 'Return' shall mean the physical return of the cultural object to the territory of the requesting Member State.

6. 'Possessor' shall mean the person physically holding the cultural object on his own account.

7. 'Holder' shall mean the person physically holding the cultural object for third parties.

Article 2. Cultural objects which have been unlawfully removed from the territory of a Member State shall be returned in accordance with the procedure and in the circumstances provided for in this Directive.

Article 3. Each Member State shall appoint one or more central authorities to carry out the tasks provided for in this Directive. ...

Article 4. Member States' central authorities shall cooperate and promote consultation between the Member States' competent national authorities. ...

Article 5.   The requesting Member State may initiate, before the competent court in the requested Member State, proceedings against the possessor or, failing him, the holder, with the aim of securing the return of a cultural object which has been unlawfully removed from its territory.

Proceedings may be brought only where the document initiating them is accompanied by:

— a document describing the object covered by the request and stating that it is a cultural object,

— a declaration by the competent authorities of the requesting Member State that the cultural object has been unlawfully removed from its territory.

Article 7.   1.   Member States shall lay down in their legislation that the return proceedings provided for in this Directive may not be brought more than one year after the requesting Member State became aware of the location of the cultural object and of the identity of its possessor or holder.

Such proceedings may, at all events, not be brought more than 30 years after the object was unlawfully removed from the territory of the requesting Member State. However, in the case of objects forming part of public collections, referred to in Article 1(1), and ecclesiastical goods in the Member States where they are subject to special protection arrangements under national law, return proceedings shall be subject to a time-limit of 75 years, except in Member States where proceedings are not subject to a time-limit or in the case of bilateral agreements between Member States laying down a period exceeding 75 years.

2.   Return proceedings may not be brought if removal from the national territory of the requesting Member State is no longer unlawful at the time when they are to be initiated.

Article 8.   Save as otherwise provided in Articles 7 and 13, the competent court shall order the return of the cultural object in question where it is found to be a cultural object within the meaning of Article 1(1) and to have been removed unlawfully from national territory.

Article 9.   Where return of the object is ordered, the competent court in the requested States shall award the possessor such compensation as it deems fair according to the circumstances of the case, provided that it is satisfied that the possessor exercised due care and attention in acquiring the object.

The burden of proof shall be governed by the legislation of the requested Member State.

In the case of a donation or succession, the possessor shall not be in a more favourable position than the person from whom he acquired the object by that means.

The requesting Member State shall pay such compensation upon return of the object.

Article 12.   Ownership of the cultural object after return shall be governed by that law of the requesting Member State.

Article 13.   This Directive shall apply only to cultural objects unlawfully removed from the territory of a Member State on or after 1 January 1993.

Article 14.   1.   Each Member State may extend its obligation to return cultural objects to cover categories of objects other than those listed in the Annex.
2.   Each Member State may apply the arrangements provided for by this Directive to requests for the return of cultural objects unlawfully removed from the territory of other Member States prior to 1 January 1993.

Article 15.   This Directive shall be without prejudice to any civil or criminal proceedings that may be brought, under the national laws of the Member States, by the requesting Member State and/or the owner of a cultural object that has been stolen.

Rights on financial instruments

A.   Council Regulation (EC) No 1346/2000 of 29 May 2000 on insolvency proceedings (OJ, L 160 of 30 June 2000): Recital 25, Articles 5, 9

See Chapter V, A.1.

B.   Directive 98/26/EC of the European Parliament and of the Council of 19 May 1998 on settlement finality in payment and securities settlement systems (OJ, L 166 of 11 June 1998): Recital 18, Articles 1–2, 8–9

See Chapter V, I.

C.1.   Directive 2002/47/EC of the European Parliament and of the Council of 6 June 2002 on financial collateral arrangements (OJ, L 168 of 27 June 2002)[1]

(1)   Directive 98/26/EC of the European Parliament and of the Council of 19 May 1998 on settlement finality in payment and securities settlement systems constituted a milestone in establishing a sound legal framework for payment and securities settlement systems. Implementation of that Directive has demonstrated the importance of limiting systemic risk inherent in such systems stemming from the different influence of several

---

[1]   As modified by Directive 2009/44/EC of the European Parliament and of the Council of 6 May 2009 (OJ, L 146 of 10 June 2009). [Note of the Editor]

jurisdictions, and the benefits of common rules in relation to collateral constituted to such systems.

(2)   In its communication of 11 May 1999 to the European Parliament and to the Council on financial services: implementing the framework for financial markets: action plan, the Commission undertook, after consultation with market experts and national authorities, to work on further proposals for legislative action on collateral urging further progress in the field of collateral, beyond Directive 98/26/EC.

(3)   A Community regime should be created for the provision of securities and cash as collateral under both security interest and title transfer structures including repurchase agreements (repos). This will contribute to the integration and cost-efficiency of the financial market as well as to the stability of the financial system in the Community, thereby supporting the freedom to provide services and the free movement of capital in the single market in financial services. This Directive focuses on bilateral financial collateral arrangements.

(4)   This Directive is adopted in a European legal context which consists in particular of the said Directive 98/26/EC as well as Directive 2001/24/EC of the European Parliament and of the Council of 4 April 2001 on the reorganisation and winding up of credit institutions, Directive 2001/17/EC of the European Parliament and of the Council of 19 March 2001 on the reorganisation and winding-up of insurance undertakings and Council Regulation (EC) No 1346/2000 of 29 May 2000 on insolvency proceedings. This Directive is in line with the general pattern of these previous legal acts and is not opposed to it. Indeed, this Directive complements these existing legal acts by dealing with further issues and going beyond them in connection with particular matters already dealt with by these legal acts.

(5)   In order to improve the legal certainty of financial collateral arrangements, Member States should ensure that certain provisions of insolvency law do not apply to such arrangements, in particular, those that would inhibit the effective realisation of financial collateral or cast doubt on the validity of current techniques such as bilateral close-out netting, the provision of additional collateral in the form of top-up collateral and substitution of collateral.

(6)   This Directive does not address rights which any person may have in respect of assets provided as financial collateral, and which arise otherwise than under the terms of the financial collateral arrangement and otherwise than on the basis of any legal provision or rule of law arising by reason of the commencement or continuation of winding-up proceedings or reorganisation measures, such as restitution arising from mistake, error or lack of capacity.

(7)   The principle in Directive 98/26/EC, whereby the law applicable to book entry securities provided as collateral is the law of the jurisdiction where the relevant register, account or centralised deposit system is located, should be extended in order to create legal certainty regarding the use of such securities held in a crossborder context and used as financial collateral under the scope of this Directive.

(8)   The *lex rei sitae* rule, according to which the applicable law for determining whether a financial collateral arrangement is properly perfected and therefore good against third parties is the law of the country where the financial collateral is located, is currently recognised by all Member States. Without affecting the application of this Directive to directly-held securities, the location of book entry securities provided as financial collateral and held through one or more intermediaries should be determined.

If the collateral taker has a valid and effective collateral arrangement according to the governing law of the country in which the relevant account is maintained, then the validity against any competing title or interest and the enforceability of the collateral should be governed solely by the law of that country, thus preventing legal uncertainty as a result of other unforeseen legislation.

(9)   In order to limit the administrative burdens for parties using financial collateral under the scope of this Directive, the only perfection requirement regarding parties which national law may impose in respect of financial collateral should be that the financial collateral is under the control of the collateral taker or of a person acting on the collateral taker's behalf while not excluding collateral techniques where the collateral provider is allowed to substitute collateral or to withdraw excess collateral. This Directive should not prohibit Member States from requiring that a credit claim be delivered by means of inclusion in a list of claims.

Article 1. Subject matter and scope.   1.   This Directive lays down a Community regime applicable to financial collateral arrangements which satisfy the requirements set out in paragraphs 2 and 5 and to financial collateral in accordance with the conditions set out in paragraphs 4 and 5.

2.   The collateral taker and the collateral provider must each belong to one of the following categories:

(a)   a public authority (excluding publicly guaranteed undertakings unless they fall under points (b) to (e)) including:

(i)   public sector bodies of Member States charged with or intervening in the management of public debt, and

(ii)   public sector bodies of Member States authorised to hold accounts for customers;

(b)   a central bank, the European Central Bank, the Bank for International Settlements, a multilateral development bank as referred to in Annex VI, Part 1, Section 4 of Directive 2006/48/EC of the European Parliament and of the Council of 14 June 2006 relating to the taking up and pursuit of the business of credit institutions (recast), the International Monetary Fund and the European Investment Bank;

(c)   a financial institution subject to prudential supervision including:

(i)   a credit institution as defined in Article 4(1) of Directive 2006/48/EC, including the institutions listed in Article 2 of that Directive;

(ii)   an investment firm as defined in Article 4(1)(1) of Directive 2004/39/EC of the European Parliament and of the Council of 21 April 2004 on markets in financial instruments;

(iii)   a financial institution as defined in Article 4(5) of Directive 2006/48/EC;

(iv)   an insurance undertaking as defined in Article 1(a) of Council Directive 92/49/EEC of 18 June 1992 on the coordination of laws, regulations and administrative provisions relating to direct insurance other than life insurance (third non-life insurance Directive) and an assurance undertaking as defined in Article 1(1)(a) of Directive 2002/83/EC of the European Parliament and of the Council of 5 November 2002 concerning life assurance;

(v)   an undertaking for collective investment in transferable securities (UCITS) as defined in Article 1(2) of Council Directive 85/611/EEC of 20 December 1985 on the coordination of laws, regulations and administrative provisions relating to undertakings for collective investment in transferable securities (UCITS);

(vi)   a management company as defined in Article 1a(2) of Directive 85/611/EEC;

(d)   a central counterparty, settlement agent or clearing house, as defined respectively in Article 2(c), (d) and (e) of Directive 98/26/EC, including similar institutions regulated under national law acting in the futures, options and derivatives markets to the extent not covered by that Directive, and a person, other than a natural person, who acts in a trust or representative capacity on behalf of any one or more persons that includes any bondholders or holders of other forms of securitised debt or any institution as defined in points (a) to (d);

(e)   a person other than a natural person, including unincorporated firms and partnerships, provided that the other party is an institution as defined in points (a) to (d).

3.   Member States may exclude from the scope of this Directive financial collateral arrangements where one of the parties is a person mentioned in paragraph 2(e).

If they make use of this option Member States shall inform the Commission which shall inform the other Member States thereof.

4.   (a)   The financial collateral to be provided shall consist of cash, financial instruments or credit claims;

(b)   Member States may exclude from the scope of this Directive financial collateral consisting of the collateral provider's own shares, shares in affiliated undertakings within the meaning of seventh Council Directive 83/349/EEC of 13 June 1983 on consolidated accounts, and shares in undertakings whose exclusive purpose is to own means of production that are essential for the collateral provider's business or to own real property.

(c)   Member States may exclude from the scope of this Directive credit claims where the debtor is a consumer as defined in Article 3(a) of Directive 2008/48/EC of the European Parliament and of the Council of 23 April 2008 on credit agreements for consumers or a micro or small enterprise as defined in Article 1 and Article 2(2) and (3) of the Annex to Commission Recommendation 2003/361/EC of 6 May 2003 concerning the definition of micro, small and medium-sized enterprises, save where the collateral taker or the collateral provider of such credit claims is one of the institutions referred under Article 1(2)(b) of this Directive.

5.   This Directive applies to financial collateral once it has been provided and if that provision can be evidenced in writing.

The evidencing of the provision of financial collateral must allow for the identification of the financial collateral to which it applies. For this purpose, it is sufficient to prove that the book entry securities collateral has been credited to, or forms a credit in, the relevant account and that the cash collateral has been credited to, or forms a credit in, a designated account. For credit claims, the inclusion in a list of claims submitted in writing, or in a legally equivalent manner, to the collateral taker is sufficient to identify the credit claim and to evidence the provision of the claim provided as financial collateral between the parties.

Without prejudice to the second subparagraph, Member States may provide that the inclusion in a list of claims submitted in writing, or in a legally equivalent manner, to the collateral taker is also sufficient to identify the credit claim and to evidence the provision of the claim provided as financial collateral against the debtor or third parties.

This Directive applies to financial collateral arrangements if that arrangement can be evidenced in writing or in a legally equivalent manner.

Article 2. Definitions.   1.   For the purpose of this Directive:

(a)   'financial collateral arrangement' means a title transfer financial collateral arrangement or a security financial collateral arrangement whether or not these are covered by a master agreement or general terms and conditions;

(b)   'title transfer financial collateral arrangement' means an arrangement, including repurchase agreements, under which a collateral provider transfers full ownership of, or full entitlement to, financial collateral to a collateral taker for the purpose of securing or otherwise covering the performance of relevant financial obligations;

(c)   'security financial collateral arrangement' means an arrangement under which a collateral provider provides financial collateral by way of security to or in favour of a collateral taker, and where the full or qualified ownership of, or full entitlement to, the financial collateral remains with the collateral provider when the security right is established;

(d)   'cash' means money credited to an account in any currency, or similar claims for the repayment of money, such as money market deposits;

(e)   'financial instruments' means shares in companies and other securities equivalent to shares in companies and bonds and other forms of debt instruments if these are negotiable on the capital market, and any other securities which are normally dealt in and which give the right to acquire any such shares, bonds or other securities by subscription, purchase or exchange or which give rise to a cash settlement (excluding instruments of payment), including units in collective investment undertakings, money market instruments and claims relating to or rights in or in respect of any of the foregoing;

(f)   'relevant financial obligations' means the obligations which are secured by a financial collateral arrangement and which give a right to cash settlement and/or delivery of financial instruments.

Relevant financial obligations may consist of or include:

(i)   present or future, actual or contingent or prospective obligations (including such obligations arising under a master agreement or similar arrangement);

(ii)   obligations owed to the collateral taker by a person other than the collateral provider; or

(iii)   obligations of a specified class or kind arising from time to time;

(g)   'book entry securities collateral' means financial collateral provided under a financial collateral arrangement which consists of financial instruments, title to which is evidenced by entries in a register or account maintained by or on behalf of an intermediary;

(h)   'relevant account' means in relation to book entry securities collateral which is subject to a financial collateral arrangement, the register or account — which may be maintained by the collateral taker — in which the entries are made by which that book entry securities collateral is provided to the collateral taker;

(i)   'equivalent collateral':

(i)   in relation to cash, means a payment of the same amount and in the same currency;

(ii)   in relation to financial instruments, means financial instruments of the same issuer or debtor, forming part of the same issue or class and of the same nominal amount, currency and description or, where a financial collateral arrangement provides for the transfer of other assets following the occurrence of any event relating to or affecting any financial instruments provided as financial collateral, those other assets;

(j)   'winding-up proceedings' means collective proceedings involving realisation of the assets and distribution of the proceeds among the creditors, shareholders or members as appropriate, which involve any intervention by administrative or judicial authorities, including where the collective proceedings are terminated by a composition or other analogous measure, whether or not they are founded on insolvency or are voluntary or compulsory;

(k)   'reorganisation measures' means measures which involve any intervention by administrative or judicial authorities which are intended to preserve or restore the financial situation and which affect pre-existing rights of third parties, including but not limited to measures involving a suspension of payments, suspension of enforcement measures or reduction of claims;

(l)   'enforcement event' means an event of default or any similar event as agreed between the parties on the occurrence of which, under the terms of a financial collateral arrangement or by operation of law, the collateral taker is entitled to realise or appropriate financial collateral or a close-out netting provision comes into effect;

(m)   'right of use' means the right of the collateral taker to use and dispose of financial collateral provided under a security financial collateral arrangement as the owner of it in accordance with the terms of the security financial collateral arrangement;

(n)   'close-out netting provision' means a provision of a financial collateral arrangement, or of an arrangement of which a financial collateral arrangement forms part, or, in the absence of any such provision, any statutory rule by which, on the occurrence of an enforcement event, whether through the operation of netting or set-off or otherwise:

(i)   the obligations of the parties are accelerated so as to be immediately due and expressed as an obligation to pay an amount representing their estimated current value, or are terminated and replaced by an obligation to pay such an amount; and/or

(ii)   an account is taken of what is due from each party to the other in respect of such obligations, and a net sum equal to the balance of the account is payable by the party from whom the larger amount is due to the other party;

(o)   'credit claims' means pecuniary claims arising out of an agreement whereby a credit institution, as defined in Article 4(1) of Directive 2006/48/EC, including the institutions listed in Article 2 of that Directive, grants credit in the form of a loan.

2.   References in this Directive to financial collateral being 'provided', or to the 'provision' of financial collateral, are to the financial collateral being delivered, transferred, held, registered or otherwise designated so as to be in the possession or under the control of the collateral taker or of a person acting on the collateral taker's behalf. Any right of substitution, right to withdraw excess financial collateral in favour of the collateral provider or, in the case of credit claims, right to collect the proceeds thereof until further notice, shall not prejudice the financial collateral having been provided to the collateral taker as mentioned in this Directive.

3.   References in this Directive to 'writing' include recording by electronic means and any other durable medium.

Article 3. Formal requirements.   1.   Member States shall not require that the creation, validity, perfection, enforceability or admissibility in evidence of a financial collateral arrangement or the provision of financial collateral under a financial collateral arrangement be dependent on the performance of any formal act.

Without prejudice to Article 1(5), when credit claims are provided as financial collateral, Member States shall not require that the creation, validity, perfection, priority, enforceability or admissibility in evidence of such financial collateral be dependent on the performance of any formal act such as the registration or the notification of the debtor of the credit claim provided as collateral. However, Member States may require the performance of a formal act, such as registration or notification, for purposes of perfection, priority, enforceability or admissibility in evidence against the debtor or third parties.

By 30 June 2014, the Commission shall report to the European Parliament and to the Council on whether this paragraph continues to be appropriate.

2.   Paragraph 1 is without prejudice to the application of this Directive to financial collateral only once it has been provided and if that provision can be evidenced in writing and where the financial collateral arrangement can be evidenced in writing or in a legally equivalent manner.

3.   Without prejudice to Council Directive 93/13/EEC of 5 April 1993 on unfair terms in consumer contracts and national provisions concerning unfair contract terms, Member States shall ensure that debtors of the credit claims may validly waive, in writing or in a legally equivalent manner:

(i)   their rights of set-off vis-à-vis the creditors of the credit claim and vis-à-vis persons to whom the creditor assigned, pledged or otherwise mobilised the credit claim as collateral; and

(ii)   their rights arising from banking secrecy rules that would otherwise prevent or restrict the ability of the creditor of the credit claim to provide information on the credit claim or the debtor for the purposes of using the credit claim as collateral.

Article 8. Certain insolvency provisions disapplied.   1.   Member States shall ensure that a financial collateral arrangement, as well as the provision of financial collateral under such arrangement, may not be declared invalid or void or be reversed on the sole basis that the financial collateral arrangement has come into existence, or the financial collateral has been provided:

(a)   on the day of the commencement of winding-up proceedings or reorganisation measures, but prior to the order or decree making that commencement; or

(b)   in a prescribed period prior to, and defined by reference to, the commencement of such proceedings or measures or by reference to the making of any order or decree or the taking of any other action or occurrence of any other event in the course of such proceedings or measures.

2.   Member States shall ensure that where a financial collateral arrangement or a relevant financial obligation has come into existence, or financial collateral has been provided on the day of, but after the moment of the commencement of, winding-up proceedings or reorganisation measures, it shall be legally enforceable and binding on third parties if the collateral taker can prove that he was not aware, nor should have been aware, of the commencement of such proceedings or measures.

3.   Where a financial collateral arrangement contains:

(a)   an obligation to provide financial collateral or additional financial collateral in order to take account of changes in the value of the financial collateral or in the amount of the relevant financial obligations, or

(b)   a right to withdraw financial collateral on providing, by way of substitution or exchange, financial collateral of substantially the same value,

Member States shall ensure that the provision of financial collateral, additional financial collateral or substitute or replacement financial collateral under such an obligation or right shall not be treated as invalid or reversed or declared void on the sole basis that:

(i)   such provision was made on the day of the commencement of winding-up proceedings or reorganisation measures, but prior to the order or decree making that commencement or in a prescribed period prior to, and defined by reference to, the commencement of winding-up proceedings or reorganisation measures or by reference to the making of any order or decree or the taking of any other action or occurrence of any other event in the course of such proceedings or measures; and/or

(ii)   the relevant financial obligations were incurred prior to the date of the provision of the financial collateral, additional financial collateral or substitute or replacement financial collateral.

4.   Without prejudice to paragraphs 1, 2 and 3, this Directive leaves unaffected the general rules of national insolvency law in relation to the voidance of transactions entered into during the prescribed period referred to in paragraph 1(b) and in paragraph 3(i).

Article 9. Conflict of laws.   1.   Any question with respect to any of the matters specified in paragraph 2 arising in relation to book entry securities collateral shall be governed by the law of the country in which the relevant account is maintained. The reference to the law of a country is a reference to its domestic law, disregarding any rule under which, in deciding the relevant question, reference should be made to the law of another country.

2.   The matters referred to in paragraph 1 are:

(a)   the legal nature and proprietary effects of book entry securities collateral;

(b)   the requirements for perfecting a financial collateral arrangement relating to book entry securities collateral and the provision of book entry securities collateral under such an arrangement, and more generally the completion of the steps necessary to render such an arrangement and provision effective against third parties;

(c)   whether a person's title to or interest in such book entry securities collateral is overridden by or subordinated to a competing title or interest, or a good faith acquisition has occurred;

(d)   the steps required for the realisation of book entry securities collateral following the occurrence of an enforcement event.

Article 9a. Directive 2008/48/EC.   The provisions of this Directive shall be without prejudice to Directive 2008/48/EC.

Article 10. Report by the Commission.   Not later than 27 December 2006, the Commission shall present a report to the European Parliament and the Council on the application of this Directive, in particular on the application of Article 1(3), Article 4(3) and Article 5, accompanied where appropriate by proposals for its revision.

Article 11. Implementation.   Member States shall bring into force the laws, regulations and administrative provisions necessary to comply with this Directive by 27 December 2003 at the latest. They shall forthwith inform the Commission thereof.

When Member States adopt those provisions, they shall contain a reference to this Directive or be accompanied by such reference on the occasion of their official publication. Member States shall determine how such reference is to be made.

C.2.   Statement of the Council's reasons attached to the Common Position (EC) No 32/2002 adopted by the Council on 5 March 2002 (OJ, C 119 E of 22 May 2002)

Point III.8.   The non application of certain insolvency provisions. – Article 8 (Article 9 of the Commission proposal).

Article 8 of the Common Position maintains the substance of Article 9 of the Commission proposal, but with different wording.

The aim is to protect a financial collateral arrangement, as well as the provision of financial collateral under such an arrangement, against certain automatic avoidance rules which would render an arrangement or the provision of collateral void on the sole basis that the collateral was provided on the day of, but before the commencement of, insolvency proceedings or in a prescribed period prior to such proceedings. This is set out in Article 8(1) of the Common Position.

The Common Position introduces a new rule in Article 8(2), not contained in the Commission proposal, protecting a collateral-taker who has acted in good faith on the day of, but after the opening of, insolvency procedures.

The second aim of this article is to protect the market practices of 'top up', whereby participants in the financial market use top-up financial collateral arrangements to manage and limit their credit risk to each other by mark-to-market calculations of the current market value of the credit exposure and the value of the financial collateral and accordingly ask for top-up financial collateral or return the surplus of financial collateral, and the market practice of substituting other assets of the same value for assets provided as financial collateral. Article 8(3) provides that these two practices should be protected against invalidation on the basis of the sole fact that the collateral was provided on the day of, but before the commencement of, insolvency proceedings or in a prescribed period prior to such proceedings, or on the basis of the sole fact that the relevant financial obligations were incurred prior to the provision of the top-up or substitute collateral.

However, this Article does not prejudice the possibility of questioning the financial collateral arrangement and the provision of financial collateral as part of the initial provision, top-up or substitution of financial collateral, under national law for other reasons, for example where this has been done intentionally to the detriment of the other creditors (this covers, *inter alia*, actions based on fraud or similar avoidance rules which may apply in a prescribed period).

Point III.9.   Conflict of laws. – Article 9 (Article 10 of the Commission proposal).

Article 9 of the Common Position covers the substance of Article 10 of the Commission proposal and introduces a provision regarding conflict of laws in relation to book entry securities. The Common Position does not include Article 9(2) of the Commission proposal since the question of conflict of laws is currently subject to ongoing international discussions in the Hague Conference, which is negotiating a Convention on the law applicable to certain rights in respect of securities held with an intermediary. In order not to bind the hands of Member States and the Commission in these discussions it is preferable simply to establish the place of the relevant intermediary (PRIMA) principle in the Directive, without going into further details at this stage. The Common Position thus includes amendment 17 proposed by the European Parliament.

The Council takes the view that it is, in principle, desirable that provisions with regard to the applicable law are in line with the ongoing discussions at the Hague Conference, but taking into account the importance of the Directive for the EU financial market, the Council nevertheless finds it impossible to postpone the passing of the Directive until the discussions in the Hague Conference have been completed. Therefore it must be kept in mind that, when the Conference has been finalised, Article 9 may have to be reviewed in the light of the outcome of the Convention.

The wording of Article 9(1) has been amended slightly to take account of the new structure, and the wording of Article 9(2) has been changed from that of Article 10(3) of the Commission proposal, to reflect more closely the current state of negotiations within the framework of the Hague conference.

Interests in goods and equipment

A.1.   Council Decision 2009/370/EC of 6 April 2009 on the accession of the European Community to the Convention on international interests in mobile equipment and its Protocol on matters specific to aircraft equipment, adopted jointly in Cape Town on 16 November 2001 (OJ, L 121 of 15 May 2009)

(1)   The Community is working towards the establishment of a common judicial area based on the principle of mutual recognition of judicial decisions.

(2)   The Convention on international interests in mobile equipment (hereinafter referred to as the 'Cape Town Convention') and its Protocol on matters specific to aircraft equipment (hereinafter referred to as the 'Aircraft Protocol'), adopted jointly in Cape Town on 16 November 2001, make a useful contribution to regulation at the international level in their respective areas. It is therefore desirable that the provisions of the two instruments which concern matters falling within the exclusive competence of the Community should be applied as soon as possible.

(3)   The Commission negotiated the Cape Town Convention and the Aircraft Protocol on behalf of the Community, for the parts falling within the exclusive competence of the Community.

(4)   Regional economic integration organisations which have competence over certain matters governed by the Cape Town Convention and the Aircraft Protocol may accede to the said Convention and the said Protocol after their entry into force.

(5)   Some of the matters governed by Council Regulation (EC) No 44/2001 of 22 December 2000 on jurisdiction and the recognition and enforcement of judgments in civil and commercial matters, Council Regulation (EC) No 1346/2000 of 29 May 2000 on insolvency proceedings and Regulation (EC) No 593/2008 of the European Parliament and of the Council of 17 June 2008 on the law applicable to contractual obligations (Rome I) are also dealt with in the Cape Town Convention and the Aircraft Protocol.

(6)   The Community has exclusive competence over some of the matters governed by the Cape Town Convention and the Aircraft Protocol, while the Member States have competence over other matters governed by these two instruments.

(7)   The Community should therefore accede to the Cape Town Convention and the Aircraft Protocol.

(8)   Article 48 of the Cape Town Convention and Article XXVII of the Aircraft Protocol provide that, at the time of accession, a regional economic integration organisation shall make a declaration specifying the matters governed by the said Convention and the said Protocol in respect of which competence has been transferred to that organisation by its Member States. The Community should therefore make such a declaration at the time of accession to the two instruments.

(9)   Article 55 of the Cape Town Convention provides that a Contracting State may declare that it will not apply the provisions of Article 13 or Article 43, or both, wholly or in part. At the time of accession to the said Convention, the Community should make such a declaration.

(10) Articles X, XI and XII of the Aircraft Protocol apply only where a Contracting State has made a declaration to that effect pursuant to Article XXX of the said Protocol and under the conditions specified by that declaration. At the time of accession to the Aircraft Protocol, the Community should declare that it will not apply Article XII and that it will not be making any declaration pursuant to Article XXX(2) and (3). The competence of the Member States concerning the rules of substantive law as regards insolvency will not be affected.

(11) The application of Article VIII of the Aircraft Protocol on choice of law is also subject to a declaration which may be made by any Contracting State pursuant to Article XXX(1). At the time of accession to the Aircraft Protocol, the Community should declare that it will not apply Article VIII.

(12) The United Kingdom will remain bound by the 1980 Rome Convention on the law applicable to contractual obligations until such time as it may be bound by the rules of Regulation (EC) No 593/2008. It is assumed that the United Kingdom, if it accedes to the Aircraft Protocol before such time, at the time of accession will make a declaration pursuant to Article XXX(1), which will not prejudice the application of the rules of the said Regulation.

(13) The United Kingdom and Ireland are taking part in the adoption and application of this Decision.

(14) In accordance with Articles 1 and 2 of the Protocol on the position of Denmark, annexed to the Treaty on European Union and to the Treaty establishing the European Community, Denmark does not take part in the adoption of this Decision and is not bound by it or subject to its application, …

Article 1. 1. The Convention on international interests in mobile equipment (hereinafter referred to as the 'Cape Town Convention') and the Protocol on matters specific to aircraft equipment (hereinafter referred to as the 'Aircraft Protocol'), adopted jointly in Cape Town on 16 November 2001, are hereby approved on behalf of the European Community. The texts of the Cape Town Convention and of the Aircraft Protocol are attached to this Decision.

2. In this Decision, 'Member State' shall mean all the Member States with the exception of Denmark.

Article 2. The President of the Council is hereby authorised to designate the person(s) empowered to deposit, on behalf of the Community, the instruments referred to in Article 47(4) of the Cape Town Convention and in Article XXVI(4) of the Aircraft Protocol.

Article 3. 1. At the time of accession to the Cape Town Convention, the Community shall make the declarations set out in points I of Annexes I and II.

2. At the time of accession to the Aircraft Protocol, the Community shall make the declarations set out in points II of Annexes I and II.

A.2. General declarations concerning the competence of the European Community to be made by the Community at the time of accession to the Convention on international interests in mobile equipment (Cape Town Convention) and the Protocol on matters specific to aircraft equipment (Aircraft Protocol), adopted jointly in Cape Town on 16 November 2001 (OJ, L 121 of 15 May 2009)

I. *Declaration made pursuant to Article 48(2) concerning the competence of the European Community over matters governed by the Convention on international interests in mobile equipment (Cape Town Convention) in respect of which the Member States have transferred their competence to the Community*

1. Article 48 of the Cape Town Convention provides that regional economic integration organisations which are constituted by sovereign States and which have competence over certain matters governed by that Convention may accede to it on condition that they make the declaration referred to in Article 48(2). The Community has decided to accede to the Cape Town Convention and is accordingly making that declaration.

2. The current Members of the Community are the Kingdom of Belgium, the Republic of Bulgaria, the Czech Republic, the Kingdom of Denmark, the Federal Republic of Germany, the Republic of Estonia, Ireland, the Hellenic Republic, the Kingdom of Spain, the French Republic, the Italian Republic, the Republic of Cyprus, the Republic of Latvia, the Republic of Lithuania, the Grand-Duchy of Luxembourg, the Republic of Hungary, Malta, the Kingdom of the Netherlands, the Republic of Austria, the Republic of Poland, the Portuguese Republic, Romania, the Republic of Slovenia, the Slovak Republic, the Republic of Finland, the Kingdom of Sweden and the United Kingdom of Great Britain and Northern Ireland.

3.   However, this Declaration does not apply to the Kingdom of Denmark, in accordance with Articles 1 and 2 of the Protocol on the position of Denmark, annexed to the Treaty on European Union and the Treaty establishing the European Community.

4.   This Declaration is not applicable in the case of the territories of the Member States in which the Treaty establishing the European Community does not apply and is without prejudice to such acts or positions as may be adopted under the Cape Town Convention by the Member States concerned on behalf and in the interests of those territories.

5.   The Member States of the European Community have transferred their competence to the Community as regards matters which affect Council Regulation (EC) No 44/2001 of 22 December 2000 on jurisdiction and the recognition and enforcement of judgments in civil and commercial matters, Council Regulation (EC) No 1346/2000 of 29 May 2000 on insolvency proceedings and Regulation (EC) No 593/2008 of the European Parliament and of the Council of 17 June 2008 on the law applicable to contractual obligations (Rome I).

6.   At the time of accession to the Cape Town Convention, the Community will not make any of the declarations permitted under the Articles referred to in Article 56 of the said Convention, with the exception of a declaration concerning Article 55. The Member States keep their competence concerning the rules of substantive law as regards insolvency.

7.   The exercise of the competence which the Member States have transferred to the Community pursuant to the Treaty establishing the European Community is, by its nature, liable to continuous development. In the framework of that Treaty, the competent institutions may take decisions which determine the extent of the competence of the Community. The latter therefore reserves the right to amend this Declaration accordingly, without this constituting a prerequisite for the exercise of its competence with regard to matters governed by the Cape Town Convention.

II.   *Declaration pursuant to Article XXVII(2) concerning the competence of the European Community over matters governed by the Protocol on matters specific to aircraft equipment (Aircraft Protocol), in respect of which the Member States have transferred their competence to the Community*

1.   Article XXVII of the Aircraft Protocol provides that regional economic integration organisations which are constituted by sovereign States and which have competence over certain matters governed by that Protocol may accede to it on condition that they make the declaration referred to in Article XXVII(2). The Community has decided to accede to the Aircraft Protocol and is accordingly making that declaration.

2.   The current Members of the Community are the Kingdom of Belgium, the Republic of Bulgaria, the Czech Republic, the Kingdom of Denmark, the Federal Republic of Germany, the Republic of Estonia, Ireland, the Hellenic Republic, the Kingdom of Spain, the French Republic, the Italian Republic, the Republic of Cyprus, the Republic of Latvia, the Republic of Lithuania, the Grand-Duchy of Luxembourg, the Republic of Hungary, Malta, the Kingdom of the Netherlands, the Republic of Austria, the Republic of Poland, the Portuguese Republic, Romania, the Republic of Slovenia, the Slovak Republic, the Republic of Finland, the Kingdom of Sweden and the United Kingdom of Great Britain and Northern Ireland.

3.   However, this Declaration does not apply to the Kingdom of Denmark, in accordance with Articles 1 and 2 of the Protocol on the position of Denmark, annexed to the Treaty on European Union and the Treaty establishing the European Community.

4.   This Declaration is not applicable in the case of the territories of the Member States in which the Treaty establishing the European Community does not apply and is without prejudice to such acts or positions as may be adopted under the Aircraft Protocol by the Member States concerned on behalf and in the interests of those territories.

5.   The Member States of the European Community have transferred their competence to the Community as regards matters which affect Council Regulation (EC) No 44/2001 of 22 December 2000 on jurisdiction and the recognition and enforcement of judgments in civil and commercial matters, Council Regulation (EC) No 1346/2000 of 29 May 2000 on insolvency proceedings and Regulation (EC) No 593/2008 of the European Parliament and of the Council of 17 June 2008 on the law applicable to contractual obligations (Rome I).

6.   At the time of accession to the Aircraft Protocol, the Community will not make a declaration pursuant to Article XXX(1) concerning the application of Article VIII nor will it make any of the declarations permitted under Article XXX(2) and (3). The Member States keep their competence concerning the rules of substantive law as regards insolvency.

7.   The exercise of competence which the Member States have transferred to the Community pursuant to the Treaty establishing the European Community is, by its nature, liable to continuous development. In the framework of that Treaty, the competent institutions may take decisions which determine the extent of the competence of the Community. The latter therefore reserves the right to amend this Declaration accordingly, without this constituting a prerequisite for the exercise of its competence with regard to matters governed by the Aircraft Protocol.

A.3.   Declarations to be made by the European Community at the time of accession to the Convention on international interests in mobile equipment (Cape Town Convention) and the Protocol on matters specific to aircraft equipment (Aircraft Protocol) concerning certain provisions and measures contained therein (OJ, L 121 of 15 May 2009)

I.   *Declaration by the European Community pursuant to Article 55 of the Convention on international interests in mobile equipment (Cape Town Convention)*

Pursuant to Article 55 of the Cape Town Convention, where the debtor is domiciled in the territory of a Member State of the Community, the Member States bound by Council Regulation (EC) No 44/2001 of 22 December 2000 on jurisdiction and the recognition and enforcement of judgments in civil and commercial matters will apply Articles 13 and 43 of the Cape Town Convention for interim relief only in accordance with Article 31 of Regulation (EC) No 44/2001 as interpreted by the Court of Justice of the European Communities in the context of Article 24 of the Brussels Convention of 27 September 1968 on jurisdiction and the enforcement of judgments in civil and commercial matters.

II.   *Declaration by the European Community pursuant to Article XXX of the Protocol on matters specific to aircraft equipment (Aircraft Protocol)*

In accordance with Article XXX(5) of the Aircraft Protocol, Article XXI of that Protocol will not apply within the Community and Council Regulation (EC) No 44/2001 of 22 December 2000 on jurisdiction and the recognition and enforcement of judgments in civil and commercial matters will apply to this matter for the Member States bound by the said Regulation or by any other agreement designed to extend its effects.

A.4.   Convention on international interests in mobile equipment (OJ, L 121 of 15 May 2009)

Chapter I — Sphere of application and general provisions

Article 1. Definitions.   In this Convention, except where the context otherwise requires, the following terms are employed with the meanings set out below:

(a)   'agreement' means a security agreement, a title reservation agreement or a leasing agreement;

(b)   'assignment' means a contract which, whether by way of security or otherwise, confers on the assignee associated rights with or without a transfer of the related international interest;

(c)   'associated rights' means all rights to payment or other performance by a debtor under an agreement which are secured by or associated with the object;

(d)   'commencement of the insolvency proceedings' means the time at which the insolvency proceedings are deemed to commence under the applicable insolvency law;

(e)   'conditional buyer' means a buyer under a title reservation agreement;

(f)   'conditional seller' means a seller under a title reservation agreement;

(g)   'contract of sale' means a contract for the sale of an object by a seller to a buyer which is not an agreement as defined in (a) above;

(h)   'court' means a court of law or an administrative or arbitral tribunal established by a Contracting State;

(i)   'creditor' means a chargee under a security agreement, a conditional seller under a title reservation agreement or a lessor under a leasing agreement;

(j)   'debtor' means a charger under a security agreement, a conditional buyer under a title reservation agreement, a lessee under a leasing agreement or a person whose interest in an object is burdened by a registrable non-consensual right or interest;

(k)   'insolvency administrator' means a person authorised to administer the reorganisation or liquidation, including one authorised on an interim basis, and includes a debtor in possession if permitted by the applicable insolvency law;

(l)   'insolvency proceedings' means bankruptcy, liquidation or other collective judicial or administrative proceedings, including interim proceedings, in which the assets and affairs of the debtor are subject to control or supervision by a court for the purposes of reorganisation or liquidation;

(m)   'interested persons' means:

    (i)   the debtor;

    (ii)   any person who, for the purpose of assuring performance of any of the obligations in favour of the creditor, gives or issues a suretyship or demand guarantee or a standby letter of credit or any other form of credit insurance;

    (iii) any other person having rights in or over the object;

    (n) 'internal transaction' means a transaction of a type listed in Article 2(2)(a) to (c) where the centre of the main interests of all parties to such transaction is situated, and the relevant object located (as specified in the Protocol), in the same Contracting State at the time of the conclusion of the contract and where the interest created by the transaction has been registered in a national registry in that Contracting State which has made a declaration under Article 50(1);

    (o) 'international interest' means an interest held by a creditor to which Article 2 applies:

    (p) 'International Registry' means the international registration facilities established for the purposes of this Convention or the Protocol;

    (q) 'leasing agreement' means an agreement by which one person (the lessor) grants a right to possession or control of an object (with or without an option to purchase) to another person (the lessee) in return for a rental or other payment;

    (r) 'national interest' means an interest held by a creditor in an object and created by an internal transaction covered by a declaration under Article 50(1);

    (s) 'non-consensual right or interest' means a right or interest conferred under the law of a Contracting State which has made a declaration under Article 39 to secure the performance of an obligation, including an obligation to a State, State entity or an intergovernmental or private organisation;

    (t) 'notice of a national interest' means notice registered or to be registered in the International Registry that a national interest has been created;

    (u) 'object' means an object of a category to which Article 2 applies;

    (v) 'pre-existing right or interest' means a right or interest of any kind in or over an object created or arising before the effective date of this Convention as defined by Article 60(2)(a);

    (w) 'proceeds' means money or non-money proceeds of an object arising from the total or partial loss or physical destruction of the object or its total or partial confiscation, condemnation or requisition;

    (x) 'prospective assignment' means an assignment that is intended to be made in the future, upon the occurrence of a stated event, whether or not the occurrence of the event is certain;

    (y) 'prospective international interest' means an interest that is intended to be created or provided for in an object as an international interest in the future, upon the occurrence of a stated event (which may include the debtor's acquisition of an interest in the object), whether or not the occurrence of the event is certain;

    (z) 'prospective sale' means a sale which is intended to be made in the future, upon the occurrence of a stated event, whether or not the occurrence of the event is certain;

    (aa) 'Protocol' means, in respect of any category of object and associated rights to which this Convention applies, the Protocol in respect of that category of object and associated rights;

    (bb) 'registered' means registered in the International Registry pursuant to Chapter V;

(cc) 'registered interest' means an international interest, a registrable non-consensual right or interest or a national interest specified in a notice of a national interest registered pursuant to Chapter V;

(dd) 'registrable non-consensual right or interest' means a non-consensual right or interest registrable pursuant to a declaration deposited under Article 40;

(ee) 'Registrar' means, in respect of the Protocol, the person or body designated by that Protocol or appointed under Article 17(2)(b);

(ff) 'regulations' means regulations made or approved by the Supervisory Authority pursuant to the Protocol;

(gg) 'sale' means a transfer of ownership of an object pursuant to a contract of sale;

(hh) 'secured obligation' means an obligation secured by a security interest:

(ii) 'security agreement' means an agreement by which a chargor grants or agrees to grant to a chargee an interest (including an ownership interest) in or over an object to secure the performance of any existing or future obligation of the chargor or a third person;

(jj) 'security interest' means an interest created by a security agreement;

(kk) 'Supervisory Authority' means, in respect of the Protocol, the Supervisory Authority referred to in Article 17(1);

(ll) 'title reservation agreement' means an agreement for the sale of an object on terms that ownership does not pass until fulfilment of the condition or conditions stated in the agreement;

(mm) 'unregistered interest' means a consensual interest or non-consensual right or interest (other than an interest to which Article 39 applies) which has not been registered, whether or not it is registrable under this Convention; and

(nn) 'writing' means a record of information (including information communicated by teletransmission) which is in tangible or other form and is capable of being reproduced in tangible form on a subsequent occasion and which indicates by reasonable means a person's approval of the record.

Article 2. The international interest.   1.   This Convention provides for the constitution and effects of an international interest in certain categories of mobile equipment and associated rights.

2.   For the purposes of this Convention, an international interest in mobile equipment is an interest, constituted under Article 7, in a uniquely identifiable object of a category of such objects listed in paragraph 3 and designated in the Protocol:

(a)   granted by the chargor under a security agreement;

(b)   vested in a person who is the conditional seller under a title reservation agreement; or

(c)   vested in a person who is the lessor under a leasing agreement. An interest falling within subparagraph (a) does not also fall within subparagraph (b) or (c).

3.   The categories referred to in the preceding paragraphs are:

(a)   airframes, aircraft engines and helicopters;

(b)   railway rolling stock; and

(c)   space assets.

4.   The applicable law determines whether an interest to which paragraph 2 applies falls within subparagraph (a), (b) or (c) of that paragraph.

5.   An international interest in an object extends to proceeds of that object.

Article 3. Sphere of application.   1.   This Convention applies when, at the time of the conclusion of the agreement creating or providing for the international interest, the debtor is situated in a Contracting State.

2.   The fact that the creditor is situated in a non-Contracting State does not affect the applicability of this Convention.

Article 4. Where debtor is situated.   1.   For the purposes of Article 3(1), the debtor is situated in any Contracting State:

(a)   under the law of which it is incorporated or formed;

(b)   where it has its registered office or statutory seat;

(c)   where it has its centre of administration; or

(d)   where it has its place of business.

2.   A reference in subparagraph (d) of the preceding paragraph to the debtor's place of business shall, if it has more than one place of business, mean its principal place of business or, if it has no place of business, its habitual residence.

Article 5. Interpretation and applicable law.   1.   In the interpretation of this Convention, regard is to be had to its purposes as set forth in the preamble, to its international character and to the need to promote uniformity and predictability in its application.

2.   Questions concerning matters governed by this Convention which are not expressly settled in it are to be settled in conformity with the general principles on which it is based or, in the absence of such principles, in conformity with the applicable law.

3.   References to the applicable law are to the domestic rules of the law applicable by virtue of the rules of private international law of the forum State.

4.   Where a State comprises several territorial units, each of which has its own rules of law in respect of the matter to be decided, and where there is no indication of the relevant territorial unit, the law of that State decides which is the territorial unit whose rules shall govern. In the absence of any such rule, the law of the territorial unit with which the case is most closely connected shall apply.

Article 6. Relationship between the Convention and the Protocol.   1.   This Convention and the Protocol shall be read and interpreted together as a single instrument.

2.   To the extent of any inconsistency between this Convention and the Protocol, the Protocol shall prevail.

Chapter VIII — *Effects of an international interest as against third parties*

Article 29. Priority of competing interests.   7.   This Convention:

(a)   does not affect the rights of a person in an item, other than an object, held prior to its installation on an object if under the applicable law those rights continue to exist after the installation; and

(b)   does not prevent the creation of rights in an item, other than an object, which has previously been installed on an object where under the applicable law those rights are created.

Article 30. Effects of insolvency.   1.   In insolvency proceedings against the debtor an international interest is effective if prior to the commencement of the insolvency proceedings that interest was registered in conformity with this Convention.

2.   Nothing in this Article impairs the effectiveness of an international interest in the insolvency proceedings where that interest is effective under the applicable law.

3.   Nothing in this Article affects:

(a)   any rules of law applicable in insolvency proceedings relating to the avoidance of a transaction as a preference or a transfer in fraud of creditors; or

(b)   any rules of procedure relating to the enforcement of rights to property which is under the control or supervision of the insolvency administrator.

Chapter IX — Assignments of associated rights and international interests; rights of subrogation

Article 31. Effects of assignment.   3.   Subject to paragraph 4, the applicable law shall determine the defences and rights of set-off available to the debtor against the assignee.

4.   The debtor may at any time by agreement in writing waive all or any of the defences and rights of set-off referred to in the preceding paragraph other than defences arising from fraudulent acts on the part of the assignee. ...

Article 35. Priority of competing assignments.   1.   Where there are competing assignments of associated rights and at least one of the assignments includes the related international interest and is registered, the provisions of Article 29 apply as if the references to a registered interest were references to an assignment of the associated rights and the related registered interest and as if references to a registered or unregistered interest were references to a registered or unregistered assignment.

2.   Article 30 applies to an assignment of associated rights as if the references to an international interest were references to an assignment of the associated rights and the related international interest.

Article 36. Assignee's priority with respect to associated rights.   1.   The assignee of associated rights and the related international interest whose assignment has been registered only has priority under Article 35(1) over another assignee of the associated rights:

(a)   if the contract under which the associated rights arise states that they are secured by or associated with the object; and

(b)   to the extent that the associated rights are related to an object.

2.   For the purposes of subparagraph (b) of the preceding paragraph, associated rights are related to an object only to the extent that they consist of rights to payment or performance that relate to:

(a)   a sum advanced and utilised for the purchase of the object;

(b)   a sum advanced and utilised for the purchase of another object in which the assignor held another international interest if the assignor transferred that interest to the assignee and the assignment has been registered;

(c)   the price payable for the object;

(d)   the rentals payable in respect of the object; or

(e)   other obligations arising from a transaction referred to in any of the preceding subparagraphs.

3.   In all other cases, the priority of the competing assignments of the associated rights shall be determined by the applicable law.

Article 37. Effects of assignor's insolvency.   The provisions of Article 30 apply to insolvency proceedings against the assignor as if references to the debtor were references to the assignor.

Article 38. Subrogation.   1.   Subject to paragraph 2, nothing in this Convention affects the acquisition of associated rights and the related international interest by legal or contractual subrogation under the applicable law.
   2.   The priority between any interest within the preceding paragraph and a competing interest may be varied by agreement in writing between the holders of the respective interests but an assignee of a subordinated interest is not bound by an agreement to subordinate that interest unless at the time of the assignment a subordination had been registered relating to that agreement.

Chapter XI — Application of the Convention to sales

Article 41. Sale and prospective sale.   This Convention shall apply to the sale or prospective sale of an object as provided for in the Protocol with any modifications therein.

Chapter XII — Jurisdiction

Article 42. Choice of forum.   1.   Subject to Articles 43 and 44, the courts of a Contracting State chosen by the parties to a transaction have jurisdiction in respect of any claim brought under this Convention, whether or not the chosen forum has a connection with the parties or the transaction. Such jurisdiction shall be exclusive unless otherwise agreed between the parties.
   2.   Any such agreement shall be in writing or otherwise concluded in accordance with the formal requirements of the law of the chosen forum.

Article 43. Jurisdiction under Article 13.   1.   The courts of a Contracting State chosen by the parties and the courts of the Contracting State on the territory of which the object is situated have jurisdiction to grant relief under Article 13(1)(a), (b), (c) and Article 13(4) in respect of that object.
   2.   Jurisdiction to grant relief under Article 13(1)(d) or other interim relief by virtue of Article 13(4) may be exercised either:
   (a)   by the courts chosen by the parties; or
   (b)   by the courts of a Contracting State on the territory of which the debtor is situated, being relief which, by the terms of the order granting it, is enforceable only in the territory of that Contracting State.
   3.   A court has jurisdiction under the preceding paragraphs even if the final determination of the claim referred to in Article 13(1) will or may take place in a court of another Contracting State or by arbitration.

Article 44. Jurisdiction to make orders against the Registrar.   1.   The courts of the place in which the Registrar has its centre of administration shall have exclusive jurisdiction to award damages or make orders against the Registrar.
   2.   Where a person fails to respond to a demand made under Article 25 and that person has ceased to exist or cannot be found for the purpose of enabling an order to be

made against it requiring it to procure discharge of the registration, the courts referred to in the preceding paragraph shall have exclusive jurisdiction, on the application of the debtor or intending debtor, to make an order directed to the Registrar requiring the Registrar to discharge the registration.

3. Where a person fails to comply with an order of a court having jurisdiction under this Convention or, in the case of a national interest, an order of a court of competent jurisdiction requiring that person to procure the amendment or discharge of a registration, the courts referred to in paragraph 1 may direct the Registrar to take such steps as will give effect to that order.

4. Except as otherwise provided by the preceding paragraphs, no court may make orders or give judgments or rulings against or purporting to bind the Registrar.

Article 45. Jurisdiction in respect of insolvency proceedings. The provisions of this Chapter are not applicable to insolvency proceedings.

Chapter XIII — Relationship with other Conventions

Article 45-bis. Relationship with the United Nations Convention on the assignment of receivables in international trade. This Convention shall prevail over the United Nations Convention on the assignment of receivables in international trade, opened for signature in New York on 12 December 2001, as it relates to the assignment of receivables which are associated rights related to international interests in aircraft objects, railway rolling stock and space assets.

Article 46. Relationship with the Unidroit Convention on international financial leasing. The Protocol may determine the relationship between this Convention and the Unidroit Convention on international financial leasing, signed at Ottawa on 28 May 1988.

Chapter XIV — Final provisions

Article 53. Determination of courts. A Contracting State may, at the time of ratification, acceptance, approval of, or accession to the Protocol, declare the relevant 'court' or 'courts' for the purposes of Article 1 and Chapter XII of this Convention.

Article 55. Declarations regarding relief pending final determination. A Contracting State may, at the time of ratification, acceptance, approval of, or accession to the Protocol, declare that it will not apply the provisions of Article 13 or Article 43, or both, wholly or in part. The declaration shall specify under which conditions the relevant Article will be applied, in case it will be applied partly, or otherwise which other forms of interim relief will be applied.

Article 56. Reservations and declarations. 1. No reservations may be made to this Convention but declarations authorised by Articles 39, 40, 50, 52, 53, 54, 55, 57, 58 and 60 may be made in accordance with these provisions. ...

A.5.   Protocol to the Convention on international interests in mobile equipment on matters specific to aircraft equipment (OJ, L 121 of 15 May 2009)

Chapter I — Sphere of application and general provisions

Article I. Defined terms.   1.   In this Protocol, except where the context otherwise requires, terms used in it have the meanings set out in the Convention.

2.   In this Protocol the following terms are employed with the meanings set out below:

(a)   'aircraft' means aircraft as defined for the purposes of the Chicago Convention which are either airframes with aircraft engines installed thereon or helicopters;

(b)   'aircraft engines' means aircraft engines (other than those used in military, customs or police services) powered by jet propulsion or turbine or piston technology and:

(i)   in the case of jet propulsion aircraft engines, have at least 1750 lb of thrust or its equivalent; and

(ii)   in the case of turbine-powered or piston-powered aircraft engines, have at least 550 rated take-off shaft horsepower or its equivalent, together with all modules and other installed, incorporated or attached accessories, parts and equipment and all data, manuals and records relating thereto;

(c)   'aircraft objects' means airframes, aircraft engines and helicopters;

(d)   'aircraft register' means a register maintained by a State or a common mark registering authority for the purposes of the Chicago Convention;

(e)   'airframes' means airframes (other than those used in military, customs or police services) that, when appropriate aircraft engines are installed thereon, are type certified by the competent aviation authority to transport:

(i)   at least eight (8) persons including crew; or

(ii)   goods in excess of 2750 kilograms, together with all installed, incorporated or attached accessories, parts and equipment (other than aircraft engines), and all data, manuals and records relating thereto;

(f)   'authorised party' means the party referred to in Article XIII(3);

(g)   'Chicago Convention' means the Convention on International Civil Aviation, signed at Chicago on 7 December 1944, as amended, and its Annexes;

(h)   'common mark registering authority' means the authority maintaining a register in accordance with Article 77 of the Chicago Convention as implemented by the Resolution adopted on 14 December 1967 by the Council of the International Civil Aviation Organisation on nationality and registration of aircraft operated by international operating agencies;

(i)   'de-registration of the aircraft' means deletion or removal of the registration of the aircraft from its aircraft register in accordance with the Chicago Convention;

(j)   'guarantee contract' means a contract entered into by a person as guarantor;

(k)   'guarantor' means a person who, for the purpose of assuring performance of any obligations in favour of a creditor secured by a security agreement or under an agreement, gives or issues a suretyship or demand guarantee or a standby letter of credit or any other form of credit insurance;

(l) 'helicopters' means heavier-than-air machines (other than those used in military, customs or police services) supported in flight chiefly by the reactions of the air on one or more power-driven rotors on substantially vertical axes and which are type certified by the competent aviation authority to transport:

(i) at least five (5) persons including crew; or

(ii) goods in excess of 450 kilograms, together with all installed, incorporated or attached accessories, parts and equipment (including rotors), and all data, manuals and records relating thereto;

(m) 'insolvency-related event' means:

(i) the commencement of the insolvency proceedings; or

(ii) the declared intention to suspend or actual suspension of payments by the debtor where the creditor's right to institute insolvency proceedings against the debtor or to exercise remedies under the Convention is prevented or suspended by law or State action;

(n) 'primary insolvency jurisdiction' means the Contracting State in which the centre of the debtor's main interests is situated, which for this purpose shall be deemed to be the place of the debtor's statutory seat or, if there is none, the place where the debtor is incorporated or formed, unless proved otherwise;

(o) 'registry authority' means the national authority or the common mark registering authority, maintaining an aircraft register in a Contracting State and responsible for the registration and de-registration of an aircraft in accordance with the Chicago Convention; and

(p) 'State of registry' means, in respect of an aircraft, the State on the national register of which an aircraft is entered or the State of location of the common mark registering authority maintaining the aircraft register.

Article II. Application of Convention as regards aircraft objects. 1. The Convention shall apply in relation to aircraft objects as provided by the terms of this Protocol.

2. The Convention and this Protocol shall be known as the Convention on international interests in mobile equipment as applied to aircraft objects.

Article III. Application of Convention to sales. The following provisions of the Convention apply as if references to an agreement creating or providing for an international interest were references to a contract of sale and as if references to an international interest, a prospective international interest, the debtor and the creditor were references to a sale, a prospective sale, the seller and the buyer respectively:

— Articles 3 and 4,

— Article 16(1)(a),

— Article 19(4),

— Article 20(1) (as regards registration of a contract of sale or a prospective sale),

— Article 25(2) (as regards a prospective sale), and

— Article 30.

In addition, the general provisions of Article 1, Article 5, Chapters IV to VII, Article 29 (other than Article 29(3) which is replaced by Article XIV(1) and (2)), Chapter X, Chapter XII (other than Article 43), Chapter XIII and Chapter XIV (other than Article 60) shall apply to contracts of sale and prospective sales.

Article IV. Sphere of application.   1.   Without prejudice to Article 3(1) of the Convention, the Convention shall also apply in relation to a helicopter, or to an airframe pertaining to an aircraft, registered in an aircraft register of a Contracting State which is the State of registry, and where such registration is made pursuant to an agreement for registration of the aircraft it is deemed to have been effected at the time of the agreement.

2.   For the purposes of the definition of 'internal transaction' in Article 1 of the Convention:

(a)   an airframe is located in the State of registry of the aircraft of which it is a part;

(b)   an aircraft engine is located in the State of registry of the aircraft on which it is installed or, if it is not installed on an aircraft, where it is physically located; and

(c)   a helicopter is located in its State of registry, at the time of the conclusion of the agreement creating or providing for the interest.

3.   The parties may, by agreement in writing, exclude the application of Article XI and, in their relations with each other, derogate from or vary the effect of any of the provisions of this Protocol except Article IX(2)-(4).

Article V. Formalities, effects and registration of contracts of sale.   1.   For the purposes of this Protocol, a contract of sale is one which:

(a)   is in writing;

(b)   relates to an aircraft object of which the seller has power to dispose; and

(c)   enables the aircraft object to be identified in conformity with this Protocol.

2.   A contract of sale transfers the interest of the seller in the aircraft object to the buyer according to its terms.

3.   Registration of a contract of sale remains effective indefinitely. Registration of a prospective sale remains effective unless discharged or until expiry of the period, if any, specified in the registration.

Article VI. Representative capacities.   A person may enter into an agreement or a sale, and register an international interest in, or a sale of, an aircraft object, in an agency, trust or other representative capacity. In such case, that person is entitled to assert rights and interests under the Convention.

Article VII. Description of aircraft objects.   A description of an aircraft object that contains its manufacturer's serial number, the name of the manufacturer and its model designation is necessary and sufficient to identify the object for the purposes of Article 7(c) of the Convention and Article V(1)(c) of this Protocol.

Article VIII. Choice of law.   1.   This Article applies only where a Contracting State has made a declaration pursuant to Article XXX(1).

2.   The parties to an agreement, or a contract of sale, or a related guarantee contract or subordination agreement may agree on the law which is to govern their contractual rights and obligations, wholly or in part.

3.   Unless otherwise agreed, the reference in the preceding paragraph to the law chosen by the parties is to the domestic rules of law of the designated State or, where that State comprises several territorial units, to the domestic law of the designated territorial unit.

Chapter II — Default remedies, priorities and assignments

Article XI. Remedies on insolvency.   1.   This Article applies only where a Contracting State that is the primary insolvency jurisdiction has made a declaration pursuant to Article XXX(3).

Alternative A

2.   Upon the occurrence of an insolvency-related event, the insolvency administrator or the debtor, as applicable, shall, subject to paragraph 7, give possession of the aircraft object to the creditor no later than the earlier of:

(a)   the end of the waiting period; and

(b)   the date on which the creditor would be entitled to possession of the aircraft object if this Article did not apply.

3.   For the purposes of this Article, the 'waiting period' shall be the period specified in a declaration of the Contracting State which is the primary insolvency jurisdiction.

4.   References in this Article to the 'insolvency administrator' shall be to that person in its official, not in its personal, capacity.

5.   Unless and until the creditor is given the opportunity to take possession under paragraph 2:

(a)   the insolvency administrator or the debtor, as applicable, shall preserve the aircraft object and maintain it and its value in accordance with the agreement; and

(b)   the creditor shall be entitled to apply for any other forms of interim relief available under the applicable law.

6.   Subparagraph (a) of the preceding paragraph shall not preclude the use of the aircraft object under arrangements designed to preserve the aircraft object and maintain it and its value.

7.   The insolvency administrator or the debtor, as applicable, may retain possession of the aircraft object where, by the time specified in paragraph 2, it has cured all defaults other than a default constituted by the opening of insolvency proceedings and has agreed to perform all future obligations under the agreement. A second waiting period shall not apply in respect of a default in the performance of such future obligations.

8.   With regard to the remedies in Article IX(1):

(a)   they shall be made available by the registry authority and the administrative authorities in a Contracting State, as applicable, no later than five working days after the date on which the creditor notifies such authorities that it is entitled to procure those remedies in accordance with the Convention; and

(b)   the applicable authorities shall expeditiously cooperate with and assist the creditor in the exercise of such remedies in conformity with the applicable aviation safety laws and regulations.

9.   No exercise of remedies permitted by the Convention or this Protocol may be prevented or delayed after the date specified in paragraph 2.

10.   No obligations of the debtor under the agreement may be modified without the consent of the creditor.

11.   Nothing in the preceding paragraph shall be construed to affect the authority, if any, of the insolvency administrator under the applicable law to terminate the agreement.

12.   No rights or interests, except for non-consensual rights or interests of a category covered by a declaration pursuant to Article 39(1), shall have priority in insolvency proceedings over registered interests.

13.   The Convention as modified by Article IX of this Protocol shall apply to the exercise of any remedies under this Article.

Alternative B

2.   Upon the occurrence of an insolvency-related event, the insolvency administrator or the debtor, as applicable, upon the request of the creditor, shall give notice to the creditor within the time specified in a declaration of a Contracting State pursuant to Article XXX(3) whether it will:

(a)   cure all defaults other than a default constituted by the opening of insolvency proceedings and agree to perform all future obligations, under the agreement and related transaction documents; or

(b)   give the creditor the opportunity to take possession of the aircraft object, in accordance with the applicable law.

3.   The applicable law referred to in subparagraph (b) of the preceding paragraph may permit the court to require the taking of any additional step or the provision of any additional guarantee.

4.   The creditor shall provide evidence of its claims and proof that its international interest has been registered.

5.   If the insolvency administrator or the debtor, as applicable, does not give notice in conformity with paragraph 2, or when the insolvency administrator or the debtor has declared that it will give the creditor the opportunity to take possession of the aircraft object but fails to do so, the court may permit the creditor to take possession of the aircraft object upon such terms as the court may order and may require the taking of any additional step or the provision of any additional guarantee.

6.   The aircraft object shall not be sold pending a decision by a court regarding the claim and the international interest.

Article XII. Insolvency assistance.   1.   This Article applies only where a Contracting State has made a declaration pursuant to Article XXX(1).

2.   The courts of a Contracting State in which an aircraft object is situated shall, in accordance with the law of the Contracting State, cooperate to the maximum extent possible with foreign courts and foreign insolvency administrators in carrying out the provisions of Article XI.

Article XVI. Debtor provisions.   2.   Nothing in the Convention or this Protocol affects the liability of a creditor for any breach of the agreement under the applicable law in so far as that agreement relates to an aircraft object.

Chapter IV — Jurisdiction

Article XXI. Modification of jurisdiction provisions.   For the purposes of Article 43 of the Convention and subject to Article 42 of the Convention, a court of a Contracting State also has jurisdiction where the object is a helicopter, or an airframe pertaining to an aircraft, for which that State is the State of registry.

Article XXII. Waivers of sovereign immunity. 1. Subject to paragraph 2, a waiver of sovereign immunity from jurisdiction of the courts specified in Article 42 or Article 43 of the Convention or relating to enforcement of rights and interests relating to an aircraft object under the Convention shall be binding and, if the other conditions to such jurisdiction or enforcement have been satisfied, shall be effective to confer jurisdiction and permit enforcement, as the case may be.

    2. A waiver under the preceding paragraph must be in writing and contain a description of the aircraft object.

Chapter V — Relationship with other Conventions

Article XXIII. Relationship with the Convention on the international recognition of rights in aircraft. The Convention shall, for a Contracting State that is a party to the Convention on the international recognition of rights in aircraft, signed at Geneva on 19 June 1948, supersede that Convention as it relates to aircraft, as defined in this Protocol, and to aircraft objects. However, with respect to rights or interests not covered or affected by the present Convention, the Geneva Convention shall not be superseded.

Article XXIV. Relationship with the Convention for the unification of certain rules relating to the precautionary attachment of aircraft. 1. The Convention shall, for a Contracting State that is a Party to the Convention for the unification of certain rules relating to the precautionary attachment of aircraft, signed at Rome on 29 May 1933, supersede that Convention as it relates to aircraft, as defined in this Protocol.

    2. A Contracting State Party to the above Convention may declare, at the time of ratification, acceptance, approval of, or accession to this Protocol, that it will not apply this Article.

Article XXV. Relationship with the Unidroit Convention on international financial leasing. The Convention shall supersede the Unidroit Convention on international financial leasing, signed at Ottawa on 28 May 1988, as it relates to aircraft objects.

Chapter VI — Final provisions

Article XXX. Declarations relating to certain provisions. 1. A Contracting State may, at the time of ratification, acceptance, approval of, or accession to this Protocol, declare that it will apply any one or more of Articles VIII, XII and XIII of this Protocol. …

    3. A Contracting State may, at the time of ratification, acceptance, approval of, or accession to this Protocol, declare that it will apply the entirety of Alternative A, or the entirety of Alternative B of Article XI and, if so, shall specify the types of insolvency proceeding, if any, to which it will apply Alternative A and the types of insolvency proceeding, if any, to which it will apply Alternative B. A Contracting State making a declaration pursuant to this paragraph shall specify the time-period required by Article XI.

    4. The courts of Contracting States shall apply Article XI in conformity with the declaration made by the Contracting State which is the primary insolvency jurisdiction.

    5. A Contracting State may, at the time of ratification, acceptance, approval of, or accession to this Protocol, declare that it will not apply the provisions of Article XXI,

wholly or in part. The declaration shall specify under which conditions the relevant Article will be applied, in case it will be applied partly, or otherwise which other forms of interim relief will be applied.

Article XXXI. Declarations under the Convention.   Declarations made under the Convention, including those made under Articles 39, 40, 50, 53, 54, 55, 57, 58 and 60 of the Convention, shall be deemed to have also been made under this Protocol unless stated otherwise.

Article XXXII. Reservations and declarations.   1.   No reservations may be made to this Protocol but declarations authorised by Articles XXIV, XXIX, XXX, XXXI, XXXIII and XXXIV may be made in accordance with these provisions. ...

A.6.   Council Decision 2009/940/EC of 30 November 2009 on the signing by the European Community of the Protocol to the Convention on International Interests in Mobile Equipment on Matters Specific to Railway Rolling Stock, adopted in Luxembourg on 23 February 2007 (OJ, L 331 of 16 December 2009)

(1)   The Community is working towards the establishment of a common judicial area based on the principle of mutual recognition of judicial decisions.

(2)   The Protocol to the Convention on International Interests in Mobile Equipment on Matters Specific to Railway Rolling Stock (hereinafter referred to as the 'Rail Protocol'), adopted in Luxembourg on 23 February 2007, makes a useful contribution to regulation at the international level in its area. It is therefore desirable that the provisions of this instrument which concern matters falling within the exclusive competence of the Community should be applied as soon as possible.

(3)   The Commission negotiated the Rail Protocol on behalf of the Community, for the parts falling within the exclusive competence of the Community.

(4)   Article XXII(1) of the Rail Protocol provides that Regional Economic Integration Organisations which have competence over certain matters governed by that Protocol may sign it.

(5)   The Rail Protocol remains open for signature until its entry into force.

(6)   Some of the matters governed by Council Regulation (EC) No 44/2001 of 22 December 2000 on jurisdiction and the recognition and enforcement of judgments in civil and commercial matters, Council Regulation (EC) No 1346/2000 of 29 May 2000 on insolvency proceedings, Regulation (EC) No 593/2008 of the European Parliament and of the Council of 17 June 2008 on the law applicable to contractual obligations (Rome I), Directive 2008/57/EC of the European Parliament and of the Council of 17 June 2008 on the interoperability of the rail system within the Community (Recast) and Regulation (EC) No 881/2004 of the European Parliament and of the Council of 29 April 2004 establishing a European Railway Agency (Agency Regulation) are also dealt with in the Rail Protocol.

(7) The Community has exclusive competence over some of the matters governed by the Rail Protocol, while the Member States have competence over other matters governed by this instrument.

(8) The Community should therefore sign the Rail Protocol.

(9) Article XXII(2) of the Rail Protocol provides that, at the time of signature, acceptance, approval or accession, a Regional Economic Integration Organisation shall make a declaration specifying the matters governed by that Protocol in respect of which competence has been transferred to that Organisation by its Member States. The Community should therefore make such a declaration at the time of signature of the Rail Protocol.

(10) The United Kingdom and Ireland are taking part in the adoption and application of this Decision.

(11) In accordance with Articles 1 and 2 of the Protocol on the position of Denmark, annexed to the Treaty on European Union and to the Treaty establishing the European Community, Denmark does not take part in the adoption of this Decision and is not bound by it or subject to its application, ...

Article 1. The signing of the Protocol to the Convention on International Interests in Mobile Equipment on Matters Specific to Railway Rolling Stock (the 'Rail Protocol'), adopted in Luxembourg on 23 February 2007, is hereby approved on behalf of the European Community, subject to its conclusion.

The text of the Rail Protocol is attached to this Decision.

Article 2. The President of the Council is hereby authorised to designate the person(s) empowered to sign the Rail Protocol on behalf of the Community, subject to the condition set out in Article 3.

Article 3. When signing the Rail Protocol, the Community shall make the declaration set out in the Annex, in accordance with Article XXII(2) thereof.

A.7. Declaration to be made pursuant to Article XXII(2) concerning the competence of the European Community over matters governed by the Protocol to the Convention on International Interests in Mobile Equipment on Matters Specific to Railway Rolling Stock (the 'Rail Protocol'), adopted in Luxembourg on 23 February 2007, in respect of which the Member States have transferred their competence to the Community (OJ, L 331 of 16 December 2009)

1. Article XXII of the Rail Protocol provides that Regional Economic Integration Organisations which are constituted by sovereign States and which have competence over certain matters governed by that Protocol may sign it on condition that they make the declaration referred to in Article XXII(2). The Community has decided to sign the Rail Protocol and is accordingly making that declaration.

2.   The current Members of the Community are the Kingdom of Belgium, the Republic of Bulgaria, the Czech Republic, the Kingdom of Denmark, the Federal Republic of Germany, the Republic of Estonia, Ireland, the Hellenic Republic, the Kingdom of Spain, the French Republic, the Italian Republic, the Republic of Cyprus, the Republic of Latvia, the Republic of Lithuania, the Grand-Duchy of Luxembourg, the Republic of Hungary, Malta, the Kingdom of the Netherlands, the Republic of Austria, the Republic of Poland, the Portuguese Republic, Romania, the Republic of Slovenia, the Slovak Republic, the Republic of Finland, the Kingdom of Sweden and the United Kingdom of Great Britain and Northern Ireland.

3.   However, this declaration does not apply to the Kingdom of Denmark, in accordance with Articles 1 and 2 of the Protocol on the position of Denmark, annexed to the Treaty on European Union and to the Treaty establishing the European Community.

4.   This declaration is not applicable in the case of the territories of the Member States in which the Treaty establishing the European Community does not apply and is without prejudice to such acts or positions as may be adopted under the Rail Protocol by the Member States concerned on behalf of and in the interests of those territories.

5.   The Member States of the European Community have transferred their competence to the Community as regards matters which affect Council Regulation (EC) No 44/2001 of 22 December 2000 on jurisdiction and the recognition and enforcement of judgments in civil and commercial matters, Council Regulation (EC) No 1346/2000 of 29 May 2000 on insolvency proceedings, Regulation (EC) No 593/2008 of the European Parliament and of the Council of 17 June 2008 on the law applicable to contractual obligations (Rome I), Directive 2008/57/EC of the European Parliament and of the Council of 17 June 2008 on the interoperability of the rail system within the Community (Recast) and Regulation (EC) No 881/2004 of the European Parliament and of the Council of 29 April 2004 establishing a European Railway Agency (Agency Regulation).

6.   As far as the numbering system of vehicles is concerned, the Community has adopted by way of Decision 2006/920/EC (Commission Decision of 11 August 2006 concerning the technical specification of interoperability relating to the subsystem Traffic Operation and Management of the trans-European conventional rail system) a numbering system which is appropriate for the purpose of identification of railway rolling stock as referred to in Article V(2) of the Rail Protocol.

Furthermore, as far as data exchange between Member States of the Community and the International Registry is concerned, the Community has made considerable progress by way of Decision 2007/756/EC (Commission Decision of 9 November 2007 adopting a common specification of the national vehicle register provided for under Articles 14(4) and (5) of Directives 96/48/EC and 2001/16/EC). Under that Decision Member States of the Community are implementing National Vehicle Registers and duplication of data with the International Registry should be avoided.

7.   The exercise of competence which the Member States have transferred to the Community pursuant to the Treaty establishing the European Community is, by its nature, liable to continuous development. In the framework of that Treaty, the competent institutions may take decisions which determine the extent of the competence of the Community. The latter therefore reserves the right to amend this Declaration accordingly, without this constituting a prerequisite for the exercise of its competence with regard to matters governed by the Rail Protocol.

A.8. Luxembourg Protocol to the Convention on International Interests in Mobile Equipment on Matters Specific to Railway Rolling Stock (OJ, L 331 of 16 December 2009)

Chapter I — Sphere of application and general provisions

Article I. Defined terms. 1. In this Protocol, except where the context otherwise requires, terms used in it have the meanings set out in the Convention.

2. In this Protocol the following terms are employed with the meanings set out below:

(a) 'guarantee contract' means a contract entered into by a person as guarantor;

(b) 'guarantor' means a person who, for the purpose of assuring performance of any obligations in favour of a creditor secured by a security agreement or under an agreement, gives or issues a suretyship or demand guarantee or a standby letter of credit or any other form of credit insurance;

(c) 'insolvency-related event' means:

(i) the commencement of the insolvency proceedings; or

(ii) the declared intention to suspend or actual suspension of payments by the debtor where the creditor's right to institute insolvency proceedings against the debtor or to exercise remedies under the Convention is prevented or suspended by law or State action;

(d) 'primary insolvency jurisdiction' means the Contracting State in which the centre of the debtor's main interests is situated, which for this purpose shall be deemed to be the place of the debtor's statutory seat or, if there is none, the place where the debtor is incorporated or formed, unless proved otherwise;

(e) 'railway rolling stock' means vehicles movable on a fixed railway track or directly on, above or below a guideway, together with traction systems, engines, brakes, axles, bogies, pantographs, accessories and other components, equipment and parts, in each case installed on or incorporated in the vehicles, and together with all data, manuals and records relating thereto.

Article II. Application of Convention as regards railway rolling stock. 1. The Convention shall apply in relation to railway rolling stock as provided by the terms of this Protocol.

2. The Convention and this Protocol shall be known as the Convention on International Interests in Mobile Equipment as applied to railway rolling stock.

Article III. Derogation. The parties may, by agreement in writing, exclude the application of Article IX and, in their relations with each other, derogate from or vary the effect of any of the provisions of this Protocol except Article VII(3) and (4).

Article IV. Representative capacities. A person may, in relation to railway rolling stock, enter into an agreement, effect a registration as defined by Article 16(3) of the Convention and assert rights and interests under the Convention, in an agency, trust or representative capacity.

Article V. Identification of railway rolling stock in the agreement. 1. For the purposes of Article 7(c) of the Convention and Article XVIII(2) of this Protocol, a description of railway rolling stock is sufficient to identify the railway rolling stock if it contains:

(a)   a description of the railway rolling stock by item;

(b)   a description of the railway rolling stock by type;

(c)   a statement that the agreement covers all present and future railway rolling stock; or

(d)   a statement that the agreement covers all present and future railway rolling stock except for specified items or types.

2.   For the purposes of Article 7 of the Convention, an interest in future railway rolling stock identified in accordance with the preceding paragraph shall be constituted as an international interest as soon as the chargor, conditional seller or lessor acquires the power to dispose of the railway rolling stock, without the need for any new act of transfer.

Article VI. Choice of law. 1. This Article applies only where a Contracting State has made a declaration pursuant to Article XXVII.

2.   The parties to an agreement or a related guarantee contract or subordination agreement may agree on the law which is to govern their contractual rights and obligations, wholly or in part.

3.   Unless otherwise agreed, the reference in the preceding paragraph to the law chosen by the parties is to the domestic rules of law of the designated State or, where that State comprises several territorial units, to the domestic law of the designated territorial unit.

Chapter II — Default remedies, priorities and assignments

Article VIII. Modification of provisions regarding relief pending final determination. 1. This Article applies only in a Contracting State which has made a declaration pursuant to Article XXVII and to the extent stated in such declaration.

2.   For the purposes of Article 13(1) of the Convention, 'speedy' in the context of obtaining relief means within such number of calendar days from the date of filing of the application for relief as is specified in a declaration made by the Contracting State in which the application is made.

3.   Article 13(1) of the Convention applies with the following being added immediately after subparagraph (d):

'(e) if at any time the debtor and the creditor specifically agree, sale of the object and application of proceeds therefrom',

and Article 43(2) applies with the insertion after the words 'Article 13(1)(d)' of the words 'and (e)'.

4.   Ownership or any other interest of the debtor passing on a sale under the preceding paragraph is free from any other interest over which the creditor's international interest has priority under the provisions of Article 29 of the Convention.

5.   The creditor and the debtor or any other interested person may agree in writing to exclude the application of Article 13(2) of the Convention.

6.   With regard to the remedies in Article VII(1):

(a)   they shall be made available by the administrative authorities in a Contracting State no later than seven calendar days after the creditor notifies such authorities that the relief specified in Article VII(1) is granted or, in the case of relief granted by a foreign court, recognised by a court of that Contracting State, and that the creditor is entitled to procure those remedies in accordance with the Convention; and

(b)   the applicable authorities shall expeditiously cooperate with and assist the creditor in the exercise of such remedies in conformity with the applicable safety laws and regulations.

7.   Paragraphs 2 and 6 shall not affect any applicable safety laws and regulations.

Article IX. Remedies on insolvency.   1.   This Article applies only where a Contracting State that is the primary insolvency jurisdiction has made a declaration pursuant to Article XXVII.

2.   References in this Article to the 'insolvency administrator' shall be to that person in its official, not in its personal, capacity.

Alternative A

3.   Upon the occurrence of an insolvency-related event, the insolvency administrator or the debtor, as applicable, shall, subject to paragraph 7, give possession of the railway rolling stock to the creditor no later than the earlier of:

(a)   the end of the waiting period; and

(b)   the date on which the creditor would be entitled to possession of the railway rolling stock if this Article did not apply.

4.   For the purposes of this Article, the 'waiting period' shall be the period specified in a declaration of the Contracting State which is the primary insolvency jurisdiction.

5.   Unless and until the creditor is given the opportunity to take possession under paragraph 3:

(a)   the insolvency administrator or the debtor, as applicable, shall preserve the railway rolling stock and maintain it and its value in accordance with the agreement; and

(b)   the creditor shall be entitled to apply for any other forms of interim relief available under the applicable law.

6.   Subparagraph (a) of the preceding paragraph shall not preclude the use of the railway rolling stock under arrangements designed to preserve the railway rolling stock and maintain it and its value.

7.   The insolvency administrator or the debtor, as applicable, may retain possession of the railway rolling stock where, by the time specified in paragraph 3, it has cured all defaults other than a default constituted by the opening of insolvency proceedings and has agreed to perform all future obligations under the agreement and related transaction documents. A second waiting period shall not apply in respect of a default in the performance of such future obligations.

8.   With regard to the remedies in Article VII(1):

(a)   they shall be made available by the administrative authorities in a Contracting State no later than seven calendar days after the date on which the creditor notifies such authorities that it is entitled to procure those remedies in accordance with the Convention; and

(b)   the applicable authorities shall expeditiously cooperate with and assist the creditor in the exercise of such remedies in conformity with the applicable safety laws and regulations.

9.   No exercise of remedies permitted by the Convention or this Protocol may be prevented or delayed after the date specified in paragraph 3.

10.   No obligations of the debtor under the agreement may be modified without the consent of the creditor.

11.   Nothing in the preceding paragraph shall be construed to affect the authority, if any, of the insolvency administrator under the applicable law to terminate the agreement.

12.   No rights or interests, except for non-consensual rights or interests of a category covered by a declaration pursuant to Article 39(1) of the Convention, shall have priority in insolvency proceedings over registered interests.

13.   The Convention as modified by Articles VII and XXV of this Protocol shall apply to the exercise of any remedies under this Article.

Alternative B

3.   Upon the occurrence of an insolvency-related event, the insolvency administrator or the debtor, as applicable, upon the request of the creditor, shall give notice to the creditor within the time specified in a declaration of a Contracting State pursuant to Article XXVII whether it will:

(a)   cure all defaults other than a default constituted by the opening of insolvency proceedings and agree to perform all future obligations, under the agreement and related transaction documents; or

(b)   give the creditor the opportunity to take possession of the railway rolling stock, in accordance with the applicable law.

4.   The applicable law referred to in subparagraph (b) of the preceding paragraph may permit the court to require the taking of any additional step or the provision of any additional guarantee.

5.   The creditor shall provide evidence of its claims and proof that its international interest has been registered.

6.   If the insolvency administrator or the debtor, as applicable, does not give notice in conformity with paragraph 3, or when the insolvency administrator or the debtor has declared that it will give the creditor the opportunity to take possession of the railway rolling stock but fails to do so, the court may permit the creditor to take possession of the railway rolling stock upon such terms as the court may order and may require the taking of any additional step or the provision of any additional guarantee.

7.   The railway rolling stock shall not be sold pending a decision by a court regarding the claim and the international interest.

Alternative C

3.   Upon the occurrence of an insolvency-related event, the insolvency administrator or the debtor, as applicable, shall within the cure period:

(a)   cure all defaults other than a default constituted by the opening of insolvency proceedings and agree to perform all future obligations, under the agreement and related transaction documents; or

(b)   give the creditor the opportunity to take possession of the railway rolling stock in accordance with the applicable law.

4.   Before the end of the cure period, the insolvency administrator or the debtor, as applicable, may apply to the court for an order suspending its obligation under subparagraph (b) of the preceding paragraph for a period commencing from the end of the cure period and ending no later than the expiration of the agreement or any renewal thereof, and on such terms as the court considers just (the 'suspension period'). Any such order shall require that all sums accruing to the creditor during the suspension period be paid from the insolvency estate or by the debtor as they become due and that the insolvency administrator or the debtor, as applicable, perform all other obligations arising during the suspension period.

5.   If an application is made to the court under the preceding paragraph, the creditor shall not take possession of the railway rolling stock pending an order of the court. If the application is not granted within such number of calendar days from the date of filing of the application for relief as is specified in a declaration made by the Contracting State in which the application is made, the application will be deemed withdrawn unless the creditor and the insolvency administrator or the debtor, as applicable, otherwise agree.

6.   Unless and until the creditor is given the opportunity to take possession under paragraph 3:

(a)   the insolvency administrator or the debtor, as applicable, shall preserve the railway rolling stock and maintain it and its value in accordance with the agreement; and

(b)   the creditor shall be entitled to apply for any other forms of interim relief available under the applicable law.

7.   Subparagraph (a) of the preceding paragraph shall not preclude the use of the railway rolling stock under arrangements designed to preserve and maintain it and its value.

8.   Where during the cure period or any suspension period the insolvency administrator or the debtor, as applicable, cures all defaults other than a default constituted by the opening of insolvency proceedings and agrees to perform all future obligations under the agreement and related transaction documents, the insolvency administrator or debtor may retain possession of the railway rolling stock and any order made by the court under paragraph 4 shall cease to have effect. A second cure period shall not apply in respect of a default in the performance of such future obligations.

9.   With regard to the remedies in Article VII(1):

(a)   they shall be made available by the administrative authorities in a Contracting State no later than seven calendar days after the date on which the creditor notifies such authorities that it is entitled to procure those remedies in accordance with the Convention; and

(b)   the applicable authorities shall expeditiously cooperate with and assist the creditor in the exercise of such remedies in conformity with the applicable safety laws and regulations.

10.   Subject to paragraphs 4, 5 and 8, no exercise of remedies permitted by the Convention may be prevented or delayed after the cure period.

11.   Subject to paragraphs 4, 5 and 8, no obligations of the debtor under the agreement and related transactions may be modified in insolvency proceedings without the consent of the creditor.

12.   Nothing in the preceding paragraph shall be construed to affect the authority, if any, of the insolvency administrator under the applicable law to terminate the agreement.

13.   No rights or interests, except for non-consensual rights or interests of a category covered by a declaration pursuant to Article 39(1) of the Convention, shall have priority in insolvency proceedings over registered interests.

14.   The Convention as modified by Articles VII and XXV of this Protocol shall apply to the exercise of any remedies under this Article.

15.   For the purposes of this Article, the 'cure period' shall be the period, commencing with the date of the insolvency-related event, specified in a declaration of the Contracting State which is the primary insolvency jurisdiction.

Article X. Insolvency assistance.   1.   This Article applies only in a Contracting State which has made a declaration pursuant to Article XXVII(1).

2.   The courts of a Contracting State in which railway rolling stock is situated shall, in accordance with the law of the Contracting State, cooperate to the maximum extent possible with foreign courts and foreign insolvency administrators in carrying out the provisions of Article IX.

Article XI. Debtor provisions.   1.   In the absence of a default within the meaning of Article 11 of the Convention, the debtor shall be entitled to the quiet possession and use of the railway rolling stock in accordance with the agreement as against:

(a)   its creditor and the holder of any interest from which the debtor takes free pursuant to Article 29(4)(b) of the Convention unless and to the extent that the debtor has otherwise agreed; and

(b)   the holder of any interest to which the debtor's right or interest is subject pursuant to Article 29(4)(a) of the Convention, but only to the extent, if any, that such holder has agreed.

2.   Nothing in the Convention or this Protocol affects the liability of a creditor for any breach of the agreement under the applicable law in so far as that agreement relates to railway rolling stock.

Chapter IV — Jurisdiction

Article XVIII. Waivers of sovereign immunity.   1.   Subject to paragraph 2, a waiver of sovereign immunity from jurisdiction of the courts specified in Article 42 or Article 43 of the Convention or relating to enforcement of rights and interests relating to railway rolling stock under the Convention shall be binding and, if the other conditions to such jurisdiction or enforcement have been satisfied, shall be effective to confer jurisdiction and permit enforcement, as the case may be.

2.   A waiver under the preceding paragraph must be in writing and contain a description of the railway rolling stock as specified in Article V(1) of this Protocol.

Chapter V — Relationship with other Conventions

Article XIX. Relationship with the Unidroit Convention on International Financial Leasing.   The Convention shall, to the extent of any inconsistency, prevail over the

Unidroit Convention on International Financial Le asing, signed in Ottawa on 28 May 1988.

Article XX. Relationship with the Convention concerning International Carriage by Rail (COTIF). The Convention shall, to the extent of any inconsistency, prevail over the Convention concerning International Carriage by Rail (COTIF) of 9 May 1980 in the version of the Protocol of Modification of 3 June 1999.

Chapter VI — Final provisions

Article XXVII. Declarations relating to certain provisions. 1. A Contracting State may, at the time of ratification, acceptance, approval of, or accession to this Protocol, declare that it will apply either or both of Articles VI and X.

    2. A Contracting State may, at the time of ratification, acceptance, approval of, or accession to this Protocol, declare that it will apply Article VIII, wholly or in part. If it so declares, it shall specify the time-period required by Article VIII(2).

    3. A Contracting State may, at the time of ratification, acceptance, approval of, or accession to this Protocol, declare that it will apply the entirety of one of Alternatives A, B and C of Article IX and, if it so declares, it shall specify the type of insolvency proceeding, if any, to which it will apply such Alternative. A Contracting State making a declaration pursuant to this paragraph shall specify the time-period required by Article IX under paragraph 4 of Alternative A, paragraph 3 of Alternative B or paragraphs 5 and 15 of Alternative C, as applicable.

    4. The courts of Contracting States shall apply Article IX in conformity with the declaration made by the Contracting State which is the primary insolvency jurisdiction.

Article XXVIII. Reservations and declarations. No reservations may be made to this Protocol but declarations authorised by Articles XIII, XIV, XXIV, XXV, XXVII, XXIX and XXX may be made in accordance with these provisions. ...

Article XXIX. Declarations under the Convention. 1. Declarations made under the Convention, including those made under Articles 39, 40, 50, 53, 54, 55, 57, 58 and 60, shall be deemed to have also been made under this Protocol unless stated otherwise.

    2. For the purposes of Article 50(1) of the Convention, an 'internal transaction' shall also mean, in relation to railway rolling stock, a transaction of a type listed in Article 2(2)(a) to (c) of the Convention where the relevant railway rolling stock is only capable, in its normal course of use, of being operated on a single railway system within the Contracting State concerned, because of track gauge or other elements of the design of such railway rolling stock.

IP rights

A.   Council Regulation (EC) No 2100/94 of 27 July 1994 on Community plant variety rights (OJ, L 227 of 1 September 1994)[1]

Whereas plant varieties pose specific problems as regards the industrial property regime which may be applicable;

Whereas industrial property regimes for plant varieties have not been harmonized at Community level and therefore continue to be regulated by the legislation of the Member States, the content of which is not uniform;

Whereas in such circumstances it is appropriate to create a Community regime which, although co-existing with national regimes, allows for the grant of industrial property rights valid throughout the Community;

Whereas it is appropriate that the implementation and application of this Community regime should not be carried out by the authorities of the Member States but by a Community Office with legal personality, the 'Community Plan Variety Office'; ...

Whereas this Regulation takes into account existing international conventions such as the International Convention for the Protection of New Varieties of Plants (UPOV Convention), the Convention of the Grant of European Patents (European Patent Convention) or the Agreement on trade-related aspects of intellectual property rights, including trade in counterfeit goods; whereas it consequently implements the ban on patenting plant varieties only to the extent that the European Patent Convention so requires, i.e. to plant varieties as such;

Whereas this Regulation should be re-examined for amendment as necessary in the light of future developments in the aforementioned Conventions, ...

Part One — General provisions

Article 1. Community plant variety rights.   A system of Community plant variety rights is hereby established as the sole and exclusive form of Community industrial property rights for plant varieties.

Article 2. Uniform effect of Community plant variety rights.   Community plant variety rights shall have uniform effect within the territory of the Community and may not be granted, transferred or terminated in respect of the abovementioned territory otherwise than on a uniform basis.

Article 3. National property rights for plant varieties.   This Regulation shall be without prejudice to the right of the Member States to grant national property rights for plant varieties, subject to the provisions of Article 92(1).

Article 4. Community Office.   For the purpose of the implementation of this Regulation a Community Plant Variety Office, hereinafter referred to as 'the Office', is hereby established.

---

[1]   As finally modified by Council Regulation (EC) No 15/2008 of 20 December 2007 (OJ, L 8 of 11 January 2008). [Note of the Editor]

Part Two — Substantive law

Chapter II — Persons entitled

Article 11. Entitlement to Community plant variety rights.   1.   The person who bred, or discovered and developed the variety, or his successor in title, both — the person and his successor — referred to hereinafter as 'the breeder', shall be entitled to the Community plant variety right.

2.   If two or more persons bred, or discovered and developed the variety jointly, entitlement shall be vested jointly in them or their respective successors in title. This provision shall also apply to two or more persons in cases where one or more of them discovered the variety and the other or the others developed it.

3.   Entitlement shall also be invested jointly in the breeder and any other person or persons, if the breeder and the other person or persons have agreed to joint entitlement by written declaration.

4.   If the breeder is an employee, the entitlement to the Community plant variety right shall be determined in accordance with the national law applicable to the employment relationship in the context of which the variety was bred, or discovered and developed.

5.   Where entitlement to a Community plant variety right is vested jointly in two or more persons pursuant to paragraphs 2 to 4, one or more of them may empower the others by written declaration to such effect to claim entitlement thereto.

Article 12. Entitlement to file an application for a Community plant variety right.   An application for a Community plant variety right may be filed by any natural or legal person, or any body ranking as a legal person under the law applicable to that body.
An application may be filed jointly by two or more such persons.

Chapter V — Community plant variety rights as object of property

Article 22. Assimilation with national laws.   1.   Save where otherwise provided in Articles 23 to 29, a Community plant variety right as an object of property shall be regarded in all respects, and for the entire territory of the Community, as a corresponding property right in the Member State in which:

(a)   according to the entry in the Register of Community Plant Variety Rights, the holder was domiciled or had his seat or an establishment on the relevant date; or

(b)   if the conditions laid down in subparagraph a are not fulfilled, the first-mentioned procedural representative of the holder, as indicated in the said Register, was domiciled or had his seat or an establishment on the date of registration.

2.   Where the conditions laid down in paragraph 1 are not fulfilled, the Member State referred to in paragraph 1 shall be the Member State in which the seat of the Office is located.

3.   Where domiciles, seats or establishments in two or more Member States are entered in respect of the holder or the procedural representatives in the Register referred to in paragraph 1, the first-mentioned domicile or seat shall apply for the purposes of paragraph 1.

4.   Where two or more persons are entered in the Register referred to in paragraph 1 as joint holders, the relevant holder for the purposes of applying paragraph 1(a) shall be the first joint holder taken in order of entry in the Register who fulfils the conditions. Where none of the joint holders fulfils the conditions laid down in paragraph 1(a), paragraph 2 shall be applicable.

Article 23. Transfer.   1.   A Community plant variety right may be the object of a transfer to one or more successors in title.

2.   Transfer of a Community plant variety right by assignment can be made only to successors who comply with the conditions laid down in Article 12 and 82. It shall be made in writing and shall require the signature of the parties to the contract, except when it is a result of a judgement or of any other acts terminating court proceedings. Otherwise it shall be void.

3.   Save as otherwise provided in Article 100, a transfer shall have no bearing on the rights acquired by third parties before the date of transfer.

4.   A transfer shall not take effect for the Office and may not be cited *vis-à-vis* third parties unless documentary evidence thereof as provided for in the implementing rules is provided and until it has been entered in the Register of Community Plant Variety Rights. A transfer that has not yet been entered in the Register may, however, be cited *vis-à-vis* third parties who have acquired rights after the date of transfer but who knew of the transfer at the date on which they acquired those rights.

Article 24. Levy of execution.   A Community plant variety right may be levied in execution and be the subject of provisional, including protective, measures within the meaning of Article 24 of the Convention on Jurisdiction and the Enforcement of Judgments in Civil and Commercial Matters, signed in Lugano on 16 September 1988, hereinafter referred to as the 'Lugano Convention'.[2]

Article 25. Bankruptcy or like proceedings.   Until such time as common rules for the Member States in this field enter into force, the only Member State in which a Community plant variety right may be involved in bankruptcy or like proceedings shall be that in which such proceedings are first brought within the meaning of national law or of conventions applicable in this field.

Article 26. The application for a Community plant variety right as an object of property.   Articles 22 to 25 shall apply to applications for Community plant variety rights. Concerning such applications, the references made in those Articles to the Register of Community Plant Variety Rights shall be regarded as references to the Register of Application for Community Plant Variety Rights.

---

[2] The provisions of the Lugano Convention which are different from the corresponding provisions of Council Regulation (EC) No 44/2001 are published in Chapter IV, General provisions, A.1. [Note of the Editor]

Part Three — The Community plant variety Office

Chapter I — General provisions

Article 33. Liability.   1.   The contractual liability of the Office shall be governed by the law applicable to the contract in question.

2.   The Court of Justice of the European Communities shall have jurisdiction to give judgment pursuant to any arbitration clause contained in a contract concluded by the Office.

3.   In the case of non-contractual liability, the Office shall, in accordance with the general principles common to the laws of the Member States, make good any damage caused by its departments or by its servants in the performance of their duties.

4.   The Court of Justice shall have jurisdiction in disputes relating to compensation for the damage referred to in paragraph 3.

5.   The personal liability of its servants towards the Office shall be governed by the provisions laid down in the Staff Regulations or Conditions of Employment applicable to them.

Part Four — Proceedings before the Office

Chapter V — Appeals

Article 67. Decisions subject to appeal.   1.   An appeal shall lie from decisions of the Office which have been taken pursuant to Articles 20, 21, 59, 61, 62, 63 and 66, as well as on decisions related to fees pursuant to Article 83, to costs pursuant to Article 85, to the entering or deletion of information in the Register pursuant to Article 87 and to the public inspection pursuant to Article 88.

2.   An appeal lodged pursuant to paragraph 1 shall have suspensory effect. The Office may, however, if it considers that circumstances so require, order that the contested decision not be suspended.

3.   An appeal may lie from decisions of the Office pursuant to Articles 29 and 100(2), unless a direct action is brought pursuant to Article 74. The appeal shall not have suspensory effect.

4.   An appeal against a decision which does not terminate proceedings as regards one of the parties may only be made in conjunction with an appeal against the final decision, unless the decision provides for separate appeal.

Article 72. Decision on appeal.   The Board of Appeal shall decide on the appeal on the basis of the examination carried out pursuant to Article 71. The Board of Appeal may exercise any power which lies within the competence of the Office, or it may remit the case to the competent body of the Office for further action. The latter one shall, in so far as the facts are the same, be bound by the *ratio decidendi* of the Board of Appeal.

Article 73. Actions against decisions of the Boards of Appeal.   1.   Actions may be brought before the Court of Justice against decisions of the Boards of Appeal on appeals.

2.   The action may be brought on grounds of lack of competence, infringement of an essential procedural requirement, infringement of the Treaty, of this Regulation or of any rule of law relating to their application, or misuse of power.

3.   The Court of Justice shall have jurisdiction to annul or to alter the contested decision.

4.   The action shall be open to any party to appeal proceedings which has been unsuccessful, in whole or in part, in its submissions.

5.   The action shall be brought before the Court of Justice within two months of the date of service of the decision of the Board of Appeal.

6.   The Office shall be required to take the necessary measures to comply with the judgment of the Court of Justice.

Article 74. Direct action.   1.   A direct action may be brought before the Court of Justice against decisions of the Office pursuant to Articles 29 and 100(2).

2.   The provisions laid down in Article 73 shall apply *mutatis mutandis.*

Chapter VII — Fees, settlement of costs

Article 86. Enforcement of decisions which determine the amount of costs.   1.   Final decisions of the Office which determine the amount of costs shall be enforceable.

2.   Enforcement shall be governed by the rules of civil procedure applicable in the Member State in which it takes place. Subject only to verification that the relevant document is authentic, the enforcement clause or endorsement shall be appended by the national authority appointed for that purpose by the Government of each Member State; the Governments shall inform the Office and the Court of Justice of the European Communities of the identity of each such national authority.

3.   When, upon application by the party seeking enforcement, these formalities have been completed, it shall be entitled to proceed to endorsement under national law by bringing the matter directly before the competent body.

4.   Enforcement shall not be suspended except by decision of the Court of Justice of the European Communities. Control as to the regularity of enforcement measures shall, however, reside with the national courts.

Chapter VIII — Registers

Article 91. Administrative and legal cooperation.   1.   Unless otherwise provided in this Regulation or in national law, the Office, Examination Offices referred to in Article 55(1) and the courts or authorities of the Member States shall on request give assistance to each other by communicating information or opening files related to the variety, and samples or growing thereof for inspection. Where the Office and the Examination Offices lay files, samples or growing thereof open to inspection by courts or public prosecutors' offices, the inspection shall not be subject to the restrictions laid down in Article 88, and the inspection given by the Examination Offices shall not be subject to a decision of the Office pursuant to that Article.

2.   Upon receipt of letters rogatory from the Office, the courts or other competent authorities of the Member States shall undertake on behalf of that Office and within the limits of their jurisdiction, any necessary enquiries or other related measures.

Part Five — Impact on other laws

Article 93. Application of national law.   Claims under Community plant variety rights shall be subject to limitations imposed by the law of the Member States only as expressly referred to in this Regulation.

Part Six — Civil law claims, infringements, jurisdiction

Article 94. Infringement.   1.   Whosoever:

(a)   effects one of the acts set out in Article 13(2) without being entitled to do so, in respect of a variety for which a Community plant variety right has been granted; or

(b)   omits the correct usage of a variety denomination as referred to in Article 17(1) or omits the relevant information as referred to in Article 17(2); or

(c)   contrary to Article 18(3) uses the variety denomination of a variety for which a Community plant variety right has been granted or a designation that may be confused with it;

may be sued by the holder to enjoin such infringement or to pay reasonable compensation or both.

2.   Whosoever acts intentionally or negligently shall moreover be liable to compensate the holder for any further damage resulting from the act in question. In cases of slight negligence, such claims may be reduced according to the degree of such slight negligence, but not however to the extent that they are less than the advantage derived therefrom by the person who committed the infringement.

Article 97. Supplementary application of national law regarding infringement.   1.   Where the party liable pursuant to Article 94 has, by virtue of the infringement, made any gain at the expense of the holder or of a person entitled to exploitation rights, the courts competent pursuant to Articles 101 or 102 shall apply their national law, including their private international law, as regards restitution.

2.   Paragraph 1 shall also apply as regards other claims that may arise in respect of the performance or omission of acts pursuant to Article 95 in the time between publication of the application for grant of a Community plant variety right and the disposal of the request.

3.   In all other respects the effects of Community plant variety rights shall be determined solely in accordance with this Regulation.

Article 101. Jurisdiction and procedure in legal actions relating to civil law claims.   1.   The Lugano Convention as well as the complementary provisions of this Article and of Articles 102 to 106 of this Regulation shall apply to proceedings relating to actions in respect of the claims referred to in Articles 94 to 100.

2.   Proceedings of the type referred to in paragraph 1 shall be brought in the courts:

(a)   of the Member State or another Contracting Party to the Lugano Convention in which the defendant is domiciled or has his seat or, in the absence of such, has an establishment; or

(b)   if this condition is not met in any of the Member States or Contracting Parties, of the Member State in which the plaintiff is domiciled or has his seat or, in the absence of such, has an establishment; or

(c)   if this condition is also not met in any of the Member States, of the Member States in which the seat of the Office is located.

The competent courts shall have jurisdiction in respect of infringements alleged to have been committed in any of the Member States.

3.   Proceedings relating to actions in respect of claims for infringement may also be brought in the courts for the place where the harmful event occured. In such cases, the court shall have jurisdiction only in respect of infringements alleged to have been committed in the territory of the Member State to which it belongs.

4.   The legal processes and the competent courts shall be those that operate under the laws of the State determined pursuant to paragraphs 2 or 3.

Article 102. Supplementary provisions.   1.   Actions for claiming entitlement pursuant to Article 98 of this Regulation shall not be considered to fall under the provisions of Article 5(3) and (4) of the Lugano Convention.

2.   Notwithstanding Article 101 of this Regulation, Articles 5(1), 17 and 18 of the Lugano Convention shall apply.

3.   For the purposes of applying Articles 101 and 102 of this Regulation, the domicile or seat of a party shall be determined pursuant to Articles 52 and 53 of the Lugano Convention.

Article 103. Rules of procedure applicable.   Where jurisdiction lies with national courts pursuant to Articles 101 and 102, the rules of procedure of the relevant State governing the same type of action relating to corresponding national property rights shall apply without prejudice to Articles 104 and 105.

Article 104. Entitlement to bring an action for infringement.   1.   Actions for infringement may be brought by the holder. Persons enjoying exploitation rights may bring such actions unless that has been expressly excluded by agreement with the holder in the case of an exclusive exploitation right or by the Office pursuant to Articles 29 or 100(2).

2.   Any person enjoying exploitation rights shall, for the purpose of obtaining compensation for damage suffered by him, be entitled to intervene in an infringement action brought by the holder.

Article 105. Obligation of national courts or other bodies.   A national court or other body hearing an action relating to a Community plant variety right shall treat the Community plant variety right as valid.

Article 106. Stay of proceedings.   1.   Where an action relates to claims pursuant to Article 98(4) and the decision depends upon the protectability of the variety pursuant to Article 6, this decision may not be given before the Office has decided on the application for a Community plant variety right.

2.   Where an action relates to a Community plant variety right that has been granted and in respect of which proceedings for revocation or cancellation pursuant to Articles 20 or 21 have been initiated, the proceedings may be stayed in so far as the decision depends upon the validity of the Community plant variety right.

Article 107. Penalties for infringement of Community plant variety rights. Member States shall take all appropriate measures to ensure that the same provisions are made applicable to penalize infringements of Community plant variety rights as apply in the matter of infringements of corresponding national rights.

B. Council Regulation (EC) No 6/2002 of 12 December 2001 on Community designs (OJ, L 3 of 5 January 2002)[1]

(1) A unified system for obtaining a Community design to which uniform protection is given with uniform effect throughout the entire territory of the Community would further the objectives of the Community as laid down in the Treaty.

(2) Only the Benelux countries have introduced a uniform design protection law. In all the other Member States the protection of designs is a matter for the relevant national law and is confined to the territory of the Member State concerned. Identical designs may be therefore protected differently in different Member States and for the benefit of different owners. This inevitably leads to conflicts in the course of trade between Member States.

(3) The substantial differences between Member States' design laws prevent and distort Community-wide competition. In comparison with domestic trade in, and competition between, products incorporating a design, trade and competition within the Community are prevented and distorted by the large number of applications, offices, procedures, laws, nationally circumscribed exclusive rights and the combined administrative expense with correspondingly high costs and fees for the applicant. Directive 98/71/EC of the European Parliament and of the Council of 13 October 1998 on the legal protection of designs contributes to remedying this situation.

(4) The effect of design protection being limited to the territory of the individual Member States whether or not their laws are approximated, leads to a possible division of the internal market with respect to products incorporating a design which is the subject of national rights held by different individuals, and hence constitutes an obstacle to the free movement of goods.

(5) This calls for the creation of a Community design which is directly applicable in each Member State, because only in this way will it be possible to obtain, through one application made to the Office for Harmonisation in the Internal Market (Trade Marks and Design) in accordance with a single procedure under one law, one design right for one area encompassing all Member States.

(27) A procedure for hearing actions concerning validity of a registered Community design in a single place would bring savings in costs and time compared with procedures involving different national courts.

(28) It is therefore necessary to provide safeguards including a right of appeal to a Board of Appeal, and ultimately to the Court of Justice. Such a procedure would assist the development of uniform interpretation of the requirements governing the validity of Community designs.

---

[1] As finally modified by Council Regulation (EC) No 1891/2006 of 18 December 2006 (OJ, L 386 of 29 December 2006). [Note of the Editor]

(29) It is essential that the rights conferred by a Community design can be enforced in an efficient manner throughout the territory of the Community.

(30) The litigation system should avoid as far as possible 'forum shopping'. It is therefore necessary to establish clear rules of international jurisdiction.

(31) This Regulation does not preclude the application to designs protected by Community designs of the industrial property laws or other relevant laws of the Member States, such as those relating to design protection acquired by registration or those relating to unregistered designs, trade marks, patents and utility models, unfair competition or civil liability.

(32) In the absence of the complete harmonisation of copyright law, it is important to establish the principle of cumulation of protection under the Community design and under copyright law, whilst leaving Member States free to establish the extent of copyright protection and the conditions under which such protection is conferred.

Title I — General provisions

Article 1. Community design.   1.   A design which complies with the conditions contained in this Regulation is hereinafter referred to as a 'Community design'.

2.   A design shall be protected:

(a)   by an 'unregistered Community design', if made available to the public in the manner provided for in this Regulation;

(b)   by a 'registered Community design', if registered in the manner provided for in this Regulation.

3.   A Community design shall have a unitary character. It shall have equal effect throughout the Community. It shall not be registered, transferred or surrendered or be the subject of a decision declaring it invalid, nor shall its use be prohibited, save in respect of the whole Community. This principle and its implications shall apply unless otherwise provided in this Regulation.

Article 2. Office.   The Office for Harmonisation in the Internal Market (Trade Marks and Designs), hereinafter referred to as 'the Office', instituted by Council Regulation (EC) No 40/94 of 20 December 1993 on the Community trade mark, hereinafter referred to as the 'Regulation on the Community trade mark', shall carry out the tasks entrusted to it by this Regulation.

Title II — The law relating to designs

Section 3 — Right to the Community design

Article 14. Right to the Community design.   1.   The right to the Community design shall vest in the designer or his successor in title.

2.   If two or more persons have jointly developed a design, the right to the Community design shall vest in them jointly.

3.   However, where a design is developed by an employee in the execution of his duties or following the instructions given by his employer, the right to the Community design shall vest in the employer, unless otherwise agreed or specified under national law.

Title III — Community designs as objects of property

Article 27. Dealing with Community designs as national design rights.   1.   Unless Articles 28, 29, 30, 31 and 32 provide otherwise, a Community design as an object of property shall be dealt with in its entirety, and for the whole area of the Community, as a national design right of the Member State in which:
   (a)   the holder has his seat or his domicile on the relevant date; or
   (b)   where point (a) does not apply, the holder has an establishment on the relevant date.
   2.   In the case of a registered Community design, paragraph 1 shall apply according to the entries in the register.
   3.   In the case of joint holders, if two or more of them fulfil the condition under paragraph 1, the Member State referred to in that paragraph shall be determined:
   (a)   in the case of an unregistered Community design, by reference to the relevant joint holder designated by them by common agreement;
   (b)   in the case of a registered Community design, by reference to the first of the relevant joint holders in the order in which they are mentioned in the register.
   4.   Where paragraphs 1, 2 and 3 do not apply, the Member State referred to in paragraph 1 shall be the Member State in which the seat of the Office is situated.

Article 29. Rights in rem on a registered Community design.   1.   A registered Community design may be given as security or be the subject of rights *in rem*.
   2.   On request of one of the parties, the rights mentioned in paragraph 1 shall be entered in the register and published.

Article 30. Levy of execution.   1.   A registered Community design may be levied in execution.
   2.   As regards the procedure for levy of execution in respect of a registered Community design, the courts and authorities of the Member State determined in accordance with Article 27 shall have exclusive jurisdiction.
   3.   On request of one of the parties, levy of execution shall be entered in the register and published.

Article 31. Insolvency proceedings.   1.   The only insolvency proceedings in which a Community design may be involved shall be those opened in the Member State within the territory of which the centre of a debtor's main interests is situated.
   2.   In the case of joint proprietorship of a Community design, paragraph 1 shall apply to the share of the joint proprietor.
   3.   Where a Community design is involved in insolvency proceedings, on request of the competent national authority an entry to this effect shall be made in the register and published in the Community Designs Bulletin referred to in Article 73(1).

Article 33. Effects vis-à-vis third parties.   1.   The effects vis-à-vis third parties of the legal acts referred to in Articles 28, 29, 30 and 32 shall be governed by the law of the Member State determined in accordance with Article 27.
   2.   However, as regards registered Community designs, legal acts referred to in Articles 28, 29 and 32 shall only have effect vis-à-vis third parties in all the Member

States after entry in the register. Nevertheless, such an act, before it is so entered, shall have effect vis-à-vis third parties who have acquired rights in the registered Community design after the date of that act but who knew of the act at the date on which the rights were acquired.

3.   Paragraph 2 shall not apply to a person who acquires the registered Community design or a right concerning the registered Community design by way of transfer of the whole of the undertaking or by any other universal succession.

4.   Until such time as common rules for the Member States in the field of insolvency enter into force, the effects vis-à-vis third parties of insolvency proceedings shall be governed by the law of the Member State in which such proceedings are first brought under the national law or the regulations applicable in this field.

Title VII — Appeals

Article 55. Decisions subject to appeal.   1.   An appeal shall lie from decisions of the examiners, the Administration of Trade Marks and Designs and Legal Division and Invalidity Divisions. It shall have suspensive effect.

2.   A decision which does not terminate proceedings as regards one of the parties can only be appealed together with the final decision, unless the decision allows separate appeal.

Article 60. Decisions in respect of appeals.   1.   Following the examination as to the merits of the appeal, the Board of Appeal shall decide on the appeal. The Board of Appeal may either exercise any power within the competence of the department which was responsible for the decision appealed against or remit the case to that department for further prosecution.

2.   If the Board of Appeal remits the case for further prosecution to the department whose decision was appealed, that department shall be bound by the *ratio decidendi* of the Board of Appeal, in so far as the facts are the same.

3.   The decisions of the Boards of Appeal shall take effect only from the date of expiry of the period referred to in Article 61(5) or, if an action has been brought before the Court of Justice within that period, from the date of rejection of such action.

Article 61. Actions before the Court of Justice.   1.   Actions may be brought before the Court of Justice against decisions of the Boards of Appeal on appeals.

2.   The action may be brought on grounds of lack of competence, infringement of an essential procedural requirement, infringement of the Treaty, of this Regulation or of any rule of law relating to their application or misuse of power.

3.   The Court of Justice has jurisdiction to annul or to alter the contested decision.

4.   The action shall be open to any party to proceedings before the Board of Appeal adversely affected by its decision.

5.   The action shall be brought before the Court of Justice within two months of the date of notification of the decision of the Board of Appeal.

6.   The Office shall be required to take the necessary measures to comply with the judgment of the Court of Justice.

Title VIII — Procedure before the Office

Section 2 — Costs

Article 71. Enforcement of decisions fixing the amount of costs. 1. Any final decision of the Office fixing the amount of costs shall be enforceable.

2. Enforcement shall be governed by the rules of civil procedure in force in the State in the territory of which it is carried out. The order for its enforcement shall be appended to the decision, without any other formality than verification of the authenticity of the decision, by the national authority which the government of each Member State shall designate for this purpose and shall make known to the Office and to the Court of Justice.

3. When these formalities have been completed on application by the party concerned, the latter may proceed to enforcement in accordance with the national law, by bringing the matter directly before the competent authority.

4. Enforcement may be suspended only by a decision of the Court of Justice. However, the courts of the Member State concerned shall have jurisdiction over complaints that enforcement is being carried out in an irregular manner.

Title IX — Jurisdiction and procedure in legal actions relating to Community designs

Section 1 — Jurisdiction and enforcement

Article 79. Application of the Convention on Jurisdiction and Enforcement.[2] 1. Unless otherwise specified in this Regulation, the Convention on Jurisdiction and the Enforcement of Judgements in Civil and Commercial Matters, signed in Brussels on 27 September 1968, hereinafter referred to as the 'Convention on Jurisdiction and Enforcement', shall apply to proceedings relating to Community designs and applications for registered Community designs, as well as to proceedings relating to actions on the basis of Community designs and national designs enjoying simultaneous protection.

2. The provisions of the Convention on Jurisdiction and Enforcement which are rendered applicable by the paragraph 1 shall have effect in respect of any Member State solely in the text which is in force in respect of that State at any given time.

3. In the event of proceedings in respect of the actions and claims referred to in Article 85:

(a) Articles 2, 4, 5(1), (3), (4) and (5), 16(4) and 24 of the Convention on Jurisdiction and Enforcement shall not apply;

(b) Articles 17 and 18 of that Convention shall apply subject to the limitations in Article 82(4) of this Regulation;

---

[2] We hereby recall that pursuant to Article 68(2) of the Council Regulation (EC) No 44/2001 (see Chapter IV, General provisions, A.1), within the limits in which it replaces the Brussels Convention, any reference to the latter is to be intended as to Regulation (EC) No 44/2001. The reference is to be intended as made to the Articles of the Regulation corresponding, as far as the matter, if not completely the contents, is concerned, to the ones indicated in this Regulation on Community designs. [Note of the Editor]

(c)   the provisions of Title II of that Convention which are applicable to persons domiciled in a Member State shall also be applicable to persons who do not have a domicile in any Member State but have an establishment therein.

4.   The provisions of the Convention on Jurisdiction and Enforcement shall not have effect in respect of any Member State for which that Convention has not yet entered into force. Until such entry into force, proceedings referred to in paragraph 1 shall be governed in such a Member State by any bilateral or multilateral convention governing its relationship with another Member State concerned, or, if no such convention exists, by its domestic law on jurisdiction, recognition and enforcement of decisions.

Section 2 — Disputes concerning the infringement and validity of Community designs

Article 80. Community design courts.   1.   The Member States shall designate in their territories as limited a number as possible of national courts and tribunals of first and second instance (Community design courts) which shall perform the functions assigned to them by this Regulation.

2.   Each Member State shall communicate to the Commission not later than 6 March 2005 a list of Community design courts, indicating their names and their territorial jurisdiction.

3.   Any change made after communication of the list referred to in paragraph 2 in the number, names or territorial jurisdiction of the Community design courts shall be notified without delay by the Member State concerned to the Commission.

4.   The information referred to in paragraphs 2 and 3 shall be notified by the Commission to the Member States and published in the *Official Journal of the European Communities.*

5.   As long as a Member State has not communicated the list as stipulated in paragraph 2, jurisdiction for any proceedings resulting from an action covered by Article 81 for which the courts of that State have jurisdiction pursuant to Article 82 shall lie with that court of the State in question which would have jurisdiction *ratione loci* and *ratione materiae* in the case of proceedings relating to a national design right of that State.

Article 81. Jurisdiction over infringement and validity.   The Community design courts shall have exclusive jurisdiction:

(a)   for infringement actions and – if they are permitted under national law – actions in respect of threatened infringement of Community designs;

(b)   for actions for declaration of non-infringement of Community designs, if they are permitted under national law;

(c)   for actions for a declaration of invalidity of an unregistered Community design;

(d)   for counterclaims for a declaration of invalidity of a Community design raised in connection with actions under (a).

Article 82. International jurisdiction.   1.   Subject to the provisions of this Regulation and to any provisions of the Convention on Jurisdiction and Enforcement applicable by virtue of Article 79, proceedings in respect of the actions and claims referred to in Article 81 shall be brought in the courts of the Member State in which the defendant is domiciled or, if he is not domiciled in any of the Member States, in any Member State in which he has an establishment.

2.   If the defendant is neither domiciled nor has an establishment in any of the Member States, such proceedings shall be brought in the courts of the Member State in which the plaintiff is domiciled or, if he is not domiciled in any of the Member States, in any Member State in which he has an establishment.

3.   If neither the defendant nor the plaintiff is so domiciled or has such an establishment, such proceedings shall be brought in the courts of the Member State where the Office has its seat.

4.   Notwithstanding paragraphs 1, 2 and 3:

(a)   Article 17 of the Convention on Jurisdiction and Enforcement shall apply if the parties agree that a different Community design court shall have jurisdiction;

(b)   Article 18 of that Convention shall apply if the defendant enters an appearance before a different Community design court.

5.   Proceedings in respect of the actions and claims referred to in Article 81(a) and (d) may also be brought in the courts of the Member State in which the act of infringement has been committed or threatened.

Article 83. Extent of jurisdiction on infringement.   1.   A Community design court whose jurisdiction is based on Article 82(1), (2) (3) or (4) shall have jurisdiction in respect of acts of infringement committed or threatened within the territory of any of the Member States.

2.   A Community design court whose jurisdiction is based on Article 82(5) shall have jurisdiction only in respect of acts of infringement committed or threatened within the territory of the Member State in which that court is situated.

Article 84. Action or counterclaim for a declaration of invalidity of a Community design.   1.   An action or a counterclaim for a declaration of invalidity of a Community design may only be based on the grounds for invalidity mentioned in Article 25.

2.   In the cases referred to in Article 25(2), (3), (4) and (5) the action or the counterclaim may be brought solely by the person entitled under those provisions.

3.   If the counterclaim is brought in a legal action to which the right holder of the Community design is not already a party, he shall be informed thereof and may be joined as a party to the action in accordance with the conditions set out in the law of the Member State where the court is situated.

4.   The validity of a Community design may not be put in issue in an action for a declaration of non-infringement.

Article 85. Presumption of validity — defence as to the merits.   1.   In proceedings in respect of an infringement action or an action for threatened infringement of a registered Community design, the Community design court shall treat the Community design as valid. Validity may be challenged only with a counterclaim for a declaration of invalidity. However, a plea relating to the invalidity of a Community design, submitted otherwise than by way of counterclaim, shall be admissible in so far as the defendant claims that the Community design could be declared invalid on account of an earlier national design right, within the meaning of Article 25(1)(d), belonging to him.

2.   In proceedings in respect of an infringement action or an action for threatened infringement of an unregistered Community design, the Community design court shall treat the Community design as valid if the right holder produces proof that the conditions

laid down in Article 11 have been met and indicates what constitutes the individual character of his Community design. However, the defendant may contest its validity by way of a plea or with a counterclaim for a declaration of invalidity.

Article 86. Judgements of invalidity.   1.   Where in a proceeding before a Community design court the Community design has been put in issue by way of a counterclaim for a declaration of invalidity:

(a)   if any of the grounds mentioned in Article 25 are found to prejudice the maintenance of the Community design, the court shall declare the Community design invalid;

(b)   if none of the grounds mentioned in Article 25 is found to prejudice the maintenance of the Community design, the court shall reject the counterclaim.

2.   The Community design court with which a counterclaim for a declaration of invalidity of a registered Community design has been filed shall inform the Office of the date on which the counterclaim was filed. The latter shall record this fact in the register.

3.   The Community design court hearing a counterclaim for a declaration of invalidity of a registered Community design may, on application by the right holder of the registered Community design and after hearing the other parties, stay the proceedings and request the defendant to submit an application for a declaration of invalidity to the Office within a time limit which the court shall determine. If the application is not made within the time limit, the proceedings shall continue; the counterclaim shall be deemed withdrawn. Article 91(3) shall apply.

4.   Where a Community design court has given a judgment which has become final on a counterclaim for a declaration of invalidity of a registered Community design, a copy of the judgment shall be sent to the Office. Any party may request information about such transmission. The Office shall mention the judgment in the register in accordance with the provisions of the implementing regulation.

5.   No counterclaim for a declaration of invalidity of a registered Community design may be made if an application relating to the same subject matter and cause of action, and involving the same parties, has already been determined by the Office in a decision which has become final.

Article 87. Effects of the judgement on invalidity.   When it has become final, a judgment of a Community design court declaring a Community design invalid shall have in all the Member States the effects specified in Article 26.

Article 88. Applicable law.   1.   The Community design courts shall apply the provisions of this Regulation.

2.   On all matters not covered by this Regulation, a Community design court shall apply its national law, including its private international law.

3.   Unless otherwise provided in this Regulation, a Community design court shall apply the rules of procedure governing the same type of action relating to a national design right in the Member State where it is situated.

Article 89. Sanctions in actions for infringement.   1.   Where in an action for infringement or for threatened infringement a Community design court finds that the defendant has infringed or threatened to infringe a Community design, it shall, unless there are special reasons for not doing so, order the following measures:

(a) an order prohibiting the defendant from proceeding with the acts which have infringed or would infringe the Community design;

(b) an order to seize the infringing products;

(c) an order to seize materials and implements predominantly used in order to manufacture the infringing goods, if their owner knew the effect for which such use was intended or if such effect would have been obvious in the circumstances;

(d) any order imposing other sanctions appropriate under the circumstances which are provided by the law of the Member State in which the acts of infringement or threatened infringement are committed, including its private international law.

2. The Community design court shall take such measures in accordance with its national law as are aimed at ensuring that the orders referred to in paragraph 1 are complied with.

Article 90. Provisional measures, including protective measures. 1. Application may be made to the courts of a Member State, including Community design courts, for such provisional measures, including protective measures, in respect of a Community design as may be available under the law of that State in respect of national design rights even if, under this Regulation, a Community design court of another Member State has jurisdiction as to the substance of the matter.

2. In proceedings relating to provisional measures, including protective measures, a plea otherwise than by way of counterclaim relating to the invalidity of a Community design submitted by the defendant shall be admissible. Article 85(2) shall, however, apply *mutatis mutandis*.

3. A Community design court whose jurisdiction is based on Article 82(1), (2), (3) or (4) shall have jurisdiction to grant provisional measures, including protective measures, which, subject to any necessary procedure for recognition and enforcement pursuant to Title III of the Convention on Jurisdiction and Enforcement, are applicable in the territory of any Member State. No other court shall have such jurisdiction.

Article 91. Specific rules on related actions. 1. A Community design court hearing an action referred to in Article 81, other than an action for a declaration of non-infringement, shall, unless there are special grounds for continuing the hearing, of its own motion after hearing the parties, or at the request of one of the parties and after hearing the other parties, stay the proceedings where the validity of the Community design is already in issue before another Community design court on account of a counterclaim or, in the case of a registered Community design, where an application for a declaration of invalidity has already been filed at the Office.

2. The Office, when hearing an application for a declaration of invalidity of a registered Community design, shall, unless there are special grounds for continuing the hearing, of its own motion after hearing the parties, or at the request of one of the parties and after hearing the other parties, stay the proceedings where the validity of the registered Community design is already in issue on account of a counterclaim before a Community design court. However, if one of the parties to the proceedings before the Community design court so requests, the court may, after hearing the other parties to these proceedings, stay the proceedings. The Office shall in this instance continue the proceedings pending before it.

3.   Where the Community design court stays the proceedings it may order provisional measures, including protective measures, for the duration of the stay.

Article 92. Jurisdiction of Community design courts of second instance — further appeal.   1.   An appeal to the Community design courts of second instance shall lie from judgments of the Community design courts of first instance in respect of proceedings arising from the actions and claims referred to in Article 81.

2.   The conditions under which an appeal may be lodged with a Community design court of second instance shall be determined by the national law of the Member State in which that court is located.

3.   The national rules concerning further appeal shall be applicable in respect of judgments of Community design courts of second instance.

Section 3 — Other disputes concerning Community designs

Article 93. Supplementary provisions on the jurisdiction of national courts other than Community design courts.   1.   Within the Member State whose courts have jurisdiction under Article 79(1) or (4), those courts shall have jurisdiction for actions relating to Community designs other than those referred to in Article 81 which would have jurisdiction *ratione loci* and *ratione materiae* in the case of actions relating to a national design right in that State.

2.   Actions relating to a Community design, other than those referred to in Article 81, for which no court has jurisdiction pursuant to Article 79(1) and (4) and paragraph 1 of this Article may be heard before the courts of the Member State in which the Office has its seat.

Article 94. Obligation of the national court.   A national court which is dealing with an action relating to a Community design other than the actions referred to in Article 81 shall treat the design as valid. Articles 85(2) and 90(2) shall, however, apply *mutatis mutandis*.

Title X — Effects on the laws of the Member States

Article 95. Parallel actions on the basis of Community designs and national design rights.   1.   Where actions for infringement or for threatened infringement involving the same cause of action and between the same parties are brought before the courts of different Member States, one seized on the basis of a Community design and the other seized on the basis of a national design right providing simultaneous protection, the court other than the court first seized shall of its own motion decline jurisdiction in favour of that court. The court which would be required to decline jurisdiction may stay its proceedings if the jurisdiction of the other court is contested.

2.   The Community design court hearing an action for infringement or threatened infringement on the basis of a Community design shall reject the action if a final judgment on the merits has been given on the same cause of action and between the same parties on the basis of a design right providing simultaneous protection.

3.   The court hearing an action for infringement or for threatened infringement on the basis of a national design right shall reject the action if a final judgment on the

merits has been given on the same cause of action and between the same parties on the basis of a Community design providing simultaneous protection.

4.　Paragraphs 1, 2 and 3 shall not apply in respect of provisional measures, including protective measures.

Article 96. Relationship to other forms of protection under national law. 1.　The provisions of this Regulation shall be without prejudice to any provisions of Community law or of the law of the Member States concerned relating to unregistered designs, trade marks or other distinctive signs, patents and utility models, typefaces, civil liability and unfair competition.

2.　A design protected by a Community design shall also be eligible for protection under the law of copyright of Member States as from the date on which the design was created or fixed in any form. The extent to which, and the conditions under which, such a protection is conferred, including the level of originality required, shall be determined by each Member State.

C.　Council Regulation (EC) No 207/2009 of 26 February 2009 on the Community trade mark (codified version) (OJ, L 78 of 24 March 2009)

(1)　Council Regulation (EC) No 40/94 of 20 December 1993 on the Community trade mark has been substantially amended several times. In the interests of clarity and rationality the said Regulation should be codified.

(2)　It is desirable to promote throughout the Community a harmonious development of economic activities and a continuous and balanced expansion by completing an internal market which functions properly and offers conditions which are similar to those obtaining in a national market. In order to create a market of this kind and make it increasingly a single market, not only must barriers to free movement of goods and services be removed and arrangements be instituted which ensure that competition is not distorted, but, in addition, legal conditions must be created which enable undertakings to adapt their activities to the scale of the Community, whether in manufacturing and distributing goods or in providing services. For those purposes, trade marks enabling the products and services of undertakings to be distinguished by identical means throughout the entire Community, regardless of frontiers, should feature amongst the legal instruments which undertakings have at their disposal.

(3)　For the purpose of pursuing the Community's said objectives it would appear necessary to provide for Community arrangements for trade marks whereby undertakings can by means of one procedural system obtain Community trade marks to which uniform protection is given and which produce their effects throughout the entire area of the Community. The principle of the unitary character of the Community trade mark thus stated should apply unless otherwise provided for in this Regulation.

(4)　The barrier of territoriality of the rights conferred on proprietors of trade marks by the laws of the Member States cannot be removed by approximation of laws. In order to open up unrestricted economic activity in the whole of the internal market for the benefit of undertakings, trade marks should be created which are governed by a uniform Community law directly applicable in all Member States.

(5)   Since the Treaty has not provided the specific powers to establish such a legal instrument, Article 308 of the Treaty should be applied.

(6)   The Community law relating to trade marks nevertheless does not replace the laws of the Member States on trade marks. It would not in fact appear to be justified to require undertakings to apply for registration of their trade marks as Community trade marks. National trade marks continue to be necessary for those undertakings which do not want protection of their trade marks at Community level.

(7)   The rights in a Community trade mark should not be obtained otherwise than by registration, and registration should be refused in particular if the trade mark is not distinctive, if it is unlawful or if it conflicts with earlier rights.

(8)   The protection afforded by a Community trade mark, the function of which is in particular to guarantee the trade mark as an indication of origin, should be absolute in the case of identity between the mark and the sign and the goods or services. The protection should apply also in cases of similarity between the mark and the sign and the goods or services. An interpretation should be given of the concept of similarity in relation to the likelihood of confusion. The likelihood of confusion, the appreciation of which depends on numerous elements and, in particular, on the recognition of the trade mark on the market, the association which can be made with the used or registered sign, the degree of similarity between the trade mark and the sign and between the goods or services identified, should constitute the specific condition for such protection.

(9)   It follows from the principle of free movement of goods that the proprietor of a Community trade mark must not be entitled to prohibit its use by a third party in relation to goods which have been put into circulation in the Community, under the trade mark, by him or with his consent, save where there exist legitimate reasons for the proprietor to oppose further commercialisation of the goods.

(10)   There is no justification for protecting Community trade marks or, as against them, any trade mark which has been registered before them, except where the trade marks are actually used.

(11)   A Community trade mark is to be regarded as an object of property which exists separately from the undertakings whose goods or services are designated by it. Accordingly, it should be capable of being transferred, subject to the overriding need to prevent the public being misled as a result of the transfer. It should also be capable of being charged as security in favour of a third party and of being the subject matter of licences.

(12)   Administrative measures are necessary at Community level for implementing in relation to every trade mark the trade mark law created by this Regulation. It is therefore essential, while retaining the Community's existing institutional structure and balance of powers, to provide for an Office for Harmonisation in the Internal Market (trade marks and designs) which is independent in relation to technical matters and has legal, administrative and financial autonomy. To this end it is necessary and appropriate that that Office should be a body of the Community having legal personality and exercising the implementing powers which are conferred on it by this Regulation, and that it should operate within the framework of Community law without detracting from the competencies exercised by the Community institutions.

(13)   It is necessary to ensure that parties who are affected by decisions made by the Office are protected by the law in a manner which is suited to the special character of trade mark law. To that end provision is made for an appeal to lie from decisions of the

examiners and of the various divisions of the Office. If the department whose decision is contested does not rectify its decision it is to remit the appeal to a Board of Appeal of the Office, which is to decide on it. Decisions of the Boards of Appeal are, in turn, amenable to actions before the Court of Justice of the European Communities, which has jurisdiction to annul or to alter the contested decision.

(14) Under the first subparagraph of Article 225(1) of the EC Treaty the Court of First Instance of the European Communities has jurisdiction to hear and determine at first instance the actions referred to in particular in Article 230 of the EC Treaty with the exception of those assigned to a judicial panel and those reserved in the Statute to the Court of Justice. The jurisdiction which this Regulation confers on the Court of Justice to cancel and alter decisions of the Boards of Appeal should accordingly be exercised at first instance by the Court.

(15) In order to strengthen the protection of Community trade marks the Member States should designate, having regard to their own national system, as limited a number as possible of national courts of first and second instance having jurisdiction in matters of infringement and validity of Community trade marks.

(16) Decisions regarding the validity and infringement of Community trade marks must have effect and cover the entire area of the Community, as this is the only way of preventing inconsistent decisions on the part of the courts and the Office and of ensuring that the unitary character of Community trade marks is not undermined. The provisions of Council Regulation (EC) No 44/2001 of 22 December 2000 on jurisdiction and the recognition and enforcement of judgments in civil and commercial matters should apply to all actions at law relating to Community trade marks, save where this Regulation derogates from those rules.

(17) Contradictory judgments should be avoided in actions which involve the same acts and the same parties and which are brought on the basis of a Community trade mark and parallel national trade marks. For this purpose, when the actions are brought in the same Member State, the way in which this is to be achieved is a matter for national procedural rules, which are not prejudiced by this Regulation, whilst when the actions are brought in different Member States, provisions modelled on the rules on *lis pendens* and related actions of Regulation (EC) No 44/2001 appear appropriate.

(18) In order to guarantee the full autonomy and independence of the Office, it is considered necessary to grant it an autonomous budget whose revenue comes principally from fees paid by the users of the system. However, the Community budgetary procedure remains applicable as far as any subsidies chargeable to the general budget of the European Communities are concerned. Moreover, the auditing of accounts should be undertaken by the Court of Auditors.

(19) Measures necessary for the implementation of this Regulation should be adopted, particularly as regards fees regulations and an Implementing Regulation, in accordance with Council Decision 1999/468/EC of 28 June 1999 laying down the procedures for the exercise of implementing powers conferred on the Commission.

Title I — General provisions

Article 1. Community trade mark.   1.   A trade mark for goods or services which is registered in accordance with the conditions contained in this Regulation and in the manner herein provided is hereinafter referred to as a 'Community trade mark'.
2.   A Community trade mark shall have a unitary character. It shall have equal effect throughout the Community: it shall not be registered, transferred or surrendered or be the subject of a decision revoking the rights of the proprietor or declaring it invalid, nor shall its use be prohibited, save in respect of the whole Community. This principle shall apply unless otherwise provided in this Regulation.

Article 2. Office.   An Office for Harmonisation in the Internal Market (trade marks and designs), hereinafter referred to as 'the Office', is hereby established.

Article 3. Capacity to act.   For the purpose of implementing this Regulation, companies or firms and other legal bodies shall be regarded as legal persons if, under the terms of the law governing them, they have the capacity in their own name to have rights and obligations of all kinds, to make contracts or accomplish other legal acts and to sue and be sued.

Title II — The law relating to trade marks

Section 1 — Definition of a Community trade mark and obtaining a Community trade mark

Article 4. Signs of which a Community trade mark may consist.   A Community trade mark may consist of any signs capable of being represented graphically, particularly words, including personal names, designs, letters, numerals, the shape of goods or of their packaging, provided that such signs are capable of distinguishing the goods or services of one undertaking from those of other undertakings.

Article 5. Persons who can be proprietors of Community trade marks.   Any natural or legal person, including authorities established under public law, may be the proprietor of a Community trade mark.

Article 6. Means whereby a Community trade mark is obtained.   A Community trade mark shall be obtained by registration.

Section 2 — Effects of Community trade marks

Article 9. Rights conferred by a Community trade mark.   A Community trade mark shall confer on the proprietor exclusive rights therein. …

Article 14. Complementary application of national law relating to infringement.   1.   The effects of Community trade marks shall be governed solely by the provisions of this Regulation. In other respects, infringement of a Community trade mark shall be governed by the national law relating to infringement of a national trade mark in accordance with the provisions of Title X.

2.   This Regulation shall not prevent actions concerning a Community trade mark being brought under the law of Member States relating in particular to civil liability and unfair competition.

3.   The rules of procedure to be applied shall be determined in accordance with the provisions of Title X.

Section 4 — Community trade marks as objects of property

Article 16. Dealing with Community trade marks as national trade marks.   1.   Unless Articles 17 to 24 provide otherwise, a Community trade mark as an object of property shall be dealt with in its entirety, and for the whole area of the Community, as a national trade mark registered in the Member State in which, according to the Register of Community trade marks:

(a)   the proprietor has his seat or his domicile on the relevant date;

(b)   where point (a) does not apply, the proprietor has an establishment on the relevant date.

2.   In cases which are not provided for by paragraph 1, the Member State referred to in that paragraph shall be the Member State in which the seat of the Office is situated.

3.   If two or more persons are mentioned in the Register of Community trade marks as joint proprietors, paragraph 1 shall apply to the joint proprietor first mentioned; failing this, it shall apply to the subsequent joint proprietors in the order in which they are mentioned. Where paragraph 1 does not apply to any of the joint proprietors, paragraph 2 shall apply.

Article 17. Transfer.   1.   A Community trade mark may be transferred, separately from any transfer of the undertaking, in respect of some or all of the goods or services for which it is registered.

2.   A transfer of the whole of the undertaking shall include the transfer of the Community trade mark except where, in accordance with the law governing the transfer, there is agreement to the contrary or circumstances clearly dictate otherwise. This provision shall apply to the contractual obligation to transfer the undertaking.

3.   Without prejudice to paragraph 2, an assignment of the Community trade mark shall be made in writing and shall require the signature of the parties to the contract, except when it is a result of a judgment; otherwise it shall be void.

4.   Where it is clear from the transfer documents that because of the transfer the Community trade mark is likely to mislead the public concerning the nature, quality or geographical origin of the goods or services in respect of which it is registered, the Office shall not register the transfer unless the successor agrees to limit registration of the Community trade mark to goods or services in respect of which it is not likely to mislead.

5.   On request of one of the parties a transfer shall be entered in the Register and published.

6.   As long as the transfer has not been entered in the Register, the successor in title may not invoke the rights arising from the registration of the Community trade mark.

7.   Where there are time limits to be observed vis-à-vis the Office, the successor in title may make the corresponding statements to the Office once the request for registration of the transfer has been received by the Office.

8.   All documents which require notification to the proprietor of the Community trade mark in accordance with Article 79 shall be addressed to the person registered as proprietor.

Article 19. Rights in rem.   1.   A Community trade mark may, independently of the undertaking, be given as security or be the subject of rights *in rem*.

2.   On request of one of the parties, rights mentioned in paragraph 1 shall be entered in the Register and published.

Article 20. Levy of execution.   1.   A Community trade mark may be levied in execution.

2.   As regards the procedure for levy of execution in respect of a Community trade mark, the courts and authorities of the Member States determined in accordance with Article 16 shall have exclusive jurisdiction.

3.   On request of one the parties, levy of execution shall be entered in the Register and published.

Article 21. Insolvency proceedings.   1.   The only insolvency proceedings in which a Community trade mark may be involved are those opened in the Member State in the territory of which the debtor has his centre of main interests.

However, where the debtor is an insurance undertaking or a credit institution as defined in Directive 2001/17/EC of the European Parliament and of the Council of 19 March 2001 on the reorganisation and winding-up of insurance undertakings and Directive 2001/24/EC of the European Parliament and of the Council of 4 April 2001 on the reorganisation and winding up of credit institutions, respectively, the only insolvency proceedings in which a Community trademark may be involved are those opened in the Member State where that undertaking or institution has been authorised.

2.   In the case of joint proprietorship of a Community trade mark, paragraph 1 shall apply to the share of the joint proprietor.

3.   Where a Community trade mark is involved in insolvency proceedings, on request of the competent national authority an entry to this effect shall be made in the Register and published in the Community Trade Marks Bulletin referred to in Article 89.

Article 23. Effects vis-à-vis third parties.   1.   Legal acts referred to in Articles 17, 19 and 22 concerning a Community trade mark shall have effects vis-à-vis third parties in all the Member States only after entry in the Register. Nevertheless, such an act, before it is so entered, shall have effect vis-à-vis third parties who have acquired rights in the trade mark after the date of that act but who knew of the act at the date on which the rights were acquired.

2.   Paragraph 1 shall not apply in the case of a person who acquires the Community trade mark or a right concerning the Community trade mark by way of transfer of the whole of the undertaking or by any other universal succession.

3.   The effects vis-à-vis third parties of the legal acts referred to in Article 20 shall be governed by the law of the Member State determined in accordance with Article 16.

4.   Until such time as common rules for the Member States in the field of bankruptcy enter into force, the effects vis-à-vis third parties of bankruptcy or like proceedings shall be governed by the law of the Member State in which such proceedings are first brought within the meaning of national law or of conventions applicable in this field.

Article 24. The application for a Community trade mark as an object of property. Articles 16 to 23 shall apply to applications for Community trade marks.

Article 65. Actions before the Court of Justice. 1. Actions may be brought before the Court of Justice against decisions of the Boards of Appeal on appeals.

2. The action may be brought on grounds of lack of competence, infringement of an essential procedural requirement, infringement of the Treaty, of this Regulation or of any rule of law relating to their application or misuse of power.

3. The Court of Justice has jurisdiction to annul or to alter the contested decision.

4. The action shall be open to any party to proceedings before the Board of Appeal adversely affected by its decision.

5. The action shall be brought before the Court of Justice within two months of the date of notification of the decision of the Board of Appeal.

6. The Office shall be required to take the necessary measures to comply with the judgment of the Court of Justice.

Article 86. Enforcement of decisions fixing the amount of costs. 1. Any final decision of the Office fixing the amount of costs shall be enforceable.

2. Enforcement shall be governed by the rules of civil procedure in force in the State in the territory of which it is carried out. The order for its enforcement shall be appended to the decision, without other formality than verification of the authenticity of the decision, by the national authority which the Government of each Member State shall designate for this purpose and shall make known to the Office and to the Court of Justice.

3. When these formalities have been completed on application by the party concerned, the latter may proceed to enforcement in accordance with the national law, by bringing the matter directly before the competent authority.

4. Enforcement may be suspended only by a decision of the Court of Justice. However, the courts of the country concerned shall have jurisdiction over complaints that enforcement is being carried out in an irregular manner.

Title X — Jurisdiction and procedure in legal actions relating to Community trade marks

Section 1 — Application of Regulation (EC) No 44/2001

Article 94. Application of Regulation (EC) No 44/2001. 1. Unless otherwise specified in this Regulation, Regulation (EC) No 44/2001 shall apply to proceedings relating to Community trade marks and applications for Community trade marks, as well as to proceedings relating to simultaneous and successive actions on the basis of Community trade marks and national trade marks.

2. In the case of proceedings in respect of the actions and claims referred to in Article 96:

(a) Articles 2 and 4, points 1, 3, 4 and 5 of Article 5 and Article 31 of Regulation (EC) No 44/2001 shall not apply;

(b) Articles 23 and 24 of Regulation (EC) No 44/2001 shall apply subject to the limitations in Article 97(4) of this Regulation;

(c) the provisions of Chapter II of Regulation (EC) No 44/2001 which are applicable to persons domiciled in a Member State shall also be applicable to persons who do not have a domicile in any Member State but have an establishment therein.

Section 2 — Disputes concerning the infringement and validity of Community trade marks

Article 95. Community trade mark courts.   1.   The Member States shall designate in their territories as limited a number as possible of national courts and tribunals of first and second instance, hereinafter referred to as 'Community trade mark courts', which shall perform the functions assigned to them by this Regulation.

2.   Each Member State shall communicate to the Commission within three years of the entry into force of Regulation (EC) No 40/94 a list of Community trade mark courts indicating their names and their territorial jurisdiction.

3.   Any change made after communication of the list referred to in paragraph 2 in the number, names or territorial jurisdiction of the courts shall be notified without delay by the Member State concerned to the Commission.

4.   The information referred to in paragraphs 2 and 3 shall be notified by the Commission to the Member States and published in the *Official Journal of the European Union.*

5.   As long as a Member State has not communicated the list as stipulated in paragraph 2, jurisdiction for any proceedings resulting from an action or application covered by Article 96, and for which the courts of that State have jurisdiction under Article 97, shall lie with that court of the State in question which would have jurisdiction *ratione loci* and *ratione materiae* in the case of proceedings relating to a national trade mark registered in that State.

Article 96. Jurisdiction over infringement and validity.   The Community trade mark courts shall have exclusive jurisdiction:

(a)   for all infringement actions and – if they are permitted under national law — actions in respect of threatened infringement relating to Community trade marks;

(b)   for actions for declaration of non-infringement, if they are permitted under national law;

(c)   for all actions brought as a result of acts referred to in Article 9(3), second sentence;

(d)   for counterclaims for revocation or for a declaration of invalidity of the Community trade mark pursuant to Article 100.

Article 97. International jurisdiction.   1.   Subject to the provisions of this Regulation as well as to any provisions of Regulation (EC) No 44/2001 applicable by virtue of Article 94, proceedings in respect of the actions and claims referred to in Article 96 shall be brought in the courts of the Member State in which the defendant is domiciled or, if he is not domiciled in any of the Member States, in which he has an establishment.

2.   If the defendant is neither domiciled nor has an establishment in any of the Member States, such proceedings shall be brought in the courts of the Member State in

which the plaintiff is domiciled or, if he is not domiciled in any of the Member States, in which he has an establishment.

3.   If neither the defendant nor the plaintiff is so domiciled or has such an establishment, such proceedings shall be brought in the courts of the Member State where the Office has its seat.

4.   Notwithstanding the provisions of paragraphs 1, 2 and 3:

(a)   Article 23 of Regulation (EC) No 44/2001 shall apply if the parties agree that a different Community trade mark court shall have jurisdiction

(b)   Article 24 of Regulation (EC) No 44/2001 shall apply if the defendant enters an appearance before a different Community trade mark court.

5.   Proceedings in respect of the actions and claims referred to in Article 96, with the exception of actions for a declaration of non-infringement of a Community trade mark, may also be brought in the courts of the Member State in which the act of infringement has been committed or threatened, or in which an act within the meaning of Article 9(3), second sentence, has been committed.

Article 98. Extent of jurisdiction.   1.   A Community trade mark court whose jurisdiction is based on Article 97(1) to (4) shall have jurisdiction in respect of:

(a)   acts of infringement committed or threatened within the territory of any of the Member States;

(b)   acts within the meaning of Article 9(3), second sentence, committed within the territory of any of the Member States.

2.   A Community trade mark court whose jurisdiction is based on Article 97(5) shall have jurisdiction only in respect of acts committed or threatened within the territory of the Member State in which that court is situated.

Article 99. Presumption of validity – Defence as to the merits.   1.   The Community trade mark courts shall treat the Community trade mark as valid unless its validity is put in issue by the defendant with a counterclaim for revocation or for a declaration of invalidity.

2.   The validity of a Community trade mark may not be put in issue in an action for a declaration of non-infringement.

3.   In the actions referred to in Article 96(a) and (c) a plea relating to revocation or invalidity of the Community trade mark submitted otherwise than by way of a counterclaim shall be admissible in so far as the defendant claims that the rights of the proprietor of the Community trade mark could be revoked for lack of use or that the Community trade mark could be declared invalid on account of an earlier right of the defendant.

Article 100. Counterclaims.   1.   A counterclaim for revocation or for a declaration of invalidity may only be based on the grounds for revocation or invalidity mentioned in this Regulation.

2.   A Community trade mark court shall reject a counterclaim for revocation or for a declaration of invalidity if a decision taken by the Office relating to the same subject matter and cause of action and involving the same parties has already become final.

3.   If the counterclaim is brought in a legal action to which the proprietor of the trade mark is not already a party, he shall be informed thereof and may be joined as a party to the action in accordance with the conditions set out in national law.

4.   The Community trade mark court with which a counterclaim for revocation or for a declaration of invalidity of the Community trade mark has been filed shall inform the Office of the date on which the counterclaim was filed. The latter shall record this fact in the Register of Community trade marks.

5.   Article 57(2) to (5) shall apply.

6.   Where a Community trade mark court has given a judgment which has become final on a counterclaim for revocation or for invalidity of a Community trade mark, a copy of the judgment shall be sent to the Office. Any party may request information about such transmission. The Office shall mention the judgment in the Register of Community trade marks in accordance with the provisions of the Implementing Regulation.

7.   The Community trade mark court hearing a counterclaim for revocation or for a declaration of invalidity may stay the proceedings on application by the proprietor of the Community trade mark and after hearing the other parties and may request the defendant to submit an application for revocation or for a declaration of invalidity to the Office within a time limit which it shall determine. If the application is not made within the time limit, the proceedings shall continue; the counterclaim shall be deemed withdrawn. Article 104(3) shall apply.

Article 101. Applicable law.   1.   The Community trade mark courts shall apply the provisions of this Regulation.

2.   On all matters not covered by this Regulation a Community trade mark court shall apply its national law, including its private international law.

3.   Unless otherwise provided in this Regulation, a Community trade mark court shall apply the rules of procedure governing the same type of action relating to a national trade mark in the Member State in which the court is located.

Article 102. Sanctions.   1.   Where a Community trade mark court finds that the defendant has infringed or threatened to infringe a Community trade mark, it shall, unless there are special reasons for not doing so, issue an order prohibiting the defendant from proceeding with the acts which infringed or would infringe the Community trade mark. It shall also take such measures in accordance with its national law as are aimed at ensuring that this prohibition is complied with.

2.   In all other respects the Community trade mark court shall apply the law of the Member State in which the acts of infringement or threatened infringement were committed, including the private international law.

Article 103. Provisional and protective measures.   1.   Application may be made to the courts of a Member State, including Community trade mark courts, for such provisional, including protective, measures in respect of a Community trade mark or Community trade mark application as may be available under the law of that State in respect of a national trade mark, even if, under this Regulation, a Community trade mark court of another Member State has jurisdiction as to the substance of the matter.

2.   A Community trade mark court whose jurisdiction is based on Article 97(1), (2), (3) or (4) shall have jurisdiction to grant provisional and protective measures which, subject to any necessary procedure for recognition and enforcement pursuant to Title III of Regulation (EC) No 44/2001, are applicable in the territory of any Member State. No other court shall have such jurisdiction.

Article 104. Specific rules on related actions. 1. A Community trade mark court hearing an action referred to in Article 96, other than an action for a declaration of non-infringement shall, unless there are special grounds for continuing the hearing, of its own motion after hearing the parties or at the request of one of the parties and after hearing the other parties, stay the proceedings where the validity of the Community trade mark is already in issue before another Community trade mark court on account of a counterclaim or where an application for revocation or for a declaration of invalidity has already been filed at the Office.

2. The Office, when hearing an application for revocation or for a declaration of invalidity shall, unless there are special grounds for continuing the hearing, of its own motion after hearing the parties or at the request of one of the parties and after hearing the other parties, stay the proceedings where the validity of the Community trade mark is already in issue on account of a counterclaim before a Community trade mark court. However, if one of the parties to the proceedings before the Community trade mark court so requests, the court may, after hearing the other parties to these proceedings, stay the proceedings. The Office shall in this instance continue the proceedings pending before it.

3. Where the Community trade mark court stays the proceedings it may order provisional and protective measures for the duration of the stay.

Article 105. Jurisdiction of Community trade mark courts of second instance — Further appeal. 1. An appeal to the Community trade mark courts of second instance shall lie from judgments of the Community trade mark courts of first instance in respect of proceedings arising from the actions and claims referred to in Article 96.

2. The conditions under which an appeal may be lodged with a Community trade mark court of second instance shall be determined by the national law of the Member State in which that court is located.

3. The national rules concerning further appeal shall be applicable in respect of judgments of Community trade mark courts of second instance.

Section 3 — Other disputes concerning Community trade marks

Article 106. Supplementary provisions on the jurisdiction of national courts other than Community trade mark courts. 1. Within the Member State whose courts have jurisdiction under Article 94(1) those courts shall have jurisdiction for actions other than those referred to in Article 96, which would have jurisdiction *ratione loci* and *ratione materiae* in the case of actions relating to a national trade mark registered in that State.

2. Actions relating to a Community trade mark, other than those referred to in Article 96, for which no court has jurisdiction under Article 94(1) and paragraph 1 of this Article may be heard before the courts of the Member State in which the Office has its seat.

Article 107. Obligation of the national court. A national court which is dealing with an action relating to a Community trade mark, other than the action referred to in Article 96, shall treat the trade mark as valid.

Section 4 — Transitional provision

Article 108. Transitional provision relating to the application of the Convention on Jurisdiction and Enforcement. The provisions of Regulation (EC) No 44/2001 which are rendered applicable by the preceding Articles shall have effect in respect of any Member State solely in the text of the Regulation which is in force in respect of that State at any given time.

Title XI — Effects on the laws of the Member States

Section 1 — Civil actions on the basis of more than one trade mark

Article 109. Simultaneous and successive civil actions on the basis of Community trade marks and national trade marks.   1.   Where actions for infringement involving the same cause of action and between the same parties are brought in the courts of different Member States, one seized on the basis of a Community trade mark and the other seized on the basis of a national trade mark:

(a)   the court other than the court first seized shall of its own motion decline jurisdiction in favour of that court where the trade marks concerned are identical and valid for identical goods or services. The court which would be required to decline jurisdiction may stay its proceedings if the jurisdiction of the other court is contested;

(b)   the court other than the court first seized may stay its proceedings where the trade marks concerned are identical and valid for similar goods or services and where the trade marks concerned are similar and valid for identical or similar goods or services.

2.   The court hearing an action for infringement on the basis of a Community trade mark shall reject the action if a final judgment on the merits has been given on the same cause of action and between the same parties on the basis of an identical national trade mark valid for identical goods or services.

3.   The court hearing an action for infringement on the basis of a national trade mark shall reject the action if a final judgment on the merits has been given on the same cause of action and between the same parties on the basis of an identical Community trade mark valid for identical goods or services.

4.   Paragraphs 1, 2 and 3 shall not apply in respect of provisional, including protective, measures.

Section 2 — Application of national laws for the purpose of prohibiting the use of Community trade marks

Article 110. Prohibition of use of Community trade marks.   1.   This Regulation shall, unless otherwise provided for, not affect the right existing under the laws of the Member States to invoke claims for infringement of earlier rights within the meaning of Article 8 or Article 53(2) in relation to the use of a later Community trade mark. Claims for infringement of earlier rights within the meaning of Article 8(2) and (4) may, however, no longer be invoked if the proprietor of the earlier right may no longer apply for a declaration that the Community trade mark is invalid in accordance with Article 54(2).

2.   This Regulation shall, unless otherwise provided for, not affect the right to bring proceedings under the civil, administrative or criminal law of a Member State or under

provisions of Community law for the purpose of prohibiting the use of a Community trade mark to the extent that the use of a national trade mark may be prohibited under the law of that Member State or under Community law.

Article 118. Liability. 1. The contractual liability of the Office shall be governed by the law applicable to the contract in question.

2. The Court of Justice shall be competent to give judgment pursuant to any arbitration clause contained in a contract concluded by the Office.

3. In the case of non-contractual liability, the Office shall, in accordance with the general principles common to the laws of the Member States, make good any damage caused by its departments or by its servants in the performance of their duties.

4. The Court of Justice shall have jurisdiction in disputes relating to compensation for the damage referred to in paragraph 3.

5. The personal liability of its servants towards the Office shall be governed by the provisions laid down in their Staff Regulations or in the Conditions of Employment applicable to them.

Section 4 — Implementation of procedures

Article 130. Competence. For taking decisions in connection with the procedures laid down in this Regulation, the following shall be competent:
   (a)   examiners;
   (b)   Opposition Divisions;
   (c)   an Administration of Trade Marks and Legal Division;
   (d)   Cancellation Divisions;
   (e)   Boards of Appeal.

Article 131. Examiners. An examiner shall be responsible for taking decisions on behalf of the Office in relation to an application for registration of a Community trade mark, including the matters referred to in Articles 36, 37 and 68, except in so far as an Opposition Division is responsible.

Article 132. Opposition Divisions. An Opposition Division shall be responsible for taking decisions on an opposition to an application to register a Community trade mark. ...

Article 133. Administration of Trade Marks and Legal Division. 1. The Administration of Trade Marks and Legal Division shall be responsible for those decisions required by this Regulation which do not fall within the competence of an examiner, an Opposition Division or a Cancellation Division.
It shall in particular be responsible for decisions in respect of entries in the Register of Community trade marks.

2. It shall also be responsible for keeping the list of professional representatives which is referred to in Article 93.

3. A decision of the Division shall be taken by one member.

Article 134. Cancellation Divisions. A Cancellation Division shall be responsible for taking decisions in relation to an application for the revocation or declaration of invalidity of a Community trade mark. ...

Article 135. Boards of Appeal.   1.   The Boards of Appeal shall be responsible for deciding on appeals from decisions of the examiners, Opposition Divisions, Administration of Trade Marks and Legal Division and Cancellation Divisions. ...

D.1.   Regulation (EC) No 733/2002 of the European Parliament and of the Council of 22 April 2002 on the implementation of the .eu Top Level Domain (OJ, L 113 of 30 April 2002)[1]

(9)   Internet management has generally been based on the principles of non-interference, self-management and self-regulation. To the extent possible and without prejudice to Community law, these principles should also apply to the .eu ccTLD. The implementation of the .eu TLD may take into consideration best practices in this regard and could be supported by voluntary guidelines or codes of conduct where appropriate.

(10) The establishment of the .eu TLD should contribute to the promotion of the European Union image on the global information networks and bring an added value to the Internet naming system in addition to the national ccTLDs.

(11) The objective of this Regulation is to establish the conditions of implementation of the .eu TLD, to provide for the designation of a Registry and establish the general policy framework within which the Registry will function. National ccTLDs are not covered by this Regulation.

(12) The Registry is the entity charged with the organisation, administration and management of the .eu TLD, including maintenance of the corresponding databases and the associated public query services, the accreditation of Registrars, the registration of domain names applied for by accredited Registrars, the operation of the TLD name servers and the dissemination of TLD zone files. Public query services associated with the TLD are referred to as 'Who is' queries. 'Who is'-type databases should be in conformity with Community law on data protection and privacy. Access to these databases provides information on a domain name holder and is an essential tool in boosting user confidence.

Article 1. Objective and scope.   1.   The objective of this Regulation is to implement the .eu country code Top Level Domain (ccTLD) within the Community. The Regulation sets out the conditions for such implementation, including the designation of a Registry, and establishes the general policy framework within which the Registry will function.

2.   This Regulation shall apply without prejudice to arrangements in Member States regarding national ccTLDs.

Article 2. Definitions.   For the purposes of this Regulation:

(a)   'Registry' means the entity entrusted with the organisation, administration and management of the .eu TLD including maintenance of the corresponding databases and the associated public query services, registration of domain names, operation of the Registry of domain names, operation of the Registry TLD name servers and dissemination of TLD zone files;

---

[1]   As modified by Regulation No 1137/2008 of the European Parliament and of the Council of 22 October 2008 (OJ, L 311 of 21 November 2008). [Note of the Editor]

(b) 'Registrar' means a person or entity that, via contract with the Registry, provides domain name registration services to registrants.

Article 3. Characteristics of the Registry. 2. The Registry shall be a non-profit organisation, formed in accordance with the law of a Member State and having its registered office, central administration and principal place of business within the Community. …

Article 4. Obligations of the Registry. 1. The Registry shall observe the rules, policies and procedures laid down in this Regulation and the contracts referred to in Article 3. The Registry shall observe transparent and non-discriminatory procedures.

2. The Registry shall:

(a) organise, administer and manage the .eu TLD in the general interest and on the basis of principles of quality, efficiency, reliability and accessibility;

(b) register domain names in the .eu TLD through any accredited .eu Registrar requested by any:

(i) undertaking having its registered office, central administration or principal place of business within the Community, or

(ii) organisation established within the Community without prejudice to the application of national law, or

(iii) natural person resident within the Community;

(c) impose fees directly related to costs incurred;

(d) implement the extra-judicial settlement of conflicts policy based on recovery of costs and a procedure to resolve promptly disputes between domain name holders regarding rights relating to names including intellectual property rights as well as disputes in relation to individual decisions by the Registry. This policy shall be adopted in accordance with Article 5(1) and take into consideration the recommendations of the World Intellectual Property Organisation. The policy shall provide adequate procedural guaranties for the parties concerned, and shall apply without prejudice to any court proceeding;

(e) adopt procedures for, and carry out, accreditation of .eu Registrars and ensure effective and fair conditions of competition among .eu Registrars;

(f) ensure the integrity of the databases of domain names.

Article 7. Reservation of rights. The Community shall retain all rights relating to the.eu TLD including, in particular, intellectual property rights and other rights to the Registry databases required to ensure the implementation of this Regulation and the right to re-designate the Registry.

D.2.   Commission Regulation (EC) No 874/2004 of 28 April 2004 laying down public policy rules concerning the implementation and functions of .eu Top Level Domain and the principles governing registration (OJ, L 162 of 30 April 2004)[1]

(5)   To ensure better protection of consumers' rights, and without prejudice to any Community rules concerning jurisdiction and applicable law, the applicable law in disputes between registrars and registrants on matters concerning Community titles should be the law of one of the Member States.

(16)   The Registry should provide for an ADR procedure which takes into account the international best practices in this area and in particular the relevant World Intellectual Property Organization (WIPO) recommendations, to ensure that speculative and abusive registrations are avoided as far as possible.

(17)   The Registry should select service providers that have appropriate expertise on the basis of objective, transparent and non-discriminatory criteria. ADR should respect a minimum of uniform procedural rules, similar to the ones set out in the Uniform Dispute Resolution Policy adopted by the Internet Corporation of Assigned Names and Numbers (ICANN).

Article 5. Provisions for registrars.   Without prejudice to any rule governing jurisdiction and applicable law, agreements between the Registrar and the registrant of a domain name cannot designate, as applicable law, a law other than the law of one of the Member States, nor can they designate a dispute-resolution body, unless selected by the Registry pursuant to Article 23, nor an arbitration court or a court located outside the Community. …

Article 18. Improper registrations.   Where a domain name is considered by a Court of a Member State to be defamatory, racist or contrary to public policy, it shall be blocked by the Registry upon notification of a Court decision and shall be revoked upon notification of a final court decision. The Registry shall block from future registration those names which have been subject to such a court order for as long as such order remains valid.

E.1.   Council Regulation (EC) No 1383/2003 of 22 July 2003 concerning customs action against goods suspected of infringing certain intellectual property rights and the measures to be taken against goods found to have infringed such rights (OJ, L 196 of 2 August 2003)

(2)   The marketing of counterfeit and pirated goods, and indeed all goods infringing intellectual property rights, does considerable damage to law-abiding manufacturers and traders and to right-holders, as well as deceiving and in some cases endangering the health and safety of consumers. Such goods should, in so far as is possible, be kept off the market and measures adopted to deal effectively with this unlawful activity without

---

[1]   As finally modified by Commission Regulation (EC) No 560/2009 of 26 June 2009 (OJ, L 166 of 27 June 2009), as rectified in OJ, L 291 of 7 November 2009. [Note of the Editor]

impeding the freedom of legitimate trade. This objective is consistent with efforts under way at international level.

(3)   In cases where counterfeit goods, pirated goods and, more generally, goods infringing an intellectual property right originate in or come from third countries, their introduction into the Community customs territory, including their transhipment, release for free circulation in the Community, placing under a suspensive procedure and placing in a free zone or warehouse, should be prohibited and a procedure set up to enable the customs authorities to enforce this prohibition as effectively as possible.

(4)   Customs authorities should also be able to take action against counterfeit goods, pirated goods and goods infringing certain intellectual property rights which are in the process of being exported, re-exported or leaving the Community customs territory.

(5)   Action by the customs authorities should involve, for the period necessary to determine whether suspect goods are indeed counterfeit goods, pirated goods or goods infringing certain intellectual property rights, suspending release for free circulation, export and re-export or, in the case of goods placed under a suspensive procedure, placed in a free zone or a free warehouse, in the process of being re-exported with notification, introduced into the customs territory or leaving that territory, detaining those goods.

(8)   Proceedings initiated to determine whether an intellectual property right has been infringed under national law will be conducted with reference to the criteria used to establish whether goods produced in that Member State infringe intellectual property rights. This Regulation does not affect the Member States' provisions on the competence of the courts or judicial procedures.

Chapter I — Subject matter and scope

Article 1.   1.   This Regulation sets out the conditions for action by the customs authorities when goods are suspected of infringing an intellectual property right in the following situations:

(a)   when they are entered for release for free circulation, export or re-export in accordance with Article 61 of Council Regulation (EC) No 2913/92 of 12 October 1992 establishing the Community Customs Code;

(b)   when they are found during checks on goods entering or leaving the Community customs territory in accordance with Articles 37 and 183 of Regulation (EEC) No 2913/92, placed under a suspensive procedure within the meaning of Article 84(1)(a) of that Regulation, in the process of being re-exported subject to notification under Article 182(2) of that Regulation or placed in a free zone or free warehouse within the meaning of Article 166 of that Regulation.

2.   This Regulation also fixes the measures to be taken by the competent authorities when the goods referred to in paragraph 1 are found to infringe intellectual property rights.

Article 2.   1.   For the purposes of this Regulation, 'goods infringing an intellectual property right' means:

(a)   'counterfeit goods', namely:

(i)   goods, including packaging, bearing without authorisation a trademark identical to the trademark validly registered in respect of the same type of goods, or which cannot be distinguished in its essential aspects from such a trademark, and which thereby infringes the trademark-holder's rights under Community law, as provided for by Council Regulation (EC) No 40/94 of 20 December 1993 on the Community trademark or the law of the Member State in which the application for action by the customs authorities is made;

(ii)   any trademark symbol (including a logo, label, sticker, brochure, instructions for use or guarantee document bearing such a symbol), even if presented separately, on the same conditions as the goods referred to in point (i);

(iii)   packaging materials bearing the trademarks of counterfeit goods, presented separately, on the same conditions as the goods referred to in point (i);

(b)   'pirated goods', namely goods which are or contain copies made without the consent of the holder of a copyright or related right or design right, regardless of whether it is registered in national law, or of a person authorised by the right-holder in the country of production in cases where the making of those copies would constitute an infringement of that right under Council Regulation (EC) No 6/2002 of 12 December 2001 on Community designs or the law of the Member State in which the application for customs action is made;

(c)   goods which, in the Member State in which the application for customs action is made, infringe:

(i)   a patent under that Member State's law;

(ii)   a supplementary protection certificate of the kind provided for in Council Regulation (EEC) No 1768/92 or Regulation (EC) No 1610/96 of the European Parliament and of the Council;

(iii)   a national plant variety right under the law of that Member State or a Community plant variety right of the kind provided for in Council Regulation (EC) No 2100/94;

(iv)   designations of origin or geographical indications under the law of that Member State or Council Regulations (EEC) No 2081/92 and (EC) No 1493/1999;

(v)   geographical designations of the kind provided for in Council Regulation (EEC) No 1576/89.

2.   For the purposes of this Regulation, 'right-holder' means:

(a)   the holder of a trademark, copyright or related right, design right, patent, supplementary protection certificate, plant variety right, protected designation of origin, protected geographical indication and, more generally, any right referred to in paragraph 1; or

(b)   any other person authorised to use any of the intellectual property rights mentioned in point (a), or a representative of the right-holder or authorised user.

3.   Any mould or matrix which is specifically designed or adapted for the manufacture of goods infringing an intellectual property right shall be treated as goods of that kind if the use of such moulds or matrices infringes the right-holder's rights under Community law or the law of the Member State in which the application for action by the customs authorities is made.

Article 3.   1.   This Regulation shall not apply to goods bearing a trademark with the consent of the holder of that trademark or to goods bearing a protected designation of origin or a protected geographical indication or which are protected by a patent or a supplementary protection certificate, by a copyright or related right or by a design right or a plant variety right and which have been manufactured with the consent of the right-holder but are placed in one of the situations referred to in Article 1(1) without the latter's consent.

It shall similarly not apply to goods referred to in the first subparagraph and which have been manufactured or are protected by another intellectual property right referred to in Article 2(1) under conditions other than those agreed with the right-holder.

2.   Where a traveller's personal baggage contains goods of a non-commercial nature within the limits of the duty-free allowance and there are no material indications to suggest the goods are part of commercial traffic, Member States shall consider such goods to be outside the scope of this Regulation.

Chapter II — Applications for action by the customs authorities

Section 1 — Measures prior to an application for action by the customs authorities

Article 4. 1.   Where the customs authorities, in the course of action in one of the situations referred to in Article 1(1) and before an application has been lodged by a right-holder or granted, have sufficient grounds for suspecting that goods infringe an intellectual property right, they may suspend the release of the goods or detain them for a period of three working days from the moment of receipt of the notification by the right-holder and by the declarant or holder of the goods, if the latter are known, in order to enable the right-holder to submit an application for action in accordance with Article 5.

2.   In accordance with the rules in force in the Member State concerned, the customs authorities may, without divulging any information other than the actual or supposed number of items and their nature and before informing the right-holder of the possible infringement, ask the right-holder to provide them with any information they may need to confirm their suspicions.

Section 2 — The lodging and processing of applications for customs action

Article 5. 1.   In each Member State a right-holder may apply in writing to the competent customs department for action by the customs authorities when goods are found in one of the situations referred to in Article 1(1) (application for action).

2.   Each Member State shall designate the customs department competent to receive and process applications for action.

3.   Where electronic data interchange systems exist, the Member States shall encourage right-holders to lodge applications electronically.

4.   Where the applicant is the right-holder of a Community trademark or a Community design right, a Community plant variety right or a designation of origin or geographical indication or a geographical designation protected by the Community, an application may, in addition to requesting action by the customs authorities of the Member State in which it is lodged, request action by the customs authorities of one or more other Member States. ... .

Chapter III — Conditions governing action by the customs authorities and by the authority competent to decide on the case

Article 9. 1.   Where a customs office to which the decision granting an application by the right-holder has been forwarded pursuant to Article 8 is satisfied, after consulting the applicant where necessary, that goods in one of the situations referred to in Article 1(1) are suspected of infringing an intellectual property right covered by that decision, it shall suspend release of the goods or detain them. ...

Article 10.   The law in force in the Member State within the territory of which the goods are placed in one of the situations referred to in Article 1(1) shall apply when deciding whether an intellectual property right has been infringed under national law.

That law shall also apply to the immediate notification of the customs department or office referred to in Article 9(1) that the procedure provided for in Article 13 has been initiated, unless the procedure was initiated by that department or office.

Article 12.   A right-holder receiving the particulars cited in the first subparagraph of Article 9(3) shall use that information only for the purposes specified in Articles 10, 11 and 13(1).

Any other use, not permitted by the national legislation of the Member State where the situation arose, may, on the basis of the law of the Member State in which the goods in question are located, cause the right-holder to incur civil liability and lead to the suspension of the application for action, for the period of validity remaining before renewal, in the Member State in which the events have taken place.

In the event of a further breach of this rule, the competent customs department may refuse to renew the application. In the case of an application of the kind provided for in Article 5(4), it must also notify the other Member States indicated on the form.

Article 14.   1.   In the case of goods suspected of infringing design rights, patents, supplementary protection certificates or plant variety rights, the declarant, owner, importer, holder or consignee of the goods shall be able to obtain the release of the goods or an end to their detention on provision of a security, provided that:

(a)   the customs office or department referred to in Article 9(1) has been notified, in accordance with Article 13(1), that a procedure has been initiated within the period provided for in Article 13(1) to establish whether an intellectual property right has been infringed under national law;

(b)   the authority empowered for this purpose has not authorised precautionary measures before the expiry of the time limit laid down in Article 13(1);

(c)   all customs formalities have been completed.

2.   The security provided for in paragraph 1 must be sufficient to protect the interests of the right-holder.

Payment of the security shall not affect the other legal remedies available to the right-holder.

Where the procedure to determine whether an intellectual property right has been infringed under national law has been initiated other than on the initiative of the holder of a design right, patent, supplementary protection certificate or plant variety right, the security shall be released if the person initiating the said procedure does not exercise his right to institute legal proceedings within 20 working days of the date on which he receives notification of the suspension of release or detention.

Where the second subparagraph of Article 13(1) applies, this period may be extended to a maximum of 30 working days.

Chapter IV — Provisions applicable to goods found to infringe an intellectual property right

Article 16.   Goods found to infringe an intellectual property right at the end of the procedure provided for in Article 9 shall not be:
— allowed to enter into the Community customs territory,
— released for free circulation,
— removed from the Community customs territory,
— exported,
— re-exported,
— placed under a suspensive procedure or
— placed in a free zone or free warehouse.

Chapter VI — Liability of the customs authorities and the right-holder

Article 19.   1.   Save as provided by the law of the Member State in which an application is lodged or, in the case of an application under Article 5(4), by the law of the Member State in which goods infringing an intellectual property right are not detected by a customs office, the acceptance of an application shall not entitle the right-holder to compensation in the event that such goods are not detected by a customs office and are released or no action is taken to detain them in accordance with Article 9(1).

2.   The exercise by a customs office or by another duly empowered authority of the powers conferred on them in order to fight against goods infringing an intellectual property right shall not render them liable towards the persons involved in the situations referred to in Article 1(1) or the persons affected by the measures provided for in Article 4 for damages suffered by them as a result of the authority's intervention, except where provided for by the law of the Member State in which the application is made or, in the case of an application under Article 5(4), by the law of the Member State in which loss or damage is incurred.

3.   A right-holder's civil liability shall be governed by the law of the Member State in which the goods in question were placed in one of the situations referred to in Article 1(1).

E.2.   Commission Regulation (EC) No 1891/2004 of 21 October 2004 laying down provisions for the implementation of Council Regulation (EC) No 1383/2003 concerning customs action against goods suspected of infringing certain intellectual property rights and the measures to be taken against goods found to have infringed such rights (OJ, L 328 of 30 October 2004)[1]

(4)   It is necessary to specify the nature of the proof of ownership of intellectual property required under the second subparagraph of Article 5(5) of Regulation (EC) No 1383/2003.

---

[1]   As modified by Commission Regulation (EC) No 1172/2007 of 5 October 2007 (OJ, L 261 of 6 October 2007). [Note of the Editor]

Article 1.   For the purposes of Article 2(2)(b) of Regulation (EC) No 1383/2003, hereinafter 'the basic Regulation', the right-holder or any other person authorised to use the right may be represented by natural or legal persons.

The persons referred to in the first paragraph shall include collecting societies which have as their sole or principal purpose the management or administration of copyrights or related rights; groups or representatives who have lodged a registration application for a protected designation of origin or a protected geographical indication; and plant breeders.

Article 2.   1.   If an application for action within the meaning of Article 5(1) of the basic Regulation is lodged by the right-holder himself, the proof required under the second subparagraph of Article 5(5) shall be as follows:

(a)   in the case of a right that is registered or for which an application has been lodged, proof of registration with the relevant office or proof that the application has been lodged;

(b)   in the case of a copyright, related right or design right which is not registered or for which an application has not been lodged, any evidence of authorship or of the applicant's status as original holder.

A copy of registration from the database of a national or international office may be considered to be proof for the purposes of point (a) of the first subparagraph.

For protected designations of origin and protected geographical indications, the proof referred to in point (a) of the first subparagraph shall, in addition, consist in proof that the right-holder is the producer or group and proof that the designation or indication has been registered. This subparagraph shall apply *mutatis mutandis* to wines and spirits.

2.   Where the application for action is lodged by any other person authorised to use one of the rights referred to in Article 2(1) of the basic Regulation, proof shall, in addition to the proof required under paragraph 1 of this Article, consist in the document by virtue of which the person is authorised to use the right in question.

3.   Where the application for action is lodged by a representative of the right-holder or of any other person authorised to use one of the rights referred to in Article 2(2) of the basic Regulation, proof shall, in addition to the proof referred to in paragraph 1 of this Article, consist in his authorisation to act.

A representative, as referred to in the first subparagraph, must produce the declaration required pursuant to Article 6 of the basic Regulation, signed by the persons referred to in paragraphs 1 and 2 of this Article, or a document authorising him to bear any costs arising from customs action on their behalf in accordance with Article 6 of the basic Regulation.

F.   Directive 2004/48/EC of the European Parliament and of the Council of 29 April 2004 on the enforcement of intellectual property rights (OJ, L 157 of 30 April 2004)[1]

(11)   This Directive does not aim to establish harmonised rules for judicial cooperation, jurisdiction, the recognition and enforcement of decisions in civil and commercial matters, or deal with applicable law. There are Community instruments which govern such matters in general terms and are, in principle, equally applicable to intellectual property.

(12)   This Directive should not affect the application of the rules of competition, and in particular Articles 81 and 82 of the Treaty. The measures provided for in this Directive should not be used to restrict unduly competition in a manner contrary to the Treaty.

G.1.   Council Directive 93/83/EEC of 27 September 1993 on the coordination of certain rules concerning copyright and rights related to copyright applicable to satellite broadcasting and cable retransmission (OJ, L 248 of 6 October 1993)

(5)   Whereas, however, the achievement of these objectives in respect of cross-border satellite broadcasting and the cable retransmission of programmes from other Member States is currently still obstructed by a series of differences between national rules of copyright and some degree of legal uncertainty; whereas this means that holders of rights are exposed to the threat of seeing their works exploited without payment of remuneration or that the individual holders of exclusive rights in various Member States block the exploitation of their rights; whereas the legal uncertainty in particular constitutes a direct obstacle in the free circulation of programmes within the Community;

(6)   Whereas a distinction is currently drawn for copyright purposes between communication to the public by direct satellite and communication to the public by communications satellite; whereas, since individual reception is possible and affordable nowadays with both types of satellite, there is no longer any justification for this differing legal treatment;

(7)   Whereas the free broadcasting of programmes is further impeded by the current legal uncertainty over whether broadcasting by a satellite whose signals can be received directly affects the rights in the country of transmission only or in all countries of reception together; whereas, since communications satellites and direct satellites are treated alike for copyright purposes, this legal uncertainty now affects almost all programmes broadcast in the Community by satellite;

(13) Whereas, therefore, an end should be put to the differences of treatment of the transmission of programmes by communications satellite which exist in the Member States, so that the vital distinction throughout the Community becomes whether works and other protected subject matter are communicated to the public; whereas this will also ensure equal treatment of the suppliers of cross-border broadcasts, regardless of whether they use a direct broadcasting satellite or a communications satellite;

---

[1]   As finally rectified in OJ, L 204 of 4 August 2007. [Note of the Editor]

(14) Whereas the legal uncertainty regarding the rights to be acquired which impedes cross-border satellite broadcasting should be overcome by defining the notion of communication to the public by satellite at a Community level; whereas this definition should at the same time specify where the act of communication takes place; whereas such a definition is necessary to avoid the cumulative application of several national laws to one single act of broadcasting; whereas communication to the public by satellite occurs only when, and in the Member State where, the programme-carrying signals are introduced under the control and responsibility of the broadcasting organization into an uninterrupted chain of communication leading to the satellite and down towards the earth; whereas normal technical procedures relating to the programme-carrying signals should not be considered as interruptions to the chain of broadcasting;

Chapter I — Definitions

Article 1. Definitions.   1.   For the purpose of this Directive, 'satellite' means any satellite operating on frequency bands which, under telecommunications law, are reserved for the broadcast of signals for reception by the public or which are reserved for closed, point-to-point communication. In the latter case, however, the circumstances in which individual reception of the signals takes place must be comparable to those which apply in the first case.

2.   (a)   For the purpose of this Directive, 'communication to the public by satellite' means the act of introducing, under the control and responsibility of the broadcasting organization, the programme-carrying signals intended for reception by the public into an uninterrupted chain of communication leading to the satellite and down towards the earth.

(b)   The act of communication to the public by satellite occurs solely in the Member State where, under the control and responsibility of the broadcasting organization, the programme-carrying signals are introduced into an uninterrupted chain of communication leading to the satellite and down towards the earth.

(c)   If the programme-carrying signals are encrypted, then there is communication to the public by satellite on condition that the means for decrypting the broadcast are provided to the public by the broadcasting organization or with its consent.

(d)   Where an act of communication to the public by satellite occurs in a non-Community State which does not provide the level of protection provided for under Chapter II;

(i)   if the programme-carrying signals are transmitted to the satellite from an uplink situation situated in a Member State, that act of communication to the public by satellite shall be deemed to have occurred in that Member State and the rights provided for under Chapter II shall be exercisable against the person operating the uplink station; or

(ii)   if there is no use of an uplink station situated in a Member State but a broadcasting organization established in a Member State has commissioned the act of communication to the public by satellite, that act shall be deemed to have occured in the Member State in which the broadcasting organization has its principal establishment in the Community and the rights provided for under Chapter II shall be exercisable against the broadcasting organization.

3.   For the purposes of this Directive, 'cable retransmission' means the simultaneous, unaltered and unabridged retransmission by a cable or microwave system

for reception by the public of an initial transmission from another Member State, by wire or over the air, including that by satellite, of television or radio programmes intended for reception by the public.

4.   For the purposes of this Directive 'collecting society' means any organization which manages or administers copyright or rights related to copyright as its sole purpose or as one of its main purposes.

5.   For the purposes of this Directive, the principal director of a cinematographic or audiovisual work shall be considered as its author or one of its authors. Member States may provide for others to be considered as its co-authors.

Chapter II — Broadcasting of programmes by satellite

Article 4. Rights of performers, phonogram producers and broadcasting organizations.   1.   For the purposes of communication to the public by satellite, the rights of performers, phonogram producers and broadcasting organizations shall be protected in accordance with the provisions of Articles 6, 7, 8 and 10 of Directive 92/100/EEC.

2.   For the purposes of paragraph 1, 'broadcasting by wireless means' in Directive 92/100/EEC shall be understood as including communication to the public by satellite.

3.   With regard to the exercise of the rights referred to in paragraph 1, Articles 2(7) and 12 of Directive 92/100/EEC shall apply.

G.2.   Directive 2006/115/EC of the European Parliament and of the Council of 12 December 2006 on rental right and lending right and on certain rights related to copyright in the field of intellectual property (codified version) (OJ, L 376 of 27 December 2006)

Chapter I — Rental and lending right

Article 1. Object of harmonisation.   1.   In accordance with the provisions of this Chapter, Member States shall provide, subject to Article 6, a right to authorise or prohibit the rental and lending of originals and copies of copyright works, and other subject matter as set out in Article 3(1).

2.   The rights referred to in paragraph 1 shall not be exhausted by any sale or other act of distribution of originals and copies of copyright works and other subject matter as set out in Article 3(1).

Chapter II — Rights related to copyright

Article 8. Broadcasting and communication to the public.   1.   Member States shall provide for performers the exclusive right to authorise or prohibit the broadcasting by wireless means and the communication to the public of their performances, except where the performance is itself already a broadcast performance or is made from a fixation.

2.   Member States shall provide a right in order to ensure that a single equitable remuneration is paid by the user, if a phonogram published for commercial purposes, or

a reproduction of such phonogram, is used for broadcasting by wireless means or for any communication to the public, and to ensure that this remuneration is shared between the relevant performers and phonogram producers. Member States may, in the absence of agreement between the performers and phonogram producers, lay down the conditions as to the sharing of this remuneration between them.

3.   Member States shall provide for broadcasting organisations the exclusive right to authorise or prohibit the rebroadcasting of their broadcasts by wireless means, as well as the communication to the public of their broadcasts if such communication is made in places accessible to the public against payment of an entrance fee.

G.3.   ECJ case-law

The Court of Justice interpreted Directives 93/83/EEC and 92/100/EEC (subsequently substituted by Directive 2006/115/EC) in case *Lagardère Active Broadcast* (14 July 2005, case C-192/04, Reports, I-7199). The company Lagardère, having its registered office in France, broadcasted by satellite its programmes, using repeater stations located in French territory as well as in German one and a digital audio terrestrial circuit. Notwithstanding, the transmissions were only directed to French public. According to the Court, Directive 93/83/EEC.

42. ... is to provide both broadcasting organisations and the holders of rights with legal certainty regarding the legislation applicable to a chain of communication.

43.   It follows from all the foregoing that a broadcast of the kind at issue in this case does not constitute a communication by satellite to the public within the meaning of Article 1(2)(a) of Directive 93/83. Consequently, it does not fall within the scope of Article 1(2)(b).

44.   Therefore, the answer to the first question must be that, in the case of a broadcast of the kind at issue in this case, Directive 93/83 does not preclude the fee for phonogram use being governed not only by the law of the Member State in whose territory the broadcasting company is established but also by the legislation of the Member State in which, for technical reasons, the terrestrial transmitter broadcasting to the first State is located.

Lagardère paid in France a royalty accruing to the performers and producers of the broadcasted phonograms, while the controlled company which managed the German plant only a flat-rate in Germany. The aforesaid amount will be automatically deducted by Lagardère from the royalties due in France. To this regard, the Court affirmed:

46.   ... from its wording and scheme that Directive 92/100 provides for minimal harmonisation regarding rights related to copyright. Thus, it does not purport to detract, in particular, from the principle of the territoriality of those rights, which is recognised in international law and also in the EC Treaty. Those rights are therefore of a territorial nature and, moreover, domestic law can only penalise conduct engaged in within national territory.

47.   Furthermore, it must be borne in mind that in this case the programmes containing the protected phonograms are broadcast using terrestrial transmitters in French territory and from a terrestrial transmitter in German territory. In so far as the broadcasting operations are thus carried out in the territory of two Member States, those rights are based on the legislation of two States.

48.   In that context, it should be noted that the Court has already held that there is no objective reason to justify the laying down by the Community judicature of specific methods for determining what constitutes uniform equitable remuneration, which would necessarily entail its acting in the place of the Member States, which are not bound by any particular criteria under Directive 92/100. It is therefore for the Member States alone to determine, in their own territory, what are the most relevant criteria for ensuring adherence to the Community concept of equitable remuneration …

49.   However, the Member States must exercise their powers in this area within the limits laid down by Community law and, in particular, by Article 8(2) of Directive 92/100, which requires that such remuneration be equitable. More specifically, they must lay down rules for equitable remuneration that enable a proper balance to be achieved between the interests of performers and producers in obtaining remuneration for the broadcast of a particular phonogram and the interests of third parties in being able to broadcast the phonogram on terms that are reasonable …

50.   Thus, whether the remuneration, which represents the consideration for the use of a commercial phonogram, in particular for broadcasting purposes, is equitable is to be assessed, in particular, in the light of the value of that use in trade …

51.   In order to determine that value, it is necessary to obtain guidance on this specific point from the criteria referred to in the 17th recital in the preamble to Directive 93/83 and therefore to take account of all the parameters of the broadcast, such as, in particular, the actual audience, the potential audience and the language version of the broadcast.

52.   The use of phonograms for a broadcasting operation in the Member State where that terrestrial transmitter is located does not in any way reduce the actual or potential audience in the State where the broadcasting company is established or, consequently, the value of that use in trade within the territory of the latter State.

53.   Moreover, it is clear from the file that the broadcasting of phonograms constitutes actual commercial exploitation only within French territory since the advertising slots are marketed only to French undertakings. Similarly, almost the entire audience is in France since, first, the broadcast at issue in this case can only be received by the public in a small area of German territory and, second, the broadcast is in the French language.

54.   However, in so far as an actual or potential audience for broadcasts in the Member State where the abovementioned terrestrial transmitter is situated is not entirely absent, a certain economic value attaches to the use of protected phonograms in that State, even though it is low. Consequently, the latter State may, in the light of the principle of territoriality referred to in paragraph 46 of this judgment, require payment of equitable remuneration for the broadcast of those phonograms within its own territory. The circumstances mentioned in the foregoing paragraph, which limit the economic value of such use, are relevant only as regards the rate of that royalty and it will be for the courts of that Member State to take them into account when determining the royalty. On the other hand, they do not detract from the fact that the royalty thus determined constitutes payment for the use of phonograms in that State and that that payment cannot be taken into account in order to calculate equitable remuneration in another Member State.

55.   In view of the foregoing considerations, the answer to the second question must be that Article 8(2) of Directive 92/100 must be interpreted as meaning that, for determination of the equitable remuneration mentioned in that provision, the

broadcasting company is not entitled unilaterally to deduct from the amount of the royalty for phonogram use payable in the Member State in which it is established the amount of the royalty paid or claimed in the Member State in whose territory the terrestrial transmitter broadcasting to the first State is located.

H.   Commission Recommendation 2005/737/EC of 18 October 2005 on collective cross-border management of copyright and related rights for legitimate online music services (OJ, L 276 of 21 October 2005)[1]

(1)   In April 2004 the Commission adopted a Communication on the Management of Copyright and Related Rights in the Internal Market.

(2)   The European Parliament, in its report of 15 January 2004, stated that right-holders should be able to enjoy copyright and related rights protection wherever such rights are established, independent of national borders or modes of use during the whole term of their validity.

(3)   The European Parliament further emphasised that any action by the Community in respect of the collective cross-border management of copyright and related rights should strengthen the confidence of artists, including writers and musicians, that the pan-European use of their creative works will be financially rewarded.

(4)   New technologies have led to the emergence of a new generation of commercial users that make use of musical works and other subject matter online. The provision of legitimate online music services requires management of a series of copyright and related rights.

(5)   One category of those rights is the exclusive right of reproduction which covers all reproductions made in the process of online distribution of a musical work. Other categories of rights are the right of communication to the public of musical works, the right to equitable remuneration for the communication to the public of other subject matter and the exclusive right of making available a musical work or other subject matter.

(6)   Pursuant to Directive 2001/29/EC of the European Parliament and of the Council of 22 May 2001 on the harmonisation of certain aspects of copyright and related rights in the information society and Council Directive 92/100/EEC of 19 November 1992 on rental right and lending right and on certain rights related to copyright in the field of intellectual property, a licence is required for each of the rights in the online exploitation of musical works. These rights may be managed by collective rights managers that provide certain management services to right-holders as agents or by individual right-holders themselves.

(7)   Licensing of online rights is often restricted by territory, and commercial users negotiate in each Member State with each of the respective collective rights managers for each right that is included in the online exploitation.

(8)   In the era of online exploitation of musical works, however, commercial users need a licensing policy that corresponds to the ubiquity of the online environment and

---

[1]   As rectified in OJ, L 284 of 27 October 2005. [Note of the Editor]

which is multi-territorial. It is therefore appropriate to provide for multi-territorial licensing in order to enhance greater legal certainty to commercial users in relation to their activity and to foster the development of legitimate online services, increasing, in turn, the revenue stream for right-holders.

(9)   Freedom to provide collective management services across national borders entails that right-holders are able to freely choose the collective rights manager for the management of the rights necessary to operate legitimate online music services across the Community. That right implies the possibility to entrust or transfer all or a part of the online rights to another collective rights manager irrespective of the Member State of residence or the nationality of either the collective rights manager or the rights-holder.

(10)   Fostering effective structures for cross-border management of rights should also ensure that collective rights managers achieve a higher level of rationalisation and transparency, with regard to compliance with competition rules, especially in the light of the requirements arising out of the digital environment.

(11)   The relationship between right-holders and collective rights managers, whether based on contract or statutory membership rules, should include a minimum protection for right-holders with respect to all categories of rights that are necessary for the provision of legitimate online music services. There should be no difference in treatment of right-holders by rights managers on the basis of the Member State of residence or nationality.

(12) Royalties collected on behalf of right-holders should be distributed equitably and without discrimination on the grounds of residence, nationality, or category of right-holder. In particular, royalties collected on behalf of right-holders in Member States other than those in which the right-holders are resident or of which they are nationals should be distributed as effectively and efficiently as possible.

(13) Additional recommendations on accountability, right-holder representation in the decision-making bodies of collective rights managers and dispute resolution should ensure that collective rights managers achieve a higher level of rationalisation and transparency and that right-holders and commercial users can make informed choices. There should be no difference in treatment on the basis of category of membership in the collective rights management society: all right-holders, be they authors, composers, publishers, record producers, performers or others, should be treated equally.

(14)   It is appropriate to continuously assess the development of the online music market …

Definitions

1.   For the purposes of this Recommendation the following definitions are applied:
(a)   'management of copyright and related rights for the provision of legitimate online music services at Community level' means the provision of the following services: the grant of licences to commercial users, the auditing and monitoring of rights, the enforcement of copyright and related rights, the collection of royalties and the distribution of royalties to right-holders;
(b)   'musical works' means any musical work or other protected subject matter;
(c)   'repertoire' means the catalogue of musical works which is administered by a collective rights manager;
(d)   'multi-territorial licence' means a licence which covers the territory of more than one Member state;

(e)   'collective rights manager' means any person providing the services set out in point (a) to several right-holders;

(f)   'online rights' means any of the following rights:

(i)   the exclusive right of reproduction that covers all reproductions provided for under Directive 2001/29/EC in the form of intangible copies, made in the process of online distribution of musical works;

(ii)   the right of communication to the public of a musical work, either in the form of a right to authorise or prohibit pursuant to Directive 2001/29/EC or a right to equitable remuneration in accordance with Directive 92/100/EEC, which includes webcasting, internet radio and simulcasting or near-on-demand services received either on a personal computer or on a mobile telephone;

(iii)   the exclusive right of making available a musical work pursuant to Directive 2001/29/EC, which includes on-demand or other interactive services;

(g)   'right-holder' means any natural or legal person that holds online rights;

(h)   'commercial user' means any person involved in the provision of online music services who needs a licence from right-holders in order to provide legitimate online music services;

(i)   'reciprocal representation agreement' means any bilateral agreement between collective rights managers whereby one collective rights manager grants to the other the right to represent its repertoire in the territory of the other.

General

2.   Member States are invited to take the steps necessary to facilitate the growth of legitimate online services in the Community by promoting a regulatory environment which is best suited to the management, at Community level, of copyright and related rights for the provision of legitimate online music services.

The relationship between right-holders, collective rights managers and commercial users

3.   Right-holders should have the right to entrust the management of any of the online rights necessary to operate legitimate online music services, on a territorial scope of their choice, to a collective rights manager of their choice, irrespective of the Member State of residence or the nationality of either the collective rights manager or the right-holder.

4.   Collective rights managers should apply the utmost diligence in representing the interests of right-holders.

5.   With respect to the licensing of online rights the relationship between right-holders and collective rights managers, whether based on contract or statutory membership rules, should, at least be governed by the following:

(a)   right-holders should be able to determine the online rights to be entrusted for collective management;

(b)   right-holders should be able to determine the territorial scope of the mandate of the collective rights managers;

(c)   right-holders should, upon reasonable notice of their intention to do so, have the right to withdraw any of the online rights and transfer the multi-territorial management of those rights to another collective rights manager, irrespective of the Member State of residence or the nationality of either the collective rights manager or the right-holder;

(d)   where a right-holder has transferred the management of an online right to another collective rights manager, without prejudice to other forms of cooperation among rights managers, all collective rights managers concerned should ensure that those online rights are withdrawn from any existing reciprocal representation agreement concluded amongst them.

6.   Collective rights managers should inform right-holders and commercial users of the repertoire they represent, any existing reciprocal representation agreements, the territorial scope of their mandates for that repertoire and the applicable tariffs.

7.   Collective rights managers should give reasonable notice to each other and commercial users of changes in the repertoire they represent.

8.   Commercial users should inform collective right managers of the different features of the services for which they want to acquire online rights.

9.   Collective rights managers should grant commercial users licences on the basis of objective criteria and without any discrimination among users.

Equitable distribution and deductions

10.   Collective rights managers should distribute royalties to all right-holders or category of right-holders they represent in an equitable manner.

11.   Contracts and statutory membership rules governing the relationship between collective rights managers and right-holders for the management, at Community level, of musical works for online use should specify whether and to what extent, there will be deductions from the royalties to be distributed for purposes other than for the management services provided.

12.   Upon payment of the royalties collective rights managers should specify vis-à-vis all the right-holders they represent, the deductions made for purposes other than for the management services provided.

Non discrimination and representation

13.   The relationship between collective rights managers and right-holders, whether based on contract or statutory membership rules should be based on the following principles:

(a)   any category of right-holder is treated equally in relation to all elements of the management service provided;

(b)   the representation of right-holders in the internal decision making process is fair and balanced.

Accountability

14.   Collective rights managers should report regularly to all right-holders they represent, whether directly or under reciprocal representation agreements, on any licences granted, applicable tariffs and royalties collected and distributed.

Dispute settlement

15.   Member States are invited to provide for effective dispute resolution mechanisms, in particular in relation to tariffs, licensing conditions, entrustment of online rights for management and withdrawal of online rights.

Follow-up

16.   Member States and collective rights managers are invited to report, on a yearly basis, to the Commission on the measures they have taken in relation to this Recommendation and on the management, at Community level, of copyright and related rights for the provision of legitimate online music services.

17.   The Commission intends to assess, on a continuous basis, the development of the online music sector and in the light of this Recommendation.

18.   The Commission will to consider, on the basis of the assessment referred to in point 17, the need for further action at Community level.

Addressees

19.   This Recommendation is addressed to the Member States and to all economic operators which are involved in the management of copyright and related rights within the Community.

I.1.   Proposal for a Council Regulation on the European Union patent (Doc. Consilium No 16113/09 Add 1 of 27 November 2009)

(1)   The activities of the European Union (hereafter 'EU') include the establishment of an internal market characterized by the abolition of obstacles to the free movement of goods and the creation of a system ensuring that competition in the internal market is not distorted. The creation of the legal conditions enabling undertakings to adapt their activities in manufacturing and distributing products to an EU dimension helps to attain these objectives. A patent to which uniform protection is given and which produces uniform effects throughout the EU should feature amongst the legal instruments which undertakings have at their disposal.

(1a)   A cost-effective, legally secure European Union patent (hereafter 'EU patent') would in particular benefit Small and Medium-Sized Enterprises (hereafter: SMEs) and would be complementary to the Small Business Act for Europe. The creation of such a unitary title should make access to the patent system easier, less costly and less risky, which would be of particular importance for SMEs.

(1b)   The availability of a unitary title providing for equal protection throughout the entire territory of the EU would enhance and help raise effectiveness of the fight against counterfeiting and patent infringement to the benefit of inventors, businesses and society at large. A complete geographical coverage without any loopholes would ensure effective patent protection at all external borders of the EU and would help to prevent the entry of counterfeit products into the European Single Market on the basis of Council Regulation (EC) No 1383/2003 of 22 July 2003 concerning customs action against goods suspected of infringing certain intellectual property rights and the measures to be taken against goods found to have infringed such rights.

(2)   The Convention on the Grant of European Patents of 5 October 1973 as amended by a revision act of 29 November 2000 (hereafter: EPC) established the European Patent Office (hereafter: EPO) and entrusted it with the task of granting European patents. The expertise offered by the EPO should be used in the granting of the EU patent.

(2a)   The EPO would play a central role in the administration of EU patents and would alone be responsible for examination of applications and the grant of EU patents. Enhanced partnership should however enable for the European Patent Office to make regular use, where appropriate, of the result of any search carried out by central industrial property offices of the member states of the European Patent Organisation on a national patent application the priority of which is claimed in a subsequent filing of a European patent application.

(2aa) All central industrial property offices, including those which do not perform searches in the course of a national patent granting procedure can have an essential role under the enhanced partnership, inter alia by giving advice and support to potential applicants for EU patents, in particular SMEs, by receiving applications, by forwarding applications to the EPO, and by disseminating patent information. National patent offices should be compensated for these activities through the distribution of annual renewal fees.

(2b)   Applications for EU patents should be filed directly with the EPO or via the national patent office of a Member State.

(2c)   The level of procedural fees for processing an application for an EU patent should be the same regardless of where the application is filed and should be related to the costs of handling the EU patent.

(3)   The accession of the EU to the EPC would enable it to be included in the system of law established by the EPC as a territory for which a unitary patent can be granted. The pre-grant stage of the EU patent should thus principally be governed by the EPC. This Regulation should in particular establish the law applicable to the EU patent once granted.

(3a)   The EPO should also be entrusted with the task of administering the EU patent in the postgrant stage, for example, as regards the collection and distribution of renewal fees to Member States and the management of the Register of EU Patents.

(4a)   To the extent that this Regulation does not provide otherwise the substantive law applicable to the EU patent, for example as regards patentability, the scope of patent protection and the limitation of the effects of the patent, should be governed by the pertinent provisions of the EPC and national law where this complies with EU law.

(4b)   The EU patent should constitute a third option. Applicants should remain free to apply instead for a national or a European patent. This Regulation is without prejudice to the right of the Member States to grant national patents and should not replace Member States' laws on patents or European patent law as established by the EPC.

(6)   Negative effects of an exclusive right created by an EU patent should be mitigable through a system of compulsory licences. This is without prejudice to the application of EU competition law by the Commission or national authorities. The [European and EU

Patents Court] should be entrusted with the grant of compulsory licences in situations not falling under EU competition law.

(7)   The jurisdictional system for the EU patent should be part of the [European and EU Patents Court] having jurisdiction for both European and EU patents. This jurisdiction is established and governed by [*quote title of the legal instrument*].

(8)   In accordance with the principles of subsidiarity and proportionality as set out in Article 5 of the Treaty, the objectives of the proposed action, in particular the creation of a unitary right with effect throughout the EU can be achieved only by the EU. This Regulation confines itself to the minimum required in order to achieve those objectives and does not go beyond what is necessary for that purpose.

(9)   Whereas the creation of the EU patent by this Regulation is part of a comprehensive patent reform, which also involves changes to the EPC and the establishment of a unified patent litigation system based upon an international agreement to be concluded between the EU, its Member States and certain other Contracting Parties to the EPC, ratified in accordance with the Member States' Constitutional requirements.

Chapter I — General provisions

Article 1. Scope of application.   This Regulation applies to all EU patents within the meaning of Article 2(1) and to all applications for such patents.

Article 2. EU patent.   1.   The EU patent is a European patent designating the EU, granted by the EPO under the provisions of the EPC 5.

2.   The EU patent shall have a unitary character. It shall have equal effect throughout the EU and may only be granted, limited, transferred, declared invalid or lapse in respect of the whole of the EU.

3.   The EU patent shall have an autonomous character. Subject to paragraph 4, it shall be subject only to this Regulation and to the general principles of EU law. The provisions of this Regulation shall be without prejudice to the application of EU competition law or the law of Member States with regard to criminal liability, unfair competition and mergers.

4.   The EPC shall apply to EU patents and to applications for EU patents to the extent that this Regulation does not provide for specific rules.

Article 3. Application to the sea and submarine areas and to space.   1.   This Regulation shall also apply to the sea and submarine areas adjacent to a Member State's territory in which that Member State exercises sovereign rights or jurisdiction in accordance with international law.

2.   This Regulation shall apply to inventions created or used in outer space, including on celestial bodies or on spacecraft, which are under the jurisdiction and control of one or more Member States in accordance with international law.

Chapter II — Patent law

Section 1 — Right to the patent

Article 4. Right to the EU patent. 1.   The right to the EU patent shall belong to the inventor or his/her successor in title.

2.   If the inventor is an employee, the right to the EU patent shall be determined in accordance with the law of the State in which the employee is mainly employed; if the State in which the employee is mainly employed cannot be determined, the law to be applied shall be that of the State in which the employer has his/her place of business to which the employee is attached.

3.   If two or more persons have made an invention independently of each other, the right to the EU patent shall belong to the person whose application for the EU patent has the earliest date of filing or, where applicable, the earliest date of priority. This provision shall apply only if the first application for the EU patent has been published under Article 93 of the EPC.

Article 5. Claiming the right to the EU patent. 1.   If the EU patent has been granted to a person who is not entitled to it under Article 4(1) and (2), the person entitled to it under that Article may, without prejudice to any other right or remedy which may be open to him/her, claim to have the patent transferred to him/her.

2.   Where a person is entitled to only part of the EU patent, that person may, in accordance with paragraph 1, claim to be made a joint proprietor.

3.   Legal proceedings in respect of the rights referred to in paragraphs 1 and 2 may be instituted only within a period of three years after the date on which the EU Patent Bulletin, referred to in Article 57, publishes the mention of the grant of the EU patent. This provision shall not apply if the proprietor of the patent knew, at the time of the grant or of the acquisition of the patent, that he/she was not entitled to the patent.

4.   The fact that legal proceedings have been instituted shall be entered in the Register of EU Patents, referred to in Article 56. The final decision in the legal proceedings or any withdrawal thereof shall also be entered.

Article 6. Effect of change of proprietorship of the EU patent. 1.   Where there is a complete change of proprietorship of an EU patent as a result of legal proceedings referred to in Article 5, licences and other rights shall lapse upon the registration of the person entitled to the patent in the Register of EU Patents.

2.   If, before the institution of legal proceedings has been registered,

(a)   the proprietor of the patent has used the invention within the territory of the EU or made effective and serious preparations to do so,

    or

(b)   a licensee of the patent has obtained his/her licence and has used the invention within the territory of the EU or made effective and serious preparations to do so, he/she may continue such use provided that he/she requests a non-exclusive licence of the patent from the new proprietor whose name is entered in the Register of EU Patents. Such request must be made within the period prescribed in the implementing regulations. A licence shall be granted for a reasonable period and upon reasonable terms.

3.   Paragraph 2 shall not apply if the proprietor of the patent or the licensee was acting in bad faith at the time when he/she began to use the invention or to make preparations to do so.

Section 2 — Effects of the EU patent and the EU patent application

Article 7. Right to prevent the direct use of the invention.   The EU patent shall confer on its proprietor the right to prevent any third party not having his/her consent from: ...

Section 3 — The EU patent as an object of property

Article 14. Dealing with the EU patent as a national patent.   1.   Unless otherwise specified in Articles 15 to 24, the EU patent as an object of property shall be dealt with in its entirety, and for the whole of the EU, as a national patent of the Member State in which, according to the Register of EU Patents:
    (a)   the applicant for the patent had his/her residence or place of business on the date of filing of the application for the EU patent;
    (b)   where subparagraph (a) does not apply, the applicant had an establishment on that date.
    In all other cases, the Member State referred to shall be that in which the EPO has its seat.
    2.   If two or more persons are mentioned in the Register of EU Patents as joint applicants, paragraph 1(a) shall apply to the joint applicant first mentioned. If this is not possible, paragraph 1(a) shall apply to the joint applicants next mentioned in order of entry. Where paragraph 1(a) does not apply to any of the joint applicants, paragraph 1(b) shall apply.

Article 15. Transfer.   1.   The transfer of the EU patent shall be made in writing and shall require the signature of the parties to the contract, except when it is a result of a judgment; otherwise it shall be void. The transfer shall be entered in the Register of EU Patents.
    2.   Subject to Article 6(1), a transfer shall not affect rights acquired by third parties before the date of transfer.
    3.   A transfer shall, to the extent to which it is verified by such written documents referred to in paragraph 1, have effect vis-à-vis third parties only after entry in the Register of EU Patents. Nevertheless, a transfer, before it is so entered, shall have effect vis-à-vis third parties who have acquired rights after the date of the transfer but who knew of the transfer on the date on which the rights were acquired.

Article 16. Rights in rem.   1.   The EU patent may, independently of the undertaking, be given as security or be the subject of rights in rem.
    2.   At the request of one of the parties, the rights referred to in paragraph 1 shall be entered in the Register of EU Patents and published in the EU Patent Bulletin.

Article 17. Levy of Execution.   1.   The EU patent may be levied in execution.
    2.   At the request of one of the parties, the levy of execution shall be entered in the Register of EU Patents of this Regulation and published in the EU Patent Bulletin.

Article 18. Insolvency proceedings.   1.   The only insolvency proceedings in which an EU patent may be involved shall be those instituted in the Member State within the territory of which the centre of a debtor's main interests is situated.

2.   In the case of joint proprietorship of an EU patent, paragraph 1 shall apply to the share of the joint proprietor.

3.   Where an EU patent is involved in insolvency proceedings, on request of the competent national authority an entry to this effect shall be made in the Register of EU Patents and published in the EU Patent Bulletin.

Article 23. Effects vis-à-vis third parties.   1.   Legal acts referred to in Articles 16 to 22 concerning an EU patent shall have effects vis-à-vis third parties in all the Member States only after entry in the Register of EU Patents. Nevertheless, such an act, before it is so entered, shall have effect vis-à-vis third parties who have acquired rights concerning the patent after the date of that act but who knew of the act at the date on which the rights were acquired.

2.   Paragraph 1 shall not apply in the case of a person who acquires the EU patent or a right concerning the EU patent by way of transfer of the whole of the undertaking or by any other universal succession.

Article 24. The application for an EU patent as an object of property.   1.   Articles 9a and 14 to 19 and Article 21(3) to (6), and Article 22 shall apply to the application for an EU patent, whereby it is understood that all references to the Register of EU Patents include references to the European Patent Register provided for by the EPC.

2.   The rights acquired by third parties in respect of an application for an EU patent referred to in paragraph 1 shall continue to be effective with regard to the EU patent granted upon that application.

I.2.   Draft Agreement on the European and Community Patents Court and Draft Statute (Doc. Consilium No 7928/09 of 23 March 2009)[1]

Considering that co-operation amongst the countries of Europe in the field of patents contributes significantly to the integration process in Europe, in particular to the establishment of an internal market within the European Economic Area characterized by the free movement of goods and services and the creation of a system ensuring that competition in the internal market is not distorted,

Considering that the fragmented market for patents and the significant variations between national court systems are detrimental for innovation, in particular for small and medium sized enterprises which have difficulties to enforce their patents and to defend themselves against unfounded claims,

---

[1]   Revised Presidency text. The Council has submitted to the ECJ a request for an opinion pursuant to Article 300 No 6 TEC (OJ, C 220 of 12 September 2009), on the compatibility of the proposed agreement creating a unified patent litigation system (currently called the 'European and Community Patent Court') with the provisions of the Treaty establishing the European Community. [Note of the Editor]

Wishing to improve the enforcement of patents and to enhance legal certainty by setting up a European and Community Patents Court for litigation related to the infringement and validity of patents,

Considering that the integrated and exclusive European and Community Patents Court shall be set up for Community patents and European patents designating one or more ... States party to this Agreement ... and that the present Agreement shall be open to accession by any Contracting State to the European Patent Convention,

Considering that the Court of Justice of the European Communities shall ensure the uniformity of the Community legal order,

Considering that the European and Community Patents Court shall be designed to ensure expeditious and high quality decisions, striking a fair balance between the interests of right holders and other parties and taking into account the need for proportionality and flexibility,

Part I — General and institutional provisions

Chapter I — General provisions

Article 1. European and Community Patents Court.   A jurisdictional system for the settlement of litigation related to Community patents and European patents is hereby established. To this end, the European and Community Patents Court is created.

Article 2. Definitions.   (1)   'Court' means the European and Community Patents Court.

(2)   'Community Patent' means a patent within the meaning of Article 2, paragraph 1, of Regulation (EC) No ... on the Community patent.

(3)   'European Patent' means a patent granted under the provisions of the European Patent Convention designating one or more Contracting States to this Agreement.

(4)   'Supplementary protection certificate' means a supplementary protection certificate granted under Regulation (EC) No 1768/922 or under Regulation (EC) No 1610/963.

(5)   'European Patent Convention' means the Convention on the Grant of European Patents of 5 October 1973, as amended.

(6)   'European Patent Office' means the organ carrying out the granting of patents as established by Article 4, paragraph 2(a), of the European Patent Convention.

(7)   'Patent' means ... a Community patent and a European patent ...

(8)   'Statute' means the Statute of the European and Community Patents Court which is attached to this Agreement.

(9)   'Rules of Procedure' means the Rules of Procedure of the European and Community Patents Court ...

(10)   'Contracting State' means any State party to this Agreement ...

(11)   'Member State' means a Member State of the European Union.

Article 3. Scope of application.   This Agreement shall apply to any:
    (a)   Community patent;
    (b)   supplementary protection certificate issued for a patent;
    (c)   compulsory licence in respect of a Community patent;

(d)   European patent which has not yet lapsed at the date referred to in Article 59 or was granted after that date, without prejudice to Article 58; and

(e)   application for a patent which is pending at the date referred to in Article 59 or filed after that date.

Chapter IIIa — Substantive law

Article 14a. Applicable law.   (1)   When hearing a case brought before it under this Agreement, the Court shall respect Community law and base its decisions on:

(a)   this Agreement;

(b)   directly applicable Community law, in particular Council Regulation (EC) No … on the Community patent, and national law of the Contracting States implementing Community law …;

(c)   the European Patent Convention and national law which has been adopted by the Contracting States in accordance with the European Patent Convention; and

(d)   any provision of international agreements applicable to patents and binding on all the Contracting Parties.

(2)   To the extent that the Court shall base its decisions on national law of the Contracting States, the applicable law shall be determined:

(a)   by directly applicable provisions of Community law, or

(b)   in the absence of directly applicable provisions of Community law, by international instruments on private international law to which all Contracting Parties are parties; or

c)   in the absence of provisions referred to in (a) and (b), by national provisions on international private law as determined by the Court.

(3)   A Contracting State which is not a party to the Agreement on the European Economic Area shall bring into force the laws, regulations and administrative provisions necessary to comply with Community law relating to substantive patent law.

Chapter IV — Jurisdiction and effects of decisions

Article 15. Jurisdiction.   (1)   The Court shall have exclusive jurisdiction in respect of:

(a)   actions for actual or threatened infringements of patents and supplementary protection certificates and related defences, including counterclaims concerning licences;

(a1)   actions for declarations of non-infringement;

(b)   actions for provisional and protective measures and injunctions;

(c)   actions or counterclaims for revocation of patents;

(d)   actions for damages or compensation derived from the provisional protection conferred by a published patent application;

(e)   actions relating to the use of the invention prior to the granting of the patent or to the right based on prior use of the patent;

(f)   actions for the grant or revocation of compulsory licences in respect of Community patents; and

(g)   actions on compensation for licences within the meaning of [Article 20, paragraph 1] of Council Regulation (EC) No … on the Community patent.

(2)   The national courts of the Contracting States shall have jurisdiction in actions related to Community patents and European patents which do not come within the exclusive jurisdiction of the Court.

Article 15a. Jurisdiction of the divisions of the Court of First Instance. (1)   Actions referred to in Article 15, paragraph 1(a), (b), (d) and (e) shall be brought before:

(a)   the local division hosted by the Contracting State where the actual or threatened infringement has occurred or may occur, or the regional division in which this Contracting State participates; or

(b)   the local division hosted by the Contracting State where the defendant is domiciled, or the regional division in which this Contracting State participates.

Actions against defendants domiciled outside the territory of the Contracting States shall be brought before the local or regional division in accordance with (a).

If the Contracting State concerned does not host a local division and does not participate in a regional division, actions shall be brought before the central division.

(2)   A counterclaim for revocation can be brought in the case of an action for infringement. The local or regional division concerned shall, after having heard the parties, have the discretion either to:

(a)   proceed with both the infringement action and with the counterclaim for revocation and request the President of the Court of First Instance to allocate from the Pool of Judges a technically qualified judge with qualifications and experience in the field of technology concerned;

(b)   refer the counterclaim for decision to the central division and suspend or proceed with the infringement proceedings; or

(c)   with agreement of the parties, refer the case for decision to the central division.

(3)   Without prejudice to paragraph 2, the actions referred to in Article 15, paragraph 1 (a1), (c), (f) and (g) shall be brought before the central division. Such actions may only be initiated if no action for infringement has been initiated between the same parties relating to the same patent before a local or a regional division.

(4)   If an action for revocation is pending before the central division, an action for infringement between the same parties on the same patent may be initiated at any division in accordance with paragraph 1. The local or regional division concerned shall have the discretion to proceed in accordance with paragraph 2.

(5)   An action for declaration of non-infringement pending before the central division shall be stayed once an infringement action related to the same patent between the same parties or between the holder of an exclusive licence and the party requesting a declaration of non-infringement is initiated within three months before a local or regional division.

(6)   Parties may agree to bring an action before the division of their choice, including the central division.

(7)   The actions referred to in paragraph 3 can be brought without the plaintiff having to initiate an opposition procedure before the European Patent Office.

(8)   Any party shall inform the Court of any pending limitation or opposition proceedings before the European Patent Office, and of any request for accelerated processing before the European Patent Office. The Court may stay its proceedings when a rapid decision may be expected from the European Patent Office.

Article 16. Territorial effects of decisions.   Decisions of the Court shall have effect, in the case of a Community patent, for the whole territory of the European Union and, in the case of a European patent, for the territory of those Contracting States for which the European patent has taken effect.

Chapter V — Patent mediation and arbitration

Article 17. Patent mediation and arbitration centre.   (1)   A patent mediation and arbitration centre is hereby established ('the Centre'). It shall have its seat in …

(2)   The Centre shall provide facilities for mediation and arbitration of patent disputes falling within the scope of this Agreement. However, a patent may not be declared fully or partially invalid or be fully or partially invalidated in mediation or arbitration proceedings.

(3)   In the interim procedure referred to in Article 32, paragraph 2, the judge acting as Rapporteur shall explore with the parties the possibilities for a settlement through mediation and arbitration, and for the use of the facilities of the Centre.

(4)   The Centre shall establish Mediation and Arbitration Rules.

(5)   The Centre shall draw up a list of mediators and arbitrators to assist the parties in the settlement of their dispute.

Part III — Organisation and procedural provisions

Chapter IV — Powers of the Court

Article 34a. General.   (1)   The Court may impose such measures, procedures and remedies as are laid down in this Agreement and may make its orders subject to other conditions, in accordance with the Statute and the Rules of Procedure.

(2)   The Court shall take due account of the interest of the parties and shall, before making an order, give any party an opportunity to present its interests unless this is incompatible with an effective enforcement of such order.

Article 35. Order to produce evidence.   (1)   Where a party has presented reasonably available evidence sufficient to support its claims and has, in substantiating those claims, specified evidence which lies in the control of the opposing party or a third party, the Court may order that party to produce such evidence. Such order shall not result in an obligation of self-incrimination.

(2)   On application by a party the Court may order, under the same conditions as specified in paragraph 1, the communication of banking, financial or commercial documents under the control of the opposing party.

Article 35a. Order to preserve evidence and to inspect property.   (1)   The Court may, even before the commencement of proceedings on the merits of the case, on application by a party who has presented reasonably available evidence to support the claim that the patent right has been infringed or is about to be infringed, order prompt and effective provisional measures to preserve relevant evidence in respect of the alleged infringement.

(2)   Such measures may include the detailed description, with or without the taking of samples, or the physical seizure of the infringing goods, and, in appropriate cases, the materials and implements used in the production and/or distribution of these goods and the documents relating thereto.

(2a)   The inspection of the premises shall be conducted by a person appointed by the Court in accordance with the Rules of Procedure.

(3)   At the inspection of the premises the requesting party shall not be present itself but may be represented by an independent professional practitioner whose name has to be specified in the Court's order.

(4)   The measures shall be taken, if necessary without the other party having been heard, in particular where any delay is likely to cause irreparable harm to the proprietor of the patent, or where there is a demonstrable risk of evidence being destroyed.

(5)   Where measures to preserve evidence are adopted without the other party having been heard, the parties affected shall be given notice, without delay and at the latest immediately after the execution of the measures. A review, including a right to be heard, shall take place upon request of the parties affected with a view to deciding, within a reasonable period after the notification of the measures, whether the measures shall be modified, revoked or confirmed.

(6)   The Court shall ensure that the measures to preserve evidence are revoked or otherwise cease to have effect, upon request of the defendant, without prejudice to the damages which may be claimed, if the applicant does not initiate, within a period not exceeding 31 calendar days, proceedings leading to a decision on the merits of the case before the Court.

(7)   Where the measures to preserve evidence are revoked, or where they lapse due to any act or omission by the applicant, or where it is subsequently found that there has been no infringement or threat of infringement of the patent right, the Court may order the applicant, upon request of the defendant, to provide the defendant appropriate compensation for any injury caused by those measures.

Article 35b. Freezing orders.   The Court may order a party to refrain from removing from its jurisdiction any assets located there, or from dealing in any assets, whether located within its jurisdiction or not.

Article 37. Provisional and protective measures.   (1)   The Court may grant injunctions against an alleged infringer or against a third party whose intermediary services are used by the alleged infringer, on a provisional basis, intended to prevent any impending infringement, to forbid the continuation of the alleged infringement or to make such continuation subject to the lodging of guarantees.

(2)   The Court shall have the discretion to weigh up the interests of the parties and in particular to take into account the potential harm for either of the parties resulting from the granting or the refusal of the injunction.

(3)   The Court may also order the seizure or delivery up of the goods suspected of infringing a patent right so as to prevent their entry into or movement within the channels of commerce. If the injured party demonstrates circumstances likely to endanger the recovery of damages, the Court may order the precautionary seizure of the movable and immovable property of the alleged infringer, including the blocking of his/her bank accounts and other assets.

(4)   The Court may, in respect of the measures referred to in paragraphs 1 and 3, require the applicant to provide any reasonable evidence in order to satisfy itself with a sufficient degree of certainty that the applicant is the right-holder and that the applicant's right is being infringed, or that such infringement is imminent.

(5)   Article 35a, paragraphs 4 to 7, shall apply by analogy to the measures referred to in this Article.

Article 37a. Permanent injunctions. (1) Where a decision is taken finding an infringement of a patent, the Court may grant an injunction aimed at prohibiting the continuation of the infringement. The Court may also grant such injunctions against an intermediary whose services are being used by a third party to infringe a patent right.

(2) Where appropriate, such injunction shall be subject to a periodic penalty payment payable to the Court with a view to ensuring compliance.

Article 38. Corrective measures in infringement proceedings. (1) Without prejudice to any damages due to the injured party by reason of the infringement, and without compensation of any sort, the Court may order, at the request of the applicant, that appropriate measures be taken with regard to goods found to be infringing patent rights and, in appropriate cases, with regard to materials and implements principally used in the creation or manufacture of those goods.

(2) Such measures shall include:

(a) declaration of the fact of infringement;

(b) recall from the channels of commerce;

(c) depriving the product from its infringing property;

(d) definitive removal from the channels of commerce; or

(e) destruction.

(3) The Court shall order that those measures be carried out at the expense of the infringer, unless particular reasons are invoked for not doing so.

(4) In considering a request for corrective measures, the need for proportionality between the seriousness of the infringement and the remedies ordered, the willingness of the party concerned to convert the materials into a non-infringing state, as well as the interests of third parties shall be taken into account.

Article 38a. Decision on the validity of a patent. (1) The Court shall decide on the validity of a patent on the basis of a direct action for revocation or a counterclaim for revocation.

(2) The Court may revoke a patent, either entirely or partly, only on the grounds referred to in Article 138, paragraph 1, of the European Patent Convention or Article 28, paragraph 1, of Council Regulation (EC) No ... on the Community patent.

(3) Without prejudice to Article 138, paragraph 3, of the European Patent Convention, if the grounds for revocation affect the patent only in part, the patent shall be limited by a corresponding amendment of the claims and revoked in part.

(4) To the extent that a patent has been revoked it shall be deemed not to have had, from the outset, in the case of a Community patent, the effects specified in Articles 7 and 8 of Council Regulation (EC) No ... on the Community patent and in the case of a European patent, the effects specified in Articles 64 and 67 of the European Patent Convention.

(5) Where the Court, in a final decision, has revoked a patent, either entirely or partly, it shall send a copy of the decision to the European Patent Office and, with respect to a European patent, to the national patent office of any Contracting State concerned.

Article 39. Power to order the communication of information. (1) The Court may, in response to a justified and proportionate request of the plaintiff and in accordance with the Rules of Procedure, order an alleged infringer to inform the plaintiff of:

(a)   the origin and distribution channels of the infringing goods or processes;

(b)   the quantities produced, manufactured, delivered, received or ordered, as well as the price obtained for the goods in question; and

(c)   the identity of any third person involved in the production or distribution of infringing goods or in the use of an infringing process.

(2)   The Court may, in accordance with the Rules of Procedure, also order any other person who, on a commercial scale:

(a)   was found in the possession of infringing goods or in the use of an infringing process;

(b)   was found to be providing services used in infringing activities; or

(c)   was indicated by the person referred to in (a) or (b) as being involved in the production, manufacture or distribution of the goods or processes or in the provision of the services, to provide the plaintiff with the information referred to in paragraph 1.

Article 41. Award of damages.   (1)   The Court may, at the request of the injured party, order the infringer who knowingly, or with reasonable grounds to know, engaged in a patent infringing activity, to pay the injured party damages appropriate to the prejudice actually suffered as a result of the infringement.

(2)   The injured party shall, to the extent possible, be restored in the position it would have been in if no infringement had taken place. The infringer shall not benefit from the infringement. However, damages shall not be punitive.

(3)   When the Court sets the damages:

(a)   it shall take into account all appropriate aspects, such as the negative economic consequences, including lost profits, which the injured party has suffered, any unfair profits made by the infringer and, in appropriate cases, elements other than economic factors, such as the moral prejudice caused to the injured party by the infringement; or

(b)   as an alternative to (a), it may, in appropriate cases, set the damages as a lump sum on the basis of elements such as at least the amount of the royalties or fees which would have been due if the infringer had requested authorisation to use the patent in question.

(4)   Where the infringer did not knowingly or with reasonable grounds to know engage in infringing activity, the Court may order the recovery of profits or the payment of compensation.

Chapter V — Appeals

Article 45. Appeal.   (1)   An appeal against a decision of the Court of First Instance may be brought before the Court of Appeal by any party which has been unsuccessful, in whole or in part, in its submissions. An appeal may be brought against a final decision of the Court of First Instance or against an order referred to in Articles [29, paragraph 4,] 35, 35a, 35b, 37 or 39.

Any other order may only be appealed together with the final decision, unless the Court of Appeal grants leave to appeal.

(2)   An appeal shall be brought within two months of the notification of a final decision of the Court of First Instance or within fifteen calendar days of the notification of an order referred to in paragraph 1.

(3)   The appeal against a decision of the Court of First Instance may be based on points of law and matters of fact.

(4)   New facts and new evidence may only be introduced if their submission by the party concerned could not reasonably have been expected during proceedings before the Court of First Instance, in accordance with the Rules of Procedure.

Article 48. Interpretation of Community law.   (1)   When a question of interpretation of the Treaty establishing the European Community or the validity and interpretation of acts of the institutions of the European Community is raised before the Court of First Instance, it may, if it considers this necessary to enable it to give a decision, request the Court of Justice of the European Communities to decide on the question. Where such question is raised before the Court of Appeal, it shall request the Court of Justice of the European Communities to decide on the question.

(2)   The decision of the Court of Justice of the European Communities on the interpretation of the Treaty establishing the European Community or the validity and interpretation of acts of the institutions of the European Community shall be binding on the Court of First Instance and the Court of Appeal.

Chapter VI — Decisions

Article 56. Enforcement of decisions.   (1)   Decisions of the Court shall be enforceable in any Contracting State without the need for a declaration of enforceability. An order for the enforcement of a decision shall be appended to the decision by the Court.

(2)   Where appropriate, the enforcement of a decision may be subject to the provision of security or an equivalent assurance to ensure compensation for any prejudice suffered, in particular in the case of injunctions.

(3)   Without prejudice to the provisions of this Agreement and the Statute, the enforcement procedures shall be governed by the law of the Contracting State where the enforcement takes place. Any decision of the Court shall be enforced under the same conditions as a decision given in the Contacting State where the enforcement takes place.

(4)   If a party does not comply with the terms of an order of the Court, it may be sanctioned with a periodic penalty payment payable to the Court. The individual penalty shall be proportionate to the importance of the order to be enforced. The periodic penalty payment shall be ordered without prejudice to the party's right to claim damages or security.

Successions

A.　Proposal for a Regulation of the European Parliament and of the Council on jurisdiction, applicable law, recognition and enforcement of decisions and authentic instruments in matters of succession and the creation of a European Certificate of Succession (COM (2009) 154 of 14 October 2009): Recitals 10, 21–22, Articles 21–22

See Chapter XII, A.

IX

Companies

General provisions on freedom of establishment and freedom to provide services

A.   Treaty on the Functioning of the European Union: Articles 49, 54, 56–58, 62

See Chapter II, Fundamental rights, A.2.

B.   General Programme for the abolition of restrictions on freedom of establishment (OJ, No 2 of 15 January 1962)

Title I: Beneficiaries

Subject to any decisions taken by the Council under the second subparagraph of Article 227(2) of the Treaty and without prejudice to subsequent provisions laying down association arrangements between the European Economic Community and the overseas countries and territories having attained independence after the entry into force of the Treaty, the persons entitled to benefit from the abolition of restrictions on freedom of establishment as set out in this General Programme are:
  — nationals of Member States or of the overseas countries and territories, and
  — companies and firms formed under the law of a Member State or of an overseas country or territory and having either the seat prescribed by their statutes, or their centre of administration, or their main establishment situated within the Community or in an overseas country or territory, who wish to establish themselves in order to pursue activities as self-employed persons in a Member State; and
  — nationals of Member States or of the overseas countries and territories who are established in a Member State or in an overseas country or territory, and
  — companies and firms as above, provided that, where only the seat prescribed by their statutes is situated within the Community or in an overseas country or territory, their activity shows a real and continuous link with the economy of a Member State or of an overseas country or territory ; such link shall not be one of nationality, whether of the members of the company or firm, or of the persons holding managerial or supervisory posts therein, or of the holders of the capital, who wish to set up agencies, branches or subsidiaries in a Member State.

C.   General Programme for the abolition of restrictions on freedom to provide services (OJ, No 2 of 15 January 1962)

Title I: Beneficiaries

The persons entitled to benefit from the abolition of restrictions on freedom to provide services as set out in this General Programme are:

— nationals of Member States who are established within the Community;

— companies or firms formed under the law of a Member State and having the seat prescribed by their statutes, or their centre of administration, or their main establishment situated within the Community, provided that where only that seat is situated within the Community their activity shows a real and continuous link with the economy of a Member State; such link shall not be one of nationality, whether of the members of the company or firm, or of the persons holding managerial or supervisory posts therein, or of the holders of the capital;

subject to the condition that the service is carried out either personally by the person contracting to provide it or by one of his agencies or branches established in the Community.

D.   Directive 2000/31/EC of the European Parliament and of the Council of 8 June 2000 on certain legal aspects of information society services, in particular electronic commerce, in the Internal Market (Directive on electronic commerce) (OJ, L 178 of 17 July 2000)

(11)   This Directive is without prejudice to the level of protection for, in particular, public health and consumer interests, as established by Community acts; amongst others, Council Directive 93/13/EEC of 5 April 1993 on unfair terms in consumer contracts and Directive 97/7/EC of the European Parliament and of the Council of 20 May 1997 on the protection of consumers in respect of distance contracts form a vital element for protecting consumers in contractual matters; those Directives also apply in their entirety to information society services; that same Community acquis, which is fully applicable to information society services, also embraces in particular Council Directive 84/450/ EEC of 10 September 1984 concerning misleading and comparative advertising, Council Directive 87/102/EEC of 22 December 1986 for the approximation of the laws, regulations and administrative provisions of the Member States concerning consumer credit, Council Directive 93/22/EEC of 10 May 1993 on investment services in the securities field, Council Directive 90/314/EEC of 13 June 1990 on package travel, package holidays and package tours, Directive 98/6/EC of the European Parliament and of the Council of 16 February 1998 on consumer production in the indication of prices of products offered to consumers, Council Directive 92/59/EEC of 29 June 1992 on general product safety, Directive 94/47/ EC of the European Parliament and of the Council of 26 October 1994 on the protection of purchasers in respect of certain aspects on contracts relating to the purchase of the right to use immovable properties on a timeshare basis, Directive 98/27/EC of the European Parliament and of the Council of 19 May 1998 on injunctions for the protection of

consumers' interests, Council Directive 85/374/EEC of 25 July 1985 on the approximation of the laws, regulations and administrative provisions concerning liability for defective products, Directive 1999/44/EC of the European Parliament and of the Council of 25 May 1999 on certain aspects of the sale of consumer goods and associated guarantees, the future Directive of the European Parliament and of the Council concerning the distance marketing of consumer financial services and Council Directive 92/28/EEC of 31 March 1992 on the advertising of medicinal products; this Directive should be without prejudice to Directive 98/43/EC of the European Parliament and of the Council of 6 July 1998 on the approximation of the laws, regulations and administrative provisions of the Member States relating to the advertising and sponsorship of tobacco products adopted within the framework of the internal market, or to directives on the protection of public health; this Directive complements information requirements established by the abovementioned Directives and in particular Directive 97/7/EC.

(14) The protection of individuals with regard to the processing of personal data is solely governed by Directive 95/46/EC of the European Parliament and of the Council of 24 October 1995 on the protection of individuals with regard to the processing of personal data and on the free movement of such data and Directive 97/66/EC of the European Parliament and of the Council of 15 December 1997 concerning the processing of personal data and the protection of privacy in the telecommunications sector which are fully applicable to information society services; these Directives already establish a Community legal framework in the field of personal data and therefore it is not necessary to cover this issue in this Directive in order to ensure the smooth functioning of the internal market, in particular the free movement of personal data between Member States; the implementation and application of this Directive should be made in full compliance with the principles relating to the protection of personal data, in particular as regards unsolicited commercial communication and the liability of intermediaries; this Directive cannot prevent the anonymous use of open networks such as the Internet.

(15) The confidentiality of communications is guaranteed by Article 5 Directive 97/66/EC; in accordance with that Directive, Member States must prohibit any kind of interception or surveillance of such communications by others than the senders and receivers, except when legally authorised.

(17) The definition of information society services already exists in Community law in Directive 98/34/EC of the European Parliament and of the Council of 22 June 1998 laying down a procedure for the provision of information in the field of technical standards and regulations and of rules on information society services and in Directive 98/84/EC of the European Parliament and of the Council of 20 November 1998 on the legal protection of services based on, or consisting of, conditional access; this definition covers any service normally provided for remuneration, at a distance, by means of electronic equipment for the processing (including digital compression) and storage of data, and at the individual request of a recipient of a service; those services referred to in the indicative list in Annex V to Directive 98/34/EC which do not imply data processing and storage are not covered by this definition.

(18) Information society services span a wide range of economic activities which take place on-line; these activities can, in particular, consist of selling goods on-line; activities such as the delivery of goods as such or the provision of services off-line are not covered; information society services are not solely restricted to services giving rise to on-line contracting but also, in so far as they represent an economic activity, extend to

services which are not remunerated by those who receive them, such as those offering on-line information or commercial communications, or those providing tools allowing for search, access and retrieval of data; information society services also include services consisting of the transmission of information via a communication network, in providing access to a communication network or in hosting information provided by a recipient of the service; television broadcasting within the meaning of Directive EEC/89/552 and radio broadcasting are not information society services because they are not provided at individual request; by contrast, services which are transmitted point to point, such as video-on-demand or the provision of commercial communications by electronic mail are information society services; the use of electronic mail or equivalent individual communications for instance by natural persons acting outside their trade, business or profession including their use for the conclusion of contracts between such persons is not an information society service; the contractual relationship between an employee and his employer is not an information society service; activities which by their very nature cannot be carried out at a distance and by electronic means, such as the statutory auditing of company accounts or medical advice requiring the physical examination of a patient are not information society services.

(19) The place at which a service provider is established should be determined in conformity with the case-law of the Court of Justice according to which the concept of establishment involves the actual pursuit of an economic activity through a fixed establishment for an indefinite period; this requirement is also fulfilled where a company is constituted for a given period; the place of establishment of a company providing services via an Internet website is not the place at which the technology supporting its website is located or the place at which its website is accessible but the place where it pursues its economic activity; in cases where a provider has several places of establishment it is important to determine from which place of establishment the service concerned is provided; in cases where it is difficult to determine from which of several places of establishment a given service is provided, this is the place where the provider has the centre of his activities relating to this particular service.

(22) Information society services should be supervised at the source of the activity, in order to ensure an effective protection of public interest objectives; to that end, it is necessary to ensure that the competent authority provides such protection not only for the citizens of its own country but for all Community citizens; in order to improve mutual trust between Member States, it is essential to state clearly this responsibility on the part of the Member State where the services originate; moreover, in order to effectively guarantee freedom to provide services and legal certainty for suppliers and recipients of services, such information society services should in principle be subject to the law of the Member State in which the service provider is established.

(23) This Directive neither aims to establish additional rules on private international law relating to conflicts of law nor does it deal with the jurisdiction of Courts; provisions of the applicable law designated by rules of private international law must not restrict the freedom to provide information society services as established in this Directive.

(24) In the context of this Directive, notwithstanding the rule on the control at source of information society services, it is legitimate under the conditions established in this Directive for Member States to take measures to restrict the free movement of information society services.

(55) This Directive does not affect the law applicable to contractual obligations relating to consumer contracts; accordingly, this Directive cannot have the result of depriving the consumer of the protection afforded to him by the mandatory rules relating to contractual obligations of the law of the Member State in which he has his habitual residence.

(56) As regards the derogation contained in this Directive regarding contractual obligations concerning contracts concluded by consumers, those obligations should be interpreted as including information on the essential elements of the content of the contract, including consumer rights, which have a determining influence on the decision to contract.

(57) The Court of Justice has consistently held that a Member State retains the right to take measures against a service provider that is established in another Member State but directs all or most of his activity to the territory of the first Member State if the choice of establishment was made with a view to evading the legislation that would have applied to the provider had he been established on the territory of the first Member State.

(58) This Directive should not apply to services supplied by service providers established in a third country; in view of the global dimension of electronic commerce, it is, however, appropriate to ensure that the Community rules are consistent with international rules; this Directive is without prejudice to the results of discussions within international organisations (amongst others WTO, OECD, Uncitral) on legal issues.

Chapter I — General provisions

Article 1. Objective and scope. 1. This Directive seeks to contribute to the proper functioning of the internal market by ensuring the free movement of information society services between the Member States.

2. This Directive approximates, to the extent necessary for the achievement of the objective set out in paragraph 1, certain national provisions on information society services relating to the internal market, the establishment of service providers, commercial communications, electronic contracts, the liability of intermediaries, codes of conduct, out-of-court dispute settlements, court actions and cooperation between Member States.

3. This Directive complements Community law applicable to information society services without prejudice to the level of protection for, in particular, public health and consumer interests, as established by Community acts and national legislation implementing them in so far as this does not restrict the freedom to provide information society services.

4. This Directive does not establish additional rules on private international law nor does it deal with the jurisdiction of Courts.

5. This Directive shall not apply to:

(a) the field of taxation;

(b) questions relating to information society services covered by Directives 95/46/EC and 97/66/EC;

(c) questions relating to agreements or practices governed by cartel law;

(d) the following activities of information society services:

— the activities of notaries or equivalent professions to the extent that they involve a direct and specific connection with the exercise of public authority,

—   the representation of a client and defence of his interests before the courts,

—   gambling activities which involve wagering a stake with monetary value in games of chance, including lotteries and betting transactions.

6.   This Directive does not affect measures taken at Community or national level, in the respect of Community law, in order to promote cultural and linguistic diversity and to ensure the defence of pluralism.

Article 2. Definitions.   For the purpose of this Directive, the following terms shall bear the following meanings:

(a)   'information society services': services within the meaning of Article 1(2) of Directive 98/34/EC as amended by Directive 98/48/EC;

(b)   'service provider': any natural or legal person providing an information society service;

(c)   'established service provider': a service provider who effectively pursues an economic activity using a fixed establishment for an indefinite period. The presence and use of the technical means and technologies required to provide the service do not, in themselves, constitute an establishment of the provider;

(d)   'recipient of the service': any natural or legal person who, for professional ends or otherwise, uses an information society service, in particular for the purposes of seeking information or making it accessible;

(e)   'consumer': any natural person who is acting for purposes which are outside his or her trade, business or profession;

(f)   'commercial communication': any form of communication designed to promote, directly or indirectly, the goods, services or image of a company, organisation or person pursuing a commercial, industrial or craft activity or exercising a regulated profession. The following do not in themselves constitute commercial communications:

—   information allowing direct access to the activity of the company, organisation or person, in particular a domain name or an electronic-mail address,

—   person compiled in an independent manner, particularly when this is without financial consideration;

(g)   'regulated profession': any profession within the meaning of either Article 1(d) of Council Directive 89/48/EEC of 21 December 1988 on a general system for the recognition of higher-education diplomas awarded on completion of professional education and training of at least three-years' duration or of Article 1(f) of Council Directive 92/51/EEC of 18 June 1992 on a second general system for the recognition of professional education and training to supplement Directive 89/48/EEC;

(h)   'coordinated field': requirements laid down in Member States' legal systems applicable to information society service providers or information society services, regardless of whether they are of a general nature or specifically designed for them.

(i)   The coordinated field concerns requirements with which the service provider has to comply in respect of:

—   the taking up of the activity of an information society service, such as requirements concerning qualifications, authorisation or notification,

—   the pursuit of the activity of an information society service, such as requirements concerning the behaviour of the service provider, requirements regarding the quality or content of the service, including those applicable to advertising and contracts, or requirements concerning the liability of the service provider;

(ii)   The coordinated field does not cover requirements such as:
— requirements applicable to goods as such,
— requirements applicable to the delivery of goods,
— requirements applicable to services not provided by electronic means.

Article 3. Internal market.   1.   Each Member State shall ensure that the information society services provided by a service provider established on its territory comply with the national provisions applicable in the Member State in question which fall within the coordinated field.

2.   Member States may not, for reasons falling within the coordinated field, restrict the freedom to provide information society services from another Member State.

3.   Paragraphs 1 and 2 shall not apply to the fields referred to in the Annex.

4.   Member States may take measures to derogate from paragraph 2 in respect of a given information society service if the following conditions are fulfilled:

(a)   the measures shall be:

(i)   necessary for one of the following reasons:
— public policy, in particular the prevention, investigation, detection and prosecution of criminal offences, including the protection of minors and the fight against any incitement to hatred on grounds of race, sex, religion or nationality, and violations of human dignity concerning individual persons,
— the protection of public health,
— public security, including the safeguarding of national security and defence,
— the protection of consumers, including investors;

(ii)   taken against a given information society service which prejudices the objectives referred to in point (i) or which presents a serious and grave risk of prejudice to those objectives;

(iii)   proportionate to those objectives;

(b)   before taking the measures in question and without prejudice to court proceedings, including preliminary proceedings and acts carried out in the framework of a criminal investigation, the Member State has:
— asked the Member State referred to in paragraph 1 to take measures and the latter did not take such measures, or they were inadequate,
— notified the Commission and the Member State referred to in paragraph 1 of its intention to take such measures.

5.   Member States may, in the case of urgency, derogate from the conditions stipulated in paragraph 4(b). Where this is the case, the measures shall be notified in the shortest possible time to the Commission and to the Member State referred to in paragraph 1, indicating the reasons for which the Member State considers that there is urgency.

6.   Without prejudice to the Member State's possibility of proceeding with the measures in question, the Commission shall examine the compatibility of the notified measures with Community law in the shortest possible time; where it comes to the conclusion that the measure is incompatible with Community law, the Commission shall ask the Member State in question to refrain from taking any proposed measures or urgently to put an end to the measures in question.

Annex — Derogations from Article 3

As provided for in Article 3(3), Article 3(1) and (2) do not apply to:

—   copyright, neighbouring rights, rights referred to in Directive 87/54/EEC(1) and Directive 96/9/EC as well as industrial property rights,

—   the emission of electronic money by institutions in respect of which Member States have applied one of the derogations provided for in Article 8(1) of Directive 2000/46/EC,

—   Article 44(2) of Directive 85/611/EEC,

—   Article 30 and Title IV of Directive 92/49/EEC, Title IV of Directive 92/96/EEC, Articles 7 and 8 of Directive 88/357/EEC and Article 4 of Directive 90/619/EEC,

—   the freedom of the parties to choose the law applicable to their contract,

—   contractual obligations concerning consumer contacts,

—   formal validity of contracts creating or transferring rights in real estate where such contracts are subject to mandatory formal requirements of the law of the Member State where the real estate is situated,

—   the permissibility of unsolicited commercial communications by electronic mail.

E.   Directive 2003/71/EC of the European Parliament and of the Council of 4 November 2003 on the prospectus to be published when securities are offered to the public or admitted to trading and amending directive 2001/34/EC (OJ, L 345 of 31 December 2003)[1]

(14)   The grant to the issuer of a single passport, valid throughout the Community, and the application of the country of origin principle require the identification of the home Member State as the one best placed to regulate the issuer for the purposes of this Directive.

Article 1. Purpose and scope.   1.   The purpose of this Directive is to harmonise requirements for the drawing up, approval and distribution of the prospectus to be published when securities are offered to the public or admitted to trading on a regulated market situated or operating within a Member State…

Article 2. Definitions.   1.   For the purposes of this Directive, the following definitions shall apply: …

(m)   'home Member State' means:

(i)   for all Community issuers of securities which are not mentioned in (ii), the Member State where the issuer has its registered office;

---

[1]   As amended by Directive 2008/11/EC of 11 March 2008 (OJ, L 76 of 19 March 2008). Directive 2010/73/EU of the European Parliament and of the Council of 24 November 2010 (OJ, L 327 of 11 December 2010), to be transposed by Member States by 1 July 2012, will amend some provisions of Directive 2003/71/EC. [Note of the Editor]

(ii)   for any issues of non-equity securities whose denomination per unit amounts to at least EUR 1 000, and for any issues of non-equity securities giving the right to acquire any transferable securities or to receive a cash amount, as a consequence of their being converted or the rights conferred by them being exercised, provided that the issuer of the non-equity securities is not the issuer of the underlying securities or an entity belonging to the group of the latter issuer, the Member State where the issuer has its registered office, or where the securities were or are to be admitted to trading on a regulated market or where the securities are offered to the public, at the choice of the issuer, the offeror or the person asking for admission, as the case may be. The same regime shall be applicable to non-equity securities in a currency other than euro, provided that the value of such minimum denomination is nearly equivalent to EUR 1 000;

(iii)   for all issuers of securities incorporated in a third country, which are not mentioned in (ii), the Member State where the securities are intended to be offered to the public for the first time after the date of entry into force of this Directive or where the first application for admission to trading on a regulated market is made, at the choice of the issuer, the offeror or the person asking for admission, as the case may be, subject to a subsequent election by issuers incorporated in a third country if the home Member State was not determined by their choice;

(n)   'host Member State' means the State where an offer to the public is made or admission to trading is sought, when different from the home Member State; ...

Article 8. Omission of information.   1.   ... The final offer price and amount of securities shall be filed with the competent authority of the home Member State and published in accordance with the arrangements provided for in Article 14(2).

2.   The competent authority of the home Member State may authorise the omission from the prospectus of certain information provided for in this Directive or in the implementing measures referred to in Article 7(1), if it considers that ...

Article 10. Information.   2.   The document shall be filed with the competent authority of the home Member State after the publication of the financial statement. Where the document refers to information, it shall be stated where the information can be obtained ...

Article 13. Approval of the prospectus.   1.   No prospectus shall be published until it has been approved by the competent authority of the home Member State ...

5.   The competent authority of the home Member State may transfer the approval of a prospectus to the competent authority of another Member State, subject to the agreement of that authority. Furthermore, this transfer shall be notified to the issuer, the offeror or the person asking for admission to trading on a regulated market within three working days from the date of the decision taken by the competent authority of the home Member State ...

Article 15. Advertisements.   6.   The competent authority of the home Member State shall have the power to exercise control over the compliance of advertising activity, relating to a public offer of securities or an admission to trading on a regulated market, with the principles referred to in paragraphs 2 to 5...

Article 17. Community scope of approvals of prospectuses.   1.   Without prejudice to Article 23, where an offer to the public or admission to trading on a regulated market is provided for in one or more Member States, or in a Member State other than the home Member State, the prospectus approved by the home Member State and any supplements thereto shall be valid for the public offer or the admission to trading in any number of host Member States, provided that the competent authority of each host Member State is notified in accordance with Article 18. Competent authorities of host Member States shall not undertake any approval or administrative procedures relating to prospectuses.

2.   If there are significant new factors, material mistakes or inaccuracies, as referred to in Article 16, arising since the approval of the prospectus, the competent authority of the home Member State shall require the publication of a supplement to be approved as provided for in Article 13(1). The competent authority of the host Member State may draw the attention of the competent authority of the home Member State to the need for any new information.

Article 18. Notification.   1.   The competent authority of the home Member State shall, at the request of the issuer or the person responsible for drawing up the prospectus and within three working days following that request or, if the request is submitted together with the draft prospectus, within one working day after the approval of the prospectus provide the competent authority of the host Member State with a certificate of approval attesting that the prospectus has been drawn up in accordance with this Directive and with a copy of the said prospectus. If applicable, this notification shall be accompanied by a translation of the summary produced under the responsibility of the issuer or person responsible for drawing up the prospectus. The same procedure shall be followed for any supplement to the prospectus...

Article 20. Issuers incorporated in third countries.   1.   The competent authority of the home Member State of issuers having their registered office in a third country may approve a prospectus for an offer to the public or for admission to trading on a regulated market, drawn up in accordance with the legislation of a third country, provided that:

(a)   the prospectus has been drawn up in accordance with international standards set by international securities commission organisations, including the IOSCO disclosure standards;

(b)   the information requirements, including information of a financial nature, are equivalent to the requirements under this Directive.

2.   In the case of an offer to the public or admission to trading on a regulated market of securities, issued by an issuer incorporated in a third country, in a Member State other than the home Member State, the requirements set out in Articles 17, 18 and 19 shall apply...

Article 23. Precautionary measures.   1.   Where the competent authority of the host Member State finds that irregularities have been committed by the issuer or by the financial institutions in charge of the public offer or that breaches have been committed of the obligations attaching to the issuer by reason of the fact that the securities are admitted to trading on a regulated market, it shall refer these findings to the competent authority of the home Member State.

2.   If, despite the measures taken by the competent authority of the home Member State or because such measures prove inadequate, the issuer or the financial institution in charge of the public offer persists in breaching the relevant legal or regulatory provisions, the competent authority of the host Member State, after informing the competent authority of the home Member State, shall take all the appropriate measures in order to protect investors. The Commission shall be informed of such measures at the earliest opportunity.

F.   Council Regulation (EC) No 139/2004 of 20 January 2004 on the control of concentrations between undertakings (the EC Merger Regulation) (OJ, L 24 of 29 January 2004)

Article 21. Application of the Regulation and jurisdiction.   1.   This Regulation alone shall apply to concentrations as defined in Article 3, and Council Regulations (EC) No 1/2003, (EEC) No 1017/68, (EEC) No 4056/86 and (EEC) No 3975/87 shall not apply, except in relation to joint ventures that do not have a Community dimension and which have as their object or effect the coordination of the competitive behaviour of undertakings that remain independent.

2.   Subject to review by the Court of Justice, the Commission shall have sole jurisdiction to take the decisions provided for in this Regulation.

3.   No Member State shall apply its national legislation on competition to any concentration that has a Community dimension.

The first subparagraph shall be without prejudice to any Member State's power to carry out any enquiries necessary for the application of Articles 4(4), 9(2) or after referral, pursuant to Article 9(3), first subparagraph, indent (b), or Article 9(5), to take the measures strictly necessary for the application of Article 9(8).

4.   Notwithstanding paragraphs 2 and 3, Member States may take appropriate measures to protect legitimate interests other than those taken into consideration by this Regulation and compatible with the general principles and other provisions of Community law.

Public security, plurality of the media and prudential rules shall be regarded as legitimate interests within the meaning of the first subparagraph.

Any other public interest must be communicated to the Commission by the Member State concerned and shall be recognised by the Commission after an assessment of its compatibility with the general principles and other provisions of Community law before the measures referred to above may be taken. The Commission shall inform the Member State concerned of its decision within 25 working days of that communication.

G.   Directive 2004/25/EC of the European Parliament and of the Council of 21 April 2004 on takeover bids (OJ, L 142 of 30 April 2004)[1]

(2)   It is necessary to protect the interests of holders of the securities of companies governed by the law of a Member State when those companies are the subject of takeover bids or of changes of control and at least some of their securities are admitted to trading on a regulated market in a Member State.

Article 1. Scope.   1.   This Directive lays down measures coordinating the laws, regulations, administrative provisions, codes of practice and other arrangements of the Member States, including arrangements established by organisations officially authorised to regulate the markets (hereinafter referred to as 'rules'), relating to takeover bids for the securities of companies governed by the laws of Member States, where all or some of those securities are admitted to trading on a regulated market within the meaning of Directive 93/22/EEC (2) in one or more Member States (hereinafter referred to as a 'regulated market').

2.   This Directive shall not apply to takeover bids for securities issued by companies, the object of which is the collective investment of capital provided by the public, which operate on the principle of risk-spreading and the units of which are, at the holders' request, repurchased or redeemed, directly or indirectly, out of the assets of those companies. Action taken by such companies to ensure that the stock exchange value of their units does not vary significantly from their net asset value shall be regarded as equivalent to such repurchase or redemption.

3.   This Directive shall not apply to takeover bids for securities issued by the Member States' central banks.

Article 4. Supervisory authority and applicable law.   1.   Member States shall designate the authority or authorities competent to supervise bids for the purposes of the rules which they make or introduce pursuant to this Directive. The authorities thus designated shall be either public authorities, associations or private bodies recognised by national law or by public authorities expressly empowered for that purpose by national law. Member States shall inform the Commission of those designations, specifying any divisions of functions that may be made. They shall ensure that those authorities exercise their functions impartially and independently of all parties to a bid.

2.   (a)   The authority competent to supervise a bid shall be that of the Member State in which the offeree company has its registered office if that company's securities are admitted to trading on a regulated market in that Member State.

(b)   If the offeree company's securities are not admitted to trading on a regulated market in the Member State in which the company has its registered office, the authority competent to supervise the bid shall be that of the Member State on the regulated market of which the company's securities are admitted to trading. If the offeree company's securities are admitted to trading on regulated markets in more than one Member State, the authority

---

[1]   As amended by Regulation (EC) No 219/2009 of 11 March 2009 (OJ, L 87 of 31 March 2009). [Note of the Editor]

competent to supervise the bid shall be that of the Member State on the regulated market of which the securities were first admitted to trading.

(c)   If the offeree company's securities were first admitted to trading on regulated markets in more than one Member State simultaneously, the offeree company shall determine which of the supervisory authorities of those Member States shall be the authority competent to supervise the bid by notifying those regulated markets and their supervisory authorities on the first day of trading. If the offeree company's securities have already been admitted to trading on regulated markets in more than one Member State on the date laid down in Article 21(1) and were admitted simultaneously, the supervisory authorities of those Member States shall agree which one of them shall be the authority competent to supervise the bid within four weeks of the date laid down in Article 21(1). Otherwise, the offeree company shall determine which of those authorities shall be the competent authority on the first day of trading following that four-week period.

(d)   Member States shall ensure that the decisions referred to in (c) are made public.

(e)   In the cases referred to in (b) and (c), matters relating to the consideration offered in the case of a bid, in particular the price, and matters relating to the bid procedure, in particular the information on the offeror's decision to make a bid, the contents of the offer document and the disclosure of the bid, shall be dealt with in accordance with the rules of the Member State of the competent authority. In matters relating to the information to be provided to the employees of the offeree company and in matters relating to company law, in particular the percentage of voting rights which confers control and any derogation from the obligation to launch a bid, as well as the conditions under which the board of the offeree company may undertake any action which might result in the frustration of the bid, the applicable rules and the competent authority shall be those of the Member State in which the offeree company has its registered office.

Article 5. Protection of minority shareholders, the mandatory bid and the equitable price.   1.   Where a natural or legal person, as a result of his/her own acquisition or the acquisition by persons acting in concert with him/her, holds securities of a company as referred to in Article 1(1) which, added to any existing holdings of those securities of his/hers and the holdings of those securities of persons acting in concert with him/her, directly or indirectly give him/her a specified percentage of voting rights in that company, giving him/her control of that company, Member States shall ensure that such a person is required to make a bid as a means of protecting the minority shareholders of that company. Such a bid shall be addressed at the earliest opportunity to all the holders of those securities for all their holdings at the equitable price as defined in paragraph 4.

2.   Where control has been acquired following a voluntary bid made in accordance with this Directive to all the holders of securities for all their holdings, the obligation laid down in paragraph 1 to launch a bid shall no longer apply.

3.   The percentage of voting rights which confers control for the purposes of paragraph 1 and the method of its calculation shall be determined by the rules of the Member State in which the company has its registered office.

Article 12. Optional arrangements.   1.   Member States may reserve the right not to require companies as referred to in Article 1(1) which have their registered offices within their territories to apply Article 9(2) and (3) and/or Article 11.

2.   Where Member States make use of the option provided for in paragraph 1, they shall nevertheless grant companies which have their registered offices within their territories the option, which shall be reversible, of applying Article 9(2) and (3) and/or Article 11, without prejudice to Article 11(7).

The decision of the company shall be taken by the general meeting of shareholders, in accordance with the law of the Member State in which the company has its registered office in accordance with the rules applicable to amendment of the articles of association. The decision shall be communicated to the supervisory authority of the Member State in which the company has its registered office and to all the supervisory authorities of Member States in which its securities are admitted to trading on regulated markets or where such admission has been requested.

3.   Member States may, under the conditions determined by national law, exempt companies which apply Article 9(2) and (3) and/or Article 11 from applying Article 9(2) and (3) and/or Article 11 if they become the subject of an offer launched by a company which does not apply the same Articles as they do, or by a company controlled, directly or indirectly, by the latter, pursuant to Article 1 of Directive 83/349/EEC.

H.   Directive 2004/39/EC of the European Parliament and of the Council of 21 April 2004 on markets in financial instruments amending Council Directives 85/611/EEC and 93/6/EEC and Directive 2000/12/EC of the European Parliament and of the Council and repealing Council Directive 93/22/EEC (OJ, L 145 of 30 April 2004)[1]

(1)   Council Directive 93/22/EEC of 10 May 1993 on investment services in the securities field sought to establish the conditions under which authorised investment firms and banks could provide specified services or establish branches in other Member States on the basis of home country authorisation and supervision. To this end, that Directive aimed to harmonise the initial authorisation and operating requirements for investment firms including conduct of business rules. It also provided for the harmonisation of some conditions governing the operation of regulated markets.

(2)   In recent years more investors have become active in the financial markets and are offered an even more complex wide-ranging set of services and instruments. In view of these developments the legal framework of the Community should encompass the full range of investor-oriented activities. To this end, it is necessary to provide for the degree of harmonisation needed to offer investors a high level of protection and to allow investment firms to provide services throughout the Community, being a Single Market, on the basis of home country supervision. In view of the preceding, Directive 93/22/EEC should be replaced by a new Directive.

(17) Persons who provide the investment services and/or perform investment activities covered by this Directive should be subject to authorisation by their home Member States in order to protect investors and the stability of the financial system.

---

[1]   As corrected by corrigendum (OJ, L 45 of 16 February 2005) and finally amended by Directive 2008/10/ EC of 11 March 2008 (OJ, L 76 of 19 March 2008). [Note of the Editor]

(22) The principles of mutual recognition and of home Member State supervision require that the Member States' competent authorities should not grant or should withdraw authorisation where factors such as the content of programmes of operations, the geographical distribution or the activities actually carried on indicate clearly that an investment firm has opted for the legal system of one Member State for the purpose of evading the stricter standards in force in another Member State within the territory of which it intends to carry on or does carry on the greater part of its activities. An investment firm which is a legal person should be authorised in the Member State in which it has its registered office. An investment firm which is not a legal person should be authorised in the Member State in which it has its head office.

In addition, Member States should require that an investment firm's head office must always be situated in its home Member State and that it actually operates there.

(23) An investment firm authorised in its home Member State should be entitled to provide investment services or perform investment activities throughout the Community without the need to seek a separate authorisation from the competent authority in the Member State in which it wishes to provide such services or perform such activities.

(32) By way of derogation from the principle of home country authorisation, supervision and enforcement of obligations in respect of the operation of branches, it is appropriate for the competent authority of the host Member State to assume responsibility for enforcing certain obligations specified in this Directive in relation to business conducted through a branch within the territory where the branch is located, since that authority is closest to the branch, and is better placed to detect and intervene in respect of infringements of rules governing the operations of the branch.

(39) Member States' competent authorities should not register or should withdraw the registration where the activities actually carried on indicate clearly that a tied agent has opted for the legal system of one Member State for the purpose of evading the stricter standards in force in another Member State within the territory of which it intends to carry on or does carry on the greater part of its activities.

(46) A Member State may decide to apply the pre- and post-trade transparency requirements laid down in this Directive to financial instruments other than shares. In that case those requirements should apply to all investment firms for which that Member State is the home Member State for their operations within the territory of that Member State and those carried out cross-border through the freedom to provide services. They should also apply to the operations carried out within the territory of that Member State by the branches established in its territory of investment firms authorised in another Member State.

Article 1. Scope. 1. This Directive shall apply to investment firms and regulated markets
...

Article 4. Definitions. 1. For the purposes of this Directive, the following definitions shall apply:

(1) 'Investment firm' means any legal person whose regular occupation or business is the provision of one or more investment services to third parties and/or the performance of one or more investment activities on a professional basis;

Member States may include in the definition of investment firms undertakings which are not legal persons, provided that:

(a)   their legal *status* ensures a level of protection for third parties' interests equivalent to that afforded by legal persons, and

(b)   they are subject to equivalent prudential supervision appropriate to their legal form.

However, where a natural person provides services involving the holding of third parties' funds or transferable securities, he may be considered as an investment firm for the purposes of this Directive only if, without prejudice to the other requirements imposed in this Directive and in Directive 93/6/EEC, he complies with the following conditions...

(14) 'Regulated market' means a multilateral system operated and/or managed by a market operator, which brings together or facilitates the bringing together of multiple third-party buying and selling interests in financial instruments — in the system and in accordance with its non-discretionary rules — in a way that results in a contract, in respect of the financial instruments admitted to trading under its rules and/or systems, and which is authorised and functions regularly and in accordance with the provisions of Title III;

(15) 'Multilateral trading facility (MTF)' means a multilateral system, operated by an investment firm or a market operator, which brings together multiple third-party buying and selling interests in financial instruments — in the system and in accordance with non-discretionary rules — in a way that results in a contract in accordance with the provisions of Title II; ...

(20) 'Home Member State' means:

(a)   in the case of investment firms:

(i)   if the investment firm is a natural person, the Member State in which its head office is situated;

(ii)   if the investment firm is a legal person, the Member State in which its registered office is situated;

(iii)   if the investment firm has, under its national law, no registered office, the Member State in which its head office is situated;

(b)   in the case of a regulated market, the Member State in which the regulated market is registered or, if under the law of that Member State it has no registered office, the Member State in which the head office of the regulated market is situated;

(21) 'Host Member State' means the Member State, other than the home Member State, in which an investment firm has a branch or performs services and/or activities or the Member State in which a regulated market provides appropriate arrangements so as to facilitate access to trading on its system by remote members or participants established in that same Member State ...

Article 5. Requirement for authorisation.   1.   Each Member State shall require that the performance of investment services or activities as a regular occupation or business on a professional basis be subject to prior authorisation in accordance with the provisions of this Chapter. Such authorisation shall be granted by the home Member State competent authority designated in accordance with Article 48...

4.   Each Member State shall require that:

—   any investment firm which is a legal person have its head office in the same Member State as its registered office,

—   any investment firm which is not a legal person or any investment firm which is a legal person but under its national law has no registered office have its head office in the Member State in which it actually carries on its business...

Article 6. Scope of authorisation.   1.   The home Member State shall ensure that the authorisation specifies the investment services or activities which the investment firm is authorised to provide. The authorisation may cover one or more of the ancillary services set out in Section B of Annex I. Authorisation shall in no case be granted solely for the provision of ancillary services...

Article 13. Organisational requirements.   1.   The home Member State shall require that investment firms comply with the organisational requirements set out in paragraphs 2 to 8...

Article 24. Transactions executed with eligible counterparties.   3.   Member States may also recognise as eligible counterparties other undertakings meeting pre-determined proportionate requirements, including quantitative thresholds. In the event of a transaction where the prospective counterparties are located in different jurisdictions, the investment firm shall defer to the *status* of the other undertaking as determined by the law or measures of the Member State in which that undertaking is established...

Chapter III — Rights of investment firms

Article 31. Freedom to provide investment services and activities.   1.   Member States shall ensure that any investment firm authorised and supervised by the competent authorities of another Member State in accordance with this Directive, and in respect of credit institutions in accordance with Directive 2000/12/EC, may freely perform investment services and/or activities as well as ancillary services within their territories, provided that such services and activities are covered by its authorisation. Ancillary services may only be provided together with an investment service and/or activity.

Member States shall not impose any additional requirements on such an investment firm or credit institution in respect of the matters covered by this Directive ...

Article 32. Establishment of a branch.   1.   Member States shall ensure that investment services and/or activities as well as ancillary services may be provided within their territories in accordance with this Directive and Directive 2000/12/EC through the establishment of a branch provided that those services and activities are covered by the authorisation granted to the investment firm or the credit institution in the home Member State. Ancillary services may only be provided together with an investment service and/or activity...

Title III — Regulated markets

Article 36. Authorisation and applicable law.   4.   Without prejudice to any relevant provisions of Directive 2003/6/EC, the public law governing the trading conducted under the systems of the regulated market shall be that of the home Member State of the regulated market...

I.   Directive 2004/109/EC of the European Parliament and of the Council of 15 December 2004 on the harmonisation of transparency requirements in relation to information about issuers whose securities are admitted to trading on a regulated market and amending Directive 2001/34/EC (OJ, L 390 of 31 December 2004)[1]

(8)   The removal of barriers on the basis of the home Member State principle under this Directive should not affect areas not covered by this Directive, such as rights of shareholders to intervene in the management of an issuer. Nor should it affect the home Member State's right to request the issuer to publish, in addition, parts of or all regulated information through newspapers.

(27)   So as to ensure the effective protection of investors and the proper operation of regulated markets, the rules relating to information to be published by issuers whose securities are admitted to trading on a regulated market should also apply to issuers which do not have a registered office in a Member State and which do not fall within the scope of Article 48 of the Treaty. It should also be ensured that any additional relevant information about Community issuers or third country issuers, disclosure of which is required in a third country but not in a Member State, is made available to the public in the Community.

Article 1. Subject matter and scope.   1.   This Directive establishes requirements in relation to the disclosure of periodic and ongoing information about issuers whose securities are already admitted to trading on a regulated market situated or operating within a Member State.

2.   This Directive shall not apply to units issued by collective investment undertakings other than the closed-end type, or to units acquired or disposed of in such collective investment undertakings.

3.   Member States may decide not to apply the provisions mentioned in Article 16(3) and in paragraphs 2, 3 and 4 of Article 18 to securities which are admitted to trading on a regulated market issued by them or their regional or local authorities.

4.   Member States may decide not to apply Article 17 to their national central banks in their capacity as issuers of shares admitted to trading on a regulated market if this admission took place before 20 January 2005.

Article 2. Definitions.   1.   For the purposes of this Directive the following definitions shall apply:…

(i)   'home Member State' means

(i)   in the case of an issuer of debt securities the denomination per unit of which is less than EUR 1 000 or an issuer of shares:

—   where the issuer is incorporated in the Community, the Member State in which it has its registered office;

---

[1]   As amended by Directive 2008/22/EC of 11 March 2008 (OJ, L 76 of 19 March 2008). Directive 2010/73/EU of the European Parliament and of the Council of 24 November 2010 (OJ, L 327 of 11 December 2010), to be transposed by Member States by 1 July 2012, will amend some provisions of Directive 2004/109/EC. [Note of the Editor]

— where the issuer is incorporated in a third country, the Member State in which it is required to file the annual information with the competent authority in accordance with Article 10 of Directive 2003/71/EC.

The definition of 'home' Member State shall be applicable to debt securities in a currency other than Euro, provided that the value of such denomination per unit is, at the date of the issue, less than EUR 1 000, unless it is nearly equivalent to EUR 1 000;

(ii) for any issuer not covered by (i), the Member State chosen by the issuer from among the Member State in which the issuer has its registered office and those Member States which have admitted its securities to trading on a regulated market on their territory. The issuer may choose only one Member State as its home Member State. Its choice shall remain valid for at least three years unless its securities are no longer admitted to trading on any regulated market in the Community;

(j) 'host Member State' means a Member State in which securities are admitted to trading on a regulated market, if different from the home Member State;

3. In order to take account of technical developments on financial markets and to ensure the uniform application of paragraph 1, the Commission shall, in accordance with the procedures referred to in Article 27(2) and (2a), adopt implementing measures concerning the definitions set out in paragraph 1.

The Commission shall, in particular:

(a) establish, for the purposes of paragraph 1(i)(ii), the procedural arrangements in accordance with which an issuer may make the choice of the home Member State;

(b) adjust, where appropriate for the purposes of the choice of the home Member State referred to in paragraph 1(i)(ii), the three-year period in relation to the issuer's track record in the light of any new requirement under Community law concerning admission to trading on a regulated market;

Article 3. Integration of securities markets. 1. The home Member State may make an issuer subject to requirements more stringent than those laid down in this Directive.

The home Member State may also make a holder of shares, or a natural person or legal entity referred to in Articles 10 or 13, subject to requirements more stringent than those laid down in this Directive.

2. A host Member State may not:

(a) as regards the admission of securities to a regulated market in its territory, impose disclosure requirements more stringent than those laid down in this Directive or in Article 6 of Directive 2003/6/EC;

(b) as regards the notification of information, make a holder of shares, or a natural person or legal entity referred to in Articles 10 or 13, subject to requirements more stringent than those laid down in this Directive.

Chapter II — Periodic information

Article 4. Annual financial reports. 1. The issuer shall make public its annual financial report at the latest four months after the end of each financial year and shall ensure that it remains publicly available for at least five years…

3. Where the issuer is required to prepare consolidated accounts according to the Seventh Council Directive 83/349/EEC of 13 June 1983 on consolidated accounts, the audited financial statements shall comprise such consolidated accounts drawn up in

accordance with Regulation (EC) No 1606/2002 and the annual accounts of the parent company drawn up in accordance with the national law of the Member State in which the parent company is incorporated.

Where the issuer is not required to prepare consolidated accounts, the audited financial statements shall comprise the accounts prepared in accordance with the national law of the Member State in which the company is incorporated.

Chapter IV — General obligations

Article 19. Home Member State control.   1.   Whenever the issuer, or any person having requested, without the issuer's consent, the admission of its securities to trading on a regulated market, discloses regulated information, it shall at the same time file that information with the competent authority of its home Member State. That competent authority may decide to publish such filed information on its Internet site.

Where an issuer proposes to amend its instrument of incorporation or statutes, it shall communicate the draft amendment to the competent authority of the home Member State and to the regulated market to which its securities have been admitted to trading. Such communication shall be effected without delay, but at the latest on the date of calling the general meeting which is to vote on, or be informed of, the amendment.

2.   The home Member State may exempt an issuer from the requirement under paragraph 1 in respect of information disclosed in accordance with Article 6 of Directive 2003/6/EC or Article 12(6) of this Directive.

3.   Information to be notified to the issuer in accordance with Articles 9, 10, 12 and 13 shall at the same time be filed with the competent authority of the home Member State.

4.   In order to ensure the uniform application of paragraphs 1, 2 and 3, the Commission shall adopt implementing measures.

The Commission shall, in particular, specify the procedure in accordance with which an issuer, a holder of shares or other financial instruments, or a person or entity referred to in Article 10, is to file information with the competent authority of the home Member State under paragraphs 1 or 3, respectively, in order to:

(a)   enable filing by electronic means in the home Member State;

(b)   coordinate the filing of the annual financial report referred to in Article 4 of this Directive with the filing of the annual information referred to in Article 10 of Directive 2003/71/EC.

The measures referred to in the first and second subparagraphs, designed to amend non-essential elements of this Directive by supplementing it, shall be adopted in accordance with the regulatory procedure with scrutiny referred to in Article 27(2a).

Article 23. Third countries.   1.   Where the registered office of an issuer is in a third country, the competent authority of the home Member State may exempt that issuer from requirements under Articles 4 to 7 and Articles 12(6), 14, 15 and 16 to 18, provided that the law of the third country in question lays down equivalent requirements or such an issuer complies with requirements of the law of a third country that the competent authority of the home Member State considers as equivalent.

However, the information covered by the requirements laid down in the third country shall be filed in accordance with Article 19 and disclosed in accordance with Articles 20 and 21.

2.   By way of derogation from paragraph 1, an issuer whose registered office is in a third country shall be exempted from preparing its financial statement in accordance with Article 4 or Article 5 prior to the financial year starting on or after 1 January 2007, provided such issuer prepares its financial statements in accordance with internationally accepted standards referred to in Article 9 of Regulation (EC) No 1606/2002.

3.   The competent authority of the home Member State shall ensure that information disclosed in a third country which may be of importance for the public in the Community is disclosed in accordance with Articles 20 and 21, even if such information is not regulated information within the meaning of Article 2(1)(k) …

6.   Undertakings whose registered office is in a third country which would have required an authorisation in accordance with Article 5(1) of Directive 85/611/EEC or, with regard to portfolio management under point 4 of section A of Annex I to Directive 2004/39/EC if it had its registered office or, only in the case of an investment firm, its head office within the Community, shall also be exempted from aggregating holdings with the holdings of its parent undertaking under the requirements laid down in Article 12(4) and (5) provided that they comply with equivalent conditions of independence as management companies or investment firms.

Article 26. Precautionary measures.   1.   Where the competent authority of a host Member State finds that the issuer or the holder of shares or other financial instruments, or the person or entity referred to in Article 10, has committed irregularities or infringed its obligations, it shall refer its findings to the competent authority of the home Member State.

2.   If, despite the measures taken by the competent authority of the home Member State, or because such measures prove inadequate, the issuer or the security holder persists in infringing the relevant legal or regulatory provisions, the competent authority of the host Member State shall, after informing the competent authority of the home Member State, take, in accordance with Article 3(2), all the appropriate measures in order to protect investors. The Commission shall be informed of such measures at the earliest opportunity.

J.   Directive 2006/48/EC of the European Parliament and of the Council of 14 June 2006 relating to the taking up and pursuit of the business of credit institutions (recast) (OJ, L 177 of 30 June 2006)[1]

(1)   Directive 2000/12/EC of the European Parliament and of the Council of 20 March 2000 relating to the taking up and pursuit of the business of credit institutions has been significantly amended on several occasions. Now that new amendments are being made to the said Directive, it is desirable, in order to clarify matters, that it should be recast.

(2)   In order to make it easier to take up and pursue the business of credit institutions, it is necessary to eliminate the most obstructive differences between the laws of the Member States as regards the rules to which these institutions are subject.

---

[1]   As finally amended by Directive 2009/110/EC of 16 September 2009 (OJ, L 267 of 10 October 2009). [Note of the Editor]

(3)   This Directive constitutes the essential instrument for the achievement of the internal market from the point of view of both the freedom of establishment and the freedom to provide financial services, in the field of credit institutions.

(5)   Measures to coordinate credit institutions should, both in order to protect savings and to create equal conditions of competition between these institutions, apply to all of them. Due regard should however be had to the objective differences in their statutes and their proper aims as laid down by national laws.

(7)   It is appropriate to effect only the essential harmonisation necessary and sufficient to secure the mutual recognition of authorisation and of prudential supervision systems, making possible the granting of a single licence recognised throughout the Community and the application of the principle of home Member State prudential supervision. Therefore, the requirement that a programme of operations be produced should be seen merely as a factor enabling the competent authorities to decide on the basis of more precise information using objective criteria. A measure of flexibility should nonetheless be possible as regards the requirements on the legal form of credit institutions concerning the protection of banking names.

(10)   The principles of mutual recognition and home Member State supervision require that Member States' competent authorities should not grant or should withdraw an authorisation where factors such as the content of the activities programmes, the geographical distribution of activities or the activities actually carried on indicate clearly that a credit institution has opted for the legal system of one Member State for the purpose of evading the stricter standards in force in another Member State within whose territory it carries on or intends to carry on the greater Part of its activities. Where there is no such clear indication, but the majority of the total assets of the entities in a banking group are located in another Member State the competent authorities of which are responsible for exercising supervision on a consolidated basis, in the context of Articles 125 and 126 responsibility for exercising supervision on a consolidated basis should be changed only with the agreement of those competent authorities. A credit institution which is a legal person should be authorised in the Member State in which it has its registered office. A credit institution which is not a legal person should have its head office in the Member State in which it has been authorised. In addition, Member States should require that a credit institution's head office always be situated in its home Member State and that it actually operates there.

(14)   Credit institutions authorised in their home Member States should be allowed to carry on, throughout the Community, any or all of the activities listed in Annex I by establishing branches or by providing services.

(15)   The Member States may also establish stricter rules than those laid down in Article 9(1), first subparagraph, Article 9(2) and Articles 12, 19 to 21, 44 to 52, 75 and 120 to 122 for credit institutions authorised by their competent authorities. The Member States may also require that Article 123 be complied with on an individual or other basis, and that the sub-consolidation described in Article 73(2) be applied to other levels within a group.

(18)   The Member States should ensure that there are no obstacles to carrying on activities receiving mutual recognition in the same manner as in the home Member State, as long as the latter do not conflict with legal provisions protecting the general good in the host Member State.

(21) Responsibility for supervising the financial soundness of a credit institution, and in particular its solvency, should lay with its home Member State. The host Member State's competent authorities should be responsible for the supervision of the liquidity of the branches and monetary policies. The supervision of market risk should be the subject of close cooperation between the competent authorities of the home and host Member States.

Title I — Subject matter, scope and definitions

Article 1. 1. This Directive lays down rules concerning the taking up and pursuit of the business of credit institutions, and their prudential supervision.

2. Article 39 and Title V, Chapter 4, Section 1 shall apply to financial holding companies and mixed-activity holding companies which have their head offices in the Community.

3. The institutions permanently excluded pursuant to Article 2, with the exception, however, of the central banks of the Member States, shall be treated as financial institutions for the purposes of Article 39 and Title V, Chapter 4, Section 1.

Article 2. This Directive shall not apply to the following:
— the central banks of Member States;
— post office giro institutions;
— in Belgium, the 'Institut de Réescompte et de Garantie/Herdiscontering-en Waarborginstituut',
— in Denmark, the 'Dansk Eksportfinansieringsfond', the 'Danmarks Skibskredit A/S' and the 'KommuneKredit',
— in Germany, the 'Kreditanstalt für Wiederaufbau', undertakings which are recognised under the 'Wohnungsgemeinnützigkeitsgesetz' as bodies of State housing policy and are not mainly engaged in banking transactions, and undertakings recognised under that law as non-profit housing undertakings;
— in Greece, the 'Ταμείο Παρακαταθηκών και Δανείων' (Tamio Parakatathikon kai Danion);
— in Spain, the 'Instituto de Crédito Oficial',
— in France, the 'Caisse des dépôts et consignations',
— in Ireland, credit unions and the friendly societies;
— in Italy, the 'Cassa depositi e prestiti',
— in Latvia, the 'krājaizdevu sabiedrības', undertakings that are recognised under the 'krājaizdevu sabiedrību likums' as cooperative undertakings rendering financial services solely to their members;
— in Lithuania, the 'kredito unijos' other than the 'Centrinė kredito unija',
— in Hungary, the 'Magyar Fejlesztési Bank Rt' and the 'Magyar Export-Import Bank Rt',
— in the Netherlands, the 'Nederlandse Investeringsbank voor Ontwikkelingslanden NV', the 'NV Noordelijke Ontwikkelingsmaatschappij', the 'NV Industriebank Limburgs Instituut voor Ontwikkeling en Financiering' and the 'Overijsselse Ontwikkelingsmaatschappij NV',
— in Austria, undertakings recognised as housing associations in the public interest and the 'Österreichische Kontrollbank AG',

—   in Poland, the 'Spółdzielcze Kasy Oszczędnościowo-Kreditowe' and the 'Bank Gospodarstwa Krajowego',

—   in Portugal, 'Caixas Económicas' existing on 1 January 1986 with the exception of those incorporated as limited companies and of the 'Caixa Económica Montepio Geral',

—   in Finland, the 'Teollisen yhteistyön rahasto Oy/Fonden för industriellt samarbete AB', and the 'Finnvera Oyj/Finnvera Abp',

—   in Sweden, the 'Svenska Skeppshypotekskassan',

—   in the United Kingdom, the National Savings Bank, the Commonwealth Development Finance Company Ltd, the Agricultural Mortgage Corporation Ltd, the Scottish Agricultural Securities Corporation Ltd, the Crown Agents for overseas governments and administrations, credit unions and municipal banks.

Article 4.   For the purposes of this Directive, the following definitions shall apply:

(1)   'credit institution' means an undertaking the business of which is to receive deposits or other repayable funds from the public and to grant credits for its own account;

(2)   'authorisation' means an instrument issued in any form by the authorities by which the right to carry on the business of a credit institution is granted;

(3)   'branch' means a place of business which forms a legally dependent Part of a credit institution and which carries out directly all or some of the transactions inherent in the business of credit institutions;

(4)   'competent authorities' means the national authorities which are empowered by law or regulation to supervise credit institutions;

(5)   'financial institution' means an undertaking other than a credit institution, the principal activity of which is to acquire holdings or to pursue one or more of the activities listed in points 2 to 12 and 15 of Annex I;

(6)   'institutions' for the purposes of Sections 2, 3 and 5 of Title V, Chapter 2, means institutions as defined in Article 3(1)(c) of Directive 2006/49/EC;

(7)   'home Member State' means the Member State in which a credit institution has been authorised in accordance with Articles 6 to 9 and 11 to 14;

(8)   'host Member State' means the Member State in which a credit institution has a branch or in which it provides services;

(9)   'control' means the relationship between a parent undertaking and a subsidiary, as defined in Article 1 of Directive 83/349/EEC, or a similar relationship between any natural or legal person and an undertaking;

(10)   'participation' for the purposes of points (o) and (p) of Article 57, Articles 71 to 73 and Title V, Chapter 4 means participation within the meaning of the first sentence of Article 17 of Fourth Council Directive 78/660/EEC of 25 July 1978 on the annual accounts of certain types of companies (1), or the ownership, direct or indirect, of 20 % or more of the voting rights or capital of an undertaking;

(11)   'qualifying holding' means a direct or indirect holding in an undertaking which represents 10 % or more of the capital or of the voting rights or which makes it possible to exercise a significant influence over the management of that undertaking;

(12)   'parent undertaking' means:

(a)   a parent undertaking as defined in Articles 1 and 2 of Directive 83/349/EEC; or

(b)   for the purposes of Articles 71 to 73, Title V, Chapter 2, Section 5 and Chapter 4, a parent undertaking within the meaning of Article 1(1) of Directive 83/349/EEC and any undertaking which, in the opinion of the competent authorities, effectively exercises a dominant influence over another undertaking;

(13) 'subsidiary' means:

(a)   a subsidiary undertaking as defined in Articles 1 and 2 of Directive 83/349/EEC; or

(b) for the purposes of Articles 71 to 73, Title V, Chapter 2, Section 5, and Chapter 4 a subsidiary undertaking within the meaning of Article 1(1) of Directive 83/349/EEC and any undertaking over which, in the opinion of the competent authorities, a parent undertaking effectively exercises a dominant influence.

All subsidiaries of subsidiary undertakings shall also be considered subsidiaries of the undertaking that is their original parent;

(14) 'parent credit institution in a Member State' means a credit institution which has a credit institution or a financial institution as a subsidiary or which holds a participation in such an institution, and which is not itself a subsidiary of another credit institution authorised in the same Member State, or of a financial holding company set up in the same Member State;

(15) 'parent financial holding company in a Member State' means a financial holding company which is not itself a subsidiary of a credit institution authorised in the same Member State, or of a financial holding company set up in the same Member State;

(16) 'EU parent credit institution' means a parent credit institution in a Member State which is not a subsidiary of another credit institution authorised in any Member State, or of a financial holding company set up in any Member State;

(17) 'EU parent financial holding company' means a parent financial holding company in a Member State which is not a subsidiary of a credit institution authorised in any Member State or of another financial holding company set up in any Member State;

(18) 'public sector entities' means non-commercial administrative bodies responsible to central governments, regional governments or local authorities, or authorities that in the view of the competent authorities exercise the same responsibilities as regional and local authorities, or non-commercial undertakings owned by central governments that have explicit guarantee arrangements, and may include selfadministered bodies governed by law that are under public supervision;

(19) 'financial holding company' means a financial institution, the subsidiary undertakings of which are either exclusively or mainly credit institutions or financial institutions, at least one of such subsidiaries being a credit institution, and which is not a mixed financial holding company within the meaning of Article 2(15) of Directive 2002/87/EC;

(20) 'mixed-activity holding company' means a parent undertaking, other than a financial holding company or a credit institution or a mixed financial holding company within the meaning of Article 2(15) of Directive 2002/87/EC, the subsidiaries of which include at least one credit institution;

(21) 'ancillary services undertaking' means an undertaking the principal activity of which consists in owning or managing property, managing data-processing services, or any other similar activity which is ancillary to the principal activity of one or more credit institutions...

Title III — Provisions concerning the freedom of establishment and the freedom to provide services

Section 1. — Credit institutions

Article 23.   The Member States shall provide that the activities listed in Annex I may be carried on within their territories, in accordance with Articles 25, 26(1) to (3), 28(1) and (2) and 29 to 37 either by the establishment of a branch or by way of the provision of services, by any credit institution authorised and supervised by the competent authorities of another Member State, provided that such activities are covered by the authorisation.

Section 2. — Financial institutions

Article 24.   1.   The Member States shall provide that the activities listed in Annex I may be carried on within their territories, in accordance with Articles 25, 26(1) to (3), 28(1) and (2) and 29 to 37, either by the establishment of a branch or by way of the provision of services, by any financial institution from another Member State, whether a subsidiary of a credit institution or the jointly-owned subsidiary of two or more credit institutions, the memorandum and Articles of association of which permit the carrying on of those activities and which fulfils each of the following conditions:
    (a)   the parent undertaking or undertakings shall be authorised as credit institutions in the Member State by the law of which the financial institution is governed;
    (b)   the activities in question shall actually be carried on within the territory of the same Member State;
    (c)   the parent undertaking or undertakings shall hold 90 % or more of the voting rights attaching to shares in the capital of the financial institution;
    (d)   the parent undertaking or undertakings shall satisfy the competent authorities regarding the prudent management of the financial institution and shall have declared, with the consent of the relevant home Member State competent authorities, that they jointly and severally guarantee the commitments entered into by the financial institution; and
    (e)   the financial institution shall be effectively included, for the activities in question in particular, in the consolidated supervision of the parent undertaking, or of each of the parent undertakings, in accordance with Title V, Chapter 4, Section 1, in particular for the purposes of the minimum own funds requirements set out in Article 75 for the control of large exposures and for purposes of the limitation of holdings provided for in Articles 120 to 122. Compliance with these conditions shall be verified by the competent authorities of the home Member State and the latter shall supply the financial institution with a certificate of compliance which shall form Part of the notification referred to in Articles 25 and 28. The competent authorities of the home Member State shall ensure the supervision of the financial institution in accordance with Articles 10(1), 19 to 22, 40, 42 to 52 and 54.
    2.   If a financial institution as referred to in the first subparagraph of paragraph 1 ceases to fulfil any of the conditions imposed, the home Member State shall notify the competent authorities of the host Member State and the activities carried on by that financial institution in the host Member State shall become subject to the legislation of the host Member State.

3.   Paragraphs 1 and 2 shall apply mutatis mutandis to subsidiaries of a financial institution as referred to in the first subparagraph of paragraph 1.

K.   Directive 2007/36/EC of the European Parliament and of the Council of 11 July 2007 on the exercise of certain rights of shareholders in listed companies (OJ, L 184 of 14 July 2007)

(5)   Significant proportions of shares in listed companies are held by shareholders who do not reside in the Member State in which the company has its registered office. Non-resident shareholders should be able to exercise their rights in relation to the general meeting as easily as shareholders who reside in the Member State in which the company has its registered office. This requires that existing obstacles which hinder the access of non-resident shareholders to the information relevant to the general meeting and the exercise of voting rights without physically attending the general meeting be removed. The removal of these obstacles should also benefit resident shareholders who do not or cannot attend the general meeting.

Chapter I — General provisions

Article 1. Subject-matter and scope.   1.   This Directive establishes requirements in relation to the exercise of certain shareholder rights attaching to voting shares in relation to general meetings of companies which have their registered office in a Member State and whose shares are admitted to trading on a regulated market situated or operating within a Member State.

2.   The Member State competent to regulate matters covered in this Directive shall be the Member State in which the company has its registered office, and references to the 'applicable law' are references to the law of that Member State...

Article 3. Further national measures.   This Directive shall not prevent Member States from imposing further obligations on companies or from otherwise taking further measures to facilitate the exercise by shareholders of the rights referred to in this Directive.

L.   Directive 2009/38/EC of the European Parliament and of the Council of 6 May 2009 on the establishment of a European Works Council or a procedure in Community-scale undertakings and Community-scale groups of undertakings for the purposes of informing and consulting employees (recast) (OJ, L 122 of 16 May 2009)[1]

(16)   The transnational character of a matter should be determined by taking account of both the scope of its potential effects, and the level of management and representation that it involves. For this purpose, matters which concern the entire undertaking or group or at least two Member States are considered to be transnational. These include matters which, regardless of the number of Member States involved, are of importance for the European workforce in terms of the scope of their potential effects or which involve transfers of activities between Member States.

Article 1. Objective.   1.   The purpose of this Directive is to improve the right to information and to consultation of employees in Community-scale undertakings and Community-scale groups of undertakings.

2.   To that end, a European Works Council or a procedure for informing and consulting employees shall be established in every Community-scale undertaking and every Community-scale group of undertakings, where requested in the manner laid down in Article 5(1), with the purpose of informing and consulting employees. The arrangements for informing and consulting employees shall be defined and implemented in such a way as to ensure their effectiveness and to enable the undertaking or group of undertakings to take decisions effectively.

3.   Information and consultation of employees must occur at the relevant level of management and representation, according to the subject under discussion. To achieve that, the competence of the European Works Council and the scope of the information and consultation procedure for employees governed by this Directive shall be limited to transnational issues.

4.   Matters shall be considered to be transnational where they concern the Community-scale undertaking or Community-scale group of undertakings as a whole, or at least two undertakings or establishments of the undertaking or group situated in two different Member States.

Article 3. Definition of 'controlling undertaking'.   1.   For the purposes of this Directive, 'controlling undertaking' means an undertaking which can exercise a dominant influence over another undertaking (the controlled undertaking) by virtue, for example, of ownership, financial participation or the rules which govern it.

2.   The ability to exercise a dominant influence shall be presumed, without prejudice to proof to the contrary, when an undertaking, in relation to another undertaking directly

---

[1]   Pursuant to Article 17, the Directive 2009/38/EC will repeal the Directive 94/45/EC on the establishment of a European Works Council or a procedure in Community-scale undertakings and Community-scale groups of undertakings for the purposes of informing and consulting employees with effect from 6 June 2011. [Note of the Editor]

or indirectly: (a) holds a majority of that undertaking's subscribed capital; (b) controls a majority of the votes attached to that undertaking's issued share capital; or (c) can appoint more than half of the members of that undertaking's administrative, management or supervisory body.

3.   For the purposes of paragraph 2, a controlling undertaking's rights as regards voting and appointment shall include the rights of any other controlled undertaking and those of any person or body acting in his or its own name but on behalf of the controlling undertaking or of any other controlled undertaking.

4.   Notwithstanding paragraphs 1 and 2, an undertaking shall not be deemed to be a 'controlling undertaking' with respect to another undertaking in which it has holdings where the former undertaking is a company referred to in Article 3(5)(a) or (c) of Council Regulation (EC) No 139/2004 of 20 January 2004 on the control of concentrations between undertakings.

5.   A dominant influence shall not be presumed to be exercised solely by virtue of the fact that an office holder is exercising his functions, according to the law of a Member State relating to liquidation, winding up, insolvency, cessation of payments, compositions or analogous proceedings.

6.   The law applicable in order to determine whether an undertaking is a controlling undertaking shall be the law of the Member State which governs that undertaking. Where the law governing that undertaking is not that of a Member State, the law applicable shall be the law of the Member State within whose territory the representative of the undertaking or, in the absence of such a representative, the central management of the group undertaking which employs the greatest number of employees is situated.

7.   Where, in the case of a conflict of laws in the application of paragraph 2, two or more undertakings from a group satisfy one or more of the criteria laid down in that paragraph, the undertaking which satisfies the criterion laid down in point (c) thereof shall be regarded as the controlling undertaking, without prejudice to proof that another undertaking is able to exercise a dominant influence.

M.   Directive 2009/65/EC of the European Parliament and of the Council of 13 July 2009 on the coordination of laws, regulations and administrative provisions relating to undertakings for collective investment in transferable securities (UCITS) (OJ, L 302 of 17 November 2009)[1]

(8)   An authorisation granted to the management company in its home Member State should ensure investor protection and the solvency of management companies, with a view to contributing to the stability of the financial system. The approach adopted in this Directive is to ensure the essential harmonisation necessary and sufficient to secure

---

[1]   See also Articles 14, 25 and 28 of Commission Directive 2010/42/EU of 1 July 2010 as regards certain provisions concerning fund mergers, master-feeder structures and notification procedure, and Article 34 of Commission Directive 2010/43/EU of 1 July 2010 as regards organisational requirements, conflicts of interest, conduct of business, risk management and content of the agreement between a depositary and a management company (both in OJ, L 176 of 1 July 2010). For the provisions concerning the mergers of UCITS, see this Chapter, Cross-border mergers, B. [Note of the Editor]

the mutual recognition of authorisation and of prudential supervision systems, making possible the grant of a single authorisation valid throughout the Community and the application of the principle of home Member State supervision.

(11) By virtue of the principle of home Member State supervision, management companies authorised in their home Member States should be permitted to provide the services for which they have received authorisation throughout the Community by establishing branches or under the freedom to provide services.

(13) With regard to the scope of activity of management companies and in order to take into account national law and permit such companies to achieve significant economies of scale, it is desirable to permit them also to pursue the activity of management of portfolios of investments on a client-by-client basis (individual portfolio management), including the management of pension funds as well as some specific non-core activities linked to the main business without prejudicing the stability of such companies. However, specific rules should be laid down in order to prevent conflicts of interest when management companies are authorised to pursue the business of both collective and individual portfolio management.

(14) The activity of management of individual portfolios of investments is an investment service covered by Directive 2004/39/EC. In order to ensure a homogeneous regulatory framework in this area, it is desirable to subject management companies, the authorisation of which also covers that service, to the operating conditions laid down in that Directive.

(15) A home Member State should be able, as a general rule, to establish rules stricter than those laid down in this Directive, in particular as regards authorisation conditions, prudential requirements and the rules on reporting and the prospectus.

(18) The principle of home Member State supervision requires that the competent authorities withdraw or refuse to grant authorisation where factors, such as the content of programmes of operations, the geographical distribution or the activities in fact pursued indicate clearly that a management company has opted for the legal system of one Member State for the purpose of evading the stricter standards in force in another Member State within the territory of which it intends to pursue or does pursue the greater part of its activities. For the purposes of this Directive, a management company should be authorised in the Member State in which it has its registered office. In accordance with the principle of home Member State supervision, only the competent authorities of the management company's home Member State should be considered competent to supervise the organisation of the management company, including all procedures and resources to perform the function of administration referred to in Annex II, which should be subject to the law of the management company's home Member State.

(21) The competent authorities of the UCITS home Member State should be competent to supervise compliance with the rules regarding the constitution and functioning of the UCITS, which should be subject to the law of the UCITS home Member State...

(27) Despite the need for consolidation between UCITS, mergers of UCITS encounter many legal and administrative difficulties in the Community. It is therefore necessary, in order to improve the functioning of the internal market, to lay down Community provisions facilitating mergers between UCITS (and investment compartments thereof). Although some Member States are likely to authorise only contractual funds, cross-border mergers between all types of UCITS (contractual, corporate and unit trusts) should be

permitted and recognised by each Member State without the need for Member States to provide for new legal forms of UCITS in their national law.

(28) This Directive concerns those merger techniques which are most commonly used in Member States. It does not require all Member States to introduce all three techniques into their national law, but each Member State should recognise a transfer of assets resulting from those merger techniques. This Directive does not prevent UCITS from using other techniques on a purely national basis, in situations where none of the UCITS concerned by the merger has been notified for cross-border marketing of its units. Those mergers will remain subject to the relevant provisions of national law. National rules on quorum should neither discriminate between national and cross-border mergers, nor be more stringent than those laid down for mergers of corporate entities.

(29) In order to safeguard investors' interests, Member States should require proposed domestic or cross-border mergers between UCITS to be subject to authorisation by their competent authorities. For cross-border mergers, the competent authorities of the merging UCITS should authorise the merger so as to ensure that the interests of the unit-holders who effectively change UCITS are duly protected. If the merger involves more than one merging UCITS and such UCITS are domiciled in different Member States, the competent authorities of each merging UCITS will need to authorise the merger, in close cooperation with each other, including through appropriate information-sharing. Since the interests of the unit-holders of the receiving UCITS also need to be adequately safeguarded, they should be taken into account by the competent authorities of the receiving UCITS home Member State.

(30) Unit-holders of both the merging and the receiving UCITS should also be able to request the repurchase or redemption of their units or, where possible, to convert them into units in another UCITS with similar investment policies and managed by the same management company or by a linked company. That right should not be subject to any additional charge, save for fees, to be retained exclusively by the respective UCITS, to cover disinvestment costs in all situations, as set out in the prospectuses of the merging and the receiving UCITS.

(31) Third-party control of mergers should also be ensured. The depositaries of each of the UCITS involved in the merger should verify the conformity of the common draft terms of the merger with the relevant provisions of this Directive and of the UCITS fund rules. Either a depositary or an independent auditor should draw-up a report on behalf of all the UCITS involved in the merger validating the valuation methods of the assets and liabilities of such UCITS and the calculation method of the exchange ratio as set out in the common draft terms of merger as well as the actual exchange ratio and, where applicable, the cash payment per unit. In order to limit costs connected with cross-border mergers, it should be possible to draw up a single report for all UCITS involved and the statutory auditor of the merging or the receiving UCITS should be enabled to do so. For investor protection reasons, unit-holders should be able to obtain a copy of such report on request and free of charge.

(32) It is particularly important that the unit-holders are adequately informed about the proposed merger and that their rights are sufficiently protected. Although the interests of the unit-holders of the merging UCITS are most concerned by the merger, those of the unit-holders of the receiving UCITS should also be safeguarded.

(33) The provisions on mergers laid down in this Directive are without prejudice to the application of the legislation on control of concentrations between undertakings,

in particular Council Regulation (EC) No 139/2004 of 20 January 2004 on the control of concentrations between undertakings (the EC Merger Regulation).

(62) UCITS should be able to market their units in other Member States subject to a notification procedure based on improved communication between the competent authorities of the Member States. Following transmission of a complete notification file by the competent authorities of the UCITS home Member State, it should not be possible for the UCITS host Member State to oppose access to its market by a UCITS established in another Member State or challenge the authorisation given by that other Member State.

(65) For the purpose of enhancing legal certainty there is a need to ensure that a UCITS which markets its units on a cross-border basis has easy access, in the form of an electronic publication and in a language customary in the sphere of international finance, to complete information on the laws, regulations and administrative provisions applicable in the UCITS host Member State, which specifically relate to the arrangements made for marketing of units of UCITS. Liabilities relating to such publications should be subject to national law.

(69) It is necessary to enhance convergence of powers at the disposal of competent authorities so as to bring about the equal enforcement of this Directive throughout the Member States. A common minimum set of powers, consistent with those conferred upon competent authorities by other Community financial services legislation should guarantee supervisory effectiveness. In addition, Member States should lay down rules on penalties, which may include criminal or administrative penalties, and administrative measures, applicable to infringements of this Directive. Member States should also take the measures necessary to ensure that those penalties are enforced.

(71) For the purpose of cross-border provision of services, clear competences should be assigned to the respective competent authorities so as to eliminate any gaps or overlaps, in accordance with the applicable law.

(73) The principle of home Member State supervision requires that the competent authorities withdraw or refuse to grant authorisation where factors such as the content of programmes of operations, the geographical distribution or the activities actually pursued indicate clearly that a UCITS or an undertaking contributing towards its business activity has opted for the legal system of one Member State for the purpose of evading the stricter standards in force in another Member State within whose territory it pursues or intends to pursue the greater part of its activities.

(83) This Directive should not affect national rules on taxation, including arrangements that may be imposed by Member States to ensure compliance with those rules in their territory.

Chapter I — Subject matter, scope and definitions

Article 1.   1.   This Directive applies to undertakings for collective investment in transferable securities (UCITS) established within the territories of the Member States.

2.   For the purposes of this Directive, and subject to Article 3, UCITS means an undertaking:

(a)   with the sole object of collective investment in transferable securities or in other liquid financial assets referred to in Article 50(1) of capital raised from the public and which operate on the principle of risk-spreading; and

(b)   with units which are, at the request of holders, repurchased or redeemed, directly or indirectly, out of those undertakings' assets. Action taken by a UCITS to ensure that the stock exchange value of its units does not significantly vary from their net asset value shall be regarded as equivalent to such repurchase or redemption.

Member States may allow UCITS to consist of several investment compartments.

3.   The undertakings referred to in paragraph 2 may be constituted in accordance with contract law (as common funds managed by management companies), trust law (as unit trusts), or statute (as investment companies).

For the purposes of this Directive:

(a)   'common funds' shall also include unit trusts;

(b)   'units' of UCITS shall also include shares of UCITS.

4.   Investment companies, the assets of which are invested through the intermediary of subsidiary companies, mainly other than in transferable securities, shall not be subject to this Directive.

5.   The Member States shall prohibit UCITS which are subject to this Directive from transforming themselves into collective investment undertakings which are not covered by this Directive.

6.   Subject to the provisions in Community law governing capital movements and subject to Articles 91 and 92 and the second subparagraph of Article 108(1), no Member State shall apply any other provisions in the field covered by this Directive to UCITS established in another Member State or to the units issued by such UCITS, where those UCITS market their units within the territory of that Member State.

7.   Without prejudice to this Chapter, a Member State may apply to UCITS established within its territory requirements which are stricter than or additional to those laid down in this Directive, provided that they are of general application and do not conflict with the provisions of this Directive.

Article 2.   1.   For the purposes of this Directive the following definitions apply:

(a)   'depositary' means an institution entrusted with the duties set out in Articles 22 and 32 and subject to the other provisions laid down in Chapter IV and Section 3 of Chapter V;

(b)   'management company' means a company, the regular business of which is the management of UCITS in the form of common funds or of investment companies (collective portfolio management of UCITS);

(c)   'management company's home Member State' means the Member State in which the management company has its registered office;

(d)   'management company's host Member State' means a Member State, other than the home Member State, within the territory of which a management company has a branch or provides services;

(e)   'UCITS home Member State' means the Member State in which the UCITS is authorised pursuant to Article 5;

(f)   'UCITS host Member State' means a Member State, other than the UCITS home Member State, in which the units of the UCITS are marketed;

(g)   'branch' means a place of business which is a part of the management company, which has no legal personality and which provides the services for which the management company has been authorised;

(h) 'competent authorities' means the authorities which each Member State designates under Article 97;

(i) 'close links' means a situation in which two or more natural or legal persons are linked by either:

(i) 'participation', which means the ownership, direct or by way of control, of 20 % or more of the voting rights or capital of an undertaking; or

(ii) 'control', which means the relationship between a 'parent undertaking' and a 'subsidiary', as defined in Articles 1 and 2 of Seventh Council Directive 83/349/EEC of 13 June 1983 based on the Article 54(3)(g) of the Treaty on consolidated accounts and in all the cases referred to in Article 1(1) and (2) of Directive 83/349/EEC, or a similar relationship between any natural or legal person and an undertaking;

(j) 'qualifying holding' means a direct or indirect holding in a management company which represents 10 % or more of the capital or of the voting rights or which makes it possible to exercise a significant influence over the management of the management company in which that holding subsists;

(k) 'initial capital' means the funds as referred to in Article 57(a) and (b) of Directive 2006/48/EC;

(l) 'own funds' means own funds as referred to in Title V, Chapter 2, Section 1 of Directive 2006/48/EC;

(m) 'durable medium' means an instrument which enables an investor to store information addressed personally to that investor in a way that is accessible for future reference for a period of time adequate for the purposes of the information and which allows the unchanged reproduction of the information stored;

(n) 'transferable securities' means:

(i) shares in companies and other securities equivalent to shares in companies (shares);

(ii) bonds and other forms of securitised debt (debt securities);

(iii) any other negotiable securities which carry the right to acquire any such transferable securities by subscription or exchange;

(o) 'money market instruments' means instruments normally dealt in on the money market which are liquid and have a value which can be accurately determined at any time;

(p) 'mergers' means an operation whereby:

(i) one or more UCITS or investment compartments thereof, the 'merging UCITS', on being dissolved without going into liquidation, transfer all of their assets and liabilities to another existing UCITS or an investment compartment thereof, the 'receiving UCITS', in exchange for the issue to their unit-holders of units of the receiving UCITS and, if applicable, a cash payment not exceeding 10% of the net asset value of those units;

(ii) two or more UCITS or investment compartments thereof, the 'merging UCITS', on being dissolved without going into liquidation, transfer all of their assets and liabilities to a UCITS which they form or an investment compartment thereof, the 'receiving UCITS', in exchange for the issue to their unit-holders of units of the receiving UCITS and, if applicable, a cash payment not exceeding 10 % of the net asset value of those units;

(iii) one or more UCITS or investment compartments thereof, the 'merging UCITS', which continue to exist until the liabilities have been discharged, transfer their net assets to another investment compartment of the same UCITS, to a UCITS which they form or to another existing UCITS or an investment compartment thereof, the 'receiving UCITS';

(q)   'cross-border merger' means a merger of UCITS:

(i)   at least two of which are established in different Member States; or

(ii)   established in the same Member State into a newly constituted UCITS established in another Member State;

(r)   'domestic merger' means a merger between UCITS established in the same Member State where at least one of the involved UCITS has been notified pursuant to Article 93.

2.   For the purposes of paragraph 1(b), the regular business of a management company shall include the functions referred to in Annex II.

3.   For the purposes of paragraph 1(g), all the places of business established in the same Member State by a management company with its head office in another Member State shall be regarded as a single branch.

4.   For the purposes of point (i)(ii) of paragraph 1, the following shall apply:

(a)   a subsidiary undertaking of a subsidiary undertaking shall also be considered to be a subsidiary of the parent undertaking which is at the head of those undertakings;

(b)   situations in which two or more natural or legal persons are permanently linked to the same person by a control relationship shall also be regarded as constituting a close links between such persons.

5.   For the purposes of paragraph 1(j), the voting rights referred to in Articles 9 and 10 of Directive 2004/109/EC of the European Parliament and of the Council of 15 December 2004 on the harmonisation of transparency requirements in relation to information about issuers whose securities are admitted to trading on a regulated market shall be taken into account.

6.   For the purposes of paragraph 1(l), Articles 13 to 16 of Directive 2006/49/EC shall apply mutatis mutandis.

7.   For the purposes of paragraph 1(n), transferable securities shall exclude the techniques and instruments referred to in Article 51.

Article 3.   The following undertakings are not subject to this Directive:

(a)   collective investment undertakings of the closed-ended type;

(b)   collective investment undertakings which raise capital without promoting the sale of their units to the public within the Community or any part of it;

(c)   collective investment undertakings the units of which, under the fund rules or the instruments of incorporation of the investment company, may be sold only to the public in third countries;

(d)   categories of collective investment undertakings prescribed by the regulations of the Member States in which such collective investment undertakings are established, for which the rules laid down in Chapter VII and Article 83 are inappropriate in view of their investment and borrowing policies.

Article 4.   For the purposes of this Directive, a UCITS shall be deemed to be established in its home Member State.

Chapter II — Authorisation of UCITS

Article 5.   1.   No UCITS shall pursue activities as such unless it has been authorised in accordance with this Directive. Such authorisation shall be valid for all Member States.

2.   A common fund shall be authorised only if the competent authorities of its home Member State have approved the application of the management company to manage that common fund, the fund rules and the choice of depositary. An investment company shall be authorised only if the competent authorities of its home Member State have approved both its instruments of incorporation and the choice of depositary, and, where relevant, the application of the designated management company to manage that investment company.

3.   Without prejudice to paragraph 2, if the UCITS is not established in the management company's home Member State, the competent authorities of the UCITS home Member State shall decide, on the application of the management company, to manage the UCITS pursuant to Article 20. Authorisation shall not be subject either to a requirement that the UCITS be managed by a management company having its registered office in the UCITS home Member State or that the management company pursue or delegate any activities in the UCITS home Member State.

Chapter III — Obligations regarding management companies

Section 1 — Conditions for taking up business

Article 6.   1.   Access to the business of management companies shall be subject to prior authorisation to be granted by the competent authorities of the management company's home Member State. Authorisation granted under this Directive to a management company shall be valid for all Member States.

Section 4 — Freedom of establishment and freedom to provide services

Article 16.   1.   Member States shall ensure that a management company, authorised by its home Member State, may pursue within their territories the activity for which it has been authorised, either by the establishment of a branch or under the freedom to provide services.

Where a management company so authorised proposes, without establishing a branch, only to market the units of the UCITS it manages as provided for in Annex II in a Member State other than the UCITS home Member State, without proposing to pursue any other activities or services, such marketing shall be subject only to the requirements of Chapter XI.

2.   Member States shall not make the establishment of a branch or the provision of the services subject to any authorisation requirement, to any requirement to provide endowment capital or to any other measure having equivalent effect.

3.   Subject to the conditions set out in this Article, a UCITS shall be free to designate, or to be managed by a management company authorised in a Member State other than the UCITS home Member State in accordance with the relevant provisions of this Directive, provided that such a management company complies with the provisions of:

(a)   Article 17 or Article 18; and
(b)   Articles 19 and 20.

Article 18. 3. A management company which pursues activities under the freedom to provide services shall comply with the rules drawn up by the management company's home Member State pursuant to Article 14.

Article 19. 1. A management company which pursues the activity of collective portfolio management on a cross-border basis by establishing a branch or under the freedom to provide services shall comply with the rules of the management company's home Member State which relate to the organisation of the management company, including delegation arrangements, risk-management procedures, prudential rules and supervision, procedures referred to in Article 12 and the management company's reporting requirements. Those rules shall be no stricter than those applicable to management companies conducting their activities only in their home Member State.

2. The competent authorities of the management company's home Member State shall be responsible for supervising compliance with paragraph 1.

3. A management company which pursues the activity of collective portfolio management on a cross-border basis by establishing a branch or in accordance with the freedom to provide services shall comply with the rules of the UCITS home Member State which relate to the constitution and functioning of the UCITS, namely the rules applicable to:

(a) the setting up and authorisation of the UCITS;

(b) the issuance and redemption of units and shares;

(c) investment policies and limits, including the calculation of total exposure and leverage;

(d) restrictions on borrowing, lending and uncovered sales;

(e) the valuation of assets and the accounting of the UCITS;

(f) the calculation of the issue or redemption price, and errors in the calculation of the net asset value and related investor compensation;

(g) the distribution or reinvestment of the income;

(h) the disclosure and reporting requirements of the UCITS, including the prospectus, key investor information and periodic reports;

(i) the arrangements made for marketing;

(j) the relationship with unit-holders;

(k) the merging and restructuring of the UCITS;

(l) the winding-up and liquidation of the UCITS;

(m) where applicable, the content of the unit-holder register;

(n) the licensing and supervision fees regarding the UCITS; and

(o) the exercise of unit-holders' voting rights and other unit-holders' rights in relation to points (a) to (m).

4. The management company shall comply with the obligations set out in the fund rules or in the instruments of incorporation, and the obligations set out in the prospectus, which shall be consistent with the applicable law as referred to in paragraphs 1 and 3.

5. The competent authorities of the UCITS home Member State shall be responsible for supervising compliance with paragraphs 3 and 4 …

8. Member States shall ensure that any management company authorised in a Member State is not subject to any additional requirement established in the UCITS home Member State in respect of the subject matter of this Directive, except in the cases expressly referred to in this Directive.

Article 24.   A depositary shall, in accordance with the national law of the UCITS home Member State, be liable to the management company and the unit-holders for any loss suffered by them as a result of its unjustifiable failure to perform its obligations or its improper performance of them.

Chapter V — Obligations regarding investment companies

Section 1 — Conditions for taking up business

Article 27.   Access to the business of an investment company shall be subject to prior authorisation to be granted by the competent authorities of the investment company's home Member State.

Member States shall determine the legal form which an investment company must take.

The registered office of the investment company shall be situated in the investment company's home Member State.

Article 34.   A depositary shall, in accordance with the national law of the investment company's home Member State, be liable to the investment company and the unit-holders for any loss suffered by them as a result of its unjustifiable failure to perform its obligations, or its improper performance of them.

Chapter XI — Special provisions applicable to UCITS which market their units in Member States other than those in which they are established

Article 91.   1.   UCITS host Member States shall ensure that UCITS are able to market their units within their territories upon notification in accordance with Article 93.

2.   UCITS host Member States shall not impose any additional requirements or administrative procedures on UCITS as referred to in paragraph 1 in respect of the field governed by this Directive.

3.   Member States shall ensure that complete information on the laws, regulations and administrative provisions which do not fall within the field governed by this Directive and which are specifically relevant to the arrangements made for the marketing of units of UCITS, established in another Member State within their territories, is easily accessible from a distance and by electronic means. Member States shall ensure that that information is available in a language customary in the sphere of international finance, is provided in a clear and unambiguous manner and is kept up to date.

4.   For the purposes of this Chapter, a UCITS shall include investment compartments thereof.

Article 92.   UCITS shall, in accordance with the laws, regulations and administrative provisions in force in the Member State where their units are marketed, take the measures necessary to ensure that facilities are available in that Member State for making payments to unit-holders, repurchasing or redeeming units and making available the information which UCITS are required to provide.

Article 93. 1. If a UCITS proposes to market its units in a Member State other than its home Member State, it shall first submit a notification letter to the competent authorities of its home Member State.

The notification letter shall include information on arrangements made for marketing units of the UCITS in the host Member State, including, where relevant, in respect of share classes. In the context of Article 16(1), it shall include an indication that the UCITS is marketed by the management company that manages the UCITS.

2. A UCITS shall enclose with the notification letter, as referred to in paragraph 1, the latest version of the following:

(a) its fund rules or its instruments of incorporation, its prospectus and, where appropriate, its latest annual report and any subsequent half-yearly report translated in accordance with the provisions of Article 94(1)(c) and (d); and

(b) its key investor information referred to in Article 78, translated in accordance with Article 94(1)(b) and (d).

3. The competent authorities of the UCITS home Member State shall verify whether the documentation submitted by the UCITS in accordance with paragraphs 1 and 2 is complete.

The competent authorities of the UCITS home Member State shall transmit the complete documentation referred to in paragraphs 1 and 2 to the competent authorities of the Member State in which the UCITS proposes to market its units, no later than 10 working days of the date of receipt of the notification letter accompanied by the complete documentation provided for in paragraph 2. They shall enclose with the documentation an attestation that the UCITS fulfils the conditions imposed by this Directive.

Upon the transmission of the documentation, the competent authorities of the UCITS home Member State shall immediately notify the UCITS about the transmission. The UCITS may access the market of the UCITS host Member State as from the date of that notification.

4. Member States shall ensure that the notification letter referred to in paragraph 1 and the attestation referred to in paragraph 3 are provided in a language customary in the sphere of international finance, unless the UCITS home and host Member States agree to that notification letter and that attestation being provided in an official language of both Member States.

5. Member States shall ensure that the electronic transmission and filing of the documents referred to in paragraph 3 is accepted by their competent authorities.

6. For the purpose of the notification procedure set out in this Article, the competent authorities of the Member State in which a UCITS proposes to market its units shall not request any additional documents, certificates or information other than those provided for in this Article.

7. The UCITS home Member State shall ensure that the competent authorities of the UCITS host Member State have access, by electronic means, to the documents referred to in paragraph 2 and, if applicable, to any translations thereof. It shall ensure that the UCITS keeps those documents and translations up to date. The UCITS shall notify any amendments to the documents referred to in paragraph 2 to the competent authorities of the UCITS host Member State and shall indicate where those documents can be obtained electronically.

8. In the event of a change in the information regarding the arrangements made for marketing communicated in the notification letter in accordance with paragraph 1,

or a change regarding share classes to be marketed, the UCITS shall give written notice thereof to the competent authorities of the host Member State before implementing the change.

Article 94.   1.   Where a UCITS markets its units in a UCITS host Member State, it shall provide to investors within the territory of such Member State all information and documents which it is required pursuant to Chapter IX to provide to investors in its home Member State.

Such information and documents shall be provided to investors in compliance with the following provisions:

(a)   without prejudice to the provisions of Chapter IX, such information or documents shall be provided to investors in the way prescribed by the laws, regulations or administrative provisions of the UCITS host Member State;

(b)   key investor information referred to in Article 78 shall be translated into the official language, or one of the official languages, of the UCITS host Member State or into a language approved by the competent authorities of that Member State;

(c)   information or documents other than key investor information referred to in Article 78 shall be translated, at the choice of the UCITS, into the official language, or one of the official languages, of the UCITS host Member State, into a language approved by the competent authorities of that Member State or into a language customary in the sphere of international finance; and

(d)   translations of information or documents under points (b) and (c) shall be produced under the responsibility of the UCITS and shall faithfully reflect the content of the original information.

2.   The requirements set out in paragraph 1 shall also be applicable to any changes to the information and documents referred therein.

3.   The frequency of the publication of the issue, sale, repurchase or redemption price of units of UCITS according to Article 76 shall be subject to the laws, regulations and administrative provisions of the UCITS home Member State.

Article 95.   1.   The Commission may adopt implementing measures specifying:

(a)   the scope of the information referred to in Article 91(3);

(b)   the facilitation of access for the competent authorities of the UCITS host Member States to the information or documents referred to in Article 93(1), (2) and (3) in accordance with Article 93(7).

Those measures, designed to amend non-essential elements of this Directive by supplementing it, shall be adopted in accordance with the regulatory procedure with scrutiny referred to in Article 112(2).

2.   The Commission may also adopt implementing measures specifying:

(a)   the form and contents of a standard model notification letter to be used by a UCITS for the purpose of notification referred to in Article 93(1), including an indication as to which documents the translations refer to;

(b)   the form and contents of a standard model attestation to be used by competent authorities of Member States referred to in Article 93(3);

(c)   the procedure for the exchange of information and the use of electronic communication between competent authorities for the purpose of notification under the provisions of Article 93.

Those measures shall be adopted in accordance with the regulatory procedure referred to in Article 112(3).

Article 96.   For the purpose of pursuing its activities, a UCITS may use the same reference to its legal form (such as investment company or common fund) in its designation in a UCITS host Member State as it uses in its home Member State.

N.   Directive 2009/138/EC of the European Parliament and of the Council of 25 November 2009 on the taking-up and pursuit of the business of Insurance and Reinsurance (Solvency II) (recast) (OJ, L 335 of 17 December 2009)[1]

(1)   A number of substantial changes are to be made to First Council Directive 73/239/EEC of 24 July 1973 on the coordination of laws, regulations and administrative provisions relating to the taking-up and pursuit of the business of direct insurance other than life assurance; Council Directive 78/473/EEC of 30 May 1978 on the coordination of laws, regulations and administrative provisions relating to Community co-insurance; Council Directive 87/344/EEC of 22 June 1987 on the coordination of laws, regulations and administrative provisions relating to legal expenses insurance; Second Council Directive 88/357/EEC of 22 June 1988 on the coordination of laws, regulations and administrative provisions relating to direct insurance other than life assurance and laying down provisions to facilitate the effective exercise of freedom to provide services; Council Directive 92/49/EEC of 18 June 1992 on the coordination of laws, regulations and administrative provisions relating to direct insurance other than life assurance (third non-life insurance Directive); Directive 98/78/EC of the European Parliament and of the Council of 27 October 1998 on the supplementary supervision of insurance undertakings in an insurance group; Directive 2001/17/EC of the European Parliament and of the Council of 19 March 2001 on the reorganisation and winding-up of insurance undertakings; Directive 2002/83/EC of the European Parliament and of the Council of 5 November 2002 concerning life assurance; and Directive 2005/68/EC of the European Parliament and of the Council of 16 November 2005 on reinsurance. In the interests of clarity those Directives should be recast.

(2)   In order to facilitate the taking-up and pursuit of the activities of insurance and reinsurance, it is necessary to eliminate the most serious differences between the laws of the Member States as regards the rules to which insurance and reinsurance undertakings are subject. A legal framework should therefore be provided for insurance and reinsurance undertakings to conduct insurance business throughout the internal market thus making it easier for insurance and reinsurance undertakings with head offices in the Community to cover risks and commitments situated therein....

(5)   Very small insurance undertakings fulfilling certain conditions, including gross premium income below EUR 5 million, are excluded from the scope of this Directive.

---

[1]   For the provisions concerning the insolvency of insurance undertakings and the law applicable to insurance contracts see Chapters V, C, and VI, Insurance contracts, B. [Note of the Editor]

However, all insurance and reinsurance undertakings which are already licensed under the current Directives should continue to be licensed when this Directive is implemented. Undertakings that are excluded from the scope of this Directive should be able to make use of the basic freedoms granted by the Treaty. Those undertakings have the option to seek authorisation under this Directive in order to benefit from the single licence provided for in this Directive.

(12) Directive 2000/26/EC of the European Parliament and of the Council of 16 May 2000 on the approximation of the laws of the Member States relating to insurance against civil liability in respect of the use of motor vehicles (Fourth motor insurance Directive) lays down rules on the appointment of claims representatives. Those rules should apply for the purposes of this Directive.

(77) Within the framework of an internal market it is in the interest of policy holders that they should have access to the widest possible range of insurance products available in the Community. The Member State in which the risk is situated or the Member State of the commitment should therefore ensure that there is nothing to prevent the marketing within its territory of all the insurance products offered for sale in the Community as long as they do not conflict with the legal provisions protecting the general good in force in that Member State and in so far as the general good is not safeguarded by the rules of the home Member State.

(105) All policy holders and beneficiaries should receive equal treatment regardless of their nationality or place of residence. For this purpose, each Member State should ensure that all measures taken by a supervisory authority on the basis of that supervisory authority's national mandate are not regarded as contrary to the interests of that Member State or of policy holders and beneficiaries in that Member State. In all situations of settling of claims and winding-up, assets should be distributed on an equitable basis to all relevant policy holders, regardless of their nationality or place of residence.

(134) Council Directive 64/225/EEC of 25 February 1964 on the abolition of restrictions on freedom of establishment and freedom to provide services in respect of reinsurance and retrocession; Council Directive 73/240/EEC of 24 July 1973 abolishing restrictions on freedom of establishment in the business of direct insurance other than life insurance; Council Directive 76/580/EEC of 29 June 1976 amending Directive 73/239/EEC on the coordination of laws, regulations and administrative provisions relating to the taking-up and pursuit of the business of direct insurance other than life assurance; and Council Directive 84/641/EEC of 10 December 1984amending, particularly as regards tourist assistance, First Directive (73/239/EEC) on the coordination of laws, regulations and administrative provisions relating to the taking-up and pursuit of the business of direct insurance other than life have become obsolete and should therefore be repealed.

Title I — *General rules on the taking-up and pursuit of direct insurance and reinsurance activities*

Chapter I — Subject matter, scope and definitions

Section 1 — Subject matter and scope

Article 1. Subject matter.   This Directive lays down rules concerning the following:

(1)   the taking-up and pursuit, within the Community, of the self-employed activities of direct insurance and reinsurance;

(2)   the supervision of insurance and reinsurance groups;

(3)   the reorganisation and winding-up of direct insurance undertakings.

Article 2. Scope.   1.   This Directive shall apply to direct life and non-life insurance undertakings which are established in the territory of a Member State or which wish to become established there.

It shall also apply to reinsurance undertakings which conduct only reinsurance activities and which are established in the territory of a Member State or which wish to become established there with the exception of Title IV.

2.   In regard to non-life insurance, this Directive shall apply to activities of the classes set out in Part A of Annex I. For the purposes of the first subparagraph of paragraph 1, non-life insurance shall include the activity which consists of assistance provided for persons who get into difficulties while travelling, while away from their home or their habitual residence. It shall comprise an undertaking, against prior payment of a premium, to make aid immediately available to the beneficiary under an assistance contract where that person is in difficulties following the occurrence of a chance event, in the cases and under the conditions set out in the contract.

The aid may comprise the provision of benefits in cash or in kind. The provision of benefits in kind may also be effected by means of the staff and equipment of the person providing them.

The assistance activity shall not cover servicing, maintenance, after-sales service or the mere indication or provision of aid as an intermediary.

3.   In regard to life insurance, this Directive shall apply:

(a)   to the following life insurance activities where they are on a contractual basis:

(i)   life insurance which comprises assurance on survival to a stipulated age only, assurance on death only, assurance on survival to a stipulated age or on earlier death, life assurance with return of premiums, marriage assurance, birth assurance;

(ii)   annuities;

(iii)   supplementary insurance underwritten in addition to life insurance, in particular, insurance against personal injury including incapacity for employment, insurance against death resulting from an accident and insurance against disability resulting from an accident or sickness;

(iv)   types of permanent health insurance not subject to cancellation currently existing in Ireland and the United Kingdom;

(b)   to the following operations, where they are on a contractual basis, in so far as they are subject to supervision by the authorities responsible for the supervision of private insurance:

(i)   operations whereby associations of subscribers are set up with a view to capitalising their contributions jointly and subsequently distributing the assets thus accumulated among the survivors or among the beneficiaries of the deceased (tontines);

(ii)   capital redemption operations based on actuarial calculation whereby, in return for single or periodic payments agreed in advance, commitments of specified duration and amount are undertaken;

(iii)   management of group pension funds, comprising the management of investments, and in particular the assets representing the reserves of bodies that effect payments on death or survival or in the event of discontinuance or curtailment of activity;

(iv)   the operations referred to in point (iii) where they are accompanied by insurance covering either conservation of capital or payment of a minimum interest;

(v)   the operations carried out by life insurance undertakings such as those referred to in Chapter 1, Title 4 of Book IV of the French 'Code des assurances';

(c)   to operations relating to the length of human life which are prescribed by or provided for in social insurance legislation, in so far as they are effected or managed by life insurance undertakings at their own risk in accordance with the laws of a Member State.

Section 2 — Exclusions from scope

SUBSECTION 1 — GENERAL

Article 3. Statutory systems.   Without prejudice to Article 2(3)(c), this Directive shall not apply to insurance forming part of a statutory system of social security.

Article 4. Exclusion from scope due to size.   1.   Without prejudice to Article 3 and Articles 5 to 10, this Directive shall not apply to an insurance undertaking which fulfils all the following conditions:

(a)   the undertaking's annual gross written premium income does not exceed EUR 5 million;

(b)   the total of the undertaking's technical provisions, gross of the amounts recoverable from reinsurance contracts and special purpose vehicles, as referred to in Article 76, does not exceed EUR 25 million;

(c)   where the undertaking belongs to a group, the total of the technical provisions of the group defined as gross of the amounts recoverable from reinsurance contracts and special purpose vehicles does not exceed EUR 25 million;

(d)   the business of the undertaking does not include insurance or reinsurance activities covering liability, credit and suretyship insurance risks, unless they constitute ancillary risks within the meaning of Article 16(1);

(e)   the business of the undertaking does not include reinsurance operations exceeding EUR 0,5 million of its gross written premium income or EUR 2,5 million of its technical provisions gross of the amounts recoverable from reinsurance contracts and special purpose vehicles, or more than 10 % of its gross written premium income or more than 10 % of its technical provisions gross of the amounts recoverable from reinsurance contracts and special purpose vehicles.

2.   If any of the amounts set out in paragraph 1 is exceeded for three consecutive years this Directive shall apply as from the fourth year.

3.   By way of derogation from paragraph 1, this Directive shall apply to all undertakings seeking authorisation to pursue insurance and reinsurance activities of which the annual gross written premium income or technical provisions gross of the amounts recoverable from reinsurance contracts and special purpose vehicles are expected to exceed any of the amounts set out in paragraph 1 within the following five years.

4.   This Directive shall cease to apply to those insurance undertakings for which the supervisory authority has verified that all of the following conditions are met:

(a)   none of the thresholds set out in paragraph 1 has been exceeded for the three previous consecutive years; and

(b)   none of the thresholds set out in paragraph 1 is expected to be exceeded during the following five years.

For as long as the insurance undertaking concerned pursues activities in accordance with Articles 145 to 149, paragraph 1 of this Article shall not apply.

5.   Paragraphs 1 and 4 shall not prevent any undertaking from applying for authorisation or continuing to be authorised under this Directive.

SUBSECTION 2 — NON-LIFE

Article 5. Operations.   In regard to non-life insurance, this Directive shall not apply to the following operations:

(1)   capital redemption operations, as defined by the law in each Member State;

(2)   operations of provident and mutual benefit institutions whose benefits vary according to the resources available and in which the contributions of the members are determined on a flat-rate basis;

(3)   operations carried out by organisations not having a legal personality with the purpose of providing mutual cover for their members without there being any payment of premiums or constitution of technical reserves; or

(4)   export credit insurance operations for the account of or guaranteed by the State, or where the State is the insurer.

Article 6. Assistance.   1.   This Directive shall not apply to an assistance activity which fulfils all the following conditions:

(a)   the assistance is provided in the event of an accident or breakdown involving a road vehicle when the accident or breakdown occurs in the territory of the Member State of the undertaking providing cover;

(b)   the liability for the assistance is limited to the following operations:

(i)   an on-the-spot breakdown service for which the undertaking providing cover uses, in most circumstances, its own staff and equipment;

(ii)   the conveyance of the vehicle to the nearest or the most appropriate location at which repairs may be carried out and the possible accompaniment, normally by the same means of assistance, of the driver and passengers to the nearest location from where they may continue their journey by other means; and

(iii) where provided for by the home Member State of the undertaking providing cover, the conveyance of the vehicle, possibly accompanied by the driver and passengers, to their home, point of departure or original destination within the same State; and

(c)   the assistance is not carried out by an undertaking subject to this Directive.

2.   In the cases referred to in points (i) and (ii) of paragraph 1(b), the condition that the accident or breakdown must have happened in the territory of the Member State of the undertaking providing cover shall not apply where the beneficiary is a member of the body providing cover and the breakdown service or conveyance of the vehicle is provided simply on presentation of a membership card, without any additional premium being paid, by a similar body in the country concerned on the basis of a reciprocal agreement, or, in the case of Ireland and the United Kingdom, where the assistance operations are provided by a single body operating in both States.

3.   This Directive shall not apply in the case of operations referred to in point (iii) of paragraph 1(b), where the accident or the breakdown has occurred in the territory of Ireland or, in the case of the United Kingdom, in the territory of Northern Ireland and the vehicle, possibly accompanied by the driver and passengers, is conveyed to their home, point of departure or original destination within either territory.

4.   This Directive shall not apply to assistance operations carried out by the Automobile Club of the Grand Duchy of Luxembourg where the accident or the breakdown of a road vehicle has occurred outside the territory of the Grand Duchy of Luxembourg and the assistance consists in conveying the vehicle which has been involved in that accident or breakdown, possibly accompanied by the driver and passengers, to their home.

Article 7. Mutual undertakings.   This Directive shall not apply to mutual undertakings which pursue non-life insurance activities and which have concluded with other mutual undertakings an agreement which provides for the full reinsurance of the insurance policies issued by them or under which the accepting undertaking is to meet the liabilities arising under such policies in the place of the ceding undertaking. In such a case the accepting undertaking shall be subject to the rules of this Directive.

Article 8. Institutions.   This Directive shall not apply to the following institutions which pursue non-life insurance activities unless their statutes or the applicable law are amended as regards capacity:
   (1)   in Denmark, Falck Danmark;
   (2)   in Germany, the following semi-public institutions:
   (a)   Postbeamtenkrankenkasse,
   (b)   Krankenversorgung der Bundesbahnbeamten;
   (3)   in Ireland, the Voluntary Health Insurance Board;
   (4)   in Spain, the Consorcio de Compensación de Seguros.

SUBSECTION 3 — LIFE

Article 9. Operations and activities.   In regard to life insurance, this Directive shall not apply to the following operations and activities:
   (1)   operations of provident and mutual-benefit institutions whose benefits vary according to the resources available and which require each of their members to contribute at the appropriate flat rate;
   (2)   operations carried out by organisations, other than undertakings referred to in Article 2, whose object is to provide benefits for employed or self-employed persons belonging to an undertaking or group of undertakings, or a trade or group of trades, in

the event of death or survival or of discontinuance or curtailment of activity, whether or not the commitments arising from such operations are fully covered at all times by mathematical provisions;

(3)   the pension activities of pension insurance undertakings prescribed in the Employees Pension Act (TyEL) and other related Finnish legislation provided that:

(a)   pension insurance companies which already under Finnish law are obliged to have separate accounting and management systems for their pension activities, as from 1 January 1995, set up separate legal entities for pursuing those activities; and

(b)   the Finnish authorities allow, in a non-discriminatory manner, all nationals and companies of Member States to perform according to Finnish legislation the activities specified in Article 2 related to that exemption whether by means of ownership or participation in an existing insurance company or group or by means of creation or participation of new insurance companies or groups, including pension insurance companies.

Article 10. Organisations, undertakings and institutions.   In regard to life insurance, this Directive shall not apply to the following organisations, undertakings and institutions:

(1)   organisations which undertake to provide benefits solely in the event of death, where the amount of such benefits does not exceed the average funeral costs for a single death or where the benefits are provided in kind;

(2)   the 'Versorgungsverband deutscher Wirtschaftsorganisationen' in Germany, unless its statutes are amended as regards the scope of its capacity;

(3)   the 'Consorcio de Compensación de Seguros' in Spain, unless its statutes are amended as regards the scope of its activities or capacity.

SUBSECTION 4 — REINSURANCE

Article 11. Reinsurance.   In regard to reinsurance, this Directive shall not apply to the activity of reinsurance conducted or fully guaranteed by the government of a Member State when that government is acting, for reasons of substantial public interest, in the capacity of reinsurer of last resort, including in circumstances where such a role is required by a situation in the market in which it is not feasible to obtain adequate commercial cover.

Article 12. Reinsurance undertakings closing their activity.   1.   Reinsurance undertakings which by 10 December 2007 ceased to conduct new reinsurance contracts and exclusively administer their existing portfolio in order to terminate their activity shall not be subject to this Directive.

2.   Member States shall draw up a list of the reinsurance undertakings concerned and communicate that list to all the other Member States.

Section 3 — Definitions

Article 13. Definitions.   For the purposes of this Directive, the following definitions shall apply:

(1)   'insurance undertaking' means a direct life or non-life insurance undertaking which has received authorisation in accordance with Article 14;

(2) 'captive insurance undertaking' means an insurance undertaking, owned either by a financial undertaking other than an insurance or reinsurance undertaking or a group of insurance or reinsurance undertakings within the meaning of Article 212(1)(c) or by a non-financial undertaking, the purpose of which is to provide insurance cover exclusively for the risks of the undertaking or undertakings to which it belongs or of an undertaking or undertakings of the group of which it is a member;

(3) 'third-country insurance undertaking' means an undertaking which would require authorisation as an insurance undertaking in accordance with Article 14 if its head office were situated in the Community;

(4) 'reinsurance undertaking' means an undertaking which has received authorisation in accordance with Article 14 to pursue reinsurance activities;

(5) 'captive reinsurance undertaking' means a reinsurance undertaking, owned either by a financial undertaking other than an insurance or reinsurance undertaking or a group of insurance or reinsurance undertakings within the meaning of Article 212(1)(c) or by a non-financial undertaking, the purpose of which is to provide reinsurance cover exclusively for the risks of the undertaking or undertakings to which it belongs or of an undertaking or undertakings of the group of which it is a member;

(6) 'third-country reinsurance undertaking' means an undertaking which would require authorisation as a reinsurance undertaking in accordance with Article 14 if its head office were situated in the Community;

(7) 'reinsurance' means either of the following:

(a) the activity consisting in accepting risks ceded by an insurance undertaking or third-country insurance undertaking, or by another reinsurance undertaking or third-country reinsurance undertaking; or

(b) in the case of the association of underwriters known as Lloyd's, the activity consisting in accepting risks, ceded by any member of Lloyd's, by an insurance or reinsurance undertaking other than the association of underwriters known as Lloyd's;

(8) 'home Member State' means any of the following:

(a) for non-life insurance, the Member State in which the head office of the insurance undertaking covering the risk is situated;

(b) for life insurance, the Member State in which the head office of the insurance undertaking covering the commitment is situated; or

(c) for reinsurance, the Member State in which the head office of the reinsurance undertaking is situated;

(9) 'host Member State' means the Member State, other than the home Member State, in which an insurance or a reinsurance undertaking has a branch or provides services; for life and non-life insurance, the Member State of the provisions of services means, respectively, the Member State of the commitment or the Member State in which the risk is situated, where that commitment or risk is covered by an insurance undertaking or a branch situated in another Member State;

(10) 'supervisory authority' means the national authority or the national authorities empowered by law or regulation to supervise insurance or reinsurance undertakings;

(11) 'branch' means an agency or a branch of an insurance or reinsurance undertaking which is located in the territory of a Member State other than the home Member State;

(12) 'establishment' of an undertaking means its head office or any of its branches;

(13) 'Member State in which the risk is situated' means any of the following:

(a)   the Member State in which the property is situated, where the insurance relates either to buildings or to buildings and their contents, in so far as the contents are covered by the same insurance policy;

(b)   the Member State of registration, where the insurance relates to vehicles of any type;

(c)   the Member State where the policy holder took out the policy in the case of policies of a duration of four months or less covering travel or holiday risks, whatever the class concerned;

(d)   in all cases not explicitly covered by points (a), (b) or (c), the Member State in which either of the following is situated:

(i)   the habitual residence of the policy holder; or

(ii)   if the policy holder is a legal person, that policy holder's establishment to which the contract relates;

(14) 'Member State of the commitment' means the Member State in which either of the following is situated:

(a)   the habitual residence of the policy holder;

(b)   if the policy holder is a legal person, that policy holder's establishment, to which the contract relates;

(15) 'parent undertaking' means a parent undertaking within the meaning of Article 1 of Directive 83/349/EEC;

(16) 'subsidiary undertaking' means any subsidiary undertaking within the meaning of Article 1 of Directive 83/349/EEC, including subsidiaries thereof;

(17) 'close links' means a situation in which two or more natural or legal persons are linked by control or participation, or a situation in which two or more natural or legal persons are permanently linked to one and the same person by a control relationship;

(18) 'control' means the relationship between a parent undertaking and a subsidiary undertaking, as set out in Article 1 of Directive 83/349/EEC, or a similar relationship between any natural or legal person and an undertaking;

(19) 'intra-group transaction' means any transaction by which an insurance or reinsurance undertaking relies, either directly or indirectly, on other undertakings within the same group or on any natural or legal person linked to the undertakings within that group by close links, for the fulfilment of an obligation, whether or not contractual, and whether or not for payment;

(20) 'participation' means the ownership, direct or by way of control, of 20 % or more of the voting rights or capital of an undertaking;

(21) 'qualifying holding' means a direct or indirect holding in an undertaking which represents 10 % or more of the capital or of the voting rights or which makes it possible to exercise a significant influence over the management of that undertaking;

(22) 'regulated market' means either of the following:

(a)   in the case of a market situated in a Member State, a regulated market as defined in Article 4(1)(14) of Directive 2004/39/EC; or

(b)   in the case of a market situated in a third country, a financial market which fulfils the following conditions:

(i)   it is recognised by the home Member State of the insurance undertaking and fulfils requirements comparable to those laid down in Directive 2004/39/EC; and

(ii)   the financial instruments dealt in on that market are of a quality comparable to that of the instruments dealt in on the regulated market or markets of the home Member State;

(23) 'national bureau' means a national insurers' bureau as defined in Article 1(3) of Directive 72/166/EEC;

(24) 'national guarantee fund' means the body referred to in Article 1(4) of Directive 84/5/EEC;

(25) 'financial undertaking' means any of the following entities:

(a)   a credit institution, a financial institution or an ancillary banking services undertaking within the meaning of Article 4(1), (5) and (21) of Directive 2006/48/EC respectively;

(b)   an insurance undertaking, or a reinsurance undertaking or an insurance holding company within the meaning of Article 212(1)(f);

(c)   an investment firm or a financial institution within the meaning of Article 4(1) (1) of Directive 2004/39/EC; or

(d)   a mixed financial holding company within the meaning of Article 2(15) of Directive 2002/87/EC

(26) 'special purpose vehicle' means any undertaking, whether incorporated or not, other than an existing insurance or reinsurance undertaking, which assumes risks from insurance or reinsurance undertakings and which fully funds its exposure to such risks through the proceeds of a debt issuance or any other financing mechanism where the repayment rights of the providers of such debt or financing mechanism are subordinated to the reinsurance obligations of such an undertaking…

Chapter II — Taking-up of business

Article 14. Principle of authorisation.   1.   The taking-up of the business of direct insurance or reinsurance covered by this Directive shall be subject to prior authorisation.

2.   The authorisation referred to in paragraph 1 shall be sought from the supervisory authorities of the home Member State by the following:

(a)   any undertaking which is establishing its head office within the territory of that Member State; or

(b)   any insurance undertaking which, having received an authorisation pursuant to paragraph 1, wishes to extend its business to an entire insurance class or to insurance classes other than those already authorised.

Article 15. Scope of authorisation.   1.   An authorisation pursuant to Article 14 shall be valid for the entire Community. It shall permit insurance and reinsurance undertakings to pursue business there, that authorisation covering also the right of establishment and the freedom to provide services…

Section 3 — Competencies of the supervisory authorities of the host Member State

SUBSECTION 1 — INSURANCE

Article 157. Taxes on premiums.   1.   Without prejudice to any subsequent harmonisation, every insurance contract shall be subject exclusively to the indirect taxes and parafiscal charges on insurance premiums in the Member State in which the risk is situated or the Member State of the commitment.

For the purposes of the first subparagraph, movable property contained in a building situated within the territory of a Member State, except for goods in commercial transit, shall be considered as a risk situated in that Member State, even where the building and its contents are not covered by the same insurance policy....

2.   The law applicable to the contract under Article 178 of this Directive and under Regulation (EC) No 593/2008 shall not affect the fiscal arrangements applicable.

3.   Each Member State shall apply its own national provisions to those insurance undertakings which cover risks or commitments situated within its territory for measures to ensure the collection of indirect taxes and parafiscal charges due under paragraph 1.

Title VI — Transitional and final provisions

Article 310. Repeal.   Directives 64/225/EEC, 73/239/EEC, 73/240/EEC, 76/580/EEC, 78/473/EEC, 84/641/EEC, 87/344/EEC, 88/357/EEC, 92/49/EEC, 98/78/EC, 2001/17/EC, 2002/83/EC and 2005/68/EC, as amended by the acts listed in Part A of Annex VI, are repealed with effect from 1 November 2012, without prejudice to the obligations of the Member States relating to the time-limits for transposition into national law and application of the Directives set out in Part B of Annex VI.

References to the repealed Directives shall be construed as references to this Directive and shall be read in accordance with the correlation table in Annex VII.

O.   Commission Interpretative Communication — Freedom to provide services and the interest of the general good in the second banking directive (OJ, C 209 of 10 July 1997)

This Communication is the product of the discussions conducted by the Commission on the questions of the freedom to provide services and the interest of the general good in the Second Banking Directive.[1]

Not only the Member States (within the Banking Advisory Committee and the Working Group on the Interpretation of the Banking Directives) but also private establishments have been involved in the discussions.

The Commission published, in the Official Journal of the European Communities,[2] a draft communication which marked the launch of a broad consultation. Following the publication of this Communication, the Commission received numerous contributions from all the circles concerned (Member States, professional associations, credit institutions, consumer organizations, lawyers, etc.). It also organized hearings with all the parties who had taken part in the written consultation.

The Commission came to realize in the course of this consultation that there was still some uncertainty regarding the interpretation of basic concepts such as freedom to provide services and the interest of the general good. This uncertainty is such as to deter certain credit institutions from exercising the very freedoms which the Second Directive

---

[1]   [Footnotes are published in the original numerical order as in OJ] Second Council Directive 89/646/EEC of 15 December 1989 on the coordination of laws, regulations and administrative provisions relating to the taking-up and pursuit of the business of credit institutions and amending Directive 77/780/EEC (OJ, L 386 of 30 December 1989, 1), as amended by Directive 92/30/EEC (OJ, L 110 of 28 April 1992, 52).

[2]   OJ, C 291of 4 November 1995, 7.

sets out to promote and, consequently, to hamper the free movement of banking services within the European Union.

The Commission therefore deems it desirable to restate in a Communication the principles laid down by the Court of Justice and to set out its position regarding the application of those principles to the specific problems raised by the Second Banking Directive.

Its objective in publishing this Communication is to explain and clarify the Community rules. It provides all the parties concerned — national administrations, traders and consumers — with a reference document defining the legal framework within which, in the view of the Commission, banking activities benefiting from mutual recognition should be pursued.

The interpretations and ideas set out in this Communication, which are confined to problems specifically related to the Second Directive, set out to cover not all possible situations, but merely the most frequent or the most likely.

They are put forward in the light of Community policy regarding the information society, which is aimed at promoting the growth and movement of information-society services between Member States and, in particular, electronic commerce.[3]

They do not necessarily represent the views of the Member States and should not, in themselves, impose any obligation on them.

Lastly, they do not prejudge the interpretation that the Court of Justice, as the final instance responsible for interpreting the Treaty and secondary legislation, might place on the matters at issue.

Part one — freedom to provide services in the second banking directive

Part One analyses in turn (A) the results of the consultations on the notification procedure, (B) the difficulties relating to the distinction between the freedom to provide services and the right of establishment and (C) the question of the time when an activity falling within the scope of the freedom to provide services may begin.

A.   Notification procedure

1.   Scope in terms of time

Article 20(1) of the Second Banking Directive provides that:
> 'Any credit institution wishing to exercise the freedom to provide services by carrying on its activities within the territory of another Member State for the first time shall notify the competent authorities of the home Member State of the activities on the list in the Annex which it intends to carry on.'

---

[3]   Council Resolution on new policy priorities regarding the information society, adopted on 8 October 1996; Commission Communication to the European Council: 'Putting services to work': CSE(96) 6 fin. of 27 November 1996; Communication to the European Parliament, the Council of the European Union and the Economic and Social Committee entitled 'Regulatory transparency in the single market for information society services'; Proposal for a European Parliament and Council Directive amending for the third time Directive 83/189/EEC laying down a procedure for the provision of information in the field of technical standards and regulations (COM(96)392 fin. of 30 August 1996; also published in OJ, C 307 of 16 October 1996, 11).

The procedure laid down in Article 20(1) thus concerns only those credit institutions (and their subsidiaries within the meaning of Article 18(2)) which intend to conduct for the first time an activity listed in the Annex. Article 23(2) provides for an exemption from notification for credit institutions which provided services before the provisions implementing the Directive came into force.

The Commission considers that, in order to benefit from acquired rights, a credit institution need only have provided a service at least once in the territory of a Member State (in accordance with the line of reasoning set out in section 2 below), regardless of when that was, but it must have carried on this activity lawfully within the territory of the Member State in question. It must also be able to furnish evidence of this previous activity if so requested by the competent authority of the country of origin.

The exemption is, however, restricted to the activity and Member State concerned.

The Commission considers that the lawful nature of the previous activity should be assessed at the time when this activity was being exercised and not at the time when the Second Directive entered into force. It is irrelevant, therefore, whether the host Member State's legislation changed after the activity was exercised by the credit institution. It is, of course, assumed that the institution complied with the host country's new legislation if it continued to carry on its activities there or that it ceased its activities under the freedom to provide services at that time.

2. Scope in terms of territory

(A) PRINCIPLES

Article 20(1) of the Second Directive makes implementation of the notification procedure conditional upon the intention to carry on activities 'within the territory of another Member State'.

It is necessary, therefore, to 'locate' the place of supply of the future banking service in order to determine whether prior notification is required.

Unlike other services, where the place of supply can give rise to no doubts (legal defence, construction of a building, etc), the banking services listed in the Annex to the Second Directive are difficult to pin down to a specific location. They are also very different from one another and are increasingly provided in an intangible form. The growth of distance services, particularly those using electronic means (Internet, home banking, etc.), will undoubtedly soon result in excessively strict criteria on location becoming obsolete.

The Commission has examined certain possibilities for locating the service (originator of the initiative, customer's place of residence, supplier's place of establishment, place where contracts are signed, etc.) and considers that none could satisfactorily apply to all the activities listed in the Annex. It considers it necessary to adhere to a simple and flexible interpretation of Article 20 of the Second Directive. Accordingly, in its opinion, only activities carried on *within the territory* of another Member State should be the subject of prior notification. In order to determine where an activity was carried on, the place of provision of what may be termed the 'characteristic performance' of the service, i.e. the essential supply for which payment is due must be determined.

This line of reasoning is aimed merely at establishing whether prior notification is necessary. It does not affect the law or tax system applicable to the banking service concerned.

(B)   APPLICATION TO THE SECOND DIRECTIVE

A bank may have non-resident customers without necessarily pursuing the activities concerned *within the territory* of the Member States where the customers have their domicile.

Consequently, the fact of temporarily visiting the territory of a Member State to carry on an activity preceding (e.g. survey of property prior to granting a loan) or following (incidental activities) the essential activity does not, in the Commission's view, constitute a situation that is liable in itself to be the subject of prior notification. The same is true of any visits which a credit institution may pay to customers if such visits do not involve the provision of the characteristic performance of the service that is the subject of the contractual relationship.

Furthermore, the Commission considers that the fact of temporarily visiting the territory of a Member State in order to conclude contracts prior to the exercise of a banking activity should not be regarded as exercising the activity itself. Prior notification would not be required in such circumstances.

If, on the other hand, the institution intends to provide the characteristic performance of a banking service by sending a member of its staff or a temporarily authorized intermediary to the territory of another Member State, prior notification should be necessary.

Conversely, if the service is supplied to a beneficiary who has gone in person, for the purpose of receiving that service, to the Member State where the institution is established, prior notification should not take place. The Commission considers, in fact, that the service is not provided by the credit institution in the territory of another Member State within the meaning of Article 20 of the Second Banking Directive.

Lastly, the provision of distance banking services, for example through the Internet, should not, in the Commission's view, require prior notification, since the supplier cannot be deemed to be pursuing its activities in the customer's territory.

The Commission is aware that this solution will require a case-by-case analysis, which could prove difficult.

It is also aware that, as long as the Court has not ruled on this issue, any credit institution is at liberty to choose, for reasons of legal certainty, to make use of the notification procedures provided for in the Second Directive even if, according to the criteria proposed above, notification may not be necessary.

The fact that certain types of supplies of services do not, according to the Commission, fall within the scope of Article 20 of the Second Directive and, consequently, should not be notified does not mean that such activities are not the subject of mutual recognition and home-country control.

The Commission considers that mutual recognition of the activities contained in the Annex, accompanied by home-country control, is established by Article 18 of the Second Directive. Article 20 is merely a procedural article, of residual scope, which is merely for the use of banks wishing to operate for the first time under the freedom to provide services in another Member State.

3.   *Advertising and offers of services*

The Commission considers that the prior existence of advertising or an offer cannot be linked with the need to comply with the notification procedure.

Such a link would be artificial in that no express provision for it is made in the Second Directive. It is not the prior offer of a service to a non-resident but merely the intention to carry on activities within the territory of another Member State that Article 20 makes conditional on notification.

Moreover, canvassing customers from a distance does not necessarily mean that an institution plans to provide services within the territory of another Member State.

Similarly, linking advertising with notification could lead to ridiculous situations in which an institution was required to notify the authorities of all the countries where its advertising might theoretically be received.

The Commission therefore considers that, for the sake of simplicity and in keeping with the Second Directive, all forms of advertising, targeted or otherwise, and all offers of a service made at a distance by any means whatsoever (e.g. post, fax, electronic mail) should be exempt from the requirement of prior notification. Only if a credit institution plans to carry on its activities *within the territory of the customer's country* under the freedom to provide services (according to the line of reasoning employed in paragraph (a)) will it be obliged to notify.

This view, which concerns only the notification requirement, does not affect the law applicable to the banking service. In accordance with the Rome Convention,[4] the existence of a specific invitation or prior advertising may, in the case of contracts concluded with consumers, have an effect on the law applicable to the contract concluded subsequently.[5]

4.   Nature of the procedure

The Commission considers that the notification procedure laid down in the Second Directive pursues a simple objective of exchange of information between supervisory authorities and is not a consumer-protection measure. It should not, in the Commission's view, be considered a procedural condition affecting the validity of a banking contract...

B.   Freedom to provide services and right of establishment

1.   Freedom to provide services

(A)   TEMPORARY NATURE

The Treaty stipulates in the third paragraph of Article 60 that a person providing a service may, in order to do so, 'temporarily' pursue his activity in the State where the service is provided. The Court considered, in a judgment of 30 November 1995,[6] that the temporary nature of the supply of services provided for by this Article: 'is to be determined in the light of its duration, regularity, periodicity and continuity.'

On the basis of this case-law, the Commission considers that, if a banking activity is exercised within a territory in a durable, frequent, regular or continuous manner by a

---

[4]   Convention on the law applicable to contractual obligations, opened for signature in Rome on 19 June 1980 and brought into force on 1 April 1991 (OJ, L 266 of 9 October 1980, 1). Ratified by all Member States except Sweden, Austria and Finland, who signed the Convention on 29 November 1996 and whose ratification procedures are still under way.

[5]   See Part Two of this Communication.

[6]   Judgment 30 November 1995, case C-55/94, *Gebhard*, Reports, I-4165.

credit institution exercising the freedom to provide services, the question must be asked whether that credit institution can still lawfully be considered to be working temporarily within the meaning of the Treaty. The question also arises whether the credit institution is not attempting to sidestep the rules on establishment by unjustifiably invoking the freedom to provide services.

(B)   PREVENTING CIRCUMVENTION OF THE RULES

The Court has acknowledged that a Member State is entitled to take steps to prevent a service provider whose activity is entirely or mainly directed towards its territory, but who has become established in another Member State in order to circumvent the rules of professional conduct that would apply to him if he were established in the territory of the State where he entirely or mainly pursues his activities, from exercising the freedom to provide services that is enshrined in Article 59 of the Treaty.[7] It adds that such instances of 'circumvention' may fall within the ambit of the chapter of the Treaty on the right of establishment and not of that on the provision of services.

However, the Commission considers that a situation where a credit institution is frequently approached within its own territory by consumers residing in other Member States could not be held to constitute 'circumvention'.

2.   *Right of establishment*

If an undertaking maintains a permanent presence in the Member State in which it provides services, it comes, in principle, under the Treaty provisions on the right of establishment.[8]

The Court has ruled that: 'A national of a Member State who pursues a professional activity on a stable and continuous basis in another Member State where he holds himself out from an established professional base to, amongst others, nationals of that State comes under the provisions of the chapter relating to the right of establishment and not those of the chapter relating to services.'[9]

However, in the same judgment, the Court ruled that a person operating under the freedom to provide services may equip himself in the host Member State with the infrastructure necessary for the purposes of performing the services in question without falling within the scope of the right of establishment.

On the basis of this case-law, an employee of a credit institution coming to work within the territory of a Member State in order to carry out a limited number of specific tasks in connection with existing customers could, therefore, have the infrastructure necessary to perform these tasks without the bank being deemed to be 'established' within the meaning laid down by Community law. If, on the other hand, he went beyond the bounds of these specific tasks by using that 'pied-à-terre' to approach nationals of the host Member State, e.g. to offer them banking services as a branch would do, the bank could fall within the scope of the right of establishment.

---

[7]   Judgments 4 December 1986, case 205/84, *Commission v. Germany*, Reports, 3755; 3 December 1974, case 33/74, *Van Binsbergen*, Reports, 1299; 3 February 1993, case C-148/91, *Veronica*, Reports, I-487; 5 October 1994, case C-23/93 *TV 10*, Reports, I-4795.

[8]   Judgment 4 December 1986, case 205/84, *Commission v Germany*, see note 7.

[9]   Judgment *Gebhard*, see note 6.

3. 'Grey' area

It is not always easy to draw the line between the concepts of provision of services and establishment, particularly since, as the case-law of the Court indicates, one may be considered in certain circumstances to be operating in a Member State under the freedom to provide services despite having some kind of infrastructure in that Member State.

Some situations are particularly difficult to classify. This is especially true of:

— recourse to independent intermediaries; and
— electronic machines (ATMs) carrying out banking activities.

(A) INDEPENDENT INTERMEDIARIES

The problem lies in determining the extent to which a credit institution having recourse to an independent intermediary in another Member State could be deemed to be pursuing a permanent activity in that Member State.

We are concerned here with intermediaries who drum up business but are not in themselves credit institutions or investment firms, and who are not operating on their own behalf.

In its judgment of 4 December 1986,[10] the Court held that: 'an insurance undertaking of another Member State which maintains a permanent presence in the Member State in question comes within the scope of the provisions of the Treaty on the right of establishment, even if that presence does not take the form of a branch or agency, but consists merely of an office managed by the undertaking's own staff or by a person who is independent but authorized to act on a permanent basis for the undertaking, as will be the case with an agency.'

The Court has therefore acknowledged that an undertaking which uses an intermediary within the territory of another Member State on a permanent basis may, on account of that fact, lose its *status* as a service provider and fall within the scope of the provisions on the right of establishment.

The Commission, therefore, suggests the following interpretations.

— INTERMEDIARIES AND FREEDOM TO PROVIDE SERVICES

In the view of the Commission, if a bank uses an intermediary to provide temporarily or from time to time a banking service within the territory of a Member State, it must first give notification within the meaning of Article 20 of the Second Directive.

It considers that if, in a given country, a bank has independent intermediaries whose duties consist solely in seeking customers for it, it cannot be considered to be necessarily intending to carry on its activities, within the meaning of Article 20, in the territory of the Member State in question. Notification would not be required in that case.

On the other hand, in certain circumstances set out below, it may be considered that a bank having one or more intermediaries permanently established in a Member State does in fact come within the rules on the right of establishment.

---

[10] See note 7.

— INTERMEDIARIES AND THE RIGHT OF ESTABLISHMENT

In its *De Bloos* ruling of 6 October 1976,[11] the Court held that: 'One of the essential characteristics of the concepts of branch or agency is the fact of being subject to the direction and control of the parent body.'

It concluded that a sole concessionaire not subject to the control and direction of a company could not be regarded as a branch, agency or establishment.

In its ruling of 18 March 1981 in *Blanckaert & Willems*,[12] the Court held that: 'An independent commercial agent who merely negotiates business, in as much as his legal *status* leaves him basically free to arrange his own work and decide what proportion of his time to devote to the interests of the undertaking which he agrees to represent and whom that undertaking may not prevent from representing at the same time several firms competing in the same manufacturing or marketing sector, and who, moreover, merely transmits orders to the parent undertaking without being involved in either their terms or their execution, does not have the character of a branch, agency or other establishment…'.

In even more pointed terms, in its *Somafer* ruling of 22 November 1978,[13] the Court held that: 'The concept of branch, agency or other establishment implies a place of business which has the appearance of permanency, such as the extension of a parent body, has a management and is materially equipped to negotiate business with third parties, so that the latter, although knowing that there will if necessary be a legal link with the parent body, the head office of which is abroad, do not have to deal directly with such parent body but may transact business at the place of business constituting the extension.'

On the basis of these precedents, the Commission considers that, for the use of an intermediary to result in a bank possibly falling within the scope of the right of establishment, three criteria must be met at one and the same time:
— the intermediary must have a permanent mandate;
— the intermediary must be subject to the management and control of the credit institution he represents. In order to ascertain whether this condition is met, it is necessary to check whether the intermediary is free to organize his own work and to decide what proportion of his time to devote to the undertaking. A final pointer is whether the intermediary can represent several firms competing to provide the service concerned or whether he is, on the contrary, bound by an exclusive agreement to one credit institution;
— the intermediary must be able to commit the credit institution. A credit institution may be committed via an intermediary even if that intermediary cannot sign contracts. For example, if the intermediary can make a complete offer on behalf of an institution but only the bank itself has the power to sign the contract, the criterion of commitment may still be met. If the credit institution can reject the proposal submitted by the intermediary and signed by the customer, the criterion of the commitment capacity is not met.

The application of these three criteria requires a detailed examination to be carried out in each specific case.

---

[11] Case 14/76, Reports, 1497.
[12] Case 139/80, Reports, 819.
[13] Case 33/78, Reports, 2183. See also judgment 6 April 1995, case C-439/93, *Lloyd's Register of Shipping v. Societé Campenon Bernard*, Reports, I-961.

The fact that an intermediary can cause a bank to fall within the scope of the right of establishment does not, however, mean that the intermediary himself constitutes a branch.

Under the Second Directive, a branch is '*a place of business which forms a legally dependent part of a credit institution (...)*'. Since the intermediary is assumed to be independent, he cannot constitute '*part*' of a credit institution. His business will normally be established in the form of a company having its own legal personality.

Finally, if a bank's services are marketed in another Member State through the intermediary of another bank, notification should not, logically speaking, be necessary. The fact that the intermediate bank is itself subject to supervision in the Member State where it is established should offer that Member State sufficient guarantees for it to consider notification unnecessary. If the intermediate bank is acting on its own behalf, notification should not take place, since such a situation does not fall within the scope of the freedom to provide cross-border services.

(B)   ELECTRONIC MACHINES

This means fixed, ATM-type electronic machines capable of performing the banking activities listed in the Annex to the Second Directive. [14]

Such machines may be covered by the right of establishment if they fulfil the criteria laid down by the Court of Justice (see above).

For such a machine to be capable of being treated as an establishment, therefore, it would have to have a management, which is by definition impossible unless the Court acknowledges that the concept can encompass not only human management but also electronic management.

However, such a machine is unlikely to be the only place of business of a credit institution in a Member State. It is likely to be attached, in the same country, to a branch or an agency. In that event, the machine is not an entity in its own right as it is covered by the rules governing the establishment to which it is attached.

If the machine does, however, constitute the only presence of a credit institution in a Member State, the Commission takes the view that it may be possible to treat it as a provision of services in the territory of that Member State.

The presence in the host country of a person or company responsible simply for maintaining the machine, equipping it and dealing with any technical problems encountered by users cannot rank as an establishment and does not deprive the credit institution of the right to operate under the freedom to provide services.

The Commission considers, however, that technological developments could, in the future, induce it to review its position.

If such developments were to make it possible for an institution to have only a machine in a given country which could 'act' as a branch, taking actual decisions which would completely obviate the need for the customer to have contact with the parent company, the Commission would be forced to consider an appropriate Community legal framework.

---

[14] It does not mean individual, mobile data-processing equipment which can provide or receive distance banking services, e.g. through the Internet.

The present legal framework in fact rests on mechanisms which are still based on a 'human' concept of a branch (for example, the programme of operations must contain the names of those responsible for the management of the branch). It is therefore not possible, under the existing rules, to consider machines as constituting a branch.

Part two — *The general good in the second banking directive*

1. *Definition of the general good*

It is the Court of Justice which originated this concept. It has consistently held that: 'Taking into account the particular nature of certain services to be provided (...) , specific requirements imposed on persons providing services cannot be considered incompatible with the Treaty where they have as their purpose the application of professional rules, justified by the general good (...)'. [22]

However, the Court has never given a definition of the general good, preferring to maintain its progressive nature. It has expressed its opinion, in individual cases, on the possibility of deeming a given national measure to be aimed at achieving an imperative objective serving the general good and has specified the line of reasoning to be followed in determining whether such a measure may be enforced by one Member State against a trader from another Member State who is operating within the territory of the first in accordance with the basic freedoms provided for by the Treaty.

The Court has, however, provided much clarification regarding the measures which can be considered to be aimed at achieving an imperative objective in the general good.

Accordingly, it has consistently held that such measures must not have been the subject of prior Community harmonization. [23]

Through its case-law, the Court has specified the areas which may be considered to be in the general good. National rules adopted in one of these areas may still, therefore, under certain circumstances outlined below, be enforced against a Community trader.

The Court has so far recognized the following objectives as being imperative reasons in the general good: [24]

—   protection of the recipient of services,[25] protection of workers,[26] including social protection,[27] consumer protection,[28] preservation of the good reputation of the national financial sector,[29] prevention of fraud,[30] social order,[31] protection of intellectual

---

[22] Judgment 18 January 1979, joined cases 110 and 111/78, *Van Wesemael*, Reports, 35.

[23] Judgments 18 March 1980, case 52/79, *Debauve*, Reports, 833; 4 December 1986, case 205/84, see note 7; 25 July 1991, case 353/89, *Mediawet*, Reports, I-4069.

[24] To this list must be added *a fortiori* the provisions of Article 56, i.e. public policy, public security and public health. "Mandatory requirements", which are recognized by the Court in its case-law on the free movement of goods (protection of the environment, fairness of commercial transactions) can probably also be invoked in connection with services.

[25] Judgment 18 January 1979, joined cases 110/78 and 111/78, *Van Wesemael*, see note 22.

[26] Judgment 17 December 1981, case 279/80, *Webb*, Reports, 3305.

[27] Judgment 28 March 1996, case C-272/94 *Guiot*, Reports, I-1905.

[28] Judgment 4 December 1986, case 205/84, *Commission v. Germany*, see note 7.

[29] Judgment 10 May 1995, case C-384/93, *Alpine Investments BV*, Reports, I-1141.

[30] Judgment 24 March 1994, case C-275/92, *Schindler*, Reports, I-1039.

[31] *Ibid.*

property,[32] cultural policy,[33] preservation of the national historical and artistic heritage,[34] cohesion of the tax system,[35] road safety,[36] protection of creditors[37] and protection of the proper administration of justice.[38]

The list is open-ended and the Court reserves the right to add to it at any time.

Most of these areas can involve banking activity. For example, a national measure aimed at protecting recipients of banking services may, if it does not come within the scope of a harmonized area, be relied upon for reasons relating to the general good by a Member State vis-à-vis a Community credit institution operating within its territory in the context of mutual recognition. For this rule to be enforceable, some additional conditions must, however, be met.

2. General-good 'tests'

In its case-law, the Court has held that: 'National measures liable to hinder or make less attractive the exercise of fundamental freedoms guaranteed by the Treaty must fulfil four conditions: they must be applied in a non-discriminatory manner; they must be justified by imperative requirements in the general interest; they must be suitable for securing the attainment of the objective which they pursue; and they must not go beyond what is necessary in order to attain it'.[39]

It has consistently held that a rule relating to the public interest is enforceable against a person providing services only if 'that interest is not protected by the rules to which the person providing the services is subject in the Member State in which he is established'.[40]

C. Interest of the general good and private international law

1. Principles

An examination of the compatibility with Community law of a national rule justified on general-good grounds may be carried out where a legal discrepancy caused by an absence of harmonization creates an obstacle to the movement of banking services.

Any national rule must be compatible with Community law irrespective of the area in which it falls. In a judgment delivered on 21 March 1972, the Court ruled that: 'The effectiveness of Community law cannot vary according to the various branches of national law which it may affect'.[65]

---

[32] Judgment 18 March 1980, case 62/79 *Coditel*, Reports, 881.
[33] Judgment 25 July 1991, case C-353/89, *Mediawet*, see note 23.
[34] Judgment 26 February 1991, case C-180/89, *Commission v. Italy*, Reports, 709.
[35] Judgment 28 February 1992, case C-204/90, *Bachmann*, Reports, 249.
[36] Judgment 5 October 1994, case 55/93, *van Schaik*, Reports, I-4837.
[37] Judgment 12 December 1996, case C-3/95, *Reisebüro Broede v. Gerd Sandker* (not yet reported).
[38] *Ibid.*
[39] Judgment *Gebhard*, see note 6.
[40] Judgment *Säger v. Dennemeyer*, see note 20.
[65] Judgment 21 March 1972, case 82/71, *SAIL*, Reports, 119. See also Judgment 1 july 1993, case 20/92, *Hubbard*, Reports, I-3777.

Where necessary, Community law takes precedence, therefore, over national private law provisions.

The Court has accordingly had to check the compatibility with Community law of national provisions of civil law[66] and civil procedure.[67]

It may be stated that most contractual rules falling within the scope of civil law or procedural law (means of extinguishing obligations, limitation periods, expiry, invalidity, etc) are unlikely to constitute barriers to the trade in banking services.

However, banking contracts do contain provisions, usually of a mandatory nature, which may well constitute rules on contractual obligations, but actually affect trade. Let us take, for example, a clause preventing any variation in a rate or relating to early repayment. The effects of such provisions may constitute a restriction if they oblige a bank to alter a service to bring it into line with the legislation of the country in which it is marketed.

The Commission considers that such provisions cannot escape the controls laid down by Community law simply on the ground that they fall within the scope of the law on contractual obligations.

In this context, a judge may be required to examine the compatibility with Community law of the results achieved by applying the rules on the choice of law governing contractual obligations contained in private international legal instruments, particularly the Rome Convention.[68]

Such choice-of-law rules do not, however, constitute restrictions in themselves. It is not, in principle, the mechanism for designating the law applicable which constitutes a barrier but the result to which it leads under substantive law.[69]

2.   Link with the Rome Convention

This Convention establishes the principle of contractual freedom, which is common to all Member States.

The parties to a banking contract may, therefore, freely choose the law which is to govern the contract and the obligations which they mutually undertake to fulfil. This may be the law of the home country, the host country or even a third country, whether or not a Member of the European Union.

The Convention lays down that, where no choice is expressed by the parties, the law applicable is that of the country with which the contract is most closely connected. Under the Convention, this is presumed to be the country where the party who is to effect the performance has his habitual residence or principal or secondary place of business, depending on whether the performance is to be effected by the parent company or a branch.

---

[66] Judgments 30 March 1993, case C-168/91, *Konstantinidis*, Reports, I-1191; 24 January 1991, case C-339/89, *Alsthom Atlantique*, Reports, I-107; 13 October 1993, case C-93/92, *Motorradcenter*, Reports, I-5009.

[67] See in this connection Judgments 10 February 1994, case C-398/92, *Mund & Fester*, Reports, I-467; 26 September 1996, case C-43/95, *Data Delecta Aktiebolag*, Reports, I-4661; 1 February 1996, case C-177/94 *Perfili*, Reports, I-161; see also 1 July 1993, case 20/92, *Hubbard*, see note 65.

[68] See note 4.

[69] See, however, Judgment 30 April 1996, case C-214/94, *Boukhalfa*, Reports, I-2253.

In the case of a contract concluded with a consumer,[70] the Convention lays down that, where the parties do not express a choice, the law applicable is that of the country of the consumer if the contract is entered into in one of the following sets of circumstances (Article 5):

— the contract was preceded by a specific invitation addressed to the consumer in his country and he had taken in that country all the steps necessary on his part for the conclusion of the contract;

— the other party or his agent received the consumer's order in that country.

Where, however, the parties have chosen the law governing the contract, this choice must not deprive the consumer of the protection afforded him by the mandatory rules[71] of the law of the country in which he has his habitual residence if one of the sets of circumstances described above is found to prevail.

In addition, under the Convention, the *'mandatory rules'* (Article 7) and *'public policy'* (Article 16)[72] of Member States may be applied at the choice of the parties or, in the absence of an express choice, according to the relevant rules contained in the Convention.

On the basis of the Rome Convention, a banking contract concluded with a consumer must, therefore, observe at least the mandatory rules of the law of the consumer's country if the consumer was first canvassed in the consumer's country or if the order for the service was received there.

If, on the other hand, the banking contract is concluded not with a consumer (contract concluded between a bank and a customer acting in the course of his business), the contract will be governed by the law chosen by the parties and, in the absence of an express choice, by the law of the country where the bank has its principal or secondary place of business.

3. *Precedence of Community law*

The Commission considers that a further level of reasoning must be added to that deriving from the application of the Rome Convention.

Thus, in accordance with the principle of the precedence of Community law, the provisions of substantive law applicable to a banking service pursuant to the choice-of-law rules laid down in the Rome Convention (it being possible for freedom of choice to be overridden by mandatory rules, mandatory requirements and public policy) may, if they constitute a restriction, be examined in the light of the general good.

Two possible situations may be envisaged:[73]

---

[70] Contract carried out for a purpose outside his trade or profession.

[71] Provisions which cannot be derogated from by contract.

[72] This concept must be understood here within its meaning under national law and private international law, which is not necessarily the meaning conferred upon it by the Court of Justice; for the latter, it is a non-economic concept, implying a serious threat to society.

[73] The Court of Justice will be responsible for interpreting the Rome Convention, particularly with a view to guaranteeing an interpretation that is compatible with Community law. However, it is not yet empowered to do so since the two protocols vesting such powers in the Court (89/128/EEC and 89/129/EEC) have not yet entered into force since not all the Member States which ratified the Rome Convention have ratified protocol 89/129/EEC.

(A)   BANKING SERVICES SUPPLIED BY A BRANCH

Article 4 of the Rome Convention lays down that the law applicable in the absence of a choice by the parties is that of the country in which the principal place of business is situated or, if the performance is to be effected through a place of business other than the principal place of business, the country in which that other place of business is situated.

The Convention therefore implies that, where a service is supplied by a bank branch, the law of the country where the branch is situated is presumed to prevail in the absence of a choice by the parties concerned.[74]

In accordance with the principle of the precedence of Community law, the Commission considers that, where the legal provisions of the country of the branch constitute a restriction, they may be put to the general-good test and, if necessary, overruled.

(B)   BANKING SERVICES SUPPLIED TO CONSUMERS UNDER THE FREEDOM TO PROVIDE SERVICES

According to the principle of the precedence of Community law, the application by a consumer's country of residence of its 'mandatory rules', 'mandatory requirements' and 'public policy' provisions to contracts entered into by the consumer may also be put to the general-good test if a restriction results.

It is necessary, therefore, to extend the line of reasoning developed on the basis of the Rome Convention and to question whether, for example, the 'mandatory rules' which the consumer's country intends to enforce satisfy the general-good tests. Since they are adopted with a view to protecting the consumer, there is a strong chance that these provisions of substantive law will pass the general-good test. The Court has in fact recognized that consumer protection is a general-good objective which justifies restrictions on fundamental freedoms. It cannot be assumed, however, that they will pass the general-good test in every case. It has been seen above that national rules which purport to have been adopted for reasons of consumer protection may be subjected to review by the Court and possibly 'disqualified' if they are, for example, unnecessary or disproportionate.

In the context of the single market, therefore, this additional level of reasoning is essential in order to ascertain whether, in the absence of harmonization, national measures are not being maintained, in the guise of consumer-protection measures, merely in order to restrict or to prevent banking services which are different or unfamiliar from gaining entry to national territory.

---

[74] Under normal circumstances, however, the parties to a banking contract would choose which law to apply.

P. Commission Interpretative Communication — Freedom to provide services and the general good in the insurance sector (OJ, C 43 of 16 February 2000)

The Third Council Directives 92/49/EEC and 92/96/EEC[1] completed the establishment of the single market in the insurance sector. They introduced a single system for the authorization and financial supervision of insurance undertakings by the Member State in which they have their head office (the home Member State). Such authorisation issued by the home Member State enables an insurance undertaking to carry on its insurance business anywhere in the European Community, either on the rules on establishment, i.e. by opening agencies or branches in all the Member States, or under the rules on the freedom to provide services. Where it carries on business in another Member State, the insurance undertaking must comply with the conditions in which, for reasons of the general good, such business must be conducted in the host Member State. Under the system set up by the Directives, the financial supervision of the business carried on by the insurance undertaking, including business carried on under the rules on establishment or on the freedom to provide services, is always a matter only for that insurance undertaking's home Member State.

In the course of its contacts with numerous economic agents, the Commission has come to realise that uncertainty surrounds the interpretation of the scope of the Treaty rules and of the provisions of the Insurance Directives, in particular the basic concepts of freedom to provide services and the general good. In many cases this results in the application by the supervisory authorities of measures or penalties in respect of insurance undertakings wishing to do business in the single market or in the imposition by them of certain constraints or conditions regarding the conduct of business on their territory. The situation in which insurance undertakings find themselves is far from clear and they thus face considerable legal uncertainty, both as regards the arrangements applicable to them in the different Member States and as regards the content of the products they wish to offer. The differences of interpretation seriously undermine the workings of the machinery set up by the Third Directives and are thus likely to deter certain insurance undertakings from exercising the freedoms created by the Treaty which the Third Directives set out to promote and, hence, to restrict the free movement of insurance services in the European Union. These differences are also preventing those seeking insurance from having access to insurance undertakings elsewhere in the Community and to the range of insurance products available within the single market in order to select the one that best fits their needs in terms of cover and cost...

In publishing this interpretative communication, the Commission is seeking to make transparent and to clarify the common rules which it is its task to see are observed. It is supplying all those concerned. national administrations, economic agents and consumers with a reference tool which explains the Commission's opinion with regard to the legal framework in which insurance business may be carried on.

---

[1] [Footnotes are published in the original numerical order as in OJ] Directives 92/49/EEC (OJ, L 228 of 11 August 1992, 1) and 92/96/EEC (OJ, L 360 of 9 December 1992, 1), as last amended by Directive 95/26/EEC of the European Parliament and of the Council (OJ, L 168 of 18 July 1995, 7).

The interpretations and ideas set out in the present communication, which concern only the specific problems of the insurance sector[7] do not claim to cover all possible situations that can arise in the functioning of the single insurance market, but merely the most frequent or most likely.

It should be pointed out straight away that the interpretations given in the present communication do not necessarily represent the often very divergent views put forward by the Member States and should not, in themselves, impose any new obligation on them.

Neither do the interpretations prejudge the Commission's subsequent interpretations of the principles of establishment and freedom to provide services with regard to the development of communication technology and its use in the insurance business. European Community policy on the information society and electronic commerce is designed to promote the expansion of information society services and their movement between the Member States, especially electronic commerce.[8] The development of electronic commerce in the insurance and financial business should become very important and should eventually change the machinery for distributing insurance products in the European Community. The current legal framework for the single market in insurance is based on machinery where consideration has not been given to how to use this new technology for carrying out insurance business in the single market, and further work may possibly have to be carried out in the area. In this connection, the proposal for a European Parliament and Council Directive concerning the distance marketing of consumer financial services[9] will provide a proper harmonised legal framework for distance transactions carried out with consumers, thereby contributing to the growing use of new remote communication techniques, such as the Internet.

It goes without saying that the Commission's interpretations do not prejudice the interpretation that the Court of Justice of the European Communities, which is responsible in the final instance for interpreting the Treaty and secondary legislation, might place on the matters at issue.

---

[7] As regards the banking sector, the Commission has published an interpretative communication on the freedom to provide service and the general good in the Second Banking Directive (SEC(97) 1193 fin. of 20 June 1997). [See, in this Chapter, O].

[8] Council resolution on the new priorities concerning the information society, adopted on 8 October 1996; Commission communication to the European Council entitled. Putting services to work. (CSE(96) fin. of 27 November 1996); Commission communication to the European Parliament, the Council and the Economic and Social Committee concerning regulatory transparency in the internal market for information society services and proposal for a European Parliament and Council Directive amending for the third time Directive 83/189/EEC laying down a procedure for the provision of information in the field of technical standards and regulations (COM(96) 392 fin. of 30 August 1996); proposal for a European Parliament and Council directive on certain legal aspects of electronic commerce in the internal market (COM (98) 586 fin. of 18 November 1998) and amended proposal (COM (1999) 427 final, 17.8.1999); and proposal for a European Parliament and Council directive on a common framework for electronic signatures (COM (98) 297 fin. of 3 May 1998) and amended proposal COM (1999) 195 of 29 April 1999).

[9] COM (98) 468 fin. of 14 October 1998, and, for the amended proposal, COM (1999) 385 fin. of 23 July 1999.

I.   Freedom to provide services and right of establishment in the insurance directives

A.   Demarcation between the right of establishment and the freedom to provide services.[10]

1.   Freedom to provide services

(a) *Temporary nature.* — Article 49 *et seq* of the Treaty establish the principle of the free movement of services. The principle acquired direct, unconditional effect on the expiry of the transitional period.[11] It confers on the parties concerned rights which the national authorities are required to observe and uphold, by refraining from applying any conflicting provision of national law, whether legislative or administrative, including specific, individual administrative decisions.[12]

It should be noted that, according to the decisions of the Court of Justice, the freedom to provide services may involve the movement of the provider of the service, as envisaged in the third paragraph of Article 50 of the Treaty, or the movement of the recipient of the service to the Member State of the provider; the service may, however, also be carried out without any movement, either of the supplier or of the recipient.[13] In other words, Article 49 *et seq* of the Treaty apply in all cases where a person providing services offers those services in a Member State other than that in which he is established, wherever the recipients of those services may be established. It is only when all the relevant elements of

---

[10] For the purposes of this communication, the terms "Member States of the provision of services", "business carried on under the freedom to provide services", "Member State where the risk is situated", "home Member State", "Member State of the branch", etc. are used in accordance with the definitions given in Directives 88/357/EEC, 90/619/EEC, 92/49/EEC and 92/96/EEC.

Member State of the provision of services: the Member State where the risk is situated pursuant to Article 2(d) of Directive 88/357/EEC in cases where it is covered by an insurance undertaking or branch situated in another Member State, or the Member State of the commitment pursuant to Article 2(e) of Directive 90/619/EEC in cases where the commitment is covered by an insurance undertaking or branch situated in another Member State (Article 1(e) of Directive 92/49/EEC and Article 1(f) of Directive 92/96/EEC).

Business carried on under the freedom to provide services: the cover by an insurance undertaking operating from one Member State of a risk or commitment situated pursuant to Article 2(d) of Directive 88/357/EEC or Article 2(e) of Directive 90/619/EEC in another
Member State.

Home Member State: the Member State in which the head office of the insurance undertkaing covering the risk or the commitment is situated (Article 1(c) of Directive 92/49/EEC and Article 1(d) of Directive 92/96/EEC).

Member State of the branch: the Member State in which the branch covering the risk or commitment is situated (Article 1(d) of Directive 92/49/EEC and Article 1(e) of Directive 92/96/EEC).

Branch: any agency or branch of an insurance undertaking. Any permanent presence of an undertaking in the territory of a Member State is treated in the same way as an agency or branch, even if that presence does not take the form of a branch or agency but consists merely of an office managed by the undertaking's own staff or by a person who is independent but has permanent authority to act for the undertaking as an agency would (Articles 1(b) of Directive 92/49/EEC and Directive 92/96/EEC, and Articles 3 of Directives 88/357/EEC and 90/619/EEC).

[11] 1 January 1970 (case 205/84, *Commission v. Germany*, Reports, 3755) or the date of accession in the case of new Member States (judgment of 29 April 1999, case C-224/97, *Ciola*, Reports, I-2517.

[12] See footnote 11, case C-224/97, *Ciola*.

[13] Joined cases 286/82 and 26/83, *Luisi and Carbone*, Reports, 377; case C-76/90, *Säger*, Reports, I-195; case C-384/93, *Alpine*, Reports, I-1141.

the activity in question are confined within a single Member State that the provisions of the Treaty on freedom to provide services do not apply.[14]

Where business is carried on under the freedom to provide services with the provider present on the territory of the Member State of provision, the concept of the provision of services is basically distinguished from that of establishment by its temporary character, while the right of establishment presupposes a lasting presence in the host country.[15] The distinction stems from the Treaty itself, where the third paragraph of Article 50 stipulates that, in cases involving movement by the service provider to another Member State, the person providing the service may, in order to do so 'temporarily' pursue his activity in the State where the service is provided. According to the case law of the Court of Justice, the temporary nature of the provision of services is to be assessed in the light of its duration, regularity, periodicity and continuity. The fact that the provision of services is temporary does not mean that the provider of services may not equip himself with some form of infrastructure in the host Member State in so far as such infrastructure is necessary for the purpose of performing the services in question.[16]

The Court has also stated that an activity which consists in providing on a lasting basis services from the home Member State and does not involve movement by the Member State.[17]

(b)   *Prohibition of circumvention of national law.* — The Court has acknowledged that a host MemberState is entitled to take steps to prevent a service provider whose activity is entirely or mainly directed towards its territory (i.e. the host Member State) from improperly exercising the freedom to provide services enshrined in Article 49 of the Treaty in order to circumvent the rules of professional conduct which would be applicable to him if he were established in the territory of that host Member State.[18] It adds that such a situation may fall within the ambit of the chapter on the right of establishment and not of that on the freedom to provide services.[19]

The criterion of frequency is important in order to determine whether there may be an attempt at 'circumvention', while exercising the freedom to provide services enshrined in Article 49, but it is not sufficient to define business as being carried on under the freedom to provide services (an establishment may also operate on an occasional basis).

---

[14] Joined cases C-225/95, C-226/95 and C-227/95, *Kapasakalis*, Reports, I-4239; judgments of the Court of 26 February 1991 in three cases concerning tourist guides: C-154/89, Reports, I-659; C-180/89, Reports, I-709 and C-198/89, Reports, I-659.

[15] Joined cases 286/82 and 26/83, *Luisi und Carbone*, Reports, 377; case C-55/94, *Gebhard*, Reports, I-4165, paragraphs 25 to 27; case C-221/89, Factortame, Reports, I-3905: "the concept of establishment within the meaning of Article 52 *et seq*" of the Treaty "involves the actual pursuit of an economic activity through a fixed establishment in another Member State for an indefinite period" (paragraph 20).

[16] Case 55/94, *Gebhard*, Reports, I-4165, paragraph 27; case C-56/96, *VT4*, Reports, I-3143 "service provider to the Member State of provision falls within the scope of the rules on the freedom to provide services".

[17] Case C-56/96, *VT4*, Reports, I-3143.

[18] Case 205/84, *Commission v. Germany*, Reports, 3755 (see footnote 6); case 33/74, *Van Binsbergen*, Reports, 1299; case C-148/91, *Veronica*, Reports, I-487; case C-23/93, *TV 10*, Reports, I-4795, paragraphs 56 and 68 of the Opinion or Mr Advocate-General Lenz; case C-56/96, *VT4* (see footnote 16). See also the Opinion of Mr Advocate-General Lenz in case C-212/97, *Centros*, Reports, I-1459, a case concerning alleged misuse of the secondary right of establishment. The Court applid its case law on circumvention developed in the context of the freedom to provide services.

[19] Case 205/84, *Commission v. Germany*, Reports, 3755, paragraph 22; case 33/74, *Van Binsbergen*, Reports, 1299, paragraph 13.

The Commission takes the view that a situation where an insurance undertaking is frequently being approached within its own territory — for example, via electronic means of communication — by consumers residing in other Member States could not be regarded as a circumvention, unless it were demonstrated that there was an intention on the part of the provider of services to circumvent the national rules of those other Member States.

2.   Right of establishment

If an undertaking carries on business in a Member State for an indefinite period via a permanent presence in that Member State, it is covered in principle by the provisions of the Treaty on the right of establishment. The Court has held that: 'A national of a Member State who pursues a professional activity on a stable and continuous basis in another Member State where he holds himself out from an established professional base to, amongst others, nationals of that State comes under the chapter relating to the right of establsihment and not the chapter relating to services'.[20]

In *Commission v. Germany*,[21] the Court held that: 'an insurance undertaking of another Member State which maintains a permanent presence in the Member State in question comes within the scope of the provisions of the Treaty on the right of establishment, even if that presence does not take the form of a branch or agency, but consists merely of an office managed by the undertaking's own staff or by a person who is independent but authorised to act on a permanent basis for the undertaking, as will be the case with an agency'.

The Court has therefore acknowledged that an undertaking which has recourse to an intermediary established on the territory of another Member State to carry on activities in that Member State on a stable and continuous basis may fall within the scope of the rules on the right of establishment. The Court sought in that judgment to avoid the freedom to provide services being misused in order to circumvent the rules that would apply in the host Member State if the undertaking were established there.[22]

Nevertheless, this risk of abuse has been eliminated to a significant degree in the insurance sector as a result of the harmonisation achieved since the above judgment by the Community directives concerning the conditions for taking up and carrying on insurance activities. The prudential and supervisory rules for insurance undertakings have been largely harmonised, whichever way insurance activities are carried out: by way of establishment or through the provision of services.

The Court of Justice recently acknowledged that the temporary character of the provision of services does not mean that the provider may not equip himself with some form of infrastructure (chambers, office, etc.) in the host Member State in so far as is necessary for the purposes of performing the services in question, without coming under the right of establishment.[23] In such cases the temporary character of the services provided should be assessed by reference to their duration, frequency, periodicity and

---

[20] Case 55/94, *Gebhard,* Reports, I-4165; case C-221/89, *Factortame,* Reports, I-3905.

[21] Case 205/84, *Commission v Germany,* Reports, 3755.

[22] Case 205/84 (see footnote 11, paragraphs 21 and 22; case C-148/91, *Veronica* (see footnote 18); case C-56/96, *VT4* (see footnote 16) (see Opinion of Mr Advocate-General Lenz).

[23] Case C-55/94, *Gebhard* (see footnote 15). It should be pointed out that, in his Opinion on case 205/84, *Commission v. Germany* (see footnote 6), the Advocate-General stated that the appointment of an agent or representative (in the host Member State) did not in itself necessarily constitute establishment.

continuity.[24]   However, the mere existence of infrastructure in a Member State does not prove straight away that the situation falls within the scope of the rules on the right of establishment. In the light of the case law of the Court of Justice,[25] The Commission considers that the Member State of the provision of services may not treat any permanent presence of the provider of services on its territory as an establishment and subject it in any event to the rules relating to the right of establishment.

3.   Grey area

It is, however, not always easy to draw the line between the two concepts of provision of services and establishment. Some situations are difficult to classify, in particular where the insurer, in order to carry on its insurance business, uses a permanent infrastructure in the Member State of provision. This arises in particular in the following cases:

(a)   recourse to independent persons established in the host Member State;

(b)   electronic machines carrying on insurance business. On the strength of the Court's case law, the Commission departments propose the following interpretations:

(a)   *Recourse to independent persons established in the host Member State.* — The problem is to determine to what extent an insurance undertaking established in Member State A which has recourse to an independent person[26] established in Member State B in order to do insurance business there could be regarded as itself carrying on an insurance activity on a permanent basis in Member State B and hence be treated as an establishment of the insurance undertaking in the host Member State, instead of being regarded as carrying on an insurance activity under the rules on the freedom to provide services.

In *De Bloos*[27] the Court held that: 'One of the essential characteristics of the concepts of branch or agency is the fact of being subject to the direction and control of the parent body'.

In even more precise terms, in *Somafer*[28] the Court held that: 'The concept of branch, agency or other establishment implies a place of business which has the appearance of permanency, such as the extension of a parent body, has a management and is materially equipped to negotiate business with third parties, so that the latter, although knowing

---

[24] Case C-55/94, *Gebhard* (see footnote 15).

[25] See, in particular, *Gebhard*, and *VT4*, (see footnote 16).

[26] It should be pointed out straightaway that the notion of "independent person" refers to structures (natural or legal persons) that are legally separate from the insurance undertaking they call on, irrespective of their form or designation. It is not used therefore in the more restrictive sense of Council Directive 77/92/EEC (OJ, L 26 of 3 January 1977) to distinguish between insurance agents (who act on behalf and for the account of, or solely on behalf of, one or more insurance undertakings) and insurance brokers (whose professional activity consists in particular in bringing together persons seeking insurance and insurance undertakings without being bound in the choice of the latter, with a view to covering risks to be insured, ans who carry out work mpreparatory to the conclusion of policies of insurance and assist in the administration and performance of such policies, in particular in the event of a claim).

[27] Case 14/76, Reports, 1497. It should be noted that this judgment and those cited in footnotes 27, 28 and 29 were delivered in cases concerning the interpretation of the concept of a branch in accordance with the Brussels Convention on juridiction and the enforcement of judgments in civil and commercial matters.

[28] Case 33/78, Reports, 2183. See also case C-439/93, *Lloyd's Register of Shipping v Société Campenon Bernard*, Reports, I-961.

that there will if necessary be a legal link with the parent body, the head office of which is abroad, do not have to deal directly with such a parent body but may transact business at the place of business constituting the extension'.

It concluded that a sole concessionaire not subject to the control and direction of a company could not be regarded as a branch, agency or establishment.

In *Blanckart & Willems*,[29] the Court held that: 'An independent commercial agent who merely negotiates business, in as much as his legal *status* leaves him basically free to arrange his own work and decide what proportion of his time to devote to the interests of the undertaking which he agrees to represent and whom that undertaking may not prevent from representing at the same time several firms competing in the same manufacturing or marketing sector, and who, moreover, merely transmits orders to the parent undertaking without being involved in either their terms or their execution, does not have the character of a branch, agency or other establishment...'.

Moreover, in his Opinion in *Shearson Lehman Hutton*[30] Mr Advocate-General Darmon stated that: 'The link of dependence vis-à-vis the company established in another signatory State[31] is not the determining criterion here. In our opinion, that criterion resides in the fact the secondary establishment has the power to enter into contracts with third parties'.

Lastly, in his report on the Brussels Convention, Mr Jenard notes that there is an agency or branch only where the foreign company is represented by a person capable of acting in a manner that is binding on its vis-à-vis third parties.[32]

On the basis of these precedents, the Commission considers that, for the links between an independent person — such as, for example, an independent intermediary — and an insurance undertaking to be regarded as meaning that the insurance undertaking falls within the scope of the rules governing the right of establishment rather than those applicable to the freedom to provide services, the independent person must meet the following three cumulative conditions:

(i)   he must be subject to the direction and control of the insurance undertaking he represents;

(ii)   he must be able to commit the insurance undertaking, and

(iii)   he must have received a permanent brief.

It is, therefore, only where the independent person acts as a genuine extension of the insurance undertaking that the insurance undertaking falls within the scope of the rules applicable to the establishment of a branch ...

Conclusion

The Commission takes the view that it is only where the above three conditions are met (i.e. where the independent person to the direction and control of the insurance undertaking, is able to commit the insurance undertaking and has received a permanent brief) that an insurance undertaking, using independent persons, e.g. intermediaries — permanently

---

[29]   Case 139/80, Reports, 819.

[30]   Case C-89/91, Reports, I-165.

[31]   The term "signatory State" is used here because the case concerned the Brussels Convention on jrusidiction and the enforcement of judgments in civil and commercial matters.

[32]   O.J., C 59 of 5 March 1979, 1.

established in the host Member State, must be treated as if it had a branch in the host Member State, with all that this implies from the legal point of view. Accordingly, the insurance undertaking will have to follow the procedure for opening a branch laid down by Article 10 of the First Insurance Directives 73/329/EEC and 79/267/EEC, as amended by Article 32 of the Third Insurance Directives 92/49/EEC and 92/96/EEC (specifying that the activities envisaged will be carried on through an independent intermediary). In addition, the independent person's activities must be carried on with due regard for the rules on branches adopted in the interest of the general good by the host State.

The fact that these conditions may involve making the insurance undertaking subject to the right of establishment does not mean that the independent person himself constitutes a branch of the insurer. A branch is. a place of business which forms a legally dependent part of an insurance undertaking.[34] Since the person is assumed to be independent, he cannot be a 'part' of an insurance undertaking. This is without prejudice to compliance, where appropriate, by that independent person with the conditions governing the taking up and exercise of his professional activity in the Member State in which he is established.

(b)   *Electronic machines.* — This means fixed, ATM-type electronic machines capable of performingthe insurance activities listed in the Annex to the First Directives.[35]

Such machines may be covered by the right of establishment if they fulfil the criteria laid down by the Court of Justice (see, *supra* point (a)).

For such a machine to be capable of being treated as an establishment, therefore, it would have to have a management, which is by definition impossible unless the Court acknowledges that the concept can encompass not only human management but also electronic management.

However, such a machine is unlikely to be the only place of business of an insurance undertaking in a Member State. It is likely to be attached in the same country to a branch or an agency. In that event, the machine is not an entity in its own right as it is covered by the rules governing the establishment to which it is attached.

If the machine does, however, constitute the only presence of an insurance undertaking in a Member State for the type of insurance transaction in question, the Commission takes the view that it may be possible to treat it as a provision of services in the territory of that Member State. The presence in the host country of a person or company responsible simply for maintaining the machine, equipping it and dealing with any technical problems encountered by users cannot rank as an establishment of the insurance undertaking and does not prevent the activity being deemed to be carried on under the freedom to provide services.

The Commission cannot rule out the possibility that technological developments might, in the future, induce it to review its position. If such developments were to make it possible for an insurance undertaking to have only a machine in a given country which could 'act' as a branch, taking actual decisions which would completely obviate the need for

---

[34] See in this respect the concept of a branch given in Article 1(3) of Second Banking Directive 89/646/EEC (O.J., L 386 of 30 December 1989) and Article 1(8) of Directive 93/22/EEC on investment services in the securities field (O.J., L 141 of 11 June 1993).

[35] It does not mean individual, mobile data-processing equipment which can provide or receive distance insurance services, e.g. through the Internet. Equipment of this kind is discussed in point 6.

the customer to have contact with the parent company, the Commission would be forced to consider an appropriate Community legal framework. The present legal framework in fact rests on mechanisms which are still based on a. human. concept of a branch (for example, the programme of operations must contain the names of those responsible for the management of the branch). It is therefore not possible, under the existing rules, to consider machines as constituting a branch...

6.   *Insurance business carried on using remote means of communication, and in particular via electronic commerce*

(*a*)   The use of remote means of communication (telephone, fax, the press, etc.) and in particular electronic commerce (e.g. via the Internet) to conclude insurance policies covering a risk (or communication) situated in a Member State other than the Member State of establishment of the insurer should be regarded as insurance business carried on under the freedom to provide services wirth no movement on the part of the contracting parties.[39] In addition, most of the cases involve services provided on a lasting basis.[40] The Member State of establishment of the insurance undertaking with which a policy is concluded in this way is the Member State of establishment of the insurer that effectively comes on the insurance activity (head office or branch) and not the place where the technological means used for providing the service are located (e.g. the place where the Internet server is installed).[41]

In most cases, the initiative for the conclusion of such insurance policies via the Internet comes from the prospective policyholder, who decides to use his own equipment in order to contact, and to seek to conclude an insurance policy electronically with, an insurance undertaking willing to do business in this way.

Under the Insurance Directives, the location of the risk (or commitment) covered by the insurance policy is the key factor for determining the rules applicable to an insurance transaction. The location of the risk or commitment is furthermore itself determined according to precise criteria laid down by the Insurance Directives themselves.[42] Consequently, if an insurance transaction is to be carried out under the freedom to provide services, the risk or commitment covered by the insurance policy must be situated in a Member State other than the Member State of establishment of the insurance undertaking covering that risk or commitment.

The Commission takes the view that, in accordance with the rules as they stand, insurance activities carried on via electronic commerce (e.g. the Internet) and covering a risk located in a Member State other than that in which the insurer covering the risk is established are subject to the provisions of the Insurance Directives relating to the freedom to provide services. An insurance undertaking operating from one Member State which

---

[39]   Joined cases 286/82 and 26/83, *Luisi and Carbone* (see footnote 13); case C-23/93, *TV10* (see footnote 18).

[40]   See Part I.1 and footnote 17.

[41]   See in this connection Article 1(c) of the amended proposal for a directive on certain legal aspects of electronic commerce in the internal market, supra; case C-221/89, *Factortame* (see footnote 20).

[42]   Non-life insurance: Article 2(d) of the Second Directive 88/357/EEC; life assurance: Article 2(e) of Directive 90/619/EEC. This is unlike the banking sector, for which the Second Banking Directive 89/646/EEC does not lay any criteria for locating banking activities carried on in the single market (see communication on the banking sector (SEC(97) 1193 fin. of 20 June 1997), which provides criteria for locating banking activities carried on under the freedom to provide services with a view to determining the rules applicable).

is prepared to conclude via the Internet insurance policies covering risks or commitments situated in other Member States should therefore follow the notification procedure for activities carried on under the freedom to provide services.[43]

The existing legal framework governing the single insurance market rets on mechanisms which did not envisage the use of information technology for carrying on insurance business in the single market. For this reason, the Commission already stated in its communication to the Council on the Financial Services Action Plan[44] that it intended to bring out a Green Paper to examine whether the existing provisions of the directives in the field of financial services provided a regulatory framework that is propitious to the development of electronic commerce in financial services while ensuring that the interests of consumers are fully protected.

(*b*)   On the other hand, the use of electronic commerce methods for the sole purposes of advertising, providing commercial information or enhancing awareness of the insurance undertaking cannot be regarded as an insurance activity. As stated in Section III below, the Insurance Directives do not make advertising activities in the host Member State subject to ther notification procedure, only the intention to carry on an insurance activity in another Member State under the freedom to provide services[45].

The Commission considers that it is out of the question to make such advertising and information activities subject to the notification procedure laid down by the Third Directives (Article 34 *et seq*), which was designed for actual insurance activities carried on under the freedom to provide services…

II.   *The general good in the third insurance directives; applicability of rules promoting the general good*

The Third Insurance Directives reflect the case law of the Court of Justice and contain several references to the concept of the general good, providing in particular that an insurance undertaking operating under a single licence must comply with host country rules adopted in the interest of the general good.

Such compliance is required either in the specific context of freedom of establishment (Article 32(4) of Directives 92/49/EEC and 92/96/EEC) or indiscriminately in connection with freedom of establishment and freedom to provide services (Articles 28 and 41 of Directives 92/49/EEC and 92/96/EEC) …

The Commission takes the view that an insurance undertaking operating under the arrangements laid down by the Insurance Directives could, therefore, be obliged to adapt its services to the host-country rules only if the measures enforced against it serve the general good, irrespective of whether it carries on its activities through a branch or under the freedom to provide services.

---

[43] See Articles 14, 16 and 17 of Directive 88/357/EEC, as amended by Articles 34, 35 and 36 of Directive 92/49/EEC (non-life insurance), and Articles 11, 14 and 17 of Directive 88/357/EEC, as amended by Articles 34, 35 and 36 of Directive 92/96/EEC (life assurance), for the procedure relating to activities under the freedom to provide services falling within the scope of these Directives.

[44] COM(1999) 232 of 11 May 1999.

[45] See Commission communication .A European initiative in electronic commerce. (COM(97) 15 fin.), proposal for a European Parliament and Council Directive on certain legal aspects of electronic commerce in the internal market (COM(98) 586 fin. of 18 November 1998) and amended proposal (COM(1999) 427 fin. 17 August 1999).

This approach is borne out by recent decisions of the Court of Justice, which held that only general-good rules can restrict or impede exercise of the two basic freedoms, namely the freedom to provide services[55] and the right of establishment.[56] However, the Insurance Directives do not contain any definition of the general good... They simply recall in their recitals the requirements imposed by the Court of Justice's case law on the concept of the general good. The reason for this is that is a judicial construction of an evolutive and open nature devised by the Court of Justice. It makes it possible to assess the conformity with Community law of a national measure that is taken in a non-harmonised area at Community level and hinders freedom of establishment and freedom to provide services. In non-harmonised areas, the level of what is regarded as the general good depends first on the assessment made by the Member States and can vary substantially from one country to another according to national traditions and the objectives of the Member States. It is necessary, therefore, to refer to the relevant case law of the Court of Justice.

2. *The concept of the general good*

(a) *Case-law principles.*[57] — The concept of the general good is based in the Court's case law. It was developed first in the context of the free movement of services and goods and was subsequently applied to the right of establishment.[58]

However, the Court has never given a definition of 'the general good', preferring to maintain its evolving nature. It has expressed its opinion in individual cases on the possibility of deeming a given national measure to be aimed at achieving an imperative objective serving the general good and has specified the line of reasoning to be followed in determining whether such a measure may be enforced by one Member State against a trader from another Member State who is operating within the territory of the former.

The Court has though spelled out the strict conditions to be met by national measures which are aimed at achieving an imperative objective serving the general good if they are to be validly enforced against that trader.[59]

---

[55] Case C-76/90, *Säger*, Reports, I-4221. See the analysis set out in the Commission interpretative communications concerning the free movement of services across frontiers (O.J., C 334 of 9 December 1993, 3) and concerning freedom to provide services and the interest of the general good in the Second Banking Directive (SEC(97)1193 of 26 June 1997).

[56] *Gebhard*, footnote 15. See also cases C-19/92, *Kraus*, Reports, I-1663 and C-212/97, *Centros* (see footnote 18).

[57] The Commission's analysis may, of course, be modified to reflect changes in the Court's case law.

[58] Case-55/94, *Gebhard* (see footnote 15). It is interesting to note that the judgment in *Gebhard* relates to an area (access to the profession of lawyer) in which harmonisation of the conditions for taking up and carrying on the activity is very limited in comparison with insurance. In the insurance sector, these conditions have been very extensively harmonised and the possibilities for relying on general-good rules are hence much more limited. On the other hand, with regard to the law of insurance policies, which is a field that has not been harmonised by secondary Community legislation, the discretion of the Member States is much wider. It is above all in this field that the test of the general good is likely to be applied.

[59] See *Gebhard* (see footnote 15), where the Court held that "...national measures liable to hinder or make less attractive the exercise of fundamental freedoms guaranteed by the Treaty must fulfil four conditions: they must be applied in a non-discriminatory manner; they must be justified by imperative requirements in the general interest; they must be suitable for securing the attainment of the objective which they pursue; and they must not go beyond what is necessary in order to attain it". This was subsequently confirmed by the Court in its judgments in cases C-415/93, *Bosman*, Reports, I-4921 and C-250/95, *Futura*, Reports, I-2471.

The Court requires that a national provision must satisfy the following requirements if it is validly to obstruct or limit exercise of the right of establishment and the freedom to provide services:

— it must come within a field which has not been harmonised,
— it must pursue an objective of the general good,
— it must be non-discriminatory,
— it must by objectively necessary,
— it must be proportionate to the objective pursued,
— it is also necessary for the general-good objective not to be safeguarded by rules to which the provider of services is already subject in the Member State where he is established.

These conditions are cumulative. A national measure which is claimed to be compatible with the principle of the freedom of movement must satisfy all the conditions. If a national measure does not meet one or other condition, it is not compatible with Community law.

The concept of general good is an exception to the fundamental principles of the Treaty with regard to free movement and must, therefore, be interpreted in a restrictive fashion so as to ensure that recourse is not had to it in an excessive or abusive manner. In the event of a dispute, the Member State imposing the restriction has anyway to show that the measure meets the aforementioned conditions…

4.   Rules relating to the law applicable to insurance contracts and the concept of the general good

The Insurance Directives[109] lay down specific rules for determining the law applicable to insurance contract covering risks situated within the European Economic Area.[110] They make it possible to define what substantive law will govern the contract. The rules apply both to insurance activities carried on under the rules on establishment and to those carried on under the freedom to provide services. The Directives also lay down provisions relating to application of the mandatory rules of the forum and of the Member State of the risk/commitment and to the public policy rules.[111]

The application, under the rules on the conflict of laws laid down by the Insurance Directives, by a Member State of its own mandatory substantive provisions and its public policy rules to insurance policies is likely, if it results in a restriction, to be examined from the viewpoint of the general good. The concept of the general good acts as a filter of national legislation. It obliges the authorities of the Member States to analyse their legislation for compliance with the Treaty's principles of free movement.

---

[109] As regards non-life assurance, see Articles 7 and 8 of the Second Directive 88/357/EEC, as amended by the Third Directive 92/49/EEC; as regards life assurance, see Article 4 of the Second Directive 90/619/EEC.

[110] It should be pointed out that the Rome Convention on the law applicable to contractual obligations (O.J., L 266 of 9 October 1980, 1) excludes from its scope insurance contracts covering risks situated in the territories of the Member States (Article 1(3)).

[111] Non-life insurance: Article 7(1)(h) of Second Directive 88/35/EEC; life assurance: Article 4(4) of Second Directive 90/619/EEC.

It is essential that any rule of national law, whatever the field it relates to, should be compatible with Community law. Thus, in a judgment dated 21 March 1972, the Court held that: 'The effectiveness of Community law cannot vary according to the various spheres of national law which it may affect.'[112]

Community law takes precedence therefore, if necessary, over national rules in the sphere of private law.

In particular, it has fallen to the Court to verify the compatibility with Community law of national rules of civil law,[113] civil procedure[114] and even of criminal law.[115]

Consequently, as has already been stated above, it is not sufficient that the host Member State's entire legislation on insurance contracts be immediately declared mandatory for the authorities to think that it must be observed in full.[116] Such provisions must also satisfy the requirements of the general good if the host Member State is to be able to require compliance with them by insurers operating through a branch or by way of freedom to provide services.

Since these are rules which were adopted in order to protect the consumer, there is a strong possibility that such rules of substantive law will pass the general-good test. The Court has recognised that consumer protection is an objective of the general good which justifies restrictions of fundamental freedoms. It cannot be presumed, however, that the test will be passed. It was seen above that national laws adopted with the declared aim of protecting the consumer can be subjected to the control of the Court and, where appropriate, disqualified, e.g. if they are not necessary or are disproportionate.

This additional level of reasoning is therefore essential, in the context of a single market, in order to verify whether, in the absence of harmonisation, national measures are not, under the pretext of consumer protection, being maintained simply to restrict or prevent the entry of insurance services which are different or unknown on the national territory.

If a Member State could invoke non-conformity with its own legislation in the case of an insurance product marketed in another Member State in order to restrict the marketing thereof on its territory, it would be hindering competition between insurance undertakings.

Q.   ECJ case-law

The ECJ issued numerous important judgments relevant to the companies' right of establishment and freedom to provide services, which provide some interpretative elements concerning the *status* of companies and legal entities in Community law. It is clear that the provisions of the Treaty on these matters do not qualify as choice-of law rules, but nevertheless they provide a useful reference and an evaluation parameter for the interpreter.

---

[112] Case C-82/71, *SAIL*, Reports, 119. See also case C-20/92, *Hubbard*, Reports, I-3777.

[113] Case C-168/91, *Konstantinidis*, Reports, I-1191; case C-399/89, *Alsthom Atlantique*, Reports, I-107; case C-93/92, *Motorradcenter*, Reports, I-5009.

[114] See in this respect case C-398/92, *Mund & Fester*, Reports, I-467; case C-43/95, *Data Delecta*, Reports, I-4661; case C-177/94, *Perfili*, Reports, I-161. See also *Hubbard* (footnote 112).

[115] Case C-348/96, Reports, I-11.

[116] See point IV(3).

The first relevant decision was given in the *Segers* case (10 July 1986, case 79/85, Reports, 2375), concerning a Dutch citizen who had incorporated a private company limited by shares under English law, even if he intended to carry out his activity mainly in the Netherlands, and solely through a branch incorporated therein. The ECJ has been asked to ascertain the compatibility with Community law of certain Dutch provisions pertaining to social security benefits, that had been refused on the grounds that the Dutch national was the director of a company incorporated under English law active in the Netherlands under the rules on freedom of establishment, but that would have been granted if the English company had its registered office in the the Netherlands. The ECJ pointed out the following:

13.   The question submitted to the Court concerns a case in which the refusal to grant benefits is based not on the nationality of the director but on the location of the registered office of the company which he directs. However, as far as companies are concerned it should be recalled that according to the judgment of the Court of 28 January 1986 (case 270/83, *Commission v. France*, Reports, 273) the right of establishment includes, pursuant to Article 58 of the EEC Treaty, the right of companies or firms formed in accordance with the law of a member State and having their registered office, central administration or principal place of business within the community to pursue their activities in another member State through an agency, branch or subsidiary. With regard to companies, it should be noted that it is their registered office in the abovementioned sense that serves as the connecting factor with the legal system of a particular State, as does nationality in the case of natural persons.

14.   In that respect the Court would observe that a company which has been formed in accordance with the law of another Member State and which conducts its business through an agency, branch or subsidiary in the member State in which it seeks to establish itself cannot be deprived of the benefit of the rule set out above. As the Court has already stated, in its judgment of 28 January 1986, cited above, acceptance of the proposition that the Member State in which a company seeks to establish itself may freely apply to it a different treatment solely by reason of the fact that its registered office is situated in another Member State would deprive Article 58 of all meaning.

16.   As regards the doubt expressed by the national court concerning the significance of the fact that the English company clearly does not conduct business in the United Kingdom, it should be noted that for the application of the provisions on the right of establishment, Article 58 requires only that the companies be formed in accordance with the law of a Member State and have their registered office, central administration or principal place of business within the Community provided that those requirements are satisfied, the fact that the company conducts its business through an agency, branch or subsidiary solely in another member State is immaterial.

With the subsequent *Factortame II* judgment (25 July 1991, case C-221/89, Reports, I-3905) the ECJ clarified the scope of Article 52 of the EEC Treaty (later Article 43 EC and now 49 TFEU) with reference to the requirements provided by UK legislation on citizenship and residence of shareholders and directors of companies.

28.   The prohibition of discrimination on grounds of nationality, which is set out in particular, as regards the right of establishment, in Article 52 of the Treaty, is concerned with differences of treatment as between natural persons who are nationals of Member States and as between companies who are treated in the same way as such persons by virtue of Article 58.

29. Consequently, in exercising its powers for the purposes of defining the conditions for the grant of its 'nationality' to a ship, each Member State must comply with the prohibition of discrimination against nationals of Member States on grounds of their nationality.

30. It follows from the foregoing that a condition of the type at issue in the main proceedings which stipulates that where a vessel is owned or chartered by natural persons they must be of a particular nationality and where it is owned or chartered by a company the shareholders and directors must be of that nationality is contrary to Article 52 of the Treaty.

31. Such a condition is also contrary to Article 221 of the Treaty, under which Member States must accord nationals of the other Member States the same treatment as their own nationals as regards participation in the capital of companies or firms within the meaning of Article 58.

32. As for the requirement for the owners, charterers, managers and operators of the vessel and, in the case of a company, the shareholders and directors to be resident and domiciled in the Member State in which the vessel is to be registered, it must be held that such a requirement, which is not justified by the rights and obligations created by the grant of a national flag to a vessel, results in discrimination on grounds of nationality. The great majority of nationals of the Member State in question are resident and domiciled in that State and therefore meet that requirement automatically, whereas nationals of other Member States would, in most cases, have to move their residence and domicile to that State in order to comply with the requirements of its legislation. It follows that such a requirement is contrary to Article 52.

33. It follows from the foregoing that it is contrary to the provisions of Community law and, in particular, to Article 52 of the EEC Treaty for a Member State to stipulate as conditions for the registration of a fishing vessel in its national register: (a) that the legal owners and beneficial owners and the charterers, managers and operators of the vessel must be nationals of that Member State or companies incorporated in that Member State, and that, in the latter case, at least 75 % of the shares in the company must be owned by nationals of that Member State or by companies fulfilling the same requirements and 75 % of the directors of the company must be nationals of that Member State; and (b) that the said legal owners and beneficial owners, charterers, managers, operators, shareholders and directors, as the case may be, must be resident and domiciled in that Member State.

More recently the ECJ has ruled over the case of a company, incorporated under English law, and whose share capital was divided into two shares held by two Danish nationals residing in Denmark, which had applied to the competent Danish Authorities for registering its own branch in Denmark (9 March 1999, case C-212/97, *Centros*, Reports, I-5459). Such company had never carried out any business since incorporation. Pursuant to Danish law, *Centros* had to be considered as a foreign limited liability company allowed to do business in Denmark through a branch. Moreover, the Danish authorities refused the abovementioned registration on the grounds that Centros was in fact seeking to establish in Denmark a principal establishment and not a branch, thus circumventing the Danish rules concerning, in particular, the paying-up of the minimum share capital. The ECJ observed that:

17. In this respect, it should be noted that a situation in which a company formed in accordance with the law of a Member State in which it has its registered office desires to set up a branch in another Member State falls within the scope of Community law.

In that regard, it is immaterial that the company was formed in the first Member State only for the purpose of establishing itself in the second, where its main, or indeed entire, business is to be conducted (see, to this effect, *Segers* paragraph 16).

18.   That Mr and Mrs Bryde formed the company Centros in the United Kingdom for the purpose of avoiding Danish legislation requiring that a minimum amount of share capital be paid up has not been denied either in the written observations or at the hearing. That does not, however, mean that the formation by that British company of a branch in Denmark is not covered by freedom of establishment for the purposes of Articles 52 and 58 of the Treaty. The question of the application of those articles of the Treaty is different from the question whether or not a Member State may adopt measures in order to prevent attempts by certain of its nationals to evade domestic legislation by having recourse to the possibilities offered by the Treaty.

19.   As to the question whether, as Mr and Mrs Bryde claim, the refusal to register in Denmark a branch of their company formed in accordance with the law of another Member State in which its has its registered office constitutes an obstacle to freedom of establishment, it must be borne in mind that that freedom, conferred by Article 52 of the Treaty on Community nationals, includes the right for them to take up and pursue activities as self-employed persons and to set up and manage undertakings under the same conditions as are laid down by the law of the Member State of establishment for its own nationals. Furthermore, under Article 58 of the Treaty companies or firms formed in accordance with the law of a Member State and having their registered office, central administration or principal place of business within the Community are to be treated in the same way as natural persons who are nationals of Member States.

20.   The immediate consequence of this is that those companies are entitled to carry on their business in another Member State through an agency, branch or subsidiary. The location of their registered office, central administration or principal place of business serves as the connecting factor with the legal system of a particular State in the same way as does nationality in the case of a natural person.

21.   Where it is the practice of a Member State, in certain circumstances, to refuse to register a branch of a company having its registered office in another Member State, the result is that companies formed in accordance with the law of that other Member State are prevented from exercising the freedom of establishment conferred on them by Articles 52 and 58 of the Treaty.

22.   Consequently, that practice constitutes an obstacle to the exercise of the freedoms guaranteed by those provisions.

23.   According to the Danish authorities, however, Mr and Mrs Bryde cannot rely on those provisions, since the sole purpose of the company formation which they have in mind is to circumvent the application of the national law governing formation of private limited companies and therefore constitutes abuse of the freedom of establishment. In their submission, the Kingdom of Denmark is therefore entitled to take steps to prevent such abuse by refusing to register the branch.

24.   It is true that according to the case-law of the Court a Member State is entitled to take measures designed to prevent certain of its nationals from attempting, under cover of the rights created by the Treaty, improperly to circumvent their national legislation or to prevent individuals from improperly or fraudulently taking advantage of provisions of Community law.

25. However, although, in such circumstances, the national courts may, case by case, take account — on the basis of objective evidence — of abuse or fraudulent conduct on the part of the persons concerned in order, where appropriate, to deny them the benefit of the provisions of Community law on which they seek to rely, they must nevertheless assess such conduct in the light of the objectives pursued by those provisions.

26. In the present case, the provisions of national law, application of which the parties concerned have sought to avoid, are rules governing the formation of companies and not rules concerning the carrying on of certain trades, professions or businesses. The provisions of the Treaty on freedom of establishment are intended specifically to enable companies formed in accordance with the law of a Member State and having their registered office, central administration or principal place of business within the Community to pursue activities in other Member States through an agency, branch or subsidiary.

27. That being so, the fact that a national of a Member State who wishes to set up a company chooses to form it in the Member State whose rules of company law seem to him the least restrictive and to set up branches in other Member States cannot, in itself, constitute an abuse of the right of establishment. The right to form a company in accordance with the law of a Member State and to set up branches in other Member States is inherent in the exercise, in a single market, of the freedom of establishment guaranteed by the Treaty.

28. In this connection, the fact that company law is not completely harmonised in the Community is of little consequence. Moreover, it is always open to the Council, on the basis of the powers conferred upon it by Article 54(3)(g) of the EC Treaty, to achieve complete harmonisation.

29. In addition, it is clear from paragraph 16 of *Segers* that the fact that a company does not conduct any business in the Member State in which it has its registered office and pursues its activities only in the Member State where its branch is established is not sufficient to prove the existence of abuse or fraudulent conduct which would entitle the latter Member State to deny that company the benefit of the provisions of Community law relating to the right of establishment.

30. Accordingly, the refusal of a Member State to register a branch of a company formed in accordance with the law of another Member State in which it has its registered office on the grounds that the branch is intended to enable the company to carry on all its economic activity in the host State, with the result that the secondary establishment escapes national rules on the provision for and the paying-up of a minimum capital, is incompatible with Articles 52 and 58 of the Treaty, in so far as it prevents any exercise of the right freely to set up a secondary establishment which Articles 52 and 58 are specifically intended to guarantee.

31. The final question to be considered is whether the national practice in question might not be justified for the reasons put forward by the Danish authorities.

32. Referring both to Article 56 of the Treaty and to the case-law of the Court on imperative requirements in the general interest, the Board argues that the requirement that private limited companies provide for and pay up a minimum share capital pursues a dual objective: first, to reinforce the financial soundness of those companies in order to protect public creditors against the risk of seeing the public debts owing to them become irrecoverable since, unlike private creditors, they cannot secure those debts by means of guarantees and, second, and more generally, to protect all creditors, whether public

or private, by anticipating the risk of fraudulent bankruptcy due to the insolvency of companies whose initial capitalisation was inadequate.

33.   The Board adds that there is no less restrictive means of attaining this dual objective. The other way of protecting creditors, namely by introducing rules making it possible for shareholders to incur personal liability, under certain conditions, would be more restrictive than the requirement to provide for and pay up a minimum share capital.

34.   It should be observed, first, that the reasons put forward do not fall within the ambit of Article 56 of the Treaty. Next, it should be borne in mind that, according to the Court's case-law, national measures liable to hinder or make less attractive the exercise of fundamental freedoms guaranteed by the Treaty must fulfil four conditions: they must be applied in a non-discriminatory manner; they must be justified by imperative requirements in the general interest; they must be suitable for securing the attainment of the objective which they pursue; and they must not go beyond what is necessary in order to attain it.

35.   Those conditions are not fulfilled in the case in the main proceedings. First, the practice in question is not such as to attain the objective of protecting creditors which it purports to pursue since, if the company concerned had conducted business in the United Kingdom, its branch would have been registered in Denmark, even though Danish creditors might have been equally exposed to risk.

36.   Since the company concerned in the main proceedings holds itself out as a company governed by the law of England and Wales and not as a company governed by Danish law, its creditors are on notice that it is covered by laws different from those which govern the formation of private limited companies in Denmark and they can refer to certain rules of Community law which protect them, such as the Fourth Council Directive 78/660/EEC of 25 July 1978 based on Article 54(3)(g) of the Treaty on the annual accounts of certain types of companies (OJ, L 222/1978, 11), and the Eleventh Council Directive 89/666/EEC of 21 December 1989 concerning disclosure requirements in respect of branches opened in a Member State by certain types of company governed by the law of another State (OJ, L 395/1989, 36).

37.   Second, contrary to the arguments of the Danish authorities, it is possible to adopt measures which are less restrictive, or which interfere less with fundamental freedoms, by, for example, making it possible in law for public creditors to obtain the necessary guarantees.

38.   Lastly, the fact that a Member State may not refuse to register a branch of a company formed in accordance with the law of another Member State in which it has its registered office does not preclude that first State from adopting any appropriate measure for preventing or penalising fraud, either in relation to the company itself, if need be in cooperation with the Member State in which it was formed, or in relation to its members, where it has been established that they are in fact attempting, by means of the formation of the company, to evade their obligations towards private or public creditors established on the territory of a Member State concerned. In any event, combating fraud cannot justify a practice of refusing to register a branch of a company which has its registered office in another Member State.

39.   The answer to the question referred must therefore be that it is contrary to Articles 52 and 58 of the Treaty for a Member State to refuse to register a branch of a company formed in accordance with the law of another Member State in which it has

its registered office but in which it conducts no business where the branch is intended to enable the company in question to carry on its entire business in the State in which that branch is to be created, while avoiding the need to form a company there, thus evading application of the rules governing the formation of companies which, in that State, are more restrictive as regards the paying up of a minimum share capital. That interpretation does not, however, prevent the authorities of the Member State concerned from adopting any appropriate measure for preventing or penalising fraud, either in relation to the company itself, if need be in cooperation with the Member State in which it was formed, or in relation to its members, where it has been established that they are in fact attempting, by means of the formation of a company, to evade their obligations towards private or public creditors established in the territory of the Member State concerned.

Another decision (*Überseering*, 5 November 2002, case C-208/00, Reports, I-9919) tackles the issue of a company's legal capacity. The questions referred to the ECJ were raised before a German judge in whose legal system, according to the settled case-law, a company's legal capacity is determined by reference to the law applicable in the place where its actual centre of administration is established (so-called 'Sitztheorie' or company seat principle), as opposed to the 'Gründungstheorie' or incorporation principle, by virtue of which legal capacity is determined in accordance with the law of the State in which the company is incorporated. That rule also applies where a company has been validly incorporated in another State and has subsequently transferred its real centre of administration to Germany. In this case the company cannot enjoy rights or be the subject of obligations or be a party to legal proceedings, unless it has been reincorporated in Germany in such a way as to acquire legal capacity under German law. In the case at stake, the company, incorporated under Dutch law, had been acquired by two German nationals, but German courts had stated that the company did not enjoy *locus standi* since it was a foreign company. The ECJ stated that the interpretation of the German courts amounted to a restriction on freedom of establishment, that was unjustified by the general interest, on the basis of the following findings:

As to whether the Treaty provisions on freedom of establishment apply

52.   *In limine* and contrary to the submissions of both NCC and the German, Spanish and Italian Governments, the Court must make clear that where a company which is validly incorporated in one Member State ('A') in which it has its registered office is deemed, under the law of a second Member State ('B'), to have moved its actual centre of administration to Member State B following the transfer of all its shares to nationals of that State residing there, the rules which Member State B applies to that company do not, as Community law now stands, fall outside the scope of the Community provisions on freedom of establishment.

56.   In that regard, it must be borne in mind that, as the Court has already had occasion to point out, the freedom of establishment, conferred by Article 43 EC on Community nationals, includes the right for them to take up and pursue activities as self-employed persons and to set up and manage undertakings under the same conditions as are laid down by the law of the Member State of establishment for its own nationals. Furthermore, according to the actual wording of Article 48 EC, companies or firms formed in accordance with the law of a Member State and having their registered office, central administration or principal place of business within the Community shall, for

the purposes of [the provisions of the Treaty concerning the right of establishment], be treated in the same way as natural persons who are nationals of Member States'.

57.   The immediate consequence of this is that those companies or firms are entitled to carry on their business in another Member State. The location of their registered office, central administration or principal place of business constitutes the connecting factor with the legal system of a particular Member State in the same way as does nationality in the case of a natural person.

59.   A necessary precondition for the exercise of the freedom of establishment is the recognition of those companies by any Member State in which they wish to establish themselves.

61.   Second, it is important to consider the argument based on the decision in *Daily Mail and General Trust*, which was central to the arguments put to the Court. It was cited in order, in some way, to assimilate the situation in *Daily Mail and General Trust* to the situation which under German law entails the loss of legal capacity and of the capacity to be a party to legal proceedings by a company incorporated under the law of another Member State.

62.   It must be stressed that, unlike *Daily Mail and General Trust*, which concerned relations between a company and the Member State under whose laws it had been incorporated in a situation where the company wished to transfer its actual centre of administration to another Member State while retaining its legal personality in the State of incorporation, the present case concerns the recognition by one Member State of a company incorporated under the law of another Member State, such a company being denied all legal capacity in the host Member State where it takes the view that the company has moved its actual centre of administration to its territory, irrespective of whether in that regard the company actually intended to transfer its seat.

63.   As the Netherlands and United Kingdom Governments and the Commission and the EFTA Surveillance Authority have pointed out, Überseering never gave any indication that it intended to transfer its seat to Germany. Its legal existence was never called in question under the law of the State where it was incorporated as a result of all its shares being transferred to persons resident in Germany. In particular, the company was not subject to any winding-up measures under Netherlands law. Under Netherlands law, it did not cease to be validly incorporated.

71.   By contrast, [in *Daily Mail and General Trust*], the Court did not rule on the question whether where, as here, a company incorporated under the law of a Member State ('A') is found, under the law of another Member State ('B'), to have moved its actual centre of administration to Member State B, that State is entitled to refuse to recognise the legal personality which the company enjoys under the law of its State of incorporation ('A').

72.   Thus, despite the general terms in which paragraph 23 of *Daily Mail and General Trust* is cast, the Court did not intend to recognise a Member State as having the power, vis-à-vis companies validly incorporated in other Member States and found by it to have transferred their seat to its territory, to subject those companies' effective exercise in its territory of the freedom of establishment to compliance with its domestic company law.

73.   There are, therefore, no grounds for concluding from *Daily Mail and General Trust* that, where a company formed in accordance with the law of one Member State and with legal personality in that State exercises its freedom of establishment in another

Member State, the question of recognition of its legal capacity and its capacity to be a party to legal proceedings in the Member State of establishment falls outside the scope of the Treaty provisions on freedom of establishment, even when the company is found, under the law of the Member State of establishment, to have moved its actual centre of administration to that State.

74.   Third, the Court rejects the Spanish Government's argument that, in a situation, such as that in point before the national court, Title I of the General Programme subordinates the benefit of the freedom of establishment guaranteed by the Treaty to the requirement that there be a real and continuous link with the economy of a Member State.

75.   It is apparent from the wording of the General Programme that it requires a real and continuous link solely in a case in which the company has nothing but its registered office within the Community. That is unquestionably not the position in the case of *Überseering* whose registered office and actual centre of administration are within the Community. As regards the situation just described, the Court found, at paragraph 19 of *Centros*, that under Article 58 of the Treaty companies formed in accordance with the law of a Member State and having their registered office, central administration or principal place of business within the Community are to be treated in the same way as natural persons who are nationals of Member States.

76.   It follows from the foregoing considerations that Überseering is entitled to rely on the principle of freedom of establishment in order to contest the refusal of German law to regard it as a legal person with the capacity to be a party to legal proceedings.

77.   Furthermore, it must be borne in mind that as a general rule the acquisition by one or more natural persons residing in a Member State of shares in a company incorporated and established in another Member State is covered by the Treaty provisions on the free movement of capital, provided that the shareholding does not confer on those natural persons definite influence over the company's decisions and does not allow them to determine its activities. By contrast, where the acquisition involves all the shares in a company having its registered office in another Member State and the shareholding confers a definite influence over the company's decisions and allows the shareholders to determine its activities, it is the Treaty provisions on freedom of establishment which apply.

As to whether there is a restriction on freedom of establishment

78.   The Court must next consider whether the refusal by the German courts to recognise the legal capacity and capacity to be a party to legal proceedings of a company validly incorporated under the law of another Member State constitutes a restriction on freedom of establishment.

79. In that regard, in a situation such as that in point in the main proceedings, a company validly incorporated under the law of, and having its registered office in, a Member State other than the Federal Republic of Germany has under German law no alternative to reincorporation in Germany if it wishes to enforce before a German court its rights under a contract entered into with a company incorporated under German law.

80. Überseering, which is validly incorporated in the Netherlands and has its registered office there, is entitled under Articles 43 EC and 48 EC to exercise its freedom of establishment in Germany as a company incorporated under Netherlands law. It is of

little significance in that regard that, after the company was formed, all its shares were acquired by German nationals residing in Germany, since that has not caused Überseering to cease to be a legal person under Netherlands law.

81.   Indeed, its very existence is inseparable from its *status* as a company incorporated under Netherlands law since, as the Court has observed, a company exists only by virtue of the national legislation which determines its incorporation and functioning. The requirement of reincorporation of the same company in Germany is therefore tantamount to outright negation of freedom of establishment.

82.   In those circumstances, the refusal by a host Member State ('B') to recognise the legal capacity of a company formed in accordance with the law of another Member State ('A') in which it has its registered office on the ground, in particular, that the company moved its actual centre of administration to Member State B following the acquisition of all its shares by nationals of that State residing there, with the result that the company cannot, in Member State B, bring legal proceedings to defend rights under a contract unless it is reincorporated under the law of Member State B, constitutes a restriction on freedom of establishment which is, in principle, incompatible with Articles 43 EC and 48 EC.

As to whether the restriction on freedom of establishment is justified

83.   Finally, it is appropriate to determine whether such a restriction on freedom of establishment can be justified on the grounds advanced by the national court and by the German Government.

92.   It is not inconceivable that overriding requirements relating to the general interest, such as the protection of the interests of creditors, minority shareholders, employees and even the taxation authorities, may, in certain circumstances and subject to certain conditions, justify restrictions on freedom of establishment.

93.   Such objectives cannot, however, justify denying the legal capacity and, consequently, the capacity to be a party to legal proceedings of a company properly incorporated in another Member State in which it has its registered office. Such a measure is tantamount to an outright negation of the freedom of establishment conferred on companies by Articles 43 EC and 48 EC.

94.   Accordingly, the answer to the first question must be that, where a company formed in accordance with the law of a Member State ('A') in which it has its registered office is deemed, under the law of another Member State ('B'), to have moved its actual centre of administration to Member State B, Articles 43 EC and 48 EC preclude Member State B from denying the company legal capacity and, consequently, the capacity to bring legal proceedings before its national courts for the purpose of enforcing rights under a contract with a company established in Member State B.

The second question referred to the Court

95.   It follows from the answer to the first question referred to the Court for a preliminary ruling that, where a company formed in accordance with the law of a Member State ('A') in which it has its registered office exercises its freedom of establishment in another Member State ('B'), Articles 43 EC and 48 EC require Member State B to recognise the legal capacity and, consequently, the capacity to be a party to legal proceedings which the company enjoys under the law of its State of incorporation ('A').

Recently, the ECJ has ruled once again on a case of a company incorporated in a Member State with the sole purpose of establishing in another Member State where its main, or indeed its entire business, is to be carried out (30 September 2003, case C-167/01, *Inspire Art*, Reports, I-10155). In fact, Inspire Art was a company incorporated by a Dutch national under England law, though it was active exclusively in the Netherlands through a branch established therein and had no plans to carry out any activities in England. According to Dutch law on formally foreign companies (WFBV), a company incorporated under a foreign law law and having legal personality, that carries out its activities entirely or almost entirely in the Netherlands and has no real link with the State of incorporation, must be registered in the Dutch commercial register, after complying with various administrative obligations related to the minimum share capital and the company's director liability. The ECJ, that had been requested to decide upon the compatibility of said Dutch provisions of law with the Community provisions on freedom of establishment, rules as follows:

95.   The Court has held that it is immaterial, having regard to the application of the rules on freedom of establishment, that the company was formed in one Member State only for the purpose of establishing itself in a second Member State, where its main, or indeed entire, business is to be conducted (*Segers*, paragraph 16, and *Centros*, paragraph 17). The reasons for which a company chooses to be formed in a particular Member State are, save in the case of fraud, irrelevant with regard to application of the rules on freedom of establishment (*Centros*, paragraph 18).

96.   The Court has also held that the fact that the company was formed in a particular Member State for the sole purpose of enjoying the benefit of more favourable legislation does not constitute abuse even if that company conducts its activities entirely or mainly in that second State (*Segers*, paragraph 16, and *Centros*, paragraph 18).

97.   It follows that those companies are entitled to carry on their business in another Member State through a branch, and that the location of their registered office, central administration or principal place of business serves as the connecting factor with the legal system of a particular Member State in the same way as does nationality in the case of a natural person (*Centros*, paragraph 20).

98.   Thus, in the main proceedings, the fact that Inspire Art was formed in the United Kingdom for the purpose of circumventing Netherlands company law which lays down stricter rules with regard in particular to minimum capital and the paying-up of shares does not mean that that company's establishment of a branch in the Netherlands is not covered by freedom of establishment as provided for by Articles 43 EC and 48 EC. As the Court held in *Centros* (paragraph 18), the question of the application of those articles is different from the question whether or not a Member State may adopt measures in order to prevent attempts by certain of its nationals improperly to evade domestic legislation by having recourse to the possibilities offered by the Treaty.

99.   The argument that freedom of establishment is not in any way infringed by the WFBV in as much as foreign companies are fully recognised in the Netherlands and are not refused registration in that Member State's business register, that law having the effect simply of laying down a number of additional obligations classified as administrative, cannot be accepted.

100.   The effect of the WFBV is, in fact, that the Netherlands company-law rules on minimum capital and directors' liability are applied mandatorily to foreign companies such as Inspire Art when they carry on their activities exclusively, or almost exclusively, in the Netherlands.

101. Creation of a branch in the Netherlands by companies of that kind is therefore subject to certain rules provided for by that State in respect of the formation of a limited-liability company. The legislation at issue in the case in the main proceedings, which requires the branch of such a company formed in accordance with the legislation of a Member State to comply with the rules of the State of establishment on share capital and directors' liability, has the effect of impeding the exercise by those companies of the freedom of establishment conferred by the Treaty.

102. The last issue for consideration concerns the arguments based on the judgment in *Daily Mail and General Trust*, namely, that the Member States remain free to determine the law applicable to a company since the rules relating to freedom of establishment have not led to harmonisation of the provisions of the private international law of the Member States. In this respect it is argued that the Member States retain the right to take action against brass-plate companies, that classification being in the circumstances of the case inferred from the lack of any real connection with the State of formation.

103. It must be stressed that, unlike the case at issue in the main proceedings, *Daily Mail and General Trust* concerned relations between a company and the Member State under the laws of which it had been incorporated in a situation where the company wished to transfer its actual centre of administration to another Member State while retaining its legal personality in the State of incorporation. In the main proceedings the national court has asked the Court of Justice whether the legislation of the State where a company actually carries on its activities applies to that company when it was formed under the law of another Member State (*Überseering*, paragraph 62).

104. It follows from the foregoing that the provisions of the WFBV relating to minimum capital (both at the time of formation and during the life of the company) and to directors' liability constitute restrictions on freedom of establishment as guaranteed by Articles 43 EC and 48 EC.

105. It must therefore be concluded that Articles 43 EC and 48 EC preclude national legislation such as the WFBV which imposes on the exercise of freedom of secondary establishment in that State by a company formed in accordance with the law of another Member State certain conditions provided for in domestic law in respect of company formation relating to minimum capital and directors' liability. The reasons for which the company was formed in that other Member State, and the fact that it carries on its activities exclusively or almost exclusively in the Member State of establishment, do not deprive it of the right to invoke the freedom of establishment guaranteed by the Treaty, save where abuse is established on a case-by-case basis.

Whether there is any justification

107. Given that those rules constitute an impediment to freedom of establishment, it must be considered whether they can be justified on one of the grounds set out in Article 46 EC or, failing that, by an overriding reason relating to the public interest.

131. It must first of all be stated that none of the arguments put forward by the Netherlands Government with a view to justifying the legislation at issue in the main proceedings falls within the ambit of Article 46 EC.

132. The justifications put forward by the Netherlands Government, namely, the aims of protecting creditors, combating improper recourse to freedom of establishment,

and protecting both effective tax inspections and fairness in business dealings, fall therefore to be evaluated by reference to overriding reasons related to the public interest.

133. It must be borne in mind that, according to the Court's case-law, national measures liable to hinder or make less attractive the exercise of fundamental freedoms guaranteed by the Treaty must, if they are to be justified, fulfil four conditions: they must be applied in a non-discriminatory manner; they must be justified by imperative requirements in the public interest; they must be suitable for securing the attainment of the objective which they pursue, and they must not go beyond what is necessary in order to attain it (*Centros*, paragraph 34).

134. In consequence, it is necessary to consider whether those conditions are fulfilled by provisions relating to minimum capital such as those at issue in the main proceedings.

135. First, with regard to protection of creditors, and there being no need for the Court to consider whether the rules on minimum share capital constitute in themselves an appropriate protection measure, it is clear that Inspire Art holds itself out as a company governed by the law of England and Wales and not as a Netherlands company. Its potential creditors are put on sufficient notice that it is covered by legislation other than that regulating the formation in the Netherlands of limited liability companies and, in particular, laying down rules in respect of minimum capital and directors' liability. They can also refer, as the Court pointed out in *Centros*, paragraph 36, to certain rules of Community law which protect them, such as the Fourth and Eleventh Directives.

136. Second, with regard to combating improper recourse to freedom of establishment, it must be borne in mind that a Member State is entitled to take measures designed to prevent certain of its nationals from attempting, under cover of the rights created by the Treaty, improperly to circumvent their national legislation or to prevent individuals from improperly or fraudulently taking advantage of provisions of Community law (*Centros*, paragraph 24, and the decisions cited therein).

137. However, while in this case Inspire Art was formed under the company law of a Member State, in the case in point the United Kingdom, for the purpose in particular of evading the application of Netherlands company law, which was considered to be more severe, the fact remains that the provisions of the Treaty on freedom of establishment are intended specifically to enable companies formed in accordance with the law of a Member State and having their registered office, central administration or principal place of business within the Community to pursue activities in other Member States through an agency, branch or subsidiary (*Centros*, paragraph 26).

138. That being so, as the Court confirmed in paragraph 27 of *Centros*, the fact that a national of a Member State who wishes to set up a company can choose to do so in the Member State the company-law rules of which seem to him the least restrictive and then set up branches in other Member States is inherent in the exercise, in a single market, of the freedom of establishment guaranteed by the Treaty.

139. In addition, it is clear from settled case-law (*Segers*, paragraph 16, and *Centros*, paragraph 29) that the fact that a company does not conduct any business in the Member State in which it has its registered office and pursues its activities only or principally in the Member State where its branch is established is not sufficient to prove the existence of abuse or fraudulent conduct which would entitle the latter Member State to deny that company the benefit of the provisions of Community law relating to the right of establishment.

142. The answer to be given to the second question referred by the national court must therefore be that the impediment to the freedom of establishment guaranteed by the Treaty constituted by provisions of national law, such as those at issue, relating to minimum capital and the personal joint and several liability of directors cannot be justified under Article 46 EC, or on grounds of protecting creditors, or combating improper recourse to freedom of establishment or safeguarding fairness in business dealings or the efficiency of tax inspections.

The notion of abuse of freedom of establishment, already addressed in *Segers*, *Centros* and *Inspire Art* judgments, has been further clarified by the ECJ in *Cadbury Schweppes* case (12 September 2006, case C-196/04, Reports, I-7995), where the parent company, Cadbury Schweppes, resident in the United Kingdom, had incorporated two subsidiaries in Dublin in order to benefit from the more favourable Irish tax regime. The ECJ had been asked to to ascertain whether the fact that a company formed in a Member State establishes and capitalises companies in another Member State, solely because of the more favourable tax regime applicable in that Member State, constitutes an abuse of freedom of establishment, and stated:

35.   It is true that nationals of a Member State cannot attempt, under cover of the rights created by the Treaty, improperly to circumvent their national legislation. They must not improperly or fraudulently take advantage of provisions of Community law (*Centros*, paragraph 24).

36.   However, the fact that a Community national, whether a natural or a legal person, sought to profit from tax advantages in force in a Member State other than his State of residence cannot in itself deprive him of the right to rely on the provisions of the Treaty.

37.   As to freedom of establishment, the Court has already held that the fact that the company was established in a Member State for the purpose of benefiting from more favourable legislation does not in itself suffice to constitute abuse of that freedom (see, to that effect, *Centros*, paragraph 27, and *Inspire Art*, paragraph 96).

38.   As noted by the applicants in the main proceedings and the Belgian Government, and by the Cypriot Government at the hearing, it follows that the fact that in this case CS decided to establish CSTS and CSTI in the IFSC for the avowed purpose of benefiting from the favourable tax regime which that establishment enjoys does not in itself constitute abuse. That fact does not therefore preclude reliance by CS on Articles 43 EC and 48 EC (see, to that effect, *Centros*, paragraph 18, and *Inspire Art*, paragraph 98).

50.   It is also apparent from case-law that the mere fact that a resident company establishes a secondary establishment, such as a subsidiary, in another Member State cannot set up a general presumption of tax evasion and justify a measure which compromises the exercise of a fundamental freedom guaranteed by the Treaty.

51.   On the other hand, a national measure restricting freedom of establishment may be justified where it specifically relates to wholly artificial arrangements aimed at circumventing the application of the legislation of the Member State concerned.

52.   It is necessary, in assessing the conduct of the taxable person, to take particular account of the objective pursued by the freedom of establishment (see, to that effect, *Centros*, paragraph 25).

53.   That objective is to allow a national of a Member State to set up a secondary establishment in another Member State to carry on his activities there and thus assist economic and social interpenetration within the Community in the sphere of activities

as self-employed persons. To that end, freedom of establishment is intended to allow a Community national to participate, on a stable and continuing basis, in the economic life of a Member State other than his State of origin and to profit therefrom.

54.   Having regard to that objective of integration in the host Member State, the concept of establishment within the meaning of the Treaty provisions on freedom of establishment involves the actual pursuit of an economic activity through a fixed establishment in that State for an indefinite period. Consequently, it presupposes actual establishment of the company concerned in the host Member State and the pursuit of genuine economic activity there.

55.   It follows that, in order for a restriction on the freedom of establishment to be justified on the ground of prevention of abusive practices, the specific objective of such a restriction must be to prevent conduct involving the creation of wholly artificial arrangements which do not reflect economic reality, with a view to escaping the tax normally due on the profits generated by activities carried out on national territory.

More recently, on the notion of the abuse of freedom of establishment, in *Lammers & Van Cleef* case (17 January 2008, case C-105/07, Reports, I-173), the ECJ has ruled as follows:

26.   In this respect, it must be pointed out that, according to established case-law, a national measure restricting freedom of establishment may be justified where it specifically targets wholly artificial arrangements designed to circumvent the legislation of the Member State concerned.

27.   The mere fact that a resident company is granted a loan by a related company which is established in another Member State cannot be the basis of a general presumption of abusive practices and justify a measure which compromises the exercise of a fundamental freedom guaranteed by the Treaty.

28.   In order for a restriction on the freedom of establishment to be justified on the ground of prevention of abusive practices, the specific objective of such a restriction must be to prevent conduct involving the creation of wholly artificial arrangements which do not reflect economic reality, with a view to escaping the tax normally due on the profits generated by activities carried out on national territory.

Nationality and law applicable to companies

A.   ECJ case-law

As far as concerns the issue of the nationality of legal entities, in *Centros* (9 March 1999, case C-212/97, *Centros*, Reports, I-5459), the ECJ, referring to its previous settled case-law, pointed out that

20.   The immediate consequence of this is that those companies are entitled to carry on their business in another Member State through an agency, branch or subsidiary. The location of their registered office, central administration or principal place of business serves as the connecting factor with the legal system of a particular State in the same way as does nationality in the case of a natural person (see, to that effect, *Segers* [10 July 1986, case 79/85, Reports, 2375] paragraph 13).

As to the issue of the law applicable to companies, with reference to the conditions for the establishment of legal personality and capacity to bring claims of a company incorporated under Italian law and having its registered office in Italy, the ECJ in *Bensider and others* (27 November 1984, case 50/84, Reports, 3991) ruled that

7.   Under the second paragraph of article 33 of the ECSC Treaty undertakings may institute proceedings for a declaration that general decisions which they consider to involve a misuse of powers affecting them are void. If the undertaking is a company in formation, that company must, in order to institute proceedings, have acquired legal personality, and that fact must necessarily be established in accordance with national law.

More recently, the ECJ addressed the issue of the legal personality and capacity to be a party to legal proceedings of a company incorporated under German law and with registered office in that Member State (11 October 2001, case C-77/99, *Oder-Plan Architektur and others*, Reports, I-7355) and it stated that

28.   According to the law of the country where it has its registered office, namely German law, Oder-Plan has legal capacity and can be a party to legal proceedings pursuant to Paragraph 13 of the *Gesetz betreffend Gesellschaften mit beschrankter Haftung* (Law on limited liability companies, hereinafter GmbHG).

In the *AMI* case (17 March 2005, case C-294/02, Reports, I-2175), concerning again a company incorporated in Germany and with registered office in that same State, the ECJ explained that

60.   ... an action against a company is inadmissible if, when the action is brought, that company had neither legal capacity nor standing to be a party to legal proceedings. The applicable law in that connection is that governing the incorporation of the company in question, which in this case is German law (see *Daily Mail and General Trust*, paragraph 19, and *Überseering*, paragraph 81).

Finally, in *Cartesio* (16 December 2008, case C-210/06, Reports, I-9641 below, in this Chapter, Cross-border transfer of seat, E), the ECJ pointed out that the choice of the connecting factor for purposes of determining the law applicable to a company falls within the sphere of national legislature.

Cross-border mergers

A.   Directive 2005/56/EC of the European Parliament and of the Council of 26 October 2005 on cross-border mergers of limited liability companies (OJ, L 310 of 25 November 2005)[1]

(1)   There is a need for cooperation and consolidation between limited liability companies from different Member States. However, as regards cross-border mergers of limited liability companies, they encounter many legislative and administrative difficulties

---

[1]   As amended by Directive 2009/109/EC of 16 September 2009 (OJ, L 259 of 2 December 2009). [Note of the Editor]

in the Community. It is therefore necessary, with a view to the completion and functioning of the single market, to lay down Community provisions to facilitate the carrying-out of cross-border mergers between various types of limited liability company governed by the laws of different Member States.

(2)   This Directive facilitates the cross-border merger of limited liability companies as defined herein. The laws of the Member States are to allow the cross-border merger of a national limited liability company with a limited liability company from another Member State if the national law of the relevant Member States permits mergers between such types of company.

(3)   In order to facilitate cross-border merger operations, it should be laid down that, unless this Directive provides otherwise, each company taking part in a cross-border merger, and each third party concerned, remains subject to the provisions and formalities of the national law which would be applicable in the case of a national merger. None of the provisions and formalities of national law, to which reference is made in this Directive, should introduce restrictions on freedom of establishment or on the free movement of capital save where these can be justified in accordance with the case-law of the Court of Justice and in particular by requirements of the general interest and are both necessary for, and proportionate to, the attainment of such overriding requirements.

(4)   The common draft terms of the cross-border merger are to be drawn up in the same terms for each of the companies concerned in the various Member States. The minimum content of such common draft terms should therefore be specified, while leaving the companies free to agree on other items.

(5)   In order to protect the interests of members and others, both the common draft terms of cross-border mergers and the completion of the cross-border merger are to be publicised for each merging company via an entry in the appropriate public register.

(6)   The laws of all the Member States should provide for the drawing-up at national level of a report on the common draft terms of the cross-border merger by one or more experts on behalf of each of the companies that are merging. In order to limit experts' costs connected with cross-border mergers, provision should be made for the possibility of drawing up a single report intended for all members of companies taking part in a cross-border merger operation. The common draft terms of the cross-border merger are to be approved by the general meeting of each of those companies.

(7)   In order to facilitate cross-border merger operations, it should be provided that monitoring of the completion and legality of the decision-making process in each merging company should be carried out by the national authority having jurisdiction over each of those companies, whereas monitoring of the completion and legality of the cross-border merger should be carried out by the national authority having jurisdiction over the company resulting from the cross-border merger. The national authority in question may be a court, a notary or any other competent authority appointed by the Member State concerned. The national law determining the date on which the cross-border merger takes effect, this being the law to which the company resulting from the cross-border merger is subject, should also be specified.

(8)   In order to protect the interests of members and others, the legal effects of the cross-border merger, distinguishing as to whether the company resulting from the cross-border merger is an acquiring company or a new company, should be specified. In the interests of legal certainty, it should no longer be possible, after the date on which a cross-border merger takes effect, to declare the merger null and void.

(9)   This Directive is without prejudice to the application of the legislation on the control of concentrations between undertakings, both at Community level, by Regulation (EC) No 139/2004, and at the level of Member States.

(10) This Directive does not affect Community legislation regulating credit intermediaries and other financial undertakings and national rules made or introduced pursuant to such Community legislation.

(11) This Directive is without prejudice to a Member State's legislation demanding information on the place of central administration or the principal place of business proposed for the company resulting from the cross-border merger.

(12) Employees' rights other than rights of participation should remain subject to the national provisions referred to in Council Directive 98/59/EC of 20 July 1998 on collective redundancies, Council Directive 2001/23/EC of 12 March 2001 on the safeguarding of employees' rights in the event of transfers of undertakings, businesses or parts of undertakings or businesses, Directive 2002/14/EC of the European Parliament and of the Council of 11 March 2002 establishing a general framework for informing and consulting employees in the European Community and Council Directive 94/45/EC of 22 September 1994 on the establishment of a European Works Council or a procedure in Community-scale undertakings and Community-scale groups of undertakings for the purposes of informing and consulting employees.

(13) If employees have participation rights in one of the merging companies under the circumstances set out in this Directive and, if the national law of the Member State in which the company resulting from the cross-border merger has its registered office does not provide for the same level of participation as operated in the relevant merging companies, including in committees of the supervisory board that have decision-making powers, or does not provide for the same entitlement to exercise rights for employees of establishments resulting from the cross-border merger, the participation of employees in the company resulting from the cross-border merger and their involvement in the definition of such rights are to be regulated. To that end, the principles and procedures provided for in Council Regulation (EC) No 2157/2001 of 8 October 2001 on the Statute for a European company (SE) and in Council Directive 2001/86/EC of 8 October 2001 supplementing the Statute for a European company with regard to the involvement of employees, are to be taken as a basis, subject, however, to modifications that are deemed necessary because the resulting company will be subject to the national laws of the Member State where it has its registered office. A prompt start to negotiations under Article 16 of this Directive, with a view to not unnecessarily delaying mergers, may be ensured by Member States in accordance with Article 3(2)(b) of Directive 2001/86/EC.

(14) For the purpose of determining the level of employee participation operated in the relevant merging companies, account should also be taken of the proportion of employee representatives amongst the members of the management group, which covers the profit units of the companies, subject to employee participation.

(15) Since the objective of the proposed action, namely laying down rules with common features applicable at transnational level, cannot be sufficiently achieved by the Member States and can therefore, by reason of the scale and impact of the proposed action, be better achieved at Community level, the Community may adopt measures in accordance with the principle of subsidiarity as set out in Article 5 of the Treaty. In accordance with the principle of proportionality as set out in that Article, this Directive does not go beyond what is necessary to achieve that objective.

(16) In accordance with paragraph 34 of the Interinstitutional Agreement on better law-making, Member States should be encouraged to draw up, for themselves and in the interest of the Community, their own tables which will, as far as possible, illustrate the correlation between this Directive and the transposition measures and to make them public, ...

Article 1. Scope. This Directive shall apply to mergers of limited liability companies formed in accordance with the law of a Member State and having their registered office, central administration or principal place of business within the Community, provided at least two of them are governed by the laws of different Member States (hereinafter referred to as cross-border mergers).

Article 2. Definitions. For the purposes of this Directive:
(1) 'limited liability company', hereinafter referred to as 'company', means:
(a) a company as referred to in Article 1 of Directive 68/151/EEC, or
(b) a company with share capital and having legal personality, possessing separate assets which alone serve to cover its debts and subject under the national law governing it to conditions concerning guarantees such as are provided for by Directive 68/151/EEC for the protection of the interests of members and others;
(2) 'merger' means an operation whereby:
(a) one or more companies, on being dissolved without going into liquidation, transfer all their assets and liabilities to another existing company, the acquiring company, in exchange for the issue to their members of securities or shares representing the capital of that other company and, if applicable, a cash payment not exceeding 10 % of the nominal value, or, in the absence of a nominal value, of the accounting par value of those securities or shares; or
(b) two or more companies, on being dissolved without going into liquidation, transfer all their assets and liabilities to a company that they form, the new company, in exchange for the issue to their members of securities or shares representing the capital of that new company and, if applicable, a cash payment not exceeding 10 % of the nominal value, or in the absence of a nominal value, of the accounting par value of those securities or shares; or
(c) a company, on being dissolved without going into liquidation, transfers all its assets and liabilities to the company holding all the securities or shares representing its capital.

Article 3. Further provisions concerning the scope. 1. Notwithstanding Article 2(2), this Directive shall also apply to cross-border mergers where the law of at least one of the Member States concerned allows the cash payment referred to in points (a) and (b) of Article 2(2) to exceed 10 % of the nominal value, or, in the absence of a nominal value, of the accounting par value of the securities or shares representing the capital of the company resulting from the cross-border merger.
2. Member States may decide not to apply this Directive to cross-border mergers involving a cooperative society even in the cases where the latter would fall within the definition of 'limited liability company' as laid down in Article 2(1).
3. This Directive shall not apply to cross-border mergers involving a company the object of which is the collective investment of capital provided by the public, which

operates on the principle of risk-spreading and the units of which are, at the holders' request, repurchased or redeemed, directly or indirectly, out of the assets of that company. Action taken by such a company to ensure that the stock exchange value of its units does not vary significantly from its net asset value shall be regarded as equivalent to such repurchase or redemption.

Article 4. Conditions relating to cross-border mergers.   1.   Save as otherwise provided in this Directive,

(a)   cross-border mergers shall only be possible between types of companies which may merge under the national law of the relevant Member States, and

(b)   a company taking part in a cross-border merger shall comply with the provisions and formalities of the national law to which it is subject. The laws of a Member State enabling its national authorities to oppose a given internal merger on grounds of public interest shall also be applicable to a cross-border merger where at least one of the merging companies is subject to the law of that Member State. This provision shall not apply to the extent that Article 21 of Regulation (EC) No 139/2004 is applicable.

2.   The provisions and formalities referred to in paragraph 1(b) shall, in particular, include those concerning the decision-making process relating to the merger and, taking into account the cross-border nature of the merger, the protection of creditors of the merging companies, debenture holders and the holders of securities or shares, as well as of employees as regards rights other than those governed by Article 16. A Member State may, in the case of companies participating in a cross-border merger and governed by its law, adopt provisions designed to ensure appropriate protection for minority members who have opposed the cross-border merger.

Article 5. Common draft terms of cross-border mergers.   The management or administrative organ of each of the merging companies shall draw up the common draft terms of cross-border merger. The common draft terms of cross-border merger shall include at least the following particulars:

(a)   the form, name and registered office of the merging companies and those proposed for the company resulting from the cross-border merger;

(b)   the ratio applicable to the exchange of securities or shares representing the company capital and the amount of any cash payment;

(c)   the terms for the allotment of securities or shares representing the capital of the company resulting from the cross-border merger;

(d)   the likely repercussions of the cross-border merger on employment;

(e)   the date from which the holding of such securities or shares representing the company capital will entitle the holders to share in profits and any special conditions affecting that entitlement;

(f)   the date from which the transactions of the merging companies will be treated for accounting purposes as being those of the company resulting from the cross-border merger;

(g)   the rights conferred by the company resulting from the cross-border merger on members enjoying special rights or on holders of securities other than shares representing the company capital, or the measures proposed concerning them;

(h)   any special advantages granted to the experts who examine the draft terms of the cross-border merger or to members of the administrative, management, supervisory or controlling organs of the merging companies;

(i)   the statutes of the company resulting from the cross-border merger;

(j)   where appropriate, information on the procedures by which arrangements for the involvement of employees in the definition of their rights to participation in the company resulting from the cross-border merger are determined pursuant to Article 16;

(k)   information on the evaluation of the assets and liabilities which are transferred to the company resulting from the cross-border merger;

(l)   dates of the merging companies' accounts used to establish the conditions of the cross-border merger.

Article 6. Publication.   1.   The common draft terms of the cross-border merger shall be published in the manner prescribed by the laws of each Member State in accordance with Article 3 of Directive 68/151/EEC for each of the merging companies at least one month before the date of the general meeting which is to decide thereon.

2.   For each of the merging companies and subject to the additional requirements imposed by the Member State to which the company concerned is subject, the following particulars shall be published in the national gazette of that Member State:

(a)   the type, name and registered office of every merging company;

(b)   the register in which the documents referred to in Article 3(2) of Directive 68/151/EEC are filed in respect of each merging company, and the number of the entry in that register;

(c)   an indication, for each of the merging companies, of the arrangements made for the exercise of the rights of creditors and of any minority members of the merging companies and the address at which complete information on those arrangements may be obtained free of charge.

Article 7. Report of the management or administrative organ.   The management or administrative organ of each of the merging companies shall draw up a report intended for the members explaining and justifying the legal and economic aspects of the cross-border merger and explaining the implications of the cross-border merger for members, creditors and employees.

The report shall be made available to the members and to the representatives of the employees or, where there are no such representatives, to the employees themselves, not less than one month before the date of the general meeting referred to in Article 9.

Where the management or administrative organ of any of the merging companies receives, in good time, an opinion from the representatives of their employees, as provided for under national law, that opinion shall be appended to the report.

Article 8. Independent expert report.   1.   An independent expert report intended for members and made available not less than one month before the date of the general meeting referred to in Article 9 shall be drawn up for each merging company. Depending on the law of each Member State, such experts may be natural persons or legal persons.

2.   As an alternative to experts operating on behalf of each of the merging companies, one or more independent experts, appointed for that purpose at the joint request of the companies by a judicial or administrative authority in the Member State of

one of the merging companies or of the company resulting from the cross-border merger or approved by such an authority, may examine the common draft terms of cross-border merger and draw up a single written report to all the members.

3.   The expert report shall include at least the particulars provided for by Article 10(2) of Council Directive 78/855/EEC of 9 October 1978 concerning mergers of public limited liability companies. The experts shall be entitled to secure from each of the merging companies all information they consider necessary for the discharge of their duties.

4.   Neither an examination of the common draft terms of cross-border merger by independent experts nor an expert report shall be required if all the members of each of the companies involved in the cross-border merger have so agreed.

Article 9. Approval by the general meeting.   1.   After taking note of the reports referred to in Articles 7 and 8, the general meeting of each of the merging companies shall decide on the approval of the common draft terms of cross-border merger.

2.   The general meeting of each of the merging companies may reserve the right to make implementation of the cross-border merger conditional on express ratification by it of the arrangements decided on with respect to the participation of employees in the company resulting from the cross-border merger.

3.   The laws of a Member State need not require approval of the merger by the general meeting of the acquiring company if the conditions laid down in Article 8 of Directive 78/855/EEC are fulfilled.

Article 10. Pre-merger certificate.   1.   Each Member State shall designate the court, notary or other authority competent to scrutinise the legality of the cross-border merger as regards that part of the procedure which concerns each merging company subject to its national law.

2.   In each Member State concerned the authority referred to in paragraph 1 shall issue, without delay to each merging company subject to that State's national law, a certificate conclusively attesting to the proper completion of the pre-merger acts and formalities.

3.   If the law of a Member State to which a merging company is subject provides for a procedure to scrutinise and amend the ratio applicable to the exchange of securities or shares, or a procedure to compensate minority members, without preventing the registration of the cross-border merger, such procedure shall only apply if the other merging companies situated in Member States which do not provide for such procedure explicitly accept, when approving the draft terms of the cross-border merger in accordance with Article 9(1), the possibility for the members of that merging company to have recourse to such procedure, to be initiated before the court having jurisdiction over that merging company. In such cases, the authority referred to in paragraph 1 may issue the certificate referred to in paragraph 2 even if such procedure has commenced. The certificate must, however, indicate that the procedure is pending. The decision in the procedure shall be binding on the company resulting from the cross-border merger and all its members.

Article 11. Scrutiny of the legality of the cross-border merger.   1.   Each Member State shall designate the court, notary or other authority competent to scrutinise the legality of the cross-border merger as regards that part of the procedure which concerns the completion of the cross-border merger and, where appropriate, the formation of a new company resulting from the cross-border merger where the company created by the cross-border merger is subject to its national law. The said authority shall in particular ensure that the merging companies have approved the common draft terms of cross-border merger in the same terms and, where appropriate, that arrangements for employee participation have been determined in accordance with Article 16.

2. To that end each merging company shall submit to the authority referred to in paragraph 1 the certificate referred to in Article 10(2) within six months of its issue together with the common draft terms of cross-border merger approved by the general meeting referred to in Article 9.

Article 12. Entry into effect of the cross-border merger. The law of the Member State to whose jurisdiction the company resulting from the cross-border merger is subject shall determine the date on which the cross-border merger takes effect. That date must be after the scrutiny referred to in Article 11 has been carried out.

Article 13. Registration. The law of each of the Member States to whose jurisdiction the merging companies were subject shall determine, with respect to the territory of that State, the arrangements, in accordance with Article 3 of Directive 68/151/EEC, for publicising completion of the cross-border merger in the public register in which each of the companies is required to file documents.

The registry for the registration of the company resulting from the cross-border merger shall notify, without delay, the registry in which each of the companies was required to file documents that the cross-border merger has taken effect. Deletion of the old registration, if applicable, shall be effected on receipt of that notification, but not before.

Article 14. Consequences of the cross-border merger. 1. A cross-border merger carried out as laid down in points (a) and (c) of Article 2(2) shall, from the date referred to in Article 12, have the following consequences:

(a) all the assets and liabilities of the company being acquired shall be transferred to the acquiring company;

(b) the members of the company being acquired shall become members of the acquiring company;

(c) the company being acquired shall cease to exist.

2. A cross-border merger carried out as laid down in point (b) of Article 2(2) shall, from the date referred to in Article 12, have the following consequences:

(a) all the assets and liabilities of the merging companies shall be transferred to the new company;

(b) the members of the merging companies shall become members of the new company;

(c) the merging companies shall cease to exist.

3. Where, in the case of a cross-border merger of companies covered by this Directive, the laws of the Member States require the completion of special formalities before the transfer of certain assets, rights and obligations by the merging companies

becomes effective against third parties, those formalities shall be carried out by the company resulting from the cross-border merger.

4.   The rights and obligations of the merging companies arising from contracts of employment or from employment relationships and existing at the date on which the cross-border merger takes effect shall, by reason of that cross-border merger taking effect, be transferred to the company resulting from the cross-border merger on the date on which the cross-border merger takes effect.

5.   No shares in the acquiring company shall be exchanged for shares in the company being acquired held either:

(a)   by the acquiring company itself or through a person acting in his or her own name but on its behalf;

(b)   by the company being acquired itself or through a person acting in his or her own name but on its behalf.

Article 15. Simplified formalities.   1.   Where a cross-border merger by acquisition is carried out by a company which holds all the shares and other securities conferring the right to vote at general meetings of the company or companies being acquired:

—   Articles 5, points (b), (c) and (e), 8 and 14(1), point (b) shall not apply,
—   Article 9(1) shall not apply to the company or companies being acquired.

2.   Where a cross-border merger by acquisition is carried out by a company which holds 90 % or more, but not all, of the shares and other securities conferring the right to vote at general meetings of the company or companies being acquired, reports by an independent expert or experts and the documents necessary for scrutiny shall be required only to the extent that the national law governing either the acquiring company or the company or companies being acquired so requires, in accordance with Directive 78/855/EEC.

Article 16. Employee participation.   1.   Without prejudice to paragraph 2, the company resulting from the cross-border merger shall be subject to the rules in force concerning employee participation, if any, in the Member State where it has its registered office.

Any of the merging companies shall be exempt from the publication requirement laid down in Article 3 of Directive 68/151/EEC if, for a continuous period beginning at least one month before the day fixed for the general meeting which is to decide on the common draft terms of cross-border merger and ending not earlier than the conclusion of that meeting, it makes the common draft terms of such merger available on its website free of charge for the public. Member States shall not subject that exemption to any requirements or constraints other than those which are necessary in order to ensure the security of the website and the authenticity of the documents and may impose such requirements or constraints only to the extent that they are proportionate in order to achieve those objectives.

By way of derogation from the second subparagraph, Member States may require that publication be effected via the central electronic platform referred to in Article 3(4) of Directive 68/151/EEC. Member States may alternatively require that such publication be made on any other website designated by them for that purpose. Where Member States avail themselves of one of those possibilities, they shall ensure that companies are not charged a specific fee for such publication.

Where a website other than the central electronic platform is used, a reference giving access to that website shall be published on the central electronic platform at least one month before the day fixed for the general meeting. That reference shall include the date of publication of the common draft terms of cross-border merger on the website and shall be accessible to the public free of charge. Companies shall not be charged a specific fee for such publication.

The prohibition precluding the charging to companies of a specific fee for publication, laid down in the third and fourth subparagraphs, shall not affect the ability of Member States to pass on to companies the costs in respect of the central electronic platform.

Member States may require companies to maintain the information for a specific period after the general meeting on their website or, where applicable, on the central electronic platform or the other website designated by the Member State concerned. Member States may determine the consequences of temporary disruption of access to the website or to the central electronic platform, caused by technical or other factors.

2.   However, the rules in force concerning employee participation, if any, in the Member State where the company resulting from the cross-border merger has its registered office shall not apply, where at least one of the merging companies has, in the six months before the publication of the draft terms of the cross-border merger as referred to in Article 6, an average number of employees that exceeds 500 and is operating under an employee participation system within the meaning of Article 2(k) of Directive 2001/86/EC, or where the national law applicable to the company resulting from the cross-border merger does not

(a)   provide for at least the same level of employee participation as operated in the relevant merging companies, measured by reference to the proportion of employee representatives amongst the members of the administrative or supervisory organ or their committees or of the management group which covers the profit units of the company, subject to employee representation, or

(b)   provide for employees of establishments of the company resulting from the cross-border merger that are situated in other Member States the same entitlement to exercise participation rights as is enjoyed by those employees employed in the Member State where the company resulting from the cross-border merger has its registered office.

3.   In the cases referred to in paragraph 2, the participation of employees in the company resulting from the cross-border merger and their involvement in the definition of such rights shall be regulated by the Member States, mutatis mutandis and subject to paragraphs 4 to 7 below, in accordance with the principles and procedures laid down in Article 12(2), (3) and (4) of Regulation (EC) No 2157/2001 and the following provisions of Directive 2001/86/EC:

(a)   Article 3(1), (2) and (3), (4) first subparagraph, first indent, and second subparagraph, (5) and (7);

(b)   Article 4(1), (2), points (a), (g) and (h), and (3);

(c)   Article 5;

(d)   Article 6;

(e)   Article 7(1), (2) first subparagraph, point (b), and second subparagraph, and (3). However, for the purposes of this Directive, the percentages required by Article 7(2), first subparagraph, point (b) of Directive 2001/86/EC for the application of the standard rules contained in part 3 of the Annex to that Directive shall be raised from 25 to 33 ⅓ %;

(f)   Articles 8, 10 and 12;

(g)   Article 13(4);

(h)   part 3 of the Annex, point (b).

4.   When regulating the principles and procedures referred to in paragraph 3, Member States:

(a)   shall confer on the relevant organs of the merging companies the right to choose without any prior negotiation to be directly subject to the standard rules for participation referred to in paragraph 3(h), as laid down by the legislation of the Member State in which the company resulting from the cross-border merger is to have its registered office, and to abide by those rules from the date of registration;

(b)   shall confer on the special negotiating body the right to decide, by a majority of two-thirds of its members representing at least two-thirds of the employees, including the votes of members representing employees in at least two different Member States, not to open negotiations or to terminate negotiations already opened and to rely on the rules on participation in force in the Member State where the registered office of the company resulting from the cross-border merger will be situated;

(c)   may, in the case where, following prior negotiations, standard rules for participation apply and notwithstanding these rules, determine to limit the proportion of employee representatives in the administrative organ of the company resulting from the cross-border merger. However, if in one of the merging companies employee representatives constituted at least one third of the administrative or supervisory board, the limitation may never result in a lower proportion of employee representatives in the administrative organ than one-third.

5.   The extension of participation rights to employees of the company resulting from the cross-border merger employed in other Member States, referred to in paragraph 2(b), shall not entail any obligation for Member States which choose to do so to take those employees into account when calculating the size of workforce thresholds giving rise to participation rights under national law.

6.   When at least one of the merging companies is operating under an employee participation system and the company resulting from the cross-border merger is to be governed by such a system in accordance with the rules referred to in paragraph 2, that company shall be obliged to take a legal form allowing for the exercise of participation rights.

7.   When the company resulting from the cross-border merger is operating under an employee participation system, that company shall be obliged to take measures to ensure that employees' participation rights are protected in the event of subsequent domestic mergers for a period of three years after the cross-border merger has taken effect, by applying mutatis mutandis the rules laid down in this Article.

Article 17. Validity.   A cross-border merger which has taken effect as provided for in Article 12 may not be declared null and void.

Article 18. Review.   Five years after the date laid down in the first paragraph of Article 19, the Commission shall review this Directive in the light of the experience acquired in applying it and, if necessary, propose its amendment.

B.   Directive 2009/65/EC of the European Parliament and of the Council of 13 July 2009 on the coordination of laws, regulations and administrative provisions relating to undertakings for collective investment in transferable securities (UCITS) (OJ, L 302 of 17 November 2009)[1]

Chapter VI — Mergers of UCITS

Section 1 — Principle, authorisation and approval

Article 37.   For the purposes of this Chapter, a UCITS shall include investment compartments thereof.

Article 38.   1.   Member States shall, subject to the conditions set out in this Chapter and irrespective of the manner in which UCITS are constituted under Article 1(3), allow for cross-border and domestic mergers as defined in Article 2(1)(q) and (r) in accordance with one or more of the merger techniques provided for in Article 2(1)(p).

2.   The merger techniques used for cross-border mergers as defined in Article 2(1) (q) must be provided for under the laws of the merging UCITS home Member State.

The merger techniques used for domestic mergers as defined in Article 2(1)(r) must be provided for under the laws of the Member State, in which the UCITS are established.

Article 39.   1.   Mergers shall be subject to prior authorisation by the competent authorities of the merging UCITS home Member State.

2.   The merging UCITS shall provide the following information to the competent authorities of its home Member State:

(a)   the common draft terms of the proposed merger duly approved by the merging UCITS and the receiving UCITS;

(b)   an up-to-date version of the prospectus and the key investor information, referred to in Article 78, of the receiving UCITS, if established in another Member State;

(c)   a statement by each of the depositaries of the merging and the receiving UCITS confirming that, in accordance with Article 41, they have verified compliance of the particulars set out in points (a), (f) and (g) of Article 40(1) with the requirements of this Directive and the fund rules or instruments of incorporation of their respective UCITS; and

(d)   the information on the proposed merger that the merging and the receiving UCITS intend to provide to their respective unit-holders.

That information shall be provided in such a manner as to enable the competent authorities of both the merging and the receiving UCITS home Member State to read

---

[1]   Concerning Directive 2009/65, see also Articles 14, 25 and 28 of Commission Directive 2010/42/EU of 1 July 2010 as regards certain provisions concerning fund mergers, master-feeder structures and notification procedure, and Article 34 of Commission Directive 2010/43/EU of 1 July 2010 as regards organisational requirements, conflicts of interest, conduct of business, risk management and content of the agreement between a depositary and a management company (both in OJ, L 176 of 1° July 2010). For the provisions concerning Chapters I, II, III, V, XI, see this Chapter, General provisions, M. [Note of the Editor]

them in the official language or one of the official languages of that Member State or those Member States, or in a language approved by those competent authorities.

3.   Once the file is complete, the competent authorities of the merging UCITS home Member State shall immediately transmit copies of the information referred to in paragraph 2 to the competent authorities of the receiving UCITS home Member State. The competent authorities of the merging and the receiving UCITS home Member State shall, respectively, consider the potential impact of the proposed merger on unit-holders of the merging and the receiving UCITS to assess whether appropriate information is being provided to unit-holders.

If the competent authorities of the merging UCITS home Member State consider it necessary, they may require, in writing, that the information to unit-holders of the merging UCITS be clarified.

If the competent authorities of the receiving UCITS home Member State consider it necessary, they may require, in writing, and no later than 15 working days of receipt of the copies of the complete information referred to in paragraph 2, that the receiving UCITS modify the information to be provided to its unit-holders.

In such a case, the competent authorities of the receiving UCITS home Member State shall send an indication of their dissatisfaction to the competent authorities of the merging UCITS home Member State. They shall inform the competent authorities of the merging UCITS home Member State whether they are satisfied with the modified information to be provided to the unit-holders of the receiving UCITS within 20 working days of being notified thereof.

4.   The competent authorities of the merging UCITS home Member State shall authorise the proposed merger if the following conditions are met:

(a)   the proposed merger complies with all of the requirements of Articles 39 to 42;

(b)   the receiving UCITS has been notified, in accordance with Article 93, to market its units in all Member States where the merging UCITS is either authorised or has been notified to market its units in accordance with Article 93; and

(c)   the competent authorities of the merging and the receiving UCITS home Member State are satisfied with the proposed information to be provided to unit-holders, or no indication of dissatisfaction from the competent authorities of the receiving UCITS home Member State has been received under the fourth subparagraph of paragraph 3.

5.   If the competent authorities of the merging UCITS home Member State consider that the file is not complete, they shall request additional information within 10 working days of receiving the information referred to in paragraph 2.

The competent authorities of the merging UCITS home Member State shall inform the merging UCITS, within 20 working days of submission of the complete information, in accordance with paragraph 2, whether or not the merger has been authorised.

The competent authorities of the merging UCITS home Member State shall also inform the competent authorities of the receiving UCITS home Member State of their decision.

6.   Member States may, in accordance with the second subparagraph of Article 57(1), provide for a derogation from Articles 52 to 55 for receiving UCITS.

Article 40.   1.   Member States shall require that the merging and the receiving UCITS draw up common draft terms of merger.

The common draft terms of merger shall set out the following particulars:

(a) an identification of the type of merger and of the UCITS involved;

(b) the background to and rationale for the proposed merger;

(c) the expected impact of the proposed merger on the unit-holders of both the merging and the receiving UCITS;

(d) the criteria adopted for valuation of the assets and, where applicable, the liabilities on the date for calculating the exchange ratio as referred to in Article 47(1);

(e) the calculation method of the exchange ratio;

(f) the planned effective date of the merger;

(g) the rules applicable, respectively, to the transfer of assets and the exchange of units; and

(h) in the case of a merger pursuant to point (p)(ii) of Article 2(1) and, where applicable, point (p)(iii) of Article 2(1), the fund rules or instruments of incorporation of the newly constituted receiving UCITS.

The competent authorities shall not require that any additional information is included in the common draft terms of mergers.

2. The merging UCITS and the receiving UCITS may decide to include further items in the common draft terms of merger.

Section 2 — Third-party control, information of unit-holders and other rights of unit-holders

Article 41. Member States shall require that the depositaries of the merging and of the receiving UCITS verify the conformity of the particulars set out in points (a), (f) and (g) of Article 40(1) with the requirements of this Directive and the fund rules or instruments of incorporation of their respective UCITS.

Article 42. 1. The law of the merging UCITS home Member States shall entrust either a depositary or an independent auditor, approved in accordance with Directive 2006/43/ EC of the European Parliament and of the Council of 17 May 2006 on statutory audits of annual accounts and consolidated accounts, to validate the following:

(a) the criteria adopted for valuation of the assets and, where applicable, the liabilities on the date for calculating the exchange ratio, as referred to in Article 47(1);

(b) where applicable, the cash payment per unit; and

(c) the calculation method of the exchange ratio as well as the actual exchange ratio determined at the date for calculating that ratio, as referred to in Article 47(1).

2. The statutory auditors of the merging UCITS or the statutory auditor of the receiving UCITS shall be considered independent auditors for the purposes of paragraph 1.

3. A copy of the reports of the independent auditor, or, where applicable, the depositary shall be made available on request and free of charge to the unit-holders of both the merging UCITS and the receiving UCITS and to their respective competent authorities.

Article 43. 1. Member States shall require merging and receiving UCITS to provide appropriate and accurate information on the proposed merger to their respective unit-holders so as to enable them to make an informed judgement of the impact of the proposal on their investment.

2.   That information shall be provided to unit-holders of the merging and of the receiving UCITS only after the competent authorities of the merging UCITS home Member State have authorised the proposed merger under Article 39.

It shall be provided at least 30 days before the last date for requesting repurchase or redemption or, where applicable, conversion without additional charge under Article 45(1).

3.   The information to be provided to unit-holders of the merging and of the receiving UCITS, shall include appropriate and accurate information on the proposed merger such as to enable them to take an informed decision on the possible impact thereof on their investment and to exercise their rights under Articles 44 and 45.

It shall include the following:

(a)   the background to and the rationale for the proposed merger;

(b)   the possible impact of the proposed merger on unit-holders, including but not limited to any material differences in respect of investment policy and strategy, costs, expected outcome, periodic reporting, possible dilution in performance, and, where relevant, a prominent warning to investors that their tax treatment may be changed following the merger;

(c)   any specific rights unit-holders have in relation to the proposed merger, including but not limited to the right to obtain additional information, the right to obtain a copy of the report of the independent auditor or the depositary on request, and the right to request the repurchase or redemption or, where applicable, the conversion of their units without charge as specified in Article 45(1) and the last date for exercising that right;

(d)   the relevant procedural aspects and the planned effective date of the merger; and

(e)   a copy of the key investor information, referred to in Article 78, of the receiving UCITS.

4.   If the merging or the receiving UCITS has been notified in accordance with Article 93, the information referred to in paragraph 3 shall be provided in the official language, or one of the official languages, of the relevant UCITS host Member State, or in a language approved by its competent authorities. The UCITS required to provide the information shall be responsible for producing the translation. That translation shall faithfully reflect the content of the original.

5.   The Commission may adopt implementing measures specifying the detailed content, format and method by which to provide the information referred to in paragraphs 1 and 3.

Those measures, designed to amend non-essential elements of this Directive by supplementing it, shall be adopted in accordance with the regulatory procedure with scrutiny referred to in Article 112(2).

Article 44.   Where the national laws of Member States require approval by the unit-holders of mergers between UCITS, Member States shall ensure that such approval does not require more than 75 % of the votes actually cast by unit-holders present or represented at the general meeting of unit-holders.

The first paragraph shall be without prejudice to any presence quorum provided for under national laws. Member States shall impose neither more stringent presence quorums for cross-border than for domestic mergers nor more stringent presence quorums for UCITS mergers than for mergers of corporate entities.

Article 45. 1. The laws of Member States shall provide that unit-holders of both the merging and the receiving UCITS have the right to request, without any charge other than those retained by the UCITS to meet disinvestment costs, the repurchase or redemption of their units or, where possible, to convert them into units in another UCITS with similar investment policies and managed by the same management company or by any other company with which the management company is linked by common management or control, or by a substantial direct or indirect holding. That right shall become effective from the moment that the unit-holders of the merging UCITS and those of the receiving UCITS, have been informed of the proposed merger in accordance with Article 43 and shall cease to exist five working days before the date for calculating the exchange ratio referred to in Article 47(1).

2. Without prejudice to paragraph 1, for mergers between UCITS and by way of derogation from Article 84(1), Member States may allow the competent authorities to require or to allow the temporary suspension of the subscription, repurchase or redemption of units provided that such suspension is justified for the protection of the unit-holders.

Section 3 — Costs and entry into effect

Article 46. Except in cases where UCITS have not designated a management company, Member States shall ensure that any legal, advisory or administrative costs associated with the preparation and the completion of the merger shall not be charged to the merging or the receiving UCITS, or to any of their unit-holders.

Article 47. 1. … For cross-border mergers, the laws of the receiving UCITS home Member State shall determine those dates. Member States shall ensure that, where applicable, those dates are after the approval of the merger by unit-holders of the receiving UCITS or the merging UCITS.

2. The entry into effect of the merger shall be made public through all appropriate means in the manner prescribed by the laws of the receiving UCITS home Member State, and shall be notified to the competent authorities of the home Member States of the receiving and the merging UCITS.

3. A merger which has taken effect as provided for in paragraph 1 shall not be declared null and void.

Article 48. 1. A merger effected in accordance with point (p)(i) of Article 2(1) shall have the following consequences:

(a) all the assets and liabilities of the merging UCITS are transferred to the receiving UCITS or, where applicable, to the depositary of the receiving UCITS;

(b) the unit-holders of the merging UCITS become unit-holders of the receiving UCITS and, where applicable, they are entitled to a cash payment not exceeding 10 % of the net asset value of their units in the merging UCITS; and

(c) the merging UCITS cease to exist on the entry into effect of the merger.

2.   A merger effected in accordance with point (p)(ii) of Article 2(1) shall have the following consequences:

(a)   all the assets and liabilities of the merging UCITS are transferred to the newly constituted receiving UCITS or, where applicable, to the depositary of the receiving UCITS;

(b)   the unit-holders of the merging UCITS become unit-holders of the newly constituted receiving UCITS and, where applicable, they are entitled to a cash payment not exceeding 10 % of the net asset value of their units in the merging UCITS; and

(c)   the merging UCITS cease to exist on the entry into effect of the merger.

3.   A merger effected in accordance with point (p)(iii) of Article 2(1) shall have the following consequences:

(a)   the net assets of the merging UCITS are transferred to the receiving UCITS or, where applicable, the depositary of the receiving UCITS;

(b)   the unit-holders of the merging UCITS become unit-holders of the receiving UCITS; and

(c)   the merging UCITS continues to exist until the liabilities have been discharged.

4.   Member States shall provide for the establishment of a procedure whereby the management company of the receiving UCITS confirms to the depositary of the receiving UCITS that transfer of assets and, where applicable, liabilities is complete. Where the receiving UCITS has not designated a management company, it shall give that confirmation to the depositary of the receiving UCITS.

C.   Proposal for a Council Regulation on the statute for a European private company (COM (2008) 396 of 25 June 2008): Articles 34(3), 39

See this Chapter, Supranational legal entities, D.

D.   ECJ case-law

In *Sevic* (13 December 2005, case C-411/03, Reports, I-10805), the ECJ has tackled for the first time the difficulties related to the execution of cross-border mergers of companies having their registered office in two different Member States. The case originated from the rejection by the court of Neuwied of the application for registration in the commercial German register, in compliance with Article 16 *et seq* of the German Law on transforming companies (Umwandlungsgesetz, hereinafter referred to as UmwG), of a merger (by absorption) between the absorbing company Sevic, a company established in Germany, and the absorbed entity, Security Vision Concept SA, a company established in Luxembourg.

The German Court opposed to such registration provisions of Paragraph 1(1)(1) of the UmwG, which state that only legal entities established in Germany may be the subject of transformation by merger and that, therefore, that law does not apply to transformations resulting from cross-border mergers. In doing so, such provisions were self precluding their application to domestic mergers, with the consequence to exclude the possibility to execute, within the German territory, cross-border mergers between companies established in different Member States, other than Germany, being above mentioned mergers effective only upon condition of the prior registration. Upon the appeal lodged by *Sevic*, the appeal court referred to the ECJ the questions as to whether UmwG's provisions on refusal of the registration in the German commercial register of the merger between German companies and companies incorporated in other Member States were contrary to freedom of establishment's principle. The ECJ ruled as follows:

16.   Contrary to the arguments of the German and Netherlands Governments, Articles 43 EC and 48 EC apply to a merger situation such as that at issue in the main proceedings.

17.   In accordance with the second paragraph of Article 43 EC, read in conjunction with Article 48 EC, the freedom of establishment for companies referred to in that latter article includes in particular the formation and management of those companies under the conditions defined by the legislation of the State of establishment for its own companies.

18.   As the Advocate General points out in point 30 of his Opinion, the right of establishment covers all measures which permit or even merely facilitate access to another Member State and the pursuit of an economic activity in that State by allowing the persons concerned to participate in the economic life of the country effectively and under the same conditions as national operators.

19.   Cross-border merger operations, like other company transformation operations, respond to the needs for cooperation and consolidation between companies established in different Member States. They constitute particular methods of exercise of the freedom of establishment, important for the proper functioning of the internal market, and are therefore amongst those economic activities in respect of which Member States are required to comply with the freedom of establishment laid down by Article 43 EC.

The existence of a restriction on the freedom of establishment

20.   In this regard, it is sufficient to note that in German law, unlike what exists for internal mergers, there is no provision for registration in the commercial register of cross-border mergers, and that, therefore, applications for the registration of such mergers are generally refused.

21.   As the Advocate General has pointed out in point 47 of his Opinion, a merger such as that at issue in the main proceedings constitutes an effective means of transforming companies in that it makes it possible, within the framework of a single operation, to pursue a particular activity in new forms and without interruption, thereby reducing the complications, times and costs associated with other forms of company consolidation such as those which entail, for example, the dissolution of a company with liquidation of assets and the subsequent formation of a new company with the transfer of assets to the latter.

22.   In so far as, under national rules, recourse to such a means of company transformation is not possible where one of the companies is established in a Member State other than the Federal Republic of Germany, German law establishes a difference in treatment between companies according to the internal or cross-border nature of the merger, which is likely to deter the exercise of the freedom of establishment laid down by the Treaty.

23.   Such a difference in treatment constitutes a restriction within the meaning of Articles 43 EC and 48 EC, which is contrary to the right of establishment and can be permitted only if it pursues a legitimate objective compatible with the Treaty and is justified by imperative reasons in the public interest. It is further necessary, in such a case, that its application must be appropriate to ensuring the attainment of the objective thus pursued and must not go beyond what is necessary to attain it.

Possible justification for the restriction

26.   It should be noted in that respect that, whilst Community harmonisation rules are useful for facilitating cross-border mergers, the existence of such harmonisation rules cannot be made a precondition for the implementation of the freedom of establishment laid down by Articles 43 EC and 48 EC.

28.   In that respect, it is not possible to exclude the possibility that imperative reasons in the public interest such as protection of the interests of creditors, minority shareholders and employees (see *Überseering*, paragraph 92), and the preservation of the effectiveness of fiscal supervision and the fairness of commercial transactions (see *Inspire Art*, paragraph 132), may, in certain circumstances and under certain conditions, justify a measure restricting the freedom of establishment.

29.   But such a restrictive measure would also have to be appropriate for ensuring the attainment of the objectives pursued and not go beyond what is necessary to attain them.

30.   To refuse generally, in a Member State, to register in the commercial register a merger between a company established in that State and one established in another Member State has the result of preventing the realisation of cross-border mergers even if the interests mentioned in paragraph 28 of this judgment are not threatened. In any event, such a rule goes beyond what is necessary to protect those interests.

31.   In those circumstances, the answer to the question referred must be that Articles 43 EC and 48 EC preclude registration in the national commercial register of the merger by dissolution without liquidation of one company and transfer of the whole of its assets to another company from being refused in general in a Member State where one of the two companies is established in another Member State, whereas such registration is possible, on compliance with certain conditions, where the two companies participating in the merger are both established in the territory of the first Member State.

Cross-border transfer of seat

A.   Council Regulation (EEC) No 2137/85 of 25 July 1985 on the European Economic Interest Grouping (EEIG) (OJ, L 199 of 31 July 1985): Articles 2, 6–8, 10, 12–14

See this Chapter, Supranational legal entities, A.

B. Council Regulation (EC) No 2157/2001 of 8 October 2001 on the Statute for a European company (SE) (OJ, L 294 of 10 November 2001): Recitals 5, 24–25, 27; Articles 7, 8, 12-14.3, 37.1-37.3, 64.1

See this Chapter, Supranational legal entities, B.1.

C.1. Council Regulation (EC) No 1435/2003 of 22 July 2003 on the Statute for a European Cooperative Society (SCE) (OJ, L 207 of 18 August 2003): Recital 14; Articles 6–7, 12-13.2, 35.2, 59.4, 73.2

See this Chapter, Supranational legal entities, C.1.

C.2. Council Directive 2003/72/EC of 22 July 2003 supplementing the Statute for a European Cooperative Society with regard to the involvement of employees (OJ, L 207 of 18 August 2003): Article 8.2

See this Chapter, Supranational legal entities, C.2.

D. Proposal for a Council Regulation on the statute for a European private company (COM/2008/396 of 25 June 2008): Recitals 4, 14–15, Articles 2, 7, 18.1, 27.4, 34.2, 35–38

See this Chapter, Supranational legal entities, D.

E. ECJ case-law

In *Daily Mail* (27 September 1988, case 81/87, Reports, 5483) the main issue concerned whether the applicant, a company incorporate under English law and with registered office in the United Kingdom, was required to obtain a consent, under English tax legislation, to cease to be resident in the United Kingdom for the purpose of establishing its residence in the Netherlands.

While on one hand, English company law allows a company, such as the applicant, incorporated under that law and having its registered office in the UK, to establish its central management and control outside the UK without losing its legal personality or ceasing to be a company incorporated in the UK, on the other hand, tax legislation of said State prohibits companies, which are resident for tax purposes in the UK, from ceasing to be so resident without the prior consent of the Treasury. In this respect, a company is resident for tax purposes in the place in which its central management and control is located.

Daily Mail had applied for the above-mentioned consent in order to transfer its central management, and control, and therefore its tax residence to the Netherlands, with the purpose of obtaining the ability consequent to the establishment of its residence in the Netherlands, to sell a significant part of its non-permanent assets and to use the proceeds from that sale to buy its own shares, without having to pay the tax to which such transactions would be subject to under the UK tax law, in regard, in particular, to the substantial capital gains on the assets which the applicant was intentioned to sell.

The debate between *Daily Mail* and the tax authorities of the UK was brought before the ECJ that was asked certain interpretative questions on Articles 52 and 58 of the EEC Treaty (ex Articles 43 and 48 EC and now 49 and 54 TFEU). In particular, the ECJ was asked to establish whether Articles 52 and 58 of the EEC Treaty give a right to a corporate body, incorporated under a Member State law and with registered office in that Member State, to transfer its central management and control in another Member State and if so, if the relevant Member State is entitled to subordinate the exercise of such a right to the prior national consent whose granting depends upon the tax company's situation. The ECJ stated that such right did not exist on the basis of the following grounds:

16.   Even though those provisions are directed mainly to ensuring that foreign nationals and companies are treated in the host Member State in the same way as nationals of that State, they also prohibit the Member State of origin from hindering the establishment in another Member State of one of its nationals or of a company incorporated under its legislation which comes within the definition contained in Article 58. As the Commission rightly observed, the rights guaranteed by Article 52 *et seq* would be rendered meaningless if the Member State of origin could prohibit undertakings from leaving in order to establish themselves in another Member State. In regard to natural persons, the right to leave their territory for that purpose is expressly provided for in Directive 73/148, which is the subject of the second question referred to the Court.

17.   In the case of a company, the right of establishment is generally exercised by the setting-up of agencies, branches or subsidiaries, as is expressly provided for in the second sentence of the first paragraph of Article 52. Indeed, that is the form of establishment in which the applicant engaged in this case by opening an investment management office in the Netherlands. A company may also exercise its right of establishment by taking part in the incorporation of a company in another Member State, and in that regard Article 221 of the Treaty ensures that it will receive the same treatment as nationals of that Member State as regards participation in the capital of the new company.

18.   The provision of United Kingdom law at issue in the main proceedings imposes no restriction on transactions such as those described above. Nor does it stand in the way of a partial or total transfer of the activities of a company incorporated in the United Kingdom to a company newly incorporated in another Member State, if necessary after winding-up and, consequently, the settlement of the tax position of the United Kingdom company. It requires Treasury consent only where such a company seeks to transfer its central management and control out of the United Kingdom while maintaining its legal personality and its *status* as a United Kingdom company.

19.   In that regard it should be borne in mind that, unlike natural persons, companies are creatures of the law and, in the present state of Community law, creatures of national law. They exist only by virtue of the varying national legislation which determines their incorporation and functioning.

20. As the Commission has emphasized, the legislation of the Member States varies widely in regard to both the factor providing a connection to the national territory required for the incorporation of a company and the question whether a company incorporated under the legislation of a Member State may subsequently modify that connecting factor. Certain States require that not merely the registered office but also the real head office, that is to say the central administration of the company, should be situated on their territory, and the removal of the central administration from that territory thus presupposes the winding-up of the company with all the consequences that winding-up entails in company law and tax law. The legislation of other States permits companies to transfer their central administration to a foreign country but certain of them, such as the United Kingdom, make that right subject to certain restrictions, and the legal consequences of a transfer, particularly in regard to taxation, vary from one Member State to another.

21. The Treaty has taken account of that variety in national legislation. In defining, in Article 58, the companies which enjoy the right of establishment, the Treaty places on the same footing, as connecting factors, the registered office, central administration and principal place of business of a company. Moreover, Article 220 of the Treaty provides for the conclusion, so far as is necessary, of agreements between the Member States with a view to securing inter alia the retention of legal personality in the event of transfer of the registered office of companies from one country to another. No convention in this area has yet come into force.

22. It should be added that none of the directives on the coordination of company law adopted under Article 54(3) (g) of the Treaty deal with the differences at issue here.

23. It must therefore be held that the Treaty regards the differences in national legislation concerning the required connecting factor and the question whether — and if so how — the registered office or real head office of a company incorporated under national law may be transferred from one Member State to another as problems which are not resolved by the rules concerning the right of establishment but must be dealt with by future legislation or conventions.

24. Under those circumstances, Articles 52 and 58 of the Treaty cannot be interpreted as conferring on companies incorporated under the law of a Member State a right to transfer their central management and control and their central administration to another Member State while retaining their *status* as companies incorporated under the legislation of the first Member State.

The difficulties related to the carrying out of cross-border transfer of seat of companies were analysed also in the recent *Cartesio* case (16 December 2008, case C-210/06, Reports, I-9641). Cartesio — a company incorporated under Hungarian law and, at the time of its incorporation, having its seat in Hungary — transferred its seat to Italy, but it wished to retain its status as a company governed by Hungarian law. The application filed by Cartesio for amending of the entry in the commercial register regarding its company seat was rejected by the court competent for maintaining that register on the ground that, under Hungarian law, a company incorporated in Hungary may not transfer its seat, as defined by the Law on the commercial register, abroad while continuing to be subject to Hungarian law as the law governing its articles of association. Such a transfer would require, first, that the company ceases to exist and, then, that the company reincorporates itself in compliance with the law of the country where it wishes to establish its new seat. In this connection, the referring court essentially asked to ECJ whether Articles 43 EC and 48 EC (former 52–58 EEC and now 49–54 TFEU) are to be interpreted as precluding legislation of a Member State under which a company incorporated under the law of that Member State may not transfer its seat to another Member State whilst retaining its status as a company governed by the law of the Member State of incorporation.

104. In that regard, the Court observed in paragraph 19 of *Daily Mail and General Trust* that companies are creatures of national law and exist only by virtue of the national legislation which determines its incorporation and functioning.

105. In paragraph 20 of *Daily Mail and General Trust*, the Court stated that the legislation of the Member States varies widely in regard to both the factor providing a connection to the national territory required for the incorporation of a company and the question whether a company incorporated under the legislation of a Member State may subsequently modify that connecting factor. Certain States require that not merely the registered office but also the real seat (*siège réel*) — that is to say, the central administration of the company — should be situated in their territory, and the removal of the central administration from that territory thus presupposes the winding-up of the company with all the consequences that winding-up entails under company law. The legislation of other States permits companies to transfer their central administration to a foreign country but certain of them make that right subject to certain restrictions, and the legal consequences of a transfer vary from one Member State to another.

106. The Court added, in paragraph 21 of *Daily Mail and General Trust*, that the EEC Treaty had taken account of that variety in national legislation. In defining, in Article 58 of that Treaty (later Article 58 of the EC Treaty, now Article 48 EC), the companies which enjoy the right of establishment, the EEC Treaty placed on the same footing, as connecting factors, the registered office, central administration and principal place of business of a company.

107. In Case C-208/00 *Überseering* (Reports I-9919, paragraph 70), the Court, whilst confirming those dicta, inferred from them that the question whether a company formed in accordance with the legislation of one Member State can transfer its registered office or its actual centre of administration to another Member State without losing its legal personality under the law of the Member State of incorporation, and, in certain circumstances, the rules relating to that transfer, are determined by the national law in accordance with which the company was incorporated. The Court concluded that a Member State is able, in the case of a company incorporated under its law, to make the company's right to retain its legal personality under the law of that Member State subject to restrictions on the transfer to a foreign country of the company's actual centre of administration.

108. It should be pointed out, moreover, that the Court also reached that conclusion on the basis of the wording of Article 58 of the EEC Treaty. In defining, in that article, the companies which enjoy the right of establishment, the EEC Treaty regarded the differences in the legislation of the various Member States both as regards the required connecting factor for companies subject to that legislation and as regards the question whether — and, if so, how — the registered office (*siège statutaire*) or real seat (*siège réel*) of a company incorporated under national law may be transferred from one Member State to another as problems which are not resolved by the rules concerning the right of establishment, but which must be dealt with by future legislation or conventions (see, to that effect, *Daily Mail and General Trust*, paragraphs 21 to 23, and *Überseering*, paragraph 69).

109. Consequently, in accordance with Article 48 EC, in the absence of a uniform Community law definition of the companies which may enjoy the right of establishment on the basis of a single connecting factor determining the national law applicable to a company, the question whether Article 43 EC applies to a company which seeks to rely on the fundamental freedom enshrined in that article — like the question whether a natural person is a national of a Member State, hence entitled to enjoy that freedom — is a preliminary matter which, as Community law now stands, can only be resolved by the applicable national law. In consequence, the question whether the company is faced with a restriction on the freedom of establishment, within the meaning of Article 43 EC, can arise only if it has been established, in the light of the conditions laid down in Article 48 EC, that the company actually has a right to that freedom.

110. Thus a Member State has the power to define both the connecting factor required of a company if it is to be regarded as incorporated under the law of that Member State and, as such, capable of enjoying the right of establishment, and that required if the company is to be able subsequently to maintain that *status*. That power includes the possibility for that Member State not to permit a company governed by its law to retain that *status* if the company intends to reorganise itself in another Member State by moving its seat to the territory of the latter, thereby breaking the connecting factor required under the national law of the Member State of incorporation.

111. Nevertheless, the situation where the seat of a company incorporated under the law of one Member State is transferred to another Member State with no change as regards the law which governs that company falls to be distinguished from the situation where a company governed by the law of one Member State moves to another Member State with an attendant change as regards the national law applicable, since in the latter situation the company is converted into a form of company which is governed by the law of the Member State to which it has moved.

112. In fact, in that latter case, the power referred to in paragraph 110 above, far from implying that national legislation on the incorporation and winding-up of companies enjoys any form of immunity from the rules of the EC Treaty on freedom of establishment, cannot, in particular, justify the Member State of incorporation, by requiring the winding-up or liquidation of the company, in preventing that company from converting itself into a company governed by the law of the other Member State, to the extent that it is permitted under that law to do so.

113. Such a barrier to the actual conversion of such a company, without prior winding-up or liquidation, into a company governed by the law of the Member State to which it wishes to relocate constitutes a restriction on the freedom of establishment of the company concerned which, unless it serves overriding requirements in the public interest, is prohibited under Article 43 EC.

Supranational legal entities

A.   Council Regulation (EEC) No 2137/85 of 25 July 1985 on the European Economic Interest Grouping (EEIG) (OJ, L 199 of 31 July 1985)

[1]   Whereas a harmonious development of economic activities and a continuous and balanced expansion throughout the Community depend on the establishment and smooth functioning of a common market offering conditions analogous to those of a national market; whereas to bring about this single market and to increase its unity a legal framework which facilitates the adaptation of their activities to the economic conditions of the Community should be created for natural persons, companies, firms and other legal bodies in particular; whereas to that end it is necessary that those natural persons, companies, firms and other legal bodies should be able to cooperate effectively across frontiers;

[2]   Whereas cooperation of this nature can encounter legal, fiscal or psychological difficulties; whereas the creation of an appropriate Community legal instrument in the form of a European Economic Interest Grouping would contribute to the achievement of the abovementioned objectives and therefore proves necessary;

[3]   Whereas the Treaty does not provide the necessary powers for the creation of such a legal instrument;

[4]   Whereas a grouping's ability to adapt to economic conditions must be guaranteed by the considerable freedom for its members in their contractual relations and the internal organization of the grouping;

[5]   Whereas a grouping differs from a firm or company principally in its purpose, which is only to facilitate or develop the economic activities of its members to enable them to improve their own results; whereas, by reason of that ancillary nature, a grouping's activities must be related to the economic activities of its members but not replace them so that, to that extent, for example, a grouping may not itself, with regard to third parties, practise a profession, the concept of economic activities being interpreted in the widest sense;

[11]   Whereas matters relating to the *status* or capacity of natural persons and to the capacity of legal persons are governed by national law;

[12]   Whereas the grounds for winding up which are peculiar to the grouping should be specific while referring to national law for its liquidation and the conclusion thereof;

[13]   Whereas groupings are subject to national laws relating to insolvency and cessation of payments; whereas such laws may provide other grounds for the winding up of groupings;

[16]   Whereas the activities of groupings are subject to the provisions of Member States' laws on the pursuit and supervision of activities; whereas in the event of abuse or circumvention of the laws of a Member State by a grouping or its members that Member State may impose appropriate sanctions;

Article 1.   1.   European Economic Interest Groupings shall be formed upon the terms, in the manner and with the effects laid down in this Regulation.

Accordingly, parties intending to form a grouping must conclude a contract and have the registration provided for in Article 6 carried out.

2.   A grouping so formed shall, from the date of its registration as provided for in Article 6, have the capacity, in its own name, to have rights and obligations of all kinds, to make contracts or accomplish other legal acts, and to sue and be sued.

3.   The Member States shall determine whether or not groupings registered at their registries, pursuant to Article 6, have legal personality.

Article 2.   1.   Subject to the provisions of this Regulation, the law applicable, on the one hand, to the contract for the formation of a grouping, except as regards matters relating to the *status* or capacity of natural persons and to the capacity of legal persons and, on the other hand, to the internal organization of a grouping shall be the internal law of the State in which the official address is situated, as laid down in the contract for the formation of the grouping.

2.   Where a State comprises several territorial units, each of which has its own rules of law applicable to the matters referred to in paragraph 1, each territorial unit shall be considered as a State for the purposes of identifying the law applicable under this Article.

Article 4.   1.   Only the following may be members of a grouping:

(a)   companies or firms within the meaning of the second paragraph of Article 58 of the Treaty and other legal bodies governed by public or private law, which have been formed in accordance with the law of a Member State and which have their registered or statutory office and central administration in the Community; where, under the law of a Member State, a company, firm or other legal body is not obliged to have a registered or statutory office, it shall be sufficient for such a company, firm or other legal body to have its central administration in the Community;

(b)   natural persons who carry on any industrial, commercial, craft or agricultural activity or who provide professional or other services in the Community.

2.   A grouping must comprise at least:

(a)   two companies, firms or other legal bodies, within the meaning of paragraph 1, which have their central administrations in different Member States, or

(b)   two natural persons, within the meaning of paragraph 1, who carry on their principal activities in different Member States, or

(c)   a company, firm or other legal body within the meaning of paragraph 1 and a natural person, of which the first has its central administration in one Member State and the second carries on his principal activity in another Member State.

3.   A Member State may provide that groupings registered at its registries in accordance with Article 6 may have no more than 20 members. For this purpose, that Member State may provide that, in accordance with its laws, each member of a legal body formed under its laws, other than a registered company, shall be treated as a separate member of a grouping.

4.   Any Member State may, on grounds of that State's public interest, prohibit or restrict participation in groupings by certain classes of natural persons, companies, firms, or other legal bodies.

Article 6.   A grouping shall be registered in the State in which it has its official address, at the registry designated pursuant to Article 39(1).

Article 7.   A contract for the formation of a grouping shall be filed at the registry referred to in Article 6.
The following documents and particulars must also be filed at that registry:...(i) any proposal totransfer the official address, as referred to in Article 14(1)...

Article 8.   The following must be published, as laid down in Article 39, in the gazette referred to in paragraph 1 of that Article:...
    (b)   the number, date and place of registration as well as notice of the termination of that registration;
    (c)   the documents and particulars referred to in Article 7(b) to (j).
    The particulars referred to in (a) and (b) must be published in full. The documents and particulars referred to in (c) may be published either in full or in extract form or by means of a reference to their filing at the registry, in accordance with the national legislation applicable.

Article 9.   1.   The documents and particulars which must be published pursuant to this Regulation may be relied on by a grouping as against third parties under the conditions laid down by the national law applicable pursuant to Article 3(5) and (7) of Council Directive 68/151/EEC of 9 March 1968 on coordination of safeguards which, for the protection of the interests of members and others, are required by Member States of companies within the meaning of the second paragraph of Article 58 of the Treaty, with a view to making such safeguards equivalent throughout the Community. ...

Article 10.   Any grouping establishment situated in a Member State other than that in which the official address is situated shall be registered in that State. For the purpose of such registration, a grouping shall file, at the appropriate registry in that Member State, copies of the documents which must be filed at the registry of the Member State in which the official address is situated, together, if necessary, with a translation which conforms with the practice of the registry where the establishment is registered.

Article 12.   The official address referred to in the contract for the formation of a grouping must be situated in the Community.
    The official address must be fixed either:
    (a)   where the grouping has its central administration, or
    (b)   where one of the members of the grouping has its central administration or, in the case of a natural person, his principal activity, provided that the grouping carries on an activity there.

Article 13.   The official address of a grouping may be transferred within the Community. When such a transfer does not result in a change in the law applicable pursuant to Article 2, thedecision to transfer shall be taken in accordance with the conditions laid down in the contract for the formation of the grouping.

Article 14. 1. When the transfer of the official address results in a change in the law applicable pursuant to Article 2, a transfer proposal must be drawn up, filed and published in accordance with the conditions laid down in Articles 7 and 8.

No decision to transfer may be taken for two months after publication of the proposal. Any such decision must be taken by the members of the grouping unanimously. The transfer shall take effect on the date on which the grouping is registered, in accordance with Article 6, at the registry for the new official address. That registration may not be effected until evidence has been produced that the proposal to transfer the official address has been published.

2. The termination of a grouping's registration at the registry for its old official address may not be effected until evidence has been produced that the grouping has been registered at the registry for its new official address.

3. Upon publication of a grouping's new registration the new official address may be relied on as against third parties in accordance with the conditions referred to in Article 9(1); however, as long as the termination of the grouping's registration at the registry for the old official address has not been published, third parties may continue to rely on the old official address unless the grouping proves that such third parties were aware of the new official address.

4. The laws of a Member State may provide that, as regards groupings registered under Article 6 in that Member State, the transfer of an official address which would result in a change of the law applicable shall not take effect if, within the two-month period referred to in paragraph 1, a competent authority in that Member State opposes it. Such opposition may be based only on grounds of public interest. Review by a judicial authority must be possible.

Article 15. 1. Where the law applicable to a grouping by virtue of Article 2 provides for the nullity of that grouping, such nullity must be established or declared by judicial decision. However, the court to which the matter is referred must, where it is possible for the affairs of the grouping to be put in order, allow time to permit that to be done.

2. The nullity of a grouping shall entail its liquidation in accordance with the conditions laid down in Article 35.

3. A decision establishing or declaring the nullity of a grouping may be relied on as against third parties in accordance with the conditions laid down in Article 9(1).

Such a decision shall not of itself affect the validity of liabilities, owed by or to a grouping, which originated before it could be relied on as against third parties in accordance with the conditions laid down in the previous subparagraph.

Article 19. 1. A grouping shall be managed by one or more natural persons appointed in the contract for the formation of the grouping or by decision of the members.

No person may be a manager of a grouping if:
— by virtue of the law applicable to him, or
— by virtue of the internal law of the State in which the grouping has its official address, or
— following a judicial or administrative decision made or recognized in a Member State he may not belong to the administrative or management body of a company, may not manage an undertaking or may not act as manager of a European Economic Interest Grouping.

2.   A Member State may, in the case of groupings registered at their registries pursuant to Article 6, provide that legal persons may be managers on condition that such legal persons designate one or more natural persons, whose particulars shall be the subject of the filing provisions of Article 7(d) to represent them. …

Article 24.   1.   The members of a grouping shall have unlimited joint and several liability for its debts and other liabilities of whatever nature. National law shall determine the consequences of such liability.

2.   Creditors may not proceed against a member for payment in respect of debts and other liabilities, in accordance with the conditions laid down in paragraph 1, before the liquidation of a grouping is concluded, unless they have first requested the grouping to pay and payment has not been made within an appropriate period.

Article 32.   3.   A Member State may provide that the court may, on application by a competent authority, order the winding up of a grouping which has its official address in the State to which that authority belongs, wherever the grouping acts in contravention of that State's public interest, if the law of that State provides for such a possibility in respect of registered companies or other legal bodies subject to it.

Article 35.   1.   The winding up of a grouping shall entail its liquidation.

2.   The liquidation of a grouping and the conclusion of its liquidation shall be governed by national law.

3.   A grouping shall retain its capacity, within the meaning of Article 1(2), until its liquidation is concluded.

4.   The liquidator or liquidators shall take the steps required as listed in Articles 7 and 8.

Article 36.   Groupings shall be subject to national laws governing insolvency and cessation of payments. The commencement of proceedings against a grouping on grounds of its insolvency or cessation of payments shall not by itself cause the commencement of such proceedings against its members.

Article 38.   Where a grouping carries on any activity in a Member State in contravention of that State's public interest, a competent authority of that State may prohibit that activity. Review of that competent authority's decision by a judicial authority shall be possible.

B.1.   Council Regulation (EC) No 2157/2001 of 8 October 2001 on the Statute for a European company (SE) (OJ, L 294 of 10 November 2001)

(1)   The completion of the internal market and the improvement it brings about in the economic and social situation throughout the Community mean not only that barriers to trade must be removed, but also that the structures of production must be adapted to

the Community dimension. For that purpose it is essential that companies the business of which is not limited to satisfying purely local needs should be able to plan and carry out the reorganisation of their business on a Community scale.

(2) Such reorganisation presupposes that existing companies from different Member States are given the option of combining their potential by means of mergers. Such operations can be carried out only with due regard to the rules of competition laid down in the Treaty.

(3) Restructuring and cooperation operations involving companies from different Member States give rise to legal and psychological difficulties and tax problems. The approximation of Member States' company law by means of Directives based on Article 44 of the Treaty can overcome some of those difficulties. Such approximation does not, however, release companies governed by different legal systems from the obligation to choose a form of company governed by a particular national law.

(4) The legal framework within which business must be carried on in the Community is still based largely on national laws and therefore no longer corresponds to the economic framework within which it must develop if the objectives set out in Article 18 of the Treaty are to be achieved. That situation forms a considerable obstacle to the creation of groups of companies from different Member States.

(5) Member States are obliged to ensure that the provisions applicable to European companies under this Regulation do not result either in discrimination arising out of unjustified different treatment of European companies compared with public limited liability companies or in disproportionate restrictions on the formation of a European company or on the transfer of its registered office.

(6) It is essential to ensure as far as possible that the economic unit and the legal unit of business in the Community coincide. For that purpose, provision should be made for the creation, side by side with companies governed by a particular national law, of companies formed and carrying on business under the law created by a Community Regulation directly applicable in all Member States.

(7) The provisions of such a Regulation will permit the creation and management of companies with a European dimension, free from the obstacles arising from the disparity and the limited territorial application of national company law.

(10) Without prejudice to any economic needs that may arise in the future, if the essential objective of legal rules governing SEs is to be attained, it must be possible at least to create such a company as a means both of enabling companies from different Member States to merge or to create a holding company and of enabling companies and other legal persons carrying on economic activities and governed by the laws of different Member States to form joint subsidiaries.

(11) In the same context it should be possible for a public limited liability company with a registered office and head office within the Community to transform itself into an SE without going into liquidation, provided it has a subsidiary in a Member State other than that of its registered office.

(12) National provisions applying to public limited-liability companies that offer their securities to the public and to securities transactions should also apply where an SE is formed by means of an offer of securities to the public and to SEs wishing to utilize such financial instruments.

(13) The SE itself must take the form of a company with share capital, that being the form most suited, in terms of both financing and management, to the needs of a company

carrying on business on a European scale. In order to ensure that such companies are of reasonable size, a minimum amount of capital should be set so that they have sufficient assets without making it difficult for small and medium-sized undertakings to form SEs.

(15) Under the rules and general principles of private international law, where one undertaking controls another governed by a different legal system, its ensuing rights and obligations as regards the protection of minority shareholders and third parties are governed by the law governing the controlled undertaking, without prejudice to the obligations imposed on the controlling undertaking by its own law, for example the requirement to prepare consolidated accounts.

(16) Without prejudice to the consequences of any subsequent coordination of the laws of the Member States, specific rules for SEs are not at present required in this field. The rules and general principles of private international law should therefore be applied both where an SE exercises control and where it is the controlled company.

(17) The rule thus applicable where an SE is controlled by another undertaking should be specified, and for this purpose reference should be made to the law governing public limited-liability companies in the Member State in which the SE has its registered office.

(18) Each Member State must be required to apply the sanctions applicable to public limited-liability companies governed by its law in respect of infringements of this Regulation.

(19) The rules on the involvement of employees in the European company are laid down in Directive 2001/86/EC, and those provisions thus form an indissociable complement to this Regulation and must be applied concomitantly.

(20) This Regulation does not cover other areas of law such as taxation, competition, intellectual property or insolvency. The provisions of the Member States' law and of Community law are therefore applicable in the above areas and in other areas not covered by this Regulation.

(23) A company the head office of which is not in the Community should be allowed to participate in the formation of an SE provided that company is formed under the law of a Member State, has its registered office in that Member State and has a real and continuous link with a Member State's economy according to the principles established in the 1962 General Programme for the abolition of restrictions on freedom of establishment. Such a link exists in particular if a company has an establishment in that Member State and conducts operations therefrom.

(24) The SE should be enabled to transfer its registered office to another Member State. Adequate protection of the interests of minority shareholders who oppose the transfer, of creditors and of holders of other rights should be proportionate. Such transfer should not affect the rights originating before the transfer.

(25) This Regulation is without prejudice to any provision which may be inserted in the 1968 Brussels Convention or in any text adopted by Member States or by the Council to replace such Convention, relating to the rules of jurisdiction applicable in the case of transfer of the registered offices of a public limited liability company from one Member State to another.

(26) Activities by financial institutions are regulated by specific directives and the national law implementing those directives and additional national rules regulating those activities apply in full to an SE.

(27) In view of the specific Community character of an SE, the 'real seat' arrangement adopted by this Regulation in respect of SEs is without prejudice to Member States' laws and does not pre-empt any choices to be made for other Community texts on company law.

Title I — General provisions

Article 1. 1. A company may be set up within the territory of the Community in the form of a European public limited-liability company (*Societas Europaea* or SE) on the conditions and in the manner laid down in this Regulation.

2. The capital of an SE shall be divided into shares. No shareholder shall be liable for more than the amount he has subscribed.

3. An SE shall have legal personality.

4. Employee involvement in an SE shall be governed by the provisions of Directive 2001/86/EC.

Article 2. 1. Public limited-liability companies such as referred to in Annex I, formed under the law of a Member State, with registered offices and head offices within the Community may form an SE by means of a merger provided that at least two of them are governed by the law of different Member States.

2. Public and private limited-liability companies such as referred to in Annex II, formed under the law of a Member State, with registered offices and head offices within the Community may promote the formation of a holding SE provided that each of at least two of them:

(a) is governed by the law of a different Member State, or

(b) has for at least two years had a subsidiary company governed by the law of another Member State or a branch situated in another Member State.

3. Companies and firms within the meaning of the second paragraph of Article 48 of the Treaty and other legal bodies governed by public or private law, formed under the law of a Member State, with registered offices and head offices within the Community may form a subsidiary SE by subscribing for its shares, provided that each of at least two of them:

(a) is governed by the law of a different Member State, or

(b) has for at least two years had a subsidiary company governed by the law of another Member State or a branch situated in another Member State.

4. A public limited-liability company, formed under the law of a Member State, which has its registered office and head office within the Community may be transformed into an SE if for at least two years it has had a subsidiary company governed by the law of another Member State.

5. A Member State may provide that a company the head office of which is not in the Community may participate in the formation of an SE provided that company is formed under the law of a Member State, has its registered office in that Member State and has a real and continuous link with a Member State's economy.

Article 3. 1. For the purposes of Article 2(1), (2) and (3), an SE shall be regarded as a public limited-liability company governed by the law of the Member State in which it has its registered office.

2.   An SE may itself set up one or more subsidiaries in the form of SEs. The provisions of the law of the Member State in which a subsidiary SE has its registered office that require a public limited-liability company to have more than one shareholder shall not apply in the case of the subsidiary SE. The provisions of national law implementing the twelfth Council Company Law Directive (89/667/EEC) of 21 December 1989 on single-member private limited-liability companies shall apply to SEs *mutatis mutandis*.

Article 4.   1.   The capital of an SE shall be expressed in euro.
    2.   The subscribed capital shall not be less than EUR 120 000.
    3.   The laws of a Member State requiring a greater subscribed capital for companies carrying on certain types of activity shall apply to SEs with registered offices in that Member State.

Article 5.   Subject to Article 4(1) and (2), the capital of an SE, its maintenance and changes thereto, together with its shares, bonds and other similar securities shall be governed by the provisions which would apply to a public limited-liability company with a registered office in the Member State in which the SE is registered.

Article 6.   For the purposes of this Regulation, 'the statutes of the SE' shall mean both the instrument of incorporation and, where they are the subject of a separate document, the statutes of the SE.

Article 7.   The registered office of an SE shall be located within the Community, in the same Member State as its head office. A Member State may in addition impose on SEs registered in its territory the obligation of locating their head office and their registered office in the same place.

Article 8.   1.   The registered office of an SE may be transferred to another Member State in accordance with paragraphs 2 to 13. Such a transfer shall not result in the winding up of the SE or in the creation of a new legal person.
    2.   The management or administrative organ shall draw up a transfer proposal and publicise it in accordance with Article 13, without prejudice to any additional forms of publication provided for by the Member State of the registered office. That proposal shall state the current name, registered office and number of the SE and shall cover:
    (a)   the proposed registered office of the SE;
    (b)   the proposed statutes of the SE including, where appropriate, its new name;
    (c)   any implication the transfer may have on employees' involvement;
    (d)   the proposed transfer timetable;
    (e)   any rights provided for the protection of shareholders and/or creditors.
    3.   The management or administrative organ shall draw up a report explaining and justifying the legal and economic aspects of the transfer and explaining the implications of the transfer for shareholders, creditors and employees.
    4.   An SE's shareholders and creditors shall be entitled, at least one month before the general meeting called upon to decide on the transfer, to examine at the SE's registered office the transfer proposal and the report drawn up pursuant to paragraph 3 and, on request, to obtain copies of those documents free of charge.

5.   A Member State may, in the case of SEs registered within its territory, adopt provisions designed to ensure appropriate protection for minority shareholders who oppose a transfer.

6.   No decision to transfer may be taken for two months after publication of the proposal. Such a decision shall be taken as laid down in Article 59.

7.   Before the competent authority issues the certificate mentioned in paragraph 8, the SE shall satisfy it that, in respect of any liabilities arising prior to the publication of the transfer proposal, the interests of creditors and holders of other rights in respect of the SE (including those of public bodies) have been adequately protected in accordance with requirements laid down by the Member State where the SE has its registered office prior to the transfer.

A Member State may extend the application of the first subparagraph to liabilities that arise (or may arise) prior to the transfer.

The first and second subparagraphs shall be without prejudice to the application to SEs of the national legislation of Member States concerning the satisfaction or securing of payments to public bodies.

8.   In the Member State in which an SE has its registered office the court, notary or other competent authority shall issue a certificate attesting to the completion of the acts and formalities to be accomplished before the transfer.

9.   The new registration may not be effected until the certificate referred to in paragraph 8 has been submitted, and evidence produced that the formalities required for registration in the country of the new registered office have been completed.

10.   The transfer of an SE's registered office and the consequent amendment of its statutes shall take effect on the date on which the SE is registered, in accordance with Article 12, in the register for its new registered office.

11.   When the SE's new registration has been effected, the registry for its new registration shall notify the registry for its old registration. Deletion of the old registration shall be effected on receipt of that notification, but not before.

12.   The new registration and the deletion of the old registration shall be publicised in the Member States concerned in accordance with Article 13.

13.   On publication of an SE's new registration, the new registered office may be relied on as against third parties. However, as long as the deletion of the SE's registration from the register for its previous registered office has not been publicised, third parties may continue to rely on the previous registered office unless the SE proves that such third parties were aware of the new registered office.

14.   The laws of a Member State may provide that, as regards SEs registered in that Member State, the transfer of a registered office which would result in a change of the law applicable shall not take effect if any of that Member State's competent authorities opposes it within the two-month period referred to in paragraph 6. Such opposition may be based only on grounds of public interest.

Where an SE is supervised by a national financial supervisory authority according to Community directives the right to oppose the change of registered office applies to this authority as well. Review by a judicial authority shall be possible.

15.   An SE may not transfer its registered office if proceedings for winding up, liquidation, insolvency or suspension of payments or other similar proceedings have been brought against it.

16.   An SE which has transferred its registered office to another Member State shall be considered, in respect of any cause of action arising prior to the transfer as determined in paragraph 10, as having its registered office in the Member States where the SE was registered prior to the transfer, even if the SE is sued after the transfer.

Article 9.   1.   An SE shall be governed:
   (a)   by this Regulation,
   (b)   where expressly authorised by this Regulation, by the provisions of its statutes
or
   (c)   in the case of matters not regulated by this Regulation or, where matters are partly regulated by it, of those aspects not covered by it, by:
   (i)   the provisions of laws adopted by Member States in implementation of Community measures relating specifically to SEs;
   (ii)   the provisions of Member States' laws which would apply to a public limited-liability company formed in accordance with the law of the Member State in which the SE has its registered office;
   (iii)   the provisions of its statutes, in the same way as for a public limited-liability company formed in accordance with the law of the Member State in which the SE has its registered office.
   2.   The provisions of laws adopted by Member States specifically for the SE must be in accordance with Directives applicable to public limited-liability companies referred to in Annex I.
   3.   If the nature of the business carried out by an SE is regulated by specific provisions of national laws, those laws shall apply in full to the SE.

Article 10.   Subject to this Regulation, an SE shall be treated in every Member State as if it were a public limitedliability company formed in accordance with the law of the Member State in which it has its registered office.

Article 12.   1.   Every SE shall be registered in the Member State in which it has its registered office in a register designated by the law of that Member State in accordance with Article 3 of the first Council Directive (68/151/EEC) of 9 March 1968 on coordination of safeguards which, for the protection of the interests of members and others, are required by Member States of companies within the meaning of the second paragraph of Article 58 of the Treaty, with a view to making such safeguards equivalent throughout the Community...

Article 13.   Publication of the documents and particulars concerning an SE which must be publicised under this Regulation shall be effected in the manner laid down in the laws of the Member State in which the SE has its registered office in accordance with Directive 68/151/EEC.

Article 14.   1.   Notice of an SE's registration and of the deletion of such a registration shall be published for information purposes in the Official Journal of the European Communities after publication in accordance with Article 13. That notice shall state the name, number, date and place of registration of the SE, the date and place of publication and the title of publication, the registered office of the SE and its sector of activity.

2.   Where the registered office of an SE is transferred in accordance with Article 8, notice shall be published giving the information provided for in paragraph 1, together with that relating to the new registration.

3.   The particulars referred to in paragraph 1 shall be forwarded to the Office for Official Publications of the European Communities within one month of the publication referred to in Article 13.

Title II — Formation

Section 1 — General

Article 15.   1.   Subject to this Regulation, the formation of an SE shall be governed by the law applicable to public limited-liability companies in the Member State in which the SE establishes its registered office.

2.   The registration of an SE shall be publicised in accordance with Article 13.

Section 2 — Formation by merger

Article 17.   1.   An SE may be formed by means of a merger in accordance with Article 2(1).

2.   Such a merger may be carried out in accordance with:

(a)   the procedure for merger by acquisition laid down in Article 3(1) of the third Council Directive (78/855/EEC) of 9 October 1978 based on Article 54(3)(g) of the Treaty concerning mergers of public limited-liability companies or

(b)   the procedure for merger by the formation of a new company laid down in Article 4(1) of the said Directive.

In the case of a merger by acquisition, the acquiring company shall take the form of an SE when the merger takes place. In the case of a merger by the formation of a new company, the SE shall be the newly formed company.

Article 18.   For matters not covered by this section or, where a matter is partly covered by it, for aspects not covered by it, each company involved in the formation of an SE by merger shall be governed by the provisions of the law of the Member State to which it is subject that apply to mergers of public limited-liability companies in accordance with Directive 78/855/EEC.

Article 24.   1.   The law of the Member State governing each merging company shall apply as in the case of a merger of public limited-liability companies, taking into account the cross-border nature of the merger, with regard to the protection of the interests of:

(a)   creditors of the merging companies;

(b)   holders of bonds of the merging companies;

(c)   holders of securities, other than shares, which carry special rights in the merging companies.

2.   A Member State may, in the case of the merging companies governed by its law, adopt provisions designed to ensure appropriate protection for minority shareholders who have opposed the merger.

Article 25.   1.   The legality of a merger shall be scrutinised, as regards the part of the procedure concerning each merging company, in accordance with the law on mergers of public limited-liability companies of the Member State to which the merging company is subject.

2.   In each Member State concerned the court, notary or other competent authority shall issue a certificate conclusively attesting to the completion of the pre-merger acts and formalities.

3.   If the law of a Member State to which a merging company is subject provides for a procedure to scrutinise and amend the share exchange ratio, or a procedure to compensate minority shareholders, without preventing the registration of the merger, such procedures shall only apply if the other merging companies situated in Member States which do not provide for such procedure explicitly accept, when approving the draft terms of the merger in accordance with Article 23(1), the possibility for the shareholders of that merging company to have recourse to such procedure. In such cases, the court, notary or other competent authorities may issue the certificate referred to in paragraph 2 even if such a procedure has been commenced. The certificate must, however, indicate that the procedure is pending. The decision in the procedure shall be binding on the acquiring company and all its shareholders.

Article 26.   1.   The legality of a merger shall be scrutinised, as regards the part of the procedure concerning the completion of the merger and the formation of the SE, by the court, notary or other authority competent in the Member State of the proposed registered office of the SE to scrutinise that aspect of the legality of mergers of public limited-liability companies.

2.   To that end each merging company shall submit to the competent authority the certificate referred to in Article 25(2) within six months of its issue together with a copy of the draft terms of merger approved by that company.

3.   The authority referred to in paragraph 1 shall in particular ensure that the merging companies have approved draft terms of merger in the same terms and that arrangements for employee involvement have been determined pursuant to Directive 2001/86/EC.

4.   That authority shall also satisfy itself that the SE has been formed in accordance with the requirements of the law of the Member State in which it has its registered office in accordance with Article 15.

Article 29.   1.   A merger carried out as laid down in Article 17(2)(a) shall have the following consequences *ipso jure* and simultaneously:

(a)   all the assets and liabilities of each company being acquired are transferred to the acquiring company;

(b)   the shareholders of the company being acquired become shareholders of the acquiring company;

(c)   the company being acquired ceases to exist;

(d)   the acquiring company adopts the form of an SE.

2.   A merger carried out as laid down in Article 17(2)(b) shall have the following consequences *ipso jure* and simultaneously:

(a)   all the assets and liabilities of the merging companies are transferred to the SE;

(b)   the shareholders of the merging companies become shareholders of the SE;

(c) the merging companies cease to exist.

3.   Where, in the case of a merger of public limited-liability companies, the law of a Member State requires the completion of any special formalities before the transfer of certain assets, rights and obligations by the merging companies becomes effective against third parties, those formalities shall apply and shall be carried out either by the merging companies or by the SE following its registration.

4.   The rights and obligations of the participating companies on terms and conditions of employment arising from national law, practice and individual employment contracts or employment relationships and existing at the date of the registration shall, by reason of such registration be transferred to the SE upon its registration.

Section 3 — Formation of a holding SE

Article 32.   1.   A holding SE may be formed in accordance with Article 2(2).

A company promoting the formation of a holding SE in accordance with Article 2(2) shall continue to exist. ...

Section 4 — Formation of a subsidiary SE

Article 35.   An SE may be formed in accordance with Article 2(3).

Article 36.   Companies, firms and other legal entities participating in such an operation shall be subject to the provisions governing their participation in the formation of a subsidiary in the form of a public limited-liability company under national law.

Section 5 — Conversion of an existing public limited-liability company into an SE

Article 37.   1.   An SE may be formed in accordance with Article 2(4).

2.   Without prejudice to Article 12 the conversion of a public limited-liability company into an SE shall not result in the winding up of the company or in the creation of a new legal person.

3.   The registered office may not be transferred from one Member State to another pursuant to Article 8 at the same time as the conversion is effected. ...

9.   The rights and obligations of the company to be converted on terms and conditions of employment arising from national law, practice and individual employment contracts or employment relationships and existing at the date of the registration shall, by reason of such registration be transferred to the SE.

Article 47.   1.   An SE's statutes may permit a company or other legal entity to be a member of one of its organs, provided that the law applicable to public limited-liability companies in the Member State in which the SE's registered office is situated does not provide otherwise.

That company or other legal entity shall designate a natural person to exercise its functions on the organ in question.

2.   No person may be a member of any SE organ or a representative of a member within the meaning of paragraph 1 who:

(a)   is disqualified, under the law of the Member State in which the SE's registered office is situated, from serving on the corresponding organ of a public limited-liability company governed by the law of that Member State, or

(b)   is disqualified from serving on the corresponding organ of a public limited-liability company governed by the law of a Member State owing to a judicial or administrative decision delivered in a Member State....

Article 51.   Members of an SE's management, supervisory and administrative organs shall be liable, in accordance with the provisions applicable to public limited-liability companies in the Member State in which the SE's registered office is situated, for loss or damage sustained by the SE following any breach on their part of the legal, statutory or other obligations inherent in their duties.

Section 6 — General meeting

Article 52.   The general meeting shall decide on matters for which it is given sole responsibility by:
(a)   this Regulation or
(b)   the legislation of the Member State in which the SE's registered office is situated adopted in implementation of Directive 2001/86/ EC.
Furthermore, the general meeting shall decide on matters for which responsibility is given to the general meeting of a public limited-liability company governed by the law of the Member State in which the SE's registered office is situated, either by the law of that Member State or by the SE's statutes in accordance with that law.

Article 53.   Without prejudice to the rules laid down in this section, the organization and conduct of general meetings together with voting procedures shall be governed by the law applicable to public limited-liability companies in the Member State in which the SE's registered office is situated.

Article 54.   1.   An SE shall hold a general meeting at least once each calendar year, within six months of the end of its financial year, unless the law of the Member State in which the SE's registered office is situated applicable to public limited-liability companies carrying on the same type of activity as the SE provides for more frequent meetings. A Member State may, however, provide that the first general meeting may be held at any time in the 18 months following an SE's incorporation.
2.   General meetings may be convened at any time by the management organ, the administrative organ, the supervisory organ or any other organ or competent authority in accordance with the national law applicable to public limited-liability companies in the Member State in which the SE's registered office is situated.

Article 56.   One or more shareholders who together hold at least 10 % of an SE's subscribed capital may request that one or more additional items be put on the agenda of any general meeting. The procedures and time limits applicable to such requests shall be laid down by the national law of the Member State in which the SE's registered office is situated or, failing that, by the SE's statutes. The above proportion may be reduced by the statutes or by the law of the Member State in which the SE's registered office is situated under the same conditions as are applicable to public limited-liability companies.

Article 57.   Save where this Regulation or, failing that, the law applicable to public limited-liability companies in the Member State in which an SE's registered office is situated requires a larger majority, the general meeting's decisions shall be taken by a majority of the votes validly cast.

Article 59.   1.   Amendment of an SE's statutes shall require a decision by the general meeting taken by a majority which may not be less than two-thirds of the votes cast, unless the law applicable to public limited-liability companies in the Member State in which an SE's registered office is situated requires or permits a larger majority. ...

Title IV — *Annual accounts and consolidated accounts*

Article 61.   Subject to Article 62 an SE shall be governed by the rules applicable to public limited-liability companies under the law of the Member State in which its registered office is situated as regards the preparation of its annual and, where appropriate, consolidated accounts including the accompanying annual report and the auditing and publication of those accounts.

Article 62.   1.   An SE which is a credit or financial institution shall be governed by the rules laid down in the national law of the Member State in which its registered office is situated in implementation of Directive 2000/12/EC of the European Parliament and of the Council of 20 March 2000 relating to the taking up and pursuit of the business of credit institutions as regards the preparation of its annual and, where appropriate, consolidated accounts, including the accompanying annual report and the auditing and publication of those accounts.

2.   An SE which is an insurance undertaking shall be governed by the rules laid down in the national law of the Member State in which its registered office is situated in implementation of Council Directive 91/674/EEC of 19 December 1991 on the annual accounts and consolidated accounts of insurance undertakings (2) as regards the preparation of its annual and, where appropriate, consolidated accounts including the accompanying annual report and the auditing and publication of those accounts.

Title V — *Winding up, liquidation, insolvency and cessation of payments*

Article 63.   As regards winding up, liquidation, insolvency, cessation of payments and similar procedures, an SE shall be governed by the legal provisions which would apply to a public limited-liability company formed in accordance with the law of the Member State in which its registered office is situated, including provisions relating to decision-making by the general meeting.

Article 64.   1.   When an SE no longer complies with the requirement laid down in Article 7, the Member State in which the SE's registered office is situated shall take appropriate measures to oblige the SE to regularise its position within a specified period either:

(a)   by re-establishing its head office in the Member State in which its registered office is situated or

(b)   by transferring the registered office by means of the procedure laid down in Article 8.

2.   The Member State in which the SE's registered office is situated shall put in place the measures necessary to ensure that an SE which fails to regularise its position in accordance with paragraph 1 is liquidated.

3.   The Member State in which the SE's registered office is situated shall set up a judicial remedy with regard to any established infringement of Article 7. That remedy shall have a suspensory effect on the procedures laid down in paragraphs 1 and 2.

4.   Where it is established on the initiative of either the authorities or any interested party that an SE has its head office within the territory of a Member State in breach of Article 7, the authorities of that Member State shall immediately inform the Member State in which the SE's registered office is situated.

Article 65.   Without prejudice to provisions of national law requiring additional publication, the initiation and termination of winding up, liquidation, insolvency or cessation of payment procedures and any decision to continue operating shall be publicised in accordance with Article 13.

Article 66.   1.   An SE may be converted into a public limited-liability company governed by the law of the Member State in which its registered office is situated. No decision on conversion may be taken before two years have elapsed since its registration or before the first two sets of annual accounts have been approved.

2.   The conversion of an SE into a public limited-liability company shall not result in the winding up of the company or in the creation of a new legal person. ...

Article 70.   This Regulation shall enter into force on 8 October 2004....

B.2.   Council Directive 2001/86/EC of 8 October 2001 supplementing the Statute for a European company with regard to the involvement of employees (OJ, L 294 of 10 November 2001)

Article 6. Legislation applicable to the negotiation procedure.   Except where otherwise provided in this Directive, the legislation applicable to the negotiation procedure provided for in Articles 3 to 5 shall be the legislation of the Member State in which the registered office of the SE is to be situated.

C.1. Council Regulation (EC) No 1435/2003 of 22 July 2003 on the Statute for a European Cooperative Society (SCE) (OJ, L 207 of 18 August 2003)[1]

(11) Cross-border cooperation between cooperatives in the Community is currently hampered by legal and administrative difficulties which should be eliminated in a market without frontiers.

(12) The introduction of a European legal form for cooperatives, based on common principles but taking account of their specific features, should enable them to operate outside their own national borders in all or part of the territory of the Community.

(13) The essential aim of this Regulation is to enable the establishment of an SCE by physical persons resident in different Member States or legal entities established under the laws of different Member States. It will also make possible the establishment of an SCE by merger of two existing cooperatives, or by conversion of a national cooperative into the new form without first being wound up, where that cooperative has its registered office and head office within one Member State and an establishment or subsidiary in another Member State.

(14) In view of the specific Community character of an SCE, the 'real seat' arrangement adopted by this Regulation in respect of SCEs is without prejudice to Member States' laws and does not preempt the choices to be made for other Community texts on company law.

(17) The rules on the involvement of employees in the European cooperative society are laid down in Directive 2003/72/EC, and those provisions thus form an indissociable complement to this Regulation and are to be applied concomitantly.

(18) Work on the approximation of national company law has made substantial progress so that certain provisions adopted by the Member State where the SCE has its registered office for the purpose of implementing directives on companies may be referred to by analogy for the SCE in areas where the functioning of the cooperative does not require uniform Community rules, such provisions being appropriate to the arrangements governing the SCE, especially:

— first Council Directive 68/151/EEC of 9 March 1968 on coordination of safeguards which, for the protection of the interests of members and others, are required by Member States of companies within the meaning of the second paragraph of Article 48 of the Treaty, with a view to making such safeguards equivalent throughout the Community,

— fourth Council Directive 78/660/EEC of 25 July 1978 on the annual accounts of certain types of companies,

— seventh Council Directive 83/349/EEC of 13 June 1983 on consolidated accounts,

— eighth Council Directive 84/253/EEC of 10 April 1984 on the approval of persons responsible for carrying out the statutory audits of accounting documents,

---

[1] As corrected by corrigendum (OJ, L 49 of 17 February 2007). Regarding Article 308 CE as the appropriate legal basis of Council Regulation (EC) No 1435/2003, see judgment ECJ, 2 May 2006, case C-436/03, *European Parliament v Council of the European Union*, Reports, I-3733. [Note of the Editor]

—   11th Council Directive 89/666/EEC of 21 December 1989 concerning disclosure requirements in respect of branches opened in a Member State by certain types of company governed by the law of another State.

Chapter I — General provisions

Article 1. Form of the SCE.   1.   A cooperative society may be set up within the territory of the Community in the form of a European Cooperative Society (SCE) on the conditions and in the manner laid down in this Regulation.

2.   The subscribed capital of an SCE shall be divided into shares.

The number of members and the capital of an SCE shall be variable.

Unless otherwise provided by the statutes of the SCE when that SCE is formed, no member shall be liable for more than the amount he/she has subscribed. Where the members of the SCE have limited liability, the name of the SCE shall end in 'limited'.

3.   An SCE shall have as its principal object the satisfaction of its members' needs and/or the development of their economic and social activities, in particular through the conclusion of agreements with them to supply goods or services or to execute work of the kind that the SCE carries out or commissions. An SCE may also have as its object the satisfaction of its members' needs by promoting, in the manner set forth above, their participation in economic activities, in one or more SCEs and/or national cooperatives. An SCE may conduct its activities through a subsidiary.

4.   An SCE may not extend the benefits of its activities to nonmembers or allow them to participate in its business, except where its statutes provide otherwise.

5.   An SCE shall have legal personality.

6.   Employee involvement in an SCE shall be governed by the provisions of Directive 2003/72/EC.

Article 2. Formation.   1.   An SCE may be formed as follows:

—   by five or more natural persons resident in at least two Member States,

—   by five or more natural persons and companies and firms within the meaning of the second paragraph of Article 48 of the Treaty and other legal bodies governed by public or private law, formed under the law of a Member State, resident in, or governed by the law of, at least two different Member States,

—   by companies and firms within the meaning of the second paragraph of Article 48 of the Treaty and other legal bodies governed by public or private law formed under the law of a Member State which are governed by the law of at least two different Member States,

—   by a merger between cooperatives formed under the law of a Member State with registered offices and head offices within the Community, provided that at least two of them are governed by the law of different Member States,

—   by conversion of a cooperative formed under the law of a Member State, which has its registered office and head office within the Community if for at least two years it has had an establishment or subsidiary governed by the law of another Member State.

2.   A Member State may provide that a legal body the head office of which is not in the Community may participate in the formation of an SCE provided that legal body is formed under the law of a Member State, has its registered office in that Member State and has a real and continuous link with a Member State's economy.

Article 3. Minimum capital. 1. The capital of an SCE shall be expressed in the national currency.

An SCE whose registered office is outside the Euro-area may also express its capital in euro.

2. The subscribed capital shall not be less than EUR 30 000.

3. The laws of the Member State requiring a greater subscribed capital for legal bodies carrying on certain types of activity shall apply to SCEs with registered offices in that Member State.

4. The statutes shall lay down a sum below which subscribed capital may not be allowed to fall as a result of repayment of the shares of members who cease to belong to the SCE. This sum may not be less than the amount laid down in paragraph 2. The date laid down in Article 16 by which members who cease to belong to the SCE are entitled to repayment shall be suspended as long as repayment would result in subscribed capital falling below the set limit.

5. The capital may be increased by successive subscriptions by members or on the admission of new members, and it may be reduced by the total or partial repayment of subscriptions, subject to paragraph 4.

Variations in the amount of the capital shall not require amendment of the statutes or disclosure.

Article 4. Capital of the SCE. 1. The subscribed capital of an SCE shall be represented by the members' shares, expressed in the national currency. An SCE whose registered office is outside of the Euro-area may also express its shares in euro. More than one class of shares may be issued.

The statutes may provide that different classes of shares shall confer different entitlements with regard to the distribution of surpluses. Shares conferring the same entitlements shall constitute one class.

2. The capital may be formed only of assets capable of economic assessment. Members' shares may not be issued for an undertaking to perform work or supply services.

3. Shares shall be held by named persons. The nominal value of shares in a single class shall be identical. It shall be laid down in the statutes. Shares may not be issued at a price lower than their nominal value.

4. Shares issued for cash shall be paid for on the day of the subscription to not less than 25 % of their nominal value. The balance shall be paid within five years unless the statutes provide for a shorter period.

5. Shares issued otherwise than for cash shall be fully paid for at the time of subscription.

6. The law applicable to public limited-liability companies in the Member State where the SCE has its registered office, concerning the appointment of experts and the valuation of any consideration other than cash, shall apply by analogy to the SCE.

7. The statutes shall lay down the minimum number of shares which must be subscribed for in order to qualify for membership. If they stipulate that the majority at general meetings shall be constituted by members who are natural persons and if they lay down a subscription requirement for members wishing to take part in the activities of the SCE, they may not make membership subject to subscription for more than one share.

8.   When it considers the accounts for the financial year, the annual general meeting shall by resolution record the amount of the capital at the end of the financial year and the variation by reference to the preceding financial year.

At the proposal of the administrative or management organ, the subscribed capital may be increased by the capitalisation of all or part of the reserves available for distribution, following a decision of the general meeting, in accordance with the quorum and majority requirements for an amendment of the statutes. New shares shall be awarded to members in proportion to their shares in the previous capital.

9.   The nominal value of shares may be increased by consolidating the shares issued. Where such an increase necessitates a call for supplementary payments from the members under provisions laid down in the statutes, the decision shall be taken by the general meeting in accordance with the quorum and majority requirements for the amendment of the statutes.

10.   The nominal value of shares may be reduced by subdividing the shares issued.

11.   In accordance with the statutes and with the agreement either of the general meeting or of the management or administrative organ, shares may be assigned or sold to a member or to anyone acquiring membership.

12.   An SCE may not subscribe for its own shares, purchase them or accept them as security, either directly or through a person acting in his/her own name but on behalf of the SCE.

An SCE's shares may, however, be accepted as security in the ordinary transactions of SCE credit institutions.

Article 5. Statutes.   1.   For the purposes of this Regulation, 'the statutes of an SCE' shall mean both the instrument of incorporation and, when they are the subject of a separate document, the statutes of the SCE.

2.   The founder members shall draw up the statutes of the SCE in accordance with the provisions for the formation of cooperative societies laid down by the law of the Member State in which the SCE has its registered office. The statutes shall be in writing and signed by the founder members.

3.   The law for the precautionary supervision applicable in the Member State in which the SCE has its registered office to public limited-liability companies during the phase of the constitution shall apply by analogy to the control of the constitution of the SCE.

4.   The statutes of the SCE shall include at least:

— the name of the SCE, preceded or followed by the abbreviation 'SCE' and, where appropriate, the word 'limited',

— a statement of the objects,

— the names of the natural persons and the names of the entities which are founder members of the SCE, indicating their objects and registered offices in the latter case,

— the address of the SCE's registered office,

— the conditions and procedures for the admission, expulsion and resignation of members,

— the rights and obligations of members, and the different categories of member, if any, and the rights and obligations of members in each category,

— the nominal value of the subscribed shares, the amount of the subscribed capital, and an indication that the capital is variable,

— specific rules concerning the amount to be allocated from the surplus, where appropriate, to the legal reserve,

— the powers and responsibilities of the members of each of the governing organs,

— provisions governing the appointment and removal of the members of the governing organs,

— the majority and quorum requirements,

— the duration of the existence of the society, where this is of limited duration.

Article 6. Registered office. The registered office of an SCE shall be located within the Community, in the same Member State as its head office. A Member State may, in addition, impose on SCEs registered in its territory the obligation of locating the head office and the registered office in the same place.

Article 7. Transfer of registered office. 1. The registered office of an SCE may be transferred to another Member State in accordance with paragraphs 2 to 16. Such transfer shall not result in the winding-up of the SCE or in the creation of a new legal person.

2. The management or administrative organ shall draw up a transfer proposal and publicise it in accordance with Article 12, without prejudice to any additional forms of publication provided for by the Member State of the registered office. That proposal shall state the current name, the registered office and number of the SCE and shall cover:

(a) the proposed registered office of the SCE;

(b) the proposed statutes of the SCE including, where appropriate, its new name;

(c) the proposed timetable for the transfer;

(d) any implication the transfer may have on employees' involvement;

(e) any rights provided for the protection of members, creditors and holders of other rights.

3. The management or administrative organ shall draw up a report explaining and justifying the legal and economic aspects as well as the employment effects of the transfer and explaining the implications of the transfer for members, creditors, employees and holders of other rights.

4. An SCE's members, creditors and the holders of other rights, and any other body which according to national law can exercise this right, shall be entitled, at least one month before the general meeting called upon to decide on the transfer, to examine, at the SCE's registered office, the transfer proposal and the report drawn up pursuant to paragraph 3 and, on request, to obtain copies of these documents free of charge.

5. Any member who opposed the transfer decision at the general meeting or at a sectorial or section meeting may tender his/her resignation within two months of the general meeting's decision. Membership shall terminate at the end of the financial year in which the resignation was tendered; the transfer shall not take effect in respect of that member. Resignation shall entitle the member to repayment of shares on the conditions laid down in Articles 3(4) and 16.

6. No decision to transfer may be taken for two months after publication of the proposal. Such a decision shall be taken as laid down in Article 61(4).

7. Before the competent authority issues the certificate mentioned in paragraph 8, the SCE shall satisfy it that, in respect of any liabilities arising prior to the publication of the transfer proposal, the interests of creditors and holders of other rights in respect of

the SCE (including those of public bodies) have been adequately protected in accordance with requirements laid down by the Member State where the SCE has its registered office prior to the transfer.

A Member State may extend the application of the first subparagraph to liabilities that arise, or may arise, prior to the transfer.

The first and second subparagraphs shall apply without prejudice to the application to SCEs of the national legislation of Member States concerning the satisfaction or securing of payments to public bodies.

8.   In the Member State in which the SCE has its registered office, the court, notary or other competent authority shall issue a certificate attesting to the completion of the acts and formalities to be accomplished before the transfer.

9.   The new registration may not be effected until the certificate referred to in paragraph 8 has been submitted and evidence has been produced that the formalities required for registration in the country of the new registered office have been completed.

10.   The transfer of an SCE's registered office and the consequent amendment of its statutes shall take effect on the date on which the SCE is registered in accordance with Article 11(1) in the register for its new registered office.

11.   When the SCE's new registration has been effected, the registry for its new registration shall notify the register for its old registration.

Deletion of the old registration shall be effected on receipt of that notification, but not before.

12.   The new registration and the deletion of the old registration shall be publicised in the Member States concerned, in accordance with Article 12.

13.   On publication of an SCE's new registration, the new registered office may be relied on as against third parties. However, as long as the deletion of the SCE's registration from the register of its previous registered office has not been publicised, third parties may continue to rely on the previous registered office unless the SCE proves that such third parties were aware of the new registered office.

14.   The laws of a Member State may provide that, as regards SCEs registered in that Member State, the transfer of a registered office which would result in a change of the law applicable shall not take effect if any of that Member State's competent authorities opposes it within the two-month period referred to in paragraph 6. Such opposition may be based only on grounds of public interest.

Where an SCE is supervised by a national financial supervisory authority according to Community directives, the right to oppose the change of registered office applies to this authority as well.

Review by a judicial authority shall be possible.

15.   An SCE may not transfer its registered office if proceedings for winding-up, including voluntary winding-up, liquidation, insolvency or suspension of payments or other similar proceedings have been brought against it.

16.   An SCE which has transferred its registered office to another Member State shall be considered, in respect of any course of action arising prior to the transfer as determined in paragraph 10, as having its registered office in the Member State where the SCE was registered prior to the transfer, even if the SCE is sued after the transfer.

Article 8. Law applicable. 1. An SCE shall be governed:
(a) by this Regulation;

(b) where expressly authorised by this Regulation, by the provisions of its statutes;

(c) in the case of matters not regulated by this Regulation or, where matters are partly regulated by it, of those aspects not covered by it, by:

(i) the laws adopted by Member States in the implementation of Community measures relating specifically to SCEs;

(ii) the laws of Member States which would apply to a cooperative formed in accordance with the law of the Member State in which the SCE has its registered office;

(iii) the provisions of its statutes, in the same way as for a cooperative formed in accordance with the law of the Member State in which the SCE has its registered office.

2. If national law provides for specific rules and/or restrictions related to the nature of business carried out by an SCE, or for forms of control by a supervisory authority, that law shall apply in full to the SCE.

Article 9. Principle of non-discrimination. Subject to this Regulation, an SCE shall be treated in every Member State as if it were a cooperative, formed in accordance with the law of the Member State in which it has its registered office.

Article 10. Particulars to be stated in the documents. 1. The law applicable, in the Member State where the SCE has its registered office, to public limited-liability companies regulating the content of the letters and documents sent to third parties shall apply by analogy to that SCE. The name of the SCE shall be preceded or followed by the abbreviation 'SCE' and, where appropriate, by the word 'limited'.

2. Only SCEs may include the acronym 'SCE' before or after their name in order to determine their legal form.

3. Nevertheless, companies, firms and other legal entities registered in a Member State before the date of entry into force of this Regulation in the names of which the acronym 'SCE' appears shall not be required to alter their names.

Article 11. Registration and disclosure requirements. 1. Every SCE shall be registered in the Member State in which it has its registered office in a register designated by the law of that Member State in accordance with the law applicable to public limited-liability companies.

2. An SCE may not be registered unless an agreement on arrangements for employee involvement pursuant to Article 4 of Directive 2003/72/EC has been concluded, or a decision pursuant to Article 3(6) of the Directive has been taken, or the period for negotiations pursuant to Article 5 of the Directive has expired without an agreement having been concluded.

3. In order for an SCE established by way of merger to be registered in a Member State which has made use of the option referred to in Article 7(3) of Directive 2003/72/EC, either an agreement pursuant to Article 4 of the Directive must have been concluded on the arrangements for employee involvement, including participation, or none of the participating cooperatives must have been governed by participation rules before registration of the SCE.

4.   The statutes of the SCE must not conflict at any time with the arrangements for employee involvement which have been so determined. Where such new arrangements determined pursuant to Directive 2003/72/EC conflict with the existing statutes, the statutes shall be amended to the extent necessary.

In this case, a Member State may provide that the management organ or the administrative organ of the SCE shall be entitled to amend the statutes without any further decision from the general meeting.

5.   The law applicable, in the Member State where the SCE has its registered office, to public limited-liability companies concerning disclosure requirements of documents and particulars shall apply by analogy to that SCE.

Article 12. Publication of documents in the Member States.   1.   Publication of documents and particulars concerning an SCE which must be made public under this Regulation shall be effected in the manner laid down in the laws of the Member State applicable to public limited-liability companies in which the SCE has its registered office.

2.   The national rules adopted pursuant to Directive 89/666/EEC shall apply to branches of an SCE opened in a Member State other than that in which it has its registered office. However, Member States may provide for derogations from the national provisions implementing that Directive to take account of the specific features of cooperatives.

Article 13. Notice in the Official Journal of the European Union.   1.   Notice of an SCE's registration and of the deletion of such a registration shall be published for information purposes in the Official Journal of the European Union after publication in accordance with Article 12. That notice shall state the name, number, date and place of registration of the SCE, the date and place of publication and the title of publication, the registered office of the SCE and its sector of activity.

2.   Where the registered office of an SCE is transferred in accordance with Article 7, notice shall be published giving the information provided for in paragraph 1, together with that relating to the new registration…

Article 14. Acquisition of membership.   1.   Without prejudice to Article 33(1)(b) the acquisition of membership of an SCE shall be subject to the approval of the management or administrative organ. Candidates refused membership may appeal to the general meeting held following the application for membership.

Where the laws of the Member State of the SCE's registered office so permit, the statutes may provide that persons who do not expect to use or produce the SCE's goods and services may be admitted as investor (non-user) members. The acquisition of such membership shall be subject to approval by the general meeting or any other organ delegated to give approval by the general meeting or the statutes.

Members who are legal bodies shall be deemed to be users by virtue of the fact that they represent their own members provided that their members who are natural persons are users.

Unless the statutes provide otherwise, membership of an SCE may be acquired by natural persons or legal bodies.

2.   The statutes may make admission subject to other conditions, in particular:
—   subscription of a minimum amount of capital,
—   conditions related to the objects of the SCE.

3. Where provided for in the statutes, applications for a supplementary stake in the capital may be addressed to members.

4. An alphabetical index of all members shall be kept at the registered office of the SCE, showing their addresses and the number and class, if appropriate, of the shares they hold. Any party having a direct legitimate interest may inspect the index on request, and may obtain a copy of the whole or any part at a price not exceeding the administrative cost thereof.

5. Any transaction which affects the manner in which the capital is ascribed or allotted, or increased or reduced, shall be entered on the index of members provided for in paragraph 4 no later than the month following that in which the change occurs.

6. The transactions referred to in paragraph 5 shall not take effect with respect to the SCE or third parties having a direct legitimate interest until they are entered on the index referred to in paragraph 4.

7. Members shall on request be given a written statement certifying that the change has been entered.

Article 15. Loss of membership. 1. Membership shall be lost:
— upon resignation,
— upon expulsion, where the member commits a serious breach of his/her obligations or acts contrary to the interests of the SCE,
— where authorised by the statutes, upon the transfer of all shares held to a member or a natural person or legal entity which has acquired membership,
— upon winding-up in the case of a member that is not a natural person,
— upon bankruptcy,
— upon death,
— in any other situation provided for in the statutes or in the legislation on cooperatives of the Member State in which the SCE has its registered office.

2. Any minority member who opposed an amendment to the statutes at the general meeting whereby:
(i) new obligations in respect of payments or other services were introduced; or
(ii) existing obligations for members were substantially extended; or
(iii) the period of notice for resignation from the SCE was extended to more than five years; may tender his/her resignation within two months of the general meeting's decision.

Membership shall terminate at the end of the current financial year in the cases referred to in points (i) and (ii) of the first subparagraph and at the end of the period of notice which applied before the statutes were amended in the case referred to in point (iii) thereof. The amendment to the statutes shall not take effect in respect of that member. Resignation shall entitle the member to repayment of shares on the conditions laid down in Articles 3(4) and 16.

3. The decision to expel a member shall be taken by the administrative or management organ, after the member has been heard. The member may appeal against such a decision to the general meeting.

Chapter II — Formation

Section 1 — General

Article 17. Law applicable during formation.   1.   Subject to this Regulation, the formation of an SCE shall be governed by the law applicable to cooperatives in the Member State in which the SCE establishes its registered office.

2.   The registration of an SCE shall be made public in accordance with Article 12.

Article 18. Acquisition of legal personality.   1.   An SCE shall acquire legal personality on the day of its registration in the Member State in which it has its registered office, in the register designated by that State in accordance with Article 11(1).

2.   If acts are performed in an SCE's name before its registration in accordance with Article 11 and the SCE does not assume the obligations arising out of such acts after its registration, the natural persons, companies, firms or other legal entities which performed those acts shall be jointly and severally liable therefore, without limit in the absence of agreement to the contrary.

Section 2 — Formation by merger

Article 19. Procedures for formation by merger.   An SCE may be formed by means of a merger carried out in accordance with:
— the procedure for merger by acquisition,
— the procedure for merger by the formation of a new legal person.
In the case of a merger by acquisition, the acquiring cooperative shall take the form of an SCE when the merger takes place. In the case of a merger by the formation of a new legal person, the latter shall take the form of an SCE.

Article 20. Law applicable in the case of merger.   For matters not covered by this section or, where a matter is partly covered by it, for aspects not covered by it, each cooperative involved in the formation of an SCE by merger shall be governed by the provisions of the law of the Member State to which it is subject that apply to mergers of cooperatives and, failing that, the provisions applicable to internal mergers of public limited-liability companies under the law of that State.

Article 22. Conditions of merger.   1.   The management or administrative organ of merging cooperatives shall draw up draft terms of merger. The draft terms of merger shall include the following particulars:

(a)   the name and registered office of each of the merging cooperatives together with those proposed for the SCE;

(b)   the share–exchange ratio of the subscribed capital and the amount of any cash payment. If there are no shares, a precise division of the assets and its equivalent value in shares;

(c)   the terms for the allotment of shares in the SCE;

(d)   the date from which the holding of shares in the SCE will entitle the holders to share in surplus and any special conditions affecting that entitlement;

(e)   the date from which the transactions of the merging cooperatives will be treated for accounting purposes as being those of the SCE;

(f)   the special conditions or advantages attached to debentures or securities other than shares, which, according to Article 64, do not confer the *status* of members;

(g)   the rights conferred by the SCE on the holders of shares to which special rights are attached and on the holders of securities other than shares, or the measures proposed concerning them;

(h)   the forms of protection of the rights of creditors of the merging cooperatives;

(i)   any special advantage granted to the experts who examine the draft terms of merger or to members of the administrative, management, supervisory or controlling organs of the merging cooperatives;

(j)   the statutes of the SCE;

(k)   information on the procedures by which arrangements for employee involvement are determined pursuant to Directive 2003/72/EC.

2.   The merging cooperatives may include further items in the draft terms of merger.

3.   The law applicable to public limited-liability companies concerning the draft terms of a merger shall apply by analogy to the cross-border merger of cooperatives for the creation of an SCE.

Article 24. Publication.   1.   The law applicable to public limited-liability companies concerning the disclosure requirements of the draft terms of mergers shall apply by analogy to each of the merging cooperatives, subject to the additional requirements imposed by the Member State to which the cooperative concerned is subject.

2.   Publication of the draft terms of merger in the national gazette shall, however, include the following particulars for each of the merging cooperatives:

(a)   the type, name and registered office of each merging cooperative;

(b)   the address of the place or of the register in which the statutes and all other documents and particulars are filed in respect of each merging cooperative, and the number of the entry in that register;

(c)   an indication of the arrangements made in accordance with Article 28 for the exercise of the rights of the creditors of the cooperative in question and the address at which complete information on those arrangements may be obtained free of charge;

(d)   an indication of the arrangements made in accordance with Article 28 for the exercise of the rights of members of the cooperative in question and the address at which complete information on those arrangements may be obtained free of charge;

(e)   the name and registered office proposed for the SCE;

(f)   the conditions determining the date on which the merger will take effect pursuant to Article 31.

Article 28. Laws applicable to formation by merger.   1.   The law of the Member State governing each merging cooperative shall apply as in the case of a merger of public limited-liability companies, taking into account the cross-border nature of the merger, with regard to the protection of the interests of:

—   creditors of the merging cooperatives,

—   holders of bonds in the merging cooperatives.

2.   A Member State may, in the case of the merging cooperatives governed by its law, adopt provisions designed to ensure appropriate protection for members who have opposed the merger.

Article 32. Publication.   For each of the merging cooperatives the completion of the merger shall be made public as laid down by the law of the Member State concerned in accordance with the laws governing mergers of public companies limited by shares.

Section 3 — Conversion of an existing cooperative into an SCE

Article 35. Procedures for formation by conversion.   1.   Without prejudice to Article 11, the conversion of a cooperative into an SCE shall not result in the winding-up of the cooperative or in the creation of a new legal person.

2.   The registered office may not be transferred from one Member State to another pursuant to Article 7 at the same time as the conversion is effected.

3.   The administrative or management organ of the cooperative in question shall draw up draft terms of conversion and a report explaining and justifying the legal and economic aspects as well as the employment effects of the conversion and indicating the implications for members and employees of the adoption of the form of an SCE.

4.   The draft terms of conversion shall be made public in the manner laid down in each Member State's law at least one month before the general meeting called upon to decide thereon.

5.   Before the general meeting referred to in paragraph 6, one or more independent experts appointed or approved, in accordance with the national provisions, by a judicial or administrative authority in the Member State to which the cooperative being converted into an SCE is subject shall certify mutatis mutandis that the rules of Article 22(1)(b) are respected.

6.   The general meeting of the cooperative in question shall approve the draft terms of conversion together with the statutes of the SCE.

7.   Member States may make a conversion conditional on a favourable vote of a qualified majority or unanimity in the controlling organ of the cooperative to be converted within which employee participation is organised.

8.   The rights and obligations of the cooperative to be converted on both individual and collective terms and conditions of employment arising from national law, practice and individual employment contracts or employment relationships and existing at the date of the registration shall, by reason of such registration, be transferred to the SCE.

Article 46. Conditions of membership.   1.   An SCE's statutes may permit a company within the meaning of Article 48 of the Treaty to be a member of one of its organs, provided that the law applicable to cooperatives in the Member State in which the SCE's registered office is situated does not provide otherwise.

That company shall designate a natural person as its representative to exercise its functions on the organ in question. The representative shall be subject to the same conditions and obligations as if he/she were personally a member of the organ.

2.   No person may be a member of any SCE organ or a representative of a member within the meaning of paragraph 1 who:

— is disqualified, under the law of the Member State in which the SCE's registered office is situated, from serving on the corresponding organ of a cooperative governed by the law of that State, or

— is disqualified from serving on the corresponding organ of a cooperative governed by the law of a Member State owing to a judicial or administrative decision delivered in a Member State.

3. An SCE's statutes may, in accordance with the law applicable to cooperatives in the Member State, lay down special conditions of eligibility for members representing the administrative organ.

Article 47. Power of representation and liability of the SCE. 1. Where the authority to represent the SCE in dealings with third parties, in accordance with Articles 37(1) and 42(1), is conferred on two or more members, those members shall exercise that authority collectively, unless the law of the Member State in which the SCE's registered office is situated allows the statutes to provide otherwise, in which case such a clause may be relied upon against third parties where it has been disclosed in accordance with Articles 11(5) and 12.

2. Acts performed by an SCE's organs shall bind the SCE vis-à-vis third parties, even where the acts in question are not in accordance with the objects of the SCE, providing they do not exceed the powers conferred on them by the law of the Member State in which the SCE has its registered office or which that law allows to be conferred on them.

Member States may, however, provide that the SCE shall not be bound where such acts are outside the objects of the SCE, if it proves that the third party knew that the act was outside those objects or could not in the circumstances have been unaware of it; disclosure of the statutes shall not of itself be sufficient proof thereof....

Article 51. Civil liability. Members of management, supervisory and administrative organs shall be liable, in accordance with the provisions applicable to cooperatives in the Member State in which the SCE's registered office is situated, for loss or damage sustained by the SCE following any breach on their part of the legal, statutory or other obligations inherent in their duties.

Section 4 — General meeting

Article 52. Competence. The general meeting shall decide on matters for which it is given sole responsibility by:
(a) this Regulation; or
(b) the legislation of the Member State in which the SCE's registered office is situated, adopted under Directive 2003/72/EC.

Furthermore, the general meeting shall decide on matters for which responsibility is given to the general meeting of a cooperative governed by the law of the Member State in which the SCE's registered office is situated, either by the law of that Member State or by the SCE's statutes in accordance with that law.

Article 53. Conduct of general meetings. Without prejudice to the rules laid down in this section, the organization and conduct of general meetings together with voting procedures shall be governed by the law applicable to cooperatives in the Member State in which the SCE's registered office is situated.

Article 54. Holding of general meetings.   1.   An SCE shall hold a general meeting at least once each calendar year, within six months of the end of its financial year, unless the law of the Member State in which the SCE's registered office is situated applicable to cooperatives carrying on the same type of activity as the SCE provides for more frequent meetings. A Member State may, however, provide that the first general meeting may be held at any time in the 18 months following an SCE's incorporation.

2.   General meetings may be convened at any time by the management organ or the administrative organ, the supervisory organ or any other organ or competent authority in accordance with the national law applicable to cooperatives in the Member State in which the SCE's registered office is situated. The management organ shall be bound to convene a general meeting at the request of the supervisory organ....

Article 56. Notice of meeting.   1.   A general meeting shall be convened by a notice in writing sent by any available means to every person entitled to attend the SCE's general meeting in accordance with Article 58(1) and (2) and the provisions of the statutes. That notice may be given by publication in the official internal publication of the SCE.

2.   The notice calling a general meeting shall give at least the following particulars:
—   the name and registered office of the SCE,
—   the venue, date and time of the meeting,
—   where appropriate, the type of general meeting,
—   the agenda, indicating the subjects to be discussed and the proposals for decisions.

3.   The period between the date of dispatch of the notice referred to in paragraph 1 and the date of the opening of the general meeting shall be at least 30 days. It may, however, be reduced to 15 days in urgent cases. Where Article 61(4) is applied, relating to quorum requirements, the time between a first and second meeting convened to consider the same agenda may be reduced according to the law of the Member State in which the SCE has its registered office.

Article 58. Attendance and proxies.   1.   Every member shall be entitled to speak and vote at general meetings on the points that are included in the agenda.

2.   Members of the SCE's organs and holders of securities other than shares and debentures within the meaning of Article 64 and, if the statutes allow, any other person entitled to do so under the law of the State in which the SCE's registered office is situated may attend a general meeting without voting rights.

3.   A person entitled to vote shall be entitled to appoint a proxy to represent him/her at a general meeting in accordance with procedures laid down in the statutes.

The statutes shall lay down the maximum number of persons for whom a proxy may act.

4.   The statutes may permit postal voting or electronic voting, in which case they shall lay down the necessary procedures.

Article 59. Voting rights. 1. Each member of an SCE shall have one vote, regardless of the number of shares he holds.

2. If the law of the Member State in which the SCE has its registered office so permits, the statutes may provide for a member to have a number of votes determined by his/her participation in the cooperative activity other than by way of capital contribution. This attribution shall not exceed five votes per member or 30 % of total voting rights, whichever is the lower.

If the law of the Member State in which the SCE has its registered office so permits, SCEs involved in financial or insurance activities may provide in their statutes for the number of votes to be determined by the members' participation in the cooperative activity including participation in the capital of the SCE. This attribution shall not exceed five votes per member or 20 % of total voting rights, whichever is the lower.

In SCEs the majority of members of which are cooperatives, if the law of the Member State in which the SCE has its registered office so permits, the statutes may provide for the number of votes to be determined in accordance with the members' participation in the cooperative activity including participation in the capital of the SCE and/or by the number of members of each comprising entity.

3. As regards voting rights which the statutes may allocate to nonuser (investor) members, the SCE shall be governed by the law of the Member State in which the SCE has its registered office. Nevertheless, non-user (investor) members may not together have voting rights amounting to more than 25 % of total voting rights.

4. If, on the entry into force of this Regulation, the law of the Member State where an SCE has its registered office so permits, the statutes of that SCE may provide for the participation of employees' representatives in the general meetings or in the section or sectorial meetings, provided that the employees' representatives do not together control more than 15 % of total voting rights. Such rights shall cease to apply as soon as the registered office of the SCE is transferred to a Member State whose law does not provide for such participation.

Article 63. Sectorial or section meetings. 1. Where the SCE undertakes different activities or activities in more than one territorial unit, or has several establishments or more than 500 members, its statutes may provide for sectorial or section meetings, if permitted by the relevant Member State legislation. The statutes shall establish the division in sectors or sections and the number of delegates thereof....

Chapter VI — Annual accounts and consolidated accounts

Article 68. Preparation of annual accounts and consolidated accounts. 1. For the purposes of drawing up its annual accounts and its consolidated accounts if any, including the annual report accompanying them and their auditing and publication, an SCE shall be subject to the legal provisions adopted in the Member State in which it has its registered office in implementation of Directives 78/660/EEC and 83/349/EEC. However, Member States may provide for amendments to the national provisions implementing those Directives to take account of the specific features of cooperatives.

2. Where an SCE is not subject, under the law of the Member State in which the SCE has its registered office, to a publication requirement such as provided for in Article 3 of Directive 68/151/EEC, the SCE must at least make the documents relating to

annual accounts available to the public at its registered office. Copies of those documents must be obtainable on request. The price charged for such copies shall not exceed their administrative cost.

3.　An SCE must draw up its annual accounts and its consolidated accounts if any in the national currency. An SCE whose registered office is outside the euro area may also express its annual accounts and, where appropriate, consolidated accounts, in euro. In that event, the bases of conversion used to express in euro those items included in the accounts which are or were originally expressed in another currency shall be disclosed in the notes on the accounts.

Article 69. Accounts of SCEs with credit or financial activities.　1.　An SCE which is a credit or financial institution shall be governed by the rules laid down in the national law of the Member State in which its registered office is situated under directives relating to the taking up and pursuit of the business of credit institutions as regards the preparation of its annual and, where appropriate, consolidated accounts, including the accompanying annual report and the auditing and publication of those accounts.

2.　An SCE which is an insurance undertaking shall be governed by the rules laid down in the national law of the Member State in which its registered office is situated under directives as regards the preparation of its annual and, where appropriate, consolidated accounts including the accompanying annual report and the auditing and publication of those accounts.

Article 70. Auditing.　The statutory audit of an SCE's annual accounts and its consolidated accounts if any shall be carried out by one or more persons authorized to do so in the Member State in which the SCE has its registered office in accordance with the measures adopted in that State pursuant to Directives 84/253/EEC and 89/48/EEC.

Article 71. System of auditing.　Where the law of a Member State requires all cooperatives, or a certain type of them, covered by the law of that State to join a legally authorised external body and to submit to a specific system of auditing carried out by that body, the arrangements shall automatically apply to an SCE with its registered office in that Member State provided that this body meets the requirements of Directive 84/253/EEC.

Chapter VII — Winding up, liquidation, insolvency and cessation of payment

Article 72. Winding-up, insolvency and similar procedures.　As regards winding-up, liquidation, insolvency, cessation of payments and similar procedures, an SCE shall be governed by the legal provisions which would apply to a cooperative formed in accordance with the law of the Member State in which its registered office is situated, including provisions relating to decision-making by the general meeting.

Article 73. Winding-up by the court or other competent authority of the Member State where the SCE has its registered office.　1.　On an application by any person with a legitimate interest or any competent authority, the court or any competent administrative authority of the Member State where the SCE has its registered office shall order the SCE to be wound up where it finds that there has been a breach of Article 2(1) and/or Article 3(2) and in the cases covered by Article 34.

The court or the competent administrative authority may allow the SCE time to rectify the situation. If it fails to do so within the time allowed, the court or the competent administrative authority shall order it to be wound up.

2.   When an SCE no longer complies with the requirement laid down in Article 6, the Member State in which the SCE's registered office is situated shall take appropriate measures to oblige the SCE to regularize its situation within a specified period either:

—   by re-establishing its head office in the Member State in which its registered office is situated, or

—   by transferring the registered office by means of the procedure laid down in Article 7.

3.   The Member State in which the SCE's registered office is situated shall put in place the measures necessary to ensure that an SCE which fails to regularise its position in accordance with paragraph 2 is liquidated.

4.   The Member State in which the SCE's registered office is situated shall set up a judicial or other appropriate remedy with regard to any established infringement of Article 6. That remedy shall have suspensory effect on the procedures laid down in paragraphs 2 and 3.

5.   Where it is established on the initiative of either the authorities or any interested party that an SCE has its head office within the territory of a Member State in breach of Article 6, the authorities of that Member State shall immediately inform the Member State in which the SCE's registered office is situated.

Article 74. Publication of winding-up.   Without prejudice to provisions of national law requiring additional publication, the initiation and termination of winding-up including voluntary winding-up, liquidation, insolvency or suspension of payment procedures and any decision to continue operating shall be publicised in accordance with Article 12.

Article 75. Distribution.   Net assets shall be distributed in accordance with the principle of disinterested distribution, or, where permitted by the law of the Member State in which the SCE has its registered office, in accordance with an alternative arrangement set out in the statutes of the SCE. For the purposes of this Article, net assets shall comprise residual assets after payment of all amounts due to creditors and reimbursement of members' capital contributions.

Article 76. Conversion into a cooperative.   1.   An SCE may be converted into a cooperative governed by the law of the Member State in which its registered office is situated. No decision on conversion may be taken before two years have elapsed since its registration or before the first two sets of annual accounts have been approved.

2.   The conversion of an SCE into a cooperative shall not result in winding-up or in the creation of a new legal person.

3.   The management or administrative organ of the SCE shall draw up draft terms of conversion and a report explaining and justifying the legal and economic aspects as well as the employment effects of the conversion and indicating the implications of the adoption of the cooperative form for members and holders of shares referred to in Article 14 and for employees.

4.   The draft terms of conversion shall be made public in the manner laid down in each Member State's law at least one month before the general meeting called to decide on conversion.

5.   Before the general meeting referred to in paragraph 6, one or more independent experts appointed or approved, in accordance with the national provisions, by a judicial or administrative authority in the Member State to which the SCE being converted into a cooperative is subject, shall certify that the latter has assets at least equivalent to its capital.

6.   The general meeting of the SCE shall approve the draft terms of conversion together with the statutes of the cooperative. The decision of the general meeting shall be passed as laid down in the provisions of national law.

Article 79. Review of the Regulation.   Five years at the latest after the entry into force of this Regulation, the Commission shall forward to the European Parliament and to the Council a report on the application of the Regulation and proposals for amendments, where appropriate. The report shall, in particular, analyse the appropriateness of:

(a)   allowing the location of an SCE's head office and registered office in different Member States;

(b)   allowing provisions in the statutes of an SCE adopted by a Member State in execution of authorisations given to the Member States by this Regulation or laws adopted to ensure the effective application of this Regulation with regard to the SCE which deviate from, or are complementary to, these laws, even when such provisions would not be authorised in the statutes of a cooperative having its registered office in the Member State;

(c)   allowing provisions which enable the SCE to split into two or more national cooperatives;

(d)   allowing for specific legal remedies in the case of fraud or error during the registration of an SCE established by way of merger.

C.2.   Council Directive 2003/72/EC of 22 July 2003 supplementing the Statute for a European Cooperative Society with regard to the involvement of employees (OJ, L 207 of 18 August 2003)

Article 2. Definitions.   For the purposes of this Directive:

(a)   'SCE' means any cooperative society established in accordance with Regulation (EC) No 1435/2003;

(b)   'participating legal entities' means companies and firms within the meaning of the second paragraph of Article 48 of the Treaty, including cooperatives, as well as legal bodies formed under, and governed by, the law of a Member State, directly participating in the establishing of an SCE; ...

Article 6. Legislation applicable to the negotiation procedure.   Except where otherwise provided in this Directive, the legislation applicable to the negotiation procedure provided for in Articles 3, 4 and 5 shall be the legislation of the Member State in which the registered office of the SCE is to be situated.

Article 7. Standard rules. 1. In order to achieve the objective described in Article 1, Member States shall lay down standard rules on employee involvement which must satisfy the provisions set out in the Annex. The standard rules as laid down by the legislation of the Member State in which the registered office of the SCE is to be situated shall apply from the date of the registration of the SCE where either:

    (a)   the parties so agree; or

    (b)   by the deadline laid down in Article 5, no agreement has been concluded, and:

    —   the competent organ of each of the participating legal entities decides to accept the application of the standard rules in relation to the SCE and so to continue with its registration of the SCE, and

    —   the special negotiating body has not taken the decision provided in Article 3(6).

    2.   Moreover, the standard rules fixed by the national legislation of the Member State of registration in accordance with part 3 of the Annex shall apply only:

    (a)   in the case of an SCE established by transformation, if the rules of a Member State relating to employee participation in the administrative or supervisory body applied to a cooperative transformed into an SCE;

    (b)   in the case of an SCE established by merger:

    —   if, before registration of the SCE, one or more forms of participation applied in one or more of the participating cooperatives covering at least 25 % of the total number of employees employed by them, or

    —   if, before registration of the SCE, one or more forms of participation applied in one or more of the participating cooperatives covering less than 25 % of the total number of employees employed by them and if the special negotiating body so decides;

    (c)   in the case of an SCE established by any other way;

    —   if, before registration of the SCE, one or more forms of participation applied in one or more of the participating legal entities covering at least 50 % of the total number of employees employed by them; or

    —   if, before registration of the SCE, one or more forms of participation applied in one or more of the participating legal entities covering less than 50 % of the total number of employees employed by them and if the special negotiating body so decides.

If there was more than one form of participation within the various participating legal entities, the special negotiating body shall decide which of those forms must be established in the SCE. Member States may fix the rules which are applicable in the absence of any decision on the matter for an SCE registered in their territory. The special negotiating body shall inform the competent organs of the participating legal entities of any decisions taken pursuant to this paragraph....

Section III — Rules applicable to SCE's established exclusively by natural persons or by a single legal entity and natural persons

Article 8. 1. In the case of an SCE established exclusively by natural persons or by a single legal entity and natural persons, which together employ at least 50 employees in at least two Member States, the provisions of Articles 3 to 7 shall apply.

    2.   In the case of an SCE established exclusively by natural persons or by a single legal entity and natural persons, which together employ fewer than 50 employees, or

employ 50 or more employees in only one Member State, employee involvement shall be governed by the following:

— in the SCE itself, the provisions of the Member State of the SCE's registered office, which are applicable to other entities of the same type, shall apply,

— in its subsidiaries and establishments, the provisions of the Member State where they are situated, and which are applicable to other entities of the same type, shall apply.

In the case of transfer from one Member State to another of the registered office of an SCE governed by participation, at least the same level of employee participation rights shall continue to apply …

D.   Proposal for a Council Regulation on the statute for a European private company (COM (2008) 396 of 25 June 2008)

(4)   In order to enable businesses to reap the full benefits of the internal market, the SPE should be able to have its registered office and principal place of business in different Member States and to transfer its registered office from one Member State to another, with or without also transferring its central administration or principal place of business.

(6)   To ensure a high degree of uniformity of the SPE, as many matters pertaining to the company form as possible should be governed by this Regulation, either through substantive rules or by reserving matters to the articles of association of the SPE. It is therefore appropriate to provide for a list of matters, to be set out in an Annex, in respect of which the shareholders of the SPE are obliged to lay down rules in the articles of association. In relation to those matters only Community law should apply, and consequently shareholders should be able to set out rules to regulate those matters, which are different from the rules prescribed by the law of the Member State where the SPE is registered, in relation to national forms of private limited-liability companies. National law should apply to matters where this is provided for by this Regulation and to all other matters that are not covered by the articles of this Regulation, such as insolvency, employment and tax, or are not reserved by it to the articles of association.

(7)   In order to make the SPE an accessible company form for individuals and small businesses, it should be capable of being created ex nihilo or of resulting from the transformation, the merger or the division of existing national companies. The creation of an SPE by way of transformation, merger or division of companies should be governed by the applicable national law.

(14)   Competent national authorities should monitor the completion and legality of the transfer of the registered office of an SPE to another Member State. The timely access of shareholders, creditors and employees to the transfer proposal and to the report of the management body should be ensured.

(15)   Employees' rights of participation should be governed by the legislation of the Member State in which the SPE has its registered office (the 'home Member State'). The SPE should not be used for the purpose of circumventing such rights. Where the national legislation of the Member State to which the SPE transfers its registered office does not provide for at least the same level of employee participation as the home Member State, the participation of employees in the company following the transfer should in certain circumstances be negotiated. Should such negotiations fail, the provisions applying in the company before the transfer should continue to apply after the transfer.

Chapter I — General provisions

Article 1. Subject matter. This Regulation lays down the conditions governing the establishment and operation within the Community of companies in the form of a European private company with limited liability (*Societas Privata Europaea*, hereinafter 'SPE').

Article 2. Definitions. 1. For the purposes of this Regulation, the following definitions shall apply:...

(f) 'home Member State' means the Member State in which the SPE has its registered office immediately before any transfer of its registered office to another Member State;

(g) 'host Member State' means the Member State to which the registered office of the SPE is transferred ...

Article 3. Requirements for the establishment of an SPE. 1. An SPE shall comply with the following requirements:

(a) its capital shall be divided into shares,

(b) a shareholder shall not be liable for more than the amount he has subscribed or agreed to subscribe,

(c) it shall have legal personality,

(d) its shares shall not be offered to the public and shall not be publicly traded,

(e) it may be formed by one or more natural persons and/or legal entities, hereinafter 'founding shareholders'....

3. For the purposes of point (e) of paragraph 1, 'legal entities' shall mean any company or firm within the meaning of the second paragraph of Article 48 of the Treaty, a European public limited-liability company as provided for in Regulation (EC) No 2001/2157, hereinafter 'European Company', a European Cooperative Society as provided for in Council Regulation (EC) No 1435/2003, a European Economic Interest Grouping as provided for in Council Regulation (EEC) No 2137/85 and an SPE.

Article 4. Rules applicable to an SPE. 1. An SPE shall be governed by this Regulation and also, as regards the matters listed in Annex I, by its articles of association.

However, where a matter is not covered by the articles of this Regulation or by Annex I, an SPE shall be governed by the law, including the provisions implementing Community law, which applies to private limited-liability companies in the Member State in which the SPE has its registered office, hereinafter 'applicable national law'. ...

Chapter II — Formation

Article 5. Materials and methods of formation. 1. Member States shall allow the formation of a SPE by any of the following methods:

(a) the creation of a SPE in accordance with this Regulation;

(b) the transformation of an existing company;

(c) the merger of existing companies;

(d) the division of an existing company.

2. Formation of the SPE by the transformation, merger or division of existing companies shall be governed by the national law applicable to the transforming

company, to each of the merging companies or to the dividing company. Formation by transformation shall not give rise to the winding up of the company or any loss or interruption of its legal personality.

    3.   For the purposes of paragraphs 1 and 2, 'company' shall mean any form of company that may be set up under the law of the Member States, a European Company and, where applicable, an SPE.

Article 7. Seat of the company.   An SPE shall have its registered office and its central administration or principal place of business in the Community.

    An SPE shall not be under any obligation to have its central administration or principal place of business in the Member State in which it has its registered office.

Article 9. Registration.   1.   Each SPE shall be registered in the Member State in which it has its registered office in a register designated by the applicable national law in accordance with Article 3 of Directive 68/151/EEC.

    2.   The SPE shall acquire legal personality on the date on which it is entered in the register.

    3.   In the case of a merger by acquisition, the acquiring company shall adopt the form of an SPE on the day the merger is registered.

    In the case of a division by acquisition, the recipient company shall adopt the form of an SPE on the day the division is registered.

Article 10. Formalities relating to registration.   1.   Application for registration shall be made by the founding shareholders of the SPE or by any person authorised by them. Such application may be made by electronic means.

    2.   Member States shall not require any particulars and documents to be supplied upon application for the registration of a SPE other than the following:

    (a)   the name of the SPE and the address of its registered office;

    (b)   the names, addresses and any other information necessary to identify the persons who are authorised to represent the SPE in dealings with third parties and in legal proceedings, or take part in the administration, supervision or control of the SPE;

    (c)   the share capital of the SPE;

    (d)   the share classes and the number of shares in each share class;

    (e)   the total number of shares;

    (f)   the nominal value or accountable par of the shares;

    (g)   the articles of association of the SPE;

    (h)   where the SPE was formed as a result of a transformation, merger or division of companies, the resolution on the transformation, merger or division that led to the creation of the SPE.

    3.   The documents and particulars referred to in paragraph 2 shall be provided in the language required by the applicable national law. ...

Article 11. Disclosure.   1.   The disclosure of the documents and particulars concerning an SPE which must be disclosed under this Regulation shall be effected in accordance with the applicable national law implementing Article 3 of Directive 68/151/EEC.

    2.   The letters and order forms of an SPE, whether they are in paper or electronic form, as well as its website, if any, shall state the following particulars:

(a) the information necessary to identify the register referred to in Article 9, with the number of entry of the SPE in that register;

(b) the name of the SPE, the address of its registered office and, where appropriate, the fact that the company is being wound up.

Article 13. Branches.   Branches of an SPE shall be governed by the law of the Member State in which the branch is located, including the relevant provisions implementing Council Directive 89/666/EEC.

Chapter III — Shares

Article 16. Transfer of shares.   5.   A transfer of shares shall be valid only if it complies with this Regulation and the articles of association. The provisions of the applicable national law concerning the protection of persons who acquire shares in good faith shall apply.

Article 18. Withdrawal of a shareholder.   A shareholder shall have the right to withdraw from the SPE if the activities of the SPE are being or have been conducted in a manner which causes serious harm to the interests of the shareholder as a result of one or more of the following events: …

b)   the registered office of the SPE has been transferred to another Member State;
…

Chapter IV — Capital

Article 20. Consideration for shares.   1.   Shareholders must pay the agreed consideration in cash or provide the agreed consideration in kind in accordance with the articles of association of the SPE.

2.   Except in the case of a reduction of the share capital, shareholders may not be released from the obligation to pay or provide the agreed consideration.

3.   Without prejudice to paragraphs 1 and 2, the liability of shareholders for the consideration paid or provided shall be governed by the applicable national law.

Article 23. Own shares.   5.   Shares acquired by the SPE in contravention of this Regulation or the articles of association shall be sold or cancelled within one year of their acquisition.

6.   Subject to paragraph 5 and to the articles of association of the SPE, the cancellation of shares shall be governed by the applicable national law....

Article 25. Accounts.   1.   An SPE shall be subject to the requirements of the applicable national law as regards preparation, filing, auditing and publication of accounts.

2.   The management body shall keep the books of the SPE. The bookkeeping of the SPE shall be governed by the applicable national law.

Chapter V — Organisation of the SPE

Article 27. Resolutions of shareholders. 4. Resolutions of the shareholders shall comply with this Regulation and the articles of association of the SPE.

The right of shareholders to challenge resolutions shall be governed by the applicable national law.

Article 30. Directors. 1. Only a natural person may be a director of an SPE.

2. A person who acts as a director without having been formally appointed shall be considered a director as regards all duties and liabilities to which the latter are subject.

3. A person who is disqualified under national law from serving as a director of a company by a judicial or administrative decision of a Member State may not become or serve as a director of an SPE.

4. Disqualification of a person serving as a director of the SPE shall be governed by the applicable national law.

Article 31. General duties and liabilities of directors. 5. Without prejudice to the provisions of this Regulation, the liability of directors shall be governed by the applicable national law.

Article 32. Related party transactions. Related party transactions shall be governed by the provisions of the applicable national law implementing Council Directives 78/660/EEC and 83/349/EEC.

Chapter VI — Employee participation

Article 34. General provisions. 1. The SPE shall be subject to the rules on employee participation, if any, applicable in the Member State in which it has its registered office, subject to the provisions of this Article.

2. In the case of the transfer of the registered office of an SPE Article 38 shall apply.

3. In the case of a cross-border merger of an SPE with an SPE or other company registered in another Member State, the provisions of the laws of the Member States implementing Directive 2005/56/EC of the European Parliament and of the Council shall apply.

Chapter VII — Transfer of the registered office of the SPE

Article 35. General provisions. 1. The registered office of an SPE may be transferred to another Member State in accordance with this Chapter.

The transfer of the registered office of an SPE shall not result in the winding-up of the SPE or in any interruption or loss of the SPEs legal personality or affect any right or obligation under any contract entered into by the SPE existing before the transfer.

2. Paragraph 1 shall not apply to SPEs against which proceedings for winding-up, liquidation, insolvency or suspension of payments have been brought, or in respect of which preventive measures have been taken by the competent authorities to avoid the opening of such proceedings.

3.   A transfer shall take effect on the date of registration of the SPE in the host Member State. From that date, for matters covered by the second paragraph of Article 4, the SPE shall be regulated by the law of the host Member State.

4.   For the purpose of judicial or administrative proceedings commenced before the transfer of the registered office, the SPE shall be considered, following the registration referred to in paragraph 3, as having its registered office in the home Member State.

Article 36. Transfer procedure.   1.   The management body of an SPE planning a transfer shall draw up a transfer proposal, which shall include at least the following particulars:

(a)   the name of the SPE and the address of its registered office in the home Member State;

(b)   the name of the SPE and the address of its proposed registered office in the host Member State;

(c)   the proposed articles of association for the SPE in the host Member State;

(d)   the proposed timetable for the transfer;

(e)   the date from which it is proposed that the transactions of the SPE are to be regarded for accounting purposes as having been carried out in the host Member State;

(f)   the consequences of the transfer for employees, and the proposed measures concerning them;

(g)   where appropriate, detailed information on the transfer of the central administration or principal place of business of the SPE.

2.   At least one month before the resolution of the shareholders referred to in paragraph 4 is taken, the management body of the SPE shall:

(a)   submit the transfer proposal to the shareholders and employee representatives, or where there are no such representatives, to the employees of the SPE for examination and make it available to the creditors for inspection;

(b)   disclose the transfer proposal.

3.   The management body of the SPE shall draw up a report to the shareholders explaining and justifying the legal and economic aspects of the proposed transfer and setting out the implications of the transfer for shareholders, creditors and employees. The report shall be submitted to the shareholders and the employee representatives, or where there are no such representatives, to the employees themselves together with the transfer proposal.

Where the management body receives in time the opinion of the employee representatives on the transfer, that opinion shall be submitted to the shareholders.

4.   The transfer proposal shall be submitted to the shareholders for approval in accordance with the rules of the articles of association of the SPE relating to the amendment of the articles of association.

5.   Where the SPE is subject to an employee participation regime, shareholders may reserve the right to make the implementation of the transfer conditional on their express ratification of the arrangements with respect to the participation of employees in the host Member State.

6.   The protection of any minority shareholders who oppose the transfer and of the creditors of the SPE shall be governed by the law of the home Member State.

Article 37. Scrutiny of the legality of the transfer.   1.   Each Member State shall designate a competent authority to scrutinise the legality of the transfer by verifying compliance with the transfer procedure laid down in Article 36.

2.   The competent authority of the home Member State shall verify, without undue delay, that the requirements of Article 36 have been met and, if that is found to be the case, shall issue a certificate confirming that all the formalities required under the transfer procedure have been completed in the home Member State.

3.   Within one month of the receipt of the certificate referred to in paragraph 2, the SPE shall present the following documents to the competent authority in the host Member State:

(a)   the certificate provided for in paragraph 2;

(b)   the proposed articles of association for the SPE in the host Member State, as approved by the shareholders;

(c)   the transfer proposal, as approved by the shareholders.

Those documents shall be deemed to be sufficient to enable the registration of the SPE in the host Member State.

4.   The competent authority in the host Member State shall, within 14 calendar days of receipt of the documents referred to in paragraph 3, verify that the substantive and formal conditions required for the transfer of the registered office are met and if that is found to be the case, take the measures necessary for the registration of the SPE.

5.   The competent authority of the host Member State may refuse to register an SPE only on the grounds that the SPE does not meet all the substantive or formal requirements under this Chapter. The SPE shall be registered when it has fulfilled all requirements under this Chapter.

6.   Using the notification form set out in Annex II, the competent authority of the host Member State shall, without undue delay, notify the competent authority responsible for removing the SPE from the register in the home Member State of the registration of the SPE in the host Member State.

Removal from the register shall be effected as soon as, but not before, a notification has been received.

7.   Registrations in the host Member State and removals from the register in the home Member State shall be disclosed.

Article 38. Arrangements for the participation of employees.   1.   The SPE shall be subject, as from the date of registration, to the rules in force in the host Member State, if any, concerning arrangements for the participation of employees.

2.   Paragraph 1 shall not apply where the employees of the SPE in the home Member State account for at least one third of the total number of employees of the SPE including subsidiaries or branches of the SPE in any Member State, and where one of the following conditions is met:

(a)   the legislation of the host Member State does not provide for at least the same level of participation as that operated in the SPE in the home Member State prior to its registration in the host Member State. The level of employee participation shall be measured by reference to the proportion of employee representatives amongst the members of the administrative or supervisory body or their committees or of the management group which covers the profit units of the SPE, subject to employee representation;

(b)   the legislation of the host Member State does not confer on the employees of establishments of the SPE that are situated in other Member States the same entitlement to exercise participation rights as such employees enjoyed before the transfer.

3.   Where one of the conditions set out in points a) or b) of paragraph 2 is met, the management body of the SPE shall take the necessary steps, as soon as possible, after disclosure of the transfer proposal, to start negotiations with the representatives of the SPE's employees with a view to reaching an agreement on arrangements for the participation of the employees.

4.   The agreement between the management body of the SPE and the representatives of the employees shall specify:

(a)   the scope of the agreement;

(b)   where, during the negotiations, the parties decide to establish arrangements for participation in the SPE following the transfer, the substance of those arrangements including, where applicable, the number of members in the company's administrative or supervisory body employees will be entitled to elect, appoint, recommend or oppose, the procedures as to how these members may be elected, appointed, recommended or opposed by employees, and their rights;

(c)   the date of entry into force of the agreement and its duration, and any cases in which the agreement should be renegotiated and the procedure for its renegotiation.

5.   Negotiations shall be limited to a period of six months. The parties may agree to extend negotiations beyond this period for an additional six-month period. The negotiations shall otherwise be governed by the law of the home Member State.

6.   In the absence of an agreement, the participation arrangements existing in the home Member State shall be maintained.

Chapter VIII — Restructuring, dissolution and nullity

Article 39. Restructuring.   The transformation, merger and division of the SPE shall be governed by the applicable national law.

Article 40. Dissolution.   1.   The SPE shall be dissolved in the following circumstances:

(a)   by expiry of the period for which it was established;

(b)   by the resolution of the shareholders;

(c)   in cases set out in the applicable national law.

2.   Winding-up shall be governed by the applicable national law.

3.   Liquidation, insolvency, suspension of payments and similar procedures shall be governed by the applicable national law and by Council Regulation (EC) No 1346/2000.

4.   Dissolution of the SPE shall be disclosed.

Article 41. Nullity.   The nullity of the SPE shall be governed by the provisions of the applicable national law implementing Article 11(1) of Directive 68/151/EEC, points (a), (b), (c) and (e), except for the reference in point (c) to the objects of the company, of Article 11(2) and Article 12 of that Directive.

X

Law Applicable to Social Security

A.1. Regulation (EC) No 883/2004 of the European Parliament and of the Council of 29 April 2004 on the coordination of social security systems (OJ, L 200 of 7 June 2004)[1]

(7) Due to the major differences existing between national legislation in terms of the persons covered, it is preferable to lay down the principle that this Regulation is to apply to nationals of a Member State, stateless persons and refugees resident in the territory of a Member State who are or have been subject to the social security legislation of one or more Member States, as well as to the members of their families and to their survivors.

(8) The general principle of equal treatment is of particular importance for workers who do not reside in the Member State of their employment, including frontier workers.

(9) The Court of Justice has on several occasions given an opinion on the possibility of equal treatment of benefits, income and facts; this principle should be adopted explicitly and developed, while observing the substance and spirit of legal rulings.

(10) However, the principle of treating certain facts or events occurring in the territory of another Member State as if they had taken place in the territory of the Member State whose legislation is applicable should not interfere with the principle of aggregating periods of insurance, employment, self-employment or residence completed under the legislation of another Member State with those completed under the legislation of the competent Member State. Periods completed under the legislation of another Member State should therefore be taken into account solely by applying the principle of aggregation of periods.

(11) The assimilation of facts or events occurring in a Member State can in no way render another Member State competent or its legislation applicable.

(17) With a view to guaranteeing the equality of treatment of all persons occupied in the territory of a Member State as effectively as possible, it is appropriate to determine as the legislation applicable, as a general rule, that of the Member State in which the person concerned pursues his/her activity as an employed or self-employed person.

(17a) Once the legislation of a Member State becomes applicable to a person under Title II of this Regulation, the conditions for affiliation and entitlement to benefits should be defined by the legislation of the competent Member State while respecting Community law.

(18) In specific situations which justify other criteria of applicability, it is necessary to derogate from that general rule.

---

[1] As finally amended by Regulation (EC) No 988/2009 of 16 September 2009 (OJ, L 284 of 30 October 2009). [Note of the Editor]

(18a) The principle of single applicable legislation is of great importance and should be enhanced. This should not mean, however, that the grant of a benefit alone, in accordance with this Regulation and comprising the payment of insurance contributions or insurance coverage for the beneficiary, renders the legislation of the Member State, whose institution has granted that benefit, the applicable legislation for that person.

Title I — General provisions

Article 1. Definitions.   For the purposes of this Regulation:

(a)   'activity as an employed person' means any activity or equivalent situation treated as such for the purposes of the social security legislation of the Member State in which such activity or equivalent situation exists;

(b)   'activity as a self-employed person' means any activity or equivalent situation treated as such for the purposes of the social security legislation of the Member State in which such activity or equivalent situation exists;

(c)   'insured person', in relation to the social security branches covered by Title III, Chapters 1 and 3, means any person satisfying the conditions required under the legislation of the Member State competent under Title II to have the right to benefits, taking into account the provisions of this Regulation;

(d)   'civil servant' means a person considered to be such or treated as such by the Member State to which the administration employing him/her is subject;

(e)   'special scheme for civil servants' means any social security scheme which is different from the general social security scheme applicable to employed persons in the Member State concerned and to which all, or certain categories of, civil servants are directly subject;

(f)   'frontier worker' means any person pursuing an activity as an employed or self-employed person in a Member State and who resides in another Member State to which he/she returns as a rule daily or at least once a week;

(g)   'refugee' shall have the meaning assigned to it in Article 1 of the Convention relating to the Status of Refugees, signed in Geneva on 28 July 1951;

(h)   'stateless person' shall have the meaning assigned to it in Article 1 of the Convention relating to the Status of Stateless Persons, signed in New York on 28 September 1954;

(i)   'member of the family' means:

1.   (i)   any person defined or recognised as a member of the family or designated as a member of the household by the legislation under which benefits are provided;

(ii)   with regard to benefits in kind pursuant to Title III, Chapter 1 on sickness, maternity and equivalent paternity benefits, any person defined or recognised as a member of the family or designated as a member of the household by the legislation of the Member State in which he/she resides;

2.   if the legislation of a Member State which is applicable under subparagraph 1 does not make a distinction between the members of the family and other persons to whom it is applicable, the spouse, minor children, and dependent children who have reached the age of majority shall be considered members of the family;

3.   if, under the legislation which is applicable under subparagraphs 1 and 2, a person is considered a member of the family or member of the household only if he/she

lives in the same household as the insured person or pensioner, this condition shall be considered satisfied if the person in question is mainly dependent on the insured person or pensioner;

(j) 'residence' means the place where a person habitually resides;

(k) 'stay' means temporary residence;

(l) 'legislation' means, in respect of each Member State, laws, regulations and otherstatutory provisions and all other implementing measures relating to the socialsecurity branches covered by Article 3(1);

This term excludes contractual provisions other than those which serve to implement an insurance obligation arising from the laws and regulations referred to in the preceding subparagraph or which have been the subject of a decision by the public authorities which makes them obligatory or extends their scope, provided that the Member State concerned makes a declaration to that effect, notified to the President of the European Parliament and the President of the Council of the European Union. Such declaration shall be published in the *Official Journal of the European Union*;

(m) 'competent authority' means, in respect of each Member State, the Minister, Ministers or other equivalent authority responsible for social security schemes throughout or in any part of the Member State in question;

(n) 'Administrative Commission' means the commission referred to in Article 71;

(o) 'Implementing Regulation' means the Regulation referred to in Article 89;

(p) 'institution' means, in respect of each Member State, the body or authority responsible for applying all or part of the legislation;

(q) 'competent institution' means:

(i) the institution with which the person concerned is insured at the time of the application for benefit; or

(ii) the institution from which the person concerned is or would be entitled to benefits if he/she or a member or members of his/her family resided in the Member State in which the institution is situated; or

(iii) the institution designated by the competent authority of the Member State concerned; or

(iv) in the case of a scheme relating to an employer's obligations in respect of the benefits set out in Article 3(1), either the employer or the insurer involved or, in default thereof, the body or authority designated by the competent authority of the Member State concerned;

(r) 'institution of the place of residence' and 'institution of the place of stay' mean respectively the institution which is competent to provide benefits in the place where the person concerned resides and the institution which is competent to provide benefits in the place where the person concerned is staying, in accordance with the legislation administered by that institution or, where no such institution exists, the institution designated by the competent authority of the Member State concerned;

(s) 'competent Member State' means the Member State in which the competent institution is situated;

(t) 'period of insurance' means periods of contribution, employment or self-employment as defined or recognised as periods of insurance by the legislation under which they were completed or considered as completed, and all periods treated as such, where they are regarded by the said legislation as equivalent to periods of insurance;

(u) 'period of employment' or 'period of self-employment' mean periods so defined or recognised by the legislation under which they were completed, and all periods treated as such, where they are regarded by the said legislation as equivalent to periods of employment or to periods of self-employment;

(v) 'period of residence' means periods so defined or recognised by the legislation under which they were completed or considered as completed;

(va) 'Benefits in kind' means:

(i) for the purposes of Title III, Chapter 1 (sickness, maternity and equivalent paternity benefits), benefits in kind provided for under the legislation of a Member State which are intended to supply, make available, pay directly or reimburse the cost of medical care and products and services ancillary to that care.

This includes long-term care benefits in kind;

(ii) for the purposes of Title III, Chapter 2 (accidents at work and occupational diseases), all benefits in kind relating to accidents at work and occupational diseases as defined in point (i) above and provided for under the Member States' accidents at work and occupational diseases schemes;

(w) 'pension' covers not only pensions but also lump-sum benefits which can be substituted for them and payments in the form of reimbursement of contributions and, subject to the provisions of Title III, revaluation increases or supplementary allowances;

(x) 'pre-retirement benefit' means: all cash benefits, other than an unemployment benefit or an early old-age benefit, provided from a specified age to workers who have reduced, ceased or suspended their remunerative activities until the age at which they qualify for an old-age pension or an early retirement pension, the receipt of which is not conditional upon the person concerned being available to the employment services of the competent State; 'early old-age benefit' means a benefit provided before the normal pension entitlement age is reached and which either continues to be provided once the said age is reached or is replaced by another old-age benefit;

(y) 'death grant' means any one-off payment in the event of death excluding the lump-sum benefits referred to in subparagraph w;

(z) 'family benefit' means all benefits in kind or in cash intended to meet family expenses, excluding advances of maintenance payments and special childbirth and adoption allowances mentioned in Annex I.

Article 2. Persons covered. 1. This Regulation shall apply to nationals of a Member State, stateless persons and refugees residing in a Member State who are or have been subject to the legislation of one or more Member States, as well as to the members of their families and to their survivors.

2. It shall also apply to the survivors of persons who have been subject to the legislation of one or more Member States, irrespective of the nationality of such persons, where their survivors are nationals of a Member State or stateless persons or refugees residing in one of the Member States.

Article 3. Matters covered. 1. This Regulation shall apply to all legislation concerning the following branches of social security:

(a) sickness benefits;

(b) maternity and equivalent paternity benefits;

(c) invalidity benefits;

(d) old-age benefits;

(e) survivors' benefits;

(f) benefits in respect of accidents at work and occupational diseases;

(g) death grants;

(h) unemployment benefits;

(i) pre-retirement benefits;

(j) family benefits.

2. Unless otherwise provided for in Annex XI, this Regulation shall apply to general and special social security schemes, whether contributory or non-contributory, and to schemes relating to the obligations of an employer or shipowner.

3. This Regulation shall also apply to the special non-contributory cash benefits covered by Article 70.

4. The provisions of Title III of this Regulation shall not, however, affect the legislative provisions of any Member State concerning a shipowner's obligations.

5. This Regulation shall not apply to:

(a) social and medical assistance or

(b) benefits in relation to which a Member State assumes the liability for damages to persons and provides for compensation, such as those for victims of war and military action or their consequences; victims of crime, assassination or terrorist acts; victims of damage occasioned by agents of the Member State in the course of their duties; or victims who have suffered a disadvantage for political or religious reasons or for reasons of descent.

Title II — Determination of the legislation applicable

Article 11. General rules. 1. Persons to whom this Regulation applies shall be subject to the legislation of a single Member State only. Such legislation shall be determined in accordance with this Title.

2. For the purposes of this Title, persons receiving cash benefits because or as a consequence of their activity as an employed or self-employed person shall be considered to be pursuing the said activity. This shall not apply to invalidity, old-age or survivors' pensions or to pensions in respect of accidents at work or occupational diseases or to sickness benefits in cash covering treatment for an unlimited period.

3. Subject to Articles 12 to 16:

(a) a person pursuing an activity as an employed or self-employed person in a Member State shall be subject to the legislation of that Member State;

(b) a civil servant shall be subject to the legislation of the Member State to which the administration employing him/her is subject;

(c) a person receiving unemployment benefits in accordance with Article 65 under the legislation of the Member State of residence shall be subject to the legislation of that Member State;

(d) a person called up or recalled for service in the armed forces or for civilian service in a Member State shall be subject to the legislation of that Member State;

(e) any other person to whom subparagraphs (a) to (d) do not apply shall be subject to the legislation of the Member State of residence, without prejudice to other provisions of this Regulation guaranteeing him/her benefits under the legislation of one or more other Member States.

4.   For the purposes of this Title, an activity as an employed or self-employed person normally pursued on board a vessel at sea flying the flag of a Member State shall be deemed to be an activity pursued in the said Member State. However, a person employed on board a vessel flying the flag of a Member State and remunerated for such activity by an undertaking or a person whose registered office or place of business is in another Member State shall be subject to the legislation of the latter Member State if he/she resides in that State. The undertaking or person paying the remuneration shall be considered as the employer for the purposes of the said legislation.

Article 12. Special rules.   1.   A person who pursues an activity as an employed person in a Member State on behalf of an employer which normally carries out its activities there and who is posted by that employer to another Member State to perform work on that employer's behalf shall continue to be subject to the legislation of the first Member State, provided that the anticipated duration of such work does not exceed 24 months and that he/she is not sent to replace another person.

2.   A person who normally pursues an activity as a self-employed person in a Member State who goes to pursue a similar activity in another Member State shall continue to be subject to the legislation of the first Member State, provided that the anticipated duration of such activity does not exceed 24 months.

Article 13. Pursuit of activities in two or more Member States.   1.   A person who normally pursues an activity as an employed person in two or more Member States shall be subject to:

(a)   the legislation of the Member State of residence if he/she pursues a substantial part of his/her activity in that Member State or if he/she is employed by various undertakings or various employers whose registered office or place of business is in different Member States, or

(b)   the legislation of the Member State in which the registered office or place of business of the undertaking or employer employing him/her is situated, if he/she does not pursue a substantial part of his/her activities in the Member State of residence.

2.   A person who normally pursues an activity as a self-employed person in two or more Member States shall be subject to

(a)   the legislation of the Member State of residence if he/she pursues a substantial part of his/her activity in that Member State; or

(b)   the legislation of the Member State in which the centre of interest of his/her activities is situated, if he/she does not reside in one of the Member States in which he/she pursues a substantial part of his/her activity.

3.   A person who normally pursues an activity as an employed person and an activity as a self-employed person in different Member States shall be subject to the legislation of the Member State in which he/she pursues an activity as an employed person or, if he/she pursues such an activity in two or more Member States, to the legislation determined in accordance with paragraph 1.

4.   A person who is employed as a civil servant by one Member State and who pursues an activity as an employed person and/or as a self-employed person in one or more other Member States shall be subject to the legislation of the Member State to which the administration employing him/her is subject.

5.   Persons referred to in paragraphs 1 to 4 shall be treated, for the purposes of the legislation determined in accordance with these provisions, as though they were pursuing all their activities as employed or self-employed persons and were receiving all their income in the Member State concerned.

Article 14. Voluntary insurance or optional continued insurance.   1.   Articles 11 to 13 shall not apply to voluntary insurance or to optional continued insurance unless, in respect of one of the branches referred to in Article 3(1), only a voluntary scheme of insurance exists in a Member State.

2.   Where, by virtue of the legislation of a Member State, the person concerned is subject to compulsory insurance in that Member State, he/she may not be subject to a voluntary insurance scheme or an optional continued insurance scheme in another Member State. In all other cases in which, for a given branch, there is a choice between several voluntary insurance schemes or optional continued insurance schemes, the person concerned shall join only the scheme of his/her choice.

3.   However, in respect of invalidity, old age and survivors' benefits, the person concerned may join the voluntary or optional continued insurance scheme of a Member State, even if he/she is compulsorily subject to the legislation of another Member State, provided that he/she has been subject, at some stage in his/her career, to the legislation of the first Member State because or as a consequence of an activity as an employed or self-employed person and if such overlapping is explicitly or implicitly allowed under the legislation of the first Member State.

4.   Where the legislation of a Member State makes admission to voluntary insurance or optional continued insurance conditional upon residence in that Member State or upon previous activity as an employed or self-employed person, Article 5(b) shall apply only to persons who have been subject, at some earlier stage, to the legislation of that Member State on the basis of an activity as an employed or self-employed person.

Article 15. Contract staff of the European Communities.   Contract staff of the European Communities may opt to be subject to the legislation of the Member State in which they are employed, to the legislation of the Member State to which they were last subject or to the legislation of the Member State whose nationals they are, in respect of provisions other than those relating to family allowances, provided under the scheme applicable to such staff. This right of option, which may be exercised once only, shall take effect from the date of entry into employment.

Article 16. Exceptions to Articles 11 to 15.   1.   Two or more Member States, the competent authorities of these Member States or the bodies designated by these authorities may by common agreement provide for exceptions to Articles 11 to 15 in the interest of certain persons or categories of persons.

2.   A person who receives a pension or pensions under the legislation of one or more Member States and who resides in another Member State may at his/her request be exempted from application of the legislation of the latter State provided that he/she is not subject to that legislation on account of pursuing an activity as an employed or self-employed person.

Article 85. Rights of institutions.   1.   If a person receives benefits under the legislation of one Member State in respect of an injury resulting from events occurring in another Member State, any rights of the institution responsible for providing benefits against a third party liable to provide compensation for the injury shall be governed by the following rules:

(a)   where the institution responsible for providing benefits is, under the legislation it applies, subrogated to the rights which the beneficiary has against the third party, such subrogation shall be recognised by each Member State;

(b)   where the institution responsible for providing benefits has a direct right against the third party, each Member State shall recognise such rights.

2.   If a person receives benefits under the legislation of one Member State in respect of an injury resulting from events occurring in another Member State, the provisions of the said legislation which determine the cases in which the civil liability of employers or of their employees is to be excluded shall apply with regard to the said person or to the competent institution. Paragraph 1 shall also apply to any rights of the institution responsible for providing benefits against employers or their employees in cases where their liability is not excluded.

3.   Where, in accordance with Article 35(3) and/or Article 41(2), two or more Member States or their competent authorities have concluded an agreement to waive reimbursement between institutions under their jurisdiction, or, where reimbursement does not depend on the amount of benefits actually provided, any rights arising against a liable third party shall be governed by the following rules:

(a)   where the institution of the Member State of residence or stay accords benefits to a person in respect of an injury sustained in its territory, that institution, in accordance with the provisions of the legislation it applies, shall exercise the right to subrogation or direct action against the third party liable to provide compensation for the injury;

(b)   for the application of (a):

(i)   the person receiving benefits shall be deemed to be insured with the institution of the place of residence or stay, and

(ii)   that institution shall be deemed to be the institution responsible for providing benefits;

(c)   paragraphs 1 and 2 shall remain applicable in respect of any benefits not covered by the waiver agreement or a reimbursement which does not depend on the amount of benefits actually provided.

Title VI — Transitional and final provisions

Article 87. Transitional provisions.   8.   If, as a result of this Regulation, a person is subject to the legislation of a Member State other than that determined in accordance with Title II of Regulation (EEC) No 1408/71, that legislation shall continue to apply while the relevant situation remains unchanged and in any case for no longer than 10 years from the date of application of this Regulation unless the person concerned requests that he/she be subject to the legislation applicable under this Regulation. The request shall be submitted within 3 months after the date of application of this Regulation to the competent institution of the Member State whose legislation is applicable under this Regulation if the person concerned is to be subject to the legislation of that Member State as of the date of application of this

Regulation. If the request is made after the time limit indicated, the change of applicable legislation shall take place on the first day of the following month.

Article 90. Repeal. 1. Council Regulation (EEC) No 1408/71 shall be repealed from the date of application of this Regulation. However, Regulation (EEC) No 1408/71 shall remain in force and shall continue to have legal effect for the purposes of:

(a) Council Regulation (EC) No 859/2003 of 14 May 2003 extending the provisions of Regulation (EEC) No 1408/71 and Regulation (EEC) No 574/72 to nationals of third countries who are not already covered by those provisions solely on the ground of their nationality, for as long as that Regulation has not been repealed or modified;

(b) Council Regulation (EEC) No 1661/85 of 13 June 1985 laying down the technical adaptations to the Community rules on social security for migrant workers with regard to Greenland, for as long as that Regulation has not been repealed or modified;

(c) the Agreement on the European Economic Area and the Agreement between the European Community and its Member States, of the one part, and the Swiss Confederation, of the other part, on the free movement of persons and other agreements which contain a reference to Regulation (EEC) No 1408/71, for as long as those agreements have not been modified in the light of this Regulation.

2. References to Regulation (EEC) No 1408/71 in Council Directive 98/49/EC of 29 June 1998 on safeguarding the supplementary pension rights of employed and self-employed persons moving within the Community are to be read as referring to this Regulation.

Article 91. Entry into force. This Regulation shall enter into force on the 20th day after its publication in the *Official Journal of the European Union.*

It shall apply from the date of entry into force of the Implementing Regulation...

A.2. Regulation (EC) No 987/2009 of the European Parliament and of the Council of 16 September 2009 laying down the procedure for implementing Regulation (EC) No 883/2004 on the coordination of social security systems (OJ, L 284 of 30 October 2009).

(20) For the purposes of provisions on mutual assistance regarding the recovery of benefits provided but not due, the recovery of provisional payments and contributions and the offsetting and assistance with recovery, the jurisdiction of the requested Member State is limited to actions regarding enforcement measures. Any other action falls under the jurisdiction of the applicant Member State.

Title I — General provisions

Chapter I — Definitions

Article 1. Definitions. 1. For the purposes of this Regulation:
   (a) 'basic Regulation' means Regulation (EC) No 883/2004;
   (b) 'implementing Regulation' means this Regulation; and

(c)   the definitions set out in the basic Regulation shall apply.

2.   In addition to the definitions referred to in paragraph 1,

(a)   'access point' means an entity providing:

(i)   an electronic contact point;

(ii)   automatic routing based on the address; and

(iii)   intelligent routing based on software that enables automatic checking and routing (for example, an artificial intelligence application) and/or human intervention;

(b)   'liaison body' means any body designated by the competent authority of a Member State for one or more of the branches of social security referred to in Article 3 of the basic Regulation to respond to requests for information and assistance for the purposes of the application of the basic Regulation and the implementing Regulation and which has to fulfil the tasks assigned to it under Title IV of the implementing Regulation;

(c)   'document' means a set of data, irrespective of the medium used, structured in such a way that it can be exchanged electronically and which must be communicated in order to enable the operation of the basic Regulation and the implementing Regulation;

(d)   'Structured Electronic Document' means any structured document in a format designed for the electronic exchange of information between Member States;

(e)   'transmission by electronic means' means the transmission of data using electronic equipment for the processing (including digital compression) of data and employing wires, radio transmission, optical technologies or any other electromagnetic means;

(f)   'Audit Board' means the body referred to in Article 74 of the basic Regulation.

Article 6. Provisional application of legislation and provisional granting of benefits.
1.   Unless otherwise provided for in the implementing Regulation, where there is a difference of views between the institutions or authorities of two or more Member States concerning the determination of the applicable legislation, the person concerned shall be made provisionally subject to the legislation of one of those Member States, the order of priority being determined as follows:

(a)   the legislation of the Member State where the person actually pursues his employment or self-employment, if the employment or self-employment is pursued in only one Member State;

(b)   the legislation of the Member State of residence where the person concerned performs part of his activity/activities or where the person is not employed or self-employed;

(c)   the legislation of the Member State the application of which was first requested where the person pursues an activity or activities in two or more Member States.

2.   Where there is a difference of views between the institutions or authorities of two or more Member States about which institution should provide the benefits in cash or in kind, the person concerned who could claim benefits if there was no dispute shall be entitled, on a provisional basis, to the benefits provided for by the legislation applied by the institution of his place of residence or, if that person does not reside on the territory of one of the Member States concerned, to the benefits provided for by the legislation applied by the institution to which the request was first submitted.

3.   Where no agreement is reached between the institutions or authorities concerned, the matter may be brought before the Administrative Commission by the competent authorities no earlier than one month after the date on which the difference

of views, as referred to in paragraph 1 or 2 arose. The Administrative Commission shall seek to reconcile the points of view within six months of the date on which the matter was brought before it.

4.   Where it is established either that the applicable legislation is not that of the Member State of provisional membership, or the institution which granted the benefits on a provisional basis was not the competent institution, the institution identified as being competent shall be deemed retroactively to have been so, as if that difference of views had not existed, at the latest from either the date of provisional membership or of the first provisional granting of the benefits concerned.

5.   If necessary, the institution identified as being competent and the institution which provisionally paid the cash benefits or provisionally received contributions shall settle the financial situation of the person concerned as regards contributions and cash benefits paid provisionally, where appropriate, in accordance with Title IV, Chapter III, of the implementing Regulation.

Benefits in kind granted provisionally by an institution in accordance with paragraph 2 shall be reimbursed by the competent institution in accordance with Title IV of the implementing Regulation.

Article 11. Elements for determining residence.   1.   Where there is a difference of views between the institutions of two or more Member States about the determination of the residence of a person to whom the basic Regulation applies, these institutions shall establish by common agreement the centre of interests of the person concerned, based on an overall assessment of all available information relating to relevant facts, which may include, as appropriate:

(a)   the duration and continuity of presence on the territory of the Member States concerned;

(b)   the person's situation, including:

(i)   the nature and the specific characteristics of any activity pursued, in particular the place where such activity is habitually pursued, the stability of the activity, and the duration of any work contract;

(ii)   his family *status* and family ties;

(iii)   the exercise of any non-remunerated activity;

(iv)   in the case of students, the source of their income;

(v)   his housing situation, in particular how permanent it is;

(vi)   the Member State in which the person is deemed to reside for taxation purposes.

2.   Where the consideration of the various criteria based on relevant facts as set out in paragraph 1 does not lead to agreement between the institutions concerned, the person's intention, as it appears from such facts and circumstances, especially the reasons that led the person to move, shall be considered to be decisive for establishing that person's actual place of residence.

Title II — Determination of the legislation applicable

Article 14. Details relating to Articles 12 and 13 of the basic Regulation.   1.   For the purposes of the application of Article 12(1) of the basic Regulation, a 'person who pursues an activity as an employed person in a Member State on behalf of an employer which normally carries out its activities there and who is posted by that employer to another Member State' shall include a person who is recruited with a view to being posted to another Member State, provided that, immediately before the start of his employment, the person concerned is already subject to the legislation of the Member State in which his employer is established.

2.   For the purposes of the application of Article 12(1) of the basic Regulation, the words 'which normally carries out its activities there' shall refer to an employer that ordinarily performs substantial activities, other than purely internal management activities, in the territory of the Member State in which it is established, taking account of all criteria characterising the activities carried out by the undertaking in question. The relevant criteria must be suited to the specific characteristics of each employer and the real nature of the activities carried out.

3.   For the purposes of the application of Article 12(2) of the basic Regulation, the words 'who normally pursues an activity as a self-employed person' shall refer to a person who habitually carries out substantial activities in the territory of the Member State in which he is established. In particular, that person must have already pursued his activity for some time before the date when he wishes to take advantage of the provisions of that Article and, during any period of temporary activity in another Member State, must continue to fulfil, in the Member State where he is established, the requirements for the pursuit of his activity in order to be able to pursue it on his return.

4.   For the purposes of the application of Article 12(2) of the basic Regulation, the criterion for determining whether the activity that a self-employed person goes to pursue in another Member State is 'similar' to the self-employed activity normally pursued shall be that of the actual nature of the activity, rather than of the designation of employed or self-employed activity that may be given to this activity by the other Member State.

5.   For the purposes of the application of Article 13(1) of the basic Regulation a person who 'normally pursues an activity as an employed person in two or more Member States' shall refer, in particular, to a person who:

(a)   while maintaining an activity in one Member State, simultaneously exercises a separate activity in one or more other Member States, irrespective of the duration or nature of that separate activity;

(b)   continuously, pursues alternating activities, with the exception of marginal activities, in two or more Member States, irrespective of the frequency or regularity of the alternation.

6.   For the purposes of the application of Article 13(2) of the basic Regulation, a person who 'normally pursues an activity as a self-employed person in two or more Member States' shall refer, in particular, to a person who simultaneously or in alternation pursues one or more separate self-employed activities, irrespective of the nature of those activities, in two or more Member States.

7.   For the purpose of distinguishing the activities under paragraphs 5 and 6 from the situations described in Article 12(1)and (2) of the basic Regulation, the duration of the activity in one or more other Member States (whether it is permanent or of an ad hoc or temporary nature) shall be decisive. For these purposes, an overall assessment shall be made of all the relevant facts including, in particular, in the case of an employed person, the place of work as defined in the employment contract.

8.   For the purposes of the application of Article 13(1) and (2) of the basic Regulation, a 'substantial part of employed or self-employed activity' pursued in a Member

State shall mean a quantitatively substantial part of all the activities of the employed or self-employed person pursued there, without this necessarily being the major part of those activities.

To determine whether a substantial part of the activities is pursued in a Member State, the following indicative criteria shall be taken into account:

(a)   in the case of an employed activity, the working time and/or the remuneration; and

(b)   in the case of a self-employed activity, the turnover, working time, number of services rendered and/or income.

In the framework of an overall assessment, a share of less than 25 % in respect of the criteria mentioned above shall be an indicator that a substantial part of the activities is not being pursued in the relevant Member State.

9.   For the purposes of the application of Article 13(2)(b) of the basic Regulation, the 'centre of interest' of the activities of a self-employed person shall be determined by taking account of all the aspects of that person's occupational activities, notably the place where the person's fixed and permanent place of business is located, the habitual nature or the duration of the activities pursued, the number of services rendered, and the intention of the person concerned as revealed by all the circumstances.

10.   For the determination of the applicable legislation under paragraphs 8 and 9, the institutions concerned shall take into account the situation projected for the following 12 calendar months.

11.   If a person pursues his activity as an employed person in two or more Member States on behalf of an employer established outside the territory of the Union and if this person resides in a Member State without pursuing substantial activity there, he shall be subject to the legislation of the Member State of residence.

Article 15. Procedures for the application of Article 11(3)(b) and (d), Article 11(4) and Article 12 of the basic Regulation (on the provision of information to the institutions concerned).   1.   Unless otherwise provided for by Article 16 of the implementing Regulation, where a person pursues his activity in a Member State other than the Member State competent under Title II of the basic Regulation, the employer or, in the case of a person who does not pursue an activity as an employed person, the person concerned shall inform the competent institution of the Member State whose legislation is applicable thereof, whenever possible in advance. That institution shall without delay make information concerning the legislation applicable to the person concerned, pursuant to Article 11(3)(b) or Article 12 of the basic Regulation, available to the person concerned and to the institution designated by the competent authority of the Member State in which the activity is pursued.

2.   Paragraph 1 shall apply mutatis mutandis to persons covered by Article 11(3)(d) of the basic Regulation.

3.   An employer within the meaning of Article 11(4) of the basic Regulation who has an employee on board a vessel flying the flag of another Member State shall inform the competent institution of the Member State whose legislation is applicable thereof whenever possible in advance. That institution shall, without delay, make information concerning the legislation applicable to the person concerned, pursuant to Article 11(4) of the basic Regulation, available to the institution designated by the competent authority of the Member State whose flag, the vessel on which the employee is to perform the activity, is flying.

Article 16. Procedure for the application of Article 13 of the basic Regulation.   1.   A person who pursues activities in two or more Member States shall inform the institution designated by the competent authority of the Member State of residence thereof.

2.   The designated institution of the place of residence shall without delay determine the legislation applicable to the person concerned, having regard to Article 13 of the basic Regulation and Article 14 of the implementing Regulation. That initial determination shall be provisional. The institution shall inform the designated institutions of each Member State in which an activity is pursued of its provisional determination.

3.   The provisional determination of the applicable legislation, as provided for in paragraph 2, shall become definitive within two months of the institutions designated by the competent authorities of the Member States concerned being informed of it, in accordance with paragraph 2, unless the legislation has already been definitively determined on the basis of paragraph 4, or at least one of the institutions concerned informs the institution designated by the competent authority of the Member State of residence by the end of this two-month period that it cannot yet accept the determination or that it takes a different view on this.

4.   Where uncertainty about the determination of the applicable legislation requires contacts between the institutions or authorities of two or more Member States, at the request of one or more of the institutions designated by the competent authorities of the Member States concerned or of the competent authorities themselves, the legislation applicable to the person concerned shall be determined by common agreement, having regard to Article 13 of the basic Regulation and the relevant provisions of Article 14 of the implementing Regulation.

Where there is a difference of views between the institutions or competent authorities concerned, those bodies shall seek agreement in accordance with the conditions set out above and Article 6 of the implementing Regulation shall apply.

5.   The competent institution of the Member State whose legislation is determined to be applicable either provisionally or definitively shall without delay inform the person concerned.

6.   If the person concerned fails to provide the information referred to in paragraph 1, this Article shall be applied at the initiative of the institution designated by the competent authority of the Member State of residence as soon as it is appraised of that person's situation, possibly via another institution concerned.

Article 17. Procedure for the application of Article 15 of the basic Regulation.   Contract staff of the European Communities shall exercise the right of option provided for in Article 15 of the basic Regulation when the employment contract is concluded. The authority empowered to conclude the contract shall inform the designated institution of the Member State for whose legislation the contract staff member of the European Communities has opted.

Article 18. Procedure for the application of Article 16 of the basic Regulation.   A request by the employer or the person concerned for exceptions to Articles 11 to 15 of the basic Regulation shall be submitted, whenever possible in advance, to the competent authority or the body designated by the authority of the Member State, whose legislation the employee or person concerned requests be applied.

Article 96. Repeal. 1. Regulation (EEC) No 574/72 is repealed with effect from 1 May 2010.

However, Regulation (EEC) No 574/72 shall remain in force and continue to have legal effect for the purposes of:

(a) Council Regulation (EC) No 859/2003 of 14 May 2003 extending the provisions of Regulation (EEC) No 1408/71 and Regulation (EEC) No 574/72 to nationals of third countries who are not already covered by those provisions solely on the grounds of their nationality, until such time as that Regulation is repealed or amended;

(b) Council Regulation (EEC) No 1661/85 of 13 June 1985 laying down the technical adaptations to the Community rules on social security for migrant workers with regard to Greenland, until such time as that Regulation is repealed or amended;

(c) the Agreement on the European Economic Area, the Agreement between the European Community and its Member States, of the one part, and the Swiss Confederation, of the other, on the free movement of persons and other agreements containing a reference to Regulation (EEC) No 574/72, until such time as those agreements are amended on the basis of the implementing Regulation.

2. In Council Directive 98/49/EC of 29 June 1998 on safeguarding the supplementary pension rights of employed and self-employed persons moving within the Community and more generally in all other Community acts, the references to Regulation (EEC) No 574/72 shall be understood as referring to the implementing Regulation.

Article 97. Publication and entry into force. This Regulation shall be published in the Official Journal of the European Union. It shall enter into force on 1 May 2010.

A.3. Regulation (EU) No 1231/2010 of the European Parliament and of the Council of 24 November 2010 extending Regulation (EC) No 883/2004 and Regulation (EC) No 987/2009 to nationals of third countries who are not already covered by these Regulations solely on the ground of their nationality (OJ, L 344 of 29 December 2010)

Article 1. Regulation (EC) No 883/2004 and Regulation (EC) No 987/2009 shall apply to nationals of third countries who are not already covered by those Regulations solely on the ground of their nationality, as well as to members of their families and to their survivors, provided that they are legally resident in the territory of a Member State and are in a situation which is not confined in all respects within a single Member State.

Article 2. Regulation (EC) No 859/2003 shall be repealed between the Member States that are bound by this Regulation.

Article 3. This Regulation shall enter into force on the third day following its publication in the Official Journal of the European Union.

B.   Decision No A2 of 12 April 2010 concerning the interpretation of Article 12 of Regulation (EC) No 883/2004 of the European parliament and of the Council on the legislation applicable to posted workers and self-employed workers temporarily working outside the competent State (OJ, L 106 of 24 April 2010)

The Administrative Commission for the coordination of social security systems… whereas:

(1)   The provisions of Article 12 of Regulation (EC) No 883/2004, which provide for an exception to the general rule laid down in Article 11(3)(a) of the said Regulation, aim in particular to facilitate the freedom to provide services for the benefit of employers which post workers to Member States other than that in which they are established, as well as the freedom of workers to move to other Member States. These provisions also aim at overcoming the obstacles likely to impede freedom of movement of workers and at encouraging economic interpenetration whilst avoiding administrative complications, especially for workers and undertakings.

(2)   The purpose of these provisions is thus to avoid, for workers, employers and social security institutions, the administrative complications which would result from the application of the general rule laid down in Article 11(3)(a) of the said Regulation where the period of employment is of short duration in a Member State other than the State in which the undertaking has its registered office or a place of business or the State in which the self-employed person normally pursues his activity.

(3)   To this end, the first decisive condition for the application of Article 12(1) of the said Regulation is the existence of a direct relationship between the employer and the worker it engages.

(4)   The protection of the worker and the legal security to which he and the institution with which he is insured are entitled require full guarantees that the direct relationship be maintained throughout the period of posting.

(5)   The second decisive condition for application of Article 12(1) of the said Regulation is the existence of ties between the employer and the Member State in which it is established. The possibility of posting should therefore be confined solely to undertakings normally carrying on their business in the territory of the Member State whose legislation remains applicable to the posted worker; assuming therefore that the above provisions apply only to undertakings which habitually carry on significant activities in the territory of the Member State in which they are established.

(6)   Indicative periods for employed persons and self-employed persons should be specified without prejudice to a case-by-case evaluation.

(7)   There can no longer be any guarantee of maintaining the direct relationship if the posted worker is made available to a third undertaking.

(8)   It is necessary to be able to carry out, throughout the period of posting, all the checks, in particular with regard to the payment of contributions and the maintenance of the direct relationship, required to prevent wrongful use of the above-mentioned provisions, and to ensure that administrative bodies, employers and workers are suitably informed.

(9)   The worker and the employer must be duly informed of the conditions under which the posted worker is allowed to remain subject to the legislation of the country from which he has been posted.

(10) The situation of undertakings and workers should be assessed and monitored by the competent institutions with the appropriate guarantees so as not to impede the freedom to provide services and the freedom of movement of workers.

(11) The principle of sincere cooperation, laid down in Article 10 of the Treaty, places a number of obligations on the competent institutions for the purpose of implementing Article 12 of Regulation (EC) No 883/2004.

Acting in accordance with the conditions laid down in Article 71(2) of Regulation (EC) No 883/2004, has decided as follows:

1. The provisions of Article 12(1) of Regulation (EC) No 883/2004 shall apply to a worker subject to the legislation of a Member State (sending State) by virtue of the pursuit of an activity in the employ of an employer and who is sent by that employer to another Member State (State of employment) in order to perform work there for that employer.

The work shall be regarded as being performed for the employer of the sending State if it has been established that this work is being performed for that employer and that there continues to exist a direct relationship between the worker and the employer that posted him.

In order to establish whether such a direct relationship continues to exist, assuming therefore that the worker continues to be under the authority of the employer which posted him, a number of elements have to be taken into account, including responsibility for recruitment, employment contract, remuneration (without prejudice to possible agreements between the employer in the sending State and the undertaking in the State of employment on the payment to the workers), dismissal, and the authority to determine the nature of the work.

For the application of Article 14(1) of Regulation (EC) No 987/2009, as an indication, having been subject to the legislation of the Member State in which the employer is established for at least one month can be considered as meeting the requirement referred to by the words 'immediately before the start of his employment'. Shorter periods would require a case-by-case evaluation taking account of all the other factors involved.

In order, where necessary and in cases of doubt, to determine whether an employer ordinarily performs substantial activities in the territory of the Member State in which he/she is established, the competent institution in the latter is required to examine all the criteria characterising the activities carried on by that employer, including the place where the undertaking has its registered office and administration, the number of administrative staff working in the Member State in which it is established and in the other Member State, the place where posted workers are recruited and the place where the majority of contracts with clients are concluded, the law applicable to the contracts concluded by the undertaking with its workers, on the one hand, and with its clients, on the other hand, the turnover during an appropriately typical period in each Member State concerned and the number of contracts performed in the sending State. This is not an exhaustive list, as the criteria should be adapted to each specific case and take account of the nature of the activities carried out by the undertaking in the State in which it is established.

2. For the application of Article 14(3) of Regulation (EC) No 987/2009, the fulfilment of the requirements in the Member State where the person is established is assessed on criteria such as having use of office space, paying taxes, having a professional card and a VAT number or being registered with chambers of commerce or professional bodies. As an indication, pursuing one's activity for at least two months can be considered

as meeting the requirement referred to by the words 'for some time before the date when he wishes to take advantage of the provisions of that Article'. Shorter periods would require a case-by-case evaluation taking account of all the other factors involved.

3. (a)   Pursuant to the provisions of paragraph 1 of this Decision, Article 12(1) of Regulation (EC) No 883/2004 shall continue to apply for posting of staff:

if the worker, posted by an undertaking in the sending State to an undertaking in the State of employment, is also posted to one or more other undertakings in the same State of employment, in so far, however, as the worker continues to carry out his work for the undertaking which posted him. This may be the case, in particular, if the undertaking posted the worker to a Member State in order to perform work there successively or simultaneously in two or more undertakings situated in the same Member State. The essential and decisive element is that the work continues to be carried out on behalf of the posting undertaking.

Posting to different Member States which immediately follow each other shall in each case give rise to a new posting within the meaning of Article 12(1) of Regulation (EC) No 883/2004.

(b)   brief interruption of the worker's activities with the undertaking in the State of employment, whatever the reason (holidays, illness, training at the posting undertaking …), shall not constitute an interruption of the posting period within the meaning of Article 12(1) of Regulation (EC) No 883/2004.

(c)   Once a worker has ended a period of posting, no fresh period of posting for the same worker, the same undertakings and the same Member State can be authorised until at least two months have elapsed from the date of expiry of the previous posting period. Derogation from this principle is, however, permissible in specific circumstances.

4.   The provisions of Article 12(1) of Regulation (EC) No 883/2004 shall not apply or shall cease to apply in particular:

(a)   if the undertaking to which the worker has been posted places him at the disposal of another undertaking in the Member State in which it is situated;

(b)   if the worker posted to a Member State is placed at the disposal of an undertaking situated in another Member State;

(c)   if the worker is recruited in a Member State in order to be sent by an undertaking situated in a second Member State to an undertaking in a third Member State.

5.   (a)   The competent institution of the Member State to whose legislation the person concerned remains subject pursuant to Article 12(1) of Regulation (EC) No 883/2004, in the cases provided for by this Decision, shall duly inform the employer and the worker concerned of the conditions under which the posted worker may continue to be subject to its legislation. The employer shall thus be informed of the possibility of checks throughout the period of posting so as to ascertain that this period has not come to an end. Such checks may relate, in particular, to the payment of contributions and the maintenance of the direct relationship.

The competent institution of the Member State in which the person concerned in established, to whose legislation the self-employed person remains subject pursuant to the aforementioned Article 12(2) of Regulation (EC) No 883/2004, shall duly inform him of the conditions under which he may continue to be subject to its legislation. The person concerned shall thus be informed of the possibility of checks throughout the period during which he pursues a temporary activity in the State in which he is active, so as to ascertain that the conditions applying to that activity have not changed. Such checks may relate, in particular, to the payment of contributions and the maintenance of the infrastructure needed to pursue his activity in the State in which he is established.

(b)   Moreover, the posted worker and his employer shall inform the competent institution of the sending State of any change occurring during the period of posting, in particular:

— if the posting applied for has in the end not taken place;

— if the activity is interrupted in a case other than that provided for in paragraph 3(b) of this Decision;

— if the posted worker has been assigned by his employer to another undertaking in the sending State, in particular in the event of merger or transfer of an undertaking.

(c)   The competent institution of the sending State shall, where appropriate and upon request, provide the institution of the State of employment with the information referred to in subparagraph (b).

(d)   The competent institutions of the sending State and of the State of employment shall cooperate in carrying out the abovementioned checks and where there is any doubt concerning the applicability of Article 12 of Regulation (EC) No 883/2004.

6.   The competent institutions shall assess and monitor the situations covered by Article 12 of Regulation (EC) No 883/2004 and provide employers and workers with all appropriate guarantees so as not to impede the freedom to provide services and the freedom of movement of workers. In particular, the criteria used for assessing whether an employer normally carries out its activities in the territory of a State, whether a direct relationship exists between the undertaking and the worker, or whether a self-employed worker maintains the infrastructure needed to pursue his activity in a State, must be applied consistently and evenly in the same or similar situations.

7.   The Administrative Commission shall encourage cooperation between the competent authorities in the Member States for the purpose of implementing Article 12 of Regulation (EC) No 883/2004 and shall facilitate follow-up work and the exchange of information, experience and good practice when fixing and grading the criteria for assessing the situations of undertakings and workers, and in connection with the control measures put in place. To this end, it shall draw up in stages, for the benefit of administrative authorities, undertakings and workers, a guide of good practice concerning the posting of workers and the pursuit by self-employed workers of a secondary activity outside the State in which they are established.

11.   This Decision ... shall apply from the entry into force of Regulation (EC) No 987/2009.

C.   ECJ case-law

The ECJ has dealt with the matter of the compulsoriness of the certificate issued by the competent institution of the Member State in which the undertaking providing temporary personnel is established, by means of which it declares, in compliance with Article 14(1)(a) of Regulation No 1408/71, that its social security system will remain applicable to the posted workers for the duration of their posting. Confirming the principles enounced in *FTS* judgment (10 February 2000, case C-202/97, Reports, I-883), the ECJ, with reference to a dispute concerning the right to the reimbursement of the contributions paid to the

Belgium National social security office by a Belgian company which, with reference to two subcontracts, avails itself of Irish workers employed by an Irish company and temporary posted in Belgium, in case *Herbosch Kiere* (26 January 2006, case C-2/05, Reports, I-1079), has stated the following:

24.   ... an E 101 certificate establishes a presumption that posted workers are properly affiliated to the social security system of the Member State in which the undertaking which posted those workers is established, such a certificate is binding on the competent institution of the Member State to which those workers are posted (see to that effect *FTS*, paragraph 53).

32.   It follows that a court of the host Member State is not entitled to scrutinise the validity of an E 101 certificate as regards the certification of the matters on the basis of which such a certificate was issued, in particular the existence of a direct relationship between the undertaking which posted the worker and the posted worker himself.

XI

Personality Rights, Status and Family Relations

Right to protection of personal data

A.1. Directive 95/46/EC of the European Parliament and of the Council of 24 October 1995 on the protection of individuals with regard to the processing of personal data and on the free movement of such data (OJ, L 281 of 23 November 1995)[1]

(1)   Whereas the objectives of the Community, as laid down in the Treaty, as amended by the Treaty on European Union, include creating an ever closer union among the peoples of Europe, fostering closer relations between the States belonging to the Community, ensuring economic and social progress by common action to eliminate the barriers which divide Europe, encouraging the constant improvement of the living conditions of its peoples, preserving and strengthening peace and liberty and promoting democracy on the basis of the fundamental rights recognised in the constitution and laws of the Member States and in the European Convention for the Protection of Human Rights and Fundamental Freedoms;

(2)   Whereas data-processing systems are designed to serve man; whereas they must, whatever the nationality or residence of natural persons, respect their fundamental rights and freedoms, notably the right to privacy, and contribute to economic and social progress, trade expansion and the well-being of individuals...

(9)   Whereas, given the equivalent protection resulting from the approximation of national laws, the Member States will no longer be able to inhibit the free movement between them of personal data on grounds relating to protection of the rights and freedoms of individuals, and in particular the right to privacy; whereas Member States will be left a margin for manoeuvre, which may, in the context of implementation of the Directive, also be exercised by the business and social partners; whereas Member States

---

[1]   The present Directive has been particularised and complemented by the provisions of Directive 2002/58/EC of 12 July 2002 concerning the processing of personal data and the protection of privacy in the electronic communications sector (Directive on privacy and electronic communications, OJ, L 201 of 31 July 2002), which has been subsequently amended by Directive 2006/24/EC of 15 March 2006 on the retention of data generated or processed in connection with the provision of publicly available electronic communications services or of public communications networks (OJ, L 105 of 13 April 2006) and lastly by Directive 2009/136/EC of 25 November 2009 amending also Directive 2002/22/EC on universal service and users' rights relating to electronic communications networks and services and Regulation (EC) No 2006/2004 on co-operation between national authorities responsible for the enforcement of consumer protection laws (OJ, L 337 of 18 December 2009). [Note of the Editor]

will therefore be able to specify in their national law the general conditions governing the lawfulness of data processing; whereas in doing so the Member States shall strive to improve the protection currently provided by their legislation; whereas, within the limits of this margin for manoeuvre and in accordance with Community law, disparities could arise in the implementation of the Directive, and this could have an effect on the movement of data within a Member State as well as within the Community;

(10) Whereas the object of the national laws on the processing of personal data is to protect fundamental rights and freedoms, notably the right to privacy, which is recognized both in Article 8 of the European Convention for the Protection of Human Rights and Fundamental Freedoms and in the general principles of Community law; whereas, for that reason, the approximation of those laws must not result in any lessening of the protection they afford but must, on the contrary, seek to ensure a high level of protection in the Community;

(11) Whereas the principles of the protection of the rights and freedoms of individuals, notably the right to privacy, which are contained in this Directive, give substance to and amplify those contained in the Council of Europe Convention of 28 January 1981 for the Protection of Individuals with regard to Automatic Processing of Personal Data;

(12) Whereas the protection principles must apply to all processing of personal data by any person whose activities are governed by Community law; whereas there should be excluded the processing of data carried out by a natural person in the exercise of activities which are exclusively personal or domestic, such as correspondence and the holding of records of addresses…

(18) Whereas, in order to ensure that individuals are not deprived of the protection to which they are entitled under this Directive, any processing of personal data in the Community must be carried out in accordance with the law of one of the Member States; whereas, in this connection, processing carried out under the responsibility of a controller who is established in a Member State should be governed by the law of that State;

(19) Whereas establishment on the territory of a Member State implies the effective and real exercise of activity through stable arrangements; whereas the legal form of such an establishment, whether simply branch or a subsidiary with a legal personality, is not the determining factor in this respect; whereas, when a single controller is established on the territory of several Member States, particularly by means of subsidiaries, he must ensure, in order to avoid any circumvention of national rules, that each of the establishments fulfils the obligations imposed by the national law applicable to its activities;

(20) Whereas the fact that the processing of data is carried out by a person established in a third country must not stand in the way of the protection of individuals provided for in this Directive; whereas in these cases, the processing should be governed by the law of the Member State in which the means used are located, and there should be guarantees to ensure that the rights and obligations provided for in this Directive are respected in practice;

(21) Whereas this Directive is without prejudice to the rules of territoriality applicable in criminal matters…

(24) Whereas the legislation concerning the protection of legal persons with regard to the processing data which concerns them is not affected by this Directive…

(56) Whereas cross-border flows of personal data are necessary to the expansion of international trade; whereas the protection of individuals guaranteed in the Community

by this Directive does not stand in the way of transfers of personal data to third countries which ensure an adequate level of protection; whereas the adequacy of the level of protection afforded by a third country must be assessed in the light of all the circumstances surrounding the transfer operation or set of transfer operations;

(57) Whereas, on the other hand, the transfer of personal data to a third country which does not ensure an adequate level of protection must be prohibited;

(58) Whereas provisions should be made for exemptions from this prohibition in certain circumstances where the data subject has given his consent, where the transfer is necessary in relation to a contract or a legal claim, where protection of an important public interest so requires, for example in cases of international transfers of data between tax or customs administrations or between services competent for social security matters, or where the transfer is made from a register established by law and intended for consultation by the public or persons having a legitimate interest; whereas in this case such a transfer should not involve the entirety of the data or entire categories of the data contained in the register and, when the register is intended for consultation by persons having a legitimate interest, the transfer should be made only at the request of those persons or if they are to be the recipients;

(59) Whereas particular measures may be taken to compensate for the lack of protection in a third country in cases where the controller offers appropriate safeguards; whereas, moreover, provision must be made for procedures for negotiations between the Community and such third countries;

(60) Whereas, in any event, transfers to third countries may be effected only in full compliance with the provisions adopted by the Member States pursuant to this Directive, and in particular Article 8 thereof...

Chapter I — General provisions

Article 1. Object of the Directive.   1.   In accordance with this Directive, Member States shall protect the fundamental rights and freedoms of natural persons, and in particular their right to privacy with respect to the processing of personal data.

2.   Member States shall neither restrict nor prohibit the free flow of personal data between Member States for reasons connected with the protection afforded under paragraph 1.

Article 2. Definitions.   For the purposes of this Directive:

(a)   'personal data' shall mean any information relating to an identified or identifiable natural person ('data subject'); an identifiable person is one who can be identified, directly or indirectly, in particular by reference to an identification number or to one or more factors specific to his physical, physiological, mental, economic, cultural or social identity;

(b)   'processing of personal data' ('processing') shall mean any operation or set of operations which is performed upon personal data, whether or not by automatic means, such as collection, recording, organization, storage, adaptation or alteration, retrieval, consultation, use, disclosure by transmission, dissemination or otherwise making available, alignment or combination, blocking, erasure or destruction;

(c)   'personal data filing system' ('filing system') shall mean any structured set of personal data which are accessible according to specific criteria, whether centralized, decentralized or dispersed on a functional or geographical basis;

(d)   'controller' shall mean the natural or legal person, public authority, agency or any other body which alone or jointly with others determines the purposes and means of the processing of personal data; where the purposes and means of processing are determined by national or Community laws or regulations, the controller or the specific criteria for his nomination may be designated by national or Community law;

(e)   'processor' shall mean a natural or legal person, public authority, agency or any other body which processes personal data on behalf of the controller;

(f)   'third party' shall mean any natural or legal person, public authority, agency or any other body other than the data subject, the controller, the processor and the persons who, under the direct authority of the controller or the processor, are authorized to process the data;

(g)   'recipient' shall mean a natural or legal person, public authority, agency or any other body to whom data are disclosed, whether a third party or not; however, authorities which may receive data in the framework of a particular inquiry shall not be regarded as recipients;

(h)   'the data subject's consent' shall mean any freely given specific and informed indication of his wishes by which the data subject signifies his agreement to personal data relating to him being processed.

Article 3. Scope.   1.   This Directive shall apply to the processing of personal data wholly or partly by automatic means, and to the processing otherwise than by automatic means of personal data which form part of a filing system or are intended to form part of a filing system.

2.   This Directive shall not apply to the processing of personal data:

—   in the course of an activity which falls outside the scope of Community law, such as those provided for by Titles V and VI of the Treaty on European Union and in any case to processing operations concerning public security, defence, State security (including the economic well-being of the State when the processing operation relates to State security matters) and the activities of the State in areas of criminal law;by a natural person in the course of a purely personal or household activity.

Article 4. National law applicable.   1.   Each Member State shall apply the national provisions it adopts pursuant to this Directive to the processing of personal data where:

(a)   the processing is carried out in the context of the activities of an establishment of the controller on the territory of the Member State; when the same controller is established on the territory of several Member States, he must take the necessary measures to ensure that each of these establishments complies with the obligations laid down by the national law applicable;

(b)   the controller is not established on the Member State's territory, but in a place where its national law applies by virtue of international public law;

(c)   the controller is not established on Community territory and, for purposes of processing personal data makes use of equipment, automated or otherwise, situated on the territory of the said Member State, unless such equipment is used only for purposes of transit through the territory of the Community.

2.   In the circumstances referred to in paragraph 1(c), the controller must designate a representative established in the territory of that Member State, without prejudice to legal actions which could be initiated against the controller himself.

Chapter II — General rules on the lawfulness of the processing of personal data

Section VI — Exemptions and restrictions

Article 13. Exemptions and restrictions. 1. Member States may adopt legislative measures to restrict the scope of the obligations and rights provided for in Articles 6(1), 10, 11(1), 12 and 21 when such a restriction constitutes a necessary measures to safeguard:

(a)   national security;

(b)   defence;

(c)   public security;

(d)   the prevention, investigation, detection and prosecution of criminal offences, or of breaches of ethics for regulated professions;

(e)   an important economic or financial interest of a Member State or of the European Union, including monetary, budgetary and taxation matters;

(f)   a monitoring, inspection or regulatory function connected, even occasionally, with the exercise of official authority in cases referred to in (c), (d) and (e);

(g)   the protection of the data subject or of the rights and freedoms of others.

2.   Subject to adequate legal safeguards, in particular that the data are not used for taking measures or decisions regarding any particular individual, Member States may, where there is clearly no risk of breaching the privacy of the data subject, restrict by a legislative measure the rights provided for in Article 12 when data are processed solely for purposes of scientific research or are kept in personal form for a period which does not exceed the period necessary for the sole purpose of creating statistics.

Section VII. — The data subject's right to object

Article 14. The data subject's right to object.   Member States shall grant the data subject the right:

(a)   at least in the cases referred to in Article 7 (e) and (f), to object at any time on compelling legitimate grounds relating to his particular situation to the processing of data relating to him, save where otherwise provided by national legislation. Where there is a justified objection, the processing instigated by the controller may no longer involve those data;

(b)   to object, on request and free of charge, to the processing of personal data relating to him which the controller anticipates being processed for the purposes of direct marketing, or to be informed before personal data are disclosed for the first time to third parties or used on their behalf for the purposes of direct marketing, and to be expressly offered the right to object free of charge to such disclosures or uses.

Member States shall take the necessary measures to ensure that data subjects are aware of the existence of the right referred to in the first subparagraph of (b).

Article 15. Automated individual decisions. 1.   Member States shall grant the right to every person not to be subject to a decision which produces legal effects concerning him or significantly affects him and which is based solely on automated processing of data intended to evaluate certain personal aspects relating to him, such as his performance at work, creditworthiness, reliability, conduct, etc.

2.   Subject to the other Articles of this Directive, Member States shall provide that a person may be subjected to a decision of the kind referred to in paragraph 1 if that decision:

(a)   is taken in the course of the entering into or performance of a contract, provided the request for the entering into or the performance of the contract, lodged by the data subject, has been satisfied or that there are suitable measures to safeguard his legitimate interests, such as arrangements allowing him to put his point of view; or

(b)   is authorized by a law which also lays down measures to safeguard the data subject's legitimate interests.

Section VIII — Confidentiality and security of processing

Article 16. Confidentiality of processing.   Any person acting under the authority of the controller or of the processor, including the processor himself, who has access to personal data must not process them except on instructions from the controller, unless he is required to do so by law.

Article 17. Security of processing.   1.   Member States shall provide that the controller must implement appropriate technical and organizational measures to protect personal data against accidental or unlawful destruction or accidental loss, alteration, unauthorized disclosure or access, in particular where the processing involves the transmission of data over a network, and against all other unlawful forms of processing.Having regard to the state of the art and the cost of their implementation, such measures shall ensure a level of security appropriate to the risks represented by the processing and the nature of the data to be protected.

2.   The Member States shall provide that the controller must, where processing is carried out on his behalf, choose a processor providing sufficient guarantees in respect of the technical security measures and organisational measures governing the processing to be carried out, and must ensure compliance with those measures.

3.   The carrying out of processing by way of a processor must be governed by a contract or legal act binding the processor to the controller and stipulating in particular that:

—   the processor shall act only on instructions from the controller;

—   the obligations set out in paragraph 1, as defined by the law of the Member State in which the processor is established, shall also be incumbent on the processor.

4.   For the purposes of keeping proof, the parts of the contract or the legal act relating to data protection and the requirements relating to the measures referred to in paragraph 1 shall be in writing or in another equivalent form.

Chapter IV — Transfer of personal data to third countries[2]

Article 25. Principles.   1.   The Member States shall provide that the transfer to a third country of personal data which are undergoing processing or are intended for processing after transfer may take place only if, without prejudice to compliance with the national provisions adopted pursuant to the other provisions of this Directive, the third country in question ensures an adequate level of protection.

2.   The adequacy of the level of protection afforded by a third country shall be assessed in the light of all the circumstances surrounding a data transfer operation or set of data transfer operations; particular consideration shall be given to the nature of the data, the purpose and duration of the proposed processing operation or operations, the country of origin and country of final destination, the rules of law, both general and sectoral, in force in the third country in question and the professional rules and security measures which are complied with in that country.

3.   The Member States and the Commission shall inform each other of cases where they consider that a third country does not ensure an adequate level of protection within the meaning of paragraph 2.

4.   Where the Commission finds, under the procedure provided for in Article 31(2), that a third country does not ensure an adequate level of protection within the meaning of paragraph 2 of this Article, Member States shall take the measures necessary to prevent any transfer of data of the same type to the third country in question.

5.   At the appropriate time, the Commission shall enter into negotiations with a view to remedying the situation resulting from the finding made pursuant to paragraph 4.

6.   The Commission may find, in accordance with the procedure referred to in Article 31(2), that a third country ensures an adequate level of protection within the meaning of paragraph 2 of this Article, by reason of its domestic law or of the international commitments it has entered into, particularly upon conclusion of the negotiations referred to in paragraph 5, for the protection of the private lives and basic freedoms and rights of individuals.

Member States shall take the measures necessary to comply with the Commission's decision.

---

[2]   On the basis of Article 25(6) an adequate level of protection has been considered ensured in the following third countries: Andorra (Commission Decision 2010/625/EU of 19 October 2010, OJ, L 277 of 21 October 2010); Argentina (Commission Decision 2003/490/EC of 30 June 2003, OJ, L 168 of 5 July 2003); Canada (Commission Decision 2002/2/EEC of 20 December 2001, OJ, L 2/13 of 4 January 2002) also with regards to the processing and transfer of Passenger Name Record (PNR) data by air carriers (Commission Decision 2006/253/EC of 6 September 2005, OJ, L 91 of 29 March 2006); Faeroe Islands (Commission Decision 2010/146/EU of 5 March 2010, OJ, L58, 9 March 2010); Guernsey (Commission Decision 2003/821/EC of 21 November 2003, OJ, L 308 of 25 November 2003); Isle of Man (Commission Decision 2004/411/EC of 28 April 2004, OJ, L 151 of 30 April 2004); Jersey (Commission Decision 2008/393/EC of 8 May 2008, OJ, L 138 of 28 May 2008); Switzerland (Commission Decision 2000/518/EC of 26 July 2000, OJ, L 215 of 25 August 2000); United States (Commission Decision 2000/520/EC of 26 July 2000, OJ, L 215 of 25 August 2000) also with regards to the processing and transfer of Passenger Name Record (PNR) data by air carriers (Commission Decision 2004/535/EC of 14 May 2004, OJ, L 235 of 6 July 2004). See also Council Decision '2008/651/CFSP/JHA of 30 June 2008 on the signing, on behalf of the European Union, of an Agreement between the European Union and Australia on the processing and transfer of European Union-sourced passenger name record (PNR) data by air carriers to the Australian Customs Service' (OJ, L 213 of 8 June 2008). [Note of the Editor]

Article 26. Derogations.   1.   By way of derogation from Article 25 and save where otherwise provided by domestic law governing particular cases, Member States shall provide that a transfer or a set of transfers of personal data to a third country which does not ensure an adequate level of protection within the meaning of Article 25(2) may take place on condition that:

(a)   the data subject has given his consent unambiguously to the proposed transfer; or

(b)   the transfer is necessary for the performance of a contract between the data subject and the controller or the implementation of precontractual measures taken in response to the data subject's request; or

(c)   the transfer is necessary for the conclusion or performance of a contract concluded in the interest of the data subject between the controller and a third party; or

(d)   the transfer is necessary or legally required on important public interest grounds, or for the establishment, exercise or defence of legal claims; or

(e)   the transfer is necessary in order to protect the vital interests of the data subject; or

(f)   the transfer is made from a register which according to laws or regulations is intended to provide information to the public and which is open to consultation either by the public in general or by any person who can demonstrate legitimate interest, to the extent that the conditions laid down in law for consultation are fulfilled in the particular case.

2.   Without prejudice to paragraph 1, a Member State may authorize a transfer or a set of transfers of personal data to a third country which does not ensure an adequate level of protection within the meaning of Article 25(2), where the controller adduces adequate safeguards with respect to the protection of the privacy and fundamental rights and freedoms of individuals and as regards the exercise of the corresponding rights; such safeguards may in particular result from appropriate contractual clauses.

3.   The Member State shall inform the Commission and the other Member States of the authorizations it grants pursuant to paragraph 2. If a Member State or the Commission objects on justified grounds involving the protection of the privacy and fundamental rights and freedoms of individuals, the Commission shall take appropriate measures in accordance with the procedure laid down in Article 31(2).

Member States shall take the necessary measures to comply with the Commission's decision.

4.   Where the Commission decides, in accordance with the procedure referred to in Article 31(2), that certain standard contractual clauses offer sufficient safeguards as required by paragraph 2, Member States shall take the necessary measures to comply with the Commission's decision.

A.2. Commission Decision 2001/497/EC of 15 June 2001 on standard contractual clauses for the transfer of personal data to third countries, under Directive 95/46/EC (OJ, L 181 of 4 July 2001)[1]

(1)   Pursuant to Directive 95/46/EC, Member States are required to provide that a transfer of personal data to a third country may only take place if the third country in question ensures an adequate level of data protection and the Member States' laws, which comply with the other provisions of the Directive, are respected prior to the transfer.

(2)   However, Article 26(2) of Directive 95/46/EC provides that Member States may authorise, subject to certain safeguards, a transfer or a set of transfers of personal data to third countries which do not ensure an adequate level of protection. Such safeguards may in particular result from appropriate contractual clauses.

(3)   Pursuant to Directive 95/46/EC, the level of data protection should be assessed in the light of all the circumstances surrounding the data transfer operation or set of data transfer operations. The Working Party on Protection of Individuals with regard to the processing of personal data established under that Directive[2] has issued guidelines to aid with the assessment.[3]

(4)   Article 26(2) of Directive 95/46/EC, which provides flexibility for an organisation wishing to transfer data to third countries, and Article 26(4), which provides for standard contractual clauses, are essential for maintaining the necessary flow of personal data between the Community and third countries without unnecessary burdens for economic operators. Those Articles are particularly important in view of the fact that the Commission is unlikely to adopt adequacy findings under Article 25(6) for more than a limited number of countries in the short or even medium term.

(5)   The standard contractual clauses are only one of several possibilities under Directive 95/46/EC, together with Article 25 and Article 26(1) and (2), for lawfully transferring personal data to a third country. It will be easier for organizations to transfer personal data to third countries by incorporating the standard contractual clauses in a contract. The standard contractual clauses relate only to data protection. The data exporter and the data importer are free to include any other clauses on business related issues, such as clauses on mutual assistance in cases of disputes with a data subject or a supervisory authority, which they consider as being pertinent for the contract as long as they do not contradict the standard contractual clauses.

---

[1]   As lastly amended by Commission Decision 2004/915/EC of 27 December 2004 (OJ, L 385 of 29 December 2004). The following footnotes are published in the original numerical order as in the OJ. [Note of the Editor]
[2]   The Internet address of the Working Party is www.europa.eu.intlcomm/internal_market/en/medial/dataprot/wpdocs/index.htm.
[3]   WP 4 (5020/97) 'First orientations on transfers of personal data to third countries working document — possible ways forward in assessing adequacy', a discussion document adopted by the Working Party on 26 June 1997. WP 7 (5057/97) 'Judging industry self regulation: when does it make a meaningful contribution to the level of data protection in a third country?', working document: adopted by the Working Party on 14 January 1998. WP 9 (3005/98) 'Preliminary views on the use of contractual provisions in the context of transfers of personal data to third countries', working document: adopted by the Working Party on 22 April 1998. WP 12: 'Transfers of personal data to third countries: applying Articles 25 and 26 of the EU data protection directive', working document adopted by the Working Party on 24 July 1998, available, in the web-working document site 'europa.eu.int/comm/internal_markt/en/media.dataprot/wpdocs/wp12/en' hosted by the European Commission.

(6)   This Decision should be without prejudice to national authorizations Member States may grant in accordance with national provisions implementing Article 26(2) of Directive 95/46/EC. The circumstances of specific transfers may require that data controllers provide different safeguards within the meaning of Article 26(2). In any case, this Decision only has the effect of requiring the Member States not to refuse to recognize as providing adequate safeguards the contractual clauses described in it and does not therefore have any effect on other contractual clauses.

(7)   The scope of this Decision is limited to establishing that the clauses in the Annex may be used by a controller established in the Community in order to adduce sufficient safeguards within the meaning of Article 26(2) of Directive 95/46/EC. The transfer of personal data to third countries is a processing operation in a Member State, the lawfulness of which is subject to national law. The data protection supervisory authorities of the Member States, in the exercise of their functions and powers under Article 28 of Directive 95/46/EC, should remain competent to assess whether the data exporter has complied with national legislation implementing the provisions of Directive 95/46/EC and, in particular, any specific rules as regards the obligation of providing information under that Directive.

(8)   This Decision does not cover the transfer of personal data by controllers established in the Community to recipients established outside the territory of the Community who act only as processors. Those transfers do not require the same safeguards because the processor acts exclusively on behalf of the controller. The Commission intends to address that type of transfer in a subsequent decision.

(9)   It is appropriate to lay down the minimum information that the parties must specify in the contract dealing with the transfer. Member States should retain the power to particularise the information the parties are required to provide. The operation of this Decision should be reviewed in the light of experience.

(10) The Commission will also consider in the future whether standard contractual clauses submitted by business organisations or other interested parties offer adequate safeguards in accordance with Directive 95/46/EC.

(11) While the parties should be free to agree on the substantive data protection rules to be complied with by the data importer, there are certain data protection principles which should apply in any event.

(12) Data should be processed and subsequently used or further communicated only for specified purposes and should not be kept longer than necessary.

(13) In accordance with Article 12 of Directive 95/46/EC, the data subject should have the right of access to all data relating to him and as appropriate to rectification, erasure or blocking of certain data.

(14) Further transfers of personal data to another controller established in a third country should be permitted only subject to certain conditions, in particular to ensure that data subjects are given proper information and have the opportunity to object, or in certain cases to withhold their consent.

(15) In addition to assessing whether transfers to third countries are in accordance with national law, supervisory authorities should play a key role in this contractual mechanism in ensuring that personal data are adequately protected after the transfer. In specific circumstances, the supervisory authorities of the Member States should retain the power to prohibit or suspend a data transfer or a set of transfers based on the standard contractual clauses in those exceptional cases where it is established that a transfer on

contractual basis is likely to have a substantial adverse effect on the guarantees providing adequate protection to the data subject.

(16) The standard contractual clauses should be enforceable not only by the organisations which are parties to the contract, but also by the data subjects, in particular, where the data subjects suffer damage as a consequence of a breach of the contract.

(17) The governing law of the contract should be the law of the Member State in which the data exporter is established, enabling a third-party beneficiary to enforce a contract. Data subjects should be allowed to be represented by associations or other bodies if they so wish and if authorised by national law.

(18) To reduce practical difficulties which data subjects could experience when trying to enforce their rights under the standard contractual clauses, the data exporter and the data importer should be jointly and severally liable for damages resulting from any violation of those provisions which are covered by the third-party beneficiary clause.

(19) The Data Subject is entitled to take action and receive compensation from the Data Exporter, the Data Importer or from both for any damage resulting from any act incompatible with the obligations contained in the standard contractual clauses. Both parties may be exempted from that liability if they prove that neither of them was responsible.

(20) Joint and several liability does not extend to those provisions not covered by the third-party beneficiary clause and does not need to leave one party paying for the damage resulting from the unlawful processing of the other party. Although mutual indemnification between the parties is not a requirement for the adequacy of the protection for the data subjects and may therefore be deleted, it is included in the standard contractual clauses for the sake of clarification and to avoid the need for the parties to negotiate indemnification clauses individually.

(21) In the event of a dispute between the parties and the data subject which is not amicably resolved and where the data subject invokes the third-party beneficiary clause, the parties agree to provide the data subject with the choice between mediation, arbitration or litigation. The extent to which the data subject will have an effective choice will depend on the availability of reliable and recognised systems of mediation and arbitration. Mediation by the supervisory authorities of a Member State should be an option where they provide such a service.

(22) The Working Party on the protection of individuals with regard to the processing of personal data established under Article 29 of Directive 95/46/EC has delivered an opinion on the level of protection provided under the standard contractual clauses annexed to this Decision, which has been taken into account in the preparation of this Decision.[4]

(23) The measures provided for in this Decision are in accordance with the opinion of the Committee established under Article 31 of Directive 95/46/EC, has adopted this Decision:

Article 1. The standard contractual clauses set out in the Annex are considered as offering adequate safeguards with respect to the protection of the privacy and fundamental rights and freedoms of individuals and as regards the exercise of the corresponding rights as required by Article 26(2) of Directive 9/46/EC.

---

[4] Opinion No 1/2001 adopted by the Working Party on 26 January 2001 (DG MARKT 5102/00 WP 38), available in the website 'Europa' hosted by the European Commission.

Data controllers may choose either of the sets I or II in the Annex. However, they may not amend the clauses nor combine individual clauses or the sets.

Article 2.   This Decision concerns only the adequacy of protection provided by the standard contractual clauses for the transfer of personal data set out in the Annex. It does not affect the application of other national provisions implementing Directive 95/46/EC that pertain to the processing of personal data within the Member States.

This Decision shall not apply to the transfer of personal data by controllers established in the Community to recipients established outside the territory of the Community who act only as processors.

Article 3.   For the purposes of this Decision:
(a)   the definitions in Directive 95/46/EC shall apply;
(b)   'special categories of data' means the data referred to in Article 8 of that Directive;
(c)   'supervisory authority' means the authority referred to in Article 28 of that Directive;
(d)   'data exporter' means the controller who transfers the personal data;
(e)   data importer' means the controller who agrees to receive from the data exporter personal data for further processing in accordance with the terms of this Decision.

Article 4.   1.   Without prejudice to their powers to take action to ensure compliance with national provisions adopted pursuant to chapters II, III, V and VI of Directive 95/46/EC, the competent authorities in the Member States may exercise their existing powers to prohibit or suspend data flows to third countries in order to protect individuals with regard to the processing of their personal data in cases where:
(a)   it is established that the law to which the data importer is subject imposes upon him requirements to derogate from the relevant data protection rules which go beyond the restrictions necessary in a democratic society as provided for in Article 13 of Directive 95/46/EC where those requirements are likely to have a substantial adverse effect on the guarantees provided by the standard contractual clauses; or
(b)   a competent authority has established that the data importer has not respected the contractual clauses; or
(c)   there is a substantial likelihood that the standard contractual clauses in the Annex are not being or will not be complied with and the continuation of transfer would create an imminent risk of grave harm to the data subjects.
2.   For the purposes of paragraph 1, where the data controller adduces adequate safeguards on the basis of the standard contractual clauses contained in set II in the Annex, the competent data protection authorities are entitled to exercise their existing powers to prohibit or suspend data flows in either of the following cases:
(a)   refusal of the data importer to cooperate in good faith with the data protection authorities, or to comply with their clear obligations under the contract;
(b)   refusal of the data exporter to take appropriate steps to enforce the contract against the data importer within the normal period of one month after notice by the competent data protection authority to the data exporter.For the purposes of the first subparagraph, refusal in bad faith or refusal to enforce the contract by the data importer shall not include cases in which co-operation or enforcement would conflict with

mandatory requirements of the national legislation applicable to the data importer which do not go beyond what is necessary in a democratic society on the basis of one of the interests listed in Article 13(1) of Directive 95/46/EC, in particular sanctions as laid down in international and/or national instruments, tax-reporting requirements or anti-money-laundering reporting requirements.

For the purposes of point (a) of the first subparagraph co-operation may include, in particular, the submission of the data importer's data processing facilities for audit or the obligation to abide by the advice of the data protection supervisory authority in the Community.

3.   The prohibition or suspension pursuant to paragraphs 1 and 2 shall be lifted as soon as the reasons for the prohibition or suspension no longer exist.

4.   When Member States adopt measures pursuant to paragraphs 1, 2 and 3, they shall without delay inform the Commission which will forward the information to the other Member States.

Article 5.   The Commission shall evaluate the operation of this Decision on the basis of available information three years after its notification and the notification of any amendment thereto to the Member States. It shall submit a report on the endings to the Committee established under Article 31 of Directive 95/46/EC. It shall include any evidence that could affect the evaluation concerning the adequacy of the standard contractual clauses in the Annex and any evidence that this Decision is being applied in a discriminatory way.

Article 6.   This Decision shall apply from 3 September 2001.

ANNEX

SET I – STANDARD CONTRACTUAL CLAUSES FOR THE PURPOSES OF ARTICLE 26(2) OF DIRECTIVE 95/46/EC FOR THE TRANSFER OF PERSONAL DATA TO THIRD COUNTRIES WHICH DO NOT ENSURE AN ADEQUATE LEVEL OF PROTECTION

Name of the data exporting organisation: ....

Address: ....

Tel. ....fax ....e-mail: ....

Other information needed to identify the organisation: ....

('the data exporter')

and

Name of the data importing organisation: . ...

Address: ....

Tel. ....fax ....e-mail: ....

Other information needed to identify the organisation: ....

('the data importer')

have agreed on the following contractual clauses ('the Clauses') in order to adduce adequate safeguards with respect to the protection of privacy and fundamental rights and freedoms of individuals for the transfer by the data exporter to the data importer of the personal data specified in Appendix 1:

Clause 1 — Definitions

For the purposes of the Clauses:

a)   'personal data', 'special categories of data', 'process/processing', 'controller', 'processor', 'data subject' and 'supervisory authority' shall have the same meaning as in Directive 95/46/EC of the European Parliament and of the Council of 24 October 1995 on the protection of individuals with regard to the processing of personal data and on the free movement of such data ('hereinafter the Directive');

b)   the 'data exporter' shall mean the controller who transfers the personal data;

c)   the 'data importer' shall mean the controller who agrees to receive from the data exporter personal data for further processing in accordance with the terms of these clauses and who is not subject to a third country's system ensuring adequate protection.

Clause 2 — Details of the transfer

The details of the transfer, and in particular the categories of personal data and the purposes for which they are transferred, are specified in Appendix 1 which forms an integral part of the Clauses.

Clause 3 — Third-party beneficiary clause

The data subjects can enforce this Clause, Clause 4(b), (c) and (d), Clause 5(a), (b), (c) and (e), Clause 6(1) and (2), and Clauses 7, 9 and 11 as third-party beneficiaries. The parties do not object to the data subjects being represented by an association or other bodies if they so wish and if permitted by national law.

Clause 4 — Obligations of the data exporter

The data exporter agrees and warrants:

(a)   that the processing, including the transfer itself, of the personal data by him has been and, up to the moment of the transfer, will continue to be carried out in accordance with the relevant provisions of the Member State in which the data exporter is established (and where applicable has been notified to the relevant authorities of that State) and does not violate the relevant provisions of that State;

(b)   that if the transfer involves special categories of data the data subject has been informed or will be informed before the transfer that this data could be transmitted to a third country not providing adequate protection;

(c)   to make available to the data subjects upon request a copy of the Clauses; and (d) to respond in a reasonable time and to the extent reasonably possible to enquiries from the supervisory authority on the processing of the relevant personal data by the data importer and to any enquiries from the data subject concerning the processing of this personal data by the data importer.

Clause 5 — Obligations of the data importer

The data importer agrees and warrants:

(a)   that he has no reason to believe that the legislation applicable to him prevents him from fulfilling his obligations under the contract and that in the event of a change in that legislation which is likely to have a substantial adverse effect on the guarantees provided by the Clauses, he will notify the change to the data exporter and to the supervisory authority where the data exporter is established, in which case the data exporter is entitled to suspend the transfer of data and/or terminate the contract;

(b)   to process the personal data in accordance with the mandatory data protection principles set out in Appendix 2; or, if explicitly agreed by the parties by ticking below and subject to compliance with the mandatory data protection principles set out in Appendix 3, to process in all other respects the data in accordance with:

—   the relevant provisions of national law (attached to these Clauses) protecting the fundamental rights and freedoms of natural persons, and in particular their right to privacy with respect to the processing of personal data applicable to a data controller in the country in which the data exporter is established, or

—   the relevant provisions of any Commission Decision under Article 25(6) of Directive 95/46/EC finding that a third country provides adequate protection in certain sectors of activity only, if the data importer is based in that third country and is not covered by those provisions, in so far as those provisions are of a nature which makes them applicable in the sector of the transfer;

(c)   to deal promptly and properly with all reasonable inquiries from the data exporter or the data subject relating to his processing of the personal data subject to the transfer and to cooperate with the competent supervisory authority in the course of all its inquiries and abide by the advice of the supervisory authority with regard to the processing of the data transferred;

(d)   at the request of the data exporter to submit its data processing facilities for audit which shall be carried out by the data exporter or an inspection body composed of independent members and in possession of the required professional qualifications, selected by the data exporter, where applicable, in agreement with the supervisory authority;

(e)   to make available to the data subject upon request a copy of the Clauses and indicate the office which handles complaints.

Clause 6 — Liability

1.   The parties agree that a data subject who has suffered damage as a result of any violation of the provisions referred to in Clause 3 is entitled to receive compensation from the parties for the damage suffered. The parties agree that they may be exempted from this liability only if they prove that neither of them is responsible for the violation of those provisions.

2.   The data exporter and the data importer agree that they will be jointly and severally liable for damage to the data subject resulting from any violation referred to in paragraph 1. In the event of such a violation, the data subject may bring an action before a court against either the data exporter or the data importer or both.

3.   The parties agree that if one party is held liable for a violation referred to in paragraph 1 by the other party, the latter will, to the extent to which it is liable, indemnify the first party for any cost, charge, damages, expenses or loss it has incurred.*

Clause 7 — Mediation and jurisdiction

1.   The parties agree that if there is a dispute between a data subject and either party which is not amicably resolved and the data subject invokes the third-party beneficiary provision in clause 3, they accept the decision of the data subject:
     (a)   to refer the dispute to mediation by an independent person or, where applicable, by the supervisory authority;
     (b)   to refer the dispute to the courts in the Member State in which the data exporter is established.
     2.   The parties agree that by agreement between a data subject and the relevant party a dispute can be referred to an arbitration body, if that party is established in a country which has ratified the New York convention on enforcement of arbitration awards.
     3.   The parties agree that paragraphs 1 and 2 apply without prejudice to the data subject's substantive or procedural rights to seek remedies in accordance with other provisions of national or international law.

Clause 8 — Co-operation with supervisory authorities

The parties agree to deposit a copy of this contract with the supervisory authority if it so requests or if such deposit is required under national law.

Clause 9 — Termination of the Clauses

The parties agree that the termination of the Clauses at any time, in any circumstances and for whatever reason does not exempt them from the obligations and/or conditions under the Clauses as regards the processing of the data transferred.

Clause 10 — Governing Law

The Clauses shall be governed by the law of the Member State in which the Data Exporter is established, namely ....

---

*   Paragraph 3 is optional.

SET II — STANDARD CONTRACTUAL CLAUSES FOR THE TRANSFER OF PERSONAL
DATA FROM THE COMMUNITY TO THIRD COUNTRIES (CONTROLLER TO
CONTROLLER TRANSFERS)

Data transfer agreement

between

.... (name)

.... (address and country of establishment)
(hereinafter "data exporter")

and

.... (name)

.... (address and country of establishment)
(hereinafter "data importer")

each a "party"; together "the parties".

Definitions

For the purposes of the clauses:

(a) 'personal data', 'special categories of data/sensitive data', 'process/processing', 'controller', 'processor', 'data subject' and 'supervisory authority/authority' shall have the same meaning as in Directive 95/46/EC of 24 October 1995 (whereby 'the authority' shall mean the competent data protection authority in the territory in which the data exporter is established):

(b) 'the data exporter' shall mean the controller who transfers the personal data;

(c) 'the data importer' shall mean the controller who agrees to receive from the data exporter personal data for further processing in accordance with the terms of these clauses and who is not subject to a third country's system ensuring adequate protection;

(d) 'clauses' shall mean these contractual clauses, which are a free-standing document that does not incorporate commercial business terms established by the parties under separate commercial arrangements.

The details of the transfer (as well as the personal data covered) are specified in Annex B, which forms an integral part of the clauses.

I. *Obligations of the data exporter*

The data exporter warrants and undertakes that:

(a) The personal data have been collected, processed and transferred in accordance with the laws applicable to the data exporter …

II. *Obligations of the data importer*

The data importer warrants and undertakes that: …

(h) It will process the personal data, at its option, in accordance with:

(i)   the data protection laws of the country in which the data exporter is established, or

(ii)   the relevant provisions[1] of any Commission decision pursuant to Article 25(6) of Directive 95/46/EC, where the data importer complies with the relevant provisions of such an authorisation or decision and is based in a country to which such an authorisation or decision pertains, but is not covered by such authorisation or decision for the purposes of the transfer(s) of the personal data,[2] or…

III.   Liability and third party rights

(a)   Each party shall be liable to the other parties for damages it causes by any breach of these clauses. Liability as between the parties is limited to actual damage suffered. Punitive damages (ie damages intended to punish a party for its outrageous conduct) are specifically excluded. Each party shall be liable to data subjects for damages it causes by any breach of third party rights under these clauses. This does not affect the liability of the data exporter under its data protection law…

IV.   Law applicable to the clauses

These clauses shall be governed by the law of the country in which the data exporter is established, with the exception of the laws and regulations relating to processing of the personal data by the data importer under clause II(h), which shall apply only if so selected by the data importer under that clause.

V.   Resolution of disputes with data subjects or the authority

(a)   In the event of a dispute or claim brought by a data subject or the authority concerning the processing of the personal data against either or both of the parties, the parties will inform each other about any such disputes or claims, and will cooperate with a view to settling them amicably in a timely fashion.

(b)   The parties agree to respond to any generally available non-binding mediation procedure initiated by a data subject or by the authority. If they do participate in the proceedings, the parties may elect to do so remotely (such as by telephone or other electronic means). The parties also agree to consider participating in any other arbitration, mediation or other dispute resolution proceedings developed for data protection disputes.

(c)   Each party shall abide by a decision of a competent court of the data exporter's country of establishment or of the authority which is final and against which no further appeal is possible…

---

[1] 'Relevant provisions' means those provisions of any authorisation or decision except for the enforcement provisions of any authorisation or decision (which shall be governed by these clauses).

[2] However, the provisions of Annex A.5 concerning rights of access, rectification, deletion and objection must be applied when this option is chosen and take precedence over any comparable provisions of the Commission Decision selected.

A.3. Commission Decision 2010/87/EU of 5 February 2010 on standard contractual clauses for the transfer of personal data to processors established in third countries under Directive 95/46/EC of the European Parliament and of the Council (OJ, L 39 of 12 February 2010)[1]

(1)   Pursuant to Directive 95/46/EC Member States are required to provide that a transfer of personal data to a third country may only take place if the third country in question ensures an adequate level of data protection and the Member States' laws, which comply with the other provisions of the Directive, are respected prior to the transfer.

(2)   However, Article 26(2) of Directive 95/46/EC provides that Member States may authorise, subject to certain safeguards, a transfer or a set of transfers of personal data to third countries which do not ensure an adequate level of protection. Such safeguards may in particular result from appropriate contractual clauses.

(3)   Pursuant to Directive 95/46/EC the level of data protection should be assessed in the light of all the circumstances surrounding the data transfer operation or set of data transfer operations. The Working Party on the protection of individuals with regard to the processing of personal data established under that Directive has issued guidelines to aid with the assessment.

(4)   Standard contractual clauses should relate only to data protection. Therefore, the data exporter and the data importer are free to include any other clauses on business related issues which they consider as being pertinent for the contract as long as they do not contradict the standard contractual clauses.

(5)   This Decision should be without prejudice to national authorisations Member States may grant in accordance with national provisions implementing Article 26(2) of Directive 95/46/EC. This Decision should only have the effect of requiring the Member States not to refuse to recognise, as providing adequate safeguards, the standard contractual clauses set out in it and should not therefore have any effect on other contractual clauses.

(6)   Commission Decision 2002/16/EC of 27 December 2001 on standard contractual clauses for the transfer of personal data to processors established in third countries, under Directive 95/46/EC was adopted in order to facilitate the transfer of personal data from a data controller established in the European Union to a processor established in a third country which does not offer adequate level of protection.

(7)   Much experience has been gained since the adoption of Decision 2002/16/EC. In addition, the report on the implementation of Decisions on standard contractual clauses for the transfers of personal data to third countries has shown that there is an increasing interest in promoting the use of the standard contractual clauses for international transfers of personal data to third countries not providing an adequate level of protection. In addition, stakeholders have submitted proposals with a view to updating the standard contractual clauses set out in Decision 2002/16/EC in order to take account of the rapidly expanding scope of data-processing activities in the world and to address some issues that were not covered by that Decision.[4]

---

[1]   All the contracts concluded before 15 May 2010 between a data exporter and a data importer pursuant to Decision 2002/16/EC on standard contractual clauses for the transfer of personal data to processors established in third countries shall remain in force *ex* Article 7 of the present Decision. [Note of the Editor]

[4]   The International Chamber of Commerce (ICC), Japan Business Council in Europe (JBCE), EU Committee of the American Chamber of Commerce in Belgium (Amcham), and the Federation of European Direct Marketing Associations (FEDMA) [Original footnote published in the OJ]

(8)   The scope of this Decision should be limited to establishing that the clauses which it sets out may be used by a data controller established in the European Union in order to adduce adequate safeguards within the meaning of Article 26(2) of Directive 95/46/EC for the transfer of personal data to a processor established in a third country.

(9)   This Decision should not apply to the transfer of personal data by controllers established in the European Union to controllers established outside the European Union which fall within the scope of Commission Decision 2001/497/EC of 15 June 2001 on standard contractual clauses for the transfer of personal data to third countries, under Directive 95/46/EC.

(10)   This Decision should implement the obligation provided for in Article 17(3) of Directive 95/46/EC and should not prejudice the content of the contracts or legal acts established pursuant to that provision. However, some of the standard contractual clauses, in particular as regards the data exporter's obligations, should be included in order to increase clarity as to the provisions which may be contained in a contract between a controller and a processor.

(11)   Supervisory authorities of the Member States play a key role in this contractual mechanism in ensuring that personal data are adequately protected after the transfer. In exceptional cases where data exporters refuse or are unable to instruct the data importer properly, with an imminent risk of grave harm to the data subjects, the standard contractual clauses should allow the supervisory authorities to audit data importers and sub-processors and, where appropriate, take decisions which are binding on data importers and sub-processors. The supervisory authorities should have the power to prohibit or suspend a data transfer or a set of transfers based on the standard contractual clauses in those exceptional cases where it is established that a transfer on contractual basis is likely to have a substantial adverse effect on the warranties and obligations providing adequate protection for the data subject.

(12)   Standard contractual clauses should provide for the technical and organisational security measures to be applied by data processors established in a third country not providing adequate protection, in order to ensure a level of security appropriate to the risks represented by the processing and the nature of the data to be protected. Parties should make provision in the contract for those technical and organisational measures which, having regard to applicable data protection law, the state of the art and the cost of their implementation, are necessary in order to protect personal data against accidental or unlawful destruction or accidental loss, alteration, unauthorised disclosure or access or any other unlawful forms of processing.

(13)   In order to facilitate data flows from the European Union, it is desirable for processors providing data-processing services to several data controllers in the European Union to be allowed to apply the same technical and organisational security measures irrespective of the Member State from which the data transfer originates, in particular in those cases where the data importer receives data for further processing from different establishments of the data exporter in the European Union, in which case the law of the designated Member State of establishment should apply.

(14)   It is appropriate to lay down the minimum information that the parties should specify in the contract dealing with the transfer. Member States should retain the power to particularise the information the parties are required to provide. The operation of this Decision should be reviewed in the light of experience.

(15) The data importer should process the transferred personal data only on behalf of the data exporter and in accordance with his instructions and the obligations contained in the clauses. In particular the data importer should not disclose the personal data to a third party without the prior written consent of the data exporter. The data exporter should instruct the data importer throughout the duration of the data-processing services to process the data in accordance with his instructions, the applicable data protection laws and the obligations contained in the clauses.

(16) The report on the implementation of Decisions on standard contractual clauses for the transfers of personal data to third countries recommended the establishment of appropriate standard contractual clauses on subsequent onwards transfers from a data processor established in a third country to another data processor (sub-processing), in order to take account of business trends and practices for more and more globalised processing activity.

(17) This Decision should contain specific standard contractual clauses on the sub-processing by a data processor established in a third country (the data importer) of his processing services to other processors (sub-processors) established in third countries. In addition, this Decision should set out the conditions that the sub-processing should fulfil to ensure that the personal data being transferred continue to be protected notwithstanding the subsequent transfer to a sub-processor.

(18) In addition, the sub-processing should only consist of the operations agreed in the contract between the data exporter and the data importer incorporating the standard contractual clauses provided for in this Decision and should not refer to different processing operations or purposes so that the purpose limitation principle set out by Directive 95/46/EC is respected. Moreover, where the sub-processor fails to fulfil his own data-processing obligations under the contract, the data importer should remain liable toward the data exporter. The transfer of personal data to processors established outside the European Union should not prejudice the fact that the processing activities should be governed by the applicable data protection law.

(19) Standard contractual clauses should be enforceable not only by the organisations which are parties to the contract, but also by the data subjects, in particular where the data subjects suffer damage as a consequence of a breach of the contract.

(20) The data subject should be entitled to take action and, where appropriate, receive compensation from the data exporter who is the data controller of the personal data transferred. Exceptionally, the data subject should also be entitled to take action, and, where appropriate, receive compensation from the data importer in those cases, arising out of a breach by the data importer or any sub-processor under it of any of its obligations referred to in the paragraph 2 of Clause 3, where the data exporter has factually disappeared or has ceased to exist in law or has become insolvent. Exceptionally, the data subject should be also entitled to take action, and, where appropriate, receive compensation from a sub-processor in those situations where both the data exporter and the data importer have factually disappeared or ceased to exist in law or have become insolvent. Such third-party liability of the sub-processor should be limited to its own processing operations under the contractual clauses.

(21) In the event of a dispute between a data subject, who invokes the third-party beneficiary clause, and the data importer, which is not amicably resolved, the data importer should offer the data subject a choice between mediation or litigation. The extent to which the data subject will have an effective choice will depend on the availability of reliable

and recognised systems of mediation. Mediation by the data protection supervisory authorities of the Member State in which the data exporter is established should be an option where they provide such a service.

(22) The contract should be governed by the law of the Member State in which the data exporter is established enabling a third-party beneficiary to enforce a contract. Data subjects should be allowed to be represented by associations or other bodies if they so wish and if authorised by national law. The same law should also govern the provisions on data protection of any contract with a sub-processor for the sub-processing of the processing activities of the personal data transferred by the data exporter to the data importer under the contractual clauses.

(23) Since this Decision applies only to subcontracting by a data processor established in a third country of his processing services to a sub-processor established in a third country, it should not apply to the situation by which a processor established in the European Union and performing the processing of personal data on behalf of a controller established in the European Union subcontracts his processing operations to a sub-processor established in a third country. In such situations, Member States are free whether to take account of the fact that the principles and safeguards of the standard contractual clauses set out in this Decision have been used to subcontract to a sub-processor established in a third country with the intention of providing adequate protection for the rights of data subjects whose personal data are being transferred for sub-processing operations.

(24) The Working Party on the protection of individuals with regard to the processing of personal data established under Article 29 of Directive 95/46/EC has delivered an opinion on the level of protection provided under the standard contractual clauses annexed to this Decision, which has been taken into account in the preparation of this Decision.

(25) Decision 2002/16/EC should be repealed.

(26) The measures provided for in this Decision are in accordance with the opinion of the Committee established under Article 31 of Directive 95/46/EC, has adopted this Decision:

Article 1.   The standard contractual clauses set out in the Annex are considered as offering adequate safeguards with respect to the protection of the privacy and fundamental rights and freedoms of individuals and as regards the exercise of the corresponding rights as required by Article 26(2) of Directive 95/46/EC.

Article 2.   This Decision concerns only the adequacy of protection provided by the standard contractual clauses set out in the Annex for the transfer of personal data to processors. It does not affect the application of other national provisions implementing Directive 95/46/EC that pertain to the processing of personal data within the Member States.

This Decision shall apply to the transfer of personal data by controllers established in the European Union to recipients established outside the territory of the European Union who act only as processors.

Article 3. For the purposes of this Decision the following definitions shall apply:

(a) 'special categories of data' means the data referred to in Article 8 of Directive 95/46/EC;

(b) 'supervisory authority' means the authority referred to in Article 28 of Directive 95/46/EC;

(c) 'data exporter' means the controller who transfers the personal data;

(d) 'data importer' means the processor established in a third country who agrees to receive from the data exporter personal data intended for processing on the data exporter's behalf after the transfer in accordance with his instructions and the terms of this Decision and who is not subject to a third country's system ensuring adequate protection within the meaning of Article 25(1) of Directive 95/46/EC;

(e) 'sub-processor' means any processor engaged by the data importer or by any other sub-processor of the data importer and who agrees to receive from the data importer or from any other sub-processor of the data importer personal data exclusively intended for the processing activities to be carried out on behalf of the data exporter after the transfer in accordance with the data exporter's instructions, the standard contractual clauses set out in the Annex, and the terms of the written contract for sub-processing;

(f) 'applicable data protection law' means the legislation protecting the fundamental rights and freedoms of individuals and, in particular, their right to privacy with respect to the processing of personal data applicable to a data controller in the Member State in which the data exporter is established;

(g) 'technical and organisational security measures' means those measures aimed at protecting personal data against accidental or unlawful destruction or accidental loss, alteration, unauthorised disclosure or access, in particular where the processing involves the transmission of data over a network, and against all other unlawful forms of processing.

Article 4. 1. Without prejudice to their powers to take action to ensure compliance with national provisions adopted pursuant to Chapters II, III, V and VI of Directive 95/46/EC, the competent authorities in the Member States may exercise their existing powers to prohibit or suspend data flows to third countries in order to protect individuals with regard to the processing of their personal data in cases where:

(a) it is established that the law to which the data importer or a sub-processor is subject imposes upon him requirements to derogate from the applicable data protection law which go beyond the restrictions necessary in a democratic society as provided for in Article 13 of Directive 95/46/EC where those requirements are likely to have a substantial adverse effect on the guarantees provided by the applicable data protection law and the standard contractual clauses;

(b) a competent authority has established that the data importer or a sub-processor has not respected the standard contractual clauses in the Annex; or

(c) there is a substantial likelihood that the standard contractual clauses in the Annex are not being or will not be complied with and the continuing transfer would create an imminent risk of grave harm to the data subjects.

2. The prohibition or suspension pursuant to paragraph 1 shall be lifted as soon as the reasons for the suspension or prohibition no longer exist.

3. When Member States adopt measures pursuant to paragraphs 1 and 2, they shall, without delay, inform the Commission which will forward the information to the other Member States.

Article 5.   The Commission shall evaluate the operation of this Decision on the basis of available information three years after its adoption. It shall submit a report on the findings to the Committee established under Article 31 of Directive 95/46/EC. It shall include any evidence that could affect the evaluation concerning the adequacy of the standard contractual clauses in the Annex and any evidence that this Decision is being applied in a discriminatory way.

Article 6.   This Decision shall apply from 15 May 2010.

Article 7.   1.   Decision 2002/16/EC is repealed with effect from 15 May 2010.
     2.   A contract concluded between a data exporter and a data importer pursuant to Decision 2002/16/EC before 15 May 2010 shall remain in force and effect for as long as the transfers and data-processing operations that are the subject matter of the contract remain unchanged and personal data covered by this Decision continue to be transferred between the parties. Where contracting parties decide to make changes in this regard or subcontract the processing operations that are the subject matter of the contract they shall be required to enter into a new contract which shall comply with the standard contractual clauses set out in the Annex.

Annex — standard contractual clauses (processors)

For the purposes of Article 26(2) of Directive 95/46/EC for the transfer of personal data to processors established in third countries which do not ensure an adequate level of data protection

Name of the data exporting organisation: ....

Address: ....

Tel. ....; fax ....; e-mail: ....

Other information needed to identify the organisation:

....

(the data exporter)

And

Name of the data importing organisation: ....

Address: ....

Tel. ....; fax ....; e-mail: ....

each a "party"; together "the parties", have agreed on the following contractual clauses (the clauses) in order to adduce adequate safeguards with respect to the protection of privacy and fundamental rights and freedoms of individuals for the transfer by the data exporter to the data importer of the personal data specified in Appendix 1.

Clause 1 — Definitions

For the purposes of the Clauses:

(a) 'personal data', 'special categories of data', 'process/processing', 'controller', 'processor', 'data subject' and 'supervisory authority' shall have the same meaning as in Directive 95/46/EC of the European Parliament and of the Council of 24 October 1995 on the protection of individuals with regard to the processing of personal data and on the free movement of such data;[1]

(b) 'the data exporter' means the controller who transfers the personal data;

(c) 'the data importer' means the processor who agrees to receive from the data exporter personal data intended for processing on his behalf after the transfer in accordance with his instructions and the terms of the Clauses and who is not subject to a third country's system ensuring adequate protection within the meaning of Article 25(1) of Directive 95/46/EC;

(d) 'the sub-processor' means any processor engaged by the data importer or by any other sub-processor of the data importer who agrees to receive from the data importer or from any other sub-processor of the data importer personal data exclusively intended for processing activities to be carried out on behalf of the data exporter after the transfer in accordance with his instructions, the terms of the Clauses and the terms of the written subcontract;

(e) 'the applicable data protection law' means the legislation protecting the fundamental rights and freedoms of individuals and, in particular, their right to privacy with respect to the processing of personal data applicable to a data controller in the Member State in which the data exporter is established;

(f) 'technical and organisational security measures' means those measures aimed at protecting personal data against accidental or unlawful destruction or accidental loss, alteration, unauthorised disclosure or access, in particular where the processing involves the transmission of data over a network, and against all other unlawful forms of processing.

Clause 2 — Details of the transfer

The details of the transfer and in particular the special categories of personal data where applicable are specified in **Appendix 1** which forms an integral part of the Clauses.

Clause 3 — Third-Party beneficiary clause

1. The data subject can enforce against the data exporter this Clause, Clause 4(b) to (i), Clause 5(a) to (e), and (g) to (j), Clause 6(1) and (2), Clause 7, Clause 8(2), and Clauses 9 to 12 as third-party beneficiary.

2. The data subject can enforce against the data importer this Clause, Clause 5(a) to (e) and (g), Clause 6, Clause 7, Clause 8(2), and Clauses 9 to 12, in cases where the data exporter has factually disappeared or has ceased to exist in law unless any successor entity

---

[1] [The following footnotes are published in the original numerical order as in the OJ] Parties may reproduce definitions and meanings contained in Directive 95/46/EC within this Clause if they considered it better for the contract to stand alone.

has assumed the entire legal obligations of the data exporter by contract or by operation of law, as a result of which it takes on the rights and obligations of the data exporter, in which case the data subject can enforce them against such entity.

3.   The data subject can enforce against the sub-processor this Clause, Clause 5(a) to (e) and (g), Clause 6, Clause 7, Clause 8, Clauses 5(a) to e and g(2), and Clauses 9 to 12, in cases where both the data exporter and the data importer have factually disappeared or ceased to exist in law or have become insolvent, unless any successor entity has assumed the entire legal obligations of the data exporter by contract or by operation of law as a result of which it takes on the rights and obligations of the data exporter, in which case the data subject can enforce them against such entity. Such third-party liability of the sub-processor shall be limited to its own processing operations under the Clauses.

4.   The parties do not object to a data subject being represented by an association or other body if the data subject so expressly wishes and if permitted by national law.

Clause 4 — Obligations of the data exporter

The data exporter agrees and warrants:

(a)   that the processing, including the transfer itself, of the personal data has been and will continue to be carried out in accordance with the relevant provisions of the applicable data protection law (and, where applicable, has been notified to the relevant authorities of the Member State where the data exporter is established) and does not violate the relevant provisions of that State;

(b)   that it has instructed and throughout the duration of the personal data-processing services will instruct the data importer to process the personal data transferred only on the data exporter's behalf and in accordance with the applicable data protection law and the Clauses;

(c)   that the data importer will provide sufficient guarantees in respect of the technical and organisational security measures specified in Appendix 2 to this contract;

(d)   that after assessment of the requirements of the applicable data protection law, the security measures are appropriate to protect personal data against accidental or unlawful destruction or accidental loss, alteration, unauthorised disclosure or access, in particular where the processing involves the transmission of data over a network, and against all other unlawful forms of processing, and that these measures ensure a level of security appropriate to the risks presented by the processing and the nature of the data to be protected having regard to the state of the art and the cost of their implementation;

(e)   that it will ensure compliance with the security measures;

(f)   that, if the transfer involves special categories of data, the data subject has been informed or will be informed before, or as soon as possible after, the transfer that its data could be transmitted to a third country not providing adequate protection within the meaning of Directive 95/46/EC;

(g)   to forward any notification received from the data importer or any sub-processor pursuant to Clause 5(b) and Clause 8(3) to the data protection supervisory authority if the data exporter decides to continue the transfer or to lift the suspension;

(h)   to make available to the data subjects upon request a copy of the Clauses, with the exception of Appendix 2, and a summary description of the security measures, as well as a copy of any contract for sub-processing services which has to be made in accordance with the Clauses, unless the Clauses or the contract contain commercial information, in which case it may remove such commercial information;

(i) that, in the event of sub-processing, the processing activity is carried out in accordance with Clause 11 by a sub-processor providing at least the same level of protection for the personal data and the rights of data subject as the data importer under the Clauses; and

(j) that it will ensure compliance with Clauses 4(a) to (i).

Clause 5 — *Obligations of the data importer*[1]

The data importer agrees and warrants:

(a) to process the personal data only on behalf of the data exporter and in compliance with its instructions and the Clauses; if it cannot provide such compliance for whatever reasons, it agrees to inform promptly the data exporter of its inability to comply, in which case the data exporter is entitled to suspend the transfer of data and/or terminate the contract;

(b) that it has no reason to believe that the legislation applicable to it prevents it from fulfilling the instructions received from the data exporter and its obligations under the contract and that in the event of a change in this legislation which is likely to have a substantial adverse effect on the warranties and obligations provided by the Clauses, it will promptly notify the change to the data exporter as soon as it is aware, in which case the data exporter is entitled to suspend the transfer of data and/or terminate the contract;

(c) that it has implemented the technical and organisational security measures specified in Appendix 2 before processing the personal data transferred;

(d) that it will promptly notify the data exporter about:

(i) any legally binding request for disclosure of the personal data by a law enforcement authority unless otherwise prohibited, such as a prohibition under criminal law to preserve the confidentiality of a law enforcement investigation;

(ii) any accidental or unauthorised access; and

(iii) any request received directly from the data subjects without responding to that request, unless it has been otherwise authorised to do so;

(e) to deal promptly and properly with all inquiries from the data exporter relating to its processing of the personal data subject to the transfer and to abide by the advice of the supervisory authority with regard to the processing of the data transferred;

(f) at the request of the data exporter to submit its data-processing facilities for audit of the processing activities covered by the Clauses which shall be carried out by the data exporter or an inspection body composed of independent members and in possession of the required professional qualifications bound by a duty of confidentiality, selected by the data exporter, where applicable, in agreement with the supervisory authority;

---

[1] Mandatory requirements of the national legislation applicable to the data importer which do not go beyond what is necessary in a democratic society on the basis of one of the interests listed in Article 13(1) of Directive 95/46/EC, that is, if they constitute a necessary measure to safeguard national security, defence, public security, the prevention, investigation, detection and prosecution of criminal offences or of breaches of ethics for the regulated professions, an important economic or financial interest of the State or the protection of the data subject or the rights and freedoms of others, are not in contradiction with the standard contractual clauses. Some examples of such mandatory requirements which do not go beyond what is necessary in a democratic society are, inter alia, internationally recognised sanctions, tax-reporting requirements or anti-money-laundering reporting requirements.

(g)   to make available to the data subject upon request a copy of the Clauses, or any existing contract for sub-processing, unless the Clauses or contract contain commercial information, in which case it may remove such commercial information, with the exception of Appendix 2 which shall be replaced by a summary description of the security measures in those cases where the data subject is unable to obtain a copy from the data exporter;

(h)   that, in the event of sub-processing, it has previously informed the data exporter and obtained its prior written consent;   (i)   that the processing services by the sub-processor will be carried out in accordance with Clause 11;   (j) to send promptly a copy of any sub-processor agreement it concludes under the Clauses to the data exporter.

Clause 6 — Liability

1.   The parties agree that any data subject, who has suffered damage as a result of any breach of the obligations referred to in Clause 3 or in Clause 11 by any party or sub-processor is entitled to receive compensation from the data exporter for the damage suffered.

2.   If a data subject is not able to bring a claim for compensation in accordance with paragraph 1 against the data exporter, arising out of a breach by the data importer or his sub-processor of any of their obligations referred to in Clause 3 or in Clause 11, because the data exporter has factually disappeared or ceased to exist in law or has become insolvent, the data importer agrees that the data subject may issue a claim against the data importer as if it were the data exporter, unless any successor entity has assumed the entire legal obligations of the data exporter by contract of by operation of law, in which case the data subject can enforce its rights against such entity.

The data importer may not rely on a breach by a sub-processor of its obligations in order to avoid its own liabilities.

3.   If a data subject is not able to bring a claim against the data exporter or the data importer referred to in paragraphs 1 and 2, arising out of a breach by the sub-processor of any of their obligations referred to in Clause 3 or in Clause 11 because both the data exporter and the data importer have factually disappeared or ceased to exist in law or have become insolvent, the sub-processor agrees that the data subject may issue a claim against the data sub-processor with regard to its own processing operations under the Clauses as if it were the data exporter or the data importer, unless any successor entity has assumed the entire legal obligations of the data exporter or data importer by contract or by operation of law, in which case the data subject can enforce its rights against such entity. The liability of the sub-processor shall be limited to its own processing operations under the Clauses.

Clause 7 — Mediation and jurisdiction

1.   The data importer agrees that if the data subject invokes against it third-party beneficiary rights and/or claims compensation for damages under the Clauses, the data importer will accept the decision of the data subject:

(a)   to refer the dispute to mediation, by an independent person or, where applicable, by the supervisory authority;

(b)   to refer the dispute to the courts in the Member State in which the data exporter is established.

2. The parties agree that the choice made by the data subject will not prejudice its substantive or procedural rights to seek remedies in accordance with other provisions of national or international law.

Clause 8 — Co-operation with supervisory authorities

1. The data exporter agrees to deposit a copy of this contract with the supervisory authority if it so requests or if such deposit is required under the applicable data protection law.
2. The parties agree that the supervisory authority has the right to conduct an audit of the data importer, and of any sub-processor, which has the same scope and is subject to the same conditions as would apply to an audit of the data exporter under the applicable data protection law.
3. The data importer shall promptly inform the data exporter about the existence of legislation applicable to it or any sub-processor preventing the conduct of an audit of the data importer, or any sub-processor, pursuant to paragraph 2. In such a case the data exporter shall be entitled to take the measures foreseen in Clause 5(b).

Clause 9 — Governing law

The Clauses shall be governed by the law of the Member State in which the data exporter is established, namely ....

Clause 10 — Variation of the contract

The parties undertake not to vary or modify the Clauses. This does not preclude the parties from adding clauses on business related issues where required as long as they do not contradict the Clause.

Clause 11 — Sub-processing

1. The data importer shall not subcontract any of its processing operations performed on behalf of the data exporter under the Clauses without the prior written consent of the data exporter. Where the data importer subcontracts its obligations under the Clauses, with the consent of the data exporter, it shall do so only by way of a written agreement with the sub-processor which imposes the same obligations on the sub-processor as are imposed on the data importer under the Clauses.[1] Where the sub-processor fails to fulfil its data protection obligations under such written agreement the data importer shall remain fully liable to the data exporter for the performance of the sub-processor's obligations under such agreement.
2. The prior written contract between the data importer and the sub-processor shall also provide for a third-party beneficiary clause as laid down in Clause 3 for cases where the data subject is not able to bring the claim for compensation referred to in

---

[1] This requirement may be satisfied by the sub-processor co-signing the contract entered into between the data exporter and the data importer under this Decision.

paragraph 1 of Clause 6 against the data exporter or the data importer because they have factually disappeared or have ceased to exist in law or have become insolvent and no successor entity has assumed the entire legal obligations of the data exporter or data importer by contract or by operation of law. Such third-party liability of the sub-processor shall be limited to its own processing operations under the Clauses.

3.   The provisions relating to data protection aspects for sub-processing of the contract referred to in paragraph 1 shall be governed by the law of the Member State in which the data exporter is established, namely ....

4.   The data exporter shall keep a list of sub-processing agreements concluded under the Clauses and notified by the data importer pursuant to Clause 5(j), which shall be updated at least once a year. The list shall be available to the data exporter's data protection supervisory authority.

Clause 12 — Obligation after the termination of personal data-processing services

1.   The parties agree that on the termination of the provision of data-processing services, the data importer and the sub-processor shall, at the choice of the data exporter, return all the personal data transferred and the copies thereof to the data exporter or shall destroy all the personal data and certify to the data exporter that it has done so, unless legislation imposed upon the data importer prevents it from returning or destroying all or part of the personal data transferred. In that case, the data importer warrants that it will guarantee the confidentiality of the personal data transferred and will not actively process the personal data transferred anymore.

2.   The data importer and the sub-processor warrant that upon request of the data exporter and/or of the supervisory authority, it will submit its data-processing facilities for an audit of the measures referred to in paragraph 1.

A.4.   Directive 2000/31/EC of the European Parliament and of the Council of 8 June 2000 on Ccertain legal aspects of information society services, in particular electronic commerce, in the Internal Market ('Directive on electronic commerce') (OJ, L 178 of 17 July 2000): Recitals 14–15

See Chapter IX, General provisions, D.

A.5.   Directive 2006/123/EC of the European Parliament and of the Council of 12 December 2006 on services in the internal market: Article 17(3)

See Chapter II, Principle of non-discrimination, A.

B.1.   Regulation (EC) No 864/2007 of the European Parliament and of the Council of 11 July 2007 on the law applicable to non-contractual obligations (Rome II) (OJ, L 199 of 31 July 2007): Articles 1(2)(g) and 30(2)

See Chapter VII, A.1.

B.2.   Commission Statement on the review clause (Article 30) (OJ, L 199 of 31 July 2007)

See Chapter VII, A.2.

C.   Council Regulation (EC) No 4/2009 of 18 December 2008 on jurisdiction, applicable law, recognition and enforcement of decisions and co-operation in matters relating to maintenance obligations (OJ, L 7, 10 January 2009): Recitals 34–35, Articles 61, 62(4), 68(4)

See this Chapter, Maintenance obligations, A.1.

D.   Directive 2009/103/EC of the European Parliament and of the Council of 16 September 2009 relating to insurance against civil liability in respect of the use of motor vehicles, and the enforcement of the obligation to insure against such liability (OJ, L 263 of 7 October 2009): Recital 46, Article 23(6)

See Chapter VII, H.

E.1.   Charter of Fundamental Rights of the European Union (OJ, C 303 of 14 December 2007): Article 8

See Chapter II, Fundamental rights, E.

E.2.   The Stockholm Programme — An open and secure Europe serving and protecting the citizens, adopted by the European Council on 10–11 December 2009 (Doc. Consilium No 17024/09): Parts 1.1, 2.5, 3.4.2, 7.4, 7.5

See Chapter I, General provisions, F.

F.   ECJ case-law

In the *Bodil Lindqvist* case (6 November 2003, case C-101/01, Reports, I-12971) the ECJ has been asked to specify the notion of 'transfer of personal data to third countries' under Article 25 of Directive 95/46. In this specific case, the ECJ has to ascertain whether the loading of personal data onto a home page stored on a server in a Member State, with the result that personal data become accessible to people in third countries, constitute a transfer of data to a third country within the meaning of the Directive. The Court ruled that:

56.   Directive 95/46 does not define the expression transfer to a third country in Article 25 or any other provision, including Article 2.

57.   In order to determine whether loading personal data onto an internet page constitutes a transfer of those data to a third country within the meaning of Article 25 of Directive 95/46 merely because it makes them accessible to people in a third country, it is necessary to take account both of the technical nature of the operations thus carried out and of the purpose and structure of Chapter IV of that directive where Article 25 appears.

58.   Information on the internet can be consulted by an indefinite number of people living in many places at almost any time. The ubiquitous nature of that information is a result inter alia of the fact that the technical means used in connection with the internet are relatively simple and becoming less and less expensive.

59.   Under the procedures for use of the internet available to individuals like Mrs Lindqvist during the 1990s, the author of a page intended for publication on the internet transmits the data making up that page to his hosting provider. That provider manages the computer infrastructure needed to store those data and connect the server hosting the site to the internet. That allows the subsequent transmission of those data to anyone who connects to the internet and seeks access to it. The computers which constitute that infrastructure may be located, and indeed often are located, in one or more countries other than that where the hosting provider is established, without its clients being aware or being in a position to be aware of it.

60.   It appears from the court file that, in order to obtain the information appearing on the internet pages on which Mrs Lindqvist had included information about her colleagues, an internet user would not only have to connect to the internet but also personally carry out the necessary actions to consult those pages. In other words, Mrs Lindqvist's internet pages did not contain the technical means to send that information automatically to people who did not intentionally seek access to those pages.

61.   It follows that, in circumstances such as those in the case in the main proceedings, personal data which appear on the computer of a person in a third country, coming from a person who has loaded them onto an internet site, were not directly transferred between those two people but through the computer infrastructure of the hosting provider where the page is stored.

62.   It is in that light that it must be examined whether the Community legislature intended, for the purposes of the application of Chapter IV of Directive 95/46, to include within the expression transfer [of data] to a third country within the meaning of Article 25 of that directive activities such as those carried out by Mrs Lindqvist. It must be stressed that the fifth question asked by the referring court concerns only those activities and not those carried out by the hosting providers.

63. Chapter IV of Directive 95/46, in which Article 25 appears, sets up a special regime, with specific rules, intended to allow the Member States to monitor transfers of personal data to third countries. That Chapter sets up a complementary regime to the general regime set up by Chapter II of that directive concerning the lawfulness of processing of personal data.

64. The objective of Chapter IV is defined in the 56th to 60th recitals in the preamble to Directive 95/46, which state inter alia that, although the protection of individuals guaranteed in the Community by that Directive does not stand in the way of transfers of personal data to third countries which ensure an adequate level of protection, the adequacy of such protection must be assessed in the light of all the circumstances surrounding the transfer operation or set of transfer operations. Where a third country does not ensure an adequate level of protection the transfer of personal data to that country must be prohibited.

65. For its part, Article 25 of Directive 95/46 imposes a series of obligations on Member States and on the Commission for the purposes of monitoring transfers of personal data to third countries in the light of the level of protection afforded to such data in each of those countries.

66. In particular, Article 25(4) of Directive 95/46 provides that, where the Commission finds that a third country does not ensure an adequate level of protection, Member States are to take the measures necessary to prevent any transfer of personal data to the third country in question.

67. Chapter IV of Directive 95/46 contains no provision concerning use of the internet. In particular, it does not lay down criteria for deciding whether operations carried out by hosting providers should be deemed to occur in the place of establishment of the service or at its business address or in the place where the computer or computers constituting the service's infrastructure are located.

68. Given, first, the state of development of the internet at the time Directive 95/46 was drawn up and, second, the absence, in Chapter IV, of criteria applicable to use of the internet, one cannot presume that the Community legislature intended the expression transfer [of data] to a third country to cover the loading, by an individual in Mrs Lindqvist's position, of data onto an internet page, even if those data are thereby made accessible to persons in third countries with the technical means to access them.

69. If Article 25 of Directive 95/46 were interpreted to mean that there is transfer [of data] to a third country every time that personal data are loaded onto an internet page, that transfer would necessarily be a transfer to all the third countries where there are the technical means needed to access the internet. The special regime provided for by Chapter IV of the directive would thus necessarily become a regime of general application, as regards operations on the internet. Thus, if the Commission found, pursuant to Article 25(4) of Directive 95/46, that even one-third country did not ensure adequate protection, the Member States would be obliged to prevent any personal data being placed on the internet.

70. Accordingly, it must be concluded that Article 25 of Directive 95/46 is to be interpreted as meaning that operations such as those carried out by Mrs Lindqvist do not as such constitute a transfer [of data] to a third country. It is thus unnecessary to investigate whether an individual from a third country has accessed the internet page concerned or whether the server of that hosting service is physically in a third country.

71.   The reply to the fifth question must therefore be that there is no transfer [of data] to a third country within the meaning of Article 25 of Directive 95/46 where an individual in a Member State loads personal data onto an internet page which is stored with his hosting provider which is established in that State or in another Member State, thereby making those data accessible to anyone who connects to the internet, including people in a third country.

Right to name

A.   ECJ case-law

European Union law does not regulate directly the measures laying down the rules for the transcription of birth, marriage and death in the registers of civil status, being the adoption of such rules of exclusive competence of the Member States. Nevertheless, the national legislature cannot prescribe provisions in contrast with EU law, as the ECJ pointed out in *Konstantinidis* (30 March 1993, case C-168/91, Reports, I-1191). The action brought by a Greek national, a self-employed worker established in Germany, dealt with a request for rectification of the transliteration transcribing his Greek name in Roman characters made by the public registrar of civil status competent for the transcription of the marriage celebrated in Germany. In this regard, answering to the preliminary ruling referred by the Amtsgericht Tübingen seeking to ascertain whether transliteration by the public registrar is in violation of individual rights or anyway in contrast with the freedom to of establishment and to provide services granted by the Treaty, the ECJ affirmed:

12.   … Article 52 of the Treaty constitutes one of the fundamental legal provisions of the Community. By prohibiting any discrimination on grounds of nationality resulting from national laws, regulations or practices, that article seeks to ensure that, as regards the right of establishment, a Member State accords to nationals of other Member States the same treatment as it accords to its own nationals…

13.   It must therefore be determined whether national rules relating to the transcription in Roman characters of the name of a Greek national in the registers of civil status of the Member State in which he is established are capable of placing him at a disadvantage in law or in fact, in comparison with the way in which a national of that Member State would be treated in the same circumstances.

14.   There is nothing in the Treaty to preclude the transcription of a Greek name in Roman characters in the registers of civil status of a Member State which uses the Roman alphabet. It is therefore for the Member State in question to adopt legislative or administrative measures laying down the detailed rules for such transcription, in accordance with the prescriptions of any international conventions relating to civil status to which it is a party.

15.   Rules of that kind are to be regarded as incompatible with Article 52 of the Treaty only in so far as their application causes a Greek national such a degree of inconvenience as in fact to interfere with his freedom to exercise the right of establishment enshrined in that article.

16.   Such interference occurs if a Greek national is obliged by the legislation of the State in which he is established to use, in the pursuit of his occupation, a spelling of his

name derived from the transliteration used in the registers of civil status if that spelling is such as to modify its pronunciation and if the resulting distortion exposes him to the risk that potential clients may confuse him with other persons.

The subsequent *Garcia Avello* case (judgment 2 October 2003, case C-148/02, Reports, I-1613; see also Chapter III, Citizenship of the Member States, A) dealt with the request of a married couple (the husband being a Spanish citizen and the wife a Belgian citizen), acting as legal representatives of their children having dual nationality, aimed at modifying their children's surname as registered on the birth act by the Belgian administrative authorities only with the father's surname pursuant to Belgian law, instead of both parents's surnames to which they would be entitled according to Spanish law. Since the principle of non-discrimination, on the basis of the settled ECJ case-law, requires that comparable situations must not be treated differently unless such treatment is based on objective considerations independent of the nationality of the persons concerned and is proportionate to the objective being legitimately pursued, and given the fact that, under Belgian law, Belgian citizens having the nationality also of another Member State are, as a general rule, treated in the same way as persons who have only Belgian nationality, the ECJ held that,

35.   In contrast to persons having only Belgian nationality, Belgian nationals who also hold Spanish nationality have different surnames under the two legal systems concerned. More specifically, in a situation such as that in issue in the main proceedings, the children concerned are refused the right to bear the surname which results from application of the legislation of the Member State which determined the surname of their father.

36.   As the Advocate General has pointed out in paragraph 56 of his Opinion, it is common ground that such a discrepancy in surnames is liable to cause serious inconvenience for those concerned at both professional and private levels resulting from, inter alia, difficulties in benefiting, in one Member State of which they are nationals, from the legal effects of diplomas or documents drawn up in the surname recognised in another Member State of which they are also nationals. As has been established in paragraph 33 of the present judgment, the solution proposed by the administrative authorities of allowing children to take only the first surname of their father does not resolve the situation of divergent surnames which those here involved are seeking to avoid.

37.   In those circumstances, Belgian nationals who have divergent surnames by reason of the different laws to which they are attached by nationality may plead difficulties specific to their situation which distinguish them from persons holding only Belgian nationality, who are identified by one surname alone.

38.   However, as has been pointed out in paragraph 33 of the present judgment, the Belgian administrative authorities refuse to treat applications for a change of surname made by Belgian nationals in a situation such as that of the children of the applicant in the main proceedings with a view to avoiding a discrepancy in surnames as being based on 'serious grounds', within the meaning of the second paragraph of Article 3 of the above-mentioned Law of 15 May 1987, solely on the ground that, in Belgium, children who have Belgian nationality assume, in accordance with Belgian law, their father's surname.

In the Court's opinion, none of the grounds on which the Belgian authorities had justified their conduct can provide valid justification for the practice in issue.

42.   First, with regard to the principle of the immutability of surnames as a means designed to prevent risks of confusion as to identity or parentage of persons, although

that principle undoubtedly helps to facilitate recognition of the identity of persons and their parentage, it is still not indispensable to the point that it could not adapt itself to a practice of allowing children who are nationals of one Member State and who also hold the nationality of another Member State to take a surname which is composed of elements other than those provided for by the law of the first Member State and which has, moreover, been entered in an official register of the second Member State. Furthermore, it is common ground that, by reason in particular of the scale of migration within the Union, different national systems for the attribution of surnames coexist in the same Member State, with the result that parentage cannot necessarily be assessed within the social life of a Member State solely on the basis of the criterion of the system applicable to nationals of that latter State. In addition, far from creating confusion as to the parentage of the children, a system allowing elements of the surnames of the two parents to be handed down may, on the contrary, contribute to reinforcing recognition of that connection with the two parents.

43.   Second, with regard to the objective of integration pursued by the practice in issue, suffice it to point out that, in view of the coexistence in the Member States of different systems for the attribution of surnames applicable to those there resident, a practice such as that in issue in the main proceedings is neither necessary nor even appropriate for promoting the integration within Belgium of the nationals of other Member States.

44.   The disproportionate nature of the refusal by the Belgian authorities to accede to requests such as that in issue in the main proceedings is all the more evident when account is taken of the fact that, as is clear from paragraph 12 of the present judgment and from the question submitted, the practice in issue already allows derogations from application of the Belgian system of handing down surnames in situations similar to that of the children of the applicant in the main proceedings.

45.   Having regard to all of the foregoing, the answer to the question submitted must be that Articles 12 EC and 17 EC must be construed as precluding, in circumstances such as those of the case in the main proceedings, the administrative authority of a Member State from refusing to grant an application for a change of surname made on behalf of minor children resident in that State and having dual nationality of that State and of another Member State, in the case where the purpose of that application is to enable those children to bear the surname to which they are entitled according to the law and tradition of the second Member State.

The ECJ addressed again the issue of the law applicable to the name of dual nationals in *Grunkin and Paul* (14 October 2008, case C-353/06, Reports, I-7639), while deciding on the action brought by two German citizens both residents in Denmark, against the Registry Office of Niebüll regarding the latter's refusal both to recognise the surname of their son, a German national, as determined and registered in Denmark pursuant to Danish conflict of law rules based on residence, and to enter that surname in the family register. The Registry Office had invoked Article 10 EGBG, according to which the surname of a person is regulated by the law of nationality and German law does not allow the son to have both parents' surname. Confirming the previous judgment rendered in *Garcia Avello*, the ECJ stated:

24.   … It matters little in that regard whether the discrepancy in surnames is the result of the dual nationality of the persons concerned or of the fact that, in the State of birth and residence, the connecting factor for determination of a surname is residence while, in the State of which those persons are nationals, it is nationality.

25.   As the Commission observes, many everyday dealings, in both the public and

the private spheres, require proof of identity, which is usually provided by a passport. As the child Leonhard Matthias has only German nationality, the issuing of that document falls within the competence of the German authorities alone. If those authorities refuse to recognise the surname as determined and registered in Denmark, the child will be issued with a passport by those authorities in a name that is different from the name he was given in Denmark.

26.   Consequently, every time the child concerned has to prove his identity in Denmark, the Member State in which he was born and has been resident since birth, he risks having to dispel doubts concerning his identity and suspicions of misrepresentation caused by the difference between the surname he has always used on a day-to-day basis, which appears in the registers of the Danish authorities and on all official documents issued in his regard in Denmark, such as, inter alia, his birth certificate, and the name in his German passport…

29.   An obstacle to freedom of movement such as that resulting from the serious inconvenience described in paragraphs 23 to 28 of this judgment could be justified only if it was based on objective considerations and was proportionate to the legitimate aim pursued…

32.   In so far as the connecting factor of nationality seeks to ensure that a person's surname may be determined with continuity and stability, in circumstances such as those in the main proceedings, as was pointed out by the Commission, that connecting factor will result in an outcome contrary to that sought. Every time the child crosses the border between Denmark and Germany, he will bear a different name…

34.   It should further be noted that the connecting factor of nationality under German private international law for the determination of a person's surname is not without exception. It is not disputed that the German conflict rules relating to the determination of a child's surname permit the connecting factor of the habitual residence of one of the parents where that habitual residence is in Germany. Therefore, a child who, like his parents, does not have German nationality may nevertheless have conferred on him in Germany a surname formed in accordance with German legislation if one of his parents has his habitual residence there. A situation similar to that of the child Leonhard Matthias could therefore also arise in Germany…

39.   In view of the foregoing considerations, the answer to the question referred to the Court must be that, in circumstances such as those of the case in the main proceedings, Article 18 EC precludes the authorities of a Member State, in applying national law, from refusing to recognise a child's surname, as determined and registered in a second Member State in which the child — who, like his parents, has only the nationality of the first Member State — was born and has been resident since birth.

Personal status

A.   Council Regulation (EEC) No 2137/85 of 25 July 1985 on the European Economic Interest Grouping (EEIG): Recital [11]

See Chapter IX, Supranational legal entities, A.

B.   ECJ case-law

Although the regulation of civil status registers and the policy on their maintenance are left to the exclusive competence of each Member State, the refusal to recognise certificates and analogous documents relative to personal status issued by the competent authorities of another Member State can represent an obstacle to the exercise of the freedom of movement granted by the Treaty, as the ECJ pointed out in the *Dafeki* judgment (2 December 1997, case C-336/94, Reports, I-6761). The question was raised in proceedings brought by a Greek national who had been working in Germany and had applied to the pension fund for the early retirement benefit for women who have reached the age of sixty pursuant to German law. Her age was resulting from the civil status documents by the competent Greek authorities rectified in accordance with the procedure applicable where archives and registers have disappeared. According to German case-law and academic legal writing, the court seised of the matter proceeded to an evaluation of the documents before it in accordance with the rule of free assessment of evidence since certificates drawn up in another country do not benefit from the presumption of accuracy which applies only to German documents. The ECJ decided that

9.   It should be borne in mind at the outset that, by virtue of Article 48(2) of the Treaty, freedom of movement for workers entails the abolition of any discrimination based on nationality between workers of the Member States as regards employment, remuneration and other conditions of work and employment.

10.   The situation of Mrs Dafeki, a national of a Member State who has been employed in another Member State where she seeks the award of a retirement pension on the basis of that employment, falls within the scope of that provision.

11.   In order to invoke the right to a social security benefit flowing from the exercise of the right of free movement for workers guaranteed by the Treaty, workers must necessarily supply proof of certain particulars entered in the registers of civil status.

12.   It is clear from the provisions of German law, as set out by the national court, that the probative value accorded by those provisions to certificates of civil status issued by the competent authorities of another Member State is lower than that accorded to certificates drawn up by the German authorities.

13.   Thus, although they apply irrespective of the nationality of the worker, those rules operate in practice to the detriment of workers who are nationals of other Member States.

14.   The German Government submits, however, that there are significant differences between the Member States as regards the provisions governing the maintenance and rectification of registers of civil status, in view of the widely varying factual circumstances and legal considerations affecting legislative decisions. In particular, the rules of authentication are not the same in the Hellenic Republic and the Federal Republic of Germany. In the former State, amongst other things, alteration of a date of birth by judgment of a single judge, for which the evidence of two witnesses suffices, is not uncommon. Not a few migrant workers of Greek nationality have availed themselves of this possibility. The competent German insurance institution has noted some hundreds of cases in which the date of birth declared on taking up employment differed significantly from the date given on application for the award of a pension. As a general rule, the alteration operates to the worker's advantage.

15.   The Commission too points out that questions relating to civil status differ considerably from one Member State to another, since the respective systems have been strongly influenced by an extremely wide variety of cultural phenomena and by various external events, such as wars and transfers of territory. It is therefore difficult to start from the premise that the factual and legal situations are identical or equivalent. There are no common measures at Community level. Moreover, the Community has no general competence to lay down rules concerning the law applicable to civil status or questions related to the probative value of documents relative to civil status. In those circumstances, the Commission considers that, as Community law now stands, it does not preclude the German practice.

16.   Account must be taken, first, of the considerable differences that exist between the national legal orders as regards the conditions and procedures for rectification of a date of birth and, second, of the fact that, for the time being, the Member States have neither harmonised the matter nor established a system of mutual recognition of such decisions, as has been done for judgments falling within the scope of the Convention of 27 September 1968 on Jurisdiction and the Enforcement of Judgments in Civil and Commercial Matters…

17.   The possibility of successfully challenging the accuracy of a certificate of civil status, such as that in issue in the main proceedings, depends to a large extent on the procedure followed and on the conditions which have to be satisfied in order for such a birth certificate to be altered. These may vary considerably from one Member State to another.

18.   Consequently, the administrative and judicial authorities of a Member State are not required under Community law to treat as equivalent subsequent rectifications of certificates of civil status made by the competent authorities of their own State and those made by the competent authorities of another Member State.

19.   Nevertheless, exercise of the rights arising from freedom of movement for workers is not possible without production of documents relative to personal status, which are generally issued by the worker's State of origin. It follows that the administrative and judicial authorities of a Member State must accept certificates and analogous documents relative to personal status issued by the competent authorities of the other Member States, unless their accuracy is seriously undermined by concrete evidence relating to the individual case in question.

20.   In those circumstances, a rule of national law which establishes a general and abstract presumption that, in the event of inconsistency between several documents of differing dates, it is the document closest in time to the event to be proved which prevails in the absence of other sufficient evidence, cannot justify refusal to take account of a rectification made by a court in another Member State.

21.   The answer to be given to the question put to the Court must therefore be that, in proceedings for determining the entitlements to social security benefits of a migrant worker who is a Community national, the competent social security institutions and the courts of a Member State must accept certificates and analogous documents relative to personal status issued by the competent authorities of the other Member States, unless their accuracy is seriously undermined by concrete evidence relating to the individual case in question.

Matrimonial matters and parental responsibility

A.1.   Council Regulation (EC) No 2201/2003 of 27 November 2003 concerning jurisdiction and the recognition and enforcement of judgments in matrimonial matters and the matters of parental responsibility, repealing Regulation (EC) No 1347/2000 (OJ, L 338 of 23 December 2003)[1]

(1)   The European Community has set the objective of creating an area of freedom, security and justice, in which the free movement of persons is ensured. To this end, the Community is to adopt, among others, measures in the field of judicial co-operation in civil matters that are necessary for the proper functioning of the internal market.

(2)   The Tampere European Council endorsed the principle of mutual recognition of judicial decisions as the cornerstone for the creation of a genuine judicial area, and identified visiting rights as a priority.

(3)   Council Regulation (EC) No 1347/2000 sets out rules on jurisdiction, recognition and enforcement of judgments in matrimonial matters and matters of parental responsibility for the children of both spouses rendered on the occasion of the matrimonial proceedings. The content of this Regulation was substantially taken over from the Convention of 28 May 1998 on the same subject matter.[2]

(4)   On 3 July 2000 France presented an initiative for a Council Regulation on the mutual enforcement of judgments on rights of access to children.

(5)   In order to ensure equality for all children, this Regulation covers all decisions on parental responsibility, including measures for the protection of the child, independently of any link with a matrimonial proceeding.

(6)   Since the application of the rules on parental responsibility often arises in the context of matrimonial proceedings, it is more appropriate to have a single instrument for matters of divorce and parental responsibility.

(7)   The scope of this Regulation covers civil matters, whatever the nature of the court or tribunal.

(8)   As regards judgments on divorce, legal separation or marriage annulment, this Regulation should apply only to the dissolution of matrimonial ties and should not deal with issues such as the grounds for divorce, property consequences of the marriage or any other ancillary measures.

(9)   As regards the property of the child, this Regulation should apply only to measures for the protection of the child, i.e. (i) the designation and functions of a person or body having charge of the child's property, representing or assisting the child, and (ii) the administration, conservation or disposal of the child's property. In this context, this Regulation should, for instance, apply in cases where the parents are in dispute as regards the administration of the child's property. Measures relating to the child's property which

---

[1]   So-called 'Brussels IIa' Regulation, as amended by Council Regulation (EC) No 2116/2004 of 2 December 2004 (OJ, L 367 of 14 December 2004). Annexes I, II, III and IV are not reproduced hereinafter. [Note of the Editor]

[2]   At the time of the adoption of Regulation (EC) No 1347/2000 the Council took note of the explanatory report concerning that Convention prepared by professor A Borrás (OJ, C 221 of 16 July 1998).

do not concern the protection of the child should continue to be governed by Council Regulation (EC) No 44/2001 of 22 December 2000 on jurisdiction and the recognition and enforcement of judgments in civil and commercial matters.

(10) This Regulation is not intended to apply to matters relating to social security, public measures of a general nature in matters of education or health or to decisions on the right of asylum and on immigration. In addition it does not apply to the establishment of parenthood, since this is a different matter from the attribution of parental responsibility, nor to other questions linked to the status of persons. Moreover, it does not apply to measures taken as a result of criminal offences committed by children.

(11) Maintenance obligations are excluded from the scope of this Regulation as these are already covered by Council Regulation No 44/2001. The courts having jurisdiction under this Regulation will generally have jurisdiction to rule on maintenance obligations by application of Article 5(2) of Council Regulation No 44/2001.

(12) The grounds of jurisdiction in matters of parental responsibility established in the present Regulation are shaped in the light of the best interests of the child, in particular on the criterion of proximity. This means that jurisdiction should lie in the first place with the Member State of the child's habitual residence, except for certain cases of a change in the child's residence or pursuant to an agreement between the holders of parental responsibility.

(13) In the interest of the child, this Regulation allows, by way of exception and under certain conditions, that the court having jurisdiction may transfer a case to a court of another Member State if this court is better placed to hear the case. However, in this case the second court should not be allowed to transfer the case to a third court.

(14) This Regulation should have effect without prejudice to the application of public international law concerning diplomatic immunities. Where jurisdiction under this Regulation cannot be exercised by reason of the existence of diplomatic immunity in accordance with international law, jurisdiction should be exercised in accordance with national law in a Member State in which the person concerned does not enjoy such immunity.

(15) Council Regulation (EC) No 1348/2000 of 29 May 2000 on the service in the Member States of judicial and extrajudicial documents in civil or commercial matters should apply to the service of documents in proceedings instituted pursuant to this Regulation.

(16) This Regulation should not prevent the courts of a Member State from taking provisional, including protective measures, in urgent cases, with regard to persons or property situated in that State.

(17) In cases of wrongful removal or retention of a child, the return of the child should be obtained without delay, and to this end the Hague Convention of 25 October 1980 would continue to apply as complemented by the provisions of this Regulation, in particular Article 11. The courts of the Member State to or in which the child has been wrongfully removed or retained should be able to oppose his or her return in specific, duly justified cases. However, such a decision could be replaced by a subsequent decision by the court of the Member State of habitual residence of the child prior to the wrongful removal or retention. Should that judgment entail the return of the child, the return should take place without any special procedure being required for recognition and enforcement of that judgment in the Member State to or in which the child has been removed or retained.

(18) Where a court has decided not to return a child on the basis of Article 13 of the 1980 Hague Convention, it should inform the court having jurisdiction or central authority in the Member State where the child was habitually resident prior to the wrongful removal or retention. Unless the court in the latter Member State has been seised, this court or the central authority should notify the parties. This obligation should not prevent the central authority from also notifying the relevant public authorities in accordance with national law.

(19) The hearing of the child plays an important role in the application of this Regulation, although this instrument is not intended to modify national procedures applicable.

(20) The hearing of a child in another Member State may take place under the arrangements laid down in Council Regulation (EC) No 1206/2001 of 28 May 2001 on co-operation between the courts of the Member States in the taking of evidence in civil or commercial matters.

(21) The recognition and enforcement of judgments given in a Member State should be based on the principle of mutual trust and the grounds for non-recognition should be kept to the minimum required.

(22) Authentic instruments and agreements between parties that are enforceable in one Member State should be treated as equivalent to 'judgments' for the purpose of the application of the rules on recognition and enforcement.

(23) The Tampere European Council considered in its conclusions (point 34) that judgments in the field of family litigation should be 'automatically recognised throughout the Union without any intermediate proceedings or grounds for refusal of enforcement'. This is why judgments on rights of access and judgments on return that have been certified in the Member State of origin in accordance with the provisions of this Regulation should be recognised and enforceable in all other Member States without any further procedure being required. Arrangements for the enforcement of such judgments continue to be governed by national law.

(24) The certificate issued to facilitate enforcement of the judgment should not be subject to appeal. It should be rectified only where there is a material error, i.e. where it does not correctly reflect the judgment.

(25) Central authorities should cooperate both in general matter and in specific cases, including for purposes of promoting the amicable resolution of family disputes, in matters of parental responsibility. To this end central authorities shall participate in the European Judicial Network in civil and commercial matters created by Council Decision 2001/470/EC of 28 May 2001 establishing a European Judicial Network in civil and commercial matters.

(26) The Commission should make publicly available and update the lists of courts and redress procedures communicated by the Member States.

(27) The measures necessary for the implementation of this Regulation should be adopted in accordance with Council Decision 1999/468/EC of 28 June 1999 laying down the procedures for the exercise of implementing powers conferred on the Commission.

(28) This Regulation replaces Regulation (EC) No 1347/2000 which is consequently repealed.

(29) For the proper functioning of this Regulation, the Commission should review its application and propose such amendments as may appear necessary.

(30) The United Kingdom and Ireland, in accordance with Article 3 of the Protocol on the position of the United Kingdom and Ireland annexed to the Treaty on European Union and the Treaty establishing the European Community, have given notice of their wish to take part in the adoption and application of this Regulation.

(31) Denmark, in accordance with Articles 1 and 2 of the Protocol on the position of Denmark annexed to the Treaty on European Union and the Treaty establishing the European Community, is not participating in the adoption of this Regulation and is therefore not bound by it nor subject to its application.

(32) Since the objectives of this Regulation cannot be sufficiently achieved by the Member States and can therefore be better achieved at Community level, the Community may adopt measures, in accordance with the principle of subsidiarity as set out in Article 5 of the Treaty. In accordance with the principle of proportionality, as set out in that Article, this Regulation does not go beyond what is necessary in order to achieve those objectives.

(33) This Regulation recognises the fundamental rights and observes the principles of the Charter of Fundamental Rights of the European Union. In particular, it seeks to ensure respect for the fundamental rights of the child as set out in Article 24 of the Charter of Fundamental Rights of the European Union, has adopted the present Regulation:

Chapter I — Scope and definitions

Article 1. Scope.   1.   This Regulation shall apply, whatever the nature of the court or tribunal, in civil matters relating to:

(a)   divorce, legal separation or marriage annulment;

(b)   the attribution, exercise, delegation, restriction or termination of parental responsibility.

2.   The matters referred to in paragraph 1(b) may, in particular, deal with:

(a)   rights of custody and rights of access;

(b)   guardianship, curatorship and similar institutions;

(c)   the designation and functions of any person or body having charge of the child's person or property, representing or assisting the child;

(d)   the placement of the child in a foster family or in institutional care;

(e)   measures for the protection of the child relating to the administration, conservation or disposal of the child's property.

3.   This Regulation shall not apply to:

(a)   the establishment or contesting of a parent–child relationship;

(b)   decisions on adoption, measures preparatory to adoption, or the annulment or revocation of adoption;

(c)   the name and forenames of the child;

(d)   emancipation;

(e)   maintenance obligations;

(f)   trusts or succession;

(g)   measures taken as a result of criminal offences committed by children.

Article 2. Definitions.   For the purposes of this Regulation: 1.   the term 'court' shall cover all the authorities in the Member States with jurisdiction in the matters falling within the scope of this Regulation pursuant to Article 1;

2.   the term 'judge' shall mean the judge or an official having powers equivalent to those of a judge in the matters falling within the scope of the Regulation;

3.   the term 'Member State' shall mean all Member States with the exception of Denmark;

4.   the term 'judgment' shall mean a divorce, legal separation or marriage annulment, as well as a judgment relating to parental responsibility, pronounced by a court of a Member State, whatever the judgment may be called, including a decree, order or decision;

5.   the term 'Member State of origin' shall mean the Member State where the judgment to be enforced was issued;

6.   the term 'Member State of enforcement' shall mean the Member State where enforcement of the judgment is sought;

7.   the term 'parental responsibility' shall mean all rights and duties relating to the person or the property of a child which are given to a natural or legal person by judgment, by operation of law or by an agreement having legal effect. The term shall include rights of custody and rights of access;

8.   the term 'holder of parental responsibility' shall mean any person having parental responsibility over a child;

9.   the term 'rights of custody' shall include rights and duties relating to the care of the person of a child, and in particular the right to determine the child's place of residence;

10.   the term 'rights of access' shall include in particular the right to take a child to a place other than his or her habitual residence for a limited period of time;

11.   the term 'wrongful removal or retention' shall mean a child's removal or retention where:

(a)   it is in breach of rights of custody acquired by judgment or by operation of law or by an agreement having legal effect under the law of the Member State where the child was habitually resident immediately before the removal or retention; and

(b)   provided that, at the time of removal or retention, the rights of custody were actually exercised, either jointly or alone, or would have been so exercised but for the removal or retention. Custody shall be considered to be exercised jointly when, pursuant to a judgment or by operation of law, one holder of parental responsibility cannot decide on the child's place of residence without the consent of another holder of parental responsibility.

Chapter II — Jurisdiction

Section 1 — Divorce, legal separation and marriage annulment

Article 3. General jurisdiction.   1.   In matters relating to divorce, legal separation or marriage annulment, jurisdiction shall lie with the courts of the Member State

(a)   in whose territory:

—   the spouses are habitually resident, or

—   the spouses were last habitually resident, in so far as one of them still resides there, or

—   the respondent is habitually resident, or

—   in the event of a joint application, either of the spouses is habitually resident, or

—   the applicant is habitually resident if he or she resided there for at least a year immediately before the application was made, or

—   the applicant is habitually resident if he or she resided there for at least six months immediately before the application was made and is either a national of the Member State in question or, in the case of the United Kingdom and Ireland, has his or her 'domicile' there;

(b)   of the nationality of both spouses or, in the case of the United Kingdom and Ireland, of the 'domicile' of both spouses.

2.   For the purpose of this Regulation, 'domicile' shall have the same meaning as it has under the legal systems of the United Kingdom and Ireland.

Article 4. Counterclaim.   The court in which proceedings are pending on the basis of Article 3 shall also have jurisdiction to examine a counterclaim, in so far as the latter comes within the scope of this Regulation.

Article 5. Conversion of legal separation into divorce.   Without prejudice to Article 3, a court of a Member State that has given a judgment on a legal separation shall also have jurisdiction for converting that judgment into a divorce, if the law of that Member State so provides.

Article 6. Exclusive nature of jurisdiction under Articles 3, 4 and 5.   A spouse who:

(a)   is habitually resident in the territory of a Member State; or

(b)   is a national of a Member State, or, in the case of the United Kingdom and Ireland, has his or her 'domicile' in the territory of one of the latter Member States, may be sued in another Member State only in accordance with Articles 3, 4 and 5.

Article 7. Residual jurisdiction.   1.   Where no court of a Member State has jurisdiction pursuant to Articles 3, 4 and 5, jurisdiction shall be determined, in each Member State, by the laws of that State.

2.   As against a respondent who is not habitually resident and is not either a national of a Member State or, in the case of the United Kingdom and Ireland, does not have his 'domicile' within the territory of one of the latter Member States, any national of a Member State who is habitually resident within the territory of another Member State may, like the nationals of that State, avail himself of the rules of jurisdiction applicable in that State.

Section 2 — Parental responsibility

Article 8. General jurisdiction.   1.   The courts of a Member State shall have jurisdiction in matters of parental responsibility over a child who is habitually resident in that Member State at the time the court is seised.

2.   Paragraph 1 shall be subject to the provisions of Articles 9, 10 and 12.

Article 9. Continuing jurisdiction of the child's former habitual residence. 1.   Where a child moves lawfully from one Member State to another and acquires a new habitual residence there, the courts of the Member State of the child's former habitual residence shall, by way of exception to Article 8, retain jurisdiction during a three-month period following the move for the purpose of modifying a judgment on access rights issued in that Member State before the child moved, where the holder of access rights pursuant to the judgment on access rights continues to have his or her habitual residence in the Member State of the child's former habitual residence.

2.   Paragraph 1 shall not apply if the holder of access rights referred to in paragraph 1 has accepted the jurisdiction of the courts of the Member State of the child's new habitual residence by participating in proceedings before those courts without contesting their jurisdiction.

Article 10. Jurisdiction in cases of child abduction.   In case of wrongful removal or retention of the child, the courts of the Member State where the child was habitually resident immediately before the wrongful removal or retention shall retain their jurisdiction until the child has acquired a habitual residence in another Member State and:

(a)   each person, institution or other body having rights of custody has acquiesced in the removal or retention; or

(b)   the child has resided in that other Member State for a period of at least one year after the person, institution or other body having rights of custody has had or should have had knowledge of the whereabouts of the child and the child is settled in his or her new environment and at least one of the following conditions is met:

(i)   within one year after the holder of rights of custody has had or should have had knowledge of the whereabouts of the child, no request for return has been lodged before the competent authorities of the Member State where the child has been removed or is being retained;

(ii)   a request for return lodged by the holder of rights of custody has been withdrawn and no new request has been lodged within the time limit set in paragraph (i);

(iii)   a case before the court in the Member State where the child was habitually resident immediately before the wrongful removal or retention has been closed pursuant to Article 11(7);

(iv)   a judgment on custody that does not entail the return of the child has been issued by the courts of the Member State where the child was habitually resident immediately before the wrongful removal or retention.

Article 11. Return of the child.   1.   Where a person, institution or other body having rights of custody applies to the competent authorities in a Member State to deliver a judgment on the basis of the Hague Convention of 25 October 1980 on the Civil Aspects of International Child Abduction (hereinafter 'the 1980 Hague Convention'), in order to obtain the return of a child that has been wrongfully removed or retained in a Member State other than the Member State where the child was habitually resident immediately before the wrongful removal or retention, paragraphs 2 to 8 shall apply.

2.   When applying Articles 12 and 13 of the 1980 Hague Convention, it shall be ensured that the child is given the opportunity to be heard during the proceedings unless this appears inappropriate having regard to his or her age or degree of maturity.

3.   A court to which an application for return of a child is made as mentioned in paragraph 1 shall act expeditiously in proceedings on the application, using the most expeditious procedures available in national law. Without prejudice to the first subparagraph, the court shall, except where exceptional circumstances make this impossible, issue its judgment no later than six weeks after the application is lodged.

4.   A court cannot refuse to return a child on the basis of Article 13b of the 1980 Hague Convention if it is established that adequate arrangements have been made to secure the protection of the child after his or her return.

5.   A court cannot refuse to return a child unless the person who requested the return of the child has been given an opportunity to be heard.

6.   If a court has issued an order on non-return pursuant to Article 13 of the 1980 Hague Convention, the court must immediately either directly or through its central authority, transmit a copy of the court order on non-return and of the relevant documents, in particular a transcript of the hearings before the court, to the court with jurisdiction or central authority in the Member State where the child was habitually resident immediately before the wrongful removal or retention, as determined by national law. The court shall receive all the mentioned documents within one month of the date of the non-return order.

7.   Unless the courts in the Member State where the child was habitually resident immediately before the wrongful removal or retention have already been seised by one of the parties, the court or central authority that receives the information mentioned in paragraph 6 must notify it to the parties and invite them to make submissions to the court, in accordance with national law, within three months of the date of notification so that the court can examine the question of custody of the child.

Without prejudice to the rules on jurisdiction contained in this Regulation, the court shall close the case if no submissions have been received by the court within the time limit.

8.   Notwithstanding a judgment of non-return pursuant to Article 13 of the 1980 Hague Convention, any subsequent judgment which requires the return of the child issued by a court having jurisdiction under this Regulation shall be enforceable in accordance with Section 4 of Chapter III below in order to secure the return of the child.

Article 12. Prorogation of jurisdiction.   1.   The courts of a Member State exercising jurisdiction by virtue of Article 3 on an application for divorce, legal separation or marriage annulment shall have jurisdiction in any matter relating to parental responsibility connected with that application where:

(a)   at least one of the spouses has parental responsibility in relation to the child; and

(b)   the jurisdiction of the courts has been accepted expressly or otherwise in an unequivocal manner by the spouses and by the holders of parental responsibility, at the time the court is seised, and is in the superior interests of the child.

2.   The jurisdiction conferred in paragraph 1 shall cease as soon as:

(a)   the judgment allowing or refusing the application for divorce, legal separation or marriage annulment has become final;

(b)   in those cases where proceedings in relation to parental responsibility are still pending on the date referred to in (a), a judgment in these proceedings has become final;

(c)   the proceedings referred to in (a) and (b) have come to an end for another reason.

3.   The courts of a Member State shall also have jurisdiction in relation to parental responsibility in proceedings other than those referred to in paragraph 1 where:

(a)   the child has a substantial connection with that Member State, in particular by virtue of the fact that one of the holders of parental responsibility is habitually resident in that Member State or that the child is a national of that Member State; and

(b)   the jurisdiction of the courts has been accepted expressly or otherwise in an unequivocal manner by all the parties to the proceedings at the time the court is seised and is in the best interests of the child.

4.   Where the child has his or her habitual residence in the territory of a third State which is not a contracting party to the Hague Convention of 19 October 1996 on jurisdiction, applicable law, recognition, enforcement and cooperation in respect of parental responsibility and measures for the protection of children, jurisdiction under this Article shall be deemed to be in the child's interest, in particular if it is found impossible to hold proceedings in the third State in question.

Article 13. Jurisdiction based on the child's presence.   1.   Where a child's habitual residence cannot be established and jurisdiction cannot be determined on the basis of Article 12, the courts of the Member State where the child is present shall have jurisdiction.

2.   Paragraph 1 shall also apply to refugee children or children internationally displaced because of disturbances occurring in their country.

Article 14. Residual jurisdiction.   Where no court of a Member State has jurisdiction pursuant to Articles 8 to 13, jurisdiction shall be determined, in each Member State, by the laws of that State.

Article 15. Transfer to a court better placed to hear the case.   1.   By way of exception, the courts of a Member State having jurisdiction as to the substance of the matter may, if they consider that a court of another Member State, with which the child has a particular connection, would be better placed to hear the case, or a specific part thereof, and where this is in the best interests of the child:

(a)   stay the case or the part thereof in question and invite the parties to introduce a request before the court of that other Member State in accordance with paragraph 4; or

(b)   request a court of another Member State to assume jurisdiction in accordance with paragraph 5.

2.   Paragraph 1 shall apply:

(a)   upon application from a party; or

(b)   of the court's own motion; or

(c)   upon application from a court of another Member State with which the child has a particular connection, in accordance with paragraph 3.

A transfer made of the court's own motion or by application of a court of another Member State must be accepted by at least one of the parties.

3.   The child shall be considered to have a particular connection to a Member State as mentioned in paragraph 1, if that Member State:

(a)   has become the habitual residence of the child after the court referred to in paragraph 1 was seised; or

(b)   is the former habitual residence of the child; or

(c)   is the place of the child's nationality; or

(d)   is the habitual residence of a holder of parental responsibility; or

(e)   is the place where property of the child is located and the case concerns measures for the protection of the child relating to the administration, conservation or disposal of this property.

4.   The court of the Member State having jurisdiction as to the substance of the matter shall set a time limit by which the courts of that other Member State shall be seised in accordance with paragraph 1.

If the courts are not seised by that time, the court which has been seised shall continue to exercise jurisdiction in accordance with Articles 8 to 14.

5.   The courts of that other Member State may, where due to the specific circumstances of the case, this is in the best interests of the child, accept jurisdiction within six weeks of their seisure in accordance with paragraph 1(a) or 1(b). In this case, the court first seised shall decline jurisdiction. Otherwise, the court first seised shall continue to exercise jurisdiction in accordance with Articles 8 to 14.

6.   The courts shall cooperate for the purposes of this Article, either directly or through the central authorities designated pursuant to Article 53.

Section 3 — Common provisions

Article 16. Seising of a court.   1.   A court shall be deemed to be seised:

(a)   at the time when the document instituting the proceedings or an equivalent document is lodged with the court, provided that the applicant has not subsequently failed to take the steps he was required to take to have service effected on the respondent; or

(b)   if the document has to be served before being lodged with the court, at the time when it is received by the authority responsible for service, provided that the applicant has not subsequently failed to take the steps he was required to take to have the document lodged with the court.

Article 17. Examination as to jurisdiction.   Where a court of a Member State is seised of a case over which it has no jurisdiction under this Regulation and over which a court of another Member State has jurisdiction by virtue of this Regulation, it shall declare of its own motion that it has no jurisdiction.

Article 18. Examination as to admissibility.   1.   Where a respondent habitually resident in a State other than the Member State where the action was brought does not enter an appearance, the court with jurisdiction shall stay the proceedings so long as it is not shown that the respondent has been able to receive the document instituting the proceedings or an equivalent document in sufficient time to enable him to arrange for his defence, or that all necessary steps have been taken to this end.

2.   Article 19 of Regulation (EC) No 1348/2000 shall apply instead of the provisions of paragraph 1 of this Article if the document instituting the proceedings or an equivalent document had to be transmitted from one Member State to another pursuant to that Regulation.

3.   Where the provisions of Regulation (EC) No 1348/2000 are not applicable, Article 15 of the Hague Convention of 15 November 1965 on the service abroad of judicial

and extrajudicial documents in civil or commercial matters shall apply if the document instituting the proceedings or an equivalent document had to be transmitted abroad pursuant to that Convention.

Article 19. Lis pendens and dependent actions.   1.   Where proceedings relating to divorce, legal separation or marriage annulment between the same parties are brought before courts of different Member States, the court second seised shall of its own motion stay its proceedings until such time as the jurisdiction of the court first seised is established.

2.   Where proceedings relating to parental responsibility relating to the same child and involving the same cause of action are brought before courts of different Member States, the court second seised shall of its own motion stay its proceedings until such time as the jurisdiction of the court first seised is established.

3.   Where the jurisdiction of the court first seised is established, the court second seised shall decline jurisdiction in favour of that court.

In that case, the party who brought the relevant action before the court second seised may bring that action before the court first seised.

Article 20. Provisional, including protective, measures.   1.   In urgent cases, the provisions of this Regulation shall not prevent the courts of a Member State from taking such provisional, including protective, measures in respect of persons or assets in that State as may be available under the law of that Member State, even if, under this Regulation, the court of another Member State has jurisdiction as to the substance of the matter.

2.   The measures referred to in paragraph 1 shall cease to apply when the court of the Member State having jurisdiction under this Regulation as to the substance of the matter has taken the measures it considers appropriate.

Chapter III — Recognition and enforcement

Section 1 — Recognition

Article 21. Recognition of a judgment.   1.   A judgment given in a Member State shall be recognised in the other Member States without any special procedure being required.

2.   In particular, and without prejudice to paragraph 3, no special procedure shall be required for updating the civil-status records of a Member State on the basis of a judgment relating to divorce, legal separation or marriage annulment given in another Member State, and against which no further appeal lies under the law of that Member State.

3.   Without prejudice to Section 4 of this Chapter, any interested party may, in accordance with the procedures provided for in Section 2 of this Chapter, apply for a decision that the judgment be or not be recognised.

The local jurisdiction of the court appearing in the list notified by each Member State to the Commission pursuant to Article 68 shall be determined by the internal law of the Member State in which proceedings for recognition or non-recognition are brought.

4.   Where the recognition of a judgment is raised as an incidental question in a court of a Member State, that court may determine that issue.

Article 22. Grounds of non-recognition for judgments relating to divorce, legal separation or marriage annulment. A judgment relating to a divorce, legal separation or marriage annulment shall not be recognised:

(a) if such recognition is manifestly contrary to the public policy of the Member State in which recognition is sought;

(b) where it was given in default of appearance, if the respondent was not served with the document which instituted the proceedings or with an equivalent document in sufficient time and in such a way as to enable the respondent to arrange for his or her defence unless it is determined that the respondent has accepted the judgment unequivocally;

(c) if it is irreconcilable with a judgment given in proceedings between the same parties in the Member State in which recognition is sought; or

(d) if it is irreconcilable with an earlier judgment given in another Member State or in a non-Member State between the same parties, provided that the earlier judgment fulfils the conditions necessary for its recognition in the Member State in which recognition is sought.

Article 23. Grounds of non-recognition for judgments relating to parental responsibility. A judgment relating to parental responsibility shall not be recognised:

(a) if such recognition is manifestly contrary to the public policy of the Member State in which recognition is sought taking into account the best interests of the child;

(b) if it was given, except in case of urgency, without the child having been given an opportunity to be heard, in violation of fundamental principles of procedure of the Member State in which recognition is sought;

(c) where it was given in default of appearance if the person in default was not served with the document which instituted the proceedings or with an equivalent document in sufficient time and in such a way as to enable that person to arrange for his or her defence unless it is determined that such person has accepted the judgment unequivocally;

(d) on the request of any person claiming that the judgment infringes his or her parental responsibility, if it was given without such person having been given an opportunity to be heard;

(e) if it is irreconcilable with a later judgment relating to parental responsibility given in the Member State in which recognition is sought.

(f) if it is irreconcilable with a later judgment relating to parental responsibility given in another Member State or in the non-Member State of the habitual residence of the child provided that the later judgment fulfils the conditions necessary for its recognition in the Member State in which recognition is sought.

or

(g) if the procedure laid down in Article 56 has not been complied with.

Article 24. Prohibition of review of jurisdiction of the court of origin. The jurisdiction of the court of the Member State of origin may not be reviewed. The test of public policy referred to in Articles 22(a) and 23(a) may not be applied to the rules relating to jurisdiction set out in Articles 3 to 14.

Article 25. Differences in applicable law. The recognition of a judgment may not be refused because the law of the Member State in which such recognition is sought would not allow divorce, legal separation or marriage annulment on the same facts.

Article 26. Non-review as to substance. Under no circumstances may a judgment be reviewed as to its substance.

Article 27. Stay of proceedings. 1. A court of a Member State in which recognition is sought of a judgment given in another Member State may stay the proceedings if an ordinary appeal against the judgment has been lodged.

2. A court of a Member State in which recognition is sought of a judgment given in Ireland or the United Kingdom may stay the proceedings if enforcement is suspended in the Member State of origin by reason of an appeal.

Section 2 — Application for a declaration of enforceability

Article 28. Enforceable judgments. 1. A judgment on the exercise of parental responsibility in respect of a child given in a Member State which is enforceable in that Member State and has been served shall be enforced in another Member State when, on the application of any interested party, it has been declared enforceable there.

2. However, in the United Kingdom, such a judgment shall be enforced in England and Wales, in Scotland or in Northern Ireland only when, on the application of any interested party, it has been registered for enforcement in that part of the United Kingdom.

Article 29. Jurisdiction of local courts. 1. An application for a declaration of enforceability shall be submitted to the court appearing in the list notified by each Member State to the Commission pursuant to Article 68.

2. The local jurisdiction shall be determined by reference to the place of habitual residence of the person against whom enforcement is sought or by reference to the habitual residence of any child to whom the application relates.

Where neither of the places referred to in the first subparagraph can be found in the Member State of enforcement, the local jurisdiction shall be determined by reference to the place of enforcement.

Article 30. Procedure. 1. The procedure for making the application shall be governed by the law of the Member State of enforcement.

2. The applicant must give an address for service within the area of jurisdiction of the court applied to. However, if the law of the Member State of enforcement does not provide for the furnishing of such an address, the applicant shall appoint a representative *ad litem*.

3. The documents referred to in Articles 37 and 39 shall be attached to the application.

Article 31. Decision of the court. 1. The court applied to shall give its decision without delay. Neither the person against whom enforcement is sought, nor the child shall, at this stage of the proceedings, be entitled to make any submissions on the application.

2. The application may be refused only for one of the reasons specified in Articles 22, 23 and 24.

3. Under no circumstances may a judgment be reviewed as to its substance.

Article 32. Notice of the decision. The appropriate officer of the court shall without delay bring to the notice of the applicant the decision given on the application in accordance with the procedure laid down by the law of the Member State of enforcement.

Article 33. Appeal against the decision. 1. The decision on the application for a declaration of enforceability may be appealed against by either party.

2. The appeal shall be lodged with the court appearing in the list notified by each Member State to the Commission pursuant to Article 68.

3. The appeal shall be dealt with in accordance with the rules governing procedure in contradictory matters.

4. If the appeal is brought by the applicant for a declaration of enforceability, the party against whom enforcement is sought shall be summoned to appear before the appellate court. If such person fails to appear, the provisions of Article 18 shall apply.

5. An appeal against a declaration of enforceability must be lodged within one month of service thereof. If the party against whom enforcement is sought is habitually resident in a Member State other than that in which the declaration of enforceability was given, the time for appealing shall be two months and shall run from the date of service, either on him or at his residence. No extension of time may be granted on account of distance.

Article 34. Courts of appeal and means of contest. The judgment given on appeal may be contested only by the proceedings referred to in the list notified by each Member State to the Commission pursuant to Article 68.

Article 35. Stay of proceedings. 1. The court with which the appeal is lodged under Articles 33 or 34 may, on the application of the party against whom enforcement is sought, stay the proceedings if an ordinary appeal has been lodged in the Member State of origin, or if the time for such appeal has not yet expired. In the latter case, the court may specify the time within which an appeal is to be lodged.

2. Where the judgment was given in Ireland or the United Kingdom, any form of appeal available in the Member State of origin shall be treated as an ordinary appeal for the purposes of paragraph 1.

Article 36. Partial enforcement. 1. Where a judgment has been given in respect of several matters and enforcement cannot be authorised for all of them, the court shall authorise enforcement for one or more of them.

2. An applicant may request partial enforcement of a judgment.

Section 3 — Provisions common to sections 1 and 2

Article 37. Documents. 1. A party seeking or contesting recognition or applying for a declaration of enforceability shall produce:

(a) a copy of the judgment which satisfies the conditions necessary to establish its authenticity;

and

(b) the certificate referred to in Article 39.

2.   In addition, in the case of a judgment given in default, the party seeking recognition or applying for a declaration of enforceability shall produce:

(a)   the original or certified true copy of the document which establishes that the defaulting party was served with the document instituting the proceedings or with an equivalent document;

or

(b)   any document indicating that the defendant has accepted the judgment unequivocally.

Article 38. Absence of documents.   1.   If the documents specified in Article 37(1)(b) or (2) are not produced, the court may specify a time for their production, accept equivalent documents or, if it considers that it has sufficient information before it, dispense with their production.

2.   If the court so requires, a translation of such documents shall be furnished. The translation shall be certified by a person qualified to do so in one of the Member States.

Article 39. Certificate concerning judgments in matrimonial matters and certificate concerning judgments on parental responsibility.   The competent court or authority of a Member State of origin shall, at the request of any interested party, issue a certificate using the standard form set out in Annex 1 (judgments in matrimonial matters) or in Annex 2 (judgments on parental responsibility).

Section 4 — Enforceability of certain judgments concerning rights of access and of certain judgments which require the return of the child

Article 40. Scope.   1.   This Section shall apply to:

(a)   rights of access;

and

(b)   the return of a child entailed by a judgment given pursuant to Article 11(8).

2.   The provisions of this Section shall not prevent a holder of parental responsibility from seeking recognition and enforcement of a judgment in accordance with the provisions in Sections 1 and 2 of this Chapter.

Article 41. Rights of access.   1.   The rights of access referred to in Article 40(1)(a) granted in an enforceable judgment given in a Member State shall be recognised and enforceable in another Member State without the need for a declaration of enforceability and without any possibility of opposing its recognition if the judgment has been certified in the Member State of origin in accordance with paragraph 2.

Even if national law does not provide for enforceability by operation of law of a judgment granting access rights, the court of origin may declare that the judgment shall be enforceable, notwithstanding any appeal.

2.   The judge of origin shall issue the certificate referred to in paragraph 1 using the standard form in Annex 3 (certificate concerning rights of access) only if:

(a)   where the judgment was given in default, the person defaulting was served with the document which instituted the proceedings or with an equivalent document in sufficient time and in such a way as to enable that person to arrange for his or her defense, or, the person has been served with the document but not in compliance with these conditions, it is nevertheless established that he or she accepted the decision unequivocally;

(b)   all parties concerned were given an opportunity to be heard; and

(c)   the child was given an opportunity to be heard, unless a hearing was considered inappropriate having regard to his or her age or degree of maturity.

The certificate shall be completed in the language of the judgment.

3.   Where the rights of access involve a cross-border situation at the time of the delivery of the judgment, the certificate shall be issued ex officio when the judgment becomes enforceable, even if only provisionally. If the situation subsequently acquires a cross-border character, the certificate shall be issued at the request of one of the parties.

Article 42. Return of the child.   1.   The return of a child referred to in Article 40(1)(b) entailed by an enforceable judgment given in a Member State shall be recognised and enforceable in another Member State without the need for a declaration of enforceability and without any possibility of opposing its recognition if the judgment has been certified in the Member State of origin in accordance with paragraph 2.

Even if national law does not provide for enforceability by operation of law, notwithstanding any appeal, of a judgment requiring the return of the child mentioned in Article 11(b)(8), the court of origin may declare the judgment enforceable.

2.   The judge of origin who delivered the judgment referred to in Article 40(1)(b) shall issue the certificate referred to in paragraph 1 only if:

(a)   the child was given an opportunity to be heard, unless a hearing was considered inappropriate having regard to his or her age or degree of maturity;

(b)   the parties were given an opportunity to be heard; and

(c)   the court has taken into account in issuing its judgment the reasons for and evidence underlying the order issued pursuant to Article 13 of the 1980 Hague Convention.

In the event that the court or any other authority takes measures to ensure the protection of the child after its return to the State of habitual residence, the certificate shall contain details of such measures.

The judge of origin shall of his or her own motion issue that certificate using the standard form in Annex IV (certificate concerning return of the child(ren)).

The certificate shall be completed in the language of the judgment.

Article 43. Rectification of the certificate.   1.   The law of the Member State of origin shall be applicable to any rectification of the certificate.

2.   No appeal shall lie against the issuing of a certificate pursuant to Articles 41(1) or 42(1).

Article 44. Effects of the certificate.   The certificate shall take effect only within the limits of the enforceability of the judgment.

Article 45. Documents.   1.   A party seeking enforcement of a judgment shall produce:

(a)   a copy of the judgment which satisfies the conditions necessary to establish its authenticity;

and

(b)   the certificate referred to in Article 41(1) or Article 42(1).

2.   For the purposes of this Article;

— the certificate referred to in Article 41(1) shall be accompanied by a translation of point 12 relating to the arrangements for exercising right of access;

— the certificate referred to in Article 42(1) shall be accompanied by a translation of its point 14 relating to the arrangements for implementing the measures taken to ensure the child's return.

The translation shall be into the official language or one of the official languages of the Member State of enforcement or any other language that the Member State of enforcement expressly accepts. The translation shall be certified by a person qualified to do so in one of the Member States.

Section 5 — Authentic instruments and agreements

Article 46.   Documents which have been formally drawn up or registered as authentic instruments and are enforceable in one Member State and also agreements between the parties that are enforceable in the Member State in which they were concluded shall be recognised and declared enforceable under the same conditions as judgments.

Section 6 — Other provisions

Article 47. Enforcement procedure.   1.   The enforcement procedure is governed by the law of the Member State of enforcement.

2.   Any judgment delivered by a court of another Member State and declared to be enforceable in accordance with Section 2 or certified in accordance with Article 41(1) or Article 42(1) shall be enforced in the Member State of enforcement in the same conditions as if it had been delivered in that Member State.

In particular, a judgment which has been certified according to Article 41(1) or Article 42(1) cannot be enforced if it is irreconcilable with a subsequent enforceable judgment.

Article 48. Practical arrangements for the exercise of rights of access.   1.   The courts of the Member State of enforcement may make practical arrangements for organising the exercise of rights of access, if the necessary arrangements have not or have not sufficiently been made in the judgment delivered by the courts of the Member State having jurisdiction as to the substance of the matter and provided the essential elements of this judgment are respected.

2.   The practical arrangements made pursuant to paragraph 1 shall cease to apply pursuant to a later judgment by the courts of the Member State having jurisdiction as to the substance of the matter.

Article 49. Costs. The provisions of this Chapter, with the exception of Section 4, shall also apply to the determination of the amount of costs and expenses of proceedings under this Regulation and to the enforcement of any order concerning such costs and expenses.

Article 50. Legal aid. An applicant who, in the Member State of origin, has benefited from complete or partial legal aid or exemption from costs or expenses shall be entitled, in the procedures provided for in Articles 21, 28, 41, 42 and 48 to benefit from the most favourable legal aid or the most extensive exemption from costs and expenses provided for by the law of the Member State of enforcement.

Article 51. Security, bond or deposit. No security, bond or deposit, however described, shall be required of a party who in one Member State applies for enforcement of a judgment given in another Member State on the following grounds:

(a) that he or she is not habitually resident in the Member State in which enforcement is sought; or

(b) that he or she is either a foreign national or, where enforcement is sought in either the United Kingdom or Ireland, does not have his or her 'domicile' in either of those Member States.

Article 52. Legalisation or other similar formalità. No legalisation or other similar formality shall be required in respect of the documents referred to in Articles 37, 38 and 45 or in respect of a document appointing a representative *ad litem*.

Chapter IV — Cooperation between central authorities in matters of parental responsibility

Article 53. Designation. Each Member State shall designate one or more central authorities to assist with the application of this Regulation and shall specify the geographical or functional jurisdiction of each. Where a Member State has designated more than one central authority, communications shall normally be sent direct to the relevant central authority with jurisdiction. Where a communication is sent to a central authority without jurisdiction, the latter shall be responsible for forwarding it to the central authority with jurisdiction and informing the sender accordingly.

Article 54. General functions. The central authorities shall communicate information on national laws and procedures and take measures to improve the application of this Regulation and strengthening their co-operation. For this purpose the European Judicial Network in civil and commercial matters created by Decision No 2001/470/EC shall be used.

Article 55. Co-operation on cases specific to parental responsibility. The central authorities shall, upon request from a central authority of another Member State or from a holder of parental responsibility, cooperate on specific cases to achieve the purposes of this Regulation. To this end, they shall, acting directly or through public authorities or other bodies, take all appropriate steps in accordance with the law of that Member State in matters of personal data protection to:

(a)   collect and exchange information:

(i)   on the situation of the child;

(ii)   on any procedures under way; or

(iii)   on decisions taken concerning the child;

(b)   provide information and assistance to holders of parental responsibility seeking the recognition and enforcement of decisions on their territory, in particular concerning rights of access and the return of the child;

(c)   facilitate communications between courts, in particular for the application of Articles 11(6) and (7) and Article 15;

(d)   provide such information and assistance as is needed by courts to apply Article 56; and

(e)   facilitate agreement between holders of parental responsibility through mediation or other means, and facilitate cross-border co-operation to this end.

Article 56. Placement of a child in another Member State.   1.   Where a court having jurisdiction under Articles 8 to 15 contemplates the placement of a child in institutional care or with a foster family and where such placement is to take place in another Member State, it shall first consult the central authority or other authority having jurisdiction in the latter State where public authority intervention in that Member State is required for domestic cases of child placement.

2.   The judgment on placement referred to in paragraph 1 may be made in the requesting State only if the competent authority of the requested State has consented to the placement.

3.   The procedures for consultation or consent referred to in paragraphs 1 and 2 shall be governed by the national law of the requested State.

4.   Where the authority having jurisdiction under Articles 8 to 15 decides to place the child in a foster family, and where such placement is to take place in another Member State and where no public authority intervention is required in the latter Member State for domestic cases of child placement, it shall so inform the central authority or other authority having jurisdiction in the latter State.

Article 57. Working method.   1.   Any holder of parental responsibility may submit, to the central authority of the Member State of his or her habitual residence or to the central authority of the Member State where the child is habitually resident or present, a request for assistance as mentioned in Article 55. In general, the request shall include all available information of relevance to its enforcement. Where the request for assistance concerns the recognition or enforcement of a judgment on parental responsibility that falls within the scope of this Regulation, the holder of parental responsibility shall attach the relevant certificates provided for in Articles 39, 41(1) or 42(1).

2.   Member States shall communicate to the Commission the official language or languages of the Community institutions other than their own in which communications to the central authorities can be accepted.

3.   The assistance provided by the central authorities pursuant to Article 55 shall be free of charge.

4.   Each central authority shall bear its own costs.

Article 58. Meetings. 1. In order to facilitate the application of this Regulation, central authorities shall meet regularly.

2. These meetings shall be convened in compliance with Decision No 2001/470/EC establishing a European Judicial Network in civil and commercial matters.

Chapter V — Relations with other instruments

Article 59. Relation with other instruments. 1. Subject to the provisions of Articles 60, 63, 64 and paragraph 2 of this Article, this Regulation shall, for the Member States, supersede conventions existing at the time of entry into force of this Regulation which have been concluded between two or more Member States and relate to matters governed by this Regulation.

2. (a) Finland and Sweden shall have the option of declaring that the Convention of 6 February 1931 between Denmark, Finland, Iceland, Norway and Sweden comprising international private law provisions on marriage, adoption and guardianship, together with the Final Protocol thereto, will apply, in whole or in part, in their mutual relations, in place of the rules of this Regulation. Such declarations shall be annexed to this Regulation and published in the Official Journal of the European Union. They may be withdrawn, in whole or in part, at any moment by the said Member States.

(b) The principle of non-discrimination on the grounds of nationality between citizens of the Union shall be respected.

(c) The rules of jurisdiction in any future agreement to be concluded between the Member States referred to in subparagraph (a) which relate to matters governed by this Regulation shall be in line with those laid down in this Regulation.

(d) Judgments handed down in any of the Nordic States which have made the declaration provided for in subparagraph (a) under a forum of jurisdiction corresponding to one of those laid down in Chapter II of this Regulation, shall be recognised and enforced in the other Member States under the rules laid down in Chapter III of this Regulation.

3. Member States shall send to the Commission:

(a) a copy of the agreements and uniform laws implementing these agreements referred to in paragraph 2(a) and (c);

(b) any denunciations of, or amendments to, those agreements or uniform laws.

Article 60. Relations with certain multilateral conventions. In relations between Member States, this Regulation shall take precedence over the following Conventions in so far as they concern matters governed by this Regulation:

(a) the Hague Convention of 5 October 1961 concerning the Powers of Authorities and the Law Applicable in respect of the Protection of Minors;

(b) the Luxembourg Convention of 8 September 1967 on the Recognition of Decisions Relating to the Validity of Marriages;

(c) the Hague Convention of 1 June 1970 on the Recognition of Divorces and Legal Separations;

(d) the European Convention of 20 May 1980 on Recognition and Enforcement of Decisions concerning Custody of Children and on Restoration of Custody of Children; and

(e) the Hague Convention of 25 October 1980 on the Civil Aspects of International Child Abduction.

Article 61. Relation with the Hague Convention of 19 October 1996 on Jurisdiction, Applicable law, Recognition, Enforcement and Co-operation in Respect of Parental Responsibility and Measures for the Protection of Children. As concerns the relation with the Hague Convention of 19 October 1996 on Jurisdiction, Applicable law, Recognition, Enforcement and Co-operation in Respect of Parental Responsibility and Measures for the Protection of Children, this Regulation shall apply:

(a) where the child concerned has his or her habitual residence on the territory of a Member State;

(b) as concerns the recognition and enforcement of a judgment given in a court of a Member State on the territory of another Member State, even if the child concerned has his or her habitual residence on the territory of a third State which is a contracting Party to the said Convention.

Article 62. Scope of effects. 1. The agreements and conventions referred to in Articles 59(1), 60 and 61 shall continue to have effect in relation to matters not governed by this Regulation.

2. The conventions mentioned in Article 60, in particular the 1980 Hague Convention, continue to produce effects between the Member States which are party thereto, in compliance with Article 60.

Article 63. Treaties with the Holy See. 1. This Regulation shall apply without prejudice to the International Treaty (Concordat) between the Holy See and Portugal, signed at the Vatican City on 7 May 1940.

2. Any decision as to the invalidity of a marriage taken under the Treaty referred to in paragraph 1 shall be recognised in the Member States on the conditions laid down in Chapter III, Section 1.

3. The provisions laid down in paragraphs 1 and 2 shall also apply to the following international treaties (Concordats) with the Holy See:

(a) 'Concordato lateranense' of 11 February 1929 between Italy and the Holy See, modified by the agreement, with additional Protocol signed in Rome on 18 February 1984;

(b) Agreement between the Holy See and Spain on legal affairs of 3 January 1979.

(c) Agreement between the Holy See and Malta on the recognition of civil effects to canonical marriages and to decisions of ecclesiastical authorities and tribunals on those marriages of 3 February 1993, including the Protocol of application of the same date, with the second Additional Protocol of 6 January 1995.

4. Recognition of the decisions provided for in paragraph 2 may, in Spain, Italy or Malta, be subject to the same procedures and the same checks as are applicable to decisions of the ecclesiastical courts handed down in accordance with the international treaties concluded with the Holy See referred to in paragraph 3.

5. Member States shall send to the Commission:

(a) a copy of the Treaties referred to in paragraphs 1 and 3;

(b) any denunciations of or amendments to those Treaties.

Chapter VI — Transitional provisions

Article 64.   1.   The provisions of this Regulation shall apply only to legal proceedings instituted, to documents formally drawn up or registered as authentic instruments and to agreements concluded between the parties after its date of application in accordance with Article 72.

2.   Judgments given after the date of application of this Regulation in proceedings instituted before that date but after the date of entry into force of Regulation (EC) No 1347/2000 shall be recognised and enforced in accordance with the provisions of Chapter III of this Regulation if jurisdiction was founded on rules which accorded with those provided for either in Chapter II or in Regulation (EC) No 1347/2000 or in a convention concluded between the Member State of origin and the Member State addressed which was in force when the proceedings were instituted.

3.   Judgments given before the date of application of this Regulation in proceedings instituted after the entry into force of Regulation (EC) No 1347/2000 shall be recognised and enforced in accordance with the provisions of Chapter III of this Regulation provided they relate to divorce, legal separation or marriage annulment or parental responsibility for the children of both spouses on the occasion of these matrimonial proceedings.

4.   Judgments given before the date of application of this Regulation but after the date of entry into force of Regulation (EC) No 1347/2000 in proceedings instituted before the date of entry into force of Regulation (EC) No 1347/2000 shall be recognised and enforced in accordance with the provisions of Chapter III of this Regulation provided they relate to divorce, legal separation or marriage annulment or parental responsibility for the children of both spouses on the occasion of these matrimonial proceedings and that jurisdiction was founded on rules which accorded with those provided for either in Chapter II of this Regulation or in Regulation (EC) No 1347/2000 or in a convention concluded between the Member State of origin and the Member State addressed which was in force when the proceedings were instituted.

Chapter VII — Final provisions

Article 65. Review.   No later than 1 January 2012, and every five years thereafter, the Commission shall present to the European Parliament, to the Council and to the European Economic and Social Committee a report on the application of this Regulation on the basis of information supplied by the Member States. The report shall be accompanied if need be by proposals for adaptations.

Article 66. Member States with two or more legal systems.   With regard to a Member State in which two or more systems of law or sets of rules concerning matters governed by this Regulation apply in different territorial units:

(a)   any reference to habitual residence in that Member State shall refer to habitual residence in a territorial unit;

(b)   any reference to nationality, or in the case of the United Kingdom 'domicile', shall refer to the territorial unit designated by the law of that State;

(c)   any reference to the authority of a Member State shall refer to the authority of a territorial unit within that State which is concerned;

(d)   any reference to the rules of the requested Member State shall refer to the rules of the territorial unit in which jurisdiction, recognition or enforcement is invoked.

Article 67. Information on central authorities and languages accepted.   The Member States shall communicate to the Commission within three months following the entry into force of this Regulation:

(a)   the names, addresses and means of communication for the central authorities designated pursuant to Article 53;

(b)   the languages accepted for communications to central authorities pursuant to Article 57(2);

and

(c)   the languages accepted for the certificate concerning rights of access pursuant to Article 45(2).

The Member States shall communicate to the Commission any changes to this information.

The Commission shall make this information publicly available.

Article 68. Information relating to courts and redress procedures.   The Member States shall notify to the Commission the lists of courts and redress procedures referred to in Articles 21, 29, 33 and 34 and any amendments thereto.

The Commission shall update this information and make it publicly available through the publication in the Official Journal of the European Union and any other appropriate means.

Article 69. Amendments to the Annexes.   Any amendments to the standard forms in Annexes I to IV shall be adopted in accordance with the consultative procedure set out in Article 70(2).

Article 70. Committee.   1.   The Commission shall be assisted by a committee (committee).

2.   Where reference is made to this paragraph, Articles 3 and 7 of Decision 1999/468/EC shall apply.

3.   The committee shall adopt its rules of procedure.

Article 71. Repeal of Regulation (EC) No 1347/2000.   1.   Regulation (EC) No 1347/2000 shall be repealed as from the date of application of this Regulation.

2.   Any reference to Regulation (EC) No 1347/2000 shall be construed as a reference to this Regulation according to the comparative table in Annex V.

Article 72. Entry into force.   This Regulation shall enter into force on 1 August 2004.

The Regulation shall apply from 1 March 2005, with the exception of Articles 67, 68, 69 and 70, which shall apply from 1 August 2004.

ANNEX V – COMPARATIVE TABLE WITH REGULATION (EC) NO 1347/2000

Articles repealed	Corresponding Articles of new text
1	1, 2
2	3
3	12
4	
5	4
6	5
7	6
8	7
9	17
10	18
11	16, 19
12	20
13	2, 49, 46
14	21
15	22, 23
16	
17	24
18	25
19	26
20	27
21	28
22	21, 29
23	30
24	31
25	32
26	33
27	34
28	35
29	36
30	50
31	51
32	37
33	39
34	38
35	52
36	59
37	60, 61
38	62
39	
40	63
41	66
42	64
43	65
44	68, 69
45	70
46	72
Annex I	68
Annex II	68
Annex III	68
Annex IV	Annex I
Annex V	Annex II

A.2.   Declarations by Sweden and Finland pursuant to Article 59(2) (a) of the Council Regulation concerning jurisdiction and the recognition and enforcement of judgments in matrimonial matters and matters of parental responsibility, repealing Regulation (EC) No 1347/2000 (OJ, L 338 of 23 December 2003)

Declaration by Sweden

Pursuant to Article 59(2)(a) of the Council Regulation concerning jurisdiction and the recognition and enforcement of judgments in matrimonial matters and matters of parental responsibility, repealing Regulation (EC) No 1347/2000, Sweden hereby declares that the Convention of 6 February 1931 between Denmark, Finland, Iceland, Norway and Sweden comprising international private law provisions on marriage, adoption and guardianship, together with the Final Protocol thereto, will apply in full in relations between Sweden and Finland, in place of the rules of the Regulation.

Declaration by Finland

Pursuant to Article 59(2)(a) of the Council Regulation concerning jurisdiction and the recognition and enforcement of judgments in matrimonial matters and matters of parental responsibility, repealing Regulation (EC) No 1347/2000, Finland hereby declares that the Convention of 6 February 1931 between Finland, Denmark, Iceland, Norway and Sweden comprising international private law provisions on marriage, adoption and guardianship, together with the Final Protocol thereto, will apply in full in relations between Finland and Sweden, in place of the rules of the Regulation.

A.3.   Statements and Declarations made at the meeting of the Council (JHA) of 29 May 2000 (Doc. Consilium No 8992/00, Add. 1)

1.   Statement by the Council

This Regulation shall not prevent a Member State from concluding agreements with non-Member States, which cover the same matter as this Regulation, where the agreement in question does not affect this Regulation.

2.   Statement by the Council

The Member States undertake to inform the Commission of any agreements which they envisage concluding with third States in accordance with Article 16 and of any changes to or repeal of such agreements.

3. Statement by the Commission on Article 16

The Commission considers that implementation of Article 16 of this Regulation cannot be contrary to the case law of the Court as regards the conclusion of agreements between a Member State and third countries or international organisations.

Consequently, without prejudice to the powers and means laid down in the Treaty, the Commission will ensure that this Regulation is implemented in accordance, both generally and on a case-by-case basis, with the case law of the Court, in particular the AETR case law.

4. Declaration by the United Kingdom

The United Kingdom wishes to record its view that, after the adoption of this Regulation, Member States should be able to conclude certain agreements with third States. The first category of such agreements would be those whereby Member States agree that their nationals courts should not be required under the Regulation to recognise and enforce certain judgments coming from the courts of other Member States. These judgments would be based on grounds of jurisdiction not laid down in the Regulation. The second broader category of agreements with third States would be all those which cover the same subject matter as the Regulation, provided that such an agreement does not interfere with, in the sense of undermine, its operation. In the view of the United Kingdom, such a proviso would be adequate to protect the legitimate interests of the Community and, subject to that proviso, Member States should be free to enter into such agreements. In particular, they should be free to decide whether to ratify the 1996 Hague Convention on the Protection of Children.

5. Statement by the United Kingdom

The United Kingdom considers that the ability of Member States to enter into such agreements would be established by Article 16 and the declaration by the Council. The importance of preserving the external competence of Member States in the context of the Regulation to replace the 1968 Brussels Convention on Jurisdiction and the Recognition and Enforcement of Judgments in Civil and Commercial Matters will make it essential to ensure that the necessary provisions in that Regulation are drafted in an explicit way.

6. Declaration by the United Kingdom

In accordance with arrangements notified in Council document 7998/00 of 19 April 2000, where decisions of a Gibraltar court are to be directly enforced by a court or other enforcement authority in another Member State under the relevant provisions of this Regulation, the documents containing such decisions of the Gibraltar court will be certified as authentic by the United Kingdom Government/Gibraltar Liaison Unit for EU Affairs of the Foreign and Commonwealth Office based in London ('the Unit'). To this effect the Gibraltar court will make the necessary request to the Unit. The certification will take the form of a note.

A.4.   Written question E-3261/01 to the Commission of 23 November 2001 and answer given by the Commission on 12 March 2002 (OJ, 28 E of 6 February 2003)

Subject: Regulation (EC) No 1347/2000 and same-sex marriages and adoption by same-sex couples in The Netherlands

On 1 March 2001, Regulation (EC) No 1347/2000 on jurisdiction and the recognition and enforcement of judgments in matrimonial matters and in matters of parental responsibility for children of both spouses entered into force. On 1 April 2001, in the Netherlands, the Same-sex Marriage Act entered into force, as did the Act concerning Adoption by Persons of the Same Sex.

By letter dated 15 May 2001, the Director-General for Personnel and Administration of the Commission, Mr Reichenbach, expressed the view that all marriages contracted under Netherlands civil law should be recognised with a view to the application of the Staff Regulations at the Commission.

1.   Was Mr Reichenbach right to invoke in his letter Article 1a of the Staff Regulations, which entitles officials to equal treatment irrespective, inter alia, of their sexual orientation, and Article 9 of the European Charter of Fundamental Rights?

2.   Does the Commission consider that, in accordance with this interpretation, marriage and spouses as referred to in Regulation (EC) No 1327/2000 includes marriages between two persons of the same sex, contracted under Netherlands civil law?

3.   Does the Commission consider that, if the intention had been to exclude from the scope of the regulation same-sex marriages, whose legalisation in the Netherlands it was already possible to foresee when the regulation was being drafted, this should have been explicitly made clear in the regulation?

4.   Does Regulation (EC) No 1347/2000 also apply to the parental responsibility of same-sex spouses, which, under Netherlands law, arises automatically for the partner of a parent who has a parental relationship with the child under the law of descent?

5.   Does the term spouse as used in the directives and regulations relating to free movement of citizens of the EU and other persons, such as Regulation (EEC) No 1612/68, include same-sex spouses under Netherlands law?

Answer given by Mr Vitorino on behalf of the Commission

As to the specific question of the recognition of Dutch same-sex marriages for the purposes of the application of the Staff Regulations, reference is made to the Commission's reply to Written Question P-32438/01 of Mrs Buitenweg. In that reply of 15 October 2001 the Commission pointed out that it had reflected on how to take account of the law modifying the Netherlands Civil Code to recognise marriage between same sex couples. Following consultations within its services, the Commission has given instructions that the marriage of an official recognised under the amended Dutch Civil Code should be treated in the same way as any other marriage recognised in a Member State. The line taken in this reply is based on Article 1a of the Staff Regulations and Article 9 of the European Charter of Fundamental Rights; it is identical with the position taken by the Director-General for Personnel and Administration in his note of 15 May 2001.

As confirmed by the consistent case law of the Court of Justice[1] which has so far only dealt with the possible assimilation of unmarried partners to spouses, there are as such no provisions of Community law which define the notions of spouse or marriage; thus, as alluded to above, the Court has held that when such notions appear in legislative instruments which are intended to have consequences throughout the Community, the interpretation must take account of the situation in all the Member States and not just in a single Member State. Further, when reference is made to social and legal developments in order to justify a dynamic interpretation of such terms, the Court has said that such developments must be visible in all the Community. On the basis of this argument, the Court concluded in the *Reed* case, cited below, that Article 10 of Regulation 1612/68 could not be interpreted to mean that a companion, in a stable relationship, of a worker who is a national of a Member State and is employed in the territory of another Member State, must in certain circumstances be treated as his spouse for the purposes of that provision.

In this context, the Honourable Member refers to Council Regulation (EC) No 1347/2000 on jurisdiction and the recognition and enforcement of judgements in matrimonial matters and in matters of parental responsibility for children of both spouses. This Regulation sets out rules on jurisdiction and the recognition and enforcement of judgements in matters of divorce, legal separation or marriage annulment, as well as in matters of parental responsibility for the children of both spouses rendered on the occasion of the matrimonial proceedings.

The Regulation is a private international law instrument. As regards the relations between spouses, its purpose is to establish rules on jurisdiction and to allow recognition in a Member State of a divorce, a separation or an annulment of marriage given in another Member State in accordance with the law which is applicable according to its private international law. Even if it cannot be excluded that the Regulation applies to procedures concerning the divorce of a same sex couple, this does not translate into an obligation on the courts neither to pronounce or recognise the divorce nor to recognise the marriage.

The Regulation also provides for the enforcement in a Member State of an order granted in another Member State in relation to parental responsibility. Therefore, parental responsibility cannot be granted by relying on its provisions. Instead, the relations between a same sex partner and the child of his or her partner are a matter of substantive family law and therefore governed by the applicable national law.

Likewise, the Honourable Member makes reference to the legislation on free movement and in particular Regulation 1612/68, which by its Article 10 creates a right of family reunion for the spouse of a worker who has exercised his right of free movement in another Member State. In line with the case law mentioned earlier, the Dutch legislation, while it can have effects on Dutch territory, does not have the consequence of extending the notion of spouse under Article 10 of Regulation 1612/68 or of imposing on other Member States an extended definition of spouse.

---

[1] [Original footnote published in the OJ] 17 April 1986, case 59/85, *Netherlands v Reed*, Reports, 1283; 31 May 2001, joined cases C-122/99 P and C-125/99 P, *D v Council of the European Union*, Reports, I-4319.

A.5.   ECJ case-law regarding Regulations (EC) No 1347/2000 and No 2201/2003

Article 1

ECJ, 27 November 2007, case C-435/06, C

Article 1(1) of Regulation No 2201/2003 is to be interpreted to the effect that a single decision ordering a child to be taken into care and placed outside his original home in a foster family is covered by the term 'civil matters' for the purposes of that provision, where that decision was adopted in the context of public law rules relating to child protection.

Regulation No 2201/2003 is to be interpreted as meaning that harmonised national legislation on the recognition and enforcement of administrative decisions on the taking into care and placement of persons, adopted in the context of Nordic Co-operation, may not be applied to a decision to take a child into care that falls within the scope of that regulation.

Subject to the factual assessment which is a matter for the national court alone, Regulation No 2201/2003 is to be interpreted as applying *ratione temporis* in a case such as that in the main proceedings.

ECJ, 2 April 2009, case C-523/07, A

Article 1(1) of Regulation No 2201/2003 must be interpreted as meaning that a decision ordering that a child be immediately taken into care and placed outside his original home is covered by the term 'civil matters', for the purposes of that provision, where that decision was adopted in the context of public law rules relating to child protection.

Where the court of a Member State does not have jurisdiction at all, it must declare of its own motion that it has no jurisdiction, but is not required to transfer the case to another court. However, in so far as the protection of the best interests of the child so requires, the national court which has declared of its own motion that it has no jurisdiction must inform, directly or through the central authority designated under Article 53 of Regulation No 2201/2003, the court of another Member State having jurisdiction.

Article 2

CJ, judgment 5 October 2010, case C-400/10 PPU, McB

The notion of 'rights of custody' as defined by Regulation No 2201/2003 is an autonomous concept which is independent of the law of Member States and must be given an autonomous and uniform interpretation. Accordingly, for the purposes of applying Regulation No 2201/2003, rights of custody include the right of the person with such rights to determine the child's place of residence.

As regards the identity of the person who has rights of custody, it is apparent from Article 2(11)(a) of Regulation No 2201/2003 that whether or not a child's removal is wrongful depends on the existence of 'rights of custody acquired by judgment or by operation of law or by an agreement having legal effect under the law of the Member

State where the child was habitually resident immediately before the removal or retention'. It follows that Regulation No 2201/2003 does not determine which person must have such rights of custody as may render a child's removal wrongful within the meaning of Article 2(11), but refers to the law of the Member State where the child was habitually resident immediately before its removal or retention the question of who has such rights of custody.

Regulation No 2201/2003 must be interpreted as meaning that whether a child's removal is wrongful for the purposes of applying that Regulation is entirely dependent on the existence of rights of custody, conferred by the relevant national law, in breach of which that removal has taken place.

This conclusion is not contrary to Articles 7 and 24 of the Charter of Fundamental Rights that should be taken into consideration solely for the purposes of interpreting Regulation No 2201/2003, and not for assessing national law as such.

Regulation No 2201/2003 must be interpreted as not precluding a Member State from providing by its law that the acquisition of rights of custody by a child's father, where he is not married to the child's mother, is dependent on the father's obtaining a judgment from a national court with jurisdiction awarding such rights to him, on the basis of which the removal of the child by its mother or the retention of that child may be considered wrongful, within the meaning of Article 2(11) of that Regulation.

Article 3

ECJ, 29 November 2007, case C-68/07, Sundelind Lopez

Articles 6 and 7 of Regulation No 2201/2003 are to be interpreted as meaning that where, in divorce proceedings, a respondent is not habitually resident in a Member State and is not a national of a Member State, the courts of a Member State cannot base their jurisdiction to hear the petition on their national law, if the courts of another Member State have jurisdiction under Article 3 of the Regulation.

ECJ, 16 July 2009, case C-168/08, Hadadi

Where the court of the Member State addressed must verify, pursuant to Article 64(4) of Regulation No 2201/2003, whether the court of the Member State of origin of a judgment would have had jurisdiction under Article 3(1)(b) of the Regulation, the latter provision precludes the court of the Member State addressed from regarding spouses who each hold the nationality both of that State and of the Member State of origin as nationals only of the Member State addressed. That court must, on the contrary, take into account the fact that the spouses also hold the nationality of the Member State of origin and that, therefore, the courts of the latter could have had jurisdiction to hear the case.

Where spouses each hold the nationality of the same two Member States, Article 3(1)(b) of Regulation No 2201/2003 precludes the jurisdiction of the courts of one of those Member States from being rejected on the ground that the applicant does not put forward other links with that State. On the contrary, the courts of those Member States of which the spouses hold the nationality have jurisdiction under that provision and the spouses may seise the court of the Member State of their choice.

Articles 6, 7

ECJ, 29 November 2007, case C-68/07, Sundelind Lopez

Articles 6 and 7 of Regulation No 2201/2003 are to be interpreted as meaning that where, in divorce proceedings, a respondent is not habitually resident in a Member State and is not a national of a Member State, the courts of a Member State cannot base their jurisdiction to hear the petition on their national law, if the courts of another Member State have jurisdiction under Article 3 of the Regulation.

Article 8

ECJ, 2 April 2009, case C-523/07, A

The concept of 'habitual residence' under Article 8(1) of Regulation No 2201/2003 must be interpreted as meaning that it corresponds to the place which reflects some degree of integration by the child in a social and family environment. To that end, in particular the duration, regularity, conditions and reasons for the stay on the territory of a Member State and the family's move to that State, the child's nationality, the place and conditions of attendance at school, linguistic knowledge and the family and social relationships of the child in that State must be taken into consideration. It is for the national court to establish the habitual residence of the child, taking account of all the circumstances specific to each individual case.

Article 10

CJ, judgment 1 July 2010, case C 211/10 PPU, Povse

Article 10(b)(iv) of Regulation No 2201/2003 must be interpreted as meaning that a provisional measure does not constitute a 'judgment on custody that does not entail the return of the child' within the meaning of that provision, and cannot be the basis of a transfer of jurisdiction to the courts of the Member State to which the child has been unlawfully removed.

Article 11

ECJ, 11 July 2008, case C-195/08 PPU, Rinau

Once a non-return decision has been taken and brought to the attention of the court of origin, it is irrelevant, for the purposes of issuing the certificate provided for in Article 42 of Regulation No 2201/2003 that that decision has been suspended, overturned, set aside or, in any event, has not become *res judicata* or has been replaced by a decision ordering return, in so far as the return of the child has not actually taken place. Since no doubt has been expressed as regards the authenticity of that certificate and since it was drawn up in accordance with the standard form set out in Annex IV to the Regulation, opposition to the recognition of the decision ordering return is not permitted and it is for the requested court only to declare the enforceability of the certified decision and to allow the immediate return of the child.

Except where the procedure concerns a decision certified pursuant to Articles 11(8) and 40–42 of Regulation No 2201/2003, any interested party can apply for non-recognition of a judicial decision, even if no application for recognition of the decision has been submitted beforehand.

CJ, judgment 1 July 2010 , case C 211/10 PPU, Povse

Article 11(8) of Regulation No 2201/2003 must be interpreted as meaning that a judgment of the court with jurisdiction ordering the return of the child falls within the scope of that provision, even if it is not preceded by a final judgment of that court relating to rights of custody of the child.

Article 14

CFI, 17 May 2006, case T-93/04, Kallianos

The automatic recognition in Belgium, pursuant to Article 14 of Regulation No 1347/2000, of a divorce judgment rendered in another Member State is not sufficient in order to stop vis-à-vis the third debtor the effects of a provisional measure adopted by a Belgian court pending the divorce proceedings abroad, according to which such third party is obliged to make payments in favour of one of the spouses as provisional maintenance. To this end the service of the foreign judgments to the third debtor is necessary, as provided by Belgian procedural law.

Article 19

CJ, judgment 9 November 2010, case C-296/10, Purrucker

Article 19(2) of Regulation No 2201/2003 does not apply if the court of a Member State first seised by one party to resolve matters of parental responsibility is called upon to grant only provisional measures under Article 20 of that Regulation and the court of another Member State competent to hear the case pursuant to the same Regulation is subsequently seised by the other party in the same cause of action in order to obtain the same measures, either provisional or final.

The fact that a court in a Member State is seised for isolated provisional measures or renders a judgment in such proceedings and that neither in the document instituting such proceedings nor in the judgment given any element is provided indicating that such court is competent under Regulation No 2201/2003 does not necessarily prevent that – eventually on the basis of the national law of said Member State – an action on the merits exists, which is linked to the request for provisional measures and provides for elements aiming at proving that the court seised is competent under that Regulation.

Where, notwithstanding efforts made by the court second seised in order to get information from the party invoking lis pendens, from the court first seised and from the central authority, the court second seised does not have any element which would allow to determine the object and the cause of action of a claim brought to another court and aiming and proving the competence of such court under Regulation No 2201/2003, and where, given the specific circumstances of the case, the interest of the child requires that a decision is given which is capable of recognition in other Member States than the country of the court second seised, this court — after waiting for the answers to its requests for information for a reasonable period of time — should carry on the exam of the action brought before it. The length of this reasonable period of time should take into account the interest of the child in the specific circumstances of the case.

Article 20

ECJ, 2 April 2009, case C-523/07, A

A protective measure, such as the taking into care of children, may be decided by a national court under Article 20 of Regulation No 2201/2003 if the following conditions are satisfied:
— the measure must be urgent;
— it must be taken in respect of persons in the Member State concerned, and
— it must be provisional.
The taking of the measure and its binding nature are determined in accordance with national law. After the protective measure has been taken, the national court is not required to transfer the case to the court of another Member State having jurisdiction. However, in so far as the protection of the best interests of the child so requires, the national court which has taken provisional or protective measures must inform, directly or through the central authority designated under Article 53 of Regulation No 2201/2003, the court of another Member State having jurisdiction.

CJ, 23 December 2009, case C-403/09 PPU, Detiček

Article 20 of Regulation No 2201/2003 must be interpreted as not allowing, in circumstances such as those of the main proceedings, a court of a Member State to take a provisional measure in matters of parental responsibility granting custody of a child who is in the territory of that Member State to one parent, where a court of another Member State, which has jurisdiction under that Regulation as to the substance of the dispute relating to custody of the child, has already delivered a judgment provisionally giving custody of the child to the other parent, and that judgment has been declared enforceable in the territory of the former Member State.

CJ, judgment 15 July 2010, case C 256/09, Purrucker

The provisions laid down in Article 21 et seq. of Regulation No 2201/2003 do not apply to provisional measures, relating to rights of custody, falling within the scope of Article 20 of that Regulation.

Article 21

CJ, judgment 15 July 2010, case C 256/09, Purrucker

The provisions laid down in Article 21 et seq. of Regulation No 2201/2003 do not apply to provisional measures, relating to rights of custody, falling within the scope of Article 20 of that Regulation.

Article 31

ECJ, 11 July 2008, case C-195/08 PPU, Rinau

Article 31(1) of Regulation No 2201/2003, in so far as it provides that neither the person against whom enforcement is sought, nor the child is, at this stage of the proceedings, entitled to make any submissions on the application, is not applicable to proceedings initiated for non-recognition of a judicial decision if no application for recognition has been lodged beforehand in respect of that decision. In such a situation, the defendant, who is seeking recognition, is entitled to make such submissions.

Article 42

ECJ, 11 July 2008, case C-195/08 PPU, Rinau

Once a non-return decision has been taken and brought to the attention of the court of origin, it is irrelevant, for the purposes of issuing the certificate provided for in Article 42 of Regulation No 2201/2003 that that decision has been suspended, overturned, set aside or, in any event, has not become *res judicata* or has been replaced by a decision ordering return, in so far as the return of the child has not actually taken place. Since no doubt has been expressed as regards the authenticity of that certificate and since it was drawn up in accordance with the standard form set out in Annex IV to the Regulation, opposition to the recognition of the decision ordering return is not permitted and it is for the requested court only to declare the enforceability of the certified decision and to allow the immediate return of the child.

Except where the procedure concerns a decision certified pursuant to Articles 11(8) and 40 to 42 of Regulation No 2201/2003, any interested party can apply for non-recognition of a judicial decision, even if no application for recognition of the decision has been submitted beforehand.

CJ, judgment 1 July 2010, case C 211/10 PPU, Povse

Enforcement of a certified judgment cannot be refused in the Member State of enforcement because, as a result of a subsequent change of circumstances, it might be seriously detrimental to the best interests of the child. Such a change must be pleaded before the court which has jurisdiction in the Member State of origin, which should also hear any application to suspend enforcement of its judgment.

Article 47

CJ, judgment 1 July 2010 , case C 211/10 PPU, Povse

The second subparagraph of Article 47(2) of Regulation No 2201/2003 must be interpreted as meaning that a judgment delivered subsequently by a court in the Member State of enforcement which awards provisional rights of custody and is deemed to be enforceable under the law of that State cannot preclude enforcement of a certified judgment delivered previously by the court which has jurisdiction in the Member State of origin and ordering the return of the child.

Enforcement of a certified judgment cannot be refused in the Member State of enforcement because, as a result of a subsequent change of circumstances, it might be seriously detrimental to the best interests of the child. Such a change must be pleaded before the court which has jurisdiction in the Member State of origin, which should also hear any application to suspend enforcement of its judgment.

Article 53

ECJ, 2 April 2009, case C-523/07, A

The taking of the measure and its binding nature are determined in accordance with national law. After the protective measure has been taken, the national court is not required to transfer the case to the court of another Member State having jurisdiction. However, in so far as the protection of the best interests of the child so requires, the national court which has taken provisional or protective measures must inform, directly or through the central authority designated under Article 53 of Regulation No 2201/2003, the court of another Member State having jurisdiction.

Where the court of a Member State does not have jurisdiction at all, it must declare of its own motion that it has no jurisdiction, but is not required to transfer the case to another court. However, in so far as the protection of the best interests of the child so requires, the national court which has declared of its own motion that it has no jurisdiction must inform, directly or through the central authority designated under Article 53 of Regulation No 2201/2003, the court of another Member State having jurisdiction.

Article 64

ECJ, 16 July 2009, case C-168/08, Hadadi

Where the court of the Member State addressed must verify, pursuant to Article 64(4) of Regulation No 2201/2003, whether the court of the Member State of origin of a judgment would have had jurisdiction under Article 3(1)(b) of the Regulation, the latter provision precludes the court of the Member State addressed from regarding spouses who each hold the nationality both of that State and of the Member State of origin as nationals only of the Member State addressed. That court must, on the contrary, take into account the fact that the spouses also hold the nationality of the Member State of origin and that, therefore, the courts of the latter could have had jurisdiction to hear the case.

Article 42 of Regulation No 1347/2000

CJ, order 17 June 2010, case C-312/09, Michalias

Regulation No 1347/2000 is not applicable to divorce proceedings brought before the courts of a State before the latter became a Member State of the European Union.

A.6. Proposal for a Council Regulation amending Regulation (EC) No 2201/2003 as regards jurisdiction and introducing rules concerning applicable law in matrimonial matters (COM(2006) 399 of 17 July 2006)[1]

(1)   The European Union has set itself the objective of maintaining and developing the European Union as an area of freedom, security and justice in which the movement of persons is ensured. For the gradual establishment of such an area, the Community is to adopt, among others, the measures relating to judicial co-operation in civil matters needed for the proper functioning of the internal market.

(2)   There are currently no Community rules in the field of applicable law in matrimonial matters. Council Regulation (EC) No 2201/2003 of 27 November 2003 sets out rules on jurisdiction, recognition and enforcement of judgments in matrimonial matters and matters of parental responsibility, but does not include rules on applicable law.

(3)   The European Council held in Vienna on 11 and 12 December 1998 invited the Commission to consider the possibility of drawing up a legal instrument on the law applicable to divorce. In November 2004, the European Council invited the Commission to present a Green Paper on conflict-of-law rules in divorce matters.

(4)   In line with its political mandate, the Commission presented a Green Paper on applicable law and jurisdiction in divorce matters on 14 March 2005. The Green Paper launched a wide public consultation on possible solutions to the problems that may arise under the current situation.

(5)   This Regulation should provide a clear and comprehensive legal framework in matrimonial matters in the European Union and ensure adequate solutions to the citizens in terms of legal certainty, predictability, flexibility and access to court.

(6)   With the aim of enhancing legal certainty, predictability and flexibility, this Regulation should introduce the possibility for spouses to agree upon the competent court in proceedings for divorce and legal separation. It also should give the parties a certain possibility to choose the law applicable to divorce and legal separation. Such possibility should not extend to marriage annulment, which is closely linked to the conditions for the validity of the marriage, and for which parties' autonomy is inappropriate.

(7)   In the absence of choice of applicable law, this Regulation should introduce harmonised conflict-of-law rules based on a scale of connecting factors to ensure legal certainty and predictability and to prevent 'rush to court'. Such connecting factors should

---

[1]   So-called 'Rome III'.

be chosen as to ensure that proceedings relating to divorce or legal separation be governed by a law with which the marriage has a close connection.

(8)   Considerations of public interest should justify the possibility in exceptional circumstances to disregard the application of the foreign law in a given case where this would be manifestly contrary to the public policy of the forum.

(9)   The residual rule on jurisdiction should be revised to enhance predictability and access to courts for spouses of different nationalities living in a third State. To this end, the Regulation should set out a harmonised rule on residual jurisdiction to enable couples of different nationalities to seise a court of a Member State with which they have a close connection by virtue of their nationality or their last common habitual residence.

(10)   Article 12 of Council Regulation (EC) No 2201/2003 should be amended to ensure that a divorce court designated pursuant to Article 3a has jurisdiction also in matters of parental responsibility connected with the divorce application provided the conditions set out in Article 12 of the same Regulation are met, in particular that the jurisdiction is in the best interests of the child.

(11)   Regulation (EC) No 2201/2003 should therefore be amended accordingly.

(12)   Since the objectives of the action to be taken, namely to enhance legal certainty, flexibility and access to court in international matrimonial proceedings, cannot be sufficiently achieved by the Member States and can therefore, by reason of scale, be better achieved at Community level, the Community may adopt measures, in accordance with the principles of subsidiarity as set out in Article 5 of the Treaty. In accordance with the principle of proportionality, as set out in that Article, this Regulation does not go beyond what is necessary to attain these objectives.

(13)   This Regulation respects the fundamental rights and observes the principles recognised in particular by the Charter of Fundamental Rights of the European Union as general principles of Community law. In particular, it seeks to ensure full respect for the right to a fair trial as recognised in Article 47 of the Charter.

(14)   [The United Kingdom and Ireland, in accordance with Article 3 of the Protocol on the position of the United Kingdom and Ireland annexed to the Treaty on European Union and the Treaty establishing the European Community, have given notice of their wish to take part in the adoption and application of this Regulation.]

(15)   Denmark, in accordance with Articles 1 and 2 of the Protocol on the position of Denmark annexed to the Treaty on European Union and the Treaty establishing the European Community, is not participating in the adoption of this Regulation, and is therefore not bound by it nor subject to its application.

Article 1.   Regulation (EC) No 2201/2003 is amended as follows: (1)   the title is replaced by the following:
    'Council Regulation (EC) No 2201/2003 concerning jurisdiction and the recognition and enforcement of judgments in matrimonial matters and the matters of parental responsibility as well as applicable law in matrimonial matters'
    (2) the following Article 3a is inserted:
    '*Article 3a.* Choice of court by the parties in proceedings relating to divorce and legal separation. 1. The spouses may agree that a court or the courts of a Member State are to have jurisdiction in a proceeding between them relating to divorce or legal separation provided they have a substantial connection with that Member State by virtue of the fact that

(a)   any of the grounds of jurisdiction listed in Article 3 applies, or

(b)   it is the place of the spouses' last common habitual residence for a minimum period of three years, or

(c)   one of the spouses is a national of that Member State or, in the case of the United Kingdom and Ireland, has his or her 'domicile' in the territory of one of the latter Member States.

2.   An agreement conferring jurisdiction shall be expressed in writing and signed by both spouses at the latest at the time the court is seised.'

(3)   In Articles 4 and 5, the terms 'Article 3' are replaced by the terms 'Article 3 and 3a'.

(4)   Article 6 is deleted;

(5)   Article 7 is replaced by the following:

'*Article 7. Residual jurisdiction.* Where none of the spouses is habitually resident in the territory of a Member State and do not have a common nationality of a Member State, or, in the case of the United Kingdom and Ireland do not have their 'domicile' within the territory of one of the latter Member States, the courts of a Member State are competent by virtue of the fact that:

(a)   the spouses had their common previous habitual residence in the territory of that Member State for at least three years; or

(b)   one of the spouses has the nationality of that Member State, or, in the case of United Kingdom and Ireland, has his or her 'domicile' in the territory of one of the latter Member States.'

(6)   In Article 12(1), the terms 'Article 3' are replaced by the terms 'Articles 3 and 3a'.

(7)   The following Chapter IIa is inserted:

'CHAPTER IIA — APPLICABLE LAW IN MATTERS OF DIVORCE AND LEGAL SEPARATION

Article 20a. Choice of law by the parties.   1.   The spouses may agree to designate the law applicable to divorce and legal separation. The spouses may agree to designate one of the following laws:

(a)   the law of the State of the last common habitual residence of the spouses in so far as one of them still resides there;

(b)   the law of the State of the nationality of either spouse, or, in the case of United Kingdom and Ireland, the 'domicile' of either spouse;

(c)   the law of the State where the spouses have resided for at least five years;

(d)   the law of the Member State in which the application is lodged.

2.   An agreement designating the applicable law shall be expressed in writing and be signed by both spouses at the latest at the time the court is seised.

Article 20b. Applicable law in the absence of choice by the parties.   In the absence of choice pursuant to Article 20a, divorce and legal separation shall be subject to the law of the State:

(a)   where the spouses have their common habitual residence, or failing that,

(b)   where the spouse had their last common habitual residence in so far as one of them still resides there, or failing that,

(c)   of which both spouses are nationals, or, in the case of United Kingdom and Ireland, both have their 'domicile', or failing that,

(d)   where the application is lodged.

Article 20c.   Application of foreign law.   Where a law of another Member State is applicable, the court may make use of the European Judicial Network in civil and commercial matters to be informed of its contents.

Article 20d.   Exclusion of renvoi.   The application of a law designated under this Regulation means the application of the rules of that law other than its rules of private international law.

Article 20e.   Public policy.   The application of a provision of the law designated by this Regulation may be refused only if such application is manifestly incompatible with the public policy of the forum.

Article 2.   Entry into force.   This Regulation shall enter into force on twentieth day following that of its publication in the Official Journal of the European Union.

It shall apply from 1 March 200…

B.1.   Council Decision 2010/405/EU of 12 July 2010 authorising enhanced cooperation in the area of the law applicable to divorce and legal separation (OJ, L 189 of 22 July 2010)

(1)   The Union has set itself the objective of maintaining and developing an area of freedom, security and justice in which the free movement of persons is ensured. For the progressive establishment of such an area, the Union is to adopt measures relating to judicial co-operation in civil matters with cross-border implications, particularly when necessary for the proper functioning of the internal market.

(2)   Pursuant to Article 81 of the Treaty on the Functioning of the European Union, those measures are to include promoting the compatibility of the rules applicable in the Member States concerning conflict of laws, including measures concerning family law with cross-border implications.

(3)   On 17 July 2006, the Commission adopted a proposal for a Council Regulation amending Regulation (EC) No 2201/2003 as regards jurisdiction and introducing rules concerning applicable law in matrimonial matters (hereinafter referred to as 'the proposed Regulation').

(4)   At its meeting on 5 and 6 June 2008 the Council adopted political guidelines which recorded that there was no unanimity to go ahead with the proposed Regulation and insurmountable difficulties existed, making unanimity impossible at the time and in the foreseeable future. It established that the objectives of the proposed Regulation could not be attained within a reasonable period by applying the relevant provisions of the Treaties.

(5)   In these circumstances, Greece, Spain, Italy, Luxembourg, Hungary, Austria, Romania and Slovenia addressed a request to the Commission by letters dated 28 July 2008 indicating that they intended to establish enhanced co-operation between themselves in the area of applicable law in matrimonial matters and that the Commission should submit

a proposal to the Council to that end. Bulgaria addressed an identical request to the Commission by letter dated 12 August 2008. France joined the request by a letter dated 12 January 2009, Germany by a letter dated 15 April 2010, Belgium by a letter dated 22 April 2010, Latvia by a letter dated 17 May 2010, Malta by a letter dated 31 May 2010 and Portugal during the Council meeting of 4 June 2010. On 3 March 2010, Greece withdrew its request. In total, fourteen Member States have requested enhanced co-operation.

(6)   The enhanced co-operation should provide a clear and comprehensive legal framework in the area of divorce and legal separation in the participating Member States and ensure adequate solutions for citizens in terms of legal certainty, predictability and flexibility and prevent a 'rush to court'.

(7)   The conditions laid down in Article 20 of the Treaty on European Union and in Articles 326 and 329 of the Treaty on the Functioning of the European Union are fulfilled.

(8)   The area of the enhanced co-operation, namely the law applicable to divorce and legal separation, is identified by Article 81(2)(c) and Article 81(3) of the Treaty on the Functioning of the European Union as one of the areas covered by the Treaties.

(9)   The requirement of last resort in Article 20(2) of the Treaty on European Union is fulfilled in that the Council established in June 2008 that the objectives of the proposed Regulation cannot be attained within a reasonable period by the Union as a whole.

(10)   Enhanced co-operation in the area of the law applicable to divorce and legal separation aims to develop judicial co-operation in civil matters having cross-border implications, based on the principle of mutual recognition of judgments, and to ensure the compatibility of the rules applicable in the Member States concerning conflict of laws. Thus, it furthers the objectives of the Union, protects its interests and reinforces its integration process as required by Article 20(1) of the Treaty on European Union.

(11)   Enhanced co-operation in the area of the law applicable to divorce and legal separation complies with the Treaties and Union law, and it does not undermine the internal market or economic, social and territorial cohesion. It does not constitute a barrier to or discrimination in trade between Member States and does not distort competition between them.

(12)   Enhanced co-operation in the area of the law applicable to divorce and legal separation respects the competences, rights and obligations of those Member States that do not participate in it. The common conflict-of-law rules in the participating Member States do not affect the rules of the non-participating Member States. The courts of the non-participating Member States continue to apply their existing domestic conflict-of-law rules to determine the law applicable to divorce or legal separation.

(13)   In particular, enhanced co-operation in the area of the law applicable to divorce and legal separation complies with Union law on judicial co-operation in civil matters, in that enhanced co-operation does not affect any pre-existing *acquis*.

(14)   This Decision respects the rights, principles and freedoms recognised in the Charter of Fundamental Rights of the European Union, and in particular Article 21 thereof.

(15)   Enhanced co-operation in the area of the law applicable to divorce and legal separation is open at any time to all Member States, in accordance with Article 328 of the Treaty on the Functioning of the European Union.

Article 1.   The Kingdom of Belgium, the Republic of Bulgaria, the Federal Republic of Germany, the Kingdom of Spain, the French Republic, the Italian Republic, the Republic of Latvia, the Grand Duchy of Luxembourg, the Republic of Hungary, Malta, the Republic of Austria, the Portuguese Republic, Romania and the Republic of Slovenia are hereby authorised to establish enhanced co-operation between themselves in the area of the law applicable to divorce and legal separation by applying the relevant provisions of the Treaties.

Article 2   This Decision shall enter into force on the day of its adoption.

B.2.   Council Regulation (EU) No 1259/2010 of 20 December 2010 implementing enhanced cooperation in the area of the law applicable to divorce and legal separation (Doc. Consilium No 17523/10 of 13 December 2010)[1]

(1)   The Union has set itself the objective of maintaining and developing an area of

---

[1]   The text has been adopted by the Council on 20 December 2010; as stated in the Council press release, 'The new rules will apply to all participating Member States as of mid-2012. Other EU Member States which are not yet ready but wish to join this pioneer group at a later stage will be able to do so' (doc. No 18149/10, presse 356). According to Doc. Consilium 17046/10 of 26 November 2010, at the adoption of the Regulation the following declarations have been made:

Declaration of the Council
The Council invites the Commission to submit at its earliest convenience to the Council and to the European Parliament a proposal for the amendment of Regulation (EC) No 2201/2003 with the aim of providing a forum in those cases where the courts that have jurisdiction are all situated in Member States whose law either does not provide for divorce or does not deem the marriage in question valid for the purposes of divorce proceedings (forum necessitatis).

Declaration of the European Commission on Article 7a
In the Commission's view, Article 7a, which permits judges of a participating Member State, whose law does not provide for divorce, not to apply the same rules as the other participating Member States, is a derogation that negates the very purpose of the enhanced cooperation authorised by Council Decision 2010/405/EU.
The European Commission stresses that the inclusion of this provision in the enacting terms of the Council Regulation implementing enhanced cooperation in the area of the law applicable to divorce and legal separation does not in any way restrict or limit the powers of the European Commission under Articles 329 and 331 of the Treaty on the Functioning of the European Union with respect to any existing or future enhanced cooperation. Furthermore, the European Commission reserves all rights under Article 263 of the Treaty on the Functioning of the European Union.
The European Commission emphasises that Article 7a is to be seen without prejudice to the obligation of a Member State whose law does not provide for divorce to assume jurisdiction and entertain a petition for divorce where it is seised in conformity with the rules of jurisdiction in Council Regulation (EC) No 2201/2003.

Declaration of Malta on the Council Regulation implementing enhanced cooperation in the area of the law applicable to divorce and legal separation
Malta welcomes the agreed text of the Council Regulation implementing enhanced cooperation in the area of the law applicable to divorce and legal separation as contained in Document 17045/10 dated 26 November 2010. In particular, Malta welcomes the text of Article 7a which makes it clear that nothing in the Regulation shall oblige the Member State whose law does not provide for divorce to pronounce a divorce by virtue of the application of the Regulation.
The area of the law applicable to divorce and legal separation is a very sensitive one and full respect should be paid to the particularities of the legal systems of all Member States. In this regard, Malta recalls that the development of the area of judicial cooperation in civil matters having cross-border implications is subject to the overarching principle enshrined in Article 67(1) of the Treaty on the Functioning of the European Union, that the Area of Freedom, Security and Justice be constituted with respect for fundamental rights and the different legal systems and traditions of the Member States. Any imposition on Malta to introduce divorce in its substantive law by virtue of a Union instrument would therefore constitute a direct breach of this Article. Without the inclu-

freedom, security and justice, in which the free movement of persons is assured. For the gradual establishment of such an area, the Union must adopt measures relating to judicial cooperation in civil matters having cross-border implications, particularly when necessary for the proper functioning of the internal market.

(2)   Pursuant to Article 81 of the Treaty on the Functioning of the European Union, those measures are to include measures aimed at ensuring the compatibility of the rules applicable in the Member States concerning conflict of laws.

(3)   On 14 March 2005 the Commission adopted a Green Paper on applicable law and jurisdiction in divorce matters. The Green Paper launched a wide-ranging public consultation on possible solutions to the problems that may arise under the current situation.

(4)   On 17 July 2006 the Commission proposed a Regulation amending Council Regulation (EC) No 2201/2003 as regards jurisdiction and introducing rules concerning applicable law in matrimonial matters.

(5)   At its meeting in Luxembourg on 5 and 6 June 2008, the Council concluded that there was a lack of unanimity on the proposal and that there were insurmountable difficulties that made unanimity impossible both then and in the near future. It established that the proposal's objectives could not be attained within a reasonable period by applying the relevant provisions of the Treaties.

(6)   Belgium, Bulgaria, Germany, Greece, Spain, France, Italy, Latvia, Luxembourg, Hungary, Malta, Austria, Portugal, Romania and Slovenia subsequently addressed a request to the Commission indicating that they intended to establish enhanced cooperation between themselves in the area of applicable law in matrimonial matters. On 3 March 2010, Greece withdrew its request.

(7)   On 12 July 2010 the Council adopted Decision 2010/405/EU authorising enhanced cooperation in the area of the law applicable to divorce and legal separation.

(8)   According to Article 328(1) of the Treaty on the Functioning of the European Union, when enhanced cooperation is being established, it is to be open to all Member

---

sion of Article 7a, the Implementing Regulation would impose on the Maltese courts the obligation to apply the institute of divorce within their jurisdiction despite the fact that this is not provided for under Maltese law. The imposition of this new obligation on Maltese courts by virtue of the Implementing Regulation would go beyond the competence of the Union in this area.

Article 20(1) of the Treaty on the European Union requires that the enhanced cooperation is open at any time to all Member States. Under Article 328(1) of the Treaty on the Functioning of the European Union, the Commission is obliged to ensure that it promotes participation by as many Member States as possible. Without the inclusion of Article 7a in the Implementing Regulation Malta would have been prevented from participating in the enhanced cooperation. In the light of these Articles Malta particularly regrets the Commission's lack of support for the inclusion of Article 7a.

Declaration of Finland on the Council Regulation implementing enhanced cooperation in the area of the law applicable to divorce and legal separation

Finland considers that enhanced cooperation is a better alternative than cooperation of unofficial groups outside the institutional system of the European Union.

However, Finland regrets that the enhanced cooperation is about to be launched for the first time in the field of family law which is closely connected with fundamental values and traditions of Member States. Finland is of the opinion that the Union should act together and seek flexible solutions which respect the judicial traditions of the different Member States. This way clear and uniform rules would be offered to the citizens living in the area of the Union.

Finland finds it unfortunate that in the negotiations on the original proposal for the Rome III Regulation not enough flexibility was found to take account in an impartial way of national differences of the Member States. In this context Finland in particular takes note of Article 7a of the now proposed draft Regulation.

States, subject to compliance with any conditions of participation laid down by the authorising decision. It is also to be open to them at any other time, subject to compliance with the acts already adopted within that framework, in addition to those conditions. The Commission and the Member States participating in enhanced cooperation shall ensure that they promote participation by as many Member States as possible. This Regulation should be binding in its entirety and directly applicable only in the participating Member States in accordance with the Treaties.

(9)   This Regulation should create a clear, comprehensive legal framework in the area of the law applicable to divorce and legal separation in the participating Member States, provide citizens with appropriate outcomes in terms of legal certainty, predictability and flexibility, and prevent a situation from arising where one of the spouses applies for divorce before the other one does in order to ensure that the proceeding is governed by a given law which he or she considers more favourable to his or her own interests.

(10)   The substantive scope and enacting terms of this Regulation should be consistent with Regulation (EC) No 2201/2003. However, it should not apply to marriage annulment. This Regulation should apply only to the dissolution or loosening of marriage ties. The law determined by the conflict-of-laws rules of this Regulation should apply to the grounds for divorce and legal separation. Preliminary questions such as legal capacity and the validity of the marriage, and matters such as the effects of divorce or legal separation on property, name, parental responsibility, maintenance obligations or any other ancillary measures should be determined by the conflict-of-laws rules applicable in the participating Member State concerned.

(11)   In order to clearly delimit the territorial scope of this Regulation, the Member States participating in the enhanced cooperation should be specified.

(12)   This Regulation should be universal, i.e. it should be possible for its uniform conflict-of-laws rules to designate the law of a participating Member State, the law of a non-participating Member State or the law of a State which is not a member of the European Union.

(13)   This Regulation should apply irrespective of the nature of the court or tribunal seized. Where applicable, a court should be deemed to be seized in accordance with Regulation (EC) No 2201/2003.

(14)   In order to allow the spouses to choose an applicable law with which they have a close connection or, in the absence of such choice, in order that that law might apply to their divorce or legal separation, the law in question should apply even if it is not that of a participating Member State. Where the law of another Member State is designated, the network created by Council Decision 2001/470/EC of 28 May 2001 establishing a European Judicial Network in civil and commercial matters, could play a part in assisting the courts with regard to the content of foreign law.

(15)   Increasing the mobility of citizens calls for more flexibility and greater legal certainty. In order to achieve that objective, this Regulation should enhance the parties' autonomy in the areas of divorce and legal separation by giving them a limited possibility to choose the law applicable to their divorce or legal separation.

(16)   Spouses should be able to choose the law of a country with which they have a special connection or the law of the *forum* as the law applicable to divorce and legal separation. The law chosen by the spouses must be consonant with the fundamental rights recognised by the Treaties and the Charter of Fundamental Rights of the European Union.

(17) Before designating the applicable law, it is important for spouses to have access to up-to-date information concerning the essential aspects of national and Union law and of the procedures governing divorce and legal separation. To guarantee such access to appropriate, good-quality information, the Commission regularly updates it in the Internet-based public information system set up by Council Decision 2001/470/EC.

(18) The informed choice of both spouses is a basic principle of this Regulation. Each spouse should know exactly what are the legal and social implications of the choice of applicable law. The possibility of choosing the applicable law by common agreement should be without prejudice to the rights of, and equal opportunities for, the two spouses. Hence judges in the participating Member States should be aware of the importance of an informed choice on the part of the two spouses concerning the legal implications of the choice-of-law agreement concluded.

(19) Rules on material and formal validity should be defined so that the informed choice of the spouses is facilitated and that their consent is respected with a view to ensuring legal certainty as well as better access to justice. As far as formal validity is concerned, certain safeguards should be introduced to ensure that spouses are aware of the implications of their choice. The agreement on the choice of applicable law should at least be expressed in writing, dated and signed by both parties. However, if the law of the participating Member State in which the two spouses have their habitual residence at the time the agreement is concluded lays down additional formal rules, those rules should be complied with. For example, such additional formal rules may exist in a participating Member State where the agreement is inserted in a marriage contract. If, at the time the agreement is concluded, the spouses are habitually resident in different participating Member States which lay down different formal rules, compliance with the formal rules of one of these States would suffice. If, at the time the agreement is concluded, only one of the spouses is habitually resident in a participating Member State which lays down additional formal rules, these rules should be complied with.

(20) An agreement designating the applicable law should be able to be concluded and modified at the latest at the time the court is seized, and even during the course of the proceeding if the law of the *forum* so provides. In that event, it should be sufficient for such designation to be recorded in court in accordance with the law of the *forum*.

(21) Where no applicable law is chosen, and with a view to guaranteeing legal certainty and predictability and preventing a situation from arising in which one of the spouses applies for divorce before the other one does in order to ensure that the proceeding is governed by a given law which he considers more favourable to his own interests, this Regulation should introduce harmonised conflict-of-laws rules on the basis of a scale of successive connecting factors based on the existence of a close connection between the spouses and the law concerned. Such connecting factors should be chosen so as to ensure that proceedings relating to divorce or legal separation are governed by a law with which the spouses have a close connection.

(22) Where this Regulation refers to nationality as a connecting factor for the application of the law of a State, the question of how to deal with cases of multiple nationality should be left to national law, in full observance of the general principles of the European Union.

(23) If the court is seized in order to convert a legal separation into divorce, and where the parties have not made any choice as to the law applicable, the law which applied to the legal separation should also apply to the divorce. Such continuity would

promote predictability for the parties and increase legal certainty. If the law applied to the legal separation does not provide for the conversion of legal separation into divorce, the divorce should be governed by the conflict-of-laws rules which apply in the absence of a choice by the parties. This should not prevent the spouses from seeking divorce on the basis of other rules in this Regulation.

(24) In certain situations, such as where the applicable law makes no provision for divorce or where it does not grant one of the spouses equal access to divorce or legal separation on grounds of their sex, the law of the court seized should nevertheless apply. This, however, should be without prejudice to the public policy clause.

(25) Considerations of public interest should allow courts in the Member States the opportunity in exceptional circumstances to disregard the application of a provision of foreign law in a given case where it would be manifestly contrary to the public policy of the *forum*. However, the courts should not be able to apply the public policy exception in order to disregard a provision of the law of another State when to do so would be contrary to the Charter of Fundamental Rights of the European Union, and in particular Article 21 thereof, which prohibits all forms of discrimination.

(26) Where this Regulation refers to the fact that the law of the participating Member State whose court is seized does not provide for divorce, this should be interpreted to mean that the law of this Member State does not have the institute of divorce. In such a case, the court should not be obliged to pronounce a divorce by virtue of this Regulation. Where this Regulation refers to the fact that the law of the participating Member State whose court is seized does not deem the marriage in question valid for the purposes of divorce proceedings, this should be interpreted to mean inter alia that such a marriage does not exist in the law of that Member State. In such a case, the court should not be obliged to pronounce a divorce or a legal separation by virtue of this Regulation.

(27) Since there are States and participating Member States in which two or more systems of law or sets of rules concerning matters governed by this Regulation coexist, there should be a provision governing the extent to which this Regulation applies in the different territorial units of those States and participating Member States or to different categories of persons of those States and participating Member States.

(28) In the absence of rules designating the applicable law, parties choosing the law of the State of the nationality of one of them should at the same time indicate which territorial unit's law they have agreed upon in case the State whose law is chosen comprises several territorial units each of which has its own system of law or a set of rules in respect of divorce.

(29) Since the objectives of this Regulation, namely the enhancement of legal certainty, predictability and flexibility in international matrimonial proceedings and hence the facilitation of the free movement of persons within the Union, cannot be sufficiently achieved by the Member States and can therefore, by reasons of the scale and effects of this Regulation be better achieved at Union level, the Union may adopt measures by means of enhanced cooperation, in accordance with the principle of subsidiarity as set out in Article 5 of the Treaty on European Union. In accordance with the principle of proportionality, as set out in that Article, this Regulation does not go beyond what is necessary in order to achieve those objectives.

(30) This Regulation respects fundamental rights and observes the principles recognized by the Charter of Fundamental Rights of the European Union, and in particular by Article 21 thereof, which states that any discrimination based on any ground

such as sex, race, colour, ethnic or social origin, genetic features, language, religion or belief, political or any other opinion, membership of a national minority, property, birth, disability, age or sexual orientation shall be prohibited. This Regulation should be applied by the courts of the participating Member States in observance of those rights and principles,

Chapter I — Scope, relation with Regulation (EC) 2201/2003, definitions and universal application

Article 1. Scope.   1.   This Regulation shall apply, in situations involving a conflict of laws, to divorce and legal separation.

  2.   This Regulation shall not apply to the following matters, even if they arise merely as a preliminary question within the context of divorce or legal separation proceedings:

  (a)   the legal capacity of natural persons;
  (b)   the existence, validity or recognition of a marriage;
  (c)   the annulment of a marriage;
  (d)   the name of the spouses;
  (e)   the property consequences of the marriage;
  (f)   parental responsibility;
  (g)   maintenance obligations;
  (h)   trusts or successions.

Article 2. Relation with Regulation (EC) No 2201/2003.   This Regulation shall not affect the application of Regulation (EC) No 2201/2003.

Article 3. Definitions.   For the purposes of this Regulation: 1.   'participating Member State' means a Member State which participates in enhanced cooperation on the law applicable to divorce and legal separation by virtue of Decision 2010/405/EU, or by virtue of a decision adopted in accordance with the second or third subparagraph of Article 331(1) of the Treaty on the Functioning of the European Union;

  2.   the term 'court' shall cover all the authorities in the participating Member States with jurisdiction in the matters falling within the scope of this Regulation.

Article 4. Universal application.   The law designated by this Regulation shall apply whether or not it is the law of a participating Member State.

Chapter II — Uniform rules on the law applicable to divorce and legal separation

Article 5. Choice of applicable law by the parties.   1.   The spouses may agree to designate the law applicable to divorce and legal separation provided that it is one of the following laws:

  (a)   the law of the State where the spouses are habitually resident at the time the agreement is concluded, or

  (b)   the law of the State where the spouses were last habitually resident, insofar as one of them still resides there at the time the agreement is concluded, or

(c) the law of the State of nationality of either spouse at the time the agreement is concluded, or

(d) the law of the *forum*.

2. Without prejudice to paragraph 3, an agreement designating the applicable law may be concluded and modified at any time, but at the latest at the time the court is seized.

3. If the law of the *forum* so provides, the spouses may also designate the law applicable before the court during the course of the proceeding. In that event, such designation shall be recorded in court in accordance with the law of the *forum*.

Article 6. Consent and material validity. 1. The existence and validity of an agreement on choice of law or of any term thereof, shall be determined by the law which would govern it under this Regulation if the agreement or term were valid.

2. Nevertheless, a spouse, in order to establish that he did not consent, may rely upon the law of the country in which he has his habitual residence at the time the court is seized if it appears from the circumstances that it would not be reasonable to determine the effect of his conduct in accordance with the law specified in paragraph 1.

Article 7. Formal validity. 1. The agreement referred to in Article 5 (1) and (2), shall be expressed in writing, dated and signed by both spouses. Any communication by electronic means which provides a durable record of the agreement shall be deemed equivalent to writing.

2. However, if the law of the participating Member State in which the two spouses have their habitual residence at the time the agreement is concluded lays down additional formal requirements for this type of agreement, those requirements shall apply.

3. If the spouses are habitually resident in different participating Member States at the time the agreement is concluded and the laws of those States provide for different formal requirements, the agreement shall be formally valid if it satisfies the requirements of either of those laws.

4. If only one of the spouses is habitually resident in a participating Member State at the time the agreement is concluded and that State lays down additional formal requirements for this type of agreement, those requirements shall apply.

Article 8. Applicable law in the absence of a choice by the parties. In the absence of a choice pursuant to Article 5, divorce and legal separation shall be subject to the law of the State:

(a) where the spouses are habitually resident at the time the court is seized; or, failing that,

(b) where the spouses were last habitually resident, provided that the period of residence did not end more than one year before the court was seized, in so far as one of the spouses still resides in that State at the time the court is seized; or, failing that,

(c) of which both spouses are nationals at the time the court is seized; or, failing that,

(d) where the court is seized.

Article 9. Conversion of legal separation into divorce. 1. Where legal separation is converted into divorce, the law applicable to divorce shall be the law applied to the legal separation, unless the parties have agreed otherwise in accordance with Article 5.

2.   However, if the law applied to the legal separation does not provide for the conversion of legal separation into divorce, Article 8 shall apply, unless the parties have agreed otherwise in accordance with Article 5.

Article 10. Application of the law of the forum.   Where the law applicable pursuant to Article 5 or Article 8 makes no provision for divorce or does not grant one of the spouses equal access to divorce or legal separation on grounds of their sex, the law of the *forum* shall apply.

Article 11. Exclusion of renvoi.   Where this Regulation provides for the application of the law of a State, it refers to the rules of law in force in that State other than its rules of private international law.

Article 12. Public policy.   Application of a provision of the law designated by virtue of this Regulation may be refused only if such application is manifestly incompatible with the public policy of the *forum*.

Article 13. Differences in national law.   Nothing in this Regulation shall oblige the courts of a participating Member State whose law does not provide for divorce or does not deem the marriage in question valid for the purposes of divorce proceedings to pronounce a divorce by virtue of the application of this Regulation.

Article 14. States with two or more legal systems — territorial conflicts of laws.   Where a State comprises several territorial units each of which has its own system of law or a set of rules concerning matters governed by this Regulation:
      (a)   any reference to the law of such State shall be construed, for the purposes of determining the law applicable under this Regulation, as referring to the law in force in the relevant territorial unit;
      (b)   any reference to habitual residence in that State shall be construed as referring to habitual residence in a territorial unit;
      (c)   any reference to nationality shall refer to the territorial unit designated by the law of that State, or, in the absence of relevant rules, to the territorial unit chosen by the parties or, in absence of choice, to the territorial unit with which the spouse or spouses has or have the closest connection.

Article 15. States with two or more legal systems — inter-personal conflicts of laws.   In relation to a State which has two or more systems of law or sets of rules applicable to different categories of persons concerning matters governed by this Regulation, any reference to the law of such a State shall be construed as referring to the legal system determined by the rules in force in that State. In the absence of such rules, the system of law or the set of rules with which the spouse or spouses has or have the closest connection applies.

Article 16. Non-application of this Regulation to internal conflicts of laws.   A participating Member State in which different systems of law or sets of rules apply to matters governed by this Regulation shall not be required to apply this Regulation to conflicts of laws arising solely between such different systems of law or sets of rules.

Chapter III — Other provisions

Article 17.   Information to be provided by participating Member States.   1.   By 21 September 2011 the participating Member States shall communicate to the Commission their national provisions, if any, concerning:

(a)   the formal requirements applicable to agreements on the choice of applicable law pursuant to Article 7 (2) to (4); and

(b)   the possibility of designating the applicable law in accordance with Article 5(3).

The participating Member States shall inform the Commission of any subsequent changes to these provisions.

2.   The Commission shall make all information communicated in accordance with paragraph 1 publicly available through appropriate means, in particular through the website of the European Judicial Network in civil and commercial matters.

Article 18. Transitional provisions.   This Regulation shall apply only to legal proceedings instituted and to agreements of the kind referred to in Article 5 concluded as from 21 June 2012.

However, effect shall also be given to an agreement on the choice of the applicable law concluded before 21 June 2012, provided that it complies with Articles 6 and 7.

2.   This Regulation shall be without prejudice to agreements on the choice of applicable law concluded in accordance with the law of a participating Member State whose court is seized before 21 June 2012.

Article 19. Relationship with existing international conventions.   1.   Without prejudice to the obligations of the participating Member States pursuant to Article 351 of the Treaty on the Functioning of the European Union, this Regulation shall not affect the application of international conventions to which one or more participating Member States are party at the time when this Regulation is adopted or when the decision pursuant to the second or third subparagraph of Article 331(1) of the Treaty on the Functioning of the European Union is adopted and which lay down conflict-of-laws rules relating to divorce or separation.

2.   However, this Regulation shall, as between participating Member States, take precedence over conventions concluded exclusively between two or more of them in so far as such conventions concern matters governed by this Regulation.

Article 20. Review clause.   1.   By 21 December 2015, and every five years thereafter, the Commission shall present to the European Parliament, the Council and the European Economic and Social Committee a report on the application of this Regulation. The report shall be accompanied, where appropriate, by proposals to adapt this Regulation.

2.   To that end, the participating Member States shall communicate to the Commission the relevant information on the application of this Regulation by their courts.

Chapter IV — Final provisions

Article 21. Entry into force and date of application.   This Regulation shall enter into force on the day following that of its publication in the Official Journal of the European Union.

It shall apply from 21 June 2012, with the exception of Article 17, which shall apply from 21 June 2011.

For those participating Member States which participate in enhanced cooperation by virtue of a decision adopted in accordance with the second or third subparagraph of Article 331(1) of the Treaty on the Functioning of the European Union, this Regulation shall apply as from the date indicated in the decision concerned.

B.3.   ECJ case-law regarding the law applicable to matrimonial matters

The ECJ has addressed incidentally the issue of Member States' competence to determine conflict of law rules on divorce while deciding, in the main proceedings, on the application of the principle of non-discrimination in respect of private international law rules adopting nationality as a connecting factor (judgment 10 June 1999, case C-430/97, *Johannes*, Reports, I-3475). The questions referred to the Court involved a divorced German couple and the compensatory adjustment of pension rights under German law. The husband, a former official of the Community, maintained that the application of German law would have been contrary to the principle of non-discrimination in respect of those officials that were citizens of other Member States in which such a rule does not exist. The Court affirmed, firstly, that the Community legislature has no competence to lay down the rights of spouses in divorce proceedings, including those resulting from any compensatory adjustment of pension rights as provided for under German law, since those rights are governed by the rules of private law and family law applying in the Member States, which fall within the competence of those Member States (paragraph 18); secondly, it stated that Community law does not regulate the financial obligations owed by an official to his former spouse under national family law, and cannot have the effect, either by virtue of the principle of the primacy of Community law or by virtue of any other principle of Community law, of rendering inapplicable a provision of the kind contained in paragraph 1587 *et seq* of the BGB (German civil code), relating to the compensatory adjustment of pension rights. Finally, while rejecting the asserted discrimination that the application of German law would have implied, the Court has so decided:

26.   It should be noted in that regard that the prohibition of all discrimination on grounds of nationality laid down by Article 12 ECT applies only within the Treaty's area of application (9 October 1997, case C-291/96, *Grado and Bashir*, Reports, I-5531, paragraph 13).

27.   Neither the national provisions of private international law determining the substantive national law applicable to the effects of a divorce nor the national provisions of civil law substantively regulating those effects fall within the scope of the Treaty.

28.   It follows that Article 12 ECT does not preclude the laws of a Member State from taking the spouses' nationality into consideration as a connecting factor for the purposes of determining the substantive national law applicable to the effects of a divorce.

29.   The answer to the second question must therefore be that Article 12 ECT does not preclude the laws of a Member State regulating the consequences of divorce between an official of the Communities and his former spouse, regard being had to the

spouses' nationality as a connecting factor, from causing the official concerned to bear a heavier burden than would be borne by an official of a different nationality in the same situation.

C.   Regulation (EC) No 864/2007 of the European Parliament and of the Council of 11 July 2007 on the law applicable to non-contractual obligations (Rome II) (OJ, L 199 of 31 July 2007): Recital 10, Article 1(2)(a) and (b)

See Chapter VII, A.1.

D.   Directive 2008/52/EC of the European Parliament and of the Council of 21 May 2008 on certain aspects of mediation in civil and commercial matters: Recitals 10, 21, Article 1(2)

See Chapter IV, General provisions, L

E.   Charter of Fundamental Rights of the European Union (OJ, C 303 of 14 December 2007): Article 24

See Chapter II, Fundamental rights, E.

F.   The Stockholm Programme — An open and secure Europe serving and protecting the citizens, adopted by the European Council on 10–11 December 2009 (doc. 17024/09): Parts 2.3.2 and 3

See Chapter I, General provisions, F.

G.   Council Regulation (EC) No 664/2009 of 7 July 2009 establishing a procedure for the negotiation and conclusion of agreements between Member States and third countries concerning jurisdiction, recognition and enforcement of judgments and decisions in matrimonial matters, matters of parental responsibility and matters relating to maintenance obligations, and the law applicable to matters relating to maintenance obligations (OJ, L 200 of 31 July 2009)

See Chapter I, The external dimension, L.

H.1.   Council Decision 2008/431/EC of 5 June 2008 authorising certain Member States to ratify, or accede to, in the interest of the European Community, the 1996 Hague Convention on Jurisdiction, Applicable Law, Recognition, Enforcement and Co-operation in Respect of Parental Responsibility and Measures for the Protection of Children and authorising certain Member States to make a declaration on the application of the relevant internal rules of Community law (OJ, L 151 of 11 June 2008)

(1)   The Community is working towards the establishment of a common judicial area based on the principle of mutual recognition of judicial decisions.

(2)   The Convention on Jurisdiction, Applicable Law, Recognition, Enforcement and Co-operation in respect of Parental Responsibility and Measures for the Protection of Children concluded on 19 October 1996 within the Hague Conference on Private International Law (hereinafter referred to as the Convention) makes a valuable contribution to the protection of children at the international level. It is therefore desirable that its provisions be applied as soon as possible.

(3)   Council Decision 2003/93/EC of 19 December 2002 authorised the Member States to sign the Convention in the interest of the Community. Those States which were Member States of the Community at that time signed the Convention on 1 April 2003, with the exception of the Netherlands which had already signed the Convention. Other Member States which were not Member States of the Community on 1 April 2003 have also signed the Convention.

(4)   Upon the adoption of Decision 2003/93/EC the Council and the Commission agreed that the Decision would be followed by a Commission proposal for a Council Decision authorising the Member States to ratify, or accede to, the Convention in the interest of the Community at the appropriate time.

(5)   Some Member States have already ratified, or acceded to, the Convention.

(6)   Certain Articles of the Convention affect secondary Community legislation on jurisdiction and recognition and enforcement of judgments, in particular Council Regulation (EC) No 2201/2003 of 27 November 2003 concerning jurisdiction and the recognition and enforcement of judgments in matrimonial matters and the matters of parental responsibility. The Member States retain their competence in the areas covered by the Convention which do not affect Community law. The Community and the Member States thus share competence to conclude the Convention.

(7)   Pursuant to the Convention, only sovereign States may be party to it. For that reason, the Community may not ratify, or accede to, the Convention.

(8)   The Council should therefore authorise the Member States, by way of exception, to ratify, or accede to, the Convention in the interest of the Community, under the conditions set out in this Decision, however not those Member States which have already ratified, or acceded to, the Convention.

(9)   In order to safeguard the application of Community rules on recognition and enforcement of judgments within the Community, Article 2 of Decision 2003/93/EC required the Member States to make a declaration when signing the Convention.

(10)   The Member States which signed the Convention on 1 April 2003 made the declaration set out in Article 2 of Decision 2003/93/EC on that occasion. Other Member

States which did not sign the Convention pursuant to Decision 2003/93/EC made the declaration after their accession to the European Union. Some Member States have, however, not made the declaration and should therefore now make the declaration set out in Article 2 of this Decision.

(11) The Member States which are authorised to ratify, or accede to, the Convention by this Decision, should do so simultaneously. Those Member States should therefore exchange information on the state of their ratification or accession procedures in order to prepare the simultaneous deposit of their instruments of ratification or accession.

(12) The United Kingdom and Ireland are taking part in the adoption and application of this Decision.

(13) In accordance with Articles 1 and 2 of the Protocol on the position of Denmark, annexed to the Treaty on European Union and to the Treaty establishing the European Community, Denmark does not take part in the adoption of this Decision and is not bound by it or subject to its application, has adopted this decision:

Article 1.   1.   The Council hereby authorises Belgium, Germany, Ireland, Greece, Spain, France, Italy, Cyprus, Luxembourg, Malta, the Netherlands, Austria, Poland, Portugal, Romania, Finland, Sweden and the United Kingdom to ratify, or accede to, the 1996 Hague Convention on Jurisdiction, Applicable Law, Recognition, Enforcement and Co-operation in respect of Parental Responsibility and Measures for the Protection of Children (hereinafter referred to as the Convention), in the interest of the Community, subject to the conditions set out in Articles 3 and 4.

2.   The text of the Convention is attached to this Decision.

Article 2.   The Council hereby authorises Bulgaria, Cyprus, Latvia, Malta, the Netherlands and Poland to make the following declaration:
'Articles 23, 26 and 52 of the Convention allow Contracting Parties a degree of flexibility in order to apply a simple and rapid regime for the recognition and enforcement of judgments. The Community rules provide for a system of recognition and enforcement which is at least as favourable as the rules laid down in the Convention. Accordingly, a judgment given in a court of a Member State of the European Union, in respect of a matter relating to the Convention, shall be recognised and enforced in ...[1] by application of the relevant internal rules of Community law[2].'
[1]   Member State making the declaration
[2]   Council Regulation (EC) No 2201/2003 plays a special role in this field since it relates to jurisdiction and recognition and enforcement of judgments in matrimonial matters and matters of parental responsibility.'

Article 3.   1.   The Member States mentioned in Article 1(1) shall take the necessary steps to deposit simultaneously their instruments of ratification or accession with the Ministry of Foreign Affairs of the Kingdom of the Netherlands, if possible before 5 June 2010.

2.   The Member States referred to in paragraph 1 shall exchange information with the Commission within the Council, before 5 December 2009, on the prospective date of completion of their parliamentary procedures required for ratification or accession. On this basis, the date and modalities of the simultaneous deposit shall be determined.

Article 4.   The Member States mentioned in Article 1(1) shall inform the Ministry of Foreign Affairs of the Kingdom of the Netherlands in writing when their parliamentary procedures required for ratification or accession have been carried out indicating that their instruments of ratification or accession will be deposited at a later stage in accordance with this Decision.

Article 5.   Decision shall apply from the day of its publication in the Official Journal of the European Union.

Article 6.   This Decision is addressed to all Member States with the exception of Denmark, the Czech Republic, Estonia, Lithuania, Hungary, Slovenia and Slovakia.

H.2.   Convention on Jurisdiction, Applicable Law, Recognition, Enforcement and Co-operation in respect of Parental Responsibility and Measures for the Protection of Children (Concluded 19 October 1996) (OJ, L 151 of 11 June 2008)[1]

The States signatory to the present Convention,

Considering the need to improve the protection of children in international situations,

Wishing to avoid conflicts between their legal systems in respect of jurisdiction, applicable law, recognition and enforcement of measures for the protection of children,

Recalling the importance of international co-operation for the protection of children,

Confirming that the best interests of the child are to be a primary consideration,

Noting that the Convention of 5 October 1961 concerning the powers of authorities and the law applicable in respect of the protection of minors is in need of revision,

Desiring to establish common provisions to this effect, taking into account the United Nations Convention on the Rights of the Child of 20 November 1989,

Have agreed on the following provisions

Chapter I — Scope of the Convention

Article 1.   (1)   The objects of the present Convention are
   a)   to determine the State whose authorities have jurisdiction to take measures directed to the protection of the person or property of the child;

---

[1]   As of 2 December 2010, the Convention is in force in the following States (the date of entry into force is within brackets): Albania (1 April 2007); Armenia (1 May 2008); Australia (1 August 2003); Bulgaria (1 February 2007); Croatia (1 January 2010); Cyprus (1 Novembre 2010); Czech Republic (1 January 2002); Dominican Republic (1 October 2010); Ecuador (1 September 2003); Estonia (1 June 2003); Hungary (1 May 2006); Latvia (1 April 2003); Lithuania (1 September 2004); Monaco (1 January 2002); Morocco (1 December 2002); Slovakia (1 January 2002); Slovenia (1 February 2005); Switzerland (1 July 2009); Ukraine (1 February 2008); Uruguay (1 March 2010). The Convention will enter into force also in the following EU Member States: Finland (1 March 2011); France (1 February 2011); Germany (1 January 2011); Ireland (1 January 2011); Romania (1 January 2011); Spain (1 January 2011). [Note of the Editor]

b)   to determine which law is to be applied by such authorities in exercising their jurisdiction;

c)   to determine the law applicable to parental responsibility;

d)   to provide for the recognition and enforcement of such measures of protection in all Contracting States;

e)   to establish such co-operation between the authorities of the Contracting States as may be necessary in order to achieve the purposes of this Convention.

(2)   For the purposes of this Convention, the term 'parental responsibility' includes parental authority, or any analogous relationship of authority determining the rights, powers and responsibilities of parents, guardians or other legal representatives in relation to the person or the property of the child.

Article 2.   The Convention applies to children from the moment of their birth until they reach the age of 18 years.

Article 3.   The measures referred to in Article 1 may deal in particular with

a)   the attribution, exercise, termination or restriction of parental responsibility, as well as its delegation;

b)   rights of custody, including rights relating to the care of the person of the child and, in particular, the right to determine the child's place of residence, as well as rights of access including the right to take a child for a limited period of time to a place other than the child's habitual residence;

c)   guardianship, curatorship and analogous institutions;

d)   the designation and functions of any person or body having charge of the child's person or property, representing or assisting the child;

e)   the placement of the child in a foster family or in institutional care, or the provision of care by *kafala* or an analogous institution;

f)   the supervision by a public authority of the care of a child by any person having charge of the child;

g)   the administration, conservation or disposal of the child's property.

Article 4.   The Convention does not apply to

a)   the establishment or contesting of a parent–child relationship;

b)   decisions on adoption, measures preparatory to adoption, or the annulment or revocation of adoption;

c)   the name and forenames of the child;

d)   emancipation;

e)   maintenance obligations;

f)   trusts or succession;

g)   social security;

h)   public measures of a general nature in matters of education or health;

i)   measures taken as a result of penal offences committed by children;

j)   decisions on the right of asylum and on immigration.

Chapter II — Jurisdiction

Article 5.   (1)   The judicial or administrative authorities of the Contracting State of the habitual residence of the child have jurisdiction to take measures directed to the protection of the child's person or property.

(2)   Subject to Article 7, in case of a change of the child's habitual residence to another Contracting State, the authorities of the State of the new habitual residence have jurisdiction.

Article 6.   (1)   For refugee children and children who, due to disturbances occurring in their country, are internationally displaced, the authorities of the Contracting State on the territory of which these children are present as a result of their displacement have the jurisdiction provided for in paragraph 1 of Article 5.

(2)   The provisions of the preceding paragraph also apply to children whose habitual residence cannot be established.

Article 7.   (1)   In case of wrongful removal or retention of the child, the authorities of the Contracting State in which the child was habitually resident immediately before the removal or retention keep their jurisdiction until the child has acquired a habitual residence in another State, and

a)   each person, institution or other body having rights of custody has acquiesced in the removal or retention; or

b)   the child has resided in that other State for a period of at least one year after the person, institution or other body having rights of custody has or should have had knowledge of the whereabouts of the child, no request for return lodged within that period is still pending, and the child is settled in his or her new environment.

(2)   The removal or the retention of a child is to be considered wrongful where

a)   it is in breach of rights of custody attributed to a person, an institution or any other body, either jointly or alone, under the law of the State in which the child was habitually resident immediately before the removal or retention; and

b)   at the time of removal or retention those rights were actually exercised, either jointly or alone, or would have been so exercised but for the removal or retention.

The rights of custody mentioned in sub-paragraph *a* above, may arise in particular by operation of law or by reason of a judicial or administrative decision, or by reason of an agreement having legal effect under the law of that State.

(3)   So long as the authorities first mentioned in paragraph 1 keep their jurisdiction, the authorities of the Contracting State to which the child has been removed or in which he or she has been retained can take only such urgent measures under Article 11 as are necessary for the protection of the person or property of the child.

Article 8.   (1)   By way of exception, the authority of a Contracting State having jurisdiction under Articles 5 or 6, if it considers that the authority of another Contracting State would be better placed in the particular case to assess the best interests of the child, may either

—   request that other authority, directly or with the assistance of the Central Authority of its State, to assume jurisdiction to take such measures of protection as it considers to be necessary, or

—   suspend consideration of the case and invite the parties to introduce such a request before the authority of that other State.

(2)   The Contracting States whose authorities may be addressed as provided in the preceding paragraph are

a)   a State of which the child is a national,

b)   a State in which property of the child is located,

c)   a State whose authorities are seised of an application for divorce or legal separation of the child's parents, or for annulment of their marriage,

d)   a State with which the child has a substantial connection.

(3)   The authorities concerned may proceed to an exchange of views.

(4)   The authority addressed as provided in paragraph 1 may assume jurisdiction, in place of the authority having jurisdiction under Article 5 or 6, if it considers that this is in the child's best interests.

Article 9.   (1)   If the authorities of a Contracting State referred to in Article 8, paragraph 2, consider that they are better placed in the particular case to assess the child's best interests, they may either

—   request the competent authority of the Contracting State of the habitual residence of the child, directly or with the assistance of the Central Authority of that State, that they be authorised to exercise jurisdiction to take the measures of protection which they consider to be necessary, or

—   invite the parties to introduce such a request before the authority of the Contracting State of the habitual residence of the child.

(2)   The authorities concerned may proceed to an exchange of views.

(3)   The authority initiating the request may exercise jurisdiction in place of the authority of the Contracting State of the habitual residence of the child only if the latter authority has accepted the request.

Article 10.   (1)   Without prejudice to Articles 5 to 9, the authorities of a Contracting State exercising jurisdiction to decide upon an application for divorce or legal separation of the parents of a child habitually resident in another Contracting State, or for annulment of their marriage, may, if the law of their State so provides, take measures directed to the protection of the person or property of such child if

a)   at the time of commencement of the proceedings, one of his or her parents habitually resides in that State and one of them has parental responsibility in relation to the child, and

b)   the jurisdiction of these authorities to take such measures has been accepted by the parents, as well as by any other person who has parental responsibility in relation to the child, and is in the best interests of the child.

(2)   The jurisdiction provided for by paragraph 1 to take measures for the protection of the child ceases as soon as the decision allowing or refusing the application for divorce, legal separation or annulment of the marriage has become final, or the proceedings have come to an end for another reason.

Article 11.   (1)   In all cases of urgency, the authorities of any Contracting State in whose territory the child or property belonging to the child is present have jurisdiction to take any necessary measures of protection.

(2) The measures taken under the preceding paragraph with regard to a child habitually resident in a Contracting State shall lapse as soon as the authorities which have jurisdiction under Articles 5 to 10 have taken the measures required by the situation.

(3) The measures taken under paragraph 1 with regard to a child who is habitually resident in a non-Contracting State shall lapse in each Contracting State as soon as measures required by the situation and taken by the authorities of another State are recognised in the Contracting State in question.

Article 12. (1) Subject to Article 7, the authorities of a Contracting State in whose territory the child or property belonging to the child is present have jurisdiction to take measures of a provisional character for the protection of the person or property of the child which have a territorial effect limited to the State in question, in so far as such measures are not incompatible with measures already taken by authorities which have jurisdiction under Articles 5 to 10.

(2) The measures taken under the preceding paragraph with regard to a child habitually resident in a Contracting State shall lapse as soon as the authorities which have jurisdiction under Articles 5 to 10 have taken a decision in respect of the measures of protection which may be required by the situation.

(3) The measures taken under paragraph 1 with regard to a child who is habitually resident in a non-Contracting State shall lapse in the Contracting State where the measures were taken as soon as measures required by the situation and taken by the authorities of another State are recognised in the Contracting State in question.

Article 13. (1) The authorities of a Contracting State which have jurisdiction under Articles 5 to 10 to take measures for the protection of the person or property of the child must abstain from exercising this jurisdiction if, at the time of the commencement of the proceedings, corresponding measures have been requested from the authorities of another Contracting State having jurisdiction under Articles 5 to 10 at the time of the request and are still under consideration.

(2) The provisions of the preceding paragraph shall not apply if the authorities before whom the request for measures was initially introduced have declined jurisdiction.

Article 14. The measures taken in application of Articles 5 to 10 remain in force according to their terms, even if a change of circumstances has eliminated the basis upon which jurisdiction was founded, so long as the authorities which have jurisdiction under the Convention have not modified, replaced or terminated such measures.

Chapter III — Applicable law

Article 15. (1) In exercising their jurisdiction under the provisions of Chapter II, the authorities of the Contracting States shall apply their own law.

(2) However, in so far as the protection of the person or the property of the child requires, they may exceptionally apply or take into consideration the law of another State with which the situation has a substantial connection.

(3)   If the child's habitual residence changes to another Contracting State, the law of that other State governs, from the time of the change, the conditions of application of the measures taken in the State of the former habitual residence.

Article 16.   (1)   The attribution or extinction of parental responsibility by operation of law, without the intervention of a judicial or administrative authority, is governed by the law of the State of the habitual residence of the child.

(2)   The attribution or extinction of parental responsibility by an agreement or a unilateral act, without intervention of a judicial or administrative authority, is governed by the law of the State of the child's habitual residence at the time when the agreement or unilateral act takes effect.

(3)   Parental responsibility which exists under the law of the State of the child's habitual residence subsists after a change of that habitual residence to another State.

(4)   If the child's habitual residence changes, the attribution of parental responsibility by operation of law to a person who does not already have such responsibility is governed by the law of the State of the new habitual residence.

Article 17.   The exercise of parental responsibility is governed by the law of the State of the child's habitual residence. If the child's habitual residence changes, it is governed by the law of the State of the new habitual residence.

Article 18.   The parental responsibility referred to in Article 16 may be terminated, or the conditions of its exercise modified, by measures taken under this Convention.

Article 19.   (1)   The validity of a transaction entered into between a third party and another person who would be entitled to act as the child's legal representative under the law of the State where the transaction was concluded cannot be contested, and the third party cannot be held liable, on the sole ground that the other person was not entitled to act as the child's legal representative under the law designated by the provisions of this Chapter, unless the third party knew or should have known that the parental responsibility was governed by the latter law.

(2)   The preceding paragraph applies only if the transaction was entered into between persons present on the territory of the same State.

Article 20.   The provisions of this Chapter apply even if the law designated by them is the law of a non-Contracting State.

Article 21.   (1)   In this Chapter the term 'law' means the law in force in a State other than its choice of law rules.

(2)   However, if the law applicable according to Article 16 is that of a non-Contracting State and if the choice of law rules of that State designate the law of another non-Contracting State which would apply its own law, the law of the latter State applies. If that other non-Contracting State would not apply its own law, the applicable law is that designated by Article 16.

Article 22.   The application of the law designated by the provisions of this Chapter can be refused only if this application would be manifestly contrary to public policy, taking into account the best interests of the child.

Chapter IV — Recognition and enforcement

Article 23.   (1)   The measures taken by the authorities of a Contracting State shall be recognised by operation of law in all other Contracting States.

(2)   Recognition may however be refused

a)   if the measure was taken by an authority whose jurisdiction was not based on one of the grounds provided for in Chapter II;

b)   if the measure was taken, except in a case of urgency, in the context of a judicial or administrative proceeding, without the child having been provided the opportunity to be heard, in violation of fundamental principles of procedure of the requested State;

c)   on the request of any person claiming that the measure infringes his or her parental responsibility, if such measure was taken, except in a case of urgency, without such person having been given an opportunity to be heard;

d)   if such recognition is manifestly contrary to public policy of the requested State, taking into account the best interests of the child;

e)   if the measure is incompatible with a later measure taken in the non-Contracting State of the habitual residence of the child, where this later measure fulfils the requirements for recognition in the requested State;

f)   if the procedure provided in Article 33 has not been complied with.

Article 24.   Without prejudice to Article 23, paragraph 1, any interested person may request from the competent authorities of a Contracting State that they decide on the recognition or non-recognition of a measure taken in another Contracting State. The procedure is governed by the law of the requested State.

Article 25.   The authority of the requested State is bound by the findings of fact on which the authority of the State where the measure was taken based its jurisdiction.

Article 26.   (1)   If measures taken in one Contracting State and enforceable there require enforcement in another Contracting State, they shall, upon request by an interested party, be declared enforceable or registered for the purpose of enforcement in that other State according to the procedure provided in the law of the latter State.

(2)   Each Contracting State shall apply to the declaration of enforceability or registration a simple and rapid procedure.

(3)   The declaration of enforceability or registration may be refused only for one of the reasons set out in Article 23, paragraph 2.

Article 27.   Without prejudice to such review as is necessary in the application of the preceding Articles, there shall be no review of the merits of the measure taken.

Article 28.   Measures taken in one Contracting State and declared enforceable, or registered for the purpose of enforcement, in another Contracting State shall be enforced in the latter State as if they had been taken by the authorities of that State. Enforcement takes place in accordance with the law of the requested State to the extent provided by such law, taking into consideration the best interests of the child.

Chapter V — Co-operation

Article 29.   (1)   A Contracting State shall designate a Central Authority to discharge the duties which are imposed by the Convention on such authorities.

(2)   Federal States, States with more than one system of law or States having autonomous territorial units shall be free to appoint more than one Central Authority and to specify the territorial or personal extent of their functions. Where a State has appointed more than one Central Authority, it shall designate the Central Authority to which any communication may be addressed for transmission to the appropriate Central Authority within that State.

Article 30.   (1)   Central Authorities shall co-operate with each other and promote co-operation amongst the competent authorities in their States to achieve the purposes of the Convention.

(2)   They shall, in connection with the application of the Convention, take appropriate steps to provide information as to the laws of, and services available in, their States relating to the protection of children.

Article 31.   The Central Authority of a Contracting State, either directly or through public authorities or other bodies, shall take all appropriate steps to

a)   facilitate the communications and offer the assistance provided for in Articles 8 and 9 and in this Chapter;

b)   facilitate, by mediation, conciliation or similar means, agreed solutions for the protection of the person or property of the child in situations to which the Convention applies;

c)   provide, on the request of a competent authority of another Contracting State, assistance in discovering the whereabouts of a child where it appears that the child may be present and in need of protection within the territory of the requested State.

Article 32.   On a request made with supporting reasons by the Central Authority or other competent authority of any Contracting State with which the child has a substantial connection, the Central Authority of the Contracting State in which the child is habitually resident and present may, directly or through public authorities or other bodies,

a)   provide a report on the situation of the child;

b)   request the competent authority of its State to consider the need to take measures for the protection of the person or property of the child.

Article 33.   (1)   If an authority having jurisdiction under Articles 5 to 10 contemplates the placement of the child in a foster family or institutional care, or the provision of care by *kafala* or an analogous institution, and if such placement or such provision of care is to take place in another Contracting State, it shall first consult with the Central Authority or other competent authority of the latter State. To that effect it shall transmit a report on the child together with the reasons for the proposed placement or provision of care.

(2)   The decision on the placement or provision of care may be made in the requesting State only if the Central Authority or other competent authority of the requested State has consented to the placement or provision of care, taking into account the child's best interests.

Article 34.   (1)   Where a measure of protection is contemplated, the competent authorities under the Convention, if the situation of the child so requires, may request any authority of another Contracting State which has information relevant to the protection of the child to communicate such information.

(2)   A Contracting State may declare that requests under paragraph 1 shall be communicated to its authorities only through its Central Authority.

Article 35.   (1)   The competent authorities of a Contracting State may request the authorities of another Contracting State to assist in the implementation of measures of protection taken under this Convention, especially in securing the effective exercise of rights of access as well as of the right to maintain direct contacts on a regular basis.

(2)   The authorities of a Contracting State in which the child does not habitually reside may, on the request of a parent residing in that State who is seeking to obtain or to maintain access to the child, gather information or evidence and may make a finding on the suitability of that parent to exercise access and on the conditions under which access is to be exercised. An authority exercising jurisdiction under Articles 5 to 10 to determine an application concerning access to the child, shall admit and consider such information, evidence and finding before reaching its decision.

(3)   An authority having jurisdiction under Articles 5 to 10 to decide on access may adjourn a proceeding pending the outcome of a request made under paragraph 2, in particular, when it is considering an application to restrict or terminate access rights granted in the State of the child's former habitual residence.

(4)   Nothing in this Article shall prevent an authority having jurisdiction under Articles 5 to 10 from taking provisional measures pending the outcome of the request made under paragraph 2.

Article 36.   In any case where the child is exposed to a serious danger, the competent authorities of the Contracting State where measures for the protection of the child have been taken or are under consideration, if they are informed that the child's residence has changed to, or that the child is present in another State, shall inform the authorities of that other State about the danger involved and the measures taken or under consideration.

Article 37.   An authority shall not request or transmit any information under this Chapter if to do so would, in its opinion, be likely to place the child's person or property in danger, or constitute a serious threat to the liberty or life of a member of the child's family.

Article 38.   (1)   Without prejudice to the possibility of imposing reasonable charges for the provision of services, Central Authorities and other public authorities of Contracting States shall bear their own costs in applying the provisions of this Chapter.

(2)   Any Contracting State may enter into agreements with one or more other Contracting States concerning the allocation of charges.

Article 39.   Any Contracting State may enter into agreements with one or more other Contracting States with a view to improving the application of this Chapter in their mutual relations. The States which have concluded such an agreement shall transmit a copy to the depositary of the Convention.

Chapter VI — General provisions

Article 40.   (1)   The authorities of the Contracting State of the child's habitual residence, or of the Contracting State where a measure of protection has been taken, may deliver to the person having parental responsibility or to the person entrusted with protection of the child's person or property, at his or her request, a certificate indicating the capacity in which that person is entitled to act and the powers conferred upon him or her.

(2)   The capacity and powers indicated in the certificate are presumed to be vested in that person, in the absence of proof to the contrary.

(3)   Each Contracting State shall designate the authorities competent to draw up the certificate.

Article 41.   Personal data gathered or transmitted under the Convention shall be used only for the purposes for which they were gathered or transmitted.

Article 42.   The authorities to whom information is transmitted shall ensure its confidentiality, in accordance with the law of their State.

Article 43.   All documents forwarded or delivered under this Convention shall be exempt from legalisation or any analogous formality.

Article 44.   Each Contracting State may designate the authorities to which requests under Articles 8, 9 and 33 are to be addressed.

Article 45.   (1)   The designations referred to in Articles 29 and 44 shall be communicated to the Permanent Bureau of the Hague Conference on Private International Law.

(2)   The declaration referred to in Article 34, paragraph 2, shall be made to the depositary of the Convention.

Article 46.   A Contracting State in which different systems of law or sets of rules of law apply to the protection of the child and his or her property shall not be bound to apply the rules of the Convention to conflicts solely between such different systems or sets of rules of law.

Article 47.   In relation to a State in which two or more systems of law or sets of rules of law with regard to any matter dealt with in this Convention apply in different territorial units

(1)   any reference to habitual residence in that State shall be construed as referring to habitual residence in a territorial unit;

(2)   any reference to the presence of the child in that State shall be construed as referring to presence in a territorial unit;

(3) any reference to the location of property of the child in that State shall be construed as referring to location of property of the child in a territorial unit;

(4) any reference to the State of which the child is a national shall be construed as referring to the territorial unit designated by the law of that State or, in the absence of relevant rules, to the territorial unit with which the child has the closest connection;

(5) any reference to the State whose authorities are seised of an application for divorce or legal separation of the child's parents, or for annulment of their marriage, shall be construed as referring to the territorial unit whose authorities are seised of such application;

(6) any reference to the State with which the child has a substantial connection shall be construed as referring to the territorial unit with which the child has such connection;

(7) any reference to the State to which the child has been removed or in which he or she has been retained shall be construed as referring to the relevant territorial unit to which the child has been removed or in which he or she has been retained;

(8) any reference to bodies or authorities of that State, other than Central Authorities, shall be construed as referring to those authorised to act in the relevant territorial unit;

(9) any reference to the law or procedure or authority of the State in which a measure has been taken shall be construed as referring to the law or procedure or authority of the territorial unit in which such measure was taken;

(10) any reference to the law or procedure or authority of the requested State shall be construed as referring to the law or procedure or authority of the territorial unit in which recognition or enforcement is sought.

Article 48. For the purpose of identifying the applicable law under Chapter III, in relation to a State which comprises two or more territorial units each of which has its own system of law or set of rules of law in respect of matters covered by this Convention, the following rules apply

a) if there are rules in force in such a State identifying which territorial unit's law is applicable, the law of that unit applies;

b) in the absence of such rules, the law of the relevant territorial unit as defined in Article 47 applies.

Article 49. For the purpose of identifying the applicable law under Chapter III, in relation to a State which has two or more systems of law or sets of rules of law applicable to different categories of persons in respect of matters covered by this Convention, the following rules apply

a) if there are rules in force in such a State identifying which among such laws applies, that law applies;

b) in the absence of such rules, the law of the system or the set of rules of law with which the child has the closest connection applies.

Article 50. This Convention shall not affect the application of the Convention of 25 October 1980 on the Civil Aspects of International Child Abduction, as between Parties to both Conventions. Nothing, however, precludes provisions of this Convention from being invoked for the purposes of obtaining the return of a child who has been wrongfully removed or retained or of organising access rights.

Article 51.   In relations between the Contracting States this Convention replaces the Convention of 5 October 1961 concerning the powers of authorities and the law applicable in respect of the protection of minors, and the Convention governing the guardianship of minors, signed at The Hague 12 June 1902, without prejudice to the recognition of measures taken under the Convention of 5 October 1961 mentioned above.

Article 52.   (1)   This Convention does not affect any international instrument to which Contracting States are Parties and which contains provisions on matters governed by the Convention, unless a contrary declaration is made by the States Parties to such instrument.

   (2)   This Convention does not affect the possibility for one or more Contracting States to conclude agreements which contain, in respect of children habitually resident in any of the States Parties to such agreements, provisions on matters governed by this Convention.

   (3)   Agreements to be concluded by one or more Contracting States on matters within the scope of this Convention do not affect, in the relationship of such States with other Contracting States, the application of the provisions of this Convention.

   (4)   The preceding paragraphs also apply to uniform laws based on special ties of a regional or other nature between the States concerned.

Article 53.   (1)   The Convention shall apply to measures only if they are taken in a State after the Convention has entered into force for that State.

   (2)   The Convention shall apply to the recognition and enforcement of measures taken after its entry into force as between the State where the measures have been taken and the requested State.

Article 54.   (1)   Any communication sent to the Central Authority or to another authority of a Contracting State shall be in the original language, and shall be accompanied by a translation into the official language or one of the official languages of the other State or, where that is not feasible, a translation into French or English.

   (2)   However, a Contracting State may, by making a reservation in accordance with Article 60, object to the use of either French or English, but not both.

Article 55.   (1)   A Contracting State may, in accordance with Article 60,

   a)   reserve the jurisdiction of its authorities to take measures directed to the protection of property of a child situated on its territory;

   b)   reserve the right not to recognise any parental responsibility or measure in so far as it is incompatible with any measure taken by its authorities in relation to that property.

   (2)   The reservation may be restricted to certain categories of property.

Article 56.   The Secretary General of the Hague Conference on Private International Law shall at regular intervals convoke a Special Commission in order to review the practical operation of the Convention.

Chapter VII — Final clauses

Article 57. (1) The Convention shall be open for signature by the States which were Members of the Hague Conference on Private International Law at the time of its Eighteenth Session.

(2) It shall be ratified, accepted or approved and the instruments of ratification, acceptance or approval shall be deposited with the Ministry of Foreign Affairs of the Kingdom of the Netherlands, depositary of the Convention.

Article 58. (1) Any other State may accede to the Convention after it has entered into force in accordance with Article 61, paragraph 1.

(2) The instrument of accession shall be deposited with the depositary.

(3) Such accession shall have effect only as regards the relations between the acceding State and those Contracting States which have not raised an objection to its accession in the six months after the receipt of the notification referred to in sub-paragraph b of Article 63. Such an objection may also be raised by States at the time when they ratify, accept or approve the Convention after an accession. Any such objection shall be notified to the depositary.

Article 59. (1) If a State has two or more territorial units in which different systems of law are applicable in relation to matters dealt with in this Convention, it may at the time of signature, ratification, acceptance, approval or accession declare that the Convention shall extend to all its territorial units or only to one or more of them and may modify this declaration by submitting another declaration at any time.

(2) Any such declaration shall be notified to the depositary and shall state expressly the territorial units to which the Convention applies.

(3) If a State makes no declaration under this Article, the Convention is to extend to all territorial units of that State.

Article 60. (1) Any State may, not later than the time of ratification, acceptance, approval or accession, or at the time of making a declaration in terms of Article 59, make one or both of the reservations provided for in Article 54, paragraphs 2, and 55. No other reservation shall be permitted.

(2) Any State may at any time withdraw a reservation it has made. The withdrawal shall be notified to the depositary.

(3) The reservation shall cease to have effect on the first day of the third calendar month after the notification referred to in the preceding paragraph.

Article 61. (1) The Convention shall enter into force on the first day of the month following the expiration of three months after the deposit of the third instrument of ratification, acceptance or approval referred to in Article 57.

(2) Thereafter the Convention shall enter into force

a) for each State ratifying, accepting or approving it subsequently, on the first day of the month following the expiration of three months after the deposit of its instrument of ratification, acceptance, approval or accession;

b) for each State acceding, on the first day of the month following the expiration of three months after the expiration of the period of six months provided in Article 58, paragraph 3;

c)   for a territorial unit to which the Convention has been extended in conformity with Article 59, on the first day of the month following the expiration of three months after the notification referred to in that Article.

Article 62.   (1)   A State Party to the Convention may denounce it by a notification in writing addressed to the depositary. The denunciation may be limited to certain territorial units to which the Convention applies.

(2)   The denunciation takes effect on the first day of the month following the expiration of Twelve months after the notification is received by the depositary. Where a longer period for the denunciation to take effect is specified in the notification, the denunciation takes effect upon the expiration of such longer period.

Article 63.   The depositary shall notify the States Members of the Hague Conference on Private International Law and the States which have acceded in accordance with Article 58 of the following

a)   the signatures, ratifications, acceptances and approvals referred to in Article 57;

b)   the accessions and objections raised to accessions referred to in Article 58;

c)   the date on which the Convention enters into force in accordance with Article 61;

d)   the declarations referred to in Articles 34, paragraph 2, and 59;

e)   the agreements referred to in Article 39;

f)   the reservations referred to in Articles 54, paragraph 2, and 55 and the withdrawals referred to in Article 60, paragraph 2;

g)   the denunciations referred to in Article 62.

H.3.   Commission Working Document — Mutual recognition of decisions on parental responsibility (COM(2001)166 fin. of 27 March 2001)

3.   The international framework for measures on parental responsibility

3.1.   International conventions on parental responsibility. The 1996 Hague Convention on parental responsibility

A new convention that has not entered into force to date, the 1996 Hague Convention on parental responsibility (Annex 2),[10] is intended to replace, in relations between the Contracting States, the 1961 Hague Convention on the protection of minors.[11] The 1996

---

[10] [The footnotes are published in the original numerical order as in the OJ] XXXIV. Convention on jurisdiction, applicable law, recognition, enforcement and co-operation in respect of parental responsibility and measures for the protection of children (concluded 19 October 1996) ('the 1996 Convention'). To date the Netherlands are the only Member State to have signed (but not ratified) the Convention.

[11] X Convention concerning the powers of authorities and the law applicable in respect of the protection of minors (concluded October 5, 1961) ('the 1961 Convention'). In force in Austria, France, Germany, Italy, Luxembourg, the Netherlands, Portugal and Spain, as well as Poland, Switzerland and Turkey. The 1961 Convention has been the subject of criticisms concerning the existence of competing bases of jurisdiction (nationality and habitual residence), the inadequacy of co-operation between authorities and the absence of provisions on enforcement.

Convention lays down rules on jurisdiction, applicable law, recognition and enforcement of judgments on parental responsibility, including rights of access. Whereas the 1961 Convention gives priority to nationality, the 1996 Convention is based on the jurisdiction of the Contracting State of the habitual residence of the child. The competent authority will in principle apply its internal law, and may transfer the case to a court better placed to hear it. Judgments benefit from automatic recognition, and Contracting States must provide a simple and rapid exequatur procedure. A mechanism is set out for co-operation between designated authorities.

The fact that jurisdiction follows a change in the child's habitual residence poses the risk of the use of force to establish artificial jurisdictional links with a view to obtaining custody of a child. To dissuade such tactics, both the Brussels II Regulation[12] and the 1996 Convention give precedence to the most successful 1980 Hague Convention on international child abduction, which is in force in 36 States including all 15 Member States (see Annex 2).[13] The objective of the 1980 Convention is the restoration of the status quo by means of the prompt return of children wrongfully removed.[14] To this end, the Convention establishes a system of co-operation among authorities for the return of a child wrongfully removed as well as for the effective exercise of custody and access rights.

However, the 1980 Convention also recognises the need for certain exceptions to the obligation to return the child, which must be narrowly construed. Thus, Article 13(b) provides an exception where there is a grave risk that return would expose the child to physical or psychological harm or otherwise place him or her in an intolerable situation. The French initiative on rights of access was in part a response to the problems encountered in practice with Article 13(b), whose application is allegedly prone to abuse.

Other related international instruments

The European Convention on custody of children also addresses the problem of improper removal through rules on recognition and enforcement of custody decisions.[15] A three-tier system allows a progressively greater number of grounds of refusal to return the child. The Convention has been ratified by all Member States, albeit with reservations, which effectively result in the maximum number of grounds of refusal being applicable in all cases.

The European Convention on the legal status of children born out of wedlock aims at progressively bringing the legal status of children born out of wedlock into line with that of children born in wedlock.[16]

---

[12] Article 4 of the Brussels II Regulation requires courts to exercise their jurisdiction in accordance with the 1980 Convention, in particular Articles 3 and 16 thereof. This means that, following a child abduction, it is the court of the child's lawful habitual residence that continues to be entitled to exercise jurisdiction rather than the court of the child's new 'de facto' residence.

[13] XXVIII. Convention on the civil aspects of international child abduction (concluded October 25, 1980). A proposal has been tabled to commence work on a protocol related to the exercise of access rights.

[14] The removal or retention of a child is deemed wrongful where in breach of custody rights under the law of the State in which the child was habitually resident immediately before the removal or retention. Most importantly, these custody rights may arise, inter alia, by operation of law, that is do not require a judicial decision.

[15] European Convention on recognition and enforcement of decisions concerning custody of children and on restoration of custody of children (Luxembourg, 20/5/80).

[16] European Convention on the legal status of children born out of wedlock (Strasbourg, 15/10/75). In force in eight Member States.

Towards a body of substantive and procedural rights for children

In addition to the above-mentioned instruments aimed at facilitating recognition and enforcement, there is a growing trend towards recognition of children as bearers of a body of both substantive and procedural rights, as exemplified by the 1989 UN Convention on the rights of the child.[17] As already indicated, an article on the rights of the child has been incorporated in the EU Charter.

One should also mention the on-going work in the Council of Europe on a draft Convention on contact concerning children.[18] This draft Convention lays down a number of general principles, such as a child's right to maintain contact with both parents, and provides for appropriate safeguards and guarantees, which may include a mechanism for recognition/enforceability in advance of contact, as well as financial guarantees or undertakings. A system of co-operation between authorities is envisaged, where authorities would be empowered not only to ensure the return of the child, but also to fix or modify the conditions for the exercise of rights of access.

The basic premise behind these substantive rights is that the 'best interests of the child' should be a primary consideration in all decisions affecting him or her.[19] Moreover, a child has the right to maintain regular contact with both parents, unless that is contrary to the child's best interests.[20] As regards the procedure, children have the right to be heard in all proceedings affecting them in accordance with their age and maturity.[21] The European Convention on the exercise of children's rights (Annex 3) further provides for the right of the child to apply for the appointment of a special representative, where the holders of parental responsibility are precluded from representing him or her.[22]

3.2.   Implications of a possible Community accession to the 1996 Convention

In accordance with the AETR case law of the Court of Justice on external competence,[23] Member States are no longer free to accede on their own to the 1996 Convention to the extent that its provisions on jurisdiction and enforcement affect Community rules (that is, the Brussels II Regulation).[24] As a result, the Convention is a mixed agreement to which the Member States and the Community can only both accede.

---

[17]   United Nations Convention on the rights of the child, November 20, 1989 ("the UN Convention").

[18]   To the extent that this draft Convention affects the Brussels II Regulation, the possibility of Community accession must be envisaged.

[19]   Article 3 of the UN Convention and Article 24(2) of the EU Charter.

[20]   Article 9 of the UN Convention and Article 24(3) of the EU Charter.

[21]   Article 12 of the UN Convention and Article 24(1) of the EU Charter.

[22]   European Convention on the exercise of children's rights (Strasbourg, 25/1/96), Article 4.

[23]   Case, 22/70, *Commission v Council*, Reports, 263. In a series of cases beginning with the AETR case, the Court of Justice developed the theory of implied external competence, namely that when the Community has acted to implement a common policy, the Member States no longer have the right to take external action in an area which would affect that common policy. Where competence is shared between the Community and the Member States, the international agreement is a 'mixed agreement', which will apply in its entirety only if both become parties.

[24]   The Brussels II Regulation mandates the recognition of all judgments, including those based on residual jurisdiction under Article 8, but also takes into account any international commitments of the Member State of recognition: Article 15(f) provides that a later judgment in the non-Member State of the habitual residence of the child constitutes a ground of non-recognition if it fulfils the conditions for recognition in the Member State of recognition. In addition, Article 16 provides that, on the basis of an international agreement, a Member State may not recognise a judgment founded on residual jurisdiction.

Consultations took place during their negotiation aimed at ensuring the harmonious interplay between the 1996 Convention and the future Brussels II Convention concluded in 1998 after which the Brussels II Regulation was subsequently tailored. First, in addition to the habitual residence of the child, a concurrent basis of jurisdiction of the divorce court was introduced in Article 10 of the 1996 Convention, which essentially corresponds to Article 3(2) of the Brussels II Regulation.[25] Second, Article 52 of the 1996 Convention, the so-called disconnection clause, authorises Contracting States to conclude agreements in respect of children habitually resident in any of the States parties to such agreements.[26]

As regards a possible Community accession to the 1996 Convention, the following options may be envisaged:

(a) accession to the 1996 Convention

This option recognises the effort already put in the negotiations and the value of a coherent international framework to address problems of parental responsibility that often transcend the boundaries of the EC.[27] However, the Community as such was not involved in these negotiations, whose aim was to reconcile two international conventions (Brussels II was at the time a third pillar instrument). Although care was admittedly exercised to take into account the then existing state of development of EU law, the 1996 Convention effectively limits the scope of future Community action with respect to children non-resident in the EC. And should the Community, after accession, wish to cover non-resident children as it further develops its policy in the area (Section 4.3 on this issue), it may be placed in the delicate position of having to denounce the Convention, if its provisions can no longer be reconciled with future Community policy.

Given that the Community is not a member of the Hague Conference at present, this option also assumes that the technical difficulties associated with accession can be overcome, for instance by means of a protocol to the Convention.

(b) re-negotiation of the 1996 Convention

The Community may request a reexamination of the provisions of the Convention before it commits itself. Two options are possible: (1) Such re-negotiation may be limited to Article 52, so as to allow for immediate commitment of the Community internationally on the basis of the agreed text, while leaving policy development at Community level unhindered. Alternatively, (2) the Community may seek to renegotiate the substantive provisions of the Convention to the extent that these rules do not adequately address the Community concerns.

A reexamination of the substantive provisions of the 1996 Convention would entail an assessment of whether the simplicity of a rule based solely on the habitual residence of the child may in certain cases produce results considered unsatisfactory. For example,

---

[25] Note that Article 10 of the 1996 Convention introduces two additional requirements: the consent of a third person having parental responsibility, and one parent being habitually resident in the divorce State at the commencement of proceedings.

[26] To such agreements are assimilated uniform laws based on special ties of a regional or other nature.

[27] The need to reinforce judicial co-operation in matters of parental responsibility also arises in the context of relations with countries which do not participate in the Hague framework, and may be addressed in the relevant regional fora, for instance in the Barcelona process for the Mediterranean countries.

consider the case where a child who has been raised by his parents in a Member State (which is also the Member State of their nationality) has recently moved with his or her grandparents retired in a third country, and as a result the Member State concerned is deprived from assuming jurisdiction even for measures of parental responsibility which will be exercised in its territory.

To the extent that a reexamination of either Article 52 or the substantive provisions of the Convention is no longer possible or does not produce a successful outcome, this option would preclude accession to the 1996 Convention. This would also raise the issue of the continued application of the 1961 Convention in half of the Member States.[28]

A final *caveat*: Irrespective of the position to be taken on accession by the Community to the 1996 Convention, one should bear in mind that such accession cannot suffice in itself neither for guaranteeing equality of treatment for all children as mandated by the Council nor for attaining the requisite degree of simplification of recognition and enforcement in a common judicial area. The 1996 Convention may nonetheless serve as an inspiration for Community rules on jurisdiction (see Section 4.3).

(1)   The Community has exclusive competence for those matters in the 1996 Convention which are covered by the Brussels II Regulation. As a result, the 1996 Convention can only be a mixed agreement.

(2)   Given the limits it would place on future Community action, the implications of a possible Community accession to the 1996 Convention must be carefully considered.

(3)   In principle, it should be both feasible and desirable for an international instrument to co-exist with a more ambitious Community instrument.

(4)   In any case, Community accession to the 1996 Convention should not prejudice a more ambitious Community instrument in the area.

I.1.   Proposal for a Council Decision on the signing by the European Community of the Council of Europe Convention on contact concerning children (COM(2002)520 fin. of 2 October 2002, OJ, C 20 E of 28 January 2003)

(1)   The Convention on contact concerning children, adopted on 3 May 2002 by the Committee of Ministers of the Council of Europe, makes a valuable contribution to reinforcing the fundamental right of children and their parents and other persons having family ties with the child to maintain contact on a regular basis. It is therefore desirable that its provisions be applied as soon as possible.

(2)   The Convention will be open for signature in Strasbourg, France, on 14 October 2002.

(3)   Article 22.1 of the Convention allows signature by the European Community.

---

[28] If the Community does not accede to the 1996 Convention, the 1961 Convention will remain in force for those Member States that have ratified it. To the extent, however, that the application of the Convention is not limited to children who are habitually resident in a Contracting State, the priority to the Member State of a child's nationality may not be consistent in certain cases with the Brussels II Regulation.

(4)   The Convention will contribute to the realisation of the aims underlying existing and future Community rules in the field of recognition and enforcement of judgments in the area of parental responsibility and covers matters of Community competence.

SOLE ARTICLE

Subject to a possible conclusion at a later date, the President of the Council is hereby authorised to designate the person empowered to sign, on behalf of the European Community, the Council of Europe Convention on contact concerning children adopted on 3 May 2002.

I.2.   Convention on contact concerning children (Strasbourg, 15 May 2003)[1]

Preamble

The member States of the Council of Europe and the other Signatories hereto…

Recognising that, as provided in the different international legal instruments of the Council of Europe as well as in Article 3 of the United Nations Convention on the Rights of the Child of 20 November 1989, the best interests of the child shall be a primary consideration;

Aware of the need for further provisions to safeguard contact between children and their parents and other persons having family ties with children, as protected by Article 8 of the Convention for the Protection of Human Rights and Fundamental Freedoms of 4 November 1950 (E.T.S. No 5);

Taking into account Article 9 of the United Nations Convention on the Rights of the Child which provides for the right of a child, who is separated from one or both parents, to maintain personal relations and direct contact with both parents on a regular basis, except when this is contrary to the child's best interests;

Taking into account paragraph 2 of Article 10 of the United Nations Convention on the Rights of the Child, which provides for the right of the child whose parents reside in different States to maintain on a regular basis, save in exceptional circumstances, personal relations and direct contacts with both parents;

Aware of the desirability of recognising not only parents but also children as holders of rights;

Agreeing consequently to replace the notion of 'access to children' with the notion of 'contact concerning children';

---

[1]   As of 20 December 2010, the Convention is in force in the following States (the date of entry into force is within brackets): Albania (1 September 2005); Croatia (1 June 2009); Czech Republic (1 September 2005); Romania (1 November 2007); San Marino (1 September 2005); Ukraine (1 April 2007). [Note of the Editor]

Taking into account the European Convention on the Exercise of Children's Rights (E.T.S. No 160) and the desirability of promoting measures to assist children in matters concerning contact with parents and other persons having family ties with children;

Agreeing on the need for children to have contact not only with both parents but also with certain other persons having family ties with children and the importance for parents and those other persons to remain in contact with children, subject to the best interests of the child;

Noting the need to promote the adoption by States of common principles with respect to contact concerning children, in particular in order to facilitate the application of international instruments in this field;

Realising that machinery set up to give effect to foreign orders relating to contact concerning children is more likely to provide satisfactory results where the principles on which these foreign orders are based are similar to the principles in the State giving effect to such foreign orders;

Recognising the need, when children and parents and other persons having family ties with children live in different States, to encourage judicial authorities to make more frequent use of transfrontier contact and to increase the confidence of all persons concerned that the children will be returned at the end of such contact;

Noting that the provision of efficient safeguards and additional guarantees is likely to ensure the return of children, in particular, at the end of transfrontier contact;

Noting that an additional international instrument is necessary to provide solutions relating in particular to transfrontier contact concerning children;

Desiring to establish co-operation between all central authorities and other bodies in order to promote and improve contact between children and their parents, and other persons having family ties with such children, and in particular to promote judicial co-operation in cases concerning transfrontier contact;

Chapter I — Objects of the convention and definitions

Article 1. Objects of the Convention.   The objects of this Convention are:
   a)   to determine general principles to be applied to contact orders;
   b)   to fix appropriate safeguards and guarantees to ensure the proper exercise of contact and the immediate return of children at the end of the period of contact;
   c)   to establish co-operation between central authorities, judicial authorities and other bodies in order to promote and improve contact between children and their parents, and other persons having family ties with children.

Article 2. Definitions.   For the purposes of this Convention:
   a)   'contact' means:
   i.   the child staying for a limited period of time with or meeting a person mentioned in Articles 4 or 5 with whom he or she is not usually living;
   ii.   any form of communication between the child and such person;

iii.   the provision of information to such a person about the child or to the child about such a person.

b)   'contact order' means a decision of a judicial authority concerning contact, including an agreement concerning contact which has been confirmed by a competent judicial authority or which has been formally drawn up or registered as an authentic instrument and is enforceable;

c)   'child' means a person under 18 years of age in respect of whom a contact order may be made or enforced in a State Party;

d)   'family ties' means a close relationship such as between a child and his or her grandparents or siblings, based on law or on a de facto family relationship;

e)   'judicial authority' means a court or an administrative authority having equivalent powers.

Chapter II — General principles to be applied to contact orders

Article 3. Application of principles.   States Parties shall adopt such legislative and other measures as may be necessary to ensure that the principles contained in this chapter are applied by judicial authorities when making, amending, suspending or revoking contact orders.

Article 4. Contact between a child and his or her parents.   1.   A child and his or her parents shall have the right to obtain and maintain regular contact with each other.

2.   Such contact may be restricted or excluded only where necessary in the best interests of the child.

3.   Where it is not in the best interests of a child to maintain unsupervised contact with one of his or her parents the possibility of supervised personal contact or other forms of contact with this parent shall be considered.

Article 5. Contact between a child and persons other than his or her parents.   1.   Subject to his or her best interests, contact may be established between the child and persons other than his or her parents having family ties with the child.

2.   States Parties are free to extend this provision to persons other than those mentioned in paragraph 1, and where so extended, States may freely decide what aspects of contact, as defined in Article 2 letter a shall apply.

Article 6. The right of a child to be informed, consulted and to express his or her views.   1.   A child considered by internal law as having sufficient understanding shall have the right, unless this would be manifestly contrary to his or her best interests:
—   to receive all relevant information;
—   to be consulted;
—   to express his or her views.

2.   Due weight shall be given to those views and to the ascertainable wishes and feelings of the child.

Article 7. Resolving disputes concerning contact.   When resolving disputes concerning contact, the judicial authorities shall take all appropriate measures:

a) to ensure that both parents are informed of the importance for their child and for both of them of establishing and maintaining regular contact with their child;

b) to encourage parents and other persons having family ties with the child to reach amicable agreements with respect to contact, in particular through the use of family mediation and other processes for resolving disputes;

c) before taking a decision, to ensure that they have sufficient information at their disposal, in particular from the holders of parental responsibilities, in order to take a decision in the best interests of the child and, where necessary, obtain further information from other relevant bodies or persons.

Article 8. Contact agreements. 1. States Parties shall encourage, by means they consider appropriate, parents and other persons having family ties with the child to comply with the principles laid down in Articles 4 to 7 when making or modifying agreements on contact concerning a child. These agreements should preferably be in writing.

2. Upon request, judicial authorities shall, except where internal law otherwise provides, confirm an agreement on contact concerning a child, unless it is contrary to the best interests of the child.

Article 9. The carrying into effect of contact orders. States Parties shall take all appropriate measures to ensure that contact orders are carried into effect.

Article 10. Safeguards and guarantees to be taken concerning contact. 1. Each State Party shall provide for and promote the use of safeguards and guarantees. It shall communicate, through its central authorities, to the Secretary-General of the Council of Europe, within three months after the entry into force of this Convention for that State Party, at least three categories of safeguards and guarantees available in its internal law in addition to the safeguards and guarantees referred to in paragraph 3 of Article 4 and in letter b of paragraph 1 of Article 14 of this Convention. Changes of available safeguards and guarantees shall be communicated as soon as possible.

2. Where the circumstances of the case so require, judicial authorities may, at any time, make a contact order subject to any safeguards and guarantees both for the purpose of ensuring that the order is carried into effect and that either the child is returned at the end of the period of contact to the place where he or she usually lives or that he or she is not improperly removed.

a) Safeguards and guarantees for ensuring that the order is carried into effect, may in particular include:

— supervision of contact;

— the obligation for a person to provide for the travel and accommodation expenses of the child and, as may be appropriate, of any other person accompanying the child;

— a security to be deposited by the person with whom the child is usually living to ensure that the person seeking contact with the child is not prevented from having such contact;

— a fine to be imposed on the person with whom the child is usually living, should this person refuse to comply with the contact order.

b) Safeguards and guarantees for ensuring the return of the child or preventing an improper removal, may in particular include:

— the surrender of passports or identity documents and, where appropriate, a document indicating that the person seeking contact has notified the competent consular authority about such a surrender during the period of contact;

— financial guarantees;

— charges on property;

undertakings or stipulations to the court;

— the obligation of the person having contact with the child to present himself or herself, with the child regularly before a competent body, such as a youth welfare authority or a police station, in the place where contact is to be exercised;

— the obligation of the person seeking contact to present a document issued by the State where contact is to take place, certifying the recognition and declaration of enforceability of a custody or a contact order or both either before a contact order is made or before contact takes place;

— the imposition of conditions in relation to the place where contact is to be exercised and, where appropriate, the registration, in any national or transfrontier information system, of a prohibition preventing the child from leaving the State where contact is to take place.

3.   Any such safeguards and guarantees shall be in writing or evidenced in writing and shall form part of the contact order or the confirmed agreement.

4.   If safeguards or guarantees are to be implemented in another State Party, the judicial authority shall preferably order such safeguards or guarantees as are capable of implementation in that State Party.

Chapter III — Measures to promote and improve transfrontier contact

Article 11. Central authorities.   1.   Each State Party shall appoint a central authority to carry out the functions provided for by this Convention in cases of transfrontier contact.

2.   Federal States, States with more than one system of law or States having autonomous territorial units shall be free to appoint more than one central authority and to specify the territorial or personal extent of their functions. Where a State has appointed more than one central authority, it shall designate the central authority to which any communication may be addressed for transmission to the appropriate central authority within that State.

3.   The Secretary-General of the Council of Europe shall be notified of any appointment under this article.

Article 12. Duties of the central authorities.   The central authorities of States Parties shall:

a)   cooperate with each other and promote co-operation between the competent authorities, including judicial authorities, in their respective countries to achieve the purposes of the Convention. They shall act with all necessary despatch;

b)   with a view to facilitating the operation of this Convention, provide each other on request with information concerning their laws relating to parental responsibilities, including contact and any more detailed information concerning safeguards and guarantees in addition to that already provided according to paragraph 1 of Article 10, and their available services (including legal services, publicly funded or otherwise) as well as information concerning any changes in these laws and services;

c)   take all appropriate steps in order to discover the whereabouts of the child;

d)   secure the transmission of requests for information coming from the competent authorities and relating to legal or factual matters concerning pending proceedings;

e)   keep each other informed of any difficulties likely to arise in applying the Convention and, as far as possible, eliminate obstacles to its application.

Article 13. International co-operation.   1.   The judicial authorities, the central authorities and the social and other bodies of States Parties concerned, acting within their respective competence, shall cooperate in relation to proceedings regarding transfrontier contact.

2.   In particular, the central authorities shall assist the judicial authorities of States Parties in communicating with each other and obtaining such information and assistance as may be necessary for them to achieve the objects of this Convention.

3.   In transfrontier cases, the central authorities shall assist children, parents and other persons having family ties with the child, in particular, to institute proceedings regarding transfrontier contact.

Article 14. Recognition and enforcement of transfrontier contact orders.   1.   States Parties shall provide, including where applicable in accordance with relevant international instruments:

a)   a system for the recognition and enforcement of orders made in other States Parties concerning contact and rights of custody;

b)   a procedure whereby orders relating to contact and rights of custody made in other States Parties may be recognised and declared enforceable in advance of contact being exercised within the State addressed.

2.   If a State Party makes recognition or enforcement or both of a foreign order conditional on the existence of a treaty or reciprocity, it may consider this Convention as such a legal basis for recognition or enforcement or both of a foreign contact order.

Article 15. Conditions for implementing transfrontier contact orders.   The judicial authority of the State Party in which a transfrontier contact order made in another State Party is to be implemented may, when recognising or declaring enforceable such a contact order, or at any later time, fix or adapt the conditions for its implementation, as well as any safeguards or guarantees attaching to it, if necessary for facilitating the exercise of this contact, provided that the essential elements of the order are respected and taking into account, in particular, a change of circumstances and the arrangements made by the persons concerned. In no circumstances may the foreign decision be reviewed as to its substance.

Article 16. Return of a child.   1.   Where a child at the end of a period of transfrontier contact based on a contact order is not returned, the competent authorities shall, upon request, ensure the child's immediate return, where applicable, by applying the relevant provisions of international instruments, of internal law and by implementing, where appropriate, such safeguards and guarantees as may be provided in the contact order.

2.   A decision on the return of the child shall be made, whenever possible, within six weeks of the date of an application for the return.

Article 17. Costs.   With the exception of the cost of repatriation, each State Party undertakes not to claim any payment from an applicant in respect of any measures taken under this Convention by the central authority itself of that State on the applicant's behalf.

Article 18. Language requirement. 1. Subject to any special agreements made between the central authorities concerned:

a) communications to the central authority of the State addressed shall be made in the official language or in one of the official languages of that State or be accompanied by a translation into that language;

b) the central authority of the State addressed shall nevertheless accept communications made in English or in French, or accompanied by a translation into one of these languages.

2. Communications coming from the central authority of the State addressed, including the results of enquiries carried out, may be made in the official language or one of the official languages of that State or in English or French.

3. However, a State Party may, by making a declaration addressed to the Secretary-General of the Council of Europe, object to the use of either French or English under paragraphs 1 and 2 of this article, in any application, communication or other documents sent to their central authorities.

Chapter IV — Relationship with other instruments

Article 19. Relationship with the European Convention on Recognition and Enforcement of Decisions concerning Custody of Children and on Restoration of Custody of Children. Paragraphs 2 and 3 of Article 11 of the European Convention of 20 May 1980 (ETS No 105) on Recognition and Enforcement of Decisions concerning Custody of Children and on Restoration of Custody of Children shall not be applied in relations between States Parties which are also States Parties of the present Convention.

Article 20. Relationships with other instruments. 1. This Convention shall not affect any international instrument to which States Parties to the present Convention are Parties or shall become Parties and which contains provisions on matters governed by this Convention. In particular, this Convention shall not prejudice the application of the following legal instruments:

a) the Hague Convention of 5 October 1961 on the competence of authorities and the applicable law concerning the protection of minors;

b) the European Convention on the recognition and enforcement of decisions concerning custody of children and on restoration of custody of children of 20 May 1980, subject to Article 19 above;

c) the Hague Convention of 25 October 1980 on the civil aspects of international child abduction;

d) the Hague Convention of 19 October 1996 on jurisdiction, applicable law, recognition, enforcement and co-operation in respect of parental responsibility and measures for the protection of children.

2. Nothing in this Convention shall prevent Parties from concluding international agreements completing or developing the provisions of this Convention or extending their field of application.

3.   In their mutual relations, States Parties which are members of the European Community shall apply Community rules and shall therefore not apply the rules arising from this Convention, except in so far as there is no Community rule governing the particular subject concerned.

Chapter V — Amendments to the Convention

Article 21. Amendments.   1.   Any proposal for an amendment to this Convention presented by a Party shall be communicated to the Secretary-General of the Council of Europe and forwarded by him or her to the member States of the Council of Europe, any signatory, any State Party, the European Community, to any State invited to sign this Convention in accordance with the provisions of Article 22 and to any State invited to accede to this Convention in accordance with the provisions of Article 23.

2.   Any amendment proposed by a Party shall be communicated to the European Committee on Legal Co-operation (CDCJ), which shall submit to the Committee of Ministers its opinion on that proposed amendment.

3.   The Committee of Ministers shall consider the proposed amendment and the opinion submitted by the CDCJ and, following consultation of the Parties to the Convention, which are not members of the Council of Europe, may adopt the amendment.

4.   The text of any amendment adopted by the Committee of Ministers in accordance with paragraph 3 of this article shall be forwarded to the Parties for acceptance.

5.   Any amendment adopted in accordance with paragraph 3 of this article shall enter into force on the first day of the month following the expiration of a period of one month after the date on which all Parties have informed the Secretary-General that they have accepted it.

Chapter VI — Final clauses

Article 22. Signature and entry into force.   1.   This Convention shall be open for signature by the member States of the Council of Europe, the non-member States which have participated in its elaboration and the European Community.

2.   This Convention is subject to ratification, acceptance or approval. Instruments of ratification, acceptance or approval shall be deposited with the Secretary-General of the Council of Europe.

3.   This Convention shall enter into force on the first day of the month following the expiration of a period of three months after the date on which three States, including at least two member States of the Council of Europe, have expressed their consent to be bound by the Convention in accordance with the provisions of the preceding paragraph.

4.   In respect of any State mentioned in paragraph 1 or the European Community, which subsequently expresses its consent to be bound by it, the Convention shall enter into force on the first day of the month following the expiration of a period of three months after the date of the deposit of its instrument of ratification, acceptance or approval.

Article 23. Accession to the Convention. 1. After the entry into force of this Convention, the Committee of Ministers of the Council of Europe may, after consultation of the Parties, invite any non-member State of the Council of Europe, which has not participated in the elaboration of the Convention, to accede to this Convention by a decision taken by the majority provided for in Article 20(d). of the Statute of the Council of Europe, and by unanimous vote of the representatives of the Contracting States entitled to sit on the Committee of Ministers.

2. In respect of any acceding State, the Convention shall enter into force on the first day of the month following the expiration of a period of three months after the date of deposit of the instrument of accession with the Secretary-General of the Council of Europe.

Article 24. Territorial application. 1. Any State or the European Community may, at the time of signature or when depositing its instrument of ratification, acceptance, approval or accession, specify the territory or territories to which this Convention shall apply.

2. Any Party may, at any later date, by a declaration addressed to the Secretary-General of the Council of Europe, extend the application of this Convention to any other territory specified in the declaration and for whose international relations it is responsible or on whose behalf it is authorised to give undertakings. In respect of such territory, the Convention shall enter into force on the first day of the month following the expiration of a period of three months after the date of receipt of such declaration by the Secretary-General.

3. Any declaration made under the two preceding paragraphs may, in respect of any territory specified in such declaration, be withdrawn by a notification addressed to the Secretary-General. The withdrawal shall become effective on the first day of the month following the expiration of a period of three months after the date of receipt of such notification by the Secretary-General.

Article 25. Reservations. No reservation may be made in respect of any provision of this Convention.

Article 26. Denunciation. 1. Any Party may, at any time, denounce this Convention by means of a notification addressed to the Secretary-General of the Council of Europe.

2. Such denunciation shall become effective on the first day of the month following the expiration of a period of three months after the date of receipt of the notification by the Secretary-General.

Article 27. Notifications. The Secretary-General of the Council of Europe shall notify the member States of the Council of Europe, any State signatory, any State Party, the European Community, to any State invited to sign this Convention in accordance with the provisions of Article 22 and to any State invited to accede to this Convention in accordance with the provisions of Article 23 of:

    a)   any signature;

    b)   the deposit of any instrument of ratification, acceptance, approval or accession;

    c)   any date of entry into force of this Convention in accordance with Articles 22 and 23;

d)　any amendment adopted in accordance with Article 21 and the date on which such an amendment enters into force;

e)　any declaration made under the provisions of Article 18;

f)　any denunciation made in pursuance of the provisions of Article 26;

g)　any other act, notification or communication, in particular relating to Articles 10 and 11 of this Convention.

Maintenance obligations

A.1.　Council Regulation (EC) No 4/2009 of 18 December 2008 on jurisdiction, applicable law, recognition and enforcement of decisions and Co-operation in matters relating to maintenance obligations (OJ, L 7 of 10 January 2009)

(1)　The Community has set itself the objective of maintaining and developing an area of freedom, security and justice, in which the free movement of persons is ensured. For the gradual establishment of such an area, the Community is to adopt, among others, measures relating to judicial co-operation in civil matters having cross-border implications, in so far as necessary for the proper functioning of the internal market.

(2)　In accordance with Article 65(b) of the Treaty, these measures must aim, inter alia, to promote the compatibility of the rules applicable in the Member States concerning the conflict of laws and of jurisdiction.

(3)　In this respect, the Community has among other measures already adopted Council Regulation (EC) No 44/2001 of 22 December 2000 on jurisdiction and the recognition and enforcement of judgments in civil and commercial matters, Council Decision 2001/470/EC of 28 May 2001 establishing a European Judicial Network in civil and commercial matters, Council Regulation (EC) No 1206/2001 of 28 May 2001 on co-operation between the courts of the Member States in the taking of evidence in civil or commercial matters, Council Directive 2003/8/EC of 27 January 2003 to improve access to justice in cross-border disputes by establishing minimum common rules relating to legal aid for such disputes, Council Regulation (EC) No 2201/2003 of 27 November 2003 on jurisdiction and the recognition and enforcement of judgments in matrimonial matters and in matters of parental responsibility, Regulation (EC) No 805/2004 of the European Parliament and of the Council of 21 April 2004 creating a European Enforcement Order for uncontested claims, and Regulation (EC) No 1393/2007 of the European Parliament and of the Council of 13 November 2007 on the service in the Member States of judicial and extrajudicial documents in civil or commercial matters (service of documents).

(4)　The European Council in Tampere on 15 and 16 October 1999 invited the Council and the Commission to establish special common procedural rules to simplify and accelerate the settlement of cross-border disputes concerning, inter alia, maintenance claims. It also called for the abolition of intermediate measures required for the recognition and enforcement in the requested State of a decision given in another Member State, particularly a decision relating to a maintenance claim.

(5)   A programme of measures for the enforcement of the principle of mutual recognition of decisions in civil and commercial matters, common to the Commission and to the Council, was adopted on 30 November 2000. That programme provides for the abolition of the exequatur procedure for maintenance claims in order to boost the effectiveness of the means by which maintenance creditors safeguard their rights.

(6)   The European Council meeting in Brussels on 4 and 5 November 2004 adopted a new programme called 'The Hague Programme: strengthening freedom, security and justice in the European Union' (hereinafter referred to as The Hague Programme).

(7)   At its meeting on 2 and 3 June 2005, the Council adopted a Council and Commission Action Plan which implements The Hague Programme in concrete actions and which mentions the necessity of adopting proposals on maintenance obligations.

(8)   In the framework of The Hague Conference on Private International Law, the Community and its Member States took part in negotiations which led to the adoption on 23 November 2007 of the Convention on the International Recovery of Child Support and other Forms of Family Maintenance (hereinafter referred to as the 2007 Hague Convention) and the Protocol on the Law Applicable to Maintenance Obligations (hereinafter referred to as the 2007 Hague Protocol). Both those instruments should therefore be taken into account in this Regulation.

(9)   A maintenance creditor should be able to obtain easily, in a Member State, a decision which will be automatically enforceable in another Member State without further formalities.

(10) In order to achieve this goal, it is advisable to create a Community instrument in matters relating to maintenance obligations bringing together provisions on jurisdiction, conflict of laws, recognition and enforceability, enforcement, legal aid and co-operation between Central Authorities.

(11) The scope of this Regulation should cover all maintenance obligations arising from a family relationship, parentage, marriage or affinity, in order to guarantee equal treatment of all maintenance creditors. For the purposes of this Regulation, the term 'maintenance obligation' should be interpreted autonomously.

(12) In order to take account of the various ways of resolving maintenance obligation issues in the Member States, this Regulation should apply both to court decisions and to decisions given by administrative authorities, provided that the latter offer guarantees with regard to, in particular, their impartiality and the right of all parties to be heard. Those authorities should therefore apply all the rules of this Regulation.

(13) For the reasons set out above, this Regulation should also ensure the recognition and enforcement of court settlements and authentic instruments without affecting the right of either party to such a settlement or instrument to challenge the settlement or instrument before the courts of the Member State of origin.

(14) It should be provided in this Regulation that for the purposes of an application for the recognition and enforcement of a decision relating to maintenance obligations the term 'creditor' includes public bodies which are entitled to act in place of a person to whom maintenance is owed or to claim reimbursement of benefits provided to the creditor in place of maintenance. Where a public body acts in this capacity, it should be entitled to the same services and the same legal aid as a creditor.

(15) In order to preserve the interests of maintenance creditors and to promote the proper administration of justice within the European Union, the rules on jurisdiction as they result from Regulation (EC) No 44/2001 should be adapted. The circumstance

that the defendant is habitually resident in a third State should no longer entail the non-application of Community rules on jurisdiction, and there should no longer be any referral to national law. This Regulation should therefore determine the cases in which a court in a Member State may exercise subsidiary jurisdiction.

(16) In order to remedy, in particular, situations of denial of justice this Regulation should provide a forum necessitatis allowing a court of a Member State, on an exceptional basis, to hear a case which is closely connected with a third State. Such an exceptional basis may be deemed to exist when proceedings prove impossible in the third State in question, for example because of civil war, or when an applicant cannot reasonably be expected to initiate or conduct proceedings in that State. Jurisdiction based on the forum necessitatis should, however, be exercised only if the dispute has a sufficient connection with the Member State of the court seised, for instance the nationality of one of the parties.

(17) An additional rule of jurisdiction should provide that, except under specific conditions, proceedings to modify an existing maintenance decision or to have a new decision given can be brought by the debtor only in the State in which the creditor was habitually resident at the time the decision was given and in which he remains habitually resident. To ensure proper symmetry between the 2007 Hague Convention and this Regulation, this rule should also apply as regards decisions given in a third State which is party to the said Convention in so far as that Convention is in force between that State and the Community and covers the same maintenance obligations in that State and in the Community.

(18) For the purposes of this Regulation, it should be provided that in Ireland the concept of 'domicile' replaces the concept of 'nationality' which is also the case in the United Kingdom, subject to this Regulation being applicable in the latter Member State in accordance with Article 4 of the Protocol on the position of the United Kingdom and Ireland annexed to the Treaty on European Union and the Treaty establishing the European Community.

(19) In order to increase legal certainty, predictability and the autonomy of the parties, this Regulation should enable the parties to choose the competent court by agreement on the basis of specific connecting factors. To protect the weaker party, such a choice of court should not be allowed in the case of maintenance obligations towards a child under the age of 18.

(20) It should be provided in this Regulation that, for Member States bound by the 2007 Hague Protocol, the rules on conflict of laws in respect of maintenance obligations will be those set out in that Protocol. To that end, a provision referring to the said Protocol should be inserted. The 2007 Hague Protocol will be concluded by the Community in time to enable this Regulation to apply. To take account of a scenario in which the 2007 Hague Protocol does not apply to all the Member States a distinction for the purposes of recognition, enforceability and enforcement of decisions needs to be made in this Regulation between the Member States bound by the 2007 Hague Protocol and those not bound by it.

(21) It needs to be made clear in this Regulation that these rules on conflict of laws determine only the law applicable to maintenance obligations and do not determine the law applicable to the establishment of the family relationships on which the maintenance obligations are based. The establishment of family relationships continues to be covered by the national law of the Member States, including their rules of private international law.

(22) In order to ensure swift and efficient recovery of a maintenance obligation and to prevent delaying actions, decisions in matters relating to maintenance obligations given in a Member State should in principle be provisionally enforceable. This Regulation should therefore provide that the court of origin should be able to declare the decision provisionally enforceable even if the national law does not provide for enforceability by operation of law and even if an appeal has been or could still be lodged against the decision under national law.

(23) To limit the costs of proceedings subject to this Regulation, the greatest possible use of modern communications technologies, particularly for hearing parties, would be helpful.

(24) The guarantees provided by the application of rules on conflict of laws should provide the justification for having decisions relating to maintenance obligations given in a Member State bound by the 2007 Hague Protocol recognised and regarded as enforceable in all the other Member States without any procedure being necessary and without any form of control on the substance in the Member State of enforcement.

(25) Recognition in a Member State of a decision relating to maintenance obligations has as its only object to allow the recovery of the maintenance claim determined in the decision. It does not imply the recognition by that Member State of the family relationship, parentage, marriage or affinity underlying the maintenance obligations which gave rise to the decision.

(26) For decisions on maintenance obligations given in a Member State not bound by the 2007 Hague Protocol, there should be provision in this Regulation for a procedure for recognition and declaration of enforceability. That procedure should be modelled on the procedure and the grounds for refusing recognition set out in Regulation (EC) No 44/2001. To accelerate proceedings and enable the creditor to recover his claim quickly, the court seised should be required to give its decision within a set time, unless there are exceptional circumstances.

(27) It would also be appropriate to limit as far as possible the formal enforcement requirements likely to increase the costs to be borne by the maintenance creditor. To that end, this Regulation should provide that a maintenance creditor ought not to be required to have a postal address or an authorised representative in the Member State of enforcement, without this otherwise affecting the internal organisation of the Member States in matters relating to enforcement proceedings.

(28) In order to limit the costs of enforcement proceedings, no translation should be required unless enforcement is contested, and without prejudice to the rules applicable to service of documents.

(29) In order to guarantee compliance with the requirements of a fair trial, this Regulation should provide for the right of a defendant who did not enter an appearance in the court of origin of a Member State bound by the 2007 Hague Protocol to apply for a review of the decision given against him at the stage of enforcement. However, the defendant must apply for this review within a set period which should start no later than the day on which, in the enforcement proceedings, his property was first made non-disposable in whole or in part. That right to apply for a review should be an extraordinary remedy granted to the defendant in default and not affecting the application of any extraordinary remedies laid down in the law of the Member State of origin provided that those remedies are not incompatible with the right to a review under this Regulation.

(30) In order to speed up the enforcement in another Member State of a decision given in a Member State bound by the 2007 Hague Protocol it is necessary to limit the grounds of refusal or of suspension of enforcement which may be invoked by the debtor on account of the cross-border nature of the maintenance claim. This limitation should not affect the grounds of refusal or of suspension laid down in national law which are not incompatible with those listed in this Regulation, such as the debtor's discharge of his debt at the time of enforcement or the unattachable nature of certain assets.

(31) To facilitate cross-border recovery of maintenance claims, provision should be made for a system of co-operation between Central Authorities designated by the Member States. These Authorities should assist maintenance creditors and debtors in asserting their rights in another Member State by submitting applications for recognition, enforceability and enforcement of existing decisions, for the modification of such decisions or for the establishment of a decision. They should also exchange information in order to locate debtors and creditors, and identify their income and assets, as necessary. Lastly, they should cooperate with each other by exchanging general information and promoting co-operation amongst the competent authorities in their Member States.

(32) A Central Authority designated under this Regulation should bear its own costs, except in specifically determined cases, and should provide assistance for all applicants residing in its Member State. The criterion for determining a person's right to request assistance from a Central Authority should be less strict than the connecting factor of 'habitual residence' used elsewhere in this Regulation. However, the 'residence' criterion should exclude mere presence.

(33) In order to provide full assistance to maintenance creditors and debtors and to facilitate as much as possible cross-border recovery of maintenance, the Central Authorities should be able to obtain a certain amount of personal information. This Regulation should therefore oblige the Member States to ensure that their Central Authorities have access to such information through the public authorities or administrations which hold the information concerned in the course of their ordinary activities. It should however be left to each Member State to decide on the arrangements for such access. Accordingly, a Member State should be able to designate the public authorities or administrations which will be required to supply the information to the Central Authority in accordance with this Regulation, including, if appropriate, public authorities or administrations already designated in the context of other systems for access to information. Where a Member State designates public authorities or administrations, it should ensure that its Central Authority is able to access the requisite information held by those bodies as provided for in this Regulation. A Member State should also be able to allow its Central Authority to access requisite information from any other legal person which holds it and controls its processing.

(34) In the context of access to personal data and the use and transmission thereof, the requirements of Directive 95/46/EC of the European Parliament and of the Council of 24 October 1995 on the protection of individuals with regard to the processing of personal data and on the free movement of such data, as transposed into the national law of the Member States, should be complied with.

(35) For the purposes of the application of this Regulation it is however necessary to define the specific conditions of access to personal data and of the use and transmission of such data. In this context, the opinion of the European Data Protection Supervisor has been taken into consideration. Notification of the data subject should take place in

accordance with national law. It should however be possible to defer the notification to prevent the debtor from transferring his assets and thus jeopardising the recovery of the maintenance claim.

(36) On account of the costs of proceedings it is appropriate to provide for a very favourable legal aid scheme, that is, full coverage of the costs relating to proceedings concerning maintenance obligations in respect of children under the age of 21 initiated via the Central Authorities. Specific rules should therefore be added to the current rules on legal aid in the European Union which exist by virtue of Directive 2003/8/EC thus setting up a special legal aid scheme for maintenance obligations. In this context, the competent authority of the requested Member State should be able, exceptionally, to recover costs from an applicant having received free legal aid and lost the case, provided that the person's financial situation so permits. This would apply, in particular, where someone well-off had acted in bad faith.

(37) In addition, for maintenance obligations other than those referred to in the preceding recital, all parties should be guaranteed the same treatment in terms of legal aid at the time of enforcement of a decision in another Member State. Accordingly, the provisions of this Regulation on continuity of legal aid should be understood as also granting such aid to a party who, while not having received legal aid in the proceedings to obtain or amend a decision in the Member State of origin, did then benefit from such aid in that State in the context of an application for enforcement of the decision. Similarly, a party who benefited from free proceedings before an administrative authority listed in Annex X should, in the Member State of enforcement, benefit from the most favourable legal aid or the most extensive exemption from costs or expenses, provided that he shows that he would have so benefited in the Member State of origin.

(38) In order to minimise the costs of translating supporting documents the court seised should only require a translation of such documents when this is necessary, without prejudice to the rights of the defence and the rules applicable concerning service of documents.

(39) To facilitate the application of this Regulation, Member States should be obliged to provide the Commission with the names and contact details of their Central Authorities and with other information. That information should be made available to practitioners and to the public through publication in the Official Journal of the European Union or through electronic access to the European Judicial Network in civil and commercial matters established by Decision 2001/470/EC. Furthermore, the use of forms provided for in this Regulation should facilitate and speed up communication between the Central Authorities and make it possible to submit applications electronically.

(40) The relationship between this Regulation and the bilateral or multilateral conventions and agreements on maintenance obligations to which the Member States are party should be specified. In this context it should be stipulated that Member States which are party to the Convention of 23 March 1962 between Sweden, Denmark, Finland, Iceland and Norway on the recovery of maintenance by the Member States may continue to apply that Convention since it contains more favourable rules on recognition and enforcement than those in this Regulation. As regards the conclusion of future bilateral agreements on maintenance obligations with third States, the procedures and conditions under which Member States would be authorised to negotiate and conclude such agreements on their own behalf should be determined in the course of discussions relating to a Commission proposal on the subject.

(41) In calculating the periods and time limits provided for in this Regulation, Regulation (EEC, Euratom) No 1182/71 of the Council of 3 June 1971 determining the rules applicable to periods, dates and time limits should apply.

(42) The measures necessary for the implementation of this Regulation should be adopted in accordance with Council Decision 1999/468/EC of 28 June 1999 laying down the procedures for the exercise of implementing powers conferred on the Commission.

(43) In particular, the Commission should be empowered to adopt any amendments to the forms provided for in this Regulation in accordance with the advisory procedure provided for in Article 3 of Decision 1999/468/EC. For the establishment of the list of the administrative authorities falling within the scope of this Regulation, and the list of authorities competent to certify the right to legal aid, the Commission should be empowered to act in accordance with the management procedure provided for in Article 4 of that Decision.

(44) This Regulation should amend Regulation (EC) No 44/2001 by replacing the provisions of that Regulation applicable to maintenance obligations. Subject to the transitional provisions of this Regulation, Member States should, in matters relating to maintenance obligations, apply the provisions of this Regulation on jurisdiction, recognition, enforceability and enforcement of decisions and on legal aid instead of those of Regulation (EC) No 44/2001 as from the date on which this Regulation becomes applicable.

(45) Since the objectives of this Regulation, namely the introduction of a series of measures to ensure the effective recovery of maintenance claims in cross-border situations and thus to facilitate the free movement of persons within the European Union, cannot be sufficiently achieved by the Member States and can therefore, by reason of the scale and effects of this Regulation, be better achieved at Community level, the Community may adopt measures in accordance with the principle of subsidiarity as set out in Article 5 of the Treaty. In accordance with the principle of proportionality as set out in that Article this Regulation does not go beyond what is necessary to achieve those objectives.

(46) In accordance with Article 3 of the Protocol on the position of the United Kingdom and Ireland, annexed to the Treaty on European Union and to the Treaty establishing the European Community, Ireland has given notice of its wish to take part in the adoption and application of this Regulation.

(47) In accordance with Articles 1 and 2 of the Protocol on the position of the United Kingdom and Ireland, annexed to the Treaty on European Union and to the Treaty establishing the European Community, the United Kingdom is not taking part in the adoption of this Regulation and is not bound by it or subject to its application. This is, however, without prejudice to the possibility for the United Kingdom of notifying its intention of accepting this Regulation after its adoption in accordance with Article 4 of the said Protocol.[1]

(48) In accordance with Articles 1 and 2 of the Protocol on the position of Denmark annexed to the Treaty on European Union and the Treaty establishing the European

---

[1]   The United Kingdom notified the Council and the Commission by letter of 15 January 2009 of its intention to accept Regulation (EC) No 4/2009 and the Commission gave a positive opinion to the Council on 21 April 2009. See Commission Decision '2009/451/EC of 8 June 2009 on the intention of the United Kingdom to accept Council Regulation (EC) No 4/2009 on jurisdiction, applicable law, recognition and enforcement of decisions and co-operation in matters relating to maintenance obligations' (OJ, L 149 of 12 June 2009). [Note of the Editor]

Community, Denmark is not taking part in the adoption of this Regulation and is not bound by it or subject to its application, without prejudice to the possibility for Denmark of applying the amendments made here to Regulation (EC) No 44/2001 pursuant to Article 3 of the Agreement of 19 October 2005 between the European Community and the Kingdom of Denmark on jurisdiction and the recognition and enforcement of judgments in civil and commercial matters, has adopted this Regulation:

Chapter I — Scope and definitions

Article 1. Scope of application.   1.   This Regulation shall apply to maintenance obligations arising from a family relationship, parentage, marriage or affinity.

2.   In this Regulation, the term 'Member State' shall mean Member States to which this Regulation applies.

Article 2. Definitions.   1.   For the purposes of this Regulation:

1.   the term 'decision' shall mean a decision in matters relating to maintenance obligations given by a court of a Member State, whatever the decision may be called, including a decree, order, judgment or writ of execution, as well as a decision by an officer of the court determining the costs or expenses. For the purposes of Chapters VII and VIII, the term 'decision' shall also mean a decision in matters relating to maintenance obligations given in a third State;

2.   the term 'court settlement' shall mean a settlement in matters relating to maintenance obligations which has been approved by a court or concluded before a court in the course of proceedings;

3.   the term 'authentic instrument' shall mean:

(a)   a document in matters relating to maintenance obligations which has been formally drawn up or registered as an authentic instrument in the Member State of origin and the authenticity of which:

(i)   relates to the signature and the content of the instrument, and

(ii)   has been established by a public authority or other authority empowered for that purpose; or,

(b)   an arrangement relating to maintenance obligations concluded with administrative authorities of the Member State of origin or authenticated by them;

4.   the term 'Member State of origin' shall mean the Member State in which, as the case may be, the decision has been given, the court settlement has been approved or concluded, or the authentic instrument has been established;

5.   the term 'Member State of enforcement' shall mean the Member State in which the enforcement of the decision, the court settlement or the authentic instrument is sought;

6.   the term 'requesting Member State' shall mean the Member State whose Central Authority transmits an application pursuant to Chapter VII;

7.   the term 'requested Member State' shall mean the Member State whose Central Authority receives an application pursuant to Chapter VII;

8.   the term '2007 Hague Convention Contracting State' shall mean a State which is a contracting party to the Hague Convention of 23 November 2007 on the International Recovery of Child Support and other Forms of Family Maintenance

(hereinafter referred to as the 2007 Hague Convention) to the extent that the said Convention applies between the Community and that State;

9.   the term 'court of origin' shall mean the court which has given the decision to be enforced;

10.   the term 'creditor' shall mean any individual to whom maintenance is owed or is alleged to be owed;

11.   the term 'debtor' shall mean any individual who owes or who is alleged to owe maintenance.

2.   For the purposes of this Regulation, the term 'court' shall include administrative authorities of the Member States with competence in matters relating to maintenance obligations provided that such authorities offer guarantees with regard to impartiality and the right of all parties to be heard and provided that their decisions under the law of the Member State where they are established:

(i)   may be made the subject of an appeal to or review by a judicial authority; and

(ii)   have a similar force and effect as a decision of a judicial authority on the same matter.

These administrative authorities shall be listed in Annex X. That Annex shall be established and amended in accordance with the management procedure referred to in Article 73(2) at the request of the Member State in which the administrative authority concerned is established.

3.   For the purposes of Articles 3, 4 and 6, the concept of 'domicile' shall replace that of 'nationality' in those Member States which use this concept as a connecting factor in family matters.

For the purposes of Article 6, parties which have their 'domicile' in different territorial units of the same Member State shall be deemed to have their common 'domicile' in that Member State.

Chapter II — Jurisdiction

Article 3. General provisions.   In matters relating to maintenance obligations in Member States, jurisdiction shall lie with:

(a)   the court for the place where the defendant is habitually resident, or

(b)   the court for the place where the creditor is habitually resident, or

(c)   the court which, according to its own law, has jurisdiction to entertain proceedings concerning the status of a person if the matter relating to maintenance is ancillary to those proceedings, unless that jurisdiction is based solely on the nationality of one of the parties, or

(d)   the court which, according to its own law, has jurisdiction to entertain proceedings concerning parental responsibility if the matter relating to maintenance is ancillary to those proceedings, unless that jurisdiction is based solely on the nationality of one of the parties.

Article 4. Choice of court.   1.   The parties may agree that the following court or courts of a Member State shall have jurisdiction to settle any disputes in matters relating to a maintenance obligation which have arisen or may arise between them:

(a)   a court or the courts of a Member State in which one of the parties is habitually resident;

(b)   a court or the courts of a Member State of which one of the parties has the nationality;

(c)   in the case of maintenance obligations between spouses or former spouses:

(i)   the court which has jurisdiction to settle their dispute in matrimonial matters; or

(ii)   a court or the courts of the Member State which was the Member State of the spouses' last common habitual residence for a period of at least one year.

The conditions referred to in points (a), (b) or (c) have to be met at the time the choice of court agreement is concluded or at the time the court is seised.

The jurisdiction conferred by agreement shall be exclusive unless the parties have agreed otherwise.

2.   A choice of court agreement shall be in writing. Any communication by electronic means which provides a durable record of the agreement shall be equivalent to 'writing'.

3.   This Article shall not apply to a dispute relating to a maintenance obligation towards a child under the age of 18.

4.   If the parties have agreed to attribute exclusive jurisdiction to a court or courts of a State party to the Convention on jurisdiction and the recognition and enforcement of judgments in civil and commercial matters, signed on 30 October 2007 in Lugano (hereinafter referred to as the Lugano Convention), where that State is not a Member State, the said Convention shall apply except in the case of the disputes referred to in paragraph 3.

Article 5. Jurisdiction based on the appearance of the defendant.   Apart from jurisdiction derived from other provisions of this Regulation, a court of a Member State before which a defendant enters an appearance shall have jurisdiction. This rule shall not apply where appearance was entered to contest the jurisdiction.

Article 6. Subsidiary jurisdiction.   Where no court of a Member State has jurisdiction pursuant to Articles 3, 4 and 5 and no court of a State party to the Lugano Convention which is not a Member State has jurisdiction pursuant to the provisions of that Convention, the courts of the Member State of the common nationality of the parties shall have jurisdiction.

Article 7. Forum necessitatis.   Where no court of a Member State has jurisdiction pursuant to Articles 3, 4, 5 and 6, the courts of a Member State may, on an exceptional basis, hear the case if proceedings cannot reasonably be brought or conducted or would be impossible in a third State with which the dispute is closely connected.

The dispute must have a sufficient connection with the Member State of the court seised.

Article 8. Limit on proceedings.   1.   Where a decision is given in a Member State or a 2007 Hague Convention Contracting State where the creditor is habitually resident, proceedings to modify the decision or to have a new decision given cannot be brought by the debtor in any other Member State as long as the creditor remains habitually resident in the State in which the decision was given.

2.   Paragraph 1 shall not apply:

(a)   where the parties have agreed in accordance with Article 4 to the jurisdiction of the courts of that other Member State;

(b)   where the creditor submits to the jurisdiction of the courts of that other Member State pursuant to Article 5;

(c)   where the competent authority in the 2007 Hague Convention Contracting State of origin cannot, or refuses to, exercise jurisdiction to modify the decision or give a new decision; or

(d)   where the decision given in the 2007 Hague Convention Contracting State of origin cannot be recognised or declared enforceable in the Member State where proceedings to modify the decision or to have a new decision given are contemplated.

Article 9. Seising of a court.   For the purposes of this Chapter, a court shall be deemed to be seised:

(a)   at the time when the document instituting the proceedings or an equivalent document is lodged with the court, provided that the claimant has not subsequently failed to take the steps he was required to take to have service effected on the defendant; or

(b)   if the document has to be served before being lodged with the court, at the time when it is received by the authority responsible for service, provided that the claimant has not subsequently failed to take the steps he was required to take to have the document lodged with the court.

Article 10. Examination as to jurisdiction.   Where a court of a Member State is seised of a case over which it has no jurisdiction under this Regulation it shall declare of its own motion that it has no jurisdiction.

Article 11. Examination as to admissibility.   1.   Where a defendant habitually resident in a State other than the Member State where the action was brought does not enter an appearance, the court with jurisdiction shall stay the proceedings so long as it is not shown that the defendant has been able to receive the document instituting the proceedings or an equivalent document in sufficient time to enable him to arrange for his defence, or that all necessary steps have been taken to this end.

2.   Article 19 of Regulation (EC) No 1393/2007 shall apply instead of the provisions of paragraph 1 of this Article if the document instituting the proceedings or an equivalent document had to be transmitted from one Member State to another pursuant to that Regulation.

3.   Where the provisions of Regulation (EC) No 1393/2007 are not applicable, Article 15 of the Hague Convention of 15 November 1965 on the service abroad of judicial and extrajudicial documents in civil or commercial matters shall apply if the document instituting the proceedings or an equivalent document had to be transmitted abroad pursuant to that Convention.

Article 12. Lis pendens.   1.   Where proceedings involving the same cause of action and between the same parties are brought in the courts of different Member States, any court other than the court first seised shall of its own motion stay its proceedings until such time as the jurisdiction of the court first seised is established.

2.   Where the jurisdiction of the court first seised is established, any court other than the court first seised shall decline jurisdiction in favour of that court.

Article 13. Related actions.   1.   Where related actions are pending in the courts of different Member States, any court other than the court first seised may stay its proceedings.

2.   Where these actions are pending at first instance, any court other than the court first seised may also, on the application of one of the parties, decline jurisdiction if the court first seised has jurisdiction over the actions in question and its law permits the consolidation thereof.

3.   For the purposes of this Article, actions are deemed to be related where they are so closely connected that it is expedient to hear and determine them together to avoid the risk of irreconcilable judgments resulting from separate proceedings.

Article 14. Provisional, including protective, measures.   Application may be made to the courts of a Member State for such provisional, including protective, measures as may be available under the law of that State, even if, under this Regulation, the courts of another Member State have jurisdiction as to the substance of the matter.

Chapter III — Applicable law

Article 15. Determination of the applicable law.   The law applicable to maintenance obligations shall be determined in accordance with the Hague Protocol of 23 November 2007 on the law applicable to maintenance obligations (hereinafter referred to as the 2007 Hague Protocol) in the Member States bound by that instrument.

Chapter IV — Recognition, enforceability and enforcement of decisions

Article 16. Scope of application of this Chapter.   1.   This Chapter shall govern the recognition, enforceability and enforcement of decisions falling within the scope of this Regulation.

2.   Section 1 shall apply to decisions given in a Member State bound by the 2007 Hague Protocol.

3.   Section 2 shall apply to decisions given in a Member State not bound by the 2007 Hague Protocol.

4.   Section 3 shall apply to all decisions.

Section 1 — Decisions given in a Member State bound by the 2007 Hague Protocol

Article 17. Abolition of exequatur.   1.   A decision given in a Member State bound by the 2007 Hague Protocol shall be recognised in another Member State without any special procedure being required and without any possibility of opposing its recognition.

2.   A decision given in a Member State bound by the 2007 Hague Protocol which is enforceable in that State shall be enforceable in another Member State without the need for a declaration of enforceability.

Article 18. Protective measures.   An enforceable decision shall carry with it by operation of law the power to proceed to any protective measures which exist under the law of the Member State of enforcement.

Article 19. Right to apply for a review.   1.   A defendant who did not enter an appearance in the Member State of origin shall have the right to apply for a review of the decision before the competent court of that Member State where:

(a)   he was not served with the document instituting the proceedings or an equivalent document in sufficient time and in such a way as to enable him to arrange for his defence; or

(b)   he was prevented from contesting the maintenance claim by reason of *force majeure* or due to extraordinary circumstances without any fault on his part;

unless he failed to challenge the decision when it was possible for him to do so.

2.   The time limit for applying for a review shall run from the day the defendant was effectively acquainted with the contents of the decision and was able to react, at the latest from the date of the first enforcement measure having the effect of making his property non-disposable in whole or in part. The defendant shall react promptly, in any event within 45 days. No extension may be granted on account of distance.

3.   If the court rejects the application for a review referred to in paragraph 1 on the basis that none of the grounds for a review set out in that paragraph apply, the decision shall remain in force.

If the court decides that a review is justified for one of the reasons laid down in paragraph 1, the decision shall be null and void. However, the creditor shall not lose the benefits of the interruption of prescription or limitation periods, or the right to claim retroactive maintenance acquired in the initial proceedings.

Article 20. Documents for the purposes of enforcement.   1.   For the purposes of enforcement of a decision in another Member State, the claimant shall provide the competent enforcement authorities with:

(a)   a copy of the decision which satisfies the conditions necessary to establish its authenticity;

(b)   the extract from the decision issued by the court of origin using the form set out in Annex I;

(c)   where appropriate, a document showing the amount of any arrears and the date such amount was calculated;

(d)   where necessary, a transliteration or a translation of the content of the form referred to in point (b) into the official language of the Member State of enforcement or, where there are several official languages in that Member State, into the official language or one of the official languages of court proceedings of the place where the application is made, in accordance with the law of that Member State, or into another language that the Member State concerned has indicated it can accept. Each Member State may indicate the official language or languages of the institutions of the European Union other than its own which it can accept for the completion of the form.

2.   The competent authorities of the Member State of enforcement may not require the claimant to provide a translation of the decision. However, a translation may be required if the enforcement of the decision is challenged.

3.   Any translation under this Article must be done by a person qualified to do translations in one of the Member States.

Article 21. Refusal or suspension of enforcement. 1. The grounds of refusal or suspension of enforcement under the law of the Member State of enforcement shall apply in so far as they are not incompatible with the application of paragraphs 2 and 3.

2. The competent authority in the Member State of enforcement shall, on application by the debtor, refuse, either wholly or in part, the enforcement of the decision of the court of origin if the right to enforce the decision of the court of origin is extinguished by the effect of prescription or the limitation of action, either under the law of the Member State of origin or under the law of the Member State of enforcement, whichever provides for the longer limitation period.

Furthermore, the competent authority in the Member State of enforcement may, on application by the debtor, refuse, either wholly or in part, the enforcement of the decision of the court of origin if it is irreconcilable with a decision given in the Member State of enforcement or with a decision given in another Member State or in a third State which fulfils the conditions necessary for its recognition in the Member State of enforcement.

A decision which has the effect of modifying an earlier decision on maintenance on the basis of changed circumstances shall not be considered an irreconcilable decision within the meaning of the second subparagraph.

3. The competent authority in the Member State of enforcement may, on application by the debtor, suspend, either wholly or in part, the enforcement of the decision of the court of origin if the competent court of the Member State of origin has been seised of an application for a review of the decision of the court of origin pursuant to Article 19.

Furthermore, the competent authority of the Member State of enforcement shall, on application by the debtor, suspend the enforcement of the decision of the court of origin where the enforceability of that decision is suspended in the Member State of origin.

Article 22. No effect on the existence of family relationships. The recognition and enforcement of a decision on maintenance under this Regulation shall not in any way imply the recognition of the family relationship, parentage, marriage or affinity underlying the maintenance obligation which gave rise to the decision.

Section 2 — Decisions given in a Member State not bound by the 2007 Hague Protocol

Article 23. Recognition. 1. A decision given in a Member State not bound by the 2007 Hague Protocol shall be recognised in the other Member States without any special procedure being required.

2. Any interested party who raises the recognition of a decision as the principal issue in a dispute may, in accordance with the procedures provided for in this Section, apply for a decision that the decision be recognised.

3. If the outcome of proceedings in a court of a Member State depends on the determination of an incidental question of recognition, that court shall have jurisdiction over that question.

Article 24. Grounds of refusal of recognition. A decision shall not be recognised:

(a) if such recognition is manifestly contrary to public policy in the Member State in which recognition is sought. The test of public policy may not be applied to the rules relating to jurisdiction;

(b)   where it was given in default of appearance, if the defendant was not served with the document which instituted the proceedings or with an equivalent document in sufficient time and in such a way as to enable him to arrange for his defence, unless the defendant failed to commence proceedings to challenge the decision when it was possible for him to do so;

(c)   if it is irreconcilable with a decision given in a dispute between the same parties in the Member State in which recognition is sought;

(d)   if it is irreconcilable with an earlier decision given in another Member State or in a third State in a dispute involving the same cause of action and between the same parties, provided that the earlier decision fulfils the conditions necessary for its recognition in the Member State in which recognition is sought.

A decision which has the effect of modifying an earlier decision on maintenance on the basis of changed circumstances shall not be considered an irreconcilable decision within the meaning of points (c) or (d).

Article 25. Staying of recognition proceedings.   A court of a Member State in which recognition is sought of a decision given in a Member State not bound by the 2007 Hague Protocol shall stay the proceedings if the enforceability of the decision is suspended in the Member State of origin by reason of an appeal.

Article 26. Enforceability.   A decision given in a Member State not bound by the 2007 Hague Protocol and enforceable in that State shall be enforceable in another Member State when, on the application of any interested party, it has been declared enforceable there.

Article 27. Jurisdiction of local courts.   1.   The application for a declaration of enforceability shall be submitted to the court or competent authority of the Member State of enforcement notified by that Member State to the Commission in accordance with Article 71.

2.   The local jurisdiction shall be determined by reference to the place of habitual residence of the party against whom enforcement is sought, or to the place of enforcement.

Article 28. Procedure.   1.   The application for a declaration of enforceability shall be accompanied by the following documents:

(a)   a copy of the decision which satisfies the conditions necessary to establish its authenticity;

(b)   an extract from the decision issued by the court of origin using the form set out in Annex II, without prejudice to Article 29;

(c)   where necessary, a transliteration or a translation of the content of the form referred to in point (b) into the official language of the Member State of enforcement or, where there are several official languages in that Member State, into the official language or one of the official languages of court proceedings of the place where the application is made, in accordance with the law of that Member State, or into another language that the Member State concerned has indicated it can accept. Each Member State may indicate the official language or languages of the institutions of the European Union other than its own which it can accept for the completion of the form.

2.   The court or competent authority seised of the application may not require the claimant to provide a translation of the decision. However, a translation may be required in connection with an appeal under Articles 32 or 33.

3.   Any translation under this Article must be done by a person qualified to do translations in one of the Member States.

Article 29. Non-production of the extract.   1.   If the extract referred to in Article 28(1)(b) is not produced, the competent court or authority may specify a time for its production or accept an equivalent document or, if it considers that it has sufficient information before it, dispense with its production.

2.   In the situation referred to in paragraph 1, if the competent court or authority so requires, a translation of the documents shall be produced. The translation shall be done by a person qualified to do translations in one of the Member States.

Article 30. Declaration of enforceability.   The decision shall be declared enforceable without any review under Article 24 immediately on completion of the formalities in Article 28 and at the latest within 30 days of the completion of those formalities, except where exceptional circumstances make this impossible. The party against whom enforcement is sought shall not at this stage of the proceedings be entitled to make any submissions on the application.

Article 31. Notice of the decision on the application for a declaration.   1.   The decision on the application for a declaration of enforceability shall forthwith be brought to the notice of the applicant in accordance with the procedure laid down by the law of the Member State of enforcement.

2.   The declaration of enforceability shall be served on the party against whom enforcement is sought, accompanied by the decision, if not already served on that party.

Article 32. Appeal against the decision on the application for a declaration.   1.   The decision on the application for a declaration of enforceability may be appealed against by either party.

2.   The appeal shall be lodged with the court notified by the Member State concerned to the Commission in accordance with Article 71.

3.   The appeal shall be dealt with in accordance with the rules governing procedure in contradictory matters.

4.   If the party against whom enforcement is sought fails to appear before the appellate court in proceedings concerning an appeal brought by the applicant, Article 11 shall apply even where the party against whom enforcement is sought is not habitually resident in any of the Member States.

5.   An appeal against the declaration of enforceability shall be lodged within 30 days of service thereof. If the party against whom enforcement is sought has his habitual residence in a Member State other than that in which the declaration of enforceability was given, the time for appealing shall be 45 days and shall run from the date of service, either on him in person or at his residence. No extension may be granted on account of distance.

Article 33. Proceedings to contest the decision given on appeal.   The decision given on appeal may be contested only by the procedure notified by the Member State concerned to the Commission in accordance with Article 71.

Article 34. Refusal or revocation of a declaration of enforceability.   1.   The court with which an appeal is lodged under Articles 32 or 33 shall refuse or revoke a declaration of enforceability only on one of the grounds specified in Article 24.

2.   Subject to Article 32(4), the court seised of an appeal under Article 32 shall give its decision within 90 days from the date it was seised, except where exceptional circumstances make this impossible.

3.   The court seised of an appeal under Article 33 shall give its decision without delay.

Article 35. Staying of proceedings.   The court with which an appeal is lodged under Articles 32 or 33 shall, on the application of the party against whom enforcement is sought, stay the proceedings if the enforceability of the decision is suspended in the Member State of origin by reason of an appeal.

Article 36. Provisional, including protective measures.   1.   When a decision must be recognised in accordance with this Section, nothing shall prevent the applicant from availing himself of provisional, including protective, measures in accordance with the law of the Member State of enforcement without a declaration of enforceability under Article 30 being required.

2.   The declaration of enforceability shall carry with it by operation of law the power to proceed to any protective measures.

3.   During the time specified for an appeal pursuant to Article 32(5) against the declaration of enforceability and until any such appeal has been determined, no measures of enforcement may be taken other than protective measures against the property of the party against whom enforcement is sought.

Article 37. Partial enforceability.   1.   Where a decision has been given in respect of several matters and the declaration of enforceability cannot be given for all of them, the competent court or authority shall give it for one or more of them.

2.   An applicant may request a declaration of enforceability limited to parts of a decision.

Article 38. No charge, duty or fee.   In proceedings for the issue of a declaration of enforceability, no charge, duty or fee calculated by reference to the value of the matter at issue may be levied in the Member State of enforcement.

Section 3 — Common provisions

Article 39. Provisional enforceability.   The court of origin may declare the decision provisionally enforceable, notwithstanding any appeal, even if national law does not provide for enforceability by operation of law.

Article 40. Invoking a recognised decision. 1. A party who wishes to invoke in another Member State a decision recognised within the meaning of Article 17(1) or recognised pursuant to Section 2 shall produce a copy of the decision which satisfies the conditions necessary to establish its authenticity.

2. If necessary, the court before which the recognised decision is invoked may ask the party invoking the recognised decision to produce an extract issued by the court of origin using the form set out in Annex I or in Annex II, as the case may be.

The court of origin shall also issue such an extract at the request of any interested party.

3. Where necessary, the party invoking the recognised decision shall provide a transliteration or a translation of the content of the form referred to in paragraph 2 into the official language of the Member State concerned or, where there are several official languages in that Member State, into the official language or one of the official languages of court proceedings of the place where the recognised decision is invoked, in accordance with the law of that Member State, or into another language that the Member State concerned has indicated it can accept. Each Member State may indicate the official language or languages of the institutions of the European Union other than its own which it can accept for the completion of the form.

4. Any translation under this Article must be done by a person qualified to do translations in one of the Member States.

Article 41. Proceedings and conditions for enforcement. 1. Subject to the provisions of this Regulation, the procedure for the enforcement of decisions given in another Member State shall be governed by the law of the Member State of enforcement. A decision given in a Member State which is enforceable in the Member State of enforcement shall be enforced there under the same conditions as a decision given in that Member State of enforcement.

2. The party seeking the enforcement of a decision given in another Member State shall not be required to have a postal address or an authorised representative in the Member State of enforcement, without prejudice to persons with competence in matters relating to enforcement proceedings.

Article 42. No review as to substance. Under no circumstances may a decision given in a Member State be reviewed as to its substance in the Member State in which recognition, enforceability or enforcement is sought.

Article 43. No precedence for the recovery of costs. Recovery of any costs incurred in the application of this Regulation shall not take precedence over the recovery of maintenance.

Chapter V — Access to justice

Article 44. Right to legal aid. 1. Parties who are involved in a dispute covered by this Regulation shall have effective access to justice in another Member State, including enforcement and appeal or review procedures, in accordance with the conditions laid down in this Chapter.

In cases covered by Chapter VII, effective access to justice shall be provided by the requested Member State to any applicant who is resident in the requesting Member State.

2.   To ensure such effective access, Member States shall provide legal aid in accordance with this Chapter, unless paragraph 3 applies.

3.   In cases covered by Chapter VII, a Member State shall not be obliged to provide legal aid if and to the extent that the procedures of that Member State enable the parties to make the case without the need for legal aid, and the Central Authority provides such services as are necessary free of charge.

4.   Entitlements to legal aid shall not be less than those available in equivalent domestic cases.

5.   No security, bond or deposit, however described, shall be required to guarantee the payment of costs and expenses in proceedings concerning maintenance obligations.

Article 45. Content of legal aid.   Legal aid granted under this Chapter shall mean the assistance necessary to enable parties to know and assert their rights and to ensure that their applications, lodged through the Central Authorities or directly with the competent authorities, are fully and effectively dealt with. It shall cover as necessary the following:

(a)   pre-litigation advice with a view to reaching a settlement prior to bringing judicial proceedings;

(b)   legal assistance in bringing a case before an authority or a court and representation in court;

(c)   exemption from or assistance with the costs of proceedings and the fees to persons mandated to perform acts during the proceedings;

(d)   in Member States in which an unsuccessful party is liable for the costs of the opposing party, if the recipient of legal aid loses the case, the costs incurred by the opposing party, if such costs would have been covered had the recipient been habitually resident in the Member State of the court seised;

(e)   interpretation;

(f)   translation of the documents required by the court or by the competent authority and presented by the recipient of legal aid which are necessary for the resolution of the case;

(g)   travel costs to be borne by the recipient of legal aid where the physical presence of the persons concerned with the presentation of the recipient's case is required in court by the law or by the court of the Member State concerned and the court decides that the persons concerned cannot be heard to the satisfaction of the court by any other means.

Article 46. Free legal aid for applications through Central Authorities concerning maintenance to children.   1.   The requested Member State shall provide free legal aid in respect of all applications by a creditor under Article 56 concerning maintenance obligations arising from a parent–child relationship towards a person under the age of 21.

2.   Notwithstanding paragraph 1, the competent authority of the requested Member State may, in relation to applications other than those under Articles 56(1)(a) and (b), refuse free legal aid if it considers that, on the merits, the application or any appeal or review is manifestly unfounded.

Article 47. Cases not covered by Article 46.   1.   Subject to Articles 44 and 45, in cases not covered by Article 46, legal aid may be granted in accordance with national law, particularly as regards the conditions for the means test or the merits test.

2.   Notwithstanding paragraph 1, a party who, in the Member State of origin, has benefited from complete or partial legal aid or exemption from costs or expenses, shall be entitled, in any proceedings for recognition, enforceability or enforcement, to benefit from the most favourable legal aid or the most extensive exemption from costs or expenses provided for by the law of the Member State of enforcement.

3.   Notwithstanding paragraph 1, a party who, in the Member State of origin, has benefited from free proceedings before an administrative authority listed in Annex X, shall be entitled, in any proceedings for recognition, enforceability or enforcement, to benefit from legal aid in accordance with paragraph 2. To that end, he shall present a statement from the competent authority in the Member State of origin to the effect that he fulfils the financial requirements to qualify for the grant of complete or partial legal aid or exemption from costs or expenses.

Competent authorities for the purposes of this paragraph shall be listed in Annex XI. That Annex shall be established and amended in accordance with the management procedure referred to in Article 73(2).

Chapter VI — Court settlements and authentic instruments

Article 48. Application of this Regulation to court settlements and authentic instruments.   1.   Court settlements and authentic instruments which are enforceable in the Member State of origin shall be recognised in another Member State and be enforceable there in the same way as decisions, in accordance with Chapter IV.

2.   The provisions of this Regulation shall apply as necessary to court settlements and authentic instruments.

3.   The competent authority of the Member State of origin shall issue, at the request of any interested party, an extract from the court settlement or the authentic instrument using the forms set out in Annexes I and II or in Annexes III and IV as the case may be.

Chapter VII — Co-operation between Central Authorities

Article 49. Designation of Central Authorities.   1.   Each Member State shall designate a Central Authority to discharge the duties which are imposed by this Regulation on such an authority.

2.   Federal Member States, Member States with more than one system of law or Member States having autonomous territorial units shall be free to appoint more than one Central Authority and shall specify the territorial or personal extent of their functions. Where a Member State has appointed more than one Central Authority, it shall designate the Central Authority to which any communication may be addressed for transmission to the appropriate Central Authority within that Member State. If a communication is sent to a Central Authority which is not competent, the latter shall be responsible for forwarding it to the competent Central Authority and for informing the sender accordingly.

3.   The designation of the Central Authority or Central Authorities, their contact details, and where appropriate the extent of their functions as specified in paragraph 2, shall be communicated by each Member State to the Commission in accordance with Article 71.

Article 50. General functions of Central Authorities.   1.   Central Authorities shall:

(a)   cooperate with each other, including by exchanging information, and promote co-operation amongst the competent authorities in their Member States to achieve the purposes of this Regulation;

(b)   seek as far as possible solutions to difficulties which arise in the application of this Regulation.

2.   Central Authorities shall take measures to facilitate the application of this Regulation and to strengthen their co-operation. For this purpose the European Judicial Network in civil and commercial matters established by Decision 2001/470/EC shall be used.

Article 51. Specific functions of Central Authorities.   1.   Central Authorities shall provide assistance in relation to applications under Article 56 and shall in particular:

(a)   transmit and receive such applications;

(b)   initiate or facilitate the institution of proceedings in respect of such applications.

2.   In relation to such applications Central Authorities shall take all appropriate measures:

(a)   where the circumstances require, to provide or facilitate the provision of legal aid;

(b)   to help locate the debtor or the creditor, in particular pursuant to Articles 61, 62 and 63;

(c)   to help obtain relevant information concerning the income and, if necessary, other financial circumstances of the debtor or creditor, including the location of assets, in particular pursuant to Articles 61, 62 and 63;

(d)   to encourage amicable solutions with a view to obtaining voluntary payment of maintenance, where suitable by use of mediation, conciliation or similar processes;

(e)   to facilitate the ongoing enforcement of maintenance decisions, including any arrears;

(f)   to facilitate the collection and expeditious transfer of maintenance payments;

(g)   to facilitate the obtaining of documentary or other evidence, without prejudice to Regulation (EC) No 1206/2001;

(h)   to provide assistance in establishing parentage where necessary for the recovery of maintenance;

(i)   to initiate or facilitate the institution of proceedings to obtain any necessary provisional measures which are territorial in nature and the purpose of which is to secure the outcome of a pending maintenance application;

(j)   to facilitate the service of documents, without prejudice to Regulation (EC) No 1393/2007.

3.   The functions of the Central Authority under this Article may, to the extent permitted under the law of the Member State concerned, be performed by public bodies, or other bodies subject to the supervision of the competent authorities of that Member State. The designation of any such public bodies or other bodies, as well as their contact details and the extent of their functions, shall be communicated by each Member State to the Commission in accordance with Article Article 71.

4.   Nothing in this Article or in Article 53 shall impose an obligation on a Central Authority to exercise powers that can be exercised only by judicial authorities under the law of the requested Member State.

Article 52. Power of attorney.   The Central Authority of the requested Member State may require a power of attorney from the applicant only if it acts on his behalf in judicial proceedings or before other authorities, or in order to designate a representative so to act.

Article 53. Requests for specific measures.   1.   A Central Authority may make a request, supported by reasons, to another Central Authority to take appropriate specific measures under points (b), (c), (g), (h), (i) and (j) of Article 51(2) when no application under Article 56 is pending. The requested Central Authority shall take such measures as are appropriate if satisfied that they are necessary to assist a potential applicant in making an application under Article 56 or in determining whether such an application should be initiated.

2.   Where a request for measures under Article 51(2)(b) and (c) is made, the requested Central Authority shall seek the information requested, if necessary pursuant to Article 61. However, the information referred to in points (b), (c) and (d) of Article 61(2) may be sought only when the creditor produces a copy of the decision, court settlement or authentic instrument to be enforced, accompanied by the extract provided for in Articles 20, 28 or 48, as appropriate.

The requested Central Authority shall communicate the information obtained to the requesting Central Authority. Where that information was obtained pursuant to Article 61, this communication shall specify only the address of the potential defendant in the requested Member State. In the case of a request with a view to recognition, declaration of enforceability or enforcement, the communication shall, in addition, specify merely whether the debtor has income or assets in that State.

If the requested Central Authority is not able to provide the information requested it shall inform the requesting Central Authority without delay and specify the grounds for this impossibility.

3.   A Central Authority may also take specific measures at the request of another Central Authority in relation to a case having an international element concerning the recovery of maintenance pending in the requesting Member State.

4.   For requests under this Article, the Central Authorities shall use the form set out in Annex V.

Article 54. Central Authority costs.   1.   Each Central Authority shall bear its own costs in applying this Regulation.

2.   Central Authorities may not impose any charge on an applicant for the provision of their services under this Regulation save for exceptional costs arising from a request for a specific measure under Article 53.

For the purposes of this paragraph, costs relating to locating the debtor shall not be regarded as exceptional.

3.   The requested Central Authority may not recover the costs of the services referred to in paragraph 2 without the prior consent of the applicant to the provision of those services at such cost.

Article 55. Application through Central Authorities.   An application under this Chapter shall be made through the Central Authority of the Member State in which the applicant resides to the Central Authority of the requested Member State.

Article 56. Available applications.   1.   A creditor seeking to recover maintenance under this Regulation may make applications for the following:

(a)   recognition or recognition and declaration of enforceability of a decision;

(b)   enforcement of a decision given or recognised in the requested Member State;

(c)   establishment of a decision in the requested Member State where there is no existing decision, including where necessary the establishment of parentage;

(d)   establishment of a decision in the requested Member State where the recognition and declaration of enforceability of a decision given in a State other than the requested Member State is not possible;

(e)   modification of a decision given in the requested Member State;

(f)   modification of a decision given in a State other than the requested Member State.

2.   A debtor against whom there is an existing maintenance decision may make applications for the following:

(a)   recognition of a decision leading to the suspension, or limiting the enforcement, of a previous decision in the requested Member State;

(b)   modification of a decision given in the requested Member State;

(c)   modification of a decision given in a State other than the requested Member State.

3.   For applications under this Article, the assistance and representation referred to in Article 45(b) shall be provided by the Central Authority of the requested Member State directly or through public authorities or other bodies or persons.

4.   Save as otherwise provided in this Regulation, the applications referred to in paragraphs 1 and 2 shall be determined under the law of the requested Member State and shall be subject to the rules of jurisdiction applicable in that Member State.

Article 57. Application contents.   1.   An application under Article 56 shall be made using the form set out in Annex VI or in Annex VII.

2.   An application under Article 56 shall as a minimum include:

(a)   a statement of the nature of the application or applications;

(b)   the name and contact details, including the address, and date of birth of the applicant;

(c)   the name and, if known, address and date of birth of the defendant;

(d)   the name and the date of birth of any person for whom maintenance is sought;

(e)   the grounds upon which the application is based;

(f)   in an application by a creditor, information concerning where the maintenance payment should be sent or electronically transmitted;

(g)   the name and contact details of the person or unit from the Central Authority of the requesting Member State responsible for processing the application.

3.   For the purposes of paragraph 2(b), the applicant's personal address may be replaced by another address in cases of family violence, if the national law of the requested Member State does not require the applicant to supply his or her personal address for the purposes of proceedings to be brought.

4.   As appropriate, and to the extent known, the application shall in addition in particular include:

(a)   the financial circumstances of the creditor;

(b)   the financial circumstances of the debtor, including the name and address of the employer of the debtor and the nature and location of the assets of the debtor;

(c)   any other information that may assist with the location of the defendant.

5.   The application shall be accompanied by any necessary supporting information or documentation including, where appropriate, documentation concerning the entitlement of the applicant to legal aid. Applications under Article 56(1)(a) and (b) and under Article 56(2)(a) shall be accompanied, as appropriate, only by the documents listed in Articles 20, 28 and 48, or in Article 25 of the 2007 Hague Convention.

Article 58. Transmission, receipt and processing of applications and cases through Central Authorities.   1.   The Central Authority of the requesting Member State shall assist the applicant in ensuring that the application is accompanied by all the information and documents known by it to be necessary for consideration of the application.

2.   The Central Authority of the requesting Member State shall, when satisfied that the application complies with the requirements of this Regulation, transmit the application to the Central Authority of the requested Member State.

3.   The requested Central Authority shall, within 30 days from the date of receipt of the application, acknowledge receipt using the form set out in Annex VIII, and inform the Central Authority of the requesting Member State what initial steps have been or will be taken to deal with the application, and may request any further necessary documents and information. Within the same 30-day period, the requested Central Authority shall provide to the requesting Central Authority the name and contact details of the person or unit responsible for responding to inquiries regarding the progress of the application.

4.   Within 60 days from the date of acknowledgement, the requested Central Authority shall inform the requesting Central Authority of the status of the application.

5.   Requesting and requested Central Authorities shall keep each other informed of:

(a)   the person or unit responsible for a particular case;

(b)   the progress of the case;

and shall provide timely responses to enquiries.

6.   Central Authorities shall process a case as quickly as a proper consideration of the issues will allow.

7.   Central Authorities shall employ the most rapid and efficient means of communication at their disposal.

8.   A requested Central Authority may refuse to process an application only if it is manifest that the requirements of this Regulation are not fulfilled. In such a case, that Central Authority shall promptly inform the requesting Central Authority of its reasons for refusal using the form set out in Annex IX.

9.   The requested Central Authority may not reject an application solely on the basis that additional documents or information are needed. However, the requested Central Authority may ask the requesting Central Authority to provide these additional documents or this information. If the requesting Central Authority does not do so within 90 days or a longer period specified by the requested Central Authority, the requested Central Authority may decide that it will no longer process the application. In this case, it shall promptly notify the requesting Central Authority using the form set out in Annex IX.

Article 59. Languages. 1. The request or application form shall be completed in the official language of the requested Member State or, if there are several official languages in that Member State, in the official language or one of the official languages of the place of the Central Authority concerned, or in any other official language of the institutions of the European Union which that Member State has indicated it can accept, unless the Central Authority of that Member State dispenses with translation.

2. The documents accompanying the request or application form shall not be translated into the language determined in accordance with paragraph 1 unless a translation is necessary in order to provide the assistance requested, without prejudice to Articles 20, 28, 40 and 66.

3. Any other communication between Central Authorities shall be in the language determined in accordance with paragraph 1 unless the Central Authorities agree otherwise.

Article 60. Meetings. 1. In order to facilitate the application of this Regulation, Central Authorities shall meet regularly.

2. These meetings shall be convened in compliance with Decision 2001/470/EC.

Article 61. Access to information for Central Authorities. 1. Under the conditions laid down in this Chapter and by way of exception to Article 51(4), the requested Central Authority shall use all appropriate and reasonable means to obtain the information referred to in paragraph 2 necessary to facilitate, in a given case, the establishment, the modification, the recognition, the declaration of enforceability or the enforcement of a decision.

The public authorities or administrations which, in the course of their ordinary activities, hold, within the requested State, the information referred to in paragraph 2 and which control the processing thereof within the meaning of Directive 95/46/EC shall, subject to limitations justified on grounds of national security or public safety, provide the information to the requested Central Authority at its request in cases where the requested Central Authority does not have direct access to it.

Member States may designate the public authorities or administrations able to provide the requested Central Authority with the information referred to in paragraph 2. Where a Member State makes such a designation, it shall ensure that its choice of authorities and administrations permits its Central Authority to have access, in accordance with this Article, to the information requested.

Any other legal person which holds within the requested Member State the information referred to in paragraph 2 and controls the processing thereof within the meaning of Directive 95/46/EC shall provide the information to the requested Central Authority at the latter's request if it is authorised to do so by the law of the requested Member State.

The requested Central Authority shall, as necessary, transmit the information thus obtained to the requesting Central Authority.

2. The information referred to in this Article shall be the information already held by the authorities, administrations or persons referred to in paragraph 1. It shall be adequate, relevant and not excessive and shall relate to:

(a) the address of the debtor or of the creditor;

(b) the debtor's income;

(c) the identification of the debtor's employer and/or of the debtor's bank account(s);

(d) the debtor's assets.

For the purpose of obtaining or modifying a decision, only the information listed in point (a) may be requested by the requested Central Authority.

For the purpose of having a decision recognised, declared enforceable or enforced, all the information listed in the first subparagraph may be requested by the requested Central Authority. However, the information listed in point (d) may be requested only if the information listed in points (b) and (c) is insufficient to allow enforcement of the decision.

Article 62. Transmission and use of information. 1. The Central Authorities shall, within their Member State, transmit the information referred to in Article 61(2) to the competent courts, the competent authorities responsible for service of documents and the competent authorities responsible for enforcement of a decision, as the case may be.

2. Any authority or court to which information has been transmitted pursuant to Article 61 may use this only to facilitate the recovery of maintenance claims.

Except for information merely indicating the existence of an address, income or assets in the requested Member State, the information referred to in Article 61(2) may not be disclosed to the person having applied to the requesting Central Authority, subject to the application of procedural rules before a court.

3. Any authority processing information transmitted to it pursuant to Article 61 may not store such information beyond the period necessary for the purposes for which it was transmitted.

4. Any authority processing information communicated to it pursuant to Article 61 shall ensure the confidentiality of such information, in accordance with its national law.

Article 63. Notification of the data subject. 1. Notification of the data subject of the communication of all or part of the information collected on him shall take place in accordance with the national law of the requested Member State.

2. Where there is a risk that it may prejudice the effective recovery of the maintenance claim, such notification may be deferred for a period which shall not exceed 90 days from the date on which the information was provided to the requested Central Authority.

Chapter VIII — Public bodies

Article 64. Public bodies as applicants. 1. For the purposes of an application for recognition and declaration of enforceability of decisions or for the purposes of enforcement of decisions, the term 'creditor' shall include a public body acting in place of an individual to whom maintenance is owed or one to which reimbursement is owed for benefits provided in place of maintenance.

2. The right of a public body to act in place of an individual to whom maintenance is owed or to seek reimbursement of benefits provided to the creditor in place of maintenance shall be governed by the law to which the body is subject.

3.   A public body may seek recognition and a declaration of enforceability or claim enforcement of:

(a)   a decision given against a debtor on the application of a public body which claims payment of benefits provided in place of maintenance;

(b)   a decision given between a creditor and a debtor to the extent of the benefits provided to the creditor in place of maintenance.

4.   The public body seeking recognition and a declaration of enforceability or claiming enforcement of a decision shall upon request provide any document necessary to establish its right under paragraph 2 and to establish that benefits have been provided to the creditor.

Chapter IX — General and final provisions

Article 65. Legalisation or other similar formality.   No legalisation or other similar formality shall be required in the context of this Regulation.

Article 66. Translation of supporting documents.   Without prejudice to Articles 20, 28 and 40, the court seised may require the parties to provide a translation of supporting documents which are not in the language of proceedings only if it deems a translation necessary in order to give a decision or to respect the rights of the defence.

Article 67. Recovery of costs.   Without prejudice to Article 54, the competent authority of the requested Member State may recover costs from an unsuccessful party having received free legal aid pursuant to Article 46, on an exceptional basis and if his financial circumstances so allow.

Article 68. Relations with other Community instruments.   1.   Subject to Article 75(2), this Regulation shall modify Regulation (EC) No 44/2001 by replacing the provisions of that Regulation applicable to matters relating to maintenance obligations.

2.   This Regulation shall replace, in matters relating to maintenance obligations, Regulation (EC) No 805/2004, except with regard to European Enforcement Orders on maintenance obligations issued in a Member State not bound by the 2007 Hague Protocol.

3.   In matters relating to maintenance obligations, this Regulation shall be without prejudice to the application of Directive 2003/8/EC, subject to Chapter V.

4.   This Regulation shall be without prejudice to the application of Directive 95/46/EC.

Article 69. Relations with existing international conventions and agreements.   1.   This Regulation shall not affect the application of bilateral or multilateral conventions and agreements to which one or more Member States are party at the time of adoption of this Regulation and which concern matters governed by this Regulation, without prejudice to the obligations of Member States under Article 307 of the Treaty.

2.   Notwithstanding paragraph 1, and without prejudice to paragraph 3, this Regulation shall, in relations between Member States, take precedence over the conventions and agreements which concern matters governed by this Regulation and to which Member States are party.

3.   This Regulation shall not preclude the application of the Convention of 23 March 1962 between Sweden, Denmark, Finland, Iceland and Norway on the recovery of maintenance by the Member States which are party thereto, since, with regard to the recognition, enforceability and enforcement of decisions, that Convention provides for:

(a)   simplified and more expeditious procedures for the enforcement of decisions relating to maintenance obligations, and

(b)   legal aid which is more favourable than that provided for in Chapter V of this Regulation.

However, the application of the said Convention may not have the effect of depriving the defendant of his protection under Articles 19 and 21 of this Regulation.

Article 70. Information made available to the public.   The Member States shall provide within the framework of the European Judicial Network in civil and commercial matters established by Decision 2001/470/EC the following information with a view to making it available to the public:

(a)   a description of the national laws and procedures concerning maintenance obligations;

(b)   a description of the measures taken to meet the obligations under Article 51;

(c)   a description of how effective access to justice is guaranteed, as required under Article 44, and

(d)   a description of national enforcement rules and procedures, including information on any limitations on enforcement, in particular debtor protection rules and limitation or prescription periods.

Member States shall keep this information permanently updated.

Article 71. Information on contact details and languages (modelled on *Article 25* of Regulation (EC) No 861/2007)   1.   By 18 September 2010, the Member States shall communicate to the Commission:

(a)   the names and contact details of the courts or authorities with competence to deal with applications for a declaration of enforceability in accordance with Article 27(1) and with appeals against decisions on such applications in accordance with Article 32(2);

(b)   the redress procedures referred to in Article 33;

(c)   the review procedure for the purposes of Article 19 and the names and contact details of the courts having jurisdiction;

(d)   the names and contact details of their Central Authorities and, where appropriate, the extent of their functions, in accordance with Article 49(3);

(e)   the names and contact details of the public bodies or other bodies and, where appropriate, the extent of their functions, in accordance with Article 51(3);

(f)   the names and contact details of the authorities with competence in matters of enforcement for the purposes of Article 21;

(g)   the languages accepted for translations of the documents referred to in Articles 20, 28 and 40;

(h)   the languages accepted by their Central Authorities for communication with other Central Authorities referred to in Article 59.

The Member States shall apprise the Commission of any subsequent changes to this information.

2.   The Commission shall publish the information communicated in accordance with paragraph 1 in the Official Journal of the European Union, with the exception of the addresses and other contact details of the courts and authorities referred to in points (a), (c) and (f).

3.   The Commission shall make all information communicated in accordance with paragraph 1 publicly available through any other appropriate means, in particular through the European Judicial Network in civil and commercial matters established by Decision 2001/470/EC.

Article 72. Amendments to the forms.   Any amendment to the forms provided for in this Regulation shall be adopted in accordance with the advisory procedure referred to in Article 73(3).

Article 73. Committee.   1.   The Commission shall be assisted by the committee established by Article 70 of Regulation (EC) No 2201/2003.

2.   Where reference is made to this paragraph, Articles 4 and 7 of Decision 1999/468/EC shall apply.

The period laid down in Article 4(3) of Decision 1999/468/EC shall be set at three months.

3.   Where reference is made to this paragraph, Articles 3 and 7 of Decision 1999/468/EC shall apply.

Article 74. Review clause.   By five years from the date of application determined in the third subparagraph of Article 76 at the latest, the Commission shall submit to the European Parliament, the Council and the European Economic and Social Committee a report on the application of this Regulation, including an evaluation of the practical experiences relating to the co-operation between Central Authorities, in particular regarding those Authorities' access to the information held by public authorities and administrations, and an evaluation of the functioning of the procedure for recognition, declaration of enforceability and enforcement applicable to decisions given in a Member State not bound by the 2007 Hague Protocol. If necessary the report shall be accompanied by proposals for adaptation.

Article 75. Transitional provisions.   1.   This Regulation shall apply only to proceedings instituted, to court settlements approved or concluded, and to authentic instruments established after its date of application, subject to paragraphs 2 and 3.

2.   Sections 2 and 3 of Chapter IV shall apply:

(a)   to decisions given in the Member States before the date of application of this Regulation for which recognition and the declaration of enforceability are requested after that date;

(b)   to decisions given after the date of application of this Regulation following proceedings begun before that date, in so far as those decisions fall with the scope of Regulation (EC) No 44/2001 for the purposes of recognition and enforcement.

Regulation (EC) No 44/2001 shall continue to apply to procedures for recognition and enforcement under way on the date of application of this Regulation.

The first and second subparagraphs shall apply mutatis mutandis to court settlements approved or concluded and to authentic instruments established in the Member States.

3.   Chapter VII on co-operation between Central Authorities shall apply to requests and applications received by the Central Authority as from the date of application of this Regulation.

Article 76. Entry into force.   This Regulation shall enter into force on the 20th day following its publication in the Official Journal of the European Union.
Articles 2(2), 47(3), 71, 72 and 73 shall apply from 18 September 2010.
Except for the provisions referred to in the second paragraph, this Regulation shall apply from 18 June 2011, subject to the 2007 Hague Protocol being applicable in the Community by that date. Failing that, this Regulation shall apply from the date of application of that Protocol in the Community.

A.2.   Council Decision 2006/325/EC of 27 April 2006 concerning the conclusion of the Agreement of 19 October 2005 between the European Community and the Kingdom of Denmark on jurisdiction and the recognition and enforcement of judgments in civil and commercial matters (OJ, L 120 of 5 May 2006): Articles 3–4

See Chapter IV, General provisions, A.3.

A.3.   Agreement between the European Community and the Kingdom of Denmark on jurisdiction and the recognition and enforcement of judgments in civil and commercial matters (OJ, L 149 of 12 June 2009)

See Chapter IV, General provisions, A.5.

B.   Regulation (EC) No 864/2007 of the European Parliament and of the Council of 11 July 2007 on the law applicable to non-contractual obligations (Rome II) (OJ, L 199 of 31 July 2007): Recital 10, Article 1(2)(a) and (b)

See Chapter VII, A.1.

C.   Directive 2008/52/EC of the European Parliament and of the Council of 21 May 2008 on certain aspects of mediation in civil and commercial matters: Recitals 10, 21, Article 1(2)

See Chapter IV, General provisions, L.

D.   Commission Decision on general implementing provisions concerning persons to be treated as dependent children (Article 2(4) of Annex VII to the Staff Regulations) (C (2004) 1364 fin. of 15 April 2004)

Section 1 — General

Article 1.   The purpose of these general provisions is to specify the conditions under which a person may be treated as a dependent child pursuant to Article 2(4) of Annex VII to the Staff Regulations.

Treatment as a dependent child may be authorised by the appointing authority provided all the conditions set out below are satisfied.

Section 2 — Legal responsibility for maintenance

Article 2.   Legal responsibility for maintenance means the obligation between relatives by blood or marriage expressly laid down by law, to the exclusion of any obligation of a contractual, moral or compensatory nature. Officials' financial obligations towards their spouse or former spouse are not covered by Article 2(4) of Annex VII to the Staff Regulations.

Article 3.   1.   Where there exist factors connecting the case with more than one law, the applicable law shall be determined in accordance with the rules concerning conflicts of laws applicable by the court having jurisdiction.

2.   The court having jurisdiction shall be determined in accordance with the rules concerning the choice of court including, where appropriate, those laid down by the relevant international agreements, notably the amended Brussels Convention of 27 September 1968 on Jurisdiction and the Enforcement of Judgments in Civil and Commercial Matters. For the purpose of the provision set out in paragraph 1, officials shall be assumed to be resident at their place of employment, in the absence of evidence to the contrary.

Article 4.   It shall be for the official to establish, on the basis of supporting documents, the existence of legal responsibility for maintenance, the expenditure stemming from it and the amount of the financial contribution actually made. Treatment as a dependent child may be authorised only if the expenditure stemming from the legal responsibility for maintenance is at least equal to the amount resulting from such authorisation.

The appropriate departments shall provide the official with any guidance needed on this Section, particularly with regard to the nature of the supporting documents required.

E.   ECJ case-law

In *Meinhardt* (17 May 1972, case 24/71, Reports, 269) the ECJ dealt with a claim brought by the ex-wife of an officer of the Community for the annulment of the decision by the Director-General for personnel of the Commission refusing to award to the applicant a share in the survivor's pension which, under the Staff Regulations of Officials, is payable to the divorced wife of a deceased official provided that the decree of divorce found that the official was solely to blame for it and as a result was obliged to pay for maintenance of his ex-spouse. The Commission claimed that the maintenance had to be awarded and its amount fixed by divorce decree. On the contrary, the ECJ stated that:

6.   The existence and extent of the obligation on the part of the official to pay maintenance to his divorced wife must in principle be determined in accordance with the law which governs the consequences of divorce. In many States, and in certain Member States in particular, the maintenance payable by a spouse as a result of divorce need not, and even in certain cases cannot, be fixed by the decree of divorce or by a subsequent judicial decision, but may, inter alia, be established by an agreement between the parties. To require proof of the existence and extent of the obligation to pay maintenance by a judicial decision, when the law governing the consequences of the divorce does not recognise or, at all events, does not require recourse to such a decision, would in certain cases frustrate the exercise of a right to a survivor's pension which the Staff Regulations confers on the divorced wife whose husband is found solely to blame for the divorce. This could not have been the intention of the authors of the Staff Regulations. Therefore, the final sentence of the first paragraph of Article 28 cannot be interpreted as excluding other means of proving the obligation to pay maintenance which are required or accepted by the law governing the consequences of divorce. The purpose of Article 28 is therefore to establish a reliable point of reference based on the internal law applicable to the parties concerned.

7.   Therefore, by refusing to award the applicant the share in the pension provided for in Article 28 of Annex VIII, without having considered whether the law governing the consequences of the divorce requires a judicial decision as proof of the right to maintenance, the defendant has infringed that article.

Maintenance obligations has been the object of other two subsequent judgments of the CFI, *Díaz García* (18 December 1992, case T-43/90, Reports, II-2619) and *Khouri* (18 December 1992, case T-85/91, Reports, II-2637). In both decisions the CFI interpreted the notion of 'legal responsibility to maintain' of family members other than a dependent child and the spouse (i.e. respectively, the *more* uxorio partner's children in *Díaz García* and the nephew in *Khouri*), excluding that the officer was required by the law to maintain them, pursuant to Article 2(4) of Annex VII of the Staff Regulations. In the *Khouri* case, in particular, the Belgian judge had stated that, although there is no legal obligation to maintain collateral relatives under national law, maintenance as between collateral relations can be regarded as a moral obligation which may become a civil obligation. The CFI stated that

31.   ... the concept of a 'legal responsibility to maintain', used in the Staff Regulations, is derived from the legal systems of the Member States, which, under their laws, impose a mutual obligation to provide maintenance on relatives by blood and/or marriage of a greater or lesser degree of proximity. By employing the concept of a legal responsibility to maintain in Article 2(4) of Annex VII, the Staff Regulations are referring exclusively to an obligation of maintenance imposed on an official by a source of law independent of the will of the parties. Maintenance obligations of a contractual, moral or compensatory nature are therefore excluded. It follows that the Commission properly applied that concept when it defined, in Article 3 of its General Implementing Provisions, legal responsibility for maintenance as 'the obligation between relatives by blood or marriage expressly laid down by the law, to the exclusion of any obligation of a contractual, moral or compensatory nature'.

32.   As the Court of Justice has consistently held ... the terms of a provision of Community law which makes no express reference to the law of the Member States for the purpose of determining its meaning and scope must normally be given an independent interpretation which must take into account the context of the provision and the purpose of the relevant regulations. The Court of First Instance considers, however, that, in the absence of an express reference, the application of Community law may sometimes necessitate reference to the laws of the Member States where the Community court cannot identify in Community law or in the general principles of Community law criteria enabling it to define the meaning and scope of such a provision by way of independent interpretation.

33.   Neither Community law nor the Staff Regulations provide the Community court with any guide as to how it should define, by way of independent interpretation, the meaning and scope of the concept of a legal responsibility to maintain, whose existence entitles an official to receive a dependent child allowance under Article 2(4) of Annex VII to the Staff Regulations. Therefore, it is necessary to determine the national legal system to which the applicant is subject and to ascertain whether that system imposes on her a legal responsibility to maintain, within the meaning of the Staff Regulations, in relation to her nephew.

In the specific case, the applicant had both Belgian and Lebanese citizenship and her nephew, who was resident in Belgium, had both Dutch and Lebanese citizenship.

35.   In those circumstances, the Court considers that it is necessary to identify the legal system relevant to the present case in the light of the conflict-of-law rules applicable by the court having jurisdiction. Article 4(1) of the General Implementing Provisions provides that: 'Where there exist factors connecting the case with more than one law, the applicable law shall be determined in accordance with the rules concerning conflicts of laws applicable by the court having jurisdiction including, where appropriate, those laid down by the relevant international agreements, notably the Convention on the Law Applicable to Maintenance Obligations signed in The Hague on 2 October 1973'.

Since the appellant had brought the matter before the Belgian judge,

37.   ...the Court considers that the applicable law must be determined in this case in accordance with the conflict-of-law rules applicable by the Belgian courts.

Even if in Belgian private international law or in the case-law of the Belgian courts any clear and precise conflict rule for determining the law applicable to maintenance relationships between an aunt and her nephew cannot be found,

40.   ...the Court considers that it is entitled to accept that, in this case, the question whether the applicant bears a legal responsibility, within the meaning of the Staff regulations, to maintain her nephew must be decided in accordance with Belgian law, by reason of the applicant's nationality and residence as well as the residence of her nephew.

41.   Under Belgian law, there is, however, no obligation of maintenance between collateral relations within the meaning defined above. At most, Belgian courts recognise the existence as between collateral relations of a natural obligation which may be transformed into a civil obligation. This is confirmed by the actual wording of the judgment of 16 May 1991, which states expressly that 'there is no legal obligation to maintain collateral relations'. It follows that the obligation which the applicant may have to maintain her nephew is not an obligation imposed by a source independent of the will of the parties and consequently cannot be treated as a legal responsibility to maintain within the meaning of the Staff Regulations.

42.   As regards the undertaking to assume financial responsibility for her nephew given to the Belgian authorities by the applicant, the Court finds that, even supposing that it could create an obligation to maintain, such an undertaking likewise cannot be treated as a legal responsibility to maintain within the meaning of the Staff Regulations since it originates from the official' s own will.

In the *M.* judgment (21 April 2004, case T-172/01, Reports, II-1075) the CFI had been asked whether an oral agreement of maintenance between ex-spouses, designed to grant a survivor's pension to the divorced spouse of an ECJ judge, could fall within the provision of the first paragraph of Article 27 of Annex VIII to the Staff Regulations. The CFI has decided that the validity of an agreement providing for payment of maintenance must be determined in accordance with the law applicable to the divorce:

68.   First, it is necessary to identify the law governing the conditions in which an agreement providing for maintenance could, in some circumstances, be validly concluded in oral form by Mr and Mrs M.

69.   The two parties agree that this question must be resolved on the basis of the relevant provisions of Greek civil law.

70.   The Court observes in that regard that the terms of a provision of Community law – such as the first paragraph of Article 27 of Annex VIII to the Staff Regulations, which is applicable in this case on account of the reference to that provision in Article 15(7) of the Emoluments Regulation – which makes no express reference to the law of the Member States for the purpose of determining its meaning and scope must normally be given an independent interpretation, which must take into account the context of the provision and the purpose of the relevant rules (CFI, 18 December 1992, case T-43/90 *Díaz García v Parliament*, Reports, II-2619, paragraph 36).

71.   However, even in the absence of such an express reference, the application of Community law may necessitate a reference to the laws of the Member States where the Community judicature cannot identify in Community law or in the general principles of Community law criteria enabling it to define the meaning and scope of a Community provision by way of independent interpretation (*Díaz García v Parliament*, cited above, paragraph 36).

72.   In this case, the concept of 'maintenance ... as a result of a settlement between herself and her former husband', within the meaning of the first paragraph of Article 27 of Annex VIII to the Staff Regulations, cannot be given an independent Community

interpretation. On the contrary, the concept of a maintenance obligation agreed between former spouses by reason of their divorce is one of the financial consequences arising from the decree of divorce pronounced on the basis of the rules of the applicable civil law.

73.   Consequently, the conditions governing the validity of an agreement providing for payment of maintenance for the divorced spouse of a servant of the Communities or, in this case, a former Member of a Community institution must, in principle, be determined in accordance with the law which governs the consequences of divorce, that is, in this instance, Greek law, pursuant to which the divorce was granted (see, to that effect, judgment of 17 May 1972, case 24/71 *Meinhardt v Commission*, Reports, 269, paragraph 6).

74.   It is common ground that the relevant provisions of the Greek Civil Code allow, in the case of divorce, the establishment of entitlement to maintenance for a former spouse by mere oral agreement between the former spouses.

75.   Mr M. could therefore validly consent to pay maintenance to Mrs M. by oral agreement.

The same law governs the rules on evidence as well:

85.   The principles governing the admissibility of types of evidence for the existence of an oral agreement providing, by reason of the divorce of the former spouses, for maintenance for Mrs M. from the deceased are governed, on the same basis as the conditions of validity of such an agreement, by Greek law (see, to that effect, the judgment in *Meinhardt v Commission*, paragraph 12).

F.   Council Regulation (EC) No 664/2009 of 7 July 2009 establishing a procedure for the negotiation and conclusion of agreements between Member States and third countries concerning jurisdiction, recognition and enforcement of judgments and decisions in matrimonial matters, matters of parental responsibility and matters relating to maintenance obligations, and the law applicable to matters relating to maintenance obligations (OJ, L 200 of 31 July 2009)

See Chapter I, The external dimension, L.

G.1.   Council Decision 2009/941/EC of 30 November 2009 on the conclusion by the European Community of the Hague Protocol of 23 November 2007 on the law applicable to maintenance obligations (OJ, L 331 of 16 December 2009)

(1)   The Community is working towards the establishment of a common judicial area based on the principle of mutual recognition of decisions.

(2)   Council Regulation (EC) No 4/2009 of 18 December 2008 on jurisdiction, applicable law, recognition and enforcement of decisions and co-operation in matters relating to maintenance obligations provides that the law applicable to maintenance

obligations shall be determined in accordance with the Hague Protocol of 23 November 2007 on the law applicable to maintenance obligations (hereinafter referred to as the Protocol) in the Member States bound by that Protocol.

(3)   The Protocol makes a valuable contribution to ensuring greater legal certainty and predictability to maintenance creditors and debtors. Application of uniform rules to determine the applicable law will allow free circulation of decisions on maintenance obligations in the Community, without any form of control in the Member State where enforcement is sought.

(4)   Article 24 of the Protocol allows Regional Economic Integration Organisations such as the Community to sign, accept, approve or accede to the Protocol.

(5)   The Community has exclusive competence over all matters governed by the Protocol. This does not affect the positions of the Member States which are not bound by this Decision or subject to its application as referred to in Recitals 11 and 12.

(6)   The Community should therefore approve the Protocol.

(7)   The Protocol should apply between the Member States at the latest on 18 June 2011, the date of application of Regulation (EC) No 4/2009.

(8)   In view of the close link between the Protocol and Regulation (EC) No 4/2009, the rules of the Protocol should be applied in the Community on a provisional basis if the Protocol has not entered into force on 18 June 2011, the date of application of Regulation (EC) No 4/2009. A unilateral declaration to this effect should be made upon conclusion of the Protocol.

(9)   The rules of the Protocol should determine the law applicable to a maintenance obligation if a decision on that obligation is to be recognised and enforceable under the rules concerning the abolition of exequatur laid down in Regulation (EC) No 4/2009. In order to ensure that the same conflict of laws rules will be applied in the Community to maintenance claims relating to a period prior to as well as posterior to the entry into force or the provisional application of the Protocol in the Community, the rules of the Protocol should also apply to claims relating to a period prior to this event, notwithstanding Article 22 thereof. A unilateral declaration to this effect should be made upon conclusion of the Protocol.

(10)   In accordance with Article 3 of the Protocol on the position of the United Kingdom and Ireland, annexed to the Treaty on European Union and to the Treaty establishing the European Community, Ireland is taking part in the adoption and application of this Decision.

(11)   In accordance with Articles 1 and 2 of the Protocol on the position of the United Kingdom and Ireland, annexed to the Treaty on European Union and to the Treaty establishing the European Community, the United Kingdom is not taking part in the adoption of this Decision and is not bound by it or subject to its application.

(12)   In accordance with Articles 1 and 2 of the Protocol on the position of Denmark, annexed to the Treaty on European Union and to the Treaty establishing the European Community, Denmark is not taking part in the adoption of this Decision and is not bound by it or subject to its application, has decided as follows:

Article 1.   The Hague Protocol of 23 November 2007 on the Law Applicable to Maintenance Obligations is hereby approved on behalf of the European Community.

The text of the Protocol is attached to this Decision.

Article 2.   The President of the Council is hereby authorised to designate the person(s) empowered to sign the Protocol in order to bind the Community.

Article 3.   When concluding the Protocol, the Community shall make the following declaration in accordance with Article 24 thereof:
> 'The European Community declares, in accordance with Article 24 of the Protocol, that it exercises competence over all the matters governed by the Protocol. Its Member States shall be bound by the Protocol by virtue of its conclusion by the European Community.
>
> For the purpose of this declaration, the term "European Community" does not include Denmark, by virtue of Articles 1 and 2 of the Protocol on the position of Denmark, annexed to the Treaty on European Union and to the Treaty establishing the European Community, and the United Kingdom, by virtue of Articles 1 and 2 of the Protocol on the position of the United Kingdom and Ireland, annexed to the Treaty on European Union and to the Treaty establishing the European Community.'

Article 4.   1.   Within the Community, the rules of the Protocol shall apply provisionally, without prejudice to Article 5 of this Decision, from 18 June 2011, the date of application of Regulation (EC) No 4/2009, if the Protocol has not yet entered into force on that date.
     2.   When concluding the Protocol, the Community shall make the following declaration to take into account the possible provisional application referred to in paragraph 1:
> 'The European Community declares that it will apply the rules of the Protocol provisionally from 18 June 2011, the date of application of Council Regulation (EC) No 4/2009 of 18 December 2008 on jurisdiction, applicable law, recognition and enforcement of decisions and co-operation in matters relating to maintenance obligations, if the Protocol has not entered into force on that date in accordance with Article 25(1) thereof.'

Article 5.   1.   Notwithstanding Article 22 of the Protocol, the rules of the Protocol shall also determine the law applicable to maintenance claimed in a Member State relating to a period prior to the entry into force or the provisional application of the Protocol in the Community in situations where, under Regulation (EC) No 4/2009, proceedings are instituted, court settlements are approved or concluded and authentic instruments are established as from 18 June 2011, the date of application of Regulation (EC) No 4/2009.
     2.   When concluding the Protocol, the Community shall make the following declaration:
> 'The European Community declares that it will apply the rules of the Protocol also to maintenance claimed in one of its Member States relating to a period prior to the entry into force or the provisional application of the Protocol in the Community in situations where, under Council Regulation (EC) No 4/2009 of 18 December 2008 on jurisdiction, applicable law, recognition and enforcement of decisions and co-operation in matters relating to maintenance obligations, proceedings are instituted, court settlements are approved or concluded and authentic instruments are established as from 18 June 2011, the date of application of the said Regulation.'

G.2.   Protocol on the law applicable to maintenance obligations (OJ, L 331 of 16 December 2009)[1]

The States signatory to this Protocol,

Desiring to establish common provisions concerning the law applicable to maintenance obligations,

Wishing to modernise the Hague Convention of 24 October 1956 on the law applicable to maintenance obligations towards children and the Hague Convention of 2 October 1973 on the Law Applicable to Maintenance Obligations,

Wishing to develop general rules on applicable law that may supplement the Hague Convention of 23 November 2007 on the International Recovery of Child Support and Other Forms of Family Maintenance,

Have resolved to conclude a Protocol for this purpose and have agreed upon the following provisions

Article 1. Scope.   (1)   This Protocol shall determine the law applicable to maintenance obligations arising from a family relationship, parentage, marriage or affinity, including a maintenance obligation in respect of a child regardless of the marital status of the parents.

(2)   Decisions rendered in application of this Protocol shall be without prejudice to the existence of any of the relationships referred to in paragraph 1.

Article 2. Universal application.   This Protocol applies even if the applicable law is that of a non-Contracting State.

Article 3. General rule on applicable law.   (1)   Maintenance obligations shall be governed by the law of the State of the habitual residence of the creditor, save where this Protocol provides otherwise.

(2)   In the case of a change in the habitual residence of the creditor, the law of the State of the new habitual residence shall apply as from the moment when the change occurs.

Article 4. Special rules favouring certain creditors.   (1)   The following provisions shall apply in the case of maintenance obligations of

a)   parents towards their children;

b)   persons, other than parents, towards persons who have not attained the age of 21 years, except for obligations arising out of the relationships referred to in Article 5; and

c)   children towards their parents.

(2)   If the creditor is unable, by virtue of the law referred to in Article 3, to obtain maintenance from the debtor, the law of the forum shall apply.

(3)   Notwithstanding Article 3, if the creditor has seised the competent authority of the State where the debtor has his habitual residence, the law of the forum shall apply. However, if the creditor is unable, by virtue of this law, to obtain maintenance from the debtor, the law of the State of the habitual residence of the creditor shall apply.

---

[1]   Not yet in force as of 20 December 2010. The EU signed and ratified the Protocol on 8 April 2010. [Note of the Editor]

(4)   If the creditor is unable, by virtue of the laws referred to in Article 3 and paragraphs 2 and 3 of this Article, to obtain maintenance from the debtor, the law of the State of their common nationality, if there is one, shall apply.

Article 5. Special rule with respect to spouses and ex-spouses.   In the case of a maintenance obligation between spouses, ex-spouses or parties to a marriage which has been annulled, Article 3 shall not apply if one of the parties objects and the law of another State, in particular the State of their last common habitual residence, has a closer connection with the marriage. In such a case the law of that other State shall apply.

Article 6. Special rule on defence.   In the case of maintenance obligations other than those arising from a parent–child relationship towards a child and those referred to in Article 5, the debtor may contest a claim from the creditor on the ground that there is no such obligation under both the law of the State of the habitual residence of the debtor and the law of the State of the common nationality of the parties, if there is one.

Article 7. Designation of the law applicable for the purpose of a particular proceeding.   (1)   Notwithstanding Articles 3 to 6, the maintenance creditor and debtor for the purpose only of a particular proceeding in a given State may expressly designate the law of that State as applicable to a maintenance obligation.
    (2)   A designation made before the institution of such proceedings shall be in an agreement, signed by both parties, in writing or recorded in any medium, the information contained in which is accessible so as to be usable for subsequent reference.

Article 8. Designation of the applicable law.   (1)   Notwithstanding Articles 3 to 6, the maintenance creditor and debtor may at any time designate one of the following laws as applicable to a maintenance obligation
    a)   the law of any State of which either party is a national at the time of the designation;
    b)   the law of the State of the habitual residence of either party at the time of designation;
    c)   the law designated by the parties as applicable, or the law in fact applied, to their property regime;
    d)   the law designated by the parties as applicable, or the law in fact applied, to their divorce or legal separation.
    (2)   Such agreement shall be in writing or recorded in any medium, the information contained in which is accessible so as to be usable for subsequent reference, and shall be signed by both parties.
    (3)   Paragraph 1 shall not apply to maintenance obligations in respect of a person under the age of 18 years or of an adult who, by reason of an impairment or insufficiency of his or her personal faculties, is not in a position to protect his or her interest.
    (4)   Notwithstanding the law designated by the parties in accordance with paragraph 1, the question of whether the creditor can renounce his or her right to maintenance shall be determined by the law of the State of the habitual residence of the creditor at the time of the designation.
    (5)   Unless at the time of the designation the parties were fully informed and aware of the consequences of their designation, the law designated by the parties shall not

apply where the application of that law would lead to manifestly unfair or unreasonable consequences for any of the parties.

Article 9. 'Domicile' instead of 'nationality'. A State which has the concept of 'domicile' as a connecting factor in family matters may inform the Permanent Bureau of the Hague Conference on Private International Law that, for the purpose of cases which come before its authorities, the word 'nationality' in Articles 4 and 6 is replaced by 'domicile' as defined in that State.

Article 10. Public bodies. The right of a public body to seek reimbursement of a benefit provided to the creditor in place of maintenance shall be governed by the law to which that body is subject.

Article 11. Scope of the applicable law. The law applicable to the maintenance obligation shall determine *inter alia*
    a)   whether, to what extent and from whom the creditor may claim maintenance;
    b)   the extent to which the creditor may claim retroactive maintenance;
    c)   the basis for calculation of the amount of maintenance, and indexation;
    d)   who is entitled to institute maintenance proceedings, except for issues relating to procedural capacity and representation in the proceedings;
    e)   prescription or limitation periods;
    f)   the extent of the obligation of a maintenance debtor, where a public body seeks reimbursement of benefits provided for a creditor in place of maintenance.

Article 12. Exclusion of renvoi. In the Protocol, the term 'law' means the law in force in a State other than its choice of law rules.

Article 13. Public policy. The application of the law determined under the Protocol may be refused only to the extent that its effects would be manifestly contrary to the public policy of the forum.

Article 14. Determining the amount of maintenance. Even if the applicable law provides otherwise, the needs of the creditor and the resources of the debtor as well as any compensation which the creditor was awarded in place of periodical maintenance payments shall be taken into account in determining the amount of maintenance.

Article 15. Non-application of the Protocol to internal conflicts. (1) A Contracting State in which different systems of law or sets of rules of law apply to maintenance obligations shall not be bound to apply the rules of the Protocol to conflicts solely between such different systems or sets of rules of law.
    (2) This Article shall not apply to a Regional Economic Integration Organisation.

Article 16. Non-unified legal systems — territorial. (1) In relation to a State in which two or more systems of law or sets of rules of law with regard to any matter dealt with in this Protocol apply in different territorial units
    a)   any reference to the law of a State shall be construed as referring, where appropriate, to the law in force in the relevant territorial unit;

b)   any reference to competent authorities or public bodies of that State shall be construed as referring, where appropriate, to those authorised to act in the relevant territorial unit;

c)   any reference to habitual residence in that State shall be construed as referring, where appropriate, to habitual residence in the relevant territorial unit;

d)   any reference to the State of which two persons have a common nationality shall be construed as referring to the territorial unit designated by the law of that State or, in the absence of relevant rules, to the territorial unit with which the maintenance obligation is most closely connected;

e)   any reference to the State of which a person is a national shall be construed as referring to the territorial unit designated by the law of that State or, in the absence of relevant rules, to the territorial unit with which the person has the closest connection.

(2)   For the purpose of identifying the applicable law under the Protocol in relation to a State which comprises two or more territorial units each of which has its own system of law or set of rules of law in respect of matters covered by this Protocol, the following rules apply

a)   if there are rules in force in such a State identifying which territorial unit's law is applicable, the law of that unit applies;

b)   in the absence of such rules, the law of the relevant territorial unit as defined in paragraph 1 applies.

(3)   This Article shall not apply to a Regional Economic Integration Organisation.

Article 17. Non-unified legal systems — inter-personal conflicts.   For the purpose of identifying the applicable law under the Protocol in relation to a State which has two or more systems of law or sets of rules of law applicable to different categories of persons in respect of matters covered by this Protocol, any reference to the law of such State shall be construed as referring to the legal system determined by the rules in force in that State.

Article 18. Coordination with prior Hague Maintenance Conventions.   As between the Contracting States, this Protocol replaces the Hague Convention of 2 October 1973 on the Law Applicable to Maintenance Obligations and the Hague Convention of 24 October 1956 on the law applicable to maintenance obligations towards children.

Article 19. Coordination with other instruments.   (1)   This Protocol does not affect any other international instrument to which Contracting States are or become Parties and which contains provisions on matters governed by the Protocol, unless a contrary declaration is made by the States Parties to such instrument.

(2)   Paragraph 1 also applies to uniform laws based on special ties of a regional or other nature between the States concerned.

Article 20. Uniform interpretation.   In the interpretation of this Protocol, regard shall be had to its international character and to the need to promote uniformity in its application.

Article 21. Review of the practical operation of the Protocol.   (1)   The Secretary General of the Hague Conference on Private International Law shall as necessary convene a Special Commission in order to review the practical operation of the Protocol.

(2)   For the purpose of such review Contracting States shall cooperate with the Permanent Bureau of the Hague Conference on Private International Law in the gathering of case law concerning the application of the Protocol.

Article 22. Transitional provisions.   This Protocol shall not apply to maintenance claimed in a Contracting State relating to a period prior to its entry into force in that State.

Article 23. Signature, ratification and accession.   (1)   This Protocol is open for signature by all States.

(2)   This Protocol is subject to ratification, acceptance or approval by the signatory States.

(3)   This Protocol is open for accession by all States.

(4)   Instruments of ratification, acceptance, approval or accession shall be deposited with the Ministry of Foreign Affairs of the Kingdom of the Netherlands, depositary of the Protocol.

Article 24. Regional Economic Integration Organisations.   (1)   A Regional Economic Integration Organisation which is constituted solely by sovereign States and has competence over some or all of the matters governed by the Protocol may equally sign, accept, approve or accede to the Protocol. The Regional Economic Integration Organisation shall in that case have the rights and obligations of a Contracting State, to the extent that the Organisation has competence over matters governed by the Protocol.

(2)   The Regional Economic Integration Organisation shall, at the time of signature, acceptance, approval or accession, notify the depositary in writing of the matters governed by the Protocol in respect of which competence has been transferred to that Organisation by its Member States. The Organisation shall promptly notify the depositary in writing of any changes to its competence as specified in the most recent notice given under this paragraph.

(3)   At the time of signature, acceptance, approval or accession, a Regional Economic Integration Organisation may declare, in accordance with Article 28, that it exercises competence over all the matters governed by the Protocol and that the Member States which have transferred competence to the Regional Economic Integration Organisation in respect of the matter in question shall be bound by the Protocol by virtue of the signature, acceptance, approval or accession of the Organisation.

(4)   For the purposes of the entry into force of the Protocol, any instrument deposited by a Regional Economic Integration Organisation shall not be counted unless the Regional Economic Integration Organisation makes a declaration under paragraph 3.

(5)   Any reference to a 'Contracting State' or 'State' in the Protocol applies equally to a Regional Economic Integration Organisation that is a Party to it, where appropriate. In the event that a declaration is made by a Regional Economic Integration Organisation under paragraph 3, any reference to a 'Contracting State' or 'State' in the Protocol applies equally to the relevant Member States of the Organisation, where appropriate.

Article 25. Entry into force.   (1)   The Protocol shall enter into force on the first day of the month following the expiration of three months after the deposit of the second instrument of ratification, acceptance, approval or accession referred to in Article 23.

(2)   Thereafter the Protocol shall enter into force

a)   for each State or each Regional Economic Integration Organisation referred to in Article 24 subsequently ratifying, accepting or approving the Protocol or acceding to it, on the first day of the month following the expiration of three months after the deposit of its instrument of ratification, acceptance, approval or accession;

b)   for a territorial unit to which the Protocol has been extended in accordance with Article 26, on the first day of the month following the expiration of three months after notification of the declaration referred to in that Article.

Article 26. Declarations with respect to non-unified legal systems.   (1)   If a State has two or more territorial units in which different systems of law are applicable in relation to matters dealt with in this Protocol, it may at the time of signature, ratification, acceptance, approval or accession declare in accordance with Article 28 that the Protocol shall extend to all its territorial units or only to one or more of them and may modify this declaration by submitting another declaration at any time.

(2)   Any such declaration shall be notified to the depositary and shall state expressly the territorial units to which the Protocol applies.

(3)   If a State makes no declaration under this Article, the Protocol is to extend to all territorial units of that State.

(4)   This Article shall not apply to a Regional Economic Integration Organisation.

Article 27. Reservations.   No reservations may be made to this Protocol.

Article 28. Declarations.   (1)   Declarations referred to in Articles 24(3) and 26(1) may be made upon signature, ratification, acceptance, approval or accession or at any time thereafter, and may be modified or withdrawn at any time.

(2)   Declarations, modifications and withdrawals shall be notified to the depositary.

(3)   A declaration made at the time of signature, ratification, acceptance, approval or accession shall take effect simultaneously with the entry into force of this Protocol for the State concerned.

(4)   A declaration made at a subsequent time, and any modification or withdrawal of a declaration, shall take effect on the first day of the month following the expiration of three months after the date on which the notification is received by the depositary.

Article 29. Denunciation.   (1)   A Contracting State to this Protocol may denounce it by a notification in writing addressed to the depositary. The denunciation may be limited to certain territorial units of a State with a non-unified legal system to which the Protocol applies.

(2)   The denunciation shall take effect on the first day of the month following the expiration of 12 months after the date on which the notification is received by the depositary. Where a longer period for the denunciation to take effect is specified in the notification, the denunciation shall take effect upon the expiration of such longer period after the date on which the notification is received by the depositary.

Article 30. Notification.   The depositary shall notify the Members of the Hague Conference on Private International Law, and other States and Regional Economic

Integration Organisations which have signed, ratified, accepted, approved or acceded in accordance with Articles 23 and 24 of the following

a) the signatures and ratifications, acceptances, approvals and accessions referred to in Articles 23 and 24;

b) the date on which this Protocol enters into force in accordance with Article 25;

c) the declarations referred to in Articles 24(3) and 26(1);

d) the denunciations referred to in Article 29.

H.1. Proposal for a Council Decision on the conclusion by the European Community of the convention on the international recovery of child support and other forms of family maintenance (COM (2009) 373 fin. of 28 July 2009)

(1) The Community is working towards the establishment of a common judicial area based on the principle of mutual recognition of decisions.

(2) The Convention of 23 November 2007 on the International Recovery of Child Support and Other Forms of Family Maintenance (hereinafter referred to as 'the Convention') constitutes a good basis for a worldwide system of cooperation and for recognition and enforcement in matters of maintenance obligations, providing for virtually free legal assistance in child support cases and a streamlined procedure for recognition and enforcement.

(3) Matters governed by the Convention are also dealt with in Council Regulation (EC) No 4/2009 on jurisdiction, applicable law, recognition and enforcement of decisions and cooperation in matters relating to maintenance obligations. The Community has gained exclusive competence over all the matters governed by the Convention and should therefore conclude the Convention alone. Member States will be bound by the Convention by virtue of its conclusion by the Community. Article 59 of the Convention allows the Community to sign, accept, approve or accede to the Convention.

(4) No reservations should be made to the Convention. All the necessary declarations should be made by the Community, as should any later modifications and withdrawals of these declarations.

(5) By declaration, the scope of the Convention should be extended so that the whole Convention would apply to all maintenance obligations arising from a family relationship, parentage, marriage or affinity, in order to guarantee effective recovery of maintenance with respect to any Contracting Parties in so far as their declarations cover the same maintenance obligations and parts of the Convention.

(6) Member States should notify the Commission, by 18 September 2010, should they wish the declarations referred to in Articles 11(1)(g), 44 (1) and 44(2) of the Convention to be made, and notify the content of any such declaration, which should be based on objective and serious grounds. If any Member State subsequently wishes a declaration to be modified or withdrawn, it should inform the Commission, so that the Commission can notify the depositary.

(7) Member States should also notify the Commission, by 18 September 2010, of its Central Authority or Central Authorities as referred to in Article 4(3) of the

Convention. The Commission should communicate this information to the Permanent Bureau of the Hague Conference on Private International Law at the time the instrument of ratification or accession is deposited, as required by the Convention. If the designated Central Authority changes, Member States should communicate this information to the Commission, which will then pass it on to the Permanent Bureau.

(8)   Member States should communicate to the Commission, by 18 September 2010, the information concerning laws, procedures and services referred to in Article 57 of the Convention. The Commission should provide the Permanent Bureau with this information by the conclusion by the Community of the Convention.

(9)   In accordance with Article 3 of the Protocol on the position of the United Kingdom and Ireland, as annexed to the Treaty on the European Union and to the Treaty establishing the European Community, [United Kingdom and Ireland are taking part in the adoption and application of this Decision.]

(10)   In accordance with Articles 1 and 2 of the Protocol on the position of Denmark, Denmark is not taking part in the adoption of this Decision and is not bound by it or subject to its application, has decided as follows:

Article 1.   The Convention of 23 November 2007 on the International Recovery of Child Support and Other Forms of Family Maintenance is hereby approved on behalf of the Community.

The President of the Council is hereby authorised to designate the person(s) empowered to deposit, on behalf of the European Community, the instrument referred to in Article 58(2) of the Convention.

The text of the Convention is attached to this Decision.

Article 2.   When concluding the Convention, the Community shall make the declarations provided for in Annex 1 to this decision.

Declarations on Articles 11(1)(g) and 44(1) of the Convention shall refer to those Member States which by 18 September 2010 have informed the Commission of their wish of such declarations, and of the content of such declarations.

Declaration on Article 44(2) of the Convention refers to Belgium, which has to inform the Commission of the content of the declaration to be made by 18 September 2010.

Article 3.   Member States shall notify the Commission, by 18 September 2010, of their Central Authority or Central Authorities as referred to in Article 4(3) of the Convention. The Commission shall communicate this information to the Permanent Bureau of the Hague Conference on Private International Law at the time the instrument referred to in Article 58(2) of the Convention is deposited.

Member States shall, by 18 September 2010, communicate to the Commission the information concerning laws, procedures and services referred to in Article 57 of the Convention. The Commission will provide the Permanent Bureau of the Hague Conference on Private International Law with this information by the time the instrument referred to in Article 58(2) of the Convention is deposited.

ANNEX 1

DECLARATIONS TO BE MADE BY THE COMMUNITY AT THE TIME OF CONCLUSION OF THE
CONVENTION ON THE INTERNATIONAL RECOVERY OF CHILD SUPPORT AND OTHER FORMS
OF FAMILY MAINTENANCE ('CONVENTION') IN ACCORDANCE WITH ARTICLE 63 OF THAT
CONVENTION

I. Declaration pursuant to Article 59(3) concerning the competence of the European Community over matters governed by the Convention

1. The European Community declares, in accordance with Article 59(3) of the Convention, that it exercises competence over all the matters governed by the Convention on the International Recovery of Child Support and Other Forms of Family Maintenance ('Convention'). Its Member States will not sign, accept, approve or accede to the Convention, but shall be bound by the Convention by virtue of its conclusion by the European Community.

2. The current Members of the European Community are the Kingdom of Belgium, the Republic of Bulgaria, the Czech Republic, the Kingdom of Denmark, the Federal Republic of Germany, the Republic of Estonia, Ireland, the Hellenic Republic, the Kingdom of Spain, the French Republic, the Italian Republic, the Republic of Cyprus, the Republic of Latvia, the Republic of Lithuania, the Grand-Duchy of Luxembourg, the Republic of Hungary, the Republic of Malta, the Kingdom of the Netherlands, the Republic of Austria, the Republic of Poland, the Portuguese Republic, Romania, the Republic of Slovenia, the Slovak Republic, the Republic of Finland, the Kingdom of Sweden and the United Kingdom of Great Britain and Northern Ireland.

3. However, this declaration does not apply to the Kingdom of Denmark, in accordance with Articles 1 and 2 of the Protocol on the position of Denmark, annexed to the Treaties.

4. This declaration is not applicable to territories of the Member States in which the Treaty establishing the European Community does not apply and is without prejudice to such acts or positions as may be adopted under the Convention by the Member States concerned on behalf of and in the interests of those territories.

II. Declarations concerning certain provisions and matters

5. The European Community declares, in accordance with Article 2(3) of the Convention, that it applies the whole Convention to maintenance obligations arising from a family relationship, parentage, marriage or affinity.

6. The European Community declares, in accordance with Article 11(1)(g) of the Convention, that in [specify the Member State/Member States] an application other than an application under Article 10(1)(a) and (2)(a) should include [specify the information or documents required].

7. The European Community declares, in accordance with Article 44(1) of the Convention, that [specify the Member State/Member States] accepts applications and related documents translated into [specify the language/languages].

8. The European Community declares, in accordance with Article 44(2) of the Convention, that in Belgium documents shall be drawn up in [specify the languages] for submission to [specify the parts of the territory].

H.2.   Convention on the international recovery of child support and other forms of family maintenance[1]

The States signatory to the present Convention,

Desiring to improve co-operation among States for the international recovery of child support and other forms of family maintenance,

Aware of the need for procedures which produce results and are accessible, prompt, efficient, cost-effective, responsive and fair,

Wishing to build upon the best features of existing Hague Conventions and other international instruments, in particular the United Nations Convention on the Recovery Abroad of Maintenance of 20 June 1956,

Seeking to take advantage of advances in technologies and to create a flexible system which can continue to evolve as needs change and further advances in technology create new opportunities,

Recalling that, in accordance with Articles 3 and 27 of the United Nations Convention on the Rights of the Child of 20 November 1989,

—   in all actions concerning children the best interests of the child shall be a primary consideration, – every child has a right to a standard of living adequate for the child's physical, mental, spiritual, moral and social development,

—   the parent(s) or others responsible for the child have the primary responsibility to secure, within their abilities and financial capacities, the conditions of living necessary for the child's development, and

—   States Parties should take all appropriate measures, including the conclusion of international agreements, to secure the recovery of maintenance for the child from the parent(s) or other responsible persons, in particular where such persons live in a State different from that of the child;

Have resolved to conclude this Convention and have agreed upon the following provisions

Chapter I — Object, scope and definitions

Article 1. Object. The object of the present Convention is to ensure the effective international recovery of child support and other forms of family maintenance, in particular by

a)   establishing a comprehensive system of co-operation between the authorities of the Contracting States;

b)   making available applications for the establishment of maintenance decisions;

c)   providing for the recognition and enforcement of maintenance decisions; and

d)   requiring effective measures for the prompt enforcement of maintenance decisions.

Article 2. Scope.   (1)   This Convention shall apply

a)   to maintenance obligations arising from a parent–child relationship towards a person under the age of 21 years;

---

[1]   Not yet in force as of December 2010. [Note of the Editor]

b)   to recognition and enforcement or enforcement of a decision for spousal support when the application is made with a claim within the scope of sub-paragraph a); and

c)   with the exception of Chapters II and III, to spousal support.

(2)   Any Contracting State may reserve, in accordance with Article 62, the right to limit the application of the Convention under sub-paragraph 1 a), to persons who have not attained the age of 18 years. A Contracting State which makes this reservation shall not be entitled to claim the application of the Convention to persons of the age excluded by its reservation.

(3)   Any Contracting State may declare in accordance with Article 63 that it will extend the application of the whole or any part of the Convention to any maintenance obligation arising from a family relationship, parentage, marriage or affinity, including in particular obligations in respect of vulnerable persons. Any such declaration shall give rise to obligations between two Contracting States only in so far as their declarations cover the same maintenance obligations and parts of the Convention.

(4)   The provisions of this Convention shall apply to children regardless of the marital status of the parents.

Article 3. Definitions.   For the purposes of this Convention

a)   'creditor' means an individual to whom maintenance is owed or is alleged to be owed;

b)   'debtor' means an individual who owes or who is alleged to owe maintenance;

c)   'legal assistance' means the assistance necessary to enable applicants to know and assert their rights and to ensure that applications are fully and effectively dealt with in the requested State. The means of providing such assistance may include as necessary legal advice, assistance in bringing a case before an authority, legal representation and exemption from costs of proceedings;

d)   'agreement in writing' means an agreement recorded in any medium, the information contained in which is accessible so as to be usable for subsequent reference;

e)   'maintenance arrangement' means an agreement in writing relating to the payment of maintenance which

i)   has been formally drawn up or registered as an authentic instrument by a competent authority; or

ii)   has been authenticated by, or concluded, registered or filed with a competent authority, and may be the subject of review and modification by a competent authority;

f)   'vulnerable person' means a person who, by reason of an impairment or insufficiency of his or her personal faculties, is not able to support him or herself.

Chapter II — Administrative co-operation

Article 4. Designation of Central Authorities.   (1)   A Contracting State shall designate a Central Authority to discharge the duties that are imposed by the Convention on such an authority.

(2)   Federal States, States with more than one system of law or States having autonomous territorial units shall be free to appoint more than one Central Authority and shall specify the territorial or personal extent of their functions. Where a State has appointed more than one Central Authority, it shall designate the Central Authority to which any communication may be addressed for transmission to the appropriate Central Authority within that State.

(3)   The designation of the Central Authority or Central Authorities, their contact details, and where appropriate the extent of their functions as specified in paragraph 2, shall be communicated by a Contracting State to the Permanent Bureau of the Hague Conference on Private International Law at the time when the instrument of ratification or accession is deposited or when a declaration is submitted in accordance with Article 61. Contracting States shall promptly inform the Permanent Bureau of any changes.

Article 5. General functions of Central Authorities.   Central Authorities shall
    a.   co-operate with each other and promote co-operation amongst the competent authorities in their States to achieve the purposes of the Convention;
    b.   seek as far as possible solutions to difficulties which arise in the application of the Convention.

Article 6. Specific functions of Central Authorities.   (1)   Central Authorities shall provide assistance in relation to applications under Chapter III. In particular they shall
    a)   transmit and receive such applications;
    b)   initiate or facilitate the institution of proceedings in respect of such applications.
    (2)   In relation to such applications they shall take all appropriate measures
    a)   where the circumstances require, to provide or facilitate the provision of legal assistance;
    b)   to help locate the debtor or the creditor;
    c)   to help obtain relevant information concerning the income and, if necessary, other financial circumstances of the debtor or creditor, including the location of assets;
    d)   to encourage amicable solutions with a view to obtaining voluntary payment of maintenance, where suitable by use of mediation, conciliation or similar processes;
    e)   to facilitate the ongoing enforcement of maintenance decisions, including any arrears;
    f)   to facilitate the collection and expeditious transfer of maintenance payments;
    g)   to facilitate the obtaining of documentary or other evidence;
    h)   to provide assistance in establishing parentage where necessary for the recovery of maintenance;
    i)   to initiate or facilitate the institution of proceedings to obtain any necessary provisional measures that are territorial in nature and the purpose of which is to secure the outcome of a pending maintenance application;
    j)   to facilitate service of documents.
    (3)   The functions of the Central Authority under this Article may, to the extent permitted under the law of its State, be performed by public bodies, or other bodies subject to the supervision of the competent authorities of that State. The designation of any such public bodies or other bodies, as well as their contact details and the extent of their functions, shall be communicated by a Contracting State to the Permanent Bureau of the Hague Conference on Private International Law. Contracting States shall promptly inform the Permanent Bureau of any changes.
    (4)   Nothing in this Article or Article 7 shall be interpreted as imposing an obligation on a Central Authority to exercise powers that can be exercised only by judicial authorities under the law of the requested State.

Article 7. Requests for specific measures. (1) A Central Authority may make a request, supported by reasons, to another Central Authority to take appropriate specific measures under Article 6(2) b), c), g), h), i) and j) when no application under Article 10 is pending. The requested Central Authority shall take such measures as are appropriate if satisfied that they are necessary to assist a potential applicant in making an application under Article 10 or in determining whether such an application should be initiated.

(2) A Central Authority may also take specific measures on the request of another Central Authority in relation to a case having an international element concerning the recovery of maintenance pending in the requesting State.

Article 8. Central Authority costs. (1) Each Central Authority shall bear its own costs in applying this Convention.

(2) Central Authorities may not impose any charge on an applicant for the provision of their services under the Convention save for exceptional costs arising from a request for a specific measure under Article 7.

(3) The requested Central Authority may not recover the costs of the services referred to in paragraph 2 without the prior consent of the applicant to the provision of those services at such cost.

Chapter III — Applications through Central Authorities

Article 9. Application through Central Authorities. An application under this Chapter shall be made through the Central Authority of the Contracting State in which the applicant resides to the Central Authority of the requested State. For the purpose of this provision, residence excludes mere presence.

Article 10. Available applications. (1) The following categories of application shall be available to a creditor in a requesting State seeking to recover maintenance under this Convention

    a) recognition or recognition and enforcement of a decision;

    b) enforcement of a decision made or recognised in the requested State;

    c) establishment of a decision in the requested State where there is no existing decision, including where necessary the establishment of parentage;

    d) establishment of a decision in the requested State where recognition and enforcement of a decision is not possible, or is refused, because of the lack of a basis for recognition and enforcement under Article 20, or on the grounds specified in Article 22 b) or e);

    e) modification of a decision made in the requested State;

    f) modification of a decision made in a State other than the requested State.

(2) The following categories of application shall be available to a debtor in a requesting State against whom there is an existing maintenance decision—

    a) recognition of a decision, or an equivalent procedure leading to the suspension, or limiting the enforcement, of a previous decision in the requested State;

    b) modification of a decision made in the requested State;

    c) modification of a decision made in a State other than the requested State.

(3) Save as otherwise provided in this Convention, the applications in paragraphs 1 and 2 shall be determined under the law of the requested State, and applications in

paragraphs 1 c) to f) and 2 b) and c) shall be subject to the jurisdictional rules applicable in the requested State.

Article 11. Application contents. (1)   All applications under Article 10 shall as a minimum include
    a)   a statement of the nature of the application or applications;
    b)   the name and contact details, including the address and date of birth of the applicant;
    c)   the name and, if known, address and date of birth of the respondent;
    d)   the name and date of birth of any person for whom maintenance is sought;
    e)   the grounds upon which the application is based;
    f)   in an application by a creditor, information concerning where the maintenance payment should be sent or electronically transmitted;
    g)   save in an application under Article 10(1) a) and (2) a), any information or document specified by declaration in accordance with Article 63 by the requested State;
    h)   the name and contact details of the person or unit from the Central Authority of the requesting State responsible for processing the application.
    (2)   As appropriate, and to the extent known, the application shall in addition in particular include
    a)   the financial circumstances of the creditor;
    b)   the financial circumstances of the debtor, including the name and address of the employer of the debtor and the nature and location of the assets of the debtor;
    c)   any other information that may assist with the location of the respondent.
    (3)   The application shall be accompanied by any necessary supporting information or documentation including documentation concerning the entitlement of the applicant to free legal assistance. In the case of applications under Article 10(1) a) and (2) a), the application shall be accompanied only by the documents listed in Article 25.
    (4)   An application under Article 10 may be made in the form recommended and published by the Hague Conference on Private International Law.

Article 12. Transmission, receipt and processing of applications and cases through Central Authorities.   (1)   The Central Authority of the requesting State shall assist the applicant in ensuring that the application is accompanied by all the information and documents known by it to be necessary for consideration of the application.
    (2)   The Central Authority of the requesting State shall, when satisfied that the application complies with the requirements of the Convention, transmit the application on behalf of and with the consent of the applicant to the Central Authority of the requested State. The application shall be accompanied by the transmittal form set out in Annex 1. The Central Authority of the requesting State shall, when requested by the Central Authority of the requested State, provide a complete copy certified by the competent authority in the State of origin of any document specified under Articles 16(3), 25(1) a), b) and d) and (3) b) and 30(3).
    (3)   The requested Central Authority shall, within six weeks from the date of receipt of the application, acknowledge receipt in the form set out in Annex 2, and inform the Central Authority of the requesting State what initial steps have been or will be taken to deal with the application, and may request any further necessary documents and information. Within the same six-week period, the requested Central Authority shall

provide to the requesting Central Authority the name and contact details of the person or unit responsible for responding to inquiries regarding the progress of the application.

(4) Within three months after the acknowledgement, the requested Central Authority shall inform the requesting Central Authority of the status of the application.

(5) Requesting and requested Central Authorities shall keep each other informed of

a) the person or unit responsible for a particular case;

b) the progress of the case, and shall provide timely responses to enquiries.

(6) Central Authorities shall process a case as quickly as a proper consideration of the issues will allow.

(7) Central Authorities shall employ the most rapid and efficient means of communication at their disposal.

(8) A requested Central Authority may refuse to process an application only if it is manifest that the requirements of the Convention are not fulfilled. In such case, that Central Authority shall promptly inform the requesting Central Authority of its reasons for refusal.

(9) The requested Central Authority may not reject an application solely on the basis that additional documents or information are needed. However, the requested Central Authority may ask the requesting Central Authority to provide these additional documents or information. If the requesting Central Authority does not do so within three months or a longer period specified by the requested Central Authority, the requested Central Authority may decide that it will no longer process the application. In this case, it shall inform the requesting Central Authority of this decision.

Article 13. Means of communication. Any application made through Central Authorities of the Contracting States in accordance with this Chapter, and any document or information appended thereto or provided by a Central Authority, may not be challenged by the respondent by reason only of the medium or means of communication employed between the Central Authorities concerned.

Article 1. Effective access to procedure. (1) The requested State shall provide applicants with effective access to procedures, including enforcement and appeal procedures, arising from applications under this Chapter.

(2) To provide such effective access, the requested State shall provide free legal assistance in accordance with Articles 14 to 17 unless paragraph 3 applies.

(3) The requested State shall not be obliged to provide such free legal assistance if and to the extent that the procedures of that State enable the applicant to make the case without the need for such assistance, and the Central Authority provides such services as are necessary free of charge.

(4) Entitlements to free legal assistance shall not be less than those available in equivalent domestic cases.

(5) No security, bond or deposit, however described, shall be required to guarantee the payment of costs and expenses in proceedings under the Convention.

Article 15. Free legal assistance for child support applications. (1) The requested State shall provide free legal assistance in respect of all applications by a creditor under this Chapter concerning maintenance obligations arising from a parent–child relationship towards a person under the age of 21 years.

(2)   Notwithstanding paragraph 1, the requested State may, in relation to applications other than those under Article 10(1) a) and b) and the cases covered by Article 20(4), refuse free legal assistance if it considers that, on the merits, the application or any appeal is manifestly unfounded.

Article 16. Declaration to permit use of child-centred means test.   (1)   Notwithstanding Article 15(1), a State may declare, in accordance with Article 63, that it will provide free legal assistance in respect of applications other than under Article 10(1) a) and b) and the cases covered by Article 20(4), subject to a test based on an assessment of the means of the child.

(2)   A State shall, at the time of making such a declaration, provide information to the Permanent Bureau of the Hague Conference on Private International Law concerning the manner in which the assessment of the child's means will be carried out, including the financial criteria which would need to be met to satisfy the test.

(3)   An application referred to in paragraph 1, addressed to a State which has made the declaration referred to in that paragraph, shall include a formal attestation by the applicant stating that the child's means meet the criteria referred to in paragraph 2. The requested State may only request further evidence of the child's means if it has reasonable grounds to believe that the information provided by the applicant is inaccurate.

(4)   If the most favourable legal assistance provided for by the law of the requested State in respect of applications under this Chapter concerning maintenance obligations arising from a parent–child relationship towards a child is more favourable than that provided for under paragraphs 1 to 3, the most favourable legal assistance shall be provided.

Article 17. Applications not qualifying under Article 15 or Article 16.   In the case of all applications under this Convention other than those under Article 15 or Article 16

    a)   the provision of free legal assistance may be made subject to a means or a merits test;

    b)   an applicant, who in the State of origin has benefited from free legal assistance, shall be entitled, in any proceedings for recognition or enforcement, to benefit, at least to the same extent, from free legal assistance as provided for by the law of the State addressed under the same circumstances.

Chapter IV — Restrictions on bringing proceedings

Article 18. Limit on proceedings.   (1)   Where a decision is made in a Contracting State where the creditor is habitually resident, proceedings to modify the decision or to make a new decision cannot be brought by the debtor in any other Contracting State as long as the creditor remains habitually resident in the State where the decision was made.

(2)   Paragraph 1 shall not apply

    a)   where, except in disputes relating to maintenance obligations in respect of children, there is agreement in writing between the parties to the jurisdiction of that other Contracting State;

    b)   where the creditor submits to the jurisdiction of that other Contracting State either expressly or by defending on the merits of the case without objecting to the jurisdiction at the first available opportunity;

c)   where the competent authority in the State of origin cannot, or refuses to, exercise jurisdiction to modify the decision or make a new decision; or

d)   where the decision made in the State of origin cannot be recognised or declared enforceable in the Contracting State where proceedings to modify the decision or make a new decision are contemplated.

Chapter V — Recognition and enforcement

Article 19. Scope of the Chapter.   (1)   This Chapter shall apply to a decision rendered by a judicial or administrative authority in respect of a maintenance obligation. The term 'decision' also includes a settlement or agreement concluded before or approved by such an authority. A decision may include automatic adjustment by indexation and a requirement to pay arrears, retroactive maintenance or interest and a determination of costs or expenses.

(2)   If a decision does not relate solely to a maintenance obligation, the effect of this Chapter is limited to the parts of the decision which concern maintenance obligations.

(3)   For the purpose of paragraph 1, 'administrative authority' means a public body whose decisions, under the law of the State where it is established

a)   may be made the subject of an appeal to or review by a judicial authority; and

b)   have a similar force and effect to a decision of a judicial authority on the same matter.

(4)   This Chapter also applies to maintenance arrangements in accordance with Article 30.

(5)   The provisions of this Chapter shall apply to a request for recognition and enforcement made directly to a competent authority of the State addressed in accordance with Article 37.

Article 20. Bases for recognition and enforcement.   (1)   A decision made in one Contracting State ('the State of origin') shall be recognised and enforced in other Contracting States if

a)   the respondent was habitually resident in the State of origin at the time proceedings were instituted;

b)   the respondent has submitted to the jurisdiction either expressly or by defending on the merits of the case without objecting to the jurisdiction at the first available opportunity;

c)   the creditor was habitually resident in the State of origin at the time proceedings were instituted;

d)   the child for whom maintenance was ordered was habitually resident in the State of origin at the time proceedings were instituted, provided that the respondent has lived with the child in that State or has resided in that State and provided support for the child there;

e)   except in disputes relating to maintenance obligations in respect of children, there has been agreement to the jurisdiction in writing by the parties; or

f)   the decision was made by an authority exercising jurisdiction on a matter of personal status or parental responsibility, unless that jurisdiction was based solely on the nationality of one of the parties.

(2)   A Contracting State may make a reservation, in accordance with Article 62, in respect of paragraph 1 c), e) or f).

(3)   A Contracting State making a reservation under paragraph 2 shall recognise and enforce a decision if its law would in similar factual circumstances confer or would have conferred jurisdiction on its authorities to make such a decision.

(4)   A Contracting State shall, if recognition of a decision is not possible as a result of a reservation under paragraph 2, and if the debtor is habitually resident in that State, take all appropriate measures to establish a decision for the benefit of the creditor. The preceding sentence shall not apply to direct requests for recognition and enforcement under Article 19(5) or to claims for support referred to in Article 2(1) b).

(5)   A decision in favour of a child under the age of 18 years which cannot be recognised by virtue only of a reservation in respect of paragraph 1 c), e) or f) shall be accepted as establishing the eligibility of that child for maintenance in the State addressed.

(6)   A decision shall be recognised only if it has effect in the State of origin, and shall be enforced only if it is enforceable in the State of origin.

Article 21. Severability and partial recognition and enforcement. (1) If the State addressed is unable to recognise or enforce the whole of the decision, it shall recognise or enforce any severable part of the decision which can be so recognised or enforced.

(2)   Partial recognition or enforcement of a decision can always be applied for.

Article 22. Grounds for refusing recognition and enforcement. Recognition and enforcement of a decision may be refused if

a)   recognition and enforcement of the decision is manifestly incompatible with the public policy ('*ordre public*') of the State addressed;

b)   the decision was obtained by fraud in connection with a matter of procedure;

c)   proceedings between the same parties and having the same purpose are pending before an authority of the State addressed and those proceedings were the first to be instituted;

d)   the decision is incompatible with a decision rendered between the same parties and having the same purpose, either in the State addressed or in another State, provided that this latter decision fulfils the conditions necessary for its recognition and enforcement in the State addressed;

e)   in a case where the respondent has neither appeared nor was represented in proceedings in the State of origin

i)   when the law of the State of origin provides for notice of proceedings, the respondent did not have proper notice of the proceedings and an opportunity to be heard; or

ii)   when the law of the State of origin does not provide for notice of the proceedings, the respondent did not have proper notice of the decision and an opportunity to challenge or appeal it on fact and law; or

f)   the decision was made in violation of Article 18.

Article 23. Procedure on an application for recognition and enforcement. (1)   Subject to the provisions of the Convention, the procedures for recognition and enforcement shall be governed by the law of the State addressed.

(2)   Where an application for recognition and enforcement of a decision has been made through Central Authorities in accordance with Chapter III, the requested Central Authority shall promptly either

a)   refer the application to the competent authority which shall without delay declare the decision enforceable or register the decision for enforcement; or

b)   if it is the competent authority take such steps itself.

(3)   Where the request is made directly to a competent authority in the State addressed in accordance with Article 19(5), that authority shall without delay declare the decision enforceable or register the decision for enforcement.

(4)   A declaration or registration may be refused only on the ground set out in Article 22 a). At this stage neither the applicant nor the respondent is entitled to make any submissions.

(5)   The applicant and the respondent shall be promptly notified of the declaration or registration, made under paragraphs 2 and 3, or the refusal thereof in accordance with paragraph 4, and may bring a challenge or appeal on fact and on a point of law.

(6)   A challenge or an appeal is to be lodged within 30 days of notification under paragraph 5. If the contesting party is not resident in the Contracting State in which the declaration or registration was made or refused, the challenge or appeal shall be lodged within 60 days of notification.

(7)   A challenge or appeal may be founded only on the following

a)   the grounds for refusing recognition and enforcement set out in Article 22;

b)   the bases for recognition and enforcement under Article 20;

c)   the authenticity or integrity of any document transmitted in accordance with Article 25(1) a), b) or d) or (3) b).

(8)   A challenge or an appeal by a respondent may also be founded on the fulfilment of the debt to the extent that the recognition and enforcement relates to payments that fell due in the past.

(9)   The applicant and the respondent shall be promptly notified of the decision following the challenge or the appeal.

(10) A further appeal, if permitted by the law of the State addressed, shall not have the effect of staying the enforcement of the decision unless there are exceptional circumstances.

(11) In taking any decision on recognition and enforcement, including any appeal, the competent authority shall act expeditiously.

Article 24. Alternative procedure on an application for recognition and enforcement. (1)   Notwithstanding Article 23(2) to (11), a State may declare, in accordance with Article 63, that it will apply the procedure for recognition and enforcement set out in this Article.

(2)   Where an application for recognition and enforcement of a decision has been made through Central Authorities in accordance with Chapter III, the requested Central Authority shall promptly either

a)   refer the application to the competent authority which shall decide on the application for recognition and enforcement; or

b)   if it is the competent authority, take such a decision itself.

(3)   A decision on recognition and enforcement shall be given by the competent authority after the respondent has been duly and promptly notified of the proceedings and both parties have been given an adequate opportunity to be heard.

(4)   The competent authority may review the grounds for refusing recognition and enforcement set out in Article 22 a), c) and d) of its own motion. It may review any grounds listed in Articles 20, 22 and 23(7) c if raised by the respondent or if concerns relating to those grounds arise from the face of the documents submitted in accordance with Article 25.

(5)   A refusal of recognition and enforcement may also be founded on the fulfilment of the debt to the extent that the recognition and enforcement relates to payments that fell due in the past.

(6)   Any appeal, if permitted by the law of the State addressed, shall not have the effect of staying the enforcement of the decision unless there are exceptional circumstances.

(7)   In taking any decision on recognition and enforcement, including any appeal, the competent authority shall act expeditiously.

Article 25. Documents.   (1)   An application for recognition and enforcement under Article 23 or Article 24 shall be accompanied by the following

a)   a complete text of the decision;

b)   a document stating that the decision is enforceable in the State of origin and, in the case of a decision by an administrative authority, a document stating that the requirements of Article 19(3) are met unless that State has specified in accordance with Article 57 that decisions of its administrative authorities always meet those requirements;

c)   if the respondent did not appear and was not represented in the proceedings in the State of origin, a document or documents attesting, as appropriate, either that the respondent had proper notice of the proceedings and an opportunity to be heard, or that the respondent had proper notice of the decision and the opportunity to challenge or appeal it on fact and law;

d)   where necessary, a document showing the amount of any arrears and the date such amount was calculated;

e)   where necessary, in the case of a decision providing for automatic adjustment by indexation, a document providing the information necessary to make the appropriate calculations;

f)   where necessary, documentation showing the extent to which the applicant received free legal assistance in the State of origin.

(2)   Upon a challenge or appeal under Article 23(7) c) or upon request by the competent authority in the State addressed, a complete copy of the document concerned, certified by the competent authority in the State of origin, shall be provided promptly–

a)   by the Central Authority of the requesting State, where the application has been made in accordance with Chapter III;

b)   by the applicant, where the request has been made directly to a competent authority of the State addressed.

(3)   A Contracting State may specify in accordance with Article 57 –

a)   that a complete copy of the decision certified by the competent authority in the State of origin must accompany the application;

b)   circumstances in which it will accept, in lieu of a complete text of the decision, an abstract or extract of the decision drawn up by the competent authority of the State of origin, which may be made in the form recommended and published by the Hague Conference on Private International Law; or

c)   that it does not require a document stating that the requirements of Article 19(3) are met.

Article 26. Procedure on an application for recognition.   This Chapter shall apply mutatis mutandis to an application for recognition of a decision, save that the requirement of enforceability is replaced by the requirement that the decision has effect in the State of origin.

Article 27. Findings of fact.   Any competent authority of the State addressed shall be bound by the findings of fact on which the authority of the State of origin based its jurisdiction.

Article 28. No review of the merits.   There shall be no review by any competent authority of the State addressed of the merits of a decision.

Article 29. Physical presence of the child or the applicant not required.   The physical presence of the child or the applicant shall not be required in any proceedings in the State addressed under this Chapter.

Article 30. Maintenance arrangements.   (1)   A maintenance arrangement made in a Contracting State shall be entitled to recognition and enforcement as a decision under this Chapter provided that it is enforceable as a decision in the State of origin.

(2)   For the purpose of Article 10(1) a) and b) and (2) a), the term 'decision' includes a maintenance arrangement.

(3)   An application for recognition and enforcement of a maintenance arrangement shall be accompanied by the following

a)   a complete text of the maintenance arrangement; and

b)   a document stating that the particular maintenance arrangement is enforceable as a decision in the State of origin.

(4)   Recognition and enforcement of a maintenance arrangement may be refused if

a)   the recognition and enforcement is manifestly incompatible with the public policy of the State addressed;

b)   the maintenance arrangement was obtained by fraud or falsification;

c)   the maintenance arrangement is incompatible with a decision rendered between the same parties and having the same purpose, either in the State addressed or in another State, provided that this latter decision fulfils the conditions necessary for its recognition and enforcement in the State addressed.

(5)   The provisions of this Chapter, with the exception of Articles 20, 22, 23(7) and 25(1) and (3), shall apply mutatis mutandis to the recognition and enforcement of a maintenance arrangement save that

a)   a declaration or registration in accordance with Article 23(2) and (3) may be refused only on the ground set out in paragraph 4 a);

b)   a challenge or appeal as referred to in Article 23(6) may be founded only on the following

i)   the grounds for refusing recognition and enforcement set out in paragraph 4;

ii)   the authenticity or integrity of any document transmitted in accordance with paragraph 3;

c)   as regards the procedure under Article 24(4), the competent authority may review of its own motion the ground for refusing recognition and enforcement set out in paragraph 4 a) of this Article. It may review all grounds listed in paragraph 4 of this Article and the authenticity or integrity of any document transmitted in accordance with paragraph 3 if raised by the respondent or if concerns relating to those grounds arise from the face of those documents.

(6)   Proceedings for recognition and enforcement of a maintenance arrangement shall be suspended if a challenge concerning the arrangement is pending before a competent authority of a Contracting State.

(7)   A State may declare, in accordance with Article 63, that applications for recognition and enforcement of a maintenance arrangement shall only be made through Central Authorities.

(8)   A Contracting State may, in accordance with Article 62, reserve the right not to recognise and enforce a maintenance arrangement.

Article 31. Decisions produced by the combined effect of provisional and confirmation orders.   Where a decision is produced by the combined effect of a provisional order made in one State and an order by an authority in another State ('the confirming State') confirming the provisional order

a)   each of those States shall be deemed for the purposes of this Chapter to be a State of origin;

b)   the requirements of Article 22 e) shall be met if the respondent had proper notice of the proceedings in the confirming State and an opportunity to oppose the confirmation of the provisional order;

c)   the requirement of Article 20(6) that a decision be enforceable in the State of origin shall be met if the decision is enforceable in the confirming State; and

d)   Article 18 shall not prevent proceedings for the modification of the decision being commenced in either State.

Chapter VI — Enforcement by the State addressed

Article 32. Enforcement under internal law.   (1)   Subject to the provisions of this Chapter, enforcement shall take place in accordance with the law of the State addressed.

(2)   Enforcement shall be prompt.

(3)   In the case of applications through Central Authorities, where a decision has been declared enforceable or registered for enforcement under Chapter V, enforcement shall proceed without the need for further action by the applicant.

(4)   Effect shall be given to any rules applicable in the State of origin of the decision relating to the duration of the maintenance obligation.

(5)   Any limitation on the period for which arrears may be enforced shall be determined either by the law of the State of origin of the decision or by the law of the State addressed, whichever provides for the longer limitation period.

Article 33. Non-discrimination. The State addressed shall provide at least the same range of enforcement methods for cases under the Convention as are available in domestic cases.

Article 34. Enforcement measures. (1) Contracting States shall make available in internal law effective measures to enforce decisions under this Convention.

(2) Such measures may include

a) wage withholding;

b) garnishment from bank accounts and other sources;

c) deductions from social security payments;

d) lien on or forced sale of property;

e) tax refund withholding;

f) withholding or attachment of pension benefits;

g) credit bureau reporting;

h) denial, suspension or revocation of various licenses (for example, driving licenses);

i) the use of mediation, conciliation or similar processes to bring about voluntary compliance.

Article 35. Transfer of funds. (1) Contracting States are encouraged to promote, including by means of international agreements, the use of the most cost-effective and efficient methods available to transfer funds payable as maintenance.

(2) A Contracting State, under whose law the transfer of funds is restricted, shall accord the highest priority to the transfer of funds payable under this Convention.

Chapter VII — Public bodies

Article 36. Public bodies as applicants. (1) For the purposes of applications for recognition and enforcement under Article 10(1) a) and b) and cases covered by Article 20(4), 'creditor' includes a public body acting in place of an individual to whom maintenance is owed or one to which reimbursement is owed for benefits provided in place of maintenance.

(2) The right of a public body to act in place of an individual to whom maintenance is owed or to seek reimbursement of benefits provided to the creditor in place of maintenance shall be governed by the law to which the body is subject.

(3) A public body may seek recognition or claim enforcement of

a) a decision rendered against a debtor on the application of a public body which claims payment of benefits provided in place of maintenance;

b) a decision rendered between a creditor and debtor to the extent of the benefits provided to the creditor in place of maintenance.

(4) The public body seeking recognition or claiming enforcement of a decision shall upon request furnish any document necessary to establish its right under paragraph 2 and that benefits have been provided to the creditor.

Chapter VIII — General provisions

Article 37. Direct requests to competent authorities. (1) The Convention shall not exclude the possibility of recourse to such procedures as may be available under the internal law of a Contracting State allowing a person (an applicant) to seise directly a competent authority of that State in a matter governed by the Convention including, subject to Article 18, for the purpose of having a maintenance decision established or modified.

(2) Articles 14(5) and 17 (b) and the provisions of Chapters V, VI, VII and this Chapter, with the exception of Articles 40(2), 42, 43(3), 44(3), 45 and 55, shall apply in relation to a request for recognition and enforcement made directly to a competent authority in a Contracting State.

(3) For the purpose of paragraph 2, Article 2(1) a) shall apply to a decision granting maintenance to a vulnerable person over the age specified in that sub-paragraph where such decision was rendered before the person reached that age and provided for maintenance beyond that age by reason of the impairment.

Article 38. Protection of personal data. Personal data gathered or transmitted under the Convention shall be used only for the purposes for which they were gathered or transmitted.

Article 39. Confidentiality. Any authority processing information shall ensure its confidentiality in accordance with the law of its State.

Article 40. Non-disclosure of information. (1) An authority shall not disclose or confirm information gathered or transmitted in application of this Convention if it determines that to do so could jeopardise the health, safety or liberty of a person.

(2) A determination to this effect made by one Central Authority shall be taken into account by another Central Authority, in particular in cases of family violence.

(3) Nothing in this Article shall impede the gathering and transmitting of information by and between authorities in so far as necessary to carry out the obligations under the Convention.

Article 41. No legalisation. No legalisation or similar formality may be required in the context of this Convention.

Article 42. Power of attorney. The Central Authority of the requested State may require a power of attorney from the applicant only if it acts on his or her behalf in judicial proceedings or before other authorities, or in order to designate a representative so to act.

Article 43. Recovery of costs. (1) Recovery of any costs incurred in the application of this Convention shall not take precedence over the recovery of maintenance.

(2) A State may recover costs from an unsuccessful party.

(3) For the purposes of an application under Article 10(1) (b) to recover costs from an unsuccessful party in accordance with paragraph 2, the term 'creditor' in Article 10(1) shall include a State.

(4) This Article shall be without prejudice to Article 8.

Article 44. Language requirements. (1) Any application and related documents shall be in the original language, and shall be accompanied by a translation into an official language of the requested State or another language which the requested State has indicated, by way of declaration in accordance with Article 63, it will accept, unless the competent authority of that State dispenses with translation.

(2) A Contracting State which has more than one official language and cannot, for reasons of internal law, accept for the whole of its territory documents in one of those languages shall, by declaration in accordance with Article 63, specify the language in which such documents or translations thereof shall be drawn up for submission in the specified parts of its territory.

(3) Unless otherwise agreed by the Central Authorities, any other communications between such Authorities shall be in an official language of the requested State or in either English or French. However, a Contracting State may, by making a reservation in accordance with Article 62, object to the use of either English or French.

Article 45. Means and costs of translation. (1) In the case of applications under Chapter III, the Central Authorities may agree in an individual case or generally that the translation into an official language of the requested State may be made in the requested State from the original language or from any other agreed language. If there is no agreement and it is not possible for the requesting Central Authority to comply with the requirements of Article 44(1) and (2), then the application and related documents may be transmitted with translation into English or French for further translation into an official language of the requested State.

(2) The cost of translation arising from the application of paragraph 1 shall be borne by the requesting State unless otherwise agreed by Central Authorities of the States concerned.

(3) Notwithstanding Article 8, the requesting Central Authority may charge an applicant for the costs of translation of an application and related documents, except in so far as those costs may be covered by its system of legal assistance.

Article 46. Non-unified legal systems — interpretation. (1) In relation to a State in which two or more systems of law or sets of rules of law with regard to any matter dealt with in this Convention apply in different territorial units

a) any reference to the law or procedure of a State shall be construed as referring, where appropriate, to the law or procedure in force in the relevant territorial unit;

b) any reference to a decision established, recognised, recognised and enforced, enforced or modified in that State shall be construed as referring, where appropriate, to a decision established, recognised, recognised and enforced, enforced or modified in the relevant territorial unit;

c) any reference to a judicial or administrative authority in that State shall be construed as referring, where appropriate, to a judicial or administrative authority in the relevant territorial unit;

d) any reference to competent authorities, public bodies, and other bodies of that State, other than Central Authorities, shall be construed as referring, where appropriate, to those authorised to act in the relevant territorial unit;

e) any reference to residence or habitual residence in that State shall be construed as referring, where appropriate, to residence or habitual residence in the relevant territorial unit;

f)   any reference to location of assets in that State shall be construed as referring, where appropriate, to the location of assets in the relevant territorial unit;

g)   any reference to a reciprocity arrangement in force in a State shall be construed as referring, where appropriate, to a reciprocity arrangement in force in the relevant territorial unit;

h)   any reference to free legal assistance in that State shall be construed as referring, where appropriate, to free legal assistance in the relevant territorial unit;

i)   any reference to a maintenance arrangement made in a State shall be construed as referring, where appropriate, to a maintenance arrangement made in the relevant territorial unit;

j)   any reference to recovery of costs by a State shall be construed as referring, where appropriate, to the recovery of costs by the relevant territorial unit.

(2) This Article shall not apply to a Regional Economic Integration Organisation.

Article 47. Non-unified legal systems — substantive rules.   (1)   A Contracting State with two or more territorial units in which different systems of law apply shall not be bound to apply this Convention to situations which involve solely such different territorial units.

(2)   A competent authority in a territorial unit of a Contracting State with two or more territorial units in which different systems of law apply shall not be bound to recognise or enforce a decision from another Contracting State solely because the decision has been recognised or enforced in another territorial unit of the same Contracting State under this Convention.

(3)   This Article shall not apply to a Regional Economic Integration Organisation.

Article 48. Co-ordination with prior Hague Maintenance Conventions.   In relations between the Contracting States, this Convention replaces, subject to Article 56(2), the Hague Convention of 2 October 1973 on the Recognition and Enforcement of Decisions Relating to Maintenance Obligations and the Hague Convention of 15 April 1958 concerning the recognition and enforcement of decisions relating to maintenance obligations towards children in so far as their scope of application as between such States coincides with the scope of application of this Convention.

Article 49. Co-ordination with the 1956 New York Convention.   In relations between the Contracting States, this Convention replaces the United Nations Convention on the Recovery Abroad of Maintenance of 20 June 1956, in so far as its scope of application as between such States coincides with the scope of application of this Convention.

Article 50. Relationship with prior Hague Conventions on service of documents and taking of evidence.   This Convention does not affect the Hague Convention of 1 March 1954 on civil procedure, the Hague Convention of 15 November 1965 on the Service Abroad of Judicial and Extrajudicial Documents in Civil or Commercial Matters and the Hague Convention of 18 March 1970 on the Taking of Evidence Abroad in Civil or Commercial Matters.

Article 51. Co-ordination of instruments and supplementary agreements.   (1)   This Convention does not affect any international instrument concluded before this Convention to which Contracting States are Parties and which contains provisions on matters governed by this Convention.

(2)   Any Contracting State may conclude with one or more Contracting States agreements, which contain provisions on matters governed by the Convention, with a view to improving the application of the Convention between or among themselves, provided that such agreements are consistent with the objects and purpose of the Convention and do not affect, in the relationship of such States with other Contracting States, the application of the provisions of the Convention. The States which have concluded such an agreement shall transmit a copy to the depositary of the Convention.

(3)   Paragraphs 1 and 2 shall also apply to reciprocity arrangements and to uniform laws based on special ties between the States concerned.

(4)   This Convention shall not affect the application of instruments of a Regional Economic Integration Organisation that is a Party to this Convention, adopted after the conclusion of the Convention, on matters governed by the Convention provided that such instruments do not affect, in the relationship of Member States of the Regional Economic Integration Organisation with other Contracting States, the application of the provisions of the Convention. As concerns the recognition or enforcement of decisions as between Member States of the Regional Economic Integration Organisation, the Convention shall not affect the rules of the Regional Economic Integration Organisation, whether adopted before or after the conclusion of the Convention.

Article 52. Most effective rule.   (1)   This Convention shall not prevent the application of an agreement, arrangement or international instrument in force between the requesting State and the requested State, or a reciprocity arrangement in force in the requested State that provides for

a)   broader bases for recognition of maintenance decisions, without prejudice to Article 22 f) of the Convention;

b)   simplified, more expeditious procedures on an application for recognition or recognition and enforcement of maintenance decisions;

c)   more beneficial legal assistance than that provided for under Articles 14 to 17; or

d)   procedures permitting an applicant from a requesting State to make a request directly to the Central Authority of the requested State.

(2)   This Convention shall not prevent the application of a law in force in the requested State that provides for more effective rules as referred to in paragraph 1 a) to c). However, as regards simplified, more expeditious procedures referred to in paragraph 1 b), they must be compatible with the protection offered to the parties under Articles 23 and 24, in particular as regards the rights of the parties to be duly notified of the proceedings and be given adequate opportunity to be heard and as regards the effects of any challenge or appeal.

Article 53. Uniform interpretation.   In the interpretation of this Convention, regard shall be had to its international character and to the need to promote uniformity in its application.

Article 54. Review of practical operation of the Convention.   (1)   The Secretary General of the Hague Conference on Private International Law shall at regular intervals convene a Special Commission in order to review the practical operation of the Convention and to encourage the development of good practices under the Convention.

(2)   For the purpose of such review, Contracting States shall co-operate with the Permanent Bureau of the Hague Conference on Private International Law in the gathering of information, including statistics and case law, concerning the practical operation of the Convention.

Article 55. Amendment of forms.   (1)   The forms annexed to this Convention may be amended by a decision of a Special Commission convened by the Secretary-General of the Hague Conference on Private International Law to which all Contracting States and all Members shall be invited. Notice of the proposal to amend the forms shall be included in the agenda for the meeting.

(2)   Amendments adopted by the Contracting States present at the Special Commission shall come into force for all Contracting States on the first day of the seventh calendar month after the date of their communication by the depositary to all Contracting States.

(3)   During the period provided for in paragraph 2 any Contracting State may by notification in writing to the depositary make a reservation, in accordance with Article 62, with respect to the amendment. The State making such reservation shall, until the reservation is withdrawn, be treated as a State not Party to the present Convention with respect to that amendment.

Article 56. Transitional provisions.   (1)   The Convention shall apply in every case where
  a)   a request pursuant to Article 7 or an application pursuant to Chapter III has been received by the Central Authority of the requested State after the Convention has entered into force between the requesting State and the requested State;
  b)   a direct request for recognition and enforcement has been received by the competent authority of the State addressed after the Convention has entered into force between the State of origin and the State addressed.

(2)   With regard to the recognition and enforcement of decisions between Contracting States to this Convention that are also Parties to either of the Hague Maintenance Conventions mentioned in Article 48, if the conditions for the recognition and enforcement under this Convention prevent the recognition and enforcement of a decision given in the State of origin before the entry into force of this Convention for that State, that would otherwise have been recognised and enforced under the terms of the Convention that was in effect at the time the decision was rendered, the conditions of that Convention shall apply.

(3)   The State addressed shall not be bound under this Convention to enforce a decision or a maintenance arrangement, in respect of payments falling due prior to the entry into force of the Convention between the State of origin and the State addressed, except for maintenance obligations arising from a parent–child relationship towards a person under the age of 21 years.

Article 57. Provision of information concerning laws, procedures and services.   (1)   A Contracting State, by the time its instrument of ratification or accession is deposited or a declaration is submitted in accordance with Article 61 of the Convention, shall provide the Permanent Bureau of the Hague Conference on Private International Law with

a) a description of its laws and procedures concerning maintenance obligations;

b) a description of the measures it will take to meet the obligations under Article 6;

c) a description of how it will provide applicants with effective access to procedures, as required under Article 14;

d) a description of its enforcement rules and procedures, including any limitations on enforcement, in particular debtor protection rules and limitation periods;

e) any specification referred to in Article 25(1) b) and (3).

(2) Contracting States may, in fulfilling their obligations under paragraph 1, utilise a country profile form recommended and published by the Hague Conference on Private International Law.

(3) Information shall be kept up to date by the Contracting States.

Chapter IX — Final provisions

Article 58. Signature, ratification and accession. (1) The Convention shall be open for signature by the States which were Members of the Hague Conference on Private International Law at the time of its Twenty-First Session and by the other States which participated in that Session.

(2) It shall be ratified, accepted or approved and the instruments of ratification, acceptance or approval shall be deposited with the Ministry of Foreign Affairs of the Kingdom of the Netherlands, depositary of the Convention.

(3) Any other State or Regional Economic Integration Organisation may accede to the Convention after it has entered into force in accordance with Article 60(1).

(4) The instrument of accession shall be deposited with the depositary.

(5) Such accession shall have effect only as regards the relations between the acceding State and those Contracting States which have not raised an objection to its accession in the 12 months after the date of the notification referred to in Article 65. Such an objection may also be raised by States at the time when they ratify, accept or approve the Convention after an accession. Any such objection shall be notified to the depositary.

Article 59. Regional Economic Integration Organisations. (1) A Regional Economic Integration Organisation which is constituted solely by sovereign States and has competence over some or all of the matters governed by this Convention may similarly sign, accept, approve or accede to this Convention. The Regional Economic Integration Organisation shall in that case have the rights and obligations of a Contracting State, to the extent that the Organisation has competence over matters governed by the Convention.

(2) The Regional Economic Integration Organisation shall, at the time of signature, acceptance, approval or accession, notify the depositary in writing of the matters governed by this Convention in respect of which competence has been transferred to that Organisation by its Member States. The Organisation shall promptly notify the depositary in writing of any changes to its competence as specified in the most recent notice given under this paragraph.

(3) At the time of signature, acceptance, approval or accession, a Regional Economic Integration Organisation may declare in accordance with Article 63 that it exercises competence over all the matters governed by this Convention and that the Member States which have transferred competence to the Regional Economic Integration

Organisation in respect of the matter in question shall be bound by this Convention by virtue of the signature, acceptance, approval or accession of the Organisation.

(4)   For the purposes of the entry into force of this Convention, any instrument deposited by a Regional Economic Integration Organisation shall not be counted unless the Regional Economic Integration Organisation makes a declaration in accordance with paragraph 3.

(5)   Any reference to a 'Contracting State' or 'State' in this Convention shall apply equally to a Regional Economic Integration Organisation that is a Party to it, where appropriate. In the event that a declaration is made by a Regional Economic Integration Organisation in accordance with paragraph 3, any reference to a 'Contracting State' or 'State' in this Convention shall apply equally to the relevant Member States of the Organisation, where appropriate.

Article 60. Entry into force.   (1)   The Convention shall enter into force on the first day of the month following the expiration of three months after the deposit of the second instrument of ratification, acceptance or approval referred to in Article 58.

(2)   Thereafter the Convention shall enter into force

a)   for each State or Regional Economic Integration Organisation referred to in Article 59(1) subsequently ratifying, accepting or approving it, on the first day of the month following the expiration of three months after the deposit of its instrument of ratification, acceptance or approval;

b)   for each State or Regional Economic Integration Organisation referred to in Article 58(3) on the day after the end of the period during which objections may be raised in accordance with Article 58(5);

c)   for a territorial unit to which the Convention has been extended in accordance with Article 61, on the first day of the month following the expiration of three months after the notification referred to in that Article.

Article 61. Declarations with respect to non-unified legal systems.   (1)   If a State has two or more territorial units in which different systems of law are applicable in relation to matters dealt with in the Convention, it may at the time of signature, ratification, acceptance, approval or accession declare in accordance with Article 63 that this Convention shall extend to all its territorial units or only to one or more of them and may modify this declaration by submitting another declaration at any time.

(2)   Any such declaration shall be notified to the depositary and shall state expressly the territorial units to which the Convention applies.

(3)   If a State makes no declaration under this Article, the Convention shall extend to all territorial units of that State.

(4)   This Article shall not apply to a Regional Economic Integration Organisation.

Article 62. Reservations.   (1)   Any Contracting State may, not later than the time of ratification, acceptance, approval or accession, or at the time of making a declaration in terms of Article 61, make one or more of the reservations provided for in Articles 2(2), 20(2), 30(8), 44(3) and 55(3). No other reservation shall be permitted.

(2)   Any State may at any time withdraw a reservation it has made. The withdrawal shall be notified to the depositary.

(3)   The reservation shall cease to have effect on the first day of the third calendar month after the notification referred to in paragraph 2.

(4)   Reservations under this Article shall have no reciprocal effect with the exception of the reservation provided for in Article 2(2).

Article 63. Declarations.   (1)   Declarations referred to in Articles 2(3), 11(1) g), 16(1), 24(1), 30(7), 44(1) and (2), 59 (3) and 61(1), may be made upon signature, ratification, acceptance, approval or accession or at any time thereafter, and may be modified or withdrawn at any time.

(2)   Declarations, modifications and withdrawals shall be notified to the depositary.

(3)   A declaration made at the time of signature, ratification, acceptance, approval or accession shall take effect simultaneously with the entry into force of this Convention for the State concerned.

(4)   A declaration made at a subsequent time, and any modification or withdrawal of a declaration, shall take effect on the first day of the month following the expiration of three months after the date on which the notification is received by the depositary.

Article 64. Denunciation.   (1)   A Contracting State to the Convention may denounce it by a notification in writing addressed to the depositary. The denunciation may be limited to certain territorial units of a multi-unit State to which the Convention applies.

(2)   The denunciation shall take effect on the first day of the month following the expiration of 12 months after the date on which the notification is received by the depositary. Where a longer period for the denunciation to take effect is specified in the notification, the denunciation shall take effect upon the expiration of such longer period after the date on which the notification is received by the depositary.

Article 65. Notification.   The depositary shall notify the Members of the Hague Conference on Private International Law, and other States and Regional Economic Integration Organisations which have signed, ratified, accepted, approved or acceded in accordance with Articles 58 and 59 of the following

a)   the signatures, ratifications, acceptances and approvals referred to in Articles 58 and 59;

b)   the accessions and objections raised to accessions referred to in Articles 58(3) and (5) and 59;

c)   the date on which the Convention enters into force in accordance with Article 60;

d)   the declarations referred to in Articles 2(3), 11(1) g), 16(1), 24(1), 30(7), 44(1) and (2), 59 (3) and 61(1):

e)   the agreements referred to in Article 51(2);

f)   the reservations referred to in Articles 2(2), 20(2), 30(8), 44(3) and 55(3), and the withdrawals referred to in Article 62(2);

g)   the denunciations referred to in Article 64.

XII

Successions

A. Proposal for a Regulation of the European Parliament and of the Council on jurisdiction, applicable law, recognition and enforcement of decisions and authentic instruments in matters of succession and the creation of a European Certificate of Succession (COM (2009) 154 of 14 October 2009)

(1) The Community has set itself the objective of maintaining and developing an area of freedom, security and justice. For the progressive establishment of such an area, it has to adopt measures relating to judicial cooperation in civil matters with a cross-border impact to the extent necessary for the proper functioning of the internal market.

(2) In accordance with Article 65(b) of the Treaty, these measures are to include those promoting the compatibility of the rules applicable in the Member States concerning the conflict of laws and of jurisdiction.

(3) The European Council meeting in Tampere on 15 and 16 October 1999 endorsed the principle of mutual recognition of judgments and other decisions of judicial authorities as the cornerstone of judicial cooperation in civil matters and invited the Council and the Commission to adopt a programme of measures to implement that principle.

(4) On 30 November 2000 the Council adopted a draft programme of measures for implementation of the principle of mutual recognition of decisions in civil and commercial matters. The programme identifies measures relating to the harmonisation of conflict-of-law rules as those facilitating the mutual recognition of decisions. It provides for the drawing up of an instrument relating to successions and wills, which were not included in Council Regulation (EC) No 44/2001 of 22 December 2000 on jurisdiction and the recognition and enforcement of judgments in civil and commercial matters.

(5) The European Council meeting in Brussels on 4 and 5 November 2004 adopted a new programme entitled 'The Hague Programme: strengthening freedom, security and justice in the European Union'. The programme underlines the need to adopt by 2011 an instrument on the law of succession which deals among other things with the issue of conflict of laws, legal jurisdiction, mutual recognition and the enforcement of decisions in this area, a European Certificate of Succession and a mechanism enabling it to be known with certainty if a resident of the European Union has left a last will or testament.

(6) The smooth functioning of the internal market should be facilitated by removing the obstacles to the free movement of persons who currently face difficulties asserting their rights in the context of an international succession. In the European area of justice, citizens must be able to organise their succession in advance. The rights of heirs

and/or legatees, other persons linked to the deceased and creditors of the succession must be effectively guaranteed.

(7)   In order to achieve these objectives, this Regulation should group together the provisions on legal jurisdiction, applicable law, recognition and enforcement of decisions and authentic instruments in this area and on the European Certificate of Succession.

(8)   The scope of this Regulation should include all questions arising in civil law in connection with succession to the estates of deceased persons, namely all forms of transfer of property as a result of death, be it by voluntary transfer, transfer in accordance with a will or an agreement as to succession, or a legal transfer of property as a result of death.

(9)   The validity and effects of gifts are covered by Regulation (EC) No 593/2008 of the European Parliament and of the Council of 17 June 2008 on the law applicable to contractual obligations (Rome I). They should therefore be excluded from the scope of this Regulation in the same way as other rights and assets created or transferred other than by succession. However, it is the law on succession determined pursuant to this Regulation which should specify if this gift or other form of provisions *inter vivos* giving rise to an immediate right *in rem* can lead to any obligation to restore or account for gifts when determining the shares of heirs or legatees in accordance with the law on succession.

(10)   While this Regulation should cover the method of acquiring a right *in rem* in respect of tangible or intangible property as provided for in the law governing the succession, the exhaustive list ('*numerus clausus*') of rights *in rem* which may exist under the national law of the Member States, which is, in principle, governed by the *lex rei sitae*, should be included in the national rules governing conflict of laws. The publication of these rights, in particular the functioning of the land registry and the effects of entry or failure to make an entry into the register, which is also governed by local law, should also be excluded.

(11)   In order to take into account the different methods of settling a succession in the Member States, this Regulation should define the jurisdiction of the courts in the broad sense, including the jurisdiction of non-judicial authorities where they exercise a jurisdictional role, in particular by delegation.

(12)   In view of the increasing mobility of European citizens and in order to encourage good administration of justice within the European Union and to ensure that a genuine connecting factor exists between the succession and the Member State exercising jurisdiction, this Regulation should provide for the competence of the courts of the Member State of the last habitual residence of the deceased for the whole of the succession. For the same reasons, it should allow the competent court, by way of exception and under certain conditions, to transfer the case to the jurisdiction where the deceased had nationality if the latter is better placed to hear the case.

(13)   In order to facilitate mutual recognition, no referral to the rules of jurisdiction under national law should be envisaged from now on. There are therefore grounds for determining in this Regulation the cases in which a court in a Member State can exercise subsidiary jurisdiction.

(14)   In order to simplify the lives of heirs and legatees living in a Member State other than that in which the courts are competent to settle the succession, the settlement should authorise them to make declarations regarding the acceptance or waiver of succession in the manner provided for under the law of their last habitual residence, if necessary before the courts of that State.

(15) The close links between the succession rules and the substantive rules mean that the Regulation should provide for the exceptional competence of the courts of the Member State where the property is located if the law of this Member State requires the intervention of its courts in order to take measures covered by substantive law relating to the transmission of this property and its recording in the land registers.

(16) The harmonious functioning of justice requires that irreconcilable decisions should not be pronounced in two Member States. To this end, this Regulation should provide for general rules of procedure based on Regulation (EC) No 44/2001.

(17) In order to allow citizens to avail themselves, with all legal certainty, of the benefits offered by the internal market, this Regulation should enable them to know in advance which law will apply to their succession. Harmonised rules governing conflict of laws should be introduced in order to avoid contradictory decisions being delivered in the Member States. The main rule should ensure that the succession is governed by a predictable law to which it is closely linked. Concern for legal certainty requires that this law should cover all of the property involved in the succession, irrespective of its nature or location, in order to avoid difficulties arising from the fragmentation of the succession.

(18) This Regulation should make it easier for citizens to organise their succession in advance by enabling them to choose the applicable law. This choice should be subject to strict rules in order to respect the legitimate expectations of the heirs and legatees.

(19) The validity of the form of dispositions of property upon death is not covered by the Regulation. For the Member States which have ratified it, its scope is governed by the provisions of the Hague Convention of 5 October 1961 on the conflicts of laws relating to the form of testamentary dispositions.

(20) In order to facilitate recognition of succession rights acquired in a Member State, the conflict-of-laws rule should favour the validity of the agreements as to succession by accepting alternative connecting factors. The legitimate expectations of third parties should be preserved.

(21) To the extent compatible with the general objective of this Regulation and in order to facilitate the transmission of a right *in rem* acquired under the law on succession, this Regulation should not present an obstacle to the application of certain mandatory rules of law of the place in which property is located that are exhaustively listed.

(22) On account of their economic, family or social purpose, some buildings, enterprises or other categories of property are subject to a particular succession regime in the Member State in which they are located. This Regulation should respect the particular regime. However, this exception to the application of the law on succession requires strict interpretation in order to remain compatible with the general objective of this Regulation. The exception does not apply in particular to the conflict-of-laws rule subjecting immovable property to a different law from that applicable to movable property or to the reserved portion of an estate.

(23) The differences between, on the one hand, national solutions as to the right of the State to seize a vacant succession and, on the other hand, the handling of a situation in which the order of death of one or more persons is not known can lead to contradictory results or, conversely, the absence of a solution. This Regulation should provide for a result consistent with the substantive law of the Member States.

(24) Considerations of public interest should allow courts in the Member States the opportunity in exceptional circumstances to disregard the application of foreign law in a given case where this would be contrary to the public policy of the forum. However, the

courts should not be able to apply the public-policy exception in order to disregard the law of another Member State or to refuse to recognise or enforce a decision, an authentic instrument, a legal transaction or a European Certificate of Succession drawn up in another Member State when this would be contrary to the Charter of Fundamental Rights of the European Union, and in particular Article 21, which prohibits all forms of discrimination.

(25) In the light of its general objective, which is the mutual recognition of decisions given in the Member States concerning succession to the estates of deceased persons, this Regulation should lay down rules relating to the recognition and enforcement of decisions on the basis of Regulation (EC) No 44/2001 and which should be adapted where necessary to meet the specific requirements of matters covered by this Regulation.

(26) In order to take into account the different methods of settling the issues regarding successions in the Member States, this Regulation should guarantee the recognition and enforcement of authentic instruments. Nevertheless, the authentic instruments cannot be treated as court decisions with regard to their recognition. The recognition of authentic instruments means that they enjoy the same evidentiary effect with regard to their contents and the same effects as in their country of origin, as well as a presumption of validity which can be eliminated if they are contested. This validity will therefore always be contestable before a court in the Member State of origin of the authentic instrument, in accordance with the procedural conditions defined by the Member State.

(27) An accelerated, manageable and efficient settlement of international successions within the European Union implies the possibility for the heir, legatee, executor of the will or administrator to prove easily on an out-of-court basis their capacity in the Member States in which the property involved in the succession is located. In order to facilitate free movement of this proof within the European Union, this Regulation should introduce a uniform model for the European Certificate of Succession and appoint the authority competent to issue it. In order to respect the principle of subsidiarity, this certificate should not replace the internal procedures of the Member States. The Regulation should specify the linkage with these procedures.

(28) The international commitments entered into by the Member States mean that this Regulation should not affect the international conventions to which one or more Member States are party when they are adopted. Consistency with the general objectives of this Regulation requires, however, that the Regulation take precedence as between Member States over the conventions.

(29) In order to facilitate the application of this Regulation, provision should be made for an obligation for Member States to communicate certain information regarding their law on succession within the framework of the European legal network in civil and commercial matters created by Council Decision 2001/470/EC of 28 May 2001.

(30) The measures necessary for the implementation of this Regulation should be adopted in accordance with Council Decision 1999/468/EC of 28 June 1999 laying down the procedures for the exercise of implementing powers conferred on the Commission.

(31) It would be particularly appropriate to enable the Commission to adopt any amendment to the forms provided for in this Regulation in accordance with the procedure laid down in Article 3 of Decision 1999/468/EC.

(32) Where the concept of 'nationality' serves to determine the law applicable, account should be taken of the fact that certain States whose legal system is based on *common law* use the concept of '*domicile*' and not 'nationality' as an equivalent connecting factor in matters of succession.

(33) Since the objectives of this Regulation, namely the free movement of persons, the organisation in advance by European citizens of their succession in an international context, the rights of heirs and legatees, and persons linked to the deceased and the creditors of the succession, cannot be satisfactorily met by the Member States and can therefore, by reason of the scale and effects of this Regulation, be better achieved at Community level, the Community may take measures in accordance with the principle of subsidiarity as set out in Article 5 of the Treaty. In accordance with the principle of proportionality, as set out in that Article, this Regulation does not go beyond what is necessary in order to achieve those objectives.

(34) This Regulation respects fundamental rights and observes the principles recognised in the Charter of Fundamental Rights of the European Union, in particular Article 21 thereof which states that any discrimination based on any ground such as sex, race, colour, ethnic or social origin, genetic features, language, religion or belief, political or any other opinion, membership of a national minority, property, birth, disability, age or sexual orientation shall be prohibited. This Regulation must be applied by the courts of the Member States in observance of these rights and principles.

(35) In accordance with Articles 1 and 2 of the Protocol on the position of the United Kingdom and Ireland annexed to the Treaty on European Union and the Treaty establishing the European Community, [the United Kingdom and Ireland have notified their wish to participate in the adoption and application of this Regulation]/ [without prejudice to Article 4 of the Protocol, the United Kingdom and Ireland will not participate in the adoption of this Regulation and will not be bound by it or be subject to its application].

(36) In accordance with Articles 1 and 2 of the Protocol on the position of Denmark annexed to the Treaty on European Union and the Treaty establishing the European Community, Denmark is not taking part in the adoption of this Regulation and is therefore not bound by it or subject to its application…

Chapter I — Scope and definitions

Article 1. Scope.   1.   This Regulation shall apply to successions to the estates of deceased persons. It shall not apply to revenue, customs or administrative matters.

2.   In this Regulation, 'Member State' means all the Member States with the exception of Denmark, [the United Kingdom and Ireland].

3.   The following shall be excluded from the scope of this Regulation:

(a)   the status of natural persons, as well as family relationships and relationships which are similar in effect;

(b)   the legal capacity of natural persons, notwithstanding Article 19(2)(c) and (d);

(c)   the disappearance, absence and presumed death of a natural person;

(d)   questions regarding the matrimonial property regime and the property regime applicable to relationships which are deemed to have comparable effects to marriage;

(e)   maintenance obligations;

(f)   rights and assets created or transferred other than by succession to the estate of deceased persons, including gifts, such as in joint ownership with right of survival, pension plans, insurance contracts and or arrangements of a similar nature, notwithstanding Article 19(2)(j);

(g)   questions covered by company law, such as clauses contained in company memoranda of association and articles of association, associations and legal persons and determining what will happen to the shares upon the death of their partners;

(h)   the dissolving, closure and merging of enterprises, associations and legal persons;

(i)   the constitution, functioning and dissolving of trusts;

(j)   the nature of rights *in rem* relating to property and publicising these rights.

Article 2. Definitions.   For the purposes of this Regulation, the following definitions shall apply:

(a)   'succession to the estates of deceased persons': all forms of transfer of property as a result of death, be it by voluntary transfer, in accordance with a will or an agreement as to succession, or a legal transfer of property as a result of death;

(b)   'court': any judicial authority or any competent authority in the Member States which carries out a judicial function in matters of succession. Other authorities which carry out by delegation of public power the functions falling within the jurisdiction of the courts as provided for in this Regulation shall be deemed to be courts.

(c)   'agreement as to succession': an agreement which confers, modifies or withdraws, with or without consideration, rights to the future succession of one or more persons who are party to the agreement;

(d)   'joint wills': wills drawn up by two or more persons in the same instrument for the benefit of a third party and/or on the basis of a reciprocal and mutual disposition;

(e)   'home Member State': the Member State in which, depending on the case, the decision has been given, the legal transaction approved or concluded and the authentic instrument drawn up;

(f)   'Member State addressed': the Member State in which recognition and/or enforcement of the decision, the legal transaction or the authentic instrument is requested;

(g)   'decision': any decision given in a matter of succession to the estate of a deceased person by a court of a Member State, whatever the decision may be called, including a decree, order, ordinance or writ of execution, as well as the determination of costs or expenses by an officer of the court;

(h)   'authentic instrument': an instrument which has been formally drawn up or registered as an authentic instrument and the authenticity of which:

—   relates to the signing and content of the authentic instrument; and

—   has been established by a public authority or other authority empowered for that purpose by the Member State in which it originates:

(i)   'European Certificate of Succession': the certificate issued by the competent court pursuant to Chapter VI of this Regulation.

Chapter II — Jurisdiction

Article 3. Courts.   The provisions of this Chapter shall apply to all courts in the Member States but shall apply to non-judicial authorities only where necessary.

Article 4. General jurisdiction. Notwithstanding the provisions of this Regulation the courts of the Member State on whose territory the deceased had habitual residence at the time of their death shall be competent to rule in matters of successions.

Article 5. Referral to a court better placed to hear the case. 1. Where the law of a Member State was chosen by the deceased to govern their succession in accordance with Article 17, the court seised in accordance with Article 4 may, at the request of one of the parties and if it considers that the courts of the Member State whose law has been chosen are better placed to rule on the succession, stay proceedings and invite the parties to seise the courts in that Member State with the application.

2. The competent court in accordance with Article 4 shall set a deadline by which the courts of the Member State whose law has been chosen must be seised in accordance with paragraph 1. If the courts are not seised by that deadline, the court seised shall continue to exercise its jurisdiction.

3. The courts of the Member State whose law has been chosen shall declare themselves competent within a maximum period of eight weeks from the date on which they were seised in accordance with paragraph 2. In this case, the court seised first shall decline jurisdiction. Otherwise, the court seised first shall continue to exercise its jurisdiction.

Article 6. Residual jurisdiction. Where the habitual residence of the deceased at the time of death is not located in a Member State, the courts of a Member State shall nevertheless be competent on the basis of the fact that succession property is located in that Member State and that:

(a) the deceased had their previous habitual residence in that Member State, provided that such residence did not come to an end more than five years before the court was deemed to be seised; or, failing that;

(b) the deceased had the nationality of that Member State at the time of their death; or, failing that;

(c) an heir or legatee has their habitual residence in the Member State; or, failing that;

(d) the application relates solely to this property.

Article 7. Counterclaim. The court before which proceedings are pending under Article 4, 5 or 6 shall also be competent to examine the counterclaim where this falls within the scope of this Regulation.

Article 8. Jurisdiction to accept or waive succession. The courts in the Member State of the habitual residence of the heir or legatee shall also be competent to receive declarations concerning the acceptance or waiver of succession or legacy or designed to limit the liability of the heir or legatee where such declarations must be made before a court.

Article 9. Competence of courts in the place in which the property is located. Where the law of the Member State of the place in which property is located requires the involvement of its courts in order to take measures under substantive law relating to the transmission of the property, its recording or transfer in the public register, the courts of the Member State shall be competent to take such measures.

Article 10. Seising of a court.   For the purposes of this Chapter, a court shall be deemed to be seised:

(a)   at the time when the document instituting the proceedings or an equivalent document is lodged with the court, provided that the applicant has not subsequently failed to take the steps they were required to take to have service effected on the defendant, or

(b)   if the document has to be served before being lodged with the court, at the time when it is formally drawn up or registered by the authority responsible for service, provided that the applicant has not subsequently failed to take the steps that they were required to take to have the document lodged with the court.

Article 11. Examination as to jurisdiction.   Where a court of a Member State is seised of a case over which it has no jurisdiction under this Regulation, it shall declare of its own motion that it has no jurisdiction.

Article 12. Examination as to admissibility.   1.   Where a defendant habitually resident in a Member State other than the Member State where the action was brought does not enter an appearance, the court with jurisdiction shall be responsible for staying the proceedings so long as it is not shown that the defendant has been able to receive the document instituting the proceedings or an equivalent document in time to defend themself or that all necessary steps have been taken to this end.

2.   Article 19 of Regulation (EC) No 1393/2007 of the European Parliament and of the Council of 13 November 2007 on the service in the Member States of judicial and extrajudicial documents in civil or commercial matters shall apply instead of the provisions of paragraph 1 of this Article if the document instituting the proceedings or an equivalent document has had to be sent from one Member State to another pursuant to that Regulation.

3.   Where the provisions of Council Regulation (EC) No 1393/2007 are not applicable, Article 15 of the Hague Convention of 15 November 1965 on the service abroad of judicial and extrajudicial documents in civil or commercial matters shall apply if the document instituting the proceedings or an equivalent document has to be sent abroad pursuant to that Convention.

Article 13. Lis pendens.   1.   Where proceedings involving the same cause of action and between the same parties are brought in the courts of different Member States, any court other than the court first seised shall of its own motion stay its proceedings until such time as the jurisdiction of the court first seised is established.

2.   Where the jurisdiction of the court first seised is established, any court other than the court first seised shall decline jurisdiction in favour of that court.

Article 14. Related actions.   1.   Where related actions are pending before courts of different Member States, any court other than the court first seised may stay its proceedings.

2.   Where these actions are pending at first instance, any court other than the court first seised may also, on the application of one of the parties, decline jurisdiction if the court first seised has jurisdiction over the actions in question and its law permits the consolidation thereof.

3. For the purposes of this Article, actions are deemed to be related where they are so closely connected that it is expedient to hear and determine them together in order to avoid the risk of irreconcilable judgments resulting from separate proceedings.

Article 15. Provisional, including protective, measures. Application may be made to the judicial authorities of a Member State for such provisional or protective measures as may be available under the law of that State, even if, under this Regulation, the courts of another Member State have jurisdiction as to the substance of the matter.

Chapter III — Applicable law

Article 16. General rule.

Unless otherwise provided for in this Regulation, the law applicable to the succession as a whole shall be that of the State in which the deceased had their habitual residence at the time of their death.

Article 17. Freedom of choice. 1. A person may choose as the law to govern the succession as a whole the law of the State whose nationality they possess.
   2. The law applicable to the succession must be expressly determined and included in a declaration in the form of a disposition of property upon death.
   3. The existence and the validity in substantive terms of the consent to this determination shall be governed by the determined law.
   4. Modification or revocation by its author of such a determination of applicable law must meet the conditions for the modification or revocation of a disposition of property upon death.

Article 18. Agreements as to succession. 1. An agreement regarding a person's succession shall be governed by the law which, under this Regulation, would have been applicable to the succession of that person in the event of their death on the day on which the agreement was concluded. If, in accordance with this law, the agreement is not valid, its validity shall nevertheless be accepted if it is in accordance with the law which, at the time of death, is applicable to the succession under this Regulation. The agreement shall therefore be governed by this law.
   2. An agreement concerning the succession of several persons shall be valid in substantive terms only if this validity is accepted by the law which, pursuant to Article 16, would have applied to the succession of one of the persons whose succession is involved in the event of death on the day on which the agreement was concluded. If the contract is valid pursuant to the law applicable to the succession of only one of those persons, that law shall apply. Where the contract is valid pursuant to the law applicable to the succession of several of these persons, the agreement shall be governed by the law with which it has the closest links.
   3. The parties may determine as the law governing their agreement the law which the person or one of the persons whose succession is involved could have chosen in accordance with Article 17.
   4. The application of the law provided for in this Article shall not prejudice the rights of any person who is not party to the agreement and who, in accordance with the

law determined in Article 16 or 17, has an indefeasible interest or another right of which it cannot be deprived by the person whose succession is involved.

Article 19. Scope of applicable law.   1.   The law determined in Chapter III shall govern the succession as a whole, from its opening to the final transfer of the inheritance to the beneficiaries.

2.   This law shall govern in particular:

(a)   the causes, time and place of the opening of succession;

(b)   the eligibility of the heirs and legatees, including the inheritance rights of the surviving spouse, determination of the respective shares of such persons, the responsibilities imposed on them by the deceased, and the other rights governing succession which have their source in the death;

(c)   the capacity to inherit;

(d)   the particular causes of the incapacity to dispose or receive;

(e)   disinheritance and debarment from succession;

(f)   the transfer of assets and rights making up the succession to the heirs and legatees, including the conditions and effects of accepting or waiving the succession or legacy;

(g)   the powers of the heirs, the executors of the wills and other administrators of the succession, in particular the sale of property and the payment of creditors;

(h)   responsibility for the debts under the succession;

(i)   the freely disposable portion, the reserved portions and the other restrictions on the freedom to dispose of property upon death, including the allocations deducted from the succession by a judicial authority or another authority for the benefit of the relatives of the deceased;

(j)   any obligation to restore or account for gifts and the taking of them into account when determining the shares of heirs;

(k)   the validity, interpretation, amendment and revocation of a disposition of property upon death, with the exception of its formal validity;

(l)   sharing the inheritance.

Article 20. Validity of the form of the acceptance or waiver.   Without prejudice to Article 19, acceptance or waiver of the succession or a legacy or a declaration made to limit the liability of the heir or legatee shall also be valid where it meets the conditions of the law of the State in which the heir or legatee has their place of habitual residence.

Article 21. Application of the law of the State in the place in which the property is located.   1.   The law applicable to the succession shall be no obstacle to the application of the law of the State in which the property is located where, for the purposes of acceptance or waiver of the succession or a legacy, it stipulates formalities subsequent to those laid down in the law applicable to the succession.

2.   The law applicable to the succession shall be no obstacle to the application of the law of the Member State in which the property is located where it:

(a)   subjects the administration and liquidation of the succession to the appointment of an administrator or executor of the will via an authority located in this Member State. The law applicable to the succession shall govern the determination of the persons, such as the heirs, legatees, executors or administrators of the will, who are likely to be appointed to administer and liquidate the succession;

(b)   subjects the final transfer of the inheritance to the beneficiaries to the prior payment of taxes relating to the succession.

Article 22. Special succession regimes.   The law applicable in accordance with this Regulation shall not prejudice the special succession regimes to which certain immovable property enterprises, enterprises or other special categories of property are subjected by the law of the Member State in which they are located on account of their economic, family or social purpose where, according to that law, this regime is applicable irrespective of the law governing the succession.

Article 23. Simultaneous death.   Where two or more persons whose successions are governed by different laws die in circumstances which do not allow the order of death to be determined and where the laws deal with the situation through provisions which are incompatible or which do not settle it at all, none of the persons shall have any rights regarding the succession of the other party or parties.

Article 24. Estate without a claimant.   Where, in accordance with the law applicable in accordance with this Regulation, there is neither an heir nor a legatee as determined by a disposition of property upon death and where no natural person is an heir by operation of law, the application of the law thereby determined shall not be an obstacle to the right of a Member State or a body appointed in accordance with the law of the Member State in question to seize the succession property located on its territory.

Article 25. Universal nature.   Any law specified by this Regulation shall apply even if it is not the law of a Member State.

Article 26. Referral.   Where this Regulation provides for the application of the law of a State, it means the rules of law in force in that State other than its rules of private international law.

Article 27. Public policy.   1.   The application of a rule of the law determined by this Regulation may be refused only if such application is incompatible with the public policy of the forum.

2.   In particular, the application of a rule of the law determined by this Regulation may not be considered to be contrary to the public policy of the forum on the sole ground that its clauses regarding the reserved portion of an estate differ from those in force in the forum.

Article 28. States with more than one legal system.   1.   Where a State comprises several territorial units each of which has its own rules of law in respect of succession to the estates of deceased persons, each territorial unit shall be considered as a State for the purpose of identifying the law applicable under this Regulation.

2.   A Member State within which different territorial units have their own rules of law in respect of successions shall not be required to apply this Regulation to conflicts of law arising between such units only.

Chapter IV — Recognition and enforcement

Article 29. Recognition of a decision.   A decision given pursuant to this Regulation shall be recognised in the other Member States without any special procedure being required.

Any interested party who raises the recognition of a decision as the principal issue in a dispute may, in accordance with the procedures provided for under Articles 38 to 56 of Regulation (EC) No 44/2001, apply for that decision to be recognised. If the outcome of the proceedings in a court of a Member State depends on the determination of an incidental question of recognition, that court shall have jurisdiction over that question.

Article 30. Grounds of non-recognition.   A decision shall not be recognised in the following cases:

(a)   where it was given in default of appearance, such recognition is manifestly contrary to public policy in the Member State in which recognition is sought, it being understood that the public policy criterion may not be applied to the rules of jurisdiction;

(b)   if the defendant was not served with the document which instituted the proceedings or with an equivalent document in sufficient time and in such a way as to enable him to arrange for his defence, unless the defendant failed to commence proceedings to challenge the decision when it was possible for him to do so;

(c)   if it is irreconcilable with a decision given in a dispute between the same parties in the Member State in which recognition is sought;

(d)   if it is irreconcilable with an earlier decision given in another Member State or in a third State involving the same cause of action and between the same parties, provided that the earlier decision fulfils the conditions necessary for its recognition in the Member State addressed.

Article 31. No review as to the substance of a decision.   Under no circumstances may a foreign decision be reviewed as to its substance.

Article 32. Stay of proceedings.   A court of a Member State in which recognition is sought of a decision given in another Member State may stay the proceedings if an ordinary appeal against the decision has been lodged.

Article 33. Enforceability of decisions.   Decisions given in a Member State and enforceable there and legal transactions shall be carried out in the other Member States in accordance with Articles 38 to 56 and 58 of Regulation (EC) No 44/2001.

Chapter V — Authentic instruments

Article 34. Recognition of authentic instruments.   Authentic instruments formally drawn up or registered in a Member State shall be recognised in the other Member States, except where the validity of these instruments is contested in accordance with the procedures provided for in the home Member State and provided that such recognition is not contrary to public policy in the Member State addressed.

Article 35. Enforceability of authentic instruments. A document which has been formally drawn up or registered as an authentic instrument and is enforceable in one Member State shall be declared enforceable in another Member State, on application made in accordance with the procedures provided for in Articles 38 to 57 of Regulation (EC) No 44/2001. The court with which an appeal is lodged in accordance with Articles 43 and 44 of this Regulation shall refuse or revoke a declaration of the enforceability if enforceability only of the authentic instrument is manifestly contrary to public policy in the Member State addressed or if contestation of the validity of the instrument is pending before a court of the home Member State of the authentic instrument.

Chapter VI — European Certificate of Succession

Article 36. Creation of a European Certificate of Succession. 1. This Regulation introduces a European Certificate of Succession, which shall constitute proof of the capacity of heir or legatee and of the powers of the executors of wills or third-party administrators. This certificate shall be issued by the competent authority pursuant to this Chapter, in accordance with the law applicable to succession pursuant to Chapter III of this Regulation.

2. The use of the European Certificate of Succession shall not be obligatory. The certificate shall not be a substitute for internal procedures. However, the effects of the certificate shall also be recognised in the Member State whose authorities have issued it in accordance with this Chapter.

Article 37. Competence to issue the certificate. 1. The certificate shall be issued upon application by any person obliged to provide proof of the capacity of heir or legatee and of the powers of the executors of wills or third-party administrators.

2. The certificate shall be drawn up by the competent court in the Member State whose courts are competent pursuant to Articles 4, 5 and 6.

Article 38. Content of the application. 1. Any person applying for the issue of a certificate of succession shall provide, via the form a model of which is provided in Annex 1, where such information is in their possession:

(a) information concerning the deceased: surname, forename(s), sex, civil status, nationality, their identification code (where possible), address of last habitual residence, date and place of their death;

(b) the claimant's details: surname, forename(s), sex, nationality, their identification code (where possible), address of last place of habitual residence and relationship to the deceased;

(c) the elements of fact or law which justify their right to succession and/or right to administer and/or execute the succession. Where they are aware of a disposition of property upon death, a copy of the disposition shall be attached to the application;

(d) if they are replacing other heirs or legatees and, if so, the proof of their death or any other event which has prevented them from making a claim to the succession;

(e) whether the deceased has stipulated a marriage contract; if so, they must attach a copy of the marriage contract;

(f) if they are aware that the succession rights are being contested.

2.   The applicant must prove the accuracy of the information provided by means of authentic instruments. If the documents cannot be produced or can be produced only with disproportionate difficulties, other forms of evidence shall be admissible.

3.   The competent court shall take the appropriate measures to guarantee the veracity of the declarations made. Where its domestic law allows, the court shall request that such declarations are made on oath.

Article 39. Partial certificate.   1.   A partial certificate may be applied for and issued to attest to:

(a)   the rights of each heir or legatee, and their share;

(b)   the devolution of a specific item of property, where this is allowed under the law applicable to the succession;

(c)   administration of the succession.

Article 40. Issue of the certificate.   1.   The certificate shall be issued only if the competent court considers that the facts which are presented as the grounds for the application are established. The competent court shall issue the certificate promptly.

2.   The competent court shall carry out, of its own accord and on the basis of the applicant's declarations and the instruments and other means of proof provided by them, the enquiries necessary to verify the facts and to search for any further proof that seems necessary.

3.   For the purposes of this Chapter, the Member States shall grant access to the competent courts in other Member States, in particular to the civil status registers, to registers recording acts and facts relating to the succession or to the matrimonial regime of the family of the deceased and to the land registers.

4.   The issuing court may summon before it any persons involved and any administrators or executors and make public statements inviting any other beneficiaries to the succession to assert their rights.

Article 41. Content of the certificate.   1.   The European Certificate of Succession shall be issued using the standard form in Annex II.

2.   The European Certificate of Succession shall contain the following information:

(a)   the issuing court, the elements of fact and law for which the court considers itself to be competent to issue the certificate and the date of issue;

(b)   information concerning the deceased: surname, forenames, sex, civil status, nationality, their identification code (where possible), address of last habitual residence, date and place of death;

(c)   any marriage contracts stipulated by the deceased;

(d)   the law applicable to the succession in accordance with this Regulation and the circumstances in fact and in law used to determine that law;

(e)   the elements in fact and law giving rise to the rights and/or powers of heirs, legatees, executors of wills or third-party administrators: legal succession and/or succession according to the will and/or arising out of agreements as to succession;

(f)   the applicant's details: surname, forename(s), sex, nationality, their identification code (where possible), address and relationship to the deceased;

(g)   where applicable, information in respect of each heir concerning the nature of the acceptance of the succession;

(h)   where there are several heirs, the share for each of them and, if applicable, the list of rights and assets for any given heir;

(i)   the list of assets or rights for legatees in accordance with the law applicable to the succession;

(j)   the restrictions on the rights of the heir in accordance with the law applicable to the succession in accordance with Chapter III and/or in accordance with the provisions contained in the will or agreement as to succession;

(k)   the list of acts that the heir, legatee, executor of the will and/or administrator may perform on the property to the succession pursuant to the law applicable to the succession.

Article 42. The effects of the European Certificate of Succession. 1.   The European Certificate of Succession shall be recognised automatically in all the Member States with regard to the capacity of the heirs, legatees, and powers of the executors of wills or third-party administrators.

2.   The content of the certificate shall be presumed to be accurate in all the Member States throughout the period of its validity. It shall be presumed that the person designated by the certificate as the heir, legatee, executor of the will or administrator shall hold the right to the succession or the powers of administration stated in the certificate and that there shall be no conditions or restrictions other than those stated therein.

3.   Any person who pays or passes on property to the bearer of a certificate who is authorised to carry out such acts on the basis of the certificate shall be released from their obligations, unless they know that the contents of the certificate are not accurate.

4.   Any person who has acquired succession property from the bearer of a certificate who is authorised to possess the property in accordance with the list attached to the certificate shall be considered to have acquired it from a person with the authority to possess the property, unless they know that the contents of the certificate are not accurate.

5.   The certificate shall constitute a valid document allowing for the transcription or entry of the inherited acquisition in the public registers of the Member State in which the property is located. Transcription shall take place in accordance with the conditions laid down in the law of the Member State in which the register is held and shall produce the effects specified therein.

Article 43. Rectification, suspension or cancellation of the European Certificate of Succession. 1.   The original of the certificate shall be retained by the issuing court, which shall issue one or more authentic copies to the applicant or to any person having a legitimate interest.

2.   The copies issued shall have the effects provided for in Article 42 for a limited period of three months. Once this period has elapsed, the bearers of the certificate or any other interested persons must request a new authentic copy from the issuing court in order to assert their rights to succession.

3.   The certificate shall, at the request of an interested party addressed to the issuing court, or spontaneously by the authority in question:

(a)   be rectified in the case of material error;

(b)   have a comment entered into its margin suspending its effects where it is contested that the certificate is accurate;

(c)   be cancelled where it is established that it is not accurate.

4.   The issuing court shall note in the margin of the original of the certificate its rectification, the suspension of its effects or its cancellation and shall notify the applicant(s) thereof.

Article 44. Methods of appeal.   Each Member State shall organise the methods of appeal against the decision to issue or not to issue, to rectify, to suspend or to cancel a certificate.

Chapter VII — General and final provisions

Article 45. Relations with existing international conventions.   1.   This Regulation shall not affect the application of the bilateral or multilateral conventions to which one or more Member States are party at the time of adoption of this Regulation and which relate to the subjects covered by this Regulation, without prejudice to the obligations of the Member States pursuant to Article 307 of the Treaty.

2.   Notwithstanding paragraph 1, this Regulation shall take precedence as between Member States over conventions which relate to subjects governed by this Regulation and to which the Member States are party.

Article 46. Information made available to the public.   The Member States shall provide within the framework of the European Judicial Network in civil and commercial matters a description of the national legislation and procedures relating to the law on succession and the relevant texts, with a view to their being made available to the public. They shall notify any subsequent amendments to these provisions.

Article 47. Amendments to the forms.   Any amendment to the forms referred to in Articles 38 and 41 shall be adopted in accordance with the consultative procedure set out in Article 48(2).

Article 48. Committee procedure.   1.   The Commission shall be assisted by the committee established by Article 75 of Regulation (EC) No 44/2001.

2.   Where reference is made to this paragraph, Articles 3 and 7 of Decision 1999/468/EC shall apply, having regard to the provisions of Article 8 thereof.

Article 49. Review clause.   By [...] at the latest, the Commission shall submit to the European Parliament, the Council and the European Economic and Social Committee a report on the application of this Regulation. The report shall be accompanied, where appropriate, by proposed amendments.

Article 50. Transitional provisions.   1.   This Regulation shall apply to the successions of persons deceased after its date of application.

2. Where the deceased had determined the law applicable to their succession prior to the date of application of this Regulation, this determination shall be considered to be valid provided that it meets the conditions listed in Article 17.

3. Where the parties to an agreement as to succession had determined the law applicable to that agreement prior to the date of application of this Regulation, this determination shall be considered to be valid provided that it meets the conditions listed in Article 18.

Article 51. Entry into force. This Regulation shall enter into force on the twentieth day following its publication in the *Official Journal of the European Union.*

This Regulation shall apply from [one year after the date of its entry into force].

B. ECJ case-law

The Court of Justice addressed the issue of the law applicable to successions in the *Fundación Gala-Salvador Dalí* case (judgment 15 April 2010, case C-518/08), concerning the claim brought by a Spanish foundation in relation to the entitlement to the resale right as per Directive 2001/84/EC on the resale right for the benefit of the author of an original work of art. In considering the notions of 'heir' and 'legatee' the CJ stated as follows,

21. ... it is not for the Court, in the context of a reference for a preliminary ruling, to give a ruling on the interpretation of provisions of national law, in particular those concerning private international law, or to decide whether the interpretation given by the national court of those provisions is correct. The Court must take account, under the division of jurisdiction between it and the national courts, of the factual and legislative context, as described in the order for reference, in which the questions put to it are set...

31. ... the adoption of that Directive forms part of the harmonisation of the Member States' laws, regulations and administrative provisions which concern the establishment and functioning of the internal market. Therefore, as is apparent from recitals 13 and 15 in the preamble to that Directive, there is no need to eliminate differences between national laws which cannot be expected to affect the functioning of the internal market and, in order to leave as much scope for national decision as possible, it is sufficient to limit the harmonisation exercise to those domestic provisions that have the most direct impact on the functioning of the internal market.

32. That analysis is reinforced by recital 27 in the preamble to Directive 2001/84, from which it is clear that while the Union legislature wanted those entitled under the author to benefit fully from the resale right after his death, it did not, in accordance with the principle of subsidiarity, consider it appropriate to take action through that Directive in relation to Member States' laws of succession, thus leaving to each Member State the task of defining the categories of persons capable of being considered, under national law, as those entitled.

33. It follows from the foregoing that, in the light of the objectives pursued by Directive 2001/84, it is permissible for Member States to make their own legislative choice in determining the categories of persons capable of benefiting from the resale right after the death of the author of a work of art.

34.   That being so, there is nothing in Directive 2001/84 to indicate that the European Union legislature intended to rule out the application of rules governing coordination between the various national laws relating to succession, in particular those of private international law which are intended to govern a conflict of laws such as that arising in the dispute in the main proceedings.

35.   It follows that it is for the referring court, for the purposes of applying the national provision transposing Article 6(1) of Directive 2001/84, to take due account of all the relevant rules for the resolution of conflicts of laws relating to the transfer on succession of the resale right.

XIII

Judicial Assistance in Civil Matters

Service of judicial and extrajudicial documents

A.1. Regulation (EC) No 1393/2007 of the European Parliament and of the Council of 13 November 2007 on the service in the Member States of judicial and extrajudicial documents in civil or commercial matters (service of documents), and repealing Council Regulation (EC) No 1348/2000 (OJ, L 324 of 10 December 2007)[1]

(1)   The Union has set itself the objective of maintaining and developing the Union as an area of freedom, security and justice, in which the free movement of persons is assured. To establish such an area, the Community is to adopt, among others, the measures relating to judicial cooperation in civil matters needed for the proper functioning of the internal market.

(2)   The proper functioning of the internal market entails the need to improve and expedite the transmission of judicial and extrajudicial documents in civil or commercial matters for service between the Member States.

(3)   The Council, by an Act dated 26 May 1997,[2] drew up a Convention on the service in the Member States of the European Union of judicial and extrajudicial documents in civil or commercial matters and recommended it for adoption by the Member States in accordance with their respective constitutional rules. That Convention has not entered into force. Continuity in the results of the negotiations for conclusion of the Convention should be ensured.

(4)   On 29 May 2000 the Council adopted Regulation (EC) No 1348/2000 on the service in the Member States of judicial and extrajudicial documents in civil or commercial matters. The main content of that Regulation is based on the Convention.

(5)   On 1 October 2004 the Commission adopted a report on the application of Regulation (EC) No 1348/2000. The report concludes that the application of Regulation (EC) No 1348/2000 has generally improved and expedited the transmission and the service of documents between Member States since its entry into force in 2001, but that nevertheless the application of certain provisions is not fully satisfactory.

(6)   Efficiency and speed in judicial procedures in civil matters require that judicial and extrajudicial documents be transmitted directly and by rapid means between local bodies designated by the Member States. Member States may indicate their intention

---

[1]   The Regulation has three annexes. The manual of receiving agencies is published and regularly updated by the European Commission at http://ec.europa.eu/justice_home/judicialatlascivil/html/ds_docs_en.htm#Manual.

[2]   OJ, C 261 of 27 August 1997, where also the Explanatory Report on the Convention is published.

to designate only one transmitting or receiving agency or one agency to perform both functions, for a period of five years. This designation may, however, be renewed every five years.

(7)   Speed in transmission warrants the use of all appropriate means, provided that certain conditions as to the legibility and reliability of the document received are observed. Security in transmission requires that the document to be transmitted be accompanied by a standard form, to be completed in the official language or one of the official languages of the place where service is to be effected, or in another language accepted by the Member State in question.

(8)   This Regulation should not apply to service of a document on the party's authorised representative in the Member State where the proceedings are taking place regardless of the place of residence of that party.

(9)   The service of a document should be effected as soon as possible, and in any event within one month of receipt by the receiving agency.

(10)   To secure the effectiveness of this Regulation, the possibility of refusing service of documents should be confined to exceptional situations.

(11)   In order to facilitate the transmission and service of documents between Member States, the standard forms set out in the Annexes to this Regulation should be used.

(12)   The receiving agency should inform the addressee in writing using the standard form that he may refuse to accept the document to be served at the time of service or by returning the document to the receiving agency within one week if it is not either in a language which he understands or in the official language or one of the official languages of the place of service. This rule should also apply to the subsequent service once the addressee has exercised his right of refusal. These rules on refusal should also apply to service by diplomatic or consular agents, service by postal services and direct service. It should be established that the service of the refused document can be remedied through the service on the addressee of a translation of the document.

(13)   Speed in transmission warrants documents being served within days of receipt of the document. However, if service has not been effected after one month has elapsed, the receiving agency should inform the transmitting agency. The expiry of this period should not imply that the request be returned to the transmitting agency where it is clear that service is feasible within a reasonable period.

(14)   The receiving agency should continue to take all necessary steps to effect the service of the document also in cases where it has not been possible to effect service within the month, for example, because the defendant has been away from his home on holiday or away from his office on business. However, in order to avoid an open-ended obligation for the receiving agency to take steps to effect the service of a document, the transmitting agency should be able to specify a time limit in the standard form after which service is no longer required.

(15)   Given the differences between the Member States as regards their rules of procedure, the material date for the purposes of service varies from one Member State to another. Having regard to such situations and the possible difficulties that may arise, this Regulation should provide for a system where it is the law of the Member State addressed which determines the date of service. However, where according to the law of a Member State a document has to be served within a particular period, the date to be taken into account with respect to the applicant should be that determined by the law of that Member State. This double date system exists only in a limited number of Member States. Those

Member States which apply this system should communicate this to the Commission, which should publish the information in the Official Journal of the European Union and make it available through the European Judicial Network in Civil and Commercial Matters established by Council Decision 2001/470/EC.

(16) In order to facilitate access to justice, costs occasioned by recourse to a judicial officer or a person competent under the law of the Member State addressed should correspond to a single fixed fee laid down by that Member State in advance which respects the principles of proportionality and non-discrimination. The requirement of a single fixed fee should not preclude the possibility for Member States to set different fees for different types of service as long as they respect these principles.

(17) Each Member State should be free to effect service of documents directly by postal services on persons residing in another Member State by registered letter with acknowledgement of receipt or equivalent.

(18) It should be possible for any person interested in a judicial proceeding to effect service of documents directly through the judicial officers, officials or other competent persons of the Member State addressed, where such direct service is permitted under the law of that Member State.

(19) The Commission should draw up a manual containing information relevant for the proper application of this Regulation, which should be made available through the European Judicial Network in Civil and Commercial Matters. The Commission and the Member States should do their utmost to ensure that this information is up to date and complete especially as regards contact details of receiving and transmitting agencies.

(20) In calculating the periods and time limits provided for in this Regulation, Regulation (EEC, Euratom) No 1182/71 of the Council of 3 June 1971 determining the rules applicable to periods, dates and time limits should apply.

(21) The measures necessary for the implementation of this Regulation should be adopted in accordance with Council Decision 1999/468/EC of 28 June 1999 laying down the procedures for the exercise of implementing powers conferred on the Commission.

(22) In particular, power should be conferred on the Commission to update or make technical amendments to the standard forms set out in the Annexes. Since those measures are of general scope and are designed to amend/delete non-essential elements of this Regulation, they must be adopted in accordance with the regulatory procedure with scrutiny provided for in Article 5a of Decision 1999/468/EC.

(23) This Regulation prevails over the provisions contained in bilateral or multilateral agreements or arrangements having the same scope, concluded by the Member States, and in particular the Protocol annexed to the Brussels Convention of 27 September 1968 and the Hague Convention of 15 November 1965 in relations between the Member States party thereto. This Regulation does not preclude Member States from maintaining or concluding agreements or arrangements to expedite or simplify the transmission of documents, provided that they are compatible with this Regulation.

(24) The information transmitted pursuant to this Regulation should enjoy suitable protection. This matter falls within the scope of Directive 95/46/EC of the European Parliament and of the Council of 24 October 1995 on the protection of individuals with regard to the processing of personal data and on the free movement of such data, and of Directive 2002/58/EC of the European Parliament and of the Council of 12 July 2002 concerning the processing of personal data and the protection of privacy in the electronic communications sector (Directive on privacy and electronic communications).

(25) No later than 1 June 2011 and every five years thereafter, the Commission should review the application of this Regulation and propose such amendments as may appear necessary.

(26) Since the objectives of this Regulation cannot be sufficiently achieved by the Member States and can therefore, by reason of the scale or effects of the action, be better achieved at Community level, the Community may adopt measures, in accordance with the principle of subsidiarity as set out in Article 5 of the Treaty. In accordance with the principle of proportionality, as set out in that Article, this Regulation does not go beyond what is necessary in order to achieve those objectives.

(27) In order to make the provisions more easily accessible and readable, Regulation (EC) No 1348/2000 should be repealed and replaced by this Regulation.

(28) In accordance with Article 3 of the Protocol on the position of the United Kingdom and Ireland, annexed to the Treaty on European Union and to the Treaty establishing the European Community, the United Kingdom and Ireland are taking part in the adoption and application of this Regulation.

(29) In accordance with Articles 1 and 2 of the Protocol on the position of Denmark, annexed to the Treaty on European Union and to the Treaty establishing the European Community, Denmark does not take part in the adoption of this Regulation and is not bound by it or subject to its application …

Chapter I — General provisions

Article 1. Scope.   1.   This Regulation shall apply in civil and commercial matters where a judicial or extrajudicial document has to be transmitted from one Member State to another for service there. It shall not extend in particular to revenue, customs or administrative matters or to liability of the State for actions or omissions in the exercise of state authority (acta iure imperii).

2.   This Regulation shall not apply where the address of the person to be served with the document is not known.

3.   In this Regulation, the term 'Member State' shall mean the Member States with the exception of Denmark.

Article 2. Transmitting and receiving agencies.   1.   Each Member State shall designate the public officers, authorities or other persons, hereinafter referred to as 'transmitting agencies', competent for the transmission of judicial or extrajudicial documents to be served in another Member State.

2.   Each Member State shall designate the public officers, authorities or other persons, hereinafter referred to as 'receiving agencies', competent for the receipt of judicial or extrajudicial documents from another Member State.

3.   A Member State may designate one transmitting agency and one receiving agency, or one agency to perform both functions. A federal State, a State in which several legal systems apply or a State with autonomous territorial units shall be free to designate more than one such agency. The designation shall have effect for a period of five years and may be renewed at five-year intervals.

4.   Each Member State shall provide the Commission with the following information:

(a)   the names and addresses of the receiving agencies referred to in paragraphs 2 and 3;

(b) the geographical areas in which they have jurisdiction;

(c) the means of receipt of documents available to them; and

(d) the languages that may be used for the completion of the standard form set out in Annex I.

Member States shall notify the Commission of any subsequent modification of such information.

Article 3. Central body. Each Member State shall designate a central body responsible for:

(a) supplying information to the transmitting agencies;

(b) seeking solutions to any difficulties which may arise during transmission of documents for service;

(c) forwarding, in exceptional cases, at the request of a transmitting agency, a request for service to the competent receiving agency.

A federal State, a State in which several legal systems apply or a State with autonomous territorial units shall be free to designate more than one central body.

Chapter II — Judicial documents

Section 1 — Transmission and service of judicial documents

Article 4. Transmission of documents. 1. Judicial documents shall be transmitted directly and as soon as possible between the agencies designated pursuant to Article 2.

2. The transmission of documents, requests, confirmations, receipts, certificates and any other papers between transmitting agencies and receiving agencies may be carried out by any appropriate means, provided that the content of the document received is true and faithful to that of the document forwarded and that all information in it is easily legible.

3. The document to be transmitted shall be accompanied by a request drawn up using the standard form set out in Annex I. The form shall be completed in the official language of the Member State addressed or, if there are several official languages in that Member State, the official language or one of the official languages of the place where service is to be effected, or in another language which that Member State has indicated it can accept. Each Member State shall indicate the official language or languages of the institutions of the European Union other than its own which is or are acceptable to it for completion of the form.

4. The documents and all papers that are transmitted shall be exempted from legalisation or any equivalent formality.

5. When the transmitting agency wishes a copy of the document to be returned together with the certificate referred to in Article 10, it shall send the document in duplicate.

Article 5. Translation of documents. 1. The applicant shall be advised by the transmitting agency to which he forwards the document for transmission that the addressee may refuse to accept it if it is not in one of the languages provided for in Article 8.

2. The applicant shall bear any costs of translation prior to the transmission of the document, without prejudice to any possible subsequent decision by the court or competent authority on liability for such costs.

Article 6. Receipt of documents by receiving agency.   1.   On receipt of a document, a receiving agency shall, as soon as possible and in any event within seven days of receipt, send a receipt to the transmitting agency by the swiftest possible means of transmission using the standard form set out in Annex I.

2.   Where the request for service cannot be fulfilled on the basis of the information or documents transmitted, the receiving agency shall contact the transmitting agency by the swiftest possible means in order to secure the missing information or documents.

3.   If the request for service is manifestly outside the scope of this Regulation or if non-compliance with the formal conditions required makes service impossible, the request and the documents transmitted shall be returned, on receipt, to the transmitting agency, together with the notice of return using the standard form set out in Annex I.

4.   A receiving agency receiving a document for service but not having territorial jurisdiction to serve it shall forward it, as well as the request, to the receiving agency having territorial jurisdiction in the same Member State if the request complies with the conditions laid down in Article 4(3) and shall inform the transmitting agency accordingly using the standard form set out in Annex I. That receiving agency shall inform the transmitting agency when it receives the document, in the manner provided for in paragraph 1.

Article 7. Service of documents.   1.   The receiving agency shall itself serve the document or have it served, either in accordance with the law of the Member State addressed or by a particular method requested by the transmitting agency, unless that method is incompatible with the law of that Member State.

2.   The receiving agency shall take all necessary steps to effect the service of the document as soon as possible, and in any event within one month of receipt. If it has not been possible to effect service within one month of receipt, the receiving agency shall:

(a)   immediately inform the transmitting agency by means of the certificate in the standard form set out in Annex I, which shall be drawn up under the conditions referred to in Article 10(2); and

(b)   continue to take all necessary steps to effect the service of the document, unless indicated otherwise by the transmitting agency, where service seems to be possible within a reasonable period of time.

Article 8. Refusal to accept a document.   1.   The receiving agency shall inform the addressee, using the standard form set out in Annex II, that he may refuse to accept the document to be served at the time of service or by returning the document to the receiving agency within one week if it is not written in, or accompanied by a translation into, either of the following languages:

(a)   a language which the addressee understands; or

(b)   the official language of the Member State addressed or, if there are several official languages in that Member State, the official language or one of the official languages of the place where service is to be effected.

2.   Where the receiving agency is informed that the addressee refuses to accept the document in accordance with paragraph 1, it shall immediately inform the transmitting agency by means of the certificate provided for in Article 10 and return the request and the documents of which a translation is requested.

3.   If the addressee has refused to accept the document pursuant to paragraph 1, the service of the document can be remedied through the service on the addressee in

accordance with the provisions of this Regulation of the document accompanied by a translation into a language provided for in paragraph 1. In that case, the date of service of the document shall be the date on which the document accompanied by the translation is served in accordance with the law of the Member State addressed. However, where according to the law of a Member State, a document has to be served within a particular period, the date to be taken into account with respect to the applicant shall be the date of the service of the initial document determined pursuant to Article 9(2).

    4.   Paragraphs 1, 2 and 3 shall also apply to the means of transmission and service of judicial documents provided for in Section 2.

    5.   For the purposes of paragraph 1, the diplomatic or consular agents, where service is effected in accordance with Article 13, or the authority or person, where service is effected in accordance with Article 14, shall inform the addressee that he may refuse to accept the document and that any document refused must be sent to those agents or to that authority or person respectively.

Article 9. Date of service.   1.   Without prejudice to Article 8, the date of service of a document pursuant to Article 7 shall be the date on which it is served in accordance with the law of the Member State addressed.

    2.   However, where according to the law of a Member State a document has to be served within a particular period, the date to be taken into account with respect to the applicant shall be that determined by the law of that Member State.

    3.   Paragraphs 1 and 2 shall also apply to the means of transmission and service of judicial documents provided for in Section 2.

Article 10. Certificate of service and copy of the document served.   1.   When the formalities concerning the service of the document have been completed, a certificate of completion of those formalities shall be drawn up in the standard form set out in Annex I and addressed to the transmitting agency, together with, where Article 4(5) applies, a copy of the document served.

    2.   The certificate shall be completed in the official language or one of the official languages of the Member State of origin or in another language which the Member State of origin has indicated that it can accept. Each Member State shall indicate the official language or languages of the institutions of the European Union other than its own which is or are acceptable to it for completion of the form.

Article 11. Costs of service.   1.   The service of judicial documents coming from a Member State shall not give rise to any payment or reimbursement of taxes or costs for services rendered by the Member State addressed.

    2.   However, the applicant shall pay or reimburse the costs occasioned by:

    (a)   recourse to a judicial officer or to a person competent under the law of the Member State addressed;

    (b)   the use of a particular method of service.

    Costs occasioned by recourse to a judicial officer or to a person competent under the law of the Member State addressed shall correspond to a single fixed fee laid down by that Member State in advance which respects the principles of proportionality and non-discrimination. Member States shall communicate such fixed fees to the Commission.

Section 2 — Other means of transmission and service of judicial documents

Article 12. Transmission by consular or diplomatic channels.   Each Member State shall be free, in exceptional circumstances, to use consular or diplomatic channels to forward judicial documents, for the purpose of service, to those agencies of another Member State which are designated pursuant to Articles 2 or 3.

Article 13. Service by diplomatic or consular agents.   1.   Each Member State shall be free to effect service of judicial documents on persons residing in another Member State, without application of any compulsion, directly through its diplomatic or consular agents.
     2.   Any Member State may make it known, in accordance with Article 23(1), that it is opposed to such service within its territory, unless the documents are to be served on nationals of the Member State in which the documents originate.

Article 14. Service by postal services.   Each Member State shall be free to effect service of judicial documents directly by postal services on persons residing in another Member State by registered letter with acknowledgement of receipt or equivalent.

Article 15. Direct service.   Any person interested in a judicial proceeding may effect service of judicial documents directly through the judicial officers, officials or other competent persons of the Member State addressed, where such direct service is permitted under the law of that Member State.

Chapter III — Extrajudicial documents

Article 16. Transmission.   Extrajudicial documents may be transmitted for service in another Member State in accordance with the provisions of this Regulation.

Chapter IV — Final provisions

Article 17. Implementing rules.   Measures designed to amend non-essential elements of this Regulation relating to the updating or to the making of technical amendments to the standard forms set out in Annexes I and II shall be adopted in accordance with the regulatory procedure with scrutiny referred to in Article 18(2).

Article 18. Committee.   1.   The Commission shall be assisted by a committee.
     2.   Where reference is made to this paragraph, Article 5a(1) to (4), and Article 7 of Decision 1999/468/EC shall apply, having regard to the provisions of Article 8 thereof.

Article 19. Defendant not entering an appearance.   1.   Where a writ of summons or an equivalent document has had to be transmitted to another Member State for the purpose of service under the provisions of this Regulation and the defendant has not appeared, judgment shall not be given until it is established that:
     (a)   the document was served by a method prescribed by the internal law of the Member State addressed for the service of documents in domestic actions upon persons who are within its territory; or

(b)   the document was actually delivered to the defendant or to his residence by another method provided for by this Regulation; and that in either of these cases the service or the delivery was effected in sufficient time to enable the defendant to defend.

2.   Each Member State may make it known, in accordance with Article 23(1), that the judge, notwithstanding the provisions of paragraph 1, may give judgment even if no certificate of service or delivery has been received, if all the following conditions are fulfilled:

(a)   the document was transmitted by one of the methods provided for in this Regulation;

(b)   a period of time of not less than six months, considered adequate by the judge in the particular case, has elapsed since the date of the transmission of the document;

(c)   no certificate of any kind has been received, even though every reasonable effort has been made to obtain it through the competent authorities or bodies of the Member State addressed.

3.   Notwithstanding paragraphs 1 and 2, the judge may order, in case of urgency, any provisional or protective measures.

4.   When a writ of summons or an equivalent document has had to be transmitted to another Member State for the purpose of service under the provisions of this Regulation and a judgment has been entered against a defendant who has not appeared, the judge shall have the power to relieve the defendant from the effects of the expiry of the time for appeal from the judgment if the following conditions are fulfilled:

(a)   the defendant, without any fault on his part, did not have knowledge of the document in sufficient time to defend, or knowledge of the judgment in sufficient time to appeal; and

(b)   the defendant has disclosed a prima facie defence to the action on the merits.

An application for relief may be filed only within a reasonable time after the defendant has knowledge of the judgment.

Each Member State may make it known, in accordance with Article 23(1), that such application will not be entertained if it is filed after the expiry of a time to be stated by it in that communication, but which shall in no case be less than one year following the date of the judgment.

5.   Paragraph 4 shall not apply to judgments concerning the status or capacity of persons.

Article 20. Relationship with agreements or arrangements to which Member States are party.   1.   This Regulation shall, in relation to matters to which it applies, prevail over other provisions contained in bilateral or multilateral agreements or arrangements concluded by the Member States, and in particular Article IV of the Protocol to the Brussels Convention of 1968 and the Hague Convention of 15 November 1965.

2.   This Regulation shall not preclude individual Member States from maintaining or concluding agreements or arrangements to expedite further or simplify the transmission of documents, provided that they are compatible with this Regulation.

3.   Member States shall send to the Commission:

(a)   a copy of the agreements or arrangements referred to in paragraph 2 concluded between the Member States as well as drafts of such agreements or arrangements which they intend to adopt; and

(b)   any denunciation of, or amendments to, these agreements or arrangements.

Article 21. Legal aid. This Regulation shall not affect the application of Article 23 of the Convention on civil procedure of 17 July 1905, Article 24 of the Convention on civil procedure of 1 March 1954 or Article 13 of the Convention on international access to justice of 25 October 1980 between the Member States party to those Conventions.

Article 22. Protection of information transmitted.   1.   Information, including in particular personal data, transmitted under this Regulation shall be used by the receiving agency only for the purpose for which it was transmitted.

2.   Receiving agencies shall ensure the confidentiality of such information, in accordance with their national law.

3.   Paragraphs 1 and 2 shall not affect national laws enabling data subjects to be informed of the use made of information transmitted under this Regulation.

4.   This Regulation shall be without prejudice to Directives 95/46/EC and 2002/58/EC.

Article 23. Communication and publication.   1.   Member States shall communicate to the Commission the information referred to in Articles 2, 3, 4, 10, 11, 13, 15 and 19. Member States shall communicate to the Commission if, according to their law, a document has to be served within a particular period as referred to in Articles 8(3) and 9(2).

2.   The Commission shall publish the information communicated in accordance with paragraph 1 in the Official Journal of the European Union with the exception of the addresses and other contact details of the agencies and of the central bodies and the geographical areas in which they have jurisdiction.

3.   The Commission shall draw up and update regularly a manual containing the information referred to in paragraph 1, which shall be available electronically, in particular through the European Judicial Network in Civil and Commercial Matters.

Article 24. Review.   No later than 1 June 2011, and every five years thereafter, the Commission shall present to the European Parliament, the Council and the European Economic and Social Committee a report on the application of this Regulation, paying special attention to the effectiveness of the agencies designated pursuant to Article 2 and to the practical application of Article 3(c) and Article 9. The report shall be accompanied if need be by proposals for adaptations of this Regulation in line with the evolution of notification systems.

Article 25. Repeal.   1.   Regulation (EC) No 1348/2000 shall be repealed as from the date of application of this Regulation.

2.   References made to the repealed Regulation shall be construed as being made to this Regulation and should be read in accordance with the correlation table in Annex III.

Article 26. Entry into force.   This Regulation shall enter into force on the 20th day following its publication in the Official Journal of the European Union.

It shall apply from 13 November 2008 with the exception of Article 23 which shall apply from 13 August 2008.

ANNEX III CORRELATION TABLE

Regulation (EC) No 1348/2000	This Regulation
Article 1(1)	Article 1(1) first sentence
—	Article 1(1) second sentence
Article 1(2)	Article 1(2)
—	Article 1(3)
Article 2	Article 2
Article 3	Article 3
Article 4	Article 4
Article 5	Article 5
Article 6	Article 6
Article 7(1)	Article 7(1)
Article 7(2) first sentence	Article 7(2) first sentence
Article 7(2) second sentence	Article 7(2) second sentence (introductory phrase) and Article 7(2)(a)
—	Article 7(2)(b)
Article 7(2) third sentence	—
Article 8(1) introductory phrase	Article 8(1) introductory phrase
Article 8(1)(a)	Article 8(1)(b)
Article 8(1)(b)	Article 8(1)(a)
Article 8(2)	Article 8(2)
—	Article 8(3) to (5)
Article 9(1) and (2)	Article 9(1) and (2)
Article 9(3)	—
—	Article 9(3)
Article 10	Article 10
Article 11(1)	Article 11(1)
Article 11(2)	Article 11(2) first subparagraph
—	Article 11(2) second subparagraph
Article 12	Article 12
Article 13	Article 13
Article 14(1)	Article 14
Article 14(2)	—
Article 15(1)	Article 15
Article 15(2)	—
Article 16	Article 16
Article 17, introductory phrase	Article 17
Article 17(a) to (c)	—
Article 18(1) and (2)	Article 18(1) and (2)
Article 18(3)	—
Article 19	Article 19
Article 20	Article 20
Article 21	Article 21
Article 22	Article 22
Article 23(1)	Article 23(1) first sentence
—	Article 23(1) second sentence
Article 23(2)	Article 23(2)
—	Article 23(3)
Article 24	Article 24
Article 25	—
—	Article 25
—	Article 26
Annex	Annex I
—	Annex II
—	Annex III

A.2. Council Decision 2006/326/EC of 27 April 2006 concerning the conclusion of the Agreement between the European Community and the Kingdom of Denmark on the service of judicial and extrajudicial documents in civil or commercial matters (OJ, L 120 of 5 May 2006)[3]

(1)   In accordance with Articles 1 and 2 of the Protocol on the position of Denmark annexed to the Treaty on European Union and the Treaty establishing the European Community, Denmark is not bound by the provisions of Council Regulation (EC) No 1348/2000 of 29 May 2000 on the service in the Member States of judicial and extrajudicial documents in civil or commercial matters, nor subject to their application.

(2)   The Commission has negotiated an Agreement between the European Community and the Kingdom of Denmark extending to Denmark the provisions of Regulation (EC) No 1348/2000.

(3)   The Agreement was signed, on behalf of the European Community, on 19 October 2005, subject to its possible conclusion at a later date, in accordance with Council Decision 2005/794/EC of 20 September 2005.

(4)   In accordance with Article 3 of the Protocol on the position of the United Kingdom and Ireland annexed to the Treaty on European Union and the Treaty establishing the European Community, the United Kingdom and Ireland are taking part in the adoption and application of this Decision.

(5)   In accordance with Articles 1 and 2 of the Protocol on the position of Denmark, Denmark is not taking part in the adoption of this Decision and is not bound by it or subject to its application.

(6)   The Agreement should be approved …

Article 1.   The Agreement between the European Community and the Kingdom of Denmark on the service of judicial and extrajudicial documents in civil or commercial matters is hereby approved on behalf of the Community.

Article 1a.   1.   For the purpose of applying Article 5(2) of the Agreement, the Commission shall assess, before taking a decision expressing the Community's agreement, whether the international agreement envisaged by Denmark would not render the Agreement ineffective and would not undermine the proper functioning of the system established by its rules.

2.   The Commission shall take a reasoned decision within 90 days of being informed by Denmark of Denmark's intention to enter into the international agreement in question.

If the international agreement in question meets the conditions referred to in paragraph 1, the decision by the Commission shall express the Community's agreement within the meaning of Article 5(2) of the Agreement.

---

[3]   As amended by Council Decision 2009/943/EC of 30 November 2009 amending Decision 2006/326/EC to provide for a procedure for the implementation of Article 5(2) of the Agreement between the European Community and the Kingdom of Denmark on the service of judicial and extrajudicial documents in civil or commercial matters, OJ, L 331 of 16 December 2009.

Article 1b.   The Commission shall inform the Member States of the international agreements which Denmark has been authorised to conclude in accordance with Article 1a.

Article 2.   The President of the Council is hereby authorised to designate the person empowered to make the notification provided for in Article 10(2) of the Agreement.

A.3.   Agreement between the European Community and the Kingdom of Denmark on the service of judicial and extrajudicial documents in civil or commercial matters (OJ, L 300 of 17 November 2005)

The European Community, hereinafter referred to as 'the Community', of the one part, and The Kingdom of Denmark, hereinafter referred to as 'Denmark', of the other part,

Desiring to improve and expedite transmission between Denmark and the other Member States of the Community of judicial and extrajudicial documents in civil or commercial matters,

Considering that transmission for this purpose is to be made directly between local bodies designated by the Contracting Parties,

Considering that speed in transmission warrants the use of all appropriate means, provided that certain conditions as to the legibility and reliability of the documents received are observed,

Considering that security in transmission requires that the document to be transmitted be accompanied by a preprinted form, to be completed in the language of the place where the service is to be effected, or in another language accepted by the receiving Member State,

Considering that to secure the effectiveness of this Agreement, the possibility of refusing service of documents should be confined to exceptional situations,

Whereas the Convention on the service in the Member States of the European Union of judicial and extrajudicial documents in civil or commercial matters drawn up by the Council of the European Union by Act of 26 May 1997 has not entered into force and that continuity in the results of the negotiations for conclusion of the Convention should be ensured,

Whereas the main content of that Convention has been taken over in Council Regulation (EC) No 1348/2000 of 29 May 2000 on the service in the Member States of judicial and extrajudicial documents in civil or commercial matters (the Regulation on the service of documents),

Referring to the Protocol on the position of Denmark annexed to the Treaty on European Union and to the Treaty establishing the European Community (the Protocol on the position of Denmark) pursuant to which the Regulation on the service of documents shall not be binding upon or applicable in Denmark,

Desiring that the provisions of the Regulation on the service of documents, future amendments hereto and the implementing measures relating to it should under international law apply to the relations between the Community and Denmark being a

Member State with a special position with respect to Title IV of the Treaty establishing the European Community,

Stressing the importance of proper coordination between the Community and Denmark with regard to the negotiation and conclusion of international agreements that may affect or alter the scope of the Regulation on the service of documents,

Stressing that Denmark should seek to join international agreements entered into by the Community where Danish participation in such agreements is relevant for the coherent application of the Regulation on the service of documents and this Agreement,

Stating that the Court of Justice of the European Communities should have jurisdiction in order to secure the uniform application and interpretation of this Agreement including the provisions of the Regulation on the service of documents and any implementing Community measures forming part of this Agreement,

Referring to the jurisdiction conferred to the Court of Justice of the European Communities pursuant to Article 68(1) of the Treaty establishing the European Community to give rulings on preliminary questions relating to the validity and interpretation of acts of the institutions of the Community based on Title IV of the Treaty, including the validity and interpretation of this Agreement, and to the circumstance that this provision shall not be binding upon or applicable in Denmark, as results from the Protocol on the position of Denmark,

Considering that the Court of Justice of the European Communities should have jurisdiction under the same conditions to give preliminary rulings on questions concerning the validity and interpretation of this Agreement which are raised by a Danish court or tribunal, and that Danish courts and tribunals should therefore request preliminary rulings under the same conditions as courts and tribunals of other Member States in respect of the interpretation of the Regulation on the service of documents and its implementing measures,

Referring to the provision that, pursuant to Article 68(3) of the Treaty establishing the European Community, the Council of the European Union, the European Commission and the Member States may request the Court of Justice of the European Communities to give a ruling on the interpretation of acts of the institutions of the Community based on Title IV of the Treaty, including the interpretation of this Agreement, and the circumstance that this provision shall not be binding upon or applicable in Denmark, as results from the Protocol on the position of Denmark,

Considering that Denmark should, under the same conditions as other Member States in respect of the Regulation on the service of documents and its implementing measures, be accorded the possibility to request the Court of Justice of the European Communities to give rulings on questions relating to the interpretation of this Agreement,

Stressing that under Danish law the courts in Denmark should — when interpreting this Agreement including the provisions of the Regulation on the service of documents and any implementing Community measures forming part of this Agreement — take due account of the rulings contained in the case law of the Court of Justice of the European Communities and of the courts of the Member States of the European Communities in respect of provisions of the Regulation on the service of documents and any implementing Community measures,

Considering that it should be possible to request the Court of Justice of the European Communities to rule on questions relating to compliance with obligations under this

Agreement pursuant to the provisions of the Treaty establishing the European Community governing proceedings before the Court,

Whereas, by virtue of Article 300(7) of the Treaty establishing the European Community, this Agreement binds Member States; it is therefore appropriate that Denmark, in the case of non-compliance by a Member State, should be able to seize the Commission as guardian of the Treaty,

Have agreed as follows:

Article 1. Aim.   1.   The aim of this Agreement is to apply the provisions of the Regulation on the service of documents and its implementing measures to the relations between the Community and Denmark, in accordance with Article 2(1) of this Agreement.

2.   It is the objective of the Contracting Parties to arrive at a uniform application and interpretation of the provisions of the Regulation on the service of documents and its implementing measures in all Member States.

3.   The provisions of Articles 3(1), 4(1) and 5(1) of this Agreement result from the Protocol on the position of Denmark.

Article 2. Cooperation on the service of documents.   1.   The provisions of the Regulation on the service of documents, which is annexed to this Agreement and forms part thereof, together with its implementing measures adopted pursuant to Article 17 of the Regulation and — in respect of implementing measures adopted after the entry into force of this Agreement — implemented by Denmark as referred to in Article 4 of this Agreement, and the information communicated by Member States under Article 23 of the Regulation, shall under international law apply to the relations between the Community and Denmark.

2.   The date of entry into force of this Agreement shall apply instead of the date referred to in Article 25 of the Regulation.

Article 3. Amendments to the Regulation on the service of documents.   1.   Denmark shall not take part in the adoption of amendments to the Regulation on the service of documents and no such amendments shall be binding upon or applicable in Denmark.

2.   Whenever amendments to the Regulation are adopted Denmark shall notify the Commission of its decision whether or not to implement the content of such amendments. Notification shall be given at the time of the adoption of the amendments or within 30 days thereafter.

3.   If Denmark decides that it will implement the content of the amendments the notification shall indicate whether implementation can take place administratively or requires parliamentary approval.

4.   If the notification indicates that implementation can take place administratively the notification shall, moreover, state that all necessary administrative measures enter into force on the date of entry into force of the amendments to the Regulation or have entered into force on the date of the notification, whichever date is the latest.

5.   If the notification indicates that implementation requires parliamentary approval in Denmark, the following rules shall apply:

(a)   legislative measures in Denmark shall enter into force on the date of entry into force of the amendments to the Regulation or within 6 months after the notification, whichever date is the latest;

(b)   Denmark shall notify the Commission of the date upon which the implementing legislative measures enter into force.

6.   A Danish notification that the content of the amendments have been implemented in Denmark, in accordance with paragraph 4 and 5, creates mutual obligations under international law between Denmark and the Community. The amendments to the Regulation shall then constitute amendments to this Agreement and shall be considered annexed hereto.

7.   In cases where:

(a)   Denmark notifies its decision not to implement the content of the amendments; or

(b)   Denmark does not make a notification within the 30-day time limit set out in paragraph 2; or

(c)   legislative measures in Denmark do not enter into force within the time limits set out in paragraph 5,

this Agreement shall be considered terminated unless the parties decide otherwise within 90 days or, in the situation referred to under (c), legislative measures in Denmark enter into force within the same period. Termination shall take effect three months after the expiry of the 90-day period.

8.   Requests that have been transmitted before the date of termination of the Agreement as set out in paragraph 7 are not affected hereby.

Article 4. Implementing measures.   1.   Denmark shall not take part in the adoption of opinions by the Committee referred to in Article 18 of the Regulation on the service of documents. Implementing measures adopted pursuant to Article 17 of that Regulation shall not be binding upon and shall not be applicable in Denmark.

2.   Whenever implementing measures are adopted pursuant to Article 17 of the Regulation, the implementing measures shall be communicated to Denmark. Denmark shall notify the Commission of its decision whether or not to implement the content of the implementing measures. Notification shall be given upon receipt of the implementing measures or within 30 days thereafter.

3.   The notification shall state that all necessary administrative measures in Denmark enter into force on the date of entry into force of the implementing measures or have entered into force on the date of the notification, whichever date is the latest.

4.   A Danish notification that the content of the implementing measures has been implemented in Denmark creates mutual obligations under international law between Denmark and the Community. The implementing measures will then form part of this Agreement.

5.   In cases where:

(a)   Denmark notifies its decision not to implement the content of the implementing measures; or

(b)   Denmark does not make a notification within the 30-day time limit set out in paragraph 2, this Agreement shall be considered terminated unless the parties decide otherwise within 90 days. Termination shall take effect three months after the expiry of the 90-day period.

6.   Requests that have been transmitted before the date of termination of the Agreement as set out in paragraph 5 are not affected hereby.

7. If in exceptional cases the implementation requires parliamentary approval in Denmark, the Danish notification under paragraph 2 shall indicate this and the provisions of Article 3(5) to (8), shall apply.

8. Denmark shall communicate to the Commission the information referred to in Articles 2, 3, 4, 9, 10, 13, 14, 15, 17(a) and 19 of the Regulation on the service of documents. The Commission shall publish this information together with the relevant information concerning the other Member States. The manual and the glossary drawn up pursuant to Article 17 of that Regulation shall include also the relevant information on Denmark.

Article 5. International agreements which affect the Regulation on the service of documents. 1. International agreements entered into by the Community when exercising its external competence based on the rules of the Regulation on the service of documents shall not be binding upon and shall not be applicable in Denmark.

2. Denmark will abstain from entering into international agreements which may affect or alter the scope of the Regulation on the service of documents as annexed to this Agreement unless it is done in agreement with the Community and satisfactory arrangements have been made with regard to the relationship between this Agreement and the international agreement in question.

3. When negotiating international agreements that may affect or alter the scope of the Regulation on the service of documents as annexed to this Agreement, Denmark will coordinate its position with the Community and will abstain from any actions that would jeopardise the objectives of a coordinated position of the Community within its sphere of competence in such negotiations.

Article 6. Jurisdiction of the Court of Justice of the European Communities in relation to the interpretation of the Agreement. 1. Where a question on the validity or interpretation of this Agreement is raised in a case pending before a Danish court or tribunal, that court or tribunal shall request the Court of Justice to give a ruling thereon whenever under the same circumstances a court or tribunal of another Member State of the European Union would be required to do so in respect of the Regulation on the service of documents and its implementing measures referred to in Article 2(1) of this Agreement.

2. Under Danish law, the courts in Denmark shall, when interpreting this Agreement, take due account of the rulings contained in the case law of the Court of Justice in respect of provisions of the Regulation on the service of documents and any implementing Community measures.

3. Denmark may, like the Council, the Commission and any Member State, request the Court of Justice to give a ruling on a question of interpretation of this Agreement. The ruling given by the Court of Justice in response to such a request shall not apply to judgments of courts or tribunals of the Member States which have become *res judicata*.

4. Denmark shall be entitled to submit observations to the Court of Justice in cases where a question has been referred to it by a court or tribunal of a Member State for a preliminary ruling concerning the interpretation of any provision referred to in Article 2(1).

5. The Protocol on the Statute of the Court of Justice of the European Communities and its Rules of Procedure shall apply.

6.   If the provisions of the Treaty establishing the European Community regarding rulings by the Court of Justice are amended with consequences for rulings in respect of the Regulation on the service of documents, Denmark may notify the Commission of its decision not to apply the amendments under this Agreement. Notification shall be given at the time of the entry into force of the amendments or within 60 days thereafter.

In such a case this Agreement shall be considered terminated. Termination shall take effect three months after the notification.

7.   Requests that have been transmitted before the date of termination of the Agreement as set out in paragraph 6 are not affected hereby.

Article 7. Jurisdiction of the Court of Justice of the European Communities in relation to compliance with the Agreement.   1.   The Commission may bring before the Court of Justice cases against Denmark concerning non-compliance with any obligation under this Agreement.

2.   Denmark may bring a complaint before the Commission as to the non-compliance by a Member State of its obligations under this Agreement.

3.   The relevant provisions of the Treaty establishing the European Community governing proceedings before the Court of Justice as well as the Protocol on the Statute of the Court of Justice of the European Communities and its Rules of Procedure shall apply.

Article 8. Territorial application.   This Agreement shall apply to the territories referred to in Article 299 of the Treaty establishing the European Community.

Article 9. Termination of the Agreement.   1.   This Agreement shall terminate if Denmark informs the other Member States that it no longer wishes to avail itself of the provisions of Part I of the Protocol on the position of Denmark, in accordance with Article 7 of that Protocol.

2.   This Agreement may be terminated by either Contracting Party giving notice to the other Contracting Party. Termination shall be effective six months after the date of such notice.

3.   Requests that have been transmitted before the date of termination of the Agreement as set out in paragraph 1 or 2 are not affected hereby.

Article 10. Entry into force.   1.   The Agreement shall be adopted by the Contracting Parties in accordance with their respective procedures.

2.   The Agreement shall enter into force on the first day of the sixth month following the notification by the Contracting Parties of the completion of their respective procedures required for this purpose.

Article 11. Authenticity of texts.   This Agreement is drawn up in duplicate in the Czech, Danish, Dutch, English, Estonian, Finnish, French, German, Greek, Hungarian, Italian, Latvian, Lithuanian, Maltese, Polish, Portuguese, Slovene, Slovak, Spanish and Swedish languages, each of these texts being equally authentic.

A.4. Green Paper on improving the efficiency of the enforcement of judgments in the European Union: the attachment of bank accounts (COM (2006) 618 of 24 October 2006): Point 5.1

See Chapter IV, General provisions, M.

A.5. ECJ case-law regarding Regulations (EC) No. 1348/2000 and No 1393/2007

Article 1

CJ, 14 January 2010, case C-233/08, Kyrian

Regulation No 1393/2007 does not apply to the assessment of the lawfulness of notification to the debtor of an instrument permitting enforcement in a Member State of a payment notice for the recovery of tax arrears rendered in another Member State under Directive 76/308/EEC of 15 March 1976 on mutual assistance for the recovery of claims relating to certain levies, duties, taxes and other measures, as amended by Council Directive 2001/44/EC of 15 June 2001. While the said Directive lays down no rules stating that the notification of an instrument permitting enforcement in a language other than that understood by the addressee or the official language, or one of the official languages of the Member State in which the requested authority is situated is unlawful, the procedure before the tax authorities or the subsequent notification of decisions are governed by the laws of the Member States. However, in the context of mutual assistance pursuant to Directive 76/308, the addressee of the instrument permitting enforcement must be placed in a position to identify with a degree of certainty at the very least the subject-matter of the claim and the cause of action.

In accordance with the settled case-law of the Court, in the absence of express Community provisions, it is for the domestic legal system of each Member State to determine the procedural conditions governing actions at law intended to ensure the protection of directly effective Community law rights. The Court has also held that those conditions cannot be less favourable than those relating to rights originating in the domestic legal order (principle of equivalence) and cannot make it impossible or excessively difficult in practice to exercise rights conferred by the Community legal order (principle of effectiveness).

Article 4

ECJ, 9 February 2006, case C-473/04, Plumex

Regulation No 1348/2000 must be interpreted as meaning that it does not establish any hierarchy between the method of transmission and service under Articles 4 to 11 thereof and that under Article 14 thereof and, consequently, it is possible to serve a judicial document by one or other or both of those methods.

Regulation No 1348/2000 must be interpreted as meaning that, where transmission and service are effected by both the method under Articles 4 to 11 thereof and the method under Article 14 thereof, in order to determine vis-à-vis the person on whom service is effected the point from which time starts to run for the purposes of a procedural time-limit linked to effecting service, reference must be made to the date of the first service validly effected.

ECJ, 25 June 2009, case C-14/08, Roda

The service of a notarial act, in the absence of legal proceedings, such as that at issue in the main proceedings, falls within the scope of Regulation No 1348/2000.

Article 8

ECJ, 8 November 2005, case C-443/03, Leffler

On a proper construction of Article 8(1) of Regulation No 1348/2000, when the addressee of a document has refused it on the ground that it is not in an official language of the Member State addressed or in a language of the Member State of transmission which the addressee understands, it is possible for the sender to remedy that by sending the translation requested.

On a proper construction of Article 8 of Regulation No 1348/2000, when the addressee of a document has refused it on the ground that it is not in an official language of the Member State addressed or in a language of the Member State of transmission which the addressee understands, that situation may be remedied by sending the translation of the document in accordance with the procedure laid down by Regulation No 1348/2000 and as soon as possible.

In order to resolve problems connected with the way in which the lack of translation should be remedied that are not envisaged by Regulation No 1348/2000 as interpreted by the Court, it is incumbent on the national court to apply national procedural law while taking care to ensure the full effectiveness of that regulation, in compliance with its objective.

ECJ, 8 May 2008, case C-14/07, Weiss und partner

Article 8(1) of Regulation No 1348/2000 to be interpreted as meaning that the addressee of a document instituting the proceedings which is to be served does not have the right to refuse to accept that document, provided that it enables the addressee to assert his rights in legal proceedings in the Member State of transmission, where annexes are attached to that document consisting of documentary evidence which is not in the language of the Member State addressed or in a language of the Member State of transmission which the addressee understands, but which has a purely evidential function and is not necessary for understanding the subject-matter of the claim and the cause of action.

It is for the national court to determine whether the content of the document instituting the proceedings is sufficient to enable the defendant to assert his rights or whether it is necessary for the party instituting the proceedings to remedy the fact that a necessary annex has not been translated.

Article 8(1)(b) of Regulation No 1348/2000 is to be interpreted as meaning that the fact that the addressee of a document served has agreed in a contract concluded with the applicant in the course of his business that correspondence is to be conducted in the language of the Member State of transmission does not give rise to a presumption of knowledge of that language, but is evidence which the court may take into account in determining whether that addressee understands the language of the Member State of transmission.

Article 8(1) of Regulation No 1348/2000 is to be interpreted as meaning that the addressee of a document served may not in any event rely on that provision in order to refuse acceptance of annexes to the document which are not in the language of the Member State addressed or in a language of the Member State of transmission which the addressee understands where the addressee concluded a contract in the course of his business in which he agreed that correspondence was to be conducted in the language of the Member State of transmission and the annexes concern that correspondence and are written in the agreed language.

Article 14

ECJ, 9 February 2006, case C-473/04, Plumex

Regulation No 1348/2000 must be interpreted as meaning that it does not establish any hierarchy between the method of transmission and service under Articles 4 to 11 thereof and that under Article 14 thereof and, consequently, it is possible to serve a judicial document by one or other or both of those methods.

Regulation No 1348/2000 must be interpreted as meaning that, where transmission and service are effected by both the method under Articles 4 to 11 thereof and the method under Article 14 thereof, in order to determine vis-à-vis the person on whom service is effected the point from which time starts to run for the purposes of a procedural time-limit linked to effecting service, reference must be made to the date of the first service validly effected.

Article 19

ECJ, 14 December 2006, Case C-283/05, ASML Netherlands

In relation to the scheme established by Regulation No 44/2001 as regards recognition and enforcement, it must be observed that the observance of the rights of defence of a defendant in default of appearance is ensured by a double review.

In the original proceedings in the State in which the judgment was given, it follows from the combined application of Article 26(2) of Regulation No 44/2001 and Article 19(1) of Regulation No 1348/2000, that the court hearing the case must stay the proceedings so long as it is not shown that the defendant has been able to receive the document which instituted the proceedings or an equivalent document in sufficient time to enable him to arrange for his defence, or that all necessary steps have been taken to this end.

B.   Council Regulation (EC) No 44/2001 of 22 December 2000 on jurisdiction and the recognition and enforcement of judgments in civil and commercial matters (OJ, L 12 of 16 January 2001): Article 26

See Chapter IV, General provisions, A.1.

C.   Council Regulation (EC) No 2201/2003 of 27 November 2003 concerning jurisdiction and the recognition and enforcement of judgments in matrimonial matters and the matters of parental responsibility, repealing Regulation (EC) No 1347/2000 (OJ, L 338 of 23 December 2003): Recital 15

See Chapter XI, Matrimonial matters, A.1.

D.   Regulation (EC) No 805/2004 of the European Parliament and of the Council of 21 April 2004 creating a European Enforcement Order for uncontested claims (OJ, L 143 of 30 April 2004): Articles 12–15

See Chapter IV, General provisions, C.

E.   Regulation (EC) No 1896/2006 of the European Parliament and of the Council of 12 December 2006 creating a European order for payment procedure (OJ, L 399 of 30 December 2006): Articles 13–15, 27–29

See Chapter IV, General provisions, D.

F.   Regulation (EC) No 861/2007 of the European Parliament and of the Council of 11 July 2007 establishing a European Small Claims Procedure (OJ, L 199 of 31 July 2007): Articles 13–14

See Chapter IV, General provisions, E.

G.   Directive 2008/52/EC of the European Parliament and of the Council of 21 May 2008 on certain aspects of mediation in civil and commercial matters (OJ, L 136 of 24 May 2008): Articles 6, 9–10

See Chapter IV, General provisions, L.

H. Council Regulation (EC) No 4/2009 of 18 December 2008 on jurisdiction, applicable law, recognition and enforcement of decisions and cooperation in matters relating to maintenance obligations (OJ, L 7 of 10 January 2010): Recitals 3, 28, 38; Articles 11, 31, 51(1)(j), 62–63

See Chapter XI, Maintenance obligations, A.1.

I. Proposal for a Regulation of the European Parliament and of the Council on jurisdiction, applicable law, recognition and enforcement of decisions and authentic instruments in matters of succession and the creation of a European Certificate of Succession (COM (2009) 154 of 14 October 2009): Article 12

See Chapter XII, A.

Taking of evidence

A.1. Council Regulation (EC) No 1206/2001 of 28 May 2001 on cooperation between the courts of the Member States in the taking of evidence in civil or commercial matters (OJ, L 174 of 27 June 2001)[4]

(1) The European Union has set itself the objective of maintaining and developing the European Union as an area of freedom, security and justice in which the free movement of persons is ensured. For the gradual establishment of such an area, the Community is to adopt, among others, the measures relating to judicial cooperation in civil matters needed for the proper functioning of the internal market.

(2) For the purpose of the proper functioning of the internal market, cooperation between courts in the taking of evidence should be improved, and in particular simplified and accelerated.

(3) At its meeting in Tampere on 15 and 16 October 1999, the European Council recalled that new procedural legislation in cross-border cases, in particular on the taking of evidence, should be prepared.

(4) This area falls within the scope of Article 65 of the Treaty.

(5) The objectives of the proposed action, namely the improvement of cooperation between the courts on the taking of evidence in civil or commercial matters, cannot be sufficiently achieved by the Member States and can therefore be better achieved at Community level. The Community may adopt measures in accordance with the principle

---

[4] As amended by Regulation (EC) No 1103/2008 of the European Parliament and of the Council of 22 October 2008 adapting a number of instruments subject to the procedure laid down in Article 251 of the Treaty to Council Decision 1999/468/EC, with regard to the regulatory procedure with scrutiny — Adaptation to the regulatory procedure with scrutiny — Part Three (OJ, L 304 of 14 November 2008).

of subsidiarity as set out in Article 5 of the Treaty. In accordance with the principle of proportionality, as set out in that Article, this Regulation does not go beyond what is necessary to achieve those objectives.

(6) To date, there is no binding instrument between all the Member States concerning the taking of evidence. The Hague Convention of 18 March 1970 on the taking of evidence abroad in civil or commercial matters applies between only 11 Member States of the European Union.

(7) As it is often essential for a decision in a civil or commercial matter pending before a court in a Member State to take evidence in another Member State, the Community's activity cannot be limited to the field of transmission of judicial and extrajudicial documents in civil or commercial matters which falls within the scope of Council Regulation (EC) No 1348/2000 of 29 May 2000 on the serving in the Member States of judicial and extrajudicial documents in civil or commercial matters. It is therefore necessary to continue the improvement of cooperation between courts of Member States in the field of taking of evidence.

(8) The efficiency of judicial procedures in civil or commercial matters requires that the transmission and execution of requests for the performance of taking of evidence is to be made directly and by the most rapid means possible between Member States' courts.

(9) Speed in transmission of requests for the performance of taking of evidence warrants the use of all appropriate means, provided that certain conditions as to the legibility and reliability of the document received are observed. So as to ensure the utmost clarity and legal certainty the request for the performance of taking of evidence must be transmitted on a form to be completed in the language of the Member State of the requested court or in another language accepted by that State. For the same reasons, forms should also be used as far as possible for further communication between the relevant courts.

(10) A request for the performance of the taking of evidence should be executed expeditiously. If it is not possible for the request to be executed within 90 days of receipt by the requested court, the latter should inform the requesting court accordingly, stating the reasons which prevent the request from being executed swiftly.

(11) To secure the effectiveness of this Regulation, the possibility of refusing to execute the request for the performance of taking of evidence should be confined to strictly limited exceptional situations.

(12) The requested court should execute the request in accordance with the law of its Member State.

(13) The parties and, if any, their representatives, should be able to be present at the performance of the taking of evidence, if that is provided for by the law of the Member State of the requesting court, in order to be able to follow the proceedings in a comparable way as if evidence were taken in the Member State of the requesting court. They should also have the right to request to participate in order to have a more active role in the performance of the taking of evidence. However, the conditions under which they may participate should be determined by the requested court in accordance with the law of its Member State.

(14) The representatives of the requesting court should be able to be present at the performance of the taking of evidence, if that is compatible with the law of the Member State of the requesting court, in order to have an improved possibility of evaluation of evidence. They should also have the right to request to participate, under the conditions

laid down by the requested court in accordance with the law of its Member State, in order to have a more active role in the performance of the taking of evidence.

(15) In order to facilitate the taking of evidence it should be possible for a court in a Member State, in accordance with the law of its Member State, to take evidence directly in another Member State, if accepted by the latter, and under the conditions determined by the central body or competent authority of the requested Member State.

(16) The execution of the request, according to Article 10, should not give rise to a claim for any reimbursement of taxes or costs. Nevertheless, if the requested court requires reimbursement, the fees paid to experts and interpreters, as well as the costs occasioned by the application of Article 10(3) and (4), should not be borne by that court. In such a case, the requesting court is to take the necessary measures to ensure reimbursement without delay. Where the opinion of an expert is required, the requested court may, before executing the request, ask the requesting court for an adequate deposit or advance towards the costs.

(17) This Regulation should prevail over the provisions applying to its field of application, contained in international conventions concluded by the Member States. Member States should be free to adopt agreements or arrangements to further facilitate cooperation in the taking of evidence.

(18) The information transmitted pursuant to this Regulation should enjoy protection. Since Directive 95/46/EC of the European Parliament and of the Council of 24 October 1995 on the protection of individuals with regard to the processing of personal data and on the free movement of such data, and Directive 97/66/EC of the European Parliament and of the Council of 15 December 1997 concerning the processing of personal data and the protection of privacy in the telecommunications sector, are applicable, there is no need for specific provisions on data protection in this Regulation.

(19) The measures necessary for the implementation of this Regulation should be adopted in accordance with Council Decision 1999/468/EC of 28 June 1999 laying down the procedures for the exercise of implementing powers conferred on the Commission.

(20) For the proper functioning of this Regulation, the Commission should review its application and propose such amendments as may appear necessary.

(21) The United Kingdom and Ireland, in accordance with Article 3 of the Protocol on the position of the United Kingdom and Ireland annexed to the Treaty on the European Union and to the Treaty establishing the European Community, have given notice of their wish to take part in the adoption and application of this Regulation.

(22) Denmark, in accordance with Articles 1 and 2 of the Protocol on the position of Denmark annexed to the Treaty on European Union and to the Treaty establishing the European Community, is not participating in the adoption of this Regulation, and is therefore not bound by it nor subject to its application;

Chapter I — General provisions

Article 1. Scope. 1. This Regulation shall apply in civil or commercial matters where the court of a Member State, in accordance with the provisions of the law of that State, requests:

(a) the competent court of another Member State to take evidence; or
(b) to take evidence directly in another Member State.

2.   A request shall not be made to obtain evidence which is not intended for use in judicial proceedings, commenced or contemplated.

3.   In this Regulation, the term 'Member State' shall mean Member States with the exception of Denmark.

Article 2. Direct transmission between the courts.   1.   Requests pursuant to Article 1(1) (a), hereinafter referred to as 'requests', shall be transmitted by the court before which the proceedings are commenced or contemplated, hereinafter referred to as the 'requesting court', directly to the competent court of another Member State, hereinafter referred to as the 'requested court', for the performance of the taking of evidence.

2.   Each Member State shall draw up a list of the courts competent for the performance of taking of evidence according to this Regulation. The list shall also indicate the territorial and, where appropriate, the special jurisdiction of those courts.

Article 3. Central body.   1.   Each Member State shall designate a central body responsible for:
   (a)   supplying information to the courts;
   (b)   seeking solutions to any difficulties which may arise in respect of a request;
   (c)   forwarding, in exceptional cases, at the request of a requesting court, a request to the competent court.

2.   A federal State, a State in which several legal systems apply or a State with autonomous territorial entities shall be free to designate more than one central body.

3.   Each Member State shall also designate the central body referred to in paragraph 1 or one or several competent authority(ies) to be responsible for taking decisions on requests pursuant to Article 17.

Chapter II — Transmission and execution of requests

Section 1 — Transmission of the request

Article 4. Form and content of the request.   1.   The request shall be made using form A or, where appropriate, form I in the Annex. It shall contain the following details:
   (a)   the requesting and, where appropriate, the requested court;
   (b)   the names and addresses of the parties to the proceedings and their representatives, if any;
   (c)   the nature and subject matter of the case and a brief statement of the facts;
   (d)   a description of the taking of evidence to be performed;
   (e)   where the request is for the examination of a person:
   —   the name(s) and address(es) of the person(s) to be examined;
   —   the questions to be put to the person(s) to be examined or a statement of the facts about which he is (they are) to be examined;
   —   where appropriate, a reference to a right to refuse to testify under the law of the Member State of the requesting court;
   —   any requirement that the examination is to be carried out under oath or affirmation in lieu thereof, and any special form to be used;

— where appropriate, any other information that the requesting court deems necessary;

(f) where the request is for any other form of taking of evidence, the documents or other objects to be inspected;

(g) where appropriate, any request pursuant to Articles 10(3) and (4), and Articles 11 and 12 and any information necessary for the application thereof.

2. The request and all documents accompanying the request shall be exempted from authentication or any equivalent formality.

3. Documents which the requesting court deems it necessary to enclose for the execution of the request shall be accompanied by a translation into the language in which the request was written.

Article 5. Language. The request and communications pursuant to this Regulation shall be drawn up in the official language of the requested Member State or, if there are several official languages in that Member State, in the official language or one of the official languages of the place where the requested taking of evidence is to be performed, or in another language which the requested Member State has indicated it can accept. Each Member State shall indicate the official language or languages of the institutions of the European Community other than its own which is or are acceptable to it for completion of the forms.

Article 6. Transmission of requests and other communications. Requests and communications pursuant to this Regulation shall be transmitted by the swiftest possible means, which the requested Member State has indicated it can accept. The transmission may be carried out by any appropriate means, provided that the document received accurately reflects the content of the document forwarded and that all information in it is legible.

Section 2 — Receipt of request

Article 7. Receipt of request. 1. Within seven days of receipt of the request, the requested competent court shall send an acknowledgement of receipt to the requesting court using form B in the Annex. Where the request does not comply with the conditions laid down in Articles 5 and 6, the requested court shall enter a note to that effect in the acknowledgement of receipt.

2. Where the execution of a request made using form A in the Annex, which complies with the conditions laid down in Article 5, does not fall within the jurisdiction of the court to which it was transmitted, the latter shall forward the request to the competent court of its Member State and shall inform the requesting court thereof using form A in the Annex.

Article 8. Incomplete request. 1. If a request cannot be executed because it does not contain all of the necessary information pursuant to Article 4, the requested court shall inform the requesting court thereof without delay and, at the latest, within 30 days of receipt of the request using form C in the Annex, and shall request it to send the missing information, which should be indicated as precisely as possible.

2.   If a request cannot be executed because a deposit or advance is necessary in accordance with Article 18(3), the requested court shall inform the requesting court thereof without delay and, at the latest, within 30 days of receipt of the request using form C in the Annex and inform the requesting court how the deposit or advance should be made. The requested Court shall acknowledge receipt of the deposit or advance without delay, at the latest within 10 days of receipt of the deposit or the advance using form D.

Article 9. Completion of the request.   1.   If the requested court has noted on the acknowledgement of receipt pursuant to Article 7(1) that the request does not comply with the conditions laid down in Articles 5 and 6 or has informed the requesting court pursuant to Article 8 that the request cannot be executed because it does not contain all of the necessary information pursuant to Article 4, the time limit pursuant to Article 10 shall begin to run when the requested court received the request duly completed.

2.   Where the requested court has asked for a deposit or advance in accordance with Article 18(3), this time limit shall begin to run when the deposit or the advance is made.

Section 3 — Taking of evidence by the requested court

Article 10. General provisions on the execution of the request.   1.   The requested court shall execute the request without delay and, at the latest, within 90 days of receipt of the request.

2.   The requested court shall execute the request in accordance with the law of its Member State.

3.   The requesting court may call for the request to be executed in accordance with a special procedure provided for by the law of its Member State, using form A in the Annex. The requested court shall comply with such a requirement unless this procedure is incompatible with the law of the Member State of the requested court or by reason of major practical difficulties. If the requested court does not comply with the requirement for one of these reasons it shall inform the requesting court using form E in the Annex.

4.   The requesting court may ask the requested court to use communications technology at the performance of the taking of evidence, in particular by using videoconference and teleconference.

The requested court shall comply with such a requirement unless this is incompatible with the law of the Member State of the requested court or by reason of major practical difficulties.

If the requested court does not comply with the requirement for one of these reasons, it shall inform the requesting court, using form E in the Annex.

If there is no access to the technical means referred to above in the requesting or in the requested court, such means may be made available by the courts by mutual agreement.

Article 11. Performance with the presence and participation of the parties.   1.   If it is provided for by the law of the Member State of the requesting court, the parties and, if any, their representatives, have the right to be present at the performance of the taking of evidence by the requested court.

2.   The requesting court shall, in its request, inform the requested court that the parties and, if any, their representatives, will be present and, where appropriate, that their participation is requested, using form A in the Annex. This information may also be given at any other appropriate time.

3.   If the participation of the parties and, if any, their representatives, is requested at the performance of the taking of evidence, the requested court shall determine, in accordance with Article 10, the conditions under which they may participate.

4.   The requested court shall notify the parties and, if any, their representatives, of the time when, the place where, the proceedings will take place, and, where appropriate, the conditions under which they may participate, using form F in the Annex.

5.   Paragraphs 1 to 4 shall not affect the possibility for the requested court of asking the parties and, if any their representatives, to be present at or to participate in the performance of the taking of evidence if that possibility is provided for by the law of its Member State.

Article 12. Performance with the presence and participation of representatives of the requesting court.   1.   If it is compatible with the law of the Member State of the requesting court, representatives of the requesting court have the right to be present in the performance of the taking of evidence by the requested court.

2.   For the purpose of this Article, the term 'representative' shall include members of the judicial personnel designated by the requesting court, in accordance with the law of its Member State. The requesting court may also designate, in accordance with the law of its Member State, any other person, such as an expert.

3.   The requesting court shall, in its request, inform the requested court that its representatives will be present and, where appropriate, that their participation is requested, using form A in the Annex. This information may also be given at any other appropriate time.

4.   If the participation of the representatives of the requesting court is requested in the performance of the taking of evidence, the requested court shall determine, in accordance with Article 10, the conditions under which they may participate.

5.   The requested court shall notify the requesting court, of the time when, and the place where, the proceedings will take place, and, where appropriate, the conditions under which the representatives may participate, using form F in the Annex.

Article 13. Coercive measures.   Where necessary, in executing a request the requested court shall apply the appropriate coercive measures in the instances and to the extent as are provided for by the law of the Member State of the requested court for the execution of a request made for the same purpose by its national authorities or one of the parties concerned.

Article 14. Refusal to execute.   1.   A request for the hearing of a person shall not be executed when the person concerned claims the right to refuse to give evidence or to be prohibited from giving evidence,

(a)   under the law of the Member State of the requested court; or

(b)   under the law of the Member State of the requesting court, and such right has been specified in the request, or, if need be, at the instance of the requested court, has been confirmed by the requesting court.

2.   In addition to the grounds referred to in paragraph 1, the execution of a request may be refused only if:

(a)   the request does not fall within the scope of this Regulation as set out in Article 1; or

(b)   the execution of the request under the law of the Member State of the requested court does not fall within the functions of the judiciary; or

(c)   the requesting court does not comply with the request of the requested court to complete the request pursuant to Article 8 within 30 days after the requested court asked it to do so; or

(d)   a deposit or advance asked for in accordance with Article 18(3) is not made within 60 days after the requested court asked for such a deposit or advance.

3.   Execution may not be refused by the requested court solely on the ground that under the law of its Member State a court of that Member State has exclusive jurisdiction over the subject matter of the action or that the law of that Member State would not admit the right of action on it.

4.   If execution of the request is refused on one of the grounds referred to in paragraph 2, the requested court shall notify the requesting court thereof within 60 days of receipt of the request by the requested court using form H in the Annex.

Article 15. Notification of delay.   If the requested court is not in a position to execute the request within 90 days of receipt, it shall inform the requesting court thereof, using form G in the Annex. When it does so, the grounds for the delay shall be given as well as the estimated time that the requested court expects it will need to execute the request.

Article 16. Procedure after execution of the request.   The requested court shall send without delay to the requesting court the documents establishing the execution of the request and, where appropriate, return the documents received from the requesting court. The documents shall be accompanied by a confirmation of execution using form H in the Annex.

Section 4 — Direct taking of evidence by the requesting court

Article 17.   1.   Where a court requests to take evidence directly in another Member State, it shall submit a request to the central body or the competent authority referred to in Article 3(3) in that State, using form I in the Annex.

2.   Direct taking of evidence may only take place if it can be performed on a voluntary basis without the need for coercive measures.

Where the direct taking of evidence implies that a person shall be heard, the requesting court shall inform that person that the performance shall take place on a voluntary basis.

3.   The taking of evidence shall be performed by a member of the judicial personnel or by any other person such as an expert, who will be designated, in accordance with the law of the Member State of the requesting court.

4.   Within 30 days of receiving the request, the central body or the competent authority of the requested Member State shall inform the requesting court if the request is accepted and, if necessary, under what conditions according to the law of its Member State such performance is to be carried out, using form J.

In particular, the central body or the competent authority may assign a court of its Member State to take part in the performance of the taking of evidence in order to ensure the proper application of this Article and the conditions that have been set out.

The central body or the competent authority shall encourage the use of communications technology, such as videoconferences and teleconferences.

5.   The central body or the competent authority may refuse direct taking of evidence only if:

(a)   the request does not fall within the scope of this Regulation as set out in Article 1;

(b)   the request does not contain all of the necessary information pursuant to Article 4; or

(c)   the direct taking of evidence requested is contrary to fundamental principles of law in its Member State.

6.   Without prejudice to the conditions laid down in accordance with paragraph 4, the requesting court shall execute the request in accordance with the law of its Member State.

Section 5 — Costs

Article 18.   1.   The execution of the request, in accordance with Article 10, shall not give rise to a claim for any reimbursement of taxes or costs.

2.   Nevertheless, if the requested court so requires, the requesting court shall ensure the reimbursement, without delay, of:
—   the fees paid to experts and interpreters, and
—   the costs occasioned by the application of Article 10(3) and(4).

The duty for the parties to bear these fees or costs shall be governed by the law of the Member State of the requesting court.

3.   Where the opinion of an expert is required, the requested court may, before executing the request, ask the requesting court for an adequate deposit or advance towards the requested costs. In all other cases, a deposit or advance shall not be a condition for the execution of a request.

The deposit or advance shall be made by the parties if that is provided for by the law of the Member State of the requesting court.

Chapter III — Final provisions

Article 19. Implementing rules.   1.   The Commission shall draw up and regularly update a manual, which shall also be available electronically, containing the information provided by the Member States in accordance with Article 22 and the agreements or arrangements in force, according to Article 21.

2.   The updating or making of technical amendments to the standard forms set out in the Annex shall be carried out by the Commission. Those measures, designed to amend non-essential elements of this Regulation, shall be adopted in accordance with the regulatory procedure with scrutiny referred to in Article 20(2).

Article 20. 1. The Commission shall be assisted by a committee.

2. Where reference is made to this paragraph, Article 5a(1) to (4) and Article 7 of Decision 1999/468/EC shall apply, having regard to the provisions of Article 8 thereof.

Article 21. Relationship with existing or future agreements or arrangements between Member States 1. This Regulation shall, in relation to matters to which it applies, prevail over other provisions contained in bilateral or multilateral agreements or arrangements concluded by the Member States and in particular the Hague Convention of 1 March 1954 on Civil Procedure and the Hague Convention of 18 March 1970 on the Taking of Evidence Abroad in Civil or Commercial Matters, in relations between the Member States party thereto.

2. This Regulation shall not preclude Member States from maintaining or concluding agreements or arrangements between two or more of them to further facilitate the taking of evidence, provided that they are compatible with this Regulation.

3. Member States shall send to the Commission:

(a) by 1 July 2003, a copy of the agreements or arrangements maintained between the Member States referred to in paragraph 2;

(b) a copy of the agreements or arrangements concluded between the Member States referred to in paragraph 2 as well as drafts of such agreements or arrangements which they intend to adopt; and

(c) any denunciation of, or amendments to, these agreements or arrangements.

Article 22. Communication. By 1 July 2003 each Member State shall communicate to the Commission the following:

(a) the list pursuant to Article 2(2) indicating the territorial and, where appropriate, the special jurisdiction of the courts;

(b) the names and addresses of the central bodies and competent authorities pursuant to Article 3, indicating their territorial jurisdiction;

(c) the technical means for the receipt of requests available to the courts on the list pursuant to Article 2(2);

(d) the languages accepted for the requests as referred to in Article 5.

Member States shall inform the Commission of any subsequent changes to this information.

Article 23. Review. No later than 1 January 2007, and every five years thereafter, the Commission shall present to the European Parliament, the Council and the Economic and Social Committee a report on the application of this Regulation, paying special attention to the practical application of Article 3(1)(c) and 3, and Articles 17 and 18.

Article 24. Entry into force. 1. This Regulation shall enter into force on 1 July 2001.

2. This Regulation shall apply from 1 January 2004, except for Articles 19, 21 and 22, which shall apply from 1 July 2001.

B. Council Directive 93/7/EEC of 15 March 1993 on the return of cultural objects unlawfully removed from the territory of a Member State (OJ, L 74 of 27 March 1993): Article 9

See Chapter VIII, Rights on cultural goods, B.

C. Council Regulation (EC) No 2100/94 of 27 July 1994 on Community plant variety rights (OJ, L 227 of 1 September 1994): Article 91

See Chapter VIII, IP rights, A.

D. Regulation (EC) No 861/2007 of the European Parliament and of the Council of 11 July 2007 establishing a European Small Claims Procedure (OJ, L 199 of 31 July 2007): Article 9

See Chapter IV, General provisions, E.

E. Council Regulation (EC) No 4/2009 of 18 December 2008 on jurisdiction, applicable law, recognition and enforcement of decisions and cooperation in matters relating to maintenance obligations (OJ, L 7 of 10 January 2010): Recital 3; Article 51(1)(g)

See Chapter XI, Maintenance obligations, A.1.

Access to justice

A. Council Directive 2003/8/EC of 27 January 2003 to improve access to justice in cross-border disputes by establishing minimum common rules relating to legal aid for such disputes (OJ, L 26 of 31 January 2003)[5]

(1) The European Union has set itself the objective of maintaining and developing an area of freedom, security and justice in which the free movement of persons is ensured. For

---

[5] Text after corrigendum (OJ, L 32 of 7 February 2003). The Commission adopted Decision 2005/630/EC of 26 August 2005 establishing a form for the transmission of legal aid applications under Council Directive 2003/8/EC (OJ, L 225 of 31 August 2005) and Decision 2004/844/EC of 9 November 2004 establishing a form for legal aid applications under Council Directive 2003/8/EC to improve access to justice in cross-border disputes by establishing minimum common rules relating to legal aid for such disputes (OJ, L 365 of 10 December 2004). See CJ, judgment 22 December 2010, case C-279/09, *DEB*.

the gradual establishment of such an area, the Community is to adopt, among others, the measures relating to judicial cooperation in civil matters having cross-border implications and needed for the proper functioning of the internal market.

(2)   According to Article 65(c) of the Treaty, these measures are to include measures eliminating obstacles to the good functioning of civil proceedings, if necessary by promoting the compatibility of the rules on civil procedure applicable in the Member States.

(3)   The Tampere European Council on 15 and 16 October 1999 called on the Council to establish minimum standards ensuring an adequate level of legal aid in cross-border cases throughout the Union.

(4)   All Member States are contracting parties to the European Convention for the Protection of Human Rights and Fundamental Freedom of 4 November 1950. The matters referred to in this Directive shall be dealt with in compliance with that Convention and in particular the respect of the principle of equality of both parties in a dispute.

(5)   This Directive seeks to promote the application of legal aid in cross-border disputes for persons who lack sufficient resources where aid is necessary to secure effective access to justice. The generally recognised right to access to justice is also reaffirmed by Article 47 of the Charter of Fundamental Rights of the European Union.

(6)   Neither the lack of resources of a litigant, whether acting as claimant or as defendant, nor the difficulties flowing from a dispute's cross-border dimension should be allowed to hamper effective access to justice.

(7)   Since the objectives of this Directive cannot be sufficiently achieved by the Member States acting alone and can therefore be better achieved at Community level, the Community may adopt measures, in accordance with the principle of subsidiarity as set out in Article 5 of the Treaty. In accordance with the principle of proportionality, as set out in that Article, this Directive does not go beyond what is necessary in order to achieve those objectives.

(8)   The main purpose of this Directive is to guarantee an adequate level of legal aid in cross-border disputes by laying down certain minimum common standards relating to legal aid in such disputes. A Council directive is the most suitable legislative instrument for this purpose.

(9)   This Directive applies in cross-border disputes, to civil and commercial matters.

(10)   All persons involved in a civil or commercial dispute within the scope of this Directive must be able to assert their rights in the courts even if their personal financial situation makes it impossible for them to bear the costs of the proceedings. Legal aid is regarded as appropriate when it allows the recipient effective access to justice under the conditions laid down in this Directive.

(11)   Legal aid should cover pre-litigation advice with a view to reaching a settlement prior to bringing legal proceedings, legal assistance in bringing a case before a court and representation in court and assistance with or exemption from the cost of proceedings.

(12)   It shall be left to the law of the Member State in which the court is sitting or where enforcement is sought whether the costs of proceedings may include the costs of the opponent imposed on the recipient of legal aid.

(13)   All Union citizens, wherever they are domiciled or habitually resident in the territory of a Member State, must be eligible for legal aid in cross-border disputes if they

meet the conditions provided for by this Directive. The same applies to third-country nationals who habitually and lawfully reside in a Member State.

(14) Member States should be left free to define the threshold above which a person would be presumed able to bear the costs of proceedings, in the conditions defined in this Directive. Such thresholds are to be defined in the light of various objective factors such as income, capital or family situation.

(15) The objective of this Directive could not, however, be attained if legal aid applicants did not have the possibility of proving that they cannot bear the costs of proceedings even if their resources exceed the threshold defined by the Member State where the court is sitting. When making the assessment of whether legal aid is to be granted on this basis, the authorities in the Member State where the court is sitting may take into account information as to the fact that the applicant satisfies criteria in respect of financial eligibility in the Member State of domicile or habitual residence.

(16) The possibility in the instant case of resorting to other mechanisms to ensure effective access to justice is not a form of legal aid. But it can warrant a presumption that the person concerned can bear the costs of the procedure despite his/her unfavourable financial situation.

(17) Member States should be allowed to reject applications for legal aid in respect of manifestly unfounded actions or on grounds related to the merits of the case in so far as pre-litigation advice is offered and access to justice is guaranteed. When taking a decision on the merits of an application, Member States may reject legal aid applications when the applicant is claiming damage to his or her reputation, but has suffered no material or financial loss or the application concerns a claim arising directly out of the applicant's trade or self-employed profession.

(18) The complexity of and differences between the legal systems of the Member States and the costs inherent in the cross-border dimension of a dispute should not preclude access to justice. Legal aid should accordingly cover costs directly connected with the cross-border dimension of a dispute.

(19) When considering if the physical presence of a person in court is required, the courts of a Member State should take into consideration the full advantage of the possibilities offered by Council Regulation (EC) No 1206/2001 of 28 May 2001 on cooperation between the courts of the Member States in the taking of evidence in civil or commercial matters.

(20) If legal aid is granted, it must cover the entire proceeding, including expenses incurred in having a judgment enforced; the recipient should continue receiving this aid if an appeal is brought either against or by the recipient in so far as the conditions relating to the financial resources and the substance of the dispute remain fulfilled.

(21) Legal aid is to be granted on the same terms both for conventional legal proceedings and for out-of-court procedures such as mediation, where recourse to them is required by the law, or ordered by the court.

(22) Legal aid should also be granted for the enforcement of authentic instruments in another Member State under the conditions defined in this Directive.

(23) Since legal aid is given by the Member State in which the court is sitting or where enforcement is sought, except pre-litigation assistance if the legal aid applicant is not domiciled or habitually resident in the Member State where the court is sitting, that Member State must apply its own legislation, in compliance with the principles of this Directive.

(24) It is appropriate that legal aid is granted or refused by the competent authority of the Member State in which the court is sitting or where a judgment is to be enforced. This is the case both when that court is trying the case in substance and when it first has to decide whether it has jurisdiction.

(25) Judicial cooperation in civil matters should be organised between Member States to encourage information for the public and professional circles and to simplify and accelerate the transmission of legal aid applications between Member States.

(26) The notification and transmission mechanisms provided for by this Directive are inspired directly by those of the European Agreement on the transmission of applications for legal aid, signed in Strasbourg on 27 January 1977, hereinafter referred to as '1977 Agreement'. A time limit, not provided for by the 1977 Agreement, is set for the transmission of legal aid applications. A relatively short time limit contributes to the smooth operation of justice.

(27) The information transmitted pursuant to this Directive should enjoy protection. Since Directive 95/46/EC of the European Parliament and of the Council of 24 October 1995 on the protection of individuals with regard to the processing of personal data and on the free movement of such data, and Directive 97/66/EC of the European Parliament and of the Council of 15 December 1997 concerning the processing of personal data and the protection of privacy in the telecommunications sector, are applicable, there is no need for specific provisions on data protection in this Directive.

(28) The establishment of a standard form for legal aid applications and for the transmission of legal aid applications in the event of cross-border litigation will make the procedures easier and faster.

(29) Moreover, these application forms, as well as national application forms, should be made available on a European level through the information system of the European Judicial Network, established in accordance with Decision 2001/470/EC.

(30) The measures necessary for the implementation of this Directive should be adopted in accordance with Council Decision 1999/468/EC of 28 June 1999 laying down the procedures for the exercise of implementing powers conferred on the Commission.

(31) It should be specified that the establishment of minimum standards in cross-border disputes does not prevent Member States from making provision for more favourable arrangements for legal aid applicants and recipients.

(32) The 1977 Agreement and the additional Protocol to the European Agreement on the transmission of applications for legal aid, signed in Moscow in 2001, remain applicable to relations between Member States and third countries that are parties to the 1977 Agreement or the Protocol. But this Directive takes precedence over provisions contained in the 1977 Agreement and the Protocol in relations between Member States.

(33) The United Kingdom and Ireland have given notice of their wish to participate in the adoption of this Directive in accordance with Article 3 of the Protocol on the position of the United Kingdom and Ireland annexed to the Treaty on European Union and to the Treaty establishing the European Community.

(34) In accordance with Articles 1 and 2 of the Protocol on the position of Denmark annexed to the Treaty on European Union and to the Treaty establishing the European Community, Denmark is not taking part in the adoption of this Directive and is not bound by it or subject to its application;

Chapter I — Scope and definitions

Article 1. Aims and scope. 1. The purpose of this Directive is to improve access to justice in cross-border disputes by establishing minimum common rules relating to legal aid in such disputes.

2. It shall apply, in cross-border disputes, to civil and commercial matters whatever the nature of the court or tribunal. It shall not extend, in particular, to revenue, customs or administrative matters.

3. In this Directive, 'Member State' shall mean Member States with the exception of Denmark.

Article 2. Cross-border disputes. 1. For the purposes of this Directive, a cross-border dispute is one where the party applying for legal aid in the context of this Directive is domiciled or habitually resident in a Member State other than the Member State where the court is sitting or where the decision is to be enforced.

2. The Member State in which a party is domiciled shall be determined in accordance with Article 59 of Council Regulation (EC) No 44/2001 of 22 December 2000 on jurisdiction and the recognition and enforcement of judgments in civil and commercial matters.

3. The relevant moment to determine if there is a cross-border dispute is the time when the application is submitted, in accordance with this Directive.

Chapter II — Right to legal aid

Article 3. Right to legal aid. 1. Natural persons involved in a dispute covered by this Directive shall be entitled to receive appropriate legal aid in order to ensure their effective access to justice in accordance with the conditions laid down in this Directive.

2. Legal aid is considered to be appropriate when it guarantees:

(a) pre-litigation advice with a view to reaching a settlement prior to bringing legal proceedings;

(b) legal assistance and representation in court, and exemption from, or assistance with, the cost of proceedings of the recipient, including the costs referred to in Article 7 and the fees to persons mandated by the court to perform acts during the proceedings.

In Member States in which a losing party is liable for the costs of the opposing party, if the recipient loses the case, the legal aid shall cover the costs incurred by the opposing party, if it would have covered such costs had the recipient been domiciled or habitually resident in the Member State in which the court is sitting.

3. Member States need not provide legal assistance or representation in the courts or tribunals in proceedings especially designed to enable litigants to make their case in person, except when the courts or any other competent authority otherwise decide in order to ensure equality of parties or in view of the complexity of the case.

4. Member States may request that legal aid recipients pay reasonable contributions towards the costs of proceedings taking into account the conditions referred to in Article 5.

5.   Member States may provide that the competent authority may decide that recipients of legal aid must refund it in whole or in part if their financial situation has substantially improved or if the decision to grant legal aid had been taken on the basis of inaccurate information given by the recipient.

Article 4. Non-discrimination.   Member States shall grant legal aid without discrimination to Union citizens and third-country nationals residing lawfully in a Member State.

Chapter III — Conditions and extent of legal id

Article 5. Conditions relating to financial resources.   1.   Member States shall grant legal aid to persons referred to in Article 3(1) who are partly or totally unable to meet the costs of proceedings referred to in Article 3(2) as a result of their economic situation, in order to ensure their effective access to justice.

2.   The economic situation of a person shall be assessed by the competent authority of the Member State in which the court is sitting, in the light of various objective factors such as income, capital or family situation, including an assessment of the resources of persons who are financially dependent on the applicant.

3.   Member States may define thresholds above which legal aid applicants are deemed partly or totally able to bear the costs of proceedings set out in Article 3(2). These thresholds shall be defined on the basis of the criteria defined in paragraph 2 of this Article.

4.   Thresholds defined according to paragraph 3 of this Article may not prevent legal aid applicants who are above the thresholds from being granted legal aid if they prove that they are unable to pay the cost of the proceedings referred to in Article 3(2) as a result of differences in the cost of living between the Member States of domicile or habitual residence and of the forum.

5.   Legal aid does not need to be granted to applicants in so far as they enjoy, in the instant case, effective access to other mechanisms that cover the cost of proceedings referred to in Article 3(2).

Article 6. Conditions relating to the substance of disputes.   1.   Member States may provide that legal aid applications for actions which appear to be manifestly unfounded may be rejected by the competent authorities.

2.   If pre-litigation advice is offered, the benefit of further legal aid may be refused or cancelled on grounds related to the merits of the case in so far as access to justice is guaranteed.

3.   When taking a decision on the merits of an application and without prejudice to Article 5, Member States shall consider the importance of the individual case to the applicant but may also take into account the nature of the case when the applicant is claiming damage to his or her reputation but has suffered no material or financial loss or when the application concerns a claim arising directly out of the applicant's trade or self-employed profession.

Article 7. Costs related to the cross-border nature of the dispute.   Legal aid granted in the Member State in which the court is sitting shall cover the following costs directly related to the cross-border nature of the dispute:

(a) interpretation:

(b) translation of the documents required by the court or by the competent authority and presented by the recipient which are necessary for the resolution of the case; and

(c) travel costs to be borne by the applicant where the physical presence of the persons concerned with the presentation of the applicant's case is required in court by the law or by the court of that Member State and the court decides that the persons concerned cannot be heard to the satisfaction of the court by any other means.

Article 8. Costs covered by the Member State of the domicile or habitual residence. The Member State in which the legal aid applicant is domiciled or habitually resident shall provide legal aid, as referred to in Article 3(2), necessary to cover:

(a) costs relating to the assistance of a local lawyer or any other person entitled by the law to give legal advice, incurred in that Member State until the application for legal aid has been received, in accordance with this Directive, in the Member State where the court is sitting;

(b) the translation of the application and of the necessary supporting documents when the application is submitted to the authorities in that Member State.

Article 9. Continuity of legal aid. 1. Legal aid shall continue to be granted totally or partially to recipients to cover expenses incurred in having a judgment enforced in the Member State where the court is sitting.

2. A recipient who in the Member State where the court is sitting has received legal aid shall receive legal aid provided for by the law of the Member State where recognition or enforcement is sought.

3. Legal aid shall continue to be available if an appeal is brought either against or by the recipient, subject to Articles 5 and 6.

4. Member States may make provision for the re-examination of the application at any stage in the proceedings on the grounds set out in Articles 3(3) and (5), 5 and 6, including proceedings referred to in paragraphs 1 to 3 of this Article.

Article 10. Extrajudicial procedures. Legal aid shall also be extended to extrajudicial procedures, under the conditions defined in this Directive, if the law requires the parties to use them, or if the parties to the dispute are ordered by the court to have recourse to them.

Article 11. Authentic instruments. Legal aid shall be granted for the enforcement of authentic instruments in another Member State under the conditions defined in this Directive.

Chapter IV — Procedure

Article 12. Authority granting legal aid. Legal aid shall be granted or refused by the competent authority of the Member State in which the court is sitting, without prejudice to Article 8.

Article 13. Introduction and transmission of legal aid applications. 1. Legal aid applications may be submitted to either:

(a)   the competent authority of the Member State in which the applicant is domiciled or habitually resident (transmitting authority); or

(b)   the competent authority of the Member State in which the court is sitting or where the decision is to be enforced (receiving authority).

2.   Legal aid applications shall be completed in, and supporting documents translated into:

(a)   the official language or one of the languages of the Member State of the competent receiving authority which corresponds to one of the languages of the Community institutions; or

(b)   another language which that Member State has indicated it can accept in accordance with Article 14(3).

3.   The competent transmitting authorities may decide to refuse to transmit an application if it is manifestly:

(a)   unfounded; or

(b)   outside the scope of this Directive.

The conditions referred to in Article 15(2) and (3) apply to such decisions.

4.   The competent transmitting authority shall assist the applicant in ensuring that the application is accompanied by all the supporting documents known by it to be required to enable the application to be determined. It shall also assist the applicant in providing any necessary translation of the supporting documents, in accordance with Article 8(b).

The competent transmitting authority shall transmit the application to the competent receiving authority in the other Member State within 15 days of the receipt of the application duly completed in one of the languages referred to in paragraph 2, and the supporting documents, translated, where necessary, into one of those languages.

5.   Documents transmitted under this Directive shall be exempt from legalisation or any equivalent formality.

6.   The Member States may not charge for services rendered in accordance with paragraph 4. Member States in which the legal aid applicant is domiciled or habitually resident may lay down that the applicant must repay the costs of translation borne by the competent transmitting authority if the application for legal aid is rejected by the competent authority.

Article 14. Competent authorities and language. 1. Member States shall designate the authority or authorities competent to send (transmitting authorities) and receive (receiving authorities) the application.

2.   Each Member State shall provide the Commission with the following information:

—   the names and addresses of the competent receiving or transmitting authorities referred to in paragraph 1,

—   the geographical areas in which they have jurisdiction,

—   the means by which they are available to receive applications, and

—   the languages that may be used for the completion of the application.

3.   Member States shall notify the Commission of the official language or languages of the Community institutions other than their own which is or are acceptable to the

competent receiving authority for completion of the legal aid applications to be received, in accordance with this Directive.

4.   Member States shall communicate to the Commission the information referred to in paragraphs 2 and 3 before 30 November 2004. Any subsequent modification of such information shall be notified to the Commission no later than two months before the modification enters into force in that Member State.

5.   The information referred to in paragraphs 2 and 3 shall be published in the Official Journal of the European Communities.

Article 15. Processing of applications.   1.   The national authorities empowered to rule on legal aid applications shall ensure that the applicant is fully informed of the processing of the application.

2.   Where applications are totally or partially rejected, the reasons for rejection shall be given.

3.   Member States shall make provision for review of or appeals against decisions rejecting legal aid applications. Member States may exempt cases where the request for legal aid is rejected by a court or tribunal against whose decision on the subject of the case there is no judicial remedy under national law or by a court of appeal.

4.   When the appeals against a decision refusing or cancelling legal aid by virtue of Article 6 are of an administrative nature, they shall always be ultimately subject to judicial review.

Article 16. Standard form.   1.   To facilitate transmission, a standard form for legal aid applications and for the transmission of such applications shall be established in accordance with the procedure set out in Article 17(2).

2.   The standard form for the transmission of legal aid applications shall be established at the latest by 30 May 2003.

The standard form for legal aid applications shall be established at the latest by 30 November 2004.

Chapter v — Final provisions

Article 17. Committee.   1.   The Commission shall be assisted by a Committee.

2.   Where reference is made to this paragraph, Articles 3 and 7 of Decision 1999/468/EC shall apply.

3.   The Committee shall adopt its Rules of Procedure.

Article 18. Information.   The competent national authorities shall cooperate to provide the general public and professional circles with information on the various systems of legal aid, in particular via the European Judicial Network, established in accordance with Decision 2001/470/EC.

Article 19. More favourable provisions.   This Directive shall not prevent the Member States from making provision for more favourable arrangements for legal aid applicants and recipients.

Article 20. Relation with other instruments.   This Directive shall, as between the Member States, and in relation to matters to which it applies, take precedence over provisions contained in bilateral and multilateral agreements concluded by Member States including:

(a)   the European Agreement on the transmission of applications for legal aid, signed in Strasbourg on 27 January 1977, as amended by the additional Protocol to the European Agreement on the transmission of applications for legal aid, signed in Moscow in 2001;

(b)   the Hague Convention of 25 October 1980 on International Access to Justice.

Article 21. Transposition into national law.   1.   Member States shall bring into force the laws, regulations and administrative provisions necessary to comply with this Directive no later than 30 November 2004 with the exception of Article 3(2)(a) where the transposition of this Directive into national law shall take place no later than 30 May 2006. They shall forthwith inform the Commission thereof.

When Member States adopt these measures, they shall contain a reference to this Directive or shall be accompanied by such a reference on the occasion of their official publication. The methods of making such a reference shall be laid down by Member States.

2.   Member States shall communicate to the Commission the text of the main provisions of national law which they adopt in the field covered by this Directive.

Article 22. Entry into force.   This Directive shall enter into force on the date of its publication in the Official Journal of the European Communities.

Article 23. Addressees.   This Directive is addressed to the Member States in accordance with the Treaty establishing the European Community.

B.   Council Regulation (EC) No 44/2001 of 22 December 2000 on jurisdiction and the recognition and enforcement of judgments in civil and commercial matters (OJ, L 12 of 16 January 2001): Article 50

See Chapter IV, General provisions, A.1.

C.   Council Regulation (EC) No 2201/2003 of 27 November 2003 concerning jurisdiction and the recognition and enforcement of judgments in matrimonial matters and the matters of parental responsibility, repealing Regulation (EC) No 1347/2000 (OJ L338 of 23 December 2003): Article 50

See Chapter XI, Matrimonial matters, A.1.

D. Regulation (EC) No 1896/2006 of the European Parliament and of the Council of 12 December 2006 creating a European order for payment procedure (OJ, L 399 of 30 December 2006): Article 24

See Chapter IV, General provisions, D.

E. Regulation (EC) No 861/2007 of the European Parliament and of the Council of 11 July 2007 establishing a European Small Claims Procedure (OJ, L 199 of 31 July 2007): Articles 13–14

See Chapter IV, General provisions, E.

F. Council Regulation (EC) No 4/2009 of 18 December 2008 on jurisdiction, applicable law, recognition and enforcement of decisions and cooperation in matters relating to maintenance obligations (OJ, L 7 of 10 January 2010): Recital 3; Articles 36–37, 44–47, 67

See Chapter XI, Maintenance obligations, A.1.

Legalisation

A. Convention abolishing the legalization of documents in the Member States of the European Communities, signed at Brussels on 25 May 1987 (OJ, No 108 of 11 May 1990)[6]

Article 1. This Convention shall apply to public documents which are drawn up in the territory of a contracting State and have to be produced in the territory of another contracting State or shown to the diplomatic or consular agents of another contracting State even if those agents are acting in the territory of a State which is not party to this Convention.

Article 2. The following are deemed to be public documents:

(a) Documents emanating from an authority or an official connected with the courts of tribunals of the State, including those emanating from a public prosecutor, a clerk of the court of a process server ('huissier de justice');

(b) Administrative documents;

---

[6] The Convention was signed by eleven Member States of the Community and is currently in force pursuant to Article 6(3) in the relationships between Belgium, Denmark, France, Ireland and Italy.

(c)   Notarial acts;

(d)   Official certificates which are placed on documents signed by persons in their private capacity, such as official certificates recording the registration of a document or the fact that it was in existence on a certain date and official and notarial authentications of signatures.

Article 3.   1.   This Convention shall also apply to documents drawn up in their official capacity by the diplomatic or consular agents of a contracting State acting in the territory of any State, where such documents have to be produced in the territory of another contracting State or shown to the diplomatic or consular agents of another contracting State acting in the territory of a State which is not party to this Convention.

2.   Each contracting State shall exempt the document to which this Convention applies from all forms of legalisation or other equivalent or similar formality.

3.   For the purposes of this Convention legalisation means only the formal procedure for certifying the authenticity of a signature, the capacity in which the person signing the document has acted and, where appropriate, the identity of the seal or stamp which it bears.

Article 4.   1.   If the authorities of the State in whose territory the document is produced have serious doubts, with good reason, as to the authenticity of the signature, the capacity in which the person signing the document has acted or the identity of the seal or stamp, they may request information directly from the relevant central authority, designated in accordance with Article 5, of the State from which the act or document emanated. Requests for information may be made only in exceptional cases and shall set out the grounds on which they are based.

2.   Whenever possible, requests for information shall be accompanied by the original document or by a photocopy thereof. Such a request and the reply thereto shall not be subject to any tax, duty or charge.

Article 5.   Each contracting State shall at the time of signature, ratification acceptance or approval of this Convention, designate the central authority responsible for receiving and forwarding the requests for information referred to in Article 4. It shall indicate the language(s) in which the authority will accept requests for information.

Article 6.   1.   This Convention shall be open for signature by the Member States. It shall be subject to ratification, acceptance or approval. The instruments of ratification, acceptance or approval shall be deposited with the Ministry of Foreign Affairs of Belgium.

2.   This Convention shall enter into force 90 days after the deposit of the instruments of ratification, acceptance or approval by all the States which are members of the European Communities on the date on which it becomes open for signature.

3.   Each State may, when depositing its instrument of ratification, acceptance or approval, or at any later date until the entry into force of the Convention, declare that the Convention will apply to it, in its relations with other States which have made the same declaration, 90 days after the date of deposit.

Article 7. 1. This Convention shall be open for accession by any State which becomes a member of the European Communities. The instruments of accession shall be deposited with the Ministry of Foreign Affairs of Belgium.

2. This Convention shall enter into force for any State acceding thereto 90 days after the deposit of its instruments of accession.

Article 8. 1. Each Member State may, at the time of signature or when depositing its instrument of ratification, acceptance or approval, specify the territory or territories to which this Convention shall apply.

2. Each Member State may, when depositing its instrument of ratification, acceptance or approval or at any later date, by declaration addressed to the Ministry of Foreign Affairs of Belgium extend this Convention to any other territory specified in the declaration and for whose international relations it is responsible or on whose behalf it is authorised to give undertakings.

3. Any declaration made in pursuance of paragraph 2 may, as regards any territory specified in that declaration, be withdrawn by means of a notification addressed to the Ministry of Foreign Affairs of Belgium.

The withdrawal shall have effect immediately or at such later date as may be specified in the notification.

Article 9. The Foreign Ministry of Belgium shall notify all the Member States of any signature, deposit of instruments, declaration or notification.

Article 10. This Convention replaces between contracting States the provisions of other treaties, conventions or agreements on the simplification or abolition of legalization of documents except when these treaties, conventions or agreements concern documents:

a) which are not covered by this Convention:

b) which have been drawn up in territories to which this Convention does not apply.

B. Council Regulation (EC) No 44/2001 of 22 December 2000 on jurisdiction and the recognition and enforcement of judgments in civil and commercial matters (OJ, L 12 of 16 January 2001): Articles 56, 57(4)

See Chapter IV, General provisions, A.1.

C.   Council Regulation (EC) No 2201/2003 of 27 November 2003 concerning jurisdiction and the recognition and enforcement of judgments in matrimonial matters and the matters of parental responsibility, repealing Regulation (EC) No 1347/2000 (OJ L338 of 23 December 2003): Article 52

See Chapter XI, Matrimonial matters, A.1.

D.   Council Regulation (EC) No 4/2009 of 18 December 2008 on jurisdiction, applicable law, recognition and enforcement of decisions and cooperation in matters relating to maintenance obligations (OJ, L 7 of 10 January 2010): Article 65

See Chapter XI, Maintenance obligations, A.1.

Judicial and administrative cooperation

A.   Council Decision 2001/470/EC of 28 May 2001 establishing a European Judicial Network in civil and commercial matters (OJ, L 174 of 27 June 2001)[1]

(1)   The European Union has set itself the objective of maintaining and developing the European Union as an area of freedom, security and justice, in which the free movement of persons is assured.

(2)   The gradual establishment of this area and the sound operation of the internal market entails the need to improve, simplify and expedite effective judicial cooperation between the Member States in civil and commercial matters.

(3)   The action plan of the Council and the Commission on how best to implement the provisions of the Treaty of Amsterdam on an area of freedom, security and justice which was adopted by the Council on 3 December 1998 and approved by the European Council on 11 and 12 December 1998 acknowledges that reinforcement of judicial cooperation in civil matters represents a fundamental stage in the creation of a European judicial area which will bring tangible benefits for every European Union citizen.

(4)   One of the measures provided for in paragraph 40 of the action plan is to examine the possibility of extending the concept of the European Judicial Network in criminal matters to embrace civil proceedings.

(5)   The conclusions of the special European Council held at Tampere on 15 and 16 October 1999 recommend the establishment of an easily accessible information system, to be maintained and updated by a Network of competent national authorities.

---

[1]   As amended by Decision No 568/2009/EC of 18 June 2009. The amended text will apply from 1 January 2011, except for the new Articles 2(5) and 20, which apply from the date of notification of this Decision to the Member States.

(6)   In order to improve, simplify and expedite effective judicial cooperation between the Member States in civil and commercial matters, it is necessary to establish at Community level a network cooperation structure — the European Judicial Network in civil and commercial matters.

(7)   This is a subject falling within the ambit of Articles 65 and 66 of the Treaty, and the measures are to be adopted in accordance with Article 67.

(8)   To ensure the attainment of the objectives of the European Judicial Network in civil and commercial matters, the rules governing its establishment should be laid down in a mandatory instrument of Community law.

(9)   The objectives of the proposed action, namely to improve effective judicial cooperation between the Member States and effective access to justice for persons engaging in cross-border litigation cannot be sufficiently achieved by the Member States and can therefore by reason of the scale or effects of the action be better achieved at Community level, the Community may adopt measures in accordance with the principle of subsidiarity as set out in Article 5 of the Treaty. In accordance with the principle of proportionality as set out in that Article, this Decision does not go beyond what is necessary in order to achieve those objectives.

(10)   The European Judicial Network in civil and commercial matters established by this Decision seeks to facilitate judicial cooperation between the Member States in civil and commercial matters both in areas to which existing instruments apply and in those where no instrument is currently applicable.

(11)   In certain specific areas, Community or international instruments relating to judicial cooperation in civil and commercial matters already provide for cooperation mechanisms. The European Judicial Network in civil and commercial matters does not set out to replace these mechanisms, and it must operate in full compliance with them. This Decision will consequently be without prejudice to Community or international instruments relating to judicial cooperation in civil or commercial matters.

(12)   The European Judicial Network in civil and commercial matters should be established in stages on the basis of the closest cooperation between the Commission and the Member States. It should be able to take advantage of modern communication and information technologies.

(13)   To attain its objectives, the European Judicial Network in civil and commercial matters needs to be supported by contact points designated by the Member States and to be sure of the participation of their authorities with specific responsibilities for judicial cooperation in civil and commercial matters. Contacts between them and periodic meetings are essential to the operation of the Network.

(14)   It is essential that efforts to establish an area of freedom, security and justice produce tangible benefits for persons engaging in cross-border litigation. It is accordingly necessary for the European Judicial Network in civil and commercial matters to promote access to justice. To this end, using the information supplied and updated by the contact points, the Network should progressively establish an information system that is accessible to the public, both the general public and specialists.

(15)   This Decision does not preclude the provision of other information than that which is provided for herein, within the European Judicial Network in civil and commercial matters and to the public. The enumeration in Title III is accordingly not to be regarded as exhaustive.

(16)   Processing of information and data should take place in compliance with

Directive 95/46/EC of the European Parliament and of the Council of 24 October 1995 on the protection of individuals with regard to the processing of personal data and of the free movement of such data and Directive 97/66/EC of the European Parliament and of the Council of 15 December 1997 concerning the processing of personal data and the protection of privacy in the telecommunications sector.

(17) To ensure that the European Judicial Network in civil and commercial matters remains an effective instrument, incorporates the best practice in judicial cooperation and internal operation and meets the public's expectations, provision should be made for periodic evaluations and for proposals for such changes as may be found necessary.

(18) The United Kingdom and Ireland, in accordance with Article 3 of the Protocol on the position of the United Kingdom and Ireland annexed to the Treaty on European Union and to the Treaty establishing the European Community, have given notice of their wish to take part in the adoption and application of this Decision.

(19) Denmark, in accordance with Articles 1 and 2 of the Protocol on the position of Denmark, annexed to the Treaty on European Union and to the Treaty establishing the European Community, is not participating in the adoption of this Decision and is therefore not bound by it nor subject to its application ...

Title I — Principles of the European Judicial Network in civil and commercial matters

Article 1. Establishment.   1.   A European Judicial Network in civil and commercial matters ('the Network') is hereby established among the Member States.

2.   In this Decision, the term 'Member State' shall mean Member States with the exception of Denmark.

Article 2. Composition.   1.   The Network shall be composed of:

(a)   contact points designated by the Member States, in accordance with paragraph 2;

(b)   central bodies and central authorities provided for in Community instruments, instruments of international law to which the Member States are parties or rules of domestic law in the area of judicial cooperation in civil and commercial matters;

(c)   the liaison magistrates to whom Joint Action 96/277/JAI of 22 April 1996 concerning a framework for the exchange of liaison magistrates to improve judicial cooperation between the Member States of the European Union applies, where they have responsibilities in cooperation in civil and commercial matters;

(d)   any other appropriate judicial or administrative authority with responsibilities for judicial cooperation in civil and commercial matters whose membership of the Network is considered to be useful by the Member State to which it belongs.

(e)   professional associations representing, at national level in the Member States, legal practitioners directly involved in the application of Community and international instruments concerning judicial cooperation in civil and commercial matters.

2.   Each Member State shall designate a contact point. Each Member State may, however, designate a limited number of other contact points if they consider this necessary on the basis of the existence of separate legal systems, the domestic distribution of jurisdiction, the tasks to be entrusted to the contact points or in order to associate

judicial bodies that frequently deal with cross-border litigation directly with the activities of the contact points.

Where a Member State designates several contact points, it shall ensure that appropriate coordination mechanisms apply between them.

If the contact point designated under this paragraph is not a judge, the Member State concerned shall provide for effective liaison with the national judiciary. To facilitate this, a Member State may designate a judge to support this function. This judge shall be a member of the Network.

2a.   Member States shall ensure that the contact points have sufficient and appropriate facilities in terms of staff, resources and modern means of communication to adequately fulfil their tasks as contact points.

3.   The Member States shall identify the authorities mentioned at points (b) and (c) of paragraph 1.

4.   The Member States shall designate the authorities mentioned at point (d) of paragraph 1.

4a.   Member States shall determine the professional associations referred to in paragraph 1(e). To that end, they shall obtain the agreement of the professional associations concerned on their participation in the Network.

Where there is more than one association representing a legal profession in a Member State, it shall be the responsibility of that Member State to provide for appropriate representation of that profession on the Network.

5.   The Member States shall notify the Commission, in accordance with Article 20, of the names and full addresses of the authorities referred to in paragraphs 1 and 2 of this Article, specifying:

(a)   the communication facilities available to them;

(b)   their knowledge of languages; and

(c)   where appropriate, their specific functions in the Network, including, where there is more than one contact point, their specific responsibilities.

Article 3. Tasks and activities of the Network.   1.   The Network shall be responsible for:

(a)   facilitating judicial cooperation between the Member States in civil and commercial matters, including devising, progressively establishing and updating an information system for the members of the Network;

(b)   facilitating effective access to justice, through measures providing information on the working of Community and international instruments concerning judicial cooperation in civil and commercial matters.

2.   Without prejudice to other Community or international instruments relating to judicial cooperation in civil or commercial matters, the Network shall develop its activities for the following purposes in particular:

(a)   the smooth operation of procedures having a cross-border impact and the facilitation of requests for judicial cooperation between the Member States, in particular where no Community or international instrument is applicable;

(b)   the effective and practical application of Community instruments or conventions in force between two or more Member States;

In particular where the law of another Member State is applicable, the courts or authorities responsible for the matter may apply to the Network for information on the content of that law;

(c)   the establishment, maintenance and promotion of an information system for the public on judicial cooperation in civil and commercial matters in the European Union, on relevant Community and international instruments and on the domestic law of the Member States, with particular reference to access to justice.

The main source of information shall be the Network's website containing up-to-date information in all the official languages of the institutions of the Union.

Article 4. Modus operandi of the Network.   The Network shall accomplish its tasks in particular by the following means:

1.   it shall facilitate appropriate contacts between the authorities of the Member States mentioned in Article 2(1) for the accomplishment of the tasks provided for by Article 3;

2.   it shall organise periodic meetings of the contact points and of the members of the Network in accordance with the rules laid down in Title II;

3.   it shall draw up and keep updated the information on judicial cooperation in civil and commercial matters and the legal systems of the Member States referred to in Title III, in accordance with the rules laid down in that Title.

Article 5. Contact points.   1.   The contact points shall be at the disposal of the authorities referred to in Article 2(1)(b) to (d) for the accomplishment of the tasks provided for by Article 3.

The contact points shall also be at the disposal of the local judicial authorities in their own Member State for the same purposes, in accordance with rules to be determined by each Member State.

2.   In particular, the contact points shall:

(a)   ensure that the local judicial authorities receive general information concerning the Community and international instruments relating to judicial cooperation in civil and commercial matters. In particular, they shall ensure that the Network, including the website of the Network, is better known to the local judicial authorities;

(b)   supply the other contact points, the authorities mentioned in Article 2(1)(b) to (d) and the local judicial authorities in their own Member State with all the information needed for sound judicial cooperation between the Member States in accordance with Article 3, in order to assist them in preparing operable requests for judicial cooperation and in establishing the most appropriate direct contacts;

(c)   supply any information to facilitate the application of the law of another Member State that is applicable under a Community or international instrument. To this end, the contact point to which such a request is addressed may draw on the support of any of the other authorities in its Member State referred to in Article 2 in order to supply the information requested. The information contained in the reply shall not be binding on the contact point, the authorities consulted or the authority which made the request;

(d)   seek solutions to difficulties arising on the occasion of a request for judicial cooperation, without prejudice to paragraph 4 of this Article and to Article 6;

(e) facilitate coordination of the processing of requests for judicial cooperation in the relevant Member State, in particular where several requests from the judicial authorities in that Member State fall to be executed in another Member State;

(f) contribute to generally informing the public, through the Network's website, on judicial cooperation in civil and commercial matters in the European Union, on relevant Community and international instruments and on the domestic law of the Member States, with particular reference to access to justice;

(g) collaborate in the organisation of, and participate in, the meetings referred to in Article 9;

(h) assist with the preparation and updating of the information referred to in Title III, and in particular with the information system for the public, in accordance with the rules laid down in that Title.

(i) ensure coordination between members of the Network at national level;

(j) draw up a two-yearly report on their activities, including, where appropriate, best practice in the Network, submit it at a meeting of the members of the Network, and draw specific attention to possible improvements in the Network.

3. Where a contact point receives a request for information from another member of the Network to which it is unable to respond, it shall forward it to the contact point or the member of the Network which is best able to respond to it. The contact point shall remain available for any such assistance as may be useful for subsequent contacts.

4. In areas where Community or international instruments governing judicial cooperation already provide for the designation of authorities responsible for facilitating judicial cooperation, contact points shall address requesters to such authorities.

Article 5a. Professional associations 1. In order to contribute to the accomplishment of the tasks provided for by Article 3, the contact points shall have appropriate contacts with the professional associations mentioned in Article 2(1)(e), in accordance with rules to be determined by each Member State.

2. In particular, the contacts referred to in paragraph 1 may include the following activities:

(a) exchange of experience and information as regards the effective and practical application of Community and international instruments;

(b) collaboration in the preparation and updating of the information sheets referred to in Article 15;

(c) participation of the professional associations in relevant meetings.

3. Professional associations shall not request information relating to individual cases from contact points.

Article 6. Relevant authorities for the purposes of Community or international instruments relating to judicial cooperation in civil and commercial matters. 1. The involvement of relevant authorities provided for by Community or international instruments relating to judicial cooperation in civil and commercial matters in the Network shall be without prejudice to the powers conferred on them by the instrument providing for their designation.

Contacts within the Network shall be without prejudice to regular or occasional contacts between these authorities.

2.   In each Member State the authorities provided for by Community or international instruments relating to judicial cooperation in civil and commercial matters and the contact points of the Network shall engage in regular exchanges of views and contacts to ensure that their respective experience is disseminated as widely as possible.

To this end, each Member State shall ensure, in accordance with the procedures to be determined by it, that the contact point(s) and competent authorities have the means to meet on a regular basis.

3.   The contact points of the Network shall be at the disposal of the authorities provided for by Community or international instruments relating to judicial cooperation in civil and commercial matters and shall assist them in all practicable ways.

Article 7. Language knowledge of the contact points.   To facilitate the practical operation of the Network, each Member State shall ensure that the contact points have adequate knowledge of an official language of the institutions of the Union other than their own, given that they need to be able to communicate with the contact points in other Member States.

Member States shall facilitate and encourage specialised language training for contact point staff and promote exchanges of staff between contact points in the Member States.

Article 8. Processing of requests for judicial cooperation.   1.   The contact points shall respond to all requests submitted to them without delay and at the latest within fifteen days of receipt thereof. If a contact point cannot reply to a request within that time limit, it shall inform the maker of the request briefly of this fact, indicating how much time it considers that it will need to reply, but this period shall not, as a rule, exceed thirty days.

2.   In order to respond as efficiently and rapidly as possible to requests referred to in paragraph 1, the contact points shall use the most appropriate technological facilities made available to them by the Member States.

3.   The Commission shall keep a secure, limited-access electronic register of the requests for judicial cooperation and replies referred to in Article 5(2)(b), (c), (d) and (e). The contact points shall ensure that the information necessary for the establishment and operation of this register is supplied regularly to the Commission.

4.   The Commission shall supply the contact points with information on the statistics relating to the judicial cooperation requests and replies referred to in paragraph 3 at least once every six months.

Title II — Meetings within the Network

Article 9. Meetings of the contact points.   1.   The contact points of the Network shall meet at least once every six months, in accordance with Article 12.

2.   Each Member State shall be represented at these meetings by one or more contact points, who may be accompanied by other members of the Network, but there shall be no more than six representatives per Member State.

3.   The first meeting of the contact points shall be held no later than 1 March 2003 without prejudice to the possibility of prior preparatory meetings.

Article 10. Purpose of periodic meetings of contact points.   1.   The purpose of the periodic meetings of contact points shall be to:

(a)   enable the contact points to get to know each other and exchange experience, in particular as regards the operation of the Network;

(b)   provide a platform for discussion of practical and legal problems encountered by the Member States in the course of judicial cooperation, with particular reference to the application of measures adopted by the European Community;

(c)   identify best practices in judicial cooperation in civil and commercial matters and ensure that relevant information is disseminated within the Network;

(d)   exchange data and views, in particular on the structure, organisation and content of and access to the available information mentioned in Title III;

(e)   draw up guidelines for progressively establishing the practical information sheets provided for by Article 15, in particular as regards the subject matter to be covered and the form of such information sheets;

(f)   identify specific initiatives other than those referred to in Title III which pursue comparable objectives.

2.   The Member States shall ensure that experience in the operation of specific cooperation mechanisms provided for by Community or international instruments is shared at meetings of the contact points.

Article 11. Meetings of members of the Network.   1.   Meetings open to all members of the Network shall be held to enable them to get to know each other and exchange experience, to provide a platform for discussion of practical and legal problems met and to deal with specific questions.

Meetings can also be held on specific issues.

2.   Meetings shall be convened, where appropriate, in accordance with Article 12.

3.   The Commission, in close cooperation with the Presidency of the Council and with the Member States, shall fix for each meeting the maximum number of participants.

Article 11a. Participation of observers in Network meetings.   1.   Without prejudice to Article 1(2), Denmark may be represented at the meetings referred to in Articles 9 and 11.

2.   Accession countries and candidate countries may be invited to attend these meetings as observers. Third countries that are party to international agreements on judicial cooperation in civil and commercial matters concluded by the Community may also be invited to attend certain Network meetings as observers.

3.   Each observer State may be represented at the meetings by one or more persons, but under no circumstances may there be more than three representatives per State.

Article 12. Organisation and proceedings of meetings of the Network.   1.   The Commission, in close cooperation with the Presidency of the Council and with the Member States, shall convene the meetings provided for by Articles 9 and 11. It shall chair them and provide secretarial services.

2.   Before each meeting the Commission shall prepare the draft agenda in agreement with the Presidency of the Council and in consultation with the Member States via their respective contact points.

3.   The contact points shall be notified of the agenda prior to the meeting. They may ask for changes to be made or for additional items to be entered.

4.   After each meeting the Commission shall prepare a record, which shall be notified to the contact points.

5.   Meetings of the contact points and of members of the Network may take place in any Member State.

Article 12a. Relations with other networks and international organisations.   1.   The Network shall maintain relations and share experience and best practice with the other European networks that share its objectives, such as the European Judicial Network in criminal matters. The Network shall also maintain relations with the European Judicial Training Network with a view to promoting, where appropriate and without prejudice to national practices, training sessions on judicial cooperation in civil and commercial matters for the benefit of the local judicial authorities of the Member States.

2.   The Network shall maintain relations with the European Consumer Centres Network (ECC-Net). In particular, in order to supply any general information on the working of Community and international instruments to facilitate consumer access to justice, the contact points of the Network shall be at the disposal of the members of ECC-Net.

3.   In order to meet its responsibilities under Article 3 concerning international instruments on judicial cooperation in civil and commercial matters, the Network shall maintain contact and exchanges of experience with the other judicial cooperation networks established between third countries and with international organisations that promote international judicial cooperation.

4.   The Commission, in close cooperation with the Presidency of the Council and the Member States, shall be responsible for implementing the provisions of this Article.

Title III — Information available within the Network, and information provided to the public

Article 13. Information disseminated within the Network.   1.   The information disseminated within the network shall include:

(a)   the information referred to in Article 2(5);

(b)   any further information deemed useful by the contact points for the proper functioning of the Network;

(c)   the information referred to in Article 8.

2.   For the purpose of paragraph 1, the Commission shall progressively establish a secure limited-access electronic information exchange-system in consultation with the contact points.

Article 13a. Provision of general information to the public.   The Network shall contribute towards providing the public with general information, using the most appropriate technological facilities to inform it about the content and working of Community or international instruments on judicial cooperation in civil and commercial matters.

To that end, and without prejudice to the provisions of Article 18, the contact points shall promote to the public the information system referred to in Article 14.

Article 14. Information systems for the public. 1. An Internet-based information system for the public, including the dedicated website for the Network, shall be progressively established in accordance with Articles 17 and 18.

2. The information system shall comprise the following elements:

(a) Community instruments in force or in preparation relating to judicial cooperation in civil and commercial matters;

(b) national measures for the domestic implementation of the instruments in force referred to in point (a);

(c) international instruments in force relating to judicial cooperation in civil and commercial matters to which the Member States are parties, and declarations and reservations made in connection with such instruments;

(d) the relevant elements of Community case-law in the area of judicial cooperation in civil and commercial matters;

(e) the information sheets provided for by Article 15.

3. For the purposes of access to the information mentioned in paragraphs 2(a) to (d), the Network should, where appropriate, in its site, make use of links to other sites where the original information is to be found.

4. The site dedicated to the Network shall likewise facilitate access to comparable public information initiatives in related matters and to sites containing information relating to the legal systems of the Member States.

Article 15. Information sheets. 1. The information sheets shall be devoted by way of priority to questions relating to access to justice in the Member States and shall include information on the procedures for bringing cases in the courts and for obtaining legal aid, without prejudice to other Community initiatives, to which the Network shall have the fullest regard.

2. Information sheets shall be of a practical and concise nature. They shall be written in easily comprehensible language and contain practical information for the public. They shall progressively be produced on at least the following subjects:

(a) principles of the legal system and judicial organisation of the Member States;

(b) procedures for bringing cases to court, with particular reference to small claims, and subsequent court procedures, including appeal possibilities and procedures;

(c) conditions and procedures for obtaining legal aid, including descriptions of the tasks of non-governmental organisations active in this field, account being taken of work already done in the Dialogue with Citizens;

(d) national rules governing the service of documents;

(e) rules and procedures for the enforcement of judgments given in other Member States;

(f) possibilities and procedures for obtaining interim relief measures, with particular reference to seizures of assets for the purposes of enforcement;

(g) alternative dispute-settlement possibilities, with an indication of the national information and advice centres of the Community-wide Network for the Extra-Judicial Settlement of Consumer Disputes;

(h) organisation and operation of the legal professions.

4. The information sheets shall, where appropriate, include elements of the relevant case-law of the Member States.

5.   The information sheets may provide more detailed information for the specialists.

Article 16. Updating of information.   All information distributed within the Network and to the public under Articles 13 to 15 shall be updated regularly.

Article 17. Role of the Commission in the public information system.   The Commission shall:
1.   be responsible for managing the information system for the public;
2.   construct, in consultation with the contact points, a dedicated website for the Network on its Internet site;
3.   provide information on relevant aspects of Community law and procedures, including Community case-law, in accordance with Article 14;
4.   (a)   ensure that the format of the information sheets is consistent and that they include all information considered necessary by the Network;
(b)   arrange for the translations into the official languages of the institutions of the Union of information on the relevant aspects of Community law and procedures, including Community case-law, and of the information system's general pages and the information sheets referred to in Article 15, and install them on the Network's dedicated website.

Article 18. Role of contact points in the public information system.   Contact points shall ensure that
1.   the appropriate information needed to create and operate the information system is supplied to the Commission;
2.   the information installed in the system is accurate;
3.   the Commission is notified forthwith of any updates as soon as an item of information requires changing;
4.   the information sheets relating to their respective Member States are established, according to the guidelines referred to in Article 10(1)(e);
5.   the broadest possible dissemination of the information sheets installed on the site dedicated to the Network is arranged in their Member State.

Title IV — Final provisions

Article 19. Reporting.   1.   No later than 1 January 2014, and every three years thereafter, the Commission shall present to the European Parliament, the Council and the Economic and Social Committee a report on the activities of the Network. The report shall be accompanied, if appropriate, by proposals aimed at adapting this Decision and shall include information on the Network's activities aimed at making progress with the design, development and implementation of European e-justice, particularly from the point of view of facilitating access to justice.
2.   The report shall consider, among other relevant matters, the question of possible direct public access to the contact points of the Network, access to and involvement of the legal professions in its activities, and synergy with the Community-wide Network for the Extra-Judicial Settlement of Consumer Disputes. It shall also consider the relationship between the contact points of the Network and the competent authorities provided for

in Community or international instruments relating to judicial cooperation in civil and commercial matters.

Article 20. Establishment of the basic components of the Network. No later than 1 July 2010, the Member States shall notify the Commission of the information referred to in Article 2(5).

Article 21. Date of application. This Decision shall apply from 1 December 2002, except for Articles 2 and 20 which shall apply from the date of notification of the Decision to the Member States to which it is addressed.

B. Regulation (EC) No 861/2007 of the European Parliament and of the Council of 11 July 2007 establishing a European Small Claims Procedure (OJ, L 199 of 31 July 2007): Article 24

See Chapter IV, General provisions, E.

C. Council Regulation (EC) No 4/2009 of 18 December 2008 on jurisdiction, applicable law, recognition and enforcement of decisions and cooperation in matters relating to maintenance obligations (OJ, L 7 of 10 January 2010): Articles 49–63

See Chapter XI, Maintenance obligations, A.1.

D. Council Regulation (EU) No 1259/2010 of 20 December 2010 implementing enhanced cooperation in the area of the law applicable to divorce and legal separation (Doc. Consilium 17523/10 of 14 December 2010): Recital 14, Article 17

See Chapter XI, Matrimonial matters, B.2.

E. Proposal for a Regulation of the European Parliament and of the Council on jurisdiction, applicable law, recognition and enforcement of decisions and authentic instruments in matters of succession and the creation of a European Certificate of Succession (COM (2009) 154 of 14 October 2009): Recital 29, Article 46

See Chapter XII, A.

Compensation to Crime Victims

A.   Council Framework Decision 2001/220/JHA of 15 March 2001 on the standing of victims in criminal proceedings (OJ, L 82 of 22 March 2001)

Article 9. Right to compensation in the course of criminal proceedings.   1.   Each Member State shall ensure that victims of criminal acts are entitled to obtain a decision within reasonable time limits on compensation by the offender in the course of criminal proceedings, except where, in certain cases, national law provides for compensation to be awarded in another manner.

2.   Each Member State shall take appropriate measures to encourage the offender to provide adequate compensation to victims.

3.   Unless urgently required for the purpose of criminal proceedings, recoverable property belonging to victims which is seized in the course of criminal proceedings shall be returned to them without delay.

Article 11. Victims resident in another Member State.   1.   Each Member State shall ensure that its competent authorities can take appropriate measures to minimise the difficulties faced where the victim is a resident of a State other than the one where the offence has occurred, particularly with regard to the organisation of the proceedings. For this purpose, its authorities should, in particular, be in a position:

—   to be able to decide whether the victim may make a statement immediately after the commission of an offence;

—   to have recourse as far as possible to the provisions on video conferencing and telephone conference calls laid down in Articles 10 and 11 of the Convention on Mutual Assistance in Criminal Matters between the Member States of the European Union of 29 May 2000(3) for the purpose of hearing victims resident abroad.

2.   Each Member State shall ensure that the victim of an offence in a Member State other than the one where he resides may make a complaint before the competent authorities of his State of residence if he was unable to do so in the Member State where the offence was committed or, in the event of a serious offence, if he did not wish to do so.

The competent authority to which the complaint is made, insofar as it does not itself have competence in this respect, shall transmit it without delay to the competent authority in the territory in which the offence was committed. The complaint shall be dealt with in accordance with the national law of the State in which the offence was committed.

B.   Council Directive 2004/80/EC of 29 April 2004 relating to compensation to crime victims (OJ, L 261 of 6 August 2004)

(1)   One of the objectives of the European Community is to abolish, as between Member States, obstacles to the free movement of persons and services.

(2)   The Court of Justice held in the Cowan case that, when Community law guarantees to a natural person the freedom to go to another Member State, the protection of that person from harm in the Member State in question, on the same basis as that of nationals and persons residing there, is a corollary of that freedom of movement. Measures to facilitate compensation to victims of crimes should form part of the realisation of this objective.

(3)   At its meeting in Tampere on 15 and 16 October 1999, the European Council called for the drawing-up of minimum standards on the protection of the victims of crime, in particular on crime victims' access to justice and their rights to compensation for damages, including legal costs.

(4)   The Brussels European Council, meeting on 25 and 26 March 2004, in the Declaration on Combating Terrorism, called for the adoption of this Directive before 1 May 2004.

(5)   On 15 March 2001 the Council adopted Framework Decision 2001/220/JHA on the standing of victims in criminal proceedings. This Decision, based on Title VI of the Treaty on the European Union, allows crime victims to claim compensation from the offender in the course of criminal proceedings.

(6)   Crime victims in the European Union should be entitled to fair and appropriate compensation for the injuries they have suffered, regardless of where in the European Community the crime was committed

(7)   This Directive sets up a system of cooperation to facilitate access to compensation to victims of crimes in cross-border situations, which should operate on the basis of Member States' schemes on compensation to victims of violent intentional crime, committed in their respective territories. Therefore, a compensation mechanism should be in place in all Member States.

(8)   Most Member States have already established such compensation schemes, some of them in fulfilment of their obligations under the European Convention of 24 November 1983 on the compensation of victims of violent crimes....

(11)   A system of cooperation between the authorities of the Member States should be introduced to facilitate access to compensation in cases where the crime was committed in a Member State other than that of the victim's residence.

(12)   This system should ensure that crime victims could always turn to an authority in their Member State of residence and should ease any practical and linguistic difficulties that occur in a cross-border situation.

(13)   The system should include the provisions necessary for allowing the crime victim to find the information needed to make the application and for allowing for efficient cooperation between the authorities involved....

Chapter I — Access to compensation in cross-border situations

Article 1. Right to submit an application in the Member State of residence.   Member States shall ensure that where a violent intentional crime has been committed in a Member State other than the Member State where the applicant for compensation is habitually resident, the applicant shall have the right to submit the application to an authority or any other body in the latter Member State.

Article 2. Responsibility for paying compensation.   Compensation shall be paid by the competent authority of the Member State on whose territory the crime was committed.

Article 3. Responsible authorities and administrative procedures.   1.   Member States shall establish or designate one or several authorities or any other bodies, hereinafter referred to as 'assisting authority or authorities', to be responsible for applying Article 1.

2.   Member States shall establish or designate one or several authorities or any other bodies to be responsible for deciding upon applications for compensation, hereinafter referred to as 'deciding authority or authorities'.

3.   Member States shall endeavour to keep to a minimum the administrative formalities required of an applicant for compensation.

Article 4. Information to potential applicants.   Member States shall ensure that potential applicants for compensation have access to essential information on the possibilities to apply for compensation, by any means Member States deem appropriate.

Article 5. Assistance to the applicant.   1.   The assisting authority shall provide the applicant with the information referred to in Article 4 and the required application forms, on the basis of the manual drawn up in accordance with Article 13(2).

2.   The assisting authority shall, upon the request of the applicant, provide him or her with general guidance and information on how the application should be completed and what supporting documentation may be required.

3.   The assisting authority shall not make any assessment of the application.

Article 6. Transmission of applications.   1.   The assisting authority shall transmit the application and any supporting documentation as quickly as possible to the deciding authority.

2.   The assisting authority shall transmit the application using the standard form referred to in Article 14.

3.   The language of the application and any supporting documentation shall be determined in accordance with Article 11(1).

Article 7. Receipt of applications.   Upon receipt of an application transmitted in accordance with Article 6, the deciding authority shall send the following information as soon as possible to the assisting authority and to the applicant:

(a)   the contact person or the department responsible for handling the matter;

(b)   an acknowledgement of receipt of the application;

(c)   if possible, an indication of the approximate time by which a decision on the application will be made.

Article 8. Requests for supplementary information.   The assisting authority shall if necessary provide general guidance to the applicant in meeting any request for supplementary information from the deciding authority.

It shall upon the request of the applicant subsequently transmit it as soon as possible directly to the deciding authority, enclosing, where appropriate, a list of any supporting documentation transmitted.

Article 9. Hearing of the applicant. 1. If the deciding authority decides, in accordance with the law of its Member State, to hear the applicant or any other person such as a witness or an expert, it may contact the assisting authority for the purpose of arranging for:

(a) the person(s) to be heard directly by the deciding authority, in accordance with the law of its Member State, through the use in particular of telephone- or video-conferencing; or

(b) the person(s) to be heard by the assisting authority, in accordance with the law of its Member State, which will subsequently transmit a report of the hearing to the deciding authority.

2. The direct hearing in accordance with paragraph 1(a) may only take place in cooperation with the assisting authority and on a voluntary basis without the possibility of coercive measures being imposed by the deciding authority.

Article 10. Communication of the decision. The deciding authority shall send the decision on the application for compensation, by using the standard form referred to in Article 14, to the applicant and to the assisting authority, as soon as possible, in accordance with national law, after the decision has been taken.

Article 11. Other provisions. 1. Information transmitted between the authorities pursuant to Articles 6 to 10 shall be expressed in:

(a) the official languages or one of the languages of the Member State of the authority to which the information is sent, which corresponds to one of the languages of the Community institutions; or

(b) another language of the Community institutions that that Member State has indicated it can accept;

with the exception of:

(i) the full text of decisions taken by the deciding authority, where the use of languages shall be governed by the law of its Member State;

(ii) reports drawn up following a hearing in accordance with Article 9(1)(b), where the use of languages shall be determined by the assisting authority, subject to the requirement that it corresponds to one of the languages of the Community institutions.

2. Services rendered by the assisting authority in accordance with Articles 1 to 10 shall not give rise to a claim for any reimbursement of charges or costs from the applicant or from the deciding authority.

3. Application forms and any other documentation transmitted in accordance with Articles 6 to 10 shall be exempted from authentication or any equivalent formality.

Chapter II — National schemes on compensation

Article 12. 1. The rules on access to compensation in cross-border situations drawn up by this Directive shall operate on the basis of Member States' schemes on compensation to victims of violent intentional crime committed in their respective territories.

2. All Member States shall ensure that their national rules provide for the existence of a scheme on compensation to victims of violent intentional crimes committed in their respective territories, which guarantees fair and appropriate compensation to victims.

Chapter III — Implementing provisions

Article 13. Information to be sent to the Commission and the manual.   1.   Member States shall, no later than 1 July 2005, send to the Commission details of:

(a)   the list of authorities established or designated in accordance with Articles 3(1) and 3(2), including, where appropriate, information on the special and territorial jurisdiction of these authorities:

(b)   the language(s) referred to in Article 11(1)(a) which the authorities can accept for the purpose of applying Articles 6 to 10 and the official language or languages other than its own which is or are acceptable to it for the transmission of applications in accordance with Article 11(1)(b).

(c)   the information established in accordance with Article 4:

(d)   the application forms for compensation:

Member States shall inform the Commission of any subsequent changes to this information.

2.   The Commission shall, in cooperation with the Member States establish and publish on the internet a manual containing the information provided by the Member States pursuant to paragraph 1. The Commission shall be responsible for arranging the necessary translations of the manual.

Article 14. Standard form for transmission of applications and decisions.   Standard forms shall be established, at the latest by 31 October 2005, for the transmission of applications and decisions in accordance with the procedure referred to in Article 15(2).

Article 15. Committee.   1.   The Commission shall be assisted by a Committee.

2.   Where reference is made to this paragraph, Articles 3 and 7 of Decision 1999/468/EC shall apply.

3.   The Committee shall adopt its Rules of Procedure.

Article 16. Central contact points.   Member States shall appoint a central contact point for the purposes of:

(a)   assisting with the implementation of Article 13(2):

(b)   furthering close cooperation and exchange of information between the assisting and deciding authorities in the Member States; and

(c)   giving assistance and seeking solutions to any difficulties that may occur in the application of Articles 1 to 10.

The contact points shall meet regularly.

Article 17. More favourable provisions.   This Directive shall not prevent Member States, in so far as such provisions are compatible with this Directive, from:

(a)   introducing or maintaining more favourable provisions for the benefit of victims of crime or any other persons affected by crime:

(b)   introducing or retaining provisions for the purpose of compensating victims of crime committed outside their territory, or any other person affected by such a crime, subject to any conditions that Member States may specify for that purpose.

Article 18. Implementation. 1.   Member States shall bring into force the laws, regulations and administrative provisions necessary to comply with this Directive by 1 January 2006 at the latest, with the exception of Article 12(2), in which case the date of compliance shall be 1 July 2005. They shall forthwith inform the Commission thereof.

2.   Member States may provide that the measures necessary to comply with this Directive shall apply only to applicants whose injuries result from crimes committed after 30 June 2005.

3.   When Member States adopt these measures, they shall contain a reference to this Directive or be accompanied by such a reference on the occasion of their official publication. The methods of making such reference shall be laid down by the Member States.

4.   Member States shall communicate to the Commission the text of the main provisions of domestic law, which they adopt in the field governed by this Directive.

Article 19. Review.   No later than by 1 January 2009, the Commission shall present to the European Parliament, the Council and the European Economic and Social Committee a report on the application of this Directive.

C.   ECJ case-law

Judgment 2 February 1989, case 186/87, *Cowan*, Reports, 195.
    See Chapter II, Principle of non-discrimination, B.